CRITICAL SURVEY
OF
LONG FICTION

CRITICAL SURVEY

OF

LONG FICTION

Second Revised Edition

Volume 4

Oscar Hijuelos - Patrick McGinley

Editor, Second Revised Edition
Carl Rollyson
Baruch College, City University of New York

Editor, First Edition, English and Foreign Language Series
Frank N. Magill

SALEM PRESS, INC.
Pasadena, California   Hackensack, New Jersey

Managing Editor: Christina J. Moose
Research Supervisor: Jeffry Jensen
Acquisitions Editor: Mark Rehn
Photograph Editor: Karrie Hyatt
Manuscript Editors: Lauren M. D'Andrea, Doug Long
Research Assistant: Jun Ohnuki
Production Editor: Cynthia Beres
Layout: William Zimmerman
Graphics: Yasmine Cordoba

Some of the essays in this work, which have been updated, originally appeared in the following Salem Press publications: *Critical Survey of Long Fiction, English Language Series, Revised Edition* (1991), *Critical Survey of Long Fiction, Foreign Language Series* (1984).

Library of Congress Cataloging-in-Publication Data

Critical survey of long fiction / editor, Carl Rollyson ; editor, English and foreign language series, Frank N. Magill.—2nd rev. ed.

p. cm.

"The current reference work both updates and substantially adds to the previous editions of the Critical survey from which it is partially drawn: the Critical survey of long fiction. English language series, revised edition (1991) and the Critical survey of long fiction. Foreign language series (1984)"—Publisher's note.

Includes bibliographical references and index.

ISBN 0-89356-886-4 (v. 4 : alk. paper) — ISBN 0-89356-882-1 (set : alk. paper)

1. Fiction—History and criticism. 2. Fiction—Bio-bibliography—Dictionaries. I. Rollyson, Carl E. (Carl Edmund) II. Magill, Frank Northen, 1907-1997.

PN3451.C75 2000
809.3—dc21

00-020195

First Printing

CONTENTS

Hijuelos, Oscar 1557	Knowles, John 1809
Himes, Chester 1561	Koestler, Arthur 1813
Hinojosa, Rolando 1565	Kosinski, Jerzy 1820
Hoagland, Edward 1569	Kundera, Milan 1828
Horgan, Paul 1574	
Howells, William Dean 1580	Lagerkvist, Pär 1836
Hudson, W. H. 1589	Lagerlöf, Selma 1844
Hugo, Victor 1595	L'Amour, Louis 1853
Hurston, Zora Neale 1605	Laurence, Margaret 1861
Huxley, Aldous 1612	Lawrence, D. H. 1868
	Le Carré, John 1889
Irving, John 1623	Lee, Harper 1900
	Le Fanu, Joseph Sheridan 1904
James, Henry 1636	Le Guin, Ursula K. 1911
James, P. D. 1648	Lehmann, Rosamond 1920
Jensen, Johannes V. 1655	Lem, Stanisław 1926
Jewett, Sarah Orne 1660	Leonard, Elmore 1937
Jhabvala, Ruth Prawer 1669	Lessing, Doris 1943
Johnson, Charles 1676	Levi, Primo 1952
Johnson, Samuel 1684	Lewis, C. S. 1956
Jolley, Elizabeth 1692	Lewis, Matthew Gregory 1964
Jones, James 1698	Lewis, Sinclair 1971
Joyce, James 1706	Lewis, Wyndham 1981
	Lispector, Clarice 1988
Kafka, Franz 1716	Lively, Penelope 1993
Kawabata, Yasunari 1724	Lodge, David 1997
Kazantzakis, Nikos 1731	London, Jack 2005
Kelley, William Melvin 1737	Lowry, Malcolm 2011
Kemal, Yashar 1742	Lurie, Alison 2021
Keneally, Thomas 1748	
Kennedy, William 1756	Macaulay, Rose 2030
Kerouac, Jack 1763	McCarthy, Cormac 2035
Kesey, Ken 1771	McCarthy, Mary 2040
Kincaid, Jamaica 1780	McCullers, Carson 2046
King, Stephen 1784	Macdonald, Ross 2054
Kingsolver, Barbara 1797	McElroy, Joseph 2062
Kipling, Rudyard 1802	McGinley, Patrick 2069

CRITICAL SURVEY
OF
LONG FICTION

OSCAR HIJUELOS

Born: New York, New York; August 24, 1951

PRINCIPAL LONG FICTION

Our House in the Last World, 1983
The Mambo Kings Play Songs of Love, 1989
The Fourteen Sisters of Emilio Montez O'Brien, 1993
Mr. Ives' Christmas, 1995
Empress of the Splendid Season, 1999

OTHER LITERARY FORMS

Although he produced several short stories, Oscar Hijuelos published only long fiction after his first book, *Our House in the Last World*, which developed from a story line written on scraps of paper as he worked as a clerk for an advertising agency.

ACHIEVEMENTS

Oscar Hijuelos attained a large audience after winning a 1990 Pulitzer Prize for his novel *The Mambo Kings Play Songs of Love*. Although Latino authors are often neglected by mainstream publishers and media, Hijuelos broke through ethnic barriers with his persistence, his style, and his Pulitzer Prize. On the strength of his first novel, Hijuelos received several grants from the National Endowment for the Arts, and the American Academy of Arts and Letters Rome Prize provided him with a stipend for living in Italy for a year of composition and reflection.

Through Hijuelos's observations, dark memories, and radiant storytelling, readers can appreciate Cuban immigrant culture. *The Mambo Kings Play Songs of Love* demonstrates the acceptance of Hispanic literature beyond the previous limited scope of small Latino presses. Critics labeled the book a breakthrough for Latino writers. Hijuelos challenges the reader to interpret the soft voices of an emerging literary culture.

BIOGRAPHY

The Hijuelos family hailed from the Oriente province of Cuba, home of entertainer Desi Arnaz and Cuban dictators Fulgencio Batista y Zaldívar and Fidel Castro—wild roots for the New York-born, iconoclastic author. At age four, Oscar and his mother Magdalena visited Cuba, and upon their return he developed nephritis, a critical-stage kidney inflammation. Bedridden, Oscar lingered in a children's hospital for two long years. This separation from family and language removed Oscar from Hispanic connections; the theme of separation would later saturate his novels.

Oscar's father Pascual drank heavily, leaving Magdalena to raise her children in a rough, lower-class neighborhood of New York. Hijuelos laments his youth, in which most fathers he knew were drunk, limousines came only for funerals, and "the working class hate[d] everyone else." He recalls the area where he played, caught between the affluence of the Columbia University campus and the habitat of muggers, thieves, and junkies of Morningside Park. Hijuelos hid from this hell by reading, watching television, and observing the traits of his family, as a partially sober father arose to cook at the Biltmore Hotel each day. Affection flooded the household, even with the dysfunction of poverty and neighborhood chaos. Forced to speak English outside his home, Hijuelos easily abandoned his Cuban tongue, although his parents expected Spanish discourse in the home. Thereby alienated, Hijuelos neglected thoughtful conversations with either parent, a theme which would recur in his work.

Frederick Tuten, director of City University of New York's creative writing program, remarked that this "intense writer" does not "create books from nothing; he's lived." Attending college while working, Hijuelos created his style and honed his skill by writing long responses to assignments, exaggerating the length to fulfill his personal need for expression. After receiving his M.A. in 1976 from the City University of New York, Oscar moved just a few blocks away from his humble childhood home to begin life as an author, supported by work as an inventory controller in an advertising agency.

Oscar Hijuelos is a mystery to some Latino writers because he chose to distance himself from their coterie. Hispanic writers must meet two differing sets

(Roberto Koch)

of standards: acceptance from the American reading public and from Latin American counterparts. With his works mostly devoid of political motives, Hijuelos has drawn criticism for not drawing sufficient attention to his Latin roots. Even with this controversy, Hijuelos was adopted by many as the voice of Latinos, the symbol of their culture in America.

ANALYSIS

Oscar Hijuelos represents a new generation of Cuban American writers. His Latino roots enrich his chronicles of the immigrant experience. Latino writers often face quandaries when choosing the language for their literary expression (Spanish or English), when committing to traditions of their descendants, and when chronicling immigrant life in their new world. Hijuelos balances the sensitivities of the American reader and the expectations of the Latino by presenting characters who, removed from the security of their Cuban homeland, are tossed into the diversity and adversity of big-city life; they survive and still bring grace to their daily existence. Hijuelos's two shorter novels, *Our House in the Last*

World, his autobiographical debut, and *Mr. Ives' Christmas*, an exploration of spirituality, provide balance to his long works. Proud of his heritage, yet conscious of the limited parameters of his youth, the author places his characters in situations that pronounce their independence but accept their assimilation into a new culture.

OUR HOUSE IN THE LAST WORLD

Our House in the Last World explores the questions of identity and perspective through the travails of the Santinio family, who are seeking fortune by moving from Cuba to New York City. The father, Alejo, expects the younger son, Héctor, to live a macho existence and to be "Cuban," while his mother, Mercedes, smothers him with her anxieties and loses her capability to develop her personality. Hijuelos offers two views of innocence: that of the wonder and confusion of a family facing a new life in an unknown world, and that of their children's bewilderment in a harsh environment.

The novel begins in the ticket office of a film house in Holguín, Cuba. Mercedes, twenty-seven, almost past the age of marriage, meets Alejo, who woos her, marries her, and moves her to New York, where they share an apartment with other Cubans who come and go. Some attain status and wealth, while the Santinios remain impoverished. Alejo becomes a sot, a gluttonous man who allows his sister to wage a harsh campaign against his wife. Mercedes transfers the memory of her father onto Alejo, and it is only after Alejo's death near the end of the novel that she is free to realize her dreams as her own.

The older son, Horatio, epitomizes the image of the man he thinks his mother demands. A womanizer and philanderer, he finally adopts a military lifestyle as an escape from fear of failure. Héctor contracts a near-fatal disease while on holiday in Cuba, and the months of hospitalization that follow embitter him toward the culture of his homeland and all things Cuban. Mercedes becomes unbearably overprotective, and his anxieties prevent him from reacting to the drunken excesses of his father and the hysteria of his mother. Castro has taken over Cuba during this time, and Mercedes and Alejo are disengaged from the lost world of their youth; New York will hold them until death.

Hijuelos embraces these characters with pure affection and gentleness, as he allows the relatives to flow through the Santinios' life. He describes their downslide from hope to resignation, from effort to insanity, and from love to harassment. Love does not conquer all, but it does provide a basis for life. The Santinios are a tribute to perseverance.

THE MAMBO KINGS PLAY SONGS OF LOVE

Oscar Hijuelos's life in the advertising agency had little to do with his passion for writing. When he first began thinking of the story that would become *The Mambo Kings Play Songs of Love*, he knew that an uncle and an elevator operator would be his models. The uncle, a musician with Xavier Cougat in the 1930's, and a building superintendent, patterned after an elevator operator and musician, merge to become Cesar Castillo, the Mambo King. Cesar's brother, Néstor, laconic, retrospective, lamenting the loss of a Latina lover he left behind in Cuba, writes a song in her memory that draws the attention of Desi Arnaz, who will change their life.

As the book opens, Cesar rots with his half-empty whiskey glass tipped at the television beaming old reruns; he seeks the *I Love Lucy* spot featuring him and Néstor as the Mambo Kings. Néstor has tragically died. Cesar pathetically reveals his aging process, the cirrhosis, the loss of flamboyant times. Cesar's old, scratchy records, black, brittle, and warped, resurrect his music stardom. He laments his brother's death by leafing through fading pictures.

In *The Mambo Kings Play Songs of Love*, Hijuelos presents pre-Castro Cubans, who, after World War II, streamed in torrents to New York, their experiences creating a historical perspective for future Third World immigration. All communities may strive for the American Dream, but in Latino quarters, music, the mainstream of a culture, sought to free the oppressed. The Castro brothers become, for a moment, cultural icons with their appearance on *I Love Lucy*. The fame short-lived, Cesar comforts his ego with debauchery, and Néstor dies ungracefully and suddenly. Ironically named, the Hotel Splendour is where Cesar commits suicide—in Cuban culture, a respectable ending to life. Latino culture encourages the machismo of men such as Cesar, and Hijuelos may be asking his countrymen to review that attitude.

THE FOURTEEN SISTERS OF EMILIO MONTEZ O'BRIEN

The Fourteen Sisters of Emilio Montez O'Brien again paints Hijuelos's theme of immigrant life in America, this time on the canvas of a small rural town. Family traditions pass down, hopes spring eternal, and sadness and attempts to assimilate fade as the book's characters meet disappointment and victories to varying degrees. Nelson O'Brien leaves Ireland, sister in tow, for the better life promised in America. Weakened by the journey and her general frailty, the sister dies, leaving Nelson to wander aimlessly, until he retreats to Cuba to take pictures of the Spanish-American War. He meets the sixteen-year-old Mariela Montez and courts her every Sunday for seven weeks. Seducing her with stories of his Pennsylvania farm and with her first sexual experiences, Nelson convinces her to marry and move to the farm, offering a telescope as a token of their future.

The Montez O'Brien household is fertile, and

fourteen magnetic sisters charge the home with a feminine aura. Finally, the lone son, Emilio, is born. Mostly told through the older daughter's eyes, the story portrays the ferocity of Nelson's ambition and character through the overbearing feminine mystique that surrounds his life, his decisions, and his focus on the future. Emilio, on the other hand, becomes a gentle soul who adores and is adored by his sisters. The sisters grow, many without mates, into expected positions in the world—entertainers, homekeepers, expectant mothers, recluses, gluttons—carrying the name and bravado of their father with them. Emilio attracts women and suffers the vanity of his charm and good looks, eventually becoming an actor in B-films. His drunken tendencies and a sordid affair with a pregnant teen turn his life sour. Scandalized, he lies in reclusiveness until finding his soulmate in an improbable café in an Alaskan fishing village. She dies before the novel's end, breaking Emilio's heart but allowing the sisters to provide him with solace. Hijuelos finishes the novel succinctly, with both realized tragedies and continuing dreams for the future.

MR. IVES' CHRISTMAS

Hijuelos somberly presents Mr. Ives, a character unlike the romanticized Cesar, the macho Mambo King. Mr. Edward Ives sensitively and sanely goes through his life with no malice toward fellow man or woman. He seeks those rewards he has become accustomed to earning, but one date, Christmas Eve, consistently seems to interfere with his life. A widowed print maker visits the orphan child Edward Ives on Christmas Eve and, a few Christmases later, adopts him. His adoptive father idyllically rears the dark-skinned child, inspires him to pursue his love for drawing, and eventually guides him to the Arts Student League, where he meets, on Christmas Eve, his future wife.

The picture-postcard family image is grotesquely distorted years later when, on Christmas Eve, the Iveses' seventeen-year-old son is gunned down as he leaves church choir practice. A fourteen-year-old Puerto Rican gunman kills the boy for ten dollars. Mr. Ives devotes his life to obsessive attempts to rehabilitate the murderer.

Symbolically, Mr. Ives's favorite book is a signed copy of Charles Dickens's *A Christmas Carol* (1843). Hijuelos strongly relies on this book to link the two tales. The author emulates Dickens's populous canvases and uses Dickens's love of coincidence and contrivance as a metaphor for God's mysterious workings. The temperance of Mr. Ives engenders his longing for grace, a gift for contemplation, and a world curiosity.

Hijuelos draws heavily on images from his New York neighborhood, his coterie of friends, and the milieu of gangs, muggers, and drug addicts at the end of his street. *Mr. Ives' Christmas* speaks of faith—a faith that mysteriously probes emotions, tested by death and the opportunity of forgiveness.

EMPRESS OF THE SPLENDID SEASON

In *Empress of the Splendid Season*, Lydia Espana is banished from her Cuban home by her father, a small-town alcalde, because she overstayed her allowed time at a dance with a young man. Disheartened, she makes her way to New York and in time marries and gains employment as a cleaning lady. In near poverty, she and her chronically ill husband, a waiter, attempt to maintain respectability and keep food on the table for their two children. Lydia resorts to fantasy as a coping mechanism, envisioning herself as the Empress of the Splendid Season, a poetic term of endearment used by her husband during the early days of their romance. Hijuelos describes Lydia's passage from privileged girlhood to a widowed old age through her relationships with family, friends, and employers. A wealthy employer sends her son to a prestigious university. He becomes a successful psychologist, but is unhappy and feels disconnected from the world. Lydia's daughter grows into a rebellious young woman who later marries an Anglo and moves to the suburbs. She chooses to rear Lydia's grandchildren far from her Cuban roots. Hijuelos again digs beneath the core of tenement life, bringing a magical mystique into his characters' lives through rich text and powerful prose.

Craig Gilbert

BIBLIOGRAPHY

Barbato, Joseph. "Latino Writers in the American Market." *Publishers Weekly* 238, no. 6 (February,

1991): 17-21. An accurate impression of Latino writers in the American market. Multiple interviews with thoughtful questions and answers.

Chávez, Lydia. "Cuban Riffs: Songs of Love." *Los Angeles Times Magazine* 112 (April, 1993): 22-28. An in-depth look at Hijuelos as a man and as a writer. Conversational style with serious revelations by this thought-provoking author.

Coffey, Michael. "Oscar Hijuelos." *Publishers Weekly* 236, no. 3 (July, 1989): 42-44. A down-to-earth discussion with the author that expands on his link to Cuba and his separation from the Cuban people.

Shirley, Paula W. "Reading Desi Arnaz in *The Mambo Kings Play Songs of Love*." *Melus* 20 (September, 1995): 69-78. An intriguing look at a fictional Desi Arnaz, relating his Cuban roots to the Castillo brothers in *The Mambo Kings Play Songs of Love*. The relationship offers some interesting comparisons between the real Arnaz and Hijuelos's fictional Cuban immigrants.

Silber, Joan. "Fiction in Review." *The Yale Review* 84, no. 4 (October, 1996): 151-157. Scholarly comparison of Hijuelos's *The Mambo Kings Play Songs of Love* to John Updike's *In the Beauty of the Lilies* (1996).

CHESTER HIMES

Born: Jefferson City, Missouri; July 29, 1909
Died: Moraira, Spain; November 12, 1984

PRINCIPAL LONG FICTION

If He Hollers Let Him Go, 1945
Lonely Crusade, 1947
Cast the First Stone, 1952 (unexpurgated edition pb. as *Yesterday Will Make You Cry*, 1998)
The Third Generation, 1954
The Primitive, 1955 (unexpurgated edition pb. as *The End of a Primitive*, 1997)
For Love of Imabelle, 1957 (revised as *A Rage in Harlem*, 1965)

Il pleut des coups durs, 1958 (*The Real Cool Killers*, 1959)
Couché dans le pain, 1959 (*The Crazy Kill*, 1959)
Dare-dare, 1959 (*Run Man, Run*, 1966)
Tout pour plaire, 1959 (*The Big Gold Dream*, 1960)
Imbroglio negro, 1960 (*All Shot Up*, 1960)
Ne nous énervons pas!, 1961 (*The Heat's On*, 1966; also pb. as *Come Back Charleston Blue*, 1974)
Pinktoes, 1961
Une affaire de viol, 1963 (*A Case of Rape*, 1980)
Retour en Afrique, 1964 (*Cotton Comes to Harlem*, 1965)
Blind Man with a Pistol, 1969 (also pb. as *Hot Day, Hot Night*, 1970)
Plan B, 1983

OTHER LITERARY FORMS

Chester Himes was primarily a writer of long fiction, but near the end of his life he published a revealing two-volume autobiography, which, if not wholly accurate about his life, nevertheless is engaging as a testament of survival of a black artist struggling to make his voice heard. Like many writers of his generation, Himes began publishing short fiction in the many periodicals of the time. As his life and career progressed—and the number of publishers declined—Himes worked less in the field. A posthumous collection of his short fiction was published in 1990. Finally, Himes also turned his hand to dramatic writing, both plays and film scripts, the most accessible of which is "Baby Sister," which was published in his book of miscellaneous writings, *Black on Black: "Baby Sister" and Selected Writings* (1973).

ACHIEVEMENTS

As the title of a biography of Chester Himes suggests, he led several lives during the seventy-five years of his troublesome career. He was the youngest son in a rising African American family, who worked his way into the middle class only to fall back again. Himes learned the craft of writing as an inmate in the Ohio correctional system, and after his release from prison he was a writer of angry and violent protest novels, which earned him a reputation as one of the more celebrated black writers in America.

Beginning in the mid-1950's Himes expatriated and became a tangential member of the community of black artists, which included Richard Wright and James Baldwin, who fled American racism to settle in Europe during the period after World War II. In his later years, he wrote a two-volume autobiography and a series of masterful crime novels, the "Harlem domestic" books. The second of the series, *The Real Cool Killers*, won in 1958 the prestigious Grand prix de la littérature policiére for best crime novel published in France. In all of his "lives" Himes struggled to come to grips with the racist American society into which he was born and to realize his place in that society as a black man and as an artist.

From the publication of his first novel, *If He Hollers Let Him Go*, Chester Himes confounded the critics, and they rarely understood his work. Was his fiction too violent or was it merely revealing the realities of American racism? Was Himes sexist or just reflecting the tensions inherent in a community where African American males were desperately searching for a sense of self? Did he compromise his art for the publishing world dominated by white editors when he wrote his Harlem domestic series, or were these hard-hitting yet more mainstream crime novels an extension of his more "artistic" but less popular protest novels? Was his autobiography merely a self-serving complaint against the slights against him or an uncompromising portrait of one black man's struggle for survival?

Perhaps it is because of the contradictions of his life that Chester Himes remains fascinating today, and it is through the mixed, often confused, responses to his work that he achieved his measure of importance, not just as a black writer but as an American writer, one who captured something of the truth of America and of its literature.

BIOGRAPHY

Chester Bomar Himes was the youngest of three sons of Joseph Sandy Himes and Estelle Bomar Himes. His father was a teacher of industrial arts and spent the years of Himes's youth as a faculty member at several black institutions predominantly in the South. By the time Himes was in his teens the family had settled in Cleveland, and after his graduation from Glenville High School he entered Ohio State University in the fall of 1926. However, his university career was short-lived, and at the end of the spring quarter, 1927, he was asked to leave because of poor grades and his participation in a speakeasy fight.

Back in Cleveland, Himes slipped into a life on the edges of the city's crime world. After several run-ins with the law he was caught for robbery, convicted, and sentenced to a lengthy term in the Ohio State Penitentiary. For the next seven-and-a-half years Himes served time, and in the enforced discipline of prison life he began to write fiction. His first publication, "His Last Day," appeared in *Abbott's Monthly* in November, 1932. Himes was paroled on April 1, 1936, and the next year he married Jean Johnson. After his prison experience Himes worked

(Library of Congress)

at a number of menial jobs while continuing to write.

On April 3, 1953, Himes embarked for Europe, and, except for several brief trips to the United States, he remained an exile for the rest of his life. During these years Himes's writing was devoted mainly to his Harlem detective series featuring Grave Digger Jones and Coffin Ed Johnson. Throughout his years in Europe Himes traveled extensively, finally settling in Alicante, Spain, with his second wife, Leslie Packard. In 1963 Himes suffered a stroke and in his later years experienced various health problems. He died on November 12, 1984, in Moraira, Spain.

ANALYSIS

In his review of *Lonely Crusade*, James Baldwin hit on the central theme of Himes's work: creating individual black characters who were many faceted and reflected the ambivalence of living in an American society full of contradictions and insecurities. Unfortunately Baldwin's grasp of the essence of Himes's fiction was not shared by all. Many of the reviewers of Himes's early "protest" fiction either criticized the violence of the books, apologized for it, or merely complained about what they saw as his awkwardness of style. Most reviews simply dismissed the books. Some acknowledged that Himes's portrait of American racism was accurate but deplored his lack of any constructive suggestions for its amelioration. Even when Himes received a certain measure of fame through the republication of his detective novels in the United States, the critical notices, with few exceptions, remained slight. After Himes's death, however, this changed. Himes's literary reputation in France undoubtedly affected his reception in the United States.

Himes once believed that in American letters there was room at the top for only one African American writer at a time, and therefore black writers were always competing against one another for that coveted spot. He felt that he always came in second, initially behind Richard Wright and then behind James Baldwin. Certainly this is no longer true (if it ever was). The proliferation of novels, drama, and poetry by such authors as Toni Morrison, Ernest J. Gaines,

Gloria Naylor, Derek Walcott, Maya Angelou, Alice Walker, and other black writers suggests that whatever constraints Himes felt as an exiled black writer seem to be loosening. Himes is now being accorded a place beside Wright, Baldwin, and Ralph Ellison, the novelists of his generation who opened the doors for African American writers to be accepted as full-fledged American writers, a part of the native grain.

IF HE HOLLERS LET HIM GO

In *If He Hollers Let Him Go* the central character, Bob Jones, is a black Everyman—as his name would suggest—who comes to represent the experience of all black males who find themselves thwarted while trying to live out their dreams. Jones is an African American who has moved to California to work in the defense plants during World War II. Here he experiences American racism in all its ugly insidiousness and spends the five days covered by the novel's narrative trying to escape the oppressions and humiliations society tries to impose on him. As an articulate man, with a few years of college, he is both better educated and more perceptive than the lower-class whites he works with in the aircraft plants. When he is elevated to the position of supervisor at work, he brings out the racism of his coworkers, who are jealous of his success. An altercation on the job, tensions with his white girlfriend, and finally the accusation of rape by a woman at work whose overtures he has rejected, convince Bob Jones that his hopes and dreams will not come true even in Los Angeles, where he thought he would be rid of the racist attitudes of his native South. After his arrest a judge strips him of his military deferment, and as the novel ends he is being sent off to join the army.

Himes's first published novel provides the basic themes he would pursue not only in his protest books but also in his crime fiction. In the course of the novel Himes explores the issues of race, class, and sexual positioning and demonstrates how Bob Jones, despite his best efforts, remains trapped within a historically determined social role as a black man trying simply to earn a living, gain some personal respect, and find love. At every turn he finds himself prevented from fulfilling the most basic of American rights and aspirations.

THE PRIMITIVE

The narrative of *The Primitive* focuses on writer Jesse Robinson and his relationship with his white girlfriend, Kriss Cummings. Again in this novel Himes uses a contained time scheme, covering only a few days in the lives of his central characters. After a chance meeting with an old acquaintance, Kriss, Jesse experiences a rapidly accelerating series of seriocomic episodes, which propel him to the novel's conclusion: In an alcoholic fog he stabs Kriss to death in her Gramercy Park apartment. The novel alternates between following Kriss's life and Jesse's thoughts as he tries, in vain, to examine his feelings about his relationship with a white woman and what she stands for in his world, as well as his growing sense of himself as a writer trying to come to grips with his experience as an African American living in a racist culture that will give him recognition as neither an artist nor a man.

The Primitive is often described as one of Himes's "confessional" novels, fiction in which he examines themes that had plagued him since the publication of *If He Hollers Let Him Go*: the rejection he felt as a writer and the obsession with white women often experienced by black men. As critics have pointed out, obsession with white women is a constant theme in Himes's writing and represents attraction, repulsion, and, because of the taboo of miscegenation, long a central anxiety of white Americans, the fear of death and social rejection. Rather than merely striking out against white society, Jesse murders Kriss out of self-hatred for his own desires to join that society, moving the murder beyond the blind killing of Bigger Thomas in Richard Wright's *Native Son* (1940). In the end, Jesse, although still a rejected author, discovers that he has the skills of a fine writer who can put into words his feelings about the conditions of his life.

COTTON COMES TO HARLEM

Cotton Comes to Harlem begins in Harlem at a "back to Africa" rally sponsored by the Reverend Deke O'Malley, who is fraudulently bilking his gullible followers. The rally is interrupted by a gang of thieves who steal the raised money and hide it in a bale of cotton, which they lose on their escape. Into this plot come two African American detectives, Grave Digger Jones and Coffin Ed Johnson, two of the toughest policemen in New York. The rest of the novel involves their attempts to recover the loot, expose the fraud, and make amends to the local residents. The ending of the novel provides an ironic twist, as a poor, old man who found the bale does go to Africa to live out the dream promised by the Reverend O'Malley at the novel's opening.

Cotton Comes to Harlem is one a series of crime novels set in New York's Harlem and featuring two African American detectives, a series Himes called his Harlem domestic books. The series began when his French publisher Marcel Duhamel contracted him to write a novel for Gallimard's La Série Noire, a notable series of crime fiction published in France. In these novels Himes concentrates as much on the social, political, and economic conditions of the people of Harlem as he does on the solving of crimes. As Himes carefully explores the racism inherent in American culture, he chronicles the world of his characters sympathetically, and without becoming didactic he demonstrates the harmful effects of almost four hundred years of oppression and exploitation of African Americans.

Charles L. P. Silet

OTHER MAJOR WORKS

SHORT FICTION: *The Collected Stories of Chester Himes*, 1990.

NONFICTION: *The Quality of Hurt: The Autobiography of Chester Himes, Volume I*, 1972; *My Life of Absurdity: The Autobiography of Chester Himes, Volume II*, 1976.

MISCELLANEOUS: *Black on Black: "Baby Sister" and Selected Writings*, 1973.

BIBLIOGRAPHY

Fabre, Michel, and Robert Skinner, eds. *Conversations with Chester Himes*. Jackson: University Press of Mississippi, 1995. This collection of interviews with Himes provides information about his life and work.

Fabre, Michel, Robert E. Skinner, and Lester Sullivan, comps. *Chester Himes: An Annotated Pri-

mary and Secondary Bibliography. Westport, Conn.: Greenwood Press, 1992. This is a comprehensive annotated bibliography of writings by and about Himes.

Lundquist, James. *Chester Himes.* New York: Frederick Ungar, 1976. Lundquist's short book is an excellent introduction to Himes's work, but it does not contain critical assessments of his writing past the 1970's.

Margolies, Edward, and Michel Fabre. *The Several Lives of Chester Himes.* Jackson: University Press of Mississippi, 1997. This full-length biography of Himes is indispensable for information about his life.

Milliken, Stephen F. *Chester Himes: A Critical Appraisal.* Columbia: University of Missouri Press, 1976. Milliken's study contains the most detailed analysis of Himes's non-crime fiction.

Muller, Gilbert H. *Chester Himes.* Boston: Twayne, 1989. A good, short introduction to Himes which comprises more material than Lundquist's book.

Skinner, Robert E. *Two Guns from Harlem: The Detective Fiction of Chester Himes.* Bowling Green, Ohio: Bowling Green State University Popular Press, 1989. Skinner's study of Himes's crime writing presents a comprehensive examination of his crime novels.

ROLANDO HINOJOSA

Born: Mercedes, Texas; January 21, 1929

PRINCIPAL LONG FICTION

Estampas del valle y otras obras/Sketches of the Valley and Other Works, 1973 (English revision, *The Valley,* 1983)

Klail City y sus alrededores, 1976 (*Klail City: A Novel,* 1987)

Mi querido Rafa, 1981 (*Dear Rafe,* 1985)

Rites and Witnesses, 1982

Partners in Crime: A Rafe Buenrostro Mystery, 1985

Claros varones de Belken, 1986 (*Fair Gentlemen of Belken County,* 1986)

Becky and Her Friends, 1990

The Useless Servants, 1993

Ask a Policeman, 1998

OTHER LITERARY FORMS

Rolando Hinojosa is known primarily for his long fiction in both English and Spanish. He has also written "verse novels," such as *Korean Love Songs from Klail City Death Trip* (1978; printed 1980). Hinojosa produced the book *Agricultural Workers of the Rio Grande and Rio Bravo Valleys* in 1984.

ACHIEVEMENTS

After the death of Tomás Rivera in 1984, Rolando Hinojosa became considered the dean of Mexican American belles lettres and selflessly advanced Mexican American literature throughout the United States, Latin America, and Europe. His works have been translated into German, French, Italian, English, and Spanish, and they have been anthologized by numerous presses. He has received many accolades, including the Premio Quinto Sol award in 1972, the Casa de las Américas Prize in 1976, and the Lon Tinkle Award for Lifetime Achievement from the Texas Institute of Letters in 1998. He has lectured and read from his work widely and has had several Ph.D. dissertations and master's theses written about his works. His distinctively concise literary style, in English and Spanish (or a combination of the two), is marked by irony, satire, stark realism, and a cutting wit. While his works are often quite experimental, Hinojosa has masterfully incorporated various genres into his novels, including sketches, reportage, poetry, and murder mysteries. Among all Mexican American authors, he is arguably the most accomplished and versatile.

BIOGRAPHY

Rolando Hinojosa was born in the Lower Rio Grande Valley of South Texas to mixed ethnic parents. On his Mexican Texan father's side, he descended from the first Spanish Mexican land-grant settlers, who settled the region in 1749. On his mother's side were Anglo-Texan settlers who arrived in South Texas in 1887. He studied English and Spanish in Texan and Mexican schools. He was therefore raised to be both bilingual and bicultural in a family fostering a rich reading environment with literature from both sides of the U.S.-Mexican border and the Atlantic. This family background influenced his future literary and cultural interests.

At seventeen, he enlisted in the U.S. army, and after serving his time he entered the University of Texas at Austin under the G.I. Bill. His education would be interrupted by the Korean War, however. After his tour of duty in Korea, he returned to Austin and in 1953 received his B.S. degree in Spanish literature. He then married, had a son, taught high school, and worked at several other jobs; he later divorced. After completing an M.A. in Spanish literature at New Mexico Highlands University in 1962, he remarried and entered a doctoral program in 1963 at the University of Illinois, Urbana. There he received a Ph.D. in 1969 in Spanish literature, writing his dissertation on the Spanish writer Benito Pérez Galdós.

Hinojosa then began his college teaching career at Trinity University in San Antonio, Texas. In 1970, he taught Spanish at Texas A&I University in Kingsville, Texas, where he later served as chair of the Spanish Department, dean of the College of Arts and Sciences in 1974, and vice president of academic affairs in 1976. His wife's decision to enter law school caused them to move to the University of Minnesota, where he chaired a Chicano studies program and taught creative writing as an English professor. In 1981 he returned to the University of Texas at Austin as a professor of English, teaching Chicano literature, literature of the Southwest, and creative writing. In 1986 he became Ellen Clayton Garwood Chair of the English department. His second wife divorced him in 1988, after raising two daughters with him. His son from his previous marriage, a graduate of the U.S. Naval Academy at Annapolis, made him a proud grandfather after the birth of a son in 1993.

ANALYSIS

Beginning in 1970, Hinojosa published fiction, nonfiction, and poetry, primarily in small Mexican American presses and journals. His major work comprises a series of short novels which he entitled The Klail City Death Trip series, after publishing *Korean Love Songs from Klail City Death Trip*, which he referred to as a novel in verse form. The Klail City Death Trip series is distinguished by Hinojosa's having published several novels in both Spanish and English. The series as of 1999 constituted nine serial works.

The different language renditions do not always represent the same narrative. Significant differences between the two versions of the same novel exist in the narrative sequence of chapters, with some chapters deleted, others added, and others rearranged. Thus, both language editions should be read for a comprehensive and more accurate understanding of The Klail City Death Trip series. Some novels, moreover, suffer from egregious publishing errors, due to Arte Público Press failing to copyedit texts before going to press, with large passages repeated and other significant passages completely left out.

The works in the series were not published in strict chronological order. *Fair Gentlemen of Belken County*, for instance, was written prior to *Dear Rafe* but was published one year after.

THE VALLEY

With *The Valley*, Hinojosa begins his serial project by introducing a host of characters, some of whom are extensively developed in succeeding novels. This novel is made up of four loosely connected sections of sketches which give readers a wide sense of the character of the Mexican Texan people inhabiting the fictional Belken County in "The Valley," the area north of the Mexican border in south Texas. Here, the people of various towns are shown at home, in their communities, carrying on with their daily lives. Two cousins, Jehú Malacara and Rafe Buenrostro, are introduced for the first time, characters whose lives are examined in greater detail in later novels. Both characters are orphans, with Jehú being raised by various people unrelated to him, while Rafe and his brothers are raised by their uncle Julian.

KLAIL CITY

Klail City continues with the same format and purpose as *The Valley*, with three sections of sketches. Hinojosa continues to develop his two main characters' lives, but with this novel, he develops a theme that permeates the entire series: the historical conflict between Anglo-Texans and Mexican Texans over the land and the laws governing their lives. In this novel, readers are informed of the cause of Rafe's father's death, murder by a member of a rival Mexican American clan, the Leguizamóns. While Jesús Buenrostro's murder is avenged by his brother Julian, the clans' animosity toward each other remains undiminished as The Klail City Death Trip series progresses. Also introduced in this novel is a greater conflict, the Korean War, which will later affect the main characters' lives, especially Rafe's.

THE USELESS SERVANTS

The Useless Servants, in prose, extensively shows Rafe's day-to-day life in the war. The masterfully written realism of the battlefield makes both *Korean Love Songs from Klail City Death Trip* and *The Useless Servants* extraordinary testaments to the horror and senselessness of war. One fact that does not escape Rafe and other Mexican Texan soldiers in Korea, however, is that even while defending their country, they are still subjected to racism by their Anglo-American counterparts.

DEAR RAFE

Dear Rafe jumps ahead in the serial narrative and portrays Jehú as a principal, though elliptical, character. Incorporating the epistolary and reportage genres, Hinojosa provides multiple perspectives from which readers see the financial, real estate, and political maneuvers enhancing the Anglo-American power structure, as represented by the Klail, Blanchard, Cook (KBC) clan. Employed as a loan officer in a Klail City bank owned by the most powerful Anglo-Texan family in the Valley, Jehú apprentices under bank president Noddy Perkins. Through liaisons Jehú has with three women, he works the system to his clan's advantage by covertly acquiring lands that would otherwise fall into the hands of the rivaling Leguizamón clan or the KBC clan.

In the first half of the novel, readers gain an understanding of the events by reading a series of letters written by Jehú to Rafe, who is interned in a veterans hospital for problems arising from wounds suffered in Korea. In the second half, readers are shown a series of interviews conducted with more than a dozen primary and secondary characters by P. Galindo, who has access to Jehú's letters. The novel's main action involves Noddy backing a Mexican Texan, Ira Escobar, against an Anglo-Texan for county commissioner, something the Anglo-American power structure had never done before. As the action progresses, Jehú comes to understand that Ira has been backed for political office because he is an easily manipulated puppet. More important, Noddy brings Ira's Anglo-Texan opponent, Roger Terry, to his knees to control him, through a political ruse, as the Valley's new U.S. congressman, which was Noddy's intention all along. Jehú, however, leaves the bank, disgusted with how local politics are run, apparently causing P. Galindo to conduct his interviews. Jehú returns to the bank three years later, as is revealed in *Partners in Crime*.

RITES AND WITNESSES

This novel's action precedes that of *Dear Rafe* and fills in gaps in the lives of both Rafe and Jehú, incorporating reportage, letters, and sketches, with chapters alternating between action in Korea and events foreshadowing *Dear Rafe*. Noddy Perkins approaches Jehú to run for county commissioner, but Jehú is wise enough to refuse the offer, causing Noddy to recruit Ira Escobar later.

PARTNERS IN CRIME

With *Partners in Crime* Hinojosa changes direction by writing a murder mystery. A lieutenant in Belken County's homicide squad, Rafe, with his squad, investigates and solves gang-land killings related to drug-running in the Valley. No longer a place where adverse race relations dominate, the Valley's economy has become corrupted by Mexican drug dealers' laundered money. The cooperation of law-enforcement agencies on both sides of the border becomes the focus of The Klail City Death Trip series. In this novel the head of the Mexican law-enforcement agency, Lisandro Solís, is responsible for the killings and the drug-running. In the end he escapes persecution but reappears in *Ask a Policeman*.

FAIR GENTLEMEN OF BELKEN COUNTY

Written before *Dear Rafe* but not published until

1986, this novel of longer sketches continues filling gaps in Rafe and Jehú's lives after their return from Korea. The texture of the Valley's Mexican Texan culture is brilliantly shown in this novel. While the life of the prominent Mexican Texan elder, Esteban Echevarría, ends, his legacy and wisdom are preserved and honored by Rafe and Jehú.

BECKY AND HER FRIENDS

Using reportage, like the second half of *Dear Rafe*, *Becky and Her Friends* provides more than two dozen interviews with various people associated with Becky Escobar, who, by her marriage to Ira, is kin to the rival Leguizamón clan. At the beginning of the novel, Becky throws out her husband Ira and asks him for a divorce. They divorce, and as the interviews progress, readers learn the circumstances surrounding her astounding transformation from an utterly anglicized and naïve Mexican Texan to a Mexicanized and independent woman. She is then employed as a business manager by Viola Barragán, a wealthy and successful Mexican Texan businesswoman who figures prominently in previous novels. Under Viola's guidance, Becky asserts her independence and marries Jehú, with whom she had an affair during the political campaigns in *Dear Rafe*. Readers also learn that Rafe has married Noddy Perkins's daughter Sammie Jo, thus cementing, through these two marriages, a resolution between formerly rivaling clans. More important, lands formerly split by these rivaling clans are reunited.

ASK A POLICEMAN

In *Ask a Policeman*, another murder mystery, Rafe has been promoted to chief inspector of the Belken County homicide squad. He and his squad again solve drug-related gangland killings, including the murder of Lisandro Solís, who escaped prosecution for his part in the drug-running and killings depicted in *Partners in Crime*. This time, the chief law-enforcement officer on the Mexican side, María Luisa (Lu) Cetina, contributes to the successful apprehension of the guilty parties, which include Lisandro's brother and Lisandro's twin sons, as well as Canadian and Central American assassins.

Jaime Armin Mejía

OTHER MAJOR WORKS

POETRY: *Korean Love Songs from Klail City Death Trip*, 1978 (printed 1980; includes some prose).

EDITED TEXTS: *Tomás Rivera, 1935-1984: The Man and His Work*, 1988 (with Gary D. Keller and Vernon E. Lattin).

MISCELLANEOUS: *Generaciones, Notas, y Brechas/ Generations, Notes, and Trails*, 1978; *Agricultural Workers of the Rio Grande and Rio Bravo Valleys*, 1984.

BIBLIOGRAPHY

Hernandez, Guillermo E. *Chicano Satire: A Study in Literary Culture*. Austin: University of Texas Press, 1991. This work explores how satire figures into the works of three Chicanos: Luis Miguel Valdez, José Montoya, and Rolando Hinojosa. It provides insights into The Klail City Death Trip series, but only some of the books.

Lee, Joyce Glover. *Rolando Hinojosa and the American Dream*. Denton: University of North Texas Press, 1997. A good book-length work in English on Hinojosa's works. Attempts to bring a biographical and psychological analysis to The Klail City Death Trip series.

Saldívar, José David, ed. *The Rolando Hinojosa Reader: Essays Historical and Critical*. Houston: Arte Publico Press, 1985. This work contains essays by Hinojosa and by a small number of scholars treating Hinojosa's works. Shows how early scholars analyzed The Klail City Death Trip series.

Saldívar, Ramón. *Chicano Narrative: The Dialectics of Difference*. Madison: University of Wisconsin Press, 1990. One of the most important works of Chicano literary criticism, this book contains a chapter treating *Korean Love Songs from Klail City Death Trip* and The Klail City Death Trip series. Saldivar's analysis covers many of the most significant Chicano literary texts.

EDWARD HOAGLAND

Born: New York, New York; December 21, 1932

PRINCIPAL LONG FICTION
Cat Man, 1956
The Circle Home, 1960
The Peacock's Tail, 1965
Seven Rivers West, 1986

OTHER LITERARY FORMS

Edward Hoagland is known primarily not for his novels but for his essays and travel books. As an essayist and reviewer, he has been published in such periodicals as *Harper's, The Village Voice, Sports Illustrated, Commentary*, and *The Atlantic Monthly*; several anthologies of his essays are now in print. His travel narratives include *Notes from the Century Before: A Journal from British Columbia* (1969) and *African Calliope: A Journey to the Sudan* (1979). During the 1960's he also wrote short stories, which appeared in publications such as *Esquire, The New Yorker, New American Review*, and *The Paris Review*; three of his short stories have been republished in *City Tales* (1986). A collection of three of his short stories, *The Final Fate of the Alligators: Stories from the City* (1992), received favorable reviews. Hoagland is the editor of the twenty-nine-volume Penguin Nature Library. He also writes book reviews and nature-based editorials for *The New York Times*.

ACHIEVEMENTS

With the publication of his first novel, *Cat Man*, in 1956, Hoagland received much favorable attention from the critics. The book won for Hoagland a Houghton Mifflin Literary Fellowship, and critics saw in him the makings of a first-rate novelist. They particularly praised his ability to capture a milieu—in this case, the seamy world of circus roustabouts, a world he presents with knowledgeable and detailed frankness. His second novel, *The Circle Home*,

(Library of Congress)

confirmed his potential. Once again, he succeeded in vividly re-creating a colorful environment, the sweaty world of a boxing gymnasium. He received several honors during this period as well, including a Longview Foundation Award in 1961, an American Academy of Arts and Letters Traveling Fellowship in 1964, and a Guggenheim Fellowship in 1964.

Hoagland received another Guggenheim in 1975 and was a nominee for the 1979 National Book Critics Circle Award for the travel book *African Calliope*. In 1971 he received an O. Henry Award and in 1972 a literary citation from the Brandeis University Creative Arts Awards Commission. He received the Harold D. Vursell Award of the American Academy of Arts and Letters in 1981, and he was elected to membership in the Academy in 1982.

With the publication of *The Peacock's Tail* in 1965, Hoagland's fiction career suffered a setback. In both the critics' and his own opinion, this book was a failure, and Hoagland, whose novels had never won for him a wide audience, turned away from long fiction. For the next twenty years, he worked primarily in nonfiction, producing essays and travel narratives to considerable acclaim. In 1986, he made a triumphal return to the novel. *Seven Rivers West* was well received, combining as it does Hoagland's ability to re-create a sense of place—here, the North American wilderness—with his impressive knowledge of the natural world.

BIOGRAPHY

Edward Hoagland was born on December 21, 1932, in New York City. His father was a financial lawyer whose employers included Standard Oil of New Jersey and the United States defense and state departments. When he was eight, his family moved to New Canaan, Connecticut, a fashionable community of country estates and exclusive clubs. He was sent off to boarding school at Deerfield Academy, where, because of his bookishness, he was assigned to a special corridor known as the Zoo, which was reserved for those whom the school deemed incorrigible misfits. Hoagland did have great difficulty fitting in as a child. In large part this was because of his stutter. Understandably, he shunned potentially embarrassing social situations, developing a love of solitude and wildlife instead. Indeed, from the age of ten onward, he became very close to nature and kept a variety of pets ranging from dogs to alligators.

He went to Harvard, where he was strongly drawn to writing, a medium in which he could speak unhampered by his stutter. He studied literature under such notables as Alfred Kazin, Archibald MacLeish, and John Berryman; encouraged by his professors, he set to work on his first novel. In his spare time he read Socialist publications and attended meetings of a Trotskyite cell in the theater district of Boston. He graduated from Harvard cum laude in 1954 with his first novel already accepted by Houghton Mifflin.

Hoagland had to put his literary career on hold, however, when he was drafted. He served in the army from 1955 to 1957, working in the medical laboratory and looking after the morgue at Valley Forge Army Hospital in Pennsylvania. Following his dis-

charge, Hoagland returned to New York City. Financially, times were very difficult. His father, who disapproved of his decision to become a writer, had cut him off. In fact, his father was so opposed to his son's career that he wrote to Houghton Mifflin's lawyer to try to stop publication of his first novel. Hoagland's annual income over the next fifteen years averaged three thousand dollars.

In 1960, his second novel was published and he married Amy Ferrara, from whom he was divorced in 1964. At about this time he also became active politically, marching in civil rights and peace demonstrations and mailing his draft card to President Lyndon Johnson. To supplement his income, he began accepting academic posts as well, teaching at such schools as Rutgers, Sarah Lawrence, the University of Iowa, and Columbia. In 1968, he married Marion Magid, the managing editor of *Commentary*, with whom he has a daughter, Molly.

For many years Hoagland lived in New York City but spent several months of each year in upper Vermont. He also traveled to diverse areas such as Yemen and the Alaskan and Canadian wilderness. He and Magid were divorced in 1993. Hoagland began teaching at Bennington College and dividing his time between Bennington and Barton, Vermont, where he lived several months of the year in an eight-room farmhouse, without electricity or telephone lines. The property adjoins an eight-thousand-acre state forest to which Hoagland has willed most of his land. Hoagland suffered blindness in the late 1990's but had his sight restored through surgery; however, it was feared that the condition might recur. Although Hoagland was essentially disinherited by his father, he was able to make a living from writing and teaching.

ANALYSIS

Edward Hoagland's novels are marked by a keen eye for detail and a remarkable sense of place. They masterfully re-create unusual and often male-dominated environments, such as that of the circus or a boxing gymnasium. His protagonists tend to be isolated and lonely men, cut off through their own actions from those they love, men who generally have failed in their relationships with women. They are misfits, drifters, or dreamers, and the novels are often organized around their journeys, which may be merely flight, as in *The Circle Home*, or a clearly focused quest, as in *Seven Rivers West*. Because of this episodic structure, the books have a looseness that can approach the discursive at times, with flashbacks and digressions slowing the pace.

CAT MAN

Many of these traits are already apparent in Hoagland's first work, *Cat Man*. Drawn from his own experience working in a circus, *Cat Man* offers a graphic and harrowing portrayal of the life of the low-paid circus roustabouts, most of whom are derelicts or social outcasts. With his usual attraction to the eccentric and offbeat, Hoagland creates a human menagerie, a gallery of grotesques such as Dogwash, who will not touch water and cleans himself by wiping his whole body as hard as he can with paper. The novel presents a brutal world in which violence threatens constantly from both the workers and the animals. In fact, the book begins with an attempted murder and ends with a lion attack. It is also a world of rampant racism, a world in which the insane are to be laughed at and women sexually used and abandoned. As sordid and disturbing as all this is, Hoagland conveys it with remarkable vividness and attention to detail. Indeed, it is the searing portrayal of this world that is the novel's great strength.

Fiddler, the main character, is a classic Hoagland protagonist. A youth who has been with the circus only seven weeks, he has been cut off from his family by his alcoholism and is very much an alienated man. Suffering from low self-esteem, he develops a foolhardy and almost obsessive fascination with the beauty and grace of his charges, the lions and tigers that it is his job, as a cat man, to tend. Hoagland's own interest in and knowledge of animals is quite evident, as he endows the cats with as much individuality as the humans. Yet while Hoagland is clearly as fascinated as Fiddler with the animals, he never sentimentalizes them. The cats may be magnificent but they can also be uncaring and deadly, a lesson that Fiddler finally and fatally learns.

Also typical of Hoagland's novels is the fact that

Cat Man has a loose structure. Ostensibly, it is the story of one tragic day in Council Bluffs, but interspersed throughout the narrative are the events of other days in other places as Fiddler travels cross-country with the circus. Many of these episodes could stand on their own as quite good short stories, but inserted as they are within the novel's main narrative they interrupt the momentum and slow the book's flow.

THE CIRCLE HOME

Hoagland's second novel, *The Circle Home*, once again features a main character who is a lonely misfit. In this work, the protagonist is an over-the-hill boxer who rightly fears that he is doomed to become a derelict like his father. Again, too, he is a man who, through his own actions, is alienated from his family. Denny Kelly, though, is a less sympathetic figure than Fiddler. He has been so abusive toward his wife, Patsy, that she has repeatedly thrown him out. In fact, Denny seems incapable of committing himself to another person and simply takes advantage of women such as his wife or Margaret, an older woman whom he exploits for whatever material and sexual comforts she can supply.

Essentially, Denny is an immature child (indeed, he is strongly attracted to children), with all the selfishness and irresponsibility that that implies. Moreover, he avoids serious introspection whenever possible and actively fights any inclination toward thought by drowning himself in sensual pleasures. If Hoagland presents animals with considerable understanding in *Cat Man*, in *The Circle Home* he focuses on an individual who exists on little more than an animal level. Denny is a man who is incapable of expressing his feelings or organizing his life, who responds simply to the need for food, shelter, and sex.

If Fiddler clung to the cats in an attempt to give his life meaning, the one element in Denny's life that gives him a sense of achievement is boxing. The novel examines his fate once that is lost to him. Completely demoralized by being brutally beaten in a training bout, Denny abandons the ring and takes to the road, drifting closer and closer to his feared future as a derelict. While the ending of *Cat Man* was utterly bleak, *The Circle Home* offers some hope:

In hitting rock bottom, Denny gains some degree of self-awareness. Although his future is far from certain, Denny does at least attempt to overcome his irresponsibility and selfishness as he tries to reconcile with his wife. He has made "the circle home," returning via a long and circuitous route of self-discovery.

Critics were generally enthusiastic about *The Circle Home*, praising in particular its convincing portrayal of the grimy world of the Better Champions' Gym. If *Cat Man* showed Hoagland's detailed knowledge of the circus, this novel shows his thorough familiarity with boxing, as he digresses on such subjects as types of fighters and gym equipment. The book's structure, however, is again quite loose, with repeated shifts in time and place and the use of an episodic journey as an organizing principle.

THE PEACOCK'S TAIL

In Hoagland's third novel, however, the problems are more than simply structural. Regarded by the critics as his weakest piece of long fiction, *The Peacock's Tail* is the rambling story of Ben Pringle, a prejudiced and maladjusted WASP who has taken up residence in a seedy New York City hotel. As usual, Hoagland's main character is a misfit isolated from those he loves. Like Denny, Ben has difficulty maintaining a lasting relationship with a woman and has just been rejected by his lover, an experience that has left him with a badly damaged ego. Indeed, like the earlier protagonists, Ben in his troubled state needs stability and support. While Fiddler clung to his cats and Denny to boxing to retain some sense of pride and avoid a total collapse, Ben turns to children, becoming a storyteller and pied piper to the hordes of youngsters who inhabit his hotel.

If Denny was attracted to children, who mirrored his own arrested development, Ben seems to turn to them out of an inability to deal with adults, using their approval to boost his crumbling sense of self-worth. Powerless and out of control with his peers, he derives a sense of power and control from the adulation of the young. Hoagland apparently intends for the reader to believe that Ben finds happiness and fulfillment leading hundreds of children through the streets of New York to the strains of his newly ac-

quired harmonica. Yet Ben's newfound role as pied piper seems less a solution to his problems than a frenzied attempt to escape them.

Once one doubts the validity of Ben's solution, however, one is also forced to question the reality of the novel's setting. While the faithful depiction of milieu was the great strength of Hoagland's earlier novels, *The Peacock's Tail* takes place in an Upper West Side welfare hotel, which is presented as if it were one large amusement park. The hotel is inhabited by vibrant, lusty blacks and Hispanics who exude an earthiness and enthusiasm that is apparently meant to balance Ben's Waspish reserve and alienation. The earlier novels portrayed their environments with a hard-edged and knowledgeable use of detail. Here the portrait is sentimentalized, a musical-comedy version of a welfare hotel.

SEVEN RIVERS WEST

This artistic and critical failure represented a setback for Hoagland's promising novelistic career, and he followed it with a twenty-year hiatus from long fiction. With his fourth novel, however, Hoagland fully redeemed himself. *Seven Rivers West* is an entertaining and dazzlingly inventive tale. Set in the North American West of the 1880's, it features the most likable incarnation of the Hoagland protagonist: Cecil Roop. Another man isolated from his loved ones, he, like Denny, has abandoned his family and is now on a journey. Yet while Denny drifted aimlessly, Cecil is on a quest: He wants to capture a grizzly bear. At least, that is his goal until he learns of the existence of Bigfoot, which then becomes his obsession. Like Fiddler's obsession with cats, however, Cecil's fascination with this mysterious creature ultimately proves tragic.

If this sounds like a tall tale, Hoagland grounds it in an utterly convincing reality, presented with documentary exactness. In fact, the novel includes a wealth of information about nature. Yet this information emerges spontaneously as the characters seek to understand their magnificent and overwhelming environment; the pace never slows as the book vigorously follows the characters' picaresque and perilous journey. Moreover, the novel includes Hoagland's most colorful assortment of eccentrics, ranging from

Cecil's companion who specializes in jumping forty feet into a tub of water to a trader celebrated for his prowess in bladder-voiding competitions.

Probably the book's greatest achievement, however, as in Hoagland's first two novels, is its stunning and detailed sense of place. The unsentimental portrayal of the unspoiled West is at times rhapsodic as Hoagland presents a world that can chill with its beauty. Hoagland depicts not only the full glory but also the full fury of nature. He offers the reader a world that is as casually violent as that of *Cat Man*, a world where creatures can almost without warning be swept away in torrents or mauled by savage beasts. With its energy, its imaginativeness, and its sheer grandeur, *Seven Rivers West* is Hoagland at his best.

Hoagland's novels, published over a period of thirty years, have a number of traits in common. One is their focus on and sympathy for the downcast and outcast, for the social misfit who finds himself alone as he journeys through a hostile and dangerous world in which his mere survival is tenuous. Isolation is a constant theme, with the protagonists having great difficulty maintaining relationships with women. Yet as harsh and as lonely as these environments are, Hoagland's ability to describe them with honesty and fidelity gives his books a vividness and immediacy that leaves a lasting impact.

Charles Trainor, updated by Margaret A. Dodson

OTHER MAJOR WORKS

SHORT FICTION: *City Tales*, 1986; *The Final Fate of the Alligators: Stories from the City*, 1992.

NONFICTION: *Notes from the Century Before: A Journal from British Columbia*, 1969; *The Courage of Turtles: Fifteen Essays About Compassion, Pain, and Love*, 1970; *Walking the Dead Diamond River*, 1973; *The Moose on the Wall: Field Notes from the Vermont Wilderness*, 1974; *Red Wolves and Black Bears*, 1976; *African Calliope: A Journey to the Sudan*, 1979; *The Tugman's Passage*, 1982; *Balancing Acts: Essays*, 1992; *Tigers and Ice: Essays on Life and Nature*, 1999.

EDITED TEXTS: *The Edward Hoagland Reader*, 1979; *Heart's Desire*, 1988.

BIBLIOGRAPHY

Ehrlich, Gretel. "An Essayist's Search for Bedrock." *Los Angeles Times Book Review*, April 30, 1995, 3-9. A review of Hoagland's *African Calliope*, *The Tugman's Passage*, and *Red Wolves and Black Bears*, occasioned by their 1995 reissue by Lyons & Burford. Discusses the lasting quality of Hoagland's personal perspective and style in his essays.

Hall, Donald. "Hoagland Was There." Review of *The Edward Hoagland Reader* and *African Calliope*, by Edward Hoagland. *National Review* 32 (May 30, 1980): 669-670. Refuses to call *African Calliope* a travel book, describing it as a fact-piece like the work of John McPhee. Hoagland is basically an autobiographer who writes of himself even when he seems to be writing about the world at large; however, he has the ability to make readers feel that they are there in the scene described. In his style of enthusiasm for daily existence, Hoagland creates exciting experiences of improvisation and speculation.

Hicks, Granville. "The Many Faces of Failure." *Saturday Review* 48 (August 14, 1965): 21-22. Many novels seem to consider adjustment to society disgraceful and misfits both admirable and pathetic. Hoagland wrote of misfits in *Cat Man* and *The Circle Home* and approaches the same subject, though differently, in *The Peacock's Tail*. The hero in this novel is from a more proper background than the circus of the *Cat Man* or the boxing world of *The Circle Home*, but his experience of unemployed drifting is in the end not very substantial. Hoagland creates splendid scenes for the novel, but the narrative is not a significant experience.

Johnson, Ronald L. Review of *Seven Rivers West*, by Edward Hoagland. *Western American Literature* 22 (November, 1987): 227-228. *Seven Rivers West*, a fictional tale after several nonfiction books, reads like a travel guide through the Canadian Rockies in 1887. It is lavish in its physical detail, with a loving response to mountain landscapes and the animals inhabiting them. Its most impressive feature is this response—which, consequently, renders the narrative about the meeting with Bigfoot less than memorable. On the other hand, the episodes of crossing a flooded river and meeting American Indians are exciting and provide much good-humored entertainment.

Mills, Nicolaus. "A Rural Life Style." *The Yale Review* 60 (June, 1971): 609-613. Looks at *The Courage of Turtles* as an expression of the rural movement in American writing. Compares Hoagland's book with those by Raymond Mungo and Helen and Scott Nearing, deciding that the city is essential to Hoagland's view of the country, providing distance and allowing him to see the comic weaknesses as well as the sober virtues of country life. He notices what others miss about rural life: that it can be uncomfortable, angry, and in need of political organization. He also shows that it is ironically inaccessible to the very people who need it the most—those who have had to move from the country to the city because they could not afford their rural lifestyle.

Sagalyn, Raphael. Review of *The Edward Hoagland Reader* and *African Calliope*, by Edward Hoagland. *The New Republic* 181 (December 19, 1979): 30-31. Claims that Hoagland has become a master of the personal essay because he has not been writing much fiction. Praises Hoagland's style and argues that he deserves a wider audience. Hoagland likes to create heroes in his short prose and stories such as Sugar Hart in "Heart's Desire" or Henri Le Mothe in the story by that name. *African Calliope* is described as an apparently disjointed travel book which becomes clearer as its people come alive and discoveries are made while journeying through the Sudan.

Updike, John. "Back to Nature." *The New Yorker* 63 (March 30, 1987): 120-124. Compares Hoagland with Elizabeth Marshall, also of the Harvard-Radcliffe class of 1954, as writers seeking rapport with animals in faraway places, writing with a refreshing sense of wonder at life in the outdoors. The focus is on *Seven Rivers West*, which Updike praises for its detailed information about frontier life. While there is much visual material, there is less sound and feeling in the novel, and the heroes' motives are not as exciting as those of the

hero in *Cat Man*. In the pursuit of Bigfoot, Updike finds an invitation to compare it with the quest for Moby Dick, and pronounces Hoagland significant in the company of the American nineteenth century Transcendentalists.

_____. "Journeyers." *The New Yorker* 56 (March 10, 1980): 150-159. *The Edward Hoagland Reader* is examined in the context of its preceding novel, *Cat Man*, and compared with other travel books of the time. Hoagland is interested in lonely places and remote terrains but can find them in the back corners of New York City as well as in the deserts of Africa. Hoagland, like Henry David Thoreau, wrote in a modest tone with a cosmic perspective; however, Hoagland sometimes forgets to be entertaining, as when he expresses the grimness of life while describing his own self-testing in *African Calliope*, a work which does not provide clarity or the comfort of understanding the journey's meaning.

PAUL HORGAN

Born: Buffalo, New York; August 1, 1903
Died: Middletown, Connecticut; March 8, 1995

PRINCIPAL LONG FICTION
The Fault of Angels, 1933
No Quarter Given, 1935
Main Line West, 1936
A Lamp on the Plains, 1937
Far from Cibola, 1938
The Habit of Empire, 1938
The Common Heart, 1942
The Devil in the Desert: A Legend of Life and Death in the Rio Grande, 1952
The Saintmaker's Christmas Eve, 1955
Give Me Possession, 1957
A Distant Trumpet, 1960
Mountain Standard Time, 1962 (includes *Main Line West*, *Far from Cibola*, and *The Common Heart*)

Things as They Are, 1964
Memories of the Future, 1966
Everything to Live For, 1968
Whitewater, 1970
The Thin Mountain Air, 1977
Mexico Bay, 1982

OTHER LITERARY FORMS

Throughout his long and meritorious career, Paul Horgan was known as widely for his short fiction and nonfiction as for his novels. Most of his short fiction is found in three collections, but the best of his stories appear in *The Peach Stone: Stories from Four Decades* (1967). Like his fiction, Horgan's histories and biographies revolve around events and people of the American Southwest. His most prestigious history is *Great River: The Rio Grande in North American History* (1954), but *The Centuries of Santa Fe* (1956) and *Conquistadors in North American History* (1963) are also important works. His biographies, most notably *Lamy of Santa Fé: His Life and Times* (1975) and *Josiah Gregg and His Visions of the Early West* (1979), vividly chronicle the struggle of individuals and the clash of Spanish and American Indian cultures on the southwestern frontier. Horgan's work in drama includes the play *Yours, A. Lincoln* (1942) and the libretto to *A Tree on the Plains: A Music Play for Americans* (1943), an American folk opera with music by Ernst Bacon. His *Approaches to Writing* (1973) is composed of three long essays explaining his craft. Horgan's novel *A Distant Trumpet* was filmed in 1964; *Things as They Are* was filmed in 1970.

ACHIEVEMENTS

As a novelist as well as a distinguished writer of nonfiction, Horgan devoted his career to the American Southwest. Although he is regarded as a regionalist, some critics have rightly pointed out that he uses regional figures and settings essentially as vehicles for universal themes, much as William Faulkner used regional materials. Horgan's work should not be identified with the popular, formulaic Western writing of such authors as Zane Grey, Louis L'Amour, and Max Brand; rather, he should be seen as a signifi-

cant figure in the tradition of literary Western fiction that has attracted the attention of critics and readers since the early 1960's.

Recognition for his writing came in many forms. He won seventy-five hundred dollars in the Harper Prize Novel Contest for *The Fault of Angels* in 1933. He was awarded two Guggenheim Fellowships (one in 1945, the other in 1958) to work on his nonfiction. For *Great River*, Horgan won the Pulitzer Prize in History and the Bancroft Prize of Columbia University. In 1957, the Campion Award for eminent service to Catholic letters was presented to him. The Western Literature Association paid tribute to Horgan with its distinguished Achievement Award (1973), and the Western Writers of America cited him with their Silver Spur Award (1976). He was twice honored by the Texas Institute of Letters (in 1954 and in 1971).

Just as important as these awards, and an indication of the wide range of his interests and abilities,

(National Archives)

are the ways in which he served his community and country. Horgan served as president of the board of the Santa Fe Opera (1958-1962) and the Roswell Museum (1946-1952). He became director of the Wesleyan Center for Advanced Studies in 1962 and remained so until 1967. President Lyndon B. Johnson made Horgan one of his first appointees to the Council of the National Endowment for the Humanities. In addition to being visiting scholar and writer-in-residence at a number of colleges and universities, Horgan served on the board of the Aspen Institute and the Book of the Month Club. Although some of his novels have sold in the millions and despite his long career, Horgan was not as well known as many of his contemporaries. Those who are familiar with his work, however, see him as a prescient figure, a writer whose concern with the complex, multicultural history of the Southwest anticipated the challenging revisionism of the 1970's and the 1980's, when scholars and fiction writers alike offered a new, critical look at the West.

BIOGRAPHY

Paul Horgan was born in Buffalo, New York, on August 1, 1903. He moved to Albuquerque, New Mexico, with his parents in 1915 and attended the New Mexico Military Institute in Roswell until 1921, when he left to be at home when his father was dying. After working for a year at the Albuquerque *Morning Journal*, he moved to the East in 1923 to study at the Eastman School of Music in Rochester, New York. He returned to Roswell in 1926 and accepted the job of librarian at the New Mexico Military Institute. He remained in Roswell until 1942 and wrote his first five novels. Horgan spent World War II in Washington, D.C., as chief of the Army Information Branch of the Information and Education Division of the War Department, where he supervised all the information that was sent to American troops all over the world. Horgan returned to New Mexico after the war and worked on his nonfiction, but after 1960 he became associated with Wesleyan University in different capacities, living and writing on the Wesleyan campus. He died in Middletown, Connecticut, in March of 1995.

ANALYSIS

Paul Horgan's fiction is dominated on one level by a skillful, aesthetic evocation of southwestern landscape and climate and a sensitive delineation of character. His novels are exceptionally well written, with sharp detail and imagery often matched by a lyrical tone perfectly suited to the basic goodness of his protagonists. Yet to dwell on this strong sense of place is to miss a basic theme in his works and to misjudge the appeal of his writing. The strength of Horgan's fiction lies in the reader's immediate and sympathetic identification with the protagonists. Curiosity is perhaps man's most distinguishing feature. This is true not only in an academic sense but in a personal way as well: To varying degrees, people take an interest in their ancestry and family histories. They want to know who they are and whence they come. It is both a peculiarity and a trademark of Horgan's fiction that this kind of knowing is its constant concern. The dramatic center in Horgan's books revolves around people learning the truth about themselves and their lives.

Horgan employs two main narrative strategies to accomplish his end. In books such as *Far from Cibola* and *A Distant Trumpet*, individuals must deal with an unexpected event upsetting the routine of everyday life and, as a result, are challenged to define their own lives more clearly. On the other hand, in novels such as *Things as They Are* and *Whitewater*, his protagonists conduct a more conscious search for an understanding of who they are and make a deliberate attempt to come to terms with their own pasts.

FAR FROM CIBOLA

Often in Horgan's fiction, discovering the truth about oneself occurs after some startling event disrupts the ordinary flow of life. Such is the case in *Far from Cibola*, which many critics regard as Horgan's best novel. This short work, set in and around a small town in New Mexico during the early years of the Great Depression, records what happens to a dozen of the local inhabitants during a day in which they are all briefly brought together as part of a large crowd protesting economic conditions. After the crowd threatens to turn into an unruly mob, the sheriff fires a warning shot above their heads into some trees and accidentally kills a teenager who had climbed up the tree to watch the excitement. The crowd disperses after the gunfire, and the remaining chapters describe what happens to the dozen characters the rest of the day. Although these figures span a broad band of the socioeconomic spectrum of the New Mexican (and American) landscape of the 1930's, *Far from Cibola* is not simply another proletarian novel of that decade. Economic problems and hardships are uppermost in the minds of almost everyone in the story, but the fate of each character hinges on his or her ability to recognize and accept reality as it suddenly appears.

The opening chapter provides a good example of what happens to all the characters in the novel. It begins with serene, pastoral images: Mountains are shimmering in the morning haze, and smoke from breakfast fires rises straight into the clear April sky. In Ellen Rood's kitchen, there is a springlike feeling of peace and well-being. As she lays wood for her own stove, Ellen listens to the sounds of her two small children out in the farmyard. Her son Donald is chopping at some wood with an ax that is too big for his hands, and her daughter Lena is washing her face from a tin dish sitting on the edge of the well. Without warning, however, smoke rolls back into her eyes and sparks sting her arms when Ellen attempts to start the fire. At about the same time, Ellen realizes that her children are strangely quiet. When she investigates, she discovers a huge rattlesnake nearby; she quickly hacks it to death before it can harm her children. There are many scenes such as this one in *Far from Cibola*, in which people suddenly have an idyllic world overturned by a more sober, often harsher reality. How they react is a good measure of their character. Not everyone can prevail as Ellen does.

The incident in the courthouse provides a social context for what happens to the novel's individuals. Until the crowd becomes violent, everything is fairly calm and orderly. There may be hunger and economic desperation in the community, but people have not yet fully faced the fact that there are no hidden food supplies and the government cannot help them. The killing underscores this bleak reality, and society as a whole must deal with this truth, as Ellen had to face the rattlesnake outside her kitchen door.

A DISTANT TRUMPET

A Distant Trumpet, written more than two decades later, shows thematic concerns similar to those of *Far from Cibola*, but Horgan achieves them in a slightly different manner. The novel's primary setting is Fort Delivery, a frontier outpost near the Mexican border in the Arizona Territory during the late 1880's. Although there are a number of characters, the story centers on a young army lieutenant named Matthew Hazard and an Apache scout called Joe Dummy. Deftly and incisively, Horgan dramatizes Hazard's and Joe Dummy's roles in helping to make peace with a rebellious band of American Indians who had escaped into Mexico, and the novel ends with Hazard, bitter and disillusioned, resigning from the army when Joe Dummy is treated no better than the Indians he helped to defeat.

Rather than using startling and often violent images, as in *Far from Cibola*, Horgan makes extensive use of flashbacks to the Civil War period and earlier as a useful device for pulling down and digging out illusion and sham and seeing the truth clearly. That Matthew Hazard is Horgan's vehicle for showing the necessity not only of recognizing but also of maintaining self-knowledge is brought out in a very short section titled "Scenes from Early Times." Consisting of a series of short questions and answers between Hazard and an unknown person, the conversation reveals the earliest and most important knowledge Matthew can recall: that he was his father's child. Indeed, it is no accident that this book often reads like a biography. To be one's father's child in *A Distant Trumpet* means being able to acknowledge the less well-known aspects of self as well as the more openly accepted parts. Tragedy occurs when individuals cannot or will not see that darker side.

One of the more striking scenes in the novel occurs when Matthew, on his way to Fort Delivery for the first time, meets White Horn. Sergeant Blickner, who has come to take Matthew to the fort, refuses to take an Indian along in his wagon, and Matthew must give him a direct order to do so. Even after this, Blickner baits White Horn on the way back and calls him "Joe Dummy," a nickname picked up later by soldiers at the fort. In previous sections, however,

White Horn's courageous and often heroic life has been described at length, so that he has become an individual to the reader. Thus, readers share the narrator's feeling of outrage and indignation that no one at the fort can see Joe Dummy as anything but another "grimy" Indian. Horgan laments bitterly the failure of these people to see clearly and suggests that they will be lost until they somehow discover the truth about themselves and their social structure. In this sense, Fort Delivery becomes an ironic name for an individual's self-imprisonment. Horgan's flashbacks in *A Distant Trumpet* force his readers to look beyond appearance and not accept the false and commonplace, in much the same way the rattlesnake and courthouse incident in *Far from Cibola* made people confront the unpleasant realities in their lives. *A Distant Trumpet* poignantly reveals what happens when individuals (and society) are unable to see worlds other than their own.

THINGS AS THEY ARE

In *Things as They Are*, perhaps the most autobiographical of all of his works, Horgan approaches the question of knowing oneself more directly. The novel is narrated by Richard, an adult writer who recounts certain events in his early childhood to help him understand the way he is now. Horgan continues Richard's story in two later novels: *Everything to Live For* and *The Thin Mountain Air*. *Things as They Are*, then, is a *Bildungsroman*, a story of growth and awakening, and through this format, Richard articulates his need to understand himself and others more clearly.

Like most stories about growing up, the boy Richard undergoes a variety of experiences that the adult Richard must then interpret if he is to make some sense of his life. Although he describes a close family life and happy summer trips to the mountains, Richard also discloses certain important conflicts and tensions for the young boy: an uncle who commits suicide, an autocratic grandfather, a well-meaning but overly protective mother, a father who is not quite strong enough. The novel's structure in its simplest terms is a delicate balancing act between Richard's honestly depicting these family tensions and then explaining both what they meant to him and how they resulted in his seeing things as they are.

WHITEWATER

Things as They Are may be regarded as a prelude to *Whitewater*, which is also about a young man, Phillipson Durham, growing up. Set in the West Texas town of Belvedere during the years 1948-1949, the novel describes what happens to Phillipson and two high school classmates (Billy Breedlove and Marilee Underwood) during his senior year. Within this framework, the novel is essentially one long flashback by a much older Phillipson, who has written it, as the last chapter makes clear, for much the same reason Richard told his story in *Things as They Are*. Phillipson is probing for clues in his past that will allow him to understand the events of his senior year and what has happened to him since. Phillipson's search is less successful than Richard's and his conclusions more tentative.

Phillipson's quest for self-knowledge is marked by three central images in the novel: Lake Whitewater, Victoria Cochran's house, and the town's water tower. Lake Whitewater is a large, man-made lake formed when Whitewater Dam went into operation. What intrigues Phillipson is that deep under the lake's surface lies an abandoned town complete with houses, yards, and streetlamps. Billy informs Phillipson that when the lake is calm, the town can still be seen. The lake and submerged town thus become a metaphor for Phillipson's own lost knowledge about himself. Like the town, his past is still there, waiting to be viewed and understood if only he can see it clearly. Linked with this image is Crystal Wells, the home of Victoria Cochran, an elderly widow who befriends Phillipson and becomes his mentor. At Crystal Wells, Phillipson escapes the dreary provincialism of Belvedere and explores his own ideas and beliefs. It becomes an intellectual oasis where he can begin to define his own life. Opposed to this image is that of Belvedere's water tower, which Horgan unmistakably identifies with unthinking and impulsive behavior. Caught up in the excitement of springtime and the end of his senior year, Billy Breedlove climbs to the top of the tower to paint the words "Beat Orpha City" on its side. He loses his footing, however, and falls ninety feet to the ground below. Billy's death and Marilee's subsequent suicide are warnings to

Phillipson that impulse and feeling by themselves threaten understanding and growth. Phillipson overcomes his grief at Crystal Wells and recognizes that his own education is only beginning. As the last section of *Whitewater* suggests, however, Phillipson years later is still growing, still trying to understand those events and himself, quite aware that there are things that he cannot and perhaps will never know completely. Nevertheless, as Richard does in *Things as They Are*, Phillipson focuses on maintaining moments of wakeful insight.

Horgan's novels are best understood by recognizing that his protagonists are driven by a need to know themselves and their pasts. Given this theme, Horgan uses two main narrative techniques. On the one hand, as in *Far from Cibola* and *A Distant Trumpet*, his characters are confronted with events suddenly disrupting their lives and their normal sense of things. In novels such as *Things as They Are* and *Whitewater*, however, his protagonists deliberately set about exploring their pasts to learn about themselves. Horgan's message is the same with either method: The truth about oneself must be pursued, no matter what the cost. Anything else is escapism, a kind of vicarious participation in life.

Terry L. Hansen

OTHER MAJOR WORKS

SHORT FICTION: *The Return of the Weed*, 1936; *Figures in a Landscape*, 1940; *The Peach Stone: Stories from Four Decades*, 1967.

PLAYS: *Yours, A. Lincoln*, pr. 1942; *A Tree on the Plains: A Music Play for Americans*, pb. 1943 (libretto; music by Ernst Bacon).

POETRY: *Lamb of God*, 1927; *Songs After Lincoln*, 1965; *The Clerihews of Paul Horgan*, 1985.

NONFICTION: *New Mexico's Own Chronicle*, 1937 (with Maurice G. Fulton); *Great River: The Rio Grande in North American History*, 1954; *The Centuries of Santa Fe*, 1956; *Rome Eternal*, 1959; *A Citizen of New Salem*, 1961; *Conquistadors in North American History*, 1963; *Peter Hurd: A Portrait Sketch from Life*, 1965; *The Heroic Triad: Essays in the Social Energies of Three Southwestern Cultures*, 1970; *Encounters with Stravinsky: A Personal Rec-*

ord, 1972; *Approaches to Writing*, 1973; *Lamy of Santa Fé: His Life and Times*, 1975; *Josiah Gregg and His Visions of the Early West*, 1979; *A Writer's Eye*, 1988; *A Certain Climate: Essays on History, Arts, and Letters*, 1988; *A Writer's Eye: Field Notes and Watercolors*, 1988; *Tracings: A Book of Partial Portraits*, 1993; *Henriette Wyeth: The Artifice of Blue Light*, 1994.

CHILDREN'S LITERATURE: *Men of Arms*, 1931.

BIBLIOGRAPHY

Erisman, Fred. "Western Regional Writers and the Uses of Place." *Journal of the West* 19 (1980): 36-44. Reprinted in *The American Literary West*, edited by Richard W. Etulain. Manhattan, Kans.: Sunflower University Press, 1980. Placing Horgan in the company of Willa Cather, John Steinbeck, and John Graves, this article presents Horgan's writings as among those which meet the challenge of Ralph Waldo Emerson for artists to use the most American of materials, the experience of the West. These writers make strong use of the visual sense of specific place but transcend the limitations of local-color writers by putting the subjectivity of human experience at the center of their visions, making place secondary. All pursue themes of human individuality developed through nature, and Horgan shows this development in the context of Indian and Spanish cultures.

Gish, Robert. *Nueva Granada: Paul Horgan and the Southwest*. College Station: Texas A & M Press, 1995. Contains short commentaries on Horgan's work and, more important, two illuminating interviews with the author.

_____. "Paul Horgan." In *A Literary History of the American West*. Fort Worth: Texas Christian University Press, 1987. Horgan receives a chapter in this important book of literary scholarship which assesses his place in American literary history as attached to the materials of Southwest regionalism, but often lifted above their limitations by his skill. His life took him from East to West, providing him with a personal model for understanding the settlement of the Southwest, and his experience in a New Mexico military academy was also an important influence. His writings are listed chronologically as to his life experiences, and a few are singled out for commentary as examples of his style, subjects, and themes. Contains a selected bibliography of primary and secondary sources.

_____. *Paul Horgan.* Boston: Twayne, 1983. Horgan's writing is not merely regionalist, but moves from East to West and back again. Chapter 2 surveys his novels with chronological sections paraphrasing the plots for each, dividing them into those written before World War II and those after. Chapter 3 is pressed to cover the great amount of shorter fiction, novellas and short stories obscurely published in magazines such as *Ladies' Home Journal* in the 1930's, classifying them regionally, with subdivisions for historical and present settings, as Southwest, Far West, or Northeast. Chapter 4 presents Horgan as a humanist historian in the biographical mode in *Great River* and *Lamy of Santa Fé* and the last chapter analyzes his essays and speeches for humanist aesthetic principles. Includes a chronology, notes and references, a selected, annotated bibliography, and an index.

Kraft, James. "No Quarter Given: An Essay on Paul Horgan." *Southwestern Historical Quarterly* 80 (July, 1976): 1-32. Represents the pattern of Horgan's life movements as a special twentieth century American phenomenon—the possibility for a creative life in the United States. He studied American Indians of the Southwest in preparation for writing *Great River*, from which he took material for *The Heroic Triad*, an excellent source for studying the three cultures of the Southwest: Indian, Spanish, and Roman Catholic. Horgan is both a writer and a painter, but also a public servant without fear of the tragic or the brutal in life. His work and his life are affirmed through the creative process.

Pilkington, William T. "Paul Horgan." In *My Blood's Country: Studies in Southwestern Literature*. Fort Worth: Texas Christian University Press, 1973. Although Horgan has been a prolific writer in a variety of forms, his best work reveals an understanding of human desires and disappointments as expressed in the concrete details of lived experi-

ence. Besides Christian values, his writing expresses features of Ralph Waldo Emerson's transcendental philosophy. Analyzes many of Horgan's books, beginning with *The Fault of Angels* and ending with *A Distant Trumpet*. Horgan's stylistic faults are outweighed by his skill in presenting believable human beings as characters with vitality.

WILLIAM DEAN HOWELLS

Born: Martin's Ferry, Ohio; March 1, 1837
Died: New York, New York; May 11, 1920

PRINCIPAL LONG FICTION
Their Wedding Journey, 1872
A Chance Acquaintance, 1873
A Foregone Conclusion, 1875
The Lady of Aroostook, 1879
The Undiscovered Country, 1880
Doctor Breen's Practice, 1881
A Modern Instance, 1882
A Woman's Reason, 1883
The Rise of Silas Lapham, 1885
Indian Summer, 1886
The Minister's Charge: Or, The Apprenticeship of Lemuel Barker, 1887
April Hopes, 1887
Annie Kilburn, 1888
A Hazard of New Fortunes, 1889
The Shadow of a Dream, 1890
An Imperative Duty, 1891
The Quality of Mercy, 1892
The World of Chance, 1893
The Coast of Bohemia, 1893
A Traveler from Altruria, 1894
The Day of Their Wedding, 1896
A Parting and a Meeting, 1896
An Open-Eyed Conspiracy: An Idyl of Saratoga, 1897
The Landlord at Lion's Head, 1897
The Story of a Play, 1898

Ragged Lady, 1899

Their Silver Wedding Journey, 1899

The Kentons, 1902

The Son of Royal Langbirth, 1904

Miss Bellard's Inspiration, 1905

Through the Eye of the Needle, 1907

Fennel and Rue, 1908

New Leaf Mills, 1913

The Leatherwood God, 1916

The Vacation of the Kelwyns, 1920

Mrs. Farrell, 1921

OTHER LITERARY FORMS

William Dean Howells was unquestionably one of the most versatile and productive writers of the nineteenth century. In addition to approximately forty novels, Howells produced several volumes of short fiction, among them *A Fearful Responsibility and Other Stories* (1881) and *Christmas Every Day and Other Stories Told for Children* (1893). He also wrote more than thirty dramas, including *The Parlor Car* (1876), *The Mouse-Trap and Other Farces* (1889), and *Parting Friends* (1911), which generally were designed to be read aloud rather than performed. In addition, one of Howells's earliest and most enduring passions was the writing of poetry. His first published collection was *Poems of Two Friends* (1860, with John J. Piatt); nearly fifty years later, he published *The Mother and the Father* (1909). The genre which first brought him to public attention was travel literature, including *Venetian Life* (1866) and *Italian Journeys* (1867); other volumes continued to appear throughout his career. Howells also continues to be renowned as a perceptive critic and literary historian. Still of literary value are *Criticism and Fiction* (1891), *My Literary Passions* (1895), *Literature and Life* (1902), and *My Mark Twain* (1910). In addition, a substantial number of Howells's critical essays appeared in *Harper's* magazine from 1886 to 1892, and between 1900 until his death in 1920. Finally, Howells wrote biographies such as *Lives and Speeches of Abraham Lincoln and Hannibal Hamlin* (1860), as well as several autobiographical works, including *My Year in a Log Cabin* (1893) and *Years of My Youth* (1916).

ACHIEVEMENTS

Howells is remembered today as an important early exponent of realism in fiction. Reacting against the highly "sentimental' novels of his day, Howells—both in his own fiction and in his criticism—advocated less reliance on love-oriented stories with formulaic plots and characters, and more interest in emphasizing real people, situations, and behavior. This is not to say that Howells shared the naturalists' interest in sex, low-life, and violence, for in fact he was quite reserved in his dealings with these aspects of life. He did, however, acknowledge their existence, and in so doing paved the way for Theodore Dreiser, Stephen Crane, and the modern realistic novel. Inspired by his reading of European literature (notably Leo Tolstoy), Howells also argued that fiction could be a tool for social reform. Finally, in his influential positions at *The Atlantic Monthly* and *Harper's*, Howells was able to offer help and encouragement to rising young American authors, including Crane and Henry James.

Howells's later years were full of recognition: He received an honorary Litt. D. from Yale University (1901), as well as from Oxford (1904) and Columbia (1905); he received the L.H.D. from Princeton in 1912. He was elected first president of the American Academy of Arts and Letters in 1908, and seven years later he received the Academy's gold medal for fiction.

BIOGRAPHY

Although early in his career he was accepted into the charmed literary circles of Boston and New York, William Dean Howells was born and reared in the Midwest, and he never fully lost touch with his midwestern background. He was born on March 1, 1837, in Martin's Ferry (then Martinsville), Ohio, the second of eight children. His early life was singularly unstable: Because his father was something of a political radical whose principles jeopardized the prosperity of every newspaper with which he was associated, the family was periodically compelled to move away from one conservative Ohio village after another. Despite such instability, Howells found the variety of experiences enriching and was able to make

(Library of Congress)

the most of the spotty formal education he received. His exposure to the written word came at an early age: When Howells was only three, his father moved the little family to Hamilton, Ohio, where he had acquired a local newspaper, the *Intelligencer*; by the age of six, the precocious William was setting type in his father's printing office, and not long after that he began to compose poems and brief sketches. In 1850, the family made one of their more fortunate moves by establishing themselves in a one-room log cabin in the utopian community at Eureka Mills near Xenia, Ohio. It was a welcome interlude in the family's struggle to find a political, economic, and social niche which would satisfy the father, and Howells would remember it fondly much later in *My Year in a Log Cabin*. The next move was to Columbus, where young Howells acquired a position as a compositor on the *Ohio State Journal*. Already beginning to diversify his literary endeavors, the fourteen-year-old Howells was also writing poetry in the manner of Alexander Pope.

In 1852, Howells's father bought a share in the Ashtabula *Sentinel* and moved it to Jefferson, Ohio.

For once, his principles did not clash with those of the community: The little newspaper was a success, and it was to remain in the Howells family for forty years. While living in Jefferson, a community composed largely of well-educated transplanted New Englanders, the teenaged Howells embarked on a plan of intensive self-education which included studies of Pope, Oliver Goldsmith, Oliver Wendell Holmes, Edgar Allan Poe, and Heinrich Heine. As much as this program compromised his social life, Howells derived enormous intellectual benefits from it, and several of the townspeople of Jefferson even offered to help finance a Harvard education for this gifted lad; his father declined the offer, however, and Howells remained at Jefferson, publishing his stories pseudonymously beginning in 1853.

As his father gradually rose in Ohio state politics (he was elected clerk of the House of Representatives in 1855), Howells rose with him, and in 1857 he was offered a permanent position as a correspondent on the Cincinnati *Gazette*. Howells, not yet twenty years old, was too emotionally dependent upon his family and too much of a hypochondriac to stay more than a few weeks at the *Gazette*, but when in the following year he received another opportunity in journalism, this time from the *Ohio State Journal*, he was able to accept the offer from his previous employer and to succeed. In addition to his duties as a reporter and editor, Howells found time to write sketches and verse, and some of his writings appeared in *The Atlantic Monthly*, the prestigious Boston-based journal of which he was to become editor-in-chief many years later.

The year 1860 was the most significant one of his life: He met Elinor Mead of Brattleboro, Vermont, whom he would marry two years later in Paris; he published his first book, *Poems of Two Friends*, coauthored with John J. Piatt; and—at the urging of the volume's Cincinnati publisher, Frank Foster—Howells prepared a campaign biography of Abraham Lincoln. Although assembled out of information Howells had gleaned from printed sources rather than from Lincoln himself, and written in only a few weeks, the book proved to be a moving and inspiring account of his fellow midwesterner. With its royalties, the resourceful and ambitious Howells financed a trip to America's two literary meccas, Boston and New York, where he arranged to meet some of the most important writers and editors of the day, and he returned to Ohio confirmed in his desire to pursue a career in literature.

Following the outbreak of the Civil War, Howells—temperamentally ill-suited to army life—decided to seek a foreign diplomatic post. Cashing in on the success of his popular Lincoln biography, the twenty-four-year-old Howells managed to be appointed as the United States Consul at Venice, a pleasant and remunerative position he held for four years. Howells was able to draw on his Italian experiences in a series of travel essays which were collected in book form as *Venetian Life* and *Italian Journeys*. When he returned to the United States in the summer of 1865, he was sufficiently established as a writer to be able to embark on a freelance writing career in New York. After a brief stint at the newly founded *The Nation*, Howells was lured to Boston and a subeditorship at *The Atlantic Monthly* under James T. Fields; after five years he became editor-in-chief (1871-1881). By the age of thirty, Howells was already a prominent member of Boston's literati. He received an honorary M.A. from Harvard in 1867 and was forging friendships with such literary figures as Henry James (whom he met in 1866) and Samuel Clemens, destined to become a lifelong friend.

At about that time (the late 1860's) Howells came to accept the fact that there was no market for his poetry; so, while he continued to write travel literature, he began to prepare descriptive sketches which would evolve rapidly into the literary form to which he was particularly well suited: the novel. The first product of this transitional period was *Their Wedding Journey*, which was serialized in *The Atlantic Monthly* in 1871 and published in book form in 1872. *Their Wedding Journey*, which manages to straddle both travel literature and fiction, features Basil and Isabel March (based upon William and Elinor Howells), characters who would recur throughout Howells's fiction, most notably in *A Hazard of New Fortunes*. After *Their Wedding Journey*, Howells produced novels with almost machinelike speed and reg-

ularity. *A Chance Acquaintance* is a psychological romance which served to demythologize the idea of the "proper Bostonian" that Howells had so admired in his youth; *A Foregone Conclusion*, in which a young American girl clashes with traditional European society, anticipates James's *Daisy Miller* by three years; two "international novels" which contrast American and Italian values and lifestyles are *The Lady of Aroostook* and *A Fearful Responsibility and Other Stories*; *The Undiscovered Country* probes spiritualism and the Shakers; *Doctor Breen's Practice* is the social and psychological study of a woman physician.

In 1881, Howells found himself caught in the dissolution of his publisher's partnership, Osgood and Houghton, so he left *The Atlantic Monthly* and began to serialize stories in the *Century* magazine. During this period, Howells began to focus increasingly on ethical problems, and in the 1880's he produced in rapid succession the novels which are generally held to be his greatest achievements in fiction. In 1882, *A Modern Instance* appeared, the so-called "divorce novel" which is now regarded as Howells's first major work in long fiction. During its composition, he suffered a breakdown, in part the result of the worsening health of his daughter Winny, who would die only a few years later at the age of twenty-six. An extended trip to Italy proved disappointing, but it enabled Howells to recover sufficiently to write another major novel, *The Rise of Silas Lapham*, followed immediately by the book he enjoyed writing most, *Indian Summer*. As a comedy of manners set in Italy, *Indian Summer* was both a reversion to Howells's earliest fictional style and subject matter, as well as a welcome change from the intense social realism which characterized his fiction in the 1880's.

By that time, Howells was living permanently in New York and was a member of the editorial staff of *Harper's*. In January, 1886, he began a regular feature in *Harper's* called the "Editor's Study," which continued until 1892 and served as the organ through which he campaigned for realism and a greater social consciousness in fiction. Howells had in fact so reoriented himself away from Boston, the cynosure of his youth, that he turned down a professorship at Harvard and wrote his first novel set in New York, *A Hazard of New Fortunes*, regarded as one of his finest works. Howells's novels in the 1890's were even more insistently illustrative of his strong social consciousness than those of the previous decade. *The Quality of Mercy* is the study of a crime (embezzlement) which is to be blamed less on the individual who committed it than on the society which created him; *An Imperative Duty* deals with miscegenation; *A Traveler from Altruria* and its belated sequel, *Through the Eye of the Needle*, were written within the literary tradition of the utopian novel. Late in his career, Howells tended to resurrect and rework earlier material (the March family of *Their Wedding Journey*, Howells's earliest novel, reappeared in *Their Silver Wedding Journey*); one of his finest character studies is that of Jeff Durgin in the late novel *The Landlord at Lion's Head*, the only work by Howells that clearly shows the influence of naturalism.

After a lecture tour through the West, Howells, in 1900, began to write a regular column, the "The Editor's Easy Chair," for *Harper's*, and continued to do so until his death in 1920. His last major works were *My Mark Twain*, an appreciative account of his friend published in 1910 (the year of the deaths of Samuel Clemens and Mrs. Howells), and the posthumous *The Vacation of the Kelwyns*, published in 1920. Howells died in New York City on May 11, 1920, still productive until his death; although he realized that his creative powers had long since dimmed, he nevertheless had managed to maintain over much of his extraordinary life his well-deserved position as the "Dean of American Letters."

ANALYSIS

Throughout his career as a fiction writer, William Dean Howells worked against the sentimentality and idealization that pervaded popular American literature in the nineteenth century. He pleaded for characters, situations, behavior, values, settings, and even speech patterns that were true to life. While twentieth century readers have come to take such elements for granted, the fact remains that in Howells's day he was regarded as something of a literary radical. One indication of his radicalism was his preference for character over plot in his fiction: He was far less interested in telling a good story (albeit his stories are good) than in presenting flesh-and-blood characters who think, feel, make mistakes, and are products of genetic, social, and economic conditions—in other words, who are as imperfect (and as interesting) as real people. Howells did not indulge in meticulous psychological analyses of his characters, as did his friend Henry James, and his plots tend to be far more linear and straightforward than are the convoluted and carefully patterned ones of James. Nevertheless, he was an innovative and influential writer who changed the quality of American fiction.

A MODERN INSTANCE

A hallmark of Howells's advocacy of realism was his interest in topics that were taboo in Victorian times. Such a topic was divorce, which in the nineteenth century was still regarded by much of society as scandalous and shameful, and which Howells utilized as the resolution of his first major novel, *A Modern Instance*. This was not a "divorce novel" per se, as was maintained by several of Howells's shocked contemporaries, but in an era when "they married and lived happily ever after" was a fictional norm, the divorce of Bartley and Marcia Hubbard was quite unpalatable. Given the situation of the characters, however, the breakup was inevitable—in a word, "realistic." As William M. Gibson explains in his excellent introduction to the Riverside edition of *A Modern Instance* (1957), the story apparently germinated when Howells saw an impressive performance of Euripides' *Medea* in Boston in the spring of 1875, and in fact the working title of the novel was *The New Medea*. The novel's genesis and working title are significant, for the story's female protagonist harbors a passion which is both overpowering and destructive.

Marcia Gaylord, the only child of Squire Gaylord and his self-effacing wife Miranda, grows up in Equity, Maine, in an era when the state's once-impressive commercial prominence has all but decayed. Her domineering but indulgent father and her ineffectual mother have failed to mold Marcia's personality in a positive way, and this lack of a strong character, interacting with an environment caught in economic, cultural, political, and spiritual decline, compels Marcia to leave Equity while rendering her utterly unequipped to deal with the outside world. Not surprisingly, she becomes enamored of the first attractive young man to happen her way: Bartley Hubbard, editor of the newspaper of Equity. Superficially, Hubbard has all the earmarks of the hero of a romantic novel: Orphaned young, he is intelligent enough to have succeeded at a country college, and with his education, charm, and diligence, he seems well on his way to a career in law. There, however, the Lincolnesque qualities end. Ambitious, manipulative, shrewd, unscrupulous, and self-centered, Bartley is the worst possible husband for the shallow Marcia, and after a courtship rife with spats, jealousy, and misunderstandings (even the short-lived engagement is the result of misinterpreted behavior), the ill-matched pair elope and settle in Boston.

The remainder of the novel is an analysis of the characters of Marcia and Bartley as they are revealed by the social, professional, and economic pressures of Boston, and a concomitant study of the deterioration of their marriage. Marcia is motivated by her sexual passion for Bartley and her deep emotional attachment to her father—an attachment so intense that she names her daughter after him and attempts to force Bartley into following in his footsteps as a lawyer. Locked into the roles of wife and daughter, Marcia has no separate identity, no concrete values, no sense of purpose. As Marcia struggles with her disordered personality, Bartley's becomes only too clear: His success as a newspaperman is the direct result of his being both shrewd in his estimation of the low level of popular taste, and unscrupulous in finding material and assuming (or disavowing) responsibility for it.

Bartley's foil is a native Bostonian and former classmate, Ben Halleck. A wealthy man without being spoiled, a trained attorney too moralistic to practice law, and a good judge of character who refuses to use that talent for ignoble ends, Halleck is all that Bartley Hubbard could have been under more favorable circumstances. Even so, Ben does not fit into the world of nineteenth century America: As is graphically symbolized by his being crippled, Ben cannot find a satisfying occupation, a meaningful religion,

or a warm relationship with a woman. In fact, it is Howells's trenchant indictment of the social, economic, and spiritual problems of nineteenth century America that not a single character in *A Modern Instance* is psychically whole. To further compound his difficulties, Ben loves Marcia, having adored her for years after noticing her from afar as a school girl in Maine. In his efforts to aid her by lending money to Bartley and pressuring her to stand by her husband, Ben unwittingly contributes to Bartley's abandonment of Marcia, to her resultant emotional crisis, and to the devastating divorce in Indiana.

Carefully avoiding the traditional happy ending, Howells completes his story with a scene of human wreckage: Bartley, unscrupulous newspaperman to the end, is shot to death by a disgruntled reader in Arizona; Squire Gaylord, emotionally destroyed by defending his daughter in the divorce suit, dies a broken man; Ben, unsuccessful as a schoolteacher in Uruguay, flees to backwoods Maine to preach; and Marcia returns to the narrow world of Equity, her beauty and spirit long vanished. Interesting, complex, and bitter, *A Modern Instance* so strained Howells's emotional and physical well-being that he suffered a breakdown while writing it. The "falling off" of energy and style in the second part of the novel which so many commentators have noticed may be attributed to the breakdown, as well as to the related stress engendered by the serious psychosomatic illness of his beloved daughter Winny; it should be borne in mind, however, that the novel's singularly unhappy ending cannot be attributed to either crisis. The book's conclusion, planned from the story's inception, was itself meant to be a commentary on a nation buffeted by spiritual, social, and economic change.

THE RISE OF SILAS LAPHAM

On a level with *A Modern Instance* is Howells's best-known novel, *The Rise of Silas Lapham*. Serialized in the *Century* magazine from November, 1884, to August, 1885, and published in book form in the late summer of 1885, *The Rise of Silas Lapham* takes a realistic look at the upheavals in late nineteenth century America by focusing on the archetypal self-made man. Colonel Silas Lapham of Lumberville, Vermont, has made a fortune in the paint business by virtue of hard work, honest dealings, and the help and guidance of a good woman, his wife, Persis. The sentimental portrait of the self-made American captain of industry is significantly compromised, however, by the fact that Lapham owes much of his success to simple luck (his father accidentally found a superb paint mine on his farm) and to an early partner's capital (Rogers, a shadowy and rather demonic figure whom Lapham "squeezed out" once his paint business began to thrive). Even more compromising is the fact that Lapham's great wealth and success cannot compensate for his personality and background: Boastful, oafish (his hands are "hairy fists"), and devoid of any aesthetic sensibility, Lapham seeks to buy his way into proper Boston society by building a fabulous mansion on the Back Bay and encouraging a romance between his daughter and Tom Corey, a Harvard graduate with "old" Boston money.

The Coreys are, in fact, foils of the Laphams: Tom's father, Bromfield Corey, is also indirectly associated with paint (he has a talent for portraiture), but having inherited substantial wealth, he has never worked, preferring instead to live off the labors of his ancestors. Ultimately, neither man is acceptable to Howells: Lapham, for all his substantial new wealth, is vulgar and ambitious; Bromfield Corey, for all his old money and polish, is lethargic and ineffectual. The wives do not fare much better. Persis Lapham is burdened with a Puritan reserve which at vital moments renders her incapable of giving her husband emotional support, and Anna Corey, despite her fine manners, is stuffy and judgmental.

The most admirable characters in the novel are two of the five children. Penelope Lapham is a quick-witted, plain girl with a passion for reading George Eliot, while Tom Corey is an educated, enterprising young man who sincerely wants an active business career. Although clearly Pen and Tom are ideally suited to each other, their relationship almost fails to materialize because virtually everyone in the novel—and the reader as well—naturally assumes Tom to be attracted to young Irene Lapham, who is strikingly pretty, beautifully attired, and considerably less intellectually endowed than her sister. In his campaign for realism in literature, Howells intentionally blurs the distinctions between the world of reality (where people like Pen and Tom fall in love) and the world of sentiment (where beautiful, empty-headed Irene is the ideal girl). The blurring is so complete that the Laphams, brainwashed by the romanticized standards of nineteenth century American life, almost deliberately scuttle Pen's relationship with Tom simply because pretty Irene had a crush on him first. The level-headed Reverend Sewell, with his realistic belief in the "economy of pain," is needed to convince the parties involved that they were acting out of "the shallowest sentimentality" rather than common sense in promoting Irene's match with Tom.

As part of his questioning of nineteenth century sentimentality, Howells specifically attacks one of its most graphic manifestations, the self-made man. In the heyday of the Horatio Alger stories, Howells presents a protagonist who to many Americans was the ultimate role model: a Vermont farm lad who became a Boston millionaire. Howells's undermining of Lapham is, however, so meticulous and so complete—he even opens the novel with Lapham being interviewed by sardonic Bartley Hubbard (of *A Modern Instance*) for the "Solid Men of Boston" series in a local pulp newspaper—that the reader is left uncertain whether to admire Lapham for his sound character and business achievements, or to laugh at him for his personality flaws and social blunders. This uncertainty is attributable to the unclear tone of the novel, as George Arms points out in his excellent introduction to *The Rise of Silas Lapham* (1949). The tone is, in fact, a major flaw in the novel, as are some episodes of dubious worth (such as the ostensible affair between Lapham and his typist) and Howells's disinclination to develop some potentially vital characters (such as Tom Corey's uncle and Lapham's financial adviser, James Bellingham). A more fundamental problem is Howells's refusal to face squarely the matter of morality: He never fully resolves the complex relationship between Lapham and his ex-partner Rogers, a relationship which raises such questions as whether good intentions can serve evil ends, and to what extent one has moral obligations toward business associates, friends, and even strangers.

Not surprisingly, the end of the novel is less than

satisfying: Tom Corey marries Pen Lapham and moves to Mexico, where presumably the disparity in their backgrounds will be less glaring; the financially ruined Laphams return to the old Vermont farm, where ostensibly they are far happier than they were as wealthy Bostonians; and pretty young Irene endures spinsterhood. Despite these problems and an overreliance on dialogue (at times the novel reads like a play), *The Rise of Silas Lapham* is indeed, as Arms remarks, "a work of competence and illumination" which rightly deserves its status as an outstanding example of late nineteenth century realistic fiction.

A HAZARD OF NEW FORTUNES

Four years after *The Rise of Silas Lapham*, Howells published the novel which he personally felt to be his best and "most vital" book: *A Hazard of New Fortunes*. A long novel (more than five hundred pages), it features a rather unwieldy number of characters who all know one another professionally or socially (indeed, the "it's a small world" motif is rather strained at times); who possess widely varying degrees of social consciousness; and who come from a number of geographical, economic, and intellectual backgrounds. This cross section of humanity resides in New York City, and the interaction among the remarkably diverse characters occurs as a result of three catalysts: a new magazine entitled *Every Other Week*; a boardinghouse run by the Leightons; and a period of labor unrest among the city's streetcar workers.

The magazine subplot nicely illustrates Howells's extraordinary ability to interweave characters, plot, and themes around a controlling element. *Every Other Week* is a new magazine to be published under the general editorship of one Fulkerson. As its literary editor, he hires Basil March, a transplanted middle-class Indianian who has left his position as an insurance agent in Boston to begin a new life at fifty in New York; as its art editor, there is young Angus Beaton, a shallow ladies' man and dilettante who cannot escape his humble background in Syracuse; the translator is Berthold Lindau, an elderly, well-read German who had befriended March as a boy and lost a hand in the Civil War; and the financial "angel" of the magazine is Jacob Dryfoos, an uncultured mid-

western farmer who has made a fortune through the natural gas wells on his land, and who forces his Christlike son, Conrad, to handle the financial aspects of the magazine as a way of learning about business. The magazine's cover artist is Alma Leighton, a feminist whom Beaton loves, and a frequent contributor of articles is Colonel Woodburn, a ruined Virginian who boards with the Leightons and whose daughter marries Fulkerson.

Each individual associated with *Every Other Week* perceives the magazine in a different light; each is attracted to it (or repulsed by it) for a different reason. As *Every Other Week* becomes a success, Howells allows it to drift out of the focus of the novel, leaving the reader to observe the interactions (usually clashes) of the various characters' personalities, interests, and motives. Lindau, whose social consciousness calls for unions and socialism, is in essential agreement with Conrad Dryfoos, although the latter disdains the German's advocacy of violence; both men clash with Jacob Dryfoos, who, no longer in touch with the earthy Indiana lifestyle of his early years, believes that pro-union workers should be shot. The artist Beaton—who loves the feline quality of Conrad's sister Christine as much as he loves the independence of Alma Leighton and the goodness of socialite worker Margaret Vance—does not care about economic and social matters one way or another, while Colonel Woodburn advocates slavery.

The character whose attitudes most closely parallel those of Howells himself is Basil March, whose social consciousness grows in the course of the novel as he witnesses the poverty of the New York slums, the senseless deaths of Lindau and Conrad, and the pathetic, belated efforts of Jacob Dryfoos to correct his mistakes through the lavish spending of money. In many respects, March is a projection of Howells's attitudes and experiences, and his tendency at the end of the novel to make speeches to his wife about labor, religion, and injustice is a reflection of Howells's reading of Tolstoy. Even so, it would be incorrect to perceive March as the story's main character. That distinction most properly belongs to Jacob Dryfoos, a sort of Pennsylvania Dutch version of Silas Lapham whose values, home, lifestyle, and attitude have been undermined forever by the finding of gas deposits on his farm.

Although much of Howells's fiction deals with social and personal upheaval in late nineteenth century America, nowhere is it more poignantly depicted than in *A Hazard of New Fortunes*. In the light of this poignancy, it is to Howells's credit that the novel does not turn into a cold social tract: The characters are flesh-and-blood rather than caricatures. The novel contains considerable humor, most notably in the early chapters dealing with the Marches house-hunting in New York. There is also a surprising emphasis on feminism and a concomitant questioning of marriage and the false behavioral ideals propagated by sentimental fiction. In addition, Howells provides psychological probing (particularly in the form of fantasizing) such as one would expect of James more readily than Howells, and above all there is the afore-mentioned interweaving of characters, incidents, and themes.

Of Howells's approximately forty novels written during his long career, at least half a dozen—including *A Modern Instance*, *The Rise of Silas Lapham*, and *A Hazard of New Fortunes*—have endured, a testament not only to their brilliant, realistic evocation of life in late nineteenth century America, but also to the distinctive skills, interests, and sensibility of the "Dean of American Letters."

Alice Hall Petry

OTHER MAJOR WORKS

SHORT FICTION: *A Fearful Responsibility and Other Stories*, 1881; *Christmas Every Day and Other Stories Told for Children*, 1893.

PLAYS: *The Parlor Car*, pb. 1876; *A Counterfeit Presentment*, pb. 1877; *Out of the Question*, pb. 1877; *The Register*, pb. 1884; *A Sea-Change*, pb. 1887; *The Albany Depot*, pb. 1892; *A Letter of Introduction*, pb. 1892; *The Unexpected Guests*, pb. 1893; *A Previous Engagement*, pb. 1897; *The Mouse-Trap and Other Farces*, pb. 1889; *Room Forty-five*, pb. 1900; *The Smoking Car*, pb. 1900; *An Indian Giver*, pb. 1900; *Parting Friends*, pb. 1911; *The Complete Plays of W. D. Howells*, pb. 1960 (Walter J. Meserve, editor).

POETRY: *Poems of Two Friends*, 1860 (with John J. Piatt); *Poems*, 1873; *Samson*, 1874; *Priscilla: A Comedy*, 1882; *A Sea Change: Or, Love's Stowaway*, 1884; *Poems*, 1886; *Stops of Various Quills*, 1895; *The Mother and the Father*, 1909.

NONFICTION: *Lives and Speeches of Abraham Lincoln and Hannibal Hamlin*, 1860; *Venetian Life*, 1866; *Italian Journeys*, 1867; *Tuscan Cities*, 1885; *Modern Italian Poets*, 1887; *A Boy's Town*, 1890; *Criticism and Fiction*, 1891; *My Year in a Log Cabin*, 1893; *My Literary Passions*, 1895; *Impressions and Experiences*, 1896; *Stories of Ohio*, 1897; *Literary Friends and Acquaintances*, 1900; *Heroines of Fiction*, 1901; *Literature and Life*, 1902; *Letters Home*, 1903; *London Films*, 1905; *Certain Delightful English Towns*, 1906; *Roman Holidays*, 1908; *Seven English Cities*, 1909; *Imaginary Interviews*, 1910; *My Mark Twain*, 1910; *Familiar Spanish Travels*, 1913; *New Leaf Mills*, 1913; *Years of My Youth*, 1916; *Eighty Years and After*, 1921; *The Life and Letters of William Dean Howells*, 1928.

BIBLIOGRAPHY

Cady, Edwin H., and Louis J. Budd, eds. *On Howells: The Best from American Literature*. Durham, N.C.: Duke University Press, 1993. Essays on materials and form in Howells's fiction, on the equalitarian principle, on individual novels such as *The Rise of Silas Lapham*, *Their Wedding Journey*, and other novels.

Cady, Edwin H., and Norma W. Cady. *Critical Essays on W. D. Howells, 1866-1920*. Boston: G. K. Hall, 1983. Gathers together important criticism on Howells, both reprints and original essays. Includes reviews by contemporaries such as Henry James, George Bernard Shaw, and Mark Twain, as well as commentaries by modern critics, such as Van Wyck Brooks, H. L. Mencken, and Wilson Follett. Contains essays by advocates and detractors of Howells.

Crowley, John W. *The Mask of Fiction: Essays on W. D. Howells*. Amherst: University of Massachusetts Press, 1989. The introduction addresses the debate among writers about Howells's contribution to American literature. The main thrust of the study, however, is the examination of Howells's unconscious in his writings, incorporating both the "probing psychologism of the 1890s" and his later light fiction with its deeper psychic integration. Explores in particular the Oedipus complex in the light of the relationship between father and son. Crowley sees his study on Howells as revisionist, not revivalist, in spirit. An important contribution to critical studies on Howells which is also useful for its extensive notes.

Eble, Kenneth E. *William Dean Howells*. 2d ed. Boston: Twayne, 1982. Contains a commentary on Howells's early life, his development as a novelist, and the later years. The chapter entitled "Fiction and Fact of the Nineties" gives valuable perspective on Howells's novels during this decade—a prolific period in his writing—including his autobiographical works.

Escholtz, Paula A., ed. *Critics on William Dean Howells*. Miami, Fla.: University of Miami Press, 1975. An accessible introduction to Howells as both author and critic, with critical essays on his major novels. The volume is designed to show how Howells's reputation has fared since the 1860's. Includes a selected bibliography.

Lynn, Kenneth S. *William Dean Howells: An American Life*. New York: Harcourt Brace Jovanovich, 1970. A highly regarded study for its blending of biographical scholarship and criticism of Howells's works.

Nettels, Elsa. *Language and Gender in American Fiction: Howells, James, Wharton, and Cather*. Charlottesville: University Press of Virginia, 1997. Explores gender roles in the fiction of male and female authors. Includes bibliographical references and an index.

Olsen, Rodney D. *Dancing in Chains: The Youth of William Dean Howells*. New York: New York University Press, 1991. Olsen provides a careful study of the middle-class roots of Howells's fiction, showing how his society shaped him and how his fiction not only appealed to that society but also was an expression of it. Very detailed notes but no bibliography.

W. H. HUDSON

Born: Quilmes, Argentina; August 4, 1841
Died: London, England; August 18, 1922

PRINCIPAL LONG FICTION

The Purple Land, 1885 (originally pb. as *The Purple Land That England Lost*)
A Crystal Age, 1887
Fan: The Story of a Young Girl's Life, 1892 (as Henry Harford)
El Ombú, 1902 (reissued as *South American Sketches*, 1909; pb. in U.S. as *Tales of the Pampas*, 1916)
Green Mansions, 1904
A Little Boy Lost, 1905

OTHER LITERARY FORMS

W. H. Hudson was most prolific as an essayist; most of his essays record his observations as a field naturalist. He was particularly fascinated by bird life; between 1888 and 1889 he compiled and published, with the aid of Professor Sclater, *Argentine Ornithology*, which was later revised as *Birds of La Plata* (1920). He followed this with books entitled *Birds in a Village* (1893) and *British Birds* (1895). More general reflections on nature can be found in such of his books as *Idle Days in Patagonia* (1893) and *Nature in Downland* (1900). Although Hudson was primarily an observer and not a theorist, his last book of this type, *A Hind in Richmond Park* (1922), is a much more philosophical work, occasionally tending to the mystical, discussing the nature of sensory experience in animals and man and linking this analysis to aesthetic theory and the "spiritualizing" of man. He also wrote an autobiography, *Far Away and Long Ago* (1918), a lyrical work recalling his childhood in South America; it deals only with his early life and refers to no incidents after 1859.

ACHIEVEMENTS

Hudson is almost a forgotten writer today, remembered primarily for *Green Mansions*. He was equally unappreciated for most of his own lifetime—

he lived in poverty and was virtually ignored by the literary public until *Green Mansions* became a best-seller in America, by which time he was well into his sixties. He seems to have had mixed feelings about this late success—it is significant that he refrained from writing any further romances, though his juvenile novel *A Little Boy Lost* appeared the following year. Hudson wanted to be known as a naturalist, and he considered his essays on nature his most important works. These books did, indeed, attract a small coterie of admirers, and for a few years before and immediately after his death they received due attention. He is commemorated by a bird sanctuary in Hyde Park, where there is a Jacob Epstein statue representing Rima, the enigmatic nature-spirit from *Green Mansions*. In 1924, J. M. Dent and Sons reissued his complete works in twenty-four volumes and his friend Morley Roberts published an appreciative memoir of him.

Hudson's nonfiction is generally more interesting and more valuable than his fiction. His essays on nature provide an unusual combination of patient and scrupulous observation with occasional speculative rhapsodies of a metaphysical character. In his visionary moments, Hudson held a view of the living world akin to that of Henri Bergson, author of *Creative Evolution* (1907), but this aspect of his work is of historical and psychological interest only. His careful and minute observations are of more enduring value, especially when he turned his attention—as he often did—from birds to men. His accounts of human life from the detached viewpoint of the field naturalist are always fascinating, and his documentation of the life of a small rural village in *A Shepherd's Life* (1910) is a rare glimpse of a world which has passed almost without record.

Hudson's fiction is interesting, and enjoys what reputation it has, because of its combination of the same contrasting traits that are to be found in his nonfiction: His descriptions of the natural world in his South American romances are delicate and scrupulous, and the same is true of his observations of the life of the inhabitants of the Banda Oriental in *The Purple Land* or the savages in *Green Mansions*. At the same time, though, the best of these stories has an

(Library of Congress)

imaginative component so ambitious that it permits the reader to see the world—and other possible and impossible worlds too—through new eyes. There is a sense in which his visions of a quasi-supernatural ecological harmony fit in better with ideas that are current today than they did with the *Zeitgeist* of Hudson's own age, and it is therefore surprising that his work does not get more attention. It is possible that he is ripe for rediscovery, and that a new assessment of his achievement may yet be made.

Biography

William Henry Hudson was born on August 4, 1841, on an *estancia* about ten miles outside Buenos Aires. His parents were both American, but he had British grandparents on both sides of the family. His parents seem to have been very devoted to their children, and Hudson apparently enjoyed an idyllic childhood on the pampas; his memories of it recorded in *Far Away and Long Ago* were fond in the extreme. During his adolescence, however, he developed solitary tendencies, drifting away from the company of his siblings. During these years, he gave himself over to the patient and lonely study of nature.

Very little is known of his later years in South America; his autobiography has nothing to say of his life after reaching adolescence, and Morley Roberts, who wrote a book about Hudson's later life, did not meet him until 1880. By the time Hudson went to England in 1869, his parents were dead and the family had dispersed. Apparently, he had spent a good deal of the previous few years wandering aimlessly in South America; it is tempting to associate certain incidents described in *The Purple Land* with experiences he may have had during these years, but to do so would be mere conjecture.

Hudson's early days in England are also undocumented. He apparently had various odd jobs, including researching genealogies for Americans, but did not settle down or make much of a living. In 1876, he met and married Emily Wingrave, who was some twenty years older than he. While he wrote, she gave singing lessons, but neither activity brought in much money, and the two had to run a boardinghouse in Bayswater for some years. Even after the publication of *The Purple Land* (which was received with indifference), they were close to desperation, but Emily inherited a large house in Bayswater which they turned into flats, retaining two rooms for themselves and living off the rents from the remainder. Though Hudson frequently went on long excursions into the country, and in later life took to wintering in Penzance, the couple stayed in Bayswater until their deaths, Emily's in 1921 and Hudson's in 1922. Hudson was naturalized in 1900, by which time he was just beginning to attract favorable attention through his essays. Sir Edward Grey procured for him a state pension in 1901, a few years before the commercial success of *Green Mansions* freed him from financial worry.

Hudson's acquaintances seem to have formed very different impressions of him. Robert Hamilton quotes summaries of his character offered by half a dozen different people which are anything but unanimous— some are flatly contradictory. If an overall impression can be gained, it is that he was usually friendly and courteous but rather reserved. More than one acquaintance suspected that he was secretly lonely and unhappy, and women seem to have formed a distinctly poorer opinion of him than men, suggesting that he was uneasy in their company. The autobiography which ceases so early in his life may provide the best insight into his character, as much by what it omits as by what it says. Hudson seems to have emerged from childhood reluctantly and with great regret; he apparently never tried particularly hard to adapt himself to the adult world, where he always felt himself to be an outsider. Although he did not marry until he was in his mid-thirties, the woman he selected as a wife probably served as a mother-substitute whose age precluded any possibility of parenthood. These details are highly significant in the consideration of his novels, especially *A Crystal Age*.

ANALYSIS

The majority of W. H. Hudson's fictions are categorized as "South American romances"—at one time a collection was issued under that title. Included under this label are the novels *The Purple Land* and *Green Mansions* and various shorter pieces from Hudson's short-story collection *El Ombú* (1902); the most important of these shorter pieces are the novellas "El Ombú" and "Marta Riquelme." All of these works make constructive use of the author's autobiographical background.

THE PURPLE LAND

The Purple Land is a documentary novel containing no plot, an imaginary travelogue set in the Banda Oriental (now Uruguay). Its protagonist, Richard Lamb, has been forced to flee to Montevideo after eloping with the daughter of a powerful Argentinean family. The story concerns Lamb's wanderings in connection with an abortive attempt to find a job managing an inland plantation. At one point, he becomes entangled in the affairs of the rebel general Santa Coloma and fights with him in an ill-fated revolution. He also attracts the attention of several women, including two very beautiful girls who mistake him for a single man and are bitterly disappointed when he informs them belatedly of his unavailability. One of these women, however, he rescues from an awkward predicament and smuggles her back to Argentina in spite of the risk to himself (the reader has already been told in the first chapter that these wanderings preceded a long spell in jail, an event that was instigated by his vengeful father-in-law and broke his wife's heart).

The attractive features of this novel are the local color and the attention to anthropological detail. It offers a convincing picture of the life of the country, and one can easily believe that some of the episodes are based on experience, and that Hudson actually heard some of the tall stories that are told to Lamb by Santa Coloma's rebel gauchos. The amorous encounters, however, fail to convince, and there is a certain perversity in hearing the protagonist's overheated expressions of devotion to a wife from whom he is willingly separated, and whom he is destined to lose. In contrast to the bleak note on which the novel begins and ends, the protestations of love are melodramatic.

"El Ombú" and "Marta Riquelme"

There is no trace of this fault in the two novellas set in the same region. "El Ombú" is a chronicle of unremitting cruelty and misfortune, detailing the sufferings of a family through the memories of an old man who loves to sit and reminisce in the shadow of an ombú tree. "Marta Riquelme," which Hudson thought the best of his stories, is even more ruthless, and it makes use of a legend connected with a species of bird called the Kakué fowl, into which men and women who experience unendurable suffering were said to change. The story is narrated by a Jesuit priest, who describes the tragic career of Marta, captured by Indians, robbed of her child, and so mutilated that when she returns to her own people they will not accept her and drive her out to find her fate.

These stories were called "romances" because their subject matter was exotic to an English audience; in fact, however, they are examples of determined narrative realism (unless one accepts the Jesuit priest's dubious allegation that Marta Riquelme really does turn into a Kakué fowl). They present a very different view of life in South America than does *The Purple Land*, a book which glosses over the plight of the common people and the cruelties visited upon them. They bear witness to the fact that Hudson, once emerged from the cocoon of his ideal childhood and initiated into the ways of the world, was deeply affected by what he discovered. He carried away from South America much fonder memories of the birds than of the people, the grotesqueness of whose lives appalled him even though he tried with all his might to sympathize with them.

In between *The Purple Land* and "El Ombú," Hudson wrote two other novels. One, the pseudonymous *Fan*, appears to have been an attempt to write a conventional three-decker novel of domestic life. The book has little to recommend it, being an entirely artificial product with little of Hudson in it, appearing when the day of the three-decker was already past. The other novel, *A Crystal Age*, also appeared without Hudson's name on it, being issued anonymously, but Hudson acknowledged authorship when it was reprinted in the wake of the success of *Green Mansions*.

A Crystal Age

A Crystal Age is a difficult work to classify: It is a vision of an earthly paradise, but it is arcadian rather than utopian in character and is by no means polemical. It carries no political message and might best be regarded as a fatalist parable lamenting the imperfections of nineteenth century man.

The narrator of the story tells the reader nothing about himself except that he is an Englishman named Smith. He is precipitated into a distant future where men live in perfect ecological harmony with their environment. Each community is a single family, based in a House which is organized around its Mother. The Mother of the House that takes Smith in is secluded because of illness, and it is some time before Smith realizes that she is an actual person rather than an imaginary goddess. When he repairs the most damaging of his many breaches of etiquette by making himself known to her, she treats him harshly but later forgives him and awards him a special place in her affections.

Smith never fully understands this peculiar world. He is passionately in love with a daughter of the House, Yoletta, whom he believes to be about seventeen years of age. Even when she tells him how old she really is, he cannot see the truth: that these people are so long-lived, and live so free from danger, that their reproductive rate has to be very slow. The Mother is revered because she really is *the* mother of the household: the only reproductive individual. When Smith tries desperately to woo Yoletta, she genuinely cannot understand him. Nor can Smith see, though the reader can, that the Mother holds him in special esteem because she plans to be followed in her role by Yoletta and is grooming him for the role of the Father. He remains lost in an anguish of uncertainty until he finds a bottle whose label promises a cure for misery. He immediately believes that it is the means by which his hosts suppress their sexual feelings, and he drinks to drown his own passion. He discovers too late that it is actually the means by which those in mortal agony achieve a merciful release.

In a sense, the world of *A Crystal Age* is the opposite of the world described in "El Ombú": It is a heaven constructed by reacting against the hellish aspects of the life of the South American peasantry. It is a world where man and nature peacefully coexist and where human society enjoys the harmonious organization of the beehive without the loss of individual identity that has made the beehive a horrific stereotype in stories of hypothetical societies. Nevertheless, *A Crystal Age* is just as misanthropic as "El Ombú," in that Smith—the book's Everyman figure— is mercilessly pilloried for being too brutal and stupid to adapt himself to the perfect world.

A LITTLE BOY LOST

In view of Hudson's personal history, it is difficult to doubt that the matricentric of the imaginary society, and Smith's own peculiar relationship with the Mother, are of some psychological significance. The same seems to be true of *A Little Boy Lost*, whose protagonist, Martin, runs away from home to follow a mirage. When he becomes homesick, it is not to his real parents that he returns (there had been a quaintly unconvincing suggestion earlier that his real father was a bird—a martin) but to a surrogate mother called the Lady of the Hills. She smothers him with affection, but he eventually leaves her, too, attracted to the distant seashore beyond the reach of her powers. When he falls into danger there, he longs for this surrogate mother rather than the real one, but there is no going back of any kind; in the end, he is picked up

by a ship which seems to be sailing to the England which his parents left before he was born. Some of Martin's other adventures—especially his encounter with savage Indians—recall elements in Hudson's other works, and it is a rather baleful world from which the Lady of the Hills temporarily rescues him. If all of this could be analyzed in the light of a more detailed knowledge of Hudson's thoughts and feelings, it might well turn out to reveal some interesting symbolic patterns.

GREEN MANSIONS

Hudson's idea of perfection, which is displayed as a whole world in *A Crystal Age*, is embodied in *Green Mansions* in a single person. In a sense, *Green Mansions* is *A Crystal Age* in reverse: It features a visitor from the imaginary world of ecological harmony cast adrift in the familiar world. Rima, the delicate refugee, can no more survive here than Smith could in the Mother's House: She is brutally murdered by savages who believe that she is an evil spirit ruining their hunting.

The story is told by a placid and gentle old man named Mr. Abel, recalling his youth when he was forced to flee from his native Venezuela because of his complicity in an abortive coup. After wandering for some time, the young Abel rests for a while in an Indian village somewhere in the remoter regions of the Orinoco River basin. In a forested area nearby, which the Indians are reluctant to enter, he hears a voice which seems to be part bird-song and part human, and he eventually discovers Rima, a tiny and somewhat ethereal girl who can communicate with birds and animals. She lives there with her adopted grandfather, Nuflo, and takes Abel in after he is bitten by a snake.

Rima is desperate to return to her half-forgotten place of origin, but Nuflo will not take her. Abel mentions a mountain chain called Riolama, and she recognizes the name, insisting that they go there. The journey is fruitless—the remote valley where Rima's people lived has been destroyed, and Abel realizes that her mother must have been the last survivor of the catastrophe. Rima decides to settle in her forest haven with Abel, but even this scheme is thwarted by the Indians, who have reclaimed the wood during

Rima's absence and who destroy her by trapping her in the branches of a solitary tree and burning it. Abel, sick and hallucinating, sets off on a phantasmagoric trip through the rain forest, back to civilization. On the way, imagined encounters with Rima's ghost instill in him the capacity to rebuild his life; he becomes convinced that he can be reunited with her after death if he accepts his situation and learns patience.

Green Mansions is a magnificently lush tragedy, and it is not difficult to understand why it captured the public imagination—at least in America—firmly enough to become established as a kind of classic. The passionate yearning which drives Abel is something with which almost everyone can identify: the yearning for an imaginary golden age of love and tranquillity which somehow seems to be located equally in the personal and prehistoric past. What Abel is chasing is a fantasy that cannot be brought down to earth, and he is bound to fail, but in his failing there is a kind of disappointment which is common to all people.

Hudson's version of this particular myth is remarkable in two ways. First of all, he was able to exploit, as he had in *The Purple Land*, "El Ombú," and "Marta Riquelme," a realism which seemed to his readers to be romanticism. This encompasses both his descriptions of the various landscapes of the story (especially the forests of Abel's last delirious journey) and his description of the way of life of the savage Indians. These are no Rousseauesque examples of a wild nobility, but of brutish individuals who are no better integrated into their environment than Abel is. (Indeed, Abel is the wiser, for he at least can appreciate, thanks to his intellect and imagination, the *possibility* of living in harmony with nature.) Second, the novel is remarkable for its characterization of the bird-girl Rima. Although not particularly convincing as a character, she is so close to the author's personal notion of perfection that his regard for her infects the novel and gives her the same status in the reader's eyes as she has in Abel's.

Again, one is tempted to look below the surface of *Green Mansions* for some psychological significance that will cast light on Hudson's enigmatic personal-

ity. It is easy enough to connect Rima with the Lady of the Hills and to observe that, in common with all the other desirable women in Hudson's fiction, she has an essential inaccessibility. Monica, Mercedes, and Demetria in *The Purple Land* are all unavailable to the hero because he is married; Yoletta in *A Crystal Age* is forbidden to Smith by social convention and cannot respond to his passion because she has no sexuality of her own; Rima is a member of a different race, more nature-spirit than human, and though there seems no obvious reason why, it is always clear that she and Abel can never be united. One "explanation" for the dearth of successful amatory ventures in Hudson's work might be found in the suggestion that all these love objects really ought to be interpreted as mother-figures rather than suitable brides, but the truth is probably more complicated. For Hudson's male characters, all feelings of sexual attraction are—or ought to be—guilt-ridden, forbidden by taboos of which they are sometimes only half aware. The possibility that Hudson suffered from a mother fixation may help to account for this but is hardly likely to be the whole story—especially when one remembers that the Lady of the Hills, in *A Little Boy Lost*, is specifically declared to be a substitute mother who displaces the real one in the child-hero's affections.

Why Hudson wrote no more significant fiction after 1905 is not altogether clear, especially as he had only just made a name for himself. He was well into his sixties, but his creative powers showed no sign of diminution. His three best books—*A Shepherd's Life, Far Away and Long Ago*, and *A Hind in Richmond Park*—were still to be written, the last when he was in his eighties. Perhaps, with the death of Rima, he laid aside his dream of a supernaturally harmonized creation—the dream which provided the imaginative fuel for *A Crystal Age* and *Green Mansions*. In *A Little Boy Lost* that same dream is displayed as a childish illusion—even on the story's own terms it is difficult to decide exactly how much takes place inside Martin's head.

The new introduction that Hudson wrote for *A Crystal Age* when it was reissued in 1906 supports this view. This brief essay is full of disillusionment, informing the reader that romances of the future are always interesting even though none of them is really any good. Hudson disparages *A Crystal Age* for being a product of its own era, and he regrets that it cannot possibly induce belief because "the ending of passion and strife is the beginning of decay." This remark echoes Hudson's ambivalent feelings about Darwinism—he was resistant to the ideas of "the struggle for existence" and "the survival of the fittest." For Hudson it was the human world, not the world of nature, that was red in tooth and claw. Despite his reluctance, though, he could not help but accept much of the Darwinian argument and was forced thereby to acknowledge the hopelessness of his own ideals. This special disenchantment is something that lurks below the surface of almost all his work; whether or not it is the cognitive reflection of a much more personal disenchantment must remain an unanswered question.

Brian Stableford

OTHER MAJOR WORKS

SHORT FICTION: *Dead Man's Plack and An Old Thorn*, 1920.

NONFICTION: *Argentine Ornithology*, 1888-1889 (with Professor Sclator); *The Naturalist in La Plata*, 1892; *Birds in a Village*, 1893; *Idle Days in Patagonia*, 1893; *British Birds*, 1895; *Nature in Downland*, 1900; *Birds and Man*, 1901; *Hampshire Days*, 1903; *The Land's End*, 1908; *Afoot in England*, 1909; *A Shepherd's Life*, 1910; *Adventures Among Birds*, 1913; *Far Away and Long Ago*, 1918; *The Book of a Naturalist*, 1919; *Birds of La Plata*, 1920; *A Traveller in Little Things*, 1921; *A Hind in Richmond Park*, 1922; *One Hundred Fifty-three Letters from W. H. Hudson*, 1923 (with Edward Garnett, editor); *Men, Books, and Birds*, 1925.

BIBLIOGRAPHY

Haymaker, Richard E. *From Pampas to Hedgerows and Downs: A Study of W. H. Hudson*. New York: Bookman Associates, 1954. Perhaps the most thorough of full-length studies to date on Hudson; a must for serious scholars of this writer.

Miller, David. *W. H. Hudson and the Elusive Paradise*. New York: St. Martin's Press, 1990. Chapters on all of Hudson's major prose fiction, exploring such themes as the supernatural, the imagination, symbolic meaning, immortality, and ideology. Includes detailed notes and a bibliography.

Roberts, Morley. *W. H. Hudson: A Portrait*. New York: E. P. Dutton, 1924. A personal, intimate account of Hudson from the perspective of Roberts's long-term relationship with this writer and naturalist.

Ronner, Amy D. *W. H. Hudson: The Man, the Novelist, the Naturalist*. New York: AMS Press, 1986. A much-needed recent addition to critical studies on Hudson, examining Hudson's work in relationship to his contemporaries, his immigration to England, and his development as a naturalist and writer. Concludes with an interesting account of Charles Darwin's influence on Hudson and consequently on his writing. Useful bibliography is also provided.

Shrubsall, Dennis. *W. H. Hudson: Writer and Naturalist*. Tisbury, England: Compton Press, 1978. Provides much useful background on Hudson's early years in Argentina and traces his development as a naturalist and his integrity as a writer on nature.

Tomalin, Ruth. *W. H. Hudson: A Biography*. London: Faber & Faber, 1982. A lively biography that has been thoroughly and painstakingly researched. Highly recommended for any serious study of Hudson. Contains excerpts of the letter which Hudson wrote in an attack on Charles Darwin and of Darwin's response.

VICTOR HUGO

Born: Besançon, France; February 26, 1802
Died: Paris, France; May 22, 1885

PRINCIPAL LONG FICTION

Han d'Islande, 1823 (*Hans of Iceland*, 1845)
Bug-Jargal, 1826 (*The Noble Rival*, 1845)

Le Dernier Jour d'un condamné, 1829 (*The Last Day of a Condemned*, 1840)

Notre-Dame de Paris, 1831 (*The Hunchback of Notre Dame*, 1833)

Claude Gueux, 1834

Les Misérables, 1862 (English translation, 1862)

Les Travailleurs de la mer, 1866 (*The Toilers of the Sea*, 1866)

L'Homme qui rit, 1869 (*The Man Who Laughs*, 1869)

Quatre-vingt-treize, 1874 (*Ninety-Three*, 1874)

OTHER LITERARY FORMS

Victor Hugo dominates nineteenth century literature in France both by the length of his writing career and by the diversity of his work. Indeed, it is difficult to think of a literary form he did not employ. Lyric, satiric, and epic poetry; drama in verse and prose; political polemic and social criticism—all are found in his oeuvre. His early plays and poetry made him a leader of the Romantic movement. His political

(Library of Congress)

writing includes the publication of a newspaper, *L'Événement*, in 1851, which contributed to his exile from the Second Empire. During his exile, he wrote vehement criticism of Napoleon III, and then his visionary works of poetry. His poetic genius ranged from light verse to profound epics; his prose works include accounts of his travels and literary criticism as well as fiction.

ACHIEVEMENTS

The complete works of Victor Hugo constitute more nearly a legend than an achievement. In poetry, he had become a national institution by the end of his life. He was a member of the Académie Française, an officer of the Légion d'Honneur, and a Peer of France under the monarchy of Louis-Philippe. When he died, he was accorded the singular honor of lying in state beneath Paris's Arc de Triomphe before his burial in the Panthéon.

During his lifetime, Hugo's novels accounted for much of his popularity with the public. Both sentimental and dramatic, they were an excellent vehicle for spreading his humanitarian ideas among large numbers of people. His two most famous novels are *The Hunchback of Notre Dame* and *Les Misérables*. The former is an example of dramatic historical romance, inspired in France by the novels of Sir Walter Scott. It is said to have created interest in and ensured the architectural preservation of the Notre Dame cathedral in Paris. It is also a study in Romanticism, with its evocation of the dark force of fate and the intricate intertwining of the grotesque and the sublime.

Les Misérables testifies to Hugo's optimistic faith in humanitarian principles and social progress. The intricate and elaborate plot confronts both social injustice and indifference. It is typical of many nineteenth century attitudes in its emphasis on education, charity, and love as powerful forces in saving the unfortunate creatures of the lower classes from becoming hardened criminals. *Les Misérables* is a novel on an epic scale both in its historical tableaux and as the story of a human soul. Thus, even though Hugo's achievements in the novel are of a lesser scale than his poetry and drama, they are enduring and worthy monuments to the author and to his century.

BIOGRAPHY

Victor-Marie Hugo was born in Besançon in 1802, the third son of Joseph-Léopold-Sigisbert Hugo and Sophie-Françoise Trébuchet. His father had been born in Nancy and his mother in Nantes. They met in the Vendée, where Léopold Hugo was serving in the Napoleonic army. His military career kept the family on the move, and it was during Major Hugo's tour of duty with the Army of the Rhine that Victor-Marie was born in Besançon.

Léopold and Sophie did not have a happy marriage, and after the birth of their third son, they were frequently separated. By 1808, Léopold had been promoted to general and was made a count in Napoleon's empire. During one reunion of Hugo's parents, Victor and his brothers joined General Hugo in Spain, a land that fascinated Victor and left its mark on his poetic imagination.

In spite of their father's desire that they should study for entrance to the École Polytechnique, Victor and his next older brother, Eugène, spent their free time writing poetry, hoping to emulate their master, François René de Chateaubriand. In 1817, Victor earned the first official recognition of his talent by winning an honorable mention in a poetry competition sponsored by the Académie Française. Because he was only fifteen, the secretary of the Académie asked to meet him, and the press displayed an interest in the young poet.

Eugène and Victor received permission from their father to study law in 1818 and left their boarding school to live with their mother in Paris. Sophie encouraged them in their ambition to become writers and never insisted that they attend lectures or study for examinations. Victor continued to receive recognition for his poems, and the brothers founded a review, *Le Conservateur littéraire*, in 1819. Unfortunately, the two brothers also shared a passion for the same young woman, Adèle Foucher. In love as well as in poetry, Eugène took second place to his younger brother. Adèle and Victor were betrothed after the death of Madame Hugo, who had opposed the marriage. The wedding took place in 1822. At the wedding feast, Eugène went insane and spent nearly all the rest of his life in institutions.

Hugo's early publications were favorably received by the avant-garde of Romanticism, and by 1824, Hugo was a dominant personality in Charles Nodier's *cénacle*, a group of Romantic poets united in their struggle against the rules of French classicism. The year 1824 also marked the birth of Léopoldine, the Hugos' second child and the first to survive infancy. She was always to have a special place in her father's heart. In 1827, the Hugos had another child, Charles.

The Hugos were acquainted with many of those writers and artists who are now considered major figures in the Romantic movement, among them Alexandre Dumas, *père*, Alfred de Vigny, and Eugène Delacroix. The sculptor David d'Anger recorded Hugo's youthful appearance on a medallion. (Decades later, sculptor Auguste Rodin would also preserve his impression of the aged poet.) The influential critic Charles-Augustin Sainte-Beuve also became a frequent visitor to the Hugos' apartment.

Momentum was building for the Romantic movement, and in December, 1827, Hugo published a play, *Cromwell* (English translation, 1896), whose preface became the manifesto of the young Romantics. Two years later, *Hernani* (1830; English translation, 1830) would provide the battleground between Romanticism and classicism. In the meantime, General Hugo had died in 1828, and a son, François-Victor, had been born to Victor and Adèle.

The famous "battle of *Hernani*" at its premiere on January 10, 1830, was an outcry against outmoded conventions in every form of art. Artists sympathetic to Romanticism had been recruited from the Latin Quarter in support of Hugo's play, which breaks the rules of versification as well as the three unities of classical drama (time, place, and action). They engaged in a battle for modern artistic freedom against the "authorities" of the past. *Hernani* therefore had political significance as well: The restoration of the Bourbons was in its final months.

Stormy performances continued at the Théâtre-Français for several months, and by the end, the tyranny of classicism had been demolished. In addition to artistic freedom for all, *Hernani* brought financial well-being to the Hugos. It also brought Sainte-Beuve increasingly into their family circle, where he kept Adèle company while Hugo was distracted by the *Hernani* affair.

In July of 1830, Victor and Adèle's last child, Adèle, came into the world to the sound of the shots of the July Revolution, which deposed Charles X, the last Bourbon "King of France." The new monarch was Louis-Philippe of the Orléans branch of the royal family, who called himself "King of the French." There was now a deep attachment between Madame Hugo and Sainte-Beuve. Although Adèle and Victor were never to separate, their marriage had become a platonic companionship.

In 1832, the Hugos moved to the Place Royale (now called the Place des Vosges), to the home that was to become the Victor Hugo museum in Paris. Scarcely a year passed without a publication by Hugo. By that time, he was able to command enormous sums for his work in comparison with other authors of his day. He was already becoming a legend, with disciples rather than friends. His ambition had always been fierce, and he was beginning to portray himself as a bard, a seer with powers to guide all France. Only in his family life was he suffering from less than complete success.

At the time, *Lucrèce Borgia* (1833; *Lucretia Borgia*, 1842) was in rehearsal, and among the cast was a lovely young actress, Juliette Drouet. Soon after opening night, she and Hugo became lovers, and they remained so for many years. Juliette had not been a brilliant actress, but she abandoned what might have been a moderately successful career to live the rest of her life in seclusion and devotion to Hugo. In *Les Chants du crépuscule* (1835; *Songs of Twilight*, 1836), Hugo included thirteen poems to Juliette and three to Adèle, expressing the deep affection he still felt for his wife.

Critics were beginning to snipe at Hugo for what seemed to be shallow emotions and facile expressions. (Sainte-Beuve deplored Hugo's lack of taste, but Sainte-Beuve was hardly a disinterested critic.) The fashion for Hugo seemed to be somewhat on the wane, although adverse criticism did not inhibit the flow of his writing. The publication of *Les Rayons et les ombres* (1840) marked the end of one phase of Hugo's poetry. The splendor of the language and the music in his verse as well as the visual imagery were richer than ever, but Hugo was still criticized for lacking genuine emotion. He had by this time decided, however, to devote himself to his political ambitions.

He was determined to become a Peer of France, having been made an officer of the Légion d'Honneur several years before. In order to obtain a peerage, a man of letters had to be a member of the Académie Française. After presenting himself for the fifth time, he was elected to the Académie in 1841, and in the spring of 1845 he was named a Peer of France, a status that protected him from arrest the following summer, when police found him *flagrante delicto* with the wife of Auguste Biard. Léonie Biard was sent to the Saint-Lazare prison, but Hugo's cordial relations with King Louis-Philippe helped calm the scandal, and Léonie retired to a convent for a short while before resuming her affair with Hugo.

An event of much deeper emotional impact had occurred in 1843, when Hugo's eldest daughter, Léopoldine, had married Charles Vacquerie. Hugo had found it difficult to be separated from his child, who went to live in Le Havre. That summer, in July, he paid a brief visit to the young couple before leaving on a journey with Juliette. In early September, while traveling, Hugo read in a newspaper that Léopoldine and Charles had been drowned in a boating accident several days before. Grief-stricken, Hugo was also beset by guilt at having left his family for a trip with his mistress. He published nothing more for nine years.

Eventually, the political events of 1848 eclipsed Hugo's complex relationship with his wife and two mistresses. During the Revolution of 1848, Louis-Philippe was forced to abdicate. The monarchy was rejected outright by the provisional government under the leadership of the Romantic poet Alphonse de Lamartine. The peerage was also abolished, and although Hugo sought political office, he was generally considered to be too dramatic and rhetorical to be of practical use in government. More than a few of his contemporary politicians viewed him as a self-interested opportunist. He seems to have longed for the glory of being a statesman without the necessary political sense.

On June 24, 1848, militant insurgents had occupied the Hugo apartment on the Place Royal. The family had fled, and Adèle had refused to live there again. One of the first visitors to their new apartment was Louis-Napoleon Bonaparte, nephew of Napoleon I. He was seeking Hugo's support of his candidacy for president of the new republic. Thereafter, Louis-Napoleon was endorsed in Hugo's newspaper, *L'Événement*, which he had founded that summer and which was edited and published by his sons.

Louis-Napoleon became president in December of 1848, but he did not long remain on good terms with Hugo. Hugo and *L'Événement* increasingly took leftist political positons, while the new government moved toward the Right. Freedom of the press was increasingly limited, and, in 1851, both of Hugo's sons were imprisoned for violating restrictions on the press and for showing disrespect to the government.

It was in this year that Juliette and Léonie attempted to force Hugo to choose between them. In the end, politics resolved the conflict. On December 2, 1851, Louis-Napoleon dissolved the National Assembly and declared himself Prince-President for ten years. When Hugo learned of the *coup d'état*, he attempted to organize some resistance. There was shooting in the streets of Paris. Juliette is given credit for saving him from violence. She hid him successfully while a false passport was prepared, and on December 11, he took the train to Brussels in disguise and under a false name. Juliette followed him into exile.

From exile, the pen was Hugo's only political weapon, and he wrote *Napoléon le petit* (1852; *Napoleon the Little*, 1852) and *Histoire d'un crime* (1877; *The History of a Crime*, 1877-1878). Having been authorized to stay in Belgium for only three months, Hugo made plans to move to Jersey, one of the Channel Islands. His family joined him, and Juliette took rooms nearby. He began work on *Les Châtiments* (1853), poems inspired by anger and pride. France remained his preoccupation while he was in exile. Indeed, it has been said that exile renewed Hugo's career. Certainly, his fame suffered neither from his banishment nor from the tone of righteous indignation with which he could thus proclaim his contempt for the Empire of Napoleon III.

There was a group of militant exiles on the island, and when, in 1855, they attacked Queen Victoria in their newspaper for visiting Napoleon III, Jersey officials informed them that they would have to leave. The Hugos moved to Guernsey, where they eventually purchased Hauteville House. At about the same time, in the spring of 1856, *Les Contemplations* was published, marking Hugo's reappearance as a lyric poet. Juliette moved to a nearby house that she called Hauteville-Féerie, where the lawn was inscribed with flowers forming a bright "V H." Although Hugo's prestige benefited immensely from his exile, his family suffered from their isolation, especially his daughter Adèle, who was in her early twenties. Eventually, she followed an army officer, Albert Pinson, to Canada, convinced that they would marry. After nine years of erratic, senseless wandering, she was brought home to end her life in a mental institution.

For her father, exile was a time to write. The first two volumes of *La Légende des siècles* (1859-1883; *The Legend of the Centuries*, 1894) was followed by *The Toilers of the Sea* and *The Man Who Laughs*, among other works. In 1859, Napoleon III offered amnesty of Republican exiles, but Hugo refused to accept it, preferring the grandeur of defiance and martyrdom on his rocky island.

After Adèle's flight, the island became intolerable for Madame Hugo. In 1865, she left for Brussels with the younger son, François-Victor, and spent most of her time there during the remainder of Hugo's exile. In his isolation, Hugo continued his work.

On the occasion of the Paris International Exposition in 1867, the imperial censors permitted a revival of *Hernani* at the Théâtre-Français. Adèle traveled to Paris to witness the great success of the play and the adulation of her husband. Another visitor to the Paris Exposition would be instrumental in ending Hugo's self-imposed banishment. Future German Chancellor Otto von Bismarck came to Paris ostensibly on a state visit from Prussia but secretly taking the measure of French armaments. Adèle died in Brussels the following year. Her sons accompanied her body to its grave in France; Hugo stopped at the French border and soon returned to Guernsey with Juliette.

One of Hugo's dreams had always been a United States of Europe, and in Lausanne in 1869, he presided over the congress of the International League for Peace and Freedom. Early in 1870, he was honored by the Second Empire with a revival of *Lucretia Borgia* and a recitation of his poetry before the Emperor by Sarah Bernhardt. On July 14 of that year, the poet planted an acorn at Hauteville House. The future tree was dedicated to "the United States of Europe." By the following day, France and Prussia were at war.

The Franco-Prussian War brought an end to the Second Empire and to Hugo's nineteen years of exile. He returned in time to participate in the siege of Paris and to witness the cataclysmic events of the Commune. His own politics, however, although idealistically liberal and Republican, did not mesh with any political group in a practical way. He refused several minor offices that were offered to him by the new government and resigned after only a month as an elected deputy for Paris to the new National Assembly.

The following years were marked by family sorrows. Soon following Hugo's resignation from active politics, his elder son, Charles, died of an apoplectic stroke. Hugo was to remain devoted to his son's widow, Alice, and to his grandchildren, Jeanne and Georges. In 1872, Adèle was brought home from Barbados, insane. The following year, his younger son, François-Victor, died of tuberculosis. Only the faithful Juliette remained as a companion to Hugo in his old age.

He continued to write unceasingly in Paris, but in 1878 he suffered a stroke. This virtually brought his writing to an end, although works he had written earlier continued to be published. On his birthday in 1881, the Republic organized elaborate festivities in his honor, including a procession of admirers who passed beneath his window for hours. In May, the main part of the avenue d'Eylau was rechristened the avenue Victor-Hugo.

Juliette died in May of 1883. On his birthday in 1885, Hugo received tributes from all quarters as a venerated symbol of the French spirit. He became seriously ill in May, suffering from a lesion of the heart and congestion of the lungs. He died on May 22, 1885. Hugo's funeral was a national ceremony, the coffin lying in state beneath the Arc de Triomphe. He was the only Frenchman to be so honored before the Unknown Soldier after World War I. While Napoleon III lay buried in exile, the remains of Victor Hugo were ceremoniously interred in the Panthéon, France's shrine to her great men of letters.

ANALYSIS

The earliest published full-length fiction by Victor Hugo was *Hans of Iceland*, begun when he was eighteen years old, although not published until three years later. In part a tribute to Adèle Foucher, who was to become his wife, it is a convoluted gothic romance in which it is not clear where the author is being serious and where he is deliberately creating a parody of the popular gothic genre. It is worthwhile to begin with this youthful work, however, because it contains many themes and images that were to remain important in Hugo's work throughout his life.

HANS OF ICELAND

The characters in *Hans of Iceland* are archetypes rather than psychologically realistic figures. In a sense, it is unfair to criticize Hugo for a lack of complexity in his characterizations, because he is a creator of myths and legends—his genius does not lie in the realm of the realistic novel. This is the reason his talent as a novelist is eclipsed by the other great novelists of his century, Stendhal, Honoré de Balzac, Gustave Flaubert, and Émile Zola. Hugo's last novels were written after Flaubert's *Madame Bovary* (1857) and after Zola's first naturalistic novels, yet Hugo's late books remain closer in tone to *Hans of Iceland* than to any contemporary novel.

It is thus more useful to consider *Hans of Iceland* as a romance, following the patterns of myths and legends, rather than as a novel with claims to psychological and historical realism. Although tenuously based on historical fact, set in seventeenth century Norway, the plot of *Hans of Iceland* closely resembles that of the traditional quest. The hero, Ordener Guldenlew (Golden Lion), disguises his noble birth and sets out to rescue his beloved, the pure maiden Ethel, from the evil forces that imprison her with her father, Jean Schumaker, Count Griffenfeld. Ordener's adventures take him through dark and fearsome settings where he must overcome the monster Hans of Iceland, a mysterious being who, although a man, possesses demoniac powers and beastly desires.

As in traditional romance, the characters in *Hans of Iceland* are all good or evil, like black and white pieces in a chess game. Ethel's father is the good former grand chancellor who has been imprisoned for some years after having been unjustly accused of treason. His counterpart is the wicked Count d'Ahlefeld, who, with the treacherous Countess, is responsible for Schumaker's downfall. Their son Frédéric is Ordener's rival for Ethel's love. The most treacherous villain is the Count's adviser, Musdoemon, who turns out to be Frédéric's real father. Opposed to everyone, good or evil, is the man-demon Hans of Iceland, who haunts the land by dark of night, leaving the marks of his clawlike nails on his victims.

Ordener's quest begins in the morgue, where he seeks a box that had been in the possession of a military officer killed by Hans. The box contains documents proving Schumaker's innocence. Believing it to be in Hans's possession, Ordener sets off through storms and danger to recover the box.

As the adventure progresses, Hugo begins to reveal his personal preoccupations and thus to depart from the traditional romance. Hans's ambiguous nature, grotesque as he is, has some unsettling sympathetic qualities. One begins to feel, as the story progresses and as the social villains become more devious and nefarious, that Hans, the social outcast, is morally superior in spite of his diabolically glowing eyes and his tendency to crunch human bones. Hugo appears to suggest the Romantic noble savage beneath a diabolic exterior. Because Ordener is a strangely passive hero, who fails to slay Hans or even to find the box, the reader's interest is transferred to Hans. In this monster with redeeming human qualities, it is not difficult to see the prefiguration of later grotesques such as Quasimodo in *The Hunchback of Notre Dame.*

The social commentary that is constant in Hugo's narratives has its beginning here in the figure of Musdoemon, the true evil figure of the work. This adviser

to the aristocracy, whose name reveals that he has the soul of a rat, betrays everyone until he is at last himself betrayed and hanged. The executioner turns out to be his brother, delighted to have revenge for Musdoemon's treachery toward him years before.

At one point, Musdoemon tricks a group of miners (the good common people) into rebelling against the King in Schumaker's name. Ordener finds himself in the midst of the angry mob as they battle the king's troops. Hans attacks both sides, increasing the confusion and slaughter. Later, at the trial of the rebels on charges of treason, Ordener takes full responsibility, thus diverting blame from Schumaker. Given the choice of execution or marriage to the daughter of the wicked d'Ahlefeld, he chooses death. He and Ethel are married in his cell and are saved by the chance discovery of the documents. Hans gives himself up and dies by his own hand.

THE NOBLE RIVAL

By comparing *Hans of Iceland* with another early novel, *The Noble Rival*, the reader can trace the preoccupations that led to *The Hunchback of Notre Dame* and *Les Misérables*. *The Noble Rival* is the story of a slave revolt in Santo Domingo, Dominican Republic. The hero of the title is a slave as well as the spiritually noble leader of his people. The Romantic hero is Léopold, a Frenchman visiting his uncle's plantation. Like Ordener, Léopold is pure but essentially passive. The heroic energy belongs to the outcast from society, Bug-Jargal. In both novels, Hugo's sympathy for the "people" is apparent. The miners and the slaves point directly to the commoners of Paris in *The Hunchback of Notre Dame*.

THE HUNCHBACK OF NOTRE DAME

At the center of *The Hunchback of Notre Dame* is the theme of fatality, a word which the author imagines to have been inscribed on the wall of one of the cathedral towers as the Greek *anankè*. The cathedral is the focus of the novel, as it was the heart of medieval Paris. It is a spiritual center with an ambiguous demoniac-grotesque spirit within. Claude Frollo, the priest, is consumed by lust for a Gypsy girl, Esmeralda. Quasimodo, the bellringer, a hunchback frighteningly deformed, is elevated by his pure love for Esmeralda, whom he attempts to save from the pernicious Frollo. In an image central to the novel and to Hugo's entire work, Frollo watches a spider and a fly caught in its web. The web, however, stretches across a pane of glass so that even if the fly should manage to escape, it will only hurl itself against the invisible barrier in its flight toward the sun. The priest will be the spider to Esmeralda, but also the fly, caught in the trap of his own consuming desire. All the characters risk entrapment in the web prepared for them by fate. Even if they somehow break free of the web, the glass will block escape until death releases them from earthly concerns.

Esmeralda believes she can "fly to the sun" in the person of the handsome military captain Phoebus, but he is interested in her only in an earthly way. Frollo's destructive passion leads him to set a trap for Esmeralda. For a fee, Phoebus agrees to hide Frollo where he can watch a rendezvous between Phoebus and Esmeralda. Unable to contain himself, the priest leaves his hiding place, stabs Phoebus, and leaves. Esmeralda is, of course, accused of the crime.

Quasimodo saves her from execution and gives her sanctuary in the cathedral, but she is betrayed again by Frollo, who orders her to choose between him and the gallows. Like the fly, Esmeralda tears herself away from the priest to collapse at the foot of the gibbet. Phoebus, who did not die of his wound, remains indifferent to her plight, but Quasimodo pushes Frollo to his death from the tower of Notre Dame as the priest gloats over Esmeralda's execution. Quasimodo, the grotesque, gains in moral stature throughout the novel, just as Frollo falls from grace. Two years later, a deformed skeleton is found in a burial vault beside that of the virtuous Esmeralda.

The Hunchback of Notre Dame and *Les Misérables* are justly Hugo's most famous novels because they combine the exposition of his social ideas with an aesthetically unified structure. By contrast, *The Last Day of a Condemned*, written in 1829, is basically a social treatise on the horrors of prison life. In the same way, *Claude Gueux*, a short work of 1834, protests against the death penalty. In both works, the writer speaks out against society's injustice to man, but it was with *Les Misérables* that the reformer's voice spoke most effectively.

LES MISÉRABLES

Les Misérables tells of the spiritual journey of Jean Valjean, a poor but honorable man, driven in desperation to steal a loaf of bread to feed his widowed sister and her children. Sent to prison, he becomes an embittered, morally deformed creature, until he is redeemed by his love for the orphan girl Cosette. The plot of the novel is quite complex, as Jean rises to respectability and descends again several times. This is true because, as a convict, he must live under an assumed name. His spiritual voyage will not end until he can stand once more as Jean Valjean. His name suggests the French verb *valoir*, "to be worth." Thus, Jean must become worthy of Jean; he cannot have value under a counterfeit name.

His first reappearance as a respectable bourgeois is as Monsieur Madeleine, Mayor of Montreuil-sur-Mer. He is soon called upon, however, to reveal his true identity in order to save another from life imprisonment for having been identified as Jean Valjean, parole breaker. He descends into society's underworld, eluding capture by his nemesis, the policeman Javert. In Hugo's works, the way down is always the way up to salvation. Just as Ordener descended into the mines, *Jean* must now pass through a valley (*Val*) in order to save *Jean*. Here, as in *The Hunchback of Notre Dame*, moral superiority is to be found among the lowly.

In order to save himself, Jean must be the savior of others. He begins by rescuing Cosette from her wicked foster parents. Later, he will save Javert from insurrectionists. His greatest test, however, will be that of saving Marius, the man Cosette loves and who will separate Jean from the girl who is his paradise. This episode is the famous flight through the sewers of Paris, a true descent into the underworld, whence Jean Valjean is reborn, his soul transfigured, clear, and serene. He still has one more trial to endure, that of regaining his own name, which, through a misunderstanding, brings a painful estrangement from Cosette and Marius. He begins to die but is reconciled with his children at the last moment and leaves this life with a soul radiantly transformed.

THE TOILERS OF THE SEA

Les Misérables was written partly in exile, and

certain episodes begin to show a preference for images of water. *The Toilers of the Sea*, written on Guernsey in 1864 and 1865, is a novel dominated by the sea. The text originally included an introductory section entitled "L'Archipel de la Manche" ("The Archipelago of the English Channel"), which Hugo's editor persuaded him to publish separately at a later date (1883). The two parts reveal that Hugo has separated sociology from fiction. It would seem that, at odds with the predominant novelistic style of his time, Hugo preferred not to communicate his social philosophy through the imagery and structure of his novels. Thus, the prologue contains Hugo's doctrine of social progress and his analysis of the geology, customs, and language of the Channel Islands. The larger section that became the published novel is once again the story of a solitary quest.

The hero, Gilliatt, is a fisherman who lives a simple, rather ordinary life with his elderly mother on the island of Guernsey. In their house, they keep a marriage chest containing a trousseau for Gilliatt's future bride. Gilliatt loves Déruchette, niece of Mess Lethierry, inventor of the steamboat *Durande*, with which he has made his fortune in commerce. When the villain, Clubin, steals Lethierry's money and wrecks his steamer, Gilliatt's adventures begin.

Like the king of myth or legend, Lethierry offers his niece's hand in marriage to whomever can salvage the *Durande*. Gilliatt sets out upon the sea. Ominously missing are the magical beasts or mysterious beings who normally appear to assist the hero as he sets off. Even Ordener, for example, had a guide, Benignus Spiagudry, at the beginning of his quest. It is entirely unaided that Gilliatt leaves shore.

He now faces nature and the unknown, completely cut off from human society. He survives a titanic struggle for the ship against the hurricane forces of nature, but he must still descend into an underwater grotto, where he is seized by a hideous octopus. Gilliatt is, in Hugo's words, "the fly of that spider." The language of the passage makes it clear that in freeing himself from the octopus, Gilliatt frees himself from evil.

Exhausted, Gilliatt prays, then sleeps. When he wakes, the sea is calm. He returns to land a savior,

bringing the engine of the ship as well as the stolen money. When he learns that Déruchette wishes to marry another, he gives her his own marriage chest and leaves to die in the rising tide. *The Toilers of the Sea* is considered by many to be the finest and purest expression of Hugo's mythic vision.

Almost immediately after *The Toilers of the Sea*, Hugo turned his attention back to history. In 1866, he began work on the first novel of what he intended to be a trilogy focusing in turn on aristocracy, monarchy, and democracy. The first, *The Man Who Laughs*, is set in England after 1688; the second would have taken place in prerevolutionary France; and the third is *Ninety-three*, a vision of France after 1789. The role of fate is diminished in these last two novels, because Hugo wished to emphasize man's conscience and free will in a social and political context.

THE MAN WHO LAUGHS

In *The Man Who Laughs*, the disfigured hero, Gwynplaine, chooses to leave his humble earthly paradise when he learns that he had been born to the aristocracy. Predictably, the way up leads to Gwynplaine's downfall. Noble society is a hellish labyrinth (another type of web), from which Gwynplaine barely manages to escape. A wolf named Homo helps him find his lost love again, a blind girl named Déa. When she dies, Gwynplaine finds salvation by letting himself sink beneath the water of the Thames.

NINETY-THREE

Hugo's vivid portrayal of a demoniac aristocratic society justified the cause of the French Revolution in 1789, preparing the way for his vision of an egalitarian future as described in his last novel, *Ninety-three*. By choosing to write about 1793 instead of the fall of the Bastille, Hugo was attempting to deal with the Terror, which he considered to have deformed the original ideals of the Revolution.

Rather than the familiar love interest, Hugo has placed the characters Michelle Fléchard and her three children at the center of the novel. In Hugo, kindness to children can redeem almost any amount of wickedness. The monstrous Hans of Iceland, for example, was partially excused because he was avenging the death of his son. It is therefore not surprising to find that each faction in the Revolution is tested and judged according to its treatment of Michelle and her children.

The extreme positions in the violent political clash are represented by the Marquis de Lantenac, the Royalist leader, and his counterpart, Cimourdain, a former priest and fanatic revolutionary. Both men are inflexible and coldly logical in their courageous devotion to their beliefs. The violent excesses of both sides are depicted as demoniac no matter how noble the cause. Human charity and benign moderation are represented in Gauvain, a general in the revolutionary army. He is Lantenac's nephew and the former pupil of Cimourdain. He is clearly also the spokesman for Hugo's point of view.

In the course of events, Lantenac redeems his inhumanity by rescuing Michelle's children from a burning tower. He is now Gauvain's prisoner and should be sent to the guillotine. Gauvain's humanity, however, responds to Lantenac's act of self-sacrifice, and Gauvain arranges for him to escape. It is now Cimourdain's turn, but he remains loyal to his principles, condemning to death his beloved disciple. Before his execution, Gauvain expounds his (Hugo's) idealistic social philosophy in a dialogue with Cimourdin's pragmatic view of a disciplined society based on strict justice.

In this final novel, Hugo's desire to express his visionary ideology overwhelms his talents as a novelist. At the age of seventy, he had become the prophet of a transfigured social order of the future. He would create no more of his compelling fictional worlds. It was time for Hugo the creator of legends to assume the legendary stature of his final decade.

Jan St. Martin

OTHER MAJOR WORKS

PLAYS: *Irtamène*, wr. 1816, pb. 1934 (verse drama); *Inez de Castro*, wr. c. 1818, pb. 1863 (verse drama); *Cromwell*, pb. 1827 (verse drama; English translation, 1896); *Amy Robsart*, pr. 1828 (English translation, 1895); *Hernani*, pr., pb. 1830 (verse drama; English translation, 1830); *Marion de Lorme*, pr., pb. 1831 (verse drama; English translation, 1895); *Le Roi s'amuse*, pr., pb. 1832 (verse drama; *The King's Fool*, 1842, also known as *The King Amuses Himself*, 1964);

Lucrèce Borgia, pr., pb. 1833 (*Lucretia Borgia*, 1842); *Marie Tudor*, pr., pb. 1833 (English translation, 1895); *Angelo, tyran de Padoue*, pr., pb. 1835 (*Angelo, Tyrant of Padua*, 1880); *Ruy Blas*, pr., pb. 1838 (verse drama; English translation, 1890); *Les Burgraves*, pr., pb. 1843 (*The Burgraves*, 1896); *La Grand-mère*, pb. 1865; *Mille Francs de Recompense*, pb. 1866; *Torquemada*, wr. 1869, pb. 1882 (English translation, 1896); *Les Deux Trouvailles de Gallus*, pb. 1881; *Théâtre en liberté*, pb. 1886 (includes *Mangeront-ils?*); *The Dramatic Works*, pb. 1887; *The Dramatic Works of Victor Hugo*, pb. 1895-1896 (4 volumes).

POETRY: *Odes et poésies diverses*, 1822, 1823; *Nouvelles Odes*, 1824; *Odes et ballades*, 1826; *Les Orientales*, 1829 (*Les Orientales: Or, Eastern Lyrics*, 1879); *Les Feuilles d'automne*, 1831; *Les Chants du crépuscule*, 1835 (*Songs of Twilight*, 1836); *Les Voix intérieures*, 1837; *Les Rayons et les ombres*, 1840; *Les Châtiments*, 1853; *Les Contemplations*, 1856; *La Légende des siècles*, 1859-1883 (5 volumes; *The Legend of the Centuries*, 1894); *Les Chansons des rues et des bois*, 1865; *L'Année terrible*, 1872; *L'Art d'être grand-père*, 1877; *Le Pape*, 1878; *La Pitié suprême*, 1879; *L'Âne*, 1880; *Les Quatre vents de l'esprit*, 1881; *The Literary Life and Poetical Works of Victor Hugo*, 1883; *La Fin de Satan*, 1886; *Toute la lyre*, 1888; *Dieu*, 1891; *Les Années funestes*, 1896; *Poems from Victor Hugo*, 1901; *Dernière Gerbe*, 1902; *Poems*, 1902; *The Poems of Victor Hugo*, 1906; *Océan*, 1942.

NONFICTION: *La Préface de Cromwell*, 1827 (English translation, 1896); *Littérature et philosophie mêlées*, 1834; *Le Rhin*, 1842 (*The Rhine*, 1843); *Napoléon le petit*, 1852 (*Napoleon the Little*, 1852); *William Shakespeare*, 1864 (English translation, 1864); *Actes et paroles*, 1875-1876; *Histoire d'un crime*, 1877 (*The History of a Crime*, 1877-1878); *Religions et religion*, 1880; *Le Théâtre en liberté*, 1886; *Choses vues*, 1887 (*Things Seen*, 1887); *En voyage: Alpes et Pyrénées*, 1890 (*The Alps and Pyrenees*, 1898); *France et Belgique*, 1892; *Correspondance*, 1896-1898.

MISCELLANEOUS: *Oeuvres complètes*, 1880-1892 (57 volumes); *Victor Hugo's Works*, 1892 (30 volumes); *Works*, 1907 (10 volumes).

BIBLIOGRAPHY

Bloom, Harold, ed. *Victor Hugo*. New York: Chelsea House, 1988. Essays on all aspects of Hugo's career—two devoted to *Les Misérables*. Includes introduction, chronology, and bibliography.

Brombert, Victor. *Victor Hugo and the Visionary Novel*. Cambridge, Mass.: Harvard University Press, 1984. A study by one of the most distinguished scholars of modern French literature. See especially the chapter on *Les Misérables*. Provides detailed notes and bibliography.

Grant, Richard D. *The Perilous Quest: Image, Myth, and Prophecy in the Narratives of Victor Hugo*. Durham, N.C.: Duke University Press, 1968. Chapters on *The Hunchback of Notre Dame* and *Les Misérables*, and on Hugo's early romances. With a useful bibliography.

Grossman, Kathryn M. *"Les Misérables": Conversion, Revolution, Redemption*. New York: Twayne, 1996. One of Twayne's masterwork studies, this volume is essential for students of the novel. Includes bibliographical references and an index.

Houston, John Porter. *Victor Hugo*. New York: Twayne, 1974. A reliable introductory study, addressing Hugo's life, his early writing, and his later novels. Includes chronology, notes, and annotated bibliography.

Josephson, Matthew. *Victor Hugo: A Realistic Biography of the Great Romantic*. Garden City, N.Y.: Doubleday, 1946. Although superseded by later biographies, Josephson is still a useful, accessible guide for the beginning student of Hugo. He has very helpful "appendix notes" on subjects such as Hugo and the Utopian Socialists and earlier biographies of Hugo.

Richardson, Joanna. *Victor Hugo*. New York: St. Martin's Press, 1976. A well-written, scholarly biography divided into three sections, "The Man," "The Prophet," "The Legend." With detailed notes and extensive bibliography.

Robb, Graham. *Victor Hugo*. New York: W. W. Norton, 1997. The most complete biography in English. See Robb's introduction for a discussion of earlier biographies. Also detailed notes and bibliography.

ZORA NEALE HURSTON

Born: Eatonville, Florida; January 7, 1891
Died: Fort Pierce, Florida; January 28, 1960

PRINCIPAL LONG FICTION
Jonah's Gourd Vine, 1934
Their Eyes Were Watching God, 1937
Moses, Man of the Mountain, 1939
Seraph on the Suwanee, 1948

OTHER LITERARY FORMS

In addition to her four novels, Zora Neale Hurston produced two collections of folklore, *Mules and Men* (1935) and *Tell My Horse* (1938), and an autobiography, *Dust Tracks on a Road* (1942). Hurston also published plays, short stories, and essays in anthologies and in magazines as diverse as *Opportunity*, the *Journal of Negro History*, the *Saturday Evening Post*, the *Journal of American Folklore*, and the *American Legion Magazine*. Finally, she wrote several articles and reviews for such newspapers as the *New York Herald Tribune* and the *Pittsburgh Courier*. Hurston's major works have only been reissued in the late twentieth century. Some of her essays and stories have also been collected and reprinted. Although the anthologies *I Love Myself When I Am Laughing . . .* (1979) and *The Sanctified Church* (1981) helped to bring her writing back into critical focus, some of her works ceased to be readily available, and her numerous unpublished manuscripts can only be seen at university archives and the Library of Congress.

ACHIEVEMENTS

Hurston was the best and most prolific black woman writer of the 1930's. Her novels were highly praised. Even so, Hurston never made more than one thousand dollars in royalties on even her most successful works, and when she died in 1960, she was penniless and forgotten. Hurston's career testifies to the difficulties of a black woman writing for a mainstream white audience whose appreciation was usually superficial and for a black audience whose responses to her work were, of necessity, politicized.

Hurston achieved recognition at a time when, as Langston Hughes declared, "the Negro was in vogue." The Harlem Renaissance, the black literary and cultural movement of the 1920's, created an interracial audience for her stories and plays. Enthusiasm for her work extended through the 1930's, although that decade also marked the beginning of critical attacks. Hurston did not portray blacks as victims stunted by a racist society. Such a view, she believed, implies that black life is only a defensive reaction to white racism. Black and left-wing critics, however, complained that her unwillingness to represent the oppression of blacks and her focus, instead, on an autonomous, unresentful black folk culture served to perpetuate minstrel stereotypes and thus fueled white racism. The radical, racial protest literature of Richard Wright, one of Hurston's strongest critics, became the model for black literature in the 1940's, and publishers on the lookout for protest works showed less and less interest in Hurston's manuscripts. Yet, when she did speak out against American racism and imperialism, her work was often censored. Her autobiography, published in 1942, as well as a number of her stories and articles were tailored by editors to please white audiences. Caught between the attacks of black critics and the censorship of the white publishing industry, Hurston floundered, struggling through the 1940's and 1950's to find other subjects. She largely dropped out of public view in the 1950's, though she continued to publish magazine and newspaper articles.

The African American and feminist political and cultural movements of the 1960's and 1970's provided the impetus for Hurston's rediscovery. The publication of Robert Hemenway's excellent book, *Zora Neale Hurston: A Literary Biography* (1977), and the reissue of her novels, her autobiography, and her folklore collections seem to promise the sustained critical recognition Hurston deserves.

BIOGRAPHY

Zora Neale Hurston was born on January 7, 1891. Her family lived in the all-black Florida town of Eatonville in an eight-room house with a five-acre garden. Her father, the Reverend John Hurston,

(Library of Congress)

mayor of Eatonville for three terms and moderator of the South Florida Baptist Association, wanted to temper his daughter's high spirits, but her intelligent and forceful mother, Lucy Potts Hurston, encouraged her to "jump at de sun." When Hurston was about nine, her mother died. That event and her father's rapid remarriage to a woman his daughter did not like prematurely ended Hurston's childhood. In the next few years, she lived only intermittently at home, spending some time at a school in Jacksonville and some time with relatives. Her father withdrew all financial support during this period, forcing her to commence what was to be a lifelong struggle to make her own living.

When Hurston was fourteen, she took a job as a wardrobe girl to a repertory company touring the South. Hurston left the troupe in Baltimore eighteen months later and finished high school there at Morgan Academy. She went on to study part-time at Howard University in 1918, taking jobs as a manicurist, a waitress, and a maid in order to support herself. At Howard, her literary talents began to emerge. She was admitted to a campus literary club, formed by Alain Locke, a Howard professor and one of the forces behind the Harlem Renaissance. Locke brought Hurston to the attention of Charles S. Johnson, another key promoter of the Harlem Renaissance. Editor of *Opportunity: A Journal of Negro Life*, he published one of her stories and encouraged her to enter the literary contest sponsored by his magazine.

With several manuscripts but little money, Hurston moved to New York City in 1925, hoping to make a career of her writing. Her success in that year's *Opportunity* contest—she received prizes for a play and a story—won her the patronage of Fanny Hurst and a scholarship to complete her education at Barnard College. She studied anthropology there under Franz Boas, leading a seemingly schizophrenic life in the next two years as an eccentric, iconoclastic artist of the Harlem Renaissance on one hand and a budding, scholarly social scientist on the other.

The common ground linking these seemingly disparate parts of Hurston's life was her interest in black folk culture. Beginning in 1927 and extending through the 1930's, she made several trips to collect black folklore in the South and in the Bahamas, Haiti, and Jamaica. Collecting trips were costly, however, as was the time to write up their results. Charlotte Osgood Mason, a wealthy, domineering white patron to a number of African American artists, supported some of that work, as did the Association for the Study of Negro Life and History and the Guggenheim Foundation. Hurston also worked intermittently during the 1930's as a drama teacher at Bethune Cookman College in Florida and at North Carolina College, as a drama coach for the WPA Federal Theatre Project in New York, and as an editor for the Federal Writers' Project in Florida.

Mules and Men and several scholarly and popular articles on folklore were the products of Hurston's collecting trips in the late 1920's and early 1930's. In 1938, she published *Tell My Horse*, the result of trips to Haiti and Jamaica to study hoodoo. As a creative writer, Hurston devised other outlets for her folk materials. Her plays, short stories, and three of her novels, *Jonah's Gourd Vine, Their Eyes Were Watching God*, and *Moses, Man of the Mountain*, make use of folklore. She also presented folk materials in theatrical revues, but even though the productions were enthusiastically received, she could never generate enough backing to finance commercially successful long-term showings.

Hurston's intense interest in black folklore prevented her from sustaining either of her two marriages. She could not reconcile the competing claims of love and work. She married Herbert Sheen, a medical student, in 1927 but separated from him a few months later. They were divorced in 1931. She married Albert Price III in 1939, and they too parted less than one year later. Other romantic relationships ended for the same reason.

In the 1940's, Hurston lost her enthusiasm for writing about black folk culture. She wrote her autobiography and in 1948 published her last novel, *Seraph on the Suwanee*, a work which turns away from black folk culture entirely. The last decade of her life took a downward turn. Falsely accused of committing sodomy with a young boy, Hurston, depressed, dropped out of public view. Through the 1950's, she lived in Florida, struggling for economic survival. She barely managed to support herself by writing newspaper and magazine articles, many of which expressed her increasing political conservatism, and by working as a maid, a substitute teacher, and a librarian. In 1959, she suffered a stroke. Too ill to nurse herself, she was forced to enter a welfare home. She died there on January 28, 1960.

ANALYSIS

For much of her career, Zora Neale Hurston was dedicated to the presentation of black folk culture. She introduced readers to hoodoo, folktales, lying contests, spirituals, the blues, sermons, children's games, riddles, playing the dozens, and, in general, a highly metaphoric folk idiom. Although she represented black folk culture in several genres, Hurston was drawn to the novel form because it could convey folklore as communal behavior. Hurston knew that much of the unconscious artistry of folklore appears in the gestures and tones in which it is expressed and that it gains much of its meaning in performance. Even *Mules and Men*, the folklore collection she completed just before embarking on her first novel (although it was published after *Jonah's Gourd Vine*), "novelizes" what could have been an anthology of disconnected folk materials. By inventing a narrator who witnesses, even participates in, the performance of folk traditions, she combated the inevitable distortion of an oral culture by its textual documentation.

Hurston's motives for presenting black folklore were, in part, political. She wanted to refute contemporary claims that African Americans lacked a distinct culture of their own. Her novels depict the unconscious creativity of the African American proletariat or folk. They represent community members participating in a highly expressive communication system which taught them to survive racial oppression and, moreover, to respect themselves and their community. At the beginning of Hurston's second novel, for example, the community's members are sitting on porches. "Mules and other brutes had occupied their skins" all day, but now it is night, work is over, and they can talk and feel "powerful and human" again: "They became lords of sounds and lesser things. They passed nations through their mouths. They sat in judgment." By showing the richness and the healthy influence of black folk culture, Hurston hoped not only to defeat racist attitudes but also to encourage racial pride among blacks. Why should African Americans wish to imitate a white bourgeoisie? The "Negro lowest down" had a richer culture.

Hurston also had a psychological motive for presenting black folk culture. She drew the folk materials for her novels from the rural, southern black life she knew as a child and subsequently recorded in folklore-collecting trips in the late 1920's and 1930's. She had fond memories of her childhood in the all-black town of Eatonville, where she did not experience poverty or racism. In her autobiographical writings, she suggests that she did not even know that

she was "black" until she left Eatonville. Finally, in Eatonville, she had a close relationship with and a strong advocate in her mother. In representing the rich culture of black rural southerners, she was also evoking a happier personal past.

Although the novel's witnessing narrator provided Hurston with the means to dramatize folklore, she also needed meaningful fictional contexts for its presentation. Her novels are a series of attempts to develop such contexts. Initially, she maintained the southern rural setting for black folk traditions. In her first novel, *Jonah's Gourd Vine*, she re-created Eatonville and neighboring Florida towns. Hurston also loosely re-created her parents' lives with the central characters, John and Lucy Pearson. Though Hurston claimed that an unhappy love affair she had had with a man she met in New York was the catalyst for her second novel, *Their Eyes Were Watching God*, the feeling rather than the details of that affair appear in the novel. The work takes the reader back to Eatonville again and to the porch-sitting storytellers Hurston knew as a child.

MOSES, MAN OF THE MOUNTAIN

With her third novel, *Moses, Man of the Mountain*, however, Hurston turned in a new direction, leaving the Eatonville milieu behind. The novel retells the biblical story of Moses via the folk idiom and traditions of southern rural blacks. Hurston leaves much of the plot of the biblical story intact—Moses does lead the Hebrews out of Egypt—but, for example, she shows Moses to be a great hoodoo doctor as well as a leader and lawgiver. In effect, Hurston simulated the creative processes of folk culture, transforming the story of Moses for modern African Americans just as slaves had adapted biblical stories in spirituals. Hurston may have reenacted an oral and communal process as a solitary writer, but she gave an imaginative rendering of the cultural process all the same.

SERAPH ON THE SUWANEE

Seraph on the Suwanee, Hurston's last novel, marks another dramatic shift in her writing. With this novel, however, she did not create a new context for the representation of folk culture. Rather, she turned away from the effort to present black folklore. *Ser-*

aph on the Suwanee is set in the rural South, but its central characters are white. Hurston apparently wanted to prove that she could write about whites as well as blacks, a desire which surfaced, no doubt, in response to the criticism and disinterest her work increasingly faced in the 1940's. Yet, even when writing of upwardly mobile southern "crackers," Hurston could not entirely leave her previous mission behind. Her white characters, perhaps unintentionally, often use the black folk idiom.

Although Hurston's novels, with the exception of the last, create contexts or develop other strategies for the presentation of folklore, they are not simply showcases for folk traditions; black folk culture defines the novels' themes. The most interesting of these thematic renderings appear in Hurston's first two novels. Hurston knew that black folk culture was composed of brilliant adaptations of African culture to American life. She admired the ingenuity of these adaptations but worried about their preservation. Would a sterile, materialistic white world ultimately absorb blacks, destroying the folk culture they had developed? Her first two novels demonstrate the disturbing influence of white America on black folkways.

JONAH'S GOURD VINE

Jonah's Gourd Vine, Hurston's first novel, portrays the tragic experience of a black preacher caught between black cultural values and the values imposed by his white-influenced church. The novel charts the life of John Pearson, laborer, foreman, and carpenter, who discovers that he has an extraordinary talent for preaching. With his linguistic skills and his wife Lucy's wise counsel, he becomes pastor of the large church Zion Hope and ultimately moderator of a Florida Baptist convention. His sexual promiscuity, however, eventually destroys his marriage and his career.

Though his verbal skills make him a success while his promiscuity ruins him, the novel shows that both his linguistic gifts and his sexual vitality are part of the same cultural heritage. His sexual conduct is pagan and so is his preaching. In praying, according to the narrator, it was as if he "rolled his African drum up to the altar, and called his Congo Gods by Christian names." Both aspects of his cultural heritage speak through him. Indeed, they speak through all members of the African American community, if most intensely through John. A key moment early in the novel, when John crosses over Big Creek, marks the symbolic beginning of his life and shows the double cultural heritage he brings to it. John heads down to the Creek, "singing a new song and stomping the beats." He makes up "some words to go with the drums of the Creek," with the animal noises in the woods, and with the hound dog's cry. He begins to think about the girls living on the other side of Big Creek: "John almost trumpeted exultantly at the new sun. He breathed lustily. He stripped and carried his clothes across, then recrossed and plunged into the swift water and breasted strongly over."

To understand why two expressions of the same heritage have such different effects on John's life, one has to turn to the community to which he belongs. Members of his congregation subscribe to differing views of the spiritual life. The view most often endorsed by the novel emerges from the folk culture. As Larry Neal, one of Hurston's best critics, explains in his introduction to the 1971 reprint of the novel, that view belongs to "a formerly enslaved communal society, non-Christian in background," which does not strictly dichotomize body and soul. The other view comes out of a white culture. It is "more rigid, being a blend of Puritan concepts and the fire-and-brimstone imagery of the white evangelical tradition." That view insists that John, as a preacher, exercise self-restraint. The cultural conflict over spirituality pervades his congregation. While the deacons, whom Hurston often portrays satirically, pressure him to stop preaching, he still has some loyal supporters among his parishioners.

White America's cultural styles and perceptions invade Pearson's community in other ways as well. By means of a kind of preaching competition, the deacons attempt to replace Pearson with the pompous Reverend Felton Cozy, whose preaching style is white. Cozy's style, however, fails to captivate most members of the congregation. Pearson is a great preacher in the folk tradition, moving his congregation to a frenzy with "barbaric thunder-poems." By contrast, Cozy, as one of the parishioners complains, does not give a sermon; he lectures. In an essay Hurston wrote on "The Sanctified Church," she explains this reaction: "The real, singing Negro derides the Negro who adopts the white man's religious ways. . . . They say of that type of preacher, 'Why he don't preach at all. He just lectures.'"

If Pearson triumphs over Cozy, he nevertheless ultimately falls. His sexual conduct destroys his marriage and leads to an unhappy remarriage with one of his mistresses, Hattie Tyson. He is finally forced to stop preaching at Zion Hope. Divorced from Hattie, he moves to another town, where he meets and marries Sally Lovelace, a woman much like Lucy. With her support, he returns to preaching. On a visit to a friend, however, he is tempted by a young prostitute and, to his dismay, succumbs. Although he has wanted to be faithful to his new wife, he will always be a pagan preacher, spirit *and* flesh. Fleeing back to Sally, he is killed when a train strikes his car.

In its presentation of folklore and its complex representation of cultural conflict, *Jonah's Gourd Vine* is a brilliant first novel, although Hurston does not always make her argument sufficiently clear. The novel lacks a consistent point of view. Though she endorses Pearson's African heritage and ridicules representatives of white cultural views, she also creates an admirable and very sympathetic character in Lucy Pearson, who is ruined by her husband's pagan behavior. Nor did Hurston seem to know how to resolve the cultural conflict she portrayed—hence, the *deus ex machina* ending. It was not until she wrote her next novel, *Their Eyes Were Watching God*, that Hurston learned to control point of view and presented a solution to the problem of white influences on black culture.

THEIR EYES WERE WATCHING GOD

The life of Janie Crawford, the heroine of *Their Eyes Were Watching God*, is shaped by bourgeois values—white in origin. She finds love and self-identity only by rejecting that life and becoming a wholehearted participant in black folk culture. Her grandmother directs Janie's entrance into adulthood. Born into slavery, the older woman hopes to find protection and materialistic comforts for Janie in a mar-

riage to the property-owning Logan Killicks. Janie, who has grown up in a different generation, does not share her grandmother's values. When she finds she cannot love her husband, she runs off with Jody Stark, who is on his way to Eatonville, where he hopes to become a "big voice," an appropriate phrase for life in a community that highly values verbal ability. Jody becomes that "big voice" as mayor of the town, owner of the general store, and head of the post office. He lives both a bourgeois and a folk life in Eatonville. He constructs a big house—the kind white people have—but he wanders out to the porch of the general store whenever he wants to enjoy the perpetual storytelling which takes place there. Even though Janie has demonstrated a talent for oratory, however, he will not let her join these sessions or participate in the mock funeral for a mule which has become a popular character in the townspeople's stories. "He didn't," the narrator suggests, "want her talking after such trashy people." As Janie tells a friend years later, Jody "classed me off." He does so by silencing her.

For several years, Janie has no voice in the community or in her private life. Her life begins to seem unreal: "She sat and watched the shadow of herself going about tending store and prostrating itself before Jody." One day, after Stark insults her in front of customers in the store, however, she speaks out and, playing the dozens, insults his manhood. The insult causes an irreconcilable break between them.

After Jody's death, Janie is courted by Tea Cake Woods, a laborer with little money. Though many of her neighbors disapprove of the match, Janie marries him. "Dis ain't no business proposition," she tells her friend Pheoby, "and no race after property and titles. Dis is uh love game. Ah done lived Grandma's way, now Ah mens tuh live mine." Marriage to Tea Cake lowers her social status but frees her from her submissive female role, from her shadow existence. Refusing to use her money, Tea Cake takes her down to the Everglades, where they become migrant workers. She picks beans with him in the fields, and he helps her prepare their dinners. With Tea Cake, she also enters into the folk culture of the Everglades, and that more than anything else enables her to shed her former submissive identity. Workers show up at their house every night to sing, dance, gamble, and, above all, to talk, like the folks in Eatonville on the front porch of the general store. Janie learns how to tell "big stories" from listening to the others, and she is encouraged to do so.

This happy phase of Janie's life ends tragically as she and Tea Cake attempt to escape a hurricane and the ensuing flood. Tea Cake saves Janie from drowning but, in the process, is bitten by a rabid dog. Sick and crazed, he tries to shoot Janie. She is forced to kill him in self-defense. Not everything she has gained during her relationship with Tea Cake, however, dies with him. The strong self-identity she has achieved while living in the Everglades enables her to withstand the unjust resentment of their black friends as well as her trial for murder in a white court. Most important, she is able to endure her own loss and returns to Eatonville, self-reliant and wise. Tea Cake, she knows, will live on in her thoughts and feelings—and in her words. She tells her story to her friend Pheoby—that storytelling event frames the novel—and allows Pheoby to bring it to the other members of the community. As the story enters the community's oral culture, it will influence it. Indeed, as the novel closes, Janie's story has already affected Pheoby. "Ah done growed ten feet higher from jus' listenin' tuh you," she tells Janie. "Ah ain't satisfied wid mahself no mo'."

In her novels, Hurston did not represent the oppression of blacks because she refused to view African American life as impoverished. If she would not focus on white racism, however, her novels do oppose white culture. In *Their Eyes Were Watching God*, Janie does not find happiness until she gives up a life governed by white values and enters into the verbal ceremonies of black folk culture. Loving celebrations of a separate black folk life were Hurston's effective political weapon; racial pride was one of her great gifts to American literature. "Sometimes, I feel discriminated against," she once told her readers, "but it does not make me angry. It merely astonishes me. How *can* any deny themselves the pleasure of my company? It's beyond me."

Deborah Kaplan

OTHER MAJOR WORKS

SHORT FICTION: *Spunk: The Selected Short Stories of Zora Neale Hurston*, 1985.

NONFICTION: *Mules and Men*, 1935; *Tell My Horse*, 1938; *Dust Tracks on a Road*, 1942; *The Sanctified Church*, 1981.

MISCELLANEOUS: *I Love Myself When I Am Laughing . . . and Then Again When I Am Looking Mean and Impressive: A Zora Neale Hurston Reader*, 1979.

BIBLIOGRAPHY

Awkward, Michael, ed. *New Essays on "Their Eyes Were Watching God."* Cambridge, England: Cambridge University Press, 1990. Essays by Robert Hemenway and Nellie McKay on the biographical roots of the novel, and by Hazel Carey on Hurston's use of anthropology. Rachel Blau DuPlessis provides a feminist perspective in "Power, Judgment, and Narrative in a Work of Zora Neale Hurston." Includes an introduction and bibliography.

Gates, Henry Louis, Jr. *The Signifying Monkey: A Theory of Afro-American Literary Criticism*. New York: Oxford University Press, 1988. The chapter on Hurston discusses her best-known novel, *Their Eyes Were Watching God*, as a conscious attempt to rebut the naturalistic view of blacks as "animalistic" that Gates claims she saw in Richard Wright's fiction.

Hemenway, Robert. *Zora Neale Hurston*. Urbana: University of Illinois Press, 1977. An excellent biography of Hurston which also provides much insight into her fiction. Perhaps the single best source of information about the author and her writings.

Hill, Lynda Marion. *Social Rituals and the Verbal Art of Zora Neale Hurston*. Washington, D.C.: Howard University Press, 1996. Chapters on Hurston's treatment of everyday life, science and humanism, folklore, and color, race, and class. Hill also considers dramatic reenactments of Hurston's writing. Includes notes, bibliography, and an appendix on "characteristics of Negro expression."

Howard, Lillie P. *Zora Neale Hurston*. Boston: Twayne, 1980. An important full-length study of Hurston's work which, nevertheless, is not as helpful as it might have been.

Johnson, Barbara. *A World of Difference*. Baltimore: The Johns Hopkins University Press, 1987. The two essays on Hurston examine how her fiction addresses the problem of the social construction of self.

ALDOUS HUXLEY

Born: Laleham, near Godalming, Surrey, England; July 26, 1894

Died: Los Angeles, California; November 22, 1963

PRINCIPAL LONG FICTION

Crome Yellow, 1921
Antic Hay, 1923
Those Barren Leaves, 1925
Point Counter Point, 1928
Brave New World, 1932
Eyeless in Gaza, 1936
After Many a Summer Dies the Swan, 1939
Time Must Have a Stop, 1944
Ape and Essence, 1948
The Genius and the Goddess, 1955
Island, 1962

OTHER LITERARY FORMS

Besides the novel, Aldous Huxley wrote in every other major literary form. He published several volumes of essays and won universal acclaim as a first-rate essayist. He also wrote poetry, plays, short stories, biographies, and travelogues.

ACHIEVEMENTS

Huxley achieved fame as a satirical novelist and essayist in the decade following World War I. In his article "Aldous Huxley: The Ultra-Modern Satirist," published in *The Nation* in 1926, Edwin Muir observed, "No other writer of our time has built up a se-

rious reputation so rapidly and so surely; compared with his rise to acceptance that of Mr. Lawrence or Mr. Eliot has been gradual, almost painful." In the 1920's and the early 1930's, Huxley became so popular that the first London editions of his books were, within a decade of their publication, held at a premium by dealers and collectors. Huxley's early readers, whose sensibilities had been hardened by the war, found his wit, his iconoclasm, and his cynicism to their taste. They were also impressed by his prophetic gifts. Bertrand Russell said, "What Huxley thinks today, England thinks tomorrow." Believing that all available knowledge should be absorbed if humanity were to survive, Huxley assimilated ideas from a wide range of fields and allowed them to find their way into his novels, which came to be variously identified as "novels of ideas," "discussion novels," or "conversation novels." His increasing store of knowledge did not, however, help him overcome his pessimistic and cynical outlook on life.

Huxley's reputation as a novelist suffered a sharp decline in his later years. In *The Novel and the Mod-*

(CORBIS/Bettmann)

ern World (1939), David Daiches took a highly critical view of Huxley's novels, and since then, many other critics have joined him. It is often asserted that Huxley was essentially an essayist whose novels frequently turn into intellectual tracts. It has also been held that his plots lack dramatic interest and his characters are devoid of real substance. Attempts were made in the late twentieth century, however, to rehabilitate him as an important novelist. In any case, no serious discussion of twentieth century fiction can afford to ignore Huxley's novels.

BIOGRAPHY

Aldous Leonard Huxley was born at Laleham, near Godalming, Surrey, on July 26, 1894. His father, Leonard Huxley, a biographer and historian, was the son of Thomas Henry Huxley, the great Darwinist, and his mother, Julia, was the niece of Matthew Arnold. Sir Julian Huxley, the famous biologist, was his brother. With this intellectual and literary family background, Huxley entered Eton at the age of fourteen. Owing to an attack of *keratitis punctata*, causing blindness, he had to withdraw from school within two years, an event which left a permanent mark on his character, evident in his reflective temperament and detached manner. He learned to read Braille and continued his studies under tutors. As soon as he was able to read with the help of a magnifying glass, he went to Balliol College, Oxford, where he studied English literature and philosophy.

Huxley started his career as a journalist on the editorial staff of *The Athenaeum* under J. Middleton Murry. He relinquished his journalistic career when he could support himself by his writing. By 1920, he had three volumes of verse and a collection of short stories to his credit. He had also become acquainted with a number of writers, including D. H. Lawrence. While in Italy in the 1920's, he met Lawrence again, and the two became close friends. Lawrence exercised a profound influence on Huxley, particularly in his distrust of intellect, against his faith in blood consciousness. Later, Huxley became a disciple of Gerald Heard, the pacifist, and took an active part in Heard's pacifist movement. In 1937, he moved to California, where he came into contact with the

Ramakrishna Mission in Hollywood. In Hinduism and Buddhism, Huxley found the means of liberation from man's bondage to the ego, a problem which had concerned him for a long time. To see if the mystical experience could be chemically induced, Huxley took drugs in 1953, and his writings concerning hallucinogenic drugs helped to popularize their use.

Huxley married Maria Nys in 1919. After her death in 1955, he married Laura Archera in 1956. On November 22, 1963, Huxley died in Los Angeles, where his body was cremated the same day. There was no funeral, but friends in London held a memorial service the next month.

ANALYSIS

Aldous Huxley's novels present, on the whole, a bitterly satirical and cynical picture of contemporary society. A recurring theme in his work is the egocentricity of the people of the twentieth century, their ignorance of any reality transcending the self, their loneliness and despair, and their pointless and sordid existence. Devoid of any sense of ultimate purpose, the world often appears to Huxley as a wilderness of apes, baboons, monkeys, and maggots, a veritable inferno, presided over by Belial himself. The dominant negativism in the novelist's outlook on life is pointedly and powerfully revealed by Will Farnaby, a character in his book *Island*, who is fond of saying that he will not take yes for an answer.

Though Huxley finds the contemporary world largely hopeless, he reveals the possibility of redemption. Little oases of humanity, islands of decency, and atolls of liberated souls generally appear in his fictional worlds. A good number of his characters transcend their egos, achieve completeness of being, recognize the higher spiritual goals of life, and even dedicate their lives to the service of an indifferent humanity. Even Will Farnaby, who will not take yes for an answer, finally casts his lot with the islanders against the corrupt and the corrupting world. It is true that these liberated individuals are not, in Huxley's novels, a force strong enough to resist the onward march of civilization toward self-destruction, but they are, nevertheless, a testimony to the author's faith in the possibilities of sanity even in the most difficult of times. No one who agrees with Huxley's assessment of the modern world will ask for a stronger affirmation of faith in human redemption.

Huxley believed that man's redemption lies in his attainment of "wholeness" and integrity. His concept of wholeness did not, however, remain the same from the beginning to the end of his career. As he matured as a novelist, Huxley's sense of wholeness achieved greater depth and clarity. Under the influence of D. H. Lawrence, Huxley viewed wholeness in terms of the harmonious blending of all human faculties. Writing under the influence of Gerald Heard, he expanded his idea of wholeness to include a mystical awareness of the unity of man with nature. Coming under the influence of the Eastern religions, especially Hinduism and Buddhism, he gave his concept of wholeness further spiritual and metaphysical depth.

CROME YELLOW

In *Crome Yellow*, his first novel, Huxley exposed the egocentricity of modern man, his inability to relate to others or recognize any reality, social or spiritual, outside himself, and the utter pointlessness of his life. Jenny Mullion, a minor character in the novel, symbolically represents the situation that prevails in the modern world by the almost impenetrable barriers of her deafness. It is difficult for anyone to carry on an intelligent conversation with her. Once early in the book, when Denis Stone, the poet, inquires if she slept well, she speaks to him, in reply, about thunderstorms. Following this ineffectual conversation, Denis reflects on the nature of Jenny Mullion.

> Parallel straight lines . . . meet only at infinity. He might talk for ever of care-charmer sleep and she of meteorology till the end of time. Did one ever establish contact with anyone? We are all parallel straight lines. Jenny was only a little more parallel than most.

Almost every character in the novel is set fast in the world that he has made for himself and cannot come out of it to establish contact with others. Henry even declaims, "How gay and delightful life would be if one could get rid of all the human contacts!" He is of the view that "the proper study of mankind is books."

His history of his family, which took him twenty-five years to write and four years to print, was obviously undertaken in order to escape human contacts. If Henry is occupied with the history of Crome, Priscilla, his wife, spends her time cultivating a rather ill-defined malady, betting, horoscope reading, and studying Barbecue-Smith's books on spiritualism. Barbecue-Smith busies himself with infinity. Bodiham, the village priest, is obsessed by the Second Coming. Having read somewhere about the dangers of sexual repression, Mary Bracegirdle hunts for a lover who will provide her with an outlet for her repressed instincts. Denis constantly broods over his failure as a writer, as a lover, and as a man. Scogan, disdainful of life, people, and the arts, finds consolation only in reason and ideas and dreams about a scientifically controlled Rational State where babies are produced in test tubes and artists are sent to a lethal chamber.

Though there is a good deal of interaction among the guests at Crome, no real meeting of minds or hearts takes place among them; this failure to connect is best illustrated by the numerous hopeless love affairs described in the novel. Denis, for example, loves Anne, but his repeated attempts to convey his love for her fail. Anne, who is four years older than Denis, talks to him as if he were a child and does not know that he is courting her. Mary falls in love with Denis only to be rebuffed. Then, she makes advances to Gombauld, the painter, with no better result. Next, she pursues Ivor, the man of many gifts and talents, and is brokenhearted to learn that she means nothing to him. She is finally seen in the embrace of a young farmer of heroic proportions, and it is anybody's guess what comes of this affair. Even the relationship between Anne and Gombauld, which showed every promise of maturation into one of lasting love, meets, at the end, the same fate as the others.

Thumbing through Jenny's red notebook of cartoons, Denis suddenly becomes conscious of points of view other than his own. He learns that there are others who are "in their way as elaborate and complete as he is in his." Denis's appreciation of the world outside himself comes, however, too late in the novel. Though he would like to abandon the plan of his intended departure from Crome, particularly when he sees that it makes Anne feel wretched, he is too proud to change his mind and stay in Crome to try again with her. Thus, the characters in *Crome Yellow* remain self-absorbed, separated from one another, and hardly concerned with the ultimate ends of life. Scogan betrays himself and others when he says, "We all know that there's no ultimate point."

Antic Hay

Antic Hay, Huxley's second novel, presents, like *Crome Yellow*, an infernolike picture of contemporary society, dominated by egocentric characters living in total isolation from society and suffering extreme loneliness, boredom, and despair. Evidence of self-preoccupation and isolation is abundant. Gumbril Junior continually dwells on his failings and on his prospects of getting rich. He retires every now and then to his private rooms at Great Russell Street, where he enjoys his stay, away from people. Lypiatt, a painter, poet, and musician, is without a sympathetic audience. "I find myself alone, spiritually alone," he complains. Shearwater, the scientist, has no interest in anything or anyone except in the study of the regulative function of the kidneys. Mercaptan is a writer whose theme is "the pettiness, the simian limitations, the insignificance and the absurd pretentiousness of *Homo* soi-disant *Sapiens*."

The men and women in *Antic Hay*, each living in his or her private universe, are unable to establish any true and meaningful relationships with one another. Myra Viveash is cold and callous toward men who come to her and offer their love: Gumbril Junior, Lypiatt, Shearwater, and others. She contemptuously lends herself to them. Lypiatt, hopelessly in love with her, finally takes his life. Gumbril, deserted by Myra, feels revengeful; in turn, he is cruelly cynical in his treatment of Mrs. Rosie Shearwater. Because of his carelessness, he loses Emily, who might have brought some happiness and meaning into his life. Engaged in his scientific research, Shearwater completely ignores his wife, with the result that she gives herself to other men. Men and women can easily find sexual partners, which does not, however, close the distance between them: They remain as distant as ever.

On the eve of Gumbril's intended departure from London for the Continent, Gumbril and Myra taxi the entire length and breadth of the West End to meet friends and invite them to a dinner that night. Their friends are, significantly enough, engaged in one way or another and shut up in their rooms—Lypiatt writing his life for Myra; Coleman sleeping with Rosie; and Shearwater cycling in a hot box in his laboratory. Despite the lovely moon above on the summer night and the poignant sorrow in their hearts, Gumbril and Myra make no attempt to take advantage of their last ride together and come closer. Instead, they aimlessly drive from place to place.

Those Barren Leaves

Huxley's next novel, *Those Barren Leaves*, shows how people who might be expected to be more enlightened are as self-centered as the mass of humanity. The setting of the novel, which deals with a circle of British intellectuals in Italy, immediately and powerfully reinforces the fact of their social isolation.

Mrs. Lilian Aldwinkle, a patroness of the arts and a votary of love, wants to believe that the whole world revolves around her. As usual, she is possessive of her guests who have assembled at her newly bought palace of Cybo Malaspina in the village of Vezza in Italy, and she wants them to do as she commands. She is unable, however, to hold them completely under her control. In spite of all her efforts, she fails to win the love of Calamy, and later of Francis Chelifer; Chelifer remains unmoved even when she goes down on her knees and begs for his love. She sinks into real despair when her niece escapes her smothering possessiveness and falls in love with Lord Hovenden. Well past her youth, Mrs. Aldwinkle finds herself left alone with nobody to blame but herself for her plight.

Miss Mary Thriplow and Francis Chelifer are both egocentric writers, cut off from the world of real human beings. Miss Thriplow is obsessed with her suffering and pain, which are mostly self-induced. Her mind is constantly busy, spinning stories on gossamer passions she experiences while moving, talking, and loving. Conscious of the unreality of the life of upper-class society, Chelifer gives up poetry and also the opportunity of receiving a fellowship at Oxford in favor of a job as editor of *The Rabbit Fanciers' Gazette* in London. The squalor, the repulsiveness, and the stupidity of modern life constitute, in Chelifer's opinion, reality. Because it is the artist's duty to live amid reality, he lives among an assorted group of eccentrics in a boardinghouse in Gog's court, which he describes as "the navel of reality." If Miss Thriplow is lost in her world of imagination and art, Chelifer is lost in "the navel of reality"—equidistant from the heart of reality.

Through the character of Calamy, Huxley suggests a way to overcome the perverse, modern world. Rich, handsome, and hedonistic, Calamy was once a part of this world, but he no longer enjoys running after women, wasting his time in futile intercourse, and pursuing pleasure. Rather, he spends his time reading, satisfying his curiosity about things, and thinking. He withdraws to a mountain retreat, hoping that his meditation will ultimately lead him into the mysteries of existence, the relationship between men, and that between man and the external world.

Calamy's withdrawal to a mountain retreat is, no doubt, an unsatisfactory solution, particularly in view of the problem of egocentricity and isolation of the individual from society raised in *Those Barren Leaves* and Huxley's two preceding novels. It may, however, be noted that Calamy's isolation is not a result of his egocentricity: He recognizes that there are spheres of reality beyond the self.

POINT COUNTER POINT

Point Counter Point, Huxley's first mature novel, is regarded by many critics as his masterpiece, a major work of twentieth century fiction. By introducing similar characters facing different situations and different characters facing a similar situation, a technique analogous to the musical device of counterpoint, Huxley presents a comprehensive and penetrating picture of the sordidness of contemporary society.

Mark Rampion, a character modeled upon D. H. Lawrence, sees the problem of modern man as one of lopsided development. Instead of achieving a harmonious development of all human faculties—reason, intellect, emotion, instinct, and body—modern man allows one faculty to develop at the expense of the others. "It's time," Rampion says, "there was a revolt in favor of life and wholeness."

Huxley makes a penetrating analysis of the failure of his characters to achieve love and understanding. Particularly acute is his analysis of Philip Quarles, a critical self-portrait of the author. Since a childhood accident, which left him slightly lame in one leg, Philip has shunned society and has developed a reflective and intellectual temperament. As a result of his constant preoccupation with ideas, the emotional side of his character atrophies, and he is unable to love even his wife with any degree of warmth. In the ordinary daily world of human contacts, he is curiously like a foreigner, not at home with his fellows, finding it difficult or impossible to enter into communication with any but those who can speak his native intellectual language of ideas. He knows his weakness, and he tries unsuccessfully to transform a detached intellectual skepticism into a way of harmonious living. It is no wonder that his wife, Lilian, feels exasperated with his coldness and unresponsiveness and feels that she could as well love a bookcase.

Philip, however, is not as hopeless a case of lopsided development as the rest of the characters who crowd the world of *Point Counter Point*. Lord Edward Tantamount, the forty-year-old scientist, is in all but intellect a child. He is engaged in research involving the transplantation of the tail of a newt onto the stump of its amputated foreleg to find out if the tail will grow into a leg or continue incongruously to grow as a tail. He shuts himself up in his laboratory most of the day and a good part of the night, avoiding all human contact. Lady Edward, his wife, and Lucy Tantamount, his daughter, live for sexual excitement. Spandril, who prides himself on being a sensualist, actually hates women. Suffering from a sense of betrayal by his mother when she remarries, he attracts women only to torture them. Burlap wears a mask of spirituality, but he is a materialist to the core. Molly, pretty and plump, makes herself desirable to men but lacks genuine emotional interest. The novel contains an assortment of barbarians (to use the language of Rampion) of the intellect, of the body, and of the spirit, suffering from "Newton's disease," "Henry

Ford's disease," "Jesus' disease," and so on—various forms of imbalance in which one human faculty is emphasized at the expense of the others.

Point Counter Point presents an extremely divided world. None of the numerous marriages, except that of the Rampions, turns out well, nor do the extramarital relationships. Both Lilian Quarles and her brother, Walter Bidlake, have problems with their spouses. Lilian plans to leave her husband, Philip Quarles, and go to Everard Webley, a political leader, who has been courting her, but the plan is terminated with Webley's murder. After leaving his wife, Walter lives with Marjorie Carling but finds her dull and unexciting within two years. Ignoring Marjorie, who is pregnant with his child, Walter begins to court Lucy Tantamount, a professional siren, who, after keeping him for a long time in a state of uncertainty, turns him away. John Bidlake, the father of Lilian and Walter, has been married three times and has had a number of love affairs. Sidney Quarles, the father of Philip, has had many secret affairs. Disharmony thus marks the marital world presented in the novel, effectively dramatized by means of parallel, contrapuntal plots.

Mark and Mary Rampion serve as a counterpoint to the gallery of barbarians and lopsided characters in the novel. Although Mary comes from an aristocratic family and Mark belongs to the working class, they do not suffer from the usual class prejudices. Transcending their origins, they have also transcended the common run of egocentric and self-divided personalities. They have achieved wholeness and integrity in personality and outlook. There is no dichotomy between what they say and what they do. Mark's art is a product of lived experience, and his concern for it is inseparable from his concern for life.

Though the dominant mood of Huxley's early novels is one of negativism and despair, the Rampions exemplify his faith in the possibility of achieving individual wholeness and loving human relationships. The Rampions may not be able to change the state of affairs in the modern world, but their presence itself is inspiring; what is more, they are, unlike Calamy of *Those Barren Leaves*, easily accessible to all those who want to meet them.

BRAVE NEW WORLD

Brave New World, Huxley's best-known work, describes a centrally administered and scientifically controlled future society in A.F. 632 (A.F. standing for After Ford), around six hundred years from the twentieth century. It is difficult to recognize the people of Huxley's future World State as human beings. Decanted from test tubes in laboratories, the population of the Brave New World comes in five standardized varieties: Alphas, Betas, Gammas, Deltas, and Epsilons. Each group is genetically conditioned to carry out different tasks. By various methods of psychological conditioning, they are trained to live in total identification with society and to shun all activities that threaten the stability of the community. The State takes full care of them, including the emotional side of their life. All their desires are satisfied; they do not want what they cannot get. With substitutes and surrogates such as the Pregnancy Substitute and the Violent Passion Surrogate, life is made happy and comfortable for everyone. Although people have nothing of which to complain, they seem to suffer pain continually. Relief from pain is, however, readily available to them in *soma*, which is distributed by the State every day.

Sentiments, ideas, and practices which liberate the human spirit find no place in Huxley's scientific utopia and are, in fact, put down as harmful to the stability of the community. Parentage, family, and home become obsolete; sex is denuded of all its mystery and significance. Small children are encouraged to indulge in erotic play so that they learn to take a strictly matter-of-fact view of sex. Men and women indulge in copulation to fill idle hours. Loyalty in sex and love is regarded as abnormal behavior. Love of nature, solitude, and meditation are looked upon as serious maladies requiring urgent medical attention. Art, science, and religion are all considered threatening. Patience, courage, self-denial, beauty, nobility, and truth become irrelevant to a society that believes in consumerism, comfort, and happiness.

Huxley shows how some people in the Brave New World, despite every care taken by the State to ensure their place in the social order, do not fall in line. Bernard Marx yearns for Lenina Crowne and wants to take her on long walks in lonely places. Helmholtz Watson's creative impulses demand poetic expression. Even Mustapha Mond, the Resident Controller of Western Europe, is somewhat regretful over his abandonment of scientific research in favor of his present position. People who stubbornly refuse to conform to the social order are removed promptly by the State to an island where they can live freely according to their wishes.

It is through the character of John, the Savage, from the Reservation, that Huxley clearly exposes the vulgarity and horror of the Brave New World. Attracted to civilization on seeing Lenina, the Savage soon comes to recoil from it. In his long conversation with Mustapha Mond, he expresses his preference for the natural world of disease, unhappiness, and death over the mechanical world of swarming indistinguishable sameness. Unable to get out of it, he retires to a lonely place where he undertakes his purification by taking mustard and warm water, doing hard labor, and resorting to self-flagellation.

In *Brave New World*, Huxley presents a world in which wholeness becomes an object of a hopeless quest. Looking back at the novel, he observed that this was the most serious defect of the story. In a foreword written in 1946, he said that if he were to rewrite the book, he would offer the Savage a third alternative: Between the utopian and the primitive horns of his dilemma would lie the possibility of sanity—a possibility already actualized, to some extent, in a community of exiles and refugees from the Brave New World, living within the borders of the Reservation.

Eyeless in Gaza

In *Eyeless in Gaza*, Huxley returns to the subject of egocentric modern man deeply buried in intellectual preoccupations, sensuality, ideology, and fanaticism. Sensualists abound in *Eyeless in Gaza*. The most notorious among them are Mrs. Mary Amberley and her daughter, Helen Ledwidge, both mistresses at different times to Anthony Beavis, the central character in the novel. Believing in "sharp, short, and exciting" affairs, Mary keeps changing her lovers until she gets prematurely old, spent, and poor. When nobody wants to have her any more, she takes to morphine to

forget her misery. Helen marries Hugh Ledwidge but soon realizes that he is incapable of taking an interest in anything except his books. To compensate for her unhappy married life, she goes from man to man in search of emotional satisfaction. Indeed, sensuality marks the lives of most of the members of the upper-class society presented in the novel.

In addition to sensualists, various other types of single-minded characters share the world of *Eyeless in Gaza*. Brian, one of Anthony's classmates and friends, suffers from a maniacal concern for chastity, and his mother shows a great possessiveness toward him. Mark, another of Anthony's classmates, becomes a cynical revolutionary. John Beavis, Anthony's father, makes philology the sole interest of his life. There are also Communists, Fascists, Fabians, and other fanatics, all fighting for their different causes.

Anthony Beavis is estranged early in his life from men and society after the death of his mother. He grows into manhood cold and indifferent to people. He finds it a disagreeable and laborious task to establish contacts; even with his own father, he maintains a distance. He does not give himself away to his friends or to the women he loves. *Elements of Sociology*, a book Beavis is engaged in writing, assumes the highest priority in his life, and he is careful to avoid the "non-job," personal relations and emotional entanglements, which might interfere with his work's progress. As he matures, however, Beavis aspires to achieve a sense of completeness above the self: "I value completeness. I think it's one's duty to develop all one's potentialities—*all* of them." At this stage, he believes in knowledge, acquired by means of intellect rather than by Laurentian intuition. He is interested only in knowing about truth, not experiencing it like a saint: "I'm quite content with only *knowing* about the way of perfection." He thinks that experience is not worth the price, for it costs one's liberty. Gradually, he realizes that knowledge is a means to an end, rather than an end in itself, a means to achieve freedom from the self. After being so enlightened, he feels genuine love for Helen, who remains unmoved, however, because of her past experiences with him. From Dr. Miller, the anthropologist,

Beavis learns how to obliterate the self and achieve wholeness through love and selfless service. He has a mystic experience of the unity of all life and becomes a pacifist to serve humankind.

AFTER MANY A SUMMER DIES THE SWAN

In *After Many a Summer Dies the Swan*, his first novel after his move to California, Huxley satirized the frenzied attempts made by men of the twentieth century to enrich their lives, stressing that the peace that comes with transcendence can bring an enduring joy. Huxley illustrates the vacuity of modern life through the character of Mr. Stoyte, an old California oil magnate living amid every conceivable luxury and comfort. With endless opportunities before him to make more money and enjoy life (he keeps a young mistress of twenty-two), Stoyte wants to live as long as he can. He finances Dr. Obispo's research on longevity in the hope that he will be able to benefit from the results of the doctor's experiments. He acquires the valuable Haubert Papers, relating to the history of an old English family, in order to discover the secret of the long life of the Fifth Earl, and he hires Jeremy Pordage, an English scholar, to arrange the papers. Dr. Obispo and his assistant, Pete, are basically no different from Mr. Stoyte in their outlooks. They believe that they will be rendering a great service to humanity by extending man's life, little realizing that growing up, as they conceive it, is really growing back into the kind of apelike existence represented by the life of the Fifth Earl. Jeremy Pordage has no real interest in anything except literature, and he too betrays a narrowness of outlook.

Propter exemplifies Huxley's dedicated search for more-than-personal consciousness. Retired from his university job, he spends his time helping poor migrant workers, trying to find ways of being self-reliant, and thinking about the timeless good. He argues that nothing good can be achieved at the human level, which is the level of "time and craving," the two aspects of evil. He disapproves most of what goes on in the name of patriotism, idealism, and spiritualism because he thinks that they are marks of man's greed and covetousness. One should, in his view, aim at the highest ideal: the liberation from personality, time, and craving into eternity.

TIME MUST HAVE A STOP

Bruno Rontini, the mystic saint in *Time Must Have a Stop*, observes that only one out of every ten thousand herrings manages to break out of his carapace completely, and few of those that break out become full-sized fish. He adds that the odds against a man's spiritual maturation today are even greater. Most people remain, according to him, spiritual children.

Time Must Have a Stop presents the obstacles that Sebastian Barnack has to face before he can reach full spiritual maturation. If egocentricity and single-mindedness were the main hurdles for Philip Quarles and Anthony Beavis, Sebastian's problems are created by his weak personality, shaped by his puritanical and idealistic father. He possesses fine poetic and intellectual endowments, but he is disappointed with his own immature appearance. Even though he is aware of his superior gifts, he looks "like a child" at seventeen. Naturally, his relatives and friends take an adoptive attitude toward him and try to influence him in different ways. Eustace, his rich and self-indulgent uncle, teaches him how to live and let live and enjoy life. Mrs. Thwale helps him to overcome his shyness in a most outrageous manner. There are many others who try to mold Sebastian's destiny and prevent him from true self-realization.

Huxley offers further insights into Propter's mystical faith through the character of Bruno Rontini, under whose guidance Sebastian finally receives enlightenment. Bruno believes that there is only one corner of the universe that one can be certain of improving, and that is one's own self. He says that a man has to begin there, not outside, not on other people, for a man has to *be* good before he can *do* good. Bruno believes that only by taking the fact of eternity into account can one free one's enslaved thoughts: "And it is only by deliberately paying our attention and our primary allegiance to eternity that we can prevent time from turning our lives into a pointless or diabolic foolery." Under the guidance of Bruno, Sebastian becomes aware of a timeless and infinite presence. After his spiritual liberation, he begins to work for world peace. He thinks that one of the indispensable conditions for peace is "a shared theology."

He evolves a "Minimum Working Hypothesis," to which all men of all countries and religions can subscribe.

APE AND ESSENCE

Huxley's increasing faith in the possibility of man's liberation in this world did not, at any time, blind him to man's immense capacity for evil. *Ape and Essence* describes how man's apelike instincts bring about the destruction of the world through a nuclear World War III. New Zealand escapes the holocaust, and in A. D. 2108, about one hundred years after the war, the country's Re-Discovery Expedition to North America reaches the coast of Southern California, at a place about twenty miles west of Los Angeles, where Dr. Poole, the Chief Botanist of the party, is taken prisoner by descendants of people who survived the war. Though some Californians have survived the war, the effects of radioactivity still show in the birth of deformed babies, who are liquidated one day of the year in the name of the Purification of the Race. Men and women are allowed free sexual intercourse only two weeks a year following the Purification ceremony so that all the deformed babies that are born in the year are taken care of at one time. Women wear shirts and trousers embroidered with the word "no" on their breasts and seats, and people who indulge in sex during any other part of the year, "Hots" as they are called, are buried alive or castrated and forced to join the priesthood, unless they are able to escape into the community of "Hots" in the north. The California survivors dig up graves to relieve the dead bodies of their clothes and other valuable items, roast bread over fires fueled by books from the Public Library, and worship Belial.

Introducing the film script of *Ape and Essence*, Huxley suggested that present society, even under normal conditions, is not basically different from the society of the survivors depicted in the novel. Gandhi's assassination, he says, had very little impact on most people, who remained preoccupied with their own petty personal problems. Under normal conditions, this unspiritual society would grow into the kind of society represented by Dr. Poole and his team. Dr. Poole is portrayed as a middle-aged child, full of inhibitions and suppressed desires, suffering under the dominance of his puritanical mother.

Ironically, Dr. Poole experiences a sense of wholeness in the satanic postatomic world, as he sheds his inhibitions and finds a free outlet for his suppressed desires during the sexual orgies following the Purification ceremony. Declining the invitation of the Arch Vicar to join his order, Dr. Poole escapes with Loola, the girl who has effected his awakening, into the land of the "Hots." Through the episode of Dr. Poole, Huxley suggests that self-transcendence is possible even in the worst of times.

THE GENIUS AND THE GODDESS

The Genius and the Goddess describes how Rivers, brought up like Dr. Poole of *Apes and Essence* in a puritanical family, undergoes a series of disturbing experiences in the household of Henry and Katy Maartens, which apparently lead him into a spiritual awakening in the end. Rivers joins the Maartens household to assist Henry, the "genius," in his scientific research. He is shocked when Katy, the "goddess," climbs into his bed and shocked again when he sees Katy, rejuvenated by her adultery, performing her wifely devotions with all earnestness, as if nothing had happened. To his further bewilderment and shock, he discovers that he is sought by the daughter as well. The mother outwits the daughter, but Katy and Rivers face the danger of being exposed before Henry. Rivers is, however, saved from disgrace when the mother and daughter both are killed in a car accident. Rivers is an old man as he narrates the story of his progress toward awareness. Though his final awakening is not described, one can safely infer from his attitude toward his past experiences that he has risen above Katy's passion and Henry's intellect to a level outside and above time and has achieved a sense of wholeness. There is, indeed, no way of telling how grace comes.

ISLAND

As previously noted, Huxley creates in almost every novel an island of decency to illustrate the possibility of achieving liberation from bondage to the ego and to time even amid the chaos of modern life. This island is generally represented by an individual or a group of individuals, or it is simply stated to be located in some remote corner of the world. In his last novel, *Island*, Huxley offers a picture of a whole society that has evolved a set of operations, such as yoga, *dhyana* (meditation), *maithuna* (yoga of love), and Zen, to achieve self-transcendence and realize the Vedantic truth, *tat tvam asi*, "thou art That."

In Huxley's island of Pala, the chief concern underlying child care, education, religion, and government is to ensure among its citizens a harmonious development of all human faculties and an achievement of a sense of completeness. To save their children from crippling influences, the parents of Pala bring up one another's children on a basis of mutual exchange. In school, children are taught the important aspects of life from biology to ecology, from sex to religion. They are taken to maternity hospitals so that they can see how children are born; they are even shown how people die. No one subject or area is given exclusive importance. The credo is that "nothing short of everything will really do." When they come of age, boys and girls freely engage in sex. Suppressed feelings and emotions are given an outlet in a vigorous type of dance. An admixture of Hinduism and Buddhism is the religion of the people, but there is no orthodoxy about it. "Karuna" or compassion and an attention to "here and now," to what is happening at any given moment, are the basic tenets of their way of life. Moksha medicines are freely available to those who want to extend their awareness and get a glimpse of the Clear Light and a knowlege of the Divine Ground. As people know how to live gracefully, they also know how to die gracefully when the time for death comes. The country has followed a benevolent monarchy for one hundred years. The nation is aligned neither with the capitalist countries nor with the communists. It is opposed to industrialization and militarization. It has rich oil resources but has refused to grant licenses to the numerous oil companies that are vying to exploit Pala. Will Farnaby, the journalist who has managed to sneak ashore the forbidden island, is so greatly impressed by the imaginative and creative Palanese way of life that he abandons the mission for which he went to the island, which was to obtain, by any means possible, a license for the South East-Asia Petroleum Company to drill for oil on the island.

Huxley fully recognizes the extreme vulnerability of the ideal of integrity and wholeness in the modern world. The state of Pala has, for example, incurred the displeasure of both the capitalist and Communist countries by its policy of nonalignment. Many big companies are resorting to bribery in an effort to get a foothold on the island. Colonel Dipa, the military dictator of the neighboring state of Randang-Lobo, has expansionist ambitions. While Pala is thus threatened by the outside world, corruption has also set in from within. Dowager Rani and Murugan, her son, disapprove of the isolationist policies of the island and want their country to march along with the rest of the world. On the day Murugan is sworn king, he invites the army from Randang-Lobo to enter the island and massacre the people who have been opposed to his progressive outlook.

Huxley's novels not only present the horrors of the modern world, but they also show ways of achieving spiritual liberation and wholeness. Huxley is among the few writers of the twentieth century who fought a brave and relentless battle against life-destroying forces. Untiringly, he sought ways of enriching life by cleansing the doors of perception, awakening his readers to the vital spiritual side of their beings.

S. Krishnamoorthy Aithal

OTHER MAJOR WORKS

SHORT FICTION: *Limbo*, 1920; *Mortal Coils*, 1922; *Little Mexican, and Other Stories*, 1924 (pb. in U. S. as *Young Archimedes, and Other Stories*, 1924); *Two or Three Graces, and Other Stories*, 1926; *Brief Candles: Stories*, 1930; *The Gioconda Smile*, 1938 (first pb. in *Mortal Coils*).

PLAYS: *The Discovery*, pb. 1924; *The World of Light*, pb. 1931; *The Gioconda Smile*, pr., pb. 1948.

POETRY: *The Burning Wheel*, 1916; *Jonah*, 1917; *The Defeat of Youth*, 1918; *Leda*, 1920; *Arabia Infelix*, 1929; *The Cicadas and Other Poems*, 1931.

NONFICTION: *On the Margin: Notes and Essays*, 1923; *Along the Road: Notes and Essays of a Tourist*, 1925; *Jesting Pilate*, 1926; *Essays New and Old*, 1926; *Proper Studies*, 1927; *Do What You Will*, 1929; *Holy Face and Other Essays*, 1929; *Vulgarity in Lit-*

erature, 1930; *Music at Night*, 1931; *Texts and Pretexts*, 1932; *Beyond the Mexique Bay*, 1934; *The Olive Tree*, 1936; *Ends and Means*, 1937; *Grey Eminence*, 1941; *The Art of Seeing*, 1942; *The Perennial Philosophy*, 1945; *Themes and Variations*, 1950; *The Devils of Loudun*, 1952; *The Doors of Perception*, 1954; *Heaven and Hell*, 1956; *Tomorrow and Tomorrow and Tomorrow*, 1956 (pb. in England as *Adonis and the Alphabet, and Other Essays*, 1956); *Brave New World Revisited*, 1958; *Collected Essays*, 1959; *Literature and Science*, 1963.

BIBLIOGRAPHY

Baker, Robert S. *The Dark Historic Page: Social Satire and Historicism in the Novels of Aldous Huxley, 1921-1939*. Madison: University of Wisconsin Press, 1982. Devotes separate chapters to close readings of Huxley's novels, which are analyzed in terms of the protagonist's conflict with the prevailing secular society. Claims that Huxley is concerned with dystopian dilemmas and the price to be paid for the protagonist's losing struggle against change and society. Includes an excellent bibliography.

Bedford, Sybille. *Aldous Huxley: A Biography*. New York: Knopf, 1974. A superbly written life of the writer by one of England's renowned authors. In addition to the well-informed narrative, Bedford includes a chronology, a chronological list of Huxley's works, and a bibliography.

Bowering, Peter. *Aldous Huxley: A Study of the Major Novels*. New York: Oxford University Press, 1969. Treats Huxley as a novelist of ideas and attempts to treat the fiction and nonfiction as a whole. Each of his nine novels is analyzed in a separate chapter, and in a concluding chapter the complex relationship between the novelist and the artist is discussed. Well indexed.

Deery, June. *Aldous Huxley and the Mysticism of Science*. New York: St. Martin's Press, 1996. Discusses Huxley's use of science in his novels. Includes bibliographical references and an index.

Firchlow, Peter. *Aldous Huxley: Satirist and Novelist.*

Minneapolis: University of Minnesota Press, 1972. Although the focus is on Huxley's novels, especially *Point Counter Point* and *Brave New World*, the book does provide a biographical chapter and one on his poetry, which is ignored by most writers. One of the highlights of the book is the parallel established between Huxley's *Island* and Jonathan Swift's book 4 of *Gulliver's Travels*.

May, Keith M. *Aldous Huxley*. New York: Barnes & Noble Books, 1972. Addresses the problem of how "novelistic" Huxley's novels are and concludes that it is language rather than structure that determines the meaning of each of his novels. The eleven novels, each of which is analyzed in a separate chapter, are divided into two chronological groups: novels of exploration and novels of certainty, with the dividing line coming between *Eyeless in Gaza* (1936) and *After Many a Summer Dies the Swan* (1939). Also contains a helpful bibliography.

Meckier, Jerome, ed. *Critical Essays on Aldous Huxley*. New York: G. K. Hall, 1996. Thoughtful essays on the author's oeuvre. Bibliographical references and an index are included.

Nance, Guinevera A. *Aldous Huxley*. New York: Continuum, 1988. Nance's introductory biographical chapter ("The Life Theoretic") reflects her emphasis on Huxley's novels of ideas. The novels, which are discussed at length, are divided into three chronological groups, with the utopian novels coming in the second group. Supplies a detailed chronology and a fairly extensive bibliography.

Watt, Donald, ed. *Aldous Huxley: The Critical Heritage*. London: Routledge & Kegan Paul, 1975. An invaluable chronological collection of book reviews and other short essays on Huxley's work and life. Among the literary contributors are Evelyn Waugh, E. M. Forster, William Inge, Stephen Spender, George Orwell, Thomas Wolfe, Ernest Hemingway, T. S. Eliot, and André Gide. The introduction traces the critical response to Huxley. Includes an extensive bibliography as well as information about translations and book sales.

I

JOHN IRVING

Born: Exeter, New Hampshire; March 2, 1942

PRINCIPAL LONG FICTION
Setting Free the Bears, 1969
The Water-Method Man, 1972
The 158-Pound Marriage, 1974
The World According to Garp, 1978
The Hotel New Hampshire, 1981
The Cider House Rules, 1985
A Prayer for Owen Meany, 1989
A Son of the Circus, 1994
A Widow for One Year, 1998

OTHER LITERARY FORMS

John Irving is best known for his long fiction. Some of his few published short stories found their way into his novels, attributed to one or another of the novel's main characters. The rest of the stories, some originally published in magazines, were collected in the volume *Trying to Save Piggy Sneed* (1996), a miscellany that also includes occasional essays and fragments of autobiography.

ACHIEVEMENTS

When *The World According to Garp* became a best-seller in 1978, prompting the reissue of his three previous novels, Irving captured the attention of literary critics as well as of the popular audience. His life and works were profiled in *Time, Saturday Review,* and *Rolling Stone,* and his novels entered what he calls in *The World According to Garp,* "that uncanny half-light where 'serious' books glow, for a time, as also 'popular' books." Various aspects of Irving's work appeal to different audiences, making him difficult to classify as either "serious" or "popular." The sometimes ribald, occasionally grotesque humor and the explicit sexuality of the novels give them a sensa-

(Marion Ettlinger)

tional appeal and made Irving—and his novelist character T. S. Garp—cult heroes. On the other hand, Irving's representation of random violence in the modern world, his emphasis on love and family responsibilities, and his use of writers as major characters have prompted serious examination of his work among academic critics. *The Hotel New Hampshire* delighted Irving fans with its continuation of established motifs and themes—bears, wrestling, Vienna, children—but critics and reviewers took a cautious approach to the novel, not certain whether to place Irving in the first rank of contemporary novelists or to chide him for reiterating his themes and allowing the trivial and the clichéd to coexist with the profound. Irving's work is of uneven quality: *Setting Free the Bears*, his first novel, is in some sections overwritten and self-indulgent, and his third novel, *The 158-Pound Marriage*, is limited in scope. He is nonetheless a figure to be reckoned with in contemporary American fiction, in part because of his confrontation with issues that occupy public attention. *The Cider House Rules* deals in large part with the issue of abortion, and Irving avoids the polemic of the debate by setting the novel in the first half of the twentieth century. *A Prayer for Owen Meany* is set against the backdrop of the Vietnam War and has a strong antiwar bias. The novel makes fresh the literary cliché of the hero as Christ figure by choosing in Owen Meany a character who seems superficially ill-suited for such heroism. The blend of contemporary issues, bizarre yet believable characters, and an old-fashioned devotion to good storytelling distinguishes Irving's novels.

BIOGRAPHY

John Winslow Irving was born on March 2, 1942, in Exeter, New Hampshire, to F. N. and Frances Winslow Irving. His father taught Russian history at Exeter Academy, where Irving attended prep school. At Exeter, he developed two lifelong interests, writing and wrestling, and became convinced that both required the same skills: practice and determination. Though not an outstanding student, he developed an appreciation of hard, steady work and a love of literature. Of his early apprenticeships Irving remarked in a *Rolling Stone* interview, "I was a very dull kid. But I really learned how to wrestle and I really learned how to write. I didn't have an idea in my head." After being graduated from Exeter at the age of nineteen, Irving spent a year at the University of Pittsburgh, where the wrestling competition convinced him that writing was a better career choice.

In 1962, Irving enrolled at the University of New Hampshire, where he began to work with authors Thomas Williams and John Yount, but a desire to see more of the world caused him to drop out. After an intensive summer course in German at Harvard University, he left for Vienna, where he enrolled at the Institute of European Studies. During his two years in Vienna, Irving married Shyla Leary, a painter whom he had met at Harvard, studied German, and became seriously devoted to writing. Living in an unfamiliar place sharpened his powers of observation; as he said in a 1981 *Time* interview, "you are made to notice even the trivial things—especially the trivial

things." He returned to the University of New Hampshire, worked again with Thomas Williams, and was graduated cum laude in 1965. From there, with his wife and son, Colin, Irving went to the University of Iowa Writers' Workshop, where he earned an M.F.A. degree in creative writing in 1967. During his time at Iowa, Irving continued wrestling with Dan Gable, the Iowa coach who won a medal at the 1976 Munich Olympics. Encouraged by writer-in-residence Kurt Vonnegut, he also completed his first published novel, *Setting Free the Bears*, which is set in Austria.

Setting Free the Bears was well received by critics and sold well (6,228 copies) for a first novel. A projected film of the book did not materialize, and Irving moved his family back to New England. After a brief period of teaching at Windham College, he taught at Mount Holyoke College until 1972, and for 1971 to 1972 was awarded a Rockefeller Foundation grant. *The Water-Method Man*, published in 1972, did not sell as well as *Setting Free the Bears*, but Irving was invited to be a writer-in-residence at the University of Iowa from 1972 to 1975, and for 1974 to 1975 he received a fellowship from the National Endowment for the Arts. During that time, Irving published his third novel, *The 158-Pound Marriage*, which was set in Iowa City. Sales of *The 158-Pound Marriage*, which Irving considers his weakest novel, were poor, and Irving returned to New England to begin a second period of teaching at Mount Holyoke.

The turning point in Irving's career came in 1978, with the publication of *The World According to Garp*. Discouraged by the seeming reluctance of Random House to promote his novels, he moved to E. P. Dutton and the guidance of Henry Robbins, its editor-in-chief. Although Dutton promoted the novel in ways that normally disenchant the serious reviewer (bumper stickers, T-shirts), the critical reaction was good and the public reception overwhelming; combined hardback and paperback sales reached three million in the first two years. In 1982, *The World According to Garp* was made into a film, with Irving playing a bit part as a wrestling referee. The success of the novel allowed Irving to devote more of his time to writing, and in 1981 Dutton published his fifth novel, *The Hotel New Hampshire*. Although some critics expressed disappointment in the novel, it was a best-seller and a Book-of-the-Month Club selection. The author of *The World According to Garp* had become a household word.

Irving's four subsequent novels—*The Cider House Rules, A Prayer for Owen Meany, A Son of the Circus*, and *A Widow for One Year*—were also bestsellers and book-club selections. As predicted by his earlier performance, he managed both to sustain a popular following and to provoke frequent scholarly interest; articles about and reviews of his work have appeared in journals as diverse as *Novel, The Sewanee Review*, and the *Journal of the American Medical Association*. In *Trying to Save Piggy Sneed*, a collection of essays and short fictional pieces originally published elsewhere, Irving updates his biography with mention of divorce, remarriage, and the birth of a third son. Like Johnny Wheelwright, the narrator of *A Prayer for Owen Meany*, Irving lived for a time in Toronto but then transferred his main residence to his native state of New Hampshire. In 1998, shortly after publication of *A Widow for One Year*, the Modern Library issued a commemorative edition of *The World According to Garp* with a new introduction by the author.

ANALYSIS

John Irving's fiction is distinguished by a highly personal fusion of seemingly incongruous elements. Irving's settings, actions, and characters are often bizarre and violent. The world he presents is frequently chaotic and unpredictable, full of sudden death and apparently meaningless collisions of people, values, ideologies, and objects. Among his characters are the Ellen Jamesians (*The World According to Garp*), who cut out their tongues to protest the rape and mutilation of a little girl; a blind bear-trainer named Freud (*The Hotel New Hampshire*); and a motorcyclist who locks a zoo attendant in a cage with an anteater (*Setting Free the Bears*). Characters die in excruciating ways: stung to death by thousands of bees, killed in airplane crashes, assassinated in parking lots. Irving himself has referred to *The World According to Garp* as "an X-rated soap opera." Balancing the sensational and pessimistic elements of

the novels, however, is a core of humane values. Irving does not posit a violent and arbitrary world, but rather one in which violence and havoc are present in sufficient quantities to demand constant vigilance. His characters may behave strangely, but their motives are usually pure. Infidelity exists, but so does real love; children deserve protection; human kindness is paramount. Despite his characterization of *The World According to Garp* as "X-rated," Irving denies that it presents an unbelievable world: "People who think *Garp* is wildly eccentric and very bizarre are misled about the real world. I can't imagine where they've been living or what they read for news."

Irving is essentially a storyteller and often uses an omniscient narrator who feels free to interrupt the narrative. In *Setting Free the Bears*, he uses elements of the tall tale and the fairy tale, and all of his novels are characterized by broad situational comedy rather than wit. At the same time, especially in *Setting Free the Bears* and *The World According to Garp*, he writes self-conscious fiction which reflects on its own making. As Michael Priestly has commented, "Irving resembles both the Victorian novelist ('dear reader') and the 'new novelist' who writes fiction about fiction." Many issues with which his novels deal are quite contemporary: feminism, sex-change operations, political assassination. Of equal importance, however, are romantic impulses such as freeing the animals in a zoo, rescuing the afflicted, and guarding one's loved ones against harm. The tension between tradition and novelty, reverence and blasphemy, contributes to the singularity of Irving's work.

A group of common motifs and images give Irving's novels coherence as a body of work. Wrestling is the dominant sport, and is the avocation of a number of characters. Bears are set free, as indicated by the title of his first novel, to reappear in a number of guises in later books. At least one character in each novel is a writer—most notably T. S. Garp in *The World According to Garp*. There are always children to be guarded from serious injury, though efforts to protect them are not always successful. Vienna is a frequent locale for Irving's fiction, as are Iowa and New Hampshire. These characters and motifs suggest a strong autobiographical current in Irving's fiction, and although the ingredients of his own life are transmuted by his imagination, his novels provide a rough outline of his progress from student in Vienna to graduate student in Iowa to successful novelist. Wary of readers believing that his novels are generally autobiographical, Irving has said that "people with limited imaginations find it hard to imagine that anyone else has an imagination. Therefore, they must think that everything they read in some way *happened*."

The enormous reality of Irving's characters, more than their possible identification with the author, is the central interest for his novels. Even his most bizarre characters are not caricatures; rather, they are believable people with extraordinary characteristics. Jenny Fields, Garp's mother, sets out to be impregnated by a terminally ill patient so that she will have to endure no further sexual contact, yet her action is presented as practical rather than perverse. Lilly, the youngest Berry child in *The Hotel New Hampshire*, never reaches four feet in height, but her family—and the reader—regards her not as a freak, but merely as small. Irving illustrates the diversity in the human family by presenting some of its most extreme members in his fiction, but instead of creating a circus, he urges tolerance. Violence is given the same matter-of-fact approach as are other extremes in Irving's fiction. It is present, if unwelcome, merely because it exists as a part of life. Irving is never sentimental or dramatic about motorcycle accidents, terrorists' bombs, bees which kill, or gearshifts which blind children; these are the risks of living.

The humor in Irving's novels serves both to make the bizarre and violent elements more acceptable and to reinforce the duality of his vision. No contemporary novelist better exemplifies Dorothy Parker's requisites for humor: "a disciplined eye and a wild mind." Early in his career, Irving relied heavily on slapstick comedy, such as the adventures of Siggy Javotnik in the Heitzinger Zoo in *Setting Free the Bears* and Bogus Trumper's duck hunt in *The Water-Method Man*. Increasingly, he turned to irony and wit as major devices of humor, but all the novels have a strong element of fantasy; dreams or nightmares become reality. Comedy and tragedy are woven closely together. Irving, always sensitive to public opinion,

built into *The World According to Garp* a defense against those who would accuse him of treating serious subjects too lightly. Mrs. Poole, of Findlay, Ohio, writes to T. S. Garp to accuse him of finding other people's problems funny; Garp replies that he has "nothing but sympathy for how people behave—and nothing but laughter to console them with." By insisting that life is both comically absurd and inevitably tragic, Irving espouses an acceptance of extremes. He has been described by Hugh Ruppersburg as a "stoic pessimist," a label which at this point seems appropriate, but his major contribution to the American novel is the product of imagination rather than philosophy: the creation of truly memorable people and situations which extend the reader's understanding of human existence. In the words of T. S. Garp, "a writer's job is to imagine everything so personally that the fiction is as vivid as our personal memories." At this job, Irving has succeeded admirably.

SETTING FREE THE BEARS

Unlike many first novels, *Setting Free the Bears* is not an autobiographical account of the author's early years. Although it is set in Austria and draws on Irving's experience there as a student, the novel is an exuberant and imaginative account of the adventures of Hannes Graff, the narrator, and his friend Siggy Javotnik as they ride a motorcycle through Austria. The middle section of the novel consists of alternating chapters of two documents written by Siggy: "The Zoo-Watch," an account of Siggy's vigil at the Heitzinger Zoo, and "The Highly Selective Autobiography of Siegfried Javotnik," which documents his family's history from the mid-1930's to the early 1960's. Siggy, who lives in the past—"I rely on prehistory for any sense and influence"—has only one dream for the future: to free the animals from the Heitzinger Zoo. After Siggy's death from multiple bee stings, Graff accomplishes Siggy's dream and, after the ensuing chaos, rides off on his motorcycle. The novel is a youthful fantasy, full of grand adventures and characters of mythic stature: The characters have no futures and only a tenuous relationship with the present.

The basic topic of the novel is freedom. Part of Siggy's "pre-history" deals with the liberation of

Austria from the Germans during World War II. In 1967, the year the frame narrative takes place, Graff frees the fairy-tale princess Gallen from her aunt's house and takes her to Vienna. Finally, Graff frees the animals from the zoo and what Siggy has assumed is their torture by the night guard, O. Schrutt. At the end of the novel, the Rare Spectacled Bears are loping across an open field to take up life in the woods, but if they survive, they will be the only ones who are free. Siggy, like the rest of his family, is dead. Gallen has sold her lovely reddish hair for money to live on while she waits for Graff to return to Vienna, and Graff is rootless and aimless on his motorcycle. In his attempt to create the perfect world denied by his ancestors by war, Siggy has become impossibly idealistic, and Graff has succumbed to his idealism, a fact he realizes at the end of the novel: "What worse awareness is there than to know there would have been a better outcome if you'd never done anything at all?" The suggestion is that freedom is best achieved by letting life run its natural course without human interference.

The nature of the novelist, however, is to interfere—that is, to impose an order on life by structuring it into novelistic form. *Setting Free the Bears* is a novel about writing. Late in his autobiography, Siggy reveals that it is more fiction than fact. Graff becomes, in a sense, Siggy's literary executor; as Graff reveals in the "P.S." at the beginning of part three, it has been his editorial decision to interleave sections of the autobiography with sections of the zoo-watch notebook. As the naïve editor-narrator, Graff does not comprehend the relationship between the two documents, though the parallels between the two types of imprisonment—war and the zoo—are apparent to the reader. Graff's attempts to impose order on Siggy's life are far more successful than Siggy's own attempts, but ultimately all that Siggy has written may be fiction—it is, of course, fiction in one sense—so Graff is left trying to order a phantom existence.

In keeping with Irving's insistence on the elusive nature of reality, the novel has a dreamlike quality. Many of the characters live fantasy lives. Graff dreams of the lovely Gallen; Siggy dreams of freeing the animals from O. Schrutt. Within Siggy's autobiography, a chicken-farmer dressed in feather-covered pie plates imagines he looks like an eagle, representing Austria's independence. Elements of fantasy, which here dominate the novel, are characteristic of Irving's later novels as well, though the line between fantasy and reality is more sharply drawn in his later work. *Setting Free the Bears* is further removed from traditional realistic fiction than any of Irving's other novels. Like "The Pension Grillparzer," T. S. Garp's first piece of fiction in *The World According to Garp*, it is a story told for the sake of telling a story. In an interview with Greil Marcus of *Rolling Stone*, Irving said, "I had no idea who the people in *Setting Free the Bears* were, or how they were going to get from A to Z." The careful plot structure of the novel suggests that at some point Irving envisioned the whole quite clearly, but the imaginative power evidenced here continued to be an important element in his fiction.

THE WATER-METHOD MAN

Deserving of more attention than has yet been given it, *The Water-Method Man* is Irving's most consistently comic novel. "I wanted," Irving has said, "to write a book that was absolutely comic: I wanted it to be intricate and funny and clever and I wanted it to go on and on and on." Fred "Bogus" Trumper, also known to various friends as "Bogge" and "Thump-Thump," is the narrator and main character of the novel, which is an account of his misadventures in Iowa, Austria, New York, and Maine. Bogus Trumper is a charming failure searching for meaning and order in his life. He has tried marriage to a skiing champion appropriately nicknamed "Biggie," fatherhood, a Ph.D. program in comparative literature, and filmmaking. In desperation one night, he begins to write a diary, which becomes the first-person portions of the novel. As he had in *Setting Free the Bears*, Irving alternates sections of two different pieces of writing, but in *The Water-Method Man* this device is simpler; the first-person autobiographical chapters tell of Trumper's past; the third-person narrative sections tell of his present.

The somewhat improbable metaphor for Bogus's wayward life is his penis. For years he has had problems with painful urination and orgasm; a urologist discovers that his urinary tract is "a narrow, winding road." Rejecting the alternative of surgery, Trumper chooses the "water method," which consists of flushing his system with large amounts of water. This treatment alleviates his problem rather than curing it and represents all the other unfinished business in his life. Also serving as an analogue to Trumper's life is the subject of his doctoral thesis, an Old Low Norse saga, *Akthelt and Gunnel*, which he is translating—or rather pretending to translate. His actual translation has stopped at the point where he realized the impending doom of the characters; after that, he began to invent a lusty saga with parallels to his own life. When Trumper finally achieves order and peace in his life, Irving signals the change with Trumper's corrective surgery and his completion of a faithful translation of *Akthelt and Gunnel*. He is able to come to terms with the people and events around him.

Any serious message in *The Water-Method Man*, however, is incidental to the comic dimensions of the novel. Much of the humor is ribald, though Irving's skill enables him to avoid obscenity. Several of the most memorable sequences involve equally memorable minor characters, such as Merrill Overturf, Trumper's diabetic friend who drowns while trying to find a Nazi tank he insists was sunk in the Danube, and Dante Calicchio, the New York limousine driver who takes Trumper to Maine. Though briefly sketched, these characters demonstrate Irving's ability to make the incidental character or situation come alive. The almost complete absence of violent or grotesque incidents makes *The Water-Method Man* unique in Irving's canon. Scenes such as the one in which Bogus Trumper skis into an Alpine parking lot, which in Irving's other novels would have some shocking, tragic outcome, are here handled as they are in comic strips: Everyone walks away unscathed. The closest approach to serious emotional involvement comes in the scenes between Trumper and his young son, Colm. The pressured responsibilities of parenthood become a major topic in Irving's later novels, as does the relationship between life and art, here represented by Bogus Trumper's attempt to find order in writing translations (both real and fake), autobiographies, letters, and making films. The fact that

Trumper is ultimately at peace with himself makes *The Water-Method Man* one of Irving's most optimistic novels.

THE 158-POUND MARRIAGE

In contrast to the boisterous comedy of *The Water-Method Man*, Irving's third novel is painfully serious. *The 158-Pound Marriage* is Irving's shortest novel to date and also the most conventional in both form and subject matter. It is the story of two couples who swap partners regularly for a period of time, an experiment which sours all the relationships involved. Irving has said that the book is about "lust and rationalization and restlessness," and it mirrors the moral floundering of the early 1970's in which it is set. Severin and Edith Winter mistakenly conceive the exchange as a means of saving their own marriage by introducing sexual variety to erase the memory of Severin's previous affair with a ballet dancer. Inevitably, the individuals become emotionally involved with their "temporary" partners, and this places both marriages in jeopardy. The first-person narrator, a novelist, considers himself a cuckold by the end of the novel (T. S. Garp's second novel in *The World According to Garp* is titled *The Second Wind of the Cuckold*), and is going to Vienna to attempt a reconciliation with his wife, Utch. Whatever the outcome of this effort, their marriage will never be the same.

Despite the significance of Irving's message about contemporary life, *The 158-Pound Marriage* is his weakest novel because he fails to take advantage of his strengths as a novelist. Instead of merging the comic and the tragic, as he does in his best work, Irving steers a course between them; as a result, the novel has a flatness rather than the peaks and valleys of emotion which Irving is capable of evoking. Only in the histories of the characters which the narrator provides at the beginning does Irving's usual inventiveness emerge. Severin and Utch have exotic yet similar backgrounds. Both were children in wartime Vienna; Severin is the son of an obscure Austrian painter and a model, and Utch is the daughter of a clever farm woman who hid Utch in the belly of a dead cow to protect her from rape at the hands of the invading Russians. Instead of being raped, the seven-year-old was christened Utchka ("calf") and virtually adopted by a Russian officer occupying Vienna. When the narrator meets Utch, she is working as a tour guide in Vienna. Edith meets Severin when she is sent by an American museum to purchase some of his father's paintings. The coincidence of the two couples' meeting and becoming intimately involved with one another years afterward lends interest to the early sections of the novel, but Irving does not manage to sustain this interest.

As the title suggests, wrestling is a major motif in *The 158-Pound Marriage*. Severin Winter is a wrestling coach as well as a professor of German, and the jargon of the sport dominates the novel as it does his speech. "Wrestling," the narrator says, "was a constant metaphor to him," and the tedious struggle of a wrestling match becomes an apt metaphor for the struggle to maintain human relationships. Were this Irving's only novel, one would have little sense of the mastery of tone and style of which he is capable; fortunately, his next two novels amply display that mastery.

THE WORLD ACCORDING TO GARP

By far Irving's most successful novel, *The World According to Garp* is the best example of his ability to wed the bizarre and the commonplace, the tragic and the comic. The novel deals with the extremes of human experience, embodying that dualism of vision which is Irving's greatest strength as a writer. Titled in the working draft *Lunacy and Sorrow*, it has been called "a manic, melancholic carnival of a book," and Irving manages to keep the reader poised between laughter and tears. The seriousness of *The World According to Garp* lies in its thematic concerns: the elusive nature of reality and the human need to find or impose order on existence. The "lunacy" in the novel derives from the extremes to which people will go to achieve order and meaning; the "sorrow" arises from the ultimate human inability to control destiny. The last line—"in the world according to Garp we are all terminal cases"—conveys the stoic acceptance of misfortune and disaster which Irving posits as necessary for survival, yet the lightly ironic tone of this concluding sentence also reflects the novel's utter lack of sentimentality or melodrama.

T. S. Garp, the main character, is an unlikely hero. On one hand he is a fairly typical twentieth century man, a husband and father who worries about his children, pursues his career, jogs regularly, and has a penchant for young female baby-sitters. He loves his wife, is good to his mother, and has a few close friends. These bare facts, however, do not explain Garp, nor, Irving suggests, would such a sketch be adequate to represent most people. Garp is the son of Jenny Fields, nurse, daughter of a wealthy family, author of an autobiography, and finally sponsor of a haven for women with special needs. Garp's father, a fatally injured ball turret gunner during World War II, enters the picture only long enough to impregnate Jenny Fields. Jenny then rears the boy at the Steering School, where she is the school nurse. After Garp is graduated from Steering, mother and son go to Vienna, where Jenny writes her autobiography, *A Sexual Suspect*, and Garp writes "The Pension Grillparzer." *A Sexual Suspect*, the beginning and end of Jenny Fields's writing career, catapults her to fame as a feminist writer and finally leads to her assassination by a reactionary gunman during a political rally. "The Pension Grillparzer" launches Garp on a career as a writer and also makes possible his marriage to Helen Holm, daughter of the wrestling coach at Steering, with whom he has two sons, Duncan and Walt. Because of his mother's fame, Garp becomes a close friend of Roberta Muldoon, a transsexual who was formerly Robert Muldoon, tight end for the Philadelphia Eagles. He also encounters the Ellen Jamesians, a radical feminist group who protest rape with self-mutilation. After an automobile accident which kills Walt and blinds Duncan in one eye, Garp and Helen adopt the real Ellen James, who eventually becomes a writer. Garp himself is killed at the age of thirty-three by an Ellen Jamesian who is angered by Garp's rejection of the group's extremist practices.

Despite this grim outline, *The World According to Garp* is often humorous and occasionally wildly comic. The humor usually grows out of human foibles: Dean Bodger catching a dead pigeon as it falls from the Steering infirmary roof and mistaking it for the body of young Garp; Jenny Fields failing to recognize a well-dressed woman as a prostitute on the streets of Vienna; Garp sprinting down the streets of his neighborhood to overtake astonished speeders who endanger the lives of his children, or dressing as a woman to attend the "feminist funeral" of his mother. When the comic and tragic merge, the result is black humor in the tradition of Nathanael West. At the climax of the novel, for example, when Garp's car crashes into that of Michael Milton, Helen, in the act of performing oral sex on Milton, bites off his penis, effectively ending the affair which she has been trying to conclude, and providing an ironic counterpoint to the tonguelessness of the Ellen Jamesians.

Humor and tragedy may coexist because the nature of reality is always in question. The title of the novel suggests that the world presented in the novel may be only Garp's idiosyncratic version of reality. The short stories and the fragment of Garp's novel *The World According to Bensenhaver* are different versions of reality—those created by T. S. Garp the novelist. Ultimately, the novel presents a version of the world according to John Irving. That things are not always what they seem is further evidenced in many of the novel's details. Garp's name is not really a name at all. The initials T. S., though echoing those of T. S. Eliot, do not stand for anything, and "Garp" is merely a sound made by Garp's brain-damaged father. Roberta Muldoon is occasionally uncertain whether to behave as a female or male. Jenny Fields does not set out to be a feminist, but is regarded as one by so many people that she takes up the cause. Given this confusion between reality and illusion, order is difficult to achieve. As a novelist, Garp can control only the worlds of his fiction; he cannot protect his family and friends from disaster. Garp is in many ways an old-fashioned knight attempting to deal with rapists in parks and speeding automobiles on suburban streets. Like his character Bensenhaver, who appoints himself special guardian of a family after he retires from the police force, Garp imagines himself the particular guardian of children and the enemy of rape.

Of particular interest to contemporary readers is the prominence of feminism in *The World According to Garp*. Irving's depiction of the movement is broad and essentially sympathetic, including not only its

extremes, such as the Ellen Jamesians, but also the changes in social and family relationships brought about by revisions in sex roles. Jenny Fields wants to be a single parent, but artificial insemination and single-parent adoptions are not available to her in the mid-1940's. Her choice of a fatally wounded patient as the father for her child is born of pragmatism rather than feminist philosophy; only later, as she writes her autobiography, is she able to articulate the need for tolerance of those with nontraditional ways. Garp himself is a house-husband. While Helen teaches at the university, he writes at home, takes care of his sons, and cooks. He therefore must deal with public suspicion that he is an unemployed failure, and his own situation enables him to understand the plight of many women and to see the damage done to the feminist cause by extremists such as the Ellen Jamesians.

The major flaw in *The World According to Garp* is its lack of a coherent structure. The examples of Garp's own writing, though interesting and thematically related to the rest of the novel, remain undigested lumps in the chronological narrative. In part, Irving has attempted too much by hoping to fuse the story of a writer's development with all the other issues in the novel. In addition, he is reluctant to let go of his characters, so that the novel continues past the point of its dramatic conclusion. Chapter 19, "Life After Garp," traces all the main characters to their inevitable ends rather than leaving the reader's imagination to envision them. Art, as the novel insists, is a way of ordering reality, but here the two become confused. There is some suggestion that Garp is a Christlike figure—his almost-virgin birth, his death at thirty-three—but the evidence is too thin to sustain a reading of the final chapter as the "lives of the disciples."

THE HOTEL NEW HAMPSHIRE

Shortly before T. S. Garp is killed in *The World According to Garp*, he has begun a new novel called *My Father's Illusions*, an apt title for *The Hotel New Hampshire*. Depending less on dreams and violence and more on the imaginative creation of real human types, the novel has a calmer, less urgent tone than *The World According to Garp*. Although themes and motifs present in Irving's earlier novels reappear in

The Hotel New Hampshire, this novel is far less dependent on autobiography and has a more cohesive focus. Critics and reviewers expressed disappointment with the novel, one calling it "a perverse *Life With Father*, a savage situation comedy." It seems likely, however, that the very absence of much of the perversity and savagery which characterized *The World According to Garp* has made it seem less vital. The tone of *The Hotel New Hampshire* is more assured, its humor more sophisticated, its presentation of life more realistic than in much of Irving's other work.

Like *The World According to Garp*, *The Hotel New Hampshire* deals with illusion and reality—specifically with one man's dreams for his family. Win Berry is a man with improbable hopes. As his son John, the narrator, says of him, "the first of my father's illusions was that bears could survive the life lived by human beings, and the second was that human beings could survive a life led in hotels." The Berry family lives in three hotels during the course of the novel, which spans the period from 1920, when Win Berry meets Mary Bates, to 1980, when the surviving Berry children are grown and have become successful at various pursuits. (Egg, the youngest, is killed in a plane crash along with his mother; Lilly, the smallest, commits suicide.) All the Berry children are marked by a childhood spent in the hotels created by their father's dreams: first a converted school in Dairy, New Hampshire, then a dubious *pension* in Vienna. Finally, Win Berry, by this time blind—as he in some ways has been all his life—returns to the Maine resort where he first met Mary Bates, shielded by his children from the knowledge that it has become a rape crisis center. The familiar Irving motifs and images are prominent in *The Hotel New Hampshire*: Win Berry's father, Iowa Bob, is a wrestling coach whose strenuous view of life contrasts sharply with his son's dreaminess; bears appear in both actual and simulated form. Near the beginning of the novel, Win Berry buys a bear named State O'Maine from a wanderer named Freud, who eventually lures Win and his family to the second Hotel New Hampshire in Vienna; there they meet Susie-the-bear, a young American who wears a bear suit as a protection against reality.

Several critics have referred to the fairy-tale quality of *The Hotel New Hampshire*, and various elements contribute to that quality: a trained bear, a dog named Sorrow who reappears in different forms, and several heroic rescues, including the Berry family's rescue of the Vienna State Opera House from terrorists who intend to bomb it. The novel partakes of the atmosphere of fantasy present in *Setting Free the Bears* and "The Pension Grillparzer"; the latter, in fact, contains the germ of this novel. Despite the premature deaths of three members of the Berry family, there is little of the bleakness or desperation of *The World According to Garp*. In part, this is the result of the narrator's point of view. John Berry, the middle child, is the keeper of the family records, and thus the one who orders their experience in writing. Though he is patient with other people's fantasies, John has few of his own, and he casts a mellow light over the experience of the family. Irving has compared him to Nick Carraway in F. Scott Fitzgerald's *The Great Gatsby* (1925), but he resembles more nearly the narrative voice in some of J. D. Salinger's work, taking the strange behavior of his family for granted and delighting in their unusual talents and proclivities. John is closest to his sister Franny (another Salinger echo); in fact, they have a brief incestuous relationship, in part intended to ease Franny back into heterosexual relationships following her rape as a teenager.

Although the tone of *The Hotel New Hampshire* is gentler than that of *The World According to Garp*, Irving presents many of the same social problems and situations: rape (which Irving has called "the most violent assault on the body and the head that can happen simultaneously"), murder, race relations, sex roles, and the modern family. The difference between this fifth novel and those which preceded it is that Irving seems to have become reconciled to the need for illusion as a means of survival. No longer are dreams only irresponsible fantasies or terrible nightmares; they are what enable most people, in the refrain of the novel, to "keep passing the open windows" rather than taking a suicidal plunge. By treating contemporary anxieties with the traditional devices of the storyteller, Irving conveys an age-old message about the purpose of art: It can provide an illusion of order which may be more important—and is certainly more readily attained—than order itself.

THE CIDER HOUSE RULES

John Irving's two novels following *The Hotel New Hampshire* deal more insistently with moral and ethical issues, although they also contain the bizarre characters and situations that have become hallmarks of his fiction. *The Cider House Rules* concerns, as the title suggests, the rules by which people are to conduct their lives, but just as the list of rules posted in the cider house ("Please don't smoke in bed or use candles") is consistently ignored, so Dr. Wilbur Larch, one of the novel's central characters, breaks the rules by performing abortions in rural Maine in the 1920's. As he dealt with the issue of rape in *The World According to Garp*, Irving here approaches the issue of abortion inventively: Wilbur Larch is no back-alley abortionist, but a skilled obstetrician who also runs an orphanage for the children whose mothers prefer to give birth, and he seeks to have the children adopted.

Homer Wells, the other central character, is an orphan who is never adopted, and who grows up in the orphanage absorbing the most basic lesson taught there: that one must "be of use." His final usefulness is to replace Dr. Larch when the elderly man dies, but even here he breaks the rules, for although he is a skilled obstetrician and abortionist, he has no medical degree, and so takes over the position with an assumed identity. Partly because of the precarious nature of his own existence, Homer has opposed abortion all his life, until he feels that he must perform one for a black teenager who has been raped by her father. Just as the illiterate apple pickers cannot read the rules of the orchard where Homer spends his young adulthood, Irving suggests that the rules that people should follow are those that are derived from human encounter rather than those that are arbitrarily imposed.

The apple orchard setting is part of a muted Garden of Eden theme in the novel. Homer falls in love with Candy, the daughter of the orchard's owner, and she gives birth to his child shortly before she marries another man. No one, however, is cast out of the garden; Irving instead creates another of his oddly mixed families when Homer moves in with Candy, her husband Wally, and the child, a boy named Angel. Here, too, Homer proves to have been "of use," because a serious illness during World War II prevents Wally from fathering children, and he and Candy rear Angel as their own. Despite its strong pro-abortion stance, *The Cider House Rules*, like Irving's previous fiction, evokes a special reverence for children. The children in Wilbur Larch's orphanage are cared for lovingly, Homer dotes on his son Angel, and it is the plight of the pregnant girl, Rose Rose, that converts Homer to the pro-choice position of Wilbur Larch.

A PRAYER FOR OWEN MEANY

As *The Cider House Rules* is set against the political and social realities of the first half of the twentieth century, *A Prayer for Owen Meany* chronicles even more directly those of the next two decades—from the escalation of the Vietnam War to the advent of heavy-metal rock music, and from the early spread of television culture to the presidency of Ronald Reagan. In its overtly religious imagery, the novel posits the need for some kind of salvation during these turbulent years. *A Prayer for Owen Meany* is more complex structurally than the straightforward storytelling of *The Cider House Rules*, features the quick juxtapositions of violence and comedy of Irving's earlier work, and is ambitious in its creation of an unlikely Christ figure.

A Prayer for Owen Meany details the friendship—from childhood in the 1950's to Owen Meany's death in the 1960's—of two boys who grow up in Gravesend, New Hampshire, at opposite ends of the social scale: Owen's reclusive family owns the local granite quarry, whereas John Wheelwright's family boasts of Mayflower origins and functions as the local gentry. Their roles are reversed and confused, however, in the course of the narrative: Owen, a diminutive boy who even as an adult is never more than five feet tall, and whose voice—rendered by Irving in capital letters—is a prepubescent squeak, becomes a Christ figure with powers over life and death, whereas John leads a rather uneventful adult life as a schoolteacher in Toronto, even remaining a virgin, as Owen does not.

Imagery and actions identifying Owen Meany with Christ begin early in the novel and accumulate rapidly to the climactic scene of his death. When he is a small child, his size and lightness seem to the other children a "miracle"; for the same reason, he is cast as the Christ child in a church Christmas pageant. Owen's father tells John that Owen's was a virgin birth—that his parents' marriage was never consummated—and Owen "plays God" to save John from being drafted during the Vietnam War by cutting off one of his fingers with a diamond wheel used to engrave granite monuments. Owen foresees the date of his own death and has a recurrent dream that he will die saving small children; the fact that both predictions are accurate lends to Owen a God-like foreknowledge.

Yet *A Prayer for Owen Meany* is far from being a solemn theological tract. Irving's characteristically ebullient humor erupts throughout the novel in slapstick scenes, in boyish pranks, and even in the ironic contrast between Owen's small voice and the large print in which it leaps authoritatively from the page. The blending of the serious and the comic reaches its apotheosis early in the novel, when the one ball that Owen Meany ever hits in Little League baseball kills John Wheelwright's mother, Tabitha. The fact that Owen Meany is the agent of John's mother's death does not mar the boys' friendship; indeed, it brings them closer together, partly because John knows that Owen worshiped his mother (and for the rest of his life keeps her dressmaker's dummy in his bedroom as a kind of ministering angel), and partly because the event has an inevitability that foretells Owen's later powers over life and death.

A Prayer for Owen Meany is a mixture of realism and fabulism, of commentary on contemporary American culture and evocation of the magic of childhood and friendship. Religious imagery permeates but does not overwhelm the novel, which takes its tone from the narrator's somewhat self-mocking stance and his obvious delight in recalling the "miracle" of Owen Meany. The novel is indeed a "prayer" for, and to, Owen, who, in refusing to flinch from his own destiny, has given John Wheelwright the courage to face his own life with equanimity.

After turning fifty, Irving published two major novels which confirmed his standing reputation, both satisfying his supporters and irritating his detractors. In *A Son of the Circus*, Irving took advantage of a recent stay in India to revisit his familiar concerns with illness, crime, violent death, and bizarre sexual practices from a somewhat different perspective; in *A Widow for One Year*, he returned to the basic premises and purview of *The World According to Garp*, this time with a female novelist as the central character. In both novels, Irving continues his investigation into the relationship of process to product in fiction.

A SON OF THE CIRCUS

In *A Son of the Circus*, Irving takes as his main character an orthopedic surgeon who, born in India and trained in postwar Vienna, has long since become a Canadian citizen, with his main practice in Toronto. As the omniscient narrator repeatedly points out, Farrokh Daruwalla, M.D., is in fact a stateless person, never "at home," regardless of where he might be. A member of the Parsi ethnic minority in India, Farrokh happened to be in Vienna studying medicine at the moment of Indian independence in 1947, when Vienna itself was partitioned among the Allied occupying forces in the aftermath of World War II. Although reasonably successful as a surgeon and medical researcher, Farrokh remains curiously adrift in life well into his late fifties due in part to the tangled legacy of his father, Lowji, who was killed by car bomb in 1969.

When the action of *A Son of the Circus* begins, Farrokh is back in India on one of his occasional extended visits, overseeing his second career as a "closet" writer of continuity for detective films starring his brother's adopted son, an actor best known by the name of his character, Inspector Dhar. One of twin sons born to a forgettable (and long forgotten) American actress who was filming on location in India in 1949, Inspector Dhar—also known as John Daruwalla or John D.—grew to maturity under the care of the entire Daruwalla family, although he was technically adopted only by Farrokh's elder brother, also a physician. Dhar's twin, it seems, was taken to California soon after birth by their mother.

A series of murders, combined with threats

against Dhar, keep deterring Farrokh from telling John D., a.k.a. Dhar, what he has come to Bombay to tell him, to wit, that John D. has a twin brother who, as a Jesuit priest in training, has been posted to Bombay, and that the brothers are likely to meet. In the meantime, the hapless Jesuit, mistaken for Dhar, is the subject of numerous assaults.

Farrokh, like his father before him, retains membership in the exclusive Duckworth Club, an anomaly left over from the days of the British Empire, and it is there that various threads of his life, including his sponsorship of Inspector Dhar, become entangled. It is there that Rahul, a *hijra* (transsexual) prostitute permanently disguised as Mrs. Dogar, threatens and commits murder; it is also at the club that Farrokh and John D., with the help of a police inspector and his American wife (who witnessed one of Rahul's murders twenty years earlier), set a trap for Rahul and bring the murders to an end. Throughout the narrative, Farrokh's active imagination keeps playing tricks on him, proposing fictional alternatives to what is actually taking place. Unlike the Inspector Dhar series, however, Farrokh's later scenarios will remain unfilmed, upstaged by equally unpredictable reality.

A WIDOW FOR ONE YEAR

In *A Widow for One Year*, Irving centers his narration around Ruth Cole, a successful American novelist whose career in some respects reflects his own, as well as that of the fictional T. S. Garp. The tale begins in 1958 when Ruth is four years old, having been conceived as the "replacement" for two adolescent brothers recently killed in a freak auto accident. Her father, Ted Cole, a successsful writer and illustrator of children's books, is also a womanizer and a borderline alcoholic; Ruth's mother Marion has put her own literary ambitions aside in favor of her husband's career. By 1958, however, a trial separation is under way; Ted has moved out of their house and hired sixteen-year-old Eddie O'Hare to serve as his driver and secretary. True to form, however, Ted has an ulterior motive: Eddie, it seems, bears a strong resemblance to the Coles' lost sons, and Ted believes Eddie might fall unwittingly into the role of Marion's lover, which he does.

Marion, meanwhile, plans simply to leave Long Island for good, destination unknown. Rearing Ruth with the help of a Latin couple formerly employed by one of his ex-mistresses, Ted has stopped writing, having depended first upon the boys and later upon Ruth for questions that would generate new stories. To stay in shape, he plays endless games of squash in a court above his detached garage. In *A Widow for One Year*, squash, for obvious reasons, replaces wrestling as the sport of choice and contest.

Eddie O'Hare, forever marked by his idyll with Marion, reaches a modest level of success with novels about the love of a young man for a woman old enough to be his mother. Throughout the novel, the implication of incest, or incest-by-proxy, is never far from the characters' minds.

By 1990, the next year of her life to be portrayed in depth, Ruth, a novelist, has long since become even better known as a writer than her father: a mainstream novelist with strong popular appeal, not unlike a female John Irving. Ted, at age seventy-seven, is still playing squash and chasing younger women. Marion, true to her word, has been out of sight since 1958 and, as far as Ruth and Ted are concerned, might well have died in the meantime. Eddie O'Hare, however, suspects that Marion is living in Canada, publishing mystery novels under her mother's maiden name. It is in 1990 that Ruth and Eddie meet again, for the first time as adults. Eddie helps to fill many of the gaps in Ruth's memory of Marion. Now in her mid-thirties, Ruth is contemplating marriage for the first time, in part to experience motherhood, and remains puzzled by her mother's disappearance from her life. Ruth emerges from the conversation inclined to accept the marriage proposal of her editor, Allan Albright, eighteen years her senior and divorced.

Ruth learns that her father has taken his own life by literally running himself to death on the squash court while his Volvo idled in the garage below. His suicide, presumably provoked by a quarrel with Ruth over his sleeping with her best friend, apparently frees Ruth to marry Allan, with whom she will soon bear a son, named Graham after the British novelist Graham Greene. Allan dies in his sleep when the boy is three years old, thus bringing Ruth a widowhood predicted by one of her angry detractors on the lecture circuit. Within a year, however, Ruth meets her second husband, an Amsterdam policeman. As it happens, the recently retired Harry Hoekstra is a voracious reader, favoring mysteries but also fond of such authors as Ruth Cole and even Eddie O'Hare. He is also familiar with the Canadian mysteries of Alice Somerset, now known by Eddie and Ruth to be the pseudonymous Marion Cole. Ruth and Eddie, meanwhile, remain concerned that nothing has managed to lure Marion out of hiding; what finally does coax her out is Ruth's decision to sell Ted's house so that she can move to Vermont with Graham and Harry. Marion does in fact come back to Eddie, with whom she will share the cost of the house, thus keeping it "in the family" for the foreseeable future.

As in *The World According to Garp*, the narrative of *A Widow for One Year* is frequently interrupted by excerpts of prose attributed to one or another of the main characters—short stories or fragments of novels by Ruth, children's books by Ted, even detective fiction ascribed to "Alice Somerset." Like other Irving protagonists, including the frustrated novelist-scenarist Farrokh Daruwalla, M.D., Ruth Cole exemplifies the creative tension between invention and experience in the writing process, a subject Irving treats at some length in the title essay of *Trying to Save Piggy Sneed*. Arguably, Ruth's childhood "reconstructions" of the lives of her dead brothers, together with her efforts to fill the void left by Marion's long absence, have turned her into a "natural" writer, a person for whom creative writing is less an option than a need.

Nancy Walker, updated by David B. Parsell

OTHER MAJOR WORKS

NONFICTION: *The Imaginary Girlfriend*, 1996; *My Movie Business: A Memoir*, 1999.

SCREENPLAY: *The Cider House Rules*, 1999.

MISCELLANEOUS: *Trying to Save Piggy Sneed*, 1996.

BIBLIOGRAPHY

Campbell, Josie R. *John Irving: A Critical Companion*. Westport, Conn.: Greenwood Press, 1998. Part of the Critical Companions to Popular Contemporary Writers series, Campbell's book covers Irving's career through *A Widow for One Year*, showing both the popular and the literary sources and appeal of his novels.

Harter, Carol C., and James R. Thompson. *John Irving*. Boston: Twayne, 1986. Part of the Twayne United States Authors series, this clearly written study of Irving's fiction through *The Cider House Rules* emphasizes the mixture of popular and artistic appeal in the novels. The volume includes an annotated bibliography.

Miller, Gabriel. *John Irving*. New York: Frederick Ungar, 1982. Part of the Ungar Modern Literature series, this is a useful biographical and critical study of Irving's career through *The Hotel New Hampshire*. It includes a chronology through 1982, a 1981 interview with Irving, and a bibliography of both primary and secondary sources.

Priestley, Michael. "Structure in the Worlds of John Irving." *Critique* 23, no. 1 (1981): 82-96. Priestley analyzes the ways the novelist—and his characters—seek to impose order on their fictional worlds in Irving's first four novels.

Reilly, Edward C. *Understanding John Irving*. Columbia: University of South Carolina Press, 1991. A concise exposition of Irving's work through *A Prayer for Owen Meany*, Reilly's volume is part of a continuing series devoted to world literature and situates Irving's work with regard to both British and continental traditions.

Van Gelder, Lindsy. Review of *A Widow for One Year*, by John Irving. *Nation* 127 (May 11, 1998): 52-55. A thoughtful feminist reading of Irving's sole novel with a female protagonist, Van Gelder's review ends on an unexpectedly positive, if still ironic, note.

J

HENRY JAMES

Born: New York, New York; April 15, 1843
Died: London, England; February 28, 1916

PRINCIPAL LONG FICTION

Roderick Hudson, 1876
The American, 1876-1877
The Europeans, 1878
Daisy Miller, 1878
An International Episode, 1878-1879
Confidence, 1879-1880
Washington Square, 1880
The Portrait of a Lady, 1880-1881
The Bostonians, 1885-1886
The Princess Casamassima, 1885-1886
The Reverberator, 1888
The Tragic Muse, 1889-1890
The Spoils of Poynton, 1897
What Maisie Knew, 1897
The Awkward Age, 1897-1899
In the Cage, 1898
The Turn of the Screw, 1898
The Sacred Fount, 1901
The Wings of the Dove, 1902
The Ambassadors, 1903
The Golden Bowl, 1904
The Outcry, 1911
The Ivory Tower, 1917
The Sense of the Past, 1917

OTHER LITERARY FORMS

Fiction was assuredly where Henry James's essential talent and interest lay, and it was the form to which he devoted almost all of his literary efforts. His more than twenty novels (the count is inexact because some of his middle-length pieces, such as *The Turn of the Screw* and *Daisy Miller*, can be categorized as novellas) and roughly 112 tales attest his lifetime of dedication to this genre. Despite this clear emphasis on fiction, however, James was seduced by his desire to regain his lost popularity with the general public and his wish to attempt a kind of writing that he had studied for many years, writing drama. For a five-year period, from 1890 to 1895, he concentrated on playwriting; during this time he wrote no novels but continued to publish short stories. While his failure to gain a public with his plays somewhat embittered James (an emotion that has been exaggerated by some biographers; he always had loyal and appreciative readers and friends), he never lost confidence in the legitimacy of his art, and he returned to fiction with what many scholars believe to be a stronger, more ambitious inspiration, resulting in what has been called the "major phase" of his writing. It is perhaps indicative of the primacy of fiction in James's career that his most successful play was *The American* (1891), an adaptation of his earlier novel.

Unlike many creative writers, James produced an enormous volume of critical writings, chiefly literary, in which he not only studied the works of other authors (the most noteworthy are Nathaniel Hawthorne, Walt Whitman, Ralph Waldo Emerson, Ivan Turgenev, Gustave Flaubert, George Eliot, Anthony Trollope, Robert Louis Stevenson, Honoré de Balzac, and Guy de Maupassant) but also performed a detailed analysis of his own work. This latter effort appears primarily in the form of the prefaces to the New York edition (1907-1909) of his novels and tales. Inasmuch as the New York edition occupies twenty-six volumes, these prefaces provide a considerable body of critical material which has proved to be of great value to James scholars. His often reprinted essay "The Art of Fiction" (1884) presents his general theories on the art. Aside from his literary criticism, James wrote numerous studies and critiques on other subjects, such as painting (which greatly interested him) and travel.

In the late twentieth century, James's books and travel sketches attained critical admiration for their graceful style and penetrating insight into times that have gone and places that will never be the same. As might be expected, his studies of Italy, France, and England (the foreign countries that most intrigued him) are detailed and entertaining. More surprising is his finest work in this genre, *The American Scene* (1907), the fruit of a long visit to the United States; he toured the country extensively (partly to visit friends and places that he had not seen and others that he had not been to for a long time, and partly to deliver lectures on literary topics). His account of America at the turn of the century fuses the poignance of a native's return with the distance and objectivity of a European perspective.

ACHIEVEMENTS

James was the first American novelist to bring to the form a sense of artistic vocation comparable to Flaubert's. Except for the wide popularity of *Daisy Miller*, which appealed to audiences both in Europe and in the United States, no work of James achieved a wide readership in his lifetime. 4This fact, though it caused him pain, did not impel this most discriminating of writers to lower his standards in order to appeal to a mass audience. Those who did appreciate his work tended to be the better educated, more sophisticated readers, though even some of these occasionally had blind spots concerning James's novels—his brother William, for example, once wrote to James that his fiction was "bloodless." Except for the disastrous essay into drama, James adhered to his principles, always convinced that what he was doing would improve the quality of the novel and even raise the standards of conscientious readers. Events after his death have proved him right.

With the growth of courses of study in modern American literature, James earned the wide readership that was denied him during his lifetime, and after World War II, critical studies and biographical works devoted to him proliferated in staggering numbers. This is not to say that James is without his critics. He has frequently been criticized for a lack of scope and feeling, for concentrating his formidable talents on the psychological maneuverings of the privileged few. His later style has often been judged impenetrable, grotesquely mannered—though some critics regard his late novels as the highest achievements of the novelist's art, unsurpassed before or since.

As to James's influence on the subsequent course of the novel, however, there can be no question. He refined the novelistic art, purified it, and gave it directions never thought of before his time. Four areas of emphasis have especially attracted scholars in their attempts to isolate the essential contributions to the art of fiction with which James can be credited: point of view, psychological realism, style, and the connection of moral and aesthetic values. Throughout his career, James experimented with the varieties of consciousness (the word can be found everywhere in his fiction and criticism) through which stories can be told. The completely objective point of view, in which the reader is presented solely with what anyone present would see and hear, and the first-person point of view, in which a character tells the story as he perceives it, were both traditional, and James used them frequently. As his writing became more complex and dense, though, he endeavored to relate the action more in terms of what goes on in people's

(Library of Congress)

minds, the most impressive example of such a "center of consciousness" being Lambert Strether in *The Ambassadors*. As Percy Lubbock noted as early as 1921 in *The Craft of Fiction*, James achieves in *The Ambassadors* a point of view remarkable for its appropriateness to the story told and astounding in its focus on Lambert Strether's consciousness, which is made possible by James's using the third-person limited point of view but relating the hero's thoughts and feelings in a way that he himself could never manage—in short, the reader sees Strether's perceptions both from the inside and from the outside, with James gently guiding attention to the more important features of Strether's cognition. This sort of advanced work in viewpoint did two important things: It helped to prepare the way for the stream-of-consciousness novel, and it deepened the psychological realism that was to be James's chief intellectual contribution to the novel form.

Realism was in the literary air when James was starting out as a writer, but he focused his attention on fidelity to the movements of consciousness in a way that no previous writer had done. In a James novel, what is most significant is not what transpires in the plot, per se, but rather the attitudes and emotions and discoveries which unfold in the consciousnesses of the characters. Even in a work in the objective mode, such as *The Awkward Age*, which consists almost entirely of dialogue, what interests the attentive reader is the tides of feeling and realization that are implied by the speech. James appreciated the realistic aspects of the novels of Stendhal, Balzac, and Flaubert, but he resisted the naturalistic emphasis on the scientific and empirical—he believed Émile Zola to be misguided and unliterary. Indeed, James became a necessary counterfoil to this powerful literary movement in the later years of the nineteenth century.

As a stylist, James introduced the scrupulous craftsmanship of Flaubert to English-language readers. Like Flaubert, he weighed every phrase, every nuance of diction and rhythm, every comma. Indeed, for James, style was a moral imperative. Joseph Conrad, a great admirer of James (the feeling was reciprocated, but with less enthusiasm), once asserted that the American writer was "the historian of fine con-

sciences." Certainly, no one who reads James closely could fail to note the delicate but constant attention paid to right and wrong in the novels. What might escape detection, however, is that James evidently believed that ethics are, in somewhat intricate ways, related to aesthetics. This does not mean that all the "good" characters are beautiful and the evil ones ugly. On the contrary, in many instances, physically attractive characters such as Christina Light (*Roderick Hudson*) and Kate Croy (*The Wings of the Dove*) are sources of much wickedness (such characters are also usually very charming); while less prepossessing ones, such as Madame Grandoni (*The Princess Casamassima*) and Henrietta Stackpole (*The Portrait of a Lady*), appear to represent the forces of virtue. The true relationship between beauty and morality in James rests on his evident conviction that those elements of life which are positive and benevolent, such as freedom and personal development, have within them great beauty—and James takes considerable pains to express these qualities fully and with impressive aesthetic form. The appreciation of Fleda Vetch, in *The Spoils of Poynton*, for the beautiful appurtenances and objets d'art of the country house in the title constitutes, to some degree, a basis for the acts of renunciation and self-effacement that provide evidence of her virtue. Ever determined not to oversimplify, James offers such concatenations cautiously. This most subtle of moralists was equally understated in his presentation of beauty, revealing the ways in which it can conceal evil as well as the ways in which it can enrich life and give it greater meaning. After reading James, one cannot doubt the sincerity of his avowal, in his 1915 letter to H. G. Wells, that "It is art that *makes* life, makes interest, makes importance, for our consideration and application of these things, and I know of no substitute whatever for the force and beauty of its process."

BIOGRAPHY

If one wished to create for oneself a background and early life that was appropriate for preparing to be an important and dedicated American novelist during the later years of the nineteenth century and the early years of the twentieth, one might very well choose just the sort of family and early experience that fate created for Henry James. The family circumstances were comfortable (his grandfather, William James, had amassed one of the three largest fortunes in New York), and his father, Henry James, Sr., his mother, Mary Robertson Walsh James, his older brother, William, and his younger siblings, Garth Wilkinson, Robertson, and Alice, were all lively, articulate, and stimulating. It has been speculated that the very effervescence of his siblings helped to develop in Henry a tendency toward observation rather than participation, a trait that may have contributed to his decision never to marry and certainly helped to lead him to the vocation to which he devoted his life.

Another important feature of James's youth was his father's belief in the merit of unsystematic but broadly based education. The future novelist thus enjoyed the benefits of instruction by tutors as well as in excellent European institutions (made possible by a four-year stay, 1855-1858, on the Continent, in Switzerland, England, and France). Early on, the elder Henry James, an unorthodox philosopher and writer, observed that "Harry is not so fond of study, properly so-called, as of reading. He is a devourer of libraries." That this parent was not insistent on a more traditional attitude toward education is to his credit; though James was largely self-educated (his only true conventional schooling was a brief period at Harvard Law School, in 1862-1863)—resulting in some ignorances of extended areas of knowledge, such as the sciences, and in specialized concentrations, represented by his phenomenally wide reading in nineteenth century fiction but in little literature written before that era—it is generally agreed that he was one of the best informed of the major literary men of his time.

Apart from several later trips to Europe, which finally led him to the decision to move there in 1875 and to remain there for the rest of his life (except for a number of trips to America, where he never established a home), James led, for his first thirty years, a largely domestic life in the family circle. In his early twenties he had decided to become a writer; his initial publication is thought to be an unsigned story that appeared in 1864. This was the first of an endless stream of tales, reviews, essays, and novels (James became so proficient at French that he also translated a few works, which achieved publication); even during the period of his attempts to write plays he was turning out short pieces regularly. He was closely attached to his older brother William, a relationship that endured until William's death, in 1910, and to Alice and his cousin Mary ("Minny") Temple, whom James thought to be "the very heroine of our common scene." This charming young lady may have been the only real romantic love of James's life—it has been suggested that her death at twenty-four, in 1870, had much to do with James's resolution never to marry—and he immortalized her in Milly Theale, the ailing heroine of *The Wings of the Dove*, and perhaps in all the bright, appealing American girls who come to grief in his novels.

James was never very close to his younger brothers, a fact that has been attributed partly to his inability to serve in the army during the Civil War (because of "an obscure hurt," which was probably nothing more dramatic than a back injury—James had a painful back for all of his early manhood), in which "Wilky" and "Bob" fought, but also to the fact that he was simply temperamentally unsuited to association with these essentially unhappy men, both of whom died before him. Alice James became an invalid. The element of sadness in these three lives underlines the note of tragedy that can be found in much of James's fiction. There is no reason to doubt that, when James wrote to a friend, in 1896, "I have the imagination of disaster—and see life indeed as ferocious and sinister," he had had this grim attitude for many years, perhaps from as far back as his youth. Certainly, touches of the sinister abound in his novels.

After James's removal to Europe, the rest of his life became chiefly a matter of hard work, important friendships with literary figures (he seems to have known nearly everyone of importance in French and English belles lettres of his time, from Stevenson to George Sand, from George Eliot to Zola—and he wrote many essays about their work), and extraordinary ranges of travel. After a year in Paris, in 1875, James decided that his art would flourish more fully in England, where he took up residence, first in London, later in Rye, Sussex. He chose this relatively re-mote location because, he claimed, the vigorous so-cial life of London was draining his energy and time from writing—typically, though, it is known that he greatly enjoyed that social contact, once boasting that during a single winter he dined out 107 times. De-spite the claims of some critics and biographers—most notably Van Wyck Brooks, in *The Pilgrimage of Henry James* (1925)—that James abandoned his na-tive land to become an uncritical lover of Europe and especially of England, a careful reading of his novels reveals that he was very clear-sighted about the weaknesses and flaws in English "high" society.

Whatever one's judgment about the validity of the reasons for James's resolve to live and work in Eu-rope, it is plain that his art was largely determined by the European experience. Abroad, James found what he believed to be lacking in America, at least for a novelist of manners interested in cultural phenom-ena. In his biography of Hawthorne, James listed, perhaps with tongue at least partly in cheek, those items that could be studied only in Europe, since they did not exist in America: "No sovereign, no court . . . no aristocracy, no church, no clergy, no army, no dip-lomatic service, no country gentlemen, no palaces, no castles, nor manors, nor old country-houses . . . no literature, no novels, no museums, no pictures, no po-litical society, no sporting class." Though this list of-fers some hint of James's sense of humor, the works themselves are sure evidence that he was convinced that Europe provided him with indispensable materi-als for his novels.

James never made a great deal of money from his writing, but he always lived comfortably (he was so confident of his financial security that he turned over his share of the estate of his father, who died in 1882, to Alice). He was a generous friend, both with money and advice, to his many acquaintances and to young writers hoping to succeed. He had what some biogra-phers call a genius for friendship, which his enor-mous correspondence attests. His fondness for con-genial associates, particularly literary ones, did not, however, blind him to their weaknesses nor subdue his pride in his accomplishments. He once wrote home that, as to his friend Flaubert, "I think I eas-ily—more than easily—see all round him intellectu-ally." Such a boast may help to explain James's re-markable adherence to his absolute belief in his powers and in the rightness of his efforts. While pub-lic taste was going in one direction (downward, in his view), James's technique was headed precisely the opposite way. This firmness has since been justified, and even in his lifetime the admiration of such re-spected writers as Conrad and William Dean Howells did much to console him for his lack of popularity. On James's seventieth birthday, April 15, 1913, some 270 friends presented him with a "golden bowl" and asked him to sit for a portrait by John Singer Sargent (which is now in the National Portrait Gallery, in London). More formal honors were an honorary de-gree from Harvard University (1911) and one from Oxford (1912); perhaps the most lofty distinction was the Order of Merit, presented to James by King George V, in 1916, the year of the author's death (from heart trouble and pneumonia). This decoration was given in recognition of James's valued service to England during the opening years of World War I; James believed that the United States was dishonor-able for not becoming involved.

As death approached—James wrote of it, "So here it is at last, the distinguished thing!"—he was still engaged in writing; he left two unfinished nov-els, *The Ivory Tower* and *The Sense of the Past*, and a number of unpublished essays and stories, all of which have since been printed. This continuation of his labors right to the end was fitting, for never be-fore, or since, was there a man of whom it is so ap-propriate to say that his work *was* his life.

ANALYSIS

Henry James's distinctive contributions to the art of the novel were developed over a long career of some fifty years. Leon Edel, possibly the most re-nowned and respected James scholar, has indicated that James's mature writing can be divided into three periods (with three subdivisions in the middle phase). Through the publication of *The Portrait of a Lady*, in 1880-1881, James was chiefly interested in the now famous "international theme," the learning experi-ences and conflicts of Americans in Europe and Europeans in America (the former situation being by far the more frequent). This first period is represented by *Roderick Hudson, The American, Daisy Miller,* and *The Portrait of a Lady*; of these *Daisy Miller* and *The Portrait of a Lady* are probably the best examples of James's early work. The more complex second period falls into three parts. The first, roughly from 1881 through 1890, displays James's concern with social issues (not the sort of topic for which he is known), as in *The Bostonians* and *The Princess Casamassima,* the former about women's rights in the United States and the latter concerning the class struggle in England. The second of these subperiods is that during which he created plays (many of which have never been performed) and produced a variety of short stories. The final subdivision is that marked by the appearance of short and midlength fictions dealing with the problems of artists in their relationships with society (he had already touched on this subject in *Roderick Hudson*) and of occasionally bizarre stories, such as *The Turn of the Screw* and "The Altar of the Dead," about men, women, and children who are obsessed, haunted, and perhaps insane. Some of these pieces were written during James's calamitous endeavor with drama. The final period, called "the major phase," from about 1896 till the close of his career, shows James returning to the international theme. The themes of this period are most obviously exhibited in the three large novels of his later years: *The Ambassadors* (which was written before the next novel but published after it), *The Wings of the Dove,* and *The Golden Bowl.*

During this extended development and shifting of interests and enthusiasms, James was continuously trying to refine his presentation of character, theme, and event. In his critical writing he stated that he finally recognized the value of "the *indirect* presentation of his main image" (he is here speaking of Milly Theale, in *The Wings of the Dove,* who is seen largely through the eyes of other characters and about whom the reader learns, even of her death, chiefly by report). Several critics, perhaps the most famous being F. R. Leavis, in *The Great Tradition* (1948), believe this "recognition" to be a grave error; they claim that James refined his presentation beyond clear compre-

hension (thus the common accusation of excessive ambiguity) and eventually beyond interest. Others—perhaps the most salient is F. W. Dupee, in *Henry James* (1951)—aver that these three late novels are James's masterpieces, works in which his study of the complexities of moral decisions reaches an elevation never attained by another author.

Two aspects of James's fiction have received little attention: Not much has been written about his humor, which is usually ironic but often gentle. A fine example is his presentation of Mrs. Lavinia Penniman, the foolish aunt of Catherine Sloper in *Washington Square* and a widow "without fortune—with nothing but the memory of Mr. Penniman's flowers of speech, a certain vague aroma of which hovered about her own conversation." This romantic, meddling woman is depicted by James humorously, but with a clear indication of the harm that her interference causes. The image of her "flowers of speech" suggests another neglected style: the repetition of certain key words and images throughout his canon. Readers can easily become distracted by frequently encountered "flower" images such as the foregoing one and key words such as "figured" (as in "it figured for him"), "lucid" or "lucidly" (as in "he said it lucidly"), "idea" (as in "he had his idea of"), and a phrase such as "She took it in" to signify an understanding of a remark. Also, "theory"—in a phrase such as "She had a theory that"—appears many times. It is not surprising that certain terms might emerge frequently in a canon as large as James's, but his evident affection for particular expressions such as the foregoing ones does seem odd in a writer whose repertoire of verbal expression appears to be boundless. It would, for example, be hard to think of another writer, who, in characterizing the grim conversation of Mrs. Bowerbank, in *The Princess Casamassima,* would be able to suggest it by noting, "her outlook seemed to abound in cheerless contingencies."

All in all, though, there is little of James's subject matter and technique that has escaped the close inspection of scholarship. Possibly the greatest shift of critical emphasis in James scholarship has been the increasing awareness of the moral thrust of his work. Early critics frequently charged that no consistent moral attitude was clearly expressed in his work. In later times, this concern evaporated, with a realization that James was an insightful moralist who understood that general rules are of little use in dealing with complex social and personal situations. He tended to treat each novel as a sort of special problem, to be worked out by the characters. From his total production, though, two "principles" have issued: The author was a firm believer in freedom and in personal development. To become a true hero or heroine in a James novel, a character must achieve a state of self-realization (again, an acute act of consciousness is needed), must recognize the truth and face it bravely, must act freely (without emotional dependence on others), and must renounce any personal gain in order to promote the welfare of others. In this way, the person attains true personal development and achieves as much freedom as James believed the world could offer—he did not subscribe to the doctrine that human liberty is unlimited. The basic moral conflict in his novels is essentially between powerful, often heartless or thoughtless, oppressors, such as Gilbert Osmond in *The Portrait of a Lady* and Olive Chancellor in *The Bostonians*, and their "victims," such as Isabel Archer, in the former work, and Verena Tarrant, in the latter.

James's reputation, already high, is continuing to rise and is likely to continue to do so. The dramatizations of several of his works in the cinema (*Daisy Miller, The Europeans, Washington Square, The Portrait of a Lady*, and *The Wings of the Dove*) and television (*The Ambassadors, The Turn of the Screw*, "The Author of Beltraffio," *The Spoils of Poynton*, and *The Golden Bowl*) are perhaps superficial indices of increasing acclaim, but the burgeoning of critical attention is not. There is no question that James belongs, in F. R. Leavis's phrase, squarely in the "great tradition" of the novel.

DAISY MILLER

Daisy Miller, which established James's reputation as a leading novelist both in England and the United States, announces several of his recurring themes and motifs. The story is an uncomplicated one, from the standpoint of plot. Frederick Winterbourne, a sophisticated young American who lives in Europe, meets Daisy Miller, who is visiting Europe with her mother and younger brother; Mr. Miller is back in Schenectady, New York, presumably making enough money to allow his family to travel comfortably. The essence of the novella is the relationship which develops between the young, cosmopolitan expatriate (a not uncommon type in James's fiction) and the pretty, naïve, and willful girl.

In *Daisy Miller* a central issue is whether Winterbourne could have prevented the tragedy that ends Daisy's life. As he gets to know her better and comes to like her, he becomes increasingly distressed at Daisy's refusal to heed the warnings of Mrs. Costello, his aunt, and Mrs. Walker, another Europeanized American society matron (it is significant that the people who most condemn Daisy are not native Europeans but expatriates). Daisy stubbornly continues to consort with the gigolo Giovanelli, who is seen with her all about Rome, much to the dismay of the society people, who are scandalized by such "loose" behavior—even the Romans joke about it in a subdued fashion, which only irritates Winterbourne the more. He tries to warn Daisy that she is seen too much with Giovanelli—"Everyone thinks so"—but she refuses to take his cautions seriously: "I don't believe a word of it. They're only pretending to be shocked. They don't really care a straw what I do." This perverse attitude finally leads to Daisy's death, when she goes, against Winterbourne's urging, to the Colosseum at night (a place that, after dark, was reputed to have a miasma often fatal to foreigners) and contracts a mortal fever. When Winterbourne angrily asks Giovanelli why he took Daisy to such a dangerous place, the Italian answers, "*she*—she did what she liked."

The complexity of the moral nuances of the story is revealed when one remembers that Winterbourne, who is regarded as quite the perfect young gentleman and is welcomed in the best society, has a mistress back in Geneva. Clearly, in that "best" society what matters is not virtue (Daisy is quite guiltless of any actual wrongdoing) but the appearance of it—Winterbourne may not be virtuous, but he is discreet. The old theme of appearance versus reality thus emerges in this story, but with social implications not found in the work of other authors. To James, one of the most difficult problems for Americans trying to come to terms with Europe is that the appearance of virtue often counts for more than the reality. This problem is seen quite plainly in *The Reverberator*, written ten years later, in which an American businessman is puzzled that a French family is upset over some scandalous things said about them in a newspaper; so far as he is concerned, such things do not matter so long as they are not true.

James's realism is most evident in the close of the story. Winterbourne is remorseful over Daisy's death. He regrets that he did not try harder to understand her and correct her misconceptions. He tells his aunt, "She would have appreciated one's esteem." Then, he applies the lesson to himself: "I've lived too long in foreign parts." So far, the story has seemed to advance a moral thesis about the corruption of innocence and the valuable truths that can be learned. James closes the novella, however, on a note that proves how realistic his vision of human nature was: "Nevertheless he soon went back to live at Geneva, whence there continue to come the most contradictory accounts of his motives of sojourn: a report that he's 'studying' hard—an intimation that he's much interested in a very clever foreign lady." James had no illusions about people.

THE PORTRAIT OF A LADY

While *Daisy Miller* is told in the first person, from Winterbourne's consciousness, *The Portrait of a Lady*, a much longer and more complicated fiction, is related through the minds of a number of characters. This book is probably the most generally admired of all James's full-length novels. It carries the "international theme" to what some consider its highest level of expression, and it offers the reader one of the most impressive characters in James's work, the delightful Isabel Archer, the "lady" of the title. Again, James is psychologically realistic: While Isabel is honest, intelligent, and sensitive, she is not without fault; she does have "an unquenchable desire to think well of herself." She is an "innocent abroad" who is "affronting her destiny." This fate is to be given, first, the chance to visit Europe (offered by Mrs. Lydia Touchett, her wealthy aunt who lives in

Europe) and, then, a great deal of money (provided by the will of Mr. Daniel Touchett, at the suggestion of his son Ralph, who becomes very fond of Isabel). This combination of high connections—Mr. Touchett associates with a number of prominent English families, most significantly that of Lord Warburton—opportunities for travel, and comfortable circumstances is common in James's novels.

In *The Portrait of a Lady*, James studies the relationships of the characters in great detail. When Lord Warburton proposes to Isabel, the situation is examined closely, and her rejection of him prepares for later plot developments and revelations of character. As is often the case with James, the money that Isabel inherits is both a blessing and a curse. It permits her to travel and to live almost lavishly, but it also attracts to her one of the few outright villains in James's fiction. Gilbert Osmond appears to be charming, modest, intelligent, and sensitive. He proves to be proud, arrogant, idle, and cruel. In a powerful enunciation of the international theme, Osmond courts Isabel cleverly, appealing to her sense of the artistic wonders of Europe, of which he seems to be a fine judge. He wins her hand, partly through the efforts of Madame Serena Merle, an American expatriate (as is Osmond) who, Isabel later discovers, was once Osmond's mistress (they could not marry, since neither was wealthy—the topic of marrying for money is one that James explored as thoroughly as any writer ever had and with greater insight). Mme Merle is eager for Osmond to marry well, since they have a daughter, Pansy, whom she wishes to see well placed in the world. With James's usual subtlety and with his use of a device that again proves effective in *The Golden Bowl*, Isabel first suspects the unacknowledged intimacy between Mme Merle and Osmond when she sees them through a window, in a room in which she is standing and he is seated—such social touches mark James's fiction repeatedly; to him, the social graces were a great deal more than simply pleasant decorations on the fringes of human intercourse.

Of course, the marriage is a failure. Osmond comes to resent Isabel, and eventually she despises him. In the famous chapter 42, Isabel examines the grim condition of her life. In an extended passage of what is clearly a precursor of the stream-of-consciousness technique, James causes Isabel to review the terrible errors she has made—"It was her deep distrust of her husband—this was what darkened her world"—and to consider how foolish her pride has made her: Ralph Touchett, among others, warned her against Osmond. Isabel's stubbornness and refusal to heed wise advice reminds one of Daisy Miller's similar folly. The plot becomes more complex when Lord Warburton directs his affections to Pansy. Naturally, Osmond is highly in favor of such a marriage, since Warburton is very rich. Isabel incurs her husband's even more intense hatred by discouraging the English peer with the simple argument that he and Pansy do not really love each other. Here, European corruption (expressed in an American expatriate, as is often the case in James's fiction) is opposed to American innocence and emotional integrity.

The conclusion of this novel is among James's most subtle and ambiguous. Isabel returns to England to visit the deathbed of Ralph Touchett. His death has been prepared for by the announcement in the first chapter that he is in poor health. In fact, Ralph is one of James's truly virtuous characters, as is shown by his renunciation of any thought of marrying Isabel, whom he loves, because of his failing physical condition. Isabel admits to Ralph that he was right and that she committed a monumental error in marrying Osmond. Ralph, typically, blames himself for having provided her with the money that tempted Osmond; Isabel refuses this excuse, recognizing that the mistake was her own. The puzzling aspect of the last pages of the novel is that Isabel determines to go back to Osmond as his wife. Several explanations have been offered, all of them proving the profound depth of James's penetration of human motives. The most dramatic is that Isabel's confrontation with her old lover from America, Casper Goodwood, is so violent—he seizes her and kisses her passionately—that it frightens her (perhaps arousing an unsettling sexuality in her nature) into returning to a life that may be despicable but is safe. Another, more likely reason for the decision is that Isabel has become fond of Pansy and has promised to come back and help her

to advance in life along sound and honorable lines. The most subtle reason may be that Isabel is simply too proud to admit her blunder openly to the world, which a separation would do, and prefers to live in misery rather than escape to what she would regard as shame. Whatever the true cause of her resolution (and they might all be operative), she starts back to Rome immediately. In the last passage of the book, however, Isabel's old friend and confidante, Henrietta Stackpole, suggests to Caspar that he must have patience—evidently a hint that this loyal friend of Isabel believes that she will not stay with Osmond forever.

Scholars who believe that James attained the peak of his treatment of the international theme in this novel point to the delicate illumination of Isabel's growing awareness of the sinister undertones of life and to the gallery of superb portraits of ineffectual innocence (as in Ralph, who is all good will and yet helps to ruin Isabel's life), black evil (in Mme Merle and Osmond), and admixtures of positive and negative traits, as in Mrs. Touchett, who is essentially well intentioned but is supremely intransigent (she does not live with the mild-mannered Mr. Touchett, and "the edges of her conduct were so very clear-cut" that they "had a knife-like effect"). Even if the reader is not quite ready to agree with the judgment of F. R. Leavis that this novel, along with *The Bostonians*, is one of "the two most brilliant novels in the language," it seems difficult to deny that *The Portrait of a Lady* is the articulate treatment of the "international theme" in American literature.

THE BOSTONIANS

James omitted *The Bostonians* from the New York edition because it deals with purely American subjects, Americans in the United States; it has no trace of the international theme. *The Bostonians* was undervalued by critics as well as by its author, and it has taken many years for readers to recognize the novel as, in Leavis's words, "a wonderfully rich, intelligent and brilliant book." Aside from focusing on a social topic, a rare instance of this emphasis in James, *The Bostonians* also treats skillfully another subject much on his mind during this era: the problems and aberrations of obsessed, disturbed people. The conflict between the old-fashioned conservative southerner, Basil Ransom, and his New England cousin, Olive Chancellor, makes for a novel full of tension and animation. Some of the modern interest in the book results from what has been judged a nearly lesbian relationship betwen Olive and Verena Tarrant, the attractive girl who is the source of the antagonism. As Irving Howe suggests in his introduction to the Modern Library edition of *The Bostonians* (1956), the fact that people of James's era did not have modern terms of reference such as "lesbian" does not mean that they knew less about these kinds of relationships.

The social problem underlined by the novel is that of women's rights, the difficulty being, of course, that women had few of them. Today, the victories that have been won for the right of women to vote, hold office, and the like are taken for granted, but a reading of *The Bostonians* makes clear how much painful and dreary effort went into creating these advances. As usual, however, James treats the issue specifically, in terms of individual people. In discussing the book later, James said that he took too long to get the story going and provided too much background for the characters. Many current readers, however, judge the background both necessary and interesting. It is, for example, important that Ransom be presented in both a positive and negative light, in order to prepare adequately for the somewhat ambiguous resolution of the plot. As a southerner who has come North to practice the law in a location that will provide him with opportunities not available in the war-ravaged South (it is a clever touch that James causes him to be a Civil War veteran, now living in the region populated by his recent enemies; in this way James emphasizes Basil's sense of alienation and loneliness), Ransom is both appealing—he has "a fine head and such magnificent eyes"—and repelling: "He was very long . . . and he looked a little hard and discouraging, like a column of figures."

Ransom proves very hard and discouraging. Once he meets Verena Tarrant, the daughter of a "mesmeric healer" of dubious integrity (James's depiction of this character is further evidence of his rich fund of humor), who has become, by some natural inspiration, an eloquent platform speaker on behalf of the movement to extend the rights of women, the stage is set for the great contention. Olive Chancellor reluctantly allows Basil to become acquainted with Verena—by this time, the well-to-do Boston spinster has already been overwhelmed by the innocent charm of the naïve girl. Thus the battle lines are drawn early. Ransom soon realizes that Verena should be married, preferably to him, instead of wasting her life on a fruitless and, in his opinion, misguided cause. Ransom believes that the highest destiny to which a woman can aspire is "to make some honest man happy." He finds a formidable opponent in Olive, whose zeal for reform inspires her widowed sister, Mrs. Luna, who believes the whole movement to be ridiculous (since she is very interested in romantic relationships with men, particularly Ransom, for a time), to remark that "she would reform the solar system if she could get hold of it." The wit that James displays at the expense of the movement may seem to indicate that he too thinks it ridiculous, but, as usual, the author is fair, offering a warm and sensitive picture of Miss Birdseye (a character who caused James to be much criticized in his own time, since many readers believed her to be based closely on a highly respected member of the Peabody family of Boston—James always denied the charge), an old reformer who has been pursuing the cause for decades.

Verena and Basil meet but a handful of times before the climax of the novel, but their dialogues are artfully designed by the author to reveal that Verena, who has been welcomed into Olive's home as a permanent guest (the Boston spinster, while having no gift for oratory herself, is fully committed to Verena's promulgation of the cause—she is also deeply and possessively committed to Verena personally, having once cried passionately, "Promise me not to marry!"), is slowly becoming interested in Ransom. Finally, when he believes that he can afford to marry, a conviction that seems somewhat optimistic, since his career has advanced very slowly, and since his belief is based on the publication of only one essay on political and social philosophy, he proposes to Verena. James has not been widely accused of depending on coincidences in his plots, as Charles Dickens and Thomas Hardy, for example, have been, but a number of them do appear. In this case, Verena turns to Olive and away from Basil chiefly because Miss Birdseye, of whom she is very fond, dies shortly after the proposal.

These circumstances lead to the highly dramatic scene at the Boston Music Hall, where Verena is scheduled to address a large crowd. Ransom, learning of the planned address, arrives, manages to get backstage (to the door of the dressing room, which is guarded by a large Boston policeman, provided by the fearful and distraught Olive), and forcefully urges Verena to go away with him. She ultimately accedes to his coercion (he seizes her and almost pushes her out the door), leaving Olive weeping and desolate. James, in his customary evenhanded dealing with themes and characters, makes it clear that the marriage of Basil and Verena will certainly be anything but "happy ever after." Verena is in tears when she is ushered from the theater by her lover, and in the last sentence of the book, James provides a typically ominous forecast of their future: "It is to be feared that with the union, so far from brilliant, into which she is about to enter, these were not the last she was destined to shed." Many readers find it astonishing that James could have so underrated this penetrating study of social movements and human beings torn between personal loyalties and abstract ideals. The climactic final scene is the most dramatic and lively that James ever wrote. This is, though, clearly not the end of the story. As Conrad has said, "One is never set at rest by Mr. Henry James's novels. His books end as an episode in life ends. You remain with the sense of the life still going on."

THE AMBASSADORS

The Ambassadors, which James considered "frankly, quite the best, 'all round,' of my productions," is now generally rated as one of his masterpieces (some critics believe it to be far and away the most accomplished work of the major phase). Like many of his novels, it was based on an incident in real life. In his notebooks, James recalls being told of a visit that his old friend William Dean Howells made to Paris in his later years. According to the anecdote, told to James by Jonathan Sturges, Howells, overcome by the beauty of Paris, remarked to his youthful friend, "Oh, you are young, you are young— be glad of it: be

glad of it and *live*. Live all you can: it's a mistake not to." This passage, and the rest of the speech, is almost word-for-word that made by the middle-aged Lambert Strether, the hero of *The Ambassadors*, to Little Bilham (a character thought to have been based on Sturges) in the beautiful Parisian garden of the artist Gloriani (a character carried over from *Roderick Hudson*; James sometimes became so interested in a character that he revived him for a later novel).

Strether is indeed an "ambassador." He has been given the unenviable assignment (by his formidable patroness, Mrs. Abel Newsome) of persuading her son, Chadwick Newsome, to return to his family and commercial responsibilities in Woollett, Massachusetts (probably representing Worcester, Massachusetts). The primary subject of this novel is *joie de vivre*; this quality is just what Strether finds when he arrives in Paris, where he has not been since he was a young man. It has been observed that one of the salient aspects of James's fiction is irony. Nowhere is this quality more in evidence than in *The Ambassadors*. Chad Newsome, Strether discovers, has been made a gracious gentleman by his life in Paris; Strether, charmed by the beauty and enchantment of the city, cannot in good conscience urge Chad to leave delightful Paris for dull Woollett. The irony lies in the fact that Chad is quite willing and, finally, eager to return home to make a great deal of money (the family business is very successful; it manufactures some useful article which is, typically, unidentified by James), while Strether longs to remain in Paris. Indeed, his delay in dispatching Chad home impels Mrs. Newsome to send her intimidating daughter, Mrs. Sarah Pocock, and her husband to take up the commission, since Strether has evidently failed. Thus the forces of philistinism are present, enlivening the conflict.

This conflict is chiefly in the mind of Strether, since, in this novel, James undertook to employ the third-person limited point of view to its fullest effect. As usual, the situation is not as simple as it appears. It is not merely residence in Paris that has "civilized" Chad; it has also been his mistress, Mme Marie de Vionnet. Strether, before he knows of the intimacy between his young friend and this sophisticated and charming lady, develops an intense admiration and affection for her. Even after he learns of the liaison, accidentally seeing the two rowing on a river near an inn where they are staying, Strether is still entranced by Marie de Vionnet. When Chad decides to return home and abandon his mistress (who has been reviled, to Strether's dismay, by Mrs. Pocock, who refers to Chad's relationship with her as "hideous"), Strether recognizes her tragedy ("You are fighting for your life!") and is extremely sympathetic. He has, however, his own problems. Thanks to Mrs. Newsome's already aroused suspicions and Sarah Pocock's expected damning report, Strether sees that his comfortable position in Woollett (and possibly eventual marriage to his widowed employer) is very likely gone: "It probably *was* all at an end."

The renunciation theme, so prominent in James's novels, is perhaps more powerfully formulated at the close of this novel than in any other of his books. Despite the appeal of Paris, and the hinted offer of an agreeable marriage to Maria Gostrey, an American expatriate who had befriended Strether when he first landed in Europe, this highly moral and responsible man resolves to return to Woollett, where he believes his duty to lie. He cannot help Mme de Vionnet. He cannot help himself. This sort of ethical resolution may seem foolish to modern readers, but it is believable in the novel, and the circumstances suggest James's belief that, in current terms, there is a price tag on everything, even happiness. The novel, then, is not only a tribute to Paris and the life of cultural elevation that it can provide but also the necessity of responsible and considerate action. James admitted that he learned a great deal from George Eliot; he shared her conviction that duty is absolute in the ethical universe. The temptation of Strether is almost overwhelming, but his New England sense of duty compels him to conquer it. It is difficult to think of another novelist, or, indeed, another novel, that illuminates so brightly the significance of conscientious moral choices.

Henry James's contributions to the evolution of the modern novel are of staggering magnitude and diversity. Perhaps his greatest contribution was best summed up by Ezra Pound shortly after James's

death: "Peace comes of communication. No man of our time has so labored to create means of communication as did the late Henry James. The whole of great art is a struggle for communication."

Fred B. McEwen

OTHER MAJOR WORKS

SHORT FICTION: *A Passionate Pilgrim*, 1875; *The Madonna of the Future*, 1879; *The Siege of London*, 1883; *Tales of Three Cities*, 1884; *The Author of Beltraffio*, 1885; *The Aspern Papers*, 1888; *The Lesson of the Master*, 1892; *The Real Thing*, 1893; *Terminations*, 1895; *Embarrassments*, 1896; *The Two Magics: The Turn of the Screw and Covering End*, 1898; *The Soft Side*, 1900; *The Better Sort*, 1903; *The Novels and Tales of Henry James*, 1907-1909 (24 volumes); *The Finer Grain*, 1910; *A Landscape Painter*, 1919; *Travelling Companions*, 1919; *Master Eustace*, 1920; *Henry James: Selected Short Stories*, 1950; *Henry James: Eight Tales from the Major Phase*, 1958; *The Complete Tales of Henry James*, 1962-1965 (12 volumes; Leon Edel, editor).

PLAYS: *Daisy Miller*, pb. 1883 (adaptation of his novel); *The American*, pr. 1891 (adaptation of his novel); *Theatricals: Tenants and Disengaged*, pb. 1894; *The Reprobate*, pb. 1894; *Guy Domville*, pb. 1894 (privately); *Theatricals, Second Series: The Album and The Reprobate*, pb. 1895; *The High Bid*, pr. 1908; *The Other House*, wr. 1909, pb. 1949; *The Outcry*, wr. 1909, pr. 1917; *The Saloon*, pr. 1911 (one act); *The Complete Plays of Henry James*, pb. 1949 (Leon Edel, editor).

NONFICTION: *Transatlantic Sketches*, 1875; *French Poets and Novelists*, 1878; *Hawthorne*, 1879; *Portraits of Places*, 1883; *A Little Tour in France*, 1884; *The Art of Fiction*, 1884; *Partial Portraits*, 1888; *Essays in London*, 1893; *William Wetmore Story and His Friends*, 1903; *English Hours*, 1905; *The American Scene*, 1907; *Views and Reviews*, 1908; *Italian Hours*, 1909; *A Small Boy and Others*, 1913 (memoirs); *Notes of a Son and Brother*, 1914 (memoirs); *Notes on Novelists*, 1914; *The Middle Years*, 1917; *The Art of the Novel: Critical Prefaces*, 1934 (R. P. Blackmur, editor); *The Notebooks of Henry James*, 1947 (F. O. Matthiessen and Kenneth B. Murdock, editors); *The Scenic Art*, 1948 (Allan Wade, editor); *Henry James Letters*, 1974-1984 (5 volumes; Leon Edel, editor); *The Art of Criticism: Henry James on the Theory and Practice of Fiction*, 1986; *The Complete Notebooks of Henry James*, 1987.

BIBLIOGRAPHY

Anderson, Charles R. *Person, Place, and Thing in Henry James's Novels*. Durham, N.C.: Duke University Press, 1977. In the introduction Anderson briefly surveys James's complete works, some sixty-five volumes. The body of this study deals with a selection of James's novels. Anderson salutes the "monumental achievement of this creative artist" and calls him the "father of the modern novel" because James opened up paths for it to flourish. The chapter "For Love or Money, *The Wings of the Dove*" is particularly recommended.

Bloom, Harold, ed. *Modern Critical Views: Henry James*. New York: Chelsea House, 1987. Bloom has compiled what he considers the best in criticism available on James, presented in order of their original publication. Contains much insight from knowledgeable sources on this important American novelist. Contributors include Carren Kaston, author of *Imagination and Desire in the Novels of Henry James* (New Brunswick, N.J.: Rutgers University Press, 1984), and Laurence Bedwell Holland, author of *The Expense of Vision: Essays on the Craft of Henry James* (Baltimore: The Johns Hopkins University Press, 1982).

Edel, Leon. *Henry James: A Life*. Rev. ed. New York: Harper & Row, 1985. An updated and revised version of the original five-volume epic and a definitive work on James. The additions to this edition are particularly useful on the subject of James's sexuality and its relationship to his writing.

Gargano, James W., ed. *Critical Essays on Henry James: The Early Novels*. Boston: G. K. Hall, 1987. An anthology of important criticism on James, including reviews and comments by James's contemporaries, as well as reprinted articles. An essay by Adeline R. Turner, "Miriam as the English Rachel: Gerome's Portrait of the Tragic Muse," was written specifically for this volume. A significant contribution to the criticism available on James's early novels.

_____, ed. *Critical Essays on Henry James: The Late Novels*. Boston: G. K. Hall, 1987. Divided into sections on reviews and contemporary comments and recent criticism. Introduction but no bibliography.

Kaplan, Fred. *Henry James: The Imagination of Genius*. New York: Morrow, 1992. A well-received, psychologically perceptive biography that extends but does not supplant Edel's.

Novick, Sheldon M. *Henry James: The Young Master*. New York: Random House, 1996. A controversial biography which provoked considerable debate between Novick and Edel. Novick explores James's career up to *The Portrait of a Lady*, delving more daringly into James's sexual life than other biographers. Includes notes and bibliography.

Pollak, Vivian R., ed. *New Essays on "Daisy Miller" and "The Turn of the Screw."* Cambridge, England: Cambridge University Press, 1993. Includes feminist and psychological approaches as well as a study of the stories in the context of the Victorian period. Contains an introduction and bibliography.

Putt, Samuel P. *Henry James: A Reader's Guide*. Ithaca, N.Y.: Cornell University Press, 1966. A well-organized commentary on most of James's major and minor works. Although this volume attempts to make James's work accessible to the beginning reader, it is better suited to the advanced reader.

P. D. JAMES

Born: Oxford, England; August 3, 1920

PRINCIPAL LONG FICTION
Cover Her Face, 1962
A Mind to Murder, 1963
Unnatural Causes, 1967
Shroud for a Nightingale, 1971

An Unsuitable Job for a Woman, 1972
The Black Tower, 1975
Death of an Expert Witness, 1977
Innocent Blood, 1980
The Skull Beneath the Skin, 1982
A Taste for Death, 1986
Devices and Desires, 1989
The Children of Men, 1992
Original Sin, 1994
A Certain Justice, 1997

OTHER LITERARY FORMS

Though P. D. James is known principally as a novelist, she is also a short-story writer and a playwright. The great bulk of James's work is in the form of the long narrative, but her short fiction has found a wide audience through its publication in *Ellery Queen's Mystery Magazine* and other popular periodicals. It is generally agreed that James requires the novel form to show her literary strengths to best advantage. Still, short stories such as "The Victim" reveal in microcosm the dominant theme of the long works. James's lone play, *A Private Treason*, was first produced in London on March 12, 1985.

ACHIEVEMENTS

James's first novel, *Cover Her Face*, did not appear until 1962, at which time the author was in her early forties. Acceptance of her as a major crime novelist, however, grew very quickly. *A Mind to Murder* appeared in 1963, and with the publication of *Unnatural Causes* in 1967 came that year's prize from the Crime Writers Association. In the novels which have followed, James has shown an increasing mastery of the labyrinthine murder-and-detection plot. This mastery is the feature of her work that most appeals to one large group of her readers, while a second group of readers would single out the subtlety and psychological validity of her characterizations. Critics have often remarked that James, more than almost any other modern mystery writer, has succeeded in overcoming the limitations of the genre. In addition, she has created one of the more memorable descendants of Sherlock Holmes. Like Dorothy Sayers's Lord Peter Wimsey and Agatha Christie's Hercule Poirot,

(Nigel Parry)

James's Adam Dalgliesh is a sleuth whose personality is more interesting than his skill in detection.

BIOGRAPHY

Phyllis Dorothy James was born in Oxford, England, on August 3, 1920. She graduated from Cambridge High School for Girls in 1937. She was married to Ernest C. B. White, a medical practitioner, from August 8, 1941, until his death in 1964. She worked as a hospital administrator from 1949 to 1968 and as a civil servant in the Department of Home Affairs, London, from 1968 to 1972. From 1972 until her retirement in 1979, she was a senior civil servant in the crime department.

Although beginning her career as a novelist rather late in life, by 1997 James had authored fourteen books, nine of which were filmed for broadcast on television. In addition, her heroine, Cordelia Gray, was featured in a series of television dramas—not adapted from stories actually written by James—produced under the overall title *An Unsuitable Job for a Woman*. The temperament informing her fiction seems to be a conservative one, but she has stated that she belongs to no political party. Although not overtly a Christian writer, James, a long-time member of the Church of England, frequently touches upon religious themes. This tendency is more marked in the later novels and is reflected in several of her titles.

Since her retirement from the Home Office, James has served as a magistrate in London and as a governor of the British Broadcasting Corporation. She has been the recipient of numerous literary prizes and other honors. In 1991, she was created Baroness James of Holland Park. Lady James is the mother of two daughters and has five grandchildren. She divides her time between homes in Oxford, her place of birth, and London, the city so intimately and lovingly described in her fiction.

ANALYSIS

P. D. James's work is solidly in the tradition of the realistic novel. Her novels are intricately plotted, as successful novels of detection must be. Through her use of extremely well-delineated characters and a wealth of minute and accurate details, however, James never allows her plot to distort the other aspects of her novel. As a result of her employment, James had extensive contact with physicians, nurses, civil servants, police officials, and magistrates. She uses this experience to devise settings in the active world where men and women busily pursue their vocations. She eschews the country weekend murders of her predecessors, with their leisure-class suspects who have little more to do than chat with the amateur detective and look guilty.

A murder requires a motive, and it is her treatment of motivation that sets James's work apart from most mystery fiction. Her suspects are frequently the emotionally maimed who, nevertheless, manage to function with an apparent normality. Beneath their veneer, dark secrets fester, producing the phobias and compulsions they take such pains to disguise. James's novels seem to suggest that danger is never far away in the most mundane setting, especially the workplace. She avoids all gothic devices, choosing instead to create a growing sense of menace just below the surface of everyday life. James's murderers rarely kill for gain; they kill to avoid exposure of some sort.

SHROUD FOR A NIGHTINGALE

The setting for *Shroud for a Nightingale* is a nursing hospital near London. The student nurses and most of the staff are in permanent residence there. In this closed society, attachments—sexual and otherwise—are formed, rivalries develop, and resentments grow. When a student nurse is murdered during a teaching demonstration, Inspector Adam Dalgliesh of Scotland Yard arrives to investigate. In the course of his investigation, Dalgliesh discovers that the murdered girl was a petty blackmailer, that a second student nurse (murdered soon after Dalgliesh's arrival) was pregnant but unmarried and had engaged in an affair with a middle-aged surgeon, that one member of the senior staff is committing adultery with a married man from the neighborhood and another is homosexually attracted to one of her charges. At the root of the murders, however, is the darkest secret of all, a terrible sin which a rather sympathetic character has been attempting both to hide and expiate for more than thirty years. The murder weapon is poison, which serves also as a metaphor for the fear and suspicion that rapidly spread through the insular world of the hospital.

Adam Dalgliesh carries a secret burden of his own. His wife and son died during childbirth. He is a sensitive and cerebral man, a poet of some reputation. These deaths have left him bereft of hope and intensely aware of the fragility of humanity's control over its own life. Only the rules that humankind has painstakingly fashioned over the centuries can ward off degeneration and annihilation. As a policeman, Dalgliesh enforces society's rules, giving himself a purpose for living and some brief respite from his memories. Those who commit murder contribute to the world's disorder and hasten the ultimate collapse of civilization. Dalgliesh will catch them and see that they are punished.

AN UNSUITABLE JOB FOR A WOMAN

In *An Unsuitable Job for a Woman*, published within a year of *Shroud for a Nightingale*, James introduces her second recurring protagonist. Cordelia

Gray's "unsuitable job" is that of private detective. Gray unexpectedly falls heir to a detective agency and, as a result, discovers her vocation. Again, James avoids the formularized characterization. Gender is the most obvious but least interesting difference between Dalgliesh and Gray. Dalgliesh is brooding and introspective; although the narratives in which he appears are the very antithesis of the gothic novel, there are aspects of the gothic hero in his behavior. Gray, on the other hand, is optimistic, outgoing, and good-natured, despite her unfortunate background (she was brought up in a series of foster homes). She is a truth seeker and, like William Shakespeare's Cordelia, a truth teller. Dalgliesh and Gray are alike in their cleverness and competence. Their paths occasionally cross, and a friendly rivalry exists between them.

DEATH OF AN EXPERT WITNESS

In *Death of an Expert Witness*, James's seventh novel, Dalgliesh again probes the secrets of a small group of coworkers and their families. The setting this time is a laboratory that conducts forensic examinations. James used her nineteen years of experience as a hospital administrative assistant to render the setting of *Shroud for a Nightingale* totally convincing, and she uses her seven years of work in the crime department of the Home Office to the same effect in *Death of an Expert Witness*. In her meticulous attention to detail, James writes in the tradition of Gustave Flaubert, Leo Tolstoy, and the nineteenth century realists. Because the setting, characterizations, and incidents of a James novel are so solidly grounded in detail, it tends to be considerably longer than the ordinary murder mystery. This fact accounts for what little adverse criticism her work has received. Some critics have suggested that so profuse is the detail, the general reader may eventually grow impatient—that the pace of the narrative is too leisurely. These objections from some contemporary critics remind the reader once more of James's affinity with the novelists of the nineteenth century.

The laboratory in which the expert witness is killed serves as a focal point for an intriguing cast of characters. Ironically, the physiologist is murdered while he is examining physical evidence from another murder. The dead man leaves behind a rather vacant, superannuated father, who lived in the house with him. The principal suspect is a high-strung laboratory assistant, whom the deceased bullied and gave an unsatisfactory performance rating. The new director of the laboratory has an attractive but cruel and wanton sister, with whom he has a relationship that is at least latently incestuous. In addition, Dalgliesh investigates a lesbian couple, one of whom becomes the novel's second murder victim; a melancholy physician, who performs autopsies for the police and whose unpleasant wife has just left him; the physician's two curious children, the elder girl being very curious indeed; a middle-aged babysitter, who is a closet tippler; and a crooked cop, who is taking advantage of a love-starved young woman of the town. In spinning her complex narrative, James draws upon her intimate knowledge of police procedure, evidential requirements in the law, and criminal behavior.

INNOCENT BLOOD

The publication in 1980 of *Innocent Blood* marked a departure for James. While the novel tells a tale of murder and vengeance, it is not a detective story. Initially, the protagonist is Philippa Rose Palfrey—later, the novel develops a second center of consciousness. Philippa is eighteen, the adopted daughter of an eminent sociologist and a juvenile court magistrate. She is obsessed with her unremembered past. She is sustained by fantasies about her real parents, especially her mother, and the circumstances which forced them to give her up for adoption. Despite these romantic notions, Philippa is intelligent, resourceful, and tenacious, as well as somewhat abrasive. She takes advantage of the Children Act of 1975 to wrest her birth record from a reluctant bureaucracy.

The record shows that she was born Rose Ducton, to a clerk and a housewife in Essex. This revelation sends Philippa rushing to the dreary eastern suburb where she was born, beginning an odyssey which will eventually lead to her mother. She discovers that her fantasies cannot match the lurid realities of her past. Her father was a child molester, who murdered a young girl in an upstairs room of his house. Her mother apparently participated in the murder and was caught trying to take the body away in her car. Her father has died in prison, and her mother is still confined. Though horrified, Philippa is now even more driven to find explanations of some sort and to rehabilitate the image of her mother. She visits Mary Ducton in prison, from which she is soon to be released, and eventually takes a small flat in London, where they will live together.

In chapter 8, James introduces the second protagonist, at which time the novel becomes as much his as it is Philippa's. Norman Scase is fifty-seven and newly retired from his job as a government accounts clerk. Scase is the widowed father of the murdered girl. He retires when he learns of Mary Ducton's impending release, for all of his time will be required to stalk her so that, at the appropriate moment, he may kill her. The murder of young Julia Mavis Scase robbed her father of the same years it stole from Philippa. Philippa is desperately trying to reclaim these lost years by learning to know, forgive, and love her mother. Scase is driven to a far more desperate act.

In form, *Innocent Blood* resembles Tolstoy's *Anna Karenina* (1875-1877). Like Anna and Levin, the dual protagonists proceed through the novel along separate paths. Philippa has no knowledge of Scase's existence, and he knows her only as the constant companion of the victim he is tracking all over London. James makes the city itself a character in the novel, and as Philippa shares her London with her mother, it is fully realized in Dickensian detail. Philippa is the more appealing protagonist, but Scase is a fascinating character study: the least likely of premeditating murderers, a little man who is insignificant in everything except his *idée fixe*. James created a similar character in "The Victim," a short story appearing seven years earlier. There, a dim and diffident assistant librarian stalks and murders the man who took his beautiful young wife away from him. The novel form, however, affords James the opportunity to develop completely this unpromising material into a memorable character. As Scase lodges in cheap hotels, monitors the women's movements with binoculars, and stares up at their window through the night, the reader realizes that the little man has found a purpose which truly animates his life for the first

time. He and Philippa will finally meet at the uncharacteristically melodramatic climax (the only blemish on an otherwise flawless novel).

A Taste for Death

Commander Adam Dalgliesh returns in *A Taste for Death* after an absence of nine years. He is heading a newly formed squad charged with investigating politically sensitive crimes. He is assisted by the aristocratic chief inspector John Massingham and a new recruit, Kate Miskin. Kate is bright, resourceful, and fiercely ambitious. Like Cordelia Gray, she has overcome an unpromising background: She is the illegitimate child of a mother who died shortly after her birth and a father she has never known. The title of the novel is evocative. A taste for death is evident in not only the psychopathic killer but also Dalgliesh and his subordinates, the principal murder victim himself, and, surprisingly, a shabby High Church Anglican priest, reminiscent of one of Graham Greene's failed clerics.

When Sir Paul Berowne, a Tory minister, is found murdered along with a tramp in the vestry of St. Matthew's Church in London, Dalgliesh is put in charge of the investigation. These murders seem linked to the deaths of two young women previously associated with the Berowne household. The long novel (more than 450 pages) contains the usual array of suspects, hampering the investigation with their evasions and outright lies, but in typical James fashion, each is portrayed in three dimensions. The case develops an additional psychological complication when Dalgliesh identifies with a murder victim for the first time in his career and a metaphysical complication when he discovers that Berowne recently underwent a profound religious experience in the church, one reportedly entailing stigmata. Perhaps the best examples of James's method of characterization are the elderly spinster and the ten-year-old boy of the streets who discover the bodies in chapter 1. In the hands of most other crime writers, these characters would have been mere plot devices, but James gives them a reality which reminds the reader how deeply a murder affects everyone associated with it in any way. Having begun the novel with Miss Wharton and Darren, James returns to them in the concluding chapter.

DEVICES AND DESIRES

Devices and Desires possesses the usual James virtues. The story is set at and around a nuclear power plant on the coast of Norfolk in East Anglia. The geographic details are convincing (even though the author states that she has invented topography to suit her purposes), and the nuclear power industry has obviously been well researched. Although the intricate plot places heavy demands of action upon the characters, the omniscient narrator analyzes even the most minor of them in such depth that they are believable. Finally, greater and more interesting than the mystery of "who did it" is the mystery of those ideas, attitudes, and experiences which have led a human being to murder. Ultimately, every James novel is a study of the devices and desires of the human heart.

In some ways, however, the novel is a departure. The setting is a brooding, windswept northern coast, the sort of gothic background which James largely eschewed in her earlier novels. *Devices and Desires* is also more of a potboiler than were any of its predecessors. As the story begins, a serial killer known as the Whistler is claiming his fourth victim (he will kill again during the course of the novel). A group of terrorists is plotting an action against the Larksoken Nuclear Power Station. The intrigue is so heavy and so many people are not what they seem that at one point the following tangled situation exists: Neil Pascoe, an antinuclear activist, has been duped by Amy Camm, whom he has taken into his trailer on the headland. Amy believes that she is acting as an agent for an animal rights group, but she has been duped by Caroline Amphlett, personal secretary to the Director of Larksoken. Caroline has, in turn, been duped by the terrorists for whom she has been spying—they plot her death when she becomes useless to them. Eventually, shadowy figures turn up from MI5, Britain's intelligence agency. In this instance, so much exposition and explication is required of James's dialogue that it is not always as convincing as in the previous books.

Adam Dalgliesh shares this novel with Chief Inspector Terry Rickards. Rickards is a mirror image of Dalgliesh. He is less intelligent and imaginative, but he has the loving wife and infant child whom Dalgliesh has lost. While Dalgliesh is on the headland, settling his aunt's estate, he stumbles upon a murder (literally—he discovers the body). Hilary Robarts, the beautiful, willful, and widely disliked and feared Acting Administrative Officer of the station, is strangled, and the Whistler's method is mimicked. As usual in a James novel, the suspects comprise a small and fairly intimate group. The author has totally mastered the detective story convention whereby at some point in the novel each of the suspects will seem the most plausible murderer.

The action of *Devices and Desires* affords James the opportunity to comment upon the use and potential misuse of nuclear power, the phenomenon of terrorism, the condition of race relations in London, even the state of Christianity in contemporary Britain. Still, what James always does best is to reveal, layer by layer, the mind which has committed itself to that most irrevocable of human actions, murder.

ORIGINAL SIN

In *Original Sin*, Commander Dalgliesh's investigative team has changed: Although he is still assisted by Kate Miskin, John Massingham has been replaced by Daniel Aaron. Inspector Aaron is a Jew who is exceedingly uncomfortable with his Jewishness—Jewishness which will become a critical factor in the last quarter of the novel. *Original Sin* is replete with religious metaphors, beginning with its title. Again, the reader is reminded that Adam Dalgliesh is the "first," the dominant human being in each of the novels (despite the fact that he makes fewer and briefer appearances in *Original Sin* than in any novel heretofore). Dalgliesh is the son of a country rector. A minor character, a sister to one of the several members of the Peverell Press to die under mysterious circumstances, is also a sister in a larger sense: She is a nun in an Anglican convent. Frances Peverell, a major character, is a devout Catholic. She is also the near namesake of Francis Peverell, whose sin 150 years earlier has placed a sort of curse upon Innocent House, a four-storey Georgian edifice on the Thames which serves as the home of the Peverell Press. Gabriel Dauntsey—a poet whose name suggests the Angel of Revelation—reveals the darkest secret of Innocent House toward the close of the novel.

Innocent House, dating from 1792, is reached by launch and exudes the atmosphere of a Venetian palace. It is the site of five deaths, all initially giving the superficial appearance of suicide. Four are eventually revealed to be murders. Thus, the very name of the building is heavily ironic. Inspectors Miskin and Aaron do most of the detecting, aided by an occasional insight shared or interview perceptively conducted by Commander Dalgliesh. Several of the characters bear the burden of original sin, the sins of their parents and ancestors. The motivation for multiple murders turns out to be events that occurred fifty years earlier in wartime France.

A CERTAIN JUSTICE

In her 1997 novel, *A Certain Justice*, P. D. James makes use of her whole bag of stylistic tricks, familiar but nevertheless effective. The appropriately ambiguous title refers to either, or both, justice of a particular sort and justice that is sure. The incidents of the novel support both interpretations. The conflicts within and between the members of Dalgliesh's investigative team continue. Kate Miskin is sexually attracted to her boss but dares not acknowledge this fact to herself. Daniel Aaron has left the force, presumably as a result of his unprofessional behavior at the conclusion of *Original Sin*, and has been replaced by Piers Tarrant. As usual, Kate is not sure that she likes her male partner. Also as usual, the murder suspects are members of a small, self-contained professional group—this time, from the Inns of Court, where London's lawyer's practice.

As in other of her later novels, James introduces religious overtones. The chief suspect in the second murder, and the victim of the third (there are four, in all), is a vicar's widow who has lost her faith. Piers Tarrant has a theology degree from Oxford; he claims the study of theology is excellent preparation for police work. Detective Sergeant Robbins, who assists Kate and Piers in their enquiries, is a Methodist of impeccable Christian virtue. He combines two apparently paradoxical qualities, a benign view of his fellow human beings and a deeply sceptical view of human nature. The second quality makes him a very good detective. A key conflict in the latter part of the novel involves Father Presteign, a High Church An-

glican priest. He initially receives crucial information about the second murder, but under the seal of the confessional.

A Certain Justice is marked by a parallel structure. As the novel begins, an accused killer is acquitted and so is free to kill again. An earlier such instance drives the main plot. Two characters, their intentions unknown to each other, set out to achieve a certain justice outside the law. Both attempts lead to violent death. James experiments with epistolary form in chapter 36, which is written in the form of a long letter left by a murder victim. In short, James continues to embellish her murder mysteries with the best features of the realistic literary novel.

Patrick Adcock

OTHER MAJOR WORKS

PLAY: *A Private Treason*, pr. 1985.

NONFICTION: *The Maul and the Pear Tree: The Ratcliff Highway Murders, 1811*, 1971 (with T. A. Critchley).

BIBLIOGRAPHY

Bakerman, Jane S. "Cordelia Gray: Apprentice and Archetype." *Clues: A Journal of Detection* 5 (Spring/Summer, 1984): 101-114. A study of *An Unsuitable Job for a Woman*, which discusses James's female detective as the heroine of a *Bildungsroman*, or apprenticeship novel. Cordelia is only twenty-two when, almost by accident, she becomes a private investigator. Her first case is her rite of passage from girlhood to maturity and professionalism.

Barber, Lynn. "The Cautious Heart of P. D. James." *Vanity Fair* 56 (March, 1993): 80. A profile of James in her seventies—commercially successful, titled, and highly honored as a literary craftsman. Includes a contemporary portrait of the novelist.

Benstock, Bernard. "The Clinical World of P. D. James." In *Twentieth-Century Women Novelists*, edited by Thomas F. Staley. Vol. 16. Totowa, N.J.: Barnes & Noble, 1982. Benstock's essay is found on pages 104-129 of the volume. He discusses James's use of setting, her narrative technique, and the relationship between the two.

Gidez, Richard B. *P. D. James*. Boston: Twayne, 1986. An entry in Twayne's English Authors series. Chapter 1 examines James's place within the tradition of the English mystery novel. Chapters 2-10 discuss in chronological order her first nine novels. Chapter 11 is devoted to her handful of short stories, and chapter 12 summarizes her work through *The Skull Beneath the Skin*.

Hubly, Erlene. "Adam Dalgliesh: Byronic Hero." *Clues: A Journal of Detection* 3 (Fall/Winter, 1982): 40-46. The brooding Dalgliesh, aloof, often forbidding, constantly bearing the pain of a deep tragedy in his personal life, has often been likened to the heroes of nineteenth century Romantic fiction. Hubly's article treats the appropriateness of this comparison.

Macintyre, Ben. Review of *A Certain Justice*, by P. D. James. *New York Times Book Review*, Dec. 7, 1997, 26. Macintyre's review, as reviews often do with James's mysteries, praises her characterization, observing that each character is himself or herself an embryonic novel. He also notes that, as in other of the later novels, the protagonist, Dalgliesh, has become a token presence in the last two-thirds of *A Certain Justice*, "oddly distant and preoccupied."

Porter, Dennis. "Detection and Ethics: The Case of P. D. James." In *The Sleuth and the Scholar: Origins, Evolution, and Current Trends in Detective Fiction*, edited by Barbara A. Rader and Howard G. Zettler. Westport, Conn.: Greenwood Press, 1988. Pages 11-18 are devoted to Porter's essay on James, a writer for whom moral principles are an integral part of the crime and detection story. Porter concentrates upon *Death of an Expert Witness, An Unsuitable Job for a Woman*, and *Innocent Blood*. Robin W. Wink, who has written elsewhere on James, contributes a foreword to the book.

Siebenheller, Norma. *P. D. James*. New York: Frederick Ungar, 1981. The first four chapters discuss the eight novels, grouped by decades, that James had produced through 1980. Chapter 5 discusses the detective protagonists Adam Dalgliesh and Cordelia Gray. Chapter 6 takes up the major themes of the novels; chapter 7, the major characters other than the two detectives. The final chapter deals with the James "style," in the sense both of her craftsmanship and of her elegance.

Stasio, Marilyn. "No Gore, Please—They're British." *The Writer* 103 (March, 1990): 15-16. The basis of this article is an interview with James. In her questions and interpretations, Stasio stresses the elegant and highly civilized nature of James's crime fiction.

JOHANNES V. JENSEN

Born: Farsø, Denmark; January 20, 1873
Died: Copenhagen, Denmark; November 25, 1950

PRINCIPAL LONG FICTION
Danskere, 1896
Einar Elkær, 1898
Kongens fald, 1900-1901 (*The Fall of the King*, 1933)
Madame d'Ora, 1904
Skovene, 1904
Hjulet, 1905
Bræen, 1908
Skibet, 1912
Norne-Gæst, 1919
Det tabte land, 1919
Christofer Columbus, 1921
Cimbrernes tog, 1922
Den lange rejse, 1908-1922 (collective title for previous 6 novels, *Bræen* through *Cimbrernes tog*; English translation, *The Long Journey*, 1922-1924, 1933, 1945 in 3 volumes: *Fire and Ice*, 1923, *The Cimbrians*, 1923, and *Christopher Columbus*, 1924)
Dr. Renaults fristelser, 1935
Gudrun, 1936

OTHER LITERARY FORMS

In addition to his novels, Johannes V. Jensen wrote an extensive number of essays dealing with

(The Nobel Foundation)

influential Danish author of the twentieth century. His reputation rests less on the ideological content of his work than on his unique power of observation and stylistic brilliancy when describing both tiny details and the vast macrocosmos with a conciseness which, in spite of its scientific precision, does not preclude artistic refinement and poetic expressiveness. With his roots in the self-centered, spiritual world of the 1890's, Jensen nevertheless began as a fanatic worshiper of progress and materialism, introducing motifs of modern technology into Scandinavian literature. After decades in which French and German philosophy and literature had been the major foreign sources of inspiration, Jensen advocated the entirely pragmatic and expansive view of life which he found in the Anglo-American world. His knowledge of American culture and society was unique. He was the first to introduce Jack London and Frank Norris in Scandinavia and Ernest Hemingway in Denmark; his translations of Walt Whitman's poetry are as yet unsurpassed. The two trends of introversion and extroversion manifest themselves in a constant process of tension and interaction, and they merge in the "mythic" aspect of Jensen's works into a sublime synthesis.

evolutionary, anthropological, and historical topics. He was also a master of the shorter prose form, primarily seen in his series of Himmerland stories and myths. The stories are principally studies of characters from the Danish countryside, rendered with humor and irony but also permeated with a tragic view of life as meaningless, whereas the myths—embodying the core concept of Jensen's aesthetics—are lyric and symbolic sketches of humankind, nature, and animals. Three volumes of exotic stories contain for the most part travel descriptions from the Far East and the United States. In addition to his prose works, Jensen was the author of several poetry collections, the first volume of which, *Digte* (1906, 1917, 1921), established him as a pioneer in modern Danish poetry.

ACHIEVEMENTS

Winner of the 1944 Nobel Prize in Literature, Jensen is generally regarded as the most prolific and

BIOGRAPHY

Johannes Vilhelm Jensen was significantly influenced by his parents. His mother had a prosaic and practical view of life, but she also possessed a vivid imagination—a double predisposition inherited by her son. His father's extensive botanical and zoological knowledge (he was a veterinarian) became an important source of information for Jensen's later studies of nature and encouraged his preoccupation with Charles Darwin's theories of evolution. A third formative element was the family's deep-rooted feeling for peasant culture.

After a few years in school in Farsø, followed by private tutoring, Jensen entered a cathedral school in Viborg in 1893. There he received his earliest contact with literature, in particular from reading Heinrich Heine, Knut Hamsun, Rudyard Kipling, and the Danish neo-Romantic poet Johannes Jørgensen. Jensen studied medicine at the University of Copenhagen from 1893 to 1898 but then decided to become a professional writer. A short trip to the United States in 1896 was the first of Jensen's extensive travels. These journeys took him five more times to the United States; to Spain in 1898 as a reporter during the Spanish-American War; to Germany, France, and England in 1898 and 1899; and to the World's Fair in Paris in 1900. In 1902 and 1903, Jensen took a long journey around the world; in 1912 and 1913, to the Far East; and in 1925 and 1926, to Egypt and Palestine. Shortly before World War II, Jensen visited the United States for the last time, a trip described in the travelogue *Fra fristaterne* (1939). During the German occupation of Denmark from 1940 to 1945, Jensen burned his diaries and most correspondence from the previous thirty years, but he continued to write until his death. In 1944 he was awarded the Nobel Prize in Literature.

ANALYSIS

"It is a force in itself, the love of my soil and my stock. . . . My entire life is a description of Himmerland." Thus does Johannes V. Jensen acknowledge the influence of his home region upon his life, and an understanding of that influence provides the key to Jensen's writing as well. The dream of the lost land of his childhood made him search both in the past and in distant places for milieus and conditions that would recall the life and traditions of his ancestors. This expansion, Jensen's mythic method, led him back to his home region and in his best works established a balance between an optimistic and a materialistic view of life, the latter influenced by Darwin's theories and the former by spiritual reflection.

This balance was not yet established when Jensen wrote his first novels. In his descriptions of students from the provinces and their confrontation with the modern metropolis, Copenhagen, both Buris in *Danskere* and the title character of *Einar Elkær* are afflicted with a paralyzing introspection. Their inability to accept life leads to cynicism and destruction. To be sure, it is suggested that Buris will escape the advancing process of disintegration, but Einar dies in a mental hospital. Preoccupation with the self

remains a major problem in the fictitious travelogue *Skovene*, written in the capricious and ironic style of Heine; here, the contrast between the white man's civilization and the native's primitive life also shows the influence of Kipling. The work tells humorously of Jensen's stay among Malaysians during his world trip of 1902 and 1903, focusing on a tiger hunt which is supposed to affirm the author as a man of action. Scattered throughout the narration is a marvelous wealth of witticisms, brilliant animal and nature descriptions, and lyric passages full of beauty and color. The predominant mood is one of homesickness and longing, which, together with a penetrating introspection, haunts the narrator throughout the book. If *Skovene*—like Jensen's other youthful works—was an attempt to escape his preoccupation during the 1890's with soul and self, the attempt did not succeed.

MADAME D'ORA

A more successful attempt can be found in Jensen's Himmerland stories, the robust realism of which is continued in two of his novels, *Madame d'Ora* and *Hjulet* (the wheel), set in the splendidly depicted milieus of New York and Chicago, respectively. These works, however, are marred by lengthy monologues and dialogues attacking metaphysical speculation. Thus, in *Madame d'Ora*, a spiritualist seance to which the Faustian scientist and neurasthenic dreamer Hall falls prey, is revealed as pure swindle. In addition, Jensen employs stereotyped suspense effects in an unsuccessful attempt to parody the detective story, as well as grotesque character delineation in accordance with his wish to portray stages in man's evolution rather than individuals. The extremes of these stages are represented by the "apeman" and religious charlatan Evanston and by his opponent, the poet Lee, a man of Nordic descent who in *Hjulet* kills Evanston, now symbolically called Cancer. Lee is thereby changed from a passive spectator to a man of action who condemns any aestheticism as an illness preventing acceptance of reality and social commitment.

The Faust theme of *Madame d'Ora* was thus replaced with social motifs, clearly influenced by Norris, an author Jensen greatly respected and admired, although it was to resurface in the novel *Dr. Renaults Fristelser*. In contrast to the famous Faust story by Johann Wolfgang von Goethe (1790-1833), Jensen's "Faust" wins over Mefisto (here called Asbest) because he is willing to accept wholeheartedly the experience of the moment—life as it is. Structurally, the novel is one of Jensen's more uneven books. The explanation lies in his intention to write a philosophical treatise disguised as fiction, a goal he had set for himself in *Madame d'Ora* and *Hjulet*. Greater artistic strength is noticeable when Jensen gives rein to his mythic imagination. Masterful are his cinematic view of modern civilization, his description of modern technology and machinery, and his evocation of the magic power of nature over the human spirit.

GUDRUN

Jensen's last novel, *Gudrun*, is a contemporary portrayal of the Copenhagen woman and thus also a novel about the Danish capital. It is, however, completely different from *Danskere* and *Einar Elkær*. The city is no longer seen through the eyes of an outsider. When he wrote *Gudrun*, Jensen had been a citizen of Copenhagen for many years—and a mature artist—and the novel delivers a splendid and profoundly personal eulogy of this city as a swarming, animated organism. As in Jensen's other realistic novels, the individualized portrait is only secondary; character delineation tends to be either caricatural or pale and blurred. Yet, typically, the portrayal of the woman is the exception: The picture of the full-blooded Gudrun is drawn with Jensen's usual gusto, which elevates it to a paean to woman as a sexual being.

THE FALL OF THE KING

A renewal of Jensen's writing had, however, already taken place in 1900 and 1901 with the novel *The Fall of the King*. Here Jensen succeeded in merging into a mythic unity two factors: the introverted and spiritual elements of his writing and the extroverted and naturalistic aspects. The book can be read as a historical novel from the early sixteenth century—the most significant period in Danish literature—that attacks skepticism and the inability to act, traits regarded by Jensen as the major components of Danish mentality. This paralyzing skepticism is ex-

emplified by the Renaissance king, Christian II, and by his companion, the mercenary Mikkel. Like the main characters of Jensen's first two novels, these men are lonely, self-divided, and therefore barren and destructive. Jensen does not, however, pay any attention to historical accuracy or detailed psychological characterization. The epic continuity is constantly disrupted either by lyric sequences of exquisite beauty or by scenes of violence and death rendered with harsh naturalism. These sequences transform the work into a magnificent, deeply pessimistic vision of man's inability to find happiness. Mikkel, who is totally unable to devote himself to enjoying the present, can act only when hatred takes possession of him. He therefore must kill his antithesis, the sensuous Axel, who has happiness in abundance and who is not plagued by doubt or reflection. Thus, all human endeavor is in vain; only death brings the sought-for peace.

THE LONG JOURNEY

This disillusionment also concludes Jensen's multivolume novel *The Long Journey*, which was intended as an evolutionary history of humankind, a modern scientific substitute for the Bible. *Det tabte land* is a Darwinian Genesis myth about the transition from animal to man, resulting from the challenges of nature in the primeval Nordic rain forests. In *Bræen*, the Ice Age has forced man toward the south. Only Dreng returns in defiance to the north, founding a large family with Moa and becoming the inventor of various tools. After Dreng's death, Hvidbjørn becomes the main character of the volume. He has inherited not only Dreng's ingenuity but also his longing for the south and the sea. This longing to travel leads to Hvidbjørn's invention of the ship and the family's voyage across the sea, bringing it to the Baltic region. There they meet the primitive people from the warm forests, modeled partly on Jonathan Swift's Yahoos and the Nietzschean *Untermensch*. In *Norne-Gæst*, Jensen follows the life of the Nordic people from the Stone Age to the era of the Great Migrations, focusing on the title character's insatiable longing to travel abroad and then to return home. This yearning drives Norne-Gæst around the world and through time, rendering him a mythic personification of "the long journey" itself. *Cimbrernes tog* takes place during the Great Migrations. Climatic deterioration sets in suddenly during the transition between the Bronze Age and the Iron Age; floods and famine threaten; and the Cimbrian tribe, living in Himmerland, sets off. We follow their everyday life on their raid down through Europe; intervening mythic scenes are observed and commented upon by the omnipresent Norne-Gœst. The Nordic longing to go abroad is represented in *Skibet* by the Vikings and their raids to the Mediterranean, and by the title character in the volume *Christopher Columbus*, whom Jensen, in *Hjulet*, had described as a Nordic type, a Goth. Like Dreng, Hvidbjørn, and Norne-Gœst, Columbus is seen as the defiant individual, the source of cultural development. Yet he is driven by more than an urge for discovery: Like his Nordic ancestors, he is searching for "the lost land." Characteristic of the northerners is the dream of warmth and sun. This dream, through which Jensen attempts to explain religious feeling, manifests itself in a longing to travel which, at the same time, is a longing for home. This search for paradise finds its concrete expression in the ship and the Gothic cathedral, but when Columbus sets out to find the India of his dreams, he discovers America, the land of reality, not an earthly paradise. The futility of his search is evident from his continued voyages of discovery, and Jensen lets him find happiness only in his memories, with life appearing in all of its splendor only in a vision illuminated by the light of eternity: the concluding prose poem "Ave Stella."

The Long Journey, therefore, does not submit to the common interpretation as a solely Darwinist epic about man's descent and the victorious march of the Nordic people through the ages. It is, rather, a collection of mythic texts, lyric fantasies with inserted essays, held together not by a pervasive plot but by a leitmotif: longing as a point of departure for the described expansion in time and space, and as an existential matter, a basic condition of life. The work stands out as a manifestation of the ages of history and of humankind, its struggle and defiance, its pain and precious dreams. It is grandiose in its concept, filled with provocative reflections and composed in a

language of unique originality. By virtue of these elements, it occupies a special position in world literature.

During the 1930's, Jensen's fictitious works became increasingly sparse. The reason was a growing antipathy toward belles lettres, which resulted outwardly in a strong involvement in the current cultural debate and, in his own writing, in a preference for the newspaper article and the essay, for the sole purpose of popularizing the theories of evolution. Jensen's numerous essays are based primarily on questionable scientific theories and deductions, but they are often written in a fluent, vigorous, yet lyric style; his mythic technique frequently emerges with a single, concrete observation as the point of departure, opening up grandiose perspectives and unsuspected inner coherences. It is precisely as a lyricist and creator of myth that Jensen reaches perfection, particularly when he is able to combine these two elements, as in *The Fall of the King, Skovene,* and *The Long Journey*—works which have shown him to be not only the greatest Danish writer of the twentieth century but also a sublime artist for all ages.

Sven H. Rossel

OTHER MAJOR WORKS

SHORT FICTION: *Himmerlandsfolk,* 1898; *Intermezzo,* 1899; *Nye Himmerlands historier,* 1904; *Myter og jagter,* 1907; *Singaporenoveller,* 1907; *Myter,* 1907-1944 (11 volumes); *Nye myter,* 1908; *Himmerlandshistorier,* 1910; *Ved livets bred,* 1928; *Kornmarken,* 1932; *Møllen,* 1944.

POETRY: *Digte,* 1906, 1917, 1921; *Den jydske blæst,* 1931.

NONFICTION: *Den gotiske Renaissance,* 1901; *Den ny verden,* 1907; *Introduktion til vor tidsalder,* 1915; *Æstetik og udvikling,* 1923; *Fra fristaterne,* 1939.

BIBLIOGRAPHY

Anderson, Frank Egholm, ed. *The Nordic Mind: Current Trends in Scandinavian Literary Criticism.* Lanham, Md.: University Press of America, 1986. Contains Per Aage Brandt's essay, "'Oedipus in Memphis': Mythic Patterns in Jensen's Poem," a valuable study of his literary sensibility. Other articles provide excellent background for assessing Jensen's work.

Fris, Oluf. "Johannes V. Jensen." *Scandinavica* 1 (1962): 114-123. Still a good introduction to Jensen.

Heitman, Annegret. "Search for Self: Aesthetics and Sexual Identity in the Early Works of Johannes V. Jensen and Thit Jensen." *Scandinavica* 24 (1985): 17-34. A good example of later scholarship on Jensen.

Houe, Poul. "Johannes V. Jensen's Long Journey or Postmodernism Under Way." *Scandinavian Studies* 64 (1992): 96-128. A very thorough, challenging article recommended for advanced students. Some grasp of literary theory is necessary to make full use of this article.

Ingwersen, Niels. "America as Setting and Symbol in Johannes V. Jensen's Early Works." *American-Novegica* 3 (1971): 272-293. Compare with Heitman.

Rossel, Sven H. *Johannes V. Jensen*. Boston: Twayne, 1984. The most comprehensive study of Jensen in English. Like other introductory volumes in this series, Rossel includes a chronology, notes, and an annotated bibliography. This is the book to use in beginning a serious study of Jensen.

Veisland, Jorgen Steen. "The Absent Father and the Inauguration of Discourse in Johannes V. Jensen's *Kongens fald*." *Scandinavian Studies* 61 (1989): 55-67. Perhaps a little difficult for the beginning student, but a perceptive account of an important theme in Jensen.

SARAH ORNE JEWETT

Born: South Berwick, Maine; September 3, 1849
Died: South Berwick, Maine; June 24, 1909

PRINCIPAL LONG FICTION
Deephaven, 1877
A Country Doctor, 1884
A Marsh Island, 1885
The Country of the Pointed Firs, 1896
The Tory Lover, 1901

OTHER LITERARY FORMS

In addition to her novels, Sarah Orne Jewett wrote several collections of short stories and sketches, most of which were published initially in periodicals such as *The Atlantic Monthly*. The best-known of these collections are *Old Friends and New* (1879), *Country By-Ways* (1881), *A White Heron and Other Stories* (1886), and *The King of Folly Island and Other People* (1888). Jewett also wrote a series of children's books, including *Play Days: A Book of Stories for Children* (1878), *The Story of the Normans* (1887), and *Betty Leicester: A Story for Girls* (1890). The posthumous *Verses: Printed for Her Friends* was published in 1916. Finally, Jewett was a voluminous writer of letters. Among the collections of her private correspondence are the *Letters of Sarah Orne Jewett* (1911), edited by Annie Fields, and the *Sarah Orne Jewett Letters* (1956), edited by Richard Cary.

ACHIEVEMENTS

Jewett is remembered today as perhaps the most successful of the dozens of so-called "local-color" or "regional" writers who flourished in the United States from approximately 1870 to 1900. She is especially noted for her remarkable depictions of the farmers and fishermen of Maine coastal villages at the end of the nineteenth century. Although Jewett was writing from firsthand observation (she was born and reared in Maine), she was not one of the common folk of whom she wrote. Wealthy, articulate, and well-read, Jewett was an avid traveler who moved within prominent literary circles. Her sophistication imbued her best work with a polish and a degree of cosmopolitanism which renders it both readable and timeless; as a result, Jewett's reputation has been preserved long after the names of most other regional writers have been forgotten. Jewett is also regarded as something of a technical innovator. As modern critics of fiction attempt to establish specific criteria for novels and short stories, Jewett's best work—notably her classic *The Country of the Pointed Firs*—is seen as straddling both fictional categories. As such, her work is of great interest to contemporary literary theorists.

BIOGRAPHY

Sarah Orne Jewett was born in South Berwick, Maine, on September 3, 1849, the second of three daughters of a country doctor. The colonial mansion in which she was born and reared had been purchased and lavishly furnished by her paternal grandfather, Theodore Furber Jewett, a sea captain turned shipowner and merchant whose fortune enabled Sarah to live in comfort and to travel and write at leisure throughout her life. Her father and maternal grandfather were both practicing physicians who early imbued Sarah with a love of science and an interest in studying human behavior, as well as a passion for literature. Her formal education was surprisingly sporadic: Since she had little patience with classroom procedures and tended to be sickly, her father generally permitted Sarah to be absent from her elementary school and to accompany him on his medical rounds in the Berwick area. This proved to be an education in itself, for her father spoke to her of literature and history, the two fields that became the great interests of her life, as well as of botany and zoology. Beginning in 1861, she attended the Berwick Academy, a private school; although for awhile she considered pursuing a career in medicine, her formal education was in fact completed with her graduation from the Academy in 1865.

Under no pressure either to earn a living or to marry, Jewett went on trips to Boston, New York, and Ohio and began to write stories and sketches under various pseudonyms, including "Alice Eliot" and "Sarah O. Sweet." Her first published story, "Jenny Garrow's Lovers," was a melodrama which appeared in Boston's *The Flag of Our Union* in 1868, and the eighteen-year-old author was sufficiently encouraged by this to begin submitting children's stories and poems to such juvenile magazines as *St. Nicholas* and the *Riverside Magazine for Young People*, as well as adult stories and sketches to *The Atlantic Monthly.* Her tale "Mr. Bruce" was published in *The Atlantic Monthly* in December, 1869. The first of her Maine sketches, "The Shore House," appeared in that maga-

(Library of Congress)

zine in 1873, and a successful series of them rapidly followed. At the urging of *The Atlantic Monthly* editor William Dean Howells, she collected and revised them for publication in book form as *Deephaven.* By that time, Jewett was beginning to establish a circle of literary friends which eventually would include James Russell Lowell, John Greenleaf Whittier, Oliver Wendell Holmes, and Harriet Beecher Stowe, whose *The Pearl of Orr's Island* (1862) that Jewett had read when she was thirteen or fourteen is believed to have inspired Jewett's attempts to record Maine life.

Unquestionably the most significant of her literary relationships was that with James T. Fields of Ticknor and Fields, the Boston publishing house. When Fields died in 1881, his widow Annie established a close lifelong friendship with Jewett. The relationship inspired long visits to Annie's Boston residence at 148 Charles Street, as well as summer vacations at the Fieldses' cottage in Manchester-by-the-Sea. In addition, Jewett and Fields traveled extensively: In 1882, they visited England, Ireland,

France, Italy, Switzerland, Belgium, and Norway, and they met Alfred, Lord Tennyson, and Christina Rossetti. On other trips to Europe in 1892 and 1898, Jewett met Samuel Clemens, Rudyard Kipling, and Henry James, and in 1900 the pair traveled to Greece and Turkey.

Meanwhile, Jewett continued to write. *A Country Doctor* was published in 1884, and a visit to Florida with Fields in 1888 led to several stories with southern settings. Jewett was strongest, however, in her fictional re-creation of Maine coastal life, as is evident from the popular and critical success of *The Country of the Pointed Firs*, published in 1896. She received an honorary Litt.D. degree from Bowdoin College in 1901, the same year she published her first (and only) historical novel, *The Tory Lover.* In 1902, an accident virtually ended her career: On her birthday, Jewett was thrown from a carriage when the horse stumbled, and she sustained serious head and spinal injuries. She never fully recovered either her physical health or her literary powers; only two brief pieces were published during the remaining few years of her life, although she was able to write letters and to encourage the literary endeavors of the young Willa Cather. In March, 1909, she had a stroke while staying at Fields's Boston home; transported to South Berwick, Jewett died on June 24 in the house where she was born.

Analysis

The proper classification of Sarah Orne Jewett's first effort at long fiction, *Deephaven*, remains problematic even after a century. In some circles it is regarded as a novel, while many literary historians regard it as a collection of short stories, a contention immediately attributable to the book's genesis. It originated as a popular series of sketches that appeared in *The Atlantic Monthly* beginning in 1873. William Dean Howells encouraged Jewett to combine the sketches and flesh them out with a suitable dramatic framework and continuity, and the result—which was entitled *Deephaven* after the composite Maine seaport in which the sketches are set—was an immediate popular success. Even if a reader were unaware of the book's origins, however, he or she still

might be inclined to perceive it as a collection of stories, for the individual chapters—and, at times, even portions of chapters—tend to function as discrete fictional units rather than as elements subsumed within a satisfying whole. *Deephaven*'s confusing fictional status is caused in part by its young author's inexperience with revision, and as such it may be perceived as a flawed book; the fictional hybrid quality of *Deephaven*, however, ultimately became Jewett's stylistic trademark, and for many readers this blurring of the traditional distinctions between the novel and the short story is precisely the source of much of the charm and uniqueness of Jewett's work.

Deephaven

Regardless of whether one reacts to *Deephaven* as seriously flawed or charmingly eclectic, the fact remains that structurally speaking it is a sort of fictional quilt: The individual chapters retain much of their original discreteness, while the fictional framework that was constructed around them is patently an afterthought; in other words, the seams show. Jewett introduces two young ladies of Boston, Kate Lancaster and Helen Denis, who spend an extended summer vacation in Deephaven, Maine, at the home of Kate's late grandaunt, Katharine Brandon. The two women are wealthy, educated, and affectionate twenty-four-year-olds: All of this background is revealed in a flurry of exposition within the first chapter or two, and in fact one learns nothing more of the women in the course of the next 250 pages. Their sole function in the story is to react to Deephaven and to record those reactions, and although Kate and Helen fulfill this function dutifully, their characterizations suffer accordingly. One has no sense of them as flesh-and-blood humans; indeed, they disappear from the text while some salty sea captain or rugged farmer, encouraged by an occasional "Please go only on!" from Kate, recounts a bit of folklore or personal history. This narrative frame, however annoying and contrived a technique it may be, suited Jewett's interests and purposes: Never skillful at portraying upperclass urbanites, she was strongest at presenting the colorful, dignified, and occasionally grim lives of common people clinging to a dying way of life in coastal Maine in the late nineteenth century. These farmers, villagers, and seafarers were a source of perennial interest to Jewett, and the rich variety of their lifestyles, skills, and experiences were elements that she lovingly recorded, even as they were dying before her eyes. Ultimately, it is this impulse to record various aspects of a cross section of American life, rather than poor judgment or technical incompetence, which must be cited as the source of Jewett's distinctive fragmentary style.

That style was rapidly being crystallized in the creation of *Deephaven*. As noted, the two outsiders who react to the coastal village almost disappear from the text despite the fact that this is a first-person narration, but frankly they are not missed. The book dissolves rapidly into a series of character studies, anecdotes, events, and descriptions of the landscape or homes. Individual characters are far more memorable than the volume in toto: The reader is inclined to recall Mrs. Kew, the lighthouse keeper; the widower Jim Patton, who repairs carpets; Danny the red-shirted fisherman, whose only friend was a stray cat; the "Kentucky Giantess," a local girl turned sideshow attraction; Captain Sands, a firm believer in thought-transference and the power of dreams; and Miss Sally Chauncey, the insane survivor of a once prosperous family. Each character is painfully aware of the passing of the economic and cultural prominence of Deephaven and, concomitantly, the passing of each one's way of life; accordingly, each (rather incredibly) recounts his or her life's high points, along with bits of folklore and anecdotes, to the two vacationing Boston ladies.

In addition to offering poignant and often penetrating studies of common folk, Jewett provides accounts of events which are symptomatic of the passing of Deephaven. These accounts include a circus full of tired performers and exhausted (or dead) animals and a lecture on the "Elements of True Manhood" written for young men but addressed to a town whose young men have all died or departed to find new lives in urban factories or in the West. Finally, Jewett provides extended descriptions, often of home interiors. As a symbol of the luxurious life of the past, she offers a chapterlong discussion of the house of the deceased Aunt Kate (an analysis so meticulous

that it mentions the tiny spiders on the wallpaper), along with a companion study of the home of the mad Miss Sally, whose crumbling, furnitureless mansion is decorated with frames without paintings. Clearly this is not the sunny, sentimental world which is generally—and erroneously—attributed to local-color writing of the late nineteenth century. Although Jewett is often accused of avoiding the less positive aspects of life, this is certainly not the case with *Deephaven*: one finds a world of despair, poverty, unemployment, disease, alcoholism, insanity, and death. This is not gratuitous misery, but life as Jewett perceived it in coastal Maine.

Despite the book's rather unexpected acknowledgement of the unpleasant in life, however, it was warmly received, not only because of the limitations Jewett set for herself (she was surely no literary naturalist when compared to Émile Zola, Stephen Crane, or Jack London), but because of the two protagonists through whose eyes the reader experiences Deephaven. Early in the book, as they giggle and kiss their way through the alien environment of Deephaven, Kate and Helen generate a sentimentalized and frankly vacuous aura which is in keeping with the book's initial focus on the superficially picturesque aspects of the town; later in the story, as Jewett progressively focuses more on the grim side of life, the two girls begin to lapse frequently into improbable dialogues. For example, it is after a poor, unemployed widower dies of alcoholism that Kate reveals the lesson she's learned: "Helen, I find that I understand better and better how unsatisfactory, how purposeless and disastrous, any life must be which is not a Christian life. It is like being always in the dark, and wandering one knows not where, if one is not learning more and more what it is to have a friendship with God." Kate and Helen are ingenuous and often preachy; they offer a romanticized counterbalance to the realistic world of Deephaven. As such, the book was rendered palatable to a Victorian audience, but as a result, it appears disjointed, dated, and sentimental to modern readers. With the notable exception of *The Country of the Pointed Firs*, these unfortunate qualities tend to pervade all of Jewett's attempts to write fiction of substantial length.

A COUNTRY DOCTOR

Jewett's second effort at long fiction, and her one book which is most amenable to classification as a novel, is *A Country Doctor*. Unfortunately, the book is marred by technical problems. Poorly proportioned, it concentrates so much on the childhood of its heroine, Nan Prince, that her adult activities as a determined medical student and successful physician are simply matters of unconvincing hearsay. Structurally unimaginative, it offers a dry chronological account and a glaring paucity of psychological depth: The strength of character which Nan ostensibly possesses is scarcely glimpsed as she facilely combats with laughter or thin logic the feeble attempts of acquaintances and townspeople to dissuade her from embarking on a "man's" career instead of assuming the more "natural" role of wife and homemaker. Even so, *A Country Doctor* was Jewett's favorite work, and it is easy to understand why. Despite its flaws, the book is in several respects representative of her finest work; its focal character, Dr. John Leslie, is a loving portrait of Jewett's own father, Dr. Theodore Herman Jewett.

The technical problems in *A Country Doctor* are apparent from even the most cursory reading. As Jewett herself acknowledged, she was far more adept at the delineation of character than at the development of plot, but even so, the characters in *A Country Doctor* are not generally handled effectively. Four of the characters to whom the reader is initially introduced—the twins Jacob and Martin Dyer and their wives (who coincidentally are sisters)—are interesting rural types and fascinating examples of the power of early sibling relationships, heredity, and environment in the determination of adult character and behavior. Also interesting is Grandmother Thacher, the death of whose troubled prodigal daughter Adeline leaves her with the infant Nan, and whose son John, a country lawyer, is old long before his time. Unfortunately, Jewett does not utilize the potential of these characters: The four Dyers are forgotten not long after they are introduced, Grandmother Thacher dies while Nan is still young, and the child's Uncle John is dispatched a few pages after he makes his belated appearance in the story.

Jewett clearly wished to devote her time and energy not to secondary characters, but to Dr. Leslie himself, and in fact she succeeded so well in this endeavor that she inadvertently blurred the focus of the novel. The very title *A Country Doctor* apparently was designed to do double duty, referring to both Dr. Leslie and Dr. Nan Prince, his ward after the deaths of her grandmother and uncle; in fact, however, Jewett's primary concern was the presentation of Dr. Leslie. His portrait is vivid and touching: A widower well into middle age, Leslie is a trusted, competent physician much loved in the community of Oldfields, Maine. If he possesses any character flaws or troubles, aside from occasional grief for his wife or qualms over the stress his ward will encounter as a doctor, he conceals them nicely. Even the transparently contrived visit from his ex-classmate and foil, the well-traveled surgeon Dr. Ferris, fails to convince Leslie that his life might have been more productive, happy, or exciting away from Oldfields.

Living with the obligatory salty housekeeper in an old house full of books and flowers, Dr. Leslie readily adopts the orphaned Nan and interprets her "wildness" as simply "natural" behavior—and in this respect he not only is in keeping with the autobiographical elements of the book but also serves to express several of Jewett's own theories. For much as Dr. Leslie is Jewett's father, young Nan is Sarah herself, and their unusual fictional relationship mimics the real one. Like Dr. Leslie, Dr. Jewett permitted his daughter to be absent from school and took her with him on his rounds, educating her with his discussions of science, literature, history, and psychology. Like Nan, Sarah was far more comfortable out of doors than in a classroom, and at an early age she decided to pursue a career as a physician rather than marry; although Sarah later abandoned her plans for medicine, the similarities between her own situation and the fictional one are quite pronounced.

Perhaps for this reason, the elements of the book that are least satisfying are those which are not derived from Jewett's personal experiences. The opening chapter, in which the wretched Adeline Thacher Prince decides against drowning herself and young Nan, and with her last breath returns home to die on her elderly mother's doorstep, is blatant melodrama. Nan's eventual reconciliation with her wealthy, long-lost aunt (also named Nan Prince) is a fairy-tale motif which does not even offer psychological tension to make it worthwhile. Finally, Nan's ostensible love affair with the milquetoast George Gerry utterly lacks credibility, let alone passion. In theory, the relationship has much literary potential: George is the son of Aunt Nancy Prince's former lover, much as Nan is the daughter of Aunt Nancy's once-beloved brother, and both young people desire to better themselves; but George is a dull, admittedly mercenary lawyer in equally dull Dunport, and he is so threatened by Nan's blithely setting a farmer's dislocated shoulder—George "felt weak and womanish, and somehow wished it had been he who could play the doctor"—that it is clear that the tension Jewett seeks to create between Nan's personal desire to become a physician and society's desire to make her a wife simply cannot materialize. George is a cipher; marriage is never a serious issue; and the single-mindedness with which Nan pursues her career, although obviously meant to demonstrate the strength of her character, compromises the chances for any development of her personality or the generation of interest in the plot. Indeed, the two elements which would have had extraordinary potential for the development of both character and plot—Nan's admission into medical school, and the difficulties she must overcome as a student—are simply ignored.

Part of the problem with *A Country Doctor* is that Jewett downplays plot in her desire to utilize the book as a sort of lecture platform. Much as the two girls in *Deephaven* (transparently speaking for Jewett herself) occasionally lapse into brief lectures on Christianity, the advantages of rural life, and the like, so too the characters in *A Country Doctor* embark on improbable discussions on behalf of the author. For example, in the chapter entitled "At Dr. Leslie's," one learns of Jewett's ideas about child rearing and heredity. As Dr. Leslie talks about young Nan at an incredible length with his old classmate Dr. Ferris, one finds that Nan's guardian seeks to rear her in a deliberately "natural" way. Leslie's interest in her "natural" growth is grounded in his scientific predisposition: He feels that "up to seven or eight years of age children are simply bundles of inheritances," and Nan presents a unique case for study: Grandmother Thacher was "an old fashioned country woman of the best stock," but there had been "a very bad streak on the other side" which led to Nan's mother being marginally insane, tubercular, and alcoholic. Whereas Dr. Leslie's desire to let Nan grow naturally stems from scientific curiosity, Nan's desire is eventually traced to a religious impulse: She feels it is her God-given (and hence "natural") duty to become a doctor, and indeed her final words in the story are "O God . . . I thank thee for my future."

In addition to injecting some of her ideas about child-rearing, heredity, and theology into the story, Jewett also presents her ideas about feminism ("It certainly cannot be the proper vocation of all women to bring up children, so many of them are dead failures at it; and I don't see why all girls should be thought failures who do not marry"), about the shortcomings of urban life (Nan's mother degenerates as a result of moving to Lowell to work), and about the economic deterioration of New England (the once-thriving Dunport is dying, albeit in a picturesque fashion). In short, *A Country Doctor* is typical of Jewett's work in that it shows her incapacity to sustain plot; her occasional inability to present and develop characters who are both believable and interesting; and her unfortunate tendency to preach or theorize. These difficulties were happily under control when Jewett came to write *The Country of the Pointed Firs*.

THE COUNTRY OF THE POINTED FIRS

The Country of the Pointed Firs is unquestionably Jewett's masterpiece: An immediate popular and critical success, it is the only one of Jewett's five volumes of long fiction that is widely known today, and it is at the center of the perennial theoretical controversy as to how one should differentiate between a true novel and a collection of related short stories. As noted above, this situation exists with regard to *Deephaven*, but with an important difference: *Deephaven* was Jewett's first book, and so its hybrid quality is generally attributed at least in part to its author's inexperience. On the other hand, *The Country of the Pointed Firs* is clearly a more mature effort: Tight in structure, consistent in tone, complex in characterization, and profound in thought, it demonstrates how two decades of writing experience had honed Jewett's judgment and technical skill. Thus, the impression that *The Country of the Pointed Firs* somehow manages to straddle the two traditionally separate fictional classifications must be regarded as intentional. Of course, *The Country of the Pointed Firs* is considerably more than a text for fictional theorists—it is a delightful book which shows Jewett at the height of her literary powers.

A comparison of *The Country of the Pointed Firs* with *Deephaven* gives some indication of the extent of those powers, for essentially *The Country of the Pointed Firs* is a masterful reworking of the earlier book. The premise is the same in both stories: A female urbanite visits a Maine coastal community for a summer and records her impressions. In *Deephaven*, the reader follows the experiences of two rather silly young women from Boston; in *The Country of the Pointed Firs*, there is only one visitor from an unspecified city, and even alone she is more than a match for Kate and Helen. A professional writer, she is by nature and training far more perceptive than the *Deephaven* girls. Well into middle age, she also has the maturity and experience to comprehend the residents of Dunnet Landing, who themselves are people who have led quite full, if not always pleasant, lives. The narrator of *The Country of the Pointed Firs* has credibility; one can believe that she enters into the world of Dunnet Landing and that people are willing to impart to her their most private and painful thoughts, whereas it is almost impossible to believe that any thinking person could be so intimate with giggly Kate and Helen. By the same token, although one knows little of the background and personal life of the narrator of *The Country of the Pointed Firs* (the reader is never told her name), one does know what goes on in her mind—her reactions, concerns, interests, misgivings—and as such she seems more like a real person than a fictional creation.

Closely aligned with this is the fact that the narrator of *The Country of the Pointed Firs* stays in focus throughout the story. Even though the book often breaks into little vignettes, character studies, or anecdotes, one never loses sight of the narrator, not only because she is the controlling consciousness who records the events at Dunnet Landing, but also because one knows how she reacts to what she sees and hears. Those reactions are not always positive: She is initially annoyed by Captain Littlepage's account of the mythical Arctic place where souls reside; she is startled (and a bit disappointed) by the modernity of Elijah Tilley's cottage; and she feels the pang of young Johnny Bowden's glance of "contemptuous surprise" as she fails to recognize a local symbol pertaining to fishing.

The narrator's revelation of her inner life is perhaps most apparent in her dealings with Mrs. Almira Todd, the owner of the house where she stays for the summer. Whereas in *Deephaven* Kate and Helen stay in a relative's mansion and bring their Boston servants to run the household for them, the narrator of *The Country of the Pointed Firs* has a close link with the community in the form of her landlady: They live, eat, visit, and occasionally work together (Mrs. Todd grows and sells medicinal herbs), a situation that enables the narrator to acquire extensive firsthand knowledge of the people and lore of Dunnet Landing. Even so, she is aware that, as a nonnative, she can never truly be admitted into the community; she feels rather out of place at Mrs. Begg's funeral and at the Bowden family reunion, and her acute awareness of her being privy to many of the more intimate or concealed aspects of the community (such as Mrs. Todd's admission that she did not love her husband), while simultaneously being denied knowledge of many others, shows her to be a more complex, perceptive, and thoughtful character than either Kate or Helen could ever be. It also shows that Jewett was able to comprehend and convey the fundamental fact that life is far less cut and dried, far more rich and contradictory, than was indicated in her earlier fiction. This is perhaps most evident in her treatment of Dunnet Landing itself.

Jewett goes to great lengths to emphasize the local aspects of Dunnet Landing that make it unique in time and place. She carefully records local dialect by spelling phonetically; she presents characters whose values, interests, and activities mark them as a dying breed living in an isolated area; she reveals the ways in which the region's unusual environment and situation result in so-called "peculiar people," including the woman who designed her life around the fantasy that she was the twin of Queen Victoria. While emphasizing the uniqueness of this late nineteenth century coastal Maine village, however, Jewett also emphasizes its universality: "There's all sorts o' folks in the country, same's there is in the city," declares Mrs. Todd, and it is clear that the reader is supposed to derive from *The Country of the Pointed Firs* a deeper comprehension of the universality of human nature and experience. It is significant in this regard that the reader is never told the year in which the events take place, and Jewett habitually draws analogies between the people of Dunnet Landing and those of biblical, classical, and medieval times.

Jewett's ability to strike a consistently happy balance between the universal and particular is quite remarkable, and equally remarkable is her talent for maintaining a tone which is profound without being obscure, touching without being sentimental. For once, Jewett also avoids preachiness: Captain Littlepage's discussion of the Arctic "waiting-place" inhabited by human souls does not lead into a lecture on Christian views of the afterlife nor a debate between matters of scientific fact and religious faith. Littlepage and his recital, like all the characters, anecdotes, and events of the novel, are allowed to speak for themselves, and the effect is a powerful one. Whether or not Willa Cather was justified in maintaining that *The Country of the Pointed Firs*, Nathaniel Hawthorne's *The Scarlet Letter* (1850), and Mark Twain's *The Adventures of Huckleberry Finn* (1884) were the only American books destined to have "a long, long life," it is true that *The Country of the Pointed Firs* does show Jewett in perfect control of her material and sure in her use of technique. Unquestionably, she had found the fictional milieu in which she functioned best. Given this achievement, it is all the more lamentable that in her next book Jewett deliberately abandoned the milieu.

THE TORY LOVER

Jewett's final attempt at long fiction proved to be her worst book. Usually classified as a historical romance or costume novel, *The Tory Lover* was transparently intended to cash in on the unprecedented and highly remunerative vogue for historical romances that characterized the American fiction market throughout the 1890's and the early years of the twentieth century; in fact, the long out-of-print book was reissued in 1975 (under the title of *Yankee Ranger*) for precisely the same reasons on the eve of the American Bicentennial. *The Tory Lover* is virtually a casebook for students of the mishandling of fictional material and technique, and as such it is a perennial embarrassment to even the most devoted advocates of Jewett's work.

As usual, Jewett demonstrates her inability to handle plot, or, as she accurately lamented to Horace Scudder in 1873, "I have no dramatic talent . . . It seems to me I can furnish the theater, and show you the actors, and the scenery, and the audience, but there never is any play!" Whereas *The Country of the Pointed Firs* is strong precisely because it lacks—and in fact does not need—a plot in the usual sense of the word, *The Tory Lover* is virtually all plot, and it suffers accordingly. Although the book is set in the opening months of the American Revolution (1777), Jewett is unable to convey the excitement and tension of that most stirring era in American history. Surprisingly, little happens in this overlong story: At the urging of his girlfriend Mary Hamilton, Roger Wallingford of Berwick, Maine, declares himself to be in support of the American cause; he ships out to England on the *Ranger* under Captain John Paul Jones, is captured during Jones's attempt to burn Whitehaven, and is imprisoned at Plymouth, eventually winning a full pardon thanks to the efforts of assorted English noblemen.

Although this story line is potentially rich with exciting scenes, none materializes. The transatlantic crossing is quite dull, despite Jewett's desperate efforts to render credible the novel's obligatory villain, Dickson. The disgruntled crew's unsuccessful attempt to overthrow Captain Jones, instead of being excitingly dramatized, is reduced to a comment: "There had been an attempt at mutiny on board, but the captain had quelled that, and mastered the deep-laid plot behind it." Similarly, Roger Wallingford's imprisonment, which lasts for much of the novel, is barely mentioned, and his daring and bloody escape is a matter of hearsay. Jewett's attempts to generate intrigue, mystery, or tension are no more successful. Wallingford's pardon is the result of the written request of a resident of Berwick, one Master Sullivan, but his relationship to the powerful noblemen who actually secure the pardon is never explained, and the effect generated is more annoyance than mystery. Likewise, the tension between Captain Jones and Wallingford which results from Jones's wearing Mary's ring is resolved a few pages later when Wallingford bluntly reveals the source of his ill temper. Finally, the book's climax—the evil Dickson's admission of his role in the thwarting of Jones and the arrest of Wallingford—is not in the least surprising or convincing: Quite simply, the drunken Dickson boasts of his deeds in a public house, and his fellow sailors toss him into the street. A few paragraphs later, the book abruptly ends.

Plot had never been Jewett's strong suit, but even the characterization in *The Tory Lover* is lamentable. The story's heroine, Mary Hamilton, is constantly described as "beautiful," "bright," and "charming"; but the repeated use of vague adjectives does not constitute characterization. The very little that she thinks, says, and does reveals virtually nothing about her. In this regard, she is perhaps ideally suited to her equally wooden lover, Roger Wallingford, who repeatedly is said to be "gentlemanly" and "handsome," but who in fact is not in the least missed as he languishes for much of the novel in a British prison. Even the historical figures who would be expected to have intrinsic interest, such as Benjamin Franklin and John Paul Jones, are nothing more than flaccid bundles of adjectives who are irritating in their very lifelessness. Jewett also introduces a series of dull, obligatory stock characters (Dickson as the villain, Madam Wallingford as the grande dame, Old Caesar as the loyal black servant), as well as a plethora of characters who are simply dropped a few pages after they first appear: Dr. Ezra Green, the *Ranger*'s literary surgeon; wealthy Colonel Jonathan Hamilton, Mary's allegedly dashing brother; Gideon Warren,

the Berwick sailor who is reunited with Wallingford in the Plymouth prison.

Ultimately, *The Tory Lover* is a cluttered, confusing pastiche of unexciting events and lifeless characters; it is to Jewett's credit that she was able to acknowledge her inability to write historical romance. There is every indication that she agreed with Henry James's negative reaction to *The Tory Lover*: "Go back to the dear Country of the Pointed Firs, *come* back to the palpable present *intimate* that throbs responsive, and that wants, misses, needs you, God knows, and suffers woefully in your absence." Jewett's devastating buggy accident occurred before she could act on James's admonition, however, and *The Tory Lover* stands as her last, but far from best, work.

Alice Hall Petry

OTHER MAJOR WORKS

SHORT FICTION: *Old Friends and New*, 1879; *Country By-Ways*, 1881; *A White Heron and Other Stories*, 1886; *The King of Folly Island and Other People*, 1888; *Tales of New England*, 1890.

POETRY: *Verses: Printed for Her Friends*, 1916.

NONFICTION: *Letters of Sarah Orne Jewett*, 1911 (Annie Fields, editor); *Sarah Orne Jewett Letters*, 1956 (Richard Cary, editor).

CHILDREN'S LITERATURE: *Play Days: A Book of Stories for Children*, 1878; *The Story of the Normans*, 1887; *Betty Leicester: A Story for Girls*, 1890.

BIBLIOGRAPHY

Cary, Richard. *Sarah Orne Jewett*. Boston: Twayne, 1962. Considered an important study because Cary maintains a balance in his approach to Jewett, appreciating her works while understanding their limitations. Contains a selected bibliography.

Church, Joseph. *Transcendent Daughters in Jewett's "Country of the Pointed Firs."* Rutherford, N.J.: Fairleigh Dickinson University Press, 1994. An excellent examination of Jewett's novel. Includes bibliographical references and an index.

Donovan, Josephine. *Sarah Orne Jewett*. New York: Frederick Ungar, 1980. A useful, but somewhat limited, survey of Jewett's writings, which focuses on how many of her works concern women's issues. The final chapter is particularly useful on Jewett's critical theories. Includes a bibliography.

Howard, June, ed. *New Essays on "The Country of the Pointed Firs."* Cambridge, England: Cambridge University Press, 1994. Essays interpreting the novel. Provides bibliographical references.

Nagel, Gwen L, ed. *Critical Essays on Sarah Orne Jewett.* Boston: G. K. Hall, 1984. A compilation of solid criticism on Jewett that contains nine original essays and an introduction providing a detailed bibliographic survey of Jewett scholarship. Among the original essays is a piece by Philip B. Eppard on two recently discovered Jewett stories. An important contribution to studies on Jewett, on whom there has been little contemporary criticism save for feminist scholarship.

Roman, Margaret. *Sarah Orne Jewett: Reconstructing Gender.* Tuscaloosa: University of Alabama Press, 1992. An exploration of how Jewett collapses gender boundaries in her fiction and breaks free of a patriarchal society. Roman discusses several of Jewett's stories that have been neglected and not previously subjected to a feminist analysis. Includes a bibliography.

Sherman, Sarah Way. *Sarah Orne Jewett: An American Persephone.* Hanover, N.H.: University Press of New England, 1989. A full-length, in-depth study of Jewett that attempts to go to the source of the mythic quality in her work. Sherman tells how Jewett came to terms with the culture that defined her womanhood, and sees the myth of Demeter and Persephone as a central symbol. Particular attention is given to the novel *The Country of the Pointed Firs.*

Silverthorne, Elizabeth. *Sarah Orne Jewett: A Writer's Life.* Woodstock, N.Y.: Overlook Press, 1993. Silverthorne describes the increasing interest in Jewett's treatment of women, ecology, and regional life. Silverthorne had access to letters and manuscripts unavailable to previous biographers, and she takes full advantage of Jewett scholarship.

Ruth Prawer Jhabvala

Born: Cologne, Germany; May 7, 1927

Principal long fiction

To Whom She Will, 1955 (pb. in U.S. as *Amrita*, 1956)
The Nature of Passion, 1956
Esmond in India, 1958
The Householder, 1960
Get Ready for Battle, 1962
A Backward Place, 1965
A New Dominion, 1972 (pb. in U.S. as *Travelers*, 1973)
Heat and Dust, 1975
In Search of Love and Beauty, 1983
Three Continents, 1987
Poet and Dancer, 1993
Shards of Memory, 1995

Other literary forms

Though Ruth Prawer Jhabvala is known mainly as a novelist, she is also an accomplished writer of short stories, film scripts, and essays. Among her collections of short stories are *Like Birds, Like Fishes, and Other Stories* (1963), *A Stronger Climate: Nine Stories* (1968), *An Experience of India* (1971), and *How I Became a Holy Mother and Other Stories* (1976); *Out of India* (1986) is a selection of stories from these volumes. *Shakespeare Wallah* (1965; with James Ivory), *Heat and Dust* (1983), and *A Room with a View* (1986; based on E. M. Forster's novel) are her best-known film scripts.

Achievements

Jhabvala has achieved remarkable distinction, both as a novelist and as a short-story writer, among writers on modern India. She has been compared to E. M. Forster, though the historical phases and settings of the India they portray are widely different. The award of the Booker Prize for *Heat and Dust* in 1975 made her internationally famous. Placing Jhabvala in a literary-cultural tradition is difficult: Her European parentage, British education, marriage to an Indian, and—after many years in her adopted country—change of residence from India to the United States perhaps reveal a lack of belonging, a recurring "refugee" consciousness. Consequently, she is not an Indian writing in English, nor a European writing on India, but perhaps a writer of the world of letters deeply conscious of being caught up in a bizarre world. She is sensitive, intense, ironic—a detached observer and recorder of the human world. Her almost clinical accuracy and her sense of the graphic, the comic, and the ironic make her one of the finest writers on the contemporary scene.

In 1984, Jhabvala won the British Award for Film and Television Arts (BAFTA) for Best Screenplay for the Ismail Merchant-James Ivory adaptation of *Heat and Dust*, and in 1986 she won an Academy Award for Best Adapted Screenplay for *A Room with a View*. In 1990, she was awarded Best Screenplay from the New York Film Critics Circle for *Mr. and Mrs.*

(Jerry Bauer)

Bridge, adapted from Evan S. Connell, Jr.'s novels. Jhabvala received an Academy Award for Best Adapted Screenplay in 1992 for Forster's *Howards End* and an Oscar nomination for her adaptation of Kazuo Ishiguro's *The Remains of the Day* in 1993. In 1984, Jhabvala won a MacArthur Foundation Award, and in 1994 she received the Writers Guild of America's Laurel Award.

Biography

Ruth Prawer was born in Cologne, Germany, on May 7, 1927, the daughter of Marcus and Eleonora Prawer; her family's heritage was German, Polish, and Jewish. She emigrated to England in 1939, became a British citizen in 1948, and obtained an M.A. in English from Queen Mary College, London, in 1951. That same year, she married C. H. S. Jhabvala, an Indian architect, and went to live in India. Jhabvala formed a profound, albeit conflicted, relationship with the country. With her Indian husband and Indian-born children, Renana, Ava, and Feroza, she has had a unique opportunity of seeing the subcontinent from the privileged position of an insider but through the eyes of an alien. Thus, rootedness in a culture and people, an issue with which she is intimate, provides a wellspring for her screenplays, novels, and stories.

The author has returned to India, to millions a place of ancient wisdom and spiritual equilibrium, time and again. Her exposure to the waves of young foreigners who descended upon India in the 1960's only to be taken advantage of by unscrupulous "mystics," influenced such books as *Three Continents*. Indeed, the theme of religious charlatans permeates much of Jhabvala's work. While she would spend three months of each year in New Delhi, Jhabvala settled in New York in 1975, living near her friends and film colleagues, the Merchant-Ivory duo. Her work on film scripts with the team, which began in the 1960's, enriched her technique as a writer of fiction and widened her vision. One may well view this move to New York as initiating the second major influence on the author's body of work, giving rise to her collection of short stories, *East into Upper East: Plain Tales from New York and New Delhi*

(1998). Jhabvala would contribute regularly to *The New Yorker*.

ANALYSIS

Ruth Prawer Jhbavala's distinctive qualities as a novelist grow from her sense of social comedy. She excels in portraying incongruities of human behavior, comic situations which are rich with familial, social, and cultural implications. Marital harmony or discord, the pursuit of wealth, family togetherness and feuds, the crisis of identity and homelessness—these are among the situations that she repeatedly explores in her fiction. She writes with sympathy, economy, and wit, with sharp irony and cool detachment.

Jhabvala's fiction has emerged out of her own experience of India. "The central fact of all my work," she once told an interviewer, "is that I am a European living permanently in India. I have lived here for most of my adult life . . . . This makes me not quite an outsider either." Much later, however, in "Myself in India," she revealed a change in her attitude toward India: "However, I must admit I am no longer interested in India. What I am interested in now is myself in India . . . my survival in India."

This shift in attitude has clearly affected Jhabvala's fiction. There is a distinct Indianness in the texture and spirit of her first five novels, which are sunny, bright, social comedies offering an affirmative view of India. The later novels, darkened by dissonance and despair, reveal a change in the novelist's perspective.

In almost all of her novels, Jhabvala assumes the role of an omniscient narrator. She stands slightly aloof from her creations, an approach which has advantages as well as disadvantages. On the one hand, she does not convey the passionate inner life of her characters, many of whom are essentially stereotypes. Even her more fully developed characters are seen largely from the outside. On the other hand, she is a consummate observer. She has a fine eye for naturalistic detail, a gift for believable dialogue, but she is also an observer at a deeper level, registering the malaise that is characteristic of the modern world: the collapse of traditional values, the incongruous

blending of diverse cultures: sometimes energizing, sometimes destructive, often bizarre. Thus, her fiction, while steeped in the particular reality of India, speaks to readers throughout the world.

AMRITA

Amrita inaugurates Jhabvala's first phase, in which reconciliation between two individuals (symbolic as well of a larger, social integration) is at the center of the action. Amrita, a young, romantic girl, has a love affair with Hari, her colleague in radio. Their affair is portrayed with a gentle comic touch: She tells Hari of her determination to marry him at all costs; he calls her a goddess and moans that he is unworthy of her. Jhabvala skillfully catches the color and rhythm of the Indian phraseology of love.

While this affair proceeds along expected lines, Pandit Ram Bahadur, Hari's grandfather, is planning to get his grandson married to Sushila, a pretty singer, in an arranged match. When Hari confesses to his brother-in-law that he loves Amrita, he is advised that first love is only a "game," and no one should take it seriously. Hari then is led to the bridal fire and married to Sushila. He forgets his earlier vows of love for Amrita, even the fact that he applied for a passport to go with her to England.

The forsaken maiden, Amrita, finds her hopes for a happy union revived when another man, Krishna Sengupta, writes her a letter full of love and tenderness. Enthralled after reading his six-page letter, she decks her hair with a beautiful flower, a sign of her happy reconciliation with life. Amrita shares in the sunshine of love that comes her way.

The original title of the novel, *To Whom She Will* (changed to *Amrita* for the American edition), alludes to a story in a classic collection of Indian fables, the *Panchatantra* (between 100 B.C.E. and 500 C.E.; *The Morall Philosophie of Doni*, 1570). In the story, which centers on a maiden in love, a Hindu sage observes that marriage should be arranged for a girl at a tender age; otherwise, "she gives herself to whom she will." This ancient injunction is dramatized in the predicaments of Hari, Amrita, Sushila, and Sengupta, the four main characters. The irony lies in the fact that Amrita does not marry "whom she will." Nevertheless, the regaining of happiness is the keynote of Jhabvala's first novel of family relations and individual predicaments.

THE NATURE OF PASSION

Alluding to Swami Paramananda's translation of the *Bhagavad Gītā* (c. fifth century B.C.E.), which Jhabvala quotes, her second novel, *The Nature of Passion*, deals with one of the three kinds of passion which are distinguished in the *Bhagavad Gītā*: that which is worldly, sensuous, pleasure-seeking. This passion, or *rajas*, rules the world of Lalaji and his tribe, who represent the rising middle class and whose debased values become the object of Jhabvala's unsparing irony. She presents a series of vignettes of the life of the affluent—such as Lalaji and the Vermas—who migrated to India after the partition and continued to prosper. Here, Jhabvala's characters are not intended to be fully rounded individuals; rather, they play their parts as embodiments of various passions.

Lalaji's role is to illustrate the contagious effects of greed and corruption. An indiscreet letter written by his older son finds its way into a government file controlled by Chandra, his second son. When Lalaji asks Chandra to remove the incriminating letter, Chandra's self-righteous wife, Kanta, objects. She soon realizes, however, that their comforts and their holidays depend upon Lalaji's tainted money, and she relents, allowing the letter to be removed. Lalaji's daughter Nimmi, too, moves from revolt to submission. Lalaji's tenderness for Nimmi is conveyed beautifully. When she cuts her hair short, Lalaji accepts this sign of modernity. Nevertheless, despite her attraction to another young man, she accepts the marriage partner chosen for her by her family.

Jhabvala's irony is cutting, but her style in this novel has an almost clinical precision, a detachment that discourages reader involvement. By concentrating on social types rather than genuinely individualized characters, she limits the appeal of the novel, which already seems badly dated.

ESMOND IN INDIA

Jhabvala's third novel, *Esmond in India*, as its title suggests, is concerned with the conflict between cultures. Esmond is an Englishman, a shallow man with a handsome face who tutors European women in

Hindi language and culture and serves as a guide to visitors. He is an egotistic, aggressive colonial, and Jhabvala is relentless in her irony in sketching him, especially in a scene at the Taj Mahal where he loses his shoes. The pretentious Esmond is cut down to size and becomes a puny figure.

Esmond's relationship with his wife, Gulab, is the novel's central focus. She is a pseudoromantic Indian girl, very fond of good food. Their marriage is in ruins: Esmond feels trapped and speaks with scorn of her dull, alien mind, while she is keenly aware of his failure to care for her. Nevertheless, Gulab, as a true Hindu wife, bears Esmond's abuse and his indulgence in love affairs, until their family servant attempts to molest her. She then packs her bag and leaves Esmond.

Is Gulab a rebel or a complete conformist? In marrying Esmond, an Englishman, she surely seems to have become a rebel. Later, however, she is subservient in response to Esmond's cruelty; the servant assaults her because he knows that Esmond does not love his wife. This sets into motion her second rebellion: separation from Esmond. Gulab is a complex, memorable character.

Esmond, too, though he is drawn with sharp irony, is no mere caricature. At the heart of the novel is his overwhelming sense of a loss of identity, a crisis which grips his soul and makes him unequal to the task of facing India, that strange land.

THE HOUSEHOLDER

The Householder is perhaps Jhabvala's most successful, least problematic, most organically conceived novel. A true social comedy, it is a direct, simple "impression of life." It centers on the maturation of its likable central character, Prem, a Hindi instructor in Mr. Khanna's private college. Prem is a shy, unassuming young man, in no way exceptional, yet his growth to selfhood, presented with insight and humor, makes for compelling fiction.

The title *The Householder* is derived from the Hindu concept of the four stages of a man's life; the second stage, that of a family man, is the one which the novel explores. Prem's relations with his wife, Indu, are most delicately portrayed. The scene of Prem loving Indu on the terrace in moonlight is both tender and touching. They both sense the space and the solitude and unite in deep intimacy. Prem realizes that Indu is pregnant and tenderly touches her growing belly—scenes which show Jhabvala at her best and most tender.

Prem's troubles are mainly economic—how to survive on a meager salary—and the comedy and the pathos which arise out of this distress constitute the real stuff of the novel. The indifference, the arrogance, and the insensitivity of the other characters are comically rendered, emphasizing Prem's seeming helplessness, as he struggles to survive and to assert his individuality. (A minor subplot is contributed by Western characters: Hans Loewe, a seeker after spiritual reality, and Kitty, his landlady, provide a contrast to Prem's struggle.) Nevertheless, Prem is finally able to overcome his inexperience and immaturity, attaining a tenderness, a human touch, and a balance which enable him to achieve selfhood and become a true "householder."

GET READY FOR BATTLE

Get Ready for Battle, Jhabvala's fifth novel, resembles *The Nature of Passion*. Like that earlier novel, it pillories the selfish, acquisitive society of postindependence India. In particular, it shows how growing urbanization affects the poor, dispossessing them of their land. Like *The Nature of Passion*, *Get Ready for Battle* derives its title from the *Bhagavad Gītā*, alluding to the scene in which Lord Krishna instructs Arjuna to "get ready for battle" without fear; similarly, Jhabvala's protagonist, Sarla Devi, urges the poor to get ready for battle to protect their rights. *Get Ready for Battle* is superior to *The Nature of Passion*, however, in its portrayal of interesting and believable characters. While the characters in the later novel still represent various social groups or points of view, they are not mere types.

The central character, Sarla Devi, deeply committed to the cause of the poor, is separated from her husband, Gulzari Lal. They represent two opposite valuations of life: She leads her life according to the tenets of the *Bhagavad Gītā*, while he, acquisitive and heartless, is a worshiper of Mammon. The main action of the novel centers on her attempt to save the poor from being evicted from their squatters' colony

and also to save her son from following her father's corrupt lifestyle. She fails in both these attempts, yet she is heroic in her failure.

Jhabvala brilliantly depicts the wasteland created by India's growing cities, which have swallowed farms and forests, at the same time destroying the value-structure of rural society. Yet *Get Ready for Battle* also includes adroitly designed domestic scenes. Kusum, Gulzari Lal's mistress, is shown with sympathy, while the relationship between two secondary characters, the married couple Vishnu and Mala, is portrayed with tenderness as well as candor. They show their disagreements (even speak of divorce), yet they are deeply in love. For them, "getting ready for battle" is a kind of game, a comic conflict, rather than a serious issue.

A BACKWARD PLACE

Jhabvala's next novel, *A Backward Place*, initiated the second phase of her career, marked by dark, despairing comedies disclosing a world out of joint. In this novel, too, Jhabvala began to focus more attention on encounters between East and West and the resulting tensions and ironies. The novel's title, which refers to a European character's condescending assessment of Delhi, suggests its pervasive irony; neither Indians nor Europeans are spared Jhabvala's scorn. While it features an appealing protagonist, the novel is too schematic, too much simply a vehicle for satire.

TRAVELERS

A Backward Place was followed by *Travelers*, a novel in the same dark mode, which presents the Western vision of contemporary India with telling irony. European girls seek a spiritual India, but the country that they actually experience is quite the opposite. Despite its satiric bite, the novel must be judged a failure: The great art of fiction seems to degenerate here into mere journalism, incapable of presenting a true vision of contemporary India.

HEAT AND DUST

This forgettable novel was followed by Jhabvala's most widely praised work, *Heat and Dust*, the complex plot of which traces parallels between the experiences of two Englishwomen in India: the unnamed narrator and her grandfather Douglas's first wife, Olivia. In the 1930's, Olivia came to India as

Douglas's wife. Bored by her prosaic, middle-class existence, Olivia is drawn to a Muslim nawab with whom she enjoys many escapades. Invited to a picnic close to a Muslim shrine, Olivia finds the nawab irresistible. They lie by a spring in a green grove, and the nawab makes her pregnant. She then leaves Douglas, aborts her child, and finally moves to a house in the hills as the nawab's mistress.

After a gap of two generations, the narrator, who has come to India to trace Olivia's life story, passes through a similar cycle of experience. Fascinated by India, she gives herself to a lower-middle-class clerk, Inder Lal, at the same place near the shrine where Olivia lay with the nawab, and with the same result. The young narrator decides to rear the baby, though she gives up her lover; she also has a casual physical relationship with another Indian, Child, who combines sexuality with a spiritual quest.

Heat and Dust is unlike many of Jhabvala's novels. It has a strong current of positive feeling beneath its surface negativism. Olivia, though she discards her baby, remains loyal to her heart's desire for the nawab, and the narrator, while not accepting her lover, wishes to rear her baby as a symbol of their love. This note of affirmation heightens the quality of human response in *Heat and Dust*, which is also notable for its fully realized characterizations.

IN SEARCH OF LOVE AND BEAUTY

In Search of Love and Beauty, set primarily in the United States but ranging widely elsewhere, centers on the experience of rootlessness which Jhabvala knows so well, and which is so widespread in the twentieth century. The novel is a multigenerational saga, beginning with refugees from Nazi Germany and Austria and concluding in contemporary times. The rootlessness of that first generation to be dislocated from their culture is passed on to their children and their children's children, all of whom go "in search of love and beauty."

The first generation, represented by Louise and Regi, wishes to retain its German heritage, concretely symbolized by their paintings and furniture. The second generation, represented by Marietta, is partly Americanized. The restless Marietta travels to India, falls in love with Ahmad, an Indian musician, and befriends Sujata, a courtesan, sketched with deft accuracy. The image of India is lovable, vital, and glorious, and seems almost a counterpart to Germany's ideal image. The third-generation refugees, represented by Natasha and Leo, are more affluent and still more Americanized, yet they are trapped in drug abuse, depression, and meaninglessness.

THREE CONTINENTS

Three Continents is the lengthiest and broadest in scope of Jhabvala's novels. Like the later *Shards of Memory*, the tale revolves around an Indian mystic and his followers. Young narrator Harriet Wishwell, the daughter of a rich but troubled American family, and her gay twin brother, Michael, are raised by their grandfather after their parents' divorce. Educated at international schools, the twins go in search of a deeper meaning to life than what their American heritage provides. Their wishes are seemingly answered when they meet Rawul, whose movement, the Fourth World, is intended to transcend racial and political divisiveness and establish a state founded on peace and love. Michael believes he has found Nirvana in Rawul's son, Crishi, while Harriet also falls under his spell. The twins and Crishi form a sexual threesome, and eventually Harriet, besotted by Crishi, weds him, only to find herself continually frustrated by his lack of devotion to her. Rawul's, and by proxy Crishi's, charismatic hold on his devotees proves Harriet and her family's ultimate undoing.

POET AND DANCER and SHARDS OF MEMORY

Poet and Dancer explores the dangers of love and commitment. Set in modern-day Manhattan, the novel explores the complex relations between two young cousins, Angel and Lara, as they become enmeshed in one another and lose touch with the realities of the outside world.

Shards of Memory concerns a young man, Henry, who has inherited all the correspondence and writings of a mysterious spiritual leader, known simply as the Master. It is with visits to his grandmother, Baby, in her Manhattan townhouse that Henry slowly uncovers bits and pieces of his family's past involvement with the Master's spiritual movement. Elsa, Baby's mother, married an Indian poet but spent her later years with her lesbian lover, Cynthia. Baby married Graeme, a standoffish British diplomat, but she later admits they had nothing besides their daughter, Renata, in common. As Graeme continues traveling the world, Baby gives over the raising of Renata to the child's grandfather, Kavi. Renata later falls in love with Carl, an idle German idealist. The son they produce, Henry, bears a striking resemblance to the Master. Baby sends young Henry from New York to London to be groomed by Elsa and Cynthia as the Master's heir. After a car accident there that kills the women and cripples Henry, he is returned to New York. As trunks full of the Master's writings arrive at the family apartment, Vera, the piano teacher's vibrant daughter, assists Henry in categorizing the vast quantities of work. There is a resurgence of interest in the Master after Henry publishes a book on his teachings, and eventually his parents purchase the Head and Heart House, which was intended as a center for the spiritual movement. Involvement with the Master, a plumb sensualist, takes over the followers' lives; parents become incapable even of rearing their children. Jhabvala's comment about such a spiritual movement has overtones of contempt. The zombie-like groupies around the Master, as well as his own shady dealings in foreign countries, provide a clear warning against placing one's well-being in the hands of self-proclaimed gurus.

Vasant A. Shahane, updated by Nika Hoffman

OTHER MAJOR WORKS

SHORT FICTION: *Like Birds, Like Fishes, and Other Stories*, 1963; *A Stronger Climate: Nine Stories*, 1968; *An Experience of India*, 1971; *How I Became a Holy Mother and Other Stories*, 1976; *Out of India*, 1986; *East into Upper East: Plain Tales from New York and New Delhi*, 1998.

SCREENPLAYS: *The Householder*, 1963; *Shakespeare Wallah*, 1965 (with James Ivory); *The Guru*, 1968; *Bombay Talkie*, 1970; *Autobiography of a Princess*, 1975 (with Ivory and John Swope); *Roseland*, 1977; *Hullabaloo over Georgie and Bonnie's Pictures*, 1978; *The Europeans*, 1979; *Quartet*, 1981; *The Courtesans of Bombay*, 1982; *Heat and Dust*, 1983 (based on her novel); *The Bostonians*, 1984 (with Ivory; based on Henry James's novel); *A Room*

with a View*, 1986 (based on E. M. Forster's novel); *Maurice*, 1987 (based on Forster's novel); *Madame Sousatzka*, 1988; *Mr. and Mrs. Bridge*, 1990 (based on Evan S. Connell, Jr's novels); *Howards End*, 1992 (based on Forster's novel); *The Remains of the Day*, 1993 (based on Kazuo Ishiguro's novel); *Jefferson in Paris*, 1995; *Surviving Picasso*, 1996; *A Soldier's Daughter Never Cries*, 1998 (based on Kaylie Jones's novel.

TELEPLAYS: *The Place of Peace*, 1975; *Jane Austen in Manhattan*, 1980; *The Wandering Company*, 1985.

BIBLIOGRAPHY

Agarwal, Ramlal G. *Ruth Prawer Jhbavala: A Study of Her Fiction*. New York: Envoy Press, 1990. Contains good criticism and interpretation of the novels. Incudes index and bibliography.

Booker, Keith M. *Colonial Texts: India in the Modern British Novel*. Ann Arbor: University of Michigan Press, 1997. Although discussion of the author is not central in this book, what proves engaging is the context into which Booker places Jhabvala's contribution to India's prominence in British literature.

Crane, Ralph J. *Ruth Prawer Jhabvala*. Boston: Twayne, 1992. Crane begins with discussion of Jhabvala's earliest novels and essays, then examines her American novels, then includes a section on Jhabvala and critics. Contains a valuable selected bibliography.

_____, ed. *Passages to Ruth Prawer Jhabvala*. New Delhi: Sterling Publishers, 1991. Features articles on Jhabvala's fiction. Includes index and bibliographic references.

Gooneratne, Yasmine. *Silence, Exile, and Cunning: The Fiction of Ruth Prawer Jhabvala*. Hyderabad, India: Orient Longman, 1983. A definitive work of Jhabvala, the title of which is taken from James Joyce's definition of a writer, with which Jhabvala concurs. Comments on the theme of loneliness and displacement that runs throughout Jhabvala's fiction as she explores the "sensibility of the Western expatriate in India." Biographical detail is interwoven with discussion of Jhabvala's fiction, including a chapter on her short stories and her writing for film. A strong critical study by an author who herself has a keen understanding of the India Jhabvala writes about.

Mason, Deborah. "Passage to America: *East into Upper East: Plain Tales from New York and New Delhi.*" *The New York Times*, November 29, 1998. An eloquent and appreciative analysis of Jhabvala's collection of stories, which squarely places her skills as a consummate storyteller at the forefront.

Pritchett, V. S. "Ruth Prawer Jhabvala: Snares and Delusions." In *The Tale Bearers*. London: Chatto & Windus, 1980. Discusses Jhabvala's novel *A New Dominion*, exploring both its satirical content and the author's role as "careful truth-teller." Hails Jhabvala as a writer who knows more about India than any other novelist writing in English. A short but interesting piece that compares Jhabvala's writing to that of Anton Chekhov.

Shahane, V. A. *Ruth Prawer Jhabvala*. New Delhi: Arnold-Heinemann, 1976. The first full-length study on Jhabvala, covering her novels up to *Heat and Dust* in 1975 and three short stories, including "An Experience of India." Shahane notes that Jhabvala's literary gift lies less on her unique insider-outsider status in India as it does on her awareness of human dilemma within the constructs of society. In a style both spirited and opinionated, Shahane contributes significant criticism to the earlier work of Jhabvala.

Sucher, Laurie. *The Fiction of Ruth Prawer Jhabvala*. New York: St. Martin's Press, 1989. In discussing Jhabvala's nine novels and four books of short stories, Sucher emphasizes Jhabvala's tragic-comic explorations of female sexuality. Cites Jhabvala as a writer who deconstructs "romantic/Gothic heroism." A valuable contribution to the literary criticism on Jhabvala. Includes bibliography.

Updike, John. "Louise in the New World, Alice on the Magic Molehill." Review of *In Search of Love and Beauty*, by Ruth Prawer Jhabvala. *The New Yorker* 59 (August 1, 1983): 85-90. Updike likens the novel to Marcel Proust's "great opus concerning the search for lost time" but says it falls short of Proust in the flatness of the prose. Updike

claims that, in spite of this, the novel contains many vivid scenes, and that "brilliance is to be found."

CHARLES JOHNSON

Born: Evanston, Illinois; April 23, 1948

PRINCIPAL LONG FICTION
Faith and the Good Thing, 1974
Oxherding Tale, 1982
Middle Passage, 1990
Dreamer, 1998

OTHER LITERARY FORMS

Believing that a writer should be able to express himself with competence in all forms of the written word, Charles Johnson has successfully published in several genres, including more than one thousand satirical comic drawings and two books of socially relevant cartoons, *Black Humor* (1970) and *Half-Past Nation Time* (1972). Six of the eight short stories in *The Sorcerer's Apprentice* (1986) were written as psychic releases from the difficulty Johnson experienced in creating a draft of *Oxherding Tale*. Two of the eight are award winners: "Popper's Disease" (receiving the 1983 *Callaloo* Creative Writing Award) and "China" (receiving the 1984 Pushcart Prize Outstanding Writer citation).

Among Johnson's screenplays are *Charlie Smith and the Fritter Tree* (which aired on *Visions* in 1978), the adventure-charged story of the oldest living American who arrived on a slaver and became a Texas cowboy; *Booker* (a 1984 *Wonderworks* premiere cowritten with John Allmann), a dramatization of the young Booker T. Washington's dogged struggle to learn at a time when education was by law denied to southern black Americans; and the award-winning *Me, Myself, Maybe* (a 1982 Public Broadcasting System *Up and Coming* episode), one of the first scripts to deal with a married black woman's process of self-determination.

A literary aesthetician, Johnson has also published articles and book reviews. *Being and Race: Black Writing Since 1970* (1988), a controversial critical analysis and winner of the 1988 Washington State Governor's Writers Award, is the product of Johnson's twenty-year exploration into the makings of black fiction.

ACHIEVEMENTS

Johnson has internationally propounded his belief that the process of fiction must have a vital, nonideological philosophical infrastructure. With several international editions of his novels as well as more than twenty grants and awards and professional and public recognition of Johnson's affirmative philosophical approach to the chaotic dualities of the Western world, his profound belief in the inexhaustible capacities of humankind is unquestionable.

Johnson has been the recipient of a 1977 Rockefeller Foundation Grant, a 1979 National Endowment for the Arts Creative Writing Fellowship, and a 1988 Guggenheim Fellowship. His screenplay *Booker* alone received four awards: against strong network competition, the 1985 Writers Guild Award for outstanding children's show script; the distinguished 1985-1987 Prix Jeunesse (International Youth Prize); the 1984 Black Film Maker's Festival Award; and the 1984 National Education Film Festival Award for Best Film in the social studies category. In addition, *Oxherding Tale* was given the 1982 Washington State Governor's Writers Award, and *The Sorcerer's Apprentice* was one of the 1987 final nominees for the prestigious PEN/Faulkner Award. In 1989, Johnson was named by a University of California study as one of the ten best American short-story writers. In 1990, his *Middle Passage* was honored with a National Book Award, making him the first male African American writer to receive this prize since Ralph Ellison won for *Invisible Man* (1952). Johnson, who received the Journalism Alumnus of the Year Award from Southern Illinois University in 1981, was again honored in 1994 when the university established the Charles Johnson Award for Fiction and Poetry. In 1998, he was awarded a coveted "genius grant" for $305,000 from the John D. and Catherine T. MacArthur Foundation in recognition of his entire body of work.

BIOGRAPHY

In 1948, Charles Richard Johnson was born to Ruby Elizabeth (Jackson) and Benjamin Lee Johnson of Evanston, Illinois. Both parents had immigrated from the South, specifically Georgia and North Carolina. Johnson's mother, an only child (as is Johnson himself), had wanted to be a schoolteacher but could not because of severe asthma. Instead, she fulfilled her artistic and aesthetic passions in the Johnson home. His father's education was cut short by the Depression, a time when all able-bodied males worked in the fields. Later, he worked with his brother, who was an Evanston general contractor.

Johnson describes his early years as a "benign upbringing" in a progressive town of unlocked doors

(AP/Wide World Photos)

and around-the-clock safety, similar to the television neighborhood of *Leave It to Beaver*. Schools had been integrated by the time Johnson became a student; therefore, he did not encounter serious racism during his childhood or adolescence. His first two short stories, "Man Beneath Rags" and "50 Cards 50" (which he also illustrated), as well as many cartoons (one award-winning), were published at Evanston Township High School, then one of the best high schools in the country. While in high school, Johnson began to work with Laurence Lariar, a cartoonist and mystery writer. In 1965, he sold his first drawing to a Chicago magazine's catalog for illustrated magic tricks. From 1965 to 1973, Johnson sold more than one thousand drawings to major magazines.

After high school graduation, Johnson had planned to attend a small art school rather than a four-year college. Nevertheless, as the first person in his extended family to attend college, he felt some obligation to fulfill his parents' hopes. This concern, combined with his art teacher's recommendation that he attend a four-year college for practical reasons, was enough to motivate Johnson to register at Southern Illinois University at Carbondale as a journalism major (with a compelling interest in philosophy). His continuing study of martial arts and, conjointly, Buddhism began in 1967. A cartoonist for the *Chicago Tribune* from 1969 to 1970, Johnson wrote and aired fifty-two fifteen-minute PBS episodes of *Charlie's Pad*, a how-to show on cartooning in 1970.

During his senior year in college, Johnson began writing novels. With his journalistic background (B.S., 1971), he saw no problem with allotting two or three months for each novel. Consequently, from 1970 to 1972, Johnson wrote six novels; three are naturalistic, while three are in the style of the Black Arts movement. Although his fourth novel was accepted for publication, Johnson withdrew it after talking with John Gardner about the implications of precipitate first publication. All six apprentice novels have been filed, unread, in a drawer. Johnson credits Gardner's tutelage on *Faith and the Good Thing* with saving him six additional years of mistakes.

In 1973, Johnson was awarded his master's degree in philosophy from Southern Illinois University with the thesis "Wilhelm Reich and the Creation of a Marxist Psychology." Following three years of doctoral work at the State University of New York at Stony Brook, Johnson began teaching at the University of Washington as well as serving as fiction editor of the *Seattle Review*. Under a 1977-1978 Rockefeller Foundation Grant, he joined the WGBH New Television Workshop as writer-in-residence. In 1982, he became a staff writer and producer for the last ten episodes of KQED's *Up and Coming* series and wrote the second season's premiere episode "Bad Business." A thirty-minute script for KCET's *Y.E.S. Inc.* aired in 1983.

From 1985 to 1987, Johnson worked on the text for *Being and Race: Black Writing Since 1970*, a project he began while guest lecturing for the University of Delaware. His 1983 draft of the first two chapters in *Middle Passage* came quickly, but Johnson worked on the novel sporadically from 1983 to 1987 before finally giving it his full attention for nine months. In addition to his continuing projects, he was a 1988 National Book Award judge and received the Lifting Up the World award and medallion presented to seventeen University of Washington faculty by Sri Chinmoy.

Beginning in 1975, Johnson practiced meditation seriously and studied many Eastern religions, including Hinduism and Taoism. Although his upbringing was Episcopalian, he became an "on-again-off-again Buddhist" in 1980. As part of his lifelong involvement with the martial arts, particularly karate and kung fu, Johnson codirected the Blue Phoenix Club, a martial arts club in Seattle. This interest is also reflected in his writing, as in the short stories "China," which appeared in *The Sorcerer's Apprentice*; "kwoon" (a training hall for students of kung fu), which was included in the O. Henry *Prize Stories* of 1993; and the teleplay *The Green Belt*, published in 1996.

He continued to teach at the University of Washington and to serve as fiction editor for the *Seattle Review*. In addition, his monthly reviews have been published in the *Los Angeles Times* and *The New York Times*. He also revisited his first love, political cartooning, and his gentle satires on racial factionalism in America appear regularly in the *Quarterly*

Black Review. Johnson was director of the University of Washington's Creative Writing Program for three years (1987-1990). In 1990, he was awarded an endowed chair, the first Pollock Professorship in Creative Writing at the University of Washington. He assumed the lifetime position in the fall of 1991.

Johnson was married to Joan New in 1970. The couple have two children: Malik, a son born in 1975, and a daughter, Elizabeth, born in 1981. His life is chronicled in Joan Walkinshaw's PBS documentary *Spirit of Place*, which aired in Seattle.

ANALYSIS

Because Charles Johnson believes implicitly in the power of language, he examines his writing line by line, word by word, to eliminate plot superfluities and to ensure verbal precision. (His drafts of *Oxherding Tale* totaled more than twenty-five hundred pages.) Token characterization to this author is "fundamentally immoral"; rather, he insists, a writer must expend the same energy with his fictional characters that he would in understanding and loving those in his physical world. Even further, Johnson identifies the committed writer as someone who cares enough about his work that it "is something he would do if a gun was held to his head and somebody was going to pull the trigger as soon as the last word of the last sentence of the last paragraph of the last page was finished." For Johnson, who thinks of himself as an artist rather than as an author, writing is a nonvolitional necessity.

A phenomenologist and metaphysician, Johnson constructs fictional universes that not only adhere to the Aristotelian concepts of coherence, consistency, and completeness but also elucidate integral life experiences in the universal search for personal identity. Moreover, the multiplicity of consciousness embodied by his characters seeks to strip the preconceptions from his readers so that they may "re-experience the world with unsealed vision." Consequently, the unrelenting integrity of his fictional vision resolutely reaffirms humanity's potential to live in a world without duality and in the process also reveals Johnson's own indefatigable regard for the unfathomable, moment-by-moment mystery of humankind.

Even though Johnson has dedicated himself to the evolution of "a genuinely systematic philosophical black American literature" and most frequently creates his *Lebenswelt* (lifeworld) within a black context, he sees the racial details as qualifiers of more universal questions. The nonlinear fictional progressions, the proliferations of synaesthetic imagery, the delicate counterbalances of comic (and cosmic) incongruities, and the philosophical underpinnings viscerally reinforced lend a Zen fluidity to the consequent shifting levels of awareness. Thus, the characters' movements toward or away from self-identity, action without ulterior motivation, and mind-body integration assume universal relevance.

FAITH AND THE GOOD THING

Written from the fall of 1972 to the early summer of 1973 under the tutelage of John Gardner, *Faith and the Good Thing* is the metaphysical journey of eighteen-year-old Faith Cross, who believes that she is following her mother's deathbed instructions and the werewitch Swamp Woman's advice by searching the external world for the "Good Thing." This quest for the key that will release her and everyone else from servitude leads from Hatten County, Georgia, to Chicago, Illinois, and home again. Despite limitations inherent in the narrative form itself, occasional lapses in viewpoint, and infrequent verbal artifice, Johnson has created a magical novel of legendary characters and metaphysical import.

The diverse characters who people Faith's life enrich her explorations on both ordinary and extraordinary levels of existence, yet none can lead her to her Good Thing. Asthmatic, stuttering, alcoholic Isaac Maxwell insists that the real power is in money. Dr. Leon Lynch, who treats her mother, believes that the purpose of human life is death and fulfills his self-prophecy by committing suicide on Christmas Eve. Nervous Arnold Tippis, a former dentist (who lost his license because of malpractice), theater usher, and male nurse, rapes her physically and spiritually. His adaptations, like Faith's initial search, are external. Richard M. Barrett, former Princeton University professor, husband, and father, is now a homeless robber who dies on a Soldiers' Field park bench. An existentialist, he believes enough in her search to will her his blank Doomsday Book and to haunt her after his death on Friday nights at midnight until her marriage. Each character shares his path to his Good Thing with Faith, thereby allowing her to choose pieces for her own.

Faith's mystical odyssey, remembered with relish by a third-person narrator addressing his listeners "children," commits every individual to his own search and, through reflection, to the potential alteration of individual consciousness. Despite identifiable elements of naturalism, romanticism, allegory, the *Bildungsroman*, and black folktales, of far greater importance is that *Faith and the Good Thing* creates its own genre of philosophical fiction in which the metaphysical and the real are integrated into a healing totality of being.

Until her return to Swamp Woman, Faith's choices for survival thrust her upon a path of intensifying alienation from herself and from her world. Her feelings of estrangement and depersonalization escalate to an existential fragmentation during her rape and subsequent periods of prostitution, chemical abuse, and marriage. With her decision to forsake her quest for the Good Thing, to manipulate the eminently unsuitable Isaac Maxwell into marriage, and to settle for a loveless middle-class existence, Faith cripples her sense of metaphysical purpose and sees herself as one of the "dead living," an "IT," her soul severed, "still as stone."

The advent of Alpha Omega Holmes, her hometown first love, enables Faith to recover vitality, but her dependence upon others since childhood for self-definition has been consistently destructive to Faith, who has lived in the past or the future and denied her present being. Holmes continues the pattern by deserting her when she announces that she is five months pregnant with his child. Rejected by Holmes and Maxwell, Faith turns to Mrs. Beasley, her former madam, who cares for her, delivers her baby daughter, and leaves the burning candle that is responsible for the fire that kills Faith's child and critically maims Faith. Repeatedly, psychic abandonment and betrayal have been the consequences of a failure to respect her own and others' process of becoming.

Nevertheless, at the summons of Swamp Woman's white cat, Faith returns to the werewitch's holy ground. Now near death, she is finally prepared to devote her total being to the search. Accepting Swamp Woman's revelations that everyone has a path and a "truth," Faith understands that all humans are the sum of their experiences and that she, as well as they, has no beginning and no end. Thus, she has the power to exchange existence with the esoteric, iconoclastic, witty magician Swamp Woman or to become anyone she wishes, thereby personifying Barrett's premise that thinking directs being. The Good Thing is the dynamic, nonpossessive, fluid freedom of the search itself.

OXHERDING TALE

After *Faith and the Good Thing*, Johnson began thinking differently about the storyteller voice. He sought a means by which he could more fully and naturally embody philosophical issues within his characters. In *Oxherding Tale*, he has realized that voice, an intriguing first-person fusion of slave narrative, picaresque, and parable. In the first of two authorial intrusions, chapters 8 and 11, Johnson explains the three existing types of slave narrative. In the second, the author defines his new voice as first-person "universal," not a "narrator who falteringly interprets the world, but a narrator who *is* that world."

Yet the eight years that Johnson worked on his second novel, a novel he believes he was born to create, were fraught with frustration as he wrote and discarded draft after draft until, in 1979, he considered never writing again. Nevertheless, his passion for writing conquered the obstructions. Following a period of extended meditation, Johnson experienced a profound catharsis and eliminated the problematic static quality of the earlier drafts by refashioning the narrator-protagonist from black to mulatto and his second master from male to female.

Oxherding Tale, inspired by Eastern artist Kakuan-Shien's "Ten Oxherding Pictures," is Andrew Hawkins's rite of passage, an often-humorous, metaphysical search for self through encounters that culminate in his nondualistic understanding of himself and the world. The narrator, born to the master's wife and the master's butler as the fruit of a comic one-night adventure, sees himself as belonging to neither the fields nor the house. Although Andrew lives with his stepmother and his father (recently demoted to herder), George and Mattie Hawkins, Master Polkinghorne arranges his classical education with an eccentric Eastern scholar. An excellent student, Andrew nevertheless expresses his recognition of the dualism when he protests that he can speak in Latin more effectively than in his own dialect. As Andrew opens his mind to the learning of the ages, George Hawkins becomes progressively more paranoid and nationalistic. This delicate counterbalance is sustained throughout the novel until, at the end, the assimilated Andrew learns from Soulcatcher that his father was shot to death as an escaped slave.

At twenty, Andrew wishes to marry the Cripplegate plantation seamstress, Minty. Instead, he is sold to Flo Hatfield, a lonely woman who considers her eleven former husbands subhuman and who has the reputation of sexually using each male slave until, discarding him to the mines or through his death, she replaces him with another. Believing that he is earning the funds for his own, his family's, and Minty's manumission, Andrew cooperates. He finds himself quickly satiated, however, with the orgiastic physical pleasures Flo demands to conceal her psychic lifelessness. Thus, neither his father's intensifying spiritual separatism nor his mistress's concupiscence is a path Andrew can accept.

Andrew proceeds to seek out Reb, the Allmuseri coffinmaker in whose Buddhist voice he finds comfort, friendship, and enlightenment. Flo's opposite, Reb (neither detached nor attached) operates not from pleasure but from duty, acting without ulterior motives simply because something needs to be done. Together, the two escape Flo's sentence to her mines as well as Bannon the Soulcatcher, a bounty hunter, with Andrew posing as William Harris, a white teacher, and Reb posing as his gentleman's gentleman. When Reb decides to leave Spartanburg for Chicago because of Bannon, Andrew, emotionally attached to the daughter of the town doctor, decides that Reb's path is not appropriate for him to follow. Instead, his dharma (Eastern soulsustaining law of conduct) is to be a homemaker married to Peggy.

During their wedding ceremony, Andrew surrenders himself to his timeless vision of all that humanity has the potential to become.

The final chapter, "Moksha," like the last of Kakuan-Shien's ten pictures, reveals the absolute integration between self and universe. "Moksha" is the Hindu concept of ultimate realization, perpetual liberation beyond dualities, of self with the Great Spirit. In an illegal slave auction, the mulatto Andrew discovers and buys his dying first love, Minty. He, Peggy, and Dr. Undercliff unite to ease her transition from this world. Thus, the three move beyond self to *arete*, "doing beautifully what needs to be done," and begin the process of healing their world.

In *Oxherding Tale*, Johnson once again offers the experience of affirmation and renewal. Through the first-person universal voice of Andrew Hawkins, he constructs a tightly interwoven, well-honed portrait of actualization. Minute details, vivid visual imagery, and delicate polarities within and among the characters achieve an exacting balance between portrayal of the process and the process itself. Once again, the search does not belong solely to Johnson's characters; the search belongs to everyone who chooses to free himself of "self-inflicted segregation from the Whole."

MIDDLE PASSAGE

Johnson deliberately depersonalized his third novel's working title, "Rutherford's Travels," to *Middle Passage*, a multiple literary allusion, to "emphasize the historical event rather than the character" and to enhance the novel's provocative content. Visual characteristics of Johnson's screenplay writing are sometimes evident in *Oxherding Tale*; however, in *Middle Passage*, scenic effect and synaesthetic detail purposefully dominate, with the narrative sections intended as scenic bridges. Johnson had already used members of the Allmuseri, a mystical African tribe reputed to be the origin of the human race, in *Oxherding Tale*, as well as in two short stories, "The Sorcerer's Apprentice" and "The Education of Mingo"; yet never before had he so masterfully drawn the portrait of this compelling tribe of Zen sorcerers.

Recently manumitted Rutherford Calhoun, a landlubbing twenty-three-year-old picaro, stows away aboard the slave ship *Republic* in order to avoid a marriage forced by his prospective bride. Discovered but allowed to remain as chef's helper by the dwarf-like captain, Ebenezer Falcon, the first-person universal narrator candidly records the brutality people unleash on one another during the forty-one-day voyage to Bangalang for forty captive Allmuseri and their living god. Later revealed as a duty assigned by the suicidal Falcon, Calhoun's log becomes a primary tool by which he processes his responses to his shipmates and to the ship's adventures.

Following an eerie storm in which the stars themselves shift in the heavens, the Allmuseri revolt and capture the ship less than one week after being confined in the *Republic*'s hold. Yet, this tribe believes that each individual is responsible for the creation of his own universe and that even the most minute action has eternal repercussions, echoing beyond this world. Therefore, that human death was involved in their freedom is a source of great sorrow, particularly for their leader, Ngonyama. Despite ceremonies of atonement, the *Republic* sinks, aided by a storm and the Allmuseri renegade Diamelo, who ignites a cannon pointed in the wrong direction.

Of captors and captives, only five survive until the *Juno*, a floating pleasure palace, rescues them: Rutherford Calhoun, his friend Josiah Squibb, and three Allmuseri children including Rutherford's female tribal ward, Baleka. On board *Juno* is Isadora Bailey, Rutherford's forceful fiancée, now scheduled to marry an underworld figure who profits by betraying his race. Instead, a transformed Rutherford, who understands that the way to deal effectively with dangerous people is to become even more dangerous than they, convinces the Créole gangster that marrying Isadora would not be in his best interest; now Rutherford can marry Isadora himself.

Against a backdrop of sea adventure, the poignancy of the characters' startling self-revelations becomes even more deeply moving. Falcon, the remorseless captain to whom human life has no value other than the price he can pocket, collects his treasures to fulfill his dead mother's dream. The first mate Peter Cringle, who responds from his heart to others' victimization, escapes his wealthy family's

mistreatment of him by offering his body as food for the *Republic*'s last survivors. Nathaniel Meadows, who murdered his own family, is so fiercely loyal to Falcon that he conditions the ships' dogs to attack those persons he believes most likely to lead a mutiny. Conversely, Diamelo, the Allmuseri insurrectionist, is so spiritually consumed by his own anger that he blinds himself to the good of his people and destroys them. Yet Ngonyama, grieving over the loss of his tribe's metaphysical connectedness to the Whole, is able to heal Rutherford before lashing himself to the helm in propitiation for the deaths that his tribe's freedom has cost.

Rutherford, self-proclaimed liar and petty thief, finds that instead of hungering for new sensory experiences, he is finally content to experience the present with acceptance and gratitude. Faced with material choices, such as those having to do with food or bed linens, he can no longer comprehend their relevance. Instead of taking, he seeks opportunities for sharing himself without expectations and in universal love. He has taken full possession of his life. He no longer needs; he simply responds.

Middle Passage employs intricately interwoven scenes appropriate to the multiplicity of levels upon which the characters exist. The Allmuseri god, a shape-shifter, is the individual personification of the living truth most fear to face. Furthermore, the anguish of each "middle passage" is uniquely reflected internally by the character and externally by all those whom the character encounters. Recognition without preconception of humanity's magnificent complexity is a significant step toward universal communion.

DREAMER

Johnson's fourth novel, *Dreamer*, begins during the summer of 1966—in the midst of the Chicago riots, the Civil Rights movement, and the Vietnam War—and continues to the fateful 1968 sanitation workers' strike in Memphis, Tennessee. The book is narrated by an observer, Matthew Bishop, a young civil rights worker in the entourage of Dr. Martin Luther King, Jr., but King's thoughts and emotions are offered indirectly in italicized sections of the narrative.

Johnson, a clear admirer of King, has re-created a time when the civil rights leader is endangered by death threats and a bounty of thirty thousand dollars on his head, and the U.S. government fears the outbreak of a race war. Even though the character of King is at the center of the novel, he is not *the* center. He shares that position with Chaym (pronounced as if spelled "Cain") Smith, a maimed Korean War veteran and heroin addict who volunteers as King's stand-in to confuse potential assassins. King is presented as an exhausted and selfless man who adheres to Gandhian nonviolence and longs for the chance to rest and renew himself. Johnson researched minute details of King's personal life, even to the brand of lye-based depilatory powder he used on his sensitive face.

Smith, King's physical double, admires and envies the minister. A spiritual enigma, Smith dreams of becoming a great preacher, yet he sets fire to his apartment building after he is evicted. He is a scholar who studied Zen Buddhism in a Japanese temple and mastered Sanskrit in three days, a practical cynic, and a wanderer. He is a descendant of the Allmuseri through Baleka Calhoun of *Middle Passage.* "I don't believe in a blessed thing, including me," he says; "[w]ork is all I got to offer."

After being wounded by a bullet meant for King, Smith moves away from his unhappy dualism, from alternating good and evil deeds, to a more inclusive unity that embraces the best of Eastern philosophy and Western *agape.* He has sacrificed himself for others, but he is not completely unselfish; rather, he is a troubled and imperfect man who grows stronger, then apparently weakens when he seems ready to betray King. He is likened to the brilliant and rebellious Lucifer; he serves as the outcast Cain to King's obedient brother Abel, but the question of whether Smith-Cain is an evil or heroic figure is posed by the novel but never directly answered. Perhaps, true to his own ambiguity, he is neither.

Once again, Johnson is writing on multiple levels. His title *Dreamer* is found in an epigraph alluding to the Old Testament betrayal of Joseph by his brothers, but it also alludes to King's famous "I have a dream" speech. In addition to the obvious biblical symbolism, Chaym Smith's eclecticism in many respects suggests an ideal metaphysical wholeness that the figure of Dr. King, with his faith and his dreams of

India, is able to embody more perfectly.

Charles Johnson's innate belief in the essential goodness of humankind and his intuitive grasp of the metaphysical empower him to create living fiction with the potential to alter human consciousness. His mastery of the English language, as well as the tight word-by-word control he exercises, heightens his characters' credibility and consequently his readers' empathic sensitivity. Employing a precise awareness of human motivation, Johnson structures his writing nonlinearly to evince tantalizing pieces of the human mystery, but he withholds consummate revelation until the metaphysical world of philosophical fiction surrounding his characters is fully realized.

Kathleen Mills, updated by Joanne McCarthy

OTHER MAJOR WORKS

SHORT FICTION: *The Sorcerer's Apprentice,* 1986.

TELEPLAYS: *Charlie Smith and the Fritter Tree,* 1978; *Booker,* 1984; *The Green Belt,* 1996.

NONFICTION: *Black Humor,* 1970 (cartoons and drawings); *Half-Past Nation Time,* 1972 (cartoons and drawings); *Being and Race: Black Writing Since 1970,* 1988; *Africans in America: America's Journey Through Slavery,* 1998 (with Patricia Smith).

BIBLIOGRAPHY

Harris, Norman. "The Black University in Contemporary Afro-American Fiction." *CLA (College Language Association) Journal* 30 (September, 1986): 1-13. Harris's discussion of the aesthetic bases in the contemporary fictional universes of Toni Morrison, Johnson, and Ishmael Reed provides a contextual overview of the black movement toward nonlinear, mythical constructions in contrast to the approaches of Richard Wright's *Native Son* (1940) and Ralph Ellison's *Invisible Man* (1952).

Johnson, Charles. Interview by Nicholas O'Connell. In *At the Field's End: Interviews with Twenty Pacific Northwest Writers.* Seattle: Madrona, 1987. Presenting a superb interview in an excellent collection, O'Connell remains discreetly in the background as Johnson reveals his thoughts about the artistry and the passion inherent in the writing process, the necessary interconnectedness of philosophy and literature, and his own intrinsically caring life view. With erudition, humor, and honesty, Johnson ranges freely over such topics as the victimization of naturalism's universe, Buddhist tenets, phenomenology, and the potency of language.

_____. "Reflections on Film, Philosophy, and Fiction." Interview by Ken McCullough. *Callaloo* 1 (October, 1978): 118-128. This interview, conducted while Johnson and McCullough were editing *Charlie Smith and the Fritter Tree*, reflects their concentration upon the film as they contrast various literary art processes with an emphasis upon the screenplay and the novel. An interesting, informal, and literate profile of a writer who lives his words.

Little, Jonathan. *Charles Johnson's Spiritual Imagination*. Columbia: University of Missouri Press, 1997. In this book-length critical study, Little examines the interplay of the ideological and the aesthetic in Johnson's work. He notes the influence of Hindu and Buddhist spirituality on the author and his rejection of the postmodern politics of difference. Johnson views the creation of art as a pathway for self-transcendence and unity rather than as a vehicle for protest.

Olderman, Raymond M. "American Fiction 1974-1976: The People Who Fell to Earth." *Contemporary Literature* 19 (Autumn, 1978): 497-527. Olderman's analysis of mutual social and spiritual reverberations expressed by the major fiction writers of the mid-1970's is excellent. His comparisons and contrasts of both form and content are so well supported that the article functions as required reading for anyone interested in this period.

Robbins, Richard. *Sidelines Activist: Charles S. Johnson and the Struggle for Civil Rights*. Jackson: University Press of Mississippi, 1996. A biographical volume of Johnson and his theme of racial equality. Includes bibliographical references and an index.

Rowell, Charles H. "An Interview with Charles Johnson." *Callaloo* 20 (Summer, 1997): 531-547. An insightful and wide-ranging interview in which

Johnson comments on his early years as a political cartoonist and his hope for an emerging body of philosophical African American fiction. He notes the limitations of naturalism and stresses the critical importance of form in fiction, explaining how he deliberately imposes form on a novel or story.

SAMUEL JOHNSON

Born: Lichfield, Staffordshire, England; September 18, 1709
Died: London, England; December 13, 1784

PRINCIPAL LONG FICTION

Rasselas, Prince of Abyssinia: A Tale by S. Johnson, 1759 (originally pb. as *The Prince of Abissinia: A Tale*)

OTHER LITERARY FORMS

As the dominant figure of the mid-eighteenth century English literary world, Samuel Johnson's published works—both what he wrote under his own name and for others under their names—ranged throughout practically every genre and form. In verse, he wrote *London: A Poem in Imitation of the Third Satire of Juvenal* (1738) and *The Vanity of Human Wishes: The Tenth Satire of Juvenal Imitated* (1749); his poem "On the Death of Dr. Robert Levet, A Practiser in Physic" appeared first in *The Gentleman's Magazine* (August, 1783) and later in the *London Magazine* (September, 1783). His *Irene: A Tragedy*, performed at the Theatre Royal in Drury Lane in February, 1749, was printed later that same year.

The prose efforts of Johnson tend to generate the highest degrees of critical analysis and commentary. Biographical studies include *The Life of Admiral Blake* (1740), *An Account of the Life of Mr. Richard Savage* (1744), and *An Account of the Life of John Philip Barretier* (1744). His critical and linguistic works are by far the most important and extensive, of which the best known are *Miscellaneous Observa-*

tions on the Tragedy of Macbeth* (1745), *The Plan of a Dictionary of the English Language* (1747), *A Dictionary of the English Language* (1755), and *Prefaces, Biographical and Critical, to the Works of the English Poets* (1779-1781). Also, Johnson's periodical essays for *The Rambler* (1750-1752), *The Adventurer* (1753-1754), and *The Idler* (1761) contain critical commentary as well as philosophical, moral, and religious observations.

A Journey to the Western Islands of Scotland (1775) comprises his major travel piece, while his political prose includes such essays as *The False Alarm* (1770), a pamphlet in support of the Ministerial majority in the House of Commons and its action in expelling a member of Parliament; *Thoughts on the Late Transactions Respecting Falkland's Islands* (1771), a seventy-five-page tract on the history of the territory and the reasons why England should not go to war with Spain; *The Patriot: Addressed to the Electors of Great Britain* (1774), in which Johnson defends the election of his friend Henry Thrale as MP for Southwark and writes to vindicate the Quebec Act; and *Taxation No Tyranny: An Answer to the Resolutions and Address of the American Congress* (1775). Finally, he edited the works of Richard Savage (1775) and the plays of William Shakespeare (1765); he also translated Father Jerome Lobo's *A Voyage to Abyssinia* (1735) and Jean Pierre de Crousaz's *Commentary on Pope's "Essay on Man"* (1738-1739).

ACHIEVEMENTS

The quantity and quality of firsthand biographical material compiled during Johnson's life and immediately following his death have helped considerably in assessing the full measure of his contributions to British life and letters. Particularly through the efforts of James Boswell, John Hawkins, Hester Lynch Thrale Piozzi, and Frances Burney, the remarkable personality began to emerge. Through his early biographers, Johnson became the property of his nation, representing the most positive qualities of the Anglo-Saxon temperament: common sense, honest realism, and high standards of performance and judgment. His critical judgments came forth as honest and rig-

orous pronouncements that left little room for the refinements and complexities of philosophical speculation; nevertheless, he must be considered a philosopher who always managed to penetrate to the essence of a given subject.

Perhaps Johnson's most significant contribution to eighteenth century thought focused upon what appeared to be a set of powerful prejudices that comprised the theses of his critical arguments. To the contrary, Johnson's so-called prejudices proved, in reality, to have been clearly defined standards or principles upon which he based his conclusions. Those criteria, in turn, originated from concrete examples from the classical and traditional past and actual experiences of the present. Johnson strived to distinguish between authority and rules on one side and nature and experience on the other. As the initial lesson of life, the individual had to realize that not all experience is of equal value—that instinctive and emotional activities, for example, cannot be placed above the authority of rational thought. In literary criticism, especially, Johnson's brand of classicism negated whim and idiosyncrasy and underscored the

(Library of Congress)

necessity for following universal nature—virtually the same criterion that gave strength to critical criteria during the earlier eighteenth century.

Johnson's domination of London intellectual life during the last half of the eighteenth century would by itself be sufficient to establish his reputation. As a writer, however, Johnson achieved distinction in several fields, and literary historians continue to cite him as a prominent poet, essayist, editor, scholar, and lexicographer. Although he failed to produce quality drama, he did succeed in writing a work of prose fiction that went through eight editions during his own lifetime and continues to be read. Certainly, his *A Dictionary of the English Language* has long since outlived its practical use; yet it, as well as *The Plan of a Dictionary of the English Language* that preceded it, remains an important work in the history and development of English lexicography. Principally, though, the achievement of Samuel Johnson focuses on his criticism, especially his sense of rhetorical balance, which causes his essays to emerge as valid critical commentary rather than as untrustworthy, emotional critical reaction.

Perhaps Johnson's greatest achievement is his prose style, which constitutes the essence of intellectual balance. The diction tends to be highly Latinate; yet, Johnson proved his familiarity with the lifeblood of his own language—its racy idiom. He possessed the ability to select the precise words with which to express exact degrees of meaning; he carefully constructed balanced sentences that rolled steadily forward, unhampered by parentheticals or excessive subordination. As writer and as thinker, Johnson nevertheless adhered to his respect for classical discipline and followed his instinct toward a just sense of proportion. His works written prior to 1760 tend to be stiff and heavy, too reliant upon classical and seventeenth century models. Later, however, in *The Lives of the Poets*, Johnson wrote with the ease and the confidence that characterized his oral, informal discussions with the famous intellectuals over whom he presided. Indeed, Johnson rose as a giant among the prose writers of his age when the strength of his style began to parallel the moral and intellectual strength of his own mind and personality.

In late February, 1907, Sir Walter Raleigh—professor of English literature at Oxford and respected scholar and critical commentator—delivered a lecture on Samuel Johnson in the Senate House at Cambridge. The final paragraph of that address is essential to any discussion of Johnson's literary and intellectual achievements. Raleigh maintained, principally, that the greatness of the man exceeded that of his works. In other words, Johnson thought of himself as a human being, not as an author; he thought of literature as a means and not as an end. "There are authors," maintained Raleigh, "who exhaust themselves in the effort to endow posterity, and distill all their virtue in a book. Yet their masterpieces have something inhuman about them, like those jewelled idols, the work of men's hands, which are worshipped by the sacrifice of man's flesh and blood." Therefore, according to Raleigh, humankind really seeks comfort and dignity in the view of literature that characterized the name of Samuel Johnson: "Books without the knowledge of life are useless; for what should books teach but the art of living?"

BIOGRAPHY

Born on September 18, 1709, in Lichfield, Staffordshire, England—the son of Michael and Sarah Ford Johnson—Samuel Johnson spent his formative years devouring the volumes in his father's bookshop. Although such acquisition of knowledge came about in haphazard fashion, the boy's tenacious memory allowed him to retain for years what he had read at a young age. Almost from birth, he evidenced those body lesions associated with scrofula; the malady affected his vision, and in 1710 or 1711, his parents took him to an oculist. Searches for cures even extended to a visit to London in 1712, where the infant received the Queen's Touch (from Anne) to rid him of the disease. The illness, however, had no serious effect upon Johnson's growth; he became a large man with enormous physical strength and, given the hazards of life during the eighteenth century, endured for a relatively long period of time.

Johnson's early education was at Lichfield and Stourbridge grammar schools, followed by his entrance to Pembroke College, Oxford, in 1728. Unfortunately, he remained at the university for only one year, since lack of funds forced him to withdraw. He then occupied a number of tutoring posts in Lichfield and Birmingham before his marriage, in 1735, to Mrs. Elizabeth Jervis Porter, a widow twenty years his senior to whom he referred as "Tetty." The following year, he attempted to establish a school at Edial, three miles to the southwest of Lichfield; despite his wife's money, the project failed. Thus, in 1737, in the company of David Garrick (a former pupil), Johnson left his home and went to London, where he found employment with Edward Cave, the publisher of *The Gentleman's Magazine*. His imitation of Juvenal's third satire, entitled *London*, appeared in 1738, and he followed that literary (but not financial) success with the biography of Richard Savage and *The Vanity of Human Wishes*, another imitation of a satire from Juvenal. By 1749, Garrick had established his reputation as an actor and then as manager of the Theatre Royal in Drury Lane, and he produced Johnson's tragedy of *Irene* as a favor to his friend and former teacher. The play, however, lasted for only nine performances and put to an abrupt end any hopes of Johnson becoming a successful dramatist.

Fortunately, Johnson's abilities could be channeled into a variety of literary forms. *The Rambler* essays appeared twice weekly during 1750-1752. In 1752, Elizabeth Johnson died, a severe loss to her husband because of his fear (terror, in fact) of being alone. Nevertheless, he continued his literary labors, particularly his dictionary, sustained in part by his sincere religious convictions and his rigorous sense of order and discipline. His adherence to the Church of England and to the Tory philosophy of government, both characterized by tradition and conservatism, grew out of that need to discover and to maintain stability and peace of mind. *A Dictionary of the English Language* was published in 1755, followed by essays for *The Idler* during 1758-1760. Another personal tragedy, the death of his mother in 1759, supposedly prompted the writing of *Rasselas* in the evenings of a week's time so that he could pay for the funeral expenses. By 1762, however, his fortunes turned for the better, motivated initially by a pension of three hun-

dred pounds per year from the Tory ministry of King George III, headed by John Stuart, third Earl of Bute. Simply, the government wished to improve its image and to appear as a sincere but disinterested patron of the arts; the fact that *A Dictionary of the English Language* had become a source of national pride no doubt provided the incentive for bestowing the sum upon Johnson.

In mid-May of 1763, Johnson met young James Boswell, the Scotsman who would become his companion, confidant, and biographer—the one person destined to become the most responsible for promoting the name of Samuel Johnson to the world. The following year, the famous literary circle over which Johnson presided was formed; its membership included the novelist/dramatist/essayist Oliver Goldsmith, the artist/essayist/philospher Sir Joshua Reynolds, the politician/philosopher Edmund Burke, and, eventually, the actor/manager David Garrick and the biographer Boswell. Johnson further solidified his reputation as a scholar/critic with his edition of Shakespeare's plays in 1765, the same year in which he began his friendship with Henry and Hester Lynch Thrale—a relationship that was to remain of utmost importance for him throughout the next fifteen years. In 1781, Henry Thrale died; shortly thereafter, his widow married an Italian music master and Roman Catholic, Gabriel Piozzi, much against the wishes of Johnson. That union and Mrs. Piozzi's frequent departures from England brought to an end one of the most noteworthy intellectual and social associations of literary history.

In 1773, Boswell convinced his friend and mentor to accompany him on a tour through Scotland. Thus, the two met in Edinburgh and proceeded on their travels, which resulted, in January, 1775, in Johnson's *A Journey to the Western Islands of Scotland*. Later that same year (in March), he received the degree of Doctor in Civil Law (LL.D.) from Oxford University, after which he spent the three months from September through November touring France with the Thrales. His last major work—*Prefaces, Biographical and Critical, to the Works of the English Poets* (known popularly as *The Lives of the Poets*)—appeared between 1779 and 1781.

Johnson died on December 13, 1784, and he received still one final honor: burial in Westminster Abbey. The poet Leigh Hunt remarked:

One thing he did, perhaps beyond any man in England before or since; he advanced by the powers of his conversation, the strictness of his veracity and the respect he exacted towards his presence, what may be called the personal dignity of literature, and has assisted men with whom he little thought of co-operating in settling the claims of truth and beneficence before all others.

ANALYSIS

Although technically a work of prose fiction, *Rasselas* belongs to the classification of literature known as the moral tale. In Samuel Johnson's specific case, the piece emerges as an essay on the vanity of human wishes, unified by a clear narrative strand. Some critics have maintained that, in *Rasselas*, Johnson simply continued the same themes that he set forth ten years earlier in his poetic *The Vanity of Human Wishes* and then later in *The Rambler* essays. Essentially, in all three efforts, the writer focused on the problem of what it means to be human and of the psychological and moral difficulties associated with the human imagination. Johnson, both a classicist and a philosophical conservative, took his cue from the poet of Ecclesiastes, particularly the idea of the mind's eye not being satisfied with seeing or the ear with hearing. Instead, whatever the human being sees or possesses causes him only to imagine something more or something entirely different. Further, to imagine more is to want more and, possibly, to lose pleasure in that which is actually possessed. The inexhaustible capacity of the imagination (including specific hopes and wishes) emerges as the principal source of most human desires, an indispensible ingredient for human happiness. According to both the poet of Ecclesiastes and Samuel Johnson, however, human happiness must be controlled by reality, which is also the primary source of most human misery. Therefore, the line dividing happiness and enjoyment from pain, suffering, and torment remains thin and sometimes even indistinct.

Johnson chose to clothe his moral speculations in a form particularly popular among fellow eighteenth century speculators: the Oriental tale, a Western genre that had come into vogue during the earlier Augustan Age. Its popularity was based on the Westerners' fascination with the Orient: Writers set down translations, pseudotranslations, and imitations of Persian, Turkish, Arabic, and Chinese tales as backdrops for brief but direct moral lessons. Although the themes of Oriental tales tended toward the theoretical and the abstract, writers of the period tried to confront real and typical issues with which the majority of readers came into contact.

RASSELAS

Originally published as *The Prince of Abissinia: A Tale*, 1759, Johnson's work of fiction is known simply as *Rasselas*. The common name, however, did not appear on the title page of any British edition published during the author's lifetime. The heading on the first page of both volumes of the 1759 edition, however, reads "The History of Rasselas, Prince of Abissinia." Not until the so-called eighth edition of 1787 does one find the title by which the work is generally known: *Rasselas, Prince of Abyssinia: A Tale by S. Johnson*.

Although Johnson once referred to *Rasselas* as merely a "little story book," the work enjoyed immediate and continuing success, which is an indication of its depth and seriousness of purpose. Literary historians agree that an English or American edition has appeared almost every year since the initial publication, while between 1760 and 1764, French, Dutch, German, Russian, and Italian editions were also released. Indeed, before long, Spanish, Hungarian, Polish, Greek, Danish, Armenian, Japanese, and Arabic translations were found, indicating clearly the universality of the piece.

The theme of the vanity of human wishes contributes heavily to the appeal of *Rasselas*, even though such a theme may tend to suffer from an emphasis on skepticism. Certainly, Johnson seems to have conveyed to his readers the idea that no single philosophy of life can sustain all cultures and that no particular lifestyle can become permanently satisfying. This philosophy might lead people to believe that life is essentially an exercise in futility and wasted energy. The vanity of human wishes theme, however, as manipulated by Johnson, also allows for considerable positive interpretations that serve to balance its darker side. In *Rasselas*, Johnson does not deny the value of human experience (including desires and hopes), but he frankly admits to its obvious complexity; man needs to move between conditions of rest and turmoil, and he further needs to experiment with new approaches to life. The admission of that need by the individual constitutes a difficult and complex decision, particularly in the light of the fact that absolute philosophies do not serve all people nor apply to all situations. In joining Prince Rasselas in his search for happiness, the experienced philosopher and poet Imlac reveals his understanding that a commitment to a single course of action constitutes a stubborn and immature attempt to settle irritating problems. Continued movement, on the other hand, is simply a form of escape. The philosopher well knows that all men require a middle ground that considers the best qualities of stability and motion.

What emerges from *Rasselas*, then, is a reinforcement of life's duality, wherein motion and rest apply to a variety of issues and problems ranging from the nature of family life to the creation of poetry. For example, the idea of the Happy Valley dominates the early chapters of the work to the extent that the reader imagines it as the fixed symbol for the life of rest and stability. Within the remaining sections, however, there exists a search for action covering a wide geographical area outside the Happy Valley. Johnson guides his reader over an unchartered realm that symbolizes the life of motion. Eventually, the two worlds unite. Before that can happen, however, Rasselas must experience the restlessness within the Happy Valley, while Pequah, the warrior's captive, must discover order in the midst of an experience charged with potential violence. In the end, Johnson offers his reader the simple but nevertheless pessimistic view that no program for the good life actually exists. In spite of that admission, though, humans will continue to perform constructive acts, realizing full well the absence of certainty. Rather than bemoan life, Johnson, through *Rasselas*, celebrates it.

Typical of the classic novel, the themes and plot of *Rasselas* are supported by its structure. The story

is about Prince Rasselas who, with his sister Nekayah, lives in the Happy Valley, where the inhabitants anticipate and satisfy every pleasure and where the external causes of grief and anxiety simply do not exist. Rasselas becomes bored with his prison-paradise, however, and with the help of Imlac, a man of the world, he escapes to search for the sources of happiness. Johnson leads his characters through the exploration of practically every condition of life. The rich suffer from anxiety, boredom, and restlessness; they seek new interests to make life attractive, yet others envy them. Believing political power to be the means for doing good, Rasselas discovers that it is both impotent and precarious in its attempts to change the human condition. Learning, which he had thought of in terms of promise and idealism, suffers, instead, from petty rivalries and vested interests. Rasselas observes a hermit who, after having fled from the social world of emptiness and idle pleasure, cannot cope with solitude, study, and meditation. Finally, Rasselas and his companions return to Abyssinia—but not to the Happy Valley—and hope that they can endure and eventually understand the meaning and responsibilities of life.

Aside from its highly subjective moral issues and the variety of questions that the themes posed, *Rasselas* proved difficult for Johnson to write. Fundamentally an essayist, he belonged to a school of rhetoric that encouraged and even demanded formal argument; the task of developing fictional characters within a variety of settings, arranging various escapes and encounters, and then returning those same characters to or near their place of origin proved bothersome for him. To his credit, however, he carefully manipulated those characters into situations that would display the best side of his peculiar literary talents. As soon as Johnson's characters began to speak, to engage in elaborate dialogues, to position themselves for argument, and to counter objections to those arguments, his style flowed easily and smoothly. Thus, *Rasselas* consists of a series of dissertations, the subjects of which scan the spectrum of human experience: learning, poetry, solitude, the natural life, social amusements, marriage versus celibacy, the art of flying, politics, philosophy. Johnson applied a thin layer of fictional episodes to unify the arguments, similar to such earlier sources as Joseph Addison's *The Spectator* essays, Voltaire's *Candide* (published in the same year as *Rasselas*), and the early seventeenth century series of travelers' tales by Samuel Purchas known as *Purchas: His Pilgrimage.*

As Johnson's spokesman, Rasselas and Imlac express the author's own fear of solitude and isolation, the supernatural, and ghosts. The Abyssinian prince and his philosopher guide also convey Johnson's horror of madness, his devotion to poetry, his thoughts on the relationship between hypocrisy and human grief, and his conviction (since the death of his wife and mother) that, although marriage can produce considerable trial and pain, celibacy evidences little or no pleasure.

In *Rasselas*, the loose fictional structure and the serious philosophic discussions combine to control the pessimism and to produce an intellectual pilgrimage upon which the travelers' questioning intellects and restless spirits seek purpose and meaning for life. In so doing, however, Johnson's Abyssinian pilgrims mistakenly associate happiness with any object or condition that suggests to them the presence of peace, harmony, or contentment. Rasselas, Nekayah, and even Imlac do not always understand that a human being cannot secure happiness simply by going out and looking for it. Johnson titled the final chapter "The Conclusion, in Which Nothing Is Concluded" probably because he sensed his own inability to suggest a solution to finding happiness, a condition he had not managed to achieve.

Outside the realm of its obvious moral considerations, *Rasselas* succeeds because of its attention to an analysis of a significant, universal, and timeless issue: education. Both Rasselas and his sister, Nekayah, are guided by the teacher, philosopher, and poet Imlac, whose principal qualification is that he has seen the world and thus knows something of it. Whether he serves as the knowledge and experience of the author does not appear as important as the reader's being able to recognize his function within the work and his contribution to the growth of the Prince and the Princess. At the outset, Imlac relates to Rasselas the story of his life, which serves as a prologue to what

the young people will eventually come to know and recognize. Johnson knew well that the experience of one individual cannot be communicated to others simply; a person can only suggest to his listeners how to respond should they be confronted with similar circumstances. The Prince and Princess go forth to acquire their own experiences. They proceed to discover at first hand, to observe and then to ask relevant questions. Imlac hovers in the background, commenting upon persons and situations. As the narrative discussion goes forward, Rasselas and his sister gain experience and even begin to resemble, in their thoughts and statements, the sound and the sense of their teacher. Naturally, Imlac's motives parallel those of the title character, which make him seem more real and more human than if he were only a teacher and commentator. Simply, Imlac believes that diligence and skill can be applied by the moral and intelligent person to help in the battle with and eventual triumph over the life of boredom, waste, and emptiness.

In the development of the eighteenth century English novel, Johnson's contemporaries did not embrace *Rasselas* and accept it on the basis of its having met or failed to meet the standards for fiction. Although not a strong example of the form, Johnson does provide his characters with sufficient substance to support the moral purpose of his effort. Nekayah appears more than adequately endowed with grace, intelligence, and the ability to communicate; in fact, stripped of the fashions and the artificial conventions of her time and place (eighteenth century London), the Princess well represents the actualities of feminine nature. Certainly, the male characters speak and act as pure Johnsonian Londoners, clothed in the intellectual habits and language of the mid-eighteenth century. Johnson's intention was to convey the essential arguments of an intellectual debate, and his contemporary readers understood that *Rasselas* existed as nothing more or less than what its author intended it to be: a fictional narrative used as a vehicle for elevated style and thought.

The noted British essayist of the first half of the nineteenth century, Thomas Babington Macaulay, in his encyclopedic essay on Johnson, observed that a number of those who read *Rasselas* "pronounced the writer a pompous pedant, who would never use a word of two syllables where it was possible to use a word of six, and who could not make a waiting-woman relate her adventures without balancing every noun with another noun, and every epithet with another epithet." When considering the size of *Rasselas*, however, it seems the epitome of compression. By composing the work quickly, Johnson forced himself to ignore doubts or hesitations regarding the vanity of human wishes theme and to depend upon his experiences (as painful as they had been) and his skill in expressing them. The entire project also stood as a challenge to Johnson's imaginative and rhetorical artistry. Thus, he again confronted the major thesis of *The Vanity of Human Wishes* and *The Rambler* essays within the context of his own moral thinking.

Walter Jackson Bate, in his biography of Samuel Johnson, claimed that *The Vanity of Human Wishes* served as the prologue to the great decade of moral writing, while *Rasselas* was the epilogue. Indeed, such is the appropriate summation for any discussion of Johnson's moral writing as well as moral thought. The wisdom found within both works—as well as in *The Rambler, The Idler*, and *The Adventurer* essays—certainly solidifies a general understanding of Johnson's religious and moral views. *Rasselas*, in particular, however, gives dimension to those views, reflects the writer's acuteness, and displays the depth and meaning of his early disillusion with life. In writing *Rasselas*, Johnson sought to expose the exact nature of human discontent as it existed in a variety of specific contexts. Each episode in *Rasselas* proved worthy of serious consideration, and each instance revealed the extent to which Johnson could creatively apply his wisdom and his experience.

Samuel J. Rogal

OTHER MAJOR WORKS

PLAY: *Irene: A Tragedy*, pr. 1749.

POETRY: *London: A Poem in Imitation of the Third Satire of Juvenal*, 1738; *The Vanity of Human Wishes: The Tenth Satire of Juvenal Imitated*, 1749; *Poems: The Yale Edition of the Works of Samuel Johnson*, 1965 (vol. 6; E. L. McAdam, Jr., and George Milne, editors).

NONFICTION: *Marmer Norfolciense*, 1739; *A Compleat Vindication of the Licensers of the Stage*, 1739; *The Life of Admiral Blake*, 1740; *An Account of the Life of John Philip Barretier*, 1744; *An Account of the Life of Mr. Richard Savage, Son of the Earl Rivers*, 1744; *Miscellaneous Observations on the Tragedy of Macbeth*, 1745; *The Plan of a Dictionary of the English Language*, 1747; essays in *The Rambler*, 1750-1752; *A Dictionary of the English Language: To Which Are Prefixed, a History of the Language, and an English Grammar*, 1755 (2 volumes); essays in *The Idler*, 1758-1760; preface and notes to *The Plays of William Shakespeare*, 1765 (8 volumes); *The False Alarm*, 1770; *Thoughts on the Late Transactions Respecting Falkland's Islands*, 1771; *The Patriot: Addressed to the Electors of Great Britain*, 1774; *Taxation No Tyranny: An Answer to the Resolutions and Address of the American Congress*, 1775; *A Journey to the Western Islands of Scotland*, 1775; *Prefaces, Biographical and Critical, to the Works of the English Poets*, 1779-1781 (10 volumes; also known as *The Lives of the Poets*); *The Critical Opinions of Samuel Johnson*, 1923, 1961 (Joseph Epes Brown, editor).

TRANSLATIONS: *A Voyage to Abyssinia*, 1735 (of Jerome Lobo's novel); *Commentary on Pope's "Essay on Man,"* 1738-1739 (of Jean Pierre de Crousaz).

BIBLIOGRAPHY

Bate, Walter Jackson. *Samuel Johnson*. New York: Harcourt Brace Jovanovich, 1977. A magisterial biography which is readable and sympathetic. Frankly Freudian, the book presents a troubled Johnson who remains lovable despite his flaws. Devotes a chapter to *Rasselas*, which is viewed as a sensible, moral treatment of life.

Greene, Donald. *The Politics of Samuel Johnson*. 2d ed. Athens: University of Georgia Press, 1990. Divided into sections on his early years, first books, London career, and the reign of George III. Greene updated the scholarship of the first edition (1960) and included detailed notes and bibliography. Indispensable background reading for the Johnson student, written by one of the great Johnson scholars of the twentieth century.

Holmes, Richard. *Dr. Johnson & Mr. Savage*. New York: Pantheon, 1993. This distinguished biographer provides a fascinating insight into the origins of Johnson's prose by conducting a keen psychological investigation of Johnson's relationship with the controversial poet Richard Savage. This short book is ideal for the beginning student of Johnson, immersing him in Johnson's period and making Johnson a vivid presence as man and writer. Holmes provides a succinct and very useful bibliography.

Keener, Frederick M. *The Chain of Becoming: The Philosophical Tale, the Novel, and a Neglected Realism of the Enlightenment; Swift, Montesquieu, Voltaire, Johnson, and Austen*. New York: Columbia University Press, 1983. Argues for the psychological realism of philosophical tales like *Rasselas* and relates such works to the novels of Jane Austen.

Lipking, Lawrence. *Samuel Johnson: The Life of an Author*. Cambridge, Mass.: Harvard University Press, 1998. In Lipking's terms, he is writing a life of an author, not the life of a man—by which he means that he concentrates on the story of how Johnson became a writer and a man of letters. A superb work of scholarship, Lipking's book reveals a sure grasp of previous biographies and should be read, perhaps, after consulting Bate.

Reinert, Thomas. *Regulating Confusion: Samuel Johnson and the Crowd*. Durham, N.C.: Duke University Press, 1996. Reinert's fascinating work of scholarship should be consulted only after perusing earlier, introductory studies, for he is reexamining Johnson's views of human nature, urban culture, and individualism. "The crowd" of the book's title refers to Elias Canetti's theories of crowds and power, which Reinert applies to his reevaluation of Johnson.

Tomarken, Edward. *Johnson, "Rasselas," and the Choice of Criticism*. Lexington: University Press of Kentucky, 1989. After surveying the various critical approaches to *Rasselas*, offers a fusion of formalist and other theories to explain *Rasselas* as a work in which life and literature confront each other. The second part of the book argues that Johnson's other writings support this view.

Wahba, Magdi, ed. *Bicentenary Essays on "Rasselas."* Cairo: Cairo Studies in English, 1959. Issued as a supplement to *Cairo Studies in English*, this work collects a number of useful essays. Included are James Clifford's comparison of Voltaire's *Candide* (1759) and *Rasselas*, Fatma Moussa Mahmoud's "*Rasselas* and *Vathek*," and C. J. Rawson's discussion of Ellis Cornelia Knight's *Dinarbas* (1790) as a continuation of Johnson's work.

Walker, Robert G. *Eighteenth-Century Arguments for Immortality and Johnson's "Rasselas."* Victoria, British Columbia: University of Victoria, 1977. Places Johnson's fiction "in the context of eighteenth century philosophical discussions on the nature of the human soul." Reads the work as an orthodox Christian defense of the soul's immortality and as a demonstration that happiness is not attainable in this world.

ELIZABETH JOLLEY

Born: Birmingham, England; June 4, 1923

PRINCIPAL LONG FICTION
Palomino, 1980
The Newspaper of Claremont Street, 1981
Mr. Scobie's Riddle, 1983
Miss Peabody's Inheritance, 1983
Milk and Honey, 1984
Foxybaby, 1985
The Well, 1986
The Sugar Mother, 1988
My Father's Moon, 1989
Cabin Fever, 1990
The Georges' Wife, 1993
The Orchard Thieves, 1995
Lovesong, 1997

OTHER LITERARY FORMS
Elizabeth Jolley's reputation was first established by her short stories, one of which, "Hedge of Rose-

mary," won an Australian prize as early as 1966. The first works she ever published were her short-story collections *Five Acre Virgin and Other Stories* (1976) and *The Travelling Entertainer and Other Stories* (1979); although her novel *Palomino* won a prize as an unpublished work in 1975, it did not appear in print until 1980. A third volume of short stories, *Woman in a Lampshade*, was published in 1983. Her radio plays have been produced on Australian radio and on the British Broadcasting Corporation (B.B.C.) World Network.

ACHIEVEMENTS

Jolley had been writing for twenty years before her first book, a volume of short stories, was published in 1976. In 1975, her novel *Palomino* was given the Con Weickhardt Award for an unfinished novel. *Palomino* was not published, however, until 1980, after a second volume of short stories had already appeared. Not until 1984 was Jolley widely reviewed in the United States. Her honors and awards include a 1986 nomination for the Booker Prize for *The Well*, the 1986 Australian Bicentennial Authority Literary Award for *The Sugar Mother*, the 1987 Miles Franklin Award for *The Well*, and the 1991 Australian Literary Society Gold Medal Award for *Cabin Fever*. She also won the 1993 inaugural France-Australia Award for Translation of a Novel for *The Sugar Mother* and the 1993 West Australian Premier's Prize for *Central Mischief*. In 1998 Jolley was named one of Australia's Living Treasures.

Sometimes compared to Muriel Spark and Barbara Pym, Jolley is unique in her characterization and tone. Critics variously refer to her novels as fantasy combined with farce, comedy of manners, moral satire, or black comedy. Although most reviewers see a moral dimension beneath the slapstick surface of her work, noting her compassion, her wisdom, and her penetration of complex human relationships, some have insisted that she is merely a comic entertainer. Yet to most thoughtful readers, it is obvious that Jolley's humor often derives from characters who refuse to be defeated by their destinies, who boldly assert their individuality, and who dare to dream and to love, however foolish they may appear to the conformists.

BIOGRAPHY

Elizabeth Monica Jolley was born in Birmingham, England, on June 4, 1923. Her mother, a German aristocrat, the daughter of a general, had married a young Englishman who had been disowned by his father because of his pacifist convictions. Privately educated for some years, Jolley and her sister were then sent to a Quaker school. Later, Jolley was trained as a nurse at Queen Elizabeth Hospital, Birmingham, and served in that capacity during World War II. In 1959, she moved to Western Australia with her husband and three children. After her move, Jolley began increasingly to divide her time between writing, tending to her farm, and conducting writing workshops.

Jolley was a tutor at the Fremantle Arts Centre and a writer-in-residence at the Western Australian Institute of Technology in the School of English. In 1996, her orchard and goose farm—the subject of her book *Diary of a Weekend Farmer* (1993)—was lost in bushfires which swept the area during the summer.

ANALYSIS

In "Self Portrait: A Child Went Forth," a personal commentary in the one-volume collection *Stories* (1984), Elizabeth Jolley muses on the frequency with which the theme of exile appears in her works. Often her major characters are lonely, physically or emotionally alienated from their surroundings, living imaginatively in a friendlier, more interesting environment. Because of their loneliness, they reach out, often to grasping or selfish partners, who inevitably disappoint them. For Jolley's lonely spinster, widow, or divorcée, the beloved may be another woman. Sometimes, however, the yearning takes a different form, and the beloved is not a person but a place, like the homes of the old men in *Mr. Scobie's Riddle*.

If there is defeat in Jolley's fiction, there is also grace in the midst of despair. Despite betrayal, her characters reach for love, and occasionally an unlikely pair or group will find it. Another redeeming quality is the power of the imagination; it is no accident that almost every work contains a writer, who may, as in *Foxybaby*, appear to be imagining events into reality and characters into existence. Finally, Jolley believes in laughter. Her characters laugh at one another and sometimes at themselves; more detached, she and her readers laugh at the outrageous characters, while at the same time realizing that the characters are only slight exaggerations of those who view them.

PALOMINO

The protagonist of Jolley's novel *Palomino* is an exile desperate for love. A physician who has been expelled from the profession and imprisoned, Laura lives on an isolated ranch, her only neighbors the shiftless, dirty tenants, who inspire her pity but provide no companionship for her. Into Laura's lonely life comes Andrea Jackson, a young woman whom the doctor noticed on her recent voyage from England but with whom she formed no relationship. Up until this point, Laura's life has been a series of unsuccessful and unconsummated love affairs with women. At one time, she adored a doctor, to whom she wrote religiously; when the doctor arrived on a visit, she brought a husband. At another period in her life, Laura loved Andrea's selfish, flirtatious mother, who eventually returned to her abusive husband. Perhaps, Laura hopes, Andrea will be different. She is delighted when Andrea agrees to run off with her, ecstatic when she can install her on the ranch, where the women live happily, talking, laughing, and making love. In her new joy, Laura does not realize that, like her other lost lovers, Andrea is obsessed with a man—her own brother, Christopher. It is Christopher's marriage and fatherhood which has driven her into Laura's arms, but Andrea continues to desire Chris, even at moments of high passion. When Andrea admits that she is pregnant with Chris's baby and tries to use Laura's love for her to obtain an abortion, Laura is forced to come to terms with the fact that the love between Andrea and her is imperfect, as it is in all relationships, doomed to change or to dwindle. Obviously, loneliness is the human condition.

Although Jolley's characters must face hard truths such as the inevitability of loneliness, often they move through suffering to new understanding. This is the pattern of *Palomino*. The novel derives its title from the horses on a nearby ranch, whose beauty Laura can appreciate even though she does not possess them. Joy is in perception, not possession; similarly, joy comes from loving, not from being loved. When Andrea and Laura agree that they must part, for fear that their brief love will dwindle into dislike or indifference, they know that they can continue to love each other, even though they will never again be together.

MR. SCOBIE'S RIDDLE

In the graphic dialogue of Laura's tenants can be seen the accuracy and the comic vigor which characterize Jolley's later works. *Mr. Scobie's Riddle*, for example, begins with a series of communications between the matron of the nursing home where the novel takes place and the poorly qualified night nurse, whose partial explanations and inadequate reports, along with her erratic spelling, infuriate her superior. At night, the nursing home comes alive with pillow fights, medicinal whiskey, and serious gambling, at which the matron's brother, a former colonel, always loses. In the daytime, the home is a prison: Old people are processed like objects, ill-fed, ill-tended by two rock-and-rolling girls, and supervised by the greedy matron, whose goal is to part her new guest, Mr. Scobie, from his property. Yet if the patients are prisoners, so are their supervisors. Having lost her husband to an old schoolmate, the matron cannot ignore the fact that the couple cavort regularly in the caravan on the grounds; in turn, the lonely matron saddles her schoolmate with as much work as possible. Meanwhile, the matron is driven constantly closer to bankruptcy by her brother's gambling and closer to a nervous breakdown by her inefficient and careless employees.

Some of the most poignant passages in *Mr. Scobie's Riddle* deal with the yearnings of two old men in Room One, who wish only to return to their homes. Unfortunately, one's has been sold and bulldozed down; the other's has been rented by a voracious niece and nephew. As the patients are driven toward their deaths, no one offers rescue or even understanding. There are, however, some triumphs. The would-be writer, Miss Hailey, never surrenders her imagination or her hope; ironically, her schoolfellow, the matron, who has taken all her money, must at last turn to Miss Hailey for understanding and companionship. In the battle for his own dignity, Mr. Scobie wins. Even though he is returned to the nursing home whenever he attempts to go home, and even though his uncaring niece and nephew finally acquire his beloved home, he wins, for he never surrenders to the matron, but dies before she can bully him into signing over his property.

MISS PEABODY'S INHERITANCE

The unique combination of farcical humor, lyrical description, pathos, and moral triumph which marks Jolley's later work is also exemplified in *Miss Peabody's Inheritance*, published, like *Mr. Scobie's Riddle*, in 1983. In this novel, a woman writer is one of the two major characters. In response to a fan letter from a middle-aged, mother-ridden London typist, the novelist regularly transmits to her the rough episodes from her new novel, a Rabelaisian story of lesbian schoolmistresses and the troublesome, innocent girl whom they escort through Europe. When at last the typist travels to Australia to meet her writer-heroine, she finds that the writer, a bed-bound invalid, has died. Yet her courage, her imagination, and her manuscript remain for Miss Peabody, an inheritance which will enable her to live as fully and as creatively as the novelist.

MILK AND HONEY

In *Milk and Honey*, there is no triumph of love, of laughter, or of the imagination. Alone among Jolley's novels, *Milk and Honey* begins and ends in despair. At the beginning, a door-to-door salesman with a poor, unhappy wife expresses his loneliness, his loss of the woman he loved and of the music he enjoyed. The rest of the novel re-creates his life, from the time when he went to live with his cello teacher and his seemingly delightful family, through the salesman's discovery that he was used and betrayed, to the final tragic climax, when his income vanished—his cellist's hand was charred in a fire—and the woman who made his life worth living was brutally murdered. Although many of the scenes in the novel are grotesque, they are devoid of the humor which is typical of Jolley and which often suggests one way of rising above despair. Nor does the protagonist's art—here, performing music, rather than creating fiction—enable him to transcend his situation. His love for his wife is

destroyed with his illusions about her, his mistress is destroyed by his wife, and he and his wife are left to live out their lives together without love.

FOXYBABY

Foxybaby, published in 1985, is as grotesque as *Milk and Honey*, but its characters move through desperation to humor, love, imagination, and hope. The setting is a campus turned into a weight-loss clinic. Typically, the characters are trapped there, in this case by the rascally bus driver, who ensures a healthy wrecker and garage business by parking so that all approaching cars plow into him. The central character of *Foxybaby* is, once again, a woman writer, Alma Porch, who along with a sculptor and a potter has been hired to take the residents' minds off food by submerging them in culture. Miss Porch's mission is to rehearse an assorted group of residents in a film which she is creating as the book progresses. Brilliantly, Jolley alternates the wildly comic events at the campus with the poignant story that Miss Porch is writing, an account of a father's attempt to rescue his young, drug-ruined, infected daughter and her sickly baby from the doom which seems to await them. From his affectionate nickname for her when she was a little girl comes the name of the book.

Like the love story in *Milk and Honey*, the plot in *Foxybaby* illustrates the destructive power of love. Well-meaning though he is, the father cannot establish communication with his daughter. The reason is unclear, even to the writer who is creating the story or, more accurately, is letting the characters she has imagined create their own story. Perhaps the father's love was crushing; perhaps in her own perverseness the daughter rejected it. At any rate, it is obvious that despite his persistence, he is making little headway in reaching the destructive stranger who is now his "Foxybaby" and who herself has a baby for whom she feels nothing.

Meanwhile, like Jolley's other protagonists, Porch considers escaping from the place which is both her prison and her exile but is prevented from doing so by the very confusion of events. Loquacious Jonquil Castle moves in with her; a Maybelle Harrow, with her lover and his lover, invites her to an orgy; and the indomitable Mrs. Viggars brings forth her private stock of wine and initiates Porch into the joys of the school-like midnight feast. Offstage, the bus driver is always heard shouting to his wife or his mistress to drop her knickers. Love, in all its variety, blooms on the campus, while it is so helpless in the story being shaped in the same place.

Although the campus trap will be easier to escape, bus or no bus, than the nursing home in *Mr. Scobie's Riddle*, Jolley stresses the courage of the residents, a courage which will be necessary in the lives to which they will return, whether those lives involve battling boredom and loneliness, like Miss Porch's, or rejection, like that of Jonquil Castle, the doting mother and grandmother, or age and the loss of love, like the lascivious Maybelle Harrow's. Just as they will survive the clinic, though probably without losing any weight, they will survive their destinies. At the end of the novel, there is a triumph of love, when Mrs. Viggars, admitting her loneliness, chooses to take a young woman and her three children into her home, in order to establish a family once again. There is also a triumph of imagination, when Miss Porch actually sees the characters whom she has created. For her loneliness, they will be companions.

At the end of the novel, the bus stops and Miss Porch awakes, to find herself at the school. Jolley does not explain: Has Porch dreamed the events of the book? Will they now take place? Or is the awakening misplaced in time, and have they already taken place? Ultimately, it does not matter. What does matter is the power of the imagination, which, along with humor and love, makes life bearable.

Hester Harper, another spinster protagonist, is somewhat like the doctor in *Palomino* in that she lives on an isolated ranch in Western Australia and yearns for love. In *The Well*, however, the beloved is an orphan girl, whom Hester takes home to be her companion. Refusing to admit her sexual desires, even to herself, Hester persuades herself that her feelings are merely friendly or perhaps maternal; yet she is so jealous of the orphan, Katherine, that she cannot bear to think of the friend who wishes to visit her or of the man who will ultimately take her away. The rival, when he appears, is mysterious, perhaps a thief, perhaps only an animal, whom Katherine hits on a late-night drive and whom Hester immediately buries in the well. Perhaps diabolical, perhaps distraught, Katherine insists that he is calling to her, demanding her love, threatening her and Hester. Although at last his voice is stilled, it is clear that Hester has lost control over Katherine, to whom the outside world of sexuality and adventure is calling with undeniable urgency. Unlike the doctor in *Palomino*, Hester cannot be contented with the memory of love. Imagination, however, once again mitigates the horror of life; at the end of the novel, Hester is making the mysterious nighttime adventure into a story to be told to children.

THE GEORGES' WIFE

In *The Georges' Wife*, Jolley repeats themes of earlier books, particularly *My Father's Moon* and *Cabin Fever*, themes of discord and harmony between brothers and sisters, husbands and wives, friends and lovers. As in earlier books, her spare prose is a dramatic contrast to the abundance of compassion and understanding she demonstrates for the complexities of human relationships. Focusing on the relationship between Vera and Mr. George, Jolley explores the life they attempt to create together, while Vera's mind continues to wander to her past and to her fear of repeating the past. The present and the past collide within her, just as the desire for peace collides with the reality of disharmony.

THE ORCHARD THIEVES

A similar theme of discord versus harmony is present in *The Orchard Thieves*. Characters in this novel are also haunted by times of discord which destroy their desire for calm. Every member of the household deals with this specter, especially the grandmother, a mother of three grown-up daughters, who understands that the unspoken and unrevealed either perplex or console people in their dealings with family. A middle sister returns home from England, with no explanations about her private life, thus jeopardizing the peace in the grandmother's house. In the face of this danger, the grandmother tries to rescue the situation and the people involved through her imagination, acceptance, and affection.

The title for this novel, the first part of which was originally published in *The New Yorker* in 1994 as

"Three Miles to One Inch," is taken from a quotation from writer Herman Melville: "The act of paying is perhaps the most uncomfortable infliction that the two orchard thieves entailed upon us." Uncomfortable inflictions do indeed intrude into the lives of Jolley's characters, especially those in this household.

LOVESONG

Another tale about uncomfortable inflictions is *Lovesong*, a novel which explores another of Jolley's exiles, Thomas Dalton, who comes reluctantly to Mrs. Porter's establishment, a Home away from Home for Homeless Gentlemen. He wants a fresh start, as does Miss Emily Vales, a fellow lodger and recipient of the predictions found in Mrs. Porter's tea leaves. The study of these two wayfarers, typical examples of Jolley's characters who are struggling with their human mixture of pathos and nobility, echoes the same struggle poet T. S. Eliot describes in his own love song, "The Love Song of J. Alfred Prufrock" (1917).

Because she deals with cruelty, indifference, lust, greed, and, above all, with loneliness, Elizabeth Jolley cannot be considered a superficial writer. The great distances of her western Australia become a metaphor for the mysterious expanses of time; the small clumps of isolated individuals, trapped together on a ranch, on a weight-loss farm, or in a nursing home, represent society, as did Joseph Conrad's microcosmic ships on an indifferent ocean. Jolley makes it clear that love is infrequent and imperfect, that childhood is endangered by cruelty, and that old age leads through indignity to death. Yet most of her works are enlivened by comic characters who defy destiny and death by their very insistence on living. Some of her characters transcend their isolation by learning to love, such as the doctor in *Palomino* or Mrs. Viggars in *Foxybaby*. Others, such as Miss Peabody and Miss Porch, triumph through their imaginations. There is redemption in nature, whether in the beauty of palomino horses or the sunlit shore where Miss Porch sees her characters. There is also triumph in the isolated courage of a human being such as Mr. Scobie, who defies institutionalized and personal greed to save the beloved home to which he can return only in memory. If Elizabeth Jolley's characters are mixtures of the pathetic, the grotesque, and the noble, it is because they are human; if her stories keep the reader off balance between confusion, laughter, and tears, it is because they reflect life.

Rosemary M. Canfield-Reisman,
updated by Marjorie Smelstor

OTHER MAJOR WORKS

SHORT FICTION: *Five Acre Virgin and Other Stories*, 1976; *The Travelling Entertainer and Other Stories*, 1979; *Woman in a Lampshade*, 1983; *Stories*, 1984.

RADIO PLAYS: *Night Report*, 1975; *The Performance*, 1976; *The Shepherd on the Roof*, 1977; *The Well-Bred Thief*, 1977; *Woman in a Lampshade*, 1979; *Two Men Running*, 1981.

NONFICTION: *Central Mischief: Elizabeth Jolley on Writing, Her Past, and Herself*, 1992 (Caroline Lurie, editor), *Diary of a Weekend Farmer*, 1993.

BIBLIOGRAPHY

Bird, Delys, and Brend Walker, eds. *Elizabeth Jolley: New Critical Essays*. North Ryde, Australia: Angus and Robertson, 1991. Criticism and interpretation of Jolley's works. Includes bibliographic references.

Daniel, Helen. "A Literary Offering, Elizabeth Jolley." In *Liars: Australian New Novelists*. New York: Penguin Books, 1988. In this comprehensive study, Jolley's fiction is compared to a musical composition by Johann Sebastian Bach, consisting of component literary fugues. While each of her novels is separate, they all blend together to form a graceful totality, and Jolley's handling of theme, time, characterization, and narrative is discussed in this light. The essay appears in a book devoted to Jolley and seven other contemporary Australian novelists, and includes a primary and selected secondary bibliography.

Howells, Coral Ann. "In Search of Lost Mothers: Margaret Laurence's *The Diviners* and Elizabeth Jolley's *Miss Peabody's Inheritance*." *Ariel* 19, no. 1 (1988): 57-70. This comparison of two novels, one Canadian, the other Australian, places them in the tradition of postcolonial writing by women who are concerned not only with their political dispossession as former colonials but with their gender dispossession as well. After a thorough discussion of the two works in this light, the conclusion is drawn that both writers claim their female literary inheritance by rejecting masculinist-inspired tradition and creating their own aesthetic.

Kirkby, Joan. "The Spinster and the Missing Mother in the Fiction of Elizabeth Jolley." In *Old Maids to Radical Spinsters: Unmarried Women in the Twentieth Century Novel*, edited by Laura L. Doan. Urbana: University of Illinois Press, 1991. Considers Jolley's use of single women in her fiction.

Manning, Gerald F. "Sunsets and Sunrises: Nursing Home as Microcosm in *Memento Mori* and *Mr. Scobie's Riddle*." *Ariel* 18, no. 2 (1987): 27-43. This comparative study takes up the similarities in Muriel Spark's *Memento Mori* and Jolley's *Mr. Scobie's Riddle*. The two novels share setting (a nursing home) and theme (age, loneliness, and alienation), and both authors make imaginative use of tragicomic devices to enrich their tone. These works attempt to discover an answer that will lead to the acceptance of death.

Salzman, Paul. *Helplessly Tangled in Female Arms and Legs: Elizabeth Jolley's Fictions*. St. Lucia, Australia: University of Queensland Press, 1993. A small but useful book containing information about Jolley's fiction. Includes bibliographic references.

Westerly 31, no. 2 (1986). Entitled "Focus on Elizabeth Jolley," this special issue of an Australian journal provides essays on various aspects of Jolley's work, including one on the way her fiction connects to form a continuum, one on her novel *Milk and Honey*, and another on her handling of displaced persons. Also includes fiction by Jolley.

Willbanks, Ray. "A Conversation with Elizabeth Jolley." *Antipodes: A North American Journal of Australian Literature* 3 (1989): 27-30. While concentrating on Jolley's fiction—its characters, themes, background, and development—this interview offers some interesting information on the author's personal background. Jolley tells about her life in England, where she was born and lived to adulthood until she moved to Australia in 1959. She also recalls the impact Australia made on her when she first arrived and discusses its effect on her writing.

JAMES JONES

Born: Robinson, Illinois; November 6, 1921
Died: Southampton, New York; May 9, 1977

PRINCIPAL LONG FICTION

From Here to Eternity, 1951
Some Came Running, 1957
The Pistol, 1959
The Thin Red Line, 1962
Go to the Widow-Maker, 1967
The Merry Month of May, 1971
A Touch of Danger, 1973
Whistle, 1978

OTHER LITERARY FORMS

James Jones published one much underrated collection of short fiction, *The Ice-Cream Headache and Other Stories*, in 1968. Despite the excellence of several of these stories, he did not return to short fiction, primarily because of the difficulty of writing openly about sex in mass circulation magazines. He wrote two book-length works of nonfiction, *Viet Journal* (1974) and *WWII* (1975). The first is an account of Jones's experiences and observations while a war correspondent in Vietnam. *WWII*, a much more important work, is an analysis of the graphic art produced during World War II. The book contains some of Jones's finest writing, as well as an extended analysis of the central concept underlying his best fiction, "the evolution of a soldier." Jones also contributed essays to *Esquire, Harper's*, and the *Saturday Evening Post*, among other journals; the subject matter of these pieces ranges widely, from theories of fiction to skin diving.

ACHIEVEMENTS

Jones's first novel, *From Here to Eternity*, was a spectacular success, both with critics and with the popular reading audience. As several reviewers pointed out, its frank treatment of sexuality and military brutality broke important new ground for American literary naturalism. While the novel had its detractors, it won the National Book Award for Fiction. *From Here to Eternity* appeared just in time to ride the crest of the new wave in paperback publishing, and in November, 1953, *Newsweek* reported that the paperback reprint of Jones's novel had gone through five printings of "1,700,000 copies . . . in the past six weeks." The popularity of the novel was augmented by its adaptation into one of the most highly regarded American films of the 1950's. Directed by Fred Zinnemann and with unforgettable performances by Montgomery Clift, Burt Lancaster, and Deborah Kerr, among others, the film version won the Best Picture award from the Motion Picture Academy of Arts and Sciences and the New York Film Critics in 1953. Jones himself became an international celebrity.

(National Archives)

During the next twenty-five years, Jones remained an enormously popular writer. He and Norman Mailer were sometimes praised for having inspired a revitalized American literary realism. Still, Jones never regained the critical acceptance he enjoyed with his first novel. His much anticipated second novel, *Some Came Running*, was denounced as a failure. Occasionally thereafter, his work received positive and intelligent reviews. His tightly constructed 1959 novella *The Pistol* was seen by some perceptive critics as refuting the recurring charge that Jones could not control his material. Such reviewers as Maxwell Geismar and Lewis Gannett emphasized the structural brilliance and emotional power of his 1962 combat novel *The Thin Red Line*. Even *Time* magazine, a perennially hostile critic of Jones's work, praised his 1975 nonfictional analysis of wartime art, *WWII*. Still, when he died in 1977, Jones had been largely ignored by the critical establishment for some

time. Academic critics especially dismissed him as an outdated naturalist no longer relevant in an age of literary innovation and experimentation. To the reading public, however, he remained quite relevant. Indeed, it seems quite likely that Jones's public acceptance was a factor in the academy's dismissal of him as a serious writer.

He was, in fact, a most serious and significant writer. Nevertheless, the critical neglect of Jones at the time of his death cannot be attributed solely to academic hostility toward popular success. The last three novels published in his lifetime, *Go to the Widow-Maker, The Merry Month of May*, and *A Touch of Danger*, added little to his total achievement. *A Touch of Danger* is a detective novel in the Dashiell Hammett-Raymond Chandler "hard-boiled" tradition. A competent work, it was never intended as anything more than popular entertainment. In contrast, *Go to the Widow-Maker*, inspired by Jones's devotion to skin diving, and *The Merry Month of May*, focusing on the 1968 Paris student rebellion, are quite ambitious civilian novels. Like *Some Came Running*, each is intended as a serious investigation of the novelist's belief that the American male is devoted to an adolescent cult of masculinity. Jones's vision of American sexual maladjustment, while honest and insightful, was simply not original enough to serve as the primary focus of a long novel, although the concept works well as a major subtheme in his army fiction.

In part because of the time he devoted to civilian novels, the major achievement of Jones's career was unrecognized at the time of his death. *From Here to Eternity* and *The Thin Red Line* were always intended as the first two volumes in a trilogy. *Whistle*, the concluding volume of the trilogy, was published posthumously in 1978 and inspired a reappraisal of Jones's lasting contribution to American literature. His army trilogy began to receive, in the late twentieth century, its proper recognition as the most important fictional treatment of American involvement in World War II. Moreover, *From Here to Eternity* has attained the status of a modern classic, and *The Thin Red Line* is frequently praised as the best American "combat novel." *The Thin Red Line* was adapted into a well-received 1998 film directed by Terrence Malick.

BIOGRAPHY

Born in Robinson, Illinois, on November 6, 1921, James Jones grew up in a proud and socially prominent family. When he was a junior in Robinson High School, however, the family's position abruptly deteriorated, largely because of the Samuel Insull stock scandal. Even though his father, Ramon, was never professionally successful and became an alcoholic before ultimately committing suicide, Jones was fond of him. In sharp contrast, he felt contemptuous of, and rejected by, his mother, Ada Blessing Jones.

After he was graduated from high school in 1939, Jones, on the advice of his father, joined the United States Air Force and was stationed in Hawaii, where he transferred to the Infantry. His army career was not distinguished; he once summarized his record of two promotions and subsequent reductions back to the lowest enlisted grade: "Apted Cpl 13 May 42 Red to Pvt 3 Dec 43, Apt Sgt 1 Mar 44 Red to Pvt 20 May 44." Still, in more than one way, Jones's military experience was crucial in his development as an artist. Primarily, he developed a complex love-hate relationship with the United States Army which later gave his military fiction a unique tension. Moreover, he was present at Schofield Barracks, Hawaii, on December 7, 1941, and witnessed the birth of a new and terrifying world. Later, Jones saw combat on Guadalcanal, the brutality of which inspired his concept of "the animal nature of man."

Wounded on Guadalcanal in 1943, he was sent back to the States and, on July 6, 1944, received his military discharge. Greatly shaken both by the combat horror he had experienced and by the continuing dissolution of his family, Jones met Mrs. Lowney Handy of Marshall, Illinois, in late 1943 or early 1944, and began one of the strangest, and ultimately most publicized, apprenticeships in the history of American letters. A 1953 *Newsweek* essay described Lowney Handy as "a more dynamic version of Sinclair Lewis's Carol Kennicott in 'Main Street,'" and she does appear to have waged a one-woman crusade against small-town midwestern provincialism. Certainly, she and her husband, Harry Handy, supported Jones during a seven-year period in which he worked at his ambition of becoming a writer.

The young soldier had discovered Thomas Wolfe at the Schofield Barracks Post Library and "realized [he] . . . had been a writer all his . . . life without knowing it or having written." With Lowney Handy's encouragement, Jones wrote a first novel, which he submitted to Maxwell Perkins, the legendary editor at Charles Scribner's Sons. Perkins rejected this first novel but encouraged Jones to concentrate on a work about the old peacetime army. After Perkins's death, Jones profited from the help and encouragement of editor Burroughs Mitchell, and when Scribner's published *From Here to Eternity* in 1951, its author became an instant celebrity. Initially, he used his new wealth to establish a writers' colony at Marshall. Lowney Handy assumed the directorship of the colony and imposed an iron discipline upon her new protégés.

Jones, however, grew bored and skeptical in Marshall, seeing the cynicism of some of the writers and the failure of Mrs. Handy's methods to create universally good writing or even cooperation among the writers. His introduction to the beautiful actress Gloria Mosolino made inevitable a bitter and painful break with the Handys. In 1957, Jones and Gloria Mosolino were married at the Olofson Hotel in Haiti. The couple lived for a few months in New York City before moving to Paris in 1958. For the next sixteen years, the Joneses were the center of the American expatriate community in Paris. Whether his books were critically praised or attacked made no difference to Jones's new status as international celebrity.

Jones's break with Lowney Handy and his love affair with Gloria are fictionalized in his autobiographical novel *Go to the Widow-Maker*, and Paris is the setting of his ambitious 1971 work *The Merry Month of May*. Still, he always wrote best about the army. In 1973, he went to Vietnam as a war correspondent and, the following year, published *Viet Journal*, a nonfictional account of what he had seen in that tragic country. Also in 1974, he and his wife and two children returned home to the United States. Jones was increasingly determined to complete what he had long envisioned as the central work of his career, a trilogy about the United States Army, of which *From Here to Eternity* and *The Thin Red Line* constituted the first two volumes.

On May 9, 1977, Jones died of congestive heart failure in Southampton, New York. He had not quite completed *Whistle*, the third volume of his trilogy. It was possible, however, for Willie Morris, a writer, editor, and longtime friend, to finish the manuscript from Jones's notes and tapes. When *Whistle* was published in February, 1978, James Jones's army trilogy took its place as the most important American fictional treatment of World War II.

ANALYSIS

Critics, especially academics, have increasingly dismissed James Jones as a "war novelist" committed to outdated naturalistic techniques. Though Ihab Hassan provides an extensive and largely favorable

discussion of *From Here to Eternity* in *Radical Innocence*, his 1961 examination of post-World War II American fiction, two important subsequent studies of the contemporary American novel, Tony Tanner's *City of Words* (1971) and Josephine Hendin's *Vulnerable People* (1978), ignore Jones completely. This neglect arises, in part, from oversimplified and incorrect perceptions of his work. For example, as the term is most commonly used, Jones is not strictly a "war novelist." Of his eight novels, only one, *The Thin Red Line*, is primarily devoted to a description of military combat, while four have peacetime civilian settings. While it is true that army life provides the background of his best fiction and World War II its controlling event, his reactions to the army and the war exhibit the complexity and ambiguity essential to meaningful art.

Especially during the 1950's, Jones often permitted himself to be depicted as an advocate of masculine toughness in life and literature. A 1957 *Life* magazine article emphasized the novelist's devotion to knives and boxing and declared his prominence in the literary cult of violence. Yet a careful reader of Jones's fiction will discover an artist deeply concerned about man's capacity for self-destruction. In a 1974 interview, Jones discussed his belief that humanity was doomed by two interrelated forces: its own animal nature and the anonymous power of modern technological society. He stressed "the ridiculous misuse of human strength which can include many subjects, not only physical strength, but technology, and all of the things that we live by." After defining morality as the refusal to give another pain "even though one suffers himself," he forecast the inevitable failure of such an idealistic ethical code:

"In all of us, there is this animal portion . . . which is not at all adverse to inflicting cruelty on others. This can be quite enjoyable at times. . . . It's in myself . . . it's in all of us."

Modern man, Jones believed, is caught in both an external and an internal trap. Human strength, which has its source in the "animal nature of man," has been translated into an awesome technology that ironically threatens the extinction of human individuality, if not the actual obliteration of humankind. In his civilian novels, Jones's characters habitually seek the few remaining "frontiers" of individualism (for example, skin diving), only to discover the impossibility of escaping their own "animal" heritage. An element of brutal and destructive competition is thereby introduced into the "frontier," which is perverted and ultimately doomed. It is in his army fiction, however, that Jones most memorably dramatizes the tragic vulnerability of contemporary man.

In a 1967 *Paris Review* interview, Jones said: "I've come to consider bravery as just about the most pernicious of virtues. Bravery is a horrible thing. The human race has it left over from the animal world and we can't get rid of it." His army fiction underscores the destructiveness of this "most pernicious of virtues." Strength and bravery are, of course, essential qualities of the traditional hero. In more romantic ages, these two virtues were often perceived as the very foundation of manhood. Today's all-pervasive technology makes such romantic concepts of heroism archaic and dangerous. The dominant social mechanism of the modern world is bureaucracy, which can hardly permit heroism, since bureaucracy denies individuality. Jones saw modern warfare as the inevitable product of a bureaucratic, highly technological society. In it, death falls from the sky in a totally "random" and "anonymous" manner. For Jones, a fundamental and dismaying truth was implicit in this impersonal rain of death: In such a technological hell, the traditional Western concepts of the individual and the self no longer hold their old importance. The question he examines throughout his most important fiction is whether they still have any validity at all.

THE ARMY TRILOGY

The major achievement of Jones's career is his army trilogy: *From Here to Eternity, The Thin Red Line*, and the posthumously published *Whistle*. His novella *The Pistol* and several of the short stories in his collection *The Ice-Cream Headache and Other Stories* also have military settings. The thematic focus in all Jones's army fiction is upon the evolution of the soldier, a concept which is given a full and convincing nonfictional elaboration in *WWII*. In Jones's view, warfare constitutes man's total capitulation to his animal nature. The traditional concepts of the individual and the self must be discarded in combat: The army trains the soldier to function on a primitive, subhuman level of consciousness. This training is a reversal of evolution; it is a process by which the army systematically dehumanizes the enlisted man. Such dehumanization is necessary for the soldier's acceptance of his own anonymity and probable death in combat. In World War II's anonymous, technological warfare, the enlisted man became more clearly expendable and anonymous than he had ever been. Throughout his military fiction, Jones is intent upon describing the manner in which the army, by using technology and its awareness of the enlisted man's inherent animalism, carried out the dehumanization process.

The three novels that constitute the army trilogy depict three major stages in the evolution of a soldier. It is important to note here that Jones intended the three novels to be seen as constituting a special kind of trilogy. He wished that each "should stand by itself as a work alone," "in a way that . . . John Dos Passos's three novels in his fine USA trilogy do not." At least in *From Here to Eternity* and *The Thin Red Line*, the first two novels in his own trilogy, Jones clearly achieved this ambition.

The army trilogy's most innovative feature is the presence of three character types in all three volumes. Of these three character types, two are of overriding importance. First Sergeant Milt Warden of *From Here to Eternity* is transformed into Sergeant "Mad" Welsh in *The Thin Red Line* and into Sergeant Mart Winch in *Whistle*. Private Robert E. Lee Prewitt of *From Here to Eternity* becomes Private Witt in *The Thin Red Line* and Private Bobby Prell in *Whistle*. John W. Aldridge, sometimes a perceptive critic of Jones's fiction, understands a more important reason than Prewitt's death in *From Here to Eternity* for the characters' different names in each of the novels: Increasingly brutal experiences, he writes, have "transformed [them] into altogether different people." In other words, as they reach new and more dehumanizing stages in the evolution of a soldier, their inner selves undergo transformation.

Still, there is a fundamental level on which the character types remain constant. Warden/Welsh/Winch is Jones's realist, who comprehends the inevitability of his own destruction as well as that of his fellow enlisted men. He is burdened by a deep concern for others, but he attempts to hide that concern behind a surface cynicism. Just as he anticipates, his inability to deny his compassion ultimately drives him mad. Private Prewitt/Witt/Prell is the determined and increasingly anachronistic individualist who regularly defies army bureaucracy in the name of his personal ethical code. In *From Here to Eternity*, which focuses on the old peacetime army, he is a romantic figure refusing to compromise with a corrupt bureaucracy. In *The Thin Red Line*, a grim account of combat on Guadalcanal, he is reduced to an animalistic level; his defiance seems insane and pointless rather than romantic. Primarily through his analysis of these two character types, Jones analyzes the contemporary validity of the interrelated concepts of the self and the individual.

FROM HERE TO ETERNITY

The central factor in the critical and popular success of *From Here to Eternity* was its vivid characterization. As Maxwell Perkins had anticipated, Sergeant Milt Warden and Private Robert E. Lee Prewitt are unforgettable figures. They are not, however, the novel's only memorable characters. Private Angelo Maggio and "the women," Alma Schmidt and Karen Holmes, are also strong individuals determined to preserve their integrity in an anonymous, bureaucratic world. *From Here to Eternity* is easily Jones's most romantic novel. In it, he depicts a world that ceased to exist on December 7, 1941; the novel's setting is Hawaii, and its climax is the Japanese attack on Pearl Harbor. For most of the novel, modern technological destruction has not made its appearance, and individualism seems a vital concept that is to be preserved in spite of "old Army" corruption. On the surface, the novel's roster of unforgettable characters seems to guarantee the survival of this traditional Western value.

Warden always knows, however, what is coming. He sees the inevitable destruction of the self and struggles to suppress his instinctive sympathy for Private Prewitt's defiance of the army. Prewitt's integrity is so strong that ultimately even Warden has to respect it. Still, the sergeant's admiration for his "bolshevik" private is a largely nostalgic response; he identifies with this defiant individualism while remaining aware that it is doomed.

Because his individualism is related to much that is crucial to Western values, Prewitt does, in fact, emerge as the dominant character in the novel. In the beginning, his quarrel with the army is almost absurdly simple. His commanding officer, Dynamite Holmes, is determined that Prewitt will become a member of the regimental boxing team; the private is equally determined not to box, even if his refusal means that he must give up playing the bugle, his "calling." Prewitt undergoes prolonged and systematic mental and physical abuse without acquiescing to Holmes's insistence that he box. Ultimately, this vicious "Treatment" does force him past his breaking point and into a mistake that enables Holmes to have him sentenced to the stockade, where he experiences further brutality at the hands of Sergeant Fatso Judson. Judson is one of the most unforgettable sadists in American literature, and Prewitt decides that he must be destroyed. The reader can hardly disagree with this decision; still, it assures Prewitt's own doom.

Much of *From Here to Eternity*'s unique power derives from the levels of symbolic meaning contained within the deceptively simple Prewitt-Holmes conflict. Boxing is a metaphor for the animal nature of man, while Prewitt's "calling" to play the bugle comes to represent that uniquely individualistic integrity that makes possible artistic creation. Throughout the novel, Prewitt is something of a romantic folk hero; he is the personification of "the good soldier," the proud enlisted man. When he plays taps on the bugle or helps in the collective composition of "The Re-Enlistment Blues," he is also giving artistic expression to the enlisted man's pain and loneliness. His desire to play the bugle symbolizes the urge to create a distinctive proletarian art. Warden sees the army's destruction of Prewitt as an illustration of animalism negating man's potential for lasting creativity. Yet, because Prewitt's death occurs just after the Japanese attack on Pearl Harbor, the sergeant has no real opportunity to mourn him. Since Warden understands that December 7, 1941, represented the end of traditional individualism and self-expression, Prewitt's death seems to him almost an anticlimax.

THE THIN RED LINE

The mood of doomed romanticism so vital to *From Here to Eternity* is completely missing from the second volume of Jones's army trilogy, *The Thin Red Line*, a grimly detailed account of brutal combat. The bolshevik private in this novel is Witt, whose defiance has no relevance to art or to any idealistic values. In a real sense, the novel's main character is "C-for-Charlie Company," all the members of which are forced to submerge themselves into an anonymous mass. *The Thin Red Line* has been called the best American combat novel, and such high praise is deserved. The novel offers an unforgettable account of the sheer animalism of war. The sexuality of all the men of Charlie Company is systematically translated into brutal aggression toward the enemy. In fact, the only meaningful difference among the characters is the degree to which they are aware that such a transformation is taking place.

The one most aware is the superficially cynical first sergeant, Edward "Mad" Welsh. Like Milt Warden in *From Here to Eternity*, "the First" continually wonders how much of his basic self can be denied without a resultant loss of sanity. He has come very close to finding an answer to this question; one source of Jones's title is an old midwestern saying: "There's only a thin red line between the sane and the mad." Welsh's sanity is still intact, but it is being severely strained by his unrelenting awareness of the dehumanization process that he and his men are undergoing. They are threatened not only by the fanatical determination of the Japanese enemy and by the deadly accidents of warfare, but also by the gross incompetence of their own officers. Writing out of a proletarian consciousness, Jones depicted the officer class as incompetent, if not actually corrupt, in all his army fiction.

The Thin Red Line is Jones's most structurally sound novel, focusing upon the American struggle to capture an area of Guadalcanal known as "The Dancing Elephant." The brutality of combat is documented in complete naturalistic detail. Still, a majority of the central characters are alive when the novel ends with Charlie Company preparing to invade New Georgia. It is only here that the reader comes to share with Mad Welsh an awful knowledge—for those men who did not die on Guadalcanal, another Japanese-occupied island awaits, and then another and another. Thus, ultimate survival seems out of the question, and madness becomes a form of escape from too much awareness.

While no one individual American soldier could confidently expect to survive the war, the majority of the soldiers did survive to return home. Such men returned to a country which, Jones believed, was being irrevocably changed by an unprecedented wave of material prosperity. Thus, men who had accepted the inevitability of their own deaths and whose sexuality had been converted into unrestrained animalism returned to a vital, challenging economy that could not afford the time for their reorientation. They faced what Jones, in *WWII*, called "The De-Evolution of a Soldier," the final and most difficult stage of the soldier's evolution: the acceptance of life and healthy sexuality by men who, after a long and excruciating process, had been converted to death-dealing and death-accepting savagery. *Whistle* focuses on this last, and nearly impossible, transformation.

WHISTLE

In large part because Jones was unable to finish it before his death in May, 1977, *Whistle* lacks the power of *From Here to Eternity* and *The Thin Red Line*. Still, as completed from Jones's notes, by Willie Morris, it stands as a memorable conclusion to the army trilogy. The novel focuses upon the return home of four characters, all members of Charlie Company and all veterans of the kind of brutal combat depicted in *The Thin Red Line*. The war is not yet over, but the stateside economic boom is well under way. Although Marion Landers is not one of Jones's three major recurring character types, he is nevertheless reminiscent of Geoffrey Fife in *The Thin Red Line* and Richard Mast in *The Pistol*. All three men are stunned by their forced realization that modern technological combat negates the heroism assigned in romantic myth to warfare. John Strange completes the least successful of the three character types introduced in *From Here to Eternity*. Like his predecessors, Maylon Stark and Mess Sergeant Storm, Strange (nicknamed Johnny Stranger) is unable to care for anyone but himself, even though he has perfected a mask of compassion. Stark/Storm/Strange is the exact opposite of First Sergeant Warden/Welsh/Winch.

Jones's bolshevik private in *Whistle* is Bobby Prell, who has recaptured much of the Prewitt quixotic idealism that had hardened into animal stubbornness in the characterization of Witt. Very seriously wounded, Prell is battling the army that wishes to give him the Congressional Medal of Honor—the army that also insists on amputating his leg. While not convinced that he deserves the medal, Prell is certain that he should keep his leg, even if refusing amputation means certain death. Certainly, his conflict is elemental and significant; still, Prell never attains a stature comparable to that of Prewitt. Given Jones's vision, Prell must, in fact, seem largely anachronistic. Pearl Harbor marked the death of the romantic rebel as hero.

The truly memorable figure in *Whistle* is Sergeant Mart Winch, the culmination of Jones's depiction of "the First." Throughout most of *Whistle*, Winch functions as Warden and Welsh did, secretly protecting his men by elaborate manipulation of army bureaucracy. He is forced to see, however, the severe limitations of his ability to protect anyone in a new and nightmarish world. After Landers and Prell are shattered by their inability to adjust to civilian society, Winch surrenders to insanity. Thus, he crosses "the thin red line" and is destroyed by the madness that had threatened to engulf Warden and Welsh. The cumulative characterization of "the First" is the most brilliant achievement in Jones's fiction; it is the heart of the army trilogy. Jones called the vision underlying his trilogy "quite tragic" and talked of the impossibility of an affirmative contemporary literature. He described a world so thoroughly converted to dehumanizing bureaucracy and technology that it drives to insanity those men who still believe in such traditional Western values as the self and individualism.

James R. Giles

OTHER MAJOR WORKS

SHORT FICTION: *The Ice-Cream Headache and Other Stories*, 1968.

NONFICTION: *Viet Journal*, 1974; *WWII*, 1975.

BIBLIOGRAPHY

Aldrich, Nelson W., ed. *Writers at Work: The Paris Review Interviews*. 3d ser. New York: Viking Press, 1967. Jones talks about his methods of composition and defends his novels and his own brand of realistic writing against critical attacks. He also believes that an academic education can hurt a writer. Although he was living in Europe at the time of the interview, he considers himself an American.

Carter, Steven R. *James Jones: An American Literary Orientalist Master*. Urbana: University of Illinois Press, 1998. A deeply probing study of Jones's spiritual evolution and philosophy and his concern with individual salvation and growth. Includes bibliography.

Giles, James R. *James Jones*. Boston: Twayne, 1981. Examines each of Jones's novels in detail and gives a brief biography of the novelist. Sees a central division between the he-man and the sophisticate in Jones's life and art. Contains an excellent bibliography.

Hassan, Ihab. *Radical Innocence*. Princeton, N.J.: Princeton University Press, 1961. Describes the hero of *From Here to Eternity*, Pruitt, as a passive sufferer and compares his alienation to that of the Negro. Hassan likes the novel but not the subliterary psychology in which Jones indulges.

Jones, Peter G. *War and the Novelist*. Columbia: University of Missouri Press, 1976. Praises James Jones's *From Here to Eternity* and *The Thin Red Line* highly, describing them as accurate portrayals of Army life and combat and as possessing psychological insights.

Morris, Willie. *James Jones: A Friendship*. Garden City, N.Y.: Doubleday, 1978. The friendship between these two writers occurred late in Jones's life. They both lived on Long Island and were drawn into conversations about life and art. Jones reveals much about his early military career.

JAMES JOYCE

Born: Dublin, Ireland; February 2, 1882
Died: Zurich, Switzerland; January 13, 1941

PRINCIPAL LONG FICTION

A Portrait of the Artist as a Young Man, 1914-1915
    (serial), 1916 (book)
Ulysses, 1922
Finnegans Wake, 1939
Stephen Hero, 1944

OTHER LITERARY FORMS

James Joyce commenced his literary career as a poet, essayist, and dramatist, under the influences of William Butler Yeats and Henrik Ibsen, respectively. His *Collected Poems* (1936) contains *Chamber Music* (1907), thirty-six lyrics written before 1904, and *Pomes Penyeach* (1927), eleven poems written after he had made his commitment to prose fiction. His first published essay, "Ibsen's New Drama" (1900), announced his admiration for the Norwegian dramatist; the same attitude is implied in his only original surviving play, *Exiles* (1918).

Miscellaneous literary essays, program and lecture notes, reviews, journalism, and two broadsides are collected in *The Critical Writings of James Joyce* (1959). Joyce's correspondence is contained in *Letters* (1957-1966), with some additions in *Selected Letters of James Joyce* (1975).

Through the compilation of fifteen short stories in *Dubliners* (1914), written between 1904 and 1907, Joyce discerned his métier. This apparently random, realistic series was the first announcement of its author's singular genius. While the volume retains a "scrupulously mean" accuracy in regard to naturalistic detail, it also incorporates a multiplicity of complex symbolic patterns. An ephemeral story, "Giacomo Joyce" (1918), was written as he completed *A Portrait of the Artist as a Young Man* and began *Ulysses* in 1914. The collaboration of several editors has produced in facsimile almost the entire Joyce "workshop"—notes, drafts, manuscripts, typescripts, and proofs—in sixty-four volumes (*The James Joyce Archives*, 1977-1979), a project of unprecedented magnitude for any twentieth century author.

ACHIEVEMENTS

From the beginning of his literary career, Joyce was the most distinctive figure in the renaissance that occurred in Irish cultural life after the death of Charles Stuart Parnell. Despite his early quarrels with Yeats, John M. Synge, and other leaders of the Irish Literary Revival, and his subsequent permanent exile, he is clearly, with Yeats, its presiding genius. From the first, he set himself to liberate Ireland, not by returning to Celtic myths or the Gaelic language and folklore, but by europeanizing its cultural institutions. His early stories are an exorcism of the spirit of paralysis he felt about himself in the Dublin of his youth. As he gained detachment from these obstacles and knowledge of his own capacities as a writer of prose fiction, he produced two of the undisputed masterworks of modern literature—*A Portrait of the Artist as a Young Man* and *Ulysses*, as well as a final work that is perhaps beyond criticism, *Finnegans Wake*.

Throughout this development, Joyce's themes and subjects remain the same, yet his means become more overtly complex: the fabulous comedy, the multivalent language, and the vast design of *Ulysses* and *Finnegans Wake* are strands in the reverse side of the sedulously restrained tapestry of *Dubliners* and *A Portrait of the Artist as a Young Man*.

Joyce's cast of characters is small, his Dublin settings barely change from work to work, he observes repeatedly certain archetypal conflicts beneath the appearances of daily life, and his fiction is marked by certain obsessions of his class, religion, and nationality. Yet his single-mindedness, his wide learning in European literature, his comprehensive grasp of the intellectual currents of the age, his broad comic vision, his vast technical skills, and above all, his unequaled mastery of language, make him at once a europeanizer of Irish literature, a hibernicizer of European literature, and a modernizer of world literature.

BIOGRAPHY

James Augustine Joyce was born in Dublin, Ireland, on February 2, 1882, the first of John Joyce's and Mary Murray's ten children. During the years of Joyce's youth, his father wasted the family's substantial resources based on properties in Cork City; Joyce, at the same time, grew to reject the pious Catholicism of his mother. Except for a brief period, his education was in the hands of the Jesuits: at Clongowes Wood College, the less exclusive Belvedere College, and finally at University College, Dublin, from where he was graduated in 1902. Joyce quickly outgrew his mentors, however, so that the early influences of the Maynooth Catechism and Saints Ignatius Loyola and Thomas Aquinas yielded to his own eclectic reading in European literature, especially Dante, Ibsen, Gerhart Hauptmann, and Gustave Flaubert. Politically, he retained his father's Parnellite Irish nationalism, modified by a moderate socialism. Despite his declared abjuration of Catholicism and the Irish political and cultural revivals, he continued to pay to each a proud and private subscription. He considered the professions of music and medicine (briefly attending the École de Medicine in Paris in 1902) before eventually leaving Ireland in October, 1904, for Europe and a literary career. He was accompanied by Nora Barnacle, a Galway-born chambermaid whom he had met the previous June, who became the mother of his two children, Georgio and Lucia, and whom he formally married in 1931.

Between 1904 and the conclusion of World War I, the Joyces lived successively in Trieste, Rome, Pola, and Zurich, where Joyce supported his wife and family by teaching English for the Berlitz schools, bank clerking, and borrowing from his brother Stanislaus, who had joined them in 1905. The *Dubliners* stories, begun shortly before he left Ireland, were finished with "The Dead" in 1907, but it was another seven years of wrangling with Irish and British publishers over details that were considered either libelous or indecent before the volume was published. By then, Joyce had fully rewritten *Stephen Hero*, a loose, naturalistic, and semiautobiographical novel, as the classic of impressionism, *A Por-*

trait of the Artist as a Young Man. Ezra Pound, then the literary editor of *The Egoist*, recognized its permanence, published the novel in serial form, and recommended its author to the patronage of Harriet Weaver, who anonymously provided Joyce with a handsome annuity for the rest of his life.

Based on this material support and the establishment of his literary reputation, Joyce worked on *Ulysses* in Trieste, Zurich, and Paris, where he moved in 1920. Meanwhile, beginning in March, 1918, Margaret Anderson and Jane Heap's *Little Review* (New York) was publishing the separate episodes of *Ulysses*. The prosecution and conviction in February, 1921, of its two publishers for obscenity gave the novel a wide notoriety which preceded its publication in Paris by Sylvia Beach's Shakespeare and Company on its author's fortieth birthday.

(Library of Congress)

Joyce then became an international celebrity and the center of literary life in Paris during the 1920's. Between 1922 and 1939, he worked on *Finnegans Wake*, which, under the title "Work in Progress," appeared in Eugene Jolas's *transition* and other avant-garde journals. During this period of his life, Joyce contended with the pirating and banning of *Ulysses* in the United States, the worsening condition of his eyes, which required eleven separate operations, his daughter's schizophrenia, and the loss of many of his earlier admirers because of their puzzlement with or hostility toward the experimentation of *Ulysses* and especially of "Work in Progress."

As World War II approached, *Finnegans Wake* was published, and the Joyces moved once again, to neutral Zurich. Following an operation for a duodenal ulcer, Joyce died there on January 13, 1941. With Nora (died 1951), he is buried in Flüntern Cemetery, Zurich, beneath Milton Hebald's sprightly statue.

ANALYSIS

The leaders of the Irish Literary Revival were born of the Anglo-Irish aristocracy. Very few were Catholics, and none was from the urban middle class, except James Joyce. The emphasis of the Revival in its early stages on legendary or peasant themes and its subsequent espousal of a vaguely nationalistic and unorthodox religious spirit kept it at a certain distance from popular pieties. It did no more than gesture toward Europe, and it registered very little of the atrophied state of middle- and lower-class city life.

The first to deal with this latter theme realistically, Joyce made a bold show as a "europeanizer" and openly criticized "patriotic" art. Despite his disdain for contemporary political and literary enthusiasms, his dismissal of Celtic myths as "broken lights," his characterization of the folk imagination as "senile," and his relative ignorance of the Gaelic language, however, his imaginative works are as thoroughly and distinctively Irish as those of William Butler Yeats, John Millington Synge, or Lady Augusta Gregory.

From his earliest childhood, Joyce was aware of the political controversies of the day, observing the conflict between the idealized Charles Stuart Parnell

and the ultramontane Church which permanently marked his outlook on Irish public affairs. His faith in Irish nationalist politics and in Catholicism was broken even as it was formed, and soon he launched himself beyond the pales of both, by exile and apostasy, proclaiming that each had betrayed his trust. The supersaturation of his consciousness with the language, attitudes, and myths of Church and State was formative, however, as all of his work documents: *Dubliners, A Portrait of the Artist as a Young Man, Ulysses*, and *Finnegans Wake* are unparalleled as a record of the "felt history" of Edwardian Dublin, or indeed of any city in modern literature.

From the beginning, Joyce's scrupulous naturalism belied his symbolist tendencies. The revisions of his early stories, and the transformation of *Stephen Hero* into the impressionistic *Bildungsroman* of *A Portrait of the Artist as a Young Man*, indicate that he recognized among his own powers of observation and language a special capacity to decode the socialization process—an aptitude, as he put it, for "epiphany." At certain moments in an otherwise continuous state of paralysis, the truth reveals itself and the spirit is liberated from a conditioned servility. The repeated use of carefully selected words can, without neglecting the obligation to realistic fidelity, have the harmonious and radiant effect of a symbol.

As Joyce's technical skills grew, he extended this principle so that in *Ulysses* the structural symbols become one, while at the same time the demands of realism were superseded. The tendencies implied in this shift have their apotheosis in *Finnegans Wake*. From 1922 to 1939, Joyce was very long removed from the Dublin he had known, and he had come to understand his own genius for language ("I find that I can do anything I like with it"). Drawing on an encyclopedic range of materials, he wrote this final, most challenging work, in which the world of the unconscious, or the sleeping mind, is represented not by realism but by multivalent language and the timeless action of archetypal characters.

In eschewing the narrow confines set by the Irish revival, Joyce turned to the masters of classical and modern European literature for his models: to Homer for his Odysseus, the hero to set against the Christian

Savior and the Irish Cuchulain; to Dante for his multiplex realization of Catholic phantasmagoria; to William Shakespeare for his language and his treatment of family relations; and to Henrik Ibsen for his disciplined criticism of modern bourgeois life. Under these influences, Joyce's art developed along highly formalist lines, and mythological antecedents stalk his modern lower-middle-class characters. The effects of such comparisons are, to various ends, ironic; the ordinary Dublin characters lack the remove, heroism, and familiarity with gods or demons of their classic counterparts. Instead, they exhibit various neurotic symptoms associated with modern urban life—repression, anxiety, fetishism, and the confusion of great and small virtue. In these four respects then—in the predeliction for formalism, mythologization, irony, and the subject of individual consciousness—Joyce establishes the methods and the subject of literary modernism.

A PORTRAIT OF THE ARTIST AS A YOUNG MAN

A Portrait of the Artist as a Young Man is a semiautobiographical *Bildungsroman* describing the development of the sensibility of Stephen Dedalus from his earliest childhood recollections to the beginnings of manhood. The work evolved from the narrative essay "A Portrait of the Artist" (January, 1904), and its expansion into *Stephen Hero*, an undisguised autobiographical novel in the naturalist tradition. The result of this evolution was a startlingly original composition: a highly structured, symbolic, impressionistic, and ironic treatment of the spiritual formation and reformation of an acutely sensitive young man. Stephen's conscience absorbs the values of his Irish Catholic family; by a progressively more complex use of language and technique through the five chapters of the novel, Joyce portrays that conscience undergoing a process of simultaneous severance and refinement. The conclusion of the process, however, is paradoxical, for as Stephen declares his determination to free himself of the claims of the formative establishments of his family, nation, and religion by setting against them the proud and defiant slogan "silence, exile and cunning," the terms by which that defiance is made have already been set. Like his language, Stephen's conflicts with the virtues advocated

by the three establishments are not different in kind but more profound than those of his fellows. It is one of Joyce's many ironies in *A Portrait of the Artist as a Young Man* that Stephen mistakes these conflicts for a radical independence of spirit. Like Icarus, his mythological antecedent, his destiny is not to escape from the paternal labyrinths, but to fall from the heights of supercilious pride.

One of the signal achievements of the novel is Joyce's management of the distance between reader and protagonist: As Stephen grows older, he becomes less amiable. This distance is achieved by a multiplicity of devices: the subtle weighing of names, the acute selection of sensuous detail, the exaggeration of language, the ironic structure, the counterpointing of incidents, and the elaborate systematizing of all devices. The endearing sensitivity and naïveté of the child slowly yield to the self-absorbed priggishness of the young man.

Chapter 1 is composed of four sections: random sensations of early childhood, Stephen's illness (at approximately seven years) at Clongowes Wood College, the Christmas dinner scene, and Stephen's first victory over injustice—Father Dolan's punishment. Each section gathers materials that dramatize the mysterious interplay of private sensation, communal constraint, and language. Each section culminates in an "epiphany," a metatheological term for "a sudden spiritual manifestation" when a response betrays its socially conditioned origin, and the true feeling or idea radiates forth with the force of a symbol.

The opening section in the language of a preschool child is the kernel out of which the entire work develops. It distinguishes in a rudimentary, purely sensory manner the symbols and themes which will preoccupy Stephen: women, road, rose, paternity, flight, creation, the relationship between experience and the representation of it, his own distinctness, guilt, and the demands of home, religion, and nation.

Stephen's illness at Clongowes Wood College causes him to meditate on the repugnance of physical life and his attraction to mysterious realms of religion and language, an association which is later to prove axial. The Christmas dinner scene, on the other hand, is a brilliant dramatization of the tension be-tween the three establishments and the threats they pose to Parnell and Stephen, heroes alike. In the final section, Stephen successfully protests an unjust school punishment.

Chapter 2 is composed of a series of some dozen epiphanies developing the themes of Stephen's grad-ual estrangement from his family, particularly his fa-ther, and his perception of sexual identification, lead-ing to his liberation from innocence in the embrace of a prostitute. Among the revelations in this chapter is the news of the Rector's real attitude toward Father Dolan's treatment of Stephen; the jocosity of this at-titude deflates the climax of chapter 1. When, in chapter 3, Stephen repents of his sin with the prosti-tute, the pattern of reversal repeats itself, and the structural irony in the novel is revealed. This chapter falls into three sections—the states of sin, repen-tance, and grace mediated by the memorable sermon on hell. This terrifying exposition (based on the pro-cedures for spiritual meditation propounded by the *Spiritual Exercises* of Ignatius Loyola) leads Stephen to contrition, confession, and communion, each treated with a certain degree of irony. Not the least of the ironies here is Stephen's dissociated sensibility, as implied in the final page of chapter 3 and ex-panded in the opening section of chapter 4. The true state of his feelings is elucidated in the course of the succeeding two sections: his consideration and rejec-tion of the priestly vocation and his ecstatic response to the call to the priesthood of the imagination. He re-jects the priesthood because of its orderliness and uniformity; the life of community is removed from the risks inherent in secular life, and it denies indi-vidual freedom. His response to the muse is, how-ever, heavily overlaid with images of the mysteries of the service of the altar. In this climactic epiphany, Stephen risks loneliness and error to transform in freedom the stuff of ordinary experience into the per-manent forms of secular art. In response to the mes-senger, girl-bird-angel, he accepts a vocation which in the cause of self expression will set him apart from all institutions.

In the final chapter, Stephen attempts an exorcism of each aspect of the culture that would possess his soul. To this end, he engages in a dialogue with a se-ries of companions who advance three claims: McCann and Davin (international and national poli-tics); Father Darlington and Lynch (servile, practical, or kinetic arts); and Cranly (conventional morality and religion). In the course of the perambulations ac-companying *apologia pro futura sua*, Stephen sets forth his aesthetic theory, which in its refusal to grant overt moral purpose to art owes more to Walter Pater than to Aquinas. The pallid "Villanelle of the Tempt-ress" comes as an anticlimax on the heels of such brilliant theorizing and raises the question of Ste-phen's capacities as a creative artist as opposed to those of an aesthete or poseur. The concluding sec-tion, comprising the diary entries from the five weeks preceding Stephen's departure, at once recapitulates the themes of the entire novel and anticipates Ste-phen's commitment to the proud and lonely life of the committed artist. The impression that this se-quence of startling entries makes is of an irony of another kind: Stephen has unknowingly stumbled upon a technique that takes him closer to his creator and to the tenor of twentieth century literature than his self-absorbed and self-conscious villanelle. Thus, at the conclusion of *A Portrait of the Artist as a Young Man*, Stephen has yet to acquire a moral awareness, develop human sympathies, or discern his own voice.

ULYSSES

The Stephen Dedalus of *Ulysses* has returned to Ireland after a brief sojourn in Paris. He has acquired a few new affectations from that experience, is in-tensely guilt-ridden over his mother's suffering and death, teaches ineffectually at a Dublin boys' school, lives with some companions in a Martello tower, makes desultory efforts at writing poetry, speculates sensitively on a variety of epistemological, theologi-cal, and metaphysical questions, theorizes ostenta-tiously on Shakespeare's psychobiography, delivers himself of cryptic remarks and oblique anecdotes, and wastes his salary on prostitutes and drink. De-spite his dissolution and moodiness, however, the Stephen of *Ulysses* is considerably more receptive to the world of ordinary experience that whirls around him than the protagonist of *A Portrait of the Artist as a Young Man*. Leopold Bloom is the personification of that world.

Bloom is a thirty-eight-year-old Irish Jew of Hungarian extraction. A family man, he has a wife, Molly, four years his junior, and a daughter Milly, age fifteen; a son, Rudy, died in infancy. Bloom is observant and intelligent despite his lack of higher education. He lives in Eccles Street and works as an advertising salesman for a daily newspaper. The key event of the day on which the action of *Ulysses* takes place—June 16, 1904—is Molly's infidelity (of which Bloom is aware) with an impresario named Blazes Boylan. During the course of the day, between 8 A.M. and approximately 3 A.M. on June 17, the reader follows Bloom's thoughts and movements as he manages to retain an equilibrium between many demands and disappointments.

Bloom serves his wife breakfast in bed, takes a bath, corresponds with an epistolary lover, attends a funeral, attempts to secure an ad from a firm by the name of Keyes, has lunch, is misunderstood over a horse race, is insulted and almost attacked in a bar, becomes sexually aroused by an exhibitionist girl on the beach, and inquires about a friend at a maternity hospital, where he encounters Stephen Dedalus carousing with sundry dissolutes. Feeling protective of Stephen, he pursues him to a brothel and subsequently rescues him from brawlers and police, taking him home for a hot drink. Bloom retires, noting the signs of Blazes Boylan's recent occupation of the marital bed. Throughout these physical events, Bloom's consciousness plays with myriad impressions and ideas serious and trivial, from his wife's infidelity to imperfectly remembered incidents from his childhood. He also proves himself to be a resilient, considerate, humorous, prudent, and even-tempered man. As the novel progresses, Bloom, certainly one of the most completely realized characters in fiction, grows in the reader's affections and estimation.

Molly, as revealed to the reader in the famous soliloquy of the final chapter, is a substantial embodiment of the anima. Born in Gibraltar of a Spanish mother and an English military father who later took her to Dublin, Molly is a superstitious Catholic, a plainspoken, amoral, fertile, sensual, passive beauty.

She is a singer of sentimental concert-stage favorites who, despite her adultery with Boylan, loves and admires her own husband. Throughout *Ulysses*, she is offstage, yet constantly on Leopold's mind.

Each of these three main figures in *Ulysses* is characterized by a distinctly individuated stream of consciousness. Stephen's bespeaks a cultivated sensibility, abounds with intellectual energy, and moves with a varying pace between considerations of language, history, literature, and theology in a private language that is learned, lyrical, morose, and laden throughout with multidirectional allusions. Bloom's stream of consciousness, on the other hand, drifts bemusedly, effortlessly, and with occasional melancholia through a catalog of received ideas, its direction easily swayed by sensual suggestion or opportunities for naïve scientific speculation, yet sometimes revealing a remarkable perspicacity. Molly's, finally, is the least ratiocinative and most fluent and even-paced, an unpunctuated mélange of nostalgia, acidity, and pragmatism.

These three fictional characters share a city with a large cast of figures, some of whom are historical, some based on actual people, and some purely imaginary. All move through the most minutely realized setting in literature. Joyce plotted the action of *Ulysses* so as to conform with the details of the day's news, the typical comings and goings in the city's various institutions, the weather report, and the precise elements of Dublin's "street furniture" on June 16, 1904: the tram schedules, addresses, advertising slogans, theatrical notices, smells and sounds of the city, topics and tone of casual conversation, and so on. At this level, the work is a virtuoso exhibition of realism that challenges the most searching literary sleuths.

On another level, *Ulysses* has an equally astounding system of mythological, historical, literary, and formal superstructures invoked by allusion and analogy. As the title implies, Leopold Bloom is a humble modern counterpart to Odysseus, the archetypal hero of Western civilization. Thus Molly corresponds to Odysseus's faithful wife Penelope, and Stephen to his devoted comrade and son Telemachus. As Joyce first revealed to Stuart Gilbert, his design for *Ulysses* called for the alignment of each of the eighteen chapters of his novel with an episode in Homer's *Odyssey* (c. 800 B.C.E.), with a particular location in the city of Dublin, with a particular hour in the day of June 16, 1904, with an organ of the human body, an art or science, a color, and an archetypal symbol. Finally, each of these chapters was to be written in a distinctive style. Two generations of readers have discerned further schemata and elucidated hundreds of ingenious and delicious ironies woven into every chapter, so that critical appreciation of Joyce's technical achievement in the writing of *Ulysses* continues to grow. Bloom's peregrinations through Dublin, his temporary usurpation from his marriage bed, his difficulties with customers and sundry citizens, and his befriending of the fatherless Stephen, under such grand auspices, become objects of simultaneous amusement and admiration. Even the most trivial actions of unremarkable modern citizens gain stature, resonance, and dignity; at the same time, a classic work and its heroic virtues are reinterpreted for this age.

In its broadest sense, *Ulysses* deals with a husband's usurpation from and repossession of his home: Rivals are routed and an ally—a son—found. From another perspective, the plot expounds the relationship of an intellectual abstraction (Stephen) and a sense experience (Bloom). This aspect has its technical analogue in the complex formal structure by which Joyce organizes the myriad material details of the novel. Joyce draws on an impressive range of masterworks from the Western cultural tradition to elaborate these themes and comparisons. Stephen's preoccupation with Shakespeare's *Hamlet* (1600-1601), especially as it is expounded in the ninth episode ("Scylla and Charybdis"), suggests the father-and-son theme in a manner that complements the Homeric. Similarly, the Blazes Boylan-Molly Bloom relationship is orchestrated by reference to Wolfgang Amadeus Mozart's *Don Giovanni* (1787). Among other major organizational devices are the Catholic Mass, Dante's *The Divine Comedy* (c. 1320), dialectical time-space progressions, Richard Wagner's Ring cycle (1854-1874), and a progression of literary techniques. Thus, for example, as one moves from

chapter to chapter under the guidance of a third-person omniscient narrator, one encounters a succession of literary procedures modeled after journalism, classical rhetoric, catechesis, popular romance, musical counterpoint, and expressionist drama.

The fourteenth chapter ("Oxen of the Sun"), for example, narrates Bloom's visit at 10 P. M. to the maternity hospital at Holles Street, the revelry of the medical students and their departure for bar and brothel. The forty-five-page chapter broadly alludes to Ulysses' visit to the Isle of the Sun (*Odyssey*, book 12) and his followers' disobediance of his orders in killing the native oxen, which brings down retribution on them that only the hero survives. Joyce's narrative around the theme of respect for the physical processes of conception, gestation, and childbirth develops as a nine-part episode tracing simultaneously the development of the human embryo and the historical growth of the English language. A complex motif of references to the successive differentiation of organs in the developing human embryo is paralleled by some two score parodies of successive English prose styles from preliteracy and Anglo-Saxon to contemporary slang and a style very like that of *Finnegans Wake*. These progressions are further enhanced by similar motifs alluding to formal evolution, the events of June 16, 1904, and symbolic identifications of Bloom, the hospital, nurse, and Stephen with the sperm, the womb, the ovum, and the embryo, respectively. The cumulative effect of this encyclopedia of procedures is paradoxical: One marvels at the grandeur, the energy, and the variety of the language and the magisterial control of the writer, while at the same time retaining skepticism about the claims of any single perspective.

On almost every aspect of this great novel, the critics are divided: the literary value of such vast systematization, the significance of Bloom's meeting with Stephen, and the very spirit of the work. Nevertheless, its impact on modern literature is immense, from specific literary influences such as that on T. S. Eliot's *The Waste Land* (1922) to all works that mythologize contemporary experience. The themes of *Ulysses*—the dignity of ordinary persons, the values of family and human brotherhood, the consolation of language and the literary tradition, the interrelationships of theological, psychological, and aesthetic language and ideas, the ambiguity of the most profound experiences and the impact of modern revolutions in politics, science, and linguistics on notions of identity—are approached in a manner of unequaled virtuosity.

FINNEGANS WAKE

For all the virtuosity of *Ulysses*, Joyce considered its form inadequate to accommodate the depth and breadth of his vision of human history, experience, and aspiration. Thus, he spent sixteen years of his life composing *Finnegans Wake*, a baffling expedition into the dream of history for which he devised a "night language" composed of scores of languages superimposed on a Hiberno-English base.

Finnegans Wake sets out to express in appropriate form and language the collective unconscious. Thus, it encompasses all of human experience through the millennia in a cycle of recurring forms through a universal language, the language of dreams. The work has five primary dreamers, is divided into four books, and employs a language with simultaneous reference to multiple tongues, expressing the major theme of the cyclical nature of history.

The title derives from the Irish-American comic ballad "Finnegan's Wake," in which Tim Finnegan, a hod carrier, has fallen to his apparent death, but under the effect of spilt whiskey, he leaps out of the bed to join the revelry. The fall of this lowly modern Irish laborer recalls previous falls—Lucifer's, Adam's, Newton's, and Humpty Dumpty's—while his resurrection suggests similar parallels, most notably with Christ and, by extension via the implied words *fin* (French for "end"), "again," and "awake," with the myth of the eternal return of all things.

The five primary dreamers are Humphrey Chimpden Earwicker (HCE), a Dublin pubkeeper, his wife Anna Livia Plurabelle (ALP), their twin sons Shem and Shaun, and their daughter Issy. HCE (Haveth Childers Everywhere/Here Comes Everybody) is the archetypal husband-father who is burdened with guilt over an obscure indiscretion in the Phoenix Park, an Original Sin, the source of all nightmares in this dreambook of history. News of this sin is carried

about by rumors and documents, lectures and arguments, accusations and recriminations. Interrogators appear in fours, and there are twelve onlookers: various jurymen, apostles, mourners, drinkers, and so on. As HCE is identified with the Dublin landscape—from Chapelizod to "Howth Castle and Environs"—his wife is the personification of the River Liffey flowing through that landscape. She is the universal wife-mother, and like all the rivers of the world, constantly in flux. Joyce lavished special care on the section of *Finnegans Wake* (book 1, chapter 8, pages 196-216) where she is featured, and he read its conclusion for a phonograph recording. Their warring twin sons, Shem and Shaun, represent the generally opposite character types of introvert and extrovert, subjective and objective, artist and man of affairs, as well as Joyce himself and various antagonists such as his brother Stanislaus, Eamon deValera, John McCormack, and St. Patrick. Issy is the femme fatale, Iseult *rediviva*, the divisive ingenue of *Finnegans Wake*, in contrast with her mother, whose influence is unitive.

The four books of *Finnegans Wake* recount human history according to the four-phase cycle of Giambattista Vico's *La Scienza Nuova* (1725, 1744): theocratic, aristocratic, democratic, anarchic, and thence via a *ricorso* to the theocratic once again and a new cycle. These four phases of history and the night comprehend the totality of individual and racial development by means of analogies with the four Evangelists of the New Testament, the four Masters of Irish history, the four compass points, and so on. Through a vast elaboration of such correspondences, the Joycean universe of *Finnegans Wake* is populated and structured.

Four decades of attempts to explicate *Finnegans Wake* appear to confirm Joyce's prediction that the work would keep the professors busy for centuries. A general opinion among those who take the work seriously is that as a dreambook and a leading expression of the twentieth century worldview, it is indeterminate, untranslatable, irreducible. It is a work in which every single element has a function: It contains no nonsense yet is finally beyond explication. Critical analyses of *Finnegans Wake* have been either macrocosmic or microcosmic, emphasizing its overall design or attempting to gloss particular passages. To date, however, neither procedure has progressed very far toward the other.

Finnegans Wake is Joyce's most ambitious literary endeavor. He anticipated, yet underestimated, the difficulties his readers would encounter, and he was disappointed that so many of those who acclaimed *A Portrait of the Artist as a Young Man* and *Ulysses* as supreme expressions of modernity were unprepared to pursue his explorations to the limits of language in *Finnegans Wake*.

Like the great masters in every discipline, Joyce enlarged the possibilities of the forms he inherited. This is indisputably true of the short story, the *Bildungsroman*, and the mythological-psychological novel. In none of these areas has his achievement been superseded, while in the case of *Finnegans Wake*, as Richard Ellmann puts it in the introduction to his classic biography, "we are still learning to be James Joyce's contemporaries, to understand our interpreter."

Cóilín Owens

OTHER MAJOR WORKS

SHORT FICTION: *Dubliners*, 1914.

PLAY: *Exiles*, pb. 1918.

POETRY: *Chamber Music*, 1907; *Pomes Penyeach*, 1927; *Collected Poems*, 1936.

NONFICTION: *The Critical Writings of James Joyce*, 1959; *Letters*, 1957-1966 (3 volumes); *Selected Letters of James Joyce*, 1975 (Richard Ellmann, editor); *The James Joyce Archives*, 1977-1979 (64 volumes).

BIBLIOGRAPHY

Attridge, Derek, ed. *The Cambridge Companion to James Joyce*. Cambridge, England: Cambridge University Press, 1990. A collection of eleven essays by the younger generation of eminent contemporary Joyce scholars, among them John Paul Riquelme, Margot Norris, Hans Walter Gabler, and Karen Lawrence. Surveys the Joyce phenomenon from cultural, textual, and critical standpoints, with *Ulysses* and *Finnegans Wake* each given a separate essay. A valuable aid and stimulus, containing a chronology of Joyce's life and an annotated bibliography.

Beja, Morris. *James Joyce: A Literary Life*. Columbus: Ohio State University Press, 1992. A succinct critical biography by a renowned scholar. Chapters on Joyce's Dublin youth, his early work, the periods of writing *A Portrait of the Artist as a Young Man*, *Ulysses*, and *Finnegans Wake*. Includes an appendix on the Joyce family, notes, and bibliography.

Benstock, Bernard, ed. *Critical Essays on James Joyce*. Boston: G. K. Hall, 1985. Divided into early assessments, mainstream critics, and later reevaluations of both the short and the long fiction. Includes an introduction but no bibliography.

_____. *Critical Essays on James Joyce's "Ulysses."* Boston: G. K. Hall, 1989. Divided into three sections: The first provides surveys of the whole novel; the second concentrates on the "Nausicaa" section; and the third takes up criticism after the 1970's, when a new generation of critics reassessed Joyce's work. Provides an introduction but no bibliography.

Blades, John. *How to Study James Joyce*. Houndmills, England: Macmillan, 1996. An excellent study guide for students of Joyce. Includes bibliographical reference, outlines, and syllabi.

Bowen, Zack R., and James F. Carens, eds. *A Companion to Joyce Studies*. Westport, Conn.: Greenwood Press, 1984. Sixteen individual essays on each of Joyce's works, with the exception of *Finnegans Wake*, to which three separate essays are devoted. For the purpose of this anthology, Joyce's works are understood to include his letters and juvenilia. Also includes a biographical sketch of Joyce, an account of his texts' history, and a history of his reputation.

Deming, Robert, ed. *A Bibliography of James Joyce Studies*. 2d rev. ed. Boston: G. K. Hall, 1977. The most important source of information for Joyce scholars.

Ellmann, Richard. *James Joyce*. 1959. Rev. ed. New York: Oxford University Press, 1982. The definitive biography, generally regarded as the last word on its subject's life and widely considered the greatest literary biography of the century. Copiously annotated and well illustrated, particularly in the 1982 edition.

Gillespie, Michael Patrick, ed. *Joyce Through the Ages: A Nonlinear View*. Gainesville: University Press of Florida, 1999. Discusses Joyce's work and themes, as well as how his writing evolved.

Hart, Clive, and David Hayman, eds. *James Joyce's "Ulysses": Critical Essays*. Berkeley: University of California Press, 1974. A compilation of eighteen essays, each devoted to a single section of *Ulysses*. The contributors are among the foremost of those who made Joyce's academic reputation in the postwar period and, while the volume's quality is variable, it is a valuable resource for students familiar with the subject matter.

Joyce, James. *"A Portrait of the Artist as a Young Man": Text, Criticism, and Notes*. Edited by Chester Anderson. New York: Viking Press, 1968. A helpful guide to Joyce's first novel, including expert critical commentary and explication of Joyce's sometimes recondite allusions.

Kenner, Hugh. *Dublin's Joyce*. London: Chatto & Windus, 1955. The first book on Joyce by a critic who has done more than any other to delimit the aesthetic and cultural terrain in which Joyce's contribution to modern literature was made. Rather acerbic and extravagant in its intellectual processes, it nevertheless has been a very influential study, containing in particular a landmark treatment of *A Portrait of the Artist as a Young Man*.

McHugh, Roland. *The Sigla of "Finnegans Wake."* Austin: University of Texas Press, 1976. A brief introduction to the compositional character of *Finnegans Wake*, with an informal, refreshing, and valuable guide to approaching Joyce's final work.

K

FRANZ KAFKA

Born: Prague, Czechoslovakia; July 3, 1883
Died: Kierling, Klosterneuburg, near Vienna, Austria; June 3, 1924

PRINCIPAL LONG FICTION

Der Prozess, 1925 (*The Trial*, 1937)
Das Schloss, 1926 (*The Castle*, 1930)
Amerika, 1927 (*America*, 1938; better known as *Amerika*, 1946)

OTHER LITERARY FORMS

In addition to long fiction, Franz Kafka wrote numerous stories, the most famous of which are *Ein Hungerkünstler: Vier Geschichten* (1924; *A Hunger Artist*, 1948) and *The Penal Colony: Stories and Short Pieces* (1948). He also left behind extensive diaries and letters.

ACHIEVEMENTS

What W. H. Auden wrote of Sigmund Freud—that he had become less a man than a climate of opinion—is equally true of Kafka. He is the twentieth century prophet of alienation, his name a household synonym for *Angst*. His stories—visionary, hallucinatory, yet very controlled artistically—have exerted their powerful influence over modern fiction. Few would dispute the assertion that he is one of the major literary figures of the twentieth century. None of this, however, could have been anticipated of a writer who was not widely known at the time of his death. Kafka's genius was difficult for him to harness: The fact is that he never completed any of his three novels. Before dying, he left instructions with Max Brod, his friend and executor, to destroy his manuscripts. Reasoning that Kafka was not committed to their destruction as much as he was ambivalent over their fate—could not he have destroyed them had he really

wished to do so?—Brod preserved the manuscripts, arranged to have them printed, wrote a biography of his friend, and generously championed his cause. Thus, *The Trial* and *The Castle*, books which so remarkably capture Kafa's paradoxical vision of human's existence, came to light.

BIOGRAPHY

Despite the strange occurrences that animate Franz Kafka's fiction, the events of his life are colorless and mundane. Like Emily Dickinson or Henry Thoreau, however, Kafka could, by sheer imagination, transform the most ordinary life into fascinating reading. Tirelessly, he penned his impressions of his life, recording the nuances of his thoughts and actions in ethical and ontological terms.

Kafka was born into a bourgeois German-Jewish family in Prague. The Czechs of Kafka's day felt oppressed by the Austrian-Germans and in turn oppressed the Jews, so from his earliest days Kafka was accustomed to the pain of a threefold prejudice—as non-Austrian, as non-Czech, and as Jew. Franz was the oldest child, the sole surviving son in a family that was later to include three girls. The father, Herrmann Kafka, struggled to achieve financial security for his family, and he succeeded, but the ordeal coarsened him; he became autocratic and irascible. Money and status were his chief passions, and he directed his considerable energy to their acquisition. Nevertheless, he had a zest for life which left its imprint on his son, who could admire though never attain it. Kafka's mother, on the other hand, came from a family of rabbis, scholars, and physicians, and from her Kafka probably inherited his sensitive nature and dreamy tendencies.

As Kafka was heir to divergent traditions in his family, so, too, the city of Prague offered him contrasting traditions. On one hand, Prague, influenced by Austria, looked westward, toward rationalism and the Enlightenment; on the other hand, it gazed eastward, toward Russia with its semimystical fervor. In his Jewish studies, too, Kafka discovered similar tensions: the casuistic flavor of the Talmud straining against the impassioned piety of the mystics. These elements ultimately recombine themselves in Kafka's fiction.

Photographs of Kafka reveal him as dark and slender, respectable in appearance, with an intense and boyish face, delicate and sensitive. Young Franz spent his school years in Prague—first at a German elementary school and later at a *gymnasium*; he ultimately was graduated from the German Karl-Ferdinand University. For two weeks, he specialized in chemistry but found it uncongenial; soon after, he succumbed to pressure from his friends and family, especially his father, and commenced the study of law. Unhappy, he described it as "living in an intellectual sense, on sawdust, which had, moreover, already been chewed for me in thousands of other people's mouths."

Kafka, however, needed some means to support himself, and the legal profession was an eminently respectable career—especially appealing to Jews. Though he never cared for the practice of law, a major consideration was the hope of winning his father's long-withheld approval. In this, he never succeeded; here was a struggle that allowed neither victory nor retreat.

Reams have been written on the subject of Kafka and his father. Are not the fathers in his fiction oversize presences that visit judgment and wrath on their sons? Are not his protagonists accused persons, judged guilty of some undefined transgression against an all-powerful and implacable force that hounds the hero and destroys him? In story after story, in all of his novels, one finds Kafka returning, irresistibly, obsessively, to the theme of the judging father in an effort to exorcise this demon—in vain. Kafka's friend and biographer, Brod, first reported and later released an amazing document penned by the twenty-six-year-old Kafka, the *Brief an den Vater* (1952, written 1919; *Letter to His Father*, 1954). The manuscript was given to Franz's mother for delivery to her spouse. Hardly a letter—it is more than one hundred pages long—the document minutely scrutinizes the son's pained relations with his father. Its tone—mingling abjectness and defiance—can be heard in Kafka's fiction as well, where it expresses his protagonists' attitudes toward their parents. One can only speculate how Herrmann Kafka might have responded to the missive: His wife never delivered the letter.

Completing his studies, Kafka gained legal experience in a district, then in a criminal court, where he observed at first hand the workings of the law, which he later fictionalized in *The Trial*. Soon after, he secured a position with the Workers' Accident Insurance Office, where he remained a respected and admired figure until illness forced his retirement in 1922. There he gained intimate knowledge of the operations of a bureaucracy, which he transferred to his novel *The Castle*.

Though Kafka never married, he did seek romance and the consolation of women. In 1912, Kafka began courting a woman he had met at Brod's house, Felice Bauer. (Her initials are echoed both in *The Trial*, in the name of Fraulein Burstner, and in *The Castle*'s Frieda.) Curiously, Kafka avoided contact with her, although he maintained a voluminous correspondence with her, sometimes writing as many as three letters a day. He feared that marriage would infringe both on his privacy and on his writing, and

(Archive Photos)

for three years the relationship waxed and waned; Kafka's ambivalence denied him the domestic peace he so desperately sought. In 1917, soon after their second engagement, Kafka discovered that he had tuberculosis, and once again he and his fiancée were disengaged. After several years of battling this disease, Kafka succumbed in June of 1924.

Though Kafka's life was marked by suffering, both intimates and casual acquaintances testify to the sweetness of his disposition, to his sympathy for others, to his unfailing humor and quiet courage. Brod's biography takes pains to overcome the impression that his friend's character was morbid; indeed, Kafka had a gift for finding wry humor both in his life and in the most dreadful predicaments of his characters. He had a gift for whimsy as well; Brod relates that once, when Kafka was about twenty years old, he came to visit Brod and inadvertently awakened Brod's father, who was napping on the sofa. "Please look upon me as a dream," murmured Franz as he glided by.

ANALYSIS

The name Franz Kafka conjures up images of a world without a center, of people alienated both from society and from themselves. Kafka lived at the threshold of the modern technological world, and his stories are prophetic of the bewilderment and anxiety that typify modern frustrations and darkest moods: humans increasingly out of touch with their essential nature or, when confronted by totalitarian oppression, out of touch with society. When Eugene O'Neill's hairy ape laments that "I ain't in heaven, and I ain't on oith, but takin' the woist from both woilds," he captured something of the spirit, if not the flavor, of Kafka's tragic vision. For Kafka, humanity has only glimmerings of its formerly blessed state yet desperately attempts to recover it.

With the story *Das Urteil* (1913, 1916; *The Sentence*, 1928; also as *The Judgment*, 1945), Kafka created the kind of fiction that characterizes his maturity, combining the unreality of dream states with images of startling vividness. In this early story, as in *The Trial* and *The Castle*, the protagonist faces a judgment on himself, a fate in which the horrible and

the absurd intertwine. In Kafka's fiction, every interpretation begets an alternative—one that may contradict its predecessor. This is partly a result of narrative technique: In limiting the narrative to the protagonist's point of view, Kafka ensures that the reader will share his character's bewilderment without benefit of an omniscient author. In terms of literary form, Kafka's stories most closely resemble the parable: simple yet enigmatic. His work may be read for its historical and social import as the reflections of a German Jew living in Czech Prague, a city under Austrian influence. Neither Austrian nor Czech but Jewish, he was trebly an outsider. His work may be viewed psychologically, as an anxious son's efforts to deal with an accusing father. (Note that all the novels' protagonists bear the author's initial, *K*.) Finally, his work may be read for its religious content, as Everyman's craving to reconcile the demands of the physical with the yearnings of the spiritual.

Characteristically, Kafka's protagonist is a man going about his normal domestic business when a violent and inexplicable eruption warns him that his life has gone astray. Often he awakens one morning to discover that some incomprehensible change has occurred. In *The Trial*, the protagonist discovers men in his room, mysterious functionaries who announce that he has been arrested on charges they will not explain. In the novella *Metamorphosis*, Gregor Samsa arises, or attempts to do so, only to discover that during the night he has been transformed into a giant dung beetle. No explanation is forthcoming. Is this a judgment on Gregor from above or from within, or is it caused by some force whose will is unknown and unknowable? Is the transformation a necessary but painful path to enlightenment or a punishment? One reads on, hoping for an explanation, a hint of rational purpose in such mysterious happenings; one watches fascinated as others respond to the protagonist's dilemma; one searches for clues in their responses; and one is disarmed at every turn by paradox piled upon paradox, an infinite regression of possibilities that welcome analysis but will never yield to it. Ultimately, the Kafka protagonist perishes or disappears, but whether he is enlightened remains obscure.

AMERIKA

In 1911, Kafka began a novel that Brod later published under the title *Amerika*. The first chapter was released during Kafka's lifetime under the title *Der Heizer* (1913; the stoker), but his journals refer to it as "The Man Who Was Lost Sight Of." The most naturalistic of Kafka's novels, *Amerika* relates the story of an innocent youth, not yet sixteen, who is forced to leave home for an indiscretion: He was seduced by an older woman, who conceived a child. Like most of Kafka's fictional parents, Karl Rossmann's, too, harshly judge their loving son, who, despite their punishment of him, yearns to be reunited with them.

Rossmann's first intimation of what the new Eden of America will be like occurs when he sees the Statue of Liberty, holding aloft not a torch but a sword (justice? wrath? expulsion from Eden?). This is not the America of Emma Lazarus's poem "The New Colossus" (1883) but rather a capitalistic/technological society replete with Mark Twain-like rogues—Robinson and Delemarche—and tycoons *à la* Frank Norris and Theodore Dreiser. At first, Rossmann seems blessed: His uncle Jacob, a politician and an industrialist, discovers him aboard a ship and takes the lad under his wing. Rossmann quickly perceives, however, that this highly industrialized state degrades all those who come in contact with it—workers, rulers, and politicians. Through the familiar device of the picaresque novel, the hero undergoes a series of adventures loosely strung together—adventures among the rich and poor, insiders and outcasts. Rossmann himself is an innocent, hopelessly entangled in a fallen world, and this is the major problem of the work. Unlike the protagonists of the later novels, Rossmann is not part of the world he observes, merely its victim. The reader can pity Rossmann, impressed with Kafka's diagnosis of a world grown increasingly bureaucratic, but one is not astonished and mesmerized, as readers of the later two novels are. The nightmare in *Amerika* is someone else's nightmare, not the reader's. When Rossmann is vilified and loses his job at the Hotel Occidental for his momentary lapse from duty, the reader is too keenly aware of the injustice, too eager to protest on his behalf.

Compare this, for example, to Kafka's novella *Metamorphosis*, in which Gregor is transformed into a giant insect. At first, one shares the protagonist's shock—how could such a thing happen, and what does it mean?—but this is quickly succeeded by a more pressing question: How does Gregor know that he is an insect? Not through his senses, for he does not need to look at himself; rather he seems to have intuited the transformation, perhaps invited it. Whether the metamorphosis is a judgment, an injustice, or a signpost to salvation, Gregor's fate, unlike Rossmann's, is part of his character.

Still, in *Amerika* many of Kafka's familiar themes are developed, however embryonically. The theme of justice is manifest in the opening chapter, when Rossmann unsuccessfully attempts to aid the confused stoker in airing his grievances. As in many scenes that follow, Rossmann will be forced to leave those he cares about without succeeding in accomplishing his aims. His departure from the ship with his uncle Jacob marks the climax of his good fortune. (Indeed, most of Kafka's fiction climaxes in the opening chapter, with the rest of the story exploring the consequences of what proves to be an irreversible judgment.) For ingratitude, Rossmann is promptly disinherited by his uncle, a capitalist/exploiter with overtones of Yahweh (the sort of paradox in which Kafka delighted). The sword that the Statue of Liberty holds aloft adds to the impression that Rossmann is being expelled from his American Eden.

Like the stoker, Rossmann will have difficulties with authority. Soon after departing from his uncle, he is employed at the Hotel Occidental in Rameses—in other words, a symbol of civilization, whether Western or Eastern. Under the patronage of the Manageress, Rossmann does well at his menial job of elevator boy, but one evening he is caught in a minor infraction. As in the case of the stoker, his efforts to obtain justice—his attempt to justify himself, to minimize his error, to benefit from the help of the Manageress—come to naught, and he is dismissed. The author here creates the kind of nightmarish scene that has become known as Kafkaesque, one in which everything that can go wrong does. The accused cannot stand before authority and state with certainty that he is truly innocent, while the officials on whom his fate depends are blasé, bored, indifferent to petitions, sometimes mocking and malicious.

Leaving the hotel in disgrace (he is even suspected by the police, though no charges have been filed against him), Rossmann is forced once more into the company of the scoundrels Delemarche and Robinson, who have taken up with the former singer Brunelda, a gross embodiment of sensuality who enslaves all three in her love nest. Usually in Kafka's works, the artist points the way to transcendence, but this singer has given up her art to satisfy her lusts. In a memorable scene, she presses her huge body against Rossmann, literally pinning him to the balcony railing while they watch a political demonstration on the streets. The scene reveals man given over to the appetites: On the balcony, Brunelda pursues carnality; on the streets, the crowd pursues drunkenness. Though this scene is vividly delineated, it reminds the reader once again of the problem Kafka faces here: What has his protagonist to do with the gross bodily appetites which indeed appall him?

At the beginning of the uncompleted final chapter, Rossmann finds himself at the nature theater of Oklahoma. What the author intended here may be inferred from Brod's report that Kafka wished to end the book on a note of reconciliation. Had Kafka realized these intentions, this work would have been unique in his fiction for its promise of hope and transcendence. The extant fragment, however, suggests that Kafka was deviating from his announced plan. The paradoxes continue: The welcoming angels blowing their horns are not angels, or even good musicians, and they are elevated above common humanity with the aid of ladders which can be seen through their gowns. Rossmann does get a job, but again it is a lowly one, far from a profession. At the novel's end, he is on a train, presumably heading westward—to a promising future or, as the title suggests, simply to vanish?

THE TRIAL

"Someone must have denounced Joseph K., for without having done anything wrong he was arrested one morning." Thus begins Kafka's second novel, *The Trial*. What are the charges? K. never learns, though he encounters several functionaries of the court, attends preliminary hearings, and hires a lawyer to defend him. This might have been the opening of a novel of political repression, but one quickly discovers that the law here, unlike its operation in Arthur Koestler's *Darkness at Noon* (1940), for example, does not represent the state judiciary system but a shadow court, one that is paradoxically both loftier and seedier. When Kafka speaks of the law, he means what the Chinese philosopher Lao-tzu called The Way—that style of living which conduces to right conduct and enlightenment. Kafka's protagonists (and his readers) grope for truth along a path circumscribed by darkness.

Has K. really done nothing "wrong"? He is certainly innocent of civil or criminal wrongdoing. A respected bank official, his conduct has been apparently irreproachable. Yet he is under arrest—a curious form of arrest, in which he is not "prevented from leading [his] ordinary life." Curiously, the "criminal" must not only defend himself but also discover his crime. Critics diverge in their efforts to understand the nature of the charge against him. According to Brod, K. is unable to love; according to another commentator, his mediocrity condemns him. A third argues that his crime lies in his suppression of his guilt. For yet another, K. is one who refuses to act in accordance with his knowledge of good and evil because he lacks the strength for such action. No easy answer emerges. Whether humanity is indeed guilty or is falsely accused by a divinity unable or unwilling to help it comprehend its own essence is never revealed. What is clear is that K. feels guilty even while defending his innocence.

What sort of man is K.? Like most Kafka protagonists, he is a bachelor, uncommitted to others. He dwells in a rooming house, ignoring both his cousin, who lives in town, and his mother, who lodges in the country. His friends are mainly business associates; his lover, a mistress visited once a week. No doubt, Kafka, in his diaries, often expressed contempt for such an existence ("My monotonous, empty, mad bachelor's life"), but is this K.'s crime? If so, he could easily have been informed of that by any number of the officials he encounters. Moreover, K. seems to be living a life similar to that of most of the officials of the court. Can the priest denounce him for bachelorhood? The Examining Magistrate or the painter Titorelli for womanizing? The Magistrates for vanity? Lawyer Huld for placing his profession before his personal life? Rather, Joseph K. is a flawed human being, flawed in some fundamental spiritual way, one who lacks self-confidence. The best clue to understanding his situation is the guilt he only halfway acknowledges. He is told: "Our officials never go hunting for guilt in the populace, but, as the Law decrees, are attracted by guilt, and must then send out us warders." The implication is that K. himself lured the warders to him in the interests of self-realization and self-extermination—the two are synonymous in Kafka's fiction.

Joseph K., respectable, even dignified in the world's eyes, experiences a number of humiliations, each of which will signify the hopelessness of his position. Arrested in his own bedroom by intruders who offer to sell his clothing (they confiscate his underwear), observed by a couple across the courtyard as well as by his landlady and three of his subordinates at the bank, K. finds his privacy, self-respect, and professional competence shredded. K. has indeed awakened to a nightmare.

Yet what authority has this court? It is independent of the civil judiciary system; K. is notified that his first hearing is to be held on a Sunday, in a shabby part of town. In fact, he discovers, he is being tried in an attic; most of the attics in the city, he learns, house divisions of this omnipresent bureaucracy. Very likely, Kafka is suggesting that most people are under indictment.

The hearing is alternately comic and maddening. At the outset, the judge mistakes the chief clerk of a bank for a house painter. Have they arrested the wrong man? Are they incompetent, or are they simply ignorant underlings blindly administering a form of justice they themselves do not comprehend?

K.'s efforts to denounce these outrageous proceedings, however, reveal that he does not grasp the nature or gravity of his situation. However clownish these officials may appear (the Examining Magistrate browses over obscene drawings throughout the hearing), their power should not be underestimated. K.'s speech mocking the court proceedings does not reveal confident self-sufficiency but swaggering ignorance. "I merely wanted to point out . . ." remarked the Examining Magistrate afterward, "that today . . . you have deprived yourself of the advantage an interrogation usually confers on an accused man." Unfortunately, this and all the other bits of information about the court that K. receives, whether valid or invalid (and how is he to distinguish between them?), are equally useless to him.

Of K.'s plight the philosopher Martin Buber remarked that, though men and women have been appointed to this world, they are forever caught in the thick vapors of a mist of absurdity. Is divinity unwilling to reveal itself? Possibly. "The highest court . . . is quite inaccessible to you, to me, and to all of us," K. is told. It is equally possible, though, that it reveals itself every moment but that people either blind themselves or are simply ill-equipped to internalize the message. Near the novel's conclusion, the priest shrieks out to him, "Can't you even see two inches in front of your nose?" K. both can and cannot: Indeed, the tragedy of human relations with divinity is the near-impossibility of communication between them.

K. can never get beyond dealing with underlings; humans lack the spiritual strength and the understanding necessary for their quest. In the often excerpted passage of the doorkeeper of the Law, the priest suggests that the petitioner might have merely stepped through the first door of justice had he the temerity and the wisdom. Presumably, the same applies to K., but all of his efforts to assert himself—to demonstrate that he is innocent or that the Law is in error—come to naught. Even the women from whom he has sought comfort have misled him. He has made many errors, and now, the priest informs him, his guilt is all but proved.

Earlier, K. had met another functionary of the court, the painter Titorelli. The name itself is a pseudonym, an amalgam of the names of famous Italian artists. In reality, he is a hack court painter, as degenerate as another artist, Brunelda, in Kafka's *Amerika*. Efforts that artists once dedicated to the glory of God, during an age of worship, Titorelli now dedicates to cynical aggrandizement of petty officials.

From the painter, K. learns of the three possible directions for his case: definite acquittal, ostensible acquittal, and indefinite postponement. Even this, however, may be merely a joke: Definite acquittals do not occur. "I have never heard of one case," avers the artist. Ostensible acquittal grants provisional freedom, which may last for years or only for an hour, followed by rearrest. Postponement seems to be the tactic another accused man, Mr. Block, has resolved to follow, but such an approach would deny K. an opportunity to face his creator and accuser; it would reduce him to the status of a beggar, more a cringing beast than a man. Are the courts merely playing with people? Possibly: Titorelli's drawing of Justice makes her look "exactly like the Goddess of the Hunt in full cry."

Exactly one year after K.'s arrest, when K. is thirty-one years old (Kafka's age at the time the novel was written), two men come for him. Garbed in black, K. is prepared for his executioners. Somber as this scene is, however, it has comically grotesque elements. "Tenth rate old actors they send for me," he muses. "Perhaps they are tenors." Joseph K. is led through the streets; at times he even does the leading, indicating acceptance of his fate. The final scene is richly textured and enigmatic. His executioners require that he lie down on the ground and intimate that he is to reach for the knife and execute himself. Wordlessly, K. refuses. Is this further evidence of his rebellious nature or his own judgment of the shameful justice rendered by the court? He is stabbed and dies "like a dog, it was as if the shame should survive him." As one critic has asked, whose shame, the man's or the court's? On this ambiguous and troubling note, Kafka's unfinished novel ceases.

THE CASTLE

Sometime in 1922, less than two years before his death, Kafka began his final novel, the longest and most thematically complex of his narratives. In *The Castle*, Kafka's settings grow even sparer than those of his earlier works, reinforcing the parablelike nature of the tale. *The Castle* is the story of K., a land surveyor, who leaves his village to live and work near the castle. Unlike Joseph K., who is summoned to trial, K. seeks out the castle of his own volition: He wishes to be the castle's land surveyor. Unable to enter the castle, he attempts to secure an interview with the Court Official in charge of land surveyors, Klamm (the letter *K* again). Like the petitioner who has come to the Law in *The Trial*, K. finds his way barred. No matter what he attempts, he is no nearer the castle at the novel's end than he was on the first day. His quest wears him out, and though Kafka never concluded this novel, he did make it clear that K. was to die, exhausted by his efforts.

Again, Kafka's enigmatic art has kindled various interpretations. Brod interprets the castle theologically, as the attempt to secure Divine Law and Divine Grace. Others assert that Kafka's novels describe human efforts to overcome limitations as physical beings in order to grapple with the spiritual self in a vain effort to unify the two sides. Another group perceives this novel as a denunciation of the bureaucracy that ruled Kafka's country. All sides can adduce strong arguments—more testimony to the paradoxical and allegorical nature of Kafka's art.

K. is an outsider, an Everyman attempting to find a meaningful life in a world that has lost its spiritual moorings. In doing so, he looks toward the castle, but whether the castle is even occupied, whether it has corporeal existence or is the inward world the narrator yearns to reach, must remain a mystery: At the novel's opening, K. stands "for a long time gazing into the apparent emptiness above him." This emptiness echoes and amplifies the spirit of T. S. Eliot's *The Waste Land* (1922) and Oswald Spengler's *Der Untergang des Abendlandes* (1918, 1923; *The Decline of the West*, 1926-1928). (The never seen owner of the castle is named Count Westwest.)

Like many of Kafka's protagonists, K. is aroused from a deep sleep to face an identity crisis. He claims at the inn where he is staying that he has been summoned by the castle, but a telephone call to the castle brings a hasty denial; then, before K. can be ejected from the inn, another call reverses the first judgment. The issue of K.'s status is further complicated when he observes that the castle "was accepting battle with a smile."

The castle accepts the intruder's invasion but its smile is not easily decipherable. Much suggests that it is mocking. The assistants assigned to him are childish and troublesome, very likely dispatched as spies. The messages he receives are so ambiguous in language, so ill-informed regarding his activities, that he despairs after receiving them, despite the fact that he wants nothing more than to be acknowledged. One official, Bürgel, even informs him that the present moment holds the key to his hopes, implying that if he were to present his petition at once, it would be accepted. Alas, K. has fallen asleep.

As in *The Trial*, the protagonist's efforts to justify himself before officialdom prove fruitless. His superior, Klamm, is perceived by K. through a peephole, but all attempts to speak to him are rebuffed. To K.'s request for an interview comes the reply: "Never. Under no conditions!" Resolutely, K. determines to intercept Klamm at his carriage, but the official will not venture forth. Stalemated, K. feels he "had won a freedom such as hardly anybody else had ever succeeded in winning, as if nobody could . . . drive him away . . . [but] at the same time there was nothing more senseless, nothing more hopeless, than this freedom." K. cannot be driven away, but he will never be recognized.

By means of subplots, mainly involving the family of K.'s messenger, Kafka reinforces his theme that humans are alienated from their society, their inner self, their God. The reader who is familiar with the Aristotelian formula of a protagonist who successfully completes an action will be disarmed by Kafka's novel, in which developments serve only to clarify the impossibility of a successful completion of the goal.

Like Joseph K. of *The Trial*, K. discovers some respite in women. Frieda (peace), the mistress of Klamm, represents domestic pleasure, the highest earth has to offer. Although she agrees to leave Klamm for K., his Faustian spirit is not satisfied. Forsaking the sensual and domestic comforts, K. continually leaves Frieda in pursuit of his goal, transcendence of the merely mundane, while maintaining that he does so in part for her. This paradoxical attitude probably mirrors Kafka's own relationship with Felice Bauer (note the two women's initials). Kafka was torn between committing himself to his fiancé

and freeing himself for his art, an ambivalence reflected in K.'s inconsistent behavior with Frieda. After losing her, K. remarks that though he "would be happy if she were to come back to me . . . I should at once begin to neglect her all over again. This is how it is." Thus we see why K. can never know peace, why he is doomed to wear himself out.

In addition to Frieda, K. is intimate with Olga, Barnabas's sister. Like K., she is desperate to reach the castle to redress a wrong done to her family by one of its officials. Olga's sister, Amalia, has been grossly propositioned by one of the castle officials. Her family has worn itself out, as K. is doing, in a fruitless attempt to justify themselves before the authorities, to gain access to the Law; even the villagers find the authorities inaccessible. From K.'s perspective, the authorities seem impersonal, aloof. In ruling, they are attentive to trivial detail but bureaucratically indifferent to human considerations.

Though Kafka did not complete *The Castle*, his intended ending was communicated to Brod: "Round [K.'s] deathbed the community assembles and from the castle comes this decision: that K. has no claim to live in the castle by right—yet taking certain auxiliary circumstances into account, it is permitted him to live and work there." How ironic! With remarkable prescience, Kafka had sketched his own epitaph. Consider the treatment accorded his memory: Czech authorities placed signs in five languages to mark his grave, yet for more than twenty years they forbid sale of his works.

Stan Sulkes

OTHER MAJOR WORKS

SHORT FICTION: *Betrachtung*, 1913 (*Meditation*, 1948); *Das Urteil*, 1913, 1916 (*The Sentence*, 1928; also as *The Judgment*, 1945); *Die Verwandlung*, 1915 (novella; *The Metamorphosis*, 1936); *Ein Landarzt: Kleine Erzählungen*, 1919 (*The Country Doctor: A Collection of Fourteen Short Stories*, 1945); *Ein Hungerkünstler: Vier Geschichten*, 1924 (*A Hunger Artist*, 1948); *Beim Bau der Chinesischen Mauer: Ungedruckte Erzählungen und Prosa aus dem Nachlass*, 1931 (*The Great Wall of China and Other Pieces*, 1933); *Erzählungen*, 1946 (*The Complete*

Stories, 1971); *The Penal Colony: Stories and Short Pieces*, 1948; *Selected Short Stories*, 1952.

NONFICTION: *The Diaries of Franz Kafka*, 1948-1949; *Tagebücher, 1910-1923*, 1951; *Brief an den Vater*, 1952 (written 1919; *Letter to His Father*, 1954); *Brief an Milena*, 1952 (*Letters to Milena*, 1953); *Briefe, 1902-1924*, 1958; *Briefe an Felice*, 1967 (*Letters to Felice*, 1974); *Briefe an Ottla und die Familie*, 1974 (*Letters to Ottla and the Family*, 1982).

MISCELLANEOUS: *Hochzeitsvorbereitungen auf dem Lande und andere Prosa aus dem Nachlass*, 1953 (*Dearest Father: Stories and Other Writings*, 1954; also known as *Wedding Preparations in the Country, and Other Posthumous Prose Writings*, 1954).

BIBLIOGRAPHY

Bloom, Harold, ed. *Franz Kafka*. New York: Chelsea House, 1986. Essays on Kafka's novels and stories, with an introduction, chronology, and bibliography.

Boa, Elizabeth. *Kafka: Gender, Class, and Race in the Letters and Fictions*. New York: Oxford University Press, 1996. An excellent study. Includes bibliographical references and an index.

Hayman, Ronald. *Kafka: A Biography*. New York: Oxford University Press, 1982. A learned and accessible biography for the general reader, with a chronological table, detailed notes, and extensive bibliography.

Heller, Erich. *Franz Kafka*. New York: Viking, 1974. A short critical study with a biographical note, separate chapters on *The Trial* and *The Castle*, and a bibliography.

Jofen, Jean. *The Jewish Mysticism of Kafka*. New York: Peter Lang, 1987. A detailed, learned examination of Kafka's connections to Jewish writers, including Y. L. Peretz, Martin Buber, Morris Rosenfeld, and other Yiddish authors. Contains notes but no bibliography.

Krauss, Karoline. *Kafka's K. Versus the Castle: The Self and the Other*. New York: Peter Lang, 1996. A good analysis of *The Castle*. Bibliographical references are included.

Robertson, Ritchie. *Kafka: Judaism, Politics, and Literature*. Oxford, England: Oxford University Press, 1987. Explores both the novels and the short fiction, with a concentration on urban themes, guilt, and religion. Includes detailed notes and bibliography.

Speirs, Ronald, and Beatrice Sandberg. *Franz Kafka*. New York: St. Martin's Press, 1997. Chapters on "a writer's life" and on *The Trial* and *The Castle*. Provides detailed notes and extensive bibliography.

Thorlby, Anthony. *Kafka: A Study*. London: Heinemann, 1972. Chapters on the life and the work, on the short stories, on the novels, and on problems of interpretation. With a biographical note and bibliography.

Udoff, Alan, ed. *Kafka and the Contemporary Critical Performance: Centenary Readings*. Bloomington: Indiana University Press, 1987. Divided into sections on "theory" and "praxis." Recommended for advanced students and Kafka scholars. No bibliography.

YASUNARI KAWABATA

Born: Osaka, Japan; June 11, 1899
Died: Zushi, Japan; April 16, 1972

PRINCIPAL LONG FICTION
Izu no odoriko, 1926 (*The Izu Dancer*, 1955)
Asakusa kurenaidan, 1930
Matsugo no me, 1930
Kinjū, 1933 (*Of Birds and Beasts*, in *The House of the Sleeping Beauties and Other Stories*, 1969)
Yukiguni, 1935-1937 (serial), 1947 (book; *Snow Country*, 1956)
Hana no warutsu, 1936
Hokura no nikki, 1940 (*The Mole*, 1955)
Meijin, 1942-1954 (serial), 1954 (book; *The Master of Go*, 1972)
Utsukushii tabi, 1947
Otome no minato, 1948

Sembazuru, 1949-1951 (serial), 1952 (book; *Thousand Cranes*, 1958)

Yama no oto, 1949-1954 (serial), 1954 (book; *The Sound of the Mountain*, 1970)

Asakusa monogatari, 1950

Hi mo tsuki mo, 1953

Saikonsha, 1953

Suigetsu, 1953 (*The Moon on the Water*, 1958)

Kawa no aru shitamachi no hanashi, 1954

Mizuumi, 1954 (serial), 1955 (book; *The Lake*, 1974)

Tokyo no hito, 1955

Nemureru bijo, 1960-1961 (serial), 1961 (book; *The House of the Sleeping Beauties*, in *The House of the Sleeping Beauties and Other Stories*, 1969)

Utsukushisa to kanashimi to, 1961-1963 (serial), 1965 (book; *Beauty and Sadness*, 1975)

Kyoto, 1962 (*The Old Capital*, 1987)

Kataude, 1965 (*One Arm*, 1967)

Shōsetsu nyumon, 1970

Aru hito no sei no naka ni, 1972

Tampopo, 1972

(The Nobel Foundation)

OTHER LITERARY FORMS

In world literature, Japan has the oldest tradition of the novel; there is, however, no significant qualitative distinction between the Japanese "novel" and the "short story." As a result, Yasunari Kawabata may be said to have been a writer of short stories, as well as novels, but the distinction is Western, arbitrary, and based merely on length. Some of the collections of works so designated are *Jōjōka* (1938), *Shiroi mangetsu* (1948), *Maihime* (1951), *Bungei tokuhon Kawabata Yasunari* (1962), *Kōgen* (1969), *Tenohira no shōsetsu* (1969), *Shui yueh* (1971), *Tenjū no ko* (1975), and *Honehiroi* (1975). His first nonfiction work was autobiographical, *Jurūkosai no nikki* (1925; diary of a sixteen-year-old), and he is well known as a literary critic. His essays have been published in *Bungakuteki jijoden* (1934), *Rakka ryusui* (1966), *Bi no sonzai to hakken/The Existence and Discovery of Beauty* (1969; bilingual), *Utsukushii nihon no watakushi/ Japan, the Beautiful, and Myself* (1969; bilingual), *Isso ikka* (1973), and *Nihon no bi no kokoro* (1973).

He also translated into modern Japanese a selection of ancient Japanese stories as *Ocho monogatari shū* (1956-1958) and *Aesop's Fables* as *Isoppu* (1968). His collected works have been published as *Kawabata Yasunari zenshū* (1948-1969).

ACHIEVEMENTS

Yasunari Kawabata has been recognized as one of Japan's major novelists, short-story writers, and critics for more than fifty years. He is the only Japanese author to have received the Nobel Prize in Literature, after having received every major Japanese literary award, including the Bungei Konwa Kai Prize (1937) and the Geijutsuin-sho Prize (1952). He also received the Goethe Medal of Frankfurt, Germany (1959), and the Ordre des Arts et Lettres (1960) and Prix du Meilleur Livre Étranger (1961) of France. In 1954, he was elected to the Japanese Academy of Arts. Early in his career, Kawabata was instrumental in founding the avant-garde neosensualist movement of the 1920's and experimented with cubism, Dadaism, Surrealism, and Futurism. He was also influenced by the stream-of-consciousness techniques of James Joyce and the "automatic writing" of the Surrealists. Later, he abandoned these experiments and reverted to more traditional Japanese forms, developing a style that was unique and difficult to translate. His works are sensitive, delicate, and often difficult for readers without a full understanding of Japanese thought and culture; he is recognized internationally as one of Japan's, and the world's, greatest twentieth century authors.

Biography

Yasunari Kawabata's childhood was dogged by sadness and loneliness. Born the son of a doctor in Osaka, he was only two when his father died and three when his mother died. He went to live with his maternal grandparents but lost his only sibling, a sister, a few years later. When he was only seven, his grandmother died, and he was left virtually alone, at age sixteen, by the death of his grandfather. The latter's death became the subject of *Jurūkosai no nikki*, a reminiscence of his sorrow-filled childhood and the affection he felt for his grandfather. In primary school, Kawabata was first interested in painting, but as he entered puberty, he became more interested in literature, especially the Buddhist writings of the Heian period of the 800's through the 1100's, valuing them more for their fantastic elements than religious teaching.

Kawabata became a secondary school student in Tokyo, where he enthusiastically read Scandinavian literature and became involved in a movement of writers interested in introducing Western artists such as Michelangelo, Leonardo da Vinci, Rembrandt, and Paul Cézanne to Japan. When Kawabata enrolled at Tokyo Imperial University in 1920, he first studied English literature but changed to Japanese literature a year later. He worked on the student literary magazine *Shinshicho* and impressed novelist and playwright Kikuchi Kan with the piece *Shokonsai ikkei* (1921; a scene of the memorial service for the war dead). He became Kikuchi's protégé and was later hired to

work for his literary magazine *Bungei shunju*. In 1924, after graduating with a degree in Japanese literature, he, with Riichi Yokomitsu and others, founded *Bungei jidai*, a literary journal which became the primary organ of the Shinkankakuha movement.

Drawing on avant-garde Western literary movements of the 1920's such as Dadaism, cubism, Surrealism, and Futurism, the Japanese Shinkankakuha movement was also known as the neosensualist, neosensationist, neoperceptionist, or neoimpressionist movement. Though the Japanese literary scene was dominated by realism and Marxism, members of the Shinkankakuha movement were primarily interested in the experiences of the senses. Kawabata himself experimented with a long interior monologue—similar to that of James Joyce's Molly Bloom—in his short story *Suishō gensō* (1934; the crystal fantasy). His main contribution to the movement, other than his writings, was to write the manifesto *Shinshin sakka no shinkeikō kaisetsu* (1925; the new tendency of the avant-garde writers), calling for new perceptions, expression, and style. It also asserts the need for a new language to replace "lifeless, objective narrative" with a more sensual expression of thought and feeling. Much of the manifesto freely uses undefined terms from the literary movements in Europe, and its arguments are largely borrowed from them. His literary reputation grew with the publication of his short novel *The Izu Dancer*, but by the middle of the 1930's, he had largely abandoned his experimental phase and was working in more traditional forms, beginning one of his major works, *Snow Country*, in 1934.

Never deeply interested in politics, Kawabata remained as aloof as possible during World War II. He traveled in Manchukuo and studied classics such as Murasaki Shikibu's *Genji monogatari* (c. 1004; *The Tale of Genji*, 1925-1933), the great traditional novel of the eleventh century, thereby retreating from the chaos of the time. Kawabata explained his detachment from politics in his essay *Bungakuteki jijoden*: "I have become a person who can never hate or grow angry at anyone." After the war, he said he was going to immerse himself in tradition and "write elegies." His most celebrated works, with their elegiac tone, appeared in the years following the war. Although he had published one version of *Snow Country* in 1937, he had never been satisfied with it, and he finished a new version in 1947. In 1949-1951, he published *Thousand Cranes* in serial form. Beginning in 1948, Kawabata became president of the International Association of Poets, Playwrights, Editors, Essayists and Novelists (PEN) of Japan; he also became the mentor of younger Japanese writers, notably Yukio Mishima.

By the mid-1950's, Kawabata's reputation had spread around the world, advanced in America by Edward G. Seidensticker's translations of *Snow Country* and *Thousand Cranes*; *The Izu Dancer* had appeared in abridged form in *The Atlantic Monthly* in 1955. Excerpts of *The Sound of the Mountain* were published in English in *Japan Quarterly* in 1962, the same year in which Kawabata published *Kyoto* (*The Old Capital*, 1987), a novel about the Western corruption of Japan, which is considered by some critics to be his masterwork. He received the major Japanese literary awards, the Bungei Konwa Kai Prize in 1937 and the Geijutsuin-sho Prize in 1952, and was elected to the Japanese Academy of Arts in 1954. In 1957, he organized the twenty-ninth congress of the PEN in Tokyo, and he was elected vice president of that organization in 1959. In that capacity, he later made many trips abroad. In 1960, he visited the United States and conducted seminars at several universities.

In 1968, on the centennial of the Meiji Restoration, Kawabata was awarded the Nobel Prize in Literature. With his usual modesty, he stated he was at a loss to know why he had been selected, crediting his translators and his background in Japanese tradition. He also expressed pleasure that Japanese literature had achieved recognition. Possibly foreshadowing his suicide, he added that for a writer "an honor becomes a burden." He spent his final years quietly with his wife, Hideko, except in 1971, when he emerged to support an unsuccessful conservative candidate for governor of Tokyo. In 1972, he took his own life by asphyxiating himself with gas in his workroom. He had been somewhat ill, though not seriously, and was sleeping poorly, but he left no explanation for the act, and there was much theorizing about the motive, including linking it to the ritual suicide of his student Yukio Mishima in 1970.

ANALYSIS

When announcing the award of the Nobel Prize in Literature to Yasunari Kawabata, Dr. Anders Osterling praised him as a "worshipper of the beautiful and melancholy pictorial language of existence" who had "contributed to spiritual bridge-spanning between East and West." He also praised Kawabata's highly refined prose for "an eminent ability to illuminate erotic episodes, an exquisite sharpness in each observation and a whole net of small secretive values that often overshadow the European techniques of the narrative." In this statement, Osterling summed up the predominant characteristics of Kawabata's fiction, as viewed by Westerners. Kawabata's novels and short stories, despite their reference to subtleties of Japanese culture and other essential Japanese elements, seem to reach across the cultural gap between East and West. As Kawabata himself remarked, Japanese literature, which constitutes an unbroken tradition between the eleventh century and the nineteenth, opened to a torrent of Western influences in the twentieth. The influence of Edgar Allan Poe, Oscar Wilde, and other Decadent writers has often been noted in the works of Jun'ichirō Tanizaki, for example, and the influence of the artistic movements of the early 1920's upon Kawabata is crucial. Therefore, in the works of these and other authors so influenced, a Western reader recognizes familiar structures and motifs which also help make the foreign works seem less alien.

Nevertheless, things that are taken for granted in Japan acquire a gloss of mysteriousness in translation. A "whole net of small secretive values" manifests itself, so that what, at first glance, is very simple prose becomes complex because of the unfamiliar, implicit Japanese cultural assumptions. Kawabata, it must be noted, is mysterious even to Japanese critics—he deliberately maintains an enigmatic aura—but this effect is intensified when the works are transported to the West.

For example, Western criticism of Tanizaki, Kawabata, and Mishima often focuses on their "eroticism" (as in the Nobel Prize citation above), yet much of what is perceived as eroticism derives from the more sexually open traditions of Japan. Kawabata is, therefore, more relaxed in dealing with the erotic, achieving a naturalness in this regard that many Western writers have found elusive. Another example is Kawabata's characteristic air of melancholy. One may point to his lonely childhood, when virtually every member of his family died before Kawabata was sixteen. One might also point to his suicide as a sign of his basic unhappiness, although no convincing reason was ever presented for it. Yet, one must also consider the cultural context. As Gwenn Boardman notes, "sadness is characteristic of much Japanese literature, the *mono-no-aware* or *aware* that is a delicate perception of transience, of sadness, of the implication of the gesture, or of the intersection of silence and time." Others have asserted that melancholy is a pleasurable mood to the Japanese. Such subtle cultural differences obviously deeply affect one's reading of Kawabata. In translation, his eroticism, his *haiku*-like effects, the implications of a simple gesture may be easily misinterpreted. At the same time, this very strangeness is a source of considerable pleasure to the Western reader of Kawabata's fiction.

SNOW COUNTRY

Snow Country, which Kawabata struggled with for some fourteen years, tells of the love of Shimamura, a jaded Tokyo writer, for Komako, a geisha at a mountain resort. Structurally, it is relatively simple. The novel begins as Shimamura is about to begin his second visit, then flashes back to their meeting the previous spring, then returns to the ground situation and progresses to his third visit, in which he takes the geisha's advice and leaves her. It is in Kawabata's suggestive imagery that *Snow Country* transcends the materials of the common love story. In particular, the theme of transience is highlighted in the novel's imagery. Despite Shimamura's desire to make the moment permanent, time passes. There is nothing he can do to slow it down. An image of a coach window early in the novel symbolizes this idea as he sees a girl reflected back to him, but the trees, mountains, and sky continue moving under her transparent face. Though the passage of time, aging, and death are in-

evitable, Shimamura feels his chest rise at the inexpressible beauty, especially when a light shines through the girl's face. Transience thus enhances the preciousness of beauty. Another striking image of impermanence is the scene in which Shimamura observes the death of a bee: "It was a quiet death that came with the change of the seasons." When he watches the bee struggle against the inevitable, he has an insight similar to that which he had at the coach window: "For such a tiny death, the empty . . . room seemed enormous." The imagery invites an existential interpretation: Even with the certain knowledge of death and impermanence, it is humankind's fate to struggle against time.

The distinctly Japanese style of *Snow Country* has caused it to be compared to *renga*, or linked verse. Like all Japanese poetry, *renga* is characterized by its affective depth and its lack of didacticism and philosophical precision. This form derives in part from characteristics of the Japanese language, such as its imagistic, concrete nouns, and in part from the traditions of Shintoism and Buddhism, which led to a poetry concerned with different states of consciousness, marked by a complexity that is tonal rather than thematic. An appreciation of these traits contributes to a greater understanding of the elements of *Snow Country* and other Kawabata novels. Like *renga*, it is a progression of images, integrated more by association than by plot. As Masao Miyoshi describes it, "The 'shape' of the novel is thus not architectural or sculptural, with a totality subsuming the parts, but musical in the sense of a continual movement generated by surprise and juxtaposition, intensification and relaxation, and the use of various rhythms and tempos." This analysis helps explain Kawabata's publication of the novel over a long period of time, in sections in different periodicals, with later substantial emendations; it also accounts for the novel's lack of traditional Western structural unity. Like all of Kawabata's works, *Snow Country* is unified not by plot or action, but by imagery, suggestion, and, to an extent, characterization.

Even the main character, Shimamura, has been described as "insubstantial." The tale is told in the third person, but the narrator seems to imply no moral judgment of Shimamura's behavior toward the women in his life. Miyoshi points out references to the legend of Kengyu and Shokujo, who loved each other so much that God made them stars and placed them at opposite ends of the Milky Way, eternally separated. This imagery is indeed suggestive but does little to explain Kawabata's attitude toward the lovers Shimamura and Komako. Perhaps a clue to Kawabata's stance is to be found in his treatment of nature imagery: When he uses images of the natural world, he does so not to mirror the inner life of the characters but to show that the world is indifferent to their affairs. This stance is curiously reminiscent of the comments made by Alain Robbe-Grillet concerning the New Novel and its need to remove the Romantic imagery that implies that nature "cares" about human beings. This would further explain why a writer as traditional as Kawabata often seems so ultramodern.

THE HOUSE OF THE SLEEPING BEAUTIES

Like Tanizaki's *Diary of a Mad Old Man* (1962), Kawabata's *The House of the Sleeping Beauties* is an exploration of an old man's sexuality. Eguchi, who is impotent, goes to a house where beautiful, drugged young girls sleep naked beside him. During these visits, he tries to understand the meaning of his existence and in drugged reveries remembers various incidents in his life. An atmosphere of doom is strongly evoked in the novel. There are locked doors and a red curtain that seem to conceal secrets. As he approaches the house, he wonders if the sleeping girl will resemble a drowned corpse. As the novel progresses, the weather turns colder, foreshadowing the approach of death, and the last section begins with Eguchi sipping warm tea to fortify himself against the winter cold. On his last visit, the conversation in the house is all about an old man who died while sleeping next to one of the girls. Eguchi sleeps between two girls this time, one symbolically dark, the other fair, but awakens to find the dark girl, whom he had called "Life itself," dead. As the novel ends, he seems paralyzed, chilled by the knowledge of inevitable death. Mishima likened the book to "a submarine in which people are trapped and the air is gradually disappearing. While in the grip of this story, the reader sweats and grows dizzy, and knows with the

greatest immediacy the terror of lust urged on by the approach of death." Particularly notable in this novel is Kawabata's use of color. As a painter, he employed it in all of his works, but the color red and the playing of light against dark stand out. The contrasting of fundamental opposites—ugliness and beauty, age and youth, life and death—is also done with extraordinary skill.

The major themes that reverberate through Kawabata's fiction are especially manifest in *The House of the Sleeping Beauties*. Loneliness, the hopelessness of love, impermanence, old age, death, and guilt all appear in evocative imagery. In keeping with Kawabata's Buddhist ethos, however, no conclusive statements on these themes emerge, except that the physical world consists of irreconcilable forces that humankind is ultimately unable to understand or transcend while in the human body. Kawabata reflects this worldview in a style that persistently hints at his meanings, particularly through visual imagery. He is a writer of suggestion. Arthur Kimball, for example, examines Kawabata's tension of opposing imagery in great detail and states that the persistent accumulation of this tension leads any reader who has identified with Eguchi to the same feeling of chilled numbness that Eguchi feels in the last scene.

Paradox follows paradox. Ugly old men sleep beside beautiful young women who are alive, yet drugged into a deathlike sleep. Though they are real, the girls are like inflatable dolls, toys for lonely men's amusement. One part of Eguchi's character is disgusted by all of this, and he thinks he will not return. Yet, these nights are as sexless—despite their obvious sexual overtones—as any night Eguchi has ever spent. On his second visit, Eguchi is given a girl described as being "more experienced," but what does her "experience" consist of? The old woman in charge makes mocking references to men she can trust. The girl's "prostitution" is apparently sexless. On his third visit, caught between his desire to stay awake to enjoy the beauty of the girl's body and his desire for a "sleep like death," he contemplates evil and thinks of the girl as a Buddha: She is a temptation to evil, yet her "young skin and scent might be forgiveness" for sad old men. In the face of death, however, Eguchi finds no answers. As Kimball remarks, "In his last extremity he stands, a chilly old man asking questions of himself."

THE SOUND OF THE MOUNTAIN

The Sound of the Mountain also uses an aging man, Ogata Shingo, as its protagonist and focuses on his meditations on the meaning of his life. Written in very brief paragraphs, the novel consists of Shingo's thoughts and relates the form of the book to the traditional *haiku* and *renga*. It does not work in the way most novels do. The character of Shingo is subservient to the succession of themes and images, just as the settings (Kamakura, Tokyo, and Shinshu) serve, as Miyoshi observes, as spatial correlatives of Shingo's present and past. The novel is an accumulation of images, many of which center on Kikuko, Shingo's daughter-in-law, who becomes a distant as well as unattainable love, similar to women in several of Kawabata's works. Although Kawabata has been praised for his insights into feminine psychology, Kikuko, like Shingo, is not a fully developed character in the usual novelistic manner. She is part of a succession of images, expressing the transience of all natural phenomena. Without a clear plot line or climax, *The Sound of the Mountain* nevertheless is powerful in evoking Shingo's nostalgia and his inward voyage of regret.

Kawabata's legacy includes some of the finest, most sensitive fiction of the twentieth century. The exact meaning of his characters' gestures is never quite clear, yet they remain strangely evocative. Like the Japanese paintings that he so admired, Kawabata's fiction reveals the shadowy nature of reality and the subjectivity of all human observation. One of the most traditionally Japanese of novelists, he is also one whose works speak with great authority to contemporary concerns.

J. Madison Davis

OTHER MAJOR WORKS

SHORT FICTION: *Shokonsai ikkei*, 1921; *Suishō gensō*, 1934; *Jōjōka*, 1938; *Shiroi mangetsu*, 1948; *Maihime*, 1951; *Bungei tokuhon Kawabata Yasunari*, 1962; *The House of the Sleeping Beauties and Other Stories*, 1969; *Kōgen*, 1969; *Tenohira no shōsetsu*,

1969; *Shui yueh*, 1971; *Honehiroi*, 1975; *Tenjū no ko*, 1975; *Palm-of-the-Hand Stories*, 1988.

NONFICTION: *Jurūkosai no nikki*, 1925; *Shinshin sakka no shinkeikō kaisetsu*, 1925; *Bungakuteki jijoden*, 1934; *Rakka ryusui*, 1966; *Bi no sonzai to hakken/The Existence and Discovery of Beauty*, 1969 (bilingual); *Utsukushii nihon no watakushi/Japan, the Beautiful, and Myself*, 1969 (bilingual); *Isso ikka*, 1973; *Nihon no bi no kokoro*, 1973.

TRANSLATIONS: *Ocho monogatari shū*, 1956-1958 (of ancient Japanese stories); *Isoppu*, 1968 (of Aesop's Fables).

MISCELLANEOUS: *Kawabata Yasunari zenshū*, 1948-1969.

BIBLIOGRAPHY

Gessel, Van C. *Three Modern Novelists: Soseki, Tanizaki, Kawabata*. New York: Kodansha International, 1993. Concentrates on Kawabata's detachment from modernity. Contains excellent biographical background and detailed notes but no bibliography.

Keene, Donald. *Dawn to the West*. New York: Holt, Rinehart and Winston, 1984. Provides excellent biographical and background material on Kawabata and his relationship to Japanese culture.

_____. *Landscapes and Portraits*. Tokyo: Kodansha International, 1971. Contains additional biographical material on Kawabata and discusses his relationship with other Japanese writers.

Napier, Susan J. *The Fantastic in Modern Japanese Literature: The Subversion of Modernity*. New York: Routledge, 1996. See chapter 3, "Woman Lost: The Dead, Damaged, or Absent Female in Postwar Fantasy," and especially the separate discussion of "Sleeping with the Dead: Kawabata's *House of Sleeping Beauties* and *One Arm*."

Peterson, Gwenn Boardman. *The Moon in the Water: Understanding Tanizaki, Kawabata, and Mishima*. Honolulu: University of Hawaii Press, 1979. The section on Kawabata concentrates on "*The Moon on the Water*: Tradition and Myth," "The Bean and the Tea Ceremony: Old Symbols and New Meanings," "The Sounds of Memory: Death and the Lonely Dance," works available in English, and a partial chronology.

Tsuruta, Kinya, and Thomas E. Swann, eds. *Approaches to the Modern Japanese Novel*. Tokyo: Sophia University, 1976. See Makota Ueda's essay, "The Virgin, the Wife, and the Nun: Kawabata's *Snow Country*."

Ueda, Makota. *Modern Japanese Writers and the Nature of Literature*. Stanford, Calif.: Stanford University Press, 1976. Contains a chapter with an excellent overview of Kawabata's career.

NIKOS KAZANTZAKIS

Born: Heraklion, Crete; February 18, 1883
Died: Freiburg, Germany; October 26, 1957

PRINCIPAL LONG FICTION

Toda Raba, 1929 (English translation, 1964)
De tuin der Rosten, 1939 (better known as *Le Jardin des rochers*; *The Rock Garden*, 1963)
Vios kai politeia tou Alexe Zormpa, 1946 (*Zorba the Greek*, 1952)
Ho Kapetan Michales, 1953 (*Freedom or Death*, 1956; also known as *Freedom and Death: A Novel*)
Ho Christos xanastauronetai, 1954 (*The Greek Passion*, 1953; also known as *Christ Recrucified*)
Ho teleutaios peirasmos, 1955 (*The Last Temptation of Christ*, 1960; also known as *The Last Temptation*)
Ho phtochoules tou Theou, 1956 (*Saint Francis*, 1962; also known as *God's Pauper: Saint Francis of Assisi*)
Aderphophades, 1963 (*The Fratricides*, 1964)

OTHER LITERARY FORMS

Long before he began writing the novels for which he won international acclaim, Nikos Kazantzakis had established a reputation in his own country and, to a lesser extent, throughout Europe as a playwright, essayist, translator, and poet. For years, he earned his living by writing about the many countries he visited and translating classics of Western civilization into his native tongue. His travelogues of Russia, Spain, and England combine vivid descriptions of these countries with observations on the political and cultural climate he found there. In addition to his original compositions, he translated a number of important works into modern Greek, among them philosophical writings of Henri Bergson and Friedrich Nietzsche, Jules Verne's novels, Dante's *La divina commedia* (c. 1320; *The Divine Comedy*), and Johann Wolfgang von Goethe's *Faust* (1808, 1833). For fourteen years, he wrote and revised *Odysseia* (1938; known in English as *The Odyssey: A Modern Sequel*, 1958), a thirty-three thousand-line continuation of Homer's *Odyssey* (c. 800 B.C.), showing Odysseus, still driven to wander in search of new experiences, traveling throughout the Mediterranean region and over the world in search of personal fulfillment.

ACHIEVEMENTS

Kazantzakis's achievements as a novelist lie in two areas: his use of native demotic Greek as a medium of fiction and his transformation of philosophical materials into art.

The most revolutionary aspect of Kazantzakis's writing is often lost in translations of his work. Early in his career, he opted to write in demotic Greek, the colloquial language spoken by Greek workers, farmers, and fishermen. This devotion to the language of the common people often caused him to meet with sharp criticism from academics and other purists, who insisted that "acceptable" literature be written in a form of Greek highly stylized and often barely readable by the masses. Though some of his travel-writing and midcareer imaginative literature was written originally in French, Kazantzakis always sided with those in his country who wanted written Greek literature to mirror the living speech of the country. *The Odyssey* and his novels beginning with *Zorba the Greek* are written in the colloquial form of his native language; in fact, *The Odyssey* has been described by Peter Bien as a repository of demotic words and phrases, a kind of gloss on modern spoken Greek. The popularity of his works among the general public in Greece attests the success he has had in achieving his aim.

Another of Kazantzakis's major achievements is his capability to transform philosophy into art. The metaphysics of Nietzsche and Bergson find life in the characters that populate Kazantzakis's fiction, poetry, and drama. While no single work stands out as a masterpiece (though some have made such claims for *Zorba the Greek*), the body of Kazantzakis's work, taken as a whole, represents a remarkable accomplishment. In almost all of his works, he focuses on the plight of people struggling to make sense of a world that is essentially meaningless. Those who continue to struggle rather than accept their fate in life are set apart from the commoners, for whom Kazantzakis has only pity or contempt. These heroes often sweep the reader along with their enthusiasm. Additionally, as Bien has noted, Kazantzakis's novels resemble those of James Joyce, Marcel Proust, Thomas Mann, Joseph Conrad, D. H. Lawrence, and William Faulkner in their fusion of the language of poetry into the medium of prose. In his novels, Kazantzakis unites his own experiences with those of his countrymen and his adopted brothers of the Western world to create fiction that illuminates the mystery of human existence.

BIOGRAPHY

Nikos Kazantzakis once described himself as a follower of Odysseus, and his life bears out his claim. Always a Cretan at heart, he nevertheless spent the better part of his adult years wandering the European continent, traveling to Asia and the Far East, storing up experiences that made their way into the many works that seemed to pour from his pen.

He was born in 1883 in Heraklion, Crete, an island strife-torn for years by a bloody war of independence. His father was a freedom fighter against the Turkish forces that ruled by might over the Greek population; Nikos himself was introduced to the struggle as a young boy when Turkish marauders invaded his village in 1889, threatening the safety and the lives of his immediate family.

At nineteen, Kazantzakis went to Athens to study at the university. Four years later, armed with his de-

gree, he went to Paris to pursue his interest in philosophy. There, he fell under the twin spells of Nietzsche and Bergson, a curious pairing but one that subsequently gave life to all of his writings. When he returned to Greece a year later, he had already become an existentialist, convinced that, though life was meaningless, great people could distinguish themselves by pursuing a meaningful existence in this meaningless world. His dissertation on Nietzsche expresses his concept of "positive nihilism." Kazantzakis saw himself as a prophet who would use his art to educate others regarding the plight of humankind. His first literary attempts were in drama, though while he was writing, he was also working actively as a businessman and minor government official. In 1917, he ran a lignite mine with the real-life Alexis Zorba; for a brief period, he was a member of the Greek government under Prime Minister Venizelos, but when Venizelos fell from power, Kazantzakis, disillusioned, returned to Paris.

The remainder of Kazantzakis's life can be described as one of constant travel. Even during periods when he was settled on the island of Aegina, he was often away, either on the mainland of Greece or in other parts of Europe. He had wed Galatea Alexiou in 1907, but their marriage lasted only a short time. Always fond of women's company, he had for his "companions" a succession of women in the various places he visited during his sojourns. Some of these relationships were merely fleeting liaisons; others developed into lifelong friendships, such as the one he formed in 1924 with Helen Samiou. They eventually were married in 1945.

After World War I, Kazantzakis began a series of journeys to countries throughout Europe and the Middle East, supporting himself by writing for magazines in his native country. At that time an active supporter of Communism, he traveled to Moscow to join other distinguished literary figures at the Soviet Union's tenth anniversary celebration in October, 1927. Though somewhat disappointed at the fate of the Russian Revolution, he nevertheless spent much time in the Soviet Union during the next three years and even considered immigrating there with Helen Samiou. From his experiences there, he produced a book in which he attempted to explain his own theory of "meta-communism."

Early in this same decade, Kazantzakis envisioned a scheme for expressing his personal philosophy in the form of a continuation of Homer's *Odyssey*. Begun in 1924, Kazantzakis's epic was to go through seven major revisions in fourteen years before he reluctantly allowed an edition of three hundred copies to be printed. While he labored over the work, he continued his wanderings and wrote other works as well. He spent a year in Gottesgab, Czechoslovakia, where he wrote his book on Russia and a novel, *Toda Raba*, also based on the Russian experience. He worked on *The Odyssey* there, moved to Paris briefly to attempt to get some of his works published, returned to Crete, then went back to Gottesgab. In 1932, he completed a translation of Dante. The following year he visited Spain, where he gathered materials for his *Ispania* (1937; *Spain*, 1963). At the end of that year, he returned to Greece, to the island of Aegina, to revise once more *The Odyssey*, but was off again in 1935 to visit Japan and China, where his experiences found expression in the novel *The Rock Garden*. The fall of 1936 found him back in Spain, observing and writing about the Spanish Civil War.

Three years later, Kazantzakis was traveling abroad again, this time to England; the outbreak of war marooned him there for several months. In 1940, he returned to Aegina, where he spent the war years writing and translating and quietly supporting the Resistance movement against the German occupation force. Despite his expressed aversion to writing novels, he found himself in 1943 turning to that form to portray another side of the complex creature called man that so fascinated him. What proved to be the first of several prose fictions was also to be his best known: *Zorba the Greek*.

The post-World War II years were far from quiet ones for Kazantzakis. He was given a minor post in the Greek government, and in 1947 he accepted a position as head of the newly created Department of Translation of the Classics for the United Nations. From that time until his death, he was a recurrent nominee for the Nobel Prize, and newfound friends Albert Schweitzer and Thomas Mann urged the trustees of the Nobel fund to select him. Bids for this honor were never successful, but Kazantzakis did not seem to mind. He worked diligently on a number of projects, including novels that raised his stature in international literary circles while bringing criticism and even condemnation in his native land.

The final years of his life were difficult ones for Kazantzakis. He refused to let physical impairment slow him down. Though diagnosed as having leukemia in 1952, he worked undaunted, slowing down only briefly to take treatment in Freiburg, Germany, on occasion. Finally, while visiting the Far East, he became ill from a bad vaccination and was forced to return to the clinic in Freiburg, where he died on October 26, 1957.

ANALYSIS

The reader interested in understanding any of the works of Nikos Kazantzakis would do well to begin by reading *Salvatores Dei: Asketike* (1927; *The Saviors of God*, 1960). In that short philosophical expostulation that Kazantzakis called his "Spiritual Exercises," he expressed succinctly his strange mixture of Nietzschean nihilism and Bergsonian optimism. For Kazantzakis, God is not dead, as Nietzsche proclaimed; rather, He is waiting to be created by people who think they need Him. The search for God becomes one of the ways that existential people seek to create meaning for their lives. Hence, Kazantzakis's heroes are often dramatizations of existential people trying to face up to the fact that God, as He has been traditionally conceived, does not exist. Rather than being overwhelmed by such knowledge, however, the hero simply posits the existence of God—one created more in his own image than in the traditional Judeo-Christian image. For example, in *The Odyssey*, Kazantzakis's Odysseus carves a harsh-looking mask that serves as the image of God, which the people who follow Odysseus revere. Odysseus, of course, knows who created the image, and he lives with the knowledge that this "god" is merely representative of his own imagination; yet he acts as if God is real, and this God is both friend and antagonist to the hero as he struggles to assert his identity and stake his claim to fame.

The actions of Odysseus in Kazantzakis's *The Odyssey* are repeated in a variety of ways by the heroes of his novels and plays. Indeed, the heavy emphasis on philosophy, and especially metaphysics, is often cause for artistic heavy-handedness in terms of plot and narration: The story is sometimes lost in the symbology, to the point where the reader not familiar with the whole of Kazantzakis's work, and especially with his nonfiction, may come away confused about the author's use of the techniques of realism to explore highly abstract philosophical issues. Indeed, his early works are often thinly disguised attempts to cloak philosophical discussion in the garb of imaginative literature.

ZORBA THE GREEK

What is surprising is that Kazantzakis's most famous novel, *Zorba the Greek*, represents an apparent reversal of the author's position that people must abandon pleasures of the flesh to achieve spiritual self-fulfillment. In this novel, the reader is forced to recognize the attractiveness of the hero Alexis Zorba, whose whole life is devoted to sensual gratification. Zorba is anti-intellectual and antireligious, having thrown off the shackles of paralyzing intellectualism that have bound the narrator, the Boss, within himself and caused him to be ineffectual in dealing with others except as "intelligences." The Boss is the consummate ascetic, a follower of Buddha who renounces the pleasures of the flesh because he believes that closeness to others only leads to pain. Zorba, on the other hand, is the epitome of Bergsonian *élan vital*. The Boss withdraws from commitment; Zorba seeks it.

The mining venture in which the two men engage is Kazantzakis's way of representing symbolically the vast differences between them and hence between the lifestyles they represent. Mining, the act of taking from the earth the materials one needs to survive, is hard work, but Zorba relishes it, getting dirty along with his fellow workers, taking chances with them, even risking his life when necessary; the Boss's involvement is that of the dilettante who occasionally pokes his nose in to see how things are going but who actually remains aloof from the work itself. Their different approaches to the mining operation character-

ize their approaches to other forms of involvement as well: Zorba is a great womanizer because he believes that only through such lovemaking can man be fulfilled (and besides, he tells the Boss, all women want a man to love them); the Boss is paralyzed by contact with women. The Boss's affection for books is paralleled by Zorba's penchant for dancing, playing the *santiri*, and womanizing; where one learns of life secondhand through the writings of others, the other experiences it fully and directly.

Zorba's power to act, even in the face of overwhelming odds and with the knowledge that his actions will be of little real value, marks him as the kind of hero whom Kazantzakis admires. Failure does not deter him from action. When his elaborate scheme to bring down timber from the top of the mountain collapses (literally as well as figuratively), he shrugs off the experience and goes on to another venture. The death of the old whore Hortense, whom Zorba has promised to marry, disturbs him only momentarily: Death is the way of the world, and Zorba understands it. By the end of the novel, the Boss, too, has come to understand the inevitability of death and the need to live vigorously in the face of that knowledge. When he receives word that his good friend Stavridakis is dead, he accepts the information stoically; when he learns that Zorba, too, has died, he chooses not to mourn but instead to turn his own talent for writing to good use by composing the story of his experiences with Zorba.

In the novels following *Zorba the Greek*, Kazantzakis moves from studying the contrast of opposing lifestyles to concentrating on the figure of the hero himself. *Freedom or Death*, based on the Cretan revolt of the 1880's, focuses on Captain Mihalis, who is torn between self-satisfaction and service to country. Kazantzakis was always fascinated by the heroes of history and literature; often his novels and plays are attempts to retell the stories of heroes whom he has met in other works, to reinterpret their struggles in the light of his own theory of positive nihilism. It is not surprising, then, to find that he chooses for his subjects Odysseus, Faust, Christopher Columbus, Saint Francis, and even Jesus Christ.

The Christ story held a special fascination for

Kazantzakis. In the early 1950's, he recast the account of Christ's Passion in a contemporary setting in *Christ Recrucified*, a novel in which the hero, a Greek peasant named Manolios, is invested with Christlike characteristics. That particular rendition apparently did not satisfy him, however, for in 1955, he returned to the subject and this time confronted the hero in his own milieu. The result is a novel that surely ranks as Kazantzakis's most controversial, *The Last Temptation of Christ*.

THE LAST TEMPTATION OF CHRIST

In *The Last Temptation of Christ*, Kazantzakis deals with the Gospel accounts directly, combining elements of mysticism with an extremely realistic treatment of the biblical characters to turn the Christ story upside down. The actors in the Gospel are humanized to a degree considered by some to be blasphemous; all are given human motives, not all of which are the highest, and the familiar characters of the Evangelists' accounts—Peter, Christ's mother Mary, Mary Magdalene, and especially Judas—are presented in a new light. The major episodes of the novel are based on biblical accounts, but these take on the particular philosophical cast that characterizes all of Kazantzakis's work: In the novel, each temptation that Jesus encounters is presented as a struggle in which the hero must choose between "flesh" and "spirit," between acquiescence to the tendencies to rest from the futile pursuit of human perfection and the drive toward self-fulfillment.

The plot of *The Last Temptation of Christ* loosely follows the Gospel stories. Structurally, the action is centered on a series of temptations, most of them drawn from the Gospels. The last temptation, which Jesus undergoes as he hangs on the cross, is the ultimate test of his commitment to "spirit" over "flesh": For an instant, he imagines himself rescued from his fate, given the opportunity to live as other men, with a wife and children, and only through a heroic act of will does he overcome the temptation and accept his own death as part of his fate as Savior. The women in the novel, even Christ's mother, become temptations of the flesh. Mary wants her son first to disassociate himself from the Romans and later to give up the messianic folly that seems to be leading only to con-

frontation with the foreign powers; she constantly yearns for him to settle down to carpentry and fatherhood. When Jesus' special nature is reported to her, she says "I don't want my son to be a saint. . . . I want him to be a man like all the rest. I want him to marry and give me grandchildren. That is God's way."

Kazantzakis also expands the meaning of and challenges the accepted responses to the parables of the Gospels. For example, in recounting the story of the wise and foolish virgins, he remains close to his source until the end of the story. In Saint Matthew's account, the foolish virgins, who were out buying oil when the bridegroom arrived, returned saying, "Lord, Lord, open to us," to which the bridegroom replies, "Verily I say unto you, I know you not." Jesus then provides a moral for the tale: "Watch, therefore, for ye know neither the day nor the hour wherein the Son of Man cometh" (Matthew 25:11-13). In Kazantzakis's version, Jesus tells essentially the same story, up to the point at which the virgins return and beg entrance, dramatizing the plea of the maidens: "'Open the door! Open the door! Open the door!' and then . . . Jesus stopped. . . . He smiled. 'And then?' said Nathanael . . . 'And then, Rabbi? What was the outcome?'" Kazantzakis's Jesus provides no "moral." Instead, he asks his disciples to supply the answer. "'What would you have done, Nathanael?' Jesus asked, pinning his large, bewitching eyes on him, 'What would you have done if you had been the bridegroom?'" Jesus repeats the question, persisting in his stare, until Nathanael finally says, "I would have opened the door." Jesus replies, "Congratulations, friend Nathanael. . . . This moment, though you are alive you enter Paradise. The bridegroom did exactly as you said." Jesus is immediately challenged by the village chief, who screeches out, "You're going contrary to the Law, Son of Mary." Jesus answers him, "The Law goes contrary to my heart." For the reader who knows the source of the story in Matthew, this scene functions in a manner similar to the original Gospel accounts, but with an ironic twist: Now it is the traditional Gospels themselves that represent the "Old Law," which Kazantzakis's hero comes to challenge with a new gospel, founded even more firmly on human interaction and human sympathy than the message of Jesus as recorded by the Evangelists. In this approach, Kazantzakis is at his most daring theologically, and the captivating power of his art has prepared the reader to side with his hero and accept the new message of salvation: People must help people if anyone is to attain paradise.

Nowhere is God's need of humanity made more apparent than in Kazantzakis's portrayal of Judas Iscariot. Where the Evangelists have portrayed Judas as a weak, self-serving coward whose disillusionment with the Messiah led him to commit the crime of betrayal, Kazantzakis depicts Judas as a strong-willed zealot, filled first with the hope that Jesus will establish a political kingdom, then infused with faith that through the Crucifixion and Resurrection, God will accomplish His messianic role. Kazantzakis's Judas is the strongest of the Apostles and the only one to whom Jesus directly reveals the way that salvation will be accomplished. Shortly before Christ's confrontation with the Sanhedrin and Pontius Pilate, he takes Judas aside and tells him, "I am the one who is going to die." When Judas appears confused and sees his dream of political rebellion slipping away, Jesus tells him "Take courage. . . . There is no other way; this is the road." To Judas, Jesus reveals the mystery of the Resurrection, because Judas is to play a key role in bringing it about. What Kazantzakis has seen in the Gospel story is a point that reinforces his own belief that God needs humanity: In order for Christ to be crucified and resurrected, he must first be betrayed. The betrayer, therefore, plays an all-important role in bringing about salvation, a role as important as that of the Messiah Himself. At first reading, such a reversal of character seems heretical, and in fact, Kazantzakis was seriously criticized by the Greek Orthodox bishops, who contemplated excommunicating him.

If one is able to approach this novel without prejudice, though, the author's achievements in characterization and exploration of theme will appear most remarkable. Kazantzakis's beliefs about the natures of humanity and of God are made most evident in the struggle of his hero, who *is* both God and man. His Christ is an unwilling savior. Presented first in a fantastical dream in which he sees himself pursued by a "tempter," Jesus is no heroic Messiah but rather a poor carpenter whose "mission" haunts him and prevents him from indulging in the pleasures of the flesh. One of his first acts is to build a cross upon which the Romans crucify a Zealot, a member of the radical Jewish group working to overthrow Roman rule. At this crucifixion, Jesus is reviled by the crowd for assisting the occupation forces in their dirty work; even his mother is disturbed by his participation and wants to rescue him from his association with the Romans. On the other hand, Kazantzakis's view of God as pure spirit is expressed by Jesus himself in his encounter with the woman at the well. "Where is God found? Enlighten me," she says; Jesus replies, "God is spirit." Jesus' own ambivalence is highlighted in this scene, as the woman continues to question him: "'Can you be the One we're waiting for?' . . . Jesus leaned his head against his breast. He seemed to be listening to his heart, as though he expected it to give him the answer." The ambivalence of the Savior toward his own mission is made evident in other places as well.

For half the novel, Christ is a man pursued by a demon, a man whose every waking moment is a struggle between the flesh and the spirit. The drama of this pursuit is heightened for the reader by the constant confusion of the demon in Christ's mind with both God and the Devil; God and Christ seem to be at war with each other. He runs away from his home to escape the Tempter, only to find himself followed and harassed wherever he goes. He seeks refuge in a monastery but is recognized by the dying abbot as the Savior and is thrust forward as the new abbot, a position he does not want. Always attracted by the prostitute Mary Magdalene, he seeks comfort at her home, but instead of losing himself in sensual gratification, he ends up leaving her, too, after engaging her in a discussion of his mission. Though others, notably the Apostles, flock to him because they recognize something in this young carpenter, Jesus himself only reluctantly accepts his role as Savior and even then is not free from the temptations of the world. Throughout his life, even when on the cross, the lures of "the flesh" are present to divert him from his redemptive mission.

The hero of *The Last Temptation of Christ* is both God and man, but throughout the novel, Kazantzakis emphasizes Jesus' humanity, often at the expense of the reader's preconceived concept of Christ's divine nature. Jesus feels the temptations of both the flesh and the intellect as fully as any character in a novel by Fyodor Dostoevski or D. H. Lawrence. He wrestles with a strong animal attraction for Mary Magdalene, desiring her body as much as he desires to save her soul. He runs from his mission as Savior because he recognizes the pain it will cause him; he wants to be like other men. In the end, however, he accepts his mission, gives in to God, and fulfills himself; spirit has won over flesh, and humankind is redeemed through the act of the hero. This is the ultimate message that Kazantzakis has for the reader in all of his novels.

Laurence W. Mazzeno

OTHER MAJOR WORKS

PLAYS: *Melissa*, pr. 1939; *Kouros*, pr. 1955; *Christophoros Kolomvos*, pr. 1956; *Three Plays: Melissa, Kouros, Christopher Columbus*, pb. 1969.

POETRY: *Odysseia*, 1938 (*The Odyssey: A Modern Sequel*, 1958); *Iliad*, 1955 (modern version; with Ioannis Kakridis); *Odysseia*, 1965 (modern version; with Kakridis).

NONFICTION: *Salvatores Dei: Asketike*, 1927 (*The Saviors of God: Spiritual Exercises*, 1960); *Ho Morias*, serial, book 1961 (*Journey to the Morea*, 1965); *Ispania*, 1937 (*Spain*, 1963); *Iaponia-Kina*, 1938 (*Japan/China*, 1963); *Anghlia*, 1941 (*England*, 1965); *Anaphora ston Greko: Mythistorema*, 1961 (autobiography; *Report to Greco*, 1965).

BIBLIOGRAPHY

Bien, Peter. *Nikos Kazantzakis.* New York: Columbia University Press, 1972. A reliable scholarly introduction to Kazantzakis's life and work, with a useful bibliography.

_____. *Nikos Kazantzakis, Novelist.* Bristol, England: Bristol Classical Press, 1989. A good study of the Greek author. Contains a bibliography.

Dombrowski, Daniel A. *Kazantzakis and God.* Albany: State University of New York Press, 1997. Chapters on the Bergsonian background, transubstantiation, eating and spiritual exercise, the new Middle Ages, theism, mysticism, method and purpose, and panexperientialism and death. Dombrowski also has an appendix on Friedrich Nietzsche's place in Kazantzakis's thought. Includes notes, bibliography, and an index of names.

Kazantzakis, Helen. *Nikos Kazantzakis: A Biography Based on His Letters.* New York: Simon and Schuster, 1968. A valuable collection of letters and photographs arranged chronologically. The letters are only lightly annotated and should be read in conjunction with Lea.

Kazantzakis, Nikos. *The Suffering God: Selected Letters to Galatea and to Papastephanou.* Edited by Katerina Anghelaki Rooke. New Rochelle, N.Y.: Caratzas Brothers, 1979. In addition to valuable biographical material, the introduction provides a reliable guide to the author's life and work. Includes useful annotations to the letters.

Lea, James F. *Kazantzakis: The Politics of Salvation.* University: University of Alabama Press, 1979. Chapter 1 presents an overview of the writer's career; chapter 2 closely examines his use of language. Chapter 3 studies his poetry, prophetic style, and political philosophy, and chapter 4 discusses his search for order in chaos. Chapter 5 concludes with his vision of freedom and hope. With detailed notes and bibliography.

Middleton, Darren J. N., and Peter Bien, eds. *God's Struggler: Religion in the Writings of Nikos Kazantzakis.* Macon, Ga.: Mercer University Press, 1996. Essays explore Kazantzakis's theme of religion in his works. Includes bibliographical references and an index.

WILLIAM MELVIN KELLEY

Born: Bronx, New York; November 1, 1937

PRINCIPAL LONG FICTION

A Different Drummer, 1962

A Drop of Patience, 1965

dem, 1967
Dunfords Travels Everywheres, 1970

OTHER LITERARY FORMS

In addition to his novels, for which he is primarily known, William Melvin Kelley is the author of a collection of short stories, *Dancers on the Shore* (1964). Some of these stories were written before his first novel, and almost all introduce characters, themes, and ideas which appear in later works. A 1997 *New Yorker* story, "Carlyle Tries Polygamy: How Many Are Too Many?," reveals that, despite almost thirty years of nearly complete fiction-publication silence, Kelley maintained interest in creatively pursuing some of the personages and ideas that appeared earlier in his short and long fiction. Anthologized selections of his fiction mostly appeared in late 1960's and 1970's anthologies of African American writers. He has been a nonfiction and fiction contributor to periodicals such as *Accent, Canto, Esquire, Jazz and Pop, Mademoiselle, Negro Digest, The New Yorker, The New York Times Magazine, The Partisan Review, Playboy, Quilt, River Styx, Urbanite*, and *Works in Progress*.

ACHIEVEMENTS

Kelley received several awards in the years in which he was actively publishing: the Dana Reed Prize from Harvard University, a Bread Loaf Scholar residency, the John Hay Whitney Foundation Award, the Rosenthal Foundation Award, the Transatlantic Review Award, and a fiction award from the Black Academy of Arts and Letters. These awards confirmed early recognition of Kelley's talent but have little to do with his enduring prominence as the creator of *A Different Drummer*, his first and most accomplished work, which brought him the accolades of such writers as Archibald MacLeish, Thomas Merton, and Frank Tuohy. As important in its own way as Ralph Ellison's *Invisible Man* (1952), James Baldwin's *Go Tell It on the Mountain* (1953), and William Demby's *Beetlecreek* (1950), *A Different Drummer* broke new ground within the confines of the subject of race in America. Visionary, grounded in myth and American history, it still confounds readers as they try to categorize and label this enduring novel of the

(Library of Congress)

civil rights era. Indeed, all Kelley's novels invite readers to consider the simple difference that race makes in America, as well as the complexity of the individual's dilemma and response in respect to this and other aspects of the human condition.

BIOGRAPHY

William Melvin Kelley is the only child of William Melvin Kelley, Sr., and Narcissa Agatha (Garcia) Kelley. His father was a journalist and an editor, for a time, at the *Amsterdam News*. When William was young, the family lived in an Italian American neighborhood in the North Bronx, but later his parents sent him to the Fieldston School, a small, predominantly white, preparatory school in New York, where he became captain of the track team and president of the student council. In 1957, the year of his mother's death, Kelley entered Harvard, intending to study law. By the following year, however, the year of his father's death, he was studying fiction writing with author John Hawkes, and later, Archibald Mac-Leish. For the rest of his career (which he left unfinished) at Harvard, no other academic subject was relevant to him. Consumed by writing, he said, "I hope only to write fiction until I die, exploring until there is no longer anything to explore . . . [about] the plight of Negroes as individual human beings in America."

In 1962, after the publication of his first novel, Kelley married Karen Isabelle Gibson, a designer, and worked as a writer, photographer, and teacher in New York, France, and the West Indies. He is the father of two children, Jessica and Ciratikaiji. Though he continued to work on a book entitled *Days of Our Lives* and occasionally appear in print and in public life, Kelley, in large part, would maintain a quiet life.

ANALYSIS

Critics often fix on the interrelatedness of Kelley's four novels (and his short stories), and, indeed, though each novel is different in style, setting, characters, and even language, the ideas that spawned them are related and grow from each other. Critic Jill Weyant sees Kelley's work as a saga, in that the "purpose of writing a serious saga . . . is to depict impressionistically a large, crowded portrait, each individual novel presenting enlarged details of the whole, each complete in itself, yet evoking a more universal picture than is possible in a single volume." Kelley admits to the possible influence of other great writers of sagas, telling Roy Newquist in an interview, "Perhaps I'm trying to follow the Faulknerian pattern—although I guess it's really Balzacian when you connect everything. I'd like to be eighty years old and look up at the shelf and see that all of my books are really one big book."

A DIFFERENT DRUMMER

A Different Drummer is Kelley's first and finest work, an enduring classic of African American literature. Kelley took his literary inspiration from American writer Henry David Thoreau's resounding celebration of individuality: "If a man does not keep pace with his companions, perhaps it is because he hears a different drummer. Let him step to the music which

he hears, however measured or far away." Kelley then adapted this idea to the plight of African Americans in a fictional narrative built on a foundation of mythic imagination, American history all the way back to the slave trade, and the racial strife of the 1960's. The black experience of being perceived as different, as a despised people with trenchantly stereotyped racial characteristics, has been anything but positive. It is here, on this ground, that Kelley develops his narrative from two basic questions rooted deeply in the history of American race relations: What would whites do without the black people they so abuse and denigrate, but to whom they are so tied? Also, who might white people be without the prison of their own prejudice?

The novel takes place in the small town of Sutton, in a nameless, imaginary southern state, in June, 1957, when, mysteriously for the white citizens, "all the state's Negro inhabitants departed." The exodus is unconsciously led by the child-sized Tucker Caliban, who, like Rosa Parks (a black woman who refused to relinquish her bus seat to a white man in 1955), simply decided one day that he could no longer comply with the way things had always been in the South. The course of history, or at least his own family history, had to be changed. For four generations the Calibans were defined and limited by their service to the Willsons, and Tucker knows that he cannot reach his full human potential living in the template of the southern racial past. Thus he salts his land, kills his farm animals, axes the grandfather clock which symbolizes all the years of his family's servitude, sets fire to his house, and walks off into the sunset with his pregnant wife and his child. This peaceful, though revolutionary, act of individual initiative and vision is a direct outgrowth of and complement to the rebellion and flight of the massive legendary African whose story begins the novel. This African prince, Tucker's great-grandfather, refused to be enslaved, and it is perhaps his spirit that propels Tucker's quiet self-reliance generations later. Ironically, it is old white Mr. Harper who keeps the memory of the African alive for the white men of Sutton, telling the story on the porch of Thomason's store as often as anyone will listen.

Kelley mixes his multiple points of view between first- and third-person narration, using flashbacks to take his readers inside the heads of the southern whites, not the blacks, who occupy the small southern town of Sutton. The whites that interest Kelley are of two classes. Harry Leland and his young son, Mister Leland, represent the poor-white southerners who wish to break with the past, who wish to know black people as individuals and not as a subjugated mass. The Willsons represent the southern aristocracy, bound by the past and the money they made from slavery, but who are also educated and morally conflicted.

Tucker's opposite, a Harvard-educated black religious leader who comes down from the North to investigate the inspiration behind the exodus, becomes the novel's sacrificial lamb. The ultimately self-seeking Reverend Bennett Bradshaw is superfluous in Sutton; the people have led themselves out of their legacy of bondage and have no need of he who is not one of their own. He becomes flotsam of the most violent of southern white rituals, ironically taking up the cross that the people have left behind.

A Different Drummer is, indeed, as critic David Bradley writes, an "elegant" little book, masterful in its balance of scenes of stunning moment, delivered in the language and points of view of the people most in need of understanding them. Within its covers there is much to understand about the nature of freedom as an individual conviction that must be realized; all social change begins with a human being's belief in his or her own equality, and no lasting social change can happen without it.

A DROP OF PATIENCE

With *A Drop of Patience*, Kelley returns to the South, to uncover the life of a blind black boy, Ludlow Washington, who is deposited in an institution and left to exist among the faceless masses that society, and particularly a segregated society, builds institutions to hide. Ludlow cannot walk away from his circumstances, like Tucker Caliban, because he is a child, and blind, so he must transcend in another way. He finds his means of self-expression and his route to finding a place in southern black society in his musical instrument, which is never identified but is clearly

some sort of horn with several keys. Extremely talented, Ludlow is released to a black bandleader, who takes him to the small southern city of New Marsails, to play with his group in a local bar. Ludlow is better than the other members of the band, however, and he has to hold his creative compulsion for avant-garde improvisation in check until he is old enough to be free of his contract, which is essentially indenture. Eventually he leaves the South and migrates to the North, becoming a leading jazz musician with his own band and enjoying relative freedom.

Though this is the framework for "one of the finest novels ever written about a jazz musician," according to critic Stanley Crouch, *A Drop of Patience* is not so much a novel about a musician as it is a novel about a blind boy coming to sexual maturity, and a black man who literally cannot see color (and is therefore able to override its coded constraints to discover deeper qualities in people) but who must come to social maturity in a superficial and pervasively race-bound society. It is a society that can drive a sane person mad, and it does this to Ludlow, who must, at bottom, be able to trust his own senses. At novel's end Ludlow chooses a course that will allow him to be a musician and to be a man among people who can see him.

DEM

If *A Drop of Patience* is an enlarged detail of the people who left the imaginary southern state in *A Different Drummer*, then *dem* is an enlarged detail of the people who are incapable of seeing Ludlow Washington as a human being beyond his racial categorization. *dem* is the black perspective on American society's "us" and "them" dichotomy, and it makes sense that this novel is both a satire and a comedy. Satire typically employs sarcasm and irony to expose human folly or vice, and not only does comedic writing provide an absurd vehicle (lighthearted treatment) to transport an absurd commodity (pervasive race prejudice), but also it provides the opportunity to temporarily "solve" this immense social problem with justice and laughter. In short, it provides catharsis.

Mitchell Pierce and his wife, Tam, are upper-middle-class white New Yorkers who are frank stereotypes. They are shallow, insular, cold, like mannequins or robots—devoid of the redeeming, individual, distinguishing features that human beings possess. Murder cannot move them, and love, to them, is a plot gleaned from soap operas. Tam gets pregnant by both her husband and her maid's black boyfriend and gives birth to twins, one white and one black. The rest of the novel is about Mitchell's ludicrous hunt through Harlem for the father of the black twin, whom he does not recognize when he sees him. For Mitchell, black people are simply a faceless race meant to serve him, and it never occurs to him that the money in his pocket cannot buy them.

DUNFORDS TRAVELS EVERYWHERES

Often dismissed by critics as "experimental," there is no doubt that *Dunfords Travels Everywheres* is a difficult book to read, but its inspiration is, after all, James Joyce's *Finnegans Wake* (1939). Critic Michael Wood notes that like Joyce, Kelley "as a black American and a writer, is caught in the language and culture of an enemy country," and Kelley's two protagonists in this novel, Chig Dunford and Carlyle Bedlow, might be understood to be acting this out. The hallucinatory dream sequences, which connect the separate adventures of these two characters, are their common ground, their realm of unconscious constructions of language with African retentions, characterized by black idiomatic expressions and dialect, phonetic sounds and spellings, puns and exuberant word plays. The Harvard-educated Chig Dunford, hanging out in an imaginary country in Europe with what amounts to imaginary white friends, blurts out two words that are revelatory. He changes his course and finds himself making a surreal transatlantic journey to America, which is, perhaps, his own "Middle Passage" to a destination of self-realization. By journey's end, he has encountered the Harriet of Ludlow Washington's healing in *A Drop of Patience* as well as his Harlem counterpart, Carlyle Bedlow, who figures prominently in *dem* and in some of Kelley's short fiction. Further, it might be argued that Chig's voyage to Harlem, to a place where he can be known, is an updated version of Tucker Caliban's journey away from "dem people's" race-based expectations of him.

Cynthia Packard Hill

OTHER MAJOR WORK

SHORT FICTION: *Dancers on the Shore*, 1964.

BIBLIOGRAPHY

Babb, Valerie M. "William Melvin Kelley." In *Afro-American Fiction Writers After 1955*. Vol. 33 in *Dictionary of Literary Biography*, edited by Thadious M. Davis. Detroit: Gale Research, 1984. In the absence of book-length secondary sources, this is a good start to learning about Kelley. The bibliography includes critical essays and an interview.

Bradley, David. Foreword to *A Different Drummer*. New York: Doubleday, 1989. A carefully researched essay that considers Kelley's first novel in the context of its time and in relation to American William Faulkner's novels, particularly *The Reivers* (1962).

Early, Gerald. Introduction to *A Drop of Patience*. Hopewell, N.J.: Ecco Press, 1996. With a short overview of the black writers of the 1950's and a brief introduction to the Black Arts movement, Early positions Kelley's "jazz novel" on the cusp, between the two eras and of neither.

Karrer, Wolfgang. "Romance as Epistemological Design: William Melvin Kelley's *A Different Drummer*." In *The Afro-American Novel Since 1960*, edited by Peter Bruck and Wolfgang Karrer. Amsterdam: Gainer, 1982. Karrer considers Kelley's novel of exodus as romantic rather than realistic and positions it among other romances by African American writers.

Ro, Sigmund. *Rage and Celebration: Essays on Contemporary Afro-American Writing*. Atlantic Highlands, N.J.: Humanities Press, 1984. Discusses African American literature, focusing on Kelley, John Alfred Williams, and James Baldwin.

Weyant, Jill. "The Kelley Saga: Violence in America." *College Language Association Journal* 19, no. 2 (December, 1975): 210-220. Weyant proposes that Kelley's fiction may be the first saga written by a black American; she examines his work in the light of what she sees as his attempt to redefine the "Complete Man."

YASHAR KEMAL
Yaşar Kemal Gökçeli

Born: Adana, Turkey; 1923

PRINCIPAL LONG FICTION

İnce Memed, 1955 (*Memed, My Hawk*, 1961)

Teneke, 1955 (novella)

Ortadirek, 1960 (*The Wind from the Plain*, 1963)

Yer demir, gök bakır, 1963 (*Iron Earth, Copper Sky*, 1974)

Ölmez otu, 1968 (*The Undying Grass*, 1977)

İnce Memed II, 1969 (*They Burn the Thistles*, 1973)

Ağrıdağsı efsanesi, 1970 (*The Legend of Ararat*, 1975)

Binboğalar efsanesi, 1971 (*The Legend of the Thousand Bulls*, 1976)

Çakırcalı efe, 1972

Demirciler çarşısı cinayeti, 1973 (*Murder in the Ironsmith's Market*, 1979)

Yusufouk Yusuf, 1975 (this novel and the previous one are collectively known as *Akçasazin Agalri* [*The Lords of Akchasaz*])

Al gözüm seyreyle Salih, 1976 (*Seagull*, 1981)

Yılanı öldürseler, 1976 (*To Crush the Serpent*, 1991)

Deniz küstü, 1978 (*The Sea-Crossed Fisherman*, 1985)

Kuşlar da gitti, 1978 (*The Birds Have Also Gone*, 1987)

Kimsecik, 1980 (*Salman the Solitary*, 1997)

Hüyükteki nar agacı, 1982

İnce Memed III, 1984

Kale kapısı, 1985

İnce Memed 4, 1987

Kanin sesi, 1991

Firat Suyu kan akiyor baksana, 1998

OTHER LITERARY FORMS

A prolific author, Yashar Kemal has published collections of journalism, essays, and short stories. His reportage appeared in *Yanan ormanlarda elli gün* (1955; fifty days in burning forests), *Çukurova yana* *yana* (1955; the Chukurova up in flames), and *Peri bacaları* (1957; fairy chimneys); these works were consolidated in *Bu diyar baştan başa* (1971). Further collections of journalism are *Bir bulut kaynıyor* (1974) and *Allahin askerleri* (1978). Kemal's essays appeared in *Taş çatlasa* (1961) and *Baldaki tuz* (1974). His short stories are collected in *Sarı sıçak* (1952), *Üç anadolu efsanesi* (1968; three Anatolian legends), and *Bütün hikâyeler* (1967, enlarged 1975; *Anatolian Tales*, 1968).

Other writings include poetry and folklore material contributed to Turkish periodicals. Kemal's first work was a collection of folk elegies, *Ağıtlar* (1943), and he has turned some of the folk material into screenplays. In addition, Kemal created stage versions of his novella *Teneke* (1965) and the novel *Iron Earth, Copper Sky* (1966).

ACHIEVEMENTS

Yashar Kemal is Turkey's most famous novelist. He has been a frequent candidate for the Nobel Prize in Literature, and his novels have been translated into some thirty languages. Kemal is the recipient of numerous awards, including the 1997 German Book Trade Peace Prize, the 1996 Hellman-Hammett Award, and several honorary degrees He is a Commander of France's Legion of Honor. He is an admirer of William Faulkner, but in his best work Kemal's imagistic description, narration of action, and tough-minded attitude are more reminiscent of Ernest Hemingway. Like Hemingway, Kemal began as a newspaper reporter, and his novels show the influence of his reportage, especially in their documentation of local color. Perhaps the most important influence on Kemal, however, has been the native tradition of songs, legends, and other folklore. In Turkey the oral tradition has remained strong, especially in rural areas, and as a child Kemal imbibed this tradition from village minstrels and storytellers.

Kemal's work reveals the strengths and weaknesses suggested by his background. His original forte was the genre called the "village novel," exemplified by the early novels *Memed, My Hawk* and *The Wind from the Plain*, which provide glimpses into the lives and minds of Anatolian peasants. As Kemal repeated himself and grew further away from village life and legend, he was faced with the need to develop. In the 1970's, he branched out into new forms and transferred his political attitudes to new settings.

BIOGRAPHY

Yashar Kemal is the anglicized form of Yaşar Kemal; the author's full name is Yaşar Kemal Gökçeli. His parents, Sadik and Nigar Gökçeli, were the only Kurdish family in the poverty-striken village of Hemite, near Adana in the southeast of Turkey, where he was born in the fall of 1923. Kemal grew up in the region of Turkey featured in his early novels, the Taurus Mountains and the coastal plain (the Chukurova) around Adana, and he personally experienced the conditions about which he writes. At the age of five, he witnessed his praying father's murder in a mosque. In the same attack, one of young Kemal's eyes was put out, and he had a severe stutter for years afterward. His stutter temporarily disappeared only when he sang, an activity at which he excelled, sometimes improvising his own songs.

There was no school in young Kemal's small village, Hemite, so at the age of nine, he began walking to the neighboring village to attend a three-class school. Later, he stayed with relatives in Kadirli, where he completed primary school and two years of secondary school (equivalent to the eighth grade) before he had to start working. He held numerous jobs—farm laborer, construction worker, factory worker, clerk, substitute teacher—but was driven out of them by the powerful landowners, the Aghas, who labeled him a Communist because he openly criticized the rural tenant-landlord system. When he became a public letter writer (a respectable type of employment in countries where most people cannot read or write and so need help with correspondence), the harassment intensified: In 1950, he was charged with disseminating Communist propaganda and was thrown in jail, where an attempt was made on his life. Although acquitted in a trial, Kemal continued to be persecuted by landowners and police. Finally, in 1951, he fled to Istanbul.

In Instanbul, he shortened his name to Yaşar Kemal, to avoid detection, and began writing for *Cum-*

huriyet, a leading daily newspaper. His journalism—reports, feature stories, travel pieces—soon caught on, and so did his short fiction. His first novel, *Memed, My Hawk*, won the 1956 Varlik Prize. His growing public esteem, which eventually became international, insulated him somewhat from persecution but also infuriated his right-wing enemies.

A one-time central committee member of the banned Workers Party and editor of the Marxist weekly *Ant* in the 1960's, Kemal has gone to jail no fewer than twenty times for his political convictions. He has been tortured "a great deal," in his own words, and evidence of this can be seen on his legs. In 1995, Kemal, in an article published in the German newsmagazine *Der Spiegel*, accused the Turkish authorities of waging genocide against the country's Kurdish minority. The article was then reprinted in a Turkish book, a collection of articles and essays by various writers called *Freedom of Expression and Turkey*. The government promptly confiscated and banned the book. Kemal received a twenty-month prison sentence, which was later suspended as a result of an in-

(AP/Wide World Photos)

ternational campaign on his behalf. Despite intimidations and harassments by the police and right-wing nationalists, Kemal continued to speak out.

On the domestic side, Kemal married Thilda Serrero in 1952; they had one son, Rasit. Thilda has translated a number of Kemal's books into English. Kemal stopped writing for *Cumhuriyet* in 1963 in order to spend his time on politics and writing fiction.

ANALYSIS

Whatever political and literary sophistication Yashar Kemal achieved after becoming a writer, his fiction grows essentially out of his village background. Until the 1970's, he specialized in village novels showing the brutal conditions of peasants in the Adana region where he grew up—the Taurus Mountains and the Chukurova. In the 1970's, Kemal moved on from the village novel to legendary tales and to novels set in the Istanbul area. Yet the legends were ones Kemal had heard as a child, and the Istanbul novels reflect political attitudes Kemal began forming based on what he saw of village life, particularly from the archetypal relationship of tenant and landlord.

Kemal's special achievement is his depiction of peasant life. In Kemal's work, the Turkish peasants are victimized by an appalling range of scourges which include the weather, hunger, hard labor, ignorance, superstition, disease, green flies, landlords, and one another. Among the few things which the peasant has to fall back on is the close-knit structure of family and village life, which can be quite helpful when things go badly. The structure has a down side to it, however, which at times can make brother turn against brother.

Another outlet is the peasants' imagination. Within their imaginations, they can daydream and fantasize, can satisfy their wishes and right wrongs. One happy result of such imagination is vigorous folk art—songs, designs on knitted socks, stories, and legends. One of the unhappy results is superstition—belief in jinn, peris, folk cures, and holy trees. Perhaps religious belief also fits in here, considering that among Kemal's peasants it so often leads to passive acceptance or fatalism—the attitude that whatever happens must have been decreed by Allah. Yet the work of the imagination does not necessarily inspire inaction, for the songs and legends sometimes speak out against oppression and glorify those who speak out and rise against the ruthless landowning overlords.

MEMED, MY HAWK

The revenge motif looms large in Kemal's first and most popular novel, *Memed, My Hawk*, which director Peter Ustinov made into a film. The story of *Memed, My Hawk* begins in the isolated little world of Dikenli, the Plateau of Thistles, where cluster the five villages owned by Abdi Agha. In the largest village, Deyirmenoluk, live both the Agha and the boy Memed, a tenant whose father is dead and who must work like a man to support his mother, Deuneh. All day long Memed plows the fields of thistles, which leave his legs bloody, and endures the unmerciful beatings of the Agha. When he is eleven, Memed runs away across the mountain but is eventually discovered and driven back home by the Agha on horseback. Thereafter, the Agha bears down harder: He takes three-fourths instead of the customary two-thirds from Memed and Deuneh's yearly harvest. Thus, Memed and his mother have even less to live on than the other tenants, who regularly starve in the winter. So it goes, Memed laboring mostly for the Agha and growing up stunted but bitter and tough as a mountain oak. Still, Memed finds some happiness in the arms of Hatche, his sweetheart since childhood.

The turning point comes when Abdi Agha tries to force Hatche to marry his nephew Veli. Memed and Hatche elope and are pursued by the Agha's gang. In a shootout, Memed kills Veli, wounds Abdi Agha, and then escapes, but Hatche is captured. Thereafter, unfairly charged with Veli's death, Hatche languishes in a terrible Turkish jail, while Memed pursues a life of brigandage. Memed also pursues Abdi Agha, who, after stomping Deuneh into the mud (she eventually dies from the beatings), fears increasingly for his own life. Memed pursues him into the Chukurova and burns a whole village around him, but the Agha miraculously escapes—only to deteriorate further psychologically. Meanwhile, Memed rescues Hatche, distributes the Agha's land to the villagers, and earns a fabulous reputation for his daring exploits and generosity toward poor people. As Memed's reputation grows, so does the Agha's paranoia. Finally, when Abdi Agha's hirelings kill Hatche, Memed rides straight into town, marches upstairs in the Agha's house, and shoots the quivering Agha. Then Memed rides off into legend.

Despite Memed's disappearance into legend, the novel has a suspiciously autobiographical cast. The reader here may be sharing one of the author's youthful fantasies—Kemal identifying with his hero and seeing himself as a sort of Robin Hood figure. With one eye missing, Kemal certainly looks enough like a brigand. In any event, *Memed, My Hawk* is full of realistic details of village life and landscape, such as the fields of thistles which, in a symbolic act of liberation, are burned at the end. Like his hero, Kemal grew up fatherless, and he no doubt heard inspiring tales from his own mother, who was descended from a family of brigands.

The political implications of brigandage in *Memed, My Hawk* are fairly clear. In a society where the law merely legitimates organized violence against the peasantry, large numbers of peasants are driven by desperation outside the law. Most of them join the brigands, who constitute a social underground. Morally, the brigands are no better than the Aghas, with whom they sometimes hire out and form political alliances, but at least they are free and empowered, as symbolized by their colorful dress bristling with daggers, cartridge belts, and grenades. They attain moral legitimacy only by following the path of Memed, turning their violence against the Aghas and becoming, in effect, guerrillas. ("Slim Memed" does not actually disappear into legend forever; he returns in a sequel, *They Burn the Thistles*, to help oppressed peasants quell another mean, greedy Agha.)

THE WIND FROM THE PLAIN

While *Memed, My Hawk* is built around legendary and realistic events, Kemal's next novel, *The Wind from the Plain*, is unrelentingly realistic throughout. It details the annual migration of Anatolian villagers across the Taurus Mountains to the Chukurova, where they hope to pick cotton and thereby earn enough to keep going for another year. The story

would be utterly depressing if the villagers' disasters did not sometimes lead to black, bitter humor.

When the villagers migrate, the whole village goes along—animals, pots and pans, the sick and old. The migration is a ritual demonstration of village solidarity, perhaps, or a return to an ancestral nomadic existence, but it is also a motley scene with its basis more in custom than in common sense. Any solidarity is only on the surface, because the migration exacerbates old frictions into inflamed sores. The villagers are trying to rebel against the *muhtar*, who is plotting as usual to sell their labor cheap in return for a fat bribe. Dredging up grudges from many years before, an old couple (who are not related but know each other well) squabble over who will ride a decrepit horse—until the horse falls dead. The old woman then spitefully blames her son, Long Ali, to whom she refuses to speak (instead, she addresses rocks or trees) and who has to travel the road three times (once in carrying his goods forward, and twice in returning to pick up the old woman and then carrying her forward, too). Scattered along the road and fearing they will be late for the harvest, Long Ali and his family fall several days behind the other villagers. When they finally come upon the others in the Chukurova, they discover that the whole village is late, that the rebellion has failed, and that the *muhtar* has sold them out to a cotton field full of weeds. Thus the novel ends, in total frustration for the villagers. (*The Wind from the Plain* is the first novel of a trilogy, followed by *Iron Earth, Copper Sky* and *The Undying Grass*; the full trilogy shows, among other things, a much better cotton harvest the next year and scores being settled with the *muhtar*.)

THE UNDYING GRASS

In *The Undying Grass*, Kemal's eighth novel in English translation, readers are once again among the poor sharecroppers of the Chukurova region who have to come down every year from their mountain homes to pick cotton in the sweltering plains below. Violence, romance, feudal oppression, and superstition are once more the common themes. Memidik, one of the pickers, has a terrible urge to kill the local tribal chief, Sefer, who is both abusive and brutal in his dealings with the cotton pickers. Each time Sefer has an opportunity to do so, he is overcome with fear. Things then begin to change quickly as the novel moves swiftly back and forth between realism and fantasy. The workers suddenly organize around a leader, Tashbash, who is both real and mythic. He has Sefer arrested and sentenced to solitary confinement. There are cries of joy and triumph, but they are short-lived as the mythic Tashbash is suddenly and unexpectedly transformed into a frail old man. Kemal's point, as he himself has said, is to help these destitute people escape, temporarily, the harsh "realities of their existence" by transplanting them in a dream world in which they, not the landlords, hold power. However, he also wishes to sharpen their understanding of the sociopolitical forces arrayed against them.

SEAGULL

A similar theme of frustration marks *Seagull*, an example of Kemal's later work. In arriving at the theme, readers of *Seagull* may experience frustrations of their own, since Kemal, following Faulkner, experiments with such techniques as flashback, interior monologue, and limited point of view. In the best Faulknerian manner, *Seagull* is narrated by an eleven-year-old boy, Salih, who seems remarkably mature for his age. Under the harsh circumstances in which Salih lives, youngsters tend to mature quite early. It is sometimes difficult to distinguish the present from flashbacks or the boy's juvenile fantasies from what is really happening. This difficulty is not necessarily a weakness on Kemal's part; such narrators are at times unsure of themselves and unreliable, and they have a lot of difficulties understanding the world around them. These qualities are exactly what make them so interesting. Like James Joyce's unnamed narrator in the short story "Araby," Salih's understanding and lack of understanding of the tensions and problems associated with growing up among adults give the novel a sense of immediacy and realism.

On a symbolic level, Salih's story is highly revealing. He lives in an unnamed Black Sea coastal town, relatively prosperous, which caters to tourists and supplies fish and smuggled goods to Istanbul. Salih's family, however, does not share in the prosperity: His father is an alchoholic, a gambler, and a beater of

wife and children, and the family exists on the earnings of Salih's mother, sister, and grandmother, who weave all day on shuttles in the home. Salih clashes constantly with his grandmother, who is embittered because her husband, Halil, left forty years before (she still meets every ship in the hope that he will return). To escape this family situation, Salih wanders about the town (he cannot afford school), watching the blacksmith and the fishing boats, helping Skipper Temel, playing with other boys, and fantasizing about his neighbor Metin (a dashing smuggler) or the snake boy. The snake boy—a boy in a huge snake's body—is an unhappy prince who kills his playmates and, later, loves his wives to death, until he meets a compatible mermaid.

Identifying with animals, especially birds, which are slaughtered for fun by the town's hunters, Salih finds his soulmate in a baby seagull with a broken wing. Told by everyone that wounded seagulls invariably die, Salih nevertheless cares for the chick and, with Skipper Temel's help, cures the broken wing. His grandmother, who had smugly predicted the bird's death, is infuriated by its recovery, especially when it actually flies. In turn, Salih's happiness is brief. For innocently wearing a Che Guevara T-shirt that a tourist gave him, Salih is beaten within an inch of his life by three teenagers, self-styled "Turkish commandos." In addition, his hero Metin is killed, which causes his grandmother to gloat. Salih taunts her back when his father joins the smugglers and leaves home: Salih announces his intentions to leave and never return, like his father and like his grandfather Halil. Enraged, the grandmother first tries to choke Salih, then twists off the head of his seagull and, still squeezing the bloody bird, dances frenziedly about the garden—like a whirling dervish—until she crumples to the ground. Salih ends up not leaving home: He misses Skipper Temel's boat to Istanbul and instead becomes the blacksmith's apprentice.

TO CRUSH THE SERPENT

In *To Crush the Serpent*, Kemal returns one more time to the rural landscape of his boyhood, where tribalism, blood feuds, superstition, and outdated social norms take a heavy toll on a people who must struggle daily just to make ends meet. This novel is considerably shorter than his early ones, but the scope and style are easily recognizable: A poetic blend of myth, folklore, and social realism is presented in a village setting through flashback, narration, and dreams. The story centers on a very attractive young woman, Esme, who is forced to marry a man, Halil, she does not love. Her lover responds to the injustice by murdering Halil shortly after Esme gives birth to a baby boy, Hasan. Halil's mother and most everyone else in the village accuse Esme of the murder. Their problem is that no one has the will to kill such a stunning beauty in revenge. What is equally troubling for these people is the belief that, if Halil's death is not avenged, then his spirit is sure to return in the form of a poisonous snake to terrorize the community. Responsibility for revenge is passed on to the young Hasan. However, Kemal, who has been an outspoken critic of tribal feuds and other forms of social oppression, will not allow Hasan to fall into the endemic trap of a blood feud: As the novel ends, Hasan leaves for the city to start a life of his own.

For Kemal, writing novels involves more than such things as technique, narration, and style. In his essay "Literature, Democracy, and Peace," which was his acceptance speech for the 1997 Peace Prize of the German Book Trade, Kemal said that his intention has always been to use his "firm commitment to the word" to expose social and political injustice. Accordingly, his novels are intended to develop in the reader a love for "fellow human beings, for all birds and beasts, for all bugs and insects, for all of nature." His writing is also intended to promote a strong sense of outrage at oppression—especially oppressive acts committed by national governments. As a case in point, he cites the Turkish state's seventy-year-old ban on the language and culture of its twenty million Kurds.

Harold Branam, updated by Sabah A. Salih

OTHER MAJOR WORKS

SHORT FICTION: *Sarı sıçak*, 1952; *Bütün hikâyeler*, 1967, enlarged 1975 (*Anatolian Tales*, 1968; includes the novella *Teneke*); *Üç anadolu efsanesi*, 1968.

PLAYS: *Teneke*, pr. 1965; *Yer demir, gök bakır*, pr. 1966.

POETRY: *Ağıtlar*, 1943; *Sari defterdekiler*, 1997.

NONFICTION: *Yanan ormanlarda elli gün*, 1955 (journalism); *Çukurova yana yana*, 1955 (journalism); *Peri bacaları*, 1957 (journalism); *Taş çatlasa*, 1961 (essays); *Bu diyar baştan başa*, 1971 (journalism); *Baldaki tuz*, 1974 (essays); *Bir bulut kaynıyor*, 1974 (journalism); *Allahin askerleri*, 1978 (journalism); *Agacin çürügü*, 1980; *Ustadir ari*, 1995; *Zulmün artsin*, 1995.

CHILDREN'S LITERATURE: *Filler sultanı ile kirmizki sakallı topal karınca*, 1977.

BIBLIOGRAPHY

Blassing, Mutlu Konuk. "The Lords of Akchasaz." *World Literature Today* 55, no. 2 (1981): 370. A review that discusses this novel's themes and Kemal's growing popularity in Europe.

_____. "Seagull." *World Literature Today* 55, no. 4 (1981): 723. A highly engaging discussion of the novel's sociopolitical themes and its protagonist's affinity with Mark Twain's Tom Sawyer.

Darnton, John. "A Prophet Tests the Honor of His Own Country." *The New York Times*, March 14, 1995, A4. Discusses Kemal's life, his literary accomplishments, and his political disagreements and troubles with the Turkish state.

Dino, Guzine. "The Turkish Peasant Novel; Or, The Anatolian Theme." *World Literature Today* 60, no. 2 (1986): 200-206. Traces the development of this type of novel and discusses Kemal's contribution to it.

Halman, Talat Sait. "Kuslar de Gitti." *World Literature Today* 52, no. 4 (1978): 689. Halman discusses the plot and themes of this novel, yet to be translated into English, in his usually clear and vivid style.

_____. "Tamberlaine Country." *The Times Literary Supplement*, May 3, 1974, 465. Though somewhat dated, this essay is a useful introduction to Kemal's early work.

_____. "To Crush the Serpent." *World Literature Today* 66, no. 2 (1992): 400-401. A detailed review of the novel by a critic who knows Kemal at first hand.

Kemal, Yashar. "Literature, Democracy, and Peace."

Translated by Talat Sait Halman. *World Literature Today* 72, no. 1 (1998), 15-17. Kemal's acceptance speech for the 1997 Peace Prize of the German Book Trade is an excellent overview of his approach as writer and political thinker.

Pollitt, Katha. "Turkish Trouble." *The New York Times Book Review*, June 18, 1978, 14, 37. Pollitt considers *Seagull* an important criticism of the Turkish state.

Pope, Nicole. "A Voice That Refuses to Be Silenced." *Guardian Weekly*, March 24, 1996, 18. Provides important and intimate insight into Kemal's thinking as a writer and political activist.

THOMAS KENEALLY

Born: Wauchope, New South Wales, Australia; October 7, 1935

PRINCIPAL LONG FICTION

The Place at Whitton, 1964
The Fear, 1965
Bring Larks and Heroes, 1967
Three Cheers for the Paraclete, 1968
The Survivor, 1969
A Dutiful Daughter, 1971
The Chant of Jimmie Blacksmith, 1972
Blood Red, Sister Rose, 1974
Gossip from the Forest, 1975
Moses the Lawgiver, 1975
Season in Purgatory, 1976
A Victim of the Aurora, 1977
Passenger, 1979
Confederates, 1979
The Cut-Rate Kingdom, 1980
Schindler's Ark, 1982 (pb. in U.S. as *Schindler's List*, 1983)
A Family Madness, 1985
The Playmaker, 1987
To Asmara, 1989
Flying Hero Class, 1991
Woman of the Inner Sea, 1992

Jacko, 1993 (pb. in England as *Jacko: The Great Intruder*)
A River Town, 1995
Bettany's Book, 1998

OTHER LITERARY FORMS

In addition to his long fiction, Thomas Keneally has written several plays: *Halloran's Little Boat* (1966), *Childermass* (1968), *An Awful Rose* (1972), and *Bullie's House* (1980). He has also written two television plays, *Essington*, produced in the United Kingdom in 1974, and *The World's Wrong End* (1981), as well as nonfiction works; *Homebush Boy* (1995) is a memoir.

ACHIEVEMENTS

Keneally has received international acclaim for his fiction; he has received the Miles Franklin Award (1967, 1968), the Captain Cook Bi-Centenary Prize (1970), the Royal Society of Literature Prize (1982), and the Booker Prize (1982). *The Chant of Jimmie Blacksmith* won for him the Heinemann Award for literature (1973), and *Schindler's Ark* won the *Los Angeles Times* Fiction Prize (1983). Keneally's other honors include the presidency of the National Book Council of Australia and membership in the Australia-China Council.

BIOGRAPHY

Thomas Michael Keneally was born in Wauchope, New South Wales, Australia, on October 7, 1935. He studied for the Roman Catholic priesthood in his youth but left the seminary two weeks before he was to take Holy Orders. He completed his education at St. Patrick's College, New South Wales. He married Judith Martin in 1965 and had two children. Before becoming a full-time novelist, he taught high school in Sydney, from 1960 to 1964; from 1968 to 1970, he was a lecturer in drama at the University of New England, New South Wales. He lived in London in 1970-1971, and from 1975 to 1977 he lived in the United States, where he lectured at New Milford, Connecticut.

In addition to writing his many novels, Keneally demonstrated his concern for Australian nationalism as a leader of the republication movement in Australia, working for separation from the British Commonwealth and recognition of national status for Australia. His political activities also demonstrate his concern for human rights. Indeed, his work as a novelist examining the human soul in the most dramatic of situations, as well as looking at Australian history and culture, is paralleled by his political activism. In 1998 Keneally was elected as one of twenty delegates from New South Wales to the Constitutional Convention. In his novels, he has focused on the individual in the midst of moral and existential chaos, on the individual's growth into heroism in the extremist of circumstances. As a prominent national figure, he was one of several who signed Community Aid Abroad's *Global Charter for Basic Rights.* Having served as distinguished professor of English and comparative literature at the University of California, Irvine, from 1991 through 1994, Keneally was awarded that university's medal for service and commitment. He has also been awarded the Order of Australia for Services to Literature and named a Fellow of the American Academy of Arts and Sciences and Fellow of the Royal Society of Literature.

(AP/Wide World Photos)

ANALYSIS

Thomas Keneally has written books on a variety of subjects. His first novel to attain international readership, *Bring Larks and Heroes*, presents the barbarous life of eighteenth century Sydney; *Three Cheers for the Paraclete* concerns a Catholic priest who attacks the Church for its indifference to social evil; *The Survivor* and *A Victim of the Aurora* are stories about Antarctic expeditions, told in flashback by an aged narrator; *A Dutiful Daughter* is a surrealistic tale of a family in which the parents are bovine from the waist down. One may, however, separate Keneally's work into two parts, albeit roughly: the novels which deal with seemingly ordinary, contemporary individuals, and the wide range of what might be called historical novels.

In a large portion of his work, Keneally concerns himself with European history, examining closely the human beings involved, seeing the past not as the present sees it, as a series of neatly wrapped, complete events, but as the participants experience it: as a jumble of occurrences that seem to have little meaning or purpose. Although some reviewers have commented on the portentousness lurking in the background of such works as *Gossip from the Forest*, a fictionalized re-creation of the 1918 peace talks that led to the disastrous Treaty of Versailles, such "damaging knowingness" is only partly Keneally's fault; after all, the present knows what happened in the past, at least in outline.

It must be emphasized that Keneally's historically based fiction is not about ordinary people set against a celebrity-filled background, in the manner of E. L. Doctorow's *Ragtime* (1975). His works deal with the historical figures themselves, presenting them as human beings embroiled in the quotidian matters from which the historical events reveal themselves gradually. The writer's knowledge of history shapes the delineation of the plot. Furthermore, the protagonist's awareness of his or her importance to posterity comes only in flashes. When such awareness occurs, it is as a result of the character's makeup; Joan of Arc, for example, was a visionary, and it is unavoidable that, as a character, she know something of her eventual fate.

It cannot be denied that what Keneally is attempting to do in his historically based novels is difficult; that he succeeds as well as he does is primarily a result of a spare, objective style that is at times brilliant, such as in the description of Yugoslav partisans from *Season in Purgatory*: "Grenades blossomed like some quaint ethnic ornamentation down the front of their coats." The third-person narration, deceptively simple, pretending to mere description, seems detached (at times too detached): *Schindler's List*, based on a German industrialist's widely successful efforts to save "his" Jews, at times suffers from an almost sprightly tone, as if the author were so determined to be objective that he expunged any sense of moral outrage from his account. At its best, however, the stark simplicity of Keneally's prose throws into sharp relief the horrors of which history is made.

GOSSIP FROM THE FOREST

The history examined by Keneally is never pretty, no matter how heroic the subject. The final terrible lesson of *Gossip from the Forest* is that well-meaning, intelligent, civilized people have no place in the twentieth century. Matthias Erzberger, liberal member of the Reichstag, has no success in his negotiations; blind self-interest thwarts his every attempt at justice for his defeated country. He is shot to death several years after the meeting at Compiègne by two young officers, proto-Nazis, as a traitor for his role in the Armistice. Erzberger himself, for all of his excellent qualities and basic decency, seems unequal to the task he has had thrust on him. He is aware of his inadequacy: "Like a cardiac spasm he suffered again the terrible bereft sense that there was nothing in his background that justified this journey. . . . At its most high-flown the true Erzberger's mind wasn't far off steak and red wine and Paula's warm and undemanding bed." His dreamy absent-mindedness and his eventual despair seem to remove him from the heroic ranks; it is only toward the end of the novel that the reader realizes the true heroism of the civilian in his struggle against the military mind.

SEASON IN PURGATORY

This gradual revelation of heroism is evident also in *Season in Purgatory*, the story of a young British physician, David Pelham, who is sent to the island of Mus to perform emergency surgery on Yugoslav partisans. Pelham arrives on Mus with all the fiery idealism of youth. After being thrust, day after day, into the results of war—both the direct results, such as graphically described wounds, and the indirect, such as Marshal Tito's order that any partisans indulging in sexual relations be summarily executed—he is worn down, no longer convinced of the rightness of any cause: "In his bloodstream were two simple propositions: that the savagery of the Germans did not excuse the savagery of the partisans: that the savagery of the partisans did not excuse the savagery of the Germans."

This final realization that "the masters of the ideologies, even the bland ideology of democracy, were blood-crazed . . . that at the core of their political fervour, there stood a desire to punish with death anyone who hankered for other systems than those approved," does not allow the story to end. It is in this moral vacuum that Pelham becomes a hero, having sacrificed the innocence and illusion of idealism for an embittered realism. Keneally continues to reveal Pelham's personal flaws, as he does with all of his heroic figures: His childishness in love and hate and his typical upper-class British attitudes survive the revelation. Therefore, the apotheosis of the physician at the end of the war comes as much as a surprise to the reader as it must to the character himself.

THE CHANT OF JIMMIE BLACKSMITH

Pelham's loss of idealism is necessary to Keneally's concept of the heroic figure; idealism bathes reality in a rosy glow that does not fit anything but the usual type of historical novel (or many types of history, for that matter). Generally, Keneally's heroes find themselves chosen to be sacrificial victims, without having wished for it. They are by turns reluctant and filled with fervor, and they are always human, at times perversely flaunting their faults. The positive aspect of their selection is generally far more ephemeral than the certitude of the doom toward which they know they are going. They are often in the situation epitomized by the half-caste protagonist of *The Chant of Jimmie Blacksmith*, the novel on which the 1978 Fred Schepisi film is based: "in tenuous elation and solid desolation between self-knowledge and delirium."

Jimmie Blacksmith has a white father, whom he does not know, and an aboriginal mother. He has been taught Christianity and ambition; he is no longer tribal, but his attempts to show the whites that a black may be as industrious and educated as they are fail to gain for him acceptance in their society. He marries a white girl who has also slept with the station cook (played by Keneally himself in the film); when their baby is born, it is white.

Jimmie has been cheated by the whites, has taken up arms against his tribe in order to be thought white, and has married white to consolidate his ambition, yet he is still rejected by the white society. The birth of the baby makes him explode, and he goes on a methodical rampage, first killing the Newby family, for whom he worked, then taking a sympathetic white schoolteacher as a hostage. He eludes his pursuers for a time, but they catch up with him. Shot in the jaw, delirious, he takes refuge in a convent, where he is eventually captured. His hanging, however, is delayed so that it will not detract from the celebration of the Federation anniversary.

Throughout, Jimmie is seen as a man who might be a bridge between the two cultures, but neither the aborigines nor the whites allow such a resolution; his killing spree seems to represent his only alternative, and while other people die, Jimmie is actually the victim. He wants to become the peaceful link, and when this course proves illusory, he becomes the avenger, knowing that he will not survive. He is doomed, in the way Keneally heroes are usually doomed.

BLOOD RED, SISTER ROSE

This sense of being the sacrificial victim is most strongly presented in Keneally's retelling of the Joan of Arc story. *Blood Red, Sister Rose* is a fictionalized account of the youth and triumph of Joan of Arc. The novel ends with the few anticlimactic months following the coronation of Charles in Rheims and an epilogue in the form of a letter from her father to the family about his daughter's death. Yet throughout the

development of Jehanne's awareness of her destiny, the certitude of her martyrdom is evident, for she is a peasant who knows that Christ's sacrifice was not enough; the king needs one, and she has been chosen. Alternately buoyed and depressed by her fate, she sees herself as a conduit for these forces, the importance of which leaves very little time or passion for Jehanne, daughter of Jacques and Zabillet, to pursue her own humanity.

Described as wide-shouldered and plain, Jehanne goes through adolescence without menstruating, which proves to her that she is not like her sister or her mother, that she is the virgin from Lorraine prophesied by Merlin. She has not chosen her fate, but she must accept it. There are moments when she resents this election: Words of tenderness spoken about another woman, for example, evoke great sadness within her, for she knows that such words will never be spoken about her. The greater part of the time, however, is consumed with her mission, not to France, not to the destruction of the English, not even to stop the slaughter of the farmers who suffered so greatly in the wars of the fifteenth century, but to ensure the consecration of the king, to whom she is mystically bound.

Through ancient ritual, Keneally presents the notion of the human sacrifice. The author's weaving of historical incident with the motivations based in archaic mythologies allows a dimension of verisimilitude to the slippery genre of historical fiction. The inclusion of certain surprising elements of fifteenth century life (for example, the mention that peasants in eastern France plowed their field with a naked woman in the harness so that the earth might be bountiful) reveals a society in which the voices heard by Jehanne cannot be casually dismissed as a frustrated spinster's wishful thinking.

Jehanne is, like her forebears, a mixture of ignorance and hardheaded shrewdness. These qualities, at the service of the obsession that invaded her at the age of nine, ensure her success in reaching the king. Furthermore, the feudal society that she opposes is rapidly approaching dissolution: The battle of Agincourt has demonstrated the impotence of armored knights, Prince Hal has taken to killing noble prisoners instead of ransoming them in the time-honored practice of chivalry, the alliances of dukes and barons have been complicated by the presence of the English, and the ongoing war has caused a near-famine in the countryside. Jehanne's clarity of purpose shines brightly through the morass of confusion and disaster that was fifteenth century France.

Once her objective is reached, however, she becomes an ordinary person again, with no voices telling her the next move. One sees her strength and influence eroding as the king is changed from a timid recluse to a confident monarch. His ingratitude is taken as a matter of course by Jehanne, for she has known all along the fate that awaits the year-king, the sacrificial victim. As if her importance has diminished for the author as well as for Charles, the ending is a mere footnote. One is left with a brilliant picture of a strange and remote past, and a sense of what heroes are—never heroes to themselves, accepting the acclaims of the populace bemusedly, as if the admirers were constantly missing the point. Although there are moments when she is elated by her specialness, more often she sees it as an onus, a word that constantly recurs in Keneally's work.

This realization, in small part exhilarating and in larger part burdensome, is one that recurs in Keneally's work. In the novel *Passenger*, for example, the narrator-fetus views the Gnome as his outside brother and protector; the Gnome is eventually killed in a plane crash, and in dying ensures the birth of the narrator. In *A Victim of the Aurora*, two explorers from a previous expedition have remained in the Antarctic, and one survives by eating the other one; their identities become mixed, so that the one who has survived identifies himself by the name of the one who was eaten. One can see plainly Keneally's Catholic background in the use of the sacrificial victim as theme or motif in many of his works: Christ's sacrifice, rendered bloodless by the sacrament of communion, is constantly reenacted in all its primal violence by either his protagonists or his supporting characters.

This theme links the historical novels with those that deal with supposedly ordinary people. In the latter category, Keneally is more experimental, particularly in the mode of narration employed. The objective third-person narration of the historical novels is replaced by various innovations, such as the second-person, self-addressed narration of *A Dutiful Daughter* or the omniscient first-person narration of *Passenger*. At first glance, there seems to be little similarity between the two types of novels, but the author's concerns form a bridge between them.

PASSENGER

Passenger's narrator is a fetus, given consciousness by a sonogram. Suddenly, the fetus is no longer happily unaware of anything save the coursing of his blood, an animal faculty that requires a certain kind of innocence; he becomes aware of everything: his mother's thoughts, the historical novel she is writing about her ne'er-do-well husband's ancestor (himself seemingly the prototype of Halloran in *Bring Larks and Heroes*), his father's fear of his birth, the existence of Warwick Jones, the Gnome—"We were Dumas' Corsican twins, the Gnome and I. It was as if we *shared* a placenta and swapped our visions and sensation." Jones feels as though he had never really been born, and that he will be born through the agency of the narrator's own birth. For Jones, however, birth means death, literal death. The narrator also sees his own eventual birth as death, and he resists it, unlike Jones, who actively seeks it.

This notion of the sacrificial double is one aspect that links the two categories of novels. The power of history is another. Keneally's fascination with history and heroes surfaces in *Passenger*. In the narrative is a character who has had the same experiences as David Pelham, the protagonist of *Season in Purgatory*. Maurice Fitzgerald, the eighteenth century ancestor of Brian, the narrator's father, was also a reluctant hero in the penal colony of Sydney. The fight against social injustice that characterizes Maurice Fitzgerald forms the thematic center of Keneally's novel *Three Cheers for the Paraclete*.

THREE CHEERS FOR THE PARACLETE

In this novel, Keneally treats directly the experience that perhaps influenced his life most strongly: the six and a half years of being a seminarian, bound to the doctrine and ideology of the Catholic Church. Again, Father Maitland, the protagonist, is a reluctant hero, unsure of the purity of his motives even as he preaches, afraid of sounding "like a fashionable priest, the glib kind." He tries earnestly to submit to the authority of his bishop, fearing the disappearance of the comforting certainties, but his conscience does not allow him a quiet life.

His working-class cousin has been cheated out of his savings by an unscrupulous housing development corporation; looking into the affair, Maitland discovers that other people had the same experience with that company, and furthermore, that his own diocese owns stock in the company. He becomes the center of controversy, a position he does not want but must take because of his own convictions. The diocese eventually rids itself of the holdings in the dishonest company on the advice of its legal staff; the question of morality has been supplanted by one of expediency for the established Church. Maitland, having indirectly succeeded, submits to the rule of his church: the censorship of his sermons, a ban on further publications, and transfer to a rural parish.

The pervasiveness of social injustice and its force makes its appearance in all of Keneally's novels, in one degree or another. Jehanne of *Blood Red, Sister Rose*, a peasant and a woman, is herself a statement against the class and gender inequities of the fifteenth century, at times bringing a modern flavor to a time when such inequities were seldom questioned. Her liberationist tendencies are diluted by the importance of her vision, but it is impossible for her to witness late medieval war without realizing who suffers the most. The farmers, the peasants who form the major part of the armies, are never held for ransom. They are killed outright when captured. The noncombatants, women and children, are raped and killed by the rampaging armies. The sexism inherent in the way she is treated makes her rage impotently.

A DUTIFUL DAUGHTER

Jehanne's story reappears in *A Dutiful Daughter*; Barbara Glover, the sister of the narrator, possesses what might be a fifteenth century transcript of Jehanne's first examination by priests, which might have saved her from the stake had it not been lost. Barbara sees in Jehanne's story elements that might explain her own life to her.

The Glover family has settled on a swampy bit of land, Campbell's Reach, and has tried to make a liv-

ing on it with only minimal success. The son, Damian, who is the narrator, has been sent to college, while Barbara has stayed behind to take care of the parents. In a flashback that is evocative of Jehanne's own awakening to the voices, Barbara runs off into the swamp, pursued by her parents; when they finally come back, the parents have undergone a bizarre metamorphosis: They have been turned into cattle from the waist down, "like centaurs, except that the horse half was a cow half." They seem not to have noticed, but Barbara tells them what has happened; they never forgive her, but from that day forward, she has complete control over them. As Damian writes, "It is the duty of a good child to let his parents know the second they turn into animals."

Barbara's control has its responsibilities, and she finds them onerous. She cannot evade them, however, any more than Jehanne can escape her destiny. She therefore perseveres, although life on Campbell's Reach is dismal at best, and in conjunction with caring for her parents, absolutely deadening. For the parents are indeed cattle from the waist down; the transformation is literal, and Keneally leaves no doubt about that fact. The mother suffers from mastitis, a bovine disease of the udder that is fatal in cows. Most farmers, it is said, kill the cows that contract it. Obviously, Barbara cannot put her mother out of her misery, so she treats her with massive doses of antibiotics, and her mother querulously suffers nearly all the time.

The father really is a bull from the waist down and goes out in search of heifers, stricken by suicidal shame every time he succeeds, but driven to repeat his quest by his animal self. It is obvious that Barbara is sacrificing herself: The only love she experiences is the incestuous passion that Damian has for her, and that is consummated only once before she puts a stop to it—for his sake. Eventually, she takes the parents with her so that they may all drown in the flood that is sweeping over Campbell's Reach, and so that her brother may finally be free of his unwholesome family ties.

A FAMILY MADNESS

Family, history, the tormented personalities of those who are present at great events, the sacrificial victim—these are the themes that are interwoven in all of Keneally's works. His novel *A Family Madness* juxtaposes two families: Terry Delaney's working-class family and that of Radislaw Kabbelski. The Delaneys seem not to be touched by history, but the Kabbelskis, Byelorussian refugees, have bathed in it for a long time. The third-person narrative, set in contemporary Australia, is interspersed with the journals of the Kabbelski family. The relative degrees of innocence or experience of the two groups are thus seen as contingent on how deeply one is embedded in history.

To Asmara

Differing perspectives, both cultural and historical, and social injustice also play definitive roles in Keneally's *To Asmara*. The product of several months spent researching at first hand in Eritrea by Keneally, *To Asmara* is a fictional account of the state of the Eritrean rebellion in 1987 (the rebellion began in 1962). Keneally uses thinly disguised characters and organizations to bring touches of reality to what is otherwise almost a philosophical tract.

Timothy Darcy is an Australian journalist whose Chinese-Australian wife, Bernadette, has left him for an Aborigine. In London, Darcy is introduced to an Eritrean rebel who wants Darcy to come to Africa to cover a special mission. Darcy accepts, hoping that by escaping to Africa, he will find his spiritual place in his coverage of the rebellion. Instead, he becomes part of a traveling party that also includes a French girl looking for her father (who had run away from his family many years before and had become a cameraman for the rebels), an English noblewoman on a crusade to end the brutal custom of female circumcision, and an aid worker trying to free his lover, who is in the hands of the Ethiopians, the Eritreans' mortal enemies. Darcy's other objective is to meet with an Ethiopian major held as a prisoner of war by the Eritreans.

The book is supposedly Darcy's journal combined with transcribed tape recordings of his thoughts and observations, with a few interjected chapters by an objective—though unidentified—third person. Ultimately, Darcy is lost, both metaphorically and physically, after he fails to connect with his fellow human beings and fails to rescue an aid truck, instead driving it over a land mine by accident. Darcy's failure reinforces the ongoing theme in Keneally's work of people divorced from their cultures and their spouses, unable to find solace or refuge in other cultures or others' spouses. With *To Asmara*, Keneally's lost generation continues.

Flying Hero Class

Revelation and realization of heroism on the part of an ordinary man, manager of a troupe of Australian native dancers, is the theme of *Flying Hero Class*. Frank McCloud is intrigued by the tribal dances of the Barramatjara, whose ancient history and beliefs in magic set them apart from the twentieth century. In their dances the Barramatjara assume the forms of creatures from the "dreamtime"—native Australian creatures such as dingos or emus. Recognizing the dancers' uniqueness, McCloud assembles and manages the troupe's tour of North America and Europe, assisted by his wife. McCloud remains an outsider to the natives, but he discovers himself and his own heroism when a jet on which they are all traveling, bound for Frankfurt, is hijacked. Middle Eastern terrorists select certain of the passengers, McCloud included, for special punishment as "criminals," forcing them to wear placards proclaiming the nature of their crimes. In the midst of chaos, death, and fear, McCloud confronts himself and discovers his ability to invoke a "revolution" among the passengers—a revolution that saves those remaining on board the aircraft.

Woman of the Inner Sea

In *Woman of the Inner Sea*, Keneally focuses on the mystery of Kate Gaffney-Kozinski, whose two children and their babysitter perish in a fire while she is away briefly. Kate flees the intrigue of Sydney and her construction-mogul husband; she takes on a new role as a barmaid in the inland town of Myambagh, surrounded by ranchers and toughs. In an improbable turn, Kate must flee again when her husband's agent appears with divorce papers; almost simultaneously, a flood occurs. On her flight into the outback, she is accompanied by a farmer, Gus, and his kangaroo and emu. Surviving the flood and drawing on the gentleness of the kangaroo, Kate (like other characters in

Keneally's fiction) finds her own heroism in endurance as she returns to Sydney to discover the reality of her tragedy. Keneally's characterization of Kate, his use of the aboriginal myth of the origin of the word "beast," and his exploration of the heroic amidst grief and chaos link this novel to others in his oeuvre, despite the melodramatic unraveling of the mystery.

A RIVER TOWN

A River Town takes the reader to turn-of-the-century Australia, where Irish immigrant Tim Shea battles the insularity and class distinctions of New South Wales. In the midst of an epidemic of bubonic plague, Tim finds himself culturally isolated. Keneally depicts the head of a young woman preserved in a jar by the local constable who seeks to identify her, Tim's rescue of two children when their father is killed in a buggy accident, Tim's being ostracized for opposition to the Boer War, and the quarantine against plague. Keneally draws on period recollections, some possibly passed down by his grandparents, who were immigrant storekeepers, to paint on a grand scale. Tension is added in Tim's own prejudice toward a Muslim medicine seller and his failure to recognize the settlers' mistreatment of the aborigines. The result is a novel of both heroism and human frailties set against the vastness of the continent and the cultural backdrop of a time of major settlement in Australia.

There is a wholeness about Keneally's work that belies one's initial impression of diversity. Not that diversity does not exist: Geographically and temporally, his work ranges from the Antarctic to Europe and America, from the dim past to the present. Yet certain themes are always prevalent. In the introduction to an interview with Keneally, Janette Turner Hospital writes, "The protagonists of the novels of Thomas Keneally are Jeremiahs of a sort, reluctant prophets or messiahs . . . prophets by random circumstance only." Keneally's fascination with circumstance and its effects stands out as the major lesson that history has taught him: Those who do great deeds, either public or private, are no better or worse than anyone else. If they are holy, they are so in the ancient sense of the word: "different from, other than." In revealing the humanity in their holiness Keneally makes his greatest contribution.

Jean-Pierre Metereau, updated by Mary Ellen Pitts

OTHER MAJOR WORKS

PLAYS: *Halloran's Little Boat*, pr. 1966; *Childermass*, pr. 1968; *An Awful Rose*, pr. 1972; *Bullie's House*, pr. 1980.

TELEPLAYS: *Essington*, 1974; *The World's Wrong End*, 1981.

NONFICTION: *Outback*, 1983; *Australia: Beyond the Dreamtime*, 1987 (with Patsy Adam-Smith and Robyn Davidson); *Now and in Time to Be: Ireland and the Irish*, 1991; *The Place Where Souls Are Born: A Journey to the Southwest*, 1992; *Memoirs from a Young Republic*, 1993; *Our Republic*, 1993; *Homebush Boy*, 1995; *The Great Shame: A Story of the Irish in the Old World and the New*, 1998 (also pb. as *The Great Shame: And the Triumph of the Irish in the English-Speaking World*).

CHILDREN'S LITERATURE: *Ned Kelly and the City of the Bees*, 1978.

BIBLIOGRAPHY

Gelder, Ken. "'Trans-what?' Sexuality and the Phallus in *A Dutiful Daughter* and *The Flesheaters* (Analysis of Novels by Thomas Keneally and David Ireland)." *Southerly* 49 (March, 1989): 3-15. Discusses Keneally's work in the light of his representation of sexuality. Includes some references.

Petersson, Irmtraud. "'White Ravens' in a World of Violence: German Connections in Thomas Keneally's Fiction." *Australian Literary Studies* 14 (October, 1989): 160-173. Addresses the question of Keneally's "cultural specificity" in his writing. Petersson discusses the historical and naturalist perspectives in Keneally's works such as *Schindler's List* and *A Family Madness*. Includes some reference information.

Pierce, Peter. *Australian Melodramas*. St. Lucia: University of Queensland Press, 1995. Arguing that Keneally uses techniques and situations of melodrama in the manner of nineteenth century writers such as Ibsen and Chekhov, Pierce finds serious melodrama basic to Australian literature. Contends that Keneally's melodrama is a source of renewal and that the extreme moral choices, exaggerated characters, and grand scale of Keneally's fiction portray Australia itself and Australia in the larger world.

Quartermaine, Peter. *Thomas Keneally*. New York: Viking Penguin, 1991. A monograph that addresses Keneally's life and major works.

Thorpe, Michael. Review of *To Asmara*, by Thomas Keneally. *World Literature Today* 64 (Spring, 1990): 360. Thorpe concentrates on Keneally as a "noncombatant novelist of war." Includes references for further information on Eritrea and on Keneally.

Willbanks, Ray. *Australian Voices*. Austin: University of Texas Press, 1992. A collection of interviews with major Australian writers that includes an interview with Keneally in which he discusses views of art and his aims as a writer.

WILLIAM KENNEDY

Born: Albany, New York; January 16, 1928

PRINCIPAL LONG FICTION

The Ink Truck, 1969
Legs, 1975
Billy Phelan's Greatest Game, 1978
Ironweed, 1983
The Albany Cycle, 1985 (includes *Legs, Billy Phelan's Greatest Game*, and *Ironweed*)
Quinn's Book, 1988
Very Old Bones, 1992
The Flaming Corsage, 1996

OTHER LITERARY FORMS

In addition to the novels cited above, William Kennedy's nonfiction *O Albany! An Urban Tapestry* (1983), pamphlets for the New York State Library, Empire State College, and the *Albany Tricentennial Guidebook* (1985) largely center on his native Al-

bany, New York. He wrote the screenplays for *The Cotton Club* (1984), with Francis Coppola and Mario Puzo, and *Ironweed* (1987), adapted from his novel of the same title. Kennedy collaborated with his son, Brendan, on the children's books *Charlie Malarkey and the Belly Button Machine* (1986) and *Charlie Malarkey and the Singing Moose* (1994).

ACHIEVEMENTS

Before becoming known as a novelist, Kennedy worked as a newspaperman in Albany, New York, a city in which politics plays an important role. He struggled at writing for years while teaching as an adjunct at the State University of New York (SUNY) at Albany. He brought all these traditions to his writing: the bite of the newsman, the literary allusions of the professor, and the mysticism of the American Irishman. His first books—*The Ink Truck, Legs*, and *Billy Phelan's Greatest Game*—drew some notice but sold sluggishly, so *Ironweed* was rejected by thirteen publishers until writer Saul Bellow, Kennedy's teacher and mentor, persuaded Viking to reconsider. Viking reissued the previous two novels along with *Ironweed* as *The Albany Cycle*, and *Ironweed* won the National Book Critics Circle Award in 1983 and the Pulitzer Prize in fiction in 1984. Kennedy received a MacArthur Foundation Fellowship in 1983. This unsolicited "genius" award freed him for creative work; he used part of the proceeds to start a writers' institute in Albany, later funded by New York State with him as director. His novels' characters are drawn from the world of bums and gangsters and have been compared in brilliance to those of James Joyce and William Faulkner. *The Albany Cycle*, with its interlocking characters and spirit of place, has been compared to Faulkner's Yoknapatawpha stories and Joyce's *Dubliners* (1914) and *Ulysses* (1922). Kennedy's style won praise as a combination of naturalism and surrealism, yet critics faulted what they call his overwriting and pandering to the public's demand for violence, explicit sex, and scatological detail. Critics generally agree that *Ironweed* is among Kennedy's best novels, fusing the style, characterization, attention to detail, and mysticism of the first two novels and focusing them with mastery.

(AP/Wide World Photos)

Kennedy would continue to add to his Albany cycle, publishing *Quinn's Book* in 1988, *Very Old Bones* in 1992, and *The Flaming Corsage* in 1996.

BIOGRAPHY

William Kennedy was born of Irish Catholic heritage in Albany, New York, on January 16, 1928. He was graduated from Siena College in 1949 and went to work for the Glens Falls, New York, *Post Star* as sports editor and columnist, followed by a stint as reporter on the Albany *Times Union* until 1956. He went to Puerto Rico to work for the *Puerto Rico World Journal*, then for the *Miami Herald* (1957), returning to Puerto Rico as founding managing editor of the San Juan *Star* from 1959 to 1961. Deciding to make fiction writing his career and Albany his literary source and center, he returned to the Albany *Times Union* as special writer and film critic from 1963 to 1970, while he gathered material and wrote columns on Albany's rich history and its often scabrous past. Upon the success of *Ironweed*, he was promoted to professor of English at State University

of New York at Albany, in 1983. The university and the city sponsored a "William Kennedy's Albany" celebration in September, 1984.

In 1993, Kennedy was elected to the American Academy of Arts and Letters. He added a sixth novel to the Albany cycle with the publication of *The Flaming Corsage* in 1996. Kennedy continued to work in other genres, writing, with his son Brendan, his second book for children, *Charlie Malarkey and the Singing Moose*.

ANALYSIS

William Kennedy's fiction is preoccupied with spirit of place, language, and style, and a mystic fusing of characters and dialogue. The place is Albany, New York, the capital city—nest of corrupt politics; heritor of Dutch, English, and Irish immigrants; home to canallers, crooks, bums and bag ladies, aristocrats, and numbers-writers. Albany, like Boston, attracted a large Irish Catholic population, which brought its churches, schools, family ties, political machine, and underworld connections.

Kennedy's style has been compared to that of sixteenth century French novelist François Rabelais for its opulent catalogs and its ribald scatology. Kennedy is not, however, a derivative writer. As his books unfold, one from another, he makes novel connections, adeptly developing the hallucinations of Bailey, the protagonist of *The Ink Truck*, the extrasensory perception of Martin Daugherty, one of the central consciousnesses of *Billy Phelan's Greatest Game*, and the ghosts of his victims visiting Francis Phelan on his quest for redemption in *Ironweed*.

THE INK TRUCK

Kennedy's first published novel, *The Ink Truck*, connects less strongly to these themes and styles than do later works. The novel focuses on the headquarters of a Newspaper Guild strike committee on the one-year anniversary of its strike against the daily newspaper of a town resembling Albany. Only four Guild members remain: Bailey, Rosenthal, Irma, and Jarvis, their leader. Bailey, the proverbial blundering Irish reporter, mixes his libido and marital problems with his earnest belief in the strike, now bogged down in trivialities.

Bailey's relationship with his wife is strained and crazed: She is madly jealous, as she has reason to be. Bailey mixes idealism about the strike with several sexual romps and psychic encounters, punctuated by savage beatings from the scabs and company agents determined to break the strike.

Bailey's fantasy is to open the valve on the ink truck coming to the newspaper plant, bleeding the newspaper's black blood into the snow of the mean streets. In the Guild room near the paper plant, Bailey attempts to revive his affair with Irma, another of the few remaining strikers. Joined by Deek, a collegiate type and an executive's son who wants to join the strike, the four members try to harass the paper's owners, whose representative, Stanley, refuses to grant their demands, which, by this time, have become niggling. As they attempt to block the ink truck in the snow and release the ink, everything goes wrong. When Bailey sets fire to the vacant store where the gypsies congregate, Putzina, the queen, is fatally burned, and she dies in the hospital amid a wild gypsy rite. Antic writing celebrates Bailey's subsequent kidnapping by the gypsies so that they seem comic despite the violence. Bailey escapes after cooperating with the company secretary in her sexual fantasy but is disillusioned when he finds that he must sign an apology to the newspaper company for the action of some members.

More setbacks emerge: Bailey takes back the apology, then finds that the motor has been taken out of his car. Rosenthal's house has been trashed viciously. Bailey, expelled from the Newspaper Guild, goes home to find that his wife, Grace, has put all of his belongings on the curb to be pilfered. His uncle Melvin refuses to help but invites him to an elaborate pet funeral for his cat. Just after this event, the cat's body disappears, a ludicrous culmination of all Bailey has lost: Guild, Guild benefits, apartment, and wife. Going literally underground, Bailey takes a job shelving books in the State Library, where Irma visits him to tell him that despite all setbacks, he, Rosenthal, and Deek are being hailed as the Ink Truck Heroes. In this aspect, Bailey prefigures the gangster hero, Legs Diamond, and the hero as transfigured bum, Francis Phelan, of the later books.

Becoming a media hero, Bailey makes one more futile try at the ink truck. In a grand finale, the orgiastic end-of-strike party hosted by Stanley becomes another humiliation for Bailey. Kennedy's low-key and inconclusive ending leaves the characters where they began: looking at the place on the wall of the Guild Room where a sign hung over the mimeograph machine saying DON'T SIT HERE. Bailey tries to make sense of his experiences, but even the reader cannot understand. Some of the richest of these experiences—a religious pilgrimage by trolley car and a trip backward in time to a cholera epidemic in 1832—seem almost gratuitous, loose ends without much relationship to the rest of the story. Bailey realizes that "all the absurd things they'd all gone through, separately or together . . . were fixed in time and space and stood only for whatever meaning he, or anyone else, cared to give them."

Legs

Kennedy's next novel, *Legs*, develops clearer patterns and meanings, though with the same mixture of realism and surrealism as in *The Ink Truck*. Kennedy demonstrates the truth of his 1975 novel's epigraph, "People like killers," a quote from Eugène Ionesco, through his portrayal of John "Jack" Diamond, also known as "Legs," an idolized, flamboyant underworld figure, a liquor smuggler during Prohibition, a careless killer, and a tough womanizer. Finally brought to justice by New York governor Franklin D. Roosevelt, Jack was mysteriously executed gangland style in Albany in December, 1931.

The story begins in a seedy Albany bar, where four of the book's characters meet in 1974 to reminisce about the assassination of their gangster-hero, Jack "Legs" Diamond. The novel is a fictionalization of Jack's life, superimposing fictional characters, fictional names for real people, and Kennedy's imagination on real events. Three of the four in the frame story are minor, therefore surviving, members of Jack's entourage. The fourth member of the group is Marcus Gorman, Jack's attorney, mouthpiece, and friend, who gave up a political career to lend respectability and a capacity for legal chicanery to Jack. Marcus is the narrator of the novel, providing a less-than-intimate portrait, yet one filtered through a legal mind accustomed to the trickery of the profession as it was practiced then in Albany.

The book is tightly crafted, with parallel scenes, apt literary allusions, well-constructed flashbacks, foreshadowing throughout, and, always, the map of Albany and its neighboring Catskills in mind. The sordid historical account is elevated with signs and coincidences: Marcus, employed by Jack after he successfully represented another gangster, visits Jack in the Catskills after speaking at a police communion breakfast in Albany; a copy of Rabelais is in the Knights of Columbus Library frequented by Marcus in Albany; one is in Jack's bookcase at his Catskills hideaway. Literary allusions combined with Bonnie-and-Clyde violence produce Kennedy's most transcendental effects. Marcus seems a divided consciousness: He regrets the straight-and-narrow life of Irish Catholic Albany and a secure role in politics, yet he has a way of suborning witnesses, getting them to pretend insanity, and ignoring obvious hints about Jack's grislier killings (such as the garage murder of an erstwhile ally).

Jack Diamond became a mythical imaginative popular hero, a "luminous" personality who appealed to the crowds and remained their darling even in his final trials. He survived assassination attempts, though his murder is foretold from the beginning. The story is interwoven with parallels and coincidences. Kiki, Jack's gorgeous mistress, engages in a monologue reminiscent of Molly Bloom's in Joyce's *Ulysses* when she learns (from a newspaper she has hidden in her closet) that Jack really kills people. Then, when Jack is shot in a hotel (he recovers), Kiki leaves for a friend's apartment and hides in her closet from both the police and the rival gangsters.

Finally, Jack comes to trial over his torture of a farmer in the matter of a still. The farmer complains, and a grand jury is called by Roosevelt. Though he is acquitted of the assault on the farmer, a federal case against him nearly succeeds because of the testimony of an aide Jack betrayed. Following this, Jack is shot and killed in a rooming house in Albany.

Part of the novel's theme relates to the legal profession. Marcus insists that he defends those who pay his fee. In Jack's second trial, he uses an old nun, a courthouse regular, telling the court in a rambling summation that this old nun came to tell him how compassionate Jack Diamond was. Though a complete fabrication, these emotional touches win juries.

Kennedy's manic touch is evident in his portrayal of scenes on an ocean liner as Jack and Marcus try to conclude a drug deal, in the Kenmore bar in Albany in its art deco heyday, and of the singing of "My Mother's Rosary" at the Elk's Club bar in Albany. The final coda is a lyrically written, but puzzling, apotheosis: Jack, dead, gradually emerges from his body, in a transfiguration worthy of a Seigfried or a Njall of Nordic sagas.

BILLY PHELAN'S GREATEST GAME

Kennedy's next novel, *Billy Phelan's Greatest Game*, tells the story of another of Albany's historical crimes—the real kidnapping of the political boss Dan O'Connell's nephew—through the framework of a series of games of chance played by a young hanger-on of the city's underside. He is Billy Phelan, son of an absent father, Francis, who will be the protagonist of *Ironweed*. The other consciousness of the book is Martin Daugherty, old neighbor of the Phelans and a newspaperman. The time frame covers several days in late October, 1938, the time of the greatest game—the kidnapping.

Family interrelationships loom importantly in this novel. Billy Phelan has lost his father, Francis, by desertion twenty-two years before; Martin's father, a writer with an insane wife and a lovely mistress, now lies senile in a nursing home. The politically powerful McCall family almost loses their only heir, the pudgy, ineffectual Charlie. Martin lusts after his father's mistress, who plays sexual games with him. Similarly, Billy's lady friend, Angie, cleverly outwits him by pretending to be pregnant, to see what Billy will do. They have never, she says, really talked about anything seriously. Billy reminisces about rowing down Broadway in a boat, during a flood in 1913, with his father and uncle. Soon, he finds his father in a seedy bar, along with his companion Helen, and gives Helen his last money for his father.

This novel frames and mirrors an unsavory crime in the lives of ordinary, yet complicated, human beings. Kennedy's wealth of language, his handiness with an anecdote, sometimes leads him to leave loose ends in his otherwise tightly constructed narratives. For example, Martin Daugherty has extrasensory perception; moreover, he lusts after his father's former mistress Melissa, who also has a taste for women. These details are interesting, yet, unlike the appearance of the vagrant Francis Phelan, these anecdotes do not further the plot or embellish the theme.

Still, Kennedy's novels unfold in a profusion of ideas, one from the other, both in language and in plot. The same time frame and some of the same characters appear in *Ironweed*, the final book of the cycle and the Pulitzer Prize winner.

IRONWEED

Ironweed takes place immediately after the events in *Billy Phelan's Greatest Game*, on Halloween and All Saint's Day, 1938, just after the radio broadcast of Orson Welles's adaptation of H. G. Wells's *The War of the Worlds* (1898). The dates are not randomly chosen: The story, though on the surface the saga of a failed, homeless man, is actually a religious pilgrimage toward redemption from sin. Ironweed is described in an epigraph as a tough-stemmed member of the sunflower family, and Francis, like the weed, is a survivor. These analogies, like the Welles broadcast, hinge on a question of belief important to this novel.

Unlike Kennedy's previous books, *Ironweed* has no narrator or central consciousness. The main character, Francis Phelan, first left home after he killed a man during a transit strike by throwing a stone during a demonstration against the hiring of scab trolley drivers. Subsequently he returned, but left for long periods when he played professional baseball. Later, he disappeared for twenty-two years after he dropped his infant son while diapering him; the child died, yet Francis's wife, Annie, never told anyone who dropped Gerald. Francis and another bum, Rudy, dying of cancer, get jobs digging in St. Agnes's Cemetery, where Gerald and other relatives are buried.

Reason and fact are supremely important in the book, yet within one page Francis's mother, a disagreeable hypocrite, twitches in her grave and eats crosses made from weeds, and the infant Gerald converses with his father and wills him to perform acts of expiation, as yet unknown, that will cease his self-destructiveness and bring forgiveness. Francis has killed several people besides the scab driver, yet it is not for these crimes that he needs forgiveness but for deserting his family. The rest of the book chronicles his redemption. Throughout, shifts to fantasy occur, triggered by passages of straight memory and detailed history. Ghosts of the men Francis killed ride the bus back to Albany, yet they do not seem as horrible to Francis as a woman he finds near the mission, freezing in the cold. He drapes a blanket around her, yet later he finds her dead, mangled and eaten by dogs.

During the night, Francis meets with his hobo "wife," Helen, a gently educated musician (she once went to Vassar) with enough energy, though dying of a tumor, to sing proudly in a pub on their rounds. In the mission, Francis gets a pair of warm socks; on the street, Helen is robbed of the money given to her by Francis's son Billy. Then follows a nightmare search through the cold streets for shelter for the delicate Helen. In desperation, Francis goes to a friend's apartment, where he washes his genital region in the toilet and begs a clean pair of shorts. The friend refuses them shelter, so Francis leaves Helen in an abandoned car with several men, though he knows she will be molested sexually.

The next day, Francis gets a job with a junkman. While making his rounds, he reads in a paper about his son Billy getting mixed up in the McCall kidnapping. Making the rounds of old neighborhoods, buying junk from housewives, releases a flood of memories for Francis: He sees his parents, his neighbors the Daughertys in their house, now burned, where one day the mad Katrina Daugherty walked out of her house naked to be rescued by the seventeen-year-old Francis. Because of this memory, he buys a shirt from the ragman to replace his filthy one. While he is buying the shirt, Helen goes to Mass, then listens to records in a record store (stealing one). Retrieving money she has hidden in her bra, Helen redeems the suitcase at the hotel. In her room, she recalls her life, her beloved father's suicide, her mother's cheating her of her inheritance, and her exploiting lover/employer in the music store. Washing herself and putting on her Japanese kimono, she prepares to die.

Francis, meanwhile, revisits his family, bringing a turkey bought with his earnings from the day's job. He bathes, dresses in his old clothing his wife has saved, looks over souvenirs, meets his grandson, gets his daughter's forgiveness as well as his wife's, and is even invited to return. He leaves, however, and finds Rudy; together they look for Helen. Finding Helen registered at Palumbo's Hotel, Francis leaves money with the clerk for her. The final violent scene occurs in a hobo jungle, as it is being raided by Legionnaires. Francis kills Rudy's attacker with his own baseball bat and carries the fatally injured Rudy to the hospital. Returning to the hotel, Francis discovers Helen dead and leaves swiftly in a freight car.

The ending, typical of Kennedy's novels, is inconclusive. The reader can assume either that Francis leaves on a southbound freight or that he returns to his wife Annie's house and lives hidden in the attic. The use of the conditional in narration of this final section lends the necessary vagueness. Nevertheless, in *Ironweed*, the intricacy of poetry combines with factual detail and hallucinatory fugues to create a tight structure, the most nearly perfect of *The Albany Cycle* and its appropriate conclusion. The parallelism, for example, of a discussion of the temptations of Saint Anthony with the name of the Italian Church of St. Anthony, where Helen hears Mass on her last day of life, shows the craftsmanship of the author. The interconnections of theme, plot, and character in the three Albany novels, their hallucinatory fantasies, their ghostly visitations, ennoble the lowest of the low into modern epic heroes.

QUINN'S BOOK

Kennedy's next novel, *Quinn's Book*, also centers on Albany. Spanning a period from the late 1840's to the mid-1860's, *Quinn's Book* is a historical novel infused with Magical Realism, deliberately extravagant in style. The narrator and protagonist, Daniel Quinn, an orphan, relates his adventures and his gradual progress toward maturity. Ultimately he becomes a writer, encouraged by his editor on the *Albany Chronicle*, Will Canady (whose name suggests that he is the author's alter ego). Coming-of-age tale, picaresque, novel of education, *Künstlerroman*: *Quinn's Book* partakes of all these genres and more, generally stopping

just short of parody. It is Kennedy's most explicit celebration of the transformative power of art.

VERY OLD BONES

In *Very Old Bones*, Kennedy focuses on the Phelan family history, his narrator a third-generation, albeit unacknowledged, Phelan. Orson Purcell, child of Peter Phelan and his landlady, Claire Purcell, has come to the family home in Albany to care for the ailing Peter. Orson brings a troubled soul to the house that was home to his father, but not to him. Uncertain of his identity, he has suffered two breakdowns and alternately mythologizes and demonizes his wife Giselle, a talented photographer.

In the house on Colonie Street, Orson composes a family history, a "memoir," while his father struggles to complete the Malachi Suite, a series of paintings that document a tragic but pivotal event in the family's past. The two artists find solutions to the mysteries of their own lives by unearthing "very old bones," not unlike the construction crews who have discovered the skeleton of a mastodon beneath Albany's old water filtration plant.

The event that provides the key to so many Phelan mysteries is the 1887 "exorcism" murder of Lizzie McIlhenny at the hands of her demented husband Malachi, brother of Kathryn Phelan. The story helps to explain the unremitting joylessness of the Phelan matriarch, an unwilling spectator of the horror. In addition, the four paintings in the suite depict the patterns of belief that have informed the behavior of successive generations of Phelans: a distrust of happiness, a keen awareness of the dark forces afoot in the world, and a conviction that the past is always buried in a very shallow grave.

THE FLAMING CORSAGE

The Flaming Corsage, the sixth novel in the Albany Cycle, begins with a cryptic account of the so-called Love Nest killings in 1908, a scandalous event in which the playwright Edward Daugherty is injured by his friend Giles Fitzroy, who then kills his own wife and himself.

The complex of causes resulting in the killings had been set in motion a generation earlier when Emmett Daugherty saved the life of his employer who, in gratitude, promised to educate Emmett's children. Thus, Edward Daugherty, a well-educated child of Albany's Irish North, is positioned not only to court the granddaughter of his patron but also to incur the envy of his colleague, Maginn, a Claggert-like figure whose machinations lead to the killings.

The union of Edward and Katrina is doomed because it defies the ethnic, religious, and class divisions of Albany, but the turning point in their marriage is the fire in the Delavan Hotel that indirectly claims the lives of Katrina's sister and father. Katrina herself is scarred when a flaming stick pierces her breast and sets her corsage afire. Finding in the accidental tragedy an indictment of her own and Edward's behavior, Katrina withdraws from her husband and unwittingly sets in motion a new train of causation that will contribute to other deaths fourteen years later.

In *The Flaming Corsage*, Kennedy's characters continue to seek "God's own symmetry" in random tragedies while failing to anticipate the consequences of their own behavior. Love, like the flaming arrow that wounds Katrina, is more often a cause of than a cure for the sadness of life.

Anne Mills King, updated by Kathleen N. Monahan

OTHER MAJOR WORKS

SHORT FICTION: "The Secrets of Creative Love," 1983; "An Exchange of Gifts," 1985; "A Cataclysm of Love," 1986.

SCREENPLAYS: *The Cotton Club*, 1984 (with Francis Coppola and Mario Puzo); *Ironweed*, 1987.

NONFICTION: *Getting It All, Saving It All: Some Notes by an Extremist*, 1978; *O Albany! An Urban Tapestry*, 1983; *Albany and the Capitol*, 1986; *Riding the Yellow Trolley Car: Selected Nonfiction*, 1993.

CHILDREN'S LITERATURE: *Charlie Malarkey and the Belly Button Machine*, 1986 (with Brendan Kennedy); *Charlie Malarkey and the Singing Moose*, 1994.

BIBLIOGRAPHY

Allen, Douglas R., and Mona Simpson. "The Art of Fiction CXI: William Kennedy." *The Paris Review* 31 (Winter, 1989): 34-59. Conducted in two sessions, in 1984 and 1988, this wide-ranging interview provides an excellent introduction to Ken-

nedy's work. He discusses his experience as a newspaper writer, the vicissitudes of his literary career, and his development as a novelist. Includes Kennedy's observation that he does not regard *Legs, Billy Phelan's Greatest Game*, and *Ironweed* as a trilogy but rather as works in an ongoing cycle that also comprises *Quinn's Book*.

Giamo, Benedict. *The Homeless of "Ironweed": Blossoms on the Crag*. Iowa City: University of Iowa Press, 1996. Giamo explores the theme of homelessness and social problems in literature, focusing on *Ironweed*. Includes bibliography.

Kennedy, Liam. "Memory and Hearsay: Ethnic History and Identity in *Billy Phelan's Greatest Game* and *Ironweed*." *Melus* 18 (Spring, 1993): 71-83. The author focuses on *Billy Phelan's Greatest Game* and *Ironweed* to explore Kennedy's presentation of ethnic identity. In a tightly knit community such as Albany's Irish North End, family, civic, and ethnic history blend into an inchoate, yet powerful, force. The author points to Kennedy's insistence on the role of the past in the motives and impulses of his characters.

Kennedy, William. *Conversations with William Kennedy*. Edited by Neila C. Seshachari. Jackson: University Press of Mississippi, 1997. Part of the Literary Conversations series, this book of interviews with Kennedy is insightful. Includes index.

Michener, Christian. *From Then into Now: William Kennedy's Albany Novels*. Scranton, Pa.: University of Scranton Press, 1998. Discusses the theme of city life in Kennedy's works. Contains bibliography and index.

Nichols, Loxley F. "William Kennedy Comes of Age." *National Review* 27 (August 9, 1985): 78-79. An excellent short piece on Kennedy with much useful information. Discusses *The Ink Truck*, which Nichols considers Kennedy's most atypical work. Also analyzes Jack Diamond's death in Kennedy's second novel, *Legs*. Explores *Ironweed* in the light of its mythical allusions and describes *O Albany!* in terms of the "pervasive vitality of the past."

Turner, Tramble T. "*Quinn's Book*: Reconstructing Irish-American History." *Melus* 18 (Spring, 1993): 31-46. This article discusses the presentation of the Irish and the African American in *Quinn's Book.* Similarities between the two outcast communities in the nineteenth century do not prevent racist outbreaks such as the Draft Riot of 1863. The author compares *Quinn's Book* to Toni Morrison's 1987 *Beloved* as commentary on America's past.

JACK KEROUAC

Born: Lowell, Massachusetts; March 12, 1922
Died: St. Petersburg, Florida; October 21, 1969

PRINCIPAL LONG FICTION
The Town and the City, 1950
On the Road, 1957
The Dharma Bums, 1958
The Subterraneans, 1958
Doctor Sax, 1959
Maggie Cassidy, 1959
Tristessa, 1960
Visions of Cody, 1960, 1972
Big Sur, 1962
Visions of Gerard, 1963
Desolation Angels, 1965
Vanity of Duluoz, 1968
Pic, 1971

OTHER LITERARY FORMS

In addition to his novels, Jack Kerouac published *Mexico City Blues* (1959), a poetry collection intended to imitate the techniques of jazz soloists. *Scattered Poems* (1971) and *Old Angel Midnight* (1976) were published posthumously. His nonfiction prose includes *The Scripture of the Golden Eternity* (1960), a homemade sutra written to Gary Snyder; *Book of Dreams* (1961), sketches that recorded his dreams; *Lonesome Traveler* (1960), travel sketches; and *Satori in Paris* (1966).

ACHIEVEMENTS

While some critics have condemned Kerouac as an incoherent, unstructured, and unsound writer, the

(Archive Photos)

prophet of a nihilistic movement, his books have continued to be read. The very qualities for which he has been criticized—wildness, sensationalism, and irresponsibility—have been sources of charm to other commentators. He has been described on one hand as pessimistic and bizarre, and on the other as optimistic and fresh. His most prestigious and enthusiastic reviewer has been Malcolm Cowley, who introduced *On the Road* to Viking after it had been turned down by Ace, Harcourt Brace, and Little, Brown. *On the Road's* respectability is evidenced by its appearance in excerpt form in *The Norton Anthology of American Literature* and its publication as a casebook in The Viking Critical Library series.

Kerouac's unofficial and unwanted title of "King of the Beats" brought him a great deal of the publicity he shunned. As with other aspects of Kerouac's life and works, there was little agreement about what a "Beat" was. Kerouac's friend, Gary Snyder, has described the Beats as a movement that gathered together the myths of freedom espoused by Henry David Thoreau and Walt Whitman, adding some of the notions of Buddhism. John Holmes defined "Beat" as a "nakedness of soul," as "feeling reduced to the bedrock of consciousness." The Beat writers, he added, recognized the need for home, for values, and for faith, and they advocated companionship, courage, and mutual confidence. To Kerouac, who is generally credited with the invention of the term, "Beat" meant "beatific"—holy and compassionate. Interviewed by Mike Wallace on television, Kerouac declared that the Beats did not fear death and that they wanted to lose themselves as Christ had advised. In *Pageant* magazine, he wrote that the Beats believed that honesty and freedom would lead to a vision of a God of Ecstasy. In a public forum, Kerouac declared that America was changing for the better and warned those who wanted to spit on the Beat generation that the wind would blow the spit back on them. Massmedia writers developed the image of a bearded "beatnik" who wore sweat shirts and jeans, played bongo drums, never bathed, and used the word "like" as a ubiquitous conjunction. Even though the beatniks were a far cry from the intellectual Beats, they became associated with them in the public eye.

Although Kerouac's public image endangered his critical reception, critics of the late twentieth century recognized him as a powerful and talented writer. His work, as he intended it to be, is one long opus.

BIOGRAPHY

Jean Louis Lebris de Kerouac was born in Lowell, Massachusetts, on March 12, 1922. His mother, Gabrielle Ange Levesque Kerouac, and his father, Leo Alcide Kerouac, were both French Canadians whose families had emigrated from Quebec. Gabrielle's father, a mill worker and an owner of a small tavern, had died when she was fourteen, and she then went to work as a machine operator in a Nashua, New Hampshire, shoe shop. From this moment, and for the rest of her life, "Memere" fought for a higher social status. Leo was an insurance salesman who became a job printer. At the time of Kerouac's birth, his sister Caroline ("Nin") was three, and Gerard, the

brother who had been weakened by rheumatic fever, was five.

The year after Kerouac's birth, Leo began publication of *The Lowell Spotlight*, which featured local political and theatrical news. The family was very close; the mother was a teller of tales, and the father was an entertainer who specialized in animal noises. At the age of nine, Gerard became so ill that he was forced to remain in bed. To his younger brother, Gerard was a saint who had once saved a mouse from a trap. As Gerard grew weaker, he grew more angelic in the eyes of everyone in the family, and the lively young Jack suffered by comparison. As Gerard's pain grew worse, Jack began to feel that he was somehow responsible. After Gerard's death, Jack tried futilely to replace him by being especially pious and sensitive.

As he grew older, Kerouac went frequently to films with passes given to Leo. The public library also became another favorite haunt, but the biggest outside influence on Kerouac's childhood was the Roman Catholic Church of his forefathers. He attended parochial school, had visions of Christ and the Virgin Mary, memorized the catechism, and worried about his sins and purgatory. When he became an altar boy, his Jesuit teachers thought that he might become a priest, but when he entered a public junior high school, Jean Kerouac became "Jacky," who could write, and whose favorite radio program was *The Shadow*—the forerunner of Dr. Sax.

As he walked to Lowell High School, where he participated in track and football, Kerouac saw the factories and the failures of his French Canadian neighbors; his father had lost his business and had even been forced to accept a job carrying water buckets for the Works Progress Administration (WPA). Memere, frustrated in her ever present ambitions, placed all her hopes in her remaining son and urged him to study and to succeed in a way that his father had not. By his senior year, Kerouac was a football star, scoring the winning touchdown for Lowell in the final game against Lawrence High.

Kerouac fell in love with Mary Carney, but he left her behind to accept Columbia University football coach Lou Little's offer to attend Horace Mann Prep

School, where he was to add the pounds and knowledge requisite for a Columbia football player. At Horace Mann, Jack wrote papers for his classmates for pay, some of which he spent on his first prostitute. He published short stories in the *Horace Mann Quarterly*, discovered the jazz world in Harlem, and adopted Whitman as his personal bard.

At Columbia, Kerouac studied William Shakespeare under Mark Van Doren, registered for the draft, found another mentor in the works of Thomas Wolfe, and broke his leg in a freshman football game. One day, to the great distress of his parents, who constantly pleaded with him to "get ahead" in the world, Kerouac left Columbia for Washington, D.C., New Haven, and Hartford, Connecticut, and a series of short-lived jobs. While he was a sportswriter for the *Lowell Sun*, he read Fyodor Dostoevski, who became his prophet. He shipped out of Boston as a merchant seaman on the *Dorchester*, where he started a novel called *The Sea Is My Brother*. In 1943, he entered the navy, which discharged him honorably three months later for "indifferent character." In 1944, Kerouac met poet Allen Ginsberg, a Columbia student until he was banned from campus, and William S. Burroughs, with whom he wrote a detective story. He also met Edie Parker, whom he married but from whom he separated shortly thereafter.

After his father died of cancer in 1946, Kerouac started taking Benzedrine and writing *The Town and the City*. He also met Neal Cassady, the "brother" he had been seeking since Gerard's death. After Cassady returned to Denver, Kerouac set out to see America, stopping in Denver before going to San Francisco, where he worked as a security guard, sending his savings to Memere. On a bus bound for Los Angeles, he met Bea Franco, with whom he took a job in Bakersfield picking cotton. From there, he took a bus to Pittsburgh and hitched a ride back to Memere's house, where she took care of him while he wrote. Cassady came East again, and he, Kerouac, and Cassady's first wife, Lu Anne, made their famous "on the road" trip.

At this time, Harcourt Brace announced that they would publish *The Town and the City*. Kerouac used the profits from *The Town and the City* to buy a house for Memere in Colorado, but she left it for New York after seven weeks of misery. Several journeys back and forth from Brooklyn to Colorado followed for Cassady and Kerouac. In 1950, Kerouac married Joan Haverty and began writing *On the Road*, typing it on rolls of teletype paper. In 1952, Janet Michele Kerouac was born to Joan, but it would be ten years before Kerouac admitted paternity.

Kerouac held jobs during the next few years as a brakeman, as a yard clerk, and as a fire watcher, but he depended mostly on his mother for support, despite the gnawing recollection that he had promised his father to take care of her. After several rejections, *On the Road* was published in 1957 and was hailed by *The New York Times* critic Gilbert Millstein as a major novel. During the next six years, Kerouac published twelve more books.

While Kerouac was in New York, he fell in love with Mardou Fox, whose American Indian and black ancestry Memere could never accept. After losing Mardou to the poet Gregory Corso, Kerouac wrote about the affair in *The Subterraneans*. In response to William Burroughs's request, Kerouac typed out "The Essentials of Spontaneous Prose," explaining the writing method he had used.

Kerouac found solace in *Walden: Or, Life in the Woods* (1854) and Thoreau, with whom he shared a rejection of civilization, and he also began to study Buddhism as part of his search for peace from the carping of Memere and the disappointments engendered by unsympathetic editors. He tried to convert the Cassadys, with whom he lived for a time in California, to Buddhism, but he also expressed to Ginsberg, once more in New York, his fear that charlatans might misuse Buddhism for aesthetic purposes. He meditated daily in an effort to reach Nirvana. When he met poet Gary Snyder, a Zen Buddhist whose approach was prayerful, Kerouac felt a harmony he had not known, even with Cassady.

By the time Kerouac married Stella Sampas, the sister of an old friend who was killed in the war, and settled down again in Lowell, he was suffering from three problems: recurring phlebitis, alcoholism, and the adulation of youngsters who invaded his privacy and made him feel old. They expected him to be

Dean Moriarty of *On the Road*, but his aging, alcoholic body rebelled.

Meanwhile, Cassady had been arrested for possession of marijuana and sentenced to prison time at San Quentin, whence he complained about Kerouac's lack of attention. After his release, Cassady drank tequila and swallowed Seconals at a Mexican wedding party; the combination caused his death. Kerouac never allowed himself to believe that Cassady was actually dead. In October, 1969, Kerouac's years of heavy drinking caused him to begin to bleed internally, and he died hours later. He had been, in spite of his bizarre habits, a gentle, loving man.

ANALYSIS

Jack Kerouac described himself as "a great rememberer redeeming life from darkness." In one sense, the Beat movement itself issued from his memory. In his June, 1959, *Playboy* essay on "The Origins of the Beat Generation," Kerouac claimed that the guts of the Beats had come from his ancestors—the independent Breton nobles who fought against the Latin French; his grandfather, Jean-Baptiste Kerouac, who used to defy God to put out his kerosene lamp during a thunderstorm; his father, who used to give such loud parties that the Lowell police came for drinks—and from his own childhood, peopled with the Shadow, the Moon Man, and the Marx Brothers.

Kerouac claimed on more than one occasion that his books were actually one book about his entire life. He had intentions to consolidate them, but these plans were not carried out before his death. The areas of life that he remembered and celebrated include the dichotomy between his family and friends in Lowell, Massachusetts, and the Beat friends with whom he carried on such a frenzied, peripatetic relationship. As a rememberer, he never separated the two entirely; the Roman Catholic Bretons and the gentle Leo and Gerard were never far from his consciousness. Kerouac declared that his father had never lifted a hand to punish his children, or even their little pets, and that Gerard had extracted from his younger brother a promise never to hurt or allow anyone else to hurt a living thing. These two strains—the fierceness of the Bretons and the gentleness of his brother

and father—culminated in the vitality and the kindness of Jack Kerouac, the ex-football player who cared so much for his pets as a grown man that his mother feared to tell him that his cat had died.

THE TOWN AND THE CITY

When he was ready to write his first published book, *The Town and the City*, Kerouac found it necessary—or more aesthetically pleasing—to use five boys to present the many facets of his own character. The Kerouac family became the Martins, and Lowell became Galloway, which had a rural setting. The Martins are wealthier than the author's own family; they are also less devout as Catholics. The mother is French, and the rest of the family is Irish. Most of the vignettes serve to illustrate the love that the Martins feel for one another and Galloway as a town of "wild, self-believing individuals," the kind about which Walt Whitman sang.

The style of the novel is romantic and sprawling, in the vein of Thomas Wolfe. While Kerouac possessed an almost uncanny aptitude for recollecting details, he enhanced his memory by reviewing his old notebooks. The book was to be more than a chronicle of the Martin/Kerouac family; it was to be a microcosm of America. There are three sisters and five brothers in the Martin family, as opposed to the daughter and two sons of the Kerouacs; the loving, compassionate Mrs. Martin recalls Kerouac's own mother. Mickey, the youngest child of the Martins, goes to dinner and the races with his father, just as the young Jack had gone to Rockingham racetrack with Leo. He also writes novels and publishes newspapers about his imaginary racehorses and baseball teams.

Two of the sisters, Rose and Ruth, have the characteristics of Kerouac's sister Nin, while the third, Liz, is more like Kerouac's high school sweetheart, Mary Carney. One story of sibling love involves Charley, who had broken a window with his slingshot and is collecting junk to pay for it. Liz and Joe pitch in to help him when they learn of his plight. Liz eventually elopes with a jazz musician, has a stillborn baby, divorces her husband, and becomes a blonde barmaid.

The central character, Peter, is thirteen when the novel begins, and the story of his most spectacular high school game is that of his creator. As a result of his prowess, Peter wins a football scholarship to the University of Pennsylvania, but he leaves to join the merchant marines. As a student, however, he meets a new circle of friends, whose habits dismay George Martin just as Kerouac's marijuana-smoking cronies had bewildered Leo. Peter tries to introduce his mistress Judie to his parents, but their meeting is interrupted by a policeman who wants Peter to identify the body of Waldo Meister, a suicide victim. The gulf between the Martin family and Peter's friends is never closed, but Peter continues to be a loving part of both groups. He nurses his father during his illness and reacts to his death with grief and disbelief.

Peter's brother Francis is a shy, studious Harvard student who fails the Officers' Candidate School aptitude test and rebels at being a soldier. When he is confined for tests, he spots a navy psychiatrist with *The New Republic* under his arm and decides that he has met a kindred spirit. Convinced that Francis is indeed incapable of taking orders, the doctor helps him obtain his discharge.

In one scene, Levinsky (the Allen Ginsberg character) lectures to Peter in a Times Square cafeteria about a "post-atomic" disease of the soul, using words taken from an actual essay by Ginsberg (with permission from Ginsberg).

The novel ends with an unhappy Peter heading West to a new life, on a lonely, rainy night. The family has figuratively died with the father, and Peter will go wherever the roads lead. According to John Clellon Holmes, the book had originally ended with the family together, and the "on the road" ending was a last-minute Kerouac addition, which would lead obviously and naturally into his next book, already in the planning stage.

The Town and the City is frequently compared with Thomas Wolfe's *Look Homeward, Angel* (1929), and, like Wolfe's book, it required considerable editing, which was accomplished by Robert Giroux, who cut one third of the manuscript. In spite of its lukewarm success, Kerouac continued to believe in his own genius. Years later, he learned that the Kerouac family crest included the motto (translated from the French), "Love, Work, and Suffer." He hap-

pily noted that these words accurately describe the Martin family.

ON THE ROAD

Both the title and the novel were incubating in Kerouac's mind for four years before he sat down to write *On the Road* on a 100-foot roll of paper, in one 120,000 word, single-spaced paragraph. Six more years passed before its publication, and in the decade between conception and birth, America had changed, and so had the writer.

Sal Paradise, the narrator and the Kerouac figure, received his name when Ginsberg wrote a poem containing the line, "Sad paradise it is I imitate." The carelessly written "d" caused "Sad" to look like "Sal." Sal, whose ideals are both romantic and personal, sets out near the beginning of the tale to search for an eden. He is at the same time leaving behind all intimacy and responsibility associated with home and family.

Like Geoffrey Chaucer's pilgrims, everyone Sal meets is described with superlatives: He hears "the greatest laugh in the world"; he observes the most smiling, cheerful face in the world; and he watches a tall Mexican roll the biggest bomber anybody ever saw. While observing these fellow pilgrims, he thinks of himself and his friends as seeking salvation and the promised land. Sal expects to find a direction and purpose on the road that his life has not previously had.

Sal has studied maps of the West, and when he begins his trip, he wants to repeat as closely as possible the path of the old wagon trains. He glories in the names of such cities as Platte and Cimarron and imagines that the unbroken red line that represents Route 6 on his map duplicates the trail of the early American settlers. After a false start on a rainy day, Sal returns to New York, where he had started, and buys a bus ticket to Chicago; the bus is a mode of travel he uses more than once. In Des Moines, Sal awakens nameless and reborn in what seems to be a turning point in his life. This moment that divides his youth from his future occurs, fittingly enough, in mid-America. He goes from Denver to California, where he meets Dean Moriarty, the central figure of the book and the figure that made Neal Cassady a legend.

Dean becomes a part of Sal's life, an extension of his personality, his alter ego; he even insists on sharing his wife with Sal. Three become a crowd, however, and Sal, after several digressions, goes back to the East and his aunt. On the last lap of the journey, he meets a shriveled old man with a paper suitcase who is called "Ghost of the Susquehanna." Sal sees him as an aging reflection of what he himself will become—a bum.

The energy of the book derives from Dean Moriarty, who is never far out of Sal's mind. Dean's accomplishments include skillful driving—often of cars he has stolen for a joyride—talking his way out of any tight situation, seducing women—frequently two at a time—and appreciating jazz. The friends Dean has met in pool halls become the minor heroes of this epic.

In Kerouac's mind, Cassady and America were one entity—vibrant, carefree, and admirable. Through Dean Moriarty, Kerouac chronicles a new kind of existence in postwar America—suggesting a life less dependent upon place and family and more tolerant of impropriety. The hedonist Dean loves and leaves his women in the manner of the stereotyped cowboy who rides off into the sunset. Dean, never complacent, ever free, can be characterized by the fact that he goes to answer his door completely naked. Even when he is employed and has a home address, he seems to be on the move; he is always planning a break from entanglements, often represented by whomever his current wife might be.

Sal sees himself as a disciple to the saint, Dean, and he exults in Dean's uniqueness and eccentricity. Dean's mysticism consists of belief in his father, in God, and IT, which can be communicated by jazz musicians and which has somehow been communicated to Dean through his missing father, who had been a drunk. The search for Dean's father is one of the book's themes, along with the search for God. The roaders are seeking someone to shelter them from life and responsibility, and they approve of those pilgrims (Montana Slim and Remi Boncoeur) who are respectful toward their own fathers.

Perhaps the story would not have been told if Dean had not been such an extraordinary driver, ab-

solutely at home on the road. Sal has no driver's license and when allowed at the wheel guides the car off the road and onto a muddy shoulder. Even though Dean's chief contribution to the conversation seems to be "Wow," he expresses himself eloquently while in control of a car. Never mind if he wears it out; he delivers the car exhausted to its owner, while he travels on jauntily in another vehicle willing to respond to his touch.

Women respond to Dean in the same way, and he sees sex as essential and holy. His problem is that he wants to love several women simultaneously. He sees them as part of his self-improvement schedule, which is not induced by remorse for crimes committed or prison terms spent, but by the demands imposed by his search for a better life. Sal forgives Dean his thefts and other transgressions, reasoning that all Americans are like that.

On the Road is a love story: Sal loves Dean Moriarty, and their movements back and forth across the continent represent in some ways their relationship. Sal sees Dean at first as a source of hope, and he moves toward him, fascinated. He finally assumes some of the responsibility for his friend, and he becomes his defender. After Dean's thumb becomes infected as a result of hitting one of his women, Sal sees him as a mad Ahab. When Dean, Sal, and a friend go to Mexico City, on what is significantly their first North-South journey, Sal becomes ill and is abandoned by Dean, who has to go home to straighten out one of his recurring domestic crises. Sal never denies Dean, but he is less enamored of his sometimes childish friend by the book's end.

Most of the characters Sal meets on the road are attractive in some way; as Huck Finn found people on the river to be sympathetic, Sal feels a communion with the hobos, who eschew competition and jobs for a sense of brotherhood and a simple life. He is disappointed, however, when he sees his first cowboy, whose apparel is his only claim to authenticity. Like Stephen Crane before him, Sal sees that the West is merely trying to perpetuate dead traditions, and that Central City is simply a tourist attraction. Nothing can be as fine as his dreams of the West, and he eventually begins to conclude that the East, after all, may be the place to find contentment and salvation. He returns home in his favorite month, October, realizing that he has acted out an adventure, but that he has experienced no rebirth.

The point of view of *On the Road* is consistently that of Sal, but as he tells the reader about his experiences as they occurred at the time, he also comments on the same events as he sees them now, with a more mature, more disillusioned, more objective eye. Saddened by the realization that the road itself is all important to Dean, he repudiates the idea of movement with no purpose.

Recognizing the vastness and shapelessness of the experience he was about to put on paper, Kerouac sought a suitable form and style. He began to write the book in a conscious imitation of Thomas Wolfe, but he finally decided to emulate Cassady's amorphous, joyous style. He added to that a new, free-association method that he called "sketching," suggested to him by Ed White, who thought it possible to paint with words. Sketching, comparable in Kerouac's view to the improvisation of the jazz musicians he greatly admired, was new, but the story he told was a repetition of the ageless initiation theme. *On the Road* is, however, not simply another *Tom Jones* (Henry Fielding, 1749) or *The Adventures of Huckleberry Finn* (Mark Twain, 1884); it reflects the confusion, the sense of search, and the troubled spirit of the Kerouac generation.

THE SUBTERRANEANS

The title of *The Subterraneans* comes from Ginsberg's name for Greenwich Villagers; its setting is New York, disguised with San Francisco place names. Kerouac claimed that the book is a full confession of the incidents surrounding his love affair with Mardou Fox, a part black, part American Indian subterranean who had been hanging out with drug addicts and musicians. Kerouac fell in love with her, he said, even before they were introduced.

The book, consciously modeled after Fyodor Dostoevski's *Notes from the Underground* (1864), contains Mardou's private thoughts as she has whispered them to Leo Percipied (the Kerouac figure). She imagines herself walking naked in the Village, crouching like a feline on a fence, experiencing a private epiphany, and then borrowing clothes and money to buy herself a symbolic brooch.

Leo (as Kerouac himself always did) sympathizes with minority races and listens to Mardou's thoughts about African Americans, American Indians, and America with a keen perception. The story carries Leo and Mardou on their frenzied movements through the Village in scenes that include meetings with bop musicians, poets, and novelists. A central scene describes Yuri Gligoric's (Gregory Corso) theft of a vendor's pushcart, in which he transports his friends to the home of Adam Moorad (Allen Ginsberg), who is angry at Yuri because of the prank.

Both Mardou and Leo become dissatisfied with their life together, and when Yuri and Leo bicker over her, Leo chooses the incident as an excuse to separate from Mardou. Afterward, he wanders alone to a freight yard, where he has a vision of his mother. Leo finally admits that he felt inadequate sexually in the presence of Mardou, and he concludes, "I go home, having lost her love, and write this book."

Fortified by Benzedrine, Kerouac sat at his typewriter with yet another teletype roll and wrote his confession in "three full moon nights of October." The style of the novel is remarkable for its faithful reproduction of Mardou's syntax and her drawn-out syllables. Kerouac heard in her speech a similarity to bop music, and he found in it what he called the "prose of the future." Impressed by this remarkable language, Burroughs and Ginsberg asked Kerouac to write a description of his spontaneous method of composition, and the result was the essay "The Essentials of Spontaneous Prose."

Reviews of *The Subterraneans* were not favorable. The only affirmation came from Henry Miller, who admired Kerouac's forthrightness. When an editor tried to cut some of the book, Kerouac refused to let him print it, and it was finally published in its original form in March of 1958.

THE DHARMA BUMS

The Dharma Bums, a book that Kerouac himself once described as a potboiler, is perhaps the most representative expression of the Beat sensibility in a work of fiction. Its focus is the close intellectual and religious relationship of Ray Smith (Kerouac) and

Japhy Ryder (Gary Snyder). Snyder called *The Dharma Bums* a real statement of synthesis, through Kerouac, of the available models and myths of freedom in America: Whitman, Thoreau, and the bums—with Buddhism added as a catalyst. Unlike *The Subterraneans*, *The Dharma Bums* is not purely confessional, and the literary hand is much more evident in the later work. For example, the author includes an encounter on a freight train with a bum who reads daily the prayers of Saint Teresa, who had been much beloved by Kerouac himself since childhood. He includes this character because the ascetic hobo adds to the book's religious ambience, but he pointedly omits mention of a meeting with an earthy, blond female that occurred the same day and is recounted in his notebook.

Ray Smith remembers an evening of peaceful happiness when he and Japhy sat together on a big glacial rock, elated, hallucinating, yet serious, and surrounded by yellow aspens. It was a cold evening in late autumn, and snow was on the ridges. It was on such an evening that Smith earned the sobriquet of the "Buddha Known as the Quitter," because he failed to climb a mountain. Ryder is another kind of coward. Because he has been a "poor guy" all of his life, he is afraid to enter a restaurant that might have an expensive menu.

The picture of Japhy is painted through faithful reproduction of Gary Snyder's speech and recollections of his poetry. The haiku Japhy composes on the mountainside are repeated verbatim, and one poem addressed to Sean Monahan (actually written by Snyder to Kerouac) is stuck on a nail of his cabin. Monahan is a twenty-two-year-old carpenter whose wife is adept at keeping him and their two children alive and happy on vegetable soup. The Monahans' life is described as "joyous," and they live in their woodland cottage furnished with Japanese straw mats, while they amuse themselves by studying sutras.

The way of life to which Ryder introduces Smith is a religious way, punctuated with prayer, laughter, and poetry, and it is espoused by the social minority who belong to the rucksack revolution. Both Smith and Ryder long to explain the dharma, or the truth of religion and life, to others. The dharma is associated with a nobility of body, mind, spirit, and speech that is surely worthy of their missionary zeal, if it can be attained.

Through Ryder, Smith learns of ecology and earth consciousness. The two discuss their own private religious beliefs. After he learns about the lifestyle of the "rucksack saints" through observation and listening, Smith delineates the mode of living for any would-be followers, listing the spiritual and physical equipment necessary: submission, acceptance, expectancy, rucksacks, tents, and sleeping bags.

Three books, then, shaped Kerouac's public image: *On the Road, The Subterraneans*, and *The Dharma Bums*. Each of them centers on a close relationship between a Kerouac figure and another person, and in each case, an intense dependency is involved. All are testaments of love, all concern America and Americans, all suggest an opportunity to develop emotional maturity, and all describe the existence of a subculture which anticipated the counterculture of the 1960's. Yet despite these similarities, there is a progression. Certainly Ray Smith of *The Dharma Bums* is a wiser figure than Sal Paradise of *On the Road*. Ray admires Japhy Ryder, who teaches him about faith, hope, and charity, whereas Sal had worshiped Dean Moriarty, whose human relationships—especially with women—had been characterized by thoughtlessness and selfishness, for all of his charm. Japhy studies Japanese and reads Ezra Pound, whereas Dean had parroted Arthur Schopenhauer, often without understanding. The Buddhist sympathy for all beings and the notion that man is but a speck in the universe are a contrast to Moriarty's selfishness and vanity. In Gary Snyder, the gentle Jack Kerouac found the brother he had lost, and *The Dharma Bums* offers a calmer, more benevolent, albeit less sweeping picture of the country Kerouac wanted his works to celebrate than does the more famous *On the Road*.

Sue L. Kimball

OTHER MAJOR WORKS

POETRY: *Mexico City Blues*, 1959; *Scattered Poems*, 1971; *Old Angel Midnight*, 1976.

NONFICTION: *Lonesome Traveler*, 1960; *The*

Scripture of the Golden Eternity, 1960; *Book of Dreams*, 1961; *Satori in Paris*, 1966.

BIBLIOGRAPHY

Amburn, Ellis. *Subterranean Kerouac: The Hidden Life of Jack Kerouac*. New York: St. Martin's Press, 1998. A fascinating biography by one of Kerouac's editors, showing how his ambivalent feelings about his sexuality influenced his work. Includes detailed notes and bibliography.

Cassady, Carolyn. *Heart Beat: My Life with Jack and Neal*. Berkeley, Calif.: Creative Arts, 1976. Chronicles Cassady's relationship with Kerouac from 1952 through 1953, and the *ménage à trois* between the Cassadys and Kerouac. Reprinted here are letters of Allen Ginsberg, Kerouac, Neal Cassady, and Carolyn Cassady.

_____. *Off the Road: My Years with Cassady, Kerouac, and Ginsberg*. New York: William Morrow, 1990. A personal account, with many anecdotes and recollections written from Carolyn Cassady's perspective. Important for its inside view of the Beat movement.

Nicosia, Gerald. *Memory Babe: A Critical Biography of Jack Kerouac*. New York: Grove Press, 1983. A comprehensive, biographical account of Kerouac's life. Highly regarded for background information on Kerouac and the process of his writing.

Turner, Steve. *Angelheaded Hipster: A Life of Jack Kerouac*. New York: Viking, 1996. Not as authoritative as Amburn, but copiously illustrated and with anecdotes that help illuminate the novels.

KEN KESEY

Born: La Junta, Colorado; September 17, 1935

PRINCIPAL LONG FICTION

One Flew over the Cuckoo's Nest, 1962
Sometimes a Great Notion, 1964
Sailor Song, 1992
Last Go Round, 1994 (with Ken Babbs)

OTHER LITERARY FORMS

When Stewart Brand was the editor of *The Last Whole Earth Catalog* in 1971, he asked Ken Kesey to edit *The Last Supplement to the Whole Earth Catalog*. Somewhat reluctant, Kesey agreed if Paul Krassner would be the coeditor. Krassner accepted, and it took almost two months to write, edit, and lay out the five-hundred-page final issue, which contained the best selections from previous issues as well as some new writings by Kesey. The final issue had a total press run of 100,000 copies and is now out of print.

Viking Press and Intrepid Trips jointly published *Kesey's Garage Sale* (1973), a volume based on an American phenomenon: the rummage, yard, or garage sale. The book is a miscellany of essays, poetry, letters, drawings, interviews, prose fiction, and a film script. Although much of the writing was Kesey's, "Hot Item Number 4: Miscellaneous Section with Guest Leftovers" contained a letter by Neal Cassady and poems by Allen Ginsberg and Hugh Romney. Kesey's "Who Flew over What," "Over the Border," and "Tools from My Chest" supply interesting insights into Kesey's beliefs and personality, and more important, they supplement the biographical details in Tom Wolfe's *The Electric Kool-Aid Acid Test* (1968), an informative biographical account of Kesey's Merry Pranksters exploits.

In "Who Flew over What," Kesey answers some of the most common questions about *One Flew over the Cuckoo's Nest*. He admitted that he wrote the novel while a night attendant at the Menlo Park Veterans Hospital, that he wrote part of it while under the influence of drugs, and that Randle Patrick Mc-Murphy, the protagonist, was a fictional character "inspired by the tragic longing of the real men" on the ward. Kesey not only included his only sketches of McMurphy but also provided interesting facts and insights into his job and the actual life on the ward.

"Over the Border" is an innovative film script based on Kesey's second arrest, his flight to Mexico, the arrival of his family and some of the Merry Pranksters, their sojourn in Mexico, and the decision to return to the United States. The characters are easily recognizable: Devlin and Betsy Deboree are

Kesey and his wife Faye; Sir Speed Houlihan is Neal Cassady; Claude and Blanch Muddle are Ken Babbs and his wife Anita; the Animal Friends are the Merry Pranksters; and Behema is Carolyn Adams. The script contains examples of Kesey's writing techniques, especially as he switches from scene to scene, as he describes the annual land-crab migration, and as he narrates Deboree's encounter with the Lizard, a Federales prison guard. Augmenting Wolfe's biographical account, the script also reveals Kesey's altered attitudes toward drugs as a means of changing society.

Another interesting section is "Tools from My Chest," parts of which were published originally in either *The Last Whole Earth Catalog* or *The Last Supplement to the Whole Earth Catalog*. These "tools" were figuratively those persons and things that had an impact on Kesey's own life and beliefs and, ultimately, on his writings. Kesey commented on such things as the Bible, the *I Ching*, mantras, the North Star, alcohol, and flowers; about such writers as Ernest Hemingway, William Faulkner (Kesey's declared favorite), Larry McMurtry, and William Burroughs; about radicals such as Malcolm X and Eldridge Cleaver; and about entertainers such as Woody Guthrie, Joan Baez, the Jefferson Airplane, and the Beatles. Finally, there are two powerfully written parables about Devlin Deboree.

Another miscellany, *Demon Box*, was published in 1986, and in 1990 Kesey and thirteen of his students published a collaborative novel, *Caverns*, under the pseudonym O. U. Levon. *The Further Inquiry*, also published in 1990, recounts the Merry Pranksters' 1964 cross-country bus trip and memorializes Neal Cassady.

ACHIEVEMENTS

Writer Tom Wolfe remarked that Kesey was one of the most charismatic men he had ever met, and others have likewise commented upon Kesey's charisma. In fact, social critics affirmed that there were two important leaders of the 1960's counterculture revolution: Timothy Leary and his devotees on the East Coast and Kesey and his Merry Pranksters on the West Coast. Leary and his Learyites took themselves seriously, advocated passively dropping out of society, and rejected much that was American, especially American gadgetry. In contrast, Kesey and his Merry Pranksters were pro-America, were more interested in the spontaneous fun of the twentieth century neo renaissance, and took LSD not to become societal dropouts but rather to lead society to new frontiers of social communality.

As a novelist, Kesey achieved both notoriety and distinction as a major voice of his generation. Yet some critics argue that his achievement goes further. They point to his complex characters, rollicking humor, and creative manipulation of point of view as Kesey's enduring contribution to American literature.

BIOGRAPHY

Ken Elton Kesey was born in La Junta, Colorado, on September 17, 1935, to Fred A. and Geneva Smith Kesey. Kesey's father shrewdly foresaw that the West Coast would be ideal for business ventures, and he moved his family to Springfield, Oregon,

(AP/Wide World Photos)

where he founded the Eugene Farmers Cooperative, the largest and most successful dairy cooperative in the Willamette Valley. The father taught his sons, Ken and Joe—the latter being called Chuck—how to wrestle, box, hunt, fish, and swim, and how to float the Willamette and McKenzie rivers on inner-tube rafts.

After attending the Springfield public schools and being voted most likely to succeed, Kesey enrolled in the University of Oregon at Eugene. In 1956, he married his high school sweetheart, Faye Haxby. During his undergraduate years, Kesey was an adept actor and seriously considered pursuing that career. He was also a champion wrestler in the 174-pound division and almost qualified for the Olympics. He received his Bachelor of Arts degree in 1957 and wrote *End of Autumn*, an unpublished novel about college athletics. In 1958, he enrolled in the graduate school at Stanford University on a creative writing scholarship and studied under Malcolm Cowley, Wallace Stegner, Frank O'Connor, and James B. Hall.

During his graduate years, two important things occurred that would influence Kesey's life and writing. The first occurred when he moved his family into one of the cottages on Perry Lane, then the bohemian quarters of Stanford. He met other writers, including Larry McMurtry, Kenneth Babbs, Robert Stone, and Neal Cassady. The second event was that Kesey met Vic Lovell, to whom he would dedicate *One Flew over the Cuckoo's Nest*. Lovell not only introduced Kesey to Freudian psychology but also told Kesey about the drug experiments at the veterans' hospital in Menlo Park, California. In 1960, Kesey volunteered, earned twenty dollars per session, and discovered mind-expanding drugs that included Ditran, IT-290, and LSD. Kesey thus experienced LSD two years before Timothy Leary and Richard Alpert began their experiment at Harvard. Lovell also suggested that Kesey become a night attendant on the Menlo Park Veterans Hospital psychiatric ward so that he could concentrate on his writing. While a night aide, Kesey completed "Zoo," an unpublished novel about San Francisco's North Beach. Kesey became intensely interested, however, in the patients and their life on the ward, and he began writing *One*

Flew over the Cuckoo's Nest during the summer of 1960 and completed it in the spring of 1961. More important, as a volunteer and an aide, Kesey stole all types of drugs—especially LSD—which he distributed to his Perry Lane friends.

In June, 1961, Kesey moved his family to Springfield, Oregon, to help his brother start the Springfield Creamery and to save enough money for researching his next novel. Having saved enough money, the Kesey family moved to Florence, Oregon, fifty miles west of Springfield, and Kesey began gathering material for *Sometimes a Great Notion*. His research included riding in the pickup trucks, called "crummies," that bussed the loggers to and from the logging sites. At night Kesey frequented the bars where the loggers drank, talked, and relaxed.

One Flew over the Cuckoo's Nest was published in 1962 and was critically acclaimed. In the late spring of 1962 the Kesey family returned to Perry Lane, where he began writing his second novel and where he renewed his drug experiments. When a developer bought the Perry Lane area for a housing development, Kesey purchased a home and land in La Honda, California, and invited a dozen or so of his closest Perry Lane friends to join him so that they could continue their drug experiments. This group would eventually become Kesey's famous Merry Pranksters or the Day-Glo Crazies.

Sometimes a Great Notion was scheduled for publication in July, 1964, and Kesey and Ken Babbs, who had just returned from Vietnam, had planned a trip to the New York World's Fair to arrive there for the publication of Kesey's second novel. Kesey bought a converted 1939 International Harvester school bus for the trip; it had all the conveniences for on-the-road living. The trip mushroomed and was the final impetus for forming the Merry Pranksters. Besides painting the bus various psychedelic colors, the Pranksters wired it with microphones, amplifiers, speakers, recorders, and motion-picture equipment: The sign on the front proclaimed "Furthur" (sic), and the sign on the back warned: "Caution: Weird Load." Prior to departing for New York, Kesey established the only rules for the trip—everyone would "do his own thing," "go with the flow," and not condemn anyone else for being himself. As an adjunct to the trip, the Pranksters recorded their entire odyssey on tape and film, which would eventually become a film entitled *The Movie*, the first acid film recorded live and spontaneously. When the journey ended, there were more than forty-five hours of color film, large portions of which were out of focus, an obvious effect of the drugs. Kesey devoted much of the 1964 spring and the 1965 fall to editing the film.

On April 23, 1965, federal narcotics agents and deputies raided Kesey's La Honda commune. Out of the seventeen people arrested, only Kesey and Page Browning were officially charged with possession of marijuana. When the San Francisco newspapers proclaimed Kesey a great writer, a new leader, and a visionary, Kesey became a celebrity, and people flocked to his La Honda commune. Jerry Rubin and the Vietnam Day Committee even invited him to speak at an antiwar rally at Berkeley in October, 1965. After the fiery speeches the protesters would march en masse to the Oakland Army Terminal and close it down. Waiting his turn to speak, Kesey realized that the speaker before him sounded like the Italian dictator Benito Mussolini, and Kesey was appalled. When he spoke, Kesey told the audience simply to turn their backs on the Vietnam War, and then he played "Home on the Range" on his harmonica. Instead of inciting the crowd, Kesey's speech had the opposite effect, and the march ended quietly in the Berkeley Civic Center Park.

Kesey later met August Owsley Stanley III, who was known as the "Ford of LSD" because he was the first mass manufacturer of quality LSD; this was, of course, before LSD was officially declared illegal. With unlimited supplies of LSD, Kesey and his Merry Pranksters could conduct their famous "Can You Pass the Acid Test" experiments. Amid rock music, Day-Glo decorations, strobe lights, and reels from *The Movie*, the Pranksters invited everyone—the straight people and the hippies—to come and try LSD.

While Kesey's lawyers were fighting the original possession charge, he was arrested in San Francisco on January 10, 1966, again for possession of marijuana; the second arrest carried an automatic five-year sentence without parole. After a clumsily planned suicide hoax (Kesey was high on drugs), he fled to Mexico and was later joined by his family and some of his Prankster friends.

Tired of being a fugitive and of life in Mexico, Kesey disguised himself and entered the United States at Brownsville, Texas. Arrested by the FBI in San Francisco on October 20, 1966, Kesey was tried twice in San Francisco, once on November 30, 1966, and again in April, 1967; both trials ended in hung juries. His lawyers appealed a *nolo contendere* sentence of ninety days, but Kesey dropped the appeal and served his sentence, first at the San Mateo Jail and then at the San Mateo County Sheriff's Honor Camp. He completed his sentence in November, 1967.

In 1968, Kesey moved his family to Pleasant Hill, Oregon, where he began a book based on his jail experiences; the book, "Cut the Mother-Fuckers Loose," was never published. In August, 1968, Tom Wolfe's *The Electric Kool-Aid Acid Test* was published, and also during this year some of Kesey's letters and other writings appeared in underground publications. Between March and June, 1969, he lived in London and wrote for *Apple*. He also revised the play version of *One Flew over the Cuckoo's Nest*, which had opened in New York but had closed after only eighty-five performances. Early in 1970, however, Lee D. Sandowich, a prominent figure in San Francisco theater circles, saw an amateur production of the play, decided it had potential, and professionally produced the play again at the Little Fox Theatre in San Francisco, where it was a success; the play reopened successfully in a New York Off-Broadway theater. During 1971, Kesey, Babbs, and Paul Foster edited selections for *Kesey's Garage Sale*, and in the spring of 1971, Kesey and Krassner coedited *The Last Supplement to the Whole Earth Catalog*. Late in 1971, the film version of *Sometimes a Great Notion* was released.

In 1974, Kesey was instrumental in organizing the Bend in the River Council, a unique people-politics experiment based on the concept of a town meeting. The council featured about two hundred delegates and various experts who discussed a variety of environmental issues in a forum carried on both radio and television, and listeners telephoned their comments and votes on certain issues. In 1976, the film version of *One Flew over the Cuckoo's Nest* was released. During 1978, Kesey edited a magazine called *Spit in the Ocean*, in which he serialized portions of a work-in-progress, a novel entitled "Seven Prayers by Grandma Whittier." Devlin Deboree is a secondary character in the work. He remained content to work on his Pleasant Hill, Oregon, farm and produce his yogurt, which was marketed in Oregon, Washington, and northern California. In the 1980's, a three-term teaching assignment with graduate students in the creative writing program at the University of Oregon resulted in the collaborative novel *Caverns* (1990).

ANALYSIS

To understand some of the ideas behind the counterculture revolution is to understand Ken Kesey's fictional heroes and some of his themes. Originating with the 1950's Beat generation, the 1960's counterculture youth were disillusioned with the vast social injustices, the industrialization, and the mass society image in their parents' world; they questioned many values and practices—the Vietnam War, the goals of higher education, the value of owning property, and the traditional forms of work. They protested by experimenting with Eastern meditation, primitive communal living, unabashed nudity, and nonpossessive physical and spiritual love. At the core of the protest was the value of individual freedom. One of the main avenues to this new type of life and freedom was mind-expanding drugs, which allowed them to *grok*, a word from Robert A. Heinlein's *Stranger in a Strange Land* (1961) that means to achieve a calm ecstasy, to contemplate the present moment. In that it emphasized some major problems in the United States, the counterculture had its merits, but it was, at best, a child's romantic dreamworld, inevitably doomed, because it did not consider answers to the ultimate question: "After the drugs, what is next?"

From Kesey's counterculture experiences, however, he learned at least two important lessons. First, he learned that drugs were not the answer to changing society and that one cannot passively drop out of life. In "Over the Border," for example, Deboree real-

izes, as he bobs up and down in the ocean's waves, that man does not become a superman by isolating himself from reality and life. Instead, he must immerse himself in the waves so that he can "ride the waves of existence" and become one with the waves.

Second, Kesey detested the mass society image which seemed to dominate life in twentieth century America. Although Kesey was pro-America and admired American democracy per se, he abhorred those things in society which seemed to deprive people of individuality and freedom. For Kesey, mass society represents big business, government, labor, communication, and religion and thus subordinates the individual, who is stripped of dignity, significance, and freedom. One of the counterculture's protest slogans underscored this plight: "I am a human being. Do not fold, spindle, or mutilate." The system, preachments, and methodologies of the twentieth century had indeed betrayed humankind and left only two choices: People could either passively conform and thus lose their individuality or find some way to exist in the modern wasteland without losing their dignity and freedom.

Kesey came to believe that people must not and cannot isolate themselves from life; they must meet life on its own terms and discover their own saving grace. Kesey's solution is similar to the solutions found in J. D. Salinger's *Catcher in the Rye* (1951), Joseph Heller's *Catch-22* (1961), Saul Bellow's *Mr. Sammler's Planet* (1970), and even John Irving's *The Hotel New Hampshire* (1981). Having their archetypes in the comic book and Western heroes, Kesey's McMurphy in *One Flew over the Cuckoo's Nest* and Hank Stamper in *Sometimes a Great Notion* are vibrant personalities who defy the overwhelming forces of life by constantly asserting their dignity, significance, and freedom as human beings. Each one learns also that no victories are ever won by passively isolating oneself from life or by being self-centered. They, therefore, immerse themselves in life, ask no quarter, and remain self-reliant. McMurphy and Stamper may not be able to save the entire world, but, Kesey believes, they can save themselves and perhaps even part of the world. Their victories may be slight, but they are, nevertheless, victories.

ONE FLEW OVER THE CUCKOO'S NEST

In *One Flew over the Cuckoo's Nest*, the oppressive power of the mass society is evident in its setting—a mental ward dominated by the tyrannical Miss Ratched, the big nurse, whom Chief Bromden, the schizophrenic narrator, describes in mechanical metaphors. Her purse is shaped like a toolbox; her lipstick and fingernail polish are "funny orange" like a glowing soldering iron; her skin and face are like an expensively manufactured baby doll's; and her ward is run like a computer. If a patient dares disrupt her smoothly running ward, Nurse Ratched has the ultimate threats—electroshock treatments—and if these fail, she has prefrontal lobotomy operations that turn people into vegetables. Bromden says that the ward is only a "factory for the Combine," a nebulous and ubiquitous force which had ruthlessly destroyed Bromden's father and which is responsible for the stereotyped housing developments along the coast.

Kesey's metaphors are clear. The Combine, the macrocosm, and the hospital ward, the microcosm, are the twentieth century world gone berserk with power; it uses the miracles of modern science not to free people and make their lives better but rather to compel them to conform. It is the mass society that will not tolerate individuality and that will fold, spindle, or mutilate any person who fails to conform.

Into the ward boils McMurphy, the former Marine, logger, gambler, and free spirit who is intimidated by neither the nurse nor her black ward attendants, and who immediately becomes a threat to Nurse Ratched and her ward policies. McMurphy has had himself committed for purely selfish reasons—he disliked the manual labor on the prison work farm, and he wants the easy gambling winnings from the patients, two facts that he candidly admits. Outraged at Ratched's power, McMurphy bets the other patients that he can get the best of her. Certain that he can win his wager, he sings and laughs on the ward, conducts poker games in the tub room, and disrupts the group therapy sessions. He finally succeeds in destroying her composure when he leads the men watching the blank television screen after Nurse Ratched cuts the power source during the first game of the World Series.

These scenes are crucial because they reveal the typical Kesey conflict. A physically powerful, free, and crucible-tested hero comes into conflict with an equally powerful force. It is simply, as most critics have noted, the classic struggle between good and evil, or the epic confrontation reminiscent of Western films. Yet the dichotomy is not so simple, because the Kesey hero must learn a further lesson. McMurphy has won his wager, but he has not yet won significant victory, because his actions are selfish ones.

Several important incidents transform McMurphy into a champion of the patients. McMurphy is *committed*, which means that Ratched can keep him on the ward as long as she wishes. Instead of jeopardizing his relatively short sentence, McMurphy conforms and does not disrupt the therapy sessions or life on the ward. When Charles Cheswick argues with the nurse about the cigarette rationing, he gets no support from McMurphy, despairs, and drowns himself in the hospital swimming pool. Cheswick's death plagues McMurphy, even though he is not actually responsible. McMurphy cannot understand why the other patients, who are there voluntarily, do not leave the hospital. Billy Bibbit finally tells McMurphy that they are not big and strong like McMurphy, that they have no "g-guts," and that it is "n-no use." McMurphy begins to realize that he must do something to convert the patients into responsible men again. At the next group therapy session, when Ratched is supposed to win her final victory over him, McMurphy rams his hand through the glass partition in the nurses' station and thereby renews the struggle.

A key passage occurs earlier that not only summarizes Kesey's view of humanity in the modern world but also provides a clue to McMurphy's actions. Scanlon, who is also committed, says that it is a "hell of a life," and that people are damned if they do and damned if they do not. Scanlon adds that this fact puts people in a "confounded bind." At this point, McMurphy is damned either way. If he does nothing, then Ratched has the final victory and McMurphy will become another victim of the Combine, a nonentity like the other patients. If he renews the struggle, he must remain on the ward until the nurse discharges him or kills him. McMurphy chooses, however, the higher damnation, selflessly to give of himself, and in so doing, he also reaffirms his own dignity and significance.

Dedicated to the patients' cause, McMurphy continues to disrupt the ward and ward policy by using what can only be termed McMurphy's therapy. He continues the poker games and organizes basketball games and even a deep-sea fishing trip, during which the men finally learn to laugh at themselves, Nurse Ratched, and the world in general. He fights with an attendant who was bullying one of the patients, and as a result he is given a series of electroshock treatments. Finally, McMurphy physically attacks the nurse when she ironically accuses him of "playing" and "gambling" with the men's lives. When a prefrontal lobotomy turns McMurphy into a vegetable, Bromden sacrificially murders him and then escapes from the hospital.

In Kesey's world, an individual may indeed be damned either way when he or she encounters the overwhelming forces of the mass society, but through accepting responsibility and acting one can still win an important victory. McMurphy's death is not futile, because he has saved his soul by losing it to a higher cause. He did not save or even change the entire world, but he did save and change part of it: The other patients are no longer cowed and intimidated by Nurse Ratched, and several of them voluntarily check out of the hospital. Bromden, as McMurphy had promised, has been "blown back up" to his full size. There is, then, a slight but significant victory.

SOMETIMES A GREAT NOTION

Kesey remarked that he wanted his style to be a "style of change," since he wished neither to write like anyone else nor to be part of any movement. Even though *One Flew over the Cuckoo's Nest* was innovative in style and technique, Kesey's second novel is even more innovative. Even though some critics faulted it for being too rambling and disjointed, *Sometimes a Great Notion* is not only much longer than but also superior to his first novel. It is Kesey at his best. Ultimately, what makes the novel superior is its technical complexity.

More than six hundred pages in length, *Sometimes a Great Notion* is reminiscent of *Light in August* (1932) and *Absalom, Absalom!* (1936) by William Faulkner, Kesey's favorite author. As did Faulkner, Kesey begins his novel at its climax, with a scene in a bus depot where Jonathan Bailey Draeger, a labor union official, asks Vivian Stamper, Hank's wife, about the nature of the Stamper family. This interview between Viv and Draeger frames the entire narrative. The narrative then shifts to the past, at times as far back as 1898, when the first Stamper left Kansas to move west. Through these past scenes, Kesey establishes the family background and relationships, which in turn provide the psychological makeup of the characters. Having rejected traditional narrative forms, Kesey thus moves freely from past to present time. Complementing the time shifts are the complex points of view. Bromden is the single narrator in *One Flew over the Cuckoo's Nest*, but in *Sometimes a Great Notion* Kesey uses several points of view. There is the traditional omniscient viewpoint, then there are the first-person points of view in the stories of Henry Stamper, Sr., Hank, and Leland Stanford Stamper, Hank's half brother. Kesey freely shifts abruptly from one viewpoint to another, and several shifts may occur in one paragraph. In addition, Kesey presents several incidents that are separated in space but are actually simultaneous actions.

Even the conflict in *Sometimes a Great Notion* is more complicated than that of *One Flew over the Cuckoo's Nest*. The forces aligned against McMurphy are clearly delineated; it is McMurphy versus Nurse Ratched and the Combine, and it is clear who is good and who is evil. On the other hand, in *Sometimes a Great Notion*, Hank confronts more subtle and complex forces. He pits himself against the logging union and the Wakonda, Oregon, community, both of which represent mass society. Hank must also contend with two natural forces—the weather and the Wakonda River, the latter being one of the major symbols in the novel. The most important conflict, however, is between Hank and Lee (Leland, his half brother).

Like McMurphy, Hank is a physically powerful man who is self-reliant, answers to no one but himself, and cherishes his freedom. Like McMurphy, Hank defies those forces of life that would strip him of his dignity, significance, and freedom. For Hank, then, the dictatorial pressures of the union and the Wakonda community are the dictates of the mass society. Having signed a contract with Wakonda Pacific, Hank becomes a strikebreaker who is harassed and threatened by union leaders and the townspeople. Literally, Hank breaks the strike to save the Stamper logging business; symbolically, he breaks the strike because to do so will assert his independence and freedom. The results of *any* action Hank chooses to take are undesirable, and he, like McMurphy, chooses the course of a higher morality.

Kesey uses three major symbols to underscore Hank's bullheaded defiance. The first is the Stamper house itself, which "protrudes" into the Wakonda River on "a peninsula of its own making." The second is the "Never Give an Inch" plaque, painted in yellow machine paint over the plaque's original message: "Blessed Are the Meek for They Shall Inherit the Earth." The plaque with its new dictum is nailed to Hank's bedroom wall by old Henry Stamper. The third symbol is old Henry's severed arm, which is a hanging pole, with all of its fingers tied down except the middle one. As part of Kesey's complex technique, these symbols fuse with the characters' historical and psychological background, with the various narrative viewpoints, and with the major conflicts.

Of the conflicts, the one between Hank and Leland is potentially the most destructive, and it is also important in terms of Hank's and Lee's character development. Through a crack in the bedroom wall, Lee watched his mother and Hank commit adultery, an act that eventually results in the mother's suicide after she and Lee move back East. Lee returns to Wakonda, not to help the Stampers' failing lumber business but actually to take revenge against Hank. Lee decides that he can best hurt Hank by having an affair with Viv, who, even though she loves Hank, cannot tolerate his "teeth-gritting stoicism in the face of pain." She wants to be both loved and needed, and Lee seems to love and need her. Ironically, after the drowning of Joe Ben, Hank swims across the Wakonda instead of using the motorboat, quietly enters the house, and through the same crack in the bedroom wall sees Lee and Viv in bed together. Tempo-

rarily overwhelmed by the death of Joe Ben, his father's horrible maiming, the bad weather, and Viv's adultery, Hank decides that he is "tired of being a villain" and that he will fight the union no longer. His surrender is implied, moreover, in the song lyrics from which the title of the novel is taken: "Sometimes I take a great notion/ To jump into the river an' drown." Immediately after the fistfight with Lee, however, Hank decides to take the logs down river, and Lee joins him.

The fight between Hank and Lee embodies the novel's central theme. Hank understands that Lee has arranged events so cleverly that Hank is damned either way, or as Hank says, "whipped if I fight and whipped if I don't." Hank chooses the greater notion and fights. During the fight, his inner strength is rekindled, and he later tells Viv that "a man is always surprised just how much he can do by himself." Concomitantly, during the fight, Lee realizes that he too has regained the strength and pride which he thought had been lost. Each has a new respect for the other, a respect that is based on love—love for the Stamper name, love for individual freedom. Lee and Hank may be defeated by the river, the weather, or the strike itself, but the significant fact is that they, like McMurphy, are acting. They have not saved the entire world, but they have saved themselves, have regained their own dignity and significance; that, in itself, is a victory.

SAILOR SONG

Sailor Song takes place in the remote little fishing village of Kuinak, Alaska, in the early twenty-first century. Largely untouched by ecological catastrophes, Kuinak attracts a big-budget Hollywood company filming a pseudomyth of aboriginal Native American life. *Sailor Song*'s protagonist, Isaak Sallas—ex-naval aviator, ex-environmental activist, ex-convict, and ex-husband—has dropped out of mainstream society and lives as a commercial fisherman. Independent, competent, and well intentioned but resolutely uninvolved, Salas is nonetheless caught up in a conflict with Nicholas Levertov, a native of Kuinak controlling the Hollywood company, which proposes not only to make a film but also to transform Kuinak into a spin-off theme park and resort. In Melvillian symbolism, Levertov is an albino, inherently bent not on creation but on desecration, destruction, and revenge.

The novel's conflict evolves against a backdrop of Kuinak's uninhibited lifestyle. Kuinak's citizens include Sallas's friend Greer, transplanted from Bimini; members of the Loyal Order of Underdogs, a rowdy but sometimes purposeful organization; Michael Carmody, a displaced English fisherman; and Carmody's wife, Alice the Angry Aleut. Into this community come the filmmakers, including Levertov, his sycophantic assistant, a figurehead director, and the Innupiat star of the film, Shoola.

The novel's loosely connected episodes come together satisfyingly in the denouement. In the opening episode, Sallas rescues a neighbor from Levertov, her vengeful ex-husband. Later Sallas rescues the marijuana-dealing president of the Underdogs from a charismatic cultist. Later still he rescues Carmody and Greer from their malfunctioning fishing boat. Most important, he saves himself, both literally and metaphorically. However, although Sallas is sometimes characterized in explicitly messianic terms, he is more modern-day Ulysses than Christ figure, while Alice Carmody is an ironically inverted Penelope.

The anticipated final confrontation between Sallas and Levertov never occurs. In the open-ended, understated denouement, a commotion of bears and wild boars may signal Levertov's end. Whether it does or not, Levertov's consuming malice not only defeats itself but also sets loose a worldwide electronic apocalypse ironically transforming civilization to a state much like Kuinak's, a transformation symbolically marked by butterfly-shaped electrical phenomena.

Technically interesting for its symbolism, fluent manipulation of point of view, and command of narrative rhythm, *Sailor Song* clearly expresses Kesey's philosophy of independence, integrity, and perseverance and counters critics' accusations against Kesey of racism or sexism. *Sailor Song* is above all an engaging and thoroughly enjoyable story.

LAST GO ROUND

Kesey wrote *Last Go Round* with Ken Babbs. Much shorter than Kesey's other novels, it is no less artfully written. *Last Go Round*, like *One Flew over the Cuckoo's Nest*, presents only a version of the truth—in this case a version told to a comatose listener by Jonathan E. Lee Spain, the story's protagonist, almost a century after the events being described. Spain's account is supplemented, if not corroborated, by a set of historical photographs of participants in the first Pendleton Round Up, held on three days in September, 1911. Spain, unlike Kesey's other heroes, is young—only seventeen—and the novel recounts his initiation into adulthood. He meets two older rodeo riders, the black cowboy George Fletcher and the Nez Perce Jackson Sundown, who make him their protégé. He rejects the corruption of the cynical showman Buffalo Bill and the malignant strongman Frank Gotch. He is attracted to a young horsewoman, Sarah Meyerhoff, whom he loses. Above all, Jonathan Spain learns. He learns the tricks of the rodeo, the trust that rodeo riders share, and the untrustworthiness of others. He learns the inconsequence of championships, the importance of excellence, and the meaningfulness of peers' approbation. He learns the unpredictability and inexorability of events. Finally, he learns to accept what comes, even while he defines himself by what he has chosen to do, however briefly.

Edward C. Reilly, updated by David W. Cole

OTHER MAJOR WORKS

PLAY: *Twister*, pr. 1994.

CHILDREN'S FICTION: *Little Tricker the Squirrel Meets Big Double the Bear*, 1990; *The Sea Lion: A Story of the Sea Cliff People*, 1991.

NONFICTION: *The Further Inquiry*, 1990.

EDITED TEXT: *The Last Supplement to the Whole Earth Catalog*, 1971 (with Paul Krassner).

MISCELLANEOUS: *Kesey's Garage Sale*, 1973; *Demon Box*, 1986.

BIBLIOGRAPHY

Kesey, Ken. *"One Flew over the Cuckoo's Nest": Text and Criticism*. Edited by John C. Pratt. New York: Viking, 1973. Contains the text of the novel, related materials, and a selection of early critical responses to the novel, together with a brief bibliography.

Porter, M. Gilbert. *The Art of Grit: Ken Kesey's Fiction.* Columbia: University of Missouri Press, 1982. In this first full-length study of Kesey, Porter penetrates Kesey's drug-culture image to reveal his accomplishments as an author in the traditional "American mold of optimism and heroism." A highly regarded critical study that offers an astute commentary on Kesey's fiction.

Searles, George J., ed. *A Casebook on Ken Kesey's "One Flew over the Cuckoo's Nest."* Albuquerque: University of New Mexico Press, 1992. A collection of critical articles, most originally published in the 1970's. Also includes a *MAD* magazine satire of the film and a bibliography.

Sherwood, Terry G. "*One Flew over the Cuckoo's Nest* and the Comic Strip." *Critique: Studies in Modern Fiction* 13, no. 1 (1971): 97-109. Sherwood explores Kesey's references to popular culture, particularly comic strip materials, which are not just "casual grace notes but clear indications of his artistic stance." Contains some appreciative criticism but faults Kesey for his belief in the escapist world of the comic strip and his oversimplification of moral dilemmas.

Tanner, Stephen L. *Ken Kesey.* Boston: Twayne, 1983. This study affirms Kesey as a significant writer and a leader of a cultural movement despite his scant output. Presents some biographical details of Kesey's early years and accomplishments, followed by a critical study of major works. Gives particular attention to *One Flew over the Cuckoo's Nest* and *Sometimes a Great Notion.* Selected bibliography is provided.

Vogler, Thomas A. "Ken Kesey." In *Contemporary Novelists,* edited by James Vinson. London: St. James Press, 1976. Describes Kesey's work as "Richly north-western and regional in quality." Presents some critical appraisal of *One Flew over the Cuckoo's Nest* and *Sometimes a Great Notion.* Also refers to *The Last Supplement to the Whole Earth Catalog,* for which Kesey wrote numerous reviews and articles.

Wolfe, Tom. *The Electric Kool-Aid Acid Test.* New York: Farrar, Straus & Giroux, 1968. A notable work in its own right. Wolfe confers on Kesey the charismatic leadership of a cultural movement. Provides important background information on Kesey, the Merry Pranksters, and the milieu of psychedelic experimentation.

Zubizarreta, John. "The Disparity of Point of View in *One Flew over the Cuckoo's Nest.*" *Literature Film Quarterly* 22 (Spring, 1994): 62-69. Contrasts the kinds of comedy produced by film's realistic third-person point of view and the novel's surrealistic, highly unreliable, and ironic first-person point of view. Bibliography.

Jamaica Kincaid
Elaine Potter Richardson

Born: St. Johns, Antigua; May 25, 1949

Principal long fiction
Annie John, 1985
Lucy, 1990
The Autobiography of My Mother, 1996

Other literary forms

Jamaica Kincaid first gained respect and admiration as the writer of *At the Bottom of the River* (1983), a collection of unconventional but thematically unified short stories. She also wrote two important memoirs, *A Small Place* (1988), about growing up in a Caribbean vacation resort, and *My Brother* (1997), the story of her brother's struggle with acquired immunodeficiency syndrome (AIDS). Additionally, as a staff writer for *The New Yorker* for twenty years, she wrote numerous "Talk of the Town" pieces and frequent articles on gardening.

Achievements

Jamaica Kincaid made writing about her life her life's work. She developed a finely honed style that highlights personal impressions and feelings over plot development. Though she allows a political dimension to emerge from her use of Caribbean settings, her fiction does not strain to be political.

(Sigrid Estrada)

Rather, the political issues relating to her colonial background are used to intensify the most important issue of her fiction: the intense bond between mother and daughter. Her spare, personal style simultaneously invites readers to enter her world and, by its toughness, challenges them to do so. Although she made no specific effort to align herself with any ideology, her first book, *At the Bottom of the River* (which in 1983 won the Morton Dauwen Zabel Award from the American Academy and Institute of Arts and Letters), quickly established her as a favorite among feminist and postcolonial critics, who lauded her personal but unsentimental presentation of the world of women and of the Caribbean.

BIOGRAPHY

Jamaica Kincaid was born Elaine Potter Richardson in St. John's, Antigua, the daughter of Annie Richardson and Roderick Potter, a taxi driver. Her father was not a significant presence in her life. The man she considered her father was David Drew, a cabinetmaker and carpenter whom her mother married shortly after Elaine's birth. Elaine learned to read at the age of three, and when she turned seven, her mother gave her a copy of the *Concise Oxford Dictionary* as a birthday gift. The birth of her three brothers, Joseph in 1958, Dalma in 1959, and Devon in 1961 (whose death from AIDS in 1996 would provide the focus for *My Brother*), changed her life, not only because it meant that she was no longer an only child but also because she began to realize that her education would never be taken as seriously as her brothers' would be. While Elaine's parents made plans for their sons' university training, Elaine was sent to study with a seamstress twice a week.

When she was seventeen, Elaine left for America to become an au pair in Scarsdale, New York. She took classes at Westchester Community College but soon left Scarsdale to take another au pair position looking after the daughters of an upper East Side, New York, couple (this experience would provide the basic material for *Lucy*). Over the course of the next few years, she would study photography at the New School for Social Research and at Franconia College in New Hampshire before returning to New York to work briefly for the magazine *Art Direction*.

In 1973 she sold her first professional publication, an interview with Gloria Steinem published in *Ingenue* on what life was like for the well-known feminist at the age of seventeen. Also in 1973, she changed her name to Jamaica Kincaid, a move probably inspired by her need to create an anonymous, authorial identity; significantly, her adopted pen name marks her as Caribbean to the American reading audience, something her birth name does not. Also in 1973, George Trow, a writer for the "Talk of the Town" column in *The New Yorker*, started incorporating quotations by her in his writing (she was his "sassy black friend"), and her writing career was started. She worked as a freelance writer until she became a staff writer for *The New Yorker* in 1976 (a position she held until a 1995 disagreement with then-editor Tina Brown over the direction of the magazine led to her resignation). In 1979, she married Allen Shawn, son of William Shawn, the editor of *The New Yorker* at the time, and the couple moved to North Bennington, Vermont, where Shawn was on the faculty of Bennington College. The couple had two children,

Annie (born in 1985) and Harold (born in 1989). Aside from being a novelist, Kincaid became a passionate gardener; she wrote on gardening for *The New Yorker* and edited a book of garden writing, *My Favorite Plant*, published in 1998.

ANALYSIS

Jamaica Kincaid is known for her impressionistic prose, which is rich with detail presented in a poetic style, her continual treatment of mother-daughter issues, and her relentless pursuit of honesty. More so than many fiction writers, she is an autobiographical writer whose life and art are inextricably woven together. She began her career by mastering the short story, the form from which her longer fiction grew. Most of the pieces that constitute *At the Bottom of the River* and *Annie John* were first published in *The New Yorker*, as were the chapters of *Lucy*. Though the individual pieces in each work have a self-contained unity, *Annie John* and *Lucy* also have a clear continuity from story to story, something less true of the impressionistic writing of *At the Bottom of the River*; thus, it is often considered a collection of short stories, while *Annie John* and *Lucy* are clearly novels. Nonetheless, it was *At the Bottom of the River* that won for Kincaid the Morton Dauwen Zabel Award for short fiction and that contained "Girl," a story written as a stream of instructions from a mother to a daughter, which is her best-known piece.

Kincaid's native Antigua is central in her writing. This colonial setting strongly relates to her mother-daughter subject matter, because the narrators Annie and Lucy of her first two novels both seem to make a connection between their Anglophile mothers and the colonial English, and also because the childhood experiences of both narrators have been shaped by a colonial background that limits their options and makes their relationships with their mothers that much more intense.

Beginning with *Lucy*, Kincaid cultivates a detachment with which she explores issues of anger and loss, carefully disallowing any easy resolution. Kincaid seems less interested in solving fictional problems than in exploring contrary states of mind that perceive problems. Admittedly, this style is not to ev-

eryone's taste, and even quite a few readers who were seduced by Kincaid's earlier works were less pleased with *Lucy* and *The Autobiography of My Mother*. However, even if her incantatory rhythms and her tight focus on bleak, emotional situations in her post-*Annie John* works are not universally appreciated, few readers deny her eye for poetic detail and her ability to achieve a shimmering honesty in her prose.

ANNIE JOHN

Kincaid's first novel, *Annie John*, is about a talented young girl in Antigua who, while growing into early womanhood, must separate herself from her mother. Fittingly, the book begins with a story of her recognition of mortality at the age of ten. Fascinated by the knowledge that she or anyone could die at any time, she begins to attend the funerals of people she does not know. At one point, she imagines herself dead and her father, who makes coffins, so overcome with grief that he cannot build one for her, a complex image suggesting her growing separation from her family. When, after attending a funeral for a child she did know, Annie neglects to bring home fish, as her mother demanded, Annie's mother punishes her before kissing her good-night. Though this ending kiss suggests a continued bond between mother and daughter, the next chapter places it in a different context. The title "The Circling Hand" refers to her mother's hand on her father's back when Annie accidentally spies her parents making love. Almost as if in contradiction to the reassuring maternal kiss of the earlier story, this chapter offers the rising specter of sexuality as a threat that will separate mother and daughter. Annie learns not only that she must stop dressing exactly like her mother but also that she must someday be married and have a house of her own. This is beyond Annie's comprehension.

Though Annie never fully understands this growing distance from her mother, she contributes to it. For instance, when she becomes friends with a girl at school named Gwen, she does not tell her mother. In part, she is transferring her affections to friends as a natural process of growing up, but as the chapters "Gwen" and "The Red Girl" make clear, she is also seeking comfort to ease the disapproval of her mother. Gwen becomes her best friend, and Annie imagines living with her, but Gwen is replaced briefly in Annie's affections by the Red Girl, who is a friend and cohort whom Annie plays marbles with, against the wishes of her mother.

The growing separation from her mother comes to a crisis in the chapter "The Long Rain," when Annie lapses into an extended depression and takes to her bed. When medicine and the cures of a local conjure woman do nothing to help, Annie's grandmother, Ma Chess, also a conjure woman, moves in with her. The weather remains damp the entire time Annie remains bedridden, and she feels herself physically cut off from other people. When she is finally well enough to return to school, she discovers she has grown so much that she needs a new uniform; symbolically, she has become a new person. Thus it is that the last chapter, "The Long Jetty," begins with Annie thinking, "My name is Annie John," an act of self-naming which is also an act of self-possession. The chapter tells of Annie's last day in Antigua as she prepares to meet the ship that will take her to England, where she plans to study to become a nurse. A sensitive, detailed portrayal of a leave-taking, this chapter serves as a poignant farewell to childhood and to the intimacy with her mother that only a child can know. This last chapter captures perfectly Kincaid's ability to tell a story sensitively without sentimentality.

LUCY

Kincaid's third novel, *Lucy*, is a thematic sequel to her first. Lucy is seventeen when the novel begins, newly arrived in the United States from Antigua to work as an au pair, watching the four girls of Lewis and Mariah, an upper-middle-class New York couple. Although the novel is set entirely outside Antigua and Lucy's mother never appears in it, Lucy's attempt to separate herself from her mother constitutes the main theme of the novel.

Mariah is presented as a loving but thoroughly ethnocentric white woman. A recurring example of this is her attempt to make Lucy appreciate the Wordsworthian beauty of daffodils, unaware that it is precisely because Lucy had to study Wordsworth's poetry about a flower that does not grow in Antigua that this flower represents the world of the colonizer to her. In fact, Mariah's unself-conscious, patronizing

goodwill is exactly what Lucy loves most and yet cannot tolerate about her employer, because it reminds her of her mother.

When Lucy learns that Lewis is having an affair with Mariah's best friend, Dinah, she understands that this idyllic marriage is falling apart. When a letter from home informs her that her father has died, she is unable to explain to Mariah that her anger toward her mother is based on mourning the perfect love she had once felt between them. At the same time, her own sexuality begins to emerge, and she develops interests in young men. Wanting more space, she moves in with her friend Peggy, a young woman who represents a more exciting world to Lucy, cutting short her one-year au pair agreement. The novel ends with Lucy writing her name, Lucy Josephine Potter, in a book and wishing that she could love someone enough to die for that love. This ending clearly signals an act of self-possession (much like the self-naming at the end of *Annie John*), but it also signifies the loneliness of breaking away from others, even to assert oneself. Though *Lucy* is a much angrier novel than *Annie John*, Lucy's anger is best understood in terms of the writer's earlier autobiographical surrogate in *Annie John*; the melancholy that debilitates Annie at the end of her novel is turned into anger by Lucy.

THE AUTOBIOGRAPHY OF MY MOTHER

The Autobiography of My Mother is a tough, bleakly ironic novel written by a writer at the full height of her powers. It follows Xuela Claudette Richardson, a Caribbean woman who aborted her only pregnancy. If this fact seems to imply that Kincaid has taken a step away from the style of autobiographical fiction, the self-contradictory title and the main character's last name, Richardson, a name she shares with Jamaica Kincaid, both suggest that this story is not very far removed from the facts of Kincaid's own family.

The novel begins with the narrator proclaiming that her mother died the moment she was born, "and so for my whole life there was nothing standing between myself and eternity." This interesting statement reveals as much about the importance of mothers in Kincaid's writing as about the character Xuela.

She lives with her father and a stepmother, who hates her and may have tried to kill her with a poisoned necklace, until she is sent at fifteen to live with a wealthy couple. Ostensibly, she is to be a student, but in fact she is to be the man's mistress.

Though the relationship between the colonizer and the colonized is important in all of Kincaid's writing, *The Autobiography of My Mother* brings it to the foreground in different ways. The first words Xuela learns to read are the words "the British Empire," written across a map. Meanwhile, her stepmother refuses to speak to Xuela in anything other than a patois, or provincial dialect, as if to reduce Xuela to the status of an illegitimate subject of the empire. When Xuela eventually marries (after many affairs with men), it is to a man she identifies as "of the victors"—the British. She takes a cruel satisfaction in refusing to love him, even though, according to her, he lived for the sound of her footsteps. Though it is never a relationship based on love, she lives with him for many years, and he becomes for her "all the children I did not allow to be born." While this is hardly an ideal relationship, it is not a completely empty one.

Toward the end, Xuela declares that her mother's death at the moment of her birth was the central facet of her life. Her ironic detachment from life seems to have been based on this, as if, devoid of the only buffer between herself and the hardship of life that she can imagine—a mother—she further rejects all other comforts and answers that people wish to propose. If Xuela is the least likable of Kincaid's main characters, her tough-as-nails approach to the world nonetheless makes her among the most compelling.

Thomas Cassidy

OTHER MAJOR WORKS

SHORT FICTION: *At the Bottom of the River*, 1983.

NONFICTION: *A Small Place*, 1988; *My Brother*, 1997; *My Garden (Book)*, 1999.

CHILDREN'S LITERATURE: *Annie, Gwen, Lilly, Pam, and Tulip*, 1986 (with illustrations by Eric Fischl).

EDITED TEXTS: *The Best American Essays 1995*, 1995; *My Favorite Plant: Writers and Gardeners on the Plants They Love*, 1998.

BIBLIOGRAPHY

Bloom, Harold, ed. *Jamaica Kincaid: Modern Critical Views*. Philadelphia: Chelsea House, 1998. A collection of some of the best essays about the author, geared primarily to an audience of graduate students and scholars.

Davies, Carole Boyce. *Black Women, Writing, and Identity: Migrations of the Subject*. New York: Routledge, 1994. Focuses on the importance of migration in the construction of identity in black women's fiction in the United States, Africa, and the Caribbean. Especially insightful regarding Kincaid's *Lucy*.

Ferguson, Moira. *Jamaica Kincaid: Where the Land Meets the Body*. Charlottesville: University Press of Virginia, 1994. In a book clearly oriented to scholars and graduate students, Ferguson provides a politically informed interpretation of Kincaid's writing that emphasizes the importance of the colonial setting in her works.

Kincaid, Jamaica. "An Interview with Jamaica Kincaid." Interview by Kay Bonetti. *Missouri Review* 15, no. 2 (Winter, 1992): 124-142. An interview in which the author talks at great length about her mother's influence on her and about her deeply ambivalent feelings about her homeland.

Simmons, Diane. *Jamaica Kincaid*. New York: Twayne, 1994. A clear, lucid critical overview of Kincaid's life and work. A good introduction to her work for nonspecialist readers.

STEPHEN KING

Born: Portland, Maine; September 21, 1947

PRINCIPAL LONG FICTION

Carrie, 1974

'Salem's Lot, 1975

The Shining, 1977

Rage, 1977 (as Richard Bachman)

The Stand, 1978, unabridged version 1990

The Dead Zone, 1979

The Long Walk, 1979 (as Bachman)

Firestarter, 1980

Roadwork, 1981 (as Bachman)

Cujo, 1981

The Running Man, 1982 (as Bachman)

The Gunslinger, 1982 (illustrated by Michael Whelan)

Christine, 1983

Pet Sematary, 1983

Cycle of the Werewolf, 1983 (novella, illustrated by Berni Wrightson)

The Talisman, 1984 (with Peter Straub)

Thinner, 1984 (as Bachman)

The Eyes of the Dragon, 1984, 1987

The Bachman Books: Four Early Novels by Stephen King, 1985 (includes *Rage, The Long Walk, Roadwork*, and *The Running Man*)

It, 1986

Misery, 1987

The Tommyknockers, 1987

The Drawing of the Three, 1987 (illustrated by Phil Hale)

The Dark Half, 1989

Needful Things, 1991

The Waste Lands, 1991 (illustrated by Ned Dameron)

Gerald's Game, 1992

Dolores Claiborne, 1993

Insomnia, 1994

Rose Madder, 1995

The Green Mile, 1996 (six-part serialized novel)

Desperation, 1996

The Regulators, 1996 (as Bachman)

Wizard and Glass, 1997 (illustrated by Dave McKean)

Bag of Bones, 1998

The Girl Who Loved Tom Gordon, 1999

OTHER LITERARY FORMS

Stephen King published more than one hundred short stories (including the collections *Night Shift*, 1978, *Skeleton Crew*, 1985, and *Nightmares and Dreamscapes*, 1993) and the eight novellas contained in *Different Seasons* (1982) and *Four Past Midnight* (1990). Two of these novellas are central to his work.

(Archive Photos)

In *The Body*, a boy's confrontation with mortality shapes his developing identity as a writer. In *The Mist*, King in his satirical and apocalyptic mode brings Armageddon to the Federal Foods Supermarket as an assortment of grade-B film monsters that inhabit a dense fog.

The relations of King's fiction with the electronic media are many and complex. Much of his fiction has been adapted to both the large and small screens, although it usually plays best in the mind's eye. Several of King's screenplays have been produced, including *Maximum Overdrive* (1986), which he directed. A relatively successful mixed-media venture was his collaboration with George Romero on *Creepshow* (1982), a film anthology inspired by the D.C. Comics' blend of camp and gore and based on King's own book version. *Creepshow II*, written by Romero and based on King's stories, appeared in 1987. King's teleplays include *The Stand* (1994), which was based on his novel, and *Storm of the Century*

(1999), which was written expressly for television broadcast. King has published numerous articles and a critical book, *Danse Macabre* (1981).

Achievements

King is perhaps the most widely known American writer of his generation, yet his distinctions include publishing as two authors at once: Beginning in 1966, he wrote novels that were published under the pseudonym Richard Bachman. He won many British Fantasy and World Fantasy Awards, including the latter for overall contributions to the genre in 1980. At first ignored and then scorned by mainstream critics, by the late 1980's his novels were reviewed regularly in *The New York Times Book Review*, with increasing favor. Beginning in 1987, most of his novels were main selections of the Book-of-the-Month Club, which in 1989 created the Stephen King Library, committed to keeping King's novels "in print in hardcover." King was *People* magazine's Writer of the Year in 1980. One of his most appropriate distinctions was the October 9, 1986, cover of *Time* magazine, which depicted a reader, hair on end, transfixed by "A Novel by Stephen King." The cover story on the "King of Horror" correctly suggested that his achievement and the "horror boom" of the 1970's and 1980's are inseparable. Yet, like Edgar Allan Poe, King turned a degenerated genre—a matter of comic-book monsters and drive-in films—into a medium embodying the primary anxieties of his age.

King's detractors attribute his success to the sensational appeal of his genre, whose main purpose, as King readily confesses, is to scare people. He is graphic, sentimental, and predictable. His humor is usually crude and campy. His novels are often long and loosely structured: *It*, for example, comprises 1,138 pages. In an environment of "exhaustion" and minimalism, King's page-turners are the summit of the garbage heap of a mass, throwaway culture. Worst of all, he is "Master of Postliterate Prose," as Paul Gray stated in 1982—writing that takes readers mentally to the films rather than making them imagine or think.

On the other hand, King's work provides the most genuine example of the storyteller's art since Charles Dickens. He has returned to the novel some of the popular appeal it had in the nineteenth century and turned out a generation of readers who vastly prefer some books to their film adaptations. As Dickens drew on the popular culture of his time, King reflects the mass-mediated culture of his own. His dark fantasies, like all good popular fiction, allow readers to express within conventional frames of reference feelings and concepts they might not otherwise consider. In imagination, King is not merely prolific; his vision articulates universal fears and desires in terms peculiar to contemporary culture.

Biography

The second son of Donald and Nellie Ruth Pillsbury King, Stephen Edwin King has lived most of his life in Maine, the setting for most of his fiction. Two childhood traumas, neither of which he remembers, may have been formative. In 1949, when he was two years old, his parents separated and his father disappeared. In 1951, he apparently saw a train dismember a neighborhood friend.

King's conservative Methodist upbringing was supplemented early with a diet of comic books and *Weird Tales*. When twelve, he began submitting stories for sale. In 1970, he was graduated from the University of Maine, Orono, with a B.S. in English and a minor in dramatics. He encountered two lasting influences, the naturalist writers and contemporary American mythology. He also met Tabitha Jane Spruce, whom he married in 1971.

After graduation, he worked in an industrial laundry until 1971, when he became an English instructor at a preparatory school in Hampden, Maine. He wrote at night in the trailer he shared with his wife and two children. In the early 1970's, he sold stories to men's magazines. Then, in 1974, he published *Carrie*, which was followed by several best-sellers and sales of motion-picture rights.

King settled in Maine with his wife Tabitha King, a novelist and the writer of *Small World* (1981), *Caretakers* (1983), and others. They had three children, Naomi, Joe, and Owen. In addition to writing daily (except Christmas and his birthday), King became active in opposing censorship, composing essays and lecturing on the topic and supporting controversial publications. He also indulged his love of rock and roll, having purchased a local radio station (renamed WZON) and occasionally performing, with writers Dave Barry, Amy Tan, and others, in the Rock-Bottom Remainders.

In 1999, King was struck by an automobile while walking along a road near his home. His injuries were quite severe, yet the famous author remained upbeat and philosophical during his lengthy recovery.

ANALYSIS

Stephen King may be known as a horror writer, but he calls himself a "brand name," describing his style as "the literary equivalent of a Big Mac and a large fries from McDonald's." His fast-food version of the "plain style" may smell of commercialism, but that may make him the contemporary American storyteller without peer. From the beginning, his dark parables spoke to the anxieties of the late twentieth century. As a surrogate author in *The Mist* explains King's mission, "when the technologies fail, when . . . religious systems fail, people have got to have something. Even a zombie lurching through the night" is a "cheerful" thought in the context of a "dissolving ozone layer."

King's fictions begin with premises accepted by middle Americans of the television generation, opening in suburban or small-town America—Derry, Maine, or Libertyville, Pennsylvania—and have the familiarity of the house next door and the 7-Eleven store. The characters have the trusted two-dimensional reality of kitsch: They originate in clichés such as the high school "nerd" or the wise child. From such premises, they move cinematically through an atmosphere resonant with a popular mythology. King applies naturalistic methods to an environment created by popular culture. This reality, already mediated, is translated easily into preternatural terms, taking on a nightmarish quality.

King's imagination is above all archetypal: His "pop" familiarity and his campy humor draw on the collective unconscious. In *Danse Macabre*, a study of the contemporary horror genre that emphasizes the cross-pollination of fiction and film, he divides his subject according to four "monster archetypes": the ghost, the "thing" (or human-made monster), the vampire, and the werewolf. As with his fiction, his sources are the classic horror films of the 1930's, inherited by the 1950's pulp and film industries. He hints at their derivations from the gothic novel, classical myth, Brothers Grimm folktales, and the oral tradition in general. In an anxious era both skeptical of and hungry for myth, horror is fundamentally reassuring and cathartic; the tale-teller combines roles of physician and priest into the witch doctor as "sin eater," who assumes the guilt and fear of his culture. In the neoprimitivism of the late twentieth century, this ancient role and the old monsters have taken on a new mystique. In *The Uses of Enchantment* (1976), psychologist Bruno Bettelheim argues that the magic and terrors of fairy tales present existential problems in forms children can understand. King's paranormal horrors have similar cathartic and educative functions for adults; they externalize the traumas of life, especially those of adolescence.

CARRIE

Stephen King's first published novel, *Carrie*, is a parable of adolescence. Sixteen-year-old Carrie White is a lonely ugly duckling, an outcast at home and at school. Her mother, a religious fanatic, associates Carrie with her own "sin"; Carrie's peers hate her in a mindless way and make her the butt of every joke. *Carrie* concerns the horrors of high school, a place of "bottomless conservatism and bigotry," as King explains, where students "are no more allowed to rise 'above their station' than a Hindu" above caste. The novel is also about the terrors of passage to womanhood. In the opening scene, in the school shower room, Carrie experiences her first menstrual period; her peers react with abhorrence and ridicule, "stoning" her with sanitary napkins, shouting "Plug it up!" Carrie becomes the scapegoat for a fear of female sexuality as epitomized in the smell and sight of blood. (The blood bath and symbolism of sacrifice will recur at the climax of the novel.) As atonement for her participation in Carrie's persecution in the shower, Susan Snell persuades her popular boyfriend Tommy Ross to invite Carrie to the Spring Ball. Carrie's conflict with her mother, who regards her emerging womanhood with loathing, is paralleled by a new plot by the girls against her, led by the rich and spoiled Chris Hargenson. They arrange to have Tommy and Carrie voted King and Queen of the Ball, only to crown them with a bucket of pig's blood. Carrie avenges her mock baptism telekinetically, destroying the school and the town, leaving Susan Snell as the only survivor.

As in most folk cultures, initiation is signified by the acquisition of special wisdom or powers. King equates Carrie's sexual flowering with the maturing of her telekinetic ability. Both cursed and empowered with righteous fury, she becomes at once victim and monster, witch and White Angel of Destruction. As King has explained, Carrie is "Woman, feeling her powers for the first time and, like Samson, pulling down the temple on everyone in sight at the end of the book."

Carrie catapulted King into the mass market; in 1976 it was adapted into a critically acclaimed film directed by Brian De Palma. The novel touched the right nerves, including feminism. William Blatty's *The Exorcist* (1971), which was adapted into a powerful and controversial film, had touched on similar social fears in the 1960's and 1970's with its subtext of the "generation gap" and the "death of God." Although Carrie's destructive power, like that of Regan in *The Exorcist*, is linked with monstrous adolescent sexuality, the similarity between the two novels ends there. Carrie's "possession" is the complex effect of her mother's fanaticism, her peers' bigotry, and her newly realized, unchecked female power. Like Anne Sexton's *Transformations* (1971), a collection of fractured fairy tales in sardonic verse, King's novel explores the social and cultural roots of its evil.

King's *Carrie* is a dark modernization of "Cinderella," with a bad mother, cruel siblings (peers), a prince (Tommy Ross), a godmother (Sue Snell), and a ball. King's reversal of the happy ending is actually in keeping with the Brothers Grimm; it recalls the tale's folk originals, which enact revenge in bloody images: The stepsisters' heels, hands, and noses are sliced off, and a white dove pecks out their eyes. As King knows, blood flows freely in the oral tradition. King represents that oral tradition in a pseudo-

documentary form that depicts the points of view of various witnesss and commentaries: newspaper accounts, case studies, court reports, and journals. Pretending to textual authenticity, he alludes to the gothic classics, especially Bram Stoker's *Dracula* (1897). *'Salem's Lot*, King's next novel, is a bloody fairy tale in which Dracula comes to Our Town.

'SALEM'S LOT

By the agnostic and sexually liberated 1970's, the vampire had been demythologized into what King called a "comic book menace." In a significant departure from tradition, he diminishes the sexual aspects of the vampire. He reinvests the archetype with meaning by basing its attraction on the human desire to surrender identity in the mass. His major innovation, however, was envisioning the mythic small town in American gothic terms and then making it the monster; the vampire's traditional victim, the populace, becomes the menace as mindless mass, plague, or primal horde. Drawing on Richard Matheson's grimly naturalistic novel *I Am Legend* (1954) and Jack Finney's novel *The Body Snatchers* (1955), King focused on the issues of fragmentation, reinvesting the vampire with contemporary meaning.

The sociopolitical subtext of *'Salem's Lot* was the ubiquitous disillusionment of the Watergate era, King has explained. Like rumor and disease, vampirism spreads secretly at night, from neighbor to neighbor, infecting men and women, the mad and the senile, the responsible citizen and the infant alike, absorbing into its zombielike horde the human population. King is especially skillful at suggesting how small-town conservatism can become inverted on itself, the harbored suspicions and open secrets gradually dividing and isolating. This picture is reinforced by the town's name, 'Salem's Lot, a degenerated form of Jerusalem's Lot, which suggests the city of the chosen reverted to a culture of dark rites in images of spreading menace.

King's other innovation was, paradoxically, a reiteration. He made his "king vampire," Barlow, an obvious reincarnation of Stoker's Dracula that functions somewhere between cliché and archetype. King uses the mythology of vampires to ask how civilization is to exist without faith in traditional authority symbols. His answer is pessimistic, turning on the abdication of Father Callahan, whose strength is undermined by secret alcoholism and a superficial adherence to form. The two survivors, Ben Mears and Mark Petrie, must partly seek, partly create their talismans and rituals, drawing on the compendium of vampire lore—the alternative, in a culture-wide crisis of faith, to conventional systems. (At one point, Mears holds off a vampire with a crucifix made with two tongue depressors.) The paraphernalia, they find, will work only if the handler has faith.

It is significant that the two survivors are, respectively, a "wise child" (Mark Petrie) and a novelist (Ben Mears); only they have the necessary resources. Even Susan Norton, Mears's lover and the gothic heroine, succumbs. As in *The Shining*, *The Dead Zone*, and *Firestarter*, the child (or childlike adult) has powers that may be used for good or for evil. Mears is the imaginative, nostalgic adult, haunted by the past. The child and the man share a naïveté, a gothic iconography, and a belief in evil. Twelve-year-old Mark worships at a shrinelike tableau of Aurora monsters that glow "green in the dark, just like the plastic Jesus" he was given in Sunday School for learning Psalm 119. Mears has returned to the town of his childhood to revive an image of the Marsten House lurking in his mythical mind's eye. Spiritual father and son, they create a community of two out of the "pop" remnants of American culture.

As in fairy tales and Dickens's novels, King's protagonists are orphans searching for their true parents, for community. His fiction may reenact his search for the father who disappeared and left behind a box of *Weird Tales*. The yearned-for bond of parent and child, a relationship signifying a unity of being, appears throughout his fiction. The weakness or treachery of a trusted parent is correspondingly the ultimate fear. Hence, the vampire Barlow is the devouring father who consumes an entire town.

THE SHINING

In *The Shining*, King domesticated his approach to the theme of parent-child relationships, focusing on the threat to the family that comes from a trusted figure within it. Jack Torrance, a writer, arranges to oversee a mountain resort during the winter months,

when it is closed due to snow. He moves his family with him to the Overlook Hotel, where he expects to break a streak of bad luck and personal problems (he is an alcoholic) by writing a play. He is also an abused child who, assuming his father's aggression, in turn becomes the abusing father. The much beloved "bad" father is the novel's monster: The environment of the Overlook Hotel traps him, as he in turn calls its power forth. As Jack metamorphoses from abusive father and husband into violent monster, King brilliantly expands the haunted-house archetype into a symbol of the accumulated sin of all fathers.

CHRISTINE

In *Christine*, the setting is Libertyville, Pennsylvania, in the late 1970's. The monster is the American Dream as embodied in the automobile. King gives *Christine* all the attributes of a fairy tale for "postliterate" adolescents. *Christine* is another fractured "Cinderella" story, *Carrie* for boys. Arnie Cunningham, a nearsighted, acne-scarred loser, falls "in love with" a car, a passionate (red and white) Christine, "one of the long ones with the big fins." An automotive godmother, she brings Arnie, in fairy-tale succession, freedom, success, power, and love: a home away from overprotective parents, a cure for acne, hit-and-run revenge on bullies, and a beautiful girl, Leigh Cabot. Soon, however, the familiar triangle emerges, of boy, girl, and car, and Christine is revealed as a femme fatale—driven by the spirit of her former owner, a malcontent named Roland LeBay. Christine is the medium for his death wish on the world, for his all-devouring, "everlasting Fury." LeBay's aggression possesses Arnie, who reverts into an older, tougher self, then into the "mythic teenaged hood" that King has called the prototype of 1950's werewolf films, and finally into "some ancient carrion eater," or primal self.

As automotive monster Christine comes from a variety of sources, including the folk tradition of the "death car" and a venerable techno-horror premise, as seen in King's "Trucks" and *Maximum Overdrive*. King's main focus, however, is the mobile youth culture that has come down from the 1950's by way of advertising, popular songs, film, and national pastimes. Christine is the car as a projection of the cultural self, Anima for the modern American Adam. To Arnie's late 1970's-style imagination, the Plymouth Fury, in 1958 a mid-priced family car, is an American Dream. Her sweeping, befinned chassis and engine re-create a fantasy of the golden age of the automobile: the horizonless future imagined as an expanding network of superhighways and unlimited fuel. Christine recovers for Arnie a prelapsarian vitality and manifest destiny.

Christine's odometer runs backward and she regenerates parts. The immortality she offers, however—and by implication, the American Dream—is really arrested development in the form of a *Happy Days* rerun and by way of her radio, which sticks on the golden oldies station. Indeed, *Christine* is a recapitulatory rock musical framed fatalistically in sections titled "Teenage Car-Songs," "Teenage Love-Songs," and "Teenage Death-Songs." Fragments of rock-and-roll songs introduce each chapter. Christine's burden, an undead 1950's youth culture, means that most of Arnie's travels are in and out of time, a deadly nostalgia trip. As Douglas Winter explains, *Christine* reenacts "the death," in the 1970's, "of the American romance with the automobile."

The epilogue from four years later presents the fairy-tale consolation in a burned-out monotone. Arnie and his parents are buried, Christine is scrap metal, and the true Americans, Leigh and Dennis, are survivors, but Dennis, the "knight of Darnell's Garage," does not woo "the lady fair"; he is a limping, lackluster junior high teacher, and they have drifted apart, grown old in their prime. Dennis narrates the story in order to file it away, all the while perceiving himself and his peers in terms of icons from the late 1950's. In his nightmares, Christine appears wearing a black vanity plate inscribed with a skull and the words, "ROCK AND ROLL WILL NEVER DIE." From Dennis's haunted perspective, *Christine* simultaneously examines and is a symptom of a cultural phenomenon: a new American gothic species of anachronism or déjà vu, which continued after *Christine*'s publication in films such as *Back to the Future* (1985), *Peggy Sue Got Married* (1986), and *Blue Velvet* (1986). The 1980's and the 1950's blur into a

seamless illusion, the nightmare side of which is the prospect of living an infinite replay.

The subtext of King's adolescent fairy tale is another coming of age, from the opposite end and the broader perspective of American culture. Written by a fortyish King in the final years of the twentieth century, *Christine* diagnoses a cultural midlife crisis and marks a turning point in King's career, a critical examination of mass culture. The dual time frame reflects his awareness of a dual audience, of writing for adolescents who look back to a mythical 1950's and also for his own generation as it relives its undead youth culture in its children. The baby boomers, King explains, "were obsessive" about childhood. "We went on playing for a long time, almost feverishly. I write for that buried child in us, but I'm writing for the grown-up too. I want grown-ups to look at the child long enough to be able to give him up. The child should be buried."

PET SEMATARY

In *Pet Sematary*, King unearthed the buried child, which is the novel's monster. *Pet Sematary* is about the "*real* cemetery," he told Winter. The focus is on the "one great fear" all fears "add up to," "the body under the sheet. It's our body." The fairy-tale subtext is the magic kingdom of our protracted American childhood, the Disney empire as mass culture—and, by implication, the comparable multimedia phenomenon represented by King himself. The grimmer, truer text-within-the-text is Mary Wollstonecraft Shelley's *Frankenstein* (1818).

The novel, which King once considered "too horrible to be published," is also his own dark night of the soul. Louis Creed, a university doctor, moves with his wife, Rachel, and their two children (five-year-old Ellie and two-year-old Gage) to Maine to work at King's alma mater; a neighbor takes the family on an outing to a pet cemetery created by the neighborhood children, their confrontation with mortality. Additionally the "sematary," whose "Druidic" rings allude to Stonehenge, is the outer circle of a Native American burial ground that sends back the dead in a state of soulless half life. Louis succumbs to temptation when the family cat Church is killed on the highway; he buries him on the sacred old Native

American burial grounds. "Frankencat" comes back with his "purr-box broken." A succession of accidents, heart attacks, strokes, and deaths—of neighbor Norma Crandall, Creed's son Gage, Norma's husband Jud, and Creed's wife Rachel—and resurrections follows.

The turning point is the death of Gage, which Creed cannot accept and which leads to the novel's analysis of modern medical miracles performed in the name of human decency and love. Louis is the father as baby boomer who cannot relinquish his childhood. The larger philosophical issue is Louis's rational, bioethical *creed*; he believes in saving the only life he knows, the material. Transferred into an immoderate love for his son, it is exposed as the narcissistic embodiment of a patriarchal lust for immortality through descendants, expressed first in an agony of sorrow and rage, then ghoulishly, as he disinters his son's corpse and makes the estranging discovery that it is like "looking at a badly made doll." Later, reanimated, Gage appears to have been "terribly hurt and then put back together again by crude, uncaring hands." Performing his task, Louis feels dehumanized, like "a subhuman character in some cheap comic-book."

The failure of Louis's creed is shown in his habit, when under stress, of taking mental trips to Orlando, Florida, where he, Church, and Gage drive a white van as Disney World's "resurrection crew." In these waking dreams, which echo the male bond of "wise child" and haunted father from as far back as *'Salem's Lot*, Louis's real creed is revealed: Its focus is on Oz the Gweat and Tewwible (a personification of death to Rachel) and Walt Disney, that "gentle faker from Nebraska"—like Louis, two wizards of science fantasy. Louis's wizardry is reflected in the narrative perspective and structure, which flashes back in part 2 from the funeral to Louis's fantasy of a heroically "long, flying tackle" that snatches Gage from death's wheels.

In this modernization of *Frankenstein*, King demythologizes death and attacks the aspirations toward immortality that typify the 1980's. King's soulless Lazaruses are graphic projections of anxieties about life-support systems, artificial hearts, organ

transplants, Baby Faye—what King has called "mechanistic miracles" that can postpone the physical signs of life almost indefinitely. The novel also indicts the "waste land" of mass culture, alluding in the same trope to George Romero's "stupid, lurching movie-zombies," T. S. Eliot's poem about the hollow men, and *The Wizard of Oz*: "headpiece full of straw." Louis worries that Ellie knows more about Ronald McDonald and "the Burger King" than the "*spiritus mundi*." If the novel suggests one source of community and culture, it is the form and ritual of the children's pet "sematary." Its concentric circles form a pattern from their "own collective unconsciousness," one that mimes "the most ancient religious symbol of all," the spiral.

It

In *It*, a group of children create a community and a mythology as a way of confronting their fears, as represented in It, the monster as a serial-murdering, shape-shifting boogey that haunts the sewers of Derry, Maine. In 1958, the seven protagonists, a cross-section of losers, experience the monster differently, for as in George Orwell's *Nineteen Eighty-Four* (1949), It derives its power through its victim's isolation and guilt and thus assumes the shape of his or her worst fear. (To Beverly Rogan It appears, in a sequence reminiscent of "Red Riding Hood," as her abusive father in the guise of the child-eating witch from "Hansel and Gretel.")

In a scary passage in *Pet Sematary*, Louis dreams of Walt Disney World, where "by the 1890s train station, Mickey Mouse was shaking hands with the children clustered around him, his big white cartoon gloves swallowing their small, trusting hands." To all of *It*'s protagonists, the monster appears in a similar archetypal or communal form, one that suggests a composite of devouring parent and mass-culture demigod, of television commercial and fairy tale, of 1958 and 1985: as Pennywise, the Clown, a cross between Bozo and Ronald McDonald. As in *Christine, Pet Sematary*, and *Thinner*, the monster is mass culture itself, the collective devouring parent nurturing its children on "imitations of immortality." Like Christine, or Louis's patched-up son, Pennywise is the dead past feeding on the future. Twenty-seven years after its original reign of terror, It resumes its seige, whereupon the protagonists, now professionally successful and, significantly, childless yuppies, must return to Derry to confront as adults their childhood fears. Led by horror writer Bill Denborough (partly based on King's friend and collaborator Peter Straub), they defeat It once more, individually as a sort of allegory of psychoanalysis and collectively as a rite of passage into adulthood and community.

It was attacked in reviews as pop psychology and by King himself as a "badly constructed novel," but the puerility was partly intended. The book summarizes King's previous themes and characters, who themselves look backward and inward, regress and take stock. The last chapter begins with an epigraph from Dickens's *David Copperfield* (1849-1850) and ends with an allusion to William Wordsworth's "Intimations of Immortality," from which King takes his primary theme and narrative device, the look back that enables one to go forward. In the 1970's, King's fiction was devoted to building a mythos out of shabby celluloid monsters to fill a cultural void; in the postmodern awareness of the late 1980's, he began a demystification process. *It* is a calling forth and ritual unmasking of motley Reagan-era monsters, the exorcism of a generation and a culture.

OTHER 1980'S NOVELS

As for King the writer, *It* was one important rite in what would be a lengthy passage. After *It*'s extensive exploration of childhood, however, he took up conspicuously more mature characters, themes, and roles. In *The Eyes of the Dragon* (written for his daughter), he returned to the springs of his fantasy, the fairy tale. He told much the same story as before but assumed the mantle of adulthood. This "pellucid" and "elegant" fairy tale, says Barbara Tritel in *The New York Times Book Review* (February 22, 1987), has the "intimate goofiness of an extemporaneous story" narrated by "a parent to a child." In *The Tommyknockers*, King again seemed to leave familiar territory for science fiction, but the novel more accurately applies technohorror themes to the 1980's infatuation with technology and televangelism. In *The Dark Tower* cycles, he combined the gothic with Western and apocalyptic fiction in a manner reminis-

cent of *The Stand*. Then with much fanfare in 1990, King returned to that novel to update and enlarge it by some 350 pages.

KING AND BACHMAN

The process of recapitulation and summing up was complicated by the disclosure, in 1984, of Richard Bachman, the pseudonym under whose cover King had published five novels over a period of eight years. Invented for business reasons, Bachman soon grew into an identity complete with a biography and photographs (he was a chicken farmer with a cancer-ravaged face), dedications, a narrative voice (of unrelenting pessimism), and if not a genre, a naturalistic mode in which sociopolitical speculation combined or alternated with psychological suspense. In 1985, when the novels (with one exception) were collected in a single volume attributed to King *as* Bachman, the mortified alter ego seemed buried. Actually Bachman's publicized demise only raised a haunting question of what "Stephen King" really was.

MISERY

Misery, which was conceived as Bachman's book, was King's first novel to explore the subject of fiction's dangerous powers. After crashing his car on an isolated road in Colorado, romance writer Paul Sheldon is "rescued," drugged, and held prisoner by a psychotic nurse named Annie Wilkes, who is also the "Number One Fan" of his heroine Misery Chastain (of whom he has tired and killed off). This "Constant Reader" becomes Sheldon's terrible "Muse," forcing him to write (in an edition especially for her) Misery's return to life. Sheldon is the popular writer imprisoned by genre and cut to fit fan expectations (signified by Annie's amputations of his foot and thumb). Like Scheherazade, the reader is reminded, Sheldon must publish or literally perish. Annie's obsession merges with the expectations of the page-turning real reader, who demands and devours each chapter, and as Sheldon struggles (against pain, painkillers, and a manual typewriter that throws keys) for his life, page by page.

Billed ironically on the dust jacket as a love letter to his fans, the novel is a witty satire on what King has called America's "cannibalistic cult of celebrity":

"[Y]ou set the guy up, and then you eat him." The monstrous Reader, however, is also the writer's muse, creation, and alter ego, as Sheldon discovers when he concludes that *Misery Returns*—not his "serious" novel *Fast Cars*—was his masterpiece. Just as ironically, *Misery* was King's first novel to please most of the critics.

THE DARK HALF

It was not a complete surprise, then, when in 1989 he examined the issue from the other side, in *The Dark Half*, an allegory of the writer's relation to his genius. The young writer-protagonist Thaddeus Beaumont has a series of headaches and seizures, and a surgeon removes from his eleven-year-old brain the incompletely absorbed fragments of a twin—including an eye, two teeth, and some fingernails. Nearly thirty years later, Beaumont is a creative writing professor and moderately successful literary novelist devoted to his family. For twelve years, however, he has been living a secret life through George Stark, the pseudonym under which he emerged from writer's block as the author of best-selling crime novels. Stark's purely instinctual genius finds its most vital expression in his protagonist, the ruthless killer Alexis Machine. Like King, Beaumont is forced to disclose and destroy his now self-destructive pseudonym, complete with gravesite service and papier mâché headstone. A series of murders (narrated in Stark's graphic prose style) soon follows. The pseudonym has materialized, risen from its fictional grave literally to take Thad's wife and children (twins, of course) hostage. What Stark wants is to live in writing, outside of which writers do not exist. Yet the writer is also a demon, vampire, and killer in this dark allegory, possessing and devouring the man, his family, friends, community.

Drawing on the motif of the double and the form of the detective story—on Robert Louis Stevenson's *The Strange Case of Dr. Jekyll and Mr. Hyde* (1886) and Sophocles' *Oedipus Rex* (c. fifth century B.C.), as well as *Misery* and *Pet Sematary*—King gluts the first half of the book with Stark/Machine's gruesome rampages. The last half is psychological suspense and metafiction in biological metaphor: the struggle of the decently introspective Beaumont against the

rawly instinctual Stark for control of both word and flesh, with the novel taking shape on the page as the true author reclaims the "third eye," King's term for both child's and artist's inward vision. Once again, the man buries the terrible child in order to possess himself and his art. The book ends in a "scene from some malign fairy tale" as that child and alter ego is borne away by flocks of sparrows to make a last appearance as a black hole in the fabric of the sky.

In dramatizing the tyrannies, perils, powers, and pleasures of reading and writing, *Misery* and *The Dark Half* might have been written by metafictionists John Fowles (to whose work King is fond of alluding) or John Barth (on whom he draws directly in *It* and *Misery*). Anything but abstract, however, *The Dark Half* is successful both as the thriller that King's fans desired and as an allegory of the writer's situation. Critic George Stade, in his review of the novel for *The New York Times Book Review* (October 29, 1989), praised King for his tact "in teasing out the implications of his parable." *The Dark Half* contains epigraphs instead to the novels of George Stark, Thad Beaumont, and "the late Richard Bachman," without whom "this novel could not have been written." Thus reworking the gothic cliché of the double, King allows the mythology of his own life story to speak wittily for itself, lending a subtle level of self-parody to this *roman à clef*. In this instance, his blunt literalness ("word become flesh, so to speak," as George Stark puts it), gives vitality to what in other hands might have been a sterile exercise.

GERALD'S GAME and DOLORES CLAIBORNE

Some have criticized negative King's depiction of women, which King himself admitted in 1983 was a weakness. A decade later, King would address, and redress, this in his paired novels *Gerald's Game* and *Dolores Claiborne*. Both present a strong but besieged female protagonist, and both feature the total solar eclipse seen in Maine in 1963, during which a moment of telepathy, the books' only supernaturalism, links the two women.

Gerald's Game is the story of Jessie Burlingame, a young wife who submits to her husband's desire for bondage in a deserted cabin, only to have him die when she unexpectedly struggles. Alone and helpless, Jessie confronts memories (including the secret reason she struck out at Gerald), her own fears and limitations, and a ghastly visitor to the cabin who may or may not be real. In a bloody scene—even by King's standards—Jessie frees herself and escapes, a victory psychological as well as physical. The aptly named Dolores Claiborne is trapped more metaphorically, by poverty and an abusive husband, and her victory too is both violent and a sign of her developing independence and strength.

Initial reaction from critics was sometimes skeptical, especially given the prurient aspect of Jessie's plight and the trendy theme of incestuous abuse in both novels. Yet King examined family dysfunction in works from *Carrie* and *The Shining* to *It*, and he continued his commitment to women's issues and realistic strong females in *Insomnia*, *Rose Madder*, and other novels. Archetypal themes also strengthen the two books: Female power must overcome male dominance, as the moon eclipses the sun; and each woman must find her own identity and strength out of travail, as the darkness gives way to light again. (King uses mythology and gender issues more explicitly in *Rose Madder*, which evenly incorporates mimetic and supernatural scenes.)

The books are daring departures for King in other ways. In contrast to King's sprawling *It* or encyclopedic *The Stand*, these books, like *Misery*, tightly focus on one setting, a shorter period of time, and a small cast—here *Misery*'s duet is replaced by intense monologues. In fact, all of *Dolores Claiborne* is her first-person narrative, without even chapter breaks, a tour de force few would attempt. Moreover, King challenges our ideas of the genre horror novel, since there is little violence, none of it supernatural and all expected, so that suspense is a function of character, not plot (done previously by King only in short fiction such as "The Body" and "The Last Rung of the Ladder").

Yet character and voice have always been essential to King's books, as Debbie Notkin, Harlan Ellison, and others have pointed out. Dolores Claiborne is especially successful, her speech authentic Mainer, and her character realistic both as the old woman telling her story and as the desperate yet indomitable wife, the past self whose story she tells. In these novels, King reaches beyond childhood and adolescence as themes; child abuse is examined, but only from an adult point of view. Dolores and Jessie—and the elderly protagonists of *Insomnia*—reveal King, perhaps having reconciled to his own history, exploring new social and psychological areas.

BAG OF BONES

Bag of Bones, which King calls a "haunted love story," opens with narrator Mike Noonan recounting the death of his wife, Jo, who collapses outside the Rite Aid pharmacy of a brain aneurysm. Both are relatively young, and Jo, Mike learns, was pregnant. Because Mike is unable to father children, he begins to question whether Jo was having an affair. As Mike slowly adjusts to life without Jo, he is forced to make another adjustment. Formerly a successful writer of gothic romance fiction, he now finds that he is unable to write even a simple sentence. In an attempt to regain his muse and put Jo's death behind him, Mike returns to Sarah Laughs (also referred to as "TR-90" or the "TR"), the vacation cabin he and Jo purchased soon after he became successful. As Mike quickly learns, Sarah Laughs is haunted by ghosts, among them the ghost of blues singer Sarah Tidwell.

While at Sarah Laughs, Mike meets Mattie Devore, her daughter Kyra, and Mattie's father-in-law, Max Devore, a withered old man of incalculable wealth who is accustomed to getting anything he wants. Having rescued Kyra from walking down the middle of Route 68, Mike quickly becomes friends with both Kyra and Mattie. Mattie is the widow of Lance Devore, Max's stuttering son. Lance had nothing to do with his father after learning that his father had tried to bribe Mattie into not marrying him. After Lance's death from a freak accident, Max returned to Mattie's life in an attempt to get acquainted with his granddaughter, Kyra. The truth is, however, that Max wants to gain custody of Kyra and take her away to California; he will do whatever it takes to accomplish that.

To help Mattie fight off Max's army of high-priced lawyers, Mike uses his own considerable resources to retain a lawyer for Mattie named John Storrow, a young New Yorker unafraid to take on someone of Max Devore's social stature. As Mike is drawn into Mattie's custody battle, he is also exposed to the ghosts that haunt the community. As Mike sleeps at night, he comes to realize that there are at least three separate spirits haunting his cabin. One, he is sure, is Jo, and one, he determines, is Sarah Tidwell. The third manifests itself only as a crying child, and Mike cannot tell whether it is Kyra or some other child. Mike and Kyra share a special psychic connection that allows them to share dreams and even to have the same ghosts haunting their homes—ghosts who communicate by rearranging magnetic letters on each of their refrigerator doors.

As Mike becomes further embroiled in the custody battle with Max Devore, his search to determine the truth about Jo's affair finally leads him to a set of journals Jo was keeping, notes from a research project that was her real reason for sneaking away to Sarah Laughs. Jo's notes explain how everyone related to the people who murdered Sarah Tidwell and her son have paid for this sin by losing a child of their own. Sarah Tidwell's ghost is exacting her revenge by murdering the children of those who murdered her own child. Mike, related to one of the people who murdered Sarah's child, has been drawn into this circle of retribution from the beginning, and the death of his unborn daughter, Kia, was not the accident it seemed to be. Mike also realizes that Kyra, the last descendant of this tragedy, is to be the final sacrifice used to put Sarah Tidwell to rest. Mike's return to the ironically named Sarah Laughs, it seems, has been a carefully orchestrated tragedy. Everything is tied to the ghost Sarah Tidwell's purposes, even Mike's writer's block. Mike's writing abilities return while he is at Sarah Laughs, but by the end of the novel he realizes it was simply to lead him to the information he needed to put Sarah's spirit to rest. Sarah's ghost may have destroyed his wife and child, but Jo's ghost gives him the means to save Kyra.

The usual King trademarks that fans have come to expect are present in *Bag of Bones*. The novel, moreover, shares much with the southern novel and its themes. Guilt is a predominant theme of many southern works, especially those of William Faulkner, Edgar Allan Poe, and Tennessee Williams. Racism, not

a theme usually associated with northern writers, has been successfully transplanted by King via the traveling Sarah Tidwell. By the end of the novel the evils of the community have become so entrenched in the soil (another similarity to Faulkner's fiction) that they begin to affect Mike himself, and he has to fight the urge to kill Kyra. Only by reburying the past—in this case, by literally reburying Sarah Tidwell's body—can matters finally be put to rest. Mike dissolves Sarah's body with lye and her spirit finally leaves Sarah Laughs. Jo's spirit also leaves, and all is quiet once more at the cabin.

By the 1980's, King had become a mass-media guru who could open an American Express commercial with the rhetorical question "Do you know me?" At first prompted to examine the "wide perceptions which light [children's] interior lives" (*Four Past Midnight*) and then the cultural roots of the empire he had created, he proceeded to explore the phenomenon of fiction, the situations of reader and writer. In the 1990's, King continued to develop as a writer of both supernatural horror and mimetic character-based fiction. His novels after *Dolores Claiborne*—from *Insomnia* through *The Girl Who Loved Tom Gordon*—all provide supernatural chills while experimenting with character, mythology, and metafiction.

Financially invulnerable, King became almost playful with publishing gambits: *The Green Mile* was a serial, six slim paperbacks, in emulation of Charles Dickens and as a self-set challenge; Richard Bachman was revived when *The Regulators* was published in 1996. While he is still thought of as having no style, actually King maintained his compelling storyteller's voice (and ability to manipulate his reader emotionally) while maturing in the depth and range of his themes and characters.

King, perhaps more than any other author since William Faulkner and his fictional Yoknapatawpha County, also creates a sense of literary history within the later novels that ties them all together. In *Bag of Bones*, King references several of his other novels, most notably *The Dark Half*, *Needful Things*, and *Insomnia*. For longtime fans, this serves both to update King's readers concerning their favorite characters and to unify King's body of work. King's ironic sense of humor is also evident. When Mike's literary agent tells him of all the other best-selling novelists who have novels coming out in the fall of 1998, the most notable name missing from the list is that of Stephen King himself.

Linda C. Badley, updated by Bernadette Lynn Bosky

OTHER MAJOR WORKS

SHORT FICTION: *Night Shift*, 1978; *Different Seasons*, 1982; *Skeleton Crew*, 1985; *Four Past Midnight*, 1990; *Nightmares and Dreamscapes*, 1993; *Hearts in Atlantis*, 1999.

SCREENPLAYS: *Creepshow*, 1982 (with George Romero; adaptation of his book); *Cat's Eye*, 1984; *Silver Bullet*, 1985 (adaptation of *Cycle of the Werewolf*); *Maximum Overdrive*, 1986 (adaptation of his short story "Trucks"); *Pet Sematary*, 1989; *Sleep Walkers*, 1992.

TELEPLAYS: *The Stand*, 1994 (based on his novel); *Storm of the Century*, 1999.

NONFICTION: *Danse Macabre*, 1981.

MISCELLANEOUS: *Creepshow*, 1982 (adaptation of the D.C. Comics).

BIBLIOGRAPHY

Beahm, George. *The Stephen King Story: A Literary Profile*. Kansas City: Andrews and McMeel, 1991. Not as stylishly written as Winter's book (below), but this complements it: It is later and contains more information on King's personal background and professional habits. Includes a good index, notes, selected bibliography, and photos.

Bloom, Harold, ed. *Stephen King: Modern Critical Views*. Philadelphia: Chelsea House, 1998. This is the best single collection of essays about King, many collected from other sources listed here, but including previously unreprinted pieces from journals or non-King specific books. High-quality pieces cover a range of themes and King's works through *Needful Things*. Good chronology, bibliography, and index.

Collings, Michael R. *The Annotated Guide to Stephen King: A Primary and Secondary Bibliography of America's Premier Horror Writer*. Mercer Island, Wash.: Starmont House, 1986. Easy to use and comprehensive to its time. Provides both a good chronology and useful descriptions of some of King's hard-to-find works, as well as a copious annotated list of secondary sources.

_____. *The Stephen King Phenomenon*. Starmont Studies in Literary Criticism 14. Mercer Island, Wash.: Starmont House, 1987. The sixth of Collings's continuing series of books on King, this study examines King from multiple perspectives, summarizing images, themes, and characters. Chapters on King as a publishing phenomenon and *It* are of special value. Collings was the first to demonstrate King's literary merits by applying scholarly textual analysis.

Hoppenstand, Gary, and Ray B. Browne, eds. *The Gothic World of Stephen King: Landscape of Nightmare*. Bowling Green, Ohio: Popular Press, 1987. The first collection of academic criticism of King includes an introduction by Hoppenstand and essays on themes ("Adolescent Revolt," "Love and Death in the American Car"), characters ("Mad Dogs and Firestarters," "The Vampire"), genres (King's "Gothic Western," techno-horror), technique ("Allegory"), and individual works.

Magistrale, Tony, ed. *The Dark Descent: Essays Defining Stephen King's Horrorscape*. Westport, Conn.: Greenwood Press, 1992. This academic collection of interpretive essays covers subjects such as homophobia, treatment of female characters, and dialogic narratives in King's work; the sixteen pieces examine most of King's novels and some short fiction. Individual essay bibliographies, book bibliography, and book index.

_____. *Landscape of Fear: Stephen King's American Gothic*. Bowling Green, Ohio: Popular Press, 1988. Placing King in an American gothic tradition with Edgar Allan Poe, Nathaniel Hawthorne, Herman Melville, and William Faulkner, this study treats sociopolitical themes such as "The Betrayal of Technology," individual accountability, innocence betrayed, and survival in the novels through *It*. The text is supplemented by a bibliography of scholarship from 1980 to 1987.

_____. *Stephen King: The Second Decade, "Danse Macabre" to "The Dark Half."* New York: Twayne,

1992. Magistrale is both careful and insightful, exploring important approaches (from King's gothic inheritance to his experiments in genre and form) and themes (from apocalypse to art) in a book-by-book examination. Full consideration of the Bachman books and a new interview with King are included, as well as a chronology of King's life, notes, selected bibliography, and index.

Reino, Joseph. *Stephen King: The First Decade.* Boston: Twayne, 1988. This book-by-book analysis, from *Carrie* to *Pet Sematary*, attempts to show King's literary merits, stressing subtle characterization and nuances of symbolism and allusion. Reino presents King as subversive. She argues that his works project a pessimistic, apocalyptic vision in fictions with a deceptive complacency of surface. The text is supplemented by a chronology, notes, and primary and secondary bibliographies.

Underwood, Tim, and Chuck Miller, eds. *Fear Itself: The Horror Fiction of Stephen King.* New York: New American Library, 1984. This first anthology of commentaries on King accounts for him as a popular genre phenomenon, bringing together notables in the field, with an introduction by Peter Straub, foreword by King, afterword by George Romero, and articles by Charles L. Grant, Alan Ryan, Douglas Winter, and King's professor Burton Hatlen. See Underwood and Miller's second anthology, *Kingdom of Fear* (1986), for essays by Robert Bloch, Ramsey Campbell, Whitley Strieber, Clive Barker, Harlan Ellison, Michael McDowell, and Leslie Fiedler. The same editors have published a collection of King interviews, *Bare Bones* (1988).

Winter, Douglas. *Stephen King: The Art of Darkness.* Rev. ed. New York: New American Library, 1986. This early book on King remains the best introduction and appreciation. Combining biography and analysis and based on exclusive interviews and correspondence, the text is supplemented with a chronology, appendices summarizing the short fiction and listing film and television adaptations, notes, primary and secondary bibliographies, and an index.

BARBARA KINGSOLVER

Born: Annapolis, Maryland; April 8, 1955

PRINCIPAL LONG FICTION
The Bean Trees, 1988
Animal Dreams, 1990
Pigs in Heaven, 1993
The Poisonwood Bible, 1998

OTHER LITERARY FORMS

Barbara Kingsolver, known primarily for her long fiction, has also written travel articles, book reviews, essays, and poetry. Her nonfiction book *Holding the Line: Women in the Great Arizona Mine Strike of 1983* (1989) presents a compelling picture of the plight of miners in southern Arizona's copper-mining "company towns." The form of her poetry collection *Another America* (1992)—with Kingsolver's poetry and its Spanish translations printed on facing pages—invites awareness of diverse perspectives. *Homeland and Other Stories* (1989), a short-story collection, contains previously published and new work, most of which depicts the vagaries and pressures of different mother/daughter relationships. Some of the stories encompass fathers, brothers, and husbands as well, but all explore how family, past and present, affects the identity and perspective of the main character or the narrator in each story. Essays included in *High Tide in Tucson: Essays from Now or Never* (1995) offer thoughts on parenting, home ownership, cultural habits, travel, and writing.

ACHIEVEMENTS

Kingsolver has won many writing awards. In 1986 the Arizona Press Club gave her its feature-writing award. She received American Library Association awards in 1989 for *The Bean Trees* and in 1990 for *Homeland*. The Edward Abbey Ecofiction Award (1990) for *Animal Dreams* and the prestigious PEN Western Fiction Award (1991) added to her reputation. In 1993 and 1994 she received the Los Angeles Book Award and Mountain and Plains Booksellers Association Award for *Pigs in Heaven*. She also received an Enoch Pratt Library Youth Book Award for *The Bean Trees*. In 1995, an honorary doctorate was conferred on her by De Pauw University. She spent two semesters as a visiting writer at Emory & Henry College. True to her activist principles, she is the founder of the Bellwether Prize, given in support of literature of social change.

BIOGRAPHY

Barbara Kingsolver was born in Annapolis, Maryland, in 1955. Her childhood was spent mostly in eastern Kentucky's rural Nicholas County. She began writing before she entered high school. In 1977 she earned a magna cum laude undergraduate degree in biology from De Pauw University in Indiana. Work toward her master of science degree at the University of Arizona in Tucson (1981) included a creative writing class. Between her stints as a student she lived for

(Seth Kantner)

a time in Greece and France. After completing her master's degree she worked as a science writer for the University of Arizona and began to write feature articles, which appeared in publications such as *Smithsonian*, *Harpers*, and *The New York Times*. In 1985 she married Joseph Hoffman. She wrote *The Bean Trees* in insomniac interludes when she was pregnant with their daughter, Camille. Kingsolver subsequently was divorced; she then married Steven Hopp, and they settled in Tucson, Arizona. Kingsolver has been a political activist all her adult life.

ANALYSIS

Kingsolver's long fiction is best characterized as contemporary versions of the *Bildungsroman* with a feminist twist. The main character ventures forth to develop herself and find her place in her community. Many books by women that incorporate such a quest portray punishment for women who explore issues of sexuality or who discover meaningful work in the world. Often these *Bildungsromane* reiterate a main female character's struggle with the patriarchal response to her journey, as in *The Awakening* (1899) by Kate Chopin, or emphasize the price in intimacy and passionate relationships a woman pays for fully developing her skills, as in Willa Cather's *O Pioneers!* (1913). In both instances, female writers highlight the tension between an individual and society to suggest women's dilemmas finding legitimate voices and strengths in their lives and times.

Kingsolver's work departs from the punitive mold. Tension emerges as her female characters seek synthesis, a coming together that will meld place, memory, and the present moment to create personal identity. Her narratives also orchestrate the play between inner and outer landscapes. In *The Bean Trees*, Taylor Greer moves across Kentucky and through Oklahoma, landing in Tucson with a baby who will change her emotional geography. On the third page of *Animal Dreams*, the still mysterious Cosima announces her destination as Grace, Arizona—the site of her early life, stage for the novel's action, and catalyst of self-knowledge. *Pigs in Heaven* includes another flight by Taylor and Turtle. Ultimately, it depicts their trek to the deep Cherokee past, which threatens Taylor's role as a mother and unlocks Taylor's and Turtle's ties to their own histories and identities. *The Poisonwood Bible* evokes the Belgian Congo of the 1960's in rich detail, juxtaposing it with the southern U.S. landscape of memory and the recent past of Nathan Price's wife and four daughters. Patriarchy, instead of creating the frame of reference as in earlier fictions, emerges referentially in Kingsolver's books as part of a female consciousness.

Kingsolver's women negotiate new places for themselves within their personal, domestic, and social contexts. They acquire self-understanding through social interaction and introspection; these things bring harmony within and without. Her main female characters weather negotiation with themselves and their environments. They display character flaws, lapses in judgment, anger, and personal fears as well as idealism, generous hearts, moral consciences, and affection. Her women reach equilibrium rather than glorious redemption. Their personal insights are fragile in the way that most real-life understandings are, remaining constant only until new discoveries or crises initiate adjustment or expansion. Such shifts do not destroy each woman's cumulative advancement toward wholeness. Kingsolver's journeying women increase their poise and certainty at a rate commensurate with their courage and individual learning curves.

Taylor, Cosima (Codi), and the Price women all passionately pursue relationships spawned by family identity. Coming into their own carries an intrinsic connection to family, community, and state. In all Kingsolver's books, the personal is acutely political. Codi, of *Animal Dreams*, discovers her true origins as she works with older Hispanic women in Grace to end toxic environmental contamination. Leah, in *The Poisonwood Bible*, redefines her cultural and religious allegiances as she takes up residence in the "liberated" Congo. Kingsolver's long fiction is overtly political, her short stories obliquely so. (Her short fiction often focused on the domestic sphere of women's lives—situations replete with social and matrimonial expectations dictated by patriarchal values before the revolutions of the 1960's began to change sensibilities.) Her women live in the real world, and her narratives include male activity in women's ruminations or the narration of events. Male perspectives surface primarily because they affect the female characters and move the plot forward. *The Poisonwood Bible*, in which the Price entourage is dragged off to Africa, seems an exception. However, the women tell the entire story of their father's and husband's misguided mission, controlling perspective and interpretation.

Kingsolver's fiction places relationships—between parents and children, spouses and families—in the foreground and sets them against the larger social milieu. Kingsolver gives no credence to the opinion that art is apolitical. The inherent inequities and racism faced by Hispanic, Native American, and African persons surface, not as the chief lament of her main characters or as the narrative frame for their lives, but as elements in their situations.

THE BEAN TREES

Marrietta Greer, the traveling woman of *The Bean Trees*, sees herself as part of life in Pittman County, Kentucky, but she has flair. She leaves town five years after high school graduation in a "'55 Volkswagen bug with no windows to speak of, and no back seat and no starter." She heads west in search of a new name and new location, believing that mysterious signs will appear to help her along. She takes her name from Taylorville, Illinois, where she runs out of gas. Deciding to go west until the car stops running, she reaches the "Great Plain," as she calls it, and finds herself in a broken-down car in Oklahoma. She appreciates the irony of landing in Cherokee territory: Her maternal grandfather had provided the one-eighth Cherokee blood required for her to qualify for tribal membership, and the idea of moving to the Cherokee Nation had become a family joke— their last hope if they face destitution. Before Taylor leaves a Cherokee bar in Oklahoma, a pleading American Indian woman deposits a child in her front seat and drives off. Taylor calls the silent child Turtle because she attaches herself to Taylor anywhere she can get a grip and holds on as fiercely as a mud turtle when it bites. Turtle has been fiercely abused. Chapter 2 introduces Lou Ann Ruiz, pregnant, living in Arizona, and struggling in a failing marriage with

Angel. Taylor arrives in Arizona in chapter 3 and, through the auspices of Mattie (a woman who runs Jesus Is Lord Used Tires), Taylor and Lou Ann form a supportive and zany household. The two friends become involved in Mattie's clandestine work with illegal Central American refugees.

The Bean Trees reorients readers toward daily experience, juxtaposing ordinary picnics, car repairs, and kitchen scenes with such events as the chilling account of Estevan and Esperanza's daughter being snatched by the Guatemalan government. Kingsolver's relatively uneducated but compassionate people live mundane lives, but many of their activities focus on the human terms of political injustice. The novel braids the stories of ordinary women following their consciences, and it gives the lie to the idea that massive amounts of money and large organizations are needed to eradicate inhumanity. The novel's end offers a typical array of Kingsolver anomalies. Turtle is illegally but justly adopted; family has been redefined, and readers accept the safe place that Taylor and Lou Ann inhabit; the politics of safe houses and churches aiding immigrants and refugees escaping crushing cruelty seems noble despite its clandestine nature; and money has nothing to do with feeling cared about and connected.

ANIMAL DREAMS

Cosima (Codi) and Homer Noline share this book in alternating sections that detail Codi's return to Grace, Arizona, to care for Homer, her physician father, who is succumbing to Alzheimer's disease. Alternation between an omniscient narrator for the Doc Homer sections and first-person narration for Codi emphasizes postmodern disjunction of perspective, but Kingsolver uses memory to create links between the sections and characters that override the break in form. The personal, communal, and global politics of *Animal Dreams* are syncopated as well. Personally, Codi discovers her tie to the nine Gracela sisters who founded Grace. She also comes to terms with a baby she had buried alone when she was fifteen. Communally, she connects with the older women of the Stitch and Bitch Club, who alert her to the Black Mountain Mining Company's toxic presence in Grace. Together they challenge and defeat the corporate pol-

luter. Hallie's letters from Nicaragua weave the theme of human rights throughout *Animal Dreams*. As usual in Kingsolver's fiction, the scenes take place in domestic and familiar public places—kitchens, attics, front yards, schools, and trains—where personal circumstances allow a focus on larger social and political issues. There are no pat answers. An ordinary woman seeking justice dies, but the Stitch and Bitch ladies triumph. Codi moves toward a full life. All Souls Day and the Corn Dance rituals unite the past and present and provide time for Codi to seek and find answers. *Animal Dreams* articulates the complicated intersection of private and public identities and offers hope.

PIGS IN HEAVEN

Pigs in Heaven revisits Taylor and Turtle's lives. They are on a road trip visiting Hoover Dam when Turtle's glimpse of a near-fatal fall that involves a spectacular rescue makes celebrities of Taylor and Turtle. Notoriety brings the Cherokee Nation into the story, and soon Taylor is traveling to keep Turtle from being "repossessed" by Cherokee lawyer Annawake Fourkiller. Taylor maintains telephone contact with her mother, Alice, and lives hand-to-mouth while avoiding Ms. Fourkiller. To expedite matters, Alice travels to Oklahoma to reestablish her tie with a Cherokee cousin. She falls in love with an American Indian man named Cash Stillwater. Telephone calls and negotiations result in Taylor and Turtle meeting with Annawake, Cash, Alice, and the Child Welfare Services. In a bizarre twist, Cash turns out to be Turtle's grandfather and proposes to Alice. The solution of joint custody and Alice and Cash's determination to be married unite everyone with their pasts, both deep and recent.

Chapters in *Pigs in Heaven* establish irregular intervals between Taylor and Turtle's adventures and accounts of Taylor's mother, who is beginning her own road trip away from her second husband as the novel starts. Taylor runs until she must return to Oklahoma, and Alice travels to Cherokee ground to reunite with her cousin. Throughout, Kingsolver relies on the threads of Cherokee blood, Alice and Taylor's telephone calls, and the history of the Cherokee Nation to bind the plot lines. She employs a style that combines an omniscient narrator in equal parts with dialogue and with sequences that seem to be half narrated and half in the voice of the character under consideration. The ritual Cherokee stomp dance and the U.S. government's mistreatment of the Cherokees make readers consider how the past carries forward as both repetition and renewal.

THE POISONWOOD BIBLE

In *The Poisonwood Bible* the ill-fated Price women follow two men, a husband and their father, to the Belgian Congo just as fighting for liberation breaks out in earnest. The *Bildungsroman* in this case involves the simultaneous creation of five separate journeys to the self within the framework of the family's African journey. The book is an ambitious undertaking, as Kingsolver creates the voices of six-year-old Ruth May, twelve-year-old twins Leah and Ada, and fifteen-year-old Rachel Price. She then follows them to adulthood (all but Ruth May, who dies of malaria), through the tumult of Congolese revolution and U.S. manipulation.

The surviving sisters fare better than their parents do. Leah Price marries the university-educated Congolese rebel who was her teacher and remains in the country. Her thoughts outline the Congo's grinding poverty and the sheer energy it takes to survive in a society preyed upon by a colonial power and then by capitalist interests. Ada becomes a doctor, and Rachel runs a hotel for the Europeans who remain in Africa fermenting unrest. Ironically, she, the most self-centered and resentful daughter, comes closest to emulating her father despite her financial success. Orleanna Price returns to America a drifting and unsteady shadow of herself.

After his family escapes, Nathan Price sinks into madness and wanders wildly for years. Kingsolver provides an intimate portrait of the stupidity of Nathan Price; his attempted exploitation of the Congolese stands as a metaphor for the plundering of the Congo. Rich details of landscape and tribal culture, including the traditional philosophy that shapes Congolese life, surface through the disparate voices of the Price girls. The tragedy of the Price family's lives, the ruin of Congolese tribal structure, and the breakdown of national order are concentric circles.

The failure of private communication within the Price family and between the Prices and their African neighbors both prefigures and contributes to the failure and destruction of an ancient society in a ruthlessly short persion of time.

Karen L. Arnold

OTHER MAJOR WORKS

SHORT FICTION: *Homeland and Other Stories*, 1989.

POETRY: *Another America*, 1992.

NONFICTION: *Holding the Line: Women in the Great Arizona Mine Strike of 1983*, 1989; *High Tide in Tucson: Essays from Now or Never*, 1995.

BIBLIOGRAPHY

Aay, Henry. "Environmental Themes in Ecofiction: *In the Center of the Nation* and *Animal Dreams*." *Journal of Cultural Geography* 14 (Spring, 1994). Aay's comparative study of Kingsolver's novel and *In the Center of the Nation* (1991) by Dan O'Brien is one of the few scholarly discussions of Kingsolver's work.

Draper, James P. "Barbara Kingsolver." In *Contemporary Literary Criticism: Yearbook 1993*. Vol. 81. Detroit: Gale Research, 1994. A collection of critical views of Kingsolver's work.

Epstein, Robin. "Barbara Kingsolver." *Progressive* 60 (February, 1996): 33-38. An informative interview with Kingsolver; Kingsolver believes that most readers do not think that her writing is overly political; she feels that she has a responsibility to discuss her beliefs with the public.

Fleischner, Jennifer, ed. *A Reader's Guide to the Fiction of Barbara Kingsolver: The Bean Trees, Homeland and Other Stories, Animal Dreams, Pigs in Heaven*. New York: Harper Perennial, 1994. Provides discussions and brief synopses of four of Kingsolver's books; HarperCollins published this guide at least partially for the benefit of book clubs reading Kingsolver's works.

Pence, Amy. "Barbara Kingsolver." *Poets and Writers* 21, no. 4 (July/August, 1993): 14-21. Pence looks at Kingsolver's writing and her commitments to political activism and family.

Ross, Jean W. "CA Interview." In *Contemporary Authors*. Vol. 134, edited by Susan M. Trotsky. Detroit: Gale Research, 1992. Brief biographical and professional information sections are followed by an interview covering Kingsolver's writing methods, the sources of some of her characters, the importance of her background, and some of her nonfiction writing.

Ryan, Maureen. "Barbara Kingsolver's Lowfat Fiction." *Journal of American Culture* 18, no. 4 (Winter, 1995): 77-23. Ryan compares Kingsolver's first three novels and first short-story collection.

RUDYARD KIPLING

Born: Bombay, India; December 30, 1865
Died: Hampstead, London, England; January 18, 1936

PRINCIPAL LONG FICTION

The Light That Failed, 1890
The Naulahka: A Story of East and West, 1892 (with Wolcott Balestier)
Captains Courageous, 1897
Kim, 1901

OTHER LITERARY FORMS

Best known for his short fiction, Rudyard Kipling wrote more than 250 stories. His style of leaving a story open-ended with the tantalizing phrase "But that's another story" established his reputation for unlimited storytelling. Although the stories are uneven in quality, W. Somerset Maugham considered Kipling to be the only British writer to equal Guy de Maupassant and Anton Chekhov in the art of short fiction.

His early stories both satisfied and glorified the Englishman in India. The empire builder, the man who devotes his life to "civilize the sullen race," comes off in glowing colors, as in the story "The Bridge Builders." Some of his best stories skillfully blend the exotic and the bizarre, and the early "The Man Who Would Be King" (1888), which is about two drifters and their fantastic dream to carve out a kingdom for themselves in Central Asia, best illustrates such a story. "A Madonna of the Trenches," with its strange, occult atmosphere; "The Children of the Zodiac," about a young poet who dreads death by cancer of the throat; and "The Gardener" (1926), with its unrelieved sadness and autobiographical reflections on the death of his son, reflect the pain, the suffering, and the dark melancholy of Kipling's later life.

The stories that make up *The Jungle Book* (1894) and *The Second Jungle Book* (1895) were written in Brattleboro, Vermont, when Kipling's mind "worked at the height of its wonderful creative power." They are in the class of animal and folktales that make up such world literary creations as the ancient folktales of *Aesop's Fables* (fourth century B.C.) and *The Jataka Tales*. Into the Jungle Book stories, Kipling incorporated not only the clear and clean discipline of the public school but also his favorite doctrine of the natural law. This law had a great impact on the Boy Scout movement and the origins of the Wolf Cub organization, found in the Mowgli tales.

Kipling was a prolific writer, and, as a journalist, he wrote a considerable number of articles, stories, and poems not only for his own newspapers but also for a variety of literary journals in England and the United States. In addition, he was a prolific letter-writer and carried on lengthy literary and political correspondence with such men as President Theodore Roosevelt, financier Cecil Rhodes, and writer H. Rider Haggard. His correspondence with Haggard has been collected in *Rudyard Kipling to Rider Haggard: The Record of a Friendship*, edited by Morton N. Cohen (1965). Two volumes of his *Uncollected Prose* were published in 1938 and even some of his desultory writing, such as *American Notes*, concerned with his travels in the United States in 1891, was reissued in the late twentieth century with editorial notes. Kipling personally supervised the publication of the Sussex edition of his work in thirty-five volumes (1937-1939). The Kipling Society, founded in 1927, publishes the quarterly *Kipling Journal*, which keeps Kipling enthusiasts informed of publications about Kipling. Biographical material on Kipling—including his autobiography, *Something of Myself: For My Friends Known and Unknown*, published posthumously in 1937—is considerable, and the record of his literary achievement is now complete.

ACHIEVEMENTS

Kipling's first book of fiction appeared in 1888. Since then, his works have undergone several editions, and several of his short stories and poems have found a permanent place in anthologies. Although England and India have both changed enormously since the turn of the twentieth century, Kipling's stories continue to attract and fascinate new readers. He was a best-selling author during his lifetime—one of his animal stories, *Thy Servant a Dog* (1930), sold 100,000 copies in six months in 1932—and he continues to be extremely popular in the English-speaking countries of the world. Several of his works, notably *Captains Courageous, Kim, The Jungle Book*, and some short stories, have been made into motion pictures.

Throughout his lifetime, and soon after his death, Kipling was associated with the British empire. He had become the laureate of England's vast imperial power, his first book was praised by the viceroy in 1888, and the king used Kipling's own words to address the empire on Christmas Day in 1932. The day Kipling's ashes were interred at Westminster Abbey—January 23, 1936—King George V's body lay in state in Westminster Hall and the comment that "the King has gone and taken his trumpeteer with him" appropriately described the image Kipling had projected.

Kipling wanted to serve the empire through the army or the civil service. Because he had neither family connections with which to obtain a civil service job nor strong eyesight, which barred him from military service, Kipling turned to writing. He wrote with a passionate intensity coupled with admiration for the soldiers, the bridge builders, the missionaries, and the civil servants in remote places who served the empire under "an alien sky." Many of the phrases

(CORBIS/Underwood & Underwood)

he used to narrate their tales—"What do they know of England who only England know?," "East is East and West is West," "the white man's burden," "somewhere east of Suez"—have become part of the English language and are often repeated by those who are unfamiliar with his writings. To have used the pen in place of a gun to serve the imperial vision and have such lasting impact on British thinking constitutes a major achievement.

In 1890, Kipling published or republished more than eighty stories, including the novelette *The Light That Failed*. At twenty-five, he had become a famous literary figure. At forty-two, he became the first Englishman to win the Nobel Prize in Literature for "the great power of observation, the original conception and also the virile comprehension and art of narrative that distinguish his literary creations." He had also become a controversial personality, since critics and readers saw in his work the effort to mix the roles of the artist and the propagandist. Kipling's writings would continue to be controversial and generate extremes of admiration or condemnation. He generates a love-hate response, and there are frequent Kipling studies that evaluate and interpret his writings from a new perspective. He is neither neglected nor ignored, which is a true testimony to his importance as a writer.

BIOGRAPHY

Rudyard Kipling was born in Bombay, India, on December 30, 1865. His father, John Lockwood Kipling of Yorkshire, was a scholar and an artist. The elder Kipling went to India as a professor of architectural sculpture in the Bombay School of Fine Arts and later became the Curator of the Lahore Museum, which Kipling was to describe meticulously in *Kim*. He also served as the Bombay correspondent of *The Pioneer* of Allahabad. In 1891, he published *Beast and Man in India* with the help of A. P. Watt, his son's literary agent. The book contains excerpts from Rudyard Kipling's newspaper reports to *The Civil and Military Gazette*. The book provided inspiration for Kipling's Jungle Books and several of his stories: "The Mark of the Beast," "The Finances of the Gods," and "Moti Guj, Mutineer" are some examples.

Kipling's mother, Alice Macdonald, was one of five Macdonald sisters, three of whom married into prominent families. Georgina Macdonald married the distinguished pre-Raphaelite painter Sir Edward Burne-Jones; Agnes Macdonald married another painter, Sir Edward Poynter, who was influential in helping John Kipling obtain a position in India; and a third sister married Alfred Baldwin, the railroad owner, whose son Stanley Baldwin became prime minister of England. Kipling was therefore connected with creative and intellectually stimulating families through his mother, while from his father, he inherited a strong Wesleyan tradition.

Rudyard and his sister, Trix, spent the first six years of their lives in India. Surrounded by Indian servants who told them Indian folktales, Kipling absorbed the Indian vocabulary and unconsciously cultivated the habit of thinking in that vocabulary, as

illustrated in his short story "Tod's Amendment." Kipling recalls these early years in his posthumously published autobiography, *Something of Myself*, in which he recalls how he and his sister had to be constantly reminded to speak English to his parents, and that he spoke English "haltingly translated out of the vernacular idiom that one thought and dreamed in." This contributed to the great facility with which he uses Indian words as part of his style. Edmund Wilson, in his essay "The Kipling That Nobody Read," writes that Kipling even looked like an Indian as a young boy.

Like other Anglo-Indian children who were sent home to England for their education, Kipling and his sister were shipped to London to live with a relative of their father in Southsea. The pain and agony of those six years under the supervision of this sadistic woman in what Kipling calls "the house of desolation" is unflinchingly re-created in the early part of his novelette *The Light That Failed* and in the short story "Baa, Baa, Blacksheep." According to Edmund Wilson, the traumatic experiences of these six years filled Kipling with hatred for the rest of his life.

Kipling studied at the United Services College, a public school for children from families with a military background or with the government civil service. Kipling served as editor of the school newspaper, *The United Services College Chronicle*, to which he contributed several youthful parodies of poets Robert Browning and Algernon Charles Swinburne. One poem, "Ave Imperatrix," however, with its note of patriotism and references to England's destiny to civilize the world, foreshadows Kipling's later imperial themes. Although Kipling makes fun of flagwaving in "The Flag of Their Country," in *Stalky and Co.* (1899), he did imbibe some of his imperial tendencies at the school because there was an almost universal desire among the boys to join either the army or the civil service for the glory of the empire.

In 1882, when Kipling was sixteen, he returned to India, and his "English years fell away" and never "came back in full strength." Through his father's connections, Kipling had no difficulty in becoming assistant editor on *The Civil and Military Gazette* of Lahore at the age of eighteen. Two horror stories written during this period, "The Phantom 'Rick-shaw" and "The Strange Ride of Morrowbie Jukes, C. E.," have found a place among his best-known stories.

After four years on *The Civil and Military Gazette*, Kipling moved to Allahabad as assistant editor to *The Pioneer*, and his writings began to appear in four major newspapers of British India. Young, unattached, with servants and horses at his disposal, enfolded in the warmth of his family, these years proved to be Kipling's happiest and most productive. He wrote to a friend, "I'm in love with the country and would sooner write about her than anything else." The poetry collection *Departmental Ditties* was published in 1886, and *Plain Tales from the Hills* in 1888. Soon, Kipling was known all over India, and a favorable review in the *Saturday Review* also created a demand for his writings in London.

In March, 1899, he left Lahore on a leisurely sea journey to London by way of Rangoon, Singapore, Hong Kong, Japan, and San Francisco. After making several stops across the United States, the twenty-four-year-old Kipling arrived in London in October, 1899. He has described this journey in *From Sea to Sea*, published the same year. In London, Kipling came into contact with the American Wolcott Balestier, whom he met in writer Mrs. Humphry Ward's drawing room. He collaborated with him on the novel *The Naulahka: A Story of East and West*. Balestier's sister Caroline was later to become Kipling's wife. Befriended by the poet W. E. Henley, Kipling published *Barrack-Room Ballads and Other Verses* in 1892. It was a completely new poetic voice in style, language, and content. Kipling won an audience, who were startled and shocked but fascinated and hypnotized by his style.

Kipling left for America in June, 1891, and the short visit brought him into conflict with certain members of the American press. He returned to England and went on a long sea voyage with a sentimental stopover in India, his last visit to the subcontinent. He returned to London hurriedly because of Wolcott Balestier's death, and a few weeks later, on January 18, 1892, he married Caroline Balestier. Henry James gave away the bride.

The newly married couple returned to the Balestier home in Brattleboro, Vermont, where Kipling wrote the Jungle Books and other stories. He also became a friend of Mark Twain. His desire for privacy, his recurrent conflicts with the press, the death of his eldest daughter, Josephine, his own illness, and the notorious publicity as a result of a quarrel with his brother-in-law all contributed to his decision to leave America in 1897, never to return.

Kipling went to South Africa during the Boer War (1899-1902) and became a good friend of another empire builder, Cecil Rhodes. It was during the war that Kipling completed his most important novel, *Kim*. Published in 1901, it was Kipling's farewell to India. In 1907, Kipling received the Nobel Prize. During World War I, Kipling lost his only son, John, and his melancholy deepened. The poem "My Boy Jack" (1916) articulates the grief and pain of that loss. In writing other works, he turned to the strange and the macabre, as in "A Madonna of the Trenches," "The Wish House," and "The Eyes of Allah."

Plagued by ill health during the last years of his life, he relied on his wife for support, but she also lost her health to the crippling effects of diabetes and rheumatism. Kipling published his last collection of stories, *Limits and Renewals*, in 1932 and continued to show interest in British and world affairs, angry at the complacency of his countrymen toward the growing fascism outside England. He died January 18, 1936, and his ashes were buried in Westminster Abbey.

ANALYSIS

Rudyard Kipling wrote four novels, one of them, *The Naulahka*, in collaboration with Wolcott Balestier. Kipling was essentially a miniaturist, and his genius was for the short story, a single event dramatized within a specific time frame. His novels reflect an episodic quality, and although Kipling brings to them a considerable amount of technical information—about cod fishing in *Captains Courageous*, army and artistic life in *The Light That Failed*, authentic topography and local color in *The Naulahka*—he fails in the development of character and in evoking an emotional response from his readers. *Kim*, however, is an exception.

THE LIGHT THAT FAILED

The Light That Failed, dedicated to his mother, has often been described by critics as "the book that failed." Kipling acknowledged a debt to the French novel *Manon Lescaut* (1731, 1733, 1753) by Abbé Prévost in writing the novel. It was first published in the January, 1891, issue of *Lippincott's Monthly Magazine* and was later dramatized and filmed. When Macmillan and Co. published it two months later, there were four new chapters, and the story concluded with a tragic ending and the note, "This is the story of *The Light That Failed* as it was originally conceived by the writer." The difference between the magazine version, with its more conventional ending, and the book version, with the sad ending, caused some consternation among readers and critics.

The Light That Failed has many autobiographical elements. The novel opens with two children brought up by a sadistic housekeeper; Kipling drew upon his own early life in "the house of desolation" for some of the harrowing experiences of Dick and Maisie in the novel. Dick and Maisie are not related but have an adolescent crush on each other. They are separated, and while Dick goes to the Far East to serve on the frontiers of the empire, Maisie pursues her dream of becoming an artist. Dick wants Maisie to travel with him, but Maisie, committed to her art, remains in England. Dick later moves to Egypt as a war artist. He returns to London, and after a period of frustration, he enjoys fame and success. Kipling draws on his familiarity with the art world to describe the life of Dick in London. He had never been to Africa, however, and for the realism of his African scenes, Kipling relied on information he obtained from his friends. When Dick expresses fury and anger at unscrupulous art dealers, Kipling is lashing out at the publishers in America who boldly pirated his works.

In Dick and Maisie's doomed love and its impact on Dick, readers see echoes of Kipling's own unrequited love for Violet Flo Garrard. Flo was a painter, like Maisie, and in the words of Kipling's sister, Flo was cold and obsessed with "her very ineffective little pictures." Writer Angus Wilson, in his study of Kipling, believes that Kipling found in Flo the quintessential *femme fatale*, "the vampire that sucks man's

life away." Kipling has transferred some of the intensity of this feeling to Dick Heldar, almost his alter ego at certain times in the novel. Dick Heldar's obsession with the single life and his desire for military life also express Kipling's own passions. When Dick goes blind after being spurned by Maisie, Kipling is again drawing upon his own anxiety about the possible loss of his own vision.

The Light That Failed ends very melodramatically with Dick's death in the Sudanese battlefield amid bloody carnage. Apart from the autobiographical elements in the novel, *The Light That Failed* has little interest for the contemporary student of Kipling.

THE NAULAHKA

Subtitled "A Story of East and West" and written in collaboration with Wolcott Balestier, *The Naulahka* compares the ways of the East, represented by the princely state of Rhatore in Central India, to those of the West, represented by the village of Topaz, Colorado. Balestier supplied the Western elements of the novel, and Kipling wrote the Eastern chapters. The result is a poorly written, melodramatic, and lackluster novel.

Naulahka is a priceless necklace owned by the Maharaja of Rhatore. Tarvin, an aggressive American entrepreneur, wants to bring the railroad to feudalistic Rhatore; he enlists the services of Mutrie, the wife of the president of the railroad company, to influence her husband. He promises to get her the Naulahka as a gift. Tarvin's fiancée, Kate, is also in India to help the Indian women. With her help, Tarvin tries to influence the Maharaja's son. Kate wants a hospital; Tarvin wants the railroad. Kate then breaks off her relationship with Tarvin; he secures the necklace but returns it in order to save Kate's life, which is threatened by a mad priest. Finally, Kate and Tarvin return to the United States.

The characters in *The Naulahka* are one dimensional, and the narrative style is very episodic. Kipling has drawn heavily from his earlier book *Letters of Marque* (1891), lifting entire passages and incidents.

CAPTAINS COURAGEOUS

A better novel than *The Light That Failed*, *Captains Courageous* is Kipling's only completely American book in character and atmosphere. Kipling made several visits to Gloucester, Massachusetts, with his friend Dr. John Conland to saturate himself with considerable technical information about cod fishing. He has used this information extravagantly in telling the story of *Captains Courageous*. The novel was published serially in *McClure's Magazine*, and Kipling was not pleased with its publication. In a letter to a friend, he wrote that the novel was really a series of sketches and that he had "crept out of the possible holes by labelling it a boy's story."

Captains Courageous is the story of Harvey Cheyne, the spoiled only son of a millionaire. On a voyage to Europe, Harvey falls overboard and is picked up by a fishing boat. He bellows out orders and insults the skipper, Disko. Disko decides to teach the boy a lesson and puts Harvey under a strict program of work and discipline. The plan succeeds, and Harvey emerges stronger and humanized. When the boat reaches Gloucester, laden with salted cod, a telegram is sent to Harvey's father, who rushes from San Francisco to retrieve his son. Harvey returns with his father to resume his studies and prepare himself for taking over his father's business empire.

"Licking a raw cub into shape," the central theme of *Captains Courageous*, is a favorite subject of Kipling. The technical knowledge about cod fishing is impressive, but the characters themselves have no individuality. Harvey Cheyne's transformation from a stubborn, spoiled young man into a mature, responsible individual is achieved too speedily. Kipling has used the story merely to illustrate what Birkenhead describes as "the virtue of the disciplined life upon a spoiled immature mind."

KIM

T. S. Eliot considered *Kim* Kipling's greatest work. Nirad C. Chaudhury, an Indian scholar, called *Kim* "not only the finest novel in English with an Indian theme but also one of the greatest of English novels in spite of the theme." Kipling wanted to write a major book about India, and he started the project in 1885, in "Mother Maturin: An Anglo-Indian Episode." That work concerned itself with the "unutterable horrors of lower class Eurasian and native life as they exist outside reports and reports and reports." It was the story of an old Irishwoman who kept an opium den in Lahore but sent her daughter to study in London, where she marries, then returns to Lahore. Kipling's father did not like it, however, and Kipling dutifully abandoned the project. *Kim* emerged instead.

Published in 1901, *Kim* is Kipling's last book set in India. In *Something of Myself*, he tells readers how he had long thought of writing about "an Irish boy born in India and mixed up with native life." Written under the influence of his demon—Kipling's word to describe his guardian muse—*Kim* takes in all of India, its rich diversity and intensity of life.

In growing old and evaluating the past, Kipling turned to the best years of his life, his years in India. In *Kim*, Kipling relives his Indian years when everything was secure and his family intact. Kim's yearning for the open road, for its smells, sights, and sounds, is part of the longing of Kipling himself for the land that quickened his creative impulse and provided his literary success.

Kim is the story of an Irish orphan boy in India, a child of the streets. He grows up among Indian children and is aware of all the subtle nuances of Indian life. Yet, at the same time, he has the spirit of adventure and energy of his Irish ancestry. His joining the Red Lama from Tibet on his quest for the River of Healing, and Kim's fascination for the British Indian secret service, "the Great Game," results in his own self-discovery.

Kim has the characteristic features of a boy's story, the lovable boy involved in a quest filled with adventure and intrigue. One is reminded of Robert Louis Stevenson's *Treasure Island* (1881-1882) and *Kidnapped* (1886) and Mark Twain's *The Adventures of Tom Sawyer* (1876). *Kim*, however, rises above the usual boy's story in that it has a spiritual dimension. By coming into contact with the Lama, Kim emerges a sadder and wiser being at the end of the novel. Kim's racial superiority is emphasized throughout the novel, but after his association with the Lama, Kim is able to say, "Thou hast said there is neither black nor white, why plague me with this talk, Holy One? Let me rub the other foot. It vexes me, I am *not* a Sahib. I am thy chela, and my head is heavy on my shoulders." This is an unusual admission for Kim and Kipling.

Many of Kipling's earlier themes are elaborated and incorporated into *Kim*. There is the vivid picture of the Indian army; the tale of "Lispeth," from *Plain Tales from the Hills*, repeated in the story of the Lady of Shamlegh; and the Anglo-Indian, the native, and the official worlds providing backgrounds as they did in the short stories. Administering medicine in the guise of a charm to soothe and satisfy the Indian native, Jat is an echo from the earlier story, "The Tomb of His Ancestors." Buddhism, whose scriptural tales—*The Jataka Tales*—supplied Kipling with a wealth of source material for his two Jungle Books and *Just So Stories* (1902), supplies the religious atmosphere in *Kim*. Even Kim's yearning for the open road had been expressed previously in the character of Strickland, who, incidentally, makes a brief appearance in *Kim*.

Both Kim and the Venerable Teshoo Lama, the two main characters in *Kim*, emerge as distinctive individual characters and not mere types of the Asian holy man and the Anglo-Indian boy. They grow and develop an awareness of themselves and their surroundings. Kim realizes that his progress depends upon the cooperation of several people: the Lama, Mukherjee, Colonel Creighton, and Mahbub Ali. The Lama too undergoes a change of character. He realizes that his physical quest for the River of Arrow has clouded his spiritual vision. The River of Arrow is at his feet if he has the faith to see it.

In selecting the Buddhist Lama as the main character, Kipling has emphasized the Middle Way. To the Lama, there is no color, no caste, no sect. He is also the tone of moderation without the extremes of Hinduism and Islam, the two main religious forces on the subcontinent.

In the relationship between Kim and the Lama, Kipling portrays an integral part of Indian spiritual life, the disciple and teacher relationship, the *guru* and *chela* interaction. It is not an ordinary relationship between a boy and a holy man; it is a special relationship, as the Lama notes, forged out of a previous association in an earlier life, the result of good karma. *Kim* is indeed a virtuoso performance; it is Kipling at his best.

K. Bhaskara Rao

OTHER MAJOR WORKS

SHORT FICTION: *In Black and White*, 1888; *Plain Tales from the Hills*, 1888; *Soldiers Three*, 1888; *The Story of the Gadsbys*, 1888; *The Phantom 'Rickshaw and Other Tales*, 1888; *Under the Deodars*, 1888; *Wee Willie Winkie*, 1888; *Life's Handicap*, 1891; *Many Inventions*, 1893; *The Jungle Book*, 1894; *The Second Jungle Book*, 1895; *Soldier Tales*, 1896; *The Day's Work*, 1898; *Stalky and Co.*, 1899; *Just So Stories*, 1902; *Traffics and Discoveries*, 1904; *Puck of Pook's Hill*, 1906; *Actions and Reactions*, 1909; *Rewards and Fairies*, 1910; *A Diversity of Creatures*, 1917; *Land and Sea Tales for Scouts and Guides*, 1923; *Debits and Credits*, 1926; *Thy Servant a Dog*, 1930; *Limits and Renewals*, 1932.

POETRY: *Departmental Ditties*, 1886; *Barrack-Room Ballads and Other Verses*, 1892; *The Seven Seas*, 1896; *Recessional and Other Poems*, 1899; *The Five Nations*, 1903; *The Years Between*, 1919; *Rudyard Kipling's Verse*, 1940 (definitive edition).

NONFICTION: *American Notes*, 1891; *Beast and Man in India*, 1891; *Letters of Marque*, 1891; *The Smith Administration*, 1891; *From Sea to Sea*, 1899; *The New Army in Training*, 1914; *France at War*, 1915; *The Fringes of the Fleet*, 1915; *Sea Warfare*, 1916; *Letters of Travel, 1892-1913*, 1920; *The Irish Guards in the Great War*, 1923; *A Book of Words*, 1928; *Something of Myself: For My Friends Known and Unknown*, 1937; *Uncollected Prose*, 1938 (2 volumes); *Rudyard Kipling to Rider Haggard: The Record of a Friendship*, 1965 (Morton N. Cohen, editor).

MISCELLANEOUS: *The Sussex Edition of the Complete Works in Prose and Verse of Rudyard Kipling*, 1937-1939 (35 volumes).

BIBLIOGRAPHY

Bauer, Helen Pike. *Rudyard Kipling: A Study of the Short Fiction*. New York: Twayne, 1994. Part 1 explores the major themes of Kipling's stories; part 2 examines his view of himself as a writer; part 3 provides examples from two particularly insightful critics. Includes chronology and bibliography.

Bloom, Harold, ed. *Rudyard Kipling*. New York:

Chelsea House, 1987. Essays on Kipling's major work, his views on art and life, and his vision of empire. Includes introduction, chronology, and bibliography.

_____. *Rudyard Kipling's "Kim."* New York: Chelsea House, 1987. Nine essays ranging from general appreciation to detailed critical analysis, with an introduction, chronology, and bibliography.

Carrington, Charles. *Rudyard Kipling: His Life and Works.* London: Macmillan, 1978. A standard biography with access to unique inside information. The appendices to the 1978 edition contain information previously suppressed by Kipling's heirs. Includes a chronology of his life and work as well as a family tree. Much stronger on his adult life than his childhood and concentrates on his life and the influences upon it rather than on literary critique.

Coates, John. *The Day's Work: Kipling and the Idea of Sacrifice.* Madison, N.J.: Fairleigh Dickinson University Press, 1997. Examines the themes of sacrifice and didacticism in Kipling's works. Includes bibliographical references and an index.

Knowles, Frederic Lawrence. *A Kipling Primer.* Reprint. New York: Haskell House, 1974. Chapter 1 concerns biographical data and includes personality traits. Chapter 2 elaborates on Kipling's literary techniques and critically examines the stages of his artistic development. Chapter 3 is an index to his major writings with brief descriptions and criticisms of Kipling's works by other authors.

Laski, Marghanita. *From Palm to Pine: Rudyard Kipling Abroad and at Home.* New York: Facts on File, 1987. A lively, well-illustrated biography with a brief chronology, appendices on Kipling's major travels and his important works, a brief bibliography, and notes.

Orel, Harold, ed. *Critical Essays on Rudyard Kipling.* Boston: G. K. Hall, 1990. Sections on Kipling's poetry, his writing on India, his work as a mature artist, his unfinished memoir, and his controversial reputation. Introduced by a distinguished critic. No bibliography.

JOHN KNOWLES

Born: Fairmont, West Virginia; September 16, 1926

PRINCIPAL LONG FICTION

A Separate Peace, 1959
Morning in Antibes, 1962
Indian Summer, 1966
The Paragon, 1971
Spreading Fires, 1974
A Vein of Riches, 1978
Peace Breaks Out, 1981
A Stolen Past, 1983
The Private Life of Axie Reed, 1986

OTHER LITERARY FORMS

John Knowles has written in several other genres besides long fiction: *Double Vision: American Thoughts Abroad*, published in 1964, is Knowles's account of his travels in essay form. The work discusses Arabian and Greek cultures and compares them to American Puritanism. Knowles also put together a collection of short stories entitled *Phineas: Six Stories* in 1968. The collection, containing the story "Phineas," on which *A Separate Peace* was based, deals with Knowles's favorite subject—the condition of humanity. In addition, Knowles contributed to such magazines as the *Saturday Evening Post*, *New World Writing*, *Holiday*, and *Reader's Digest*. A collection of Knowles's manuscripts is housed at Yale University.

ACHIEVEMENTS

John Knowles, author of one of the most popularly taught novels, *A Separate Peace*, received appropriate acclaim for his work. For his first work he was awarded both the William Faulkner Foundation award and the Richard and Hinda Rosenthal Foundation award in 1960. A year later he was presented with the National Association of Independent Schools Award. Knowles's ability to paint a visual picture for his readers helps to build his characters in terms of form and content. His narratives are insightful and free-flowing throughout all his novels, though none compares to his first work, his masterpiece, *A Separate Peace*.

BIOGRAPHY

John Knowles was born in 1926, in the small town of Fairmont, West Virginia, a declining coal-based town. He was the third of four children born to James Myron and Mary Beatrice Shaw Knowles. At age fifteen he left home and attended Phillips Exeter Academy in New Hampshire. After an early graduation, Knowles enlisted in the U.S. Army Air Forces Aviation Cadet Program and qualified as a pilot. Discharged in 1945, Knowles attended Yale University, majored in English, and served as editor of the *Yale Daily News*. After receiving his diploma, Knowles worked as a reporter for the *Hartford Courant* and later as a correspondent and editor for *Holiday* magazine. For several years he traveled and lived in southern Europe. Returning to the United States in 1955, he began to write several short stories, which eventually became the foundation for his first novel. After the death of his father in 1970, Knowles relocated to

(Kimberly Dawson Kurnizki)

Long Island, where he began writing a novel about his late friend, novelist Truman Capote.

ANALYSIS

All John Knowles's novels deal with one major theme: that of men finding themselves, without destroying too much of themselves, and eventually coming to discover the ability to love. The author uses surroundings and issues that touched his own life at one time or another. Several works are set at the Devon School, a boys' preparatory school, much like the school Knowles attended in his youth. Other novels, such as *Indian Summer*, *A Stolen Past*, and *The Paragon*, are set at Yale, Knowles's alma mater.

A SEPARATE PEACE

Known as Knowles's greatest work, *A Separate Peace* is considered a classic and has become widely read in the American school system. It has sold more than eight million copies. Unfortunately, none of the author's later works acquired critical acclaim equaling that of his first work. Many critics consider this novel to be a perfect piece of writing, one of precision and craftsmanship. *A Separate Peace* was derived from Knowles's own schoolboy experiences at Phillips Exeter and is a traditional coming-of-age story. The title is taken from writer Ernest Hemingway's *A Farewell to Arms* (1929), and the work itself has been compared to J. D. Salinger's *The Catcher in the Rye* (1951).

The setting is the Devon School, a boys' private school in New Hampshire. Devon educates its young men to become soldiers for World War II. The novel is set in the year 1942, and patriotism is at an all-time high. Gene Forrester arrives at Devon believing that there he will develop his manhood and his moral identity. His roommate Phineas, known as Finny to his friends, is a bright, athletic boy who seems to conquer any obstacle that is placed before him. The boys develop a close friendship, but surrounding it is an atmosphere of jealousy and mixed emotions.

Readers experience the story through the eyes of Gene, the narrator. He is the intellectual, while Phineas is the natural athlete destined for greatness. At the beginning of the novel, the boys are considered insignificant by the older students preparing for the war. The two still have time to live and gather lessons learned by others before them. Finny is a master of high jinks who enjoys continually testing the system. Not liking to play alone, Finny draws Gene into his world. Finny does everything with grace and style, while Gene, trying to keep up, flounders in his fear. Finny subjects Gene to all sorts of physical tests, even inventing a new game with Gene as the target. Although the mischief is fun at first, Gene begins to believe that Finny is trying to reduce the academic competition and corrupt Gene's chances to become valedictorian. In an impulsive move, Gene causes Finny to fall out of a tree and injures him severely enough to end Finny's hopes of an athletic career. Living with his guilt is difficult for Gene: Eventually this leads to a half-confession, which Finny refuses to believe.

Rumors fly through the school; accusations are spoken. Fortunately for Gene, another boy has caused a stir by suffering a mental breakdown while at war and deserting back to Devon. However, this story diverts the students' young minds only for a while, that is, until Finny returns to school. With his entrance back to Devon, Finny is confronted by others about his accident. Some of the boys decide to have their own mock trial, with Gene as the defendant. As questions and accusations are batted about the room, Finny becomes upset by some of the questions asked but not answered. He storms out of the room, only to fall down the steps leading outside. Injured again, he is rushed to the infirmary, but this time he does not survive his injury.

Many critics have touted this novel as a great exploration of early manhood and the competition that goes with it, the battle of the athlete versus the scholar. Critic Jay L. Halio wrote that "the prevailing attitude seems to be that before man can be redeeemed back into social life, he must first come to terms with himself." Gene coming to peace within himself is the issue at the heart of *A Separate Peace*. Gene experiences many conflicting emotions toward Finny—admiration, jealousy, even love. Indeed, whether or not it was Knowles's intention, his masterpiece is suffused with covert sexuality. His descriptions of Phineas reveal the underlying problem that Gene

may be facing—being in love with Finny. While preparing to go out, Finny is described in the novel by Gene as a boy whose "nose to cheekbones had the sharp look of a prow." Even at the moment of Finny's announcement that Gene is his best friend, Gene cannot openly reply, for he is "stopped by that level of feeling, deeper than thought, which contains the truth." Gene is threatened by Finny not only as a competitor but also as a man who has made him see himself differently. Only by eliminating his obstacle to success and emotional stability—Finny—can Gene come to terms with himself and achieve a separate peace.

Morning in Antibes

Three years after *A Separate Peace*, Knowles produced *Morning in Antibes*. The novel is set during the Algerian War of 1954-1962 and deals with the Algerian struggle to be liberated from French colonization. The main character's inner struggle for freedom does not compare in dramatic intensity to the protagonist's struggle in *A Separate Peace*.

Indian Summer, Spreading Fires, and A Vein of Riches

Knowles's next work of fiction, after a travel book, came in 1966. *Indian Summer* repeats the kind of tragic friendships betweeen two males of *A Separate Peace*, only here the boys are replaced by men. The story has been criticized as too fragmented and too unbelievable. *Spreading Fires* has been considered Knowles's attempt at bringing sexual emotions to the table. Set in southern France, the novel explores deeply rooted sexual attitudes, leaving one critic, Christopher Lehmann-Haupt, to label the piece an "unresolved Oedipal rage."

A Vein of Riches emerged on the literary scene to poor reviews; some critics stated that the novel held no redeeming virtue. The book uses a series of letters written by a minor character to convey information, turning the novel into a sort of documentary. The work lacks all Knowles's previous gifts for language, becoming a flat, uncompelling vision of life.

Peace Breaks Out

Knowles's next work, *Peace Breaks Out*, is a companion to *A Separate Peace*. Set four years later, the reader is once again at the Devon School. This time, a former student and World War II veteran, Pete Hallam, has returned to teach, only to find that the innocence of his school days has faded. He is told upon arrival that the students he will confront are "aware" of life much more than when he was at Devon. The book focuses on several of Pete's history and physical-education students: Eric Hochschwender, indifferent to others and a believer in the good done by the Nazi Party; Wexford (never called by his first name), school editor and antagonist; and Tug Blackburn, school athlete and daredevil. The characters are classified by the author as the "Lost Generation" and the "Just Missed."

The year is 1946, and Devon will be producing its first class of graduates who will have the opportunity to expand their minds, not just their manhood. Pete is grateful that his students will not have to prepare to fight a war, unaware that the absence of war abroad does not mean that conflict cannot be manufactured at home. The lack of wartime conflict confuses the boys as to their purposes in life. Traditionally, boys would prepare for war, then fight for their country. Now, with no concrete foreign enemy, the boys create one at home. Hochschwender provokes many of the boys with his unpatriotic views, to the extent of asking for morning chapel attendance to be voluntary instead of mandatory. In retaliation, and enraged by his callousness toward the investment men have placed in patriotism, Wexford uses the school paper to voice his views. He proposes a stained-glass window be placed in the chapel as a memorial to all those who died in the war. Soon after, the window is mysteriously broken, and trouble begins. Accusations are made, and lines are drawn. Students are categorized by their ethnicity; "war" is taking place at Devon.

First Tug is accused of breaking the window, due to his being drugged in the infirmary and not remembering his whereabouts at the time of the vandalism. After he is ruled out as a suspect, the students turn their attention to Hochschwender. With his outspoken views of the chapel and of the United States, Hochschwender is interrogated by the boys. He is repeatedly dunked in the river and beaten. Unaware of his health problem, the boys are startled when Hochschwender stops breathing. Rushed to the infir-

mary, Hochschwender cannot be saved, and he dies. Weaving a web of deceit, the boys lie about the incident and take no responsibility for their actions. Unknown to the boys, they have become pawns for someone else: Wexford had broken the window himself to even the score with Hochschwender and to have others dirty their hands for his views. Pete exposes Wexford's actions and the boys' part in Hochschwender's death, but he cannot prove that a crime has been committed. Alas, the most frightening part is Wexford's inability to take personal blame for his actions. Pete realizes that new monsters are being created around the world, even at Devon, and it will be these monsters who may one day give a new generation a more clearly labeled enemy.

A STOLEN PAST and THE PRIVATE LIFE OF AXIE REED

In 1983, *A Stolen Past* brought the reader back to Yale and the struggle between the rich and the middle class. A *Bildungsroman*, the work examines the life of a writer, Allan Prieston, as he struggles to find his literary voice. His constant battle to free himself of others' opinions, especially that of his mentor, famed novelist Reeves Lockhart, is resolved only by the acceptance of others' failings.

The Private Life of Axie Reed is a memoir in which the narrator reminisces about his cousin Axie. Like most of Knowles's novels, it met with mixed reviews. Many critics felt that Knowles reached his peak performance level with his first novel, and the rest of his novels missed the mark. Even so, John Knowles's collection is certainly worth attention, for the stories are laced with meticulously detailed reality and reflection on the human condition.

Anita M. Eckhardt

OTHER MAJOR WORKS

SHORT FICTION: *Phineas: Six Stories*, 1968.

NONFICTION: *Double Vision: American Thoughts Abroad*, 1964.

BIBLIOGRAPHY

Baker, Margaret Ann. *Popular World Fiction 1900-Present*. Washington, D.C.: Beacham, 1987. Provides publishing history, critical reception, and honors; analysis of *A Separate Peace* and *A Stolen Past.*

Bryant, Hallman Bell. *"A Separate Peace": The War Within.* Boston: Twayne, 1990. One of Twayne's masterwork studies, this is a helpful guide for the student of the novel. Includes bibliographical references and an index.

Holborn, David G. "A Rationale for Reading John Knowles' *A Separate Peace.*" In *Censored Books: Critical Viewpoints*, edited by Nicholas J. Karolides, Lee Burress, and John M. Kean. Metuchen, N.J.: Scarecrow Press, 1993. An essay championing the novel and its importance in the literary canon.

McEwen, Fred. "John Knowles: Overview." In *Twentieth-Century Young Adult Writers*, edited by Laura Standley Berger. London: St. James Press, 1994. A standard introduction to the author and his works.

Selthaug, Gordon E. "John Knowles." In *Contemporary Authors.* Vol. 40. Detroit: Gale Research, 1993. An extensive look at the majority of Knowles's work; includes a copious list of periodicals.

Weber, Ronald. "Narrative Method in a Separate Peace." *Studies in Short Fiction* 3. (Fall, 1965): 63-72. Comparison of Knowles's *A Separate Peace* with J. D. Salinger's *The Catcher in the Rye.* Explanation of Knowles's ability to make clear statements on life.

ARTHUR KOESTLER

Born: Budapest, Hungary; September 5, 1905
Died: London, England; March 3, 1983

PRINCIPAL LONG FICTION
The Gladiators, 1939
Darkness at Noon, 1940
Arrival and Departure, 1943

(National Archives)

Thieves in the Night: Chronicle of an Experiment, 1946
The Age of Longing, 1951
The Call Girls: A Tragi-Comedy with Prologue and Epilogue, 1972

OTHER LITERARY FORMS

Arthur Koestler's first five novels, along with most of his other books, have been reissued in the Danube edition, published in England by Hutchinson and Company and in America by Macmillan Publishing Company. His nonfiction works include four autobiographical volumes—*Spanish Testament* (1937), abridged in the Danube edition as *Dialogue with Death* (1942); *Scum of the Earth* (1941); *Arrow in the Blue: The First Volume of an Autobiography, 1905-1931* (1952); and *The Invisible Writing: The Second Volume of an Autobiography, 1932-1940* (1954)—as well as an autobiographical essay on his disillusionment with Communism found in *The God That Failed* (1950), edited by Richard Crossman with additional essays by Richard Wright, Ignazio Silone, Stephen Spender, Louis Fischer, and André Gide. Koestler's nonfiction works exceed twenty-five volumes, divided roughly between social-historical commentary and the history of science. He also wrote one play, *Twilight Bar: An Escapade in Four Acts* (1945).

Achievements

Koestler will be remembered as an apostate to the Left who dramatized in *Darkness at Noon* and in his autobiographical works the integrity of many Communist intellectuals in the 1930's and the anguish they suffered under Soviet leader Joseph Stalin. As a novelist, he is generally a skilled storyteller, putting conventional techniques to the service of philosophical themes. Although none of his novels have been best-sellers in the usual sense, *Darkness at Noon*—translated into thirty-three languages—has been reprinted many times, and its appeal shows no sign of slackening. It continues to be read widely in college courses and is probably one of the most influential political novels of the twentieth century, despite the fact that comparatively little academic literary criticism has been devoted to it. Indeed, Koestler's novels—even *Darkness at Noon*—are perhaps kept alive more by political scientists and historians than by professional students of literature.

Besides being an accomplished novelist of ideas, Koestler was one of the finest journalists of his age, often producing works as controversial as his political fiction. Typical of his best essays is the piece in *The Lotus and the Robot* (1960) on "Yoga Unexpurgated" (noted as being "far too horrible for me to read" by William Empson in his review); like many other of his best essays, "Yoga Unexpurgated" will maintain its readability. *The Sleepwalkers: A History of Man's Changing Vision of the Universe* (1959), a survey of early scientific thought with emphasis on Renaissance astronomy, is part of a trilogy (with *The Act of Creation*, 1964, and *The Ghost in the Machine*, 1967) on the understanding of the human mind, and it ranks as Koestler's most suggestive effort at research and speculation. Even more controversial than

his psychological studies, although a wholly different kind of work, is *The Thirteenth Tribe* (1976), which revived the thesis that the Jews of Eastern Europe are descended from the ancient Khazar Empire. Scholarly reviews of Koestler's research tended to be severe. *The Case of the Midwife Toad* (1971) reveals sympathies for neo-Lamarckian philosophy, and *The Roots of Coincidence* (1972) surveys the claims of parapsychology, ending with a plea "to get out of the straitjacket which nineteenth-century materialism imposed on any philosophical outlook."

Although he flirted with crank notions, to the detriment of his credibility, Koestler was neither a crank nor a dilettante. His renegade vision has enlivened contemporary arts and letters for several decades, and it is likely that this force will continue to be felt for several more.

Biography

Arthur Koestler was born on September 5, 1905, in Budapest, Hungary, the only child of middle-class Jewish parents. He was precocious in math and science and closer to his mother than to his father, an eccentric, self-taught businessman. When Koestler was in his teens, the family moved to Vienna, and he attended the university there as a science student. After four years, he left school without a degree and went to Palestine, where he joined a Zionist movement for a while before obtaining a correspondent's job with the Ullstein newspapers of Germany. He advanced rapidly in journalism, becoming, in 1930, the foreign editor of *B.Z. am Mittag* and the science editor of *Vossische Zeitung* in Berlin, partly as a result of his success as a reporter on the *Graf Zeppelin* flight to the North Pole in 1931.

In December, 1931, Koestler became a member of the German Communist Party, and less than one year later he gave up his position with Ullstein and spent several weeks traveling in the Soviet Union. He then spent three years in Paris working for the Comintern, leaving for Spain at the outbreak of the Spanish Civil War in 1936. His marriage to Dorothy Asher in 1935 lasted only two years before they were separated, eventually to be divorced in 1950. While in Spain for the Comintern in 1937, Koestler was captured by the

Nationalists and sentenced to execution. Thanks to the British press, he was freed after three months, and he published an account of his experiences, *Spanish Testament* (1937). By the next year, he was in France again, where he resigned from the Communist Party in disillusionment with Stalinism and the show trials. During that time, he wrote *Darkness at Noon*. After escaping from Nazi internment in France, he fled to Britain and spent 1941 to 1942 in the British Pioneer Corps.

After *Darkness at Noon* was published, Koestler was in Paris at the center of the uproar it caused among members of the French Left. (Simone de Beauvoir's *roman à clef*, *The Mandarins*, in 1954, makes vivid this period in French intellectual life.) In the late 1940's, Koestler became a leader among anti-Communist voices in the West, twice visiting America to lecture, as well as enjoying an appointment between 1950 and 1951 as a Chubb Fellow at Yale University. After his divorce in 1950, he married Mamaine Paget. In 1952, he took up residence in America for two years, during which time he published his autobiographical volumes *Arrow in the Blue* and *The Invisible Writing*. He was divorced in 1953. One phase in his career ended in 1955, when he indicated in *Trial of the Dinosaur and Other Essays* that he was through writing about politics. At that time, his interest turned to mysticism and science, and he tried in his writings on extrasensory perception (ESP) to narrow the gap between natural and extrasensory phenomena. He married Cynthia Jefferies in 1965. After World War II, Koestler became a naturalized citizen of England, and his adopted country honored him by making him a Commander of the Order of the British Empire (C.B.E.) in 1972 and a Companion of Literature (C.Lit.) in 1974.

Koestler died in London, England, on March 3, 1983. His wife was found beside him, both victims of apparent suicide.

ANALYSIS

All of Arthur Koestler's works, both fiction and nonfiction, reveal a struggle to escape from the oppressiveness of nineteenth century positivism and its later offshoots. *The Yogi and the Commissar and Other Essays* (1945) sums up the moral paradox of political action. The Yogi, at one extreme, represents a life lived by values that are grounded in idealism. The Yogi scorns utilitarian goals and yields to quietism; his refusal to intervene leads to passive toleration of social evil. The Commissar, committed to dialectical materialism, ignores the shallow ethical concerns of the historically benighted middle class and seeks to function as an instrument of historical progress. History replaces God, and human suffering is seen as an inevitable step toward the ultimate historical synthesis rather than as an element of God's mysterious purpose. For the Commissar, the end justifies the means, and it is this ethical position that is debated most effectively in *The Gladiators, Darkness at Noon*, and *Arrival and Departure*.

In his postscript to the Danube edition of *The Gladiators*, Koestler points out that these novels form a trilogy "whose leitmotif is the central question of revolutionary ethics and of political ethics in general: the question whether, or to what extent, the end justifies the means." The question "obsessed" him, he says, during the seven years in which he belonged to the Communist Party and for several years afterward. It was his answer to this question that caused him to break with the Party, as he explains eloquently in his essay in *The God That Failed*. The city built by the rebellious slaves in *The Gladiators* fails because Spartacus does not carry out the stern measures necessary to insure the city's successful continuation. In *Darkness at Noon*, the old revolutionary Rubashov is depicted as trying to avoid the error Spartacus made, but ending up lost in a maze of moral and ethical complications that destroy him.

Behaviorist psychology is congenial to the materialism of Communist revolutionary ethics, and Koestler attacks its claims heatedly. Indeed, Koestler's interest in mysticism, the occult, and parapsychology was an attempt to find an escape route from the deadly rationalism that makes humans a mere clockwork orange. As far back as 1931, Koestler was investigating psychometry with as much curiosity as he brought to his journalistic accounts of the exploding universe. His answer to the behaviorists is laid out in

The Ghost in the Machine, and it is clearly a theological answer. Koestler implies here that evolution is purposive, hence the theological nature of his understanding of life. A problem remains, however; Koestler argues that the limbic system of the brain is at odds with its neocortex, resulting in irrational decisions much of the time. Humans are thus as likely to speed to their own destruction as they are to their fulfillment. Koestler's unorthodox answer to humans' Manichaean internal struggle is deliberate mutation by chemical agents. The same topic is fictionalized quite successfully in *The Call Girls*.

THE GLADIATORS

Koestler's first novel, *The Gladiators*, was written in German and translated into English by Edith Simon (his later novels were published in his own English). The source of the novel is the sketchy account—fewer than four thousand words all together—of the Slave War of 73-71 B.C. found in Livy, Plutarch, Appian, and Florus. Koestler divides his narrative into four books. The first, entitled "Rise," imagines the revolt led by the Thracian gladiator Spartacus and a fat, cruel Gaul named Crixus. They march through Campania looting and adding more defectors to their band. In book 2, "The Law of Detours," after the destruction of the towns Nola, Suessula, and Calatia, the rebels are twenty thousand strong, or more, and approaching the peak of their power. The unruly faction, however, has spoiled the movement's idealism by its ransacking of these towns, and Spartacus is faced with a decision: Should he let this group go blindly into a foolhardy battle with the forces of the Roman general Varinius, or should he counsel them and enforce a policy of prudence? In his deliberations he is aided by a wise Essene, a type of the imminent Christ, who tells him that of all God's curses on man, "the worst curse of all is that he must tread the evil road for the sake of the good and right, that he must make detours and walk crookedly so that he may reach the straight goal." He further tells Spartacus that for what the leader wants to do now, he needs other counselors.

Despite the Essene's warning, Spartacus follows the "law of detours." Later that night, he confers with Crixus, and although no details of their talk are given, it is clear that Crixus is going to lead the lawless to their unwitting deaths in a confrontation with Varinius. This sacrifice of the unruly faction, however justified, is a cynical detour from honor. Later, however, when the Thracian Spartacus, already pressed by food shortages in the Sun State after a double cross by the neighboring city, is faced with a rebellion against his policies by the Celts, he proves to be insufficiently ruthless: He still retains the idealism with which he began the revolution. Koestler sums it up in his 1965 postscript: "Yet he shrinks from taking the last step—the purge by crucifixion of the dissident Celts and the establishment of a ruthless tyranny; and through this refusal he dooms his revolution to defeat." Book 3, "The Sun State," recounts the conflicts that lead up to Spartacus's defeat, and the gladiators' humiliation and crucifixion are narrated in book 4, "Decline." Although Koestler's characters are wooden, *The Gladiators* is a satisfying historical novel; the milieu is well sketched, and Spartacus's dilemmas are rendered convincingly.

DARKNESS AT NOON

Darkness at Noon, Koestler's masterpiece, is the story of an old Bolshevik, Rubashov, who is called before his Communist inquisitors on charges of heresy against the Party. He is interrogated first by Ivanov, who is himself executed, and then by Gletkin, and at the end he is killed by the inevitable bullet in the back of the neck. The novel is divided into three sections, one for each hearing Rubashov is given, and a short epilogue entitled "The Grammatical Fiction." Besides the confrontations between Rubashov and his questioners, there are flashbacks from Rubashov's past and extracts from his diary; the latter provide occasions for Koestler's meditations on history. The narrative is tight and fast moving, and its lucid exposition has surely made it one of the most satisfyingly pedagogic novels of all time. Many readers shared the experience of Leslie Fiedler, who referred to *Darkness at Noon* in his review of *The Ghost in the Machine*, admitting that "Koestler helped to deliver me from the platitudes of the Thirties, from those organized self-deceptions which, being my first, were especially dear and difficult to escape."

Speaking of the "historical circumstances" of *Darkness at Noon*, Koestler explains that Rubashov is "a synthesis of the lives of a number of men who were victims of the so-called Moscow Trials." Rubashov's thinking is closest to that of Nikolai Bukharin, a real purge victim, and Rubashov's tormentor, Gletkin, had a counterpart of sorts in the actual trial prosecutor Andrei Vishinsky. (Robert Conquest's *The Great Terror*, 1968, provides useful details of the real trials.)

Two main theses are argued in *Darkness at Noon:* that the end does not justify the means; and that the individual ego, the *I*, is not a mere "grammatical fiction" whose outline is blurred by the sweep of the historical dialectic. The events that cause Rubashov great pain and guilt involve two party workers whose devotion is sacrificed to the law of detours. Little Loewy is the local leader of the dockworkers' section of the Party in Belgium, a likable man whom Rubashov takes to immediately. Little Loewy is a good Communist, but he is ill used by the Party and eventually destroyed in an act of expediency. When the Party calls for the workers to resist the spreading Nazi menace, Little Loewy's dockworkers refuse to handle cargoes going out from and coming into Germany. The crisis comes when five cargo ships from Russia arrive in the port. The workers start to unload these boats until they discover the contents: badly needed materials for the German war effort. The workers strike, the Party orders them back to the docks, and most of the workers defect. Two years later, Mussolini ventures into Africa, and again a boycott is called, but this time Rubashov is sent in advance to explain to the dockworkers that more Russian cargo is on its way and the Party wants it unloaded. Little Loewy rejects the duplicity, and six days later he hangs himself.

In another tragedy of betrayal, Rubashov abandons his secretary, Arlova, a woman who loves him and with whom he has had an affair. When Arlova's brother in Russia marries a foreigner, they all come under suspicion, Arlova included. Soon after, she is called back to oblivion in Russia, and all of this happens without a word from Rubashov. As these perfidies run through his mind, Rubashov's toothache rages intensely. Ivanov senses Rubashov's human sympathies and lectures him on the revolutionary ethic: "But you must allow that we are as convinced that you and they would mean the end of the Revolution as you are of the reverse. That is the essential point. The methods follow by logical deduction. We can't afford to lose ourselves in political subtleties." Thus, Rubashov's allegiance to the law of detours leads him into a moral labyrinth. He fails to heed that small voice that gives dignity to the self in its resistance to the degrading impersonality of all-devouring history and the behaviorist conception of human beings.

ARRIVAL AND DEPARTURE

In *Arrival and Departure*, Koestler's third novel, Peter Slavek, twenty-two, stows away on a freighter coming from Eastern Europe and washes up in Neutralia (Portugal) in 1940. He is a former Communist who has been tortured by Fascists in his home country, and he is faced in Neutralia with four possibilities: reunion with the Party, with whom he is disillusioned; joining the Fascists, who present themselves as the shapers of the true brave new world; flight to America; or, finally, enlistment with the British, whose culture is maimed but still represents a "brake" on the madness overtaking Europe. Homeless and confused, he meets two women. Dr. Sonia Bolgar, a native of his country and friend of his family, gives him a room and looks after him while she is waiting for the visa that will take her to America. Her lover, Odette, is a young French war widow with whom Peter has a brief affair until Odette leaves for America. Her departure precipitates a psychosomatic paralysis of one of Peter's legs, symbolic of the paralysis of will brought on by his conflicting urges to follow her and to commit himself again to political action. Sonia, who is an analyst and reduces all behavior to the terms of her profession, leads Peter through a deconstruction of his motives that exposes their origins in childhood guilt feelings. His self-insight cures his paralysis, just as his visa for America is granted. He prepares to leave, but at the last moment he dashes off the ship and joins the British, who parachute him back into his own country in their service.

Much of *Arrival and Departure* is artistically inert, but it does have a solid point to make. Although Fyodor Dostoevski's name is never mentioned in *Arrival and Departure*, the novel is Koestler's response to Dostoevski's *The Possessed* (1871-1872), which depicts revolutionaries as warped personalities, dramatizing their neuroses and grudges in political action. For Koestler, human motives are more complex:

> "You can explain the messages of the Prophets as epileptical foam and the Sistine Madonna as the projection of an incestuous dream. The method is correct and the picture in itself complete. But beware of the arrogant error of believing that it is the only one."

Arrival and Departure is, then, a subtle commentary on the motivation of revolutionaries, rejecting any claims to exclusivity by psychoanalysis and psychobiography.

THIEVES IN THE NIGHT

A far more absorbing novel than *Arrival and Departure*, *Thieves in the Night* is an account of the establishment of the commune of Ezra's Tower in Palestine. Many of the events are seen from the perspective of one of the commune's settlers, a young man named Joseph who was born and educated in England. His father was Jewish, his mother English, and this mixed heritage justifies Koestler's use of him as a voice to meditate on the Jewish character and the desirability of assimilation. As a novelistic study of a single character, *Thieves in the Night* is incomplete, but as a depiction of the personal tensions within a commune and as an essay on the international politics wracking Palestine in the period from 1937 to 1939, it is excellent. The British policy formulated in the 1939 White Paper is exposed in all its cruelty. This policy—perhaps influenced by romantic conceptions of the Arab world—shut down the flow of immigrants into Palestine, leaving the Jews exposed and helpless in Europe. At the novel's end, Joseph has joined the terrorist movement and is engaged in smuggling Polish Jews off the Romanian cattle boats that are forbidden to unload their homeless cargo. In its musings on terrorism, *Thieves in the Night* seems to back off from the repudiation of the doctrine that the end justifies the means. Koestler always faced these issues honestly, and *Thieves in the Night* is as engrossing—and as cogent—in the twenty-first century as it was in 1946.

THE AGE OF LONGING

Published in 1951 and set in Paris in the mid-1950's, *The Age of Longing* describes a time of spiritual disillusionment and longing for an age of faith. The narrative opens on Bastille Day and focuses on three characters: Hydie, a young American apostate from Catholicism, who kneels on her prie-dieu and laments, "LET ME BELIEVE IN SOMETHING"; Fedya Nikitin, a security officer with a rigid commissar mentality; and Julien Delattre, poet and former Party member. The relationship between Hydie and Fedya occupies much of the novel, with Hydie's ache for religious solace played off against Fedya's unquestioning faith in Communism. Hydie is American, naïve, and innocent; she is seeking experience on which to base faith. Fedya is the son of proletarian revolutionaries from Baku, Azerbaijan, a son of the Revolution with the instincts of a true commissar. He seems to have been programmed with Party clichés. When the two become lovers, Fedya humiliates Hydie by treating her as a mere collocation of conditioned responses. She then turns against Fedya and, finally understanding his true assignment as a spy, tries to shoot him but botches the job. Regardless of whether their relationship has allegorical significance, the unfeeling commissar is one of Koestler's most effective characterizations. At one point, Fedya asks a young school friend why she likes him, and the answer is, "Because you are clean and simple and hard like an effigy of 'Our Proletarian Youth' from a propaganda poster."

The third main character, Julien Delattre, is in many ways Koestler's self-portrait. Delattre has given up his allegiance to the "God that failed," and he tells Hydie that "My generation turned to Marx as one swallows acid drops to fight off nausea." He finds his mission in warning others about the ideological traps that he has successfully escaped, and one of the best scenes in the novel comes when he takes Hydie to an evening meeting of the Rally for Peace and Progress. The centerpiece of the session is Koestler's satirical depiction of Jean-Paul Sartre, who appears as the pompous theoretician Professor

Pontieux. Author of a fashionable work of postwar despair, "Negation and Position," Professor Pontieux "can prove everything he believes, and he believes everything he can prove." *The Age of Longing* ends with an image appropriate to its theme. A funeral party is proceeding past the graves of Jean de La Fontaine, Victor Hugo, and others when air-raid sirens start screaming. "The siren wailed, but nobody was sure: it could have meant the Last Judgment, or just another air-raid exercise."

THE CALL GIRLS

More than twenty years passed between the publication of *The Age of Longing* and that of *The Call Girls*, Koestler's last novel. During those two decades, Koestler's interests had shifted from ideology to science and human behavior. The "call girls" of the title are prominent intellectuals—mostly scientists but including a poet and a priest—nomads of the international conference circuit. Koestler puts them all together in a Swiss mountain setting and sets them to talking about ideas. They have been summoned by one of their members, Nikolai Solovief, a physicist, to consider "approaches to survival" and to send a message to the president of the United States. Unfortunately, the meeting degenerates into a series of uncompromising exchanges between behaviorists and nonbehaviorists. Only Nikolai and Tony, the priest, are able to accommodate themselves to the claims of both reason and faith, and rancor replaces the objective search for truth. *The Call Girls* is an entertaining exposition of the various options available to those seeking enlightenment today. Readers of *The Ghost in the Machine* and Koestler's work on ESP will recognize in the arguments of Nikolai and Tony those of Koestler himself. Koestler always staged his intellectual dramas in the dress of irreconcilable opposites—the Yogi and the Commissar, ends versus means—and here the protagonist is clearly spirit and the antagonist matter. His call girls demonstrate that there is still life in this old conflict.

Frank Day

OTHER MAJOR WORKS

PLAY: *Twilight Bar: An Escapade in Four Acts*, pb. 1945.

NONFICTION: *Spanish Testament*, 1937; *Scum of the Earth*, 1941; *Dialogue with Death*, 1942; *The Yogi and the Commissar and Other Essays*, 1945; *Promise and Fulfillment: Palestine, 1917-1949*, 1949; *Insight and Outlook: An Inquiry into the Common Foundations of Science, Art, and Social Ethics*, 1949; *Arrow in the Blue: The First Volume of an Autobiography, 1905-1931*, 1952; *The Invisible Writing: The Second Volume of an Autobiography, 1932-1940*, 1954; *Trial of the Dinosaur and Other Essays*, 1955; *Reflections on Hanging*, 1956; *The Sleepwalkers: A History of Man's Changing Vision of the Universe*, 1959; *The Lotus and the Robot*, 1960; *Hanged by the Neck: An Exposure of Capital Punishment in England*, 1961 (with C. H. Rolph); *The Act of Creation*, 1964; *The Ghost in the Machine*, 1967; *The Case of the Midwife Toad*, 1971; *The Roots of Coincidence*, 1972; *The Challenge of Chance: Experiments and Speculations*, 1973 (with Sir Alister Hardy and Robert Harvie); *The Heel of Achilles: Essays, 1968-1973*, 1974; *The Thirteenth Tribe*, 1976; *Life After Death*, 1976 (with Arthur Toynbee, et al.); *Janus: A Summing Up*, 1978; *Bricks to Babel: Selected Writings with Comments*, 1981.

EDITED TEXTS: *Suicide of a Nation? An Enquiry into the State of Britain Today*, 1963; *Drinkers of Infinity: Essays, 1955-1967*, 1968 (with J. R. Smythies); *Beyond Reductionism: New Perspectives in the Life Sciences*, 1969 (with Smythies).

BIBLIOGRAPHY

Cesarani, David. *Arthur Koestler: The Homeless Mind*. London: William Heineman, 1998. A good examination of the writer and his works. Includes bibliographical references and an index.

Day, Frank. *Arthur Koestler: A Guide to Research*. New York: Garland, 1987. In addition to a listing of Koestler's publications, there are 518 entries for writings about him, many of them from newspapers and journals. Includes some foreign-language items, and the latest materials are from 1985.

Hamilton, Iain. *Koestler: A Biography*. New York: Macmillan, 1982. This lengthy biography, favorable to Koestler, is arranged year by year in the fashion of a chronicle and breaks off around 1970. Many events have been retold partly on the basis of interviews, Koestler's papers, and firsthand accounts.

Harris, Harold, ed. *Astride the Two Cultures: Arthur Koestler at Seventy*. London: Hutchinson University Library, 1975. This collection of essays by authors sympathetic to Koestler provides approximately equal coverage of the writer's involvement in literary and in scientific concerns.

Levene, Mark. *Arthur Koestler*. New York: Frederick Ungar, 1984. Koestler's own life is discussed in the first chapter, and his major literary works are considered in detail, but relatively little attention is given to his scientific writings. The chronology and bibliography are useful.

Pearson, Sidney A., Jr. *Arthur Koestler*. Boston: Twayne, 1978. Although a bit sketchy on matters of biography, this work deals with basic issues in Koestler's writings and has some trenchant and interesting discussion of political themes. Also helpful are the chronology and a selected annotated bibliography.

Perez, Jane, and Wendell Aycock, eds. *The Spanish Civil War in Literature*. Lubbock: Texas Tech University Press, 1990. Contains Peter I. Barta's essay "The Writing of History: Authors Meet on the Soviet-Spanish Border," which provides an excellent grounding in the political history from which Koestler's fiction evolved.

Sperber, Murray A., ed. *Arthur Koestler: A Collection of Critical Essays*. Englewood Cliffs, N.J.: Prentice-Hall, 1977. Both positive and negative reactions appear in this fine sampling of critical work about Koestler's literary and scientific writings. Among those commentators represented by excerpts here are George Orwell, Saul Bellow, Edmund Wilson, Stephen Spender, and A. J. Ayer, as well as others. A chronology and bibliography have also been included.

Sterne, Richard Clark. *Dark Mirror: The Sense of Injustice in Modern European and American Literature*. New York: Fordham University Press, 1994. Contains a substantial discussion of *Darkness at Noon*.

JERZY KOSINSKI

Born: Lodz, Poland; June 14, 1933
Died: New York, New York; May 3, 1991

PRINCIPAL LONG FICTION

The Painted Bird, 1965
Steps, 1968
Being There, 1971
The Devil Tree, 1973, 1981 (revised)
Cockpit, 1975
Blind Date, 1977
Passion Play, 1979
Pinball, 1982
The Hermit of 69th Street: The Working Papers of Norbert Kosky, 1988

OTHER LITERARY FORMS

Jerzy Kosinski was a professional sociologist, educated in Poland and the Soviet Union. His first two books in English were studies of collectivized life in Soviet Russia, *The Future Is Ours, Comrade* (1960) and *No Third Path* (1962), both published under the pen name "Joseph Novak." Kosinski discussed some of his critical views in two short booklets, *Notes of the Author on "The Painted Bird"* (1965) and *The Art of the Self: Essays à Propos "Steps"* (1968).

ACHIEVEMENTS

Kosinski is among that small group of serious, difficult, absolutely uncompromising writers who attained critical acclaim and, at the same time, great popular success; his novels regularly appeared on best-seller lists and have won such prizes as the National Book Award (1969) and the French Prix du Meilleur Livre Étranger (best foreign book, 1966). His first, most popular, and probably best, novel, *The Painted Bird*, about a child growing up through sheer determination in a very hostile world, is one of those works, such as Daniel Defoe's *Robinson Crusoe* (1719) or Mark Twain's *The Adventures of Huckleberry Finn* (1884), that immediately touch some basic part of every reader. His later novels expressed contemporary experiences so directly that they seem to have been written out of the day's headlines. The charges of excessive violence and sensationalism are sometimes directed against Kosinski's work, but he argued cogently that life, no matter how much people have numbed themselves to it, is violent and sensational, and it is better to face the implications of those realities than to run and hide from them. In fact, it is only in experiencing life fully that one can extract value from it. His existential theme is that only when one lives conscious of the knowledge of one's coming death is one fully alive. Kosinski's reputation will continue to grow as critics and thoughtful readers better understand his intentions.

BIOGRAPHY

Jerzy Nikodem Kosinski was born in Lodz, Poland, on June 14, 1933. His life was as incredible as any of his novels, which are, to some degree, autobiographical. In 1939, when he was six, World War II began. He was Jewish, and his parents, believing he would be safer in the remote eastern provinces of Poland, paid a large sum of money to have him taken there. He reached eastern Poland, where he was immediately abandoned; his parents thought he was dead. Instead, at this very young age, he learned to live by his wits in an area where the peasants were hostile and the Nazis were in power. The extreme experiences of that time were given artistic expression in his first novel, *The Painted Bird*. Kosinski survived the ordeal, and his parents found him in an orphanage at the end of the war. The stress of his experience had rendered him mute, and his irregular, wandering life had left him unfit to live normally with other people. Finally, in the care of his family, Kosinski regained his speech, and, studying with his philologist father, he completed his entire basic formal education in a year and entered the University of Lodz, where he eventually earned advanced degrees in history and political science.

By that time, Poland was an Iron Curtain country with a collectivized society. Kosinski, after his youthful years of lone wandering, had developed a fierce independence and could not endure communal life in which the individual was under scrutiny at every step. He knew he could not remain without getting into serious trouble with the government, so he put together an elaborate scheme to escape. Making the cumbersome bureaucracy work in his favor, Kosinski invented a series of sponsors, all highly regarded scientists according to the documents he forged for them, to write him letters of recommendation, which eventually enabled him to get a passport to study in the United States. He arrived in New York on December 20, 1957, twenty-four years old, with $2.80 in his pocket and a good textbook knowledge of English, though little experience in speaking the language. He lived any way he could, stealing food when necessary and constantly studying English. By March, he was fluent in the language, and within three years he had published *The Future Is Ours, Comrade*, a study of Soviet life that sold extremely well. Suddenly he was moderately wealthy, but that was only the beginning. Mary Hayward Weir, the young widow of steel magnate Ernest Weir and one of the wealthiest women in the United States, read his book and wrote him a letter of praise. They met and were soon married. All at once he was wealthy beyond his own dreams, owning villas in several countries, a vast yacht, a private jet. "I had lived the American nightmare,"

(National Archives)

he said, "now I was living the American dream."

Five years later, in 1968, Mary Weir died of a brain tumor. The wealth, held by her in trust, went back to the estate. Kosinski had, during his marriage, written his first two novels, *The Painted Bird* and *Steps*, and he was a well-known, celebrated author. Needing to earn a living, he taught at Yale, Princeton, and Wesleyan Universities. He continued to write novels; they continued to sell well, so that he was able to leave teaching to write fulltime. He was re-married, to Katherina von Frauenhofer, in 1987.

Kosinski's life then fell into an active but regular and disciplined pattern. In season, he traveled to Switzerland to ski or to the Caribbean to play polo, and he made extensive American tours, granting innumerable interviews and publicizing his books. He was also internationally active in civil rights cases and served for two terms (the maximum allowed) as president of the International Association of Poets, Playwrights, Editors, Essayists, and Novelists (PEN). The rest of the time he spent working in his small apartment in Manhattan.

On May 3, 1991, Jerzy Kosinski, suffering from a serious heart disorder and discouraged by a growing inability to work, apparently chose to end his own life.

Kosinski often wrote that the world is an arena of violence and pure chance, which was certainly true of his own life. In addition to the numerous violent fluctuations of his early life, on a 1969 trip his baggage was misplaced, by chance, delaying his plane flight. His eventual destination was the home of his friends Roman Polanski and Sharon Tate; had it not been for the delay, he would have been there the fateful night the Charles Manson gang murdered everyone in that house.

Always a highly visible figure, Kosinski became in the early 1980's the subject of unwelcome publicity. In an article in *The Village Voice* (June 29, 1982), Geoffrey Stokes and Eliot Fremont-Smith charged that a number of Kosinski's novels had been written in part by various editorial assistants whose contributions he failed to acknowledge and indeed systematically concealed. Stokes and Fremont-Smith further charged that Kosinski's accounts to interviewers

of his traumatic childhood experiences, his escape from Poland, and his first years in America have been contradictory and in some cases verifiably untrue. Finally, they suggested that Kosinski's acclaimed first novel, *The Painted Bird*, was actually written in Polish and then rendered into English by an unacknowledged translator. Kosinski denied all the charges. In *The Hermit of 69th Street*, which its protagonist calls a *"roman à tease,"* he responds indirectly to the controversy by reflecting on the writer's craft, which, he concludes, is largely a process of borrowing and recasting narrative material.

Analysis

The themes and techniques of Jerzy Kosinski's fiction are adumbrated in the sociological studies he published within five years of his arrival in the United States. As a highly regarded Polish sociology student in the mid-1950's, Kosinski was granted permission to travel widely in the Soviet Union to interview people about their experiences in collectivized living. It was assumed by the authorities that he would write a thesis praising Communism, but, in fact, he found it abhorrent; his notes provided material for *No Third Path* and *The Future Is Ours, Comrade*, indictments of the system that he could never have published had he remained behind the Iron Curtain. The studies are diaries of his travels and consist mainly of his interviews with the people he met, people from every walk of life, some of whom were thriving in conformity within the system while others were in trouble because of their opposition to it. The interviews are not arranged chronologically; rather, each is located at the point where it can best support the theme under discussion.

This arrangement is typical of the structure of Kosinski's novels. The protagonist, who often has a great deal in common with Kosinski himself, is a loner, able to travel freely through all walks of life. Because he is secretly at war with his society, he is unable to stop and settle or to have more than a fleeting relationship with each person he encounters. The brief scenes in the novels are not arranged chronologically, but each vignette is one more stone in a mosaic; taken together, these vignettes constitute a powerful statement of Kosinski's recurring theme.

That theme is exactly the same as that of the sociological studies on collective life: the struggle of the individual to retain his or her individuality in a mass society. Central to Kosinski's novels are the ideas of the German philosopher Martin Heidegger, who profoundly influenced the existentialists. Heidegger said that one has no control over what is given one in life—where and when one is born, whether one is healthy or the reverse, intelligent or the reverse—that it is all a matter of chance. It is one's responsibility, however, to make the most of the particular life one is given. Daily life, petty responsibilities, the routine of work and family life, all have the effect of dulling one to the passage of time, and with it, the passage of one's opportunity to make the most of one's brief life. It is soothing, in a way, to be lulled and numbed into inattentiveness to coming pain and dissolution, yet to live in such a state is really not to live at all. According to Heidegger, one only lives fully when confronted by the terror of approaching death. The Kosinski hero purposely and unflaggingly thrusts himself into the terror-ridden present moment of his life, heroically refusing the deceptive and deadening temptations of his society to give up his lonely individuality and crawl under the umbrella of its collective "safety."

THE PAINTED BIRD

While Kosinski was living in immense wealth with his wife Mary Hayward Weir, he began writing *The Painted Bird*, a novel which, in its details, closely parallels his own experience as an orphaned outcast. "It was an attempt to somehow balance the reality of my past with the reality of my present. She [Mary], in turn, learned of my past through my writing." This statement suggests an autobiographical impulse for writing *The Painted Bird*; in other statements, however, Kosinski has made it clear that it was a novel, a work of art he was writing, not a memoir.

The child protagonist of the novel, never named, is dark haired and dark eyed, and he speaks the educated dialect. The peasants among whom he is abandoned are blond and blue eyed and speak a barely comprehensible peasant dialect. He stands out from them at a glance, and they suspect he is a gypsy or a Jew; the penalty for hiding such a person from the Nazis is severe, so they are not pleased to have him around. Further, the peasants are suspicious of strangers, and superstitious, and they believe his dark coloring indicates an evil eye. He has no choice, however, but to live among them, suffer their unmotivated violence, and take the blame for any natural catastrophes, surviving in any way he can.

At one point he lives with Lekh, the birdcatcher. When Lekh is angry, he takes out his anger by capturing a bird, the strongest and handsomest of the flock, painting it in brilliant rainbow colors, and then releasing it among its drab brown congeners. They fall on it at once and peck it to death. The examples of the perils of being a "painted bird" are constantly brought home to the boy, who is aware that his visible difference from the others marks him as a painted bird. In one of Kosinski's nonfiction works, *No Third Path*, he describes a man he met in the Soviet Union who survives because he is able to remain as one of the masses, always staying in the exact center of the crowd, never calling attention to himself. In that way, life could be "waited through," as he phrased it, without too much inconvenience. There is safety, then, in not being a painted bird, yet it is safety gained through a denial of life.

In the winter there is no work for the boy to do in the villages. He is simply another mouth to feed, and his presence is unwelcome. Instead, he wanders freely over the countryside, wrapped in his collection of rags and bits of fur. He is warmed and protected by his "comet," a tin can with a wire handle. The can is punched full of holes so that by swinging it he can force air through it, thus keeping alight the sticks and bits of dry moss he uses to fuel it. No one else ventures out in the deep snow; he can easily break into barns and steal potatoes and other vegetables, then find shelter for the night under the roots of a tree and cook his food with his comet. At these times, even though he is only seven or eight years old, he feels a marvelous happiness at his freedom and independence, his ability to face life directly and survive. In the summer, he is forced to move back into the village, and his torments begin again. His only hope is to try to blend into the society—valuable months of his life need to be "waited through."

Toward the end of the war, when the Germans have retreated, he is found and briefly adopted by a Soviet army battalion. The stresses of his experience have left him mute; he has psychically cut himself off from communication with others. Two soldiers in the army have particularly taken him under their care: Gavrila, the political officer, and Mitka the Cuckoo, the sharpshooting instructor. They are the first human beings in memory to treat him kindly, and he worships them and wants to model his life after theirs. He cannot, however, because they are diametrically opposite to each other. Gavrila lectures him daily on the advantages of the collective: No one stands alone, but the entire society is a unit. Individuals can make mistakes, but not when they give themselves up to the wise decisions of the community. As long as they are careful to remain within the center of the collective, they will march ahead to a marvelous new future. The boy wants to believe what his hero Gavrila tells him, but he is uneasy. His experiences in the villages, putting himself in the power of the mass, have all been unfortunate, whereas his life seemed fullest and most satisfying when he was by himself, making his own decisions. Mitka the Cuckoo—his name suggesting that he, like the boy, is a painted bird—was a sniper behind enemy lines; because of this, he had to develop to the fullest his instincts to be solitary and to depend on no one but himself. Like the boy, he has always been a loner in a hostile world but able to take care of himself. In the end, of course, it is this philosophy that wins the boy.

The boy survives, when so many other children did not, because of his miraculously tough emotional health. He does not despair or curse his fate. Instead, he accepts his world as it is and desperately tries to learn how to survive in it. In this respect, *The Painted Bird* is a *Bildungsroman* in which the boy, always an empiricist, struggles to find the underlying principle of life. He believes at one time that it might be love, at another time religion, and finally that it might be evil, but each time he is disillusioned. At the end, his speech gone, he believes that hatred and revenge against one's enemies are the keys to survival. The war is over, and his parents have found him in an or-

phanage; it seems he has survived. Yet, hatred and cynicism possess him completely. They give him a certain power: the power to have survived. Yet, one wonders whether he really is a survivor if he has been so deeply scarred that he can no longer relate to other human beings.

How can this story about experiences apparently so remote from those of most of its readers have moved those readers so deeply? Perhaps a clue to this can be found in a statement Kosinski made: "I think it is childhood that is often traumatic, not this or that war." Perhaps the novel is best read as an allegory of childhood, and the war—as so often occurs in works of fiction—as symbolic of the struggle and engagement with life. Children—who are small, weak, powerless, and ignorant of adult ways—are often deeply alienated from the ruling adult society (adults, after all, may be the prototypes for the terrifying giants found in the most powerful children's tales). Learning to live in a society, in enemy territory, can be a deeply scarring struggle. Reconciliation and the reopening of communications come, if at all, with the slow painful dawning of maturity.

STEPS

Steps was the first novel Kosinski began writing, but feeling too close in time to some of the experiences he was recording in it, he set it aside and instead wrote *The Painted Bird*. *Steps*, which won a National Book Award, is engrossing but puzzling for the reader. The book consists of nearly fifty brief vignettes. Many of the scenes report perverse or violent sexual encounters or ruthless acts of revenge. Each scene is brief, and each has little or no connection with the successive scenes. There is no certain indication that the main character in one scene will reappear in the next one. Kosinski never comments on the action, forcing readers to decide for themselves how they are to judge the characters.

These puzzling features are explained by Kosinski's aesthetic and philosophical principles. The short vignettes force readers to concentrate their attention on the individual scenes themselves, rather than, as in a conventionally plotted book, taking the scene as a whole. Society tries to "plot" one's life, Kosinski suggests, in such a way as to make one look to the future, but while one waits for the future to come, one has missed one's real life, which takes place in the present moment. The protean narrator of the scenes presents another philosophical point. He is different each time he appears; indeed, some critics have claimed that there are several different protagonists, but Kosinski has specifically stated that one protagonist links all the scenes: Identity, the nature of the self, is fluid. Finally, there is no authorial judgment of the actions of the protagonist. Kosinski makes it a point in all his novels to give the absolute minimum of advice to readers, thus implicating readers continuously in the action, forcing them to examine their own values.

Perhaps an exception to this system is in the scenes of revenge. In many of his novels, Kosinski seems to advocate an ethic of revenge. If a person has hurt one, physically or spiritually, that individual must hurt him or her back or lose his or her sense of self. Selfhood seems to be very much an absolute value to Kosinski. It must be defended against the collective and in personal encounters as well, particularly in sexual encounters. Kosinski believes that human beings reveal themselves most completely in their sexual relations, and therefore these relations play a large role in his novels. The longest series of repeated, connected scenes in *Steps* is a series of thirteen italicized passages, sprinkled throughout the novel, which consist of elaborate pre- and postcoital dialogues between a man and a woman who are trying desperately to sort out their relationship. The difficulty in a relationship is to find the means by which one may give him- or herself to another while still retaining one's selfhood. Kosinski presents this problem in terms reminiscent of Jean-Paul Sartre's existential psychology: In any relationship between two people, one must be the subject, and the other the object. To be the object is to give up one's selfhood and be nothing. To be the subject is to manipulate and diminish the other. There is a desperate struggle then for each to retain his or her selfhood—in other words, to become the subject and make the other the object. If one is successful in the struggle, he or she survives as an individual, but only at the cost of destroying the other. Relationships in this novel, and in all of Kosinski's novels, tend to

be manipulative and destructive. Though the characters do not seem to find a way out of their dilemma, and though the novel offers no solutions, it seems that Kosinski is critical of his characters for their failure, for he has elsewhere defined love as "the attempt to be simultaneously subject and object . . . the willing relinquishment of the single subject to a new subject created from two single ones, each subject enhanced into one heightened self."

Steps is thus Kosinski's purest novel. It has no "plot," but instead it draws the reader's attention to the present moment of each incident as it unfolds; it has a protean narrator who is a new person in relation to each new set of experiences with which he is confronted; it presents human life as a struggle to maintain selfhood, to avoid being diluted into some larger mass, or, on the individual level, to avoid being dominated and made into an object in personal relationships; and finally, it offers no authorial judgments, throwing the reader entirely to his or her own resources.

BEING THERE

Being There, at twenty-three thousand words, is a novella rather than a novel. Short in length, stripped and pure in language, and simple in outline, the story is told as a parable or moral allegory, which indeed it is. Chance, the protagonist, is consistent as a character because he has no character. Since he is mentally retarded, he is incapable of change or growth. No situation makes an impression on him, and therefore no situation alters him. He has never in his life been outside a rich man's estate, where he has remained to tend the garden. He works in the garden by day and watches television by night. When the rich man dies, however, the executors of the estate release Chance. He is tall, handsome, soft-spoken, and wears his former employer's cast-off suits. The wife of a billionaire financier invites Chance into her house thinking he must be a rich businessman. That night, the president of the United States visits the financier and is introduced to Chance. In every situation, Chance acts the way he has seen someone on television act in a similar situation. Every question he is asked, he answers in terms of gardening, since that is what he knows. His simple statements about flowers growing are taken as profound metaphorical statements about the economy. The president quotes him in his national speech that night, and he is immediately pursued by all the media, invited to talk shows, and courted by foreign ambassadors; by novel's end, there are plans to run him for high office, since he looks good on television and does not seem to have a past which might prove an embarrassment.

This amusingly absurd tale is in fact Kosinski's indictment of the mass media, especially television, which, as a sociologist, he frequently attacked in lectures and essays. The first evil of television, according to Kosinski, is that it presents viewers with an immediately accessible image and therefore does not induce them to do any thinking for themselves (an infant child, Kosinski reminds his readers, can watch the same programs they do). This mindless image is ultimately deadly, because it suggests that experience is *outside*, something that happens only to other people. Through lulling viewers into believing that wrecks and bombings and deaths can happen only to others, television robs them of the angst needed to live life fully. Further, television can make mere images so attractive that it can convince viewers to vote for any well-made-up puppet it puts before them. Into the empty, simplified, television image, viewers pour all their hopes and wishes, as the characters around Chance fill in his blank personality, making him into the person they want him to be. The comedy loses its humor when Kosinski suggests how easily this completely empty puppet could find itself sitting in the Oval Office, world destruction within the push of a single button.

Unlike television or films, which present the audience directly with an external image, novels, when they are read properly, force readers to re-create the scenes inside their heads, to generate their own images. This act of re-creation allows the reader to experience directly the action of the novel; when a character dies, the reader must, to an extent, experience that death. Kosinski was so opposed to the way the image falsifies and separates people from experience that he long refused to have any of his novels made into films. Under extraordinary and repeated persuasion from Peter Sellers, he at last agreed to allow *Being There* to be made into a film, starring Sellers, in 1979. There is a kind of ironic appropriateness in a story dealing entirely with the effect of visual images being portrayed in visual images.

BLIND DATE

Blind Date is typical, and indeed is probably the best, of a later group of Kosinski novels (the others in this group are *Cockpit, Passion Play,* and *Pinball*). The novel is presented in what can be called a standard Kosinski format: a series of incidents that finds the mobile lone-wolf protagonist in various countries, frequently flashing back to the past, moving from adventure to adventure, from woman to woman. In this group of novels, Kosinski begins to move toward more conventional plotting, and his protagonists are softened and made more human, more vulnerable. They are growing older and are no longer capable of some of the feats of their youth. Human relationships become less of a battleground, and at least the possibility of love is present. The theme of revenge, so prominent in earlier novels, begins to diminish. Where it is still present, it has been sublimated. The protagonist, giving up acts of personal revenge, raises himself to be a sort of "scourge of God," taking impersonal revenge against enemies of humanity. The earlier novels made frequent use of autobiographical materials, which these later novels continue to do, but there is a new element. The later novels come more programmatically to represent Kosinski's spiritual biography, and the protagonist, for all the indirection of art, comes more and more to stand for Kosinski himself.

The novel *Blind Date* and its protagonist Levanter are transitional in this scheme. Levanter as a young man is just as egotistic and manipulative as earlier Kosinski heroes have been. In summer camp, for example, he binds and brutally rapes a girl with whom he is infatuated, but he refuses to talk to her because he is too shy. That event, however, is seen in flashback. When the novel opens, Levanter is middle aged, and though he is still capable of violence, the violence has a social dimension. When he learns that the minister of internal affairs of a small dictatorship, a man famous for tortures and murders, is staying incognito at the same ski resort he is, Levanter manages, through an elaborate scheme, to have him killed. When a champion fencer from an Iron Curtain country is imprisoned because of information given against him by an informant, Levanter kills the informer by skewering him on just such a sword as the fencer has used.

Levanter, particularly as he grows older, is not so ruthlessly manipulative in his personal relationships as previous protagonists. If Tarden, the protagonist of the previous novel, *Cockpit*, had raped a girl, he would never have looked back. Instead, Levanter again meets the girl he had raped a year later (she had never seen his face), and their relationship continues to the point of true love; when he kisses her in the way the rapist had, however, she recognizes him and leaves in a rage. He feels then that he has missed a real opportunity and regrets his earlier action.

Levanter had met the girl the second time through sheer chance, another in a series of chance events in the novel. For example, in the novel's opening, Levanter meets a woman whose piano playing reminds him of the way his mother once played. By chance, that woman had been instructed under the same teacher as his mother, and Levanter and the woman feel this establishes a link between them. They go their separate ways, but toward the end of the novel, by sheer chance, Levanter meets her again; this time they complete the relationship begun earlier, one of total fulfillment for both. These chance meetings, which have the ironic effect of giving the novel a conventional plot, seem like the most banal and improbable coincidences until the reader realizes that chance is actually the governing principle of the novel. The novel's epigraph is a quotation from Jacques Monod's *Chance and Necessity* (1972) in which he argues that every moment in life is the chance convergence of completely unrelated chains of random events, and therefore there is no "plot" to life, no inevitability, no prediction. *Blind Date* reiterates more directly than any of Kosinski's other novels the Heideggerian notion that human beings are on earth only through sheer chance, that their time here, whether long or short, must end with death, and therefore they must get the most possible out of each moment as it is lived. What is new in the novel is the

social dimension: One way human beings make their life meaningful is by trying to make the lives of those around them meaningful as well. The earlier Kosinski protagonists fought desperately and ruthlessly to preserve the self, even if it meant destroying their closest personal relationships. The later protagonists, among whom Levanter again is a transitional figure, take more risks with the self, even hesitantly offering it in love. As a sign of this mellowing, Levanter actually seeks to rectify the cruelty he had practiced as a youth. As a first step he dedicates himself to punishing totalitarians; later, he seeks to undo his own totalitarian act of raping the girl at summer camp. In the novel's greatest coincidence, he realizes that the pianist is that very girl from the summer camp, who, as a result of the rape, has never been able to achieve sexual fulfillment. He binds her now, gently, and, this time with her permission, reenacts the rape, at last freeing her to be fully herself.

At this point a romantic novel might have ended, but such an end would be a falsification. Life can only end with death, which is the only predictable and inevitable conclusion to life's "plot." An aging Levanter is skiing when an unexpected late-season surge of bad weather catches him inadequately dressed. He is lost in the fog and slowly gives in to the cold, feeling he has played life's game very well and is now perhaps entitled to a rest.

Norman Lavers

OTHER MAJOR WORKS

NONFICTION: *The Future Is Ours, Comrade*, 1960 (as Joseph Novak); *No Third Path*, 1962 (as Joseph Novak); *Notes of the Author on "The Painted Bird,"* 1965; *The Art of the Self: Essays à Propos "Steps,"* 1968; *Passing By: Selected Essays, 1962-1991*, 1992.

EDITED TEXT: *Sociologia Amerykánska: Wybór Prae, 1950-1960*, 1962.

BIBLIOGRAPHY

Bruss, Paul. *Victims: Textual Strategies in Recent American Fiction*. Lewisburg, Pa.: Bucknell University Press, 1981. Explores the strategies of three writers, including Kosinski, and their alliance with the idealist tradition. Examines Kosinski's early fiction with regard to his use of language, as well as his novels *Steps, Cockpit,* and *Blind Date.* A selected bibliography of primary and secondary sources is provided.

Fein, Richard J. "Jerzy Kosinski." In *Contemporary Novelists,* edited by James Vinson. London: St. James Press, 1976. Includes comments by Kosinski and critical appraisal of his most distinguished novels. Fein honors the vision of Kosinski and sees his works as "strange hymns to suffering."

Lavers, Norman. *Jerzy Kosinski.* Boston: Twayne, 1982. An appreciative critical study that considers Kosinski a major writer. Discusses his fiction and nonfiction novels with some biographical information and provides considerable critical commentary on *The Painted Bird.* Contains a selected bibliography. A useful introduction to the beginning reader of Kosinski.

Lilly, Paul R., Jr. *Words in Search of Victims: The Achievement of Jerzy Kosinski.* Kent, Ohio: Kent State University Press, 1988. A full-length appreciative critical study of Kosinski's novels with much of interest and value for the Kosinski scholar. Includes a discussion of the controversy with *The Village Voice,* which attacked Kosinski's authenticity and compositional methods.

Sloan, James Park. *Jerzy Kosinski: A Biography.* New York: Dutton, 1996. An excellent, updated biography of the author.

Tepa Lupack, Barbara, ed. *Critical Essays on Jerzy Kosinski.* New York: G. K. Hall, 1998. Thoughtful essays on Kosinski's writing. Includes bibliographical references and an index.

MILAN KUNDERA

Born: Brno, Czechoslovakia; April 1, 1929

PRINCIPAL LONG FICTION

Žert, 1967 (*The Joke,* 1969, rev. 1982)
La Vie est ailleurs, 1973 (*Life Is Elsewhere,* 1974; in Czech as *Život je jinde,* 1979)

La Valse aux adieux, 1976 (*The Farewell Party,* 1976; in Czech as *Valčik no rozloučenou,* 1979; rev. as *Farewell Waltz,* 1998)
Le Livre du rire et de l'oubli, 1979 (*The Book of Laughter and Forgetting,* 1980; in Czech as *Kniha smíchu a zapomnění,* 1981)
L'Insoutenable Légèreté de l'être, 1984 (*The Unbearable Lightness of Being,* 1984; in Czech as *Nesnesitelná lehkost bytí,* 1985)
Nesmrtelnost, 1990 (*Immortality,* 1991)
La Lenteur, 1995 (*Slowness,* 1996)
L'Identité, 1997 (*Identity,* 1998)

OTHER LITERARY FORMS

Apart from Milan Kundera's novels, of particular interest are his three linked volumes of short stories, *Směšné lásky* (1963; laughable loves), *Druhy sešit směšných lásek* (1965; the second book of laughable loves), and *Třetí sešit směšných lásek* (1968; the third book of laughable loves), which were published together in a definitive edition, *Směšne lásky* (1969); seven of these stories appear in English translation in *Laughable Loves* (1974). Kundera started his literary career with poetry, publishing three collections of that genre. His first important contribution to literary criticism was his study of the Czech novelist Vladislav Vančura, *Umění románu: Cesta Vladislava Vančury za velkou epikou* (1960; the art of the novel: Vladislav Vančura's search for the great epic). Kundera contributed to the revival of Czech drama with *Majitelé klíčů* (1961; the keys), *Ptákovina* (1968), and *Jacques et son maître: Hommage à Denis Diderot* (1970; *Jacques and His Master,* 1985). Kundera's speech to the Union of Czechoslovak Writers' Congress of 1967 was one of the high points of the cultural-political movement known as the Prague Spring; the essayistic talent revealed there has since been put to use in a series of striking essays, among the best known of which are "The Tragedy of Central Europe" (*The New York Review of Books,* April 26, 1984) and "The Novel and Europe" (*The New York Review of Books,* July 19, 1984). Finally, Kundera has also collaborated on a number of screenplays, the most notable of which was written for the film *Žert* (1969), based on his novel of the same title.

ACHIEVEMENTS

Kundera became well known quite early in his career on account of his poetry. However, he denounced poetry in *Life Is Elsewhere*, and he later switched to prose, experimented in drama, and finally, took a lively interest in the literary-political scene in Prague at the time of great excitement caused by the liberalization of the Communist regime. As far as Kundera was concerned, the time of his great breakthrough in literature and on the cultural scene that involved him also in politics came in 1967, following the publication of *The Joke*, a novel exemplifying the cultural and political sophistication of its author as well as of his country. This confluence of art and life, private and public and philosophical and political domains is the principal characteristic of Kundera's fiction, refined and finely honed in his subsequent novels.

(Vera Kundera)

Kundera has been the recipient of many prestigious literary prizes, including the Czechoslovak State Prize (1964), the Union of Czechoslovak Writers' Prize (1968), the Czechoslovak Writers' Publishing House Prize (1969), the Prix Médicis (1973), the Premio Mondello (1978), the Common Wealth Award for Distinguished Service in Literature (1980), the Jerusalem Prize (1985), the Académie Française Prize (1986), the Nelly Sachs Prize, and the Austrian State Prize (both 1987). He has also received nominations for a Nobel Prize. Awarded an honorary doctorate by the University of Michigan (1983), in 1986 he became a member of the American Academy of Arts.

BIOGRAPHY

Milan Kundera was born into a highly cultured and sophisticated family of a Brno pianist, Milada Janosikova, and a distinguished professor of Janáček's Academy of Music, Ludvík Kundera. Thus, among those early interests that he took seriously was music as well as literature. In 1948, the year of a Communist coup in Czechoslovakia, Kundera began his study at the Charles University in Prague and simultaneously attended the famous film school of the Prague Academy of 4Music and Dramatic Arts, from which he graduated in 1958 after being forced to withdraw from 1950 to 1956 because of his expulsion from the Communist Party. During that hiatus, he composed poetry (a genre in which he had been publishing since 1949) and music, including "Composition for Four Instruments" and a setting of verses by Guillaume Apollinaire, an author who much influenced Kundera's own poetry. The Prague film school also became his employer: There, he taught world literature. In 1963, he married Vera Hrabankova and joined the editorial board of the journal *Literarni noviny*.

Having associated himself strongly with the movement known variously as the Prague Spring or "socialism with a human face," Kundera fell into disfavor following the invasion of Czechoslovakia by the Soviet Union. His works were put on the censor's index and withdrawn from the libraries, and he was left without any means of support when forced out of his professorship in 1970. Because of a request by the president of the French parliament, he was allowed to go to France, in 1975, as a visiting professor at the university in Rennes, and it was in France that he learned, in 1979, of the Czechoslovak government's decision to take his citizenship from him. Hence, Kundera continued to teach and write in Paris, where he became a French citizen in 1981.

Beginning in 1985, Kundera spent much time revising French and English translations of his work. His 1990 sojourn to Martinique and Haiti led to his publishing a 1991 essay on the culture of French-speaking Caribbean natives of African descent. A victim of explosive politics from Czechoslovakia to the Caribbean, he strove to detach himself from public life, as he demonstrated in his 1985 address delivered upon reception of the Jerusalem Prize. He said that the novel can rise to more than personal and national wisdom only through novelists' humbly absenting themselves from celebrity, so that they can ridicule the kitsch and sentimentality spread by public figures, who fear offending the masses.

ANALYSIS

None of Milan Kundera's novels fits into the traditional concept of the novel. Each is an experimental foray into the unknown, even though well prepared and supported by the literary legacy of Jaroslav Hašek, Karel Čapek, and Vančura. This is particularly visible in the structure of Kundera's novels, which strikes one as that of a loosely organized group of short stories which have in common not so much recurring characters as a central theme of which each story illustrates a single facet.

Each of his five novels—as well as his cycle of short stories, *Laughable Loves*—is a fresh approach to his abiding concern: his search for authenticity defined as an unmasked, demythologized, yet philosophical parable of the existence of a Czech intellectual in a given historical time. Against the background of modern Czech fiction, Kundera appears as a worthy follower of the three main directions of Czech prose, associated with the names of Jaroslav Hašek, Karel Čapek, and Vladislav Vančura. It is the mark of Kundera's genius that he has been able to alchemize the best that these authors had to offer him into his own original prose, surpassing them all.

THE JOKE

Thus, Kundera's first novel, *The Joke*, seems to grow out of the short-story collection *Laughable Loves*. They have in common the central device of a "joke"—that is, an intended and performed hoax, a prank—which misfires and, like a boomerang, hurts the perpetrator rather than the intended victim. Consequently, in one of the stories in *Laughable Loves*, "I, the Mournful God," the narrator wants to punish a pretty girl who has resisted his advances by punishing her vanity. He approaches his Greek friend, who acts the role of a foreign impresario attracted by the talent of the girl, who happens to be a music student. The girl is easily seduced, and the affair is consummated the same day on the narrator's couch, to the narrator's wrenching and never-ending dismay. Hoist with his own petard, the narrator waxes philosophical about the important lesson he has learned about life.

This device becomes central in the novel *The Joke*, wherein it is enriched and used to probe deeply into the realms of character motivation past and present, the political order (with the attendant zigzags of the Party line), and the sensitive area of emotional and erotic relationships, the highs and lows of which Kundera captures with singular detachment bordering on misanthropy and misogyny.

The Joke consists of four narratives of the same event, or rather a set of events, centering on the "joke": Ludvík Jahn, the central character, sends his naïve activist girlfriend a postcard that is politically compromising; his intention is to make fun of her seriousness and steer her toward erotic rather than political interests. The girlfriend reports him to the Party organization, and Ludvík is thrown out of the university as a politically unreliable element, his life derailed for years during which he has to work as a mine laborer, first as a draftee in a punishment battalion, then as a volunteer without much choice. In revenge, the "rehabilitated" Ludvík, now a scientist in Prague, decides to seduce the wife of his archenemy who engineered his dismissal from the university. Like the first joke, the second misfires: The enemy's wife falls in love with Ludvík at a time when her husband is estranged from her; to add insult to injury, the enemy, Zemánek, is a thoroughly reformed man, now as fond of ideas as is Ludvík and embarrassed for his past—all in all, a different man, one who is involved with a young woman and glad that Ludvík is interested in his unwanted wife. Philosophically, the novel explores the fluidity, the inconstancy of people's characters and ideas; Kundera also suggests that the nature of justice is undermined by the element of time. Perhaps in some timeless corner of the universe, an exact justice prevails, but how can one implement it in a world crucified by time?

Ludvík Jahn is also an ideal personification of the reformist ideas sweeping Czechoslovakia in 1967 and 1968. Historically, the novel is a literary summing up of the Czechoslovak experience with socialism from its very outset, in 1948. The sensational quality of *The Joke*, from the political point of view—and it is clear that this point of view is relevant to the understanding of the novel—stems from the near-documentary quality with which Kundera depicts successive stages of modern Czech history, taking into account the many different moves and countermoves of cultural, social, and existential aspects of the Czech reality. What each of the four character-narrators documents, Kundera the author transcends, so powerfully does one feel the controlling intelligence behind the scene pulling the strings that direct the literary "god game."

While the novel was immediately praised for its literary qualities, it also served to polarize Czech critics along political lines, dividing them into dogmatists and reformists: The former decried Kundera's wholly irreverent attitude toward Communist taboos, while the latter praised his candor.

Kundera himself has noted the danger of ideological interpretations of the novel that obscure the more subtle love story between Ludvík and the tender girl, Lucie, whom he met while he was a laborer—a love story at the center of the complex novel but for that very reason easily overlooked when weightier and more topical concerns clamor for attention. In the novel's first reception, few critics noted Ludvík's failure to lead an authentic existence. Imprisoned by his grudge and his ambiguous attitude toward women as a result of the decisive, treacherous act by the female Party activist, Ludvík blinds himself even to

such timeless aids as Moravian folk music—which, in a key passage omitted from the original English translation, opens his eyes to the authenticity he missed.

LIFE IS ELSEWHERE

This powerful concern with authentic life is developed masterfully in *Life Is Elsewhere*. Where, then, is life? Rather, what is life? Kundera's second novel answers this question by way of a negative example of a young poet living the life of precocious maturity conventionally found admirable in Arthur Rimbaud, Vladimir Mayakovsky, Sergei Esenin, or the Czechs Jiří Wolker and Jiří Orten, embodying Romantic conventions of the genius and of the indivisibility of art and life. Is it then possible for the Poet, this higher being, to become a wretched masturbator and police informer, as well as a clumsy bungler of everything but his verses?

Kundera magisterially answers these and other questions by giving an indecent history of the young poet Jaromil: his life, beginning with his conception, all the way up to his pathetic and bathetic death. On the way, Kundera demolishes the Romantic myth of the poet as the truth-seeker, or truth-sayer. Instead of a prophet, he shows us a pervert. That, however, is only the consequence of Jaromil's inability to lead an authentic life, precisely because he is and remains all the time a poet. The lyric quality so necessary for a poet is seen as the greatest obstacle to authenticity, to life as it should be lived.

The unlikely counterpart of Jaromil is a man with whom Jaromil shares a girlfriend. The authentic man, however, is selfless, whereas Jaromil is possessive; he is attached to timeless traditional art, whereas Jaromil seeks absolute modernity. Needless to say, in the political sphere, Jaromil repeats Communist inanities, though he is sufficiently intelligent to see how flawed they are. Lyricism *contra* logic: This is the conflict at the heart of the painful demolition of the poet. He, the poet Jaromil, even dies without understanding the harm he has done to others and himself through his fateful lyricism.

THE FAREWELL PARTY

So much for the poet; but what if Jaromil's condition is generally present among people at large? Kundera turns to this question in the wry, tragicomic novel *The Farewell Party*. Instead of following one causal chain, he traces several, crisscrossing them in order to show how, like billiard balls, individual fates meet and are bounced in a yet more unexpected direction. Though the plot is too complex to recount in detail, in simplified form, *The Farewell Party* deals with the issue of self-deception on a group scale, up from the previous novel's individual scale.

A musician is arranging his mistress's abortion with a doctor who heads a fertilization clinic in an unorthodox manner: He impregnates his patients artificially, using his own semen. The man whose mission it is to fertilize then kills, and the man who wants to free himself supplies poison to a woman, the same musician's mistress who, not knowing about the poison, kills herself. Further complications follow. This novel is far more dramatic than anything else written by Kundera, but it does have the operatic quality of some of his early tales. The obvious tragic aspect of the happenings is countered step by step with genuinely comic happenings, accidents, and a jovial set of characters, almost all of whom preclude the kind of tragic tension that the mere plot implies.

Without any doubt, *The Farewell Party* is Kundera's most cynical and misanthropic literary performance. At the same time, it announces the arrival of supernatural elements in his fiction, in the guise of an American, Bartleff. Without the somewhat absurd supernaturalism of Bartleff, which injects into the novel a modicum of warmth, the novel would be hard to bear. Thematically, it is possible to place the work into the tense, Kafkaesque atmosphere of postinvasion Bohemia with its ever-growing demoralization.

THE BOOK OF LAUGHTER AND FORGETTING

Kundera's next novel was like a breath of fresh air. A daring experiment, *The Book of Laughter and Forgetting* features the return of a more aggressive narrative with documentary elements, more authorial intrusion and manipulation of the narrative with autobiographical elements, quotations from an eccentric array of thinkers, attempts at the theory of laughter, and incursions into the domains of musicology and philosophy of history.

First, Kundera manages to introduce and establish very successfully the plight of a dissident and an émigré, though in ways that run contrary to political clichés. There is then a considerable dose of "reality": Historical events are recounted; politicians—dead and alive—are quoted and described; and snippets of what purports to be Kundera's life are offered in a very appetizing smorgasbord, where the wound of history is treated with the balm of a new mythology, created by Kundera in a feat of magic to vanquish the old—people dance the hypnotic circle and rise into thin air. Finally, there is a "theory of laughter" that distinguishes between the laughter of the Devil and the laughter of angels. At the same time, structurally, the novel solidifies around seven key tales with a limited number of characters, some of whom are present in more than one tale; the tales themselves are introduced as variations (in musical fashion) on the common themes of laughter and forgetting. The dangers of forgetting and the necessity of laughter are often illustrated roughly, subtlety being reserved for a sustained criticism of the modern malaise of indifference, lack of compassion, and the frittering away of a precious cultural heritage.

Above all, Kundera's concern with authenticity is present here in force, as is his attempt to do away with the sentimental glorification of youth, of childhood even—as if he believed that he had not finished the job properly in *Life Is Elsewhere*. To get his message across in a definitive fashion, he places his favorite heroine, Tamina, on an island inhabited by children who ogle her, pounce on her, take away her privacy, rape her, and finally kill her—naïvely, sincerely, purely, without malice, but full of curiosity. The island of children, the children's paradise, is a beautiful parable of the horrors of totalitarianism.

Kundera wanted to impress the Western reader with the issue of totalitarianism, and the avenue he chose was a parable. The totalitarian system, however imperfect, tries to turn adults into children in yet another parody of a perfectly legitimate and profound traditional idea found in many sacred traditions—above all, in Christianity. The primitivism of the totalitarian ideology, the simplicity of its propaganda, has thus acquired a profound meaning: It harks back to the children imprisoned within adults, and therein lies its success, no matter how banal, how simple, how trivial.

To resist the totalitarian temptation, to become a "dissident," is desirable, but in Kundera's world, the dissident is a person who exemplifies in miniature the larger political processes existing on a large scale in society, for one is but a part of the whole. Thus, even a dissident feels the need to tamper with his or her past in order to bring it more in line with his or her present: The past embarrasses him or her. Kundera justifiably resents labels such as "dissident" or "émigré" as applied to him, for he has spent his entire adult life peering at what is hidden behind the label, behind the mask, knowing that a label—any label— does not absolve one from anything. At the depths at which Kundera operates, such labels are meaningless.

THE UNBEARABLE LIGHTNESS OF BEING

It is curious to see, then, in Kundera's *The Unbearable Lightness of Being*, an attempt to present a character who, according to all indications, does lead an authentic life. Yet when Kundera portrays someone who is living an authentic life, as his main character Tomas and Tomas's love Tereza do, it is only to suggest that ultimately life itself has been emptied of meaning, of authenticity. The novel begins by stating that if humanity believed (as in German philosopher Friedrich Nietzsche's idea of eternal return) that everything, including the horrors of the past, would occur again and again forever, every act would be "heavy" with consequence. Instead, however, many people now assume that their acts will have no eternal result (in heaven or hell); thus, life becomes "light"—perhaps unbearably so.

Tomas and Tereza, as authentic and as unobjectionable as Kundera could make them, are frustrated by the accidents of history. They understand the personal and the social tragedy which they witness. They feel compassion. When the great traumatic event of their life happens, the Soviet invasion of Czechoslovakia in 1968, they decide to emigrate to Switzerland. Because Tomas is a natural Don Juan, Tereza, who loves him deeply, decides to return to Czechoslovakia, unable to share Tomas with other women. Tereza's absence weighs heavily on Tomas, and he returns to Czechoslovakia to join her, though

the price is high: A skillful surgeon, he is fired from his hospital and forced to work as a window washer. Yet he does not mind, feeling even more free, and the new occupation seems especially useful from the point of view of his easier access to potential erotic adventures. Finally, Tomas and Tereza move into a benighted village, where Tomas works as a truck driver. During a weekend outing, Tomas and Tereza are accidentally killed in the truck.

Far away from Tomas, in America, lives his former love, Sabina, who also suffers from the burden of "lightness." She influences one of her lovers, Franz, a Swiss professor, into adopting a more authentic life and then drops him. Franz looks for a cause, is attracted to a humanitarian mission in Southeast Asia, and while there is killed in a mugging. Tomas, Sabina, and Franz all have something in common, irrespective of their accomplishments as authentic beings, inasmuch as the meaning has been decanted from life itself. This common feature is the Nietzschean *amor fati*, love of life as it is in all its merciless fatefulness. Kundera never announces this theme, but after his Nietzschean opening, it is only logical to translate the surrender of all these characters to life as it is, without preconditions, as a literary adaptation of this Nietzschean conceit.

Mention should be made of Kundera's superlative satire of leftism and its kitsch. In this connection, the conclusion serves as a magnificent counterpoint to Kundera's discussion of many varieties of kitsch, including the political. What could promise more in the way of kitsch than the death of a dog improbably named Karenin? After all, pets, whatever kind, are the beneficiaries of the most absurd type of maudlin sentimentality and kitsch. It takes courage to lecture about kitsch and then, in a truly inspired and unforgettable passage, after showing why the death of millions of human beings no longer has power to move people, describe the death of Tomas and Tereza's dog Karenin as a genuinely moving event that restores, through acceptance of tragedy, meaningfulness to life. This is the most unbearable event of the novel. As such, it pokes a hole through the all-embracing curtain of Tomas's *amor fati* and reestablishes the primary importance of authenticity.

SLOWNESS

In all Kundera's major works there is complex counterpoint between essaylike lecture and narrative. The distance between the two, however, narrows beginning with *Slowness*. It juxtaposes a leisurely, eighteenth century journey through beautiful countryside with a modern motor trip, where people distance themselves from nature and time in an "ecstasy" of speed. Representing the earlier century is a character simply called the Chevalier, who enjoys a night of love at the climax of Vivant Denon's 1777 novella *Point de lendemain* (*No Tomorrow*). Wandering out of that book and into Kundera's, this Chevalier meets Vincent, a man who also spends a night with a beautiful woman, but who is rendered impotent by trying to perform in public. Indeed, throughout *Slowness*, one modern character after another acts ridiculously because of exhibitionism, a metaphor for quickly traversed open spaces in contrast to the unhurried pace and privacy cherished in the eighteenth century. A Czech scientist, for instance, rushes to a foreign conference, only to forget to give his lecture because he is deeply moved by the grandstanding remarks he makes as his introduction. More comically lamentable is a French politician so addicted to ostentatious globe-trotting that he long ago renounced any private life.

IDENTITY

Even more than *Slowness*, Kundera's next novel, *Identity*, takes advantage of a French milieu, where ideas permeate conversation. In the former work, the essays have been reduced to short asides by a narrator who witnesses the events. In *Identity*, however, the essayistic elements are confined to the dialogue and thus are integrated into the action. They all spring from a vision of life as boring because people are no longer distinguished from one another by passionate attachment to their occupations. Instead, there has been homogenization, even of gender: The women occupy previously male-held professions, in which they feel detached and two-faced, and the men become effeminate "daddies" instead of authoritative "fathers." Kundera's assignment of these ideas to his characters leaves tantalizingly open the question of whether male chauvinism is part of his defense of old-world values or a satire of the stereotypes into which European culture has crumbled.

The character Chantal first laughs at the "daddies" she meets because they lack the masculinity to give her a second glance. Almost immediately, though, their neglect makes her feel old and unattractive. She tries to joke about this depression to her lover, Jean-Marc, but her blush betrays to him that she is deeply hurt. To rekindle her self-esteem, he begins writing her anonymous letters, as from a secret admirer. Then, he becomes jealous of their success, and the couple's life slips toward a nightmare of identity loss and boredom. According to Jean-Marc, boredom is the direct experience of time without the protection offered by friendship and occupation (both of which modern life vitiates). In fifty-one short sections, the novel provides so many variations on the theme of identity loss that *The New York Times Book Review* likened it to a fugue. Kundera has always achieved a music-like structure in his works, but his later novels have attained a new delicacy and harmony, even if perhaps with some loss of volume.

Peter Petro, updated by James Whitlark

OTHER MAJOR WORKS

SHORT FICTION: *Směšne lásky: Tri melancholicke anekdoty*, 1963; *Druhy sešit směšných lásek*, 1965; *Třetí sešit směšných lásek*, 1968; *Směšne lásky*, 1969 (partial trans. *Laughable Loves*, 1974).

PLAYS: *Majitelé klíčů*, pr. 1961; *Ptákovina, čili dvojí uši—dvoji svatba*, pr. 1968; *Jacques et son maître: Hommage à Denis Diderot*, pr. 1970 (*Jacques and His Master*, 1985).

SCREENPLAY: *Žert*, 1969.

POETRY: *Člověk zahrada širá*, 1953; *Poslední máj*, 1955, rev. 1963; *Monology*, 1957, rev. 1964.

NONFICTION: *Umění románu: Cesta Vladislava Vančury za velkou epikou*, 1960; *L'Art du roman*, 1986 (*The Art of the Novel*, 1988); *Les testaments trahis*, 1993 (*Testaments Betrayed*, 1995).

BIBLIOGRAPHY

Banerjee, Maria Nemcová. *Terminal Paradox: The Novels of Milan Kundera*. New York: Grove Weidenfeld, 1990. This is not only useful for its analysis of Kundera's humor and paradox but also for its extensive, scholarly notes.

Brand, Glen. *Milan Kundera: An Annotated Bibliography.* New York: Garland, 1988. Brand's annotation is valuable, although the list does not include enough of Kundera's French texts.

Hamsik, Dusan. *Writers Against Rulers.* Translated by D. Orpington. New York: Random House, 1971. In addition to providing necessary political background, it also contains Kundera's important speech to the 1967 Czech Writers' Congress.

Misurella, Fred. *Milan Kundera: Public Events, Private Affairs.* Columbia: University of South Carolina, 1993. Notable for its chronology and bibliography, this study mediates between aesthetic and political readings of Kundera.

O'Brien, John. *Milan Kundera and Feminism: Dangerous Intersections.* New York: St. Martin's Press, 1995. O'Brien contrasts the surface sexism of Kundera's novels with Kundera's deconstruction of that sexism.

L

PÄR LAGERKVIST

Born: Växjö, Sweden; May 23, 1891
Died: Lidingö, Sweden; July 11, 1974

PRINCIPAL LONG FICTION
Människor, 1912 (novella)
Det eviga leendet, 1920 (novella; *The Eternal Smile*, 1934)
Gäst hos verkligheten, 1925 (novella; *Guest of Reality*, 1936)
Bödeln, 1933 (novella; *The Hangman*, 1936)
Dvärgen, 1944 (*The Dwarf*, 1945)
Barabbas, 1950 (English translation, 1951)
Sibyllan, 1956 (*The Sibyl*, 1958)
Ahasverus död, 1960 (*The Death of Ahasuerus*, 1960)
Pilgrim på havet, 1962 (*Pilgrim at Sea*, 1964)
Det heliga landet, 1964 (*The Holy Land*, 1966)
Pilgrimen, 1966 (collective title for previous 3 novels)
Mariamne, 1967 (*Herod and Mariamne*, 1968)

OTHER LITERARY FORMS
Though he is known primarily for the full-length novels that began appearing near the end of World War II, Pär Lagerkvist has also achieved great recognition in Scandinavia for his numerous short stories, novellas, poems, and plays. Little of this early work is available in translation. Lagerkvist's short fiction and miscellaneous prose have been collected in *Prosa I-V* (1956). Some of the pieces in this work have appeared in translation in *The Eternal Smile and Other Stories* (1954), *The Marriage Feast and Other Stories* (1955), and *The Eternal Smile: Three Stories* (1971). Lagerkvist's nine volumes of poetry have been collected in *Dikter* (1941). This portion of his work is the least known outside Scandinavia; only one volume, *Aftonland* (1953; *Evening Land*, 1975),

has been translated in its entirety. Lagerkvist also wrote plays, as well as dramatic adaptations of two of his fictional pieces: *Bödeln* (1933; *The Hangman*, 1966) and *Barabbas* (1953). A selection of his plays has been translated in *Modern Theatre: Seven Plays and an Essay* (1966). His diaries and unpublished notes were edited by his daughter, Elin Lagerkvist, under the title *Antecknat* (1977).

ACHIEVEMENTS
Lagerkvist is perhaps the most important figure of Swedish modernism, a tradition which is little known outside Scandinavia itself. Though Lagerkvist's influence on literature outside this region has been slight, his work has exerted a great influence on the Nordic tradition of which he is a part.

Despite Lagerkvist's relative unfamiliarity to readers of modern European literature, he is the most widely translated Swedish author since August Strindberg. Though various portions of his work have been translated into at least thirty-four languages, large portions remain inaccessible. Only one other Swedish writer, Ingmar Bergman, rivals the degree of international recognition Lagerkvist has achieved, and Bergman is not so much a literary artist as a filmmaker.

Lagerkvist's importance to literary history lies in his influence on the development of the unique characteristics of Swedish modernism which distinguish it from the modern literature of other countries. Lagerkvist's influence in this regard has not been limited to his role as a leading novelist but applies to his poetry and drama as well.

In 1941, Lagerkvist received an honorary doctorate from the University of Gothenburg. In addition to being elected to the Swedish Academy of Literature in 1940, Lagerkvist received the Nobel Prize in Literature in 1951, the year following the publication of his novel *Barabbas*.

BIOGRAPHY
Pär Fabian Lagerkvist was born on May 23, 1891, in Växjö, Sweden, a small town in the southern region of Småland. His father, Anders Johan Lagerkvist, was the railway agent at the station in Växjö,

and the family lived in a small apartment above the station's restaurant. His mother, Johanna Blad, was, like her husband, from a simple peasant family. Lagerkvist was the youngest of seven children, and like the others, he attended the local primary and secondary schools, spending summer vacations with his maternal grandparents in the country. Though normally reticent about biographical disclosure, Lagerkvist described his early environment as a mixture of the fundamentalist conservatism of his parents with the radical nonconforming Calvinism of his maternal grandparents. Between these two competing religious attitudes, the young Lagerkvist was torn, and his inability to reconcile their contradictions eventually resulted in his abandonment of both.

During his secondary education at the Växjö gymnasium, Lagerkvist's rebellious attitude toward his family's conservative influence began to surface. Together with four of his friends, he formed a study group named the Red Circle. Wearing the broad-brimmed hat and flowing bow tie that indicated their affiliation with the growing Socialist movement, they met each Sunday morning at eleven o'clock—the precise hour that services were held at the nearby cathedral. With the Red Circle, Lagerkvist studied the works of Charles Darwin, Camille Flammarion, Thomas Huxley, Pyotr Kropotkin, Strindberg, and Henrik Ibsen—purveyors of a new view of the world which, Lagerkvist later said, "was sweeping God and all hope aside . . . laying life open and raw in all its nakedness, all its systematic absurdity."

Following his graduation from the gymnasium in 1910, Lagerkvist left home, going to live with his older brother, Gunnar, who was a schoolteacher in western Sweden. In the fall of 1911, Lagerkvist entered the University of Uppsala, where he studied art history and literature briefly, leaving in dissatisfaction after only one semester.

In this prewar period, from 1908 to 1914, Lagerkvist's lifelong attitude of rebellion against conformity in thought and traditional values in literature became increasingly apparent. Among his earliest published works are the idealistic "revolutionary songs of struggle," in which he identified with the developing Swedish workers' movements. Many of these early poems, essays, and prose sketches—which were first published in *Fram* and *Stormklockan*, two Socialist journals—were later collected in *Motiv* (1914). In 1912, Lagerkvist's first novella, *Människor*, appeared, and the following year, in the spring of 1913, he forsook the artistic isolation of Sweden for the avant-garde fashions of Paris, where he was much impressed by cubism. After a few months, he returned home and began to write the reviews of modern European novelists in which the earliest expression of his own personal aesthetic is to be found. Later in 1913, he published "Ordkonst och bildkonst"—his first important polemical work—in which he presented his critique of "the decadence of modern fiction" against "the vitality of modern art."

With the outbreak of World War I, Lagerkvist fled to Denmark, settling in Copenhagen in 1915, where he remained until the armistice was declared in 1918.

(The Nobel Foundation)

During this period, he became intensely involved in the theater and began reviewing drama for the local newspapers. In 1915, *Järn och människor*, his first volume of short stories, appeared, and in 1917, *Sista mänskan*, his first published play, appeared.

In 1918, Lagerkvist published the essay "Modern teater: Synpunkter och angrepp" ("Modern Theatre: Points of View and Attack," 1966), which attacked the dominant mode of naturalism in drama at that time, emulating August Strindberg's powerful experiments with symbolism and ritual in his later plays. In the same year, he married a Danish woman, Karen Sörensen, with whom he returned to Sweden after the armistice, where he served as drama critic for *Svenska dagbladet*, a Stockholm newspaper, during 1919. The following year, he traveled to Italy, France, and North Africa and published *The Eternal Smile*, a novella. Three years later, *Onda sagor* (1924; evil tales), his most famous collection of stories, appeared.

In 1925, Lagerkvist divorced his first wife and married Elaine Hallberg, a Swedish widow. The same year, his autobiographical novella *Guest of Reality* appeared. Lagerkvist was also active in the Swedish theater following the war, and in 1930, he and his wife settled permanently in Lidingö, an island community near Stockholm. In 1933, Lagerkvist published *The Hangman* and in the same year traveled to Palestine and Greece. This journey resulted in the publication of *Den knutna näven* (1934; *The Clenched Fist*, 1982), a volume of travel essays which reflect Lagerkvist's intense interest in the early history of the religions of the Mediterranean region. Also in 1933, his dramatic adaptation of *The Hangman* was produced with great success—first in Norway and then in Sweden. In 1940, he was chosen to succeed Verner von Heidenstam as one of the "Eighteen Immortals" of the Swedish Academy of Literature, and in 1941, he received an honorary doctorate from the University of Gothenburg.

In 1944, *The Dwarf* appeared. This work was the first of a series of full-length novels that, through their translation into many other languages, brought Lagerkvist increasing recognition outside his own country. His growing international reputation was se-cured by the appearance in 1950 of *Barabbas*, which was immediately published in several translations. The following year, he was awarded the Nobel Prize in Literature. *Barabbas* has been the most popular of Lagerkvist's novels and has reached the widest audience by far. A dramatic version, which appeared in 1953, and a film version, released in 1960, were both very successful. Another novel, *The Sibyl*, which appeared in 1956, drew on Lagerkvist's interest in ancient Greek religion. In 1960, Lagerkvist began publishing a series of novels which critics later called "the Tobias trilogy." Comprising *The Death of Ahasuerus, Pilgrim at Sea*, and *The Holy Land*, the trilogy was later published in a single volume entitled *Pilgrimen*. Lagerkvist's last novel, *Herod and Mariamne*, appeared in 1967, the year of Elaine's death. On July 11, 1974, Lagerkvist died in Lidingö at the age of eighty-three.

ANALYSIS

In his first critical work, *Ordkonst och bildkonst* (1913; *Literary Art and Pictorial Art*, 1982), Pär Lagerkvist argues, as Thomas Buckman says, "that the naturalistic portrayal of reality in literature is completely inadequate for the representation of modern experience." The argument of this programmatic essay is divided into two parts—"On the Decadence of Modern Fiction" and "On the Vitality of Modern Art"—which indicate Lagerkvist's approach to his subject. Emulating the treatment of "simple thoughts" in literature—the themes of timeless, universal application which he found in the Bible, the Koran, the Egyptian Book of the Dead, the *Kalevala*, and the *Eddas*—he attacked what he called "the planless improvisations" of the psychological realism that dominated Swedish fiction at the beginning of the twentieth century. To escape the state of lifeless decadence into which literature had fallen, Lagerkvist suggested modern fiction should appropriate the nonrepresentational methods of modern art. He was particularly interested in the strongly stylized picture of reality in the works of the cubist painters, whose compositions he had just seen in Paris. In these works, he found a clear example of what he believed to be the most important aspect of art: the element of "constructivity"—which he placed in opposition to the mechanical imitation of reality practiced by the naturalists and realists.

The aesthetic reform proposed in *Ordkonst och bildkonst* was elaborated in "Modern Theatre," an essay which appeared together with a series of three one-act plays entitled *Den svåra stunden* (*The Difficult Hour, I-III*, 1966) in the volume *Teater* (1918). In "Modern Theatre," Lagerkvist presented more fully his analysis of the situation of art in the modern world:

> Our time, in its lack of balance, its heterogeneity . . . is baroque and fantastic. . . . What a sea of brutality has broken over us, sweeping away and recreating! Is not every inner problem of mankind . . . now suddenly transformed into objective, threatening realities?

In such a world, with its "violent and abrupt contrasts," naturalistic and realistic means of expression seemed increasingly inadequate. Lagerkvist attempts to convey this new experience of the world as both fantastic and threatening in *The Difficult Hour*, the three brief plays which make up the remainder of the volume. It is in these plays that the portrayal of the human experience of bewilderment before the "violent and abrupt contrasts" of modern life is successfully accomplished in mature and complex symbolic terms.

Equally important to Lagerkvist's work is the effect of this symbolic aesthetic upon the content and form of his fiction. In looking for symbolic analogues of modern human experience and forms in which to express these experiences, Lagerkvist plunders many different mythological systems. Predominant among these, of course, is the Judeo-Christian heritage, though he also draws on the symbolic heritage of such diverse traditions as the dualistic and polytheistic religions of the ancient Near East, the Osirian religion of the ancient Egyptians, the mystery religions of the Hellenistic world, and the Norse mythology of his native Scandinavia.

Lagerkvist, in drawing on myths and legends from humanity's past, employs the material he finds there not to reconstruct that past so much as to reinterpret it from the perspective of life in the twentieth century. For Lagerkvist, the remote past in which nearly all of his novels are set is a symbolic world, as opposed to a historical one. It is through the activity of shaping the historical material to this purpose that Lagerkvist reveals the worldview that underlies his work.

Lagerkvist seems to prefer to treat legendary subjects about which the reader knows little, thus allowing himself greater freedom in shaping the material. Many times during his career, he demonstrated the ability to take one of the marginal characters of a well-known story—about whom the original source provides only a bare minimum of facts—and then fabricate around it a plausible psychological and social context into which those few details are carefully woven. By an act of imagination, Lagerkvist provides marginal figures from the Bible and from the Apocrypha—figures such as Barabbas, Lazarus, Ahasuerus, Tobias, and Mariamne—with a past, with complex motivation arising out of that past, and, above all, with an individual consciousness which is both appropriate to the character in question and distinctively modern in its sensibility. It is this latter quality of Lagerkvist's characters that has led critics to call them "mouthpieces" for their author; this twentieth century sensibility in historical characters has also encouraged critics to read the stories themselves as allegories or fables of people's experience in the modern world.

Of all the important elements of Lagerkvist's work, however, it is not the aesthetic values, the subject matter, or the form of his work that has attracted the most attention, but rather the philosophical ideas and patterns of thought that they express. The questing protagonists whom he portrays in his novels are alienated outsiders who wander through life as strangers trapped in a world to which they do not belong. As many critics have pointed out, Lagerkvist's response to spiritual questions is a curiously ambivalent one. While seeming to accept the objective truth of nineteenth century determinism—which swept God aside as an unnecessary appendage to a purely material universe—he continues to probe humanity's relentless quest for God in a world stripped of spiritual values.

Within this philosophical framework—which many critics have described as a form of religious existentialism—two particular tendencies of thought are prominent. The first of them is Largerkvist's dualistic perspective on the world, which leads him to characterize himself, in *Den knutna näven*, the account of his travels to Greece and Palestine, as "a believer without a faith, a religious atheist."

For Lagerkvist, the god that most people worship is a false, inferior, and evil deity—which his character Ahasuerus in *The Death of Ahasuerus* describes as a twisted abortion of the human imagination. Beyond this god is the true God, an absolutely transcendent deity who is wholly alien to human beings and, in his separation from the world, equally dissatisfying. This characteristic of Lagerkvist's thought has created much confusion among many of his critics, who, being unfamiliar with this type of theology, attempt to force the dualistic ideas and paradoxes expressed in his work into a more conventional Christian theological framework.

The second pattern of thought which is prominent in Lagerkvist's work is that of dialectical reasoning, which affects not only the arrangement of characters in the plot but also the structure of the novels themselves. This dialectical tendency is apparent in Lagerkvist's practice of presenting contrasting pairs of characters; examples of such contrasting pairs are the Sibyl and the Wandering Jew in *The Sibyl*, Barabbas and Sahak in *Barabbas*, and Tobias and Ahasuerus in *The Death of Ahasuerus*. Though there are frequently minor characters that are also contrasted in this way, Lagerkvist's novels almost always focus on a central pair of contrasting characters.

Typically, these contrasting characters become involved in debates as they tell their life stories to one another. As many critics and readers have observed, Lagerkvist is a novelist of ideas, and the argument and counterargument of these contrasting characters is typical of the way in which he engages his readers' indecision about such questions as the goodness of God, the origin of evil, the justification of earthly suffering, and the forgiveness of sins. In his trilogy comprising *The Death of Ahasuerus, Pilgrim*

at Sea, and *The Holy Land*, this dialectic is carried on not only within the individual novels themselves but also from one novel to the next, much like what critics have seen in *The Sibyl*, an antithesis to *Barabbas*. Of this continuation of the dialectic from one volume to the next, Lagerkvist said: "I constantly conduct a dialogue with myself; one book answers the other."

For many readers, Lagerkvist's portrayal of human existence in his novels is the supreme expression of the mood of Nordic despair which pervades the last plays of Strindberg, Lagerkvist's direct literary ancestor, and the mature films of Ingmar Bergman, his best-known descendant. Prominent in this somber view of life is a Manichaean strain, a metaphysical dualism in which good and evil are eternally warring principles. In some of Lagerkvist's novels, these forces exist simultaneously within the same character, while in other novels, the forces are represented by contending groups or individuals. Regardless of how they are distributed, however, their opposition is not resolved, for the world that Lagerkvist portrays in his fiction is not, despite its historical trappings, a dynamic one capable of change; it is a profoundly static world composed of symbolic forms that move in an unchanging pattern of eternal conflict.

THE DWARF

Lagerkvist's novel *The Dwarf* is in many ways the most atypical of his novels. Of the many novels he published, it is the only one that does not draw upon biblical sources. *The Dwarf*, moreover, marks an important turning point in Lagerkvist's career, for in it one can see both where he has been and where he is going. The subject matter of *The Dwarf* is drawn from the Middle Ages, as was his most successful novella, *The Hangman*, a decade before. In form, however, *The Dwarf* approaches the dialectical method of his mature novels. Unlike most of his earlier fables and satires, which employ an omniscient perspective, *The Dwarf* uses the first-person point of view, allowing the dwarf Piccoline to tell his own story in the form of a memoir. Piccoline's account of his experiences is told after the fact; he tells his story from the confines of a dungeon where he has been imprisoned by his master, Prince Leone.

The debates about the nature of power, the relativity of good and evil, and the effects of conscience upon human behavior in which the dwarf engages are, by necessity, arguments with himself—since he is alone in the dungeon. Through the device of retrospection, however—a technical strategy which Lagerkvist uses in all of his subsequent novels—Piccoline is able to re-create his scenes of conflict with Prince Leone, Princess Angelica, his rival, the dwarf Jehoshaphat, and many others. The outcome of all of these conflicts is always the same: The dwarf is triumphant—though it is important for the reader to remember that he is an unreliable narrator and that his account of the events is clearly distorted by egotism. He strangles the rival Jehoshaphat during a wrestling match; he repays Angelica's innocent curiosity about his condition by killing her favorite cat; and he "helps" the prince to overcome his vacillating conscience by poisoning his enemies for him.

In all of these actions, the dwarf comes to embody the force of evil loose in the world; yet, as Piccoline comes to realize, the malevolent, destructive impulses embodied in himself are present in all humans as part of our earthly heritage: "They think I scare them, but it is the dwarf within them, the apefaced manlike being who sticks up its head from the depths of their souls." The deformity of the dwarf externalizes this intrinsic evil. As the dwarf concludes his story, he reminds the reader of the eternal nature of the conflicts that he has described: "I shall have an opportunity of continuing my chronicle by the light of day as before, and my services will be required again. If I know anything of my lord, he cannot spare his dwarf for long."

In this novel, then, one sees not only the dualistic character of Lagerkvist's thought but also the beginnings of his search for an adequate form in which to convey these ideas. For some readers, the cyclical movement displayed here—the suggestion that nothing has really changed—is very dissatisfying, since it violates the expectations they have about the dynamic character of the world derived from their experience with novels of psychological realism. This is perhaps the greatest ideological challenge Lagerkvist's work presents to its reader.

BARABBAS

Lagerkvist's second novel, *Barabbas*, introduces important changes in subject matter and technique that influenced the remainder of his career. In this novel, he uses for the first time the body of legends surrounding the life of Christ, upon which all of his subsequent novels draw. He also begins to develop the complex narrative strategy of alternating first-person accounts spoken by the characters themselves with detached omniscient commentary. Such shifts in point of view are employed with increasing sophistication in his later novels.

Considered from the perspective of subject and form, then, *Barabbas* is the first of Lagerkvist's novels to combine successfully all the essential features of his mature style within a single work. Certainly, it is by far his most popular novel—though that is only in part the result of its aesthetic qualities. Of all of his novels, it has captured the largest and most diverse reading audience—who, attracted for the most part by its biblical subject matter, treat it as a conventional work of religious devotion.

Regardless of the reasons for its success, *Barabbas* was the first of Lagerkvist's novels to reach a large international audience, to whom his work was previously unknown. Within a year after its appearance in Sweden, *Barabbas* had been translated into nine languages, and on the strength of its appeal to this huge new audience, Lagerkvist was awarded the Nobel Prize in Literature in 1951.

Perhaps the two most interesting features of the novel are the method of extrapolation Lagerkvist has employed in telling the story of Barabbas and the persistent ambiguity with which the facts of that story are presented to the reader. Taken together, these elements reveal the intense irony which pervades the book, a quality often missed by readers who, unfamiliar with the attitudes and patterns of thought reflected in Lagerkvist's other works, read the book as a pious, factual narrative.

The plot of *Barabbas* is almost entirely fabricated. The central character, Barabbas, is little more than a name in the biblical sources upon which Lagerkvist draws: The reader of the Gospel accounts is told only that Barabbas was the name of a notorious criminal of the time, who was pardoned at the Passover feast instead of Jesus. Building around this minimal core of information, Lagerkvist carefully arranges a grouping of characters designed to reveal the personality of the protagonist, whom he provides—by the method of extrapolation from the legendary material—with a personal history and a symbolic destiny.

In developing the character of Barabbas, Lagerkvist divides his novel into three discontinuous episodes, each of which presents an important stage of Barabbas's symbolic journey through life. The first section of the novel focuses on the consequences of his unexpected release from prison. Though he immediately returns to his old way of life when he is freed, his friends notice that he has lost the brash self-assurance which characterized his former life as a criminal. During this episode, he witnesses at first hand the Crucifixion and the mysterious darkness that falls upon the city at the last hour of Christ's Passion. As he is considering the rumors he has heard that this man who died in his place is the Son of God, he encounters a harelipped woman who is a faithful follower of this self-proclaimed Messiah. Her unquestioning faith in the authenticity of this Savior—who allowed himself to be crucified in order that humankind might be redeemed—has an ironically literal application for Barabbas, the man who was pardoned at Christ's expense. The ironic interplay between the details of Barabbas's seemingly random experiences in the world and the symbols of the Christian doctrine of salvation is a pervasive element in the novel, which abounds with such surprising coincidences.

This dramatic irony arising from the plot is intensified by the verbal ambiguity with which Lagerkvist calls the very facts of Barabbas's story into question. In the majority of instances, this is done by inserting hypothetical qualifications into the statements of the omniscient narrator. This stylistic strategy forces the reader to participate consciously in the imaginative construction of the text by constantly requiring judgments concerning the validity of the narrator's inferences about the perceptions, actions, and motivations of the characters described in this manner. The most hotly debated of these ambiguous statements is the concluding sentence of the novel, which describes the last thoughts of the dying protagonist, Barabbas: "When he felt death approaching, that which he had always been so afraid of, he said out into the darkness, as though he were speaking to it: 'To thee I deliver up my soul.'" Though many critics, in their zeal to discover the religious or existential meaning of the story of Barabbas, have tried to resolve the ambiguity of this statement, upon which the validity of their particular interpretation usually depends, the "as though" bracketing of the facts of the story resists all attempts at final reduction to such a meaning. In *Barabbas*, the potential of these complex strategies of verbal and dramatic irony is fully explored for the first time.

THE SIBYL

In *The Sibyl*, his third novel, Lagerkvist develops the technique of the narrative debate that reaches its perfected form in the Tobias trilogy. Of all Lagerkvist's novels, *The Sibyl* has the most self-conscious formal structure, alternating a detached omniscient narration with the first-person accounts of the two principal characters.

The novel begins with an omniscient expository prologue reminiscent of the opening formula of traditional fairy tales—a generic similarity which is apparent throughout the entire course of the novel. The prologue is followed by a brief expository introduction in which Ahasuerus, the Wandering Jew of biblical legend, arrives at the Sibyl's hut; in the section that follows, he recounts his experiences to her. Having completed his story, Ahasuerus engages the Sibyl in a debate about its significance, and then the Sibyl tells him the story of her experiences as the Delphic Pythia. In the epilogue, they again engage in a debate about the meaning of their experiences, and the novel is brought to a close by the comments of the moralizing narrator, who sorts out the objective "truth" of the characters' situation by means of his privileged position of omniscience, completing the circular pattern of the novel's formal movement.

In form, then, *The Sibyl* is a balanced compromise between the total objective detachment of the omniscient narrators employed in Lagerkvist's early fables and satires and the total subjectivity of the viewpoint employed in *The Dwarf*, with its unreliable narrator. By mingling the two modes of narration to tell a single story, Lagerkvist found a satisfying novelistic form that enabled him to present human experience in all of its complex ambiguity. In this way, he managed to avoid the abstraction into which his desire to treat human experience in symbolic terms constantly threatened to fall. On the other hand, he was not limited by the technical restrictions of psychological realism—a "realism" incapable of expressing the baroque and fantastic quality of experience in the modern world.

The questing protagonist of the novel, Ahasuerus, who later reappears in *The Death of Ahasuerus*, the first of the Tobias novels, is never identified by name in *The Sibyl*, where he is simply referred to as "the stranger." It is clear from the story he tells, however, that he is the legendary Wandering Jew, supposedly condemned to this fate by Jesus, the Christian "savior" who cursed Ahasuerus for refusing to let him rest against his house on his way to Calvary. Reflecting on the misfortunes this curse has brought upon him, Ahasuerus comes to see the contradiction between the compassionate image of God as Christ and the vengeful malice that this curse of eternal retribution reveals in his nature. As he considers this contradiction in his discussion with the Sibyl—which follows the tale of his misfortunes—he relates it to the paradox of the Crucifixion, about which he has heard many puzzling rumors: "I can't make out either what good it was supposed to do. But I've heard it said that his father wanted him to suffer."

In his questioning of the justice and benevolence of a deity who could treat people in such a vengeful fashion as he has treated the Wandering Jew, and who is apparently so jealous of the forces of evil loose in the world that he would send down a son to recapture those who had rejected him, Ahasuerus is posing questions which are at the heart of Lagerkvist's dualistic view of the world, questions which are echoed by the dwarf, by Barabbas, and by the protagonists of all of his subsequent novels.

Whatever the challenges and difficulties presented to the reader by the aesthetic values that inform his work, Lagerkvist has, for many readers, successfully challenged the dominant mode of psychological realism in modern literature. In restoring the symbolic, mythic function to modern literature through the example of his own work, he has no doubt provided inspiration for many others.

Steven E. Colburn

OTHER MAJOR WORKS

SHORT FICTION: *Två sagor om livet*, 1913; *Järn och människor*, 1915; *Onda sagor*, 1924; *Kämpande ande*, 1930; *I den tiden*, 1935; *The Eternal Smile and Other Stories*, 1954; *The Marriage Feast and Other Stories*, 1955; *Prosa I-V*, 1956; *The Eternal Smile: Three Stories*, 1971.

PLAYS: *Sista mänskan*, pb. 1917; *Den svåra stunden*, pr., pb. 1918 (*The Difficult Hour, I-III*, 1966); *Himlens hemlighet*, pb. 1919 (*The Secret of Heaven*, 1966); *Den osynlige*, pb. 1923; *Han som fick leva om sitt liv*, pr., pb. 1928 (*The Man Who Lived His Life Over*, 1971); *Konungen*, pb. 1932 (*The King*, 1966); *Bödeln*, pb. 1933 (adaptation of his novella; *The Hangman*, 1966); *Mannen utan själ*, pb. 1936 (*The Man Without a Soul*, 1944); *Seger i mörker*, pb. 1939; *Midsommardröm i fattighuset*, pr., pb. 1941 (*Midsummer Dream in the Workhouse*, 1953); *De vises sten*, pb. 1947 (*The Philosopher's Stone*, 1966); *Låt människan leva*, pr., pb. 1949 (*Let Man Live*, 1951); *Barabbas*, pr., pb. 1953 (adaptation of his novel); *Dramatik*, pb. 1956.

POETRY: *Ångest*, 1916; *Den lyckliges väg*, 1921; *Hjärtats sånger*, 1926; *Vid lägereld*, 1932; *Genius*, 1937; *Sång och strid*, 1940; *Dikter*, 1941; *Hemmet och stjärnan*, 1942; *Aftonland*, 1953 (*Evening Land*, 1975).

NONFICTION: *Ordkonst och bildkonst*, 1913 (*Literary Art and Pictorial Art*, 1982); *Teater*, 1918; "Modern teater: Synpunkter och angrepp," 1918 ("Modern Theatre: Points of View and Attack," 1966); *Det besegrade livet*, 1927; *Den knutna näven*, 1934 (*The Clenched Fist*, 1982); *Den befriade människan*, 1939; *Antecknat*, 1977.

MISCELLANEOUS: *Motiv*, 1914 (poetry, essays, and prose sketches); *Kaos*, 1919 (poetry and the play *The Secret of Heaven*); *Modern Theatre: Seven Plays and an Essay*, 1966.

BIBLIOGRAPHY

Gustafson, Alrik. *A History of Swedish Literature.* Minneapolis: University of Minnesota Press, 1961. Contains a useful introduction to Lagerkvist.

Ryberg, Anders. *Pär Lagerkvist in Translation: A Bibliography.* Stockholm: Bonniers, 1964. Still a useful guide to Lagerkvist in English.

Scobbie, Irene. *Pär Lagerkvist: An Introduction.* Stockholm: Senska Institute, 1963. Competent discussion of the major work.

Sjoberg, Leif. *Pär Lagerkvist.* New York: Columbia University Press, 1976. A long biographical and critical essay. Includes a helpful bibliography.

Spector, Robert Donald. *Pär Lagerkvist.* New York: Twayne, 1973. Concentrates on short fiction and major novels: *Barabbas, The Sibyl, Herod and Mariamne,* and Lagerkvist's trilogy. Includes chronology, notes, and bibliography.

Weathers, Winston. *Pär Lagerkvist: A Critical Essay.* Grand Rapids, Mich.: William B. Eerdmans, 1968. Emphasizes Christian themes and is divided into chapters on "The Secular World," "God, Christ, and the Church," "The Limited Resurrection," and "The Holy Land." With a brief bibliography.

White, Ray Lewis. *Pär Lagerkvist in America.* Atlantic Highlands, N.J.: Humanities Press, 1979. Chapters on *The Dwarf, Barabbas, The Eternal Smile and Other Stories, The Sibyl, The Death of Ahasuerus, Pilgrim at Sea, The Holy Land,* and *Herod and Mariamne.* In his introduction, White gives a succinct account of the reviews and the reception of Lagerkvist in America. Includes a bibliography of books in English about Pär Lagerkvist.

SELMA LAGERLÖF

Born: Mårbacka, Sweden; November 20, 1858
Died: Mårbacka, Sweden; March 16, 1940

PRINCIPAL LONG FICTION

Gösta Berlings saga, 1891 (*The Story of Gösta Berling*, 1898; also as *Gösta Berling's Saga*, 1918)

Antikrists mirakler, 1897 (*The Miracles of Antichrist*, 1899)

Jerusalem I: I Dalarne, 1901 (*Jerusalem*, 1915)

Jerusalem II: I det heliga landet, 1902 (*The Holy City: Jerusalem II*, 1918)

Herr Arnes penningar, 1904 (*The Treasure*, 1925)

En saga om en saga, 1908 (*The Girl from the Marshcroft*, 1910)

Liljecronas hem, 1911 (*Liliecrona's Home*, 1914)

Körkarlen, 1912

Kejsaren av Portugallien, 1914 (*The Emperor of Portugallia*, 1916)

Bannlyst, 1918 (*The Outcast*, 1922)

Löwensköldska ringen, 1925 (*The General's Ring*, 1928)

Charlotte Löwensköld, 1925 (English translation, 1928)

Anna Svärd, 1928 (English translation, 1928)

Löwensköldska ringen, 1925-1928 (collective title for previous 3 novels; *The Ring of the Löwenskölds: A Trilogy*, 1928)

Höst, 1933 (*Harvest*, 1935)

OTHER LITERARY FORMS

Selma Lagerlöf's first novel, *Gösta Berling's Saga*, is a cycle of stories with a common setting and a shared cast of characters; short stories, particularly tales drawn from oral traditions of her native Värmland, are Lagerlöf's most characteristic form. Lagerlöf published several volumes of stories, and two of her works, *The Treasure* and the trilogy *The Ring of the Löwenskölds*, could be classified as tales. Two of Lagerlöf's major story collections, *Osynliga länkar* (1894; *Invisible Links*, 1899) and *Drottningar i Kungahälla* (1899; *From a Swedish Homestead*, 1901; also in *The Queens of Kungahälla and Other Sketches*, 1917), followed the publication of her first novel. In *Invisible Links*, Lagerlöf relies on plots from Swedish folk legends. *The Queens of Kungahälla* is based on the Norwegian royal sagas—the *Heimskringla* (twelfth century) and others—which record the careers and legends of medieval Scandinavian kings. Lagerlöf has presented these well-known stories from the point of view of the women in them.

Lagerlöf is also the author of the classic of Swedish children's literature, *Nils Holgerssons underbara resa genom Sverige* (1906-1907; *The Wonderful Adventures of Nils*, 1907; *The Further Adventures of Nils*, 1911). Commissioned by the National Teachers' Association of Sweden, this work was "to present in story form the geography, folklore, flora and fauna of the various Swedish provinces." Lagerlöf chose to do that through a story of a lazy and mischievous boy who is brought down to size by elves he has troubled. Nils becomes acquainted with a barnyard goose, much larger than he, and the two join a migrating flock of wild geese, Nils traveling on the gander's back.

Lagerlöf's *Kristuslegender* (1904; *Christ Legends*, 1908), although not explicitly a children's book, has had a worldwide response from children. Clemence Dane once called this work "the truest Christmas book of all." The simple, compassionate stories of Christ's life are described as if they might be ordinary neighborhood occurrences. The Christmas season is central to many of Lagerlöf's stories and novels. Of the eleven stories in *Christ Legends*, seven of them deal with Christ's birth and childhood.

In 1915, Lagerlöf wrote a volume of short stories entitled *Troll och människor* and completed a second volume of the same title in 1921. The subjects of most of these tales are drawn from Värmland lore. In 1920, Lagerlöf wrote a book-length biography of Zachris Topelius, the Finnish poet who had been a major influence on the author's literary development.

Several of Lagerlöf's later works are autobiographical, among them her memoirs, which are collected in the three so-called Mårbacka volumes: *Mårbacka* (1922; English translation, 1924), *Ett barns memoarner* (1930; *Memories of My Childhood*, 1934), and *Dagbok, Mårbacka III* (1932; *The Diary of Selma Lagerlöf*, 1936). *Liliecrona's Home*, Lagerlöf's novel published in 1911, also has an autobiographical basis.

ACHIEVEMENTS

Lagerlöf spent years searching for the right poetic form in which to present the stories that became *Gösta Berling's Saga*. In an age dominated by Henrik Ibsen, August Strindberg, and other realists whose

(The Nobel Foundation)

plays and novels were strongly naturalistic and often addressed current social issues, Lagerlöf found her own artistic energies frustrated. She did try writing for a time in a realistic style and, for many years, conceived of all of her works as poems. Her talent, however, was not to be realized as a debater of contemporary problems, nor was she to become an explorer of psychological consciousness. Rather, Lagerlöf yearned to express what she believed were the heroic, elemental, and spiritual strains running through daily life. Thomas Carlyle's *On Heroes, Hero-Worship, and the Heroic in History* (1841) gave her a sense of what was to become the epic fairy-tale atmosphere so characteristic of her mature work. In contrast to her contemporaries, many of whom examined their characters' psychological sensibilities in elaborate and often painful detail, Lagerlöf created characters marked by tragedy, sorrow, and joy, but who move through their lives with a stately dignity given to them by an author who, as a matter of decorum and aesthetic choice, does not violate a character's privacy.

With the appearance of her first book, Lagerlöf's distinctly unmodern aesthetic, perhaps more at home in the ninth century than the nineteenth, was warmly received by her countrymen, who, time and time again, communicated to her their gratitude that she expressed her subject matter in a mode entirely absent from contemporary literature.

In 1909, the Swedish Academy awarded to her the Nobel Prize in Literature, commending her noble idealism, the richness of her imagination, and the generosity and beauty of forms that characterize her work. She was the first woman to win the prize. In characteristic fashion, her speech to the Nobel Commission took the form of a story: of a journey she made to Heaven to tell her father about winning the prize. In the course of this address, Lagerlöf reviewed the several influences that had kindled her imagination, particularly honoring the "old country folk" who had taught her "to cast the glamour of poetry over grim rocks and grey waters." Five years later, Selma Lagerlöf became the first woman to be elected to the Swedish Academy. Her works are widely translated.

BIOGRAPHY

Selma Ottiliana Lovisa Lagerlöf was born on November 20, 1858, at Mårbacka in Värmland, Sweden. Her parents, both members of aristocratic families, had moved to the estate of Mårbacka after Selma's father, Lieutenant Erik Gustav Lagerlöf, had failed to inherit the important post of Regimental Paymaster from his father. Lieutenant Lagerlöf became a gentleman farmer with many progressive ideas, few of which proved practical. Lack of success at farming seemed relatively unimportant to the Lieutenant, who, according to various memoirs, was a true son of the gay-hearted Värmland gentry. Among other celebrations held at Mårbacka, Lieutenant Lagerlöf's annual birthday party, enlivened by pageants, theatricals, poetry recitations, dancing, and singing, became a social affair famous throughout the province. Adolph Noreen, later a noted philologist, attended

some of these holiday affairs at Mårbacka and remembers how Lieutenant Lagerlöf, in his office as host, made everyone feel "what an unspeakable happiness [it was] just to live!" Selma herself, as her fiction widely attests, shared this exuberant perspective. Her father's character plays a part in her creation of the cavaliers in *Gösta Berling's Saga*.

As a child, the future writer was more aware of such doings than other children because she was more observer than participant. At the age of four, the little girl had been stricken by a paralysis that left her lame, although she regained the ability to walk. The special care dictated by her condition allowed her to ripen her natural inclination for intellectual and imaginative pursuits. Lagerlöf later noted that the greatest sorrow of her childhood came with the death of her grandmother, who, as she remembered, had told her stories "from morning until evening." Other family members, particularly a sister of Lagerlöf's father, were also gifted storytellers.

Tales told from memory and read aloud at night—from local legend, from Hans Christian Andersen, and from Scandinavian sagas—were the essence of Selma Lagerlöf's early education; neither she nor her sister attended school. By early adolescence, Lagerlöf had determined that she would be a writer. During the next several years, she wrote novels, plays, and poems. In 1880, she attracted the notice of Eva Fryxell, a young author of the day, when she read an occasional poem at a friend's wedding. Despite Fryxell's sponsorship, Lagerlöf failed to place any of her work in literary journals. Fryxell encouraged the girl to broaden her education, a plan to which Lagerlöf eagerly subscribed. After a year's preparation at Sjöberg's Lyceum in Stockholm, Lagerlöf entered a teachers' college. During her years of training there, the idea of cavaliers living at a manor house, the germ of what was to become *Gösta Berling's Saga*, first came to her. It was to be ten years before it attained final form.

In 1885, Selma Lagerlöf began a career as a teacher at a high school for girls at Landskrona. According to students' reports, Lagerlöf was an unusually gifted teacher. She taught school for ten years, during which time she wrote several stories which became part of *Gösta Berling's Saga*. In 1888, three years after her father's death, Mårbacka was sold. It was while she was at the homestead, watching her childhood home and family heirlooms sold, that she finally realized that her story of the cavaliers should be told in a series of tales. With the five chapters she had completed by July of 1890, Lagerlöf won a competition sponsored by the women's paper *Idun*. She finished *Gösta Berling's Saga* by December of 1891, and it was published. While sales in Sweden were at first sluggish, the Danish version attracted the attention of the Danish critic and literary historian Georg Brandes, who immediately recognized it as a work of genius. His critical acclaim won widespread recognition for the book. By the time the second Swedish edition appeared, in 1895, recognition had come to Lagerlöf from all quarters.

In 1895 and 1896, Lagerlöf visited Italy, Switzerland, Germany, and Belgium, supported by a Royal Traveling Scholarship. Her visit to Sicily provided inspiration for *The Miracles of Antichrist*. Other travels followed. Of particular importance was Lagerlöf's journey to the East, partly in response to her desire to learn about a group of peasants from Dalecarlia who had immigrated to the Holy Land in pursuit of a fundamentalist Christian vision. While in Palestine, Lagerlöf gathered material for the second volume of *Jerusalem*, the plot of which is based on the Dalecarlian colony.

Lagerlöf's growing reputation as a writer never discouraged her from offering her talents in support of causes in which she believed. In June, 1911, she delivered a speech before the World Congress on Women's Suffrage; during World War I, she gave her full support to relief work; and after the war, she wrote on behalf of the Red Cross.

After Lagerlöf was awarded the Nobel Prize in 1909, nearly all other literary honors offered in Sweden were awarded to her. The income associated with her success allowed her to repurchase the estate of Mårbacka, to which she moved with her mother. Until Lagerlöf's death in 1940, she oversaw the estate, entertained admirers and visitors from all over Europe and America, and sustained a large correspondence. She died at Mårbacka on March 16, 1940.

ANALYSIS

Although Selma Lagerlöf wrote many distinguished novels, her countrymen have always considered the first to be her masterpiece. Whatever other merits later novels have—and they are more sophisticated in plot construction and theme—none compares to *Gösta Berling's Saga* for sheer concentration of vitality and idealism. The paeans of praise to Värmland's landscape and the detailed knowledge of Sweden's natural history, hallmarks of Lagerlöf's prose style, first appear here.

GÖSTA BERLING'S SAGA

As in later novels, the narrative voice in *Gösta Berling's Saga* is more prominent than those of the characters. The narrator is a storyteller; the raconteur never fades unobtrusively into the background. A reader knows that he or she is but a listener: The teller will make the story and say what it signifies. Characters do not, as in more realistic fiction, resemble living persons with lives of their own; rather, they are like marionettes, pulled up to their feet to dance only when the storyteller commands. One would never speculate about what a Lagerlöf character might be thinking when that character is not in the immediate scene. Characters, because they are so fully bound to the scenes in which they appear, simply do not exist when they are not "onstage." In Lagerlöf's novels, an air of reality surrounds the story but not the individual characters in it. In turn, the reader must listen, accept as final what information the narrator provides, and, above all, agree to be entertained.

The opening scene of *Gösta Berling's Saga* is characteristic of Lagerlöf's epic sweep, her comic tone, and, particularly, her eccentric character portraits. Gösta Berling, a young pastor, mounts the pulpit and pauses momentarily for inspiration, giving his congregation time to notice his exquisite features. His voice grows rich and strong as his images of God's glories ring through the chancel. At sermon's end, he has convinced the visiting bishop of his extraordinary merit; Gösta's triumph is particularly notable because on the previous Sunday he was not in church, nor was he there for many Sundays before that—each time he had been too drunk to preach.

This day appears to be his redemption. One of Gösta's overzealous drinking companions, however—fearing that the bishop might still dismiss Gösta—takes the bishop on a carriage ride over ditches and half-plowed fields, counting on physical coercion to accomplish what the brilliant sermon may have fallen short of accomplishing. Hearing of his friend's misplaced loyalty, Gösta despairs of his future as a preacher and runs away. When next seen, he is stealing a sled loaded with grain from a child in another village.

In Lagerlöf's novels, human destiny is prey to violent turns of the sort Gösta's takes; the sheer speed with which a woman loses her beauty or a pastor becomes a derelict gives the work the flavor of fairy tale or allegory. This is particularly true in this first novel, in which Lagerlöf was finding a style suitable to her Carlylean vision. Later novels possess a greater aura of realism but operate essentially upon the same premises.

Gösta is rescued by the Mistress of Ekeby, the pipe-smoking, gracious, and powerful owner of seven mines and hostess to a group of pensioners. She makes Gösta one of her cavaliers. (This situation is based on an actual custom prevalent in Sweden after the Napoleonic Wars, when families on the great estates often did take in war veterans who had little to do. They were given room and board in exchange for their appearance at social functions in the district. A cavalier was expected to sing, dance, or be socially charming in some other way.)

Although the novel does have a plot of sorts, the power of the story is primarily its ability to render the life at the manor houses of a Sweden which was vanishing during Lagerlöf's childhood. The beautifully embellished descriptions of great balls and sleigh rides suggest a nostalgic longing for a life more elegant in manner and more mythic in perception than that of later eras.

The main body of *Gösta Berling's Saga* loosely centers on Gösta's reformation as he endures his humbled station as a pensioner. Gösta, "the strongest and weakest of men," is the center of provincial society, winning the affection of four of the district's loveliest women. The gentle influence of these good women and the subtler chastening of the Almighty lead Gösta from his impetuous youth to the verge of maturity.

The *Bildungsroman* begins on Christmas Eve, when the cavaliers—Gösta signing for them—make a pact with Sintram, a jealous blacksmith who comes to the cavaliers disguised as the Devil. Sintram's predictions of doom are realized when the cavaliers take over the estate, bringing it to the brink of ruin through their wild dissipations and neglect of the industries. In turn, the district is blighted; unemployment, drunkenness, and general stagnation reign. In the novel's terms, God's Storm Year breaks over the countryside.

Nearly every main character—most are treated in separate vignettes—suffers a life-changing tragedy or loss, and these events represent a kind of spiritual cleansing. In the end, Sintram is arrested, and the Mistress of Ekeby returns home to die.

The thirty-six chapters of the book divide roughly into three sections. The first is dominated by Gösta's love affairs and the prosperous days the cavaliers enjoy before Ekeby slides toward destruction. The second section, centered on the sorrowful fate of the Countess Elizabeth, records the ongoing brilliant exploits of the cavaliers against scenes of impending doom. The cavaliers are in the background in the third section, which features great crowd scenes, emphasizing the desperate plight of the people during the year of devastation. This desolate course is altered at last by the noble Lennaert, who gives his life to defend a group of children and women. In the end, the chastened Mistress of Ekeby dies peacefully, and Gösta sets forth with his new wife to rebuild the district's fortunes.

In *Gösta Berling's Saga*, as in all of Selma Lagerlöf's novels, dramatic scenes of daily life give way to mythical, epic moments or insights. Neither mode prevails for long, and it is the tension between them that is the hallmark of Lagerlöf's style in this early novel. No event, however small, is conceived apart from the metaphysical claim that God's Storm Year has broken over the land. The morality implicit in such an idea emanates with epic force from natural causes—wind, storms, ice, and blizzard—and from the lake, invoked by the narrator as the district's guardian muse. Handsome Gösta is little more than a human embodiment of the same idea.

JERUSALEM

In the two-part novel *Jerusalem*, Lagerlöf employs another native Swedish setting but peoples it with sober, pious Dalecarlian peasants, profoundly unlike their lighthearted counterparts from Värmland. In their ability to see visions and interpret dreams, and in their earnest regard for life, the Dalecarlians resemble Old Testament Hebrews. While it is the narrator in *Gösta Berling's Saga* who gives voice to mythical and epic components at work, in *Jerusalem* it is the characters themselves. Many have the power to see from one world into the other, and they pass easily between the two. The point of view in this novel is more specifically religious but is as undoctrinaire and humane as the one in *Gösta Berling's Saga*.

The first book opens as Ingmar Ingarsson is plowing his fields, engaged in contemplation. His farm is prosperous and the activity salutary, but Ingmar has much on his mind. Several years before, Ingmar's fiancée, Brita, troubled because the wedding she never wanted had been postponed until "after the christening," ran away, gave birth to a child, and strangled it. After years in prison, she is due to be released, and Ingmar must decide if he will meet her. After "deliberating" with his dead father and making a conscious decision not to meet her, Ingmar nevertheless brings Brita home, and the two share a long, happy life. Ingmar and Brita's children become the central subjects of the second half of the first volume.

Even while Ingmar is still living, various fundamentalist religious sects spring up within the district. Efforts are made to counteract the movement, but to little avail. Hellgum, the husband of one of the Ingarsson daughters, forms one communal society. Another daughter is convinced to join when a paralysis she has suffered is miraculously cured as her little daughter is about to wander into a fire. In a scene reminiscent of the God's Storm Year motif from *Gösta Berling's Saga*, a cataclysmic storm, known as the Wild Hunt, breaks over the district one night, convincing many doubters to join the sect.

The group of believers, to the great sorrow of their families, decides to go to Jerusalem to live in closer concord with their beliefs. The departure of the group breaks up the community, splits homes, and parts lovers. One of the most powerful scenes is the final one in the first volume, in which the train of pilgrims sets forth, leaving their ancestral homes. Lagerlöf said she modeled this portion of the story on the Scandinavian sagas; the profound attachment to the soil and the determination visible in the lives of the simple farmers are depicted in heroic terms.

THE HOLY CITY

Volume 2, *The Holy City*, is set primarily in Jerusalem. It opens with an imaginary dialogue between the Dome of the Rock and the Holy Sepulchre, which summarizes the long history of the country that was once fertile and flowering and now is barren, that once was a religious center for many religions and now is cruelly divided between competing religious factions. Much of this book is devoted to a history of the colonists, who eventually reach a deeper understanding of their purpose in Jerusalem when young Ingmar arrives and encourages them to take up their old livelihoods. In a scene not unlike the one in which the smithy is fired up and the mill wheels set in motion at Ekeby, the colonists in Jerusalem begin making cloth, shoes, and bread, the wares of their old livelihoods. Ingmar's purpose in traveling to Jerusalem is to rescue his former love, Gertrude, from madness. Like many colonists, Gertrude suffers from fevers, and her desire for rapturous experiences is bound up with delirium. In the end, she and her new fiancé return to Sweden with Ingmar, where Ingmar is reunited with his estranged wife.

In the Jerusalem books, Lagerlöf's fictional treatment of the fundamentalist ideas which divide the Dalecarlian community is a balanced one. While the most compelling scenes are set in Sweden, not Jerusalem, the sympathy Lagerlöf creates for the fervent pilgrims is considerable. In the trilogy of her maturity, *The Ring of the Löwenskölds*, she attempts with less success to achieve the same tone of compelling objectivity.

THE RING OF THE LÖWENSKÖLDS

The General's Ring, the first novel of the Löwenskölds trilogy, is a ghost story, generically similar to Lagerlöf's novella *The Treasure* but less violent. This tale traces the fate of a ring given to the district hero by Charles XII and stolen from his grave by a simple country farm couple. Disaster follows immediately: The couple's house burns and they lose all their possessions. Nevertheless, they are afraid to return the ring, and it passes to the next generation. Three men who find a former owner dead in the woods are accused of his murder. Although they are innocent and pass an ordeal to prove it, they are all put to death. Unknown to them, the ring was sewn into a cap that one of the men picked up in the woods near the dead man's body. A young servant girl eventually frees the Löwenskölds from the curse.

This first part, the shortest segment of the trilogy, is a story replete with fairy-tale motifs and repetitions. It ends with a romantic and comic moment. After the servant girl saves the young master of the house from the general's ghost by returning the ring to the general's grave, the two seem destined for each other. Yet when the girl appears in the baron's room to receive his thanks, she learns that he is engaged to another. She herself is relatively untroubled by this turn of events and continues to serve the household for years. In a rather unbelievable twist of plot, her daughter, Thea Sundler, emerges in the sequel books to take revenge on later generations of Löwenskölds. This tenuous connection is all that links *The General's Ring* to the later books of the trilogy, which are among Lagerlöf's finer realistic novels.

The whole of *Charlotte Löwensköld* and the first two-thirds of *Anna Svärd* form a compelling story of a young minister and the two women he courts. The final third of *Anna Svärd* reverts from realism to the fairy-tale tone that opens the trilogy. When the storyteller attributes Thea Sundler's jealousy of Charlotte Löwensköld and Anna Svärd to the ring's curse, the realistic development of the novel is broken. To achieve this unity with the first book, Lagerlöf systematically dismantles characters, sending them into the final pages as two-dimensional versions of themselves. Anna disappears from view to reappear in a single scene in which we are to believe she has forgotten what she learned during hard years of experi-

ence; Charlotte lingers, but her character is of little consequence.

Such narrative oddities serve to point up the fact that, although Lagerlöf wrote "novels," she was preeminently a teller of tales. Her plot structures are simple ones, based on reversals of fate and the characters' growing awareness of the larger cosmic design against which all human events play. Lagerlöf's strengths as a novelist are most obvious in the openings and development of her works. She is unmatched at setting a scene; there, the storyteller finds her natural medium. She creates in the reader the sense that he or she is present at an oral rendition of the story. Each chapter begins afresh, as if the storyteller has been out for air and has returned to address a band of eager listeners. Her confidence allows her to risk a long, pregnant suspension. The introductory material might be a scrap of folk philosophy pertinent to the tale, a description of a landscape, or a bantering dialogue between narrator and an imaginary audience.

After such a lead, the action typically springs forward, the author weaving into an unforgettable spectacle precise descriptions of housewares, blossoming hedges, or the contents of a peddler's pack. Information about a character and his or her motives is invariably sketchier. In *Charlotte Löwensköld*, for example, one chapter is devoted to the preparations the manorial staff make for the arrival of Schagerström and Charlotte on their wedding day. Floors are scrubbed, great arches of flowers are braided and hung along the road, and the manor folk, dressed in costumes appropriate to their trades, line the pathway to cheer the new bride. Yet for all the attention devoted to the advent of Charlotte's tenure as mistress of Schagerström's manor, the theme is never mentioned again. Characters may be at the heart of the action in one scene but may then disappear with little ado; likewise, a scene may be drawn with an exactitude that commands the reader's attention but may have little to do with the direction of the plot. To a modern novelist, this shuttling of characters in and out, combined with the care taken to create lavish background scenes for their own sakes, is an eccentric narrative habit. As noted, this aesthetic is defined by the persona of the omniscient storyteller. She and she alone determines what belongs to the story. Motives are revealed as the narrator sees fit; otherwise, the reader has no access to them.

Something of Lagerlöf's development as a novelist can be understood by comparing Gösta Berling and Karl Arthur Ekenstedt. Despite the titles *Charlotte Löwensköld* and *Anna Svärd*, the two novels are primarily the story of Karl Arthur Ekenstedt. Charlotte is his fiancée for five years and Anna Svärd is his wife; Thea Sundler is his confidante and later his illicit companion. Karl Arthur's mother, the Baroness, is the fourth woman whose life is interwoven with Karl Arthur's.

In many ways, Karl Arthur is a more realistic Gösta Berling. The four women in his life are interwoven throughout the story and are not simply a string of romantic attachments, as Gösta's women are. While Karl Arthur has a more believable biography, he is neither as lovable nor as intrinsically capable of reform as is Gösta. Ekenstedt's characterization embodies a mature and realistic version of a theme touched on only lightly in *Gösta Berling's Saga*. In the early novel, it is primarily a comic invention to have Gösta appear as a drunken preacher. Once he runs from his parish, Gösta's spiritual life is left behind, simply a passing stage of his youth. On the other hand, in Lagerlöf's more realistically conceived later work, Karl Arthur's concept of religion and his identity as a pietist are given a much larger part, and Lagerlöf, the most devout and optimistic of novelists, treats this theme both seriously and severely.

Karl Arthur Ekenstedt is a Löwensköld, a distant cousin to Charlotte. He is the youngest of three children, the apple of his mother's eye. Because she is the Baroness, the most popular woman in the district, outshining her daughters in all ways, her adoration of Karl Arthur becomes a district affair. Everyone knows that Karl Arthur is off at the university taking Latin examinations or preparing for this or that degree. In fact, he is an ordinary boy, utterly spoiled by his mother's attentions. His extreme handsomeness, like Gösta's, attracts others to him, particularly women. While carrying out a mediocre study pro-

gram at the university, Karl Arthur becomes acquainted with a young pietist who initiates him into the religion of austerity. Because Karl Arthur is unable to succeed in other ways, he determines to become a man of God. In subsequent years, his destructive jealousies, fired by a religious fanaticism, become the cover for his own weakness and also threaten to destroy others. Like Gösta, Karl Arthur is a gifted preacher under certain inspirations. More often, however, he is confused and quick to believe that he must reform those near him in order to become more devout and thus more popular.

Despite his family's position and the possibility of acquiring a prestigious parish, Karl Arthur is content to remain at the deanery as curate. While there, he meets Charlotte, who is companion to the dean and his wife. Although Charlotte is amused by Karl Arthur's pietism, they become friends and Karl Arthur proposes. Five years pass, and Karl Arthur has made no attempt to take his career in hand. Not knowing that Charlotte is engaged, a wealthy gentleman from the countryside asks for Charlotte's hand. Charlotte, a spirited and loyal woman, refuses him. When Karl Arthur hears about the proposal, he remembers a single occasion when Charlotte suggested that he might try to find a post of his own, and he is furious at the thought. He uses what he terms Charlotte's "ambition" as an excuse for breaking with her, and she attempts to bring about a reconciliation. After Charlotte offers to accompany him to the poorest parish and to live in a humble hut, Karl Arthur is calmed, but a jealous thought sends him swiftly out the door, vowing that he will marry the first woman he sees.

Karl Arthur tells himself that he is submitting completely to God's will, but once out on the road, he begins to regret his rash vow. The moment is one of Lagerlöf's most comic. The woman Karl Arthur meets is (to his great relief) a pretty Dalecarlian peasant girl, Anna Svärd, unschooled in the ways of the gentry but a skillful peddler woman, both bright and goodhearted—an acceptable alternative to Charlotte. Meanwhile, Karl Arthur's fierce jealousy of Charlotte and his overweening pride are both encouraged by Thea Sundler, wife of the church organist. Thea, who is herself in love with Karl Arthur, manages to convince him that Charlotte is unfaithful to him.

In the opening pages of *Anna Svärd*, Lagerlöf delineates life in the northern village where Anna lives, and the segment is as sympathetic and beautifully drawn as that describing Charlotte's life among the gentry. Lagerlöf lavishes scene after scene on Anna's wedding preparations, her acquisition of manners fitting to a minister's wife, and her innocent adoration of her handsome fiancé in the south. Great plans are made for the wedding, which Anna's uncle, a man of some means, will provide. Anna is believed to be favored above all peasant women; she will have "horse and cow, manservant and maidservant."

Karl Arthur has something quite different in mind. He arrives in the village one day, insisting that the marriage take place immediately, without ceremony. As the bailiff's wife quickly perceives, Karl Arthur is looking for a wife who *is* both manservant and maidservant. Anna, too stunned and too enamored of Karl Arthur to protest, sets off with him. Anna arrives at her new home to find that it is no more than a hut refurbished for the couple by Thea Sundler. To help keep Karl Arthur true to his pietist ways, Thea has prepared a comfortable couch for Karl Arthur in his study and a narrow cot for Anna in the kitchen. As she will do many times over the next several years, Anna outwits Thea and has her wedding bed. Years later, however, after Karl Arthur has callously ignored her feelings again and again, Anna finally leaves him. Karl Arthur himself, his preaching not going well, determines that God wants him to be out on the road preaching to the traveling folk, so he decides to take God's Word to the markets and fairs.

At this point, the novel loses its realistic foundation. Thea runs away to follow Karl Arthur, and the two become derelicts of the road; Anna, pregnant with Karl Arthur's child, finds a group of ten orphans, adopts them, and buys a farm with money from Karl Arthur's parents. Charlotte has long since married the country gentleman whose proposal she rejected when she was engaged to Karl Arthur.

Karl Arthur's pietism is equivalent to weakness of character. His absorption in himself, disguised as an ongoing search for God's way, is brilliantly portrayed and satirized. His is a more complex portrait than

Gösta Berling's. At the depth of his misfortune, Karl Arthur says, "I hate mankind"—given his behavior, an apt and honest summation. Lagerlöf's description is sure and revealing. In the end, however, the narrator does not take her theme to a fittingly dismal conclusion. She attempts in the last chapters to thread Karl Arthur's tragedy and the deaths of other Löwensköld barons back to the ring's curse. The portrayal of a flawed man surrounded by good women is finally more memorable than the cursed ring motif; nevertheless, it is typical of the storyteller's mode not to wish any of her characters ill. In the final scene, Karl Arthur is planning to go to Africa to preach. Anna goes to church to hear him make his appeal and, recalling her youthful love, drops her wedding ring into the collection plate. The novel closes as Karl Arthur arrives at Anna's door, the storyteller asking, "How shall she answer him?"

In characteristic Lagerlöf style, then, the story resolves itself with a suggestion of enlightenment and joy. In this case, the ending and much of the narrative are also comic. Lagerlöf's use of comedy bypasses her more serious themes rather than bringing them to a resolution. Even so, *Charlotte Löwensköld* and *Anna Svärd* are Lagerlöf's masterworks of character portrayal; they have been favorably compared to those of Jane Austen.

Helen Mundy Hudson

OTHER MAJOR WORKS

SHORT FICTION: *Osynliga länkar*, 1894 (*Invisible Links*, 1899); *Drottningar i Kungahälla*, 1899 (*From a Swedish Homestead*, 1901; also in *The Queens of Kungahälla and Other Sketches*, 1917); *Kristuslegender*, 1904 (*Christ Legends*, 1908); *Troll och människor*, 1915, 1921 (2 volumes).

NONFICTION: *Zachris Topelius*, 1920; *Mårbacka*, 1922 (English translation, 1924); *Ett barns memoarner*, 1930 (*Memories of My Childhood*, 1934); *Dagbok, Mårbacka III*, 1932 (*The Diary of Selma Lagerlöf*, 1936).

CHILDREN'S LITERATURE: *Nils Holgerssons underbara resa genom Sverige*, 1906-1907 (2 volumes; *The Wonderful Adventures of Nils*, 1907, and *The Further Adventures of Nils*, 1911).

BIBLIOGRAPHY

Berendsohn, Walter A. *Selma Lagerlöf: Her Life and Work*. London: Ivor Nicholson & Watson, 1931. An early study still valuable for situating Lagerlöf in her homeland and ancestry. Berendsohn explains the development of *Gösta Berling's Saga* and Lagerlöf's handling of folklore and legend.

Edstrom, Vivi. *Selma Lagerlöf*. Boston: Twayne, 1984. An introductory study offering chapters of "biographical perspective," discussions of Lagerlöf's stories and short novels, the novels of the 1910's, the Löwensköld trilogy, and Lagerlöf and the role of the writer. Includes chronology, notes, and bibliography.

Gustafson, Alrik. *A History of Swedish Literature*. Minneapolis: University of Minnesota Press, 1961. Still cited as a classic introduction to Lagerlöf.

_____. *Six Scandinavian Novelists*. Princeton, N.J.: Princeton University Press, 1971. An expanded and more wide-ranging discussion than Gustafson's essay in *A History of Swedish Literature*.

Johannesson, Eric O. "Isak Dinesen and Selma Lagerlöf." *Scandinavian Studies* 32 (1960): 18-26. A succinct comparison of two great novelists.

Lagerroth, Erland. "The Narrative Art of Selma Lagerlöf: Two Problems." *Scandinavian Studies* 33 (1961): 10-17. One of the few discussions in English of Lagerlöf's narrative technique.

Olson-Buckner, Elsa. *The Epic Tradition in "Gösta Berling's Saga."* New York: Theodore Gans, 1979. An in-depth study.

Popp, Danie, and E. C. Barksdale. "Selma Lagerlöf: The Taleteller's Fugues." *Scandinavian Studies* 53 (1981): 405-412. A good discussion of structural principles in Lagerlöf's fiction.

LOUIS L'AMOUR

Born: Jamestown, North Dakota; March 22, 1908
Died: Los Angeles, California; June 10, 1988

PRINCIPAL LONG FICTION

Westward the Tide, 1950
Hondo, 1953
Sitka, 1957
Last Stand at Papago Wells, 1957
The First Fast Draw, 1959
The Daybreakers, 1960
Sackett, 1961
Shalako, 1962
Lando, 1962
Mojave Crossing, 1964
The Sackett Brand, 1965
The Broken Gun, 1966
Mustang Man, 1966
The Sky-Liners, 1967
Down the Long Hills, 1968
The Lonely Men, 1969
The Man Called Noon, 1970
Galloway, 1970
North to the Rails, 1971
Ride the Dark Trail, 1972
Treasure Mountain, 1972
The Ferguson Rifle, 1973
The Man from Skibbereen, 1973
Sackett's Land, 1974
Rivers West, 1975
The Man from the Broken Hills, 1975
Over on the Dry Side, 1975
To the Far Blue Mountains, 1976
Borden Chantry, 1977
Fair Blows the Wind, 1978
Bendigo Shafter, 1979
The Iron Marshal, 1979
The Warrior's Path, 1980
Lonely on the Mountain, 1980
Comstock Lode, 1981
Milo Talon, 1981
The Cherokee Trail, 1982
The Lonesome Gods, 1983
Ride the River, 1983
Son of a Wanted Man, 1984
The Walking Drum, 1984
Jubal Sackett, 1985
Last of the Breed, 1986
The Haunted Mesa, 1987

OTHER LITERARY FORMS

Although Louis L'Amour has achieved his greatest success as a Western novelist, he began his career as a writer of short pulp fiction, later assembled in a number of collections. He also wrote some hard-boiled detective stories, and early in his career he issued a book of undistinguished poetry. In 1988, the year of his death, a collection of L'Amour quotations entitled *A Trail of Memories* was issued. The following year saw the publication of *Education of a Wandering Man*, an autobiographical work.

ACHIEVEMENTS

L'Amour was the most phenomenal Western writer America has ever produced. Each of his eighty-five novels, mostly traditional Westerns, has sold at least a million copies; ten of his novels have doubled that figure. His books have been translated into more than a dozen foreign languages. More than thirty of his plots have been made into motion-

(Ken Howard)

picture and television dramas. In 1981, with *Comstock Lode*, L'Amour became a formidable presence in the hardbound-book market; he immediately made the best-seller list; all of his subsequent hardbound novels matched this performance. By 1977, L'Amour had sold fifty million copies of his books. In 1987, the figure was 175 million.

L'Amour also received important awards and honors. He won the Western Writers of America (WWA) Golden Spur Award in 1969 for *Down the Long Hills* and the Western Writers of America Golden Saddleman Award in 1981 for overall achievement and contribution to an understanding of the American West. When, in 1985, the WWA published a list of the twenty-six best Western novels of all time, L'Amour's *Hondo* made the list. In 1982, the United States Congress awarded him a National Gold Medal, and one year later, President Ronald Reagan awarded him the United States Medal of Freedom.

L'Amour was not averse to peddling his own wares. In June of 1980, he cruised the Midwest and the South in a leased luxury bus, meeting fans and selling autographed copies of his seventy-five books then available. He also appeared on television to promote his Louis L'Amour Collection of novels. His publisher (Bantam Books) offered L'Amour calendars, audiotape dramas (multivoiced, with sound effects) of certain L'Amour stories, and an audio-cassette of their star author's personal reminiscences.

BIOGRAPHY

Louis L'Amour was born Louis Dearborn LaMoore in Jamestown, North Dakota, on March 22, 1908, into a rugged, French-Irish pioneering family. His father, Louis Charles LaMoore, reared by his paternal grandparents in Ontario, was a veterinarian, a Jamestown police chief, and a civic leader. The novelist's mother, Emily, whose father was a Civil War veteran and an Indian fighter, attended the normal school at St. Cloud, Minnesota, and married L. C. LaMoore in 1892. Louis was the youngest of the couple's seven children, four of whom survived to distinguished maturity.

After a healthy early boyhood of outdoor activity and voracious reading, L'Amour moved in 1923 with his family to Oklahoma but soon struck out on his own. An incredible sequence of knockabout jobs followed: sailor, longshoreman, lumberjack, boxer, circus worker, cattle skinner, fruit picker, hay shocker, miner, friend of bandits in China, book reviewer in Oklahoma, lecturer there and in Texas, neophyte writer, and a United States Army tank-destroyer and transportation officer in World War II in France and Germany.

In 1946, L'Amour decided to live in Los Angeles and became a professional writer. Some of his short-story pulps and slicks into the mid-1950's were under the pen names Tex Burns and Jim Mayo. A turning point for L'Amour came with the publication of "The Gift of Cochise" in *Collier's*, the story which formed the basis for *Hondo* a year later. This was not, however, L'Amour's first Western novel, which was the competent *Westward the Tide*, published in London in 1950.

The biography of Louis L'Amour from 1953 onward is largely an account of one popular success after another, adaptations of his plots to the screen, fine efforts at versatility in a career which too many regard as merely capitalizing on the formulaic Western, and steady personal happiness.

With the publication of *Night over the Solomons* (a collection of old prewar stories) in 1986, L'Amour saw his one-hundredth book into print. Of the many films made from his fiction, the most notable are *Hondo* (1953), *The Burning Hills* (1956), *Apache Territory* (1958), *Heller in Pink Tights* (1960), *Shalako* (1968), and *Catlow* (1971). The best television adaptation from L'Amour fiction was called *The Sacketts* (based on *The Daybreakers* and *Sackett*), which first aired in 1979. Beginning in 1960, L'Amour started the first of three family sagas, novels in multiple numbers featuring generations of families. *The Daybreakers* opened the ongoing Sackett saga, which by 1986 had grown to eighteen volumes. The 1971 publication of *North to the Rails* began another ongoing series, the Chantry family series. In 1975, *Rivers West* began the Talon family sequence.

Abetting L'Amour was the former Kathy Adams, who relinquished her career as an actress to marry him in a gala 1956 ceremony at the Los Angeles

Beverly Hilton. In the 1960's, she bore him a daughter, Angelique, and then a son, Beau, and she served as his business manager, informal editor, and chauffeur. L'Amour wrote early in the morning, six hours a day, seven days a week, combining this spartan routine with tough afternoon workouts using a punching bag and weights. Throughout his long career, he lectured and traveled widely and personally scouted locales to make his work more authentic. L'Amour died in Los Angeles in 1988.

ANALYSIS

Louis L'Amour will be remembered for his action-filled Western novels, especially his family sagas. He is appreciated by readers from all walks of life who want to follow the exploits and suffering of heroic men, attractive and dutiful women, and manifestly evil villains, in exciting, well-knit plots, against a backdrop of accurately painted scenery. L'Amour extols the old American virtues of patriotism, respect for the land, go-it-alone courage, stoicism, and family loyalty. He offers his updated vision of the Old West as the locus of increasingly endangered humankind's last, best hope.

Critics should not look to L'Amour for aesthetic subtleties. His unvaried boast was that he was an old-fashioned storyteller of the sort that sits by a campfire after a hard day's work and spins his tales in a straightforward manner. He did not worry, then, about critics who categorized Western fiction into formulaic narratives, romantic-historical reconstructions, or historical reconstructions. Such critics would probably define his *Hondo* as formulaic, his *Sitka* as romantic-historical, and nothing he wrote as genuinely historical (though he meticulously researched *The Walking Drum*, for example). In addition, critics complain to no avail when they claim that L'Amour's slapdash, unrevised writing betrays compositional errors by the gross.

L'Amour was pleased to be put in the same company as James Fenimore Cooper, Honoré de Balzac, Émile Zola, Jules Romains, and William Faulkner. L'Amour's Tell Sackett bears comparison with Cooper's Natty Bumppo. L'Amour follows Balzac's habit of creating reappearing characters who help produce both unified, multivolumed fiction and loyal readers. The hero of L'Amour's *Shalako*, between wars in Paris, meets Zola, whose Rougon-Macquart cycle may have inspired L'Amour to build his Sackett/ Chantry/Talon series. Romains employed historical figures, real events, and even specific dates to augment the verisimilitude of his monumental *Men of Good Will* (1932-1946); L'Amour, to be sure, deals with three centuries of American frontier Sacketts rather than France in a mere quarter century, but he uses Romains-like details in doing so. Moreover, Faulkner's love of his native soil, his combination of different races together in weal and woe, his praise of the old virtues of enduring and prevailing, and his construction of interlocked families are echoed in L'Amour's novels.

Since it is impossible to discuss all or even most of L'Amour's fiction, long and short, in a few pages, it seems best to concentrate on several salient titles, which illustrate his peaks of accomplishment, and also to consider his monumental three-family saga. In "Ride, You Tonto Raiders!" (*New Western Magazine*, August 6, 1949; reprinted in *Law of the Desert Born*, 1983), L'Amour prophetically introduced many of his books' most typical features. The broad-shouldered hero is a hard-bitten adventurer with a military, cosmopolitan, cattleman background, and he is now a gunslinger. He kills a bad man in Texas, then delivers the victim's money to his sweet widow and small son. She owns some Arizona land and is aided but also jeopardized by an assortment of L'Amouresque types: rich man, gunslinger, bumbling lawman, codger, literary drunk, Europe-trained pianist, loyal ranch hand, half-breed, and Hispanic. Other ingredients include surrogate fatherhood, dawning love for a red-haired heroine, the taking of the law into one's own hands, berserker fighting lust, hidden documents, place-names aplenty, the dating of the action by reference to historical events, cinematic alternation of close-up and wide-angle lens scenes, the use of key words (especially "alone," "eye," "home," "land," "patience," "shoulder," "silence," and "trouble"), and compositional infelicities. In short, this story is a fine introduction to L'Amour and, in addition, incidentally prefigures *Hondo*.

Hondo

Hondo remains L'Amour's best Western. It features a typical loner hero, torn between moving on and settling down. It is datable and placeable: Hondo Lane scouts for General George Crook in the Arizona of 1874. Hondo cannot quickly woo and win the fetchingly home-loving heroine, not only because he killed her husband but also because Vittorio's Apaches grab and torture him. Hondo is half in favor of the white people's progress and half in love with violence in Apacheria; similarly, L'Amour mediates between the twentieth century and starker, earlier American epochs.

Last Stand at Papago Wells

Last Stand at Papago Wells has an unusually complex set of narrative lines, neatly converging at a desert well and featuring a gallery of characters in varied movement: hero heading west, couple eloping, outraged father of bride-to-be in hot pursuit, survivor of party butchered by Apaches, near-rape victim, frustrated Apaches and two of their chronic enemies, posse remnants, fat woman with heavy saddlebags (is she hiding gold?), and rogue Apache-Yaquis circling and then attacking the forted-up well occupants.

Sitka

Sitka is L'Amour's first big romantic-historical novel and has a refreshingly different setting. It concerns the Alaska Purchase, features real-life figures such as Secretary of the Treasury Robert Walker and Russian Ambassador Édouard de Stoeckl, and moves scenically from Pennsylvania to the Far West to Pacific Ocean waters (even to Russia)—Jean LaBarge, the hero, is L'Amour's first important fictional sailor—and up by Jean's wheat-laden schooner to Sitka, Alaska. L'Amour charmingly delays an indispensable love affair by having stalwart Jean be smitten by a beautiful Russian princess who is demurely wed to a nice old Russian count, whose greasy enemy, another Russian, is Jean's enemy as well. Toward the end of *Sitka*, the plot takes on comic-book coloration, with interludes in Czar Alexander II's court, Washington, D.C., Siberia, and a Sitka prison.

The First Fast Draw

The First Fast Draw never deserved its best-selling celebrity. It is supposedly based on the well-documented life of Cullen Montgomery Baker, the infamous Texas gunman whose bloody career got its impetus from Texas Governor Edmund Davis's vicious Reconstruction laws. L'Amour includes so many other real-life characters and events that naïve readers may think they are reading a historical reconstruction—but this is not so. L'Amour ignores the real Baker's first two marriages, his Quantrill-like antiblack and anti-Union army conduct, and even his death in 1869. L'Amour was enamored enough of thug Baker to shove him tangentially into five later books.

THE SACKETT NOVELS

The Daybreakers is the first volume of L'Amour's tremendous, million-word Sackett sequence. It introduces the most famous Sacketts. They are five Tennessee-born brothers: William Tell, Orrin, Tyrel, Bob, and Joe Sackett. An 1866 feud with the evil Higgins family, during which a Higgins kills Orrin's fiancée and is hastily gunned down by narrator Tyrel, obliges both brothers to head out. They go west to gather wild cattle, in spite of dramatic adversities, along the Santa Fe Trail. Once in New Mexico, Orrin marries disastrously: His vicious wife is the daughter of a dishonest and anti-Hispanic politician and land grabber from New England. Tyrel, on the other hand, while on the trail is taught to read by an ex-army officer who later turns alcoholic, jealous, and lethal; Tyrel becomes the gun-handy marshal of Mora and marries a lovely heiress of an old Spanish land grant there. Orrin and Tyrel send for their widowed Ma and younger brothers Bob and Joe. The plot is energized by much violence, though not involving offstage Tell Sackett; having fought in the Civil War, he is now campaigning against the Sioux in the Northwest and is soon to leave Montana for Mora. (Incidentally, Tell was first presented in the story "Booty for a Bad Man," *Saturday Evening Post*, July 30, 1960; reprinted in *War Party*, 1975.) Even while writing much else, L'Amour continued his narrative of these Sackett brothers in six more novels, which, not in order of publication (1961 to 1980) but in chronological order of events (1867 through 1878 or so), are *Lonely on the Mountain*, *Sackett*, *Mojave Crossing*, *The Sackett Brand*, *The Lonely Men*, and *Treasure Mountain*.

During this time, L'Amour was turning his Sackett clock back more than two centuries. In 1974, he published *Sackett's Land*, which introduces Barnabas Sackett of the Welsh fenlands, in 1599. The first of the Sackett dynasty, he and his wife Abigail, daughter of an Elizabethan sea captain, generate a wild brood in the Carolinas: sons Kin Ring, Brian, Yance, and Jubal Sackett, and daughter Noelle Sackett. In the later novels, the three brothers, Kin, Yance, and Jubal (in *To the Far Blue Mountains*, *The Warrior's Path*, and *Jubal Sackett*, respectively), are shown to be different, and their stories shift from the Eastern seaboard, New England, and the Caribbean to the Far West, and advance to the year 1630 or so. In 1983 came *Ride the River*, which tells how a feisty Tennessee girl named Echo Sackett (destined to become the aunt of Tell and his brothers) ventures to Philadelphia to claim an inheritance as Kin Sackett's youngest descendant and gets it home again.

L'Amour wrote six other Sackett novels (*Lando*, *Mustang Man*, *The Sky-Liners*, *Galloway*, *Ride the Dark Trail*, and *The Man from the Broken Hills*), which star a dusty array of cousins of Tell and his brothers and bring in still more Sacketts. These cousins, from different parts of Tennessee, Arizona, and New Mexico, include Lando, twins Logan and Nolan, brothers Flagan and Galloway, and Parmalee. The action, ranging through the Southwest and into Mexico, may be dated 1867-1878.

There are about sixty Sacketts in the ambitious Sackett sequence, amid a gallery of more than 750 characters in all. The Chantry/Talon novels, less expansive than the Sackett saga, are usually independent of it but occasionally connect with it. They may be most sensibly read in the chronological order of events narrated. *Fair Blows the Wind* concerns a swashbuckling, Rafael Sabatini-like hero-narrator called Tatton Chantry (not his real name, L'Amour oddly insists), in the very late sixteenth century, in Ireland, England, Spain, France, the southern colonies in America, and back to Ireland. *The Ferguson Rifle* tells about a Chantry named Ronan, in the newly acquired lands of the Louisiana Purchase. The picaresque *Rivers West* introduces an early Talon (in the year 1821). He is Jean, hinted to be a descendant of legendary Talon the Claw, a rich old pirate of the glorious Gaspé Peninsula. Western rivers take ambitious builder, lover-manqué Jean Talon to the Louisiana Purchase regions roamed by Ronan Chantry. Enter scholarly, verbose, often violent Owen Chantry in *Over on the Dry Side*, searching in Utah (1866) for his lost brother Clive (dead) and a reputed treasure (really a historical manuscript). The next Talon segment stars Milo Talon, one of Tell Sackett's countless cousins, in *Milo Talon*, a detective story fashioned largely from earlier Western mystery novels by L'Amour, specifically *The Man Called Noon, The Man from Skibbereen*, and *The Iron Marshal*, but rendered weird by ridiculous plot improbabilities. Milo does nothing for L'Amour's Talon saga. Then, in 1977, came *Borden Chantry*, perhaps his best Western mystery, because it is direct and gripping. Cleverly, L'Amour makes the victim in the puzzle Joe Sackett, who is the long-unmentioned younger brother of Tell and Tyrell and whose mysterious murder in Colorado (c. 1882) Borden Chantry, storm-ruined cattleman turned town marshal, must solve—or else Tyrel Sackett, who gallops in, will take the law into his own rough hands. The unexceptional *North to the Rails* already featured Borden Chantry's East-softened son Tom and reported that the father had been murdered about 1890, before the action starts, after which young Tom elects to drive cattle from Cimarron, near Santa Fe, north to a railhead for transport east. Obstacles to the hero in his *rites de passage* are varied and absorbing, but the novel is marred by much silliness and an improbable villainess.

As early as 1974, in his preface to *Sackett's Land*, L'Amour informed his public of plans to tell the epic of the American frontier through the westward movement of generations of three families, in forty or so novels. In 1981, he added that he had traced his Sacketts back to the fifteenth century and planned ten more Sackett, five more Chantry, and five more Talon books; further, that his Talons are builders, his Chantrys, educated statesmen, and his Sacketts, frontiersmen. (It has already been seen that L'Amour's practice has often blurred his theoretical distinctions.) Finally, in 1983, the author explained that he

saw his three families as periodically linking and splitting. Two examples, in addition to what has already been noted are: In *Ride the River* may be found strong but spoiled Dorian Chantry, whom his splendid old uncle, Philadelphia lawyer Finian Chantry, orders to help heroine Echo Sackett; in the popular but flawed *Son of a Wanted Man*, Borden Chantry is revived and joins forces with Tyrell Sackett in gunning for law and order.

Brief mention may be made of seven of L'Amour's best works, simply to suggest his versatility and undiminished professional ambition. They are *The Broken Gun, Down the Long Hills, Bendigo Shafter, The Cherokee Trail, The Lonesome Gods, The Walking Drum*, and *Last of the Breed*.

THE BROKEN GUN, DOWN THE LONG HILLS, and BENDIGO SHAFTER

The Broken Gun offers a brilliant translation of nineteenth century Western ingredients—rugged hero, mysterious murder, Hispanic friend, admirable lawman, land-hungry villains, sweet heroine, and villainess—all into twentieth century terms. In addition, the protagonist, a combat veteran and a writer, is partly autobiographical. *Down the Long Hills* is unique in L'Amour's canon: It has strict Aristotelian unities and features a seven-year-old hero saving a three-year-old girl from an assortment of dangers, in a diagrammable plot of villains avoided and rescuers frustrated. *Bendigo Shafter* is L'Amour's classic Western blockbuster—in balanced, numbered thirds, nicely structured, and huge. The admirable hero-narrator describes the establishment in Wyoming's South Pass region (starting about 1862) of a Western community whose inhabitants represent everything from saintly to depraved, young and old, married and single, gauche and nubile. Nearby are Indians good and evil, and assorted white renegades. Nature here can be cruel but rewards those who surrender to its potent beauty. Notable are the hero's return to the East and meeting Horace Greeley there; his rejuvenating visit to the sacred Indian Medicine Wheel in the Big Horns; and L'Amour's skillful depiction of nineteen varied females.

THE CHEROKEE TRAIL and THE LONESOME GODS

The Cherokee Trail also dramatizes assorted

women's activities: A young widow takes over the management of a Colorado stagecoach station, protects a daughter and an Irish maid there, and has a rich rancher's spoiled daughters for neighbors nearby. *The Lonesome Gods* is epic in its sweep, with a varied plot and such bizarre effects as a disowning, the attempted murder of a little boy, gigantism, an uncannily svelte heroine with an unnecessary Russian background, a wild stallion, ghostly visitations, and—best of all—the loneliness of sad, patient gods in need of human adoration.

THE WALKING DRUM

The Walking Drum, L'Amour's most ambitious novel, is a sprawling, episodic romp from Brittany through Europe to the Black Sea and beyond, in the years 1176-1180, starring an impossibly talented hero. He is Mathurin Kerbouchard, sailor, horseman, fighter, scientist, magician, caravan merchant, linguist, scholar, and lover. It must be added at once that L'Amour, in days of depraved adult Westerns, is restraint itself: He limns no torrid love scenes on either side of any ocean. In addition, his violence is never offered in splashes of current cinematic gore.

LAST OF THE BREED

Finally, *Last of the Breed*, another innovative effort, is nothing less than an eastern Siberian Western, cast in contemporary times (Mikhail S. Gorbachev is mentioned). Pitted are a Sioux-Cheyenne United States Air Force superpilot and squabbling Soviet secret police. It has the most elaborately detailed escape since *The Count of Monte-Cristo* (1844-1845) by Alexandre Dumas, *père:* here, from a prison camp east of Lake Baikal. Though crafted with care, this novel smacks of the film character Rambo, most of its more than forty characters have hard-to-remember names, the pages are dotted with twice that number of place names, and the hero's success depends on protracted good luck. Sympathetic readers will accept his exploits, however, because they accept the true hero of the novel—hauntingly rendered Siberia.

Louis L'Amour's two most admirable traits were his troubadour wizardry as a narrator and his profound love of Mother Nature and American derring-do. His late-career ambition to broaden his fictive scope, while admirable, can never diminish the sig-nificance of what will probably remain his most lasting contribution—namely, his best Westerns, among which the Sackett saga retains a high place. It is certainly to those works that one can attribute his immense popularity.

Robert L. Gale

OTHER MAJOR WORKS

SHORT FICTION: *War Party*, 1975; *Bowdrie*, 1983; *The Hills of Homicide*, 1983; *Law of the Desert Born*, 1983; *Riding for the Brand*, 1986; *The Rider of the Ruby Hills*, 1986; *Night over the Solomons*, 1986; *The Outlaws of Mesquite*, 1990.

POETRY: *Smoke from This Altar*, 1939.

NONFICTION: *Frontier*, 1984 (with photographs by David Muench); *A Trail of Memories: The Quotations of Louis L'Amour*, 1988; *Education of a Wandering Man*, 1989.

BIBLIOGRAPHY

Gale, Robert L. *Louis L'Amour*. Rev. ed. Boston: Twayne, 1992. Investigates L'Amour as a phenomenon who outsells all competitors with fiction that is low on sex and violence and high on patriotism and family. After sketching L'Amour's life, Gale surveys the range of his fiction from formulaic narrative to historical reconstruction. Presents a chronological perspective on his many novels, which were standard formulas with variations, written to satisfy public demand, from *Westward the Tide* in 1950 to *The Walking Drum* in 1984. Examines in detail the seventeen novels following the Sackett family's adventures, with special attention given to the best five. L'Amour is compared (unfavorably) with predecessors such as James Fenimore Cooper and William Faulkner. Evaluates his strengths (scenic description and character variety) and weaknesses (narrative structure, stereotypes, and clichés). Includes a chronology, notes and references, a selected, annotated bibliography, and an index.

Marsden, Michael T. "The Concept of the Family in the Fiction of Louis L'Amour." *North Dakota Quarterly* 46 (Summer, 1978): 12-21. Claims that the concept of the family is a unifying theme in

L'Amour's work and his commercial success in America. The Sacketts show how a family can retain its civilized values even when repeatedly uprooted and transplanted in migrations. Although some of L'Amour's heroes are loners, they always act for the good of society in a search for family. The Sacketts, the Talons, and the Chantrys are family groups analyzed in terms of their regions of settlement and the four concepts which make up the family in a L'Amour novel: the Male Principle, the Female Principle, the Hearth (of the Focused Family), and the Family Unit (the Enlarged Family).

_____. "Louis L'Amour (1908-)." In *Fifty Western Writers: A Bio-Bibliographical Sourcebook*, edited by Fred Erisman and Richard Etulain. Westport, Conn.: Greenwood Press, 1982. Explains L'Amour's reception of a congressional gold medallion, sketches his biography, and outlines his major themes. L'Amour emphasizes the importance of history, evoked through descriptions of landscape, and the concept of the family, which provides narrative structure and texture. His treatment of women is sensitive but inconsistent, as he changed his characterizations in response to pressures for women's rights. Other concerns of L'Amour are the environment, the purgatorial value of violence, and the plight of the Indian. Calls for more critical attention for L'Amour and other popular Western writers, and ends with a bibliography of his works and a list of the few critical studies which have been made of them.

_____. "The Modern Western." In *The American Literary West*, edited by Richard W. Etulain. Manhattan, Kans.: Sunflower University Press, 1980. Sets L'Amour's fiction in the tradition of the American Western novels and films. Despite tendencies of the genre since World War II to insist on accuracy of psychology and history, L'Amour continues to emphasize innocence and individual courage as ideals of the old West for modern imitation. Because he thinks of himself as a storyteller in the oral tradition, his novels can best be read aloud, one of the reasons for his suc-cess. Another is the strong family ties, expressed through the tales of the Sacketts, the Talons, and the Chantrys. L'Amour continues to write in the spirit of idealism, even as his genre is attacked and changed by many modern revisionists.

Nesbitt, John D. "Change of Purpose in the Novels of Louis L'Amour." *Western American Literature* 13 (Spring, 1978): 65-81. Reprinted in *Critical Essays on the Western American Novel*, edited by William T. Pilkington. Boston: G. K. Hall, 1980. There were three changes in the moral and historical purpose of L'Amour's writing in his career. In the first phase (1953 to the late 1950's), he wrote stories of naked violence and advocated conventional morality. His middle phase (late 1950's to the early 1970's) included more than half of his sixty or so novels, which contain either heroes who meet women who walk beside, not behind, them or heroic gentlemen who have been to Europe. In his late phase (1974-1975), L'Amour is chronicler of the movement west and apologist for the settlement of the West, as his heroes become more temperate in character and in their means of solving problems.

_____. "Louis L'Amour: Papier-Mâché Homer?" *South Dakota Review* 19 (Autumn, 1981): 37-48. Criticizes L'Amour's Homeric claims as a maker of epics, a product of advertising which critics have taken seriously. Insists on judging him by the literary tradition of well-crafted narratives, concluding that L'Amour is not rich or deep in vision or method. As he attempted to make his work more serious, he padded his lean narratives with thin philosophy, moralizing, and historical details, but his story remained the same: A superior white man overcomes adversity, wins a virtuous woman, and settles into a community. His compositions and character motivations contain little complexity, but are still valuable for studying Western American literature and showing how popular literature can achieve popular versions of the epic.

Weinberg, Robert E. *The Louis L'Amour Companion*. Kansas City: Andrews and McMeel, 1992. A good guide to the writer's works. Essential for students of L'Amour.

MARGARET LAURENCE

Born: Neepawa, Manitoba, Canada; July 18, 1926
Died: Lakefield, Ontario, Canada; January 5, 1987

PRINCIPAL LONG FICTION

This Side Jordan, 1960
The Stone Angel, 1964
A Jest of God, 1966
The Fire-Dwellers, 1969
The Diviners, 1974

OTHER LITERARY FORMS

Margaret Laurence published two short-story collections, *The Tomorrow-Tamer* (1963) and *A Bird in the House* (1970), and two children's books, *Jason's Quest* (1970) and *The Christmas Birthday Story* (1980). She also produced a translation of Somali folktales and poems, *A Tree for Poverty: Somali Poetry and Prose* (1954); a travelogue, *The Prophet's Camel Bell* (1963); and a study of Nigerian novelists and playwrights, *Long Drums and Cannons: Nigerian Dramatists and Novelists, 1952-1966* (1968). A collection of her essays, *Heart of a Stranger*, appeared in 1976. Because of her work on Nigerian fiction and drama, she is well known to students of African literature.

ACHIEVEMENTS

From the beginning of her writing career, Laurence received much popular and critical recognition. *This Side Jordan* won the Beta Sigma Phi prize for a first novel by a Canadian; *The Stone Angel* received both critical and popular acclaim; *A Jest of God* was awarded the Governor General's Medal in 1966 and was adapted for motion pictures as *Rachel, Rachel; The Diviners*, despite less than universal critical acclaim, was at the top of the best-seller list for more than sixty consecutive weeks. Along with her popularity, Laurence enjoyed an international reputation as a consistently accomplished fiction writer. Her special contribution to the novel was recognized by Jack McClelland of the Canadian publishing house of McClelland and Stewart when he first read

This Side Jordan. The stories that were gathered in *The Tomorrow-Tamer* and *A Bird in the House* originally appeared separately in such Canadian, American, and British journals as *Prism, The Atlantic Monthly*, and *Queen's Quarterly*. Laurence also won respect as a lecturer and critic. United College, University of Winnipeg, made her an Honorary Fellow, the first woman and the youngest to be so honored. She received honorary degrees from McMaster, Dalhousie, Trent, University of Toronto, and Carleton University and served as writer-in-residence at several Canadian universities. Her works have been translated into French, German, Italian, Spanish, Dutch, Norwegian, Danish, and Swedish.

BIOGRAPHY

Margaret Laurence was born Jean Margaret Wemyss on July 18, 1926, in Neepawa, Manitoba. Laurence's mother's family was of Irish descent and her father's Scottish. Although she was separated from the "old country" on both sides by at least two generations, her early memories, like those of Vanessa MacLeod in the short stories in *A Bird in the House* and of Morag Gunn in *The Diviners*, are of a proud and lively Scottish ancestry.

When Laurence was four, her mother died, and her aunt, Margaret Simpson, left a respected teaching career in Calgary and went home to care for her niece. A year later, she and Robert Wemyss were married. They had one son, Robert, born only two years before his father died of pneumonia. In 1938, Margaret Simpson Wemyss took the two children and moved in with her father, the owner of a furniture store. This domestic situation in slightly altered form provides the setting for the Vanessa MacLeod stories in *A Bird in the House*. Laurence lived in Grandfather Simpson's house until she went to United College, University of Winnipeg, in 1944.

John Simpson was a fierce and autocratic man of eighty-two when his widowed daughter and her two children moved in with him. Laurence resented his authority over her and her stepmother; this relationship fostered Laurence's empathy with women struggling toward freedom. All of her heroines—Hagar

Shipley, Rachel Cameron, Vanessa MacLeod, Stacey MacAindra, and Morag Gunn—struggle against oppressive forces, and Laurence's recurring theme of the lack of communication between men and women, as well as between women and women, is rooted in the domestic situation in Grandfather Simpson's house. It appears in her first novel, *This Side Jordan*, as the problem between the colonialists and the Africans, between husbands and wives, and between relatives. At the beginning of her last novel, *The Diviners*, the problem of communication—searching for the right words—is a major frustration that Morag, the protagonist, faces as a writer.

The encouragement and honest criticism given to Laurence by her stepmother were a great help to the girl, who started writing at an early age. At United College, she took honors in English, while her involvement with "The Winnipeg Old Left" during and after her college years reflected her dedication to social reform. Social awareness—the realization that men and women are constrained by social structures and exploit and are exploited by others through these systems—developed from her awareness that the hopes of her parents' generation had been crushed by the Depression and that her own generation's prospects were altered radically by World War II. After she was graduated, she worked for one year as a reporter for the *Winnipeg Citizen*. Her experience covering the local labor news consolidated her social and political convictions and advanced theoretical problems to personal ones.

In 1948, Laurence married Jack Laurence, a civil engineer from the University of Manitoba. They left Canada for England in 1949 and went to the British Protectorate of Somaliland in 1950, where he was in charge of a dam-building project. In 1952, they moved to the Gold Coast, now Ghana, where they lived until 1957. A daughter, Jocelyn, was born when they were on leave in England in 1952, and a son, David, was born in Ghana in 1955. Out of these African years came several early works, including *The Tomorrow-Tamer, This Side Jordan*, the translations of folktales, and the travel journal *The Prophet's Camel Bell*. Of the last, Laurence said that it was the most difficult work she ever wrote because it was not

fiction. The importance of this work lies in its theme—the growth in self-knowledge and humility in an alien environment. During the years in Africa, Laurence read the Pentateuch for the first time, and these books of the Bible became a touchstone for her, especially pertinent to the African works and to a lesser extent to her Manawaka fiction. Here she developed the patience and discipline of a professional writer.

In 1962, Laurence and her children left Jack Laurence in Vancouver and moved to London. They remained in England until 1968, when Laurence returned to Canada to be writer-in-residence at Massey College, University of Toronto. She was affiliated with several other Canadian universities in the years that followed. In 1987, Laurence died in Lakefield, Ontario.

ANALYSIS

The major emphasis of Margaret Laurence's fiction changed considerably between her early and later works. In a 1969 article in *Canadian Literature*, "Ten Years' Sentences," she notes that after she had grown out of her obsession with the nature of freedom, the theme of the African writings and *The Stone Angel*, her concern "had changed to that of survival, the attempt of the personality to survive with some dignity, toting the load of excess mental baggage that everyone carries. . . ." In the same article, she remarks that she became increasingly involved with novels of character, that her viewpoint altered from modified optimism to modified pessimism, and that she had become more concerned with form in writing.

The more profound psychological realism of her later novels developed after a general awareness of the intractable problems of emerging African nations had matured both the Africans and their observers. The characters in the African works were products of a now dated optimism which forced them into preconceived molds. The later novels reveal modified pessimism, but their vitality comes from Laurence's developing concern with psychological realism, which authenticates the characters and their voices. After *This Side Jordan*, the point of view is consistently in the first person, the protagonist's, and is strictly limited to the protagonist's consciousness. Although Hagar in *The Stone Angel* and Stacey in *The Fire-Dwellers* are stereotypes, a stubborn old lady and a frantic middle-aged housewife, Laurence makes them both compelling protagonists through accurate psychological portrayals.

A theme of major importance which Laurence did not fully develop until *The Diviners* is the nature of language. Rachel's concern with name calling in *A Jest of God* anticipates the larger exploration in *The Fire-Dwellers*, in which Laurence experiments with a variety of voices, using language in a variety of ways. Exterior voices, many of them bizarre, interrupt and are interrupted by Stacey's inner voices—her monologues, her memories of voices from the past, her challenges, threats, and prayers to God. The exterior voices include radio and television news, snatches of her children's conversations, the characteristic dialects of various socioeconomic groups, the half-truthful promotions of her husband's company, and the meaningfully unfinished conversations between her and her husband. In order to allow language to be discussed explicitly, Laurence makes the protagonist of *The Diviners* a novelist.

In her first three novels Laurence uses biblical allusions to provide a mythic framework for a psychological study of character and situation. All these allusions are from the Old Testament, which made a lasting impression on her when she read it for the first time in Africa. The names she chooses for the characters in the early fiction—Adamo, Jacob, Abraham, Nathaniel, Joshua, Hagar, Ishmael, and Rachel—provide readymade dilemmas whose traditional solutions appear contrived and psychologically unrealistic. In *This Side Jordan*, Joshua's Ghanian father proclaims that his son will cross the Jordan into the Promised Land, confidently assumed to be both an independent, prosperous Ghana and a Christian heaven. These allusions contribute to the sacramental overtones in the early works, particularly at the end of *The Stone Angel*.

Biblical myth is replaced in *A Bird in the House* and *The Diviners* by the myths of Scottish immigrants and Canadian pioneers and Indians. Vanessa in

A Bird in the House lives with the sentimentally mythologized memories of her grandparents. The dispossessed Scots and the dispossessed Metis Indians provide a personal mythology for young Morag Gunn in *The Diviners*, which her foster father, Christie Logan, embellishes to give the orphan girl an identity. Christie himself becomes mythologized in the mind of Morag's daughter Pique. The theme of the search for one's true origins plays a prominent part throughout Laurence's fiction, but the issues become increasingly complex. Whereas a clear dichotomy between his Christian and African backgrounds divides Nathaniel Amegbe in *This Side Jordan*, Morag in *The Diviners*, a recognized novelist who was an orphan brought up by a garbage collector, is seriously perplexed by the bases of her identity. Nathaniel hopes for, and apparently receives, both worldly and spiritual rewards in a successful if simplistic reconciliation of his dual heritage. In contrast, Morag painfully learns to reject the heroic Scottish ancestress Christie had invented for her without rejecting him; she realizes that she has invented a hopelessly confused web of self-fabricated personal myth which she has to reconcile with her Canadian roots in her search for self-identity.

Throughout all her works, Laurence explores themes concerning the role of women, the injustices of sex-role stereotyping, and the inequality of opportunity. The changing roles of women in the late twentieth century are a problem for Morag, who is jealous of her daughter's sexual freedom. Although the protagonists of Laurence's later novels are women—women who have not always been treated well by the men in their lives—men are never treated harshly in her work, even though the point of view is limited to the female protagonist's consciousness. Stacey generously concludes that perhaps her uncommunicative husband is tormented by fears and doubts much like her own. Morag never speculates about Jules Tonnerre's motives—a strange lack of curiosity for a novelist. Although Laurence's protagonists are oppressed, they never simply blame the men in their lives or the male-dominated society for their oppression. Men, almost to a man, are given the benefit of the doubt.

THIS SIDE JORDAN

Laurence's first novel, *This Side Jordan*, was begun in Ghana in 1955, finished in Vancouver, and published in 1960. The setting of the novel is Ghana just before independence. The protagonist, Nathaniel Amegbe, had boarded at a Roman Catholic mission school since he was seven and is now caught between two cultures, between loyalty to the fading memory of tribal customs and loyalty to the Christian mission that educated him and gave him the opportunity to better himself, in a European sense, by teaching in the city. His predicament is balanced by that of Johnnie Kestoe, a newly arrived employee of an English-based export-import firm who is trying to forget his slum-Irish background and to rise in the firm despite his antipathy for Africans. Both men have wives expecting their first child. Many of Nathaniel's dilemmas are resolved in the end, even his fears that his father's soul might be assigned to hell. In part, his resolution results from the salvation metaphor of "crossing the Jordan," a feat he hopes his newborn son will accomplish.

Nathaniel's interior monologues reveal the conflicts his dual loyalties have produced. Laurence uses this device more and more in the ensuing novels, and it culminates in *The Diviners* with its complex narrative techniques. Both Johnnie and Nathaniel move through the novel to a greater realization of self by means of humbling experiences, and both achieve worldly success, a naïvely optimistic conclusion made at the expense of psychological realism.

THE STONE ANGEL

The Stone Angel was published in 1964, two years after Laurence and her children moved to London. Laurence, in "A Place to Stand On" from *Heart of a Stranger*, states that the dominant theme of this novel is survival, "not just physical survival, but the preservation of some human dignity and in the end some human warmth and ability to reach out and touch others." The monument Hagar Shipley's father had built for her mother's tomb in the Manawaka cemetery is a stone angel, gouged out by stonemasons who were accustomed to filling the needs of "fledgling pharaohs in an uncouth land." Laurence's horror at the extravagance of the pharaohs' monuments at Luxor,

recorded in "Good Morning to the Grandson of Rameses the Second" in *Heart of a Stranger*, is similar to her reaction to the material ambitions of the stern Scotch-Irish prairie pioneers.

The story of Hagar Shipley is told in the first person and covers the three weeks before her death, but in these weeks, long flashbacks depict scenes of Hagar's life in chronological order. Laurence gives sacramental overtones to the events of Hagar's last days: She confesses to a most unlikely priest in a deserted cannery over a jug of wine; in the hospital where she dies, she is able to overcome her pride and to enjoy and empathize with her fellow patients; after she accepts a previously despised minister sent by her son, she has an epiphany—"Pride was my wilderness, and the demon that led me there was fear"; and just before her death, she wrests from her daughter-in-law her last drink. Such sacramental overtones are not unusual in Laurence's works, but in her later works they become more subtle and complex than they are here.

Hagar Shipley is an old woman, an enormously fat, physically feeble old woman, grotesque and distorted in both body and spirit. She is mean spirited as well as mean about her money and her possessions—almost a stereotype, an unlikely heroine, certainly not one who would seem to attract the sympathy of the reader. Hagar does, however, attract the reader; the genuineness of her portrayal makes her believable because of her total honesty, and the reader empathizes with her plight, which she finally recognizes as self-made. The reader feels compassion for her in spite of and because of her pettiness. Her voice, even in her old age, is still strong, willful, and vital, and the development of her self-awareness and self-knowledge is gripping.

The Stone Angel is the first work in which Manawaka, Laurence's fictionalized hometown of Neepawa, Manitoba, serves as the childhood setting of the protagonist. She makes Manawaka a microcosmic world, the childhood home of all her later protagonists, whose memories and friends carry over from one work to another. The mythic heritage of Hagar in *The Stone Angel*—the Scotch-Irish pioneers and Metis Indians in Manitoba—is shared by

Vanessa in *A Bird in the House*, Rachel in *A Jest of God*, Stacey in *The Fire-Dwellers*, and Morag in *The Diviners*, although Hagar is old enough to be the grandmother of the other four. Every one of these women leaves Manawaka in a search for identity and spiritual freedom, but none is able to escape her heredity and childhood environment entirely. The effects of environment and heredity were increasingly explored as Laurence became more and more concerned with the nature of identity. The Manawaka setting gave Laurence the opportunity to develop characters whose parents or grandparents engaged in a strenuous battle to open the frontier, founded what they hoped would be dynasties, and lived to see them fall because of the Depression. These stubborn and proud people begot children who had to find their own identities without the visible mansions their parents had built to proclaim theirs. Pride in personal success became in the next generation pride in family and origin, and Hagar's inheritance from her father showed that the strength of the pioneer generation could destroy as well as build. The recognition of the double-edged nature of this strength enables Hagar, a stone angel in her former blindness, to feel at the end some human warmth for those around her.

A JEST OF GOD

A Jest of God was written in Buckinghamshire, England, in 1964 and 1965, and was published the next year. The action takes place during a summer and fall in the 1960's in Manawaka. Laurence creates a woman protagonist learning to break through the entrapments oppressing her.

Only through the first-person point of view could Laurence manage to reenact Rachel Cameron's fearful responses to everything around her and her self-mocking evaluations of her responses; she is afraid even of herself. When she reflects upon the way she thinks, upon her paranoia and her imagination, she warns herself that through her own distortions of reality she will become strange, weird, an outcast. She continues to tell herself that she must stop thinking that way. Her fear about her own responses to ordinary life keeps her in a state near hysteria. Except for the recognizable quality of her perceptions and the color and richness of her imagination, she could in-

deed be dismissed as a stereotyped old-maid schoolteacher, the butt of the town's jokes. She lives with her widowed mother, renting the upper story of her dead father's former funeral parlor.

The mythic framework for the psychological study of Rachel is the Old Testament story in which Rachel is "mourning for her children"—in the novel, the children she has never had. When she is confident enough to love Nick Kazlik, whom she needs more as a father for her children than as a lover, he tells her that he is not God; he cannot solve her problems. Neither he nor the possibility of the child he might give her can overcome her sense of isolation, of which the lack of children is only the symbol; her sense of isolation seems to be based on her lack of spiritual fulfillment, isolation from God. God's word is evaded in the church she and her mother attend, and she is totally horrified by fundamentalist irrationality. In the end, Rachel recognizes her own self-pity to be a horrendous sort of pride, and she starts to learn instead to feel compassion for others because they are as isolated as she.

Rachel's situation could set the stage for a tragedy, but Laurence's heroines do not become tragic. They live through their crises, endure, and in enduring gain strength. Rachel gains strength from the loss of Nick, which she never understands, and from the loss of what she hoped and feared would be Nick's baby. After Rachel has decided not to commit suicide when she thinks she is pregnant, she discovers that what she had thought was a baby was a meaningless tumor, not even malignant—a jest of God. Despite, or perhaps because of, this grotesque anticlimax, Rachel is able to make the decision to leave Manawaka; she applies for and earns a teaching position in Vancouver. At the end, she is traveling with her mother, her "elderly child," to a new life in Vancouver.

THE FIRE-DWELLERS

The Fire-Dwellers was written in England between 1966 and 1968; the protagonist of the novel, Stacey MacAindra, is Rachel Cameron's sister. She is an ordinary woman—a middle-class contemporary housewife in Manawaka, anxious over all the possible and impossible perils waiting for her and her family. She overcomes stereotyping through the recognizable, likable, and spontaneous qualities of her narrative voice. Laurence's narrative technique is more complex in *The Fire-Dwellers* than in any of her earlier works. The first-person narration is fragmented by a variety of interruptions—Stacey's inner voices, snatches of Stacey's memories set to the side of the page, italicized dreams and fantasies, incomplete conversations with Mac, her husband, and radio and television news. At times, she is concentrating so completely on her inner voice that she feels a physical jolt when external reality breaks into her inner fantasies.

The title refers, as Stacey's lover Luke implies, to Stacey: She is the ladybird of the nursery rhyme who must fly away home because her house is on fire and her children will burn. Although Sir James Frazer's *The Golden Bough* (1890-1915) lies unopened beside Stacey's bed at the end of the book, as it did in the beginning, Stacey seems to understand intuitively the explanation of the primitive sexuality of fire. Stacey burns from sexual frustration and fears the burning of an atomic bomb, a threat ever present on the news. Newspaper pictures from Vietnam of a horrified mother trying to remove burning napalm from her baby's face appear again and again in Stacey's mind. Counterpointing the fire metaphor is that of water, here regenerative as well as destructive, which foreshadows its more important position in *The Diviners*.

Unlike the other Manawaka protagonists, Stacey could never be considered grotesque; she considers herself quite ordinary, and, at first glance, most people would agree, despite her apocalyptic fears. The world around her, however, is grotesque. The frightening events in the lives of Stacey's neighbors and friends are counterpointed by the daily news from the Vietnam War. Almost a symbol of Stacey's inability to communicate her fears, her two-year-old, Jen, cannot or will not speak. No wonder Stacey hides her drinks in the Mix-Master. Her interior dialogue convincingly portrays a compassionate woman with a stabilizing sense of humor that makes the limited affirmation of the conclusion believable; Mac and his equally uncommunicative son Duncan are brought together by Duncan's near-death, and Jen speaks her first words: "Hi, Mum. Want tea?"

THE DIVINERS

Laurence worked on *The Diviners* from 1969 to 1973, at the old house she bought on the Otonabee River near Peterborough, Ontario. Unlike the earlier Laurence protagonists, apparently ordinary women, almost stereotypes who turn out to be extraordinary in their own way, Morag Gunn is an extraordinarily gifted writer who has quite ordinary and common concerns. She is also unlike her Manawaka "sisters" in that she is an orphan reared by the town's garbage collector; thus she is an outsider who bears the scorn and taunts of the town's wealthier children such as Stacey Cameron and Vanessa MacLeod. She shares her humble status with the disreputable half-breed Indians, the Tonnerres, and learns the injustice of the inequality of opportunity at first hand.

The title, *The Diviners*, refers explicitly to gifted individuals, artists such as Morag who contribute to a greater understanding of life, as well as to her friend, Royland, a true water diviner. Indeed, Morag discovers that many of her acquaintances are, in some way, themselves diviners. At the end of the book, when Royland tells Morag he has lost the gift of divining, Morag muses, "At least Royland knew he had been a true diviner. . . . The necessity of doing the thing—that mattered."

The Diviners is the longest and the most tightly structured of Laurence's novels; it has three long parts framed by a prologue and epilogue. The plot is commonplace; Morag spends a summer worrying about her eighteen-year-old daughter Pique, who has gone west to "find" herself. In this action, Morag is only an observer, as all mothers must be in this situation. Her own story is enclosed within the action in the present, with chronological flashbacks such as those in *The Stone Angel*. The novel is presented in the first person, but with two new techniques: "Snapshots," meditations on the few snapshots Morag has from her youth; and "Memorybank Movies," Morag's memories from her past. The snapshots cover the lives of her parents, before Morag was born through her early childhood and their deaths. Aware that she embroidered stories about the snapshots as a child, Morag looks at a snapshot, remembers her make-believe story, and then muses, "I don't recall when I invented that one." This comment, early in the novel, establishes the mythologizing of one's past as an important motif.

Morag's future as a writer is foreshadowed by her retelling of Christie Logan's tales when just a girl, adapting them to her own needs. In the prologue, Morag the novelist worries about diction, the choice of the proper words: "How could that colour be caught in words? A sort of rosy peach colour, but that sounded corny and was also inaccurate." Morag uses her hometown for setting and characters, just as Laurence herself does; the theme of where one belongs is as important to Morag as a writer as it is to Laurence.

The title of Morag's second novel, *Prospero's Child*, foreshadows the motif of the end-frame. Royland loses his gift of witching for water and hopes to pass it on to A-Okay Smith. Morag realizes that she will pass on to Pique her gift, just as Christie Logan's manic prophecies influenced her creativity. Among all Laurence's heroines, Morag Gunn is the closest in experience and interests to Laurence herself. Each successive protagonist, from Hagar and Rachel and Vanessa to Stacy, came closer and closer to Laurence's own identity. She said that she realized how difficult it would be to portray a protagonist so much like herself, but *The Diviners* is a risky novel, an ambitious book which only an established writer could afford to produce.

Because Laurence depicts human problems in terms of sex roles, the gender of the characters in the Manawaka novels is particularly important. The women protagonists of all of these novels clearly demonstrate Laurence's persistent investigation of the role of women in society. The sex lives of Laurence's women are fully integrated parts of their identities without becoming obsessive or neurotic. All of her protagonists enjoy their sexuality but, at the same time, suffer guiltily for it. Laurence did not admit a connection with the women's liberation movement. Morag Gunn, however, a single head of a household with an illegitimate dependent child, could not have been as readily accepted and admired before the feminist movement as she was after.

Similarly, although Laurence employs Christian motifs and themes throughout her fiction, she did not embrace institutional Christianity. Like psychologist Carl Jung, Laurence seems to find God in the human soul, defining religion in terms of a Jungian "numinous experience" which can lead to a psychological change. Salvation is redefined as discovery of self, and grace is given to find a new sense of life direction.

Presenting her characters as beings caught between the determinism of history and their free will, as individuals who are torn between body and spirit, fact and illusion, Laurence portrays life as a series of internal crises. Through the development of her protagonists, Laurence celebrates even the crises as she celebrates her protagonists' progress. The search for self involves both the liberation from and the embracing of the past. Survival with dignity and the ability to love, she remarks in *Heart of a Stranger*, are themes inevitable for a writer of her stern Scotch-Irish background. Since these themes are of immense contemporary importance, her works explore problems which have universal appeal, a fact that goes far to explain her tremendous popularity.

Judith Weise

OTHER MAJOR WORKS

SHORT FICTION: *The Tomorrow-Tamer*, 1963; *A Bird in the House*, 1970.

NONFICTION: *The Prophet's Camel Bell*, 1963 (pb. in U.S. as *New Wind in a Dry Land*, 1964); *Long Drums and Cannons: Nigerian Dramatists and Novelists, 1952-1966*, 1968; *Heart of a Stranger*, 1976.

CHILDREN'S LITERATURE: *Jason's Quest*, 1970; *The Christmas Birthday Story*, 1980.

EDITED TEXT: *A Tree for Poverty: Somali Poetry and Prose*, 1954.

BIBLIOGRAPHY

Gunnars, Kristjana, ed. *Crossing the River: Essays in Honour of Margaret Laurence*. Winnipeg, Manitoba: Turnstone Press, 1988. Twelve previously unpublished essays by Canadian and international writers and critics pay tribute to Laurence's life and work. Includes some interesting new insights.

Irvine, Lorna M. *Critical Spaces: Margaret Laurence and Janet Frame*. Columbia, S.C.: Camden House, 1995. Irvine provides chapters on early reviews and critiques, maturing opinions, biographical and critical studies, and the role of politics, gender, and literary study. Includes a detailed bibliography.

Kertzer, J. M. "Margaret Laurence and Her Works." In *Canadian Writers and Their Works: Fiction Series*, edited by Robert Lecker, Jack David, and Ellen Quigley. Toronto: ECW Press, 1987. This study is divided into the four parts, "Laurence's Works" being the longest and most thorough section. Despite its scholarliness, this study's clear style and extensive bibliography make it invaluable.

King, James. *The Life of Margaret Laurence*. Toronto.: A. A. Knopf Canada, 1997. A good, updated biography of the author. Includes bibliographical references and an index.

Riegel, Christian, ed. *The Writing of Margaret Laurence: Challenging Territory*. Edmonton: University of Alberta Press, 1997. Essays on Laurence's African stories, *The Stone Angel* as a feminist confessional novel, *A Bird in the House*, *The Diviners*, *A Jest of God*, *The Fire-Dwellers*, as well as on Laurence's Scotch Presbyterian heritage and other early influences. Includes a bibliography.

Sorfleet, John R., ed. "The Work of Margaret Laurence." *Journal of Canadian Fiction* 27 (1980). This issue, devoted to Laurence, comprises four stories, a letter and an essay by Laurence, and nine essays by Canadian critics on various aspects of her fiction.

Thomas, Clara. *Margaret Laurence*. Canadian Writers 3. Toronto: McClelland and Stewart, 1969. Thomas's admiring assessment of Laurence's writing covers in five chronologically arranged chapters the African books, two Manawaka novels, and some of the stories later collected in *A Bird in the House*. This study is still relevant and Thomas's unadorned style is highly readable. The introduction includes illuminating biographical material, and the selected bibliography is thorough.

Verduyn, Christl, ed. *Margaret Laurence: An Appreciation*. Peterborough, Ontario: Broadview Press, 1988. The eighteen essays in this invaluable book chronicle the evolution of Laurence's vision in both her fiction and the chief social concerns of her life. The essay topics range from studies of her early African-experience stories to Laurence's own address/essay, "My Final Hour," in which she movingly states her commitments as a writer and a person.

Woodcock, George, ed. *A Place to Stand On: Essays By and About Margaret Laurence*. Western Canadian Literary Documents Series 4. Edmonton: NeWest Press, 1983. A thorough, rich exploration of Laurence's craft and works, containing essays by Laurence and various critics published over more than twenty years. The book is highlighted by interviews with Laurence. Also includes a useful bibliography.

D. H. LAWRENCE

Born: Eastwood, Nottinghamshire, England; September 11, 1885
Died: Vence, France; March 2, 1930

PRINCIPAL LONG FICTION

The White Peacock, 1911
The Trespasser, 1912
Sons and Lovers, 1913
The Rainbow, 1915
Women in Love, 1920
The Lost Girl, 1920
Aaron's Rod, 1922
The Ladybird, The Fox, The Captain's Doll, 1923
Kangaroo, 1923
The Boy in the Bush, 1924 (with M. L. Skinner)
The Plumed Serpent, 1926
Lady Chatterley's Lover, 1928
The Escaped Cock, 1929 (best known as *The Man Who Died*)
The Virgin and the Gipsy, 1930
Mr. Noon, 1984 (wr. 1920-1922)

OTHER LITERARY FORMS

D. H. Lawrence was among the most prolific and wide-ranging of modern writers, a fact all the more remarkable considering that he spent so much time on the move, battling chronic tuberculosis, which cut short his life in his forty-fifth year. In addition to his novels, he published more than a dozen books of poetry, collected in *The Complete Poems of D. H. Lawrence* (1964); eight volumes of short fiction, including half a dozen novellas, collected in *The Complete Short Stories of D. H. Lawrence* (1961); and seven plays, collected in *The Complete Plays of D. H. Lawrence* (1965). He also wrote a wide range of nonfiction, including four fine travel books (*Twilight in Italy*, 1916; *Sea and Sardinia*, 1921; *Mornings in Mexico*, 1927; and *Etruscan Places*, 1932). *Movements in European History* (1921), published under the pseudonym Lawrence H. Davison, is a subjective meditation on historical cycles and Europe's decline, while *Psychoanalysis and the Unconscious* (1921) is a highly original and influential volume of literary criticism. Lawrence's religious vision, in the guise of a commentary on the Book of Revelation, is offered in *Apocalypse* (1931). Many other essays on diverse subjects appeared in periodicals during the last two decades of his life and were collected posthumously by Edward McDonald in *Phoenix* (1936), and by Warren Roberts and Harry T. Moore in *Phoenix II* (1968). Lawrence was also a formidable correspondent, and his letters are invaluable aids to understanding the man and the writer. Some 1,257 of the more than 5,500 known letters are available in a collection edited by Harry T. Moore. Several of Lawrence's fictional works—*Sons and Lovers, Lady Chatterley's Lover*, "The Rocking-Horse Winner," *Women in Love*, and *The Virgin and the Gipsy*—have been adapted to the motion picture medium, while his life is the subject of the 1981 film *The Priest of Love*.

ACHIEVEMENTS

The running battle against censorship in which Lawrence engaged throughout most of his career undoubtedly performed a valuable service to subsequent writers and the reading public, though it cost him dearly both emotionally and financially. The es-

(D.C. Public Library)

sentially symbolic role of sexuality in his writing resembles somewhat that found in Walt Whitman's, but Lawrence's more overt treatment of it—liberating as it was to a generation whose Victorian upbringing had been castigated by the Freudians—led to a general misunderstanding of his work that persisted for almost three decades after his death. The thirty-year suppression of *Lady Chatterley's Lover* backfired, as censorship so often does, attracting the public's attention to the object of the prohibition. Unfortunately this notoriety made the novel, far from Lawrence's greatest, the one most commonly associated with his name in the popular mind. His reputation among more serious readers was not helped by the series of sensationalistic memoirs published by some of his more ardent followers in the 1930's and early 1940's. Championed as a prophet of free love and utopianism, repudiated as a crazed homosexual and protofascist, Lawrence the artist all but disappeared from view.

The appearance of several serious and sympathetic studies of Lawrence in the middle and late 1950's, by presenting a more accurate record of his life and a more discriminating assessment of his work, largely succeeded in salvaging Lawrence's stature as a major writer. Among those most responsible for the Lawrence revival were F. R. Leavis, Harry T. Moore, Edward Nehls, and Grahm Hough. Subsequent readers have been able to recognize more readily in the best of Lawrence's work what Leavis described as its "marked moral intensity," its "reverent openness before life."

In addition to his prophetic themes, Lawrence's technical innovations are now acknowledged as among the most important in modern fiction. He could convey a "ripping yarn" and portray lifelike characters when he chose, and parts of *Sons and Lovers* and *The Lost Girl*, among many other works, demonstrate his mastery of traditional realism in the representation of his native Midlands. More fundamentally, however, Lawrence's novels are triumphs of mood and sensibility; they seek (as Frank Kermode has said) less to represent life than to enact it. He has no peer in the evocative rendering of place, introducing poetic symbols that carry the meaning without losing sight of their basis in intensely observed, concrete details. His approach to characterization following *The Rainbow* was unconventional in that he avoided "the old stable ego" and pattern-imposed character types in an effort to go beneath the rational and articulate levels of consciousness to the nonhuman being in his characters. As Walter Allen has observed, for Lawrence "the value of people . . . consisted in how far mystery resided in them, how far they were conscious of mystery." The linear, cause-and-effect development of characters controlled by the rational intellect was for him a hindrance. He focused instead on the surging, dynamic forces—sexual impulses, the potency of nature and animals, the terrible allure of death—which in their purest form defy rationality and are communicated by a kind of unmediated intuition. His prose style was similarly subjective in emphasis. The frequent repetitiveness and inflated rhetoric can be tiresome, but at its best the prose is supple and sensuous, its dynamic rhythms incantatory, a powerful vehicle of Lawrence's vision. Further, he avoided the neat resolution of closure of traditional narratives, typically preferring the "open end" in which the vital forces operating in his characters are felt to be continuously and dynamically in process rather than subdued by the authorial imposition of finality. His comment on the bustling activities of Indian peasants on market day, in *Mornings in Mexico*, epitomizes his fictional method as well as his vitalist doctrine: "In everything, the shimmer of creation and never the finality of the created."

Lawrence's approach to fiction involved considerable risks, and many of his novels are seriously flawed. There are those who cannot read him at all. Nevertheless, the integrity of his vision and the sheer power with which he communicated it have made E. M. Forster's estimate (written shortly after Lawrence's death) stand up: "He was the greatest imaginative novelist of his generation."

BIOGRAPHY

David Herbert Lawrence was born on September 11, 1885, in the Midlands coal-mining village of Eastwood, Nottinghamshire. The noise and grime of the pits dominated Eastwood, but the proximity of fabled Sherwood Forest was a living reminder of what Lawrence would later call "the old England of the forest and agricultural past" upon which industrialization had been so rudely imposed. The contrast was to remain an essential element in his makeup. Allied to it was the equally sharp contrast between his parents. Arthur John Lawrence, the father, had worked in the coal pits from the age of seven. Coarse, semiliterate, intensely physical, a hail-fellow popular with his collier mates, he was prone to drink and to near poverty. Lydia (née Beardsall) Lawrence, his wife, was a former schoolteacher from a pious middle-class Methodist family, which counted among its forebears a noted composer of Wesleyan hymns. Along with his four siblings, young Lawrence was inevitably caught up in the frequent and sometimes violent strife between his mother and father. Delicate and sickly as a child, he could scarcely have emulated his father—not that he was inclined to do so. Instead, he sided with his mother. She in turn doted on him and encouraged him in his studies as a means of escape from the working-class life, thus further alienating him from his father. Only in later life would Lawrence come to see the dangerous liabilities of this overweening maternal bond and the counterbalancing attractiveness of his father's unassuming strength and vitality.

Lawrence was an outstanding student in school and at the age of twelve won a scholarship to Nottingham High School. After graduation in 1901, he worked for three unhappy months as a clerk in a surgical-appliance factory in Nottingham, until he fell seriously ill with pneumonia. About this time, he met Jessie Chambers, whose family lived on a small farm outside Eastwood. Over the next ten years his close relationship with the "spiritual" Jessie (the "Miriam" of *Sons and Lovers*) and her sympathetic family offered further stimulus to his fondness for the beauties of nature, for reading, and for ideas; eventually, with Jessie's encouragement and partial collaboration, he began to write stories and verse. The Chamberses' way of life and the bucolic scenery of Haggs farm, so tellingly unlike the ambience of Lawrence's own home, would later provide him with materials for his first novel, *The White Peacock*. After his prolonged convalescence from pneumonia, in 1903 he found a position as a "pupil-teacher" at an elementary school in nearby Ilkeston, Derbyshire. Two years there were followed by a third as an uncertified teacher in the Eastwood British School. In 1906, having won a King's Scholarship competition, he began a two-year course of study for his teachers' certificate at Nottingham University College. By 1908, he qualified to teach at Davidson Road School, a boys' elementary school in the London suburb of Croydon, where he remained until 1911.

Meanwhile Lawrence had published several poems in 1909 in the *English Review*, edited by Ford Madox Hueffer (later Ford), who introduced him to such established writers as H. G. Wells, Ezra Pound, and William Butler Yeats. Soon Lawrence was busily working at two novels, *The White Peacock* and the autobiographical *Paul Morel* (the working title of *Sons and Lovers*). While the former was still in press in De-

cember, 1910, his mother died of cancer, an event whose profound impact on him is duly commemorated in his poems and in *Paul Morel*, which he had already begun to rewrite. By this time his relationship with Jessie Chambers had diminished considerably, and he had had several brief affairs with other women. His ill health and his increasing commitment to writing (*The Trespasser*, his second novel, was to appear the following year) induced him to forego teaching in the winter of 1911-1912. Back in Eastwood, in April, he met and fell in love with Frieda von Richthoven Weekley, the high-spirited daughter of a German baron, wife of a professor of philology at Nottingham University, and at thirty-two the mother of three small children. In May, Lawrence and Frieda eloped to the Continent. There, for the next six months, Lawrence wrote poems, stories, travel sketches (most of which were later collected in *Twilight in Italy*), and his final revision of the autobiographical novel. This writing, particularly the metamorphosis of *Paul Morel* into *Sons and Lovers* (with which Frieda assisted him by discussing her own maternal feelings and the theories of Freud), marked the true beginning of Lawrence's artistic maturity.

The advent of World War I coincided with what in many ways was the most crucial period of his development as a writer. By the end of 1914, Lawrence and Frieda had married, the critical success of *Sons and Lovers* had established his reputation, he had formed important associations with Edward Garnett, John Middleton Murry, and Katherine Mansfield, and he had begun to work on what many now consider his greatest novels, *The Rainbow* and *Women in Love* (originally conceived as a single work, *The Sisters*). Yet the triumph that might have been his soon turned to ashes. The official suppression of *The Rainbow* in November, 1916—the charge of "immorality" was leveled on both political and sexual grounds—was followed by a series of nightmarish episodes in which, largely because of Frieda's German origins, the Lawrences were hounded and persecuted as supposed enemy spies. Lawrence was reviled in the "patriotic" English press, and, after *The Rainbow* fiasco, in which many of his literary associates had failed to come to his defense, he found it increasingly difficult to publish his work and hence to make a living. Though he completed *Women in Love* in 1917, it did not appear until 1920 in the United States. Events seemed to conspire against him so that, by the end of the war, he could never again feel at home in his native land. This bitter severance motivated the "savage pilgrimage" that dominated the last decade of his life, driving him feverishly around the globe in search of some "ideal centre" in which to live and work in hope for the future.

Lawrence's travels were as much spiritual as geographical in character, and his quest became the primary focus of his writing after the war. The more than two years he spent in Italy and Sicily (1919-1921) provided him with the materials for the concluding chapters of *The Lost Girl* (which he had begun before the war and set aside to work on *The Sisters*) and for *Aaron's Rod*. Heading for America by way of Asia, the Lawrences briefly visited Ceylon and then Australia, where he wrote *Kangaroo* in just six weeks. In September, 1922, they arrived in the United States and soon settled near Taos, New Mexico, on a mountain ranch that was to be "home" for them during most of the next three years. Here Lawrence rewrote *Studies in Classic American Literature* (1923; begun in 1917) and produced such important works as "Eagle in New Mexico" and "Spirits Summoned West" (poems), "The Woman Who Rode Away," "The Princess," "St. Mawr," and half of the travel sketches that comprise *Mornings in Mexico*. During this period Lawrence also made three trips to Mexico, staying there a total of about ten months; his travel experiences, embellished by his rather extensive readings in Aztec history and archaeology, provided the sources for his novel of Mexico, *The Plumed Serpent*, his most ambitious creative undertaking of the postwar years. On the day he finished the novel in Oaxaca, he fell gravely ill with acute tuberculosis and nearly died. After convalescing in Mexico City and on the ranch in New Mexico, he returned with Frieda to Europe in the late fall of 1925, settling first in Spotorno on the Italian Riviera and later in a villa outside Florence.

Lawrence's last years were clouded by the inevitable encroachment of his disease, but he remained remarkably active. He toured the ancient Etruscan ruins; took up painting, producing some strikingly original works; and wrote three complete versions of what would become, in its final form, his most famous novel, *Lady Chatterley's Lover*. The book's banning and confiscation in 1928, reviving the old outcry of "obscenity," prompted several of his most eloquent essays on the subject of pornography and censorship. It was his final battle, save that which could not be won. Lawrence died in Vence, France, on March 2, 1930, at the age of forty-four.

ANALYSIS

D. H. Lawrence occupies an ambiguous position with respect to James Joyce, Marcel Proust, T. S. Eliot, and the other major figures of the modernist movement. While, on the one hand, he shared their feelings of gloom about the degeneration of modern European life and looked to ancient mythologies for prototypes of the rebirth all saw as necessary, on the other he keenly distrusted the modernists' veneration of traditional culture and their classicist aesthetics. The modernist ideal of art as "an escape from personality," as a finished and perfected creation sufficient unto itself, was anathema to Lawrence, who once claimed that his motto was not art for art's sake but "art for my sake." For him, life and art were intertwined, both expressions of the same quest: "To be alive, to be man alive, to be whole man alive: that is the point." The novel realized its essential function best when it embodied and vitally enacted the novelist's mercurial sensibility. His spontaneity, his limitations and imperfections, and his fleeting moments of intuition were directly transmitted to the reader, whose own "instinct for life" would be thereby quickened. Lawrence believed that at its best "the novel, and the novel supremely," could and should perform this important task. That is why he insisted that the novel is "the one bright book of life." One way of approaching his own novels—and the most significant, by general consensus, are *Sons and Lovers, The Rainbow, Women in Love, The Plumed Serpent*, and *Lady Chatterley's Lover*—is to consider the extent to which the form and content of each in turn rises to this vitalist standard.

To be "whole man alive," for Lawrence, involved first of all the realization of *wholeness*. The great enemy of human (and of aesthetic) wholeness, he believed, was modern life itself. Industrialization had cut man off from the past, had mechanized his daily life and transformed human relations into a power struggle to acquire material commodities, thereby alienating man from contact with the divine potency residing in both nature and other men and women. Modern Europe was therefore an accumulation of dead or dying husks, fragmented and spiritually void, whose inevitable expression was mass destruction. For Lawrence, World War I was the apotheosis of modernization.

Yet contemporary history provided only the end result of a long process of atomization and dispersion whose seeds lay in ancient prehistory. In *Fantasia of the Unconscious* (1922), Lawrence formulated a myth of origins that sheds light on his quest for wholeness in his travels among "primitive" peoples as well as in his novels. He describes a kind of golden age before the flood, when the pagan world, both geographically and culturally, was a single, unified entity. This *Ur*-culture, unlike the modern fragmented age, had developed a holistic knowledge or "science in terms of life." The primal wisdom did not differentiate among body, mind, and spirit; the objective and the subjective were one, as the reason and the passions were one; man and nature and the cosmos lived in harmonious relation with one another. Men and women all over the earth shared this knowledge. They "wandered back and forth from Atlantis to the Polynesian Continent. . . . The interchange was complete, and knowledge, science, was universal over the earth." Then the glaciers melted, whole continents were drowned, and the monolithic world fragmented into isolated races, each developing its own culture, its own "science." A few refugees from the lost continents fled to the high ground of Europe, Asia, and America. There they "refused to forget, but taught the old wisdom, only in its half-forgotten, symbolic forms. More or less forgotten, as knowledge: remembered as ritual, gesture, and myth-story."

In modern Europe, even these vestiges of the old universal knowledge had largely become extinct, and with them died what was left of the unitary being of man. First Christianity, with its overemphasis on bodiless spirituality, and then modern science, with its excessive dependence upon finite reason as the instrument of control over a merely mechanistic world, had killed it. After the war Lawrence hoped, in traveling to lands where Christianity, modern science, and industrialization had not yet fully taken hold, to uncover the traces of the primal knowledge, if only "in its half-forgotten, symbolic forms." By somehow establishing a vital contact with "primitive" men and women and fusing his "white consciousness" with their "dark-blood consciousness," he hoped to usher in the next phase in the development of the human race. His novels would sound the clarion call—awakening the primordial memory by means of "ritual, gesture, and myth-story"—summoning "whole man alive" to cross over the threshold into the New World of regenerated being.

Although this myth of apocalypse and rebirth was fully articulated during Lawrence's "wander years" after the war, it was clearly anticipated in his earlier works. There the horror of the modern world's "drift toward death" and the yearning for some "holy ground" on which to begin anew were keenly felt. The initial experience of fragmentation in Lawrence's life was obviously the primal conflict between his mother and father, which among other things resulted in a confusion in his own sexual identity. In the fiction of this period, the stunting of life by fragmentation and imbalance is evident in the portrayal of such characters as Miriam Leivers in *Sons and Lovers*, Anton Skrebensky in *The Rainbow*, and Gerald Crich in *Women in Love*, just as the quest for vital wholeness is exemplified in the same novels by Paul Morel, Ursula Brangwen, and Rupert Birkin, respectively. If the secondary characters in Lawrence's novels tend in general to be static types seen from without, his protagonists, beginning with Ursula in *The Rainbow* and continuing through Constance Chatterley in *Lady Chatterley's Lover*, are anything but static. Rather, they are volatile, inconsistent, and sometimes enigmatic. In *The Plumed Serpent*, Kate Leslie vacillates between intellectual abstraction and immediate sensuous experience; between egotistic willfulness and utter self-abandonment to another; between with-drawal behind the boundaries of the safe and the known, and the passionate yearning for metamorpho-sis; and so on. There is a constant ebb and flow in Kate's behavior, even a rough circularity, that creates a spontaneous, improvisatory feeling in her narrative. Lawrence's protagonists are always in flux, realizing by turns the various aspects of their natures, and this dynamism is largely what makes them so alive. They are open to life: in themselves, in their natural envi-ronment, and in other vital human beings.

Lawrence believed that the novel was the one form of human expression malleable enough to artic-ulate and dramatize the dynamic process of living. In his essay "Why the Novel Matters," he celebrates the novelist's advantage over the saint, the scientist, and the philosopher, all of whom deal only with parts of the composite being of humankind. The nov-elist alone, says Lawrence, is capable of rendering the whole of "man alive." He alone, by so doing, "can make the whole man alive [that is, the reader] tremble."

The priestly or prophetic function of the novelist is clearly central to this aesthetic doctrine. Lawrence is one of the very few modern writers to assume this role and to do so explicitly. At times, this very explic-itness becomes problematic. His novels are quite un-even; most are marred in varying degrees by hector-ing didacticism that is less evident in his short fiction. Nevertheless, he needed the amplitude of an extended narrative to give voice to the several sides of his complex sensibility, as if to discover himself in the process. Perhaps that, as much as anything else, was the object of his quest. Collectively his novels represent a restless search for a form capable of ren-dering that sensibility fully and honestly.

SONS AND LOVERS

In a letter written a few months after the publica-tion of *Sons and Lovers*, Lawrence made an admis-sion which suggests that "art for my sake" could have been a cathartic as well as a heuristic function. "One sheds one's sickness in books," he wrote, "repeats and presents one's emotions, to be master of them." *Sons and Lovers*, his third novel, was the work that enabled Lawrence to come to terms, at least provi-sionally, with the traumas of his formative years. The more than two years he spent working and reworking the book amounted to an artistic and psychological rite of passage essential to his development as a man and as a writer.

The novel spans the first twenty-six years in the life of Paul Morel. Because of the obvious similari-ties between Paul's experiences and Lawrence's, and because the story in part concerns Paul's apprentice-ship as an artist—or, more accurately, the obstacles he must overcome to be an artist—the novel has been seen as an example of a subspecies of the *Bildungs-roman*, the *Künstlerroman*. Comparison with James Joyce's *Portrait of the Artist as a Young Man* (1916) suggests, however, how loosely the term applies to Lawrence's novel. Where Joyce scrupulously selects only those scenes and episodes of Stephen Dedalus's life that directly contribute to the young artist's de-velopment (his first use of language, his schooling, his imaginative transcendence of sex, religion, and politics, his aesthetic theories), Lawrence's focus is far more diffuse. The novel opens with a conven-tional set-piece description of the town of Bestwood (modeled on Eastwood) as it has been affected by the arrival and growth of the mining industry during the last half century. This is followed by an account of the courtship and early married life of Walter and Gertrude Morel, Paul's parents. Even after Paul's birth, the main emphasis remains for many chapters on the mother and father, and considerable space is devoted to their first child, William, whose sudden death and funeral conclude part 1 of the novel. Paul's interest in drawing is mentioned halfway through part 1, but it is not a major concern until he becomes friends with Miriam Leivers in part 2, and there the companionship itself actually receives more atten-tion. Though the comparison does an injustice to the nature of Lawrence's real achievement in the novel, perhaps *Sons and Lovers* more nearly resembles *Ste-phen Hero* (1944), the earlier and more generally au-tobiographical version of Joyce's novel, than it does the tightly constructed *A Portrait of the Artist as a Young Man*.

Yet, when in the late stages of revision Lawrence changed his title from *Paul Morel* to *Sons and*

Lovers, his motive was akin to Joyce's when the Irishman discarded *Stephen Hero* and began to rewrite. The motive was form—form determined by a controlling idea. The subject of *Sons and Lovers* is not simply Paul's development but his development as an instance of the pattern suggested by the title; that pattern involves the Morels' unhappy marriage, the fateful experiences of Paul's brother William, Paul's frustrated relationship with Miriam, and his later encounters with Clara and Baxter Dawes, as well as Paul's own maturation. For Lawrence, the pattern clearly had wide application. Indeed, in a letter to Edward Garnett, his editor, written a few days after completing the revised novel, Lawrence claimed that his book sounded "the tragedy of thousands of young men in England."

This claim, along with the change in title and the late revisions designed to underscore a theme already present in the narrative, was probably influenced by the discussions that Lawrence and Frieda had in 1912 regarding Freud's theories, of which Frieda was then an enthusiastic proponent. (There is no evidence of Lawrence's awareness of Freud before this.) In a more general sense, the "tragedy" was rooted historically, as the novel shows, in the disruption of natural human relationships that was one of the by-products of modernization. Directly or indirectly, the characters in the novel are entrapped by the materialistic values of their society, unable even when they consciously reject those values to establish true contact with one another. Instead they tend to treat one another as objects to be possessed or manipulated for the purpose of self-gratification.

Thus Mrs. Morel, frustrated by her marriage to her coal-miner husband, transfers her affections to her sons, first to William, the eldest, and then to Paul after William's death. Walter Morel, the father, becomes a scapegoat and an outcast in his own home. Whether consciously or not, Mrs. Morel uses her sons as instruments to work out her own destiny vicariously, encouraging them in pursuits that will enable them to escape the socially confining life that she herself cannot escape, yet resenting it when the sons do begin to make a life away from her. Paul's fixation upon his mother—and his hatred of his fa-

ther—contributes to a confusion of his sexual identity and to his inability to love girls his own age in a normal, healthy way. In the same letter to Edward Garnett, Lawrence characterized this inability to love as a "split," referring to the rupture in the son's natural passions caused by the mother's possessive love. The split causes Paul to seek out girls who perform the psychological role of mother-surrogates: Miriam, an exaggerated version of the spiritual, Madonna-like aspect of the mother image; and the buxom Clara Dawes, who from a Freudian viewpoint represents the "degraded sex-object," the fallen woman, equally a projection of the son's prohibited erotic desires for his mother. Because Paul's feeling for Miriam and Clara are thus compartmentalized and unbalanced, both relationships are unfulfilling, a fact which only reinforces his Oedipal bondage. At the same time, part of the responsibility for the unsatisfactory relationships belongs to Miriam and Clara themselves, both of whom exploit Paul to help them fulfill their own private fantasy lives. The world of *Sons and Lovers* is populated by isolated, fragmentary souls not unlike the inhabitants of T. S. Eliot's 1922 *The Waste Land* ("We think of the key, each in his prison/ Thinking of the key, each confirms a prison").

A decade after the appearance of *Sons and Lovers*, Lawrence declared that of all his books, it was the one he would like to rewrite, because in it he had treated his father unfairly. By then, of course, he was overtly committed to finding embodiments of "whole man alive" and, in retrospect, his father seemed to offer such an embodiment. When he wrote *Sons and Lovers*, however, he had not yet fully come to appreciate the importance of his father's unaffected male vitality. Although occasionally Walter Morel appears in a favorable light, the novel generally emphasizes his ineffectuality as a husband and father. The Oedipal conflict on which the story hinges perhaps made this unavoidable. In any event, the struggle to attain wholeness is centered in Paul Morel.

Because Paul's mother is "the pivot and pole of his life, from which he could not escape," her death amounts to the great crisis of the novel. The terrible spectacle of her agony as she lies dying slowly of cancer torments Paul until, by giving her an overdose of morphine, he commits a mercy killing. Unconsciously, the act seems to be motivated by his desire to release her from her debilitating "bondage" as wife and mother, the roles that have made her erotically unattainable to Paul. Her death is followed by an eerie, Poe-like scene in which the shaken Paul, momentarily imagining his mother as a beautiful young sleeping maiden, stoops and kisses her "passionately," as if to waken her like the handsome prince in a fairy tale, only to be horrified by her cold and unresponsive lips. It is a key moment, adumbrating as it does the writer's subsequent shift in allegiances to the "sensuous flame of life" associated with his father. For Paul, however, the loss of his mother induces a period of deep depression (interestingly enough, guilt is not mentioned) in which his uppermost desire is to reunite with his mother in death. This "drift towards death" was what Lawrence believed made Paul's story symptomatic of the times, "the tragedy of thousands of young men in England."

Nevertheless, the novel does not end tragically. Paul, on the verge of suicide, decides instead to turn his back on the "immense dark silence" where his lover/mother awaits him and to head toward the "faintly humming, glowing town"—and beyond it, to the Continent, where he plans to continue his artistic endeavors (just as Lawrence did). Some readers have found this last-minute turnabout implausible, a breakdown in the novel's form. Yet Lawrence anticipates Paul's "rebirth" by having him realize, after his mother's death, that he must finally sever his ties to both Miriam and Clara. For him to have returned to them then for consolation and affection would have meant that, inwardly, he was still cherishing some hope of preserving the maternal bond, even if only through his mother's unsatisfactory substitutes. When Paul effects a reconciliation between Clara and her estranged husband Baxter Dawes, who has been presented throughout in terms strongly reminiscent of Walter Morel, he is (as Daniel A. Weiss and others have observed) tacitly acting out a reversal of the original Oedipal conflict. If the primary emphasis of *Sons and Lovers* is on the tragic split in the emotional lives of the Morels, its conclusion finds Paul taking

the steps necessary to begin to heal the split in himself. Only by so doing would Paul, like Lawrence, be able to undertake a quest for vital wholeness. That quest would become the chief subject of the novels following *Sons and Lovers*.

As sometimes happens to a writer after he has successfully struggled to transform autobiography into art, Lawrence reacted against *Sons and Lovers* almost as soon as he had finished it. The process of revaluating the influence of his parents, begun in his revisions of the novel and particularly evident in its concluding chapters, continued apace. His nonfiction of the period exhibits a growing hostility to women as spawners of intellectual and spiritual abstraction and the early traces of his interest in the reassertion of the vital male. Lawrence reacted also against certain aspects of the narrative technique used in *Sons and Lovers*. As he worked on his next novel, initially called *The Sisters*, he found that he was no longer interested in "visualizing" or "creating vivid scenes" in which characters revealed themselves through dramatic encounters and dialogue. The conventions of plot and the "furniture" of realistic exposition bored him. Moreover, the traditional methods of characterization were positively a hindrance to the kind of novel he felt he must write.

Lawrence had in fact embarked on a long and difficult struggle to create a new kind of novel, unprecedented in English fiction. When his publisher balked, Lawrence defended his experiment in an important letter that clarifies his intentions not only in what would eventually become *The Rainbow* and *Women in Love* but in most of his subsequent fiction:

> You mustn't look in my novel for the old stable *ego* of the character. There is another *ego*, according to whose action the individual is unrecognizable, and passes through, as it were, allotropic states which it needs a deeper sense than any we've been used to exercise, to discover are states of the same radically unchanged element. (Like as diamond and coal are the same pure single element of carbon.)

What all this suggests, and what is implicit in the novels themselves, is that the conventions of realism, which were developed preeminently in the English novel of the nineteenth century, are inadequate tools for use by a writer whose aim is the transformation of the very society whose values were embodied in realism. The "old-fashioned human element," "the old stable ego," the "certain moral scheme" prescribing "consistency" and linear development—these were relics of positivism, bourgeois humanism, and other ideologies of a dying culture. Lawrence gropes a bit in the attempt to describe their successors, but it is clear enough that the "other ego," the "physic" or nonhuman in humanity, and the "radically unchanged element" whose "allotropic" transformations determine a "rhythmic form" along lines unknown, are references to the mysterious source of vital energies capable (he believed) of regenerating both art and society.

THE RAINBOW

The Rainbow applies these ideas in a most interesting way. It is an elegiac study of the dying culture, written in Lawrence's revolutionary "new" manner. The story spans three generations of the Brangwen family, beginning with the advent of industrialism around 1840 in the rural Erewash valley—signaled by the construction of canals, the collieries, and the railroad—and continuing up to the first decade of the twentieth century. The theme is the destruction of the traditional way of life and the attempt, by the Brangwens, either to accommodate themselves to that loss or to transcend it by discovering a new basis for being.

The novel opens with a rhapsodic prose poem telescoping two hundred years of Brangwens into archetypal male and female figures living in "blood intimacy" with one another and with the land: "The pulse of the blood of the teats of the cows beat into the pulse of the hands of the men. [The men] mounted their horses and held life between the grip of their knees." Despite their "vital connection," however, there are opposing impulses in the male and the female principles that become increasingly important as the story proceeds. The Brangwen men, laboring in the fields of the Marsh Farm, are compared with the rim of a wheel revolving around the still center that is hearth and home; the women, like the axle of the wheel, live in the still center but always

direct their gaze outward, beyond the wheel's rim toward the road, the village, the church steeple, "the spoken world" that is encroaching on the horizon. This tension between centripetal and centrifugal forces, the rim and the axle, is fruitful so long as the Brangwens live in harmony with the land, for it is a reflection of the cyclical processes of nature in which the clash of opposites generates change and growth. With the second generation, however, the principal Brangwen couple, Will and Anna, leaves the land and moves to the industrial town of Beldover, where Will works in a shop that produces machine-made lace. The seasonal cycle is replaced by the Christian liturgical calendar, in Lawrence's view a step toward abstraction. The old male-female opposition, having lost its former function as the means by which men and women participate in the dynamic rhythms of nature, becomes a destructive force. The marriage of contraries loses impetus because it now reflects not nature but the mechanisms that are dividing society. Husband and wife settle into a fixed domestic routine, typically Victorian, of piety (on Will's side) and child-rearing (on Anna's). Anna's "outward" impulse is thus sublimated, and, like Gertrude Morel in *Sons and Lovers*, she counts on her children to act out her frustrated quest beyond the pale.

Most important of these children is the oldest daughter, Ursula, who, with her sister Gudrun, will also figure prominently in *Women in Love*. Ursula has been called "the first complete modern woman" (Marvin Mudrick) and, even more sweepingly, "the first 'free soul'" (Keith Sagar) in the English novel. It is Ursula, a member of Lawrence's own generation, who finally breaks out of the old circle of life. As she grows into womanhood she challenges and ultimately rejects traditional views of religion, democracy, education, free enterprise, love, and marriage. She is the first Brangwen female to enter a profession and support herself (as a schoolteacher); she attends the university; she travels to London and the Continent. On several levels, then, her "centrifugal" movement takes her far afield. Yet despite her explorations she has no sense of who she really is. The traditional order, which formerly provided a living relationship with nature and with other men and women, has all but collapsed. Motivated only by her isolate will and unreciprocated by any meaningful male contrary—as is amply demonstrated by her unsatisfying love affairs with Winifred Inger, her schoolmistress, and the shallow Anton Skrebensky—Ursula's quest becomes a desperate exercise in redundancy and futility, her vital energies randomly dispersed.

The novel ends as it began, symbolically. In the last of a series of "ritual scenes," in which characters are suddenly confronted with the "physic" or nonhuman "ego" that is the mysterious life force, Ursula encounters a herd of stampeding horses. Whether hallucinatory or actual, the horses seem to represent the "dark" potencies which she has tried so long to discover on her quest and which have so far eluded her. Now, terrified, she escapes. Soon after, she falls ill with pneumonia, miscarries a child by Skrebensky, and lies delirious with fever for nearly a fortnight. All this is fitting as the culmination of Ursula's abortive, well-driven quest. Her "drift toward death," more like a plunge finally, is even more representative of her generation's crisis than Paul Morel's was in *Sons and Lovers*. As in the earlier novel, furthermore, Lawrence attempts to end *The Rainbow* on a hopeful note. After her convalescence, Ursula awakes one morning on the shores of what appears to be a new world, "as if a new day had come on the earth." Having survived the deluge, she is granted a vision of the rainbow—a symbol related to but superseding the old closed circle—which seems to offer hope for the regeneration not only of Ursula but also of her world.

On both levels, however, the symbolic promise is less than convincing. Unlike Paul Morel, Ursula has not performed any action or had any insight which suggests that her final "rebirth" is more than wishful thinking. As for the modern world's regeneration, when the novel appeared, in September, 1915, nothing could have been less likely. Lawrence hated the war, but like many other modern writers he saw it as the harbinger of the apocalypse, accelerating the advent of a new age. Before long he realized that he had "set my rainbow in the sky too soon, before, instead of after, the deluge." The furor provoked by the novel must have made the irony of his premature hopeful-

ness all the more painful. In the teeth of that furor and the public persecution waged against Frieda and himself as supposed German spies, Lawrence set about writing *Women in Love*, considered by many today his greatest novel and one of the half-dozen or so masterpieces of modern fiction.

WOMEN IN LOVE

Whatever their differences with respect to the emphasis placed upon the operations of the "physic," or nonhuman, forces in humanity, *Sons and Lovers* and *The Rainbow* share several important traits that set them apart from most of Lawrence's subsequent novels, beginning with *Women in Love*. For one, they have in common a narrative structure that, by locating the action firmly within a social context spanning generations, subscribes to the novelistic convention of rendering the story of individuals continuous with the larger movements of history. *Women in Love* takes up the story of the "modern" Brangwens about three and one-half years after the end of *The Rainbow* but, in contrast to the earlier novel's sixty-six-year span, concentrates attention onto a series of loosely connected episodes occurring within a ten-month period, from spring to winter of 1909 or 1910. One result of this altered focus, at once narrower and relatively looser than that of the earlier novels, is that the social background seems far more static than before. The great transformation of society known as modernization has already occurred, and the characters move within a world whose ostensible change is the slow, inward process of decay. The shift of emphasis is evident also in the protagonists' attitudes toward society. The conclusions of the earlier novels—Paul's turning away from death toward the "humming, glowing town," and Ursula's vision of the rainbow offering hope that a corrupt world would "issue to a new germination"—imply that Western civilization could still respond to the most urgent needs of the individual. In *Women in Love* that assumption has completely vanished. Thus, although Lawrence originally conceived of *The Rainbow* and *Women in Love* as a single work and would later describe them as forming together "an organic artistic whole," the latter novel embodies a far darker view of the world. As Lawrence once said, *Women in Love* "actually does contain the results in one's soul of the war: it is purely destructive, not like *The Rainbow*, destructive-consummating."

The phrase "purely destructive" only slightly exaggerates the despairing nature of the novel's apocalyptic vision. Certainly its depiction of modern society as a dying tree "infested with little worms and dry-rot" suggests that the impetus toward death and destruction is so pervasive as to make the war all but inevitable. In the novel, the working class, far from resisting the dehumanizing mechanism of the industrial system, is "satisfied to belong to the great wonderful machine, even whilst it destroyed them." The leisure class is seen as similarly deluded and doomed. Hermione Roddice's chic gatherings at Breadalby, her country estate (modeled on Lady Ottoline Morrell's Garsington), offer no genuine alternative to the dying world but only a static image of the "precious past," where all is formed and final and accomplished—a "horrible, dead prison" of illusory peace. Meanwhile contemporary art has abdicated its time-honored role as naysayer to a corrupt social order. Indeed, in the homosexual artist Halliday, the promiscuous Minette, and the other decadent bohemians who congregate at the Pompadour Café in London, Lawrence clearly implicates intellectual and artistic coteries such as Bloomsbury in the general dissolution of modern society. That the pandering of the modern artist to the death-drive of mechanistic society was a general phenomenon and not limited to England is emphasized near the end of the novel with the appearance of Loerke, a German sculptor whose work adorns "a great granite factory in Cologne." Loerke, who asserts on the one hand that art should interpret industry as it had formerly interpreted religion and on the other that a work of art has no relation to anything but itself, embodies the amorality of modernist aesthetics from Lawrence's viewpoint. Dominated by "pure unconnected will," Loerke is, like Hermione, sexually perverse, and, like the habitués of the Pompadour, he "lives like a rat in the river of corruption."

All of these secondary characters in *Women in Love* exemplify the results of the displacement of the traditional order by industrialization, or what Lawrence terms "the first great phase of chaos, the substitution of the mechanical principle for the organic." Except for Hermione, they are consistently presented from without, in static roles prescribed for them by a static society. Against this backdrop move the four principal characters: Ursula and Gudrun Brangwen, who are sisters, and Rupert Birkin and Gerald Crich, who are friends. The interweaving relationships of these four, highlighted in scenes of great emotional intensity and suggestiveness, provide the "rhythmic form" of the novel. Notwithstanding their interactions with external society and their long philosophical arguments, they are chiefly presented in terms of a continuous struggle among the elemental energies vying for expression within them. Mark Schorer aptly describes the book as "a drama of primal compulsions." The "drama" concerns the conflict between the mechanical will and the organic oneness of being, between the "flux of corruption" or death and the regenerative forces of life, as these are variously embodied in the four main characters and their constantly shifting relationships.

Birkin, full of talk about spontaneity and "pure being" and the "blood-knowledge" available in sensuality, is clearly a spokesman for certain of Lawrence's favorite ideas. Considering this, it is interesting that from the outset the novel emphasizes his involvement in the death-fixation of modern society at large. He has been one of the "mud-flowers" at the Café Pompadour. In addition, he has been for several years involved in an affair with the perverse socialite Hermione, an affair that has degenerated into a hysterical battle of wills, sapping Birkin of his male vitality. As he tells Gerald, he wants above all to center his life on "the finality of love" for one woman and close relationships with a few other friends, but his goal is frustrated by the lingering parody of it represented in Hermione and the London bohemians. It is therefore significant that he is frequently ill and once goes to the south of France for several weeks to recuperate. His sickness is as much spiritual as physical. Dissatisfied with his prosaic career as a school inspector and frustrated in his relationships, he often finds himself "in pure opposition to everything." In this depressed state he becomes preoccupied with death and dissolution, "that dark river" (as he calls it) which seethes through all modern reality, even love. Not until after his violent break with Hermione, during which she nearly kills him, does Birkin begin to find his way back to life.

Unlike Birkin, Gerald does not believe that love can form the center of life. Instead he maintains that there is no center to life but simply the "social mechanism" which artificially holds it together; as for loving, Gerald is incapable of it. Indeed the novel everywhere implies that his inability to love derives from his abdication of vital, integrated being in favor of mere social fulfillment. As an industrial magnate (he is the director of the local coal mines and has successfully modernized them), Gerald advocates what Birkin calls the "ethics of productivity," the "pure instrumentality of mankind," being for him the basis of social cohesion and progress. If society is essentially mechanistic, Gerald's ambition is to be "the God of the machine" whose will is "to subjugate Matter to his own ends. The subjugation itself," Lawrence adds significantly, "was the point." This egotistic obsession is illustrated in a powerful scene in which Gerald rides a young Arab mare up to a railroad track and, while Gudrun and Ursula look on aghast, he violently forces the terrified mare to stay put as the train races noisily by them. The impact of this cruel assertion of will to power registers forcefully on Ursula, who is duly horrified and outraged, and on Gudrun, who is mesmerized by the "unutterable subordination" of the mare to the "indomitable" male.

After abortive affairs with other women, Birkin and Gerald are inevitably attracted to the Brangwen sisters. The protracted ebb and flow of the two relationships is tellingly juxtaposed in a series of scenes richly symbolic of the central dialectic of life and death. Meanwhile, not content with the romantic promise of finding love with a woman only, Birkin proposes to Gerald that they form a vital male bond as of blood brothers pledged to mutual love and fidelity. Whatever its unconscious origins, the intent of the offer is clearly not sexual. As the rest of the novel demonstrates (anticipating a theme that becomes more central and explicit in subsequent novels such as *Aaron's Rod* and *The Plumed Serpent*), Birkin is

searching for a kind of pure intimacy in human relationships. He seeks with both men and women a bond of blood and mind and spirit—the integrated wholeness of being that for Lawrence was sacred—that when realized might form the nucleus of a new, vital human community. Because of Gerald's identification with the mechanism of industrial society, Birkin's repeated offer of a *Blutbrüderschaft* amounts to an invitation to a shared rebirth emblematic of epochal transfiguration, an apocalypse in microcosm. Because of that same identification, of course, Gerald, confused and threatened, must refuse the offer. Instead he chooses to die.

The choice of death is brilliantly dramatized in Gerald's impassioned encounters with Gudrun. Despite her earlier identification with the mare he brutally "subordinated," Gudrun might still have offered him the sort of vital relationship that both so desperately need. At any rate, had they been able to pursue their potential for love, the sort of shared commitment to mutual "being" that Birkin offers Gerald and that he eventually discovers with Ursula, regeneration, however painful and difficult, could have been realized. Rather than accept this challenge, however, Gerald falls back on his usual tactics and tries to subjugate Gudrun to his will. After his father's death, he becomes acutely aware of the void in his life and turns at once to Gudrun—walking straight from the cemetery in the rain to her house, up to her bedroom, his shoes still heavy with mud from the grave—not out of love but desperate need: the need to assert himself, heedless of the "otherness" of another, as if in so doing he could verify by sheer force of will that he exists. Yet, because this egotistic passion is a perversion of love as Lawrence saw it and because Gerald's yearning for ontological security is a perversion of the quest for true being, Gerald's anxieties are only made worse by his contact with Gudrun. For her part, Gudrun, unlike the helplessly dominated mare, never yields herself fully to Gerald. In fact, she does all she can to thwart and humiliate him, and their relationship soon becomes a naked battle of wills. It is redundant to say that this is a battle to the death, for, on the grounds that it is fought, the battle itself is death in Lawrencian terms. In the end, Gerald, whose aim all along as "God of the machine" had been to subjugate Matter to his will, becomes literally a frozen corpse whose expression terrifies Birkin with its "last terrible look of cold, mute Matter." Gudrun, headed at the end for a rendezvous with the despicable Loerke, arrives at a like consummation.

Whatever Lawrence might say about the "purely destructive" forces at work in *Women in Love*, in the relationship of Birkin and Ursula he finds a seed of new life germinating, albeit precariously, within the "dark river of dissolution." After the severance of his nearly fatal tie with Hermione, Birkin finds himself for a time in a quandary. Believing as he still does that the only means of withstanding dissolution is to center his life on close human ties, he casts about him to discover precisely the kind of relationship that will best serve or enact his quest for being. The "purely sensual, purely unspiritual knowledge" represented by a primitive statue of an African woman impresses Birkin but finally proves too remote a mystery for him to emulate; in any event, the modern female embodiments of this "mystic knowledge" of the senses are, like Hermione and Gudrun, will-dominated and murderous. A second way is that represented by the proposed bond with Gerald, the "Nordic" machine-god who for Birkin represents "the vast abstraction of ice and snow, . . . snow-abstract annihilation." When these alternatives both reveal themselves as mere "allotropic" variations of the flux of corruption from which he seeks release, Birkin finally hits upon a third way, "the way of freedom." He conceives of it in idealistic terms, as

> the paradisal entry into pure, single being, the individual soul taking precedence over love and desire for union, stronger than any pangs of emotion, a lovely state of free proud singleness, which accepted the obligation of the permanent connection with others, and with the other, submits to the yoke and leash of love, but never forfeits its own proud individual singleness, even while it loves and yields.

It is a difficult and elusive ideal, and when Birkin tries, laboriously, to describe it to Ursula—inviting her to join him in a new, strange relationship, "not meeting and mingling . . . but an equilibrium, a pure

balance of two single beings" dynamically counter-poised as two stars are—she mocks him for dissimulating. Why does he not simply declare his love for her without "dragging in the stars"? She has a point, and Lawrence's art only benefits from such moments of self-criticism. Still, these paradoxical images of separateness in union, of a bond that finds its strength in the reciprocal affirmation of "otherness," do express, like the wheel's axle and rim in *The Rainbow*, Lawrence's essential vision of integrated, dynamic relationships. Furthermore, only by actively pursuing such a marriage of opposites, in which the separateness of each partner is necessary to the indissolubility of the bond, can both parties be caught up in something altogether new: "the third," which transcends individual selves in the oneness of pure being. For Lawrence this is the true consummation, springing up from "the source of the deepest life-force."

So polluted had the river of life become in modern Europe, however, that Lawrence could no longer bring himself to believe that this transcendence, ephemeral as it was to begin with, could survive the general cataract of dissolution. Moreover, even when Birkin and Ursula do find fulfillment together, it is not enough; for Birkin, at any rate, the new dispensation must involve other people as well as themselves. For both reasons, the quest for integrated wholeness of being, a mystery into which Birkin and Ursula are only new initiates, becomes translated into a pilgrimage through space. They must depart from the old, dying world and, like Lawrence and Frieda after the war, proceed in search of holy ground. The primary focus of subsequent novels, this quest is defined in *Women in Love* simply as "wandering to nowhere, . . . away from the world's somewheres." As *nowhere* is the translation of the word *utopia*, the social impetus of the search is implicit. "It isn't really a locality, though," Birkin insists. "It's a perfected relation between you and me, and others . . . so that we are free together." With this ideal before him, Lawrence was poised at the crossroads of his career.

In the postwar novels, which present fictionalized versions of his and Frieda's experiences in Italy (*Aaron's Rod*), Australia (*Kangaroo*), and Mexico (*The Plumed Serpent*), the quest translates increasingly into a sociopolitical doctrine projected onto whole societies. The bond between men and the fascination of powerful male leaders became more and more of an obsession in these novels. Lawrence tried mightily to remain faithful to the notion that the regeneration of societies should correspond to the "perfected relations" between individuals. The analogy presented difficulties, however, and the struggle to express his essentially religious vision in political terms proved fatal to his art. There are brilliant moments in all of these novels, especially in *The Plumed Serpent*, yet the alien aspects of the foreign lands he visited finally obscured the central issues in what was, at bottom, a quest for self-discovery. *Women in Love*, still in touch with the real motives of that quest and yielding immediate access to its first (and, as it turned out, finest) fruits, offers the richest rendering of both the modern drift toward death and its Lawrencian antidote, "whole man alive."

However ill-defined the object of his protagonists' plans for flight from Europe, ever since the cataclysm of 1914-1918, Lawrence himself had determined to relocate in the United States. Florida, California, upstate New York, New Mexico—all at one time or another figured as proposed sites of his American dream. In one of these areas, apart from the great urban centers, he would establish a utopian colony to be called Rananim. There he would start over again, free from the runaway entropy of modern Europe. In America, and more particularly aboriginal America, he believed that the Tree of Life remained intact, its potency still issuing "up from the roots, crude but vital." Nevertheless, when the war ended he did not go to America straightaway but headed east, not to arrive in the Western Hemisphere until late in 1922. During this prolonged period of yearning, his vision of America as the New World of the soul, the locus of the regeneration of humankind, took on an increasingly definite form. He was imaginatively committed to it even before settling near Taos, New Mexico, where he and Frieda lived on a mountain ranch for most of the next three years.

After studying the classic works of early American literature, he decided that he would write an "American novel," that is, a novel which would in-

voke and adequately respond to the American "spirit of place." For Lawrence the continent's daemon was the old "blood-and-vertebrate consciousness" embodied in the Mesoamerican Indian and his aboriginal religion. Because of four centuries of white European domination, that spirit had never been fully realized, yet despite the domination it still lay waiting beneath the surface for an annunciation. The terms of this vision, even apart from other factors having to do with his frustrating contacts with Mable Dodge Luhan and her coterie of artists in Taos, all but made it inevitable that Lawrence would sooner or later situate his American novel in a land where the Indian presence was more substantial than it was in the southwestern United States. The Pueblo Indian religion impressed him deeply with its "revelation of life," but he realized that for a genuine, large-scale rebirth to occur in America, "a vast death-happening must come first" to break the hold of the degenerate white civilization. It was natural enough that he turned his eyes south to Mexico, a land which actually had been caught up in revolution for more than a decade—a revolution moreover in which the place of the Indian (who constituted more than 30 percent of the population) in the national life was a central issue. Reading pre-Columbian history and archaeology, Lawrence found in Aztec mythology a ready-made source of symbols and in the story of the Spanish conquest an important precedent for his narrative of contemporary counterrevolution and religious revival.

THE PLUMED SERPENT

Yet the writing of his *Quetzalcoatl*, the working title of what would become *The Plumed Serpent*, proved unusually difficult. *Kangaroo* had taken him only six weeks to write; *Aaron's Rod* and *The Lost Girl* were also composed in sudden, if fitful, bursts. In contrast, he worked on his "American novel" off and on for nearly two years, even taking the precaution of writing such tales as "The Woman who Rode Away," "The Princess," and "St. Mawr" (all of which have much in common with the novel), and the Mexican travel sketches in *Mornings in Mexico*, as a kind of repeated trial run for his more ambitious project.

One reason the novel proved recalcitrant was that Lawrence became increasingly aware during his three journeys into the Mexican interior that his visionary Mexico and the real thing were far from compatible. The violence of the country appalled him; its revolution, which he soon dismissed as "self-serving Bolshevism," left him cold; and most important, its Roman Catholic Indians were demonstrably uninterested and seemingly incapable of responding to the sort of pagan revival called for by Lawrence's apocalyptic scheme. Yet, so committed was he to his American "Rananim" that he was unwilling or unable to entertain the possibility of its failure. Rather than qualify his program for world regeneration in the light of the widening breach between his long-cherished dream and the disappointing reality, he elaborated the dream more fully and explicitly than ever, inflating his claims for it in a grandiose rhetoric that only called its sincerity into question. Had he been content with a purely visionary, symbolic tale, a prose romance comparable in motive with W. B. Yeats's imaginary excursions to "Holy Byzantium," such questions would probably not have arisen. Lawrence, however, could not let go of his expectation that in Mexico the primordial spirit of place would answer to his clarion call. At the same time, the realist in Lawrence allowed evidence to the contrary to appear in the form of his extraordinarily vivid perceptions of the malevolence of the Mexican landscape and its dark-skinned inhabitants. Yet, even these were forced into the pattern of New World Apocalypse. In his desperation to have it both ways, doggedly asserting the identity of his own spiritual quest and the course of events in the literal, external world, he contrived a kind of symbolic or mythic formula in which sexual, religious, and political rebirth are not only equated but also presented as mutually dependent. The result, according to most critics, is a complicated muddle in which the parts, some of which are as fine as anything he ever wrote, do not make a whole. Yet for Lawrence the muddle itself would ultimately prove instructive.

In a sense *The Plumed Serpent* begins where *Women in Love* ends. The flow of Birkin and Ursula's relationship in the earlier novel is directed centrifu-gally away from England toward a nameless "nowhere" of shared freedom in pure being. In *The Plumed Serpent*, the protagonist, Kate Leslie, having heard the death-knell of her spirit in Europe, has arrived at the threshold of the New World of mystery, where a rebirth awaits her "like a doom." That the socialist revolution has addressed only the material needs of Mexicans and left their dormant spirit untouched suggests that Mexico is also in need of rebirth. Disgusted by the tawdry imitation of a modern European capital that is Mexico City, the seat of the failed revolution, Kate journeys westward to the remote lakeside village of Sayula. Sayula also happens to be the center of a new-Aztec religious revival led by Don Ramón Carrasco, who calls himself "the living Quetzalcoatl." The boat trip down the "sperm-like" lake to Sayula begins Kate's centripetal movement toward her destiny, and also Mexico's movement toward an indigenous spiritual reawakening; both movements are directed, gradually but inexorably, toward an "immersion in a sea of living blood."

Unlike Birkin and Ursula of *Women in Love*, Kate, a middle-aged Irish widow, wants at first only to be "alone with the unfolding flower of her own soul." Her occasional contacts with the provincial Indians inspire in her a sense of wonder at their "dark" mystery, but at the same time she finds their very alienness oppressive and threatening. She feels that the country wants to pull her down, "with a slow, reptilian insistence," to prevent her "free" spirit from soaring. Since Kate values her freedom and her solitude, she retreats periodically from the "ponderous, down-pressing weight" which she associates with the coils of the old Aztec feathered serpent, Quetzalcoatl.

Don Ramón explains to her that she must submit to this weight upon the spirit, for by pulling her down into the earth it may bring her into contact with the deep-rooted Tree of Life, which still thrives in the volcanic soil of primordial Mexico beneath the "pale-face overlay" on the surface. This injunction is aimed not only at Kate but also at contemporary Mexico itself, which, beckoned by the pulsating drumbeats and hymns of the Men of Quetzalcoatl, is urged to turn its back on the imported white creeds (Catholicism and Bolshevism) and rediscover its indigenous roots.

Only by yielding their hold on the conscious will can the "bound" egos of the Mexicans as well as of Kate achieve a transfiguration, symbolized in the novel by the Morning Star. Indeed, as a representative of white "mental consciousness," Kate is destined to perform an important role in the new dispensation in Mexico. Ramón's aim is to forge a new mode of consciousness emerging from the dynamic tension between the white and dark sensibilities. The new mode is embodied by Ramón himself, in his capacity to "see both ways" without being absorbed by either, just as the ancient man-god Quetzalcoatl united the sky and the earth, and as the Morning Star (associated with Quetzalcoatl) partakes of both night and day, moon and sun, yet remains itself.

Thus described, this doctrine may seem a welcome elaboration of the star-equilibrium theory of human relationships advanced by Birkin in the earlier novel. The transcendent emergence of "the third," at best an elusive idea of divine immanence in *Women in Love*, seems to be clarified by the Aztec cosmogonic symbolism of *The Plumed Serpent*. Undoubtedly the latter novel is the fullest statement of Lawrence's vitalist religion. Yet there is something in the very explicitness of the religion in the novel that renders it suspect. As if in tacit acknowledgment of this, Lawrence, impatient with the slow progress of Don Ramón's appeal to the spirit, introduces a more overt form of conquest. When both Kate and Mexico fail to respond unequivocally to the invitation to submit voluntarily, Ramón reluctantly resorts to calling on the assistance of Don Cipriano Viedma, a full-blooded Indian general who commands a considerable army. Though Lawrence attempts to legitimize this move by having Ramón induct Cipriano into the neo-Aztec pantheon as "the living Huitzilopochtli" (the Aztec god of war) and by having Kate envision Cipriano as the Mexican Indian embodiment of "the ancient phallic mystery, . . . the god-devil of the male Pan" before whom she must "swoon," the novel descends into a pathological nightmare from which it never quite recovers.

It is not simply that Cipriano politicizes the religious movement, reducing it to yet another Latin American literary adventure which ends by imposing Quetzalcoatlism as the institutional religion of Mexico; nor is it simply that Cipriano, with Ramón's blessing, dupes Kate into a kind of sexual subservience that puts Gerald Crich's machine-god efforts with Gudrun (in *Women in Love*) to shame. The nadir of the novel is reached when Cipriano performs a public execution, stabbing to death three blindfolded prisoners who have betrayed Ramón. This brutal act is given priestly sanction by Ramón and even accepted by Kate, in her new role as Malintzi, fertility goddess in the nascent religion. "Why should I judge him?" asks Kate. "He is of the gods. . . . What do I care if he kills people. His flame is young and clean. He is Huitzilopochtli, and I am Malintzi." Their "godly" union is consummated at the foot of the altar in the new temple of Quetzalcoatl. At this point, if not before, the threefold quest for "immersion in a sea of living blood" ceases to serve a metaphorical function and becomes all too chillingly literal.

With its rigidified "mystical" doctrine, its hysterical rhetoric, and its cruelly inhuman advocacy of "necessary" bloodshed and supermasculine dominance, *The Plumed Serpent* offers what amounts to a perfect Lawrencian hell but persists in celebrating it as if it were the veritable threshold of paradise. The novel has found a few defenders among critics enamored of "mythic design," but Harry T. Moore is surely correct in calling it "a tremendous volcano of a failure." Though for a short time he thought it his best novel, by March, 1928, Lawrence himself repudiated *The Plumed Serpent* and the militaristic "leader of men" idea that it embodies.

Nevertheless, *The Plumed Serpent* marks a crucial phase in Lawrence's development, for it carries to their ultimate conclusion the most disturbing implications of the ideas that had vexed his mind ever since the war. Submersion in the "dark blood," as the novel demonstrates, could lead as readily to wholesale murder in the name of religion as to vital and spontaneous relations between men and women. By courageously following his chimerical "Rananim" dream through to its end in a horrific, palpable nightmare, Lawrence accepted enormous risks, psychological as well as artistic. The effort nearly cost him his life, bringing on a severe attack of tuberculosis complicated by malaria. Yet, in the few years that remained to him, he was in a real sense a man reborn, able to return in imagination (in *The Virgin and the Gipsy* and *Lady Chatterley's Lover*, among other works) to his native Midlands, where he could once again take up the quest for "whole man alive," happily unencumbered by the grandiose political imperatives of world regeneration. Purging him of this ideological sickness, the writing of *The Plumed Serpent* proved as salutary to his later career as *Sons and Lovers* had been to his period of greatest accomplishment.

When Lawrence settled in southern Europe after leaving America in late 1925, he began to reshape his spiritual map in ways suggestive of his shifting outlook during his last years. The problem with the United States, he decided, was that everyone was too tense. Americans took themselves and their role in the world far too seriously and were unable to slacken their grip on themselves for fear that the world would collapse as a result. In contrast, the Europeans (he was thinking chiefly of southern Europeans rather than his own countrymen) were freer and more spontaneous because they were not controlled by will and could therefore let themselves go. At bottom, the European attitude toward life was characterized by what Lawrence called "insouciance." Relaxed, essentially free from undue care or fret, Europeans were open to "a sort of bubbling-in of life," whereas the Americans' more forthright pursuit of life only killed it.

Whether this distinction between America and Europe has any validity for others, for the post-America Lawrence it meant a great deal. In *The Plumed Serpent*, his "American novel," instead of realizing the free and spontaneous life flow made accessible by insouciance, he engaged in an almost hysterical striving after life writ large, resorting to political demagoguery and a formalized religion fully armed with rifles as well as rites. Apparently aware in retrospect of his error, he eschewed the strong-leader/submissive-follower relationship as the keynote to regeneration. In its place he would focus on a new relationship: a "sort of tenderness, sensitive, between men and men and men and women, and not the

one up one down, lead on I follow, *ich dien* sort of business." Having discovered the virtues of insouciance and tenderness, Lawrence began to write *Lady Chatterley's Lover*, one of his most poignant, lyrical treatments of individual human relations.

LADY CHATTERLEY'S LOVER

As always in Lawrence, the physical setting offers a crucial barometer of sensibility. In this case the treatment of setting is indicative of the novelist's loss of faith in the "spirit of place" as a valid embodiment of his quest. In comparison with his other novels, *Lady Chatterley's Lover* presents a scene much reduced in richness and complexity. Wragby Hall, the baronial seat of the Chatterleys, is described as "a warren of a place without much distinction." Standing on a hill and surrounded by oak trees, Wragby offers a view dominated by the smokestacks of the mines in and around the Midlands village of Tevershall. Like Shortlands, the Criches' estate in *Women in Love*, Wragby and its residents attempt through formal artifice to deny the existence of the pits from which the family income derives. The attempt is futile, however, for "when the wind was that way, which was often, the house was full of the stench of this sulphurous combustion of the earth's excrement," and smuts settle on the gardens "like black manna from skies of doom." As for Tevershall ("'tis now and 'tever shall be"), the mining village offers only the appalling prospect of "the utter negation of natural beauty, the utter negation of the gladness of life, . . . the utter death of the human intuitive faculty." Clearly Wragby and Tevershall are two sides of the same coin minted by the godless machine age. Between the two is a tiny, ever-diminishing remnant of old Sherwood Forest. The wood is owned by the Chatterleys, and many of its trees were "patriotically" chopped down during the Great War for timber for the allies' trenches.

It is here that Constance (Connie) Chatterley and her lover, Oliver Mellors, the gamekeeper, find—or rather create—life together. As Julian Moynihan has observed, the little wood symbolizes "the beleaguered and vulnerable status to which the vital career has been reduced" at the hands of modern civilization. The old centrifugal impulse for a faraway "nowhere" has yielded to a desperate centripetal flight toward refuge from the industrial wasteland. Yet try as they might to find sanctuary within the wood, the lovers must recognize that there is no longer any room in the world for true sanctuary, much less for a "Rananim." "The industrial noises broke the solitude," Lawrence writes; "the sharp lights, though unseen, mocked it. A man could no longer be private and withdrawn. The world allows no hermits." The geographical focus of the Lawrencian quest is no longer able to provide a modicum of hope and so yields to a new, scaled-down, more intimate image: the human body.

The sterility and spiritual paralysis of the modern world are embodied by Clifford Chatterley, Connie's husband. A paraplegic victim of the war, Clifford is both literally and symbolically deadened to the life of the passions. All his energy is directed to verbal, abstract, or social undertakings in which actual contact is minimal. Clifford believes in the form and apparatus of the social life and is indifferent to private feelings. A director of mines, he sees the miners as objects rather than men, mere extensions of the pit machinery. For him, "the function determines the individual," who hardly matters otherwise. Clifford also writes fashionably shallow stories and entertains other writers and critics to curry favor. He modernizes the coal mines with considerable success. Thus in broad outline he resembles Gerald Crich of *Women in Love*. Yet, in the far simpler world of *Lady Chatterley's Lover*, Lawrence chooses not to cloud matters by giving his antagonist any redeeming qualities. The reader is never invited to sympathize with Clifford's plight. Motoring around Wragby Hall in his mechanical wheelchair, Clifford coolly urges Connie to have a child by another man—the "sex thing" having been of no particular importance to him even before the war—so that he can have an heir to Wragby. By the end of the novel, he turns to his attendant Mrs. Bolton for the only intimacy left to him: a regressive, perverse form of contact. Such heaping of abuse onto Clifford, far in excess of what is needed to establish his symbolic role, undoubtedly detracts from the novel.

So long as she remains with Clifford, Connie

finds herself in a condition of static bondage in which her individuality is circumscribed by the function identified in her title. A "lady" by virtue of her marriage, she is not yet truly a woman. Sex for her is merely a "thing" as it is for Clifford, an instrument of tacit control over men. She is progressively gripped by malaise. Physically she is "old at twenty-seven, with no gleam and sparkle in the flesh"; spiritually she is unborn. Her affair with Mellors is of course the means of her metamorphosis, which has been compared (somewhat ironically) with the awakening of Sleeping Beauty at the handsome prince's magical kiss. Less obvious is the overlapping of this fairy-tale pattern with a counterpattern of male transformation such as that found in the tale of the Frog Prince. For Mellors, too, is trapped in a kind of bondage, alone in his precarious refuge in the wood. The "curse" on him is his antipathy to intimate contacts, especially with women, after his disastrous marriage to the promiscuous Bertha Coutts.

The initial encounters between Connie and Mellors in the wood result only in conflict and hostility, as both, particularly Mellors, cling to their socially prescribed roles and resist the challenge of being "broken open" by true contact with another. Yet, when they finally do begin to respond to that challenge, it is Mellors who takes the lead in conducting Connie through her initiation into the mysteries of "phallic" being. With his "tender" guidance she learns the necessity of letting go her hold on herself, yielding to the "palpable unknown" beyond her conscious will. She discovers the importance of their "coming off together" rather than the merely "frictional" pleasures of clitoral orgasm (a notion acceptable within Lawrence's symbolic context if not widely endorsed by the "how-to" manuals of the Masters and Johnson generation, of which Lawrence would no doubt have disapproved). When she tries to get Mellors to tell her that he loves her, he rejects the abstract, overused word in favor of the earthier Anglo-Saxon language of the body and its functions. On one occasion he even introduces her to sodomy so as to "burn out the shames, the deepest, oldest shames, in the most secret places." The result of all this, paradoxically, is that the couple arrives at the state of "chastity." Having broken their ties to the sterile world, they are able to accept an imposed separation until it is possible, after a period of waiting for Mellors's divorce to occur, for them to live together in hope for their future.

In an aside in chapter 9, Lawrence, asserting that it is "the way our sympathy flows and recoils that really determines our lives," affirms that the great function of a novel is precisely to "inform and lead into new places the flow of our sympathetic consciousness" and to "lead our sympathies away in recoil from things gone dead." As a statement of intention, this will do for all of Lawrence's novels. Of course, even the best of intentions do not necessarily lead to artistic achievement. *Lady Chatterley's Lover*, though in many respects a remarkable recovery after the dead end that was the "leadership novels," is nevertheless flawed by the very directness with which it follows the "flow and recoil" idea. For one thing, the deck is too obviously stacked against Clifford. Lawrence never takes him seriously as a man; by making him the stationary target of so much scorn simply for what he represents, Lawrence in effect replicates Clifford's own treatment of people as mere objects or functions.

Because the "recoil" against Clifford as a "thing gone dead" seems facile and almost glib, Connie's counterflow toward Mellors seems also too easy, despite Lawrence's efforts to render her conflicting, vacillating feelings. Another part of the problem lies in the characterization of Mellors, who, after his initial reluctance, proves to be a tiresomely self-satisfied, humorless, "knowing" spokesman for the gospel according to Lawrence. Connie, however, is a marvelous creation, far more complex than even Mellors seems to realize. She is a worthy successor to Lawrence's other intriguing female characters: Gertrude Morel, Ursula and Gudrun Brangwen, Alvina Houghton (of *The Lost Girl*), and Kate Leslie.

At his best, in *Sons and Lovers, The Rainbow*, and especially *Women in Love*, Lawrence manages to enact the flow and counterflow of consciousness, the centrifugal dilation and the centripetal contraction of sympathies, in a far more complex and convincing way than he does in his last novel. Notwithstanding

his battles with Mrs. Grundy, the underlying impulse of all his work is unquestionably moral: the passionate yearning to discover, celebrate, and *become* "whole man alive." The desperateness with which he pursued that elusive ideal in both his life and his art sometimes led him to resort to a bullying, declamatory didacticism, which took the chance of alienating his readers' sympathies.

Lawrence's moral vision was most compelling when embodied and rendered in dramatic or symbolic terms rather than externally imposed by "oracular" utterance and rhetorical bombast. Yet "art for my sake" necessarily involved him in these risks, of which he was fully aware. At a time when aesthetic objectivity and the depersonalization of the artist were the dominant aims of the modernists, Lawrence courageously pursued his vision wherever it might lead.

Through his capacity for outrage against what he considered a dying civilization, his daring to risk failure and humiliation in the ongoing struggle to find and make known the "vital quick" which alone could redeem humanity and to relocate humankind's lost spiritual roots, Lawrence performed the essential role of seer or prophetic conscience for his age. Moreover, because subsequent events in the twentieth century more than confirmed his direst forebodings, his is a voice which readers today cannot afford to ignore. While many are decrying the death of the novel amidst the proliferation of the much-ballyhooed "literature of exhaustion," one could do worse than turn to Lawrence to find again the "one bright book of life."

Ronald G. Walker

OTHER MAJOR WORKS

SHORT FICTION: *The Prussian Officer and Other Stories*, 1914; *England, My England*, 1922; *St. Mawr: Together with the Princess*, 1925; *The Woman Who Rode Away and Other Stories*, 1928; *Love Among the Haystacks and Other Stories*, 1930; *The Lovely Lady and Other Stories*, 1933; *A Modern Lover*, 1934; *The Complete Short Stories of D. H. Lawrence*, 1961.

PLAYS: *The Widowing of Mrs. Holroyd*, pb. 1914;

Touch and Go, pb. 1920; *David*, pb. 1926; *A Collier's Friday Night*, pb. 1934; *The Complete Plays of D. H. Lawrence*, pb. 1965.

POETRY: *Love Poems and Others*, 1913; *Amores*, 1916; *Look! We Have Come Through*, 1917; *New Poems*, 1918; *Bay*, 1919; *Tortoises*, 1921; *Birds, Beasts, and Flowers*, 1923; *The Collected Poems of D. H. Lawrence*, 1928; *Pansies*, 1929; *Nettles*, 1930; *The Triumph of the Machine*, 1931; *Last Poems*, 1932; *Fire and Other Poems*, 1940; *Phoenix Edition of Complete Poems*, 1957; *The Complete Poems of D. H. Lawrence*, 1964 (Vivian de Sola Pinto and Warren Roberts, editors).

NONFICTION: *Twilight in Italy*, 1916; *Movements in European History*, 1921; *Psychoanalysis and the Unconscious*, 1921; *Sea and Sardinia*, 1921; *Fantasia of the Unconscious*, 1922; *Studies in Classic American Literature*, 1923; *Reflections on the Death of a Porcupine and Other Essays*, 1925; *Mornings in Mexico*, 1927; *Pornography and Obscenity*, 1929; *À Propos of Lady Chatterley's Lover*, 1930; *Assorted Articles*, 1930; *Apocalypse*, 1931; *Etruscan Places*, 1932; *The Letters of D. H. Lawrence*, 1932 (Aldous Huxley, editor); *Phoenix: The Posthumous Papers of D. H. Lawrence*, 1936 (Edward McDonald, editor); *The Collected Letters of D. H. Lawrence*, 1962 (2 volumes; Harry T. Moore, editor); *Phoenix II*, 1968 (Moore and Roberts, editors).

BIBLIOGRAPHY

Bloom, Harold, ed. *D. H. Lawrence*. New York: Chelsea House, 1986. A major compilation of critical commentary on Lawrence's writings, this collection of essays deals largely with his major novels and short stories and makes available varying assessments of philosophical and psychological concerns implicit in Lawrence's works. A chronology and short bibliography are also provided.

Ellis, David. *D. H. Lawrence: Dying Game 1922-1930*. Cambridge, England: Cambridge University Press, 1998. Volume 2 of the Cambridge biography of Lawrence (each volume is written by a different author). Ellis, like his Cambridge colleagues, has been criticized for use of excessive detail, but this biography is indispensable for students of specific periods of his life and work who wish a meticulous, accurate account. As Ellis remarks in his preface, more than most writers, Lawrence drew directly from his daily life, and only a minutely detailed biography can trace his creative process.

Heywood, Christopher, ed. *D. H. Lawrence: New Studies*. New York: St. Martin's Press, 1987. This work includes chapters on Lawrence's social origins, his poetry, his major novels, political thought, and "blood consciousness," but no bibliography.

Jackson, Dennis, and Fleda Brown Jackson, eds. *Critical Essays on D. H. Lawrence*. Boston: G. K. Hall, 1988. Various critical insights may be found in this collection of twenty essays, which includes articles by scholars and by well-known writers such as Anaïs Nin and Sean O'Casey. All literary genres in which Lawrence was involved are represented by one or more contributions here. Also of note is the editors' introduction, which deals with trends in critical and biographical literature about Lawrence.

Kinkead-Weekes, Mark. *D. H. Lawrence: Triumph to Exile 1912-1922*. Cambridge, England: Cambridge University Press, 1996. Volume 2 of the Cambridge biography of Lawrence. This is a massively detailed work, including chronology, maps, and notes.

Maddox, Brenda. *D. H. Lawrence: The Story of a Marriage*. New York: Simon & Schuster, 1994. As the subtitle indicates, Maddox focuses on Lawrence and his wife Frieda. A lively, deft writer, Maddox is not as meticulous as Lawrence's more scholarly biographers.

Meyers, Jeffrey. *D. H. Lawrence: A Biography*. New York: Alfred A. Knopf, 1990. The emphasis in this substantial and well-informed biography is on Lawrence's literary milieu and his development of themes and ideas in the broader intellectual context of his own time. Also provides some new interpretations of events in Lawrence's personal life.

Preston, Peter, and Peter Hoare, eds. *D. H. Lawrence*

in the Modern World. Cambridge, England: Cambridge University Press, 1989. The worldwide dimensions of Lawrence's reputation are illustrated by this collection of papers from an international symposium which included scholars from France, Italy, Israel, and Korea, as well as from English-speaking countries.

Sagar, Keith. *D. H. Lawrence: Life into Art.* Athens: University of Georgia Press, 1985. This important literary biography by a specialist who has written several books about Lawrence sets forth the events of Lawrence's life alongside an exposition of themes and techniques which characterized the writer's work in several genres.

Schneider, Daniel J. *The Consciousness of D. H. Lawrence: An Intellectual Biography.* Lawrence: University Press of Kansas, 1986. Major themes in Lawrence's works reflected values and subjective responses developed over the course of the writer's life. Traces psychological concerns and modes of belief as they arose during Lawrence's career, without indulging in undue speculation or reductionism.

Squires, Michael, and Keith Cushman, eds. *The Challenge of D. H. Lawrence.* Madison: University of Wisconsin Press, 1990. This group of essays, which deal both with individual works and with broader literary contexts, supplies some interesting and provocative insights. Of particular note is the first article, by Wayne C. Booth, a self-confessed "lukewarm Lawrentian" who maintains that Lawrence's works are better appreciated upon rereading and reconsideration.

Thornton, Weldon. *D. H. Lawrence: A Study of the Short Fiction.* New York: Twayne, 1993. Part 1 provides interpretations of Lawrence's most important stories; part 2 introduces Lawrence's own criticism; part 3 gives a sampling of important Lawrence critics. Includes a chronology and bibliography.

Worthen, John. *D. H. Lawrence: The Early Years, 1885-1912.* Cambridge, England: Cambridge University Press, 1991. This first volume in the Cambridge biography of Lawrence includes a family tree, chronology, and notes.

JOHN LE CARRÉ
David John Moore Cornwell

Born: Poole, England; October 19, 1931

PRINCIPAL LONG FICTION
Call for the Dead, 1960
A Murder of Quality, 1962
The Spy Who Came in from the Cold, 1963
The Looking-Glass War, 1965
A Small Town in Germany, 1968
The Naive and Sentimental Lover, 1971
Tinker, Tailor, Soldier, Spy, 1974
The Honourable Schoolboy, 1977
Smiley's People, 1980
The Quest for Karla, 1982 (trilogy, includes *Tinker, Tailor, Soldier, Spy, The Honourable Schoolboy,* and *Smiley's People*)
The Little Drummer Girl, 1983
A Perfect Spy, 1986
The Russia House, 1989
The Secret Pilgrim, 1991

(The Douglas Brothers)

The Night Manager, 1993
Our Game, 1995
The Tailor of Panama, 1996
Single and Single, 1999

OTHER LITERARY FORMS

John le Carré's reputation rests exclusively on his novels. He has published a handful of articles and reviews and two short stories but no book-length works in other forms.

ACHIEVEMENTS

Espionage fiction, the spy thriller, has a large, worldwide audience; at the end of the twentieth century one out of every four contemporary works of fiction published in the United States belonged to this genre. Le Carré is preeminent among writers of espionage fiction. John Gardner, himself an espionage novelist and the author of the continuing James Bond saga, has called le Carré "the British *guru* of literary espionage fiction."

Le Carré not only constructs the intricate plots which have made his works international best-sellers but also raises complex and fundamental questions about human nature. Most espionage fiction has a rather simplistic frame of reference: right and wrong, good and evil, us and them. The hero battles it out, his victory assured as he prepares to take on another assignment to save the free world from total collapse. He is a superman, and his adventures are narrated with all the razzle-dazzle and pyrotechnics of escapist fiction.

Le Carré's novels undermine all the stereotypes of spy fiction. Instead of a clear-cut conflict between right and wrong, le Carré's novels offer subtle shades of grey. Instead of a dashing James Bond figure, le Carré's most representative hero is George Smiley, fat, short, and balding, who "entered middle age without ever being young." In novel after novel, le Carré is concerned with ends and means, with love and betrayal. He is concerned with character and motive, probing the agony and tragedy of the person who betrays his or her country not for personal profit but for a cause in which he or she believes. He dramatizes the dilemma faced by men and women involved in the monotonous and often inhuman work of espionage, which leads him to raise the uncomfortable yet fundamental question: How is it possible to defend humanity in inhuman ways? Like Graham Greene, le Carré compels one to go on a journey of self-exploration, to come to grips with one's own self-delusions, fears, and anxieties. In the words of George Grella (*The New Republic*, July 31, 1976), the novels of le Carré "are not so much spy thrillers as thoughtful, compassionate meditations on deception, illusion and defeat." Le Carré's major achievement is his remarkable ability to transform espionage fiction from cliché-ridden, escapist fare to the level of great literature.

Le Carré's novels take his readers to the nerve center of the secret world of espionage. His is an authentic voice, drawing upon his own experiences. Whether it is the minutiae about an agent's training in combat and radio transmitting technique in *The Looking-Glass War*, the subtleties of the "memory man" shredding classified documents in *A Small Town in Germany*, or the meticulous psychological and physical details involved in delivering a clandestine message in *Smiley's People*, le Carré's novels have, in the words of Melvyn Bragg, "the smell of insider lore . . . like a good wax polish." He gives a complete portrait of the intelligence community with all its warts and wrinkles, conveying the sheer monotony and the "measureless tedium of diplomatic life" which form the background of the deadly game of espionage. There is nothing glamorous in this limbo world of spies and double agents, a world chillingly described by Alec Leamas in *The Spy Who Came in from the Cold*: "What do you think spies are? They're a squalid procession of vain fools, traitors too, yes; pansies, sadists and drunkards, people who play cowboys and Indians to brighten their rotten lives." The British Foreign Service is involved not only in plots and counterplots to outwit the Soviets, but also in its own interdepartmental plots and counterplots within the Circus, the London headquarters of the intelligence establishment. In presenting such an uncompromisingly realistic portrait of the spy profession, le Carré has scored a significant achievement.

Finally, in his portrait of George Smiley, le Carré has created a major character in contemporary world literature. Smiley is "one of life's losers." A notorious cuckold who continues to love his beautiful, unfaithful wife, he "looks like a frog, dresses like a bookie," but has a brilliant mind. His vision of retirement is to be left alone to complete his monograph on the German baroque poet Martin Optiz. When he travels on a highly sensitive life-and-death mission, his fellow passengers think of him as "the tired executive out for a bit of fun." Smiley, however, is not one face but "a whole range of faces. More your patchwork of different ages, people and endeavours. Even . . . of different faiths." He is "an abbey, made up of all sorts of conflicting ages and styles and convictions." In spite of all the "information" the reader possesses about Smiley, he remains an elusive personality, thus reflecting a mark of great literary creations: a sense of mystery, of a life beyond the boundaries of the text.

BIOGRAPHY

John le Carré was born David John Moore Cornwell, the son of Ronald and Olive (Glassy) Cornwell, on October 19, 1931, in Poole, Dorset, England, "in a mouldering, artless house with a `for sale' notice in the garden." He went to Sherborne School—where James Hilton's *Goodbye, Mr. Chips*, was filmed—but did not like Sherborne and attempted to run away. "I was not educated at all," le Carré writes in his essay "In England Now" (*The New York Times Magazine*, October 23, 1977), and speaks of his school as a prison. He spent much of his time "planning escapes across moonlit playing fields," thereby finding release from "those huge and lonely dormitories." He remembers the severity of the school crystallized in his being "sprawled inelegantly over the arm of the headmaster's small chair," to smart under blows from a small riding whip. Since young le Carré's father seldom paid the school fees, he was singled out even more for punishment. He was struck by the hand as well as whipped, and le Carré attributes his "partial deafness in one ear to a Mr. Farnsworth," a teacher in school at that time. The school atmosphere was violent: rugger wars were

fought "almost literally to death," boxing was a religious obligation, and instructors drummed into their pupils the notion that "to die in battle" was the highest achievement to which they could aspire.

Le Carré's father was determined to make his two sons grow up independent, so he sent them to schools thirty miles apart. Young David and his brother Tony, two years his senior, made arduous journeys to meet each other on Sundays to find the emotional nourishment they so desperately needed. Le Carré quit Sherborne two years later.

Le Carré's father had dropped out of school at the age of fourteen and ever after, as le Carré said in an interview with *Time* magazine (October 3, 1977), "lived in a contradictory world," full of credit but no cash with a "Micawberlike talent for messing up his business adventures." He finally ended up in prison for fraud. Le Carré's mother abandoned the children to live with a business associate of her husband. Le Carré did not see his mother until he was twenty-one. His father died in 1975 without reconciling with his sons. Without the support of his parents, le Carré had to depend on his elder brother. As children, they were ignorant of the whereabouts of their parents, and the young le Carré often wondered if his father were a spy on a crucial mission for England. False promises by his father made him distrustful of people, and he confesses that "duplicity was inescapably bred" into him. His childhood was therefore traumatic, and he draws upon this painful experience in *The Naive and Sentimental Lover* when he makes Aldo Cassidy, one of the heroes of the novel, tell Shamus how his mother abandoned him when he was a child. The loss "robbed him of his childhood," denying him "normal growth."

Le Carré's father was angry that his son had left Sherborne and, to punish him, sent him to Berne University, Switzerland; le Carré was sixteen at the time. At Berne, he studied German, French, and skiing. After completing his military service in Vienna with the army intelligence corps, he went to Lincoln College, Oxford, and studied modern languages, taking an honors degree in 1956. From 1956 to 1958, he taught languages at England's most prestigious public school, Eton.

Le Carré is fond of quoting Graham Greene's observation that "a writer's capital is his childhood." In his own case, the circumstances of his childhood led him to accept the "condition of subterfuge" as a way of life. In an interview with Melvyn Bragg (*The New York Times Book Review*, March 13, 1983), le Carré speaks again of the manner in which his childhood contributed to his secretive nature; he "began to think that [he] was, so to speak, born into occupied territory." Like the boy Bill Roach in *Tinker, Tailor, Soldier, Spy*, le Carré is the perennial clandestine watcher, observing, noting, analyzing, and piecing together the parts of the puzzle.

In 1954, le Carré married Alison Ann Veronica Sharp, daughter of a R.A.F. Marshall. He has three sons from this marriage, which ended in divorce in 1971. He is now married to Jane Eustace, formerly an editor at his British publisher, Hodder and Stoughton; they have a son, Nicholas.

In 1960, le Carré entered the British Foreign Service and served as second secretary in Bonn from 1960 to 1963, and as consul in Hamburg from 1963 to 1964. Le Carré has been reticent about his actual work in the Foreign Office, and has been noncommittal about whether his Bonn and Hamburg posts were covers for duties as a secret agent. As Melvyn Bragg writes, "He used to deny having been a spy, but now it's out. He gives in gracefully—caught but too late for it to matter. His new line is a line in charming resignation, an admission of nothing very much." The tension, the drama, and the intense human conflict that pervade all his novels undoubtedly derive from le Carré's "insider lore."

Le Carré experimented with writing while he was a student at Sherborne, but abandoned it because he was discouraged in his creative attempts. After getting married and living in Great Missenden, he once again started writing. Frequently, he used the two-hour train journey he had to make every day to London to plot his stories and overcome his "restlessness as a diplomat." He chose the pseudonym "John le Carré" in order to satisfy the regulation of the British Foreign Service which forbids its employees to publish under their own names. Appropriately, the origin of le Carré's pseudonym is itself obscured in mystery

and possible deception. Long ago, le Carré told interviewers that he had seen the name "Le Carré" ("The Square") on the window of a London shop, but diligent researchers have been unable to find any record of such a shop in the registry of London's businesses.

Le Carré's first two novels, *Call for the Dead*, which makes use of his German experience, and *A Murder of Quality*, which draws upon his Eton experience, had moderate success. It was with his third novel, however, *The Spy Who Came in from the Cold*, that le Carré won both fame and financial security. He gave up his job in the Foreign Office and became a full-time writer.

Le Carré leads a very private life in an elegantly furnished cliff house in Cornwall, near Land's End. He is a slow but eclectic reader and avoids novels in his own genre. He follows no writer as a model, but admires and enjoys good prose, clear, lucid, and full of subtle nuances. Joseph Conrad, Graham Greene, and V. S. Naipaul are among his favorite authors.

Le Carré emerged from the shadows somewhat in the 1990's, making himself available for interviews and addressing public issues. Of his time as a member of the secret world, he said in 1996: "I did nothing of significance. . . . I didn't alter the world order." He continued to travel extensively while researching his novels. When at home, he writes in the early morning and often walks along the beaches of Cornwall in the afternoons. He has grappled with the problem of writing novels about espionage in a post-Cold War world and has wondered how much he was affected by the great ideological clash of the superpowers—a clash that he helped to mythologize in his novels.

Concurrent with the release of his 1996 novel, *The Tailor of Panama*, le Carré treated the British reading public to a vituperative literary feud with the novelist Salman Rushdie. Speaking about his book to the Anglo-Israel Association in 1995, le Carré defended himself against charges of anti-Semitism, claiming that he "had become the victim of a witch-hunt by zealots of 'political correctness.'" Rushdie said that he wished le Carré had voiced a similar concern when his book *The Satanic Verses* (1988) prompted the Iranian regime of Ayatollah Ruhollah Khomeini to issue a *fatwa*, or death sentence, against him. Both writers quickly directed very personal attacks against each other in the letters section of the venerable British newspaper *The Guardian*. Le Carré wrote that "there is no law in life or nature that says that great religions may be insulted with impunity." Le Carré added in a later riposte that Rushdie's comments were "cultural intolerance masquerading as free speech."

ANALYSIS

In his first novel, *Call for the Dead* (which took second place in the Crime Writers Association awards for 1961), John le Carré introduced George Smiley, not only his most important character, but also one of the most fascinating and complex characters in the world of fictional espionage. In the very first chapter of the novel, aptly entitled "A Brief History of George Smiley," the reader is offered more information about Smiley than is provided in any other novel in which he appears.

CALL FOR THE DEAD

Cast in the form of a detective story, even though the theme—the control of Samuel Fennan, a British Foreign Service official, by East Germany—is one of international intrigue and espionage, *Call for the Dead* is a tight, short, well-constructed novel written against the background of Britain's postwar security crisis. There is a need for men of Smiley's experience because "a young Russian cypher-clerk in Ottawa" had defected. (The cypher-clerk to whom le Carré referred was Igor Gouzenko, author of *The Fall of a Titan*, 1954; his defection set in motion a number of arrests and other defections, including the notorious cases of Guy Burgess and Kim Philby, who were revealed to have been Soviet agents.)

Smiley, who "could reduce any color to grey," and who "spent a lot of money on bad clothes," has interviewed Samuel Fennan on the basis of an anonymous letter charging Fennan with Communist party affiliations. Soon after the interview, Fennan commits suicide in suspicious circumstancs. In investigating Fennan's death, Smiley investigates himself. Smiley's self-exploration and the moral responsibility he accepts for having indirectly contributed to Fennan's death add strength to the novel. Years earlier, during

a year in Germany in the Nazi era, Smiley had recruited a young man named Dieter Frey because the handsome young German had "a natural genius for the nuts and bolts of espionage." Smiley now has to confront Dieter, who turns out to be an East German agent involved in the Fennan case. When the confrontation takes place, Dieter, out of respect for their past friendship, does not fire his gun to kill Smiley, as he could. After that momentary hesitation, Dieter and Smiley struggle, and Smiley kills his former pupil. Ever the scholar-spy, Smiley recalls a line from Hermann Hesse, "Strange to wander in the mist, each is alone," and realizes that however closely one lives with another, "we know nothing."

Call for the Dead introduces and makes reference to a number of characters who become permanent citizens of le Carré's espionage world. There is Steed-Asprey, Smiley's boss, whose secretary, the Lady Ann Sercombe, Smiley married and lost. Le Carré makes a practice of alluding to Steed-Asprey in each subsequent novel, rewarding his faithful readers with sly bits of information; in *A Small Town in Germany*, for example, a character remarks with seeming irrelevance that Steed-Asprey has become ambassador to Peru. When Smiley is on his final hunt for Karla in *Smiley's People*, it is Steed-Asprey's training he recalls. The reader is also introduced to Peter Guillam, who plays a prominent part in assisting Smiley with tracking down the Soviet mole in *Tinker, Tailor, Soldier, Spy*. Mundt, who is a key character in *The Spy Who Came in from the Cold*, also makes a diabolical appearance in *Call for the Dead*. Le Carré's first novel makes it very clear that he was working to create a design, an oeuvre, and his later novels demonstrate that he succeeded in that attempt.

A MURDER OF QUALITY

Set in an English public school, le Carré's second novel, *A Murder of Quality* (which was a finalist for the Crime Writers Association Award for 1962), is a straight mystery novel with no element of espionage or international intrigue, except that the unofficial "detective" is George Smiley, brought into the case by a friend.

Stella, the wife of Stanley Rode, a teacher at Carne, a posh public school, feels threatened by her husband. Before Smiley can meet her and inquire as to the basis for her fear, Stella is murdered. In investigating Stella's death, Smiley meets a variety of characters both within and outside the school, reflecting the rigid class structure of British society. Le Carré draws upon his own teaching experience at Eton to present a convincing picture of a public school, with its inner tensions and nuances of snobbery and cruelty. "We are not democratic. We close the door on intelligence without parentage," says one of the characters. Stanley Rode is not considered a gentleman because he did not go to the right school. Life at the school is an intensely closed society, and hence, there has not been "an original thought . . . . for the last fifty years."

The least likely suspect turns out to be the murderer. Smiley faces a dilemma because the murderer is the brother of one of his best friends, a fellow agent who disappeared on a mission and is presumed dead. The irony of the situation makes Smiley say, "We just don't know what people are like, we can never tell. . . . We're the chameleons."

THE SPY WHO CAME IN FROM THE COLD

Le Carré's third novel, *The Spy Who Came in from the Cold*, became an international best-seller and brought him fame and financial independence. Graham Greene called it "the best spy story I have ever read." Malcolm Muggeridge praised it for "the cold war setting, so acutely conveyed." It was made into a successful film, with Richard Burton as Alec Leamas. The novel was translated into more than a dozen languages and was called a masterpiece.

Le Carré has said that the novel was inspired by the sight of the Berlin Wall, which drew him "like a magnet." The plot was "devised in the shadow of the Wall." Written in a spare, athletic style (the first draft of 120,000 words was reduced to 70,000, while more than a dozen characters present in the first draft were eliminated in the final version), *The Spy Who Came in from the Cold* is the story of fifty-year-old Alec Leamas, "built like a swimmer," a veteran British agent who has lost his most important agent in East Germany. He is asked to take on one more assignment before coming "in from the cold." Tired and weary, almost burned out, Leamas accepts his termi-

nal assignment: to get a British agent, "a mole," out of East Germany. It is, however, not until the very end that Leamas, a master spy himself, realizes that he is not involved in a mere double cross, but in a triple cross, and that *he* is to be sacrificed. *The Spy Who Came in from the Cold* is also a touching love story of two of society's outcasts, Leamas and Liz. Both are betrayed by the men and institutions in whom they have faith and hope, and to whom they have given their loyalty.

The moves and countermoves in the novel are plotted with the intricacy of a masterly chess game. "I wanted to make an equation and reverse it," le Carré has said, "make another equation and reverse that. Finally, let him think he's got nearly to the solution of the main equation, and then reverse the whole thing."

In Alec Leamas, le Carré creates a stunning portrait of an antihero. "Not accustomed to living on dreams," Leamas is a citizen of the amoral world of espionage, who practices the art of self-deception so completely that he is unable to distinguish where his life begins and his deception ends. "Even when he was alone he compelled himself to live with the person he had assumed." Leamas is needed by the British Foreign Service because he is the expendable man. His boss asks him if he is tired of spying because "in our world we pass so quickly out of the register of hate or love. . . . All that is left in the end is a kind of nausea." Leamas has a sharp-edged cynicism, but when he meets Liz, a devoted but naïve Communist, in the London Library, he feels for her, believing that she can give him "faith in ordinary life." She is his tender spot; she also becomes his Achilles heel. The Service has no qualms about using her to discredit and destroy Leamas, because "In the acquisition of intelligence, the weak and even the innocent must suffer."

Le Carré makes the telling point that in condoning the sacrifice of the individual, without his consent, for the good of the masses, both East and West use the same weapons of deceit and even the same spies. Le Carré's judgment on this murky world is not reassuring: "There is no victory and no virtue in the cold war, only a condition of human illness and misery."

Mundt, whom the reader met in *A Call for the Dead*, has a prominent role in the novel as the second man in the *Abteilung*, the East German Secret Service. A loathsome figure, an ex-Nazi, he turns out to be a double agent serving the British. To rescue him is Leamas's task, and in the process, two decent human beings, both Jews, are destroyed. "I used Jewish people," le Carré writes in his article "To Russia, with Greetings" (*Encounter*, May, 1966), "because I felt that after Stalin and Hitler they should particularly engage our protective instincts." Smiley makes a brief appearance in the novel in a somewhat menacing role, the only such appearance in all of le Carré's novels—Smiley without his humane personality. There are other references to Steed-Asprey, Peter Guillam, and to the Samuel Fennan case, echoes from *A Call for the Dead*.

THE LOOKING-GLASS WAR

The time frame of le Carré's next novel, *The Looking-Glass War*, is twenty years after that of *The Spy Who Came in from the Cold*. The British Military Intelligence unit, which during World War II has been vibrant, proud, and respectable, now exists as a mere remnant. Its officers and agents, nostalgic for the old days, wait for an incident to happen that could summon them to relive the past glory and regain their identity and honor. The head of this outfit is Le Clerc, a bland "precise cat of a man." When one of his agents stumbles across evidence pointing to the possible Soviet smuggling of nuclear rockets to the East Germans, Le Clerc is overjoyed. It is a British version of the Bay of Pigs. Le Clerc wants to stage an overflight to photograph the incriminating evidence. He goes about his mission with messianic zeal, because to him, the enemy is not only the Soviet Union, but the Circus—the rival British intelligence agency—as well. The Circus could take the mission away from him and destroy his unit's moment of glory. In *The Looking-Glass War*, le Carré reveals the Cold War professionals' lack of "ideological involvement." In his own words, "Half the time they are fighting the enemy, a good deal of the time they are fighting rival departments."

Taylor, the man sent to pick up the secret film, is killed, and Le Clerc recruits Avery, untrained for such work, to go undercover to bring back Taylor's body. Avery is a true believer; he attributes legendary qualities to his unit. He is faced with reality when he bungles the recovery mission and is saved only by a seasoned and contemptuous British diplomat, but he falls under Le Clerc's spell again in an ambitious project to train an agent—one of their own, not a Circus man—to send into East Germany to gather evidence of the rockets. His true moment of disillusionment comes when Fred Leiser, the agent in whose training he has participated, is caught inside East Germany. The Department refuses to help Leiser, who is left to fend for himself because of "some squalid diplomatic reason."

Leiser, an immigrant from Poland with wartime espionage experience, is another one of le Carré's rootless spies who is given a prepackaged identity and then discarded. Leiser's training provides the Department with its "carefree exciting days," yet in spite of his loyalty and his gentlemanly dress, Leiser is not considered by the Oxonians who run the show as "one of us." "He is a man to be handled, not known," says Haldane, a friend of Smiley. Leiser is not from the proper class nor from the proper school and hence cannot be a member of the privileged caste to which Haldane and Smiley belong. Through the character of Leiser, le Carré again analyzes the subtle nuances of the British class system.

A SMALL TOWN IN GERMANY

The "town" of *A Small Town in Germany* is Bonn, "a very metaphysical spot" where "dreams have quite replaced reality." Britain is eager to get into the Common Market, so eager that she is prepared to shake hands with the devil. The devil in this case is Karfeld, a demogogue with Hitlerian overtones, fanatically anti-British and involved in forging a Russo-German alliance. Of more immediate concern to the British, however, is Leo Harting, second secretary in the political section of the British embassy. Because of his refugee background—like that of Leiser in *The Looking-Glass War*—Harting is in an "unpromotable, unpostable, unpensionable position."

At the beginning of the book, Harting is missing along with some top-secret files. Information in these files could destroy British chances to join the Common Market and compromise British-German relations. Harting must be found, but the files are more important than the man. To lead this urgent manhunt, Alan Turner is sent from London. Most of the events in the novel are seen through Turner's eyes.

"A big lumbering man," Turner walks "with the thrusting slowness of a barge; a broad aggressive policeman's walk." Like Leamas, Turner is a professional. Tough, acerbic, with a passionate obsession to get the job done, Turner shakes up the inefficient officials of the British embassy. In his pursuit of Harting, Turner begins to see a mirror image of himself. Both are underground men. "I'll chase you, you chase me and each of us will chase ourselves," Turner soliloquizes. In Turner's view, Harting must not only be found but also protected, because he is "our responsibility." To the Oxonians, Harting, although he dresses in British style and "uses our language," is "only half tamed." He is, like Leamas and Leiser, expendable. In his minute analysis of the British embassy officials in Bonn, le Carré portrays what Raymond Sokolov aptly calls "an encyclopedia of the English class system."

Both as an exciting tale of suspense and as a novel exploring the moral dilemma confronting men and women involved in defending Western freedom, *A Small Town in Germany* further advanced le Carré's reputation as an able chronicler of a murky world.

TINKER, TAILOR, SOLDIER, SPY

Tinker, Tailor, Soldier, Spy, the first volume in the trilogy concerning Smiley's pursuit of his Soviet counterpart, Karla, is the story of the exposure of a Soviet "mole" burrowed deep within the Circus. Smiley, who has been fired (officially, he has "retired") because of his close association with Control, the former head of the Circus, now dead, who was discredited by the mole because he was coming too close to the truth, is summoned "to come out of his retirement and root out as unobtrusively as possible" the Soviet mole. Smiley begins his meticulous search through the "long dark tunnel." Proust-like, he indulges in remembrance of things past to trace the identity of the mole. He even questions his own motives, part of the subtle pressure exerted on him by

his adversary Karla. The search in memory takes him to Delhi, India, where the reader meets Karla for the first time. Karla, "a little wiry chap, with silvery hair and bright brown eyes and plenty of wrinkles," is imprisoned under the name of Gerstman. With characteristic frankness, Smiley tells Karla, "I can see through Eastern values just as you can through our Western ones." Trying vainly to persuade Karla to defect, Smiley offers him cigarettes and hands him his lighter, a gift inscribed with love from his wife, Ann. Karla keeps the lighter when he returns, unpersuaded, to his cell. Echoes of this prison meeting between Karla and Smiley reverberate effectively in *The Honourable Schoolboy* and *Smiley's People*.

Smiley finally captures the mole: He is suave, handsome Bill Haydon, who comes from the right background and the right school. Haydon has turned mole because he could no longer be an empire builder. Haydon not only has betrayed his country, but also has betrayed his friend Jim Prideaux by setting him up for Soviet cruelty. Further, at the command of Karla, Haydon has slept with Smiley's wife, Ann, thereby creating a doubt in Smiley's mind concerning his own motives for ferreting out Haydon. The bureaucratic world of official secrets is linked with the private world of emotional betrayal, giving le Carré's work a universality which transcends its genre.

Kim Philby, the British defector, was the prototype of Bill Haydon. In his introduction to *The Philby Conspiracy* (1968), le Carré writes that the British secret services are "microcosms of the British condition, of our social attitudes and vanities." *Tinker, Tailor, Soldier, Spy* portrays such a microcosm.

Tinker, Tailor, Soldier, Spy was a successful television miniseries with Alec Guinness as George Smiley. Le Carré admired the production, but he has remarked that Guinness "took the character away from me. Writing Smiley after Smiley-through-Guinness had entered the public domain was very difficult. In a sense his screen success blew it for me."

THE HONOURABLE SCHOOLBOY

Set in Southeast Asia at the time of America's disastrous retreat from Vietnam, *The Honourable Schoolboy*, the second volume in the trilogy *The*

Quest for Karla, is a stunning novel of contemporary history. In *The Honourable Schoolboy*, Smiley steps out of Europe: The action of the novel ranges across Southeast Asia and is centered in Hong Kong. There are two spheres of action: the Circus, where one encounters the familiar faces of Peter Guillam, Sam Collins, and Toby Esterhase; and Southeast Asia, where Smiley has sent Jerry Westerby to track down a high-ranking Chinese who is a top Soviet agent. As the novel progresses Smiley must also contend with the machinations of the "cousins" (the American Central Intelligence Agency).

Jerry Westerby is the honorable schoolboy, so called because he was called "schoolboy" in the Tuscan village where he was trying to write a novel, and given the honorific "the Honorable" because he is the son of a Press Lord. Le Carré had introduced Westerby in *Tinker, Tailor, Soldier, Spy*, and in making him the major figure in *The Honourable Schoolboy*, he demonstrated one of his techniques for developing characters. In an interview with Michael Barber (*The New York Times Book Review*, September 25, 1977), le Carré explained that he gives some of his minor characters "a variety of qualifications" so that he can later "turn them from two dimensional characters into three dimensional characters." He had provided Westerby with a Far Eastern background in the earlier novel, making him a natural for a leading role in a novel with that setting.

In *The Honourable Schoolboy*, Smiley feels compelled to restore the dignity of the Circus, lost in the aftermath of the exposure of Bill Haydon. When he spots large amounts of money from Russia pouring into Southeast Asia, his curiosity is aroused. He recruits Westerby, a newspaper writer and an "occasional" for the Circus, to go to Hong Kong. Westerby's targets are two Chinese brothers, Drake Ko and Nelson Ko. In dealing with them, Westerby is fatally attracted to Drake Ko's mistress Lizzi Worthington. Westerby, by allowing his passion—and compassion—to intrude on his sense of duty, pays a heavy price for his weakness.

The Honourable Schoolboy is a very complex novel, and there are plots within plots like ingenious Chinese boxes. Any attempt at a synopsis would be futile, and it is difficult to capture the rich texture of the novel. Le Carré peoples it with a multitude of characters, each bursting with possibilities for a separate novel. There is Craw, the Australian journalist, an old China hand, based on the London *Sunday Times* correspondent Richard Hughes (who also appears as Dikko Henderson in Ian Fleming's *You Only Live Twice*, 1964); Connie Sachs, the Circus Sovietologist; Fawn, the professional killer; and the mercenary pilot Ricardo, to mention but a few. They interact with one another in a variety of ways to dramatize a labyrinthine maze of involved relationships, both personal and political. Within this framework, le Carré again poses the questions with which he continues to be concerned: What is honor? What is loyalty? These questions, as Eliot Fremont-Smith noted, "provide the tension in the book, and are its engines of suspense."

SMILEY'S PEOPLE

Smiley's People, the final volume in the trilogy *The Quest for Karla*, opens with the knowledge that one of Smiley's most valued and loyal "people," Vladimir, alias Colonel Miller, has been murdered. He had a message for Smiley concerning the Sandman (a code name for Karla). Once again, Smiley is called back from retirement. Smiley's quest is to find a weak spot in Karla, his Soviet counterpart. In Karla, Smiley sees his own dark and mysterious side. As Connie Sachs says to him, "You and Karla, two halves of the same apple."

In this novel, Smiley is the detective *par excellence*. He stalks Vladimir's killer with the skill and acumen of Sherlock Holmes. No James Bond, Smiley is the philosopher-spy who wants to find Karla's Achilles heel. He is convinced that Karla is not "fireproof." The tender spot turns out to be Karla's mentally defective daughter, Alexandra. Smiley plays upon this weakness, this aspect of a Karla "flawed by humanity."

Karla yields, and the final tense scene of *Smiley's People* is acted out on the same site as le Carré's masterpiece, *The Spy Who Came in from the Cold*—the Berlin Wall. Smiley sees the face of the man whose photograph had hung on the wall in the Circus, constantly reminding him of his unfinished business.

They face each other, "perhaps a yard apart," Smiley hears the sound of Ann's gold cigarette lighter fall to the ground, and Karla crosses over to give Smiley the victory he has sought for so long.

In *Smiley's People*, the reader meets Ann for the first time, "beautiful and Celtic." When Smiley sees her, "Haydon's shadow" falls "between them like a sword." In the end, Smiley is alone, as he had been in his first appearance in *A Call for the Dead*, "without school, parents, regiment or trade," a man who has invested his life in institutions and realizes philosophically that all he is "left with is myself."

The women in *Smiley's People* are more fully delineated than in le Carré's previous novels. He attributes this to his second marriage. After completing *Smiley's People*, le Carré expressed the hope that the "emergence of female strength" in that novel could be carried into later writing. In *The Little Drummer Girl*, he fulfilled that ambition.

THE LITTLE DRUMMER GIRL

Charmian ("Charlie"), an English actress—incidentally inspired by le Carré's own sister Charlotte, a Shakespearean actress—is the heroine of *The Little Drummer Girl*. Charlie is a promoter of many causes, a grab-bag of the serious and the fashionable, "a passionate opponent of apartheid . . . a militant pacifist, a Sufist, a nuclear marcher, an anti-vivisectionist, and until she went back to smoking again, a champion of campaigns to eliminate tobacco from theatres and on the public underground." The resemblances to Vanessa Redgrave are unmistakable.

Kurtz, an Israeli intelligence agent, offers Charlie the most spectacular role of her career—an opportunity to perform in "the theatre of the real." She is transformed into a successful double agent with the task of cracking "the terror target." The target is Khalil, a Palestinian guerrilla who is bombing Jews and Israelis in Bonn and various other European cities. In her attempt to get Khalil out into the open, Charlie undergoes an astonishing change in her own character. It is hard to think of another novel that has so masterfully portrayed the destruction and reconstruction of the psyche of a person in the process of being turned into a double agent.

The Little Drummer Girl is a departure for le Carré. There are no moles here, but rather terrorists, and Britain and the Soviet Union are replaced by Israelis and Palestinians. Le Carré made several trips to the Middle East, talking with members of Israeli intelligence and with Yasser Arafat to soak up the atmosphere and allow his characters to develop and determine the action of the novel. The characters are not only authentic but also credible. In Charlie's switching of roles and loyalties, le Carré has the opportunity to present both viewpoints, the Israeli and the Palestinian. While le Carré admires all that Israel stands for, in this book he is a partisan for the needs of the Palestinians. In *The Little Drummer Girl*, le Carré skillfully weaves a suspense tale taken from newspaper headlines, seeking out the universal themes of loneliness, alienation, exile, love, and betrayal of human beings behind those headlines. The result is a great novel.

A PERFECT SPY

In his next two novels, le Carré returned to the world of British espionage. *A Perfect Spy* centers on Magnus Pym, a British double agent. Here, as in previous works, le Carré considers the meaning of loyalty and betrayal, not only among spies but also in everyday life; in much of the book, espionage is peripheral. The character of Rick Pym, Magnus's charming but untrustworthy father, is clearly based on le Carré's own father, and the novel is his most autobiographical to date.

THE RUSSIA HOUSE

With *The Russia House*, le Carré became one of the first masters of espionage fiction to reckon with the changes wrought by Mikhail Gorbachev's policy of *glasnost*. Published in the spring of 1989, shortly before the momentous events in Germany and Eastern Europe, *The Russia House* suggests that powerful factions in the United States intelligence community and military establishment might well contrive to keep the Cold War going.

A Perfect Spy and *The Russia House* demonstrate le Carré's continuing determination to extend the boundaries of the espionage novel. Indeed, le Carré's career offers proof—if further proof is needed—that great fiction can be written in any genre, that genius is no respecter of critical categories.

THE SECRET PILGRIM

The occasion of le Carré's next novel, *The Secret Pilgrim*, is the end-of-term dinner at the Circus's training center, Sarratt. The guest of honor, the legendary George Smiley, makes his last appearance in le Carré's work, imparting his wisdom to the spies in training and to Ned, previously Barley Blair's case officer in *The Russia House*. Ned listens to Smiley's recollections, feeling "that he was speaking straight into my heretical heart."

Smiley's comments propel Ned into a deep retrospection of the thirty years of secrecy and betrayal that have constituted his life in the Service. *The Secret Pilgrim* progresses not so much as an integrated whole but as a series of short stories. At the end of the evening's celebration, Smiley flatly states that "It's over, and so am I. . . . Time you rang down the curtain on yesterday's cold warrior. . . . The worst thing you can do is imitate us." Jauntily, as a parting note, Smiley says to "tell them to spy on the ozone layer, will you, Ned?"

THE NIGHT MANAGER

A problem that le Carré faced in the 1990's was what to write about after the end of the Cold War, which had been so central to his work. He solved this problem in his next novel, *The Night Manager*, his mostly richly textured and intricately plotted book since *The Honorable Schoolboy*. Jonathan Pine, onetime British soldier and itinerant hotelier, is haunted by the death of Sophie, an Egyptian woman he had tried to save from her brutal arms-dealing lover. Pine volunteers his services to British intelligence after he encounters Dicky Roper, the man who is ultimately responsible for Sophie's death. Pine becomes a pawn in a struggle between the "enforcement" operatives who control him, and who wish to prosecute Roper, and the "Pure Intelligence" services of the "River House" who have a secret understanding with Roper. A further complication is Pine's love for Roper's mistress, Jemima. Infiltrating Roper's household, Pine eventually becomes involved in Roper's arms deals until his cover is blown. The conclusion of the novel is a clear homage to Joseph Conrad's "The Secret Sharer"; Pine and Jemima are helped off Roper's yacht, while Roper sadly watches from the rail.

OUR GAME

Our Game, a play on the British expression "the Great Game," pits two Cold War colleagues against each other. Timothy Cranmer, a retired case officer, now a winemaker, pursues his agent, Larry, who has disappeared with Cranmer's girlfriend, Emma. Tracing Emma to Paris, Cranmer continues to follow Larry, first to Moscow, then to Chechnya during its civil war. While he arrives too late to confront his former colleague, Cranmer is not too late to redeem his own and Larry's legacy. He joins the Chechen guerrillas.

THE TAILOR OF PANAMA

Le Carré's only comic novel, *The Tailor of Panama*, recalls Graham Greene's *Our Man in Havana*. Harry Pendel, a former convict and "bespoken tailor," is suborned as a source by British intelligence. Unfortunately he has no intelligence to impart, so he invents it. Fueled by this source, the intelligence community in Panama contrives an American coup, while the British ambassador elopes with his secretary. Le Carré's darkly humorous vision of intelligence gathering is juxtaposed against the real problems of contemporary Panamanians.

K. Bhaskara Rao, updated by James Barbour

BIBLIOGRAPHY

Barley, Tony. *Taking Sides: The Fiction of John le Carré*. Philadelphia: Open University Press, 1986. This work applies a somewhat esoteric critical examination to the problems of morality and reality in le Carré's work up to *The Little Drummer Girl*. It is a thorough text, but it suffers from being too academic.

Beene, Lynn Diane. *John le Carré*. New York: Twayne, 1992. This is a very useful biography of David Cornwell's life before he adopted the pseudonym John le Carré and his career since becoming a writer. Following the biography, the author provides a detailed and well-referenced analysis of le Carré's novels through *Smiley's People*.

Cobbs, John, L. *Understanding John le Carré*. Columbia: University of South Carolina Press, 1998. This is a thorough and comprehensive critical work about John le Carré's novels, all of which through *The Tailor of Panama* are analyzed.

Lewis, Peter E. *John le Carré*. New York: Frederick Ungar, 1985. An extensive critique of John le Carré's work, with special mention of its political context. The material is well organized and includes a useful bibliography.

Monaghan, David. *The Novels of John le Carré: The Art of Survival*. New York: Basil Blackwell, 1985. Provides book-by-book coverage of all of le Carré's novels through *The Little Drummer Girl*. Also includes an insightful chapter on George Smiley.

————. *Smiley's Circus*. London: Orbis Press, 1986. A wonderful illustrated index of characters from all the novels through *A Perfect Spy*, particularly focusing on the Karla trilogy of novels. Includes chronologies of the plots of the novels, maps, and photographs of some of the more famous British landmarks featured in le Carré's work. This is an invaluable tool for untangling the byzantine complexity of George Smiley's world. Its careful compilation of characters is testament not only to Monaghan's skill as a researcher but also to le Carré's deeply textured work.

Sauerberg, Lars Ole. *Secret Agents in Fiction*. New York: St. Martin's Press, 1984. A criticism and comparison of John le Carré, Ian Fleming, and Len Deighton. Although there are references to le Carré throughout the text, one chapter, "The Enemy Within," is devoted solely to his work.

Wolfe, Peter. *Corridors of Deceit: The World of John le Carré*. Bowling Green, Ohio: Bowling Green University Popular Press, 1987. An in-depth probing of le Carré's writing, this work contains many interesting insights into the author's characters but lacks a bibliography.

HARPER LEE

Born: Monroeville, Alabama; April 28, 1926

PRINCIPAL LONG FICTION
To Kill a Mockingbird, 1960

OTHER LITERARY FORMS

In addition to the novel that made her famous, Lee wrote for magazines, including *Vogue* and *McCall's*.

ACHIEVEMENTS

Based entirely on her first and only novel, Lee's success has been phenomenal. According to a survey of reading habits conducted in 1991 by the Book-of-the-Month Club and the Library of Congress's Center for the Book, researchers found that *To Kill a Mockingbird* was "most often cited as making a difference in people's lives, second only to the Bible." In 1961, *To Kill a Mockingbird* won a Pulitzer Prize for fiction, the Brotherhood Award of the National Conference of Christians and Jews, the Alabama Library Association Award, and the British Book Society Award. By 1962 it had become a Literary Guild selection and a Book-of-the-Month-Club choice, it had won the Bestsellers' Magazine Paperback of the Year award, and it was featured in the *Reader's Digest* series of condensed books. In the same year Lee was given an honorary doctorate by Mount Holyoke College. She would receive another honorary doctorate in 1990 from the University of Alabama.

Initially enjoying seventy-three weeks on the national best-seller lists, *To Kill a Mockingbird* has been translated into at least ten languages. In 1962 it was made into a motion picture starring Gregory Peck, which won several Academy Awards. President Lyndon Johnson appointed Lee to the National Council on the Arts in 1966, on which she served for five years. In 1970 playwright Christopher Sergel published a stage version of Lee's novel, *Harper Lee's To Kill a Mockingbird: A Full-Length Play*, with Dramatic Publications. The play was professionally performed on both sides of the Atlantic Ocean during the 1980's and 1990's.

BIOGRAPHY

The third daughter and youngest child of Amasa Coleman Lee, an attorney and newspaper publisher, and Frances Finch Lee, reportedly a somewhat eccentric pianist, Nelle Harper Lee grew up in Monroeville, Alabama, attended public school there, then went to Huntington College for Women in

Montgomery for a year, before transferring to the University of Alabama in 1945. Lee edited the college newspaper, the *Rammer Jammer*, and spent a year as an exchange student at Oxford University.

In 1950 she entered law school, no doubt with the intention of following in her father's footsteps. However, after one year she decided to abandon the study of law and go to New York City to pursue a career in writing. Throughout the early 1950's Lee worked by day as a reservation clerk for Eastern Airlines and British Overseas Airways, living in a cramped flat with no hot water, and writing in her free time. During this period she also made many trips to Monroeville to be with her ailing father, who died in 1962. Happily, Amasa Lee did live long enough to see *To Kill a Mockingbird* become a hugely successful book.

In a short article published in *McCall's* in December, 1961, called "Christmas to Me," Lee recounts how she missed her home and family, contrasting New York City with memories of Monroeville during the Christmas season. However, she made some very close friends in her adopted home, and she spent Christmas with one of these families, who surprised her with a monetary gift. On the accompanying card were the words, "You have one year off from your job to write whatever you please. Merry Christmas." She was overwhelmed, but her benefactors felt that their faith in Lee's ability was well founded.

Lee used this time carefully: A methodical writer, she composed a few pages each day and revised them carefully, completing three short fictional sketches by 1957. After being advised that she must do more to transform this work into a novel, she continued to write for two and a half years, until *To Kill a Mockingbird* went to press in 1960, dedicated to her father and to her older sister, Alice, a partner in the family law firm.

Writer Truman Capote spent a great part of his childhood in Monroeville, staying each summer with relatives whose house was in close proximity to the Lees'. The character of Charles Baker Harris, nicknamed Dill, in *To Kill a Mockingbird* is an accurate portrait of the young Capote, who remained close to Lee throughout his life. In the early 1960's Lee went

(CORBIS/Bettmann)

with Capote to Kansas to help him research *In Cold Blood* (1966), which chronicles the murders of the Clutter family in Holcomb, Kansas; Capote dedicated the book to Lee and another lifelong friend, Jack Dunphy. Much of what is known about Lee is revealed in Capote's works and in those written about him by others.

Lee was invited to write the screenplay for the film version of *To Kill a Mockingbird*, but she declined. She was, however, very pleased with screenwriter Horton Foote's script, about which she said, "If the integrity of a film adaptation is measured by the degree to which the novelist's intent is preserved, Mr. Foote's screenplay should be studied as a classic." She was so delighted by Gregory Peck's portrayal of Atticus Finch that she honored his performance and resemblance to her father by giving him Amasa Lee's gold pocket watch, which was inscribed, "To Gregory from Harper, 1962."

Although *To Kill a Mockingbird* has sold more than fifteen million copies, Harper Lee never produced another book. As she told her cousin Richard Williams, when he questioned her about this, "When you have a hit like that, you can't go anywhere but down." Although known in her hometown as a friendly and jovial woman, Lee consistently refused all attempts to interview her. In 1995, when Harper-Collins released the thirty-fifth-anniversary edition of *To Kill a Mockingbird*, Lee declined to write an introduction, stating, "The book still says what it has to say: it has managed to survive the years without preamble." She continued to divide her time between a New York apartment and a modest house in Monroeville, which she shared with her sister, Miss Alice.

Analysis

To Kill a Mockingbird

To Kill a Mockingbird has gained stature over the years, becoming thought of as more than merely a skillful depiction of small-town Southern life during the 1930's with a coming-of-age theme. Claudia Durst Johnson, who has published two books of analysis on *To Kill a Mockingbird*, suggests that the novel is universally compelling because Lee's overall theme of "threatening boundaries" covers a wide spectrum, from law to social standing, from childhood innocence to racism.

The narrator of the book is Scout (Jean Louise) Finch, who is discussing childhood events with her adult brother, Jem, as the story begins. She then slips effortlessly into the role of the six-year-old tomboy who matures over the three years of the book's action. In the first half of the novel, Scout and Jem, along with their childhood companion, Dill, are fascinated by their mysterious neighbor, Boo (Arthur) Radley. Because no one has seen Boo in many years, the youngsters construct a gothic stereotype of him, imagining him as huge and ugly, a monster who dines on raw squirrels, sports a jagged scar, and has rotten yellowing teeth and bulging eyes. They make plans to lure Boo from his "castle" (in reality the dark, shuttered Radley house), but in the course of their attempts to breach the boundaries of his life, they begin to discover the real Boo, an extremely shy man who has attempted to reach out to the children in a number of ways, and who, in the final chapters of the book, saves their lives.

The second half of the book is principally concerned with the trial of Tom Robinson, a young African American unfairly accused of raping a white woman. Racial tensions in the neighborhood explode; Scout and Jem are shocked to find that not only their peers but also adults they have known their whole lives are harshly critical of their father, Atticus, who provides the legal defense for the innocent man.

Throughout both sections of *To Kill a Mockingbird* Lee skillfully shows other divisions among people and how these barriers are threatened. Obviously, it is not a matter of race alone that sets societal patterns in this provincial Alabama town. For example, when Atticus's sister, Alexandria, visits the family, she makes it clear that she is displeased by Scout's tomboyish appearance, since she feels a future "Southern belle" should be interested in more lady-like clothing and more feminine behavior. Furthermore, as Jem tells Scout later, there is a strict caste system in Maycomb, with each group threatened by any possible abridgements of the social order. As Jem suggests, there are the "old" families—the gentry, who are usually educated, frequently professional, but, given the era, often cash-poor. On the next level down are the "poor but proud" people, such as the Cunninghams. They are country folk who pay their bills with crops and adamantly refuse all charity. Beneath them is the group commonly called "poor white trash," amply represented by Bob Ewell, "the only man ever fired by the WPA for laziness," and his pitiful daughter Mayella, the supposed victim of the rape. At the lowest rung of the social ladder are African Americans, although many are clearly superior to some of the poor white trash, who have only their skin color as their badge of superiority. They are represented by Tom Robinson, the accused rapist, and Calpurnia, the housekeeper for the motherless Finch family.

In addition to the clearly defined social castes, there are deviants, such as Dolphus Raymond, a white man involved in a long relationship with a black woman. He pretends to be an alcoholic to "give himself an excuse with the community" for his lifestyle. There is Mrs. Henry Lafayette Dubose, a member of the upper class who became a morphine addict, whose one desire is to overcome her habit before her death. Also featured is Miss Maudie, the friendly neighbor who seems to represent, along with Atticus, the best hope for change in the community.

Lee uses many symbols in the book, none more pervasive than the mockingbird of the title. The bird is characterized as an innocent singer who lives only to give pleasure to others. Early in the novel, when Atticus gives Jem and Scout air rifles, he makes it clear that it would be a sin to harm a mockingbird, a theme reiterated by Miss Maudie. Two of the main characters are subtly equated with the birds: Boo Radley and Tom Robinson, both innocents "caged for crimes they never committed." Atticus himself is a symbol of conscience. Unlike his sister, he is a nonconformist, an atypical Southerner, a thoughtful, bookish man at odds with his environment. He constantly tells his children that they can understand other people only by walking in their shoes. He is mindful of majority opinion but asserts, "The one thing that doesn't abide by majority rule is a person's conscience."

Sometimes, of course, violent action is necessary to alter boundaries. This is foreshadowed early in the novel when Atticus finds it necessary to shoot a rabid dog. However, later, when he faces the mob from Old Sarum, who are intent on lynching Tom Robinson, he simply sits in front of the jail, ostensibly reading a newspaper. Atticus seems very calm, upset only by the appearance of the children and Jem's refusal to take Dill and Scout home, not by the men who threaten violence. After Scout recognizes Mr. Cunningham and mentions Walter, his son, as her school friend, the group leaves. Braxton Underwood, owner of the *Maycomb Tribune*, leans out of his window above the office holding a double-barreled shotgun, saying, "I had you covered all the time, Atticus," suggesting that there may well be occasions in which force is appropriate.

Tried before a jury of white men, in an echo of the 1931 *Scottsboro Nine* case, which convicted nine innocent black men of raping two white women, Tom

Robinson is found guilty in spite of proof that he could not have committed the crime. Yet even here there is a bit of hope for change to come, because the jury does not reach a quick decision, deliberating for three hours in a case involving the strongest taboo in the South, a black man sexually molesting a white woman. Tom, however, does not believe that Atticus's legal appeals will save him, and again violence erupts when he is shot and killed while trying to escape from the prison exercise yard.

Although Lee set her novel in a very isolated locale, which she calls Maycomb, in an era when her notion of crossing racial and social boundaries does not always seem imminently attainable, the world of 1960, when *To Kill a Mockingbird* appeared, was radically different. The Civil Rights movement had begun: The United States Supreme Court had ruled against school segregation in the 1954 *Brown v. Board of Education* decision, and there had been a successful bus boycott in Montgomery, Alabama, in 1955-1956, which brought activist Martin Luther King, Jr., to public attention. Finally, people who believed in the importance of applying law fairly and breaking racial boundaries (as Atticus Finch did) were being heard.

There was some criticism of the melodramatic ending of the novel, in which Bob Ewell attacks the Finch children, who are in costume returning from a school Halloween pageant. Jem's arm is broken in the scuffle, and Scout is saved from the attacker by Boo Radley, who kills Ewell with his own knife. However, in addition to providing closure for the plot, Lee uses this ending to confirm her view of Atticus and his moral character. At first, when Sheriff Heck Tate comes to the Finch home to learn the details of the evening's happenings, Atticus mistakenly assumes that Jem has killed Bob while defending Scout. Heck tries to reassure Atticus, saying, "Bob Ewell fell on his knife. He killed himself." Atticus believes that the sheriff is suggesting a cover-up for Jem, which he refuses, saying, "I can't live one way in town and another way in my home." Finally he realizes that it was Boo Radley who had stabbed Bob with a kitchen knife, not Jem. Atticus then agrees out of kindness to the reclusive Boo to go along with the sheriff's version of the death. When he tells Scout that Mr. Tate was right, she says, "Well, [telling the truth would] be sort of like shootin' a mockingbird, wouldn't it?"

Most literary critics have written of *To Kill a Mockingbird* in glowing terms. One critic has suggested that Atticus is the symbol of the future, of the "new" South that will arise when it takes into account all human experience, discarding the old romantic notions of an isolated regionalism in favor of a wider Emersonian view of the world.

Edythe M. McGovern

BIBLIOGRAPHY

Bloom, Harold, ed. *To Kill a Mockingbird*. Philadelphia: Chelsea House, 1999. Part of the Modern Critical Interpretations series, this volume includes a number of critical essays concerning the novel.

Johnson, Claudia Durst. *To Kill a Mockingbird: Threatening Boundaries*. New York: Twayne, 1994. A thesis regarding Lee's feelings about the South.

_____. *Understanding "To Kill a Mockingbird": A Casebook to Issues, Sources and Historical Documents*. Westport, Conn.: Greenwood Press, 1994. Useful for those doing in-depth studies of the novel.

Moates, Marianne M. *A Bridge of Childhood: Truman Capote's Southern Years*. New York: Holt, 1989. Clearly shows Capote as character Dill Harris, reiterating childhood episodes which Lee used in the book.

JOSEPH SHERIDAN LE FANU

Born: Dublin, Ireland; August 28, 1814
Died: Dublin, Ireland; February 7, 1873

PRINCIPAL LONG FICTION

The Cock and Anchor, 1845
Torlogh O'Brien, 1847
The House by the Churchyard, 1863
Wylder's Hand, 1864
Uncle Silas, 1864
Guy Deverell, 1865
All in the Dark, 1866
The Tenants of Malory: A Novel, 1867 (3 volumes)
A Lost Name, 1868
The Wyvern Mystery, 1869
Checkmate, 1871
The Rose and the Key, 1871
Morley Court, 1873
Willing to Die, 1873 (3 volumes)

OTHER LITERARY FORMS

Joseph Sheridan Le Fanu is better known today as a short-story writer than as a novelist. His many tales first appeared in periodicals, later to be combined into collections. In addition to having genuine intrinsic merit, the stories are important to an understanding of Le Fanu the novelist, for in them he perfected the techniques of mood, characterization, and plot construction that make his later novels so obviously superior to his early efforts. Indeed, Le Fanu seems to have recognized little distinctive difference between the novel and the tale; his novels are often expansions of earlier stories, and stories reissued in collections might be loosely linked by a frame created to give them some of the unity of a novel. The major collections, *Ghost Stories and Tales of Mystery* (1851), *Chronicles of Golden Friars* (1871), *In a Glass Darkly* (1872), and *The Purcell Papers* (1880), reveal an artist who ranks with Edgar Allan Poe, Ambrose Bierce, M. R. James, and Algernon Blackwood as one of the masters of supernatural fiction in the English language. One story from *In A Glass Darkly*, "Carmilla," is reprinted in almost every anthology of horror stories and has inspired numerous film versions, the most famous being Carl-Theodore Dreyer's *Vampyr* (1931).

Le Fanu wrote verse throughout his literary career. While unknown as a poet to modern audiences, in his own day at least one of his compositions achieved great popularity in both Ireland and the United States. "Shamus O'Brien" (1850) is a fine ballad that relates the adventures of the title character in the uprising of 1798.

(CORBIS/Hulton-Deutsch Collection)

Achievements

In the preface to his most famous novel, *Uncle Silas*, Le Fanu rejects the claim of critics that he is a mere writer of "sensational novels." Pointing out that the great novels of Sir Walter Scott have sensational elements of violence and horror, he denies that his own work, any more than Scott's, should be characterized by the presence of such elements; like Scott, Le Fanu too has "moral aims."

To see the truth in this self-appraisal requires familiarity with more than one of Le Fanu's novels. Singly, each of the major works overwhelms the reader with the cleverness of its plot, the depravity of its villain, the suspense evoked by its carefully controlled tone. Several novels together, however, recollected in tranquility, reveal a unity of theme. Moreover, each novel can then be seen as not merely a variation on the theme but also as a deliberate next logical step toward a more comprehensive and definitive statement. The intricacies of plot, the kinds of

evil represented by the villains, the pervasive gothic gloom are to Le Fanu more than story elements; they are themselves his quite serious comment on the nature of human existence, driven by natural and social forces that leave little room for the effective assertion of free will toward any beneficial end.

In Le Fanu's short stories, more often than in his novels, those forces are embodied in tangible supernatural agents. "Carmilla," for example, is the tale of a real female vampire's attack on a young woman, but seen in the context of the larger theme, it is more than a bit of occult fiction calculated to give its readers a scare. With her intense sexuality and lesbian tendencies, the vampire is nothing less than the embodiment of a basic human drive out of control, and that drive—like the others that move society: self-preservation, physical comfort—can quite unpredictably move toward destruction. Le Fanu's most significant achievement as a novelst was to show how the horror genre could be used for serious purposes—to show that monsters are not as horrible as minds that beget monsters, and that ghosts are not as interesting as people who are haunted.

Biography

Joseph Sheridan Le Fanu was descended from a Huguenot family that had left France for Ireland in the seventeenth century. Both his grandfather, Joseph, and great uncle, Henry, had married sisters of the famous playwright, Richard Brinsley Sheridan. His father, Philip Le Fanu, was a noted scholar and clergyman who served as rector at the Royal Hibernian School, where Le Fanu was born, and later as Dean of Emly. His mother was from all accounts a most charming and gentle person, an essayist on philanthropic subjects and a leader in the movement for humane treatment of animals. With loving and indulgent parents and the excitement of life at the school, where military reviews were frequent, Le Fanu's childhood was a happy one.

In 1826, the family moved to Abington in county Limerick. Le Fanu and his brother, William, were not sent to a formal school but were tutored by their father with the help of an elderly clergyman, who gladly excused the boys from their lessons so he could pursue the passion of his life: fishing. Walking tours through the wild Irish countryside, conversations with friendly peasants, who told of fairies and pookhas and banshees, shaped very early the imagination of the boy who would become the creator of so many tales of the mysterious and supernatural. The Tithe Wars of 1831 and the resulting animosity of the peasants to the Le Fanus, who were seen as representative of the Anglo-Irish establishment, forced the young Le Fanu to examine his own Irishness. On the one hand, he was intellectually supportive of the union and convinced that the British rule was in the best interests of the Irish people; on the other, the courage and sacrifices of the bold Irish nationalists filled him with admiration and respect.

In 1837, Le Fanu was graduated from Trinity College, Dublin. He took honors in classics and was well-known for his fine orations before the College Historical Society. Called to the Irish Bar in 1839, he never practiced law but entered a productive career in journalism. His first published work, "The Ghost and the Bonesetter," appeared in the *Dublin University Magazine* in January, 1838. That magazine was to publish serially eight of Le Fanu's fourteen novels after he became its owner and editor in 1861. During the early 1840's, Le Fanu became proprietor or part-owner of a number of journals, including *The Warder, The Statesman, The Protestant Guardian*, and the *Evening Mail*.

In 1844, Le Fanu married Susan Bennett. The union was a happy one; the Le Fanus had two sons and two daughters. One son, George, became an artist and illustrated some of his father's works. Le Fanu's novels published in the 1840's, *The Cock and Anchor* and *Torlogh O'Brien*, received poor reviews, and Le Fanu turned from writing fiction to concentrate on his journalistic work. With the death of his beloved wife in 1858, he withdrew from society and became a recluse. Only a few close friends were allowed to visit "the invisible prince" at his elegant home at Merrion Square, Dublin. Emerging only occasionally to visit booksellers for volumes on ghosts and the occult, Le Fanu established a daily routine he was to follow for the remaining years of his life: writing in bed by candlelight from midnight till dawn,

rising at noon, and writing all afternoon at a prized, small desk once owned by Richard Brinsley Sheridan. In this manner was produced the greatest share of a literary canon that rivals in quantity the output of the most prolific authors of the Victorian age.

At the end, under treatment for heart disease, troubled by nightmares—especially one recurring scene of a gloomy, old mansion on the verge of collapsing on the terrified dreamer—Le Fanu refused the company of even his closest friends. On the night of February 7, 1873, his doctor found him in bed, his arms flung wide, his unseeing eyes fixed in terror at something that could no longer do him harm. "I feared this," the doctor said; "that house fell at last."

ANALYSIS

After writing two novels that failed to impress the critics, Joseph Sheridan Le Fanu left that genre for approximately fifteen years. In his reclusive later life, he returned to long fiction to produce the fine work for which he is remembered. Le Fanu's career as a novelist reveals a marked change in his perception of humanity and the very nature of the universe itself. The development of the author's major theme can be illustrated by a survey of the major novels in his quite extensive canon.

THE COCK AND ANCHOR

The early works, *The Cock and Anchor* and *Torlogh O'Brien*, are both historical novels dealing with the Ireland of the late seventeenth and early eighteenth centuries, the turbulent time of the Williamite wars (1689-1691). *The Cock and Anchor* presents a slice of Irish life that cuts across events and persons of real historical significance and the personal misfortunes of one fictional couple, Mary Ashewoode and Edmund O'Connor. The story of these ill-fated lovers has nothing special to recommend it. Mary is kept from Edmund first by her father, Sir Richard, who would marry her for a fortune to Lord Aspenly, a conventional fop, and then by her brother, Henry, who would see her wed to one Nicholas Blarden, a conventional villain. Mary escapes these nefarious designs and flees to the protection of Oliver French, the conventional benevolent uncle. There is, however, no happy ending: Mary dies before Edmund can reach her. The designing Sir Richard suffers a fatal stroke; brother Henry finally finds the destiny for which he was born, the hangman's noose; and even Edmund's unlucky life ends on the battlefield of Denain in 1712. More interesting to the modern reader are the historical characters. The haughty Lord Warton, Viceroy of Dublin, personifies power and Machiavellian self-interest. Joseph Addison and young Jonathan Swift are also here in well-drawn portraits that demonstrate considerable historical research. Still, the novel is at best uneven, the work of an author with promise who has more to learn about his craft.

The technical obstructions, however, cannot hide Le Fanu's message: The problems of Ireland are profound and rooted deep in a history of conflict. The Anglo-Irish establishment, represented by the Ashewoode family, has lost sight of the values needed to end the strife and move the society toward peace and prosperity, values such as personal responsibility, compassion, and even love within the family. Le Fanu was unwilling to risk clouding his theme by allowing the happy marriage of Mary and Edmund, the conventional ending to which the conventional plot could be expected to lead. They die to prove the point. The Ashewoodes's decay is really Ireland's decay, and the wage is death.

Torlogh O'Brien

Torlogh O'Brien, Le Fanu's second novel and the last he was to write for sixteen years, is set a few years before *The Cock and Anchor*, during the Williamite war. Again, most critics have found little to admire in the work. The historical scenes and characters show that once more Le Fanu thoroughly researched his subject, but the fictional characters reveal little improvement in their creator's art. The plot, except for some unusually violent scenes, would hold no surprises for a reader of romances. The villainous Miles Garret, a traitor to the Protestant cause, wishes to take Glindarragh Castle from Sir Hugh Willoughby, a supporter of William of Orange. Arrested on false charges created by Garret, Sir Hugh and his daughter, Grace, are taken to Dublin for trial. Their escort is Torlogh O'Brien, a soldier in the army of King James II, whose family originally held the

estate. O'Brien and Sir Hugh, both honorable men, rise above their political differences to gain mutual respect. Finally, it is O'Brien who intervenes to save the Willoughbys from the designs of Garret, and of course his bravery is rewarded by the love of Grace.

From the first novel to the second, villainy—Nicholas Blarden or Miles Garret—remains a constant, and the agony of a torn Ireland is the common background against which Edmund O'Connor and Torlogh O'Brien act out their parts. The social cancer that blighted the love of Mary and Edmund is, however, allowed a possible cure in *Torlogh O'Brien*. As the deaths of the lovers in the first novel showed Ireland as a sterile wasteland, so the union of the Willoughbys and O'Briens in the second promises restoring rain, but when after the long hiatus Le Fanu returned to novel writing, he chose to let the promise go unfulfilled.

The House by the Churchyard

Held by many critics to be Le Fanu's finest work, *The House by the Churchyard*, the first novel of his later period, appeared in the *Dublin University Magazine* in 1861; two years later, it was published in London as a book. The story is set in late eighteenth century Chapelizod, a suburb of Dublin. As in the earlier historical romances, there are villains, lovers, and dispossessed heirs. A major plot concerns the righting of an old wrong. Eighteen years after the death of Lord Dunoran, executed for a murder he did not commit, his son, using the name Mr. Mervyn, returns to the confiscated family lands hoping to establish his father's innocence. The real murderer, Charles Archer, has also returned to Chapelizod under the alias of Paul Dangerfield. He is soon recognized by a former accomplice, Zekiel Irons, and a witness, Dr. Barnaby Sturk. Sturk attempts blackmail, only to have Archer beat him severely. His victim in a coma, Archer plays benefactor and arranges for a surgeon he knows to be incompetent to perform a brain operation, supposedly to restore Sturk to health. To Archer's surprise, the operation gives Sturk a period of consciousness before the expected death. Irons joins Sturk in revealing Archer as the murderer, Lord Dunoran's lands and title are restored to Mervyn, and the family name is cleared at last.

This, however, is only one of several interrelated plots that make *The House by the Churchyard* a marvel of Victorian complexity. To label the Archer mystery as the major story line would be to mislead the reader who has yet to discover the book. More accurately, the novel is about Chapelizod itself. The discovery of a murderer stands out in the plot as, to be sure, it would in any small community, but Le Fanu is reminding his readers that what immediately affects any individual—for example, Mervyn's need to clear his father's name—no matter how urgently, is of limited interest to other individuals, who are in turn preoccupied with their own concerns. Mrs. Nutter has her own problem with protecting her inheritance from wicked Mary Matchwell. Captain Devereux and Lilias Walsingham have their doomed romance to concern them, as, on a more humorous note, Captain Cuffe is preoccupied with his love for Rebecca Chattesworth, who is finally joined with Lieutenant Puddock, the former suitor of Gertrude Chattesworth, who in turn has a secret romance with Mervyn. Indeed, the unsolved murder cannot totally dominate even the life of Lord Dunoran's son.

Some of the characters serve a comic purpose, and with so many complex entanglements, the comic could easily slide into complete farce. Le Fanu avoids caricature, however, by providing each comic figure with some other distinguishing quality—wit, compassion, bravery. In *The House by the Churchyard*, Le Fanu, already a master of description and mood, added the one needed skill so obviously absent in his early novels, the art of characterization.

The characterization of Archer, alias Dangerfield, is by itself sufficient to demonstrate Le Fanu's growth as a novelist. Dangerfield's evil is almost supernatural; he describes himself as a corpse and a vampire, a werewolf and a ghoul. He is incapable not only of love but also of hate, and he calmly announces before his suicide that he "never yet bore any man the least ill-will." He has had to "remove two or three" merely to insure his own safety. The occult imagery used to define Dangerfield also links him to the microcosm of Chapelizod, for Mervyn's Tiled House is reputedly haunted; the specter of a ghostly hand has frightened more than one former resident. Le Fanu allows Mervyn, like Torlogh O'Brien, his happy ending, but so powerful is the hold of Dangerfield on the novel that the possibility of colossal evil that he personifies is not totally exorcised even by his death. The fact that he was not really supernatural but was the embodiment of human depravity in no way diminishes the horror.

WYLDER'S HAND

With his fourth novel, *Wylder's Hand*, Le Fanu left historical romances and social panoramas to study evil with a closer eye. The story, certainly Le Fanu's finest mystery, concerns the strange disappearance of young Mark Wylder, a lieutenant in the navy and rival of Captain Stanley Lake for the hand of Dorcas Brandon, a rich heiress. From several locations in Europe, Wylder has sent letters containing instructions for the conduct of his business and releasing Dorcas to marry Lake. The suspicions of Larkin, a family attorney, are aroused by a problem with the dating of certain letters, but then Wylder returns to Brandon Hall, where he is actually seen in conversation with Lake. The very next day, however, Lake is thrown from his horse as the animal is startled by the pointing hand of Mark Wylder's corpse protruding from the ground, exposed by a heavy rain. Dying, Lake confesses to having murdered his rival and arranging for the posting of forged letters. In fact, it was not Wylder who appeared the preceding night at Brandon but one James Dutton, the unwitting accomplice who had posted the letters and who happens to resemble Wylder. Only one person knew of Wylder's fate, having witnessed his midnight burial: Rachel Lake, the murderer's sister. Devotion to her brother and to Dorcas Brandon, who really loves Lake, compelled her silence.

The plot is a masterpiece of suspense, but still more impressive are the characterizations. Each figure is finely drawn and fits into a mosaic of human types which together pictures a species ill equipped to deal with evil. Wylder is a swaggering braggart, crude, unfeeling, with a general air of disreputability that seems to promise some future act of monstrous brutality had not a violent death cut short his career. Like two vicious dogs claiming the same territory, Wylder and Lake cannot exist in the same world without one destroying the other. Lake's evil, however, is of a quite different nature. In many respects, he is Le Fanu's most interesting study. Wylder's is a rather directionless evil; it could as easily manifest itself in one abhorrent action as another. Dangerfield was simply amoral. Born without any sense of restraint, his natural selfishness led to murder for convenience. Lake's evil is weakness. Greed for property and position seems almost an outside force, a part of human society that can compel even murder in those who lack the strength to resist. He experiences guilt and fear and never is able to derive satisfaction from his villainy. Considering that the murdered man was certainly no credit to the human race, the reader may actually feel sympathy for Lake. In him, Le Fanu presents the criminal as victim, but the consequences of Lake's weakness affect others as well. Rachel's knowledge of the secret and Dorcas's ignorance isolate them from the man they love, much as Lake is himself isolated. Gloom, a sense of a scheme of things not quite right, permeates the texture of the entire novel. There is no happy ending. Years later, Rachel and Dorcas are seen in Venice, sad and alone.

UNCLE SILAS

In *Uncle Silas*, Le Fanu continued his investigation of the terrible yet tragic evil represented by Lake. Two earlier tales, "An Episode in the Secret History of an Irish Countess" (1838) and "The Murdered Cousin" (1851) provided a basic plot structure for the study, and in 1864, the same year that *Wylder's Hand* was published, a bound edition in three volumes with the title *Uncle Silas: A Tale of Bartram-Haugh* appeared. Considered by most critics Le Fanu's finest novel, it brings all the skill acquired over a productive career to a definitive study of the themes that interested its author most: the nature of evil, and the hereditary aristocracy as a paradigm for the effects of that destructive force. As usual, the study is conducted through carefully drawn characters and a plot filled with mystery and suspense.

In compliance with the will of the deceased Austin Ruthyn, his daughter, Maud, is made the ward of Austin's brother, Silas, a sinister man suspected but never convicted of a past murder. The suspicions are well founded, for Uncle Silas will stop at nothing to gain full ownership of Maud's estate. When an arranged marriage between Maud and Silas's son, Dudley, proves impossible—the scoundrel is discovered to be already married—murder seems the only solution. Dudley botches the job, however, and kills Madame de la Rougierra, another of Silas's agents, by mistake. Maud flees to a kindly relative; Dudley flees to Australia; and Uncle Silas dies that same night from an overdose of opium.

Le Fanu called *Uncle Silas* a "tragic English romance," and indeed the novel does depict a truly tragic situation. The Ruthyns stumble blindly through situations and realities they can hardly perceive, much less understand. Austin Ruthyn, heedless of the suspicions surrounding his brother, sends his daughter into the wolf's lair. Dudley, purposeless and crude, sees only the moment, and this he addresses with instinct rather than intelligent consideration of consequences. Even Maud Ruthyn, the heroine and narrator, is unaware of her perilous situation until it is almost too late. Gothic heroines are expected to be naïve, and Le Fanu uses that trait in his narrator to good advantage. Maud often tells more than she realizes, and the reader sensitive to the unspoken messages that careful diction can convey sees the closing circle of predators before she does. The rhetorical effect is a sense of foreboding, a tension that charges the entire novel.

Despite his avoidance of prosecution for an earlier crime and his careful designs for his niece's downfall, Silas is as blind as any of the lesser characters. His lust for wealth and property is virtually inherited: Similar drives have directed his family for generations. His body a slave to narcotics, his mind to religious fanaticism, he is the aristocracy in decay. Le Fanu surrounds him with appropriate death imagery, and his loutish son, Dudley, married without Silas's knowledge to a barmaid, is final evidence of the collapse of the Ruthyn line. Silas's first murder victim had been a Mr. Charke, to whom he owed gambling debts, but with the planned murder of Maud, the violence turns in upon the Ruthyns themselves. Austin's blind trust puts Maud in harm's way, and Silas's blind greed would destroy her; *Uncle Silas* is ultimately nothing less than a portrait of the aristocratic class cannibalizing itself. Maud survives and eventually marries a young lord, but her concluding words speak more of hope for happiness than happiness realized, and the death of her first child, sorrowfully remembered, strikes at the last the same note sounded throughout the novel.

WILLING TO DIE

That note of futility is heard most clearly in Le Fanu at the end of his career as a novelist. *Willing to Die*, first published serially in *All the Year Round* (1872-1873), is by no means his finest effort. The story, while complex, lacks the gothic excitement of the works for which he is remembered. Still, the novel is important in a thematic study.

Ethel Ware, the heroine, is allowed to sample a full range of life's possibilities. Poverty, loneliness, love, all contribute to the growth of her character; she surmounts all obstacles to achieve great material wealth and an understanding of the meaning of life. This is a new picture; in Ethel, the reader does not meet yet another aristocrat beaten by an ignorance of the forces at work in human society. Ethel wins, in the sense that Silas Ruthyn and Stanley Lake would have liked to win, but the mature vision that comes with the material victory only shows that the quest is pointless and the victory hollow. Isolated in her accomplishment as the protagonists of earlier novels were most often isolated in their failures, Ethel sees that the human struggle is manipulated by forces of society and chance, and whether the struggle culminates in a moment that might be called success or failure is finally irrelevant, for the last force to affect the struggle, death, affects the Wares and the Ruthyns alike.

The novels of Le Fanu are the record of an artist exploring social structures and individual minds in quest of horrors natural and supernatural. With his final entry in that often brilliant record, *Willing to Die*, he penetrated at last to the very heart of darkness to discover the ultimate horror: the utter futility of it all.

William J. Heim

OTHER MAJOR WORKS

SHORT FICTION: *Ghost Stories and Tales of Mystery*, 1851; *Chronicles of Golden Friars*, 1871; *In a Glass Darkly*, 1872; *The Purcell Papers*, 1880; *The Watcher and Other Weird Stories*, 1894; *A Chronicle of Golden Friars*, 1896; *Madam Crowl's Ghost and Other Tales of Mystery*, 1923 (M. R. James, editor); *Green Tea and Other Ghost Stories*, 1945; *Best Ghost Stories of J. S. Le Fanu*, 1964.

POETRY: *The Poems of Joseph Sheridan Le Fanu*, 1896.

BIBLIOGRAPHY

Begnal, Michael. *Joseph Sheridan Le Fanu*. Lewisburg, Pa.: Bucknell University Press, 1971. Sketches Le Fanu's life up to the death of his wife in 1858 and the beginning of his seclusion in Dublin. Analyzes his work as part of the gothic tradition to which Le Fanu makes a serious contribution, though he breaks from it to relate his ideas to his contemporary society. Focuses on his last four novels, presented as his best, which he published after emerging from his seclusion, beginning with *The House by the Churchyard*, in 1863. A brief study with a chronology and a selected bibliography.

Crawford, Gary William. *J. Sheridan Le Fanu: A Bio-Bibliography*. Westport, Conn.: Greenwood Press, 1995. Part 1 discusses Le Fanu's biography; part 2 is a primary, annotated bibliography of magazines, books, anthologies, and manuscripts; part 3 is an annotated secondary bibliography. The beginning student of Le Fanu will find this book an indispensable tool, which includes an appendix on films and plays based on Le Fanu's work. Also contains two useful indexes.

McCormack, W. J. *Dissolute Characters: Irish Literary History Through Balzac, Sheridan Le Fanu, Yeats, and Bowen*. Manchester: Manchester University Press, 1993. The section on Le Fanu discusses his relationship to the English novel, the development of his fiction, his treatment of characters, and his drawing on history. Includes notes but no bibliography.

_____. *Sheridan Le Fanu and Victorian Ireland*. Oxford, England: Clarendon Press, 1980. After a short introductory note, analyzes Le Fanu's life and career, examining the special conditions in

Victorian Ireland behind his writing. These include the clerical world of Dublin during the struggles for Catholic emancipation, his Irish political background, and his own changing opinions with regard to the repeal of the Act of Union. Includes a close analysis of the symbolism of *Uncle Silas* as his most complex novel. McCormack acknowledges that his late writing is not good, but argues that study of his entire career is fundamental to study of Anglo-Irish literature. Contains illustrations, two appendices, a substantial bibliography with manuscript sources, and an index.

Melada, Ivan. *Sheridan Le Fanu*. Boston: Twayne, 1987. After summarizing Le Fanu's life, concentrates on his writing and concludes with an assessment of his literary achievements. Discusses Le Fanu's early short fiction, then his historical novels, followed by a sustained analysis of *Uncle Silas*, and then the late short fiction; Le Fanu's poetry and periodical fiction are saved for a final word on the variety of his work. Estimates his achievement by arguing that *Uncle Silas* shows him to be a master of terror literature, that his cinematic style should be attractive to a modern audience, and that his canon makes Le Fanu a major author in the gothic tradition. Provides a prefatory chronology, supplementary notes, a selected annotated bibliography, and an index.

Ursula K. Le Guin

Born: Berkeley, California; October 21, 1929

PRINCIPAL LONG FICTION

Rocannon's World, 1966
Planet of Exile, 1966
City of Illusions, 1967
A Wizard of Earthsea, 1968
The Left Hand of Darkness, 1969
The Tombs of Atuan, 1971
The Lathe of Heaven, 1971
The Farthest Shore, 1972

The Dispossessed: An Ambiguous Utopia, 1974
Very Far Away from Anywhere Else, 1976
The Eye of the Heron, 1978
Malafrena, 1979
Leese Webster, 1979
The Beginning Place, 1980
Always Coming Home, 1985
Tehanu: The Last Book of Earthsea, 1990
Searoad: Chronicles of Klatsand, 1991
Four Ways to Forgiveness, 1995 (four linked novellas)

OTHER LITERARY FORMS

In Ursula K. Le Guin's body of work are many books written for children and young adults, among them *A Wizard of Earthsea*, *The Tombs of Atuan*, and *The Farthest Shore* (the first three books of the Earthsea series); *Very Far Away from Anywhere Else*; *Leese Webster*; and *The Beginning Place*. Her other publications include novellas, such as *The Word for World Is Forest* (1972); several volumes of poetry, *Wild Angels* (1975), *Hard Words and Other Poems* (1981), *In the Red Zone* (1983), and *Wild Oats and Fireweed: New Poems* (1988); and a number of volumes of short stories, including *The Wind's Twelve Quarters* (1975), *Orsinian Tales* (1976), *The Compass Rose* (1982), *Buffalo Gals and Other Animal Presences* (1987), *A Fisherman of the Inland Sea* (1994), and *Unlocking the Air and Other Stories* (1996). Le Guin's essays on the nature and meaning of fantasy, her own creative process, science fiction, and gender politics are collected in *From Elfland to Poughkeepsie* (1973), *The Language of the Night: Essays on Fantasy and Science Fiction* (1979; edited by Susan Wood), *Dancing at the Edge of the World: Thoughts on Words, Women, and Places* (1988), and *Napa: The Roots and Springs of the Valley* (1989). Her numerous book reviews have appeared in *The New York Times Book Review*, *The Washington Post Book World*, *The New Republic*, and other respected publications. Her collaboration with the photographer Roger Dorband, *Blue Moon over Thurman Street* (1993), documents in words and pictures the human ecology of the city street on which she lived for more than a quarter of a century.

(Margaret Chodos)

Achievements

The high quality of Le Guin's work was apparent from the beginning of her writing career. Brian Attebery, a fellow writer, has stated that even her first published novels are superior to most works of science fiction written at that time. Public recognition of Le Guin's work began with the *Boston Globe* Horn Book Award for *A Wizard of Earthsea* in 1969. Le Guin soon amassed numerous prestigious awards. They include Nebula and Hugo Awards for *The Left Hand of Darkness* (1969, 1970); the Newbery Silver Medal Award for *The Tombs of Atuan* (1972); a Hugo Award for *The Word for World Is Forest* (1973); a National Book Award for Children's Books for *The Farthest Shore* (1973); a Hugo Award for "The Ones Who Walk Away from Omelas" (1974); a Nebula Award for "The Day Before the Revolution" (1974); Nebula, Jupiter, and Hugo Awards for *The Dispossessed* (1974, 1975); a Jupiter Award for "The Diary of the Rose" (1976); a Gandalf Award for achievement in fantasy (1979); and the Kafka Award in 1986. Le Guin also won a Hugo Award for "Buffalo

Gals, Won't You Come Out Tonight?" (1988); a Pilgrim Award for body of work, awarded by the Science Fiction Research Association (1989); a Pushcart Prize for "Bill Weisler" (1991-1992); a Nebula Award for *Tehanu* (1990); and a Nebula Award for "Solitude" (1995). In addition to receiving these honors, Le Guin was a writer-in-residence at the Clarion West workshop at the University of Washington and a teaching participant in a science-fiction workshop at Portland State University. A number of science-fiction conventions, literary conferences, and universities recognized her literary stature by inviting her to teach and speak.

Biography

Ursula Kroeber Le Guin was born into a close, intellectual family in Berkeley, California, on October 21, 1929. Her father, Alfred, was an anthropologist distinguished for his studies of native California tribes and was curator of the Museum of Anthropology and Ethnology of the University of California. Her mother, Theodora Krackaw Kroeber, was a respected writer with an advanced degree in psychology and a special affinity for Native American subjects and sensibilities. It was Le Guin's father who befriended Ishi, the last survivor of the native Californian Yahi people, and it was her mother who wrote *Ishi in Two Worlds* (1961), an anthropological study of Ishi's life and times, as well as the simpler popular narrative *Ishi, Last of His Tribe* (1964). The interest that Le Guin's fiction shows in communication across great barriers of culture, language, gender, and ideology is a natural branching-off from her parents' lifelong passion for understanding worldviews other than the dominant Euro-American competitive materialism. Her use of songs, stories, folktales, maps, and depictions of material culture to flesh out fictional worlds is also congruent with her parents' professional focus.

The Kroeber family seems to have enjoyed an enviable degree of closeness, reasonable financial security, and an abundance of intellectual stimulation. During the academic year, they lived in a large, airy house in Berkeley. Their summers were spent in their Napa Valley home, Kishamish. To these forty acres flocked writers, scholars, graduate students, relatives, and American Indians.

Living among so many people rich in knowledge and curiosity, and having access to an almost unlimited supply of books, Le Guin began writing and reading quite young. She did not discover science fiction, however, until she was twelve. When she found, while reading Lord Dunsany one day, that people were still creating myths, Le Guin felt liberated, for this discovery validated her own creative efforts.

In 1947, Le Guin entered Radcliffe College in Cambridge, Massachusetts. After she was graduated magna cum laude in 1951, she entered Columbia University, where she majored in French and Italian Renaissance literature. After completing her master's degree in 1952, she began work on a doctoral program. En route to France as a Fulbright fellow, she met Charles Le Guin, a historian from Georgia also on a Fulbright. They were married in Paris on December 22, 1953.

When they returned from France, the Le Guins lived in Georgia. Ursula taught French at Mercer University in Macon, and Charles completed his Ph.D. in French history at Emory University. Afterward, they moved to Idaho, where their first child, Elisabeth, was born in 1957. Caroline, their second daughter, arrived in 1959, the year Charles accepted a position at Portland State University and the family moved to a permanent home in Oregon. A third child, Theodore, would be born in 1964.

Ursula, who had never stopped writing but had yet to find a proper market for her efforts, became reacquainted with science fiction when a friend encouraged her to borrow from his library. Cordwainer Smith's story "Alpha Ralpha Boulevard" proved to be a catalyst, a type of fiction approaching Le Guin's own attempts. Le Guin began thinking, not only about writing, but also about publishing her work in something other than obscure magazines.

Since she had begun to write, she had been trying to get her work published, but except for one story, "An die Musick," and a few poems, her work was returned, some of it characterized as "remote." Her breakthrough came when *Fantastic* published "April in Paris" in September, 1962. The following year,

Fantastic published her first genuine science-fiction story, "The Masters." After that time, Le Guin's literary output steadily increased, and her recognition as one of America's outstanding writers was assured.

Throughout her career, Le Guin has been reserved about the details of her personal life, maintaining that they are expressed best through her fiction. Although she has been involved in political activities, most of Le Guin's efforts are devoted to writing. As her recognition has increased, she has become a strong advocate for improving the quality of fantasy and science fiction. She seems determined that readers of this genre will not be cheated on their voyages of discovery. She has also become a firmer, more definite advocate for feminism as she has matured as a writer and a woman. Early works (such as *The Left Hand of Darkness*) may have grappled delicately with gender issues through "gender-bending" imagination; later works (such as *Tehanu* and *Four Ways to Forgiveness*) have dealt quite explicitly with the impossibility of real love in the absence of equality, the oppression of unshared housework, and the importance of language itself in creating freedom or bondage.

During her writing career, however, Le Guin's work expanded significantly outside the genre of science fiction. From "pro-choice" parables reprinted in *Ms.* magazine to advice to fellow authors, both from her book of essays *Dancing at the Edge of the World*, Le Guin was prolifically diverse in her output.

ANALYSIS

When Ursula K. Le Guin has Genly Ai state in *The Left Hand of Darkness* that "truth is a matter of the imagination," she is indirectly summarizing the essential focus of her fiction: explorations of the ambiguous nature of truth through imaginative means. Few other contemporary authors have described this process with the force and clarity of Le Guin. Her subject is always humankind and, by extension, the human environment, since humanity cannot survive in a vacuum; her technique is descriptive, and her mode is metaphoric. The worlds Le Guin creates are authentic in a profoundly moral sense as her characters come to experience truth in falsehood, return in separation, unity in variety. Frequently using a journey motif, Le Guin sends her characters in search of shadows, rings, theories, or new worlds—all of which are metaphors for undiscovered elements of the self. Along the way, Le Guin demands that they learn the paradoxes inherent in life, the ambiguous nature of creation, and the interrelatedness of all that seems to be opposed. Once made, these discoveries allow her characters to be integrated into themselves and their worlds.

In the end, her characters stand for no one, no concrete meaning; they simply are. Le Guin offers her readers characters motivated by intellectual curiosity, humanism, and self-determination, a nonviolent, nonexploitative philosophy capable of encompassing the unknown and complex cultures in relation to one another.

Unity is what Le Guin's characters seek: not a simple sense of belonging but a complex sense of wholeness. Much of her outlook is derived from the Taoist philosopher Lao-tzu, who maintained that scientific, ethical, and aesthetic laws, instead of being imposed by any authority, "exist in things and are to be discovered." Thus, Le Guin's characters must learn to recognize the true natures (or true names) of people or objects—none of which yields easily to the protagonist—before apprehending their essence and role in the world. Tao is the ultimate unity of the universe, encompassing all and nothing. Built upon paradox, Taoist philosophy proposes that apparently opposing forces actually complete each other. Discovering this in a world enamored of dualist thought, however, requires attaining an attitude of actionless activity, an emptying of the self and at the same time the fullest self-awareness. This compassionate attitude establishes a state of attraction, not compulsion: a state of being, not doing. Indeed, because the cycle of cause and effect is so strong, the Taoist sage never tries to do good at all, for a good action implies an evil action. Discovering the correlation of life/death, good/evil, light/dark, male/female, and self/other requires a relativist judgment. The Native American lore Le Guin absorbed as a child also contributed to her sense of unity. In her writing, she has drawn upon her rich knowledge of myths and the work of C. G. Jung as well as her own fertile imagination to create

intricate metaphors for psychic realities. In her own words, "Outer Space, and the Inner Lands, are still, and will always be, my country."

Rocannon's World

Le Guin has described *Rocannon's World*, her first published novel, as "definitely purple," an odd mixture of space age and bronze age, the product of an author unsure of her direction and materials. Drawing heavily on Norse mythology, the novel originated from a short story, "Dowry of the Angyar," published in 1964. The story begins when a woman named Semley leaves her husband and child to claim her dowry, a gold and sapphire necklace. During her search, Semley time-travels to another planet, where Rocannon, an ethnologist, struck by her beauty and bearing, gives her the necklace, a museum piece on his planet. Semley returns home, believing that she has been gone only overnight. To her dismay, though, she discovers that she has been gone for sixteen years. Her husband is dead; her daughter a grown stranger.

The remainder of the novel concerns Rocannon's exploration of Semley's planet, known to him as Formalhaut II, with the aid of Semley's grandson Mogien. After his ship is destroyed by rebels from the planet Farady, Rocannon must warn the League of All Nations of their rebellion. To do so, he must locate the rebel ship in order to use their ansible, an instantaneous transmitter, since his has been destroyed.

This episodic tale moves from adventure to adventure, as Rocannon learns that appearance often belies reality, that knowledge is not gained without sacrifice. The price he pays for increased understanding (the gift of mind-speech through which he can hear the voices of his enemy) is costly: Mogien's life. Through his efforts, however, the planet is saved. Rocannon, a man changed forever by his knowlege, never returns to his own planet, and he dies without knowing that the planet he rescues is given his name.

Often her own best critic, Le Guin has cited this novel to illustrate the flaws of mixing science fiction with fantasy, of ignoring the limitations imposed by plausibility, of excessive caution in creating a new myth, and of reliance on stereotyped characters and situations. While this novel lacks the rich complexity of her later works, it does contain elements Le Guin develops in subsequent novels. A readily apparent trait is that her focus is not on theoretical or applied science but rather on social science: how different individuals, races, and cultures perpetuate diffusion through lack of communication and how her main character surmounts these genuine yet arbitrary barriers. For example, as an ethnologist, Rocannon is interested in learning about all kinds of human behavior; nevertheless, he assumes superiority over his "primitive" guides. Experience, however, leads him to admire the individual qualities of Mogien, Kyo, and the Fiians. During their journey, his admiration of and loyalty to them increase to such an extent that loyalty becomes a prominent theme, one developed more thoroughly in *The Left Hand of Darkness*, with the relationship of Mogien and Rocannon prefiguring that of Genly Ai and Estraven (as well as other pairs of characters).

The most important goal in the novel, though, is to locate the other, often presented as the enemy, unify it with the self, and thus receive personal gain. The mindspeech Rocannon learns to hear expresses his fear. Though once he listens to the voices of his enemies he will never regain the self-sufficient confidence he had before embarking on his journey, he earns a vital awareness of his human limitations. Rocannon's sense of adventure is tempered by responsibility; his gain requires loss. In the end, Rocannon feels that he is a temporary resident on an alien planet. His sense of displacement denotes his lack of completion as a character. The novel ends without any resolution. In her next two novels, Le Guin shows greater control over her materials: less dependence upon others' stories and more considered ideas and direction. Where *Rocannon's World* indicates a major theme of self-exploration, *City of Illusions* develops this theme, bringing it closer to its fullest realization in *The Dispossessed*.

CITY OF ILLUSIONS

City of Illusions begins dramatically in the blank terror of mental darkness experienced by Ramarren and ends in an even larger exterior darkness when Falk-Ramarren, returning to his home planet, departs

for his unknown future. In the intervening time, Le Guin presents vivid scenes of an America largely undeveloped and peopled by disparate tribes, all of whom distrust one another and are united only in their universal fear of the Shing, an alien group who maintain division through that terror. Themes of communication, truth, self-discovery, and self-unification are central to this novel.

Using the quest motif, Le Guin has Falk nurtured by the pacific Forest Dwellers, who instill in him their set of values. When he leaves to discover his former identity, Falk confronts differing values, conflicting truths. Along the way, he receives the same warning from those who befriend him: trust no one; go alone. While he neglects to heed this advice always, these warnings prepare him in part to withstand the considerable powers of the Shing, whose authority depends on self-doubt. Falk is able to recover his past self and retain his present self when he discovers that "there is in the long run no disharmony, only misunderstanding, no chance of mischance but only the ignorant eye." Once he achieves this state of understanding, his two identities merge; he becomes Falk-Ramarren to return to his world with the truth—or rather truths—he apprehends.

Le Guin's Taoist beliefs are given full exposure in this novel, where Falk-Ramarren not only reads the *Tao Te Ching* (late third century B.C.), called the Old Canon, and looks for The Way, but also demonstrates the strength of passivity and enters a state of actionless activity to find himself. Stoical and silent, he prefigures Shevek of *The Dispossessed*. Le Guin's use of setting is also significant as it is employed to reflect psychological states. Her description of the Shing buildings in Es Toch suggests the illusory quality of this alien race and Falk's ambiguous state of mind. This novel fails, however, to measure up to later works. The Shing, for example, meant to personify evil, are all but unbelievable. Their ambiguity lapses into confusion; their "power" is unsubstantiated. Falk's sudden compassion for them is thus rather surprising. Another mark of this novel's early place in Le Guin's career is her heavy-handedness regarding her source. Not only does she thinly disguise the *Tao Te Ching*, but she also employs puns and even paraphrases passages to stress her meaning. In her later novels, she achieves better results through greater restraint and insight.

The Left Hand of Darkness

Le Guin arrived at a denser, more original expression of Taoist thought in *The Left Hand of Darkness*. In this novel, she brings together previously expressed themes in a striking metaphor. Time levels, separate in former books, coexist in this novel, as do polarized political systems, philosophies, and genders. Genly Ai, the man sent to bring the planet of Genthen into the Ekumen (formerly the League of All Worlds), must, like Falk, come to see the relativity of truth. To do so, he must cross barriers of thought, barriers he is at first incapable of recognizing. Even when he does, Ai is reluctant to cross, for he must abandon his masculine-scientific-dualist training to become a relativist. He must believe that "truth is a matter of the imagination."

Ai's difficulty in arriving at this conclusion is complicated by his alien existence on Genthen, where he is not merely an outsider; he is a sexual anomaly, a pervert as far as the natives are concerned. Being a heterosexual male in an androgynous culture adds immeasurably to Ai's sense of distrust, for he cannot bring himself to trust "a man who is a woman, a woman who is a man." The theme of androgyny enriches this novel, not simply because it develops the complex results of an androgynous culture, but also because it demonstrates how gender affects—indeed prejudices—thought and explores the cultural effects of this bias. Initially, Ai can see only one gender, one side at a time. This limited vision leaves him vulnerable to betrayal, both by himself and by others. Through his friendship with Estraven, Ai begins to respect, even require, those qualities he at first denigrates until he and Estraven become one, joined in mindspeech. Ai's varied experiences on Genthen teach him that apparently polarized qualities of light/ dark, male/female, rational/irrational, patriot/traitor, life/death are necessary complements. The order of the universe requires both.

The Left Hand of Darkness consolidates Taoist ideas expressed in Le Guin's previous books, places them in a dramatically unique culture, and develops them with a finesse lacking in her earlier novels. Ai discovers what Falk does: a fuller recognition of self through merger with the other. He does so, however, in a much more complete way because Le Guin complicates *The Left Hand of Darkness* with questions of opposing political systems, the nature and consequences of sexism, the issue of personal and political loyalty, and the interrelatedness of different periods of time. While retaining her basic quest structure, Le Guin has Genly Ai construct his "report" by using multiple sources: Estraven's diary, folktales, ancient myths, reports from previous investigatory teams. This adds texture and depth by dramatizing the multiplicity of truth and the unity of time. In a sense, this mixture of sources, added to the seasonlessness of Genthen, where it is always winter, and the relentless journey over the Gobrin Ice, constructs a center of time for the reader, an objective correlative to Ai's state of mind. Within a circular framework, a sense of wholeness is achieved. Ai will set the keystone in the arch, the image which opens *The Left Hand of Darkness*, by adding Genthen to the Ekumen. Later, he cements his personal bond to Estraven by visiting his home, ostensibly to return Estraven's diary but actually to assuage a sense of betrayal for not having Estraven publicly absolved of his "crime" of supporting the Ekumen instead of his king. At the novel's end, however, when Ai meets in Estraven's son the father's limitless curiosity, Ai's journey begins anew.

Robert Scholes stated that one of the great strengths of *The Left Hand of Darkness* is that it "asks us to broaden our perspectives toward something truly ecumenical, beyond racism and sexism, and even speciesism." Clearly, Le Guin opened up new territory for science-fiction writers to explore.

The Dispossessed

In *The Dispossessed*, her next novel in what is called her Hainish cycle, she presses even further, bringing to full realization her heroic figure of the Taoist sage in the protagonist Shevek. Stoic, persistent, curious, and humane, he shares qualities with Falk, Estraven, and Genly Ai. Shevek's character and journey, however, differ from his predecessors' in several important respects. Shevek's sense of alienation is tempered by his mature love for his partner

Takver. No matter how alone he is on his journey, Shevek can and does turn to their mutually supportive relationship for solace. Shevek's sense of individual integrity is also more conscious than that of previous characters. Already aware of himself and his value, he is able to expand beyond both. Most important, Shevek has a clearly defined sense of purpose—a need to unbuild walls through communication—and a certainty of return. Early in the novel, Le Guin assures her readers that "he would most likely not have embarked on that years-long enterprise had he not had profound assurance that return was possible . . . that the very nature of the voyage . . . implied return." Buttressed by this conviction, Shevek goes forth, his empty hands signifying his spiritual values, and effects a revolution in both senses of the word: a completed cycle and a dynamic change. When he discovers his theory of temporal simultaneity, Shevek gives it away, for he knows that its value is not in its scarcity, but in its general use.

The Dispossessed is not simply a vehicle for Taoist philosophy; it is just as significantly a political novel. Le Guin subtitles the novel *An Ambiguous Utopia*, indicating her focus, and she directs her reader's attention by alternating chapters on Anarres, Shevek's home planet, and Urras, where he resides throughout much of the novel. Scenes from Anarres are recalled through flashback as Shevek, surrounded by an alien political and social system repugnant to much in his nature, reflects upon himself in relation to his culture. Anarres, founded by libertarian followers of Odo, a radical Urrasti thinker, is at once dedicated to individual freedom and to the good of the whole. There is no formal government, only a system of individually initiated syndicates, a Division of Labor to keep track of job needs, and the Production Distribution Committee to oversee production loosely. On Anarres nothing is owned; everything is shared. Since everyone is equal, there is no discrimination, no exploitation, but there are stringent societal responsibilities which all Anarresti share. Because Anarres is virtually a desert, with plant life so scarce that no animals are indigenous, careful conservation, voluntary labor, and a sense of duty to the whole are required of everyone.

By contrast, Urras is wealthy, lush with water, teeming with life. Its capitalistic system, however, encourages exploitation because profit is the motivating force. As a result, Urras has an entrenched class system, with women and workers considered inferior to the intellectual and governing classes, and a power structure intent on maintaining control. While much of this authority is exerted by custom, some is imposed by force. Shevek, unaccustomed to any type of exploitation, violence, discrimination, or conspicuous waste, needs to experience fully the benefits and detriments of Urras before he can make necessary connections. Once he recognizes that the seeds of his freedom germinated in the rich soil of Urras, he can declare his brotherhood with the Urrasti and offer them what he can: a way to the only future he knows, that of Anarres. Speaking from deep within himself, Shevek tells Urrasti rebels "You must come to it alone, and naked, as the child comes into his future, without any past, without any property, wholly dependent on other people for his life. . . . You cannot make the Revolution. You can only be the Revolution."

THE EARTHSEA SERIES

The Earthsea series has been categorized by many as "young adult fiction." Le Guin does write often and well for young audiences, and the fact that the three original books of the series (*A Wizard of Earthsea*, *The Tombs of Atuan*, and *The Farthest Shore*) were quite short, were populated by sorcerers and dragons, and used the vocabulary and syntax of high fantasy, tended to identify them as children's literature, at least on the surface. However, their subtle spiritual, mythic, psychological, and philosophical underpinnings and the elegant simplicity of the writing make the books challenging and satisfying to adult readers as well.

In *A Wizard of Earthsea*, Le Guin introduces Ged, a natural-born wizard whose insensitive family does not realize his innate gift. Ged becomes a sorcerer's apprentice to the mage Ogion but ultimately is forced to leave before completing his studies because he keeps casting spells before learning their complications. His inner conflicts are revealed through his struggle to find and to name what he believes to be a mysterious shadow pursuing him. Le Guin's essay "The Child and the Shadow" (in *The Language of the Night*) discusses her depiction of this archetypal Jungian "dark brother of the conscious mind."

In *The Tombs of Atuan*, Ged meets Tenar (known as Arha), the child-priestess of the dark Nameless Ones. Ged has gone to the Labyrinth of the Nameless Ones to recover a Ring that is necessary to the well-being of Earthsea, but he becomes a prisoner in the Labyrinth. Ged and Tenar help each other out of their different sorts of darkness and bondage, return the Ring to its rightful place, and become firm friends. Tenar finds a refuge with Ged's old master, Ogion. Tenar is as powerful as Ged in her own way. Yet, she too leaves her apprenticeship with Ogion before completing her training, though for a different reason. Ged is forced to leave; Tenar chooses to leave for the fulfillment of married life.

Le Guin's understanding of identity and its relationship to naming is revealed in the theme that runs throughout the Earthsea series: To know the true name of someone gives power over him. Hence, characters have "use" names as well as real names. Real names are usually only told at the moment of death or to someone who is completely trusted.

TEHANU

In 1990, *Tehanu: The Last Book of Earthsea* was published, formally (or so Le Guin has said) bringing the adventures of Tenar and Ged to an end. *Tehanu* is markedly different from the earlier books in the series, however, in that it is written unequivocally for adults. Perhaps Le Guin wanted to aim it at the audience who had grown up reading her books and was now older and mature—like Tenar and Ged, no longer rash in their actions and fearless with the immortality of youth.

In *Tehanu*, the fourth book of Le Guin's Earthsea series, Tenar has been widowed. She is called to assist in the treatment of a badly burned and sexually abused young girl, whom Tenar adopts and names Therru. A visit to the now-dying mage Ogion elicits the information that there is a powerful and dangerous presence in Therru. The dramatic return of Ged aboard the back of the dragon Kalessin, however, occupies Tenar's mind, as she must nurse him. He has

lost the powers of archmagery and is now an ordinary man, vulnerable to violence, grief, depression, aging, and sexual love.

Tehanu is, like much of Le Guin's work, a careful compendium of names, spells, and physical transformations. (As a venture in world-making, *Tehanu* resembles *Always Coming Home*, a work intended primarily for adults. Purporting to write the history of several peoples in the distant future, *Always Coming Home* is accompanied by tape-recordings of poems and stories, and the text is supplemented by illustrations and glossaries of terms.) *Tehanu*, however, deals more directly with the dark themes of child molestation and abuse and death than do the earlier volumes in the series.

FOUR WAYS TO FORGIVENESS

Just as *Tehanu* deepens Earthsea to include the difficult realities of violence, oppression, sex, and aging, *Four Ways to Forgiveness* deepens Le Guin's exploration of the ways that power creates deep gulfs between the powerful and the powerless. As in *The Dispossessed*, Le Guin again uses the device of two planets, Werel and Yeowe, connected by kinship and history, to illustrate the separate "worlds" created by privilege and exploitation. *Four Ways to Forgiveness* is a novel in the form of four interconnected novellas. Each of the four sections is, in its own way, a love story and could stand alone as a tale of alienation healed. Taken together, the four tales present the larger story of an entire society mending, a new whole being conceived through the union of opposites, and the whole being born through blood and pain.

The first story, "Betrayals," tells of two aging survivors of Yeowe's long, bitter struggle for emancipation. They each have retreated to live in seclusion and "turn to silence, as their religion recommended them to do" in old age. When the man becomes ill, the woman nurses him. When her house burns down, he takes her in. In helping each other, they learn to see each other. Seeing each other, they learn to love each other. Like *Tehanu*, "Betrayals" explores the issues of what loves and graces are left for old age, after the many inevitable losses of life.

The second section, "Forgiveness Day," is the love story of a brash young Ekumenical diplomat on

Werel and a stolid, traditional soldier of the ruling class. Their path to partnership gives the author a chance to examine sexism and racism from the point of view of a woman who has been raised in an egalitarian society and from the point of view of a male military defender of the privileged group. To the woman, the rules of behavior that enforce power and powerlessness seem bizarre; to the man, they seem completely natural. Through sharing a difficult ordeal, the two learn to appreciate each other and build a lasting loving partnership. As they work through the difficulties in their relationship, the author demonstrates for the reader how mental practices of power and privilege make true friendship and love impossible.

The third section, "A Man of the People," follows the career of a Hainish historian as he leaves the comfortable provincial village in which he was born. He studies the history of the diverse cultures of the universe, travels widely, and finally goes to Yeowe as an Ekumenical observer. On Yeowe, he commits himself to the struggle for the long-delayed liberation of women, and in this commitment to a community, he finally experiences the sense of belonging he left behind him when he first left his pueblo. The meditations of the historian on his discipline allow the author to present her ideas on the difference between local cultural knowledge and universal cross-cultural knowledge (both of which she honors), education as revolution, and the interplay between historical observation and activism.

The final piece, "A Woman's Liberation," tells the life story of the Werelian woman who becomes the Hainish historian's wife. This simple first-person telling, reminiscent of the slave narratives collected to support the abolition of slavery in the United States, details the life of an owned woman from childhood in the slave compound to service in the big "House" to the day when she is technically "freed" through the difficulties of staying free and gaining equality. Le Guin uses the final two sections of the book to depict, explicitly and realistically, many of the ugly inhumanities that accompany slavery, such as sexual abuse and other violence. To this author, power and exploitation are not merely theoretical subjects; she seeks to portray the real human suffering that is an essential component of institutionalized privilege.

Karen Carmean, updated by Donna Glee Williams

OTHER MAJOR WORKS

SHORT FICTION: *The Word for World Is Forest*, 1972; *The Wind's Twelve Quarters*, 1975; *Orsinian Tales*, 1976; *The Compass Rose*, 1982; *Buffalo Gals and Other Animal Presences*, 1987; *Fish Soup*, 1992; *A Fisherman of the Inland Sea: Science Fiction Stories*, 1994; *Unlocking the Air and Other Stories*, 1996.

POETRY: *Wild Angels*, 1975; *Hard Words and Other Poems*, 1981; *In the Red Zone*, 1983; *Wild Oats and Fireweed: New Poems*, 1988; *Blue Moon over Thurman Street*, 1993; *Going Out with Peacocks and Other Poems*, 1994; *Sixty Odd: New Poems*, 1999.

NONFICTION: *From Elfland to Poughkeepsie*, 1973; *The Language of the Night: Essays on Fantasy and Science Fiction*, 1979 (Susan Wood, editor); *Dancing at the Edge of the World: Thoughts on Words, Women, and Places*, 1988; *Napa: The Roots and Springs of the Valley*, 1989.

CHILDREN'S LITERATURE: *The Visionary*, 1984; *Solomon Leviathan's 931st Trip Around the World*, 1988; *A Visit from Dr. Katz*, 1988; *Catwings*, 1988; *Catwings Return*, 1989; *Fire and Stone*, 1989; *A Ride on the Red Mare's Back*, 1992; *Tom Mouse and Mrs. Howe*, 1998; *Jane on Her Own: A Catwings Tale*, 1999.

BIBLIOGRAPHY

Bittner, James W. *Approaches to the Fiction of Ursula K. Le Guin*. Ann Arbor, Mich.: UMI Research Press, 1984. A revised version of Bittner's 1979 doctoral thesis. Discusses the difference between Le Guin's fantasy and science-fiction writing, taking into account her work up to *Orsinian Tales*. Includes notes to chapters, primary and secondary bibliographies, and an index.

Bloom, Harold, ed. *Ursula K. Le Guin*. New York: Chelsea House, 1986. A compilation of eighteen essays by different authors on Le Guin's work.

Also contains a brief biographical and publishing chronology, a general bibliography, and an index.

Bucknall, Barbara J. *Ursula K. Le Guin*. New York: Frederick Ungar, 1981. Contains information about both Le Guin's life and her literary output. Includes a useful detailed chronology up to 1980, notes, primary and secondary bibliographies, and an index.

Cogell, Elizabeth Cummins. *Ursula K. Le Guin: A Primary and Secondary Bibliography*. Boston: Hall, 1983. Lists early works by and about Le Guin.

Keulen, Margarete *Radical Imagination: Feminist Conceptions of the Future in Ursula Le Guin, Marge Piercy, and Sally Miller Gearhart*. New York: Peter Lang, 1991. Explores science fiction from a feminist viewpoint in the three authors. Includes bibliographical references and an index.

Reid, Suzanne Elizabeth. *Presenting Ursula K. Le Guin*. New York: Twayne, 1997. This critical biography helps young readers to understand how her childhood, family, and life have helped to shape Le Guin's work.

Selinger, Bernard. *Le Guin and Identity in Contemporary Fiction*. Ann Arbor, Mich.: UMI Research Press, 1988. Covers the works missed by the earlier Bittner volume, *Approaches to the Fiction of Ursula K. Le Guin*. Discusses Le Guin's work as breaking the bounds of "realistic" fiction, placing her in the same category as Stanisław Lem, Italo Calvino, and John Barth. Annotated references, primary and secondary bibliographies, and an index are included.

Spivack, Charlotte. *Ursula K. Le Guin*. Boston: Twayne, 1984. Begins with a brief chronology of important personal and professional milestones in Le Guin's life up to 1981, and then examines her background and her literary contributions. Includes annotated references, primary and secondary bibliographies, and an index.

White, Donna R. *Dancing with Dragons: Ursula K. Le Guin and the Critics*. Columbia, S.C.: Camden House, 1999. Part of the Studies in English and American Literature, Linguistics, and Culture series, this volume examines Le Guin's works and critical reaction to them.

ROSAMOND LEHMANN

Born: Bourne End, England; February 3, 1901
Died: London, England; March 12, 1990

PRINCIPAL LONG FICTION

Dusty Answer, 1927
A Note in Music, 1930
Invitation to the Waltz, 1932
The Weather in the Streets, 1936
The Ballad and the Source, 1944
The Echoing Grove, 1953
A Sea-Grape Tree, 1976

OTHER LITERARY FORMS

Rosamond Lehmann's preferred art form was the novel, but in addition, she published a volume of short stories, *The Gipsy's Baby and Other Short Stories* (1946), and a play, *No More Music* (1939). Her autobiography, *The Swan in the Evening: Fragments of an Inner Life*, appeared in 1967, and a memoir, *Rosamond Lehmann's Album*, in 1985.

ACHIEVEMENTS

Lehmann's first novel, *Dusty Answer*, appeared in 1927, when the author was twenty-six years old. The novel struck a responsive chord with the post-World War I generation, and Lehmann soon found herself famous. Her subsequent novels and other works found a considerable audience, especially in England, where her writing was highly regarded by the reading public as well as critics. In 1982, Lehmann was honored as a recipient of the Order of the British Empire. Those of her novels that had been out of print were republished by Virago Press.

BIOGRAPHY

Rosamond Nina Lehmann was born near London on February 3, 1901. On the same day, Queen Victoria was buried, a fact that would later strike Lehmann as having symbolic significance. She received her early education at home, partly through the use of the enormous library of her father, Rudolph Lehmann, an editor of *Punch* magazine. Her later education was at Girton College of Cambridge University.

An early marriage ended in divorce, attributable, Lehmann believed, to the upheaval arising from her sudden fame. A second marriage, to the Honorable Wogan Philipps, also ended in divorce; a long relationship with the poet Cecil Day Lewis also ended unhappily. Lehmann's primary bonds were with family: her brother, poet-critic John Lehmann; her sister, actress Beatrix Lehmann; and her two children, Hugo and Sally. Sally's sudden death from polio in 1958 ended Lehmann's writing for some time; when she began to write again, her works reflected her new interest in what may imprecisely be called spiritualism. In her eighties, she served as vice president of the British College of Psychic Studies, and she counseled other parents who had lost children. Lehmann died in London in 1990, at the age of eighty-nine.

ANALYSIS

The great theme of Rosamond Lehmann's fiction is the evanescent quality of love in a world where love is the only thing worth having. This emphasis on love and on female characters has sometimes caused her to be considered a "women's novelist," an evaluation which would have surprised her audience early in her career. To many of her contemporaries in the 1920's, Lehmann was part of the vanguard, a peer of Virginia Woolf, Dorothy Richardson, and May Sinclair, writers who chose female characters as the voices of a new fictional style which these women, along with James Joyce and others, were creating. This style is generally called "stream of consciousness," although the term is somewhat imprecise: Lehmann's style requires neither the intense, allusive language of Joyce nor the changing viewpoints of Woolf. Lehmann learned from her contemporaries to stay within the mind of one character and to show the sensibilities and sensitivities of that character.

DUSTY ANSWER

Lehmann's first novel, *Dusty Answer*, is a fine achievement as a novel of consciousness, especially of the special consciousness of adolescence. The novelist stays within the mind of the young Judith Earle as she grows into early adulthood. Like other popular novels of the 1920's (Michael Arlen's *The*

Green Hat, 1924, is a good example), the novel traces the character's development by her relationship with a person or group of people whom the central character views as somehow enchanted. That the enchanted ones are also destructive constitutes the fascination and also the growth experience for the central character.

Judith grows up in a wealthy home, in an isolation that creates her bookishness and romantic turn of mind. Her loneliness is broken occasionally by a family of five cousins who visit next door; Judith sees them as a closed unit, incredibly mysterious and desirable. Her fascination with them continues even when she goes off to Cambridge University (Lehmann herself was at Girton College, Cambridge) and meets a fellow undergraduate, Jennifer Baird, to whom she is also drawn. The novel traces Judith's intense friendship with Jennifer and with each of the cousins. As the book ends, she has been separated from all of them by the differing courses of their maturity. She believes that enchantment is gone from the world and that she must now live in the cold light of reality.

Dusty Answer had an immediate and intense popularity. For some readers, it powerfully evoked their university days, and in this regard the book bears comparison with Evelyn Waugh's *Brideshead Revisited* (1945, 1959), which is set at Oxford in the same time period, the early 1920's. A reader desiring a portrait of those days could do no better than to read these two novels. A second reason for the novel's popularity is its relative frankness with regard to sexual attitudes; Lehmann shows her heroine eager to "give herself" to the man she loves. Homoerotic relationships also abound. Although there are no explicit sexual scenes, the novel was considered shocking by many critics. Some of her contemporaries thought that *Dusty Answer* was a flash in the pan which would both begin and end Lehmann's career. On the contrary, as she continued to write, maturity deepened her powers of observation.

INVITATION TO THE WALTZ

Lehmann's third novel, *Invitation to the Waltz*, shows her mastery of atmosphere in a novel. The main character is Olivia Curtis, an adolescent on the verge of adulthood, and it is primarily through her that Lehmann conveys a wonderful atmosphere of expectation and anticipation. The story opens on the morning of Olivia's seventeenth birthday. Her upper-middle-class home in the snug village of Little Compton is carefully described. A gentle air of mystery, however, is developed: "Something is going on. The kettle's boiling, the cloth is spread, the windows are flung open. Come in, come in! Here dwells the familiar mystery. Come and find it! Each room is active, fecund, brimming over with it." The invitation to the reader is explicit: Enter this novel, this home, to watch the dance of life. What one finds is both common and marvelous—common in the easy familiarity and give-and-take of family life and marvelous in the recurring mystery of girl growing to young woman. That Lehmann can have it both ways, in both its common and its marvelous aspects, testifies to her growth as a novelist.

An invitation necessarily inculcates expectation. At the opening of the novel, the invitation to the Spencers' dance, one week hence, has already been extended. Even as she lies in bed, reveling in its delicious warmth and in the slow, pleasant moments before the hectic day must begin in earnest, Olivia anticipates the dance. Indeed, thoughts about the dance subsume Olivia's anticipation of a more immediate event, breakfast with the family—the presents to be opened and the good wishes to be received. That the prized gift of the day turns out to be some flame-colored fabric for a new dress to wear to the Spencers' dance indicates something of Lehmann's skill in developing a sense of expectation in ever expanding circles of anticipation. Mundane events of plot resonate with increasingly meaningful, open-ended implications, all circumferences being blurred in the subjective consciousness, the magical visionary world, of an innocent, naïve, alert, and sensitive seventeen-year-old.

After the early-morning anticipation of the birthday breakfast, the plot points to the big dance, a week away. The dress is to be readied. An escort is to be speculated on. On the night itself, Olivia and her sister Kate are to prepare themselves carefully—with long baths and manicures and attentive dressing of hair. Kate, the older sister who is at once rival and best friend, does much better in the business of appearance than Olivia, but having turned Olivia's dress around and suggested how to fashion her hair, she and Olivia are finally ready for the dance. Part 2 of the novel explains the day's preparation for the dance, while part 3 focuses on the dance itself. Thus, the structure of the novel supports the atmosphere of anticipation.

If this were all there were to it, however, part 3 of the novel would be something of a disappointment to the reader, as it surely seems to be at times for Olivia. Reggie Kershaw, the man Olivia and Kate have invited to escort them, first asks Marigold Spencer for a dance. Olivia's dance program gradually fills, but her predominant emotion is gratitude that she will not be humiliated by being a wallflower rather than excitement over the young men with whom she will be dancing. She feels clumsy and awkward when she finally dances with Reggie; she feels intellectually inferior and unstylish with Peter Jenkin; she feels very much out of her social class with George; she feels crude and unsophisticated with Podge; and so the evening goes. She feels surprise, shock, pity, sorrow, resentment, and even repulsion at her various partners through the evening. Yet there are minor triumphs, too. When dashing Rollo Spencer returns from walking the dogs, he invites her into his father's library, where Olivia meets Sir John Spencer himself. As Olivia leaves the library, she is overwhelmed with good feeling and a sense of accomplishment: Far "from being outcast, flung beyond the furthest rim, she had penetrated suddenly to the innermost core of the house, to be in their home." At the end of the evening, sitting in the armchair, waiting for the last dancers to finish and for Kate and Reggie to appear, she reflects on the evening: "Nothing for myself really," yet "to have come to the place of not caring was very soothing, very peaceful." She anticipates "with longing . . . her dark bedroom, her bed waiting for her at home."

The power of the novel lies in the wider implications of Olivia's anticipations, for the events of the story are only the pretext for the grand anticipation of Olivia's life, the fulfillment of which the reader is left to imagine. Early in the novel, Olivia had looked at herself in the mirror, wondering if this would be one of those days when the mirror reflected back not what was familiar, but a new Olivia, a new self, a different person, a beginning life. Throughout the novel, the people whom Olivia meets and the episodes she experiences resonate as options for Olivia in her adult life. Will she become bitter and poor, like the spinster dressmaker Miss Robinson? Will scandal rob her of simple companionship and neighborly friendship, as it did Major Skinner? Will she be a victim of calculated pathos, as she is with the lace maker, who takes advantage of her pity so that she wastes the ten shillings given to her by Uncle Oswald for her birthday? Will her life be reduced to a tragedy of isolation, restriction, and emptiness, as is the life of blind Timmy Douglas, married to a former nurse in an arrangement of convenience rather than of passion?

As one anticipates Olivia's adult life, one realizes that not all options are equally available to her. The Spencers represent an aristocratic lifestyle that is clearly beyond the Curtises. Marigold and Rollo live in a world made brilliant and dashing by their parents' social status; theirs is a self-confidence that comes from solid and long-standing foundation in the bedrock of social place. Kate, too, may represent an option that proves not to be viable for Olivia, for Kate, during the course of the evening, becomes separated from Olivia, each sister following her individual pathway to the future. Kate falls in love with Tony Heriot and secretly makes plans to meet him in Paris; they share a vision to which Olivia is not party.

At the end of the novel, though, Olivia, too, has a vision. Running out beyond the garden, recognizing that every woman makes the trip to adulthood by herself, Olivia feels a sense of new beginning. Her future, in the image of a winged gigantic runner, hastens toward her from a great distance: "On it came, over ploughed field and fallow. The rooks flashed sharply, the hare and his shadow swerved in sudden sunlight. In a moment it would be everywhere. Here it was. She ran into it." The future is now. The girl is a young woman with a full life ahead. The dance of life is beginning.

THE BALLAD AND THE SOURCE

With good reason, Lehmann's fifth novel, *The Ballad and the Source*, is widely considered her best. It has an evocative power and strength of characterization that linger long after the book has been read. Furthermore, the narrative technique is at once complex and suggestive: Rebecca Landon tells the tale of a period during her childhood, between the ages of ten and fifteen, the years 1912 to 1917, when she first came to know a neighbor, Mrs. Jardine, and Mrs. Jardine's grandchildren. As she recalls the long afternoons at tea with Mrs. Jardine and the conversations with Maisie, the grandchild with whom she developed the closest of friendships, she seems at times to be reliving the experience, to return again to those childhood days of innocence threatened only sporadically by glimpses into the adult world of evil. Occasionally, the adult consciousness reflects on the limitations of the child's awareness, and the reader is reminded of the retrospective perspective, but the child's consciousness prevails, and the movement between today's adult and yesterday's child is blurred and inconsistent.

This is not to say that the shifting consciousness is a flaw in the novel. Indeed, it is one of the novel's triumphs, for like others of Lehmann's novels, *The Ballad and the Source* creates a highly subjective consciousness that colors what it encounters. Rebecca is a sensitive, romantic child, strongly attracted to the unusual situation and the magnetic personality of the suspect Mrs. Jardine. The novel presents Rebecca's attempt to solve the puzzle that is Mrs. Jardine. In rehearsing those preadolescent years, Rebecca is even now trying to reach some resolution, some recognition that ever eludes her. The novel gains in immediacy because one is not presented with the adult's conclusions but learns the pieces of information as the child did many years ago, and one can follow her engaged understanding through the maze of hints and innuendos, biased accounts and tortured confessions, shadings and concealments to which she is subject.

The amazing thing about this novel is that Rebecca is not ultimately the main character, even though her consciousness and experience govern the reader's access to information. She is an observer of the developments in the Jardine/Thomson family and a receiver of information about their past, not an involved participant in the ongoing drama of their lives. What Rebecca says or does or thinks relative to the Jardines and Thomsons is ultimately of little importance. Sibyl Anstey Herbert Jardine is really the main character, the source, and the subject of all the ballads. It is her strong personality that so attracts the love of Rebecca and the hatred of her granddaughter Maisie.

The novel is a detective story of sorts, including all the material of high drama—adultery, abandoned children, runaway wives, insanity, lifelong hatred, empty and wasted lives, early death, kidnaping, jealousy, secrecy, plots, shifting conspiracies, and passion, as well as loyalty, dedication to truth, independence, and love. Young Rebecca has led far too sheltered a life to be able to take in what she hears, but the reader is not hindered by Rebecca's limitations. The reader may have greater understanding than does the narrator of the story because of Lehmann's strategy of allowing several different people to reveal what they know. Rebecca learns something about Mrs. Jardine first from Mrs. Jardine herself. In fact, Mrs. Jardine at times actually confides in Rebecca, using her as the "listener" she always needs. It is largely because Rebecca is so fascinated by Mrs. Jardine that she has difficulty accepting some of the other accounts she subsequently hears. Rebecca recognizes good qualities in Mrs. Jardine— a strong maternal instinct, a fondness for children, courage, loyalty, and strength. These are not the traits about Mrs. Jardine that most impress other people.

Tilly, for example, the poor, elderly seamstress who makes a yearly visit to the Landon family to do necessary work and who formerly was employed by Rebecca's grandmother, certainly does not share Rebecca's fondness for the woman. When Rebecca discovers that Tilly knew Mrs. Jardine years ago, she pumps her to tell her story of Mrs. Jardine's life. Part 2 of the novel is a long narration by Tilly, interrupted by prompts and questions from Rebecca. To Tilly, Mrs. Jardine is an evil woman who violated her friendship with Rebecca's grandmother by asking her to assist her in deceiving her former husband, Charles Herbert, in order to gain access to their

daughter, Ianthe. Despite her loyalties toward her grandmother, Rebecca still sides with the cause of the mother deprived of her only child. When Sibyl Anstey Herbert (later Mrs. Jardine) left her husband, she had never intended to leave the child Ianthe behind as well, but Charles Herbert insisted on total estrangement between Ianthe and her mother, an estrangement Sibyl was never able to overcome, despite a life dedicated to winning Ianthe back.

Part 3 is a long conversation between Mrs. Jardine and Rebecca, during which Rebecca learns much about the life of Ianthe. In veiled suggestions of incest that Rebecca cannot quite grasp, Mrs. Jardine tells of the "sick" relationship between Charles Herbert and his daughter, when they are everything to each other. After his death, Ianthe moves in with a Mr. and Mrs. Connor. Again, there are suggestions in the narrative of illicit sex and corruption that young Rebecca does not understand; an adult world is being opened up to a child. Mrs. Jardine, aware that her daughter is involved in a scandalous situation but still unable to approach her directly, sends a male relative to Ianthe, and they run away together. Later, Mrs. Jardine admits that sending this young man was a mistake. Ianthe conceives a child and goes to Bohemia with Tilly to bear it. The long-standing enmity between Tilly and Mrs. Jardine stems from Tilly's refusal even at this point to allow Mrs. Jardine access to her daughter.

The story covers three generations, and the sins of the one are visited upon the next. As Sibyl left her child, so Ianthe, having married Thomson, leaves him and ultimately must abandon her children, Maisie, Malcolm, and Cherry, Mrs. Jardine's three grandchildren who became friends with Rebecca and Rebecca's sister Jess. Their father, Mr. Thomson, develops an intense hatred of both Ianthe and her mother, Mrs. Jardine—Ianthe for leaving him and Mrs. Jardine for having ruined Ianthe. As another husband with custody of children, he refuses to allow any contact between his children and either their mother or grandmother. Maisie tells Rebecca that her mother Ianthe is beautiful and that she loves the children very much, although she cannot be with them. It is Mrs. Jardine who tells Rebecca that Ianthe never cared for the children. As with every aspect of this complicated web of right and wrong, love and hate, Rebecca receives different and sometimes flatly contradictory information. Despite Mr. Thomson's hatred for Mrs. Jardine, he allows the children to live with her when he becomes too ill to care for them himself. Finally, upon his death, Mrs. Jardine recovers what had always eluded her with Ianthe; she gains custody of her grandchildren.

The influence of Henry James is sometimes noted in connection with this novel, and surely no more so than in the almost demonic passion with which Mrs. Jardine seeks to gain possession of the soul first of her own child, Ianthe, and then, when that fails, of her grandchildren. Jamesian, too, is the immature consciousness accosted with hints and suggestions, indirectness and obscurity, contradiction and variety. The quest for truth is not an easy one. The success of this novel depends in large measure on the reader's willingness to bear the burden of judgment and opinion, to make his or her own distillation of the facts and arrive at truth, and then to make a moral judgment if necessary, for Lehmann does not make the moral judgment for the reader. Indeed, the need for the rights of women and their freedom from the bondage of marriage comes across strongly, especially from the mouth of Mrs. Jardine. Yet the novel also unremittingly insists that the consequences of such freedom are devastating and evil. Rebecca is drawn to this saga because she is one of those intelligent, sensitive, strong women who may find social restrictions too binding to tolerate. An awareness of the plight of such women and a recognition of the confused and incremental way in which one learns truth are the main accomplishments of Lehmann's fifth novel.

Creating and interweaving the experiences and attitudes of both Rebecca and Mrs. Jardine, *The Ballad and the Source* attains a power that is unique in Lehmann's fiction. Her other novels are likelier to be regarded as "period pieces." Such a label does not discount the value of her work: Lehmann had the gift, shared by many other minor writers, of being able to populate a time and place—her own closely observed day, whether the 1920's or 1950's. Reading her novels, one senses instinctively that she has "gotten it

right," shown the university, the seaside villa, the run-down flat, all as they must have been. The inhabitants of those locales have life in her fiction. To create such portraits is no small feat. Lehmann's work may lack the resonance and depth of that of some of her more famous contemporaries, but she contributed significantly to the British novel: All of her novels represent some experiments with the representation of consciousness, they add to the tradition of realism, and several give powerful portrayals of the anxieties of youth and love.

Deborah Core and Paula Kopacz

OTHER MAJOR WORKS

SHORT FICTION: *The Gipsy's Baby and Other Short Stories*, 1946.

PLAY: *No More Music*, pb. 1939.

NONFICTION: *The Swan in the Evening: Fragments of an Inner Life*, 1967 (autobiography); *Letters from Our Daughters*, 1972 (with C. H. Sandys); *Rosamond Lehmann's Album*, 1985.

BIBLIOGRAPHY

Lehmann, John. *In My Own Time*. Boston: Little, Brown, 1969. Probably the most important source of information on Rosamond Lehmann's life, consisting of the three volumes of her brother's memoirs published separately in earlier editions during the 1960's. The description of Rosamond's childhood is especially revealing. Lehmann includes accounts of his sister's numerous friendships, ranging from Bernard Berenson to Guy Burgess.

Le Stourgeon, Diana E. *Rosamond Lehmann*. New York: Twayne, 1969. A standard brief survey of Lehmann's work, handicapped because it appeared before her brother's memoirs. Notes her concentration on female characters; males are relegated to minor positions. Conflicts among different generations of women often figure at the center of Lehmann's novels, which are reviewed in detail. Includes a bibliography of criticism of Lehmann with skimpy annotations.

Siegel, Ruth. *Rosamond Lehmann: A Thirties Writer*. New York: Peter Lang, 1989. The first two chapters provide a grounding in Lehmann's life and the sources of her fiction. Subsequent chapters deal with her major novels. Includes family tree, notes, and bibliography.

Simons, Judy. *Rosamond Lehmann*. New York: St. Martin's Press, 1992. Chapters on Lehmann's life and background, women and modernism, the early novels, and realism. Separate chapters on *Invitation to the Waltz*, *The Weather in the Streets*, and *The Ballad and the Source*. One chapter on later works. Includes notes and bibliography.

Tindall, Gillian. *Rosamond Lehmann: An Appreciation*. London: Chatto & Windus, 1985. The most comprehensive critical study. Behind the surface readability of her novels, Lehmann is a "deep writer" who writes frequently of death, trying to puzzle out its meaning. Abortion and the death of the very young, in particular, figure often in her novels, as does rivalry between children and parents and relations between sisters. Discusses each of the novels, and many of the short stories, in elaborate detail. Contains no footnotes or index.

STANISŁAW LEM

Born: Lvov, Poland; September 12, 1921

PRINCIPAL LONG FICTION

Astronauci, 1951

Obłok Magellana, 1955

Czas nieutracony, 1955 (includes *Szpital przemienienia* [*Hospital of the Transfiguration*, 1988], *Wśród umarłych*, and *Powrót*)

Eden, 1959 (English translation, 1989)

Śledztwo, 1959 (*The Investigation*, 1974)

Pamiętnik znaleziony w wannie, 1961 (*Memoirs Found in a Bathtub*, 1973)

Powrót z gwiazd, 1961 (*Return from the Stars*, 1980)

Solaris, 1961 (English translation, 1970)

Niezwyciężony i inne opowiadania, 1964 (*The Invincible*, 1973)

Polowanie, 1965 (*The Hunt*, in *Mortal Engines*, 1977)

Głos pana, 1968 (*His Master's Voice*, 1983)

Bezsenność, 1971 (partial translation, *The Futurological Congress*, 1974)

Ze wspomnień Ijona Tichego: Kongres futurologiczny, 1971 (*The Futurological Congress [from the Memoirs of Ijon Tichy]*, 1974)

Katar, 1976 (*The Chain of Chance*, 1978)

Wizja lokalna, 1982

Fiasko, 1986 (*Fiasco*, 1987)

Pokoj na Ziemi, 1987 (*Peace on Earth*, 1994)

OTHER LITERARY FORMS

Stanisław Lem's work defies definition. He has written both realistic and utopian novels, a detective novel with the theory of probability a leading murder suspect, reviews of nonexistent books, private poetry, Kafkaesque parables, and acid social commentary and anti-totalitarian statements in ingeniously nonsensical comic form. He has written science fiction in which extraterrestrial life takes such forms as a living ocean, weird fungi, or totally invisible and unknowable entities. Though best known for his science fiction, Lem has regularly written impressive works in other genres; all of them leap the boundaries of single forms. Many of his books are odd collections of related (or semirelated) short stories that incorporate the scientific, the philosophical, the literary, and the critical.

His principal works of nonfiction are *Wejście na orbitę* (1962; getting into orbit), *Summa technologiae* (1964; technological treatise), *Filozofia przypadku* (1968; the philosophy of chance), *Fantastyka i futurologia* (1970; science fiction and futurology), *Dialogi* (dialogues), which first appeared in 1957 and was reissued in 1984 with appendices twice the length of the original, and *Microworlds: Writings on Science Fiction and Fantasy* (1984; essays). *Summa technologiae* examines such future possibilities as the genetic remodeling of humankind and the reconstruction of reality, and *Dialogi* uses Socratic dialogues to consider the potentials of cybernetics. These works establish Lem's underlying absurdist attitudes regarding the human search for meaning amid meaninglessness.

Some of Lem's books are neither nonfiction nor science fiction; in *Hospital of the Transfiguration*, a young doctor employed in a provincial Polish insane asylum discovers in the inhumanity, cruelty, and corruption of the medical bureaucracy a foretaste of the madness of the Third Reich—which is then observed firsthand when Nazis turn the asylum into a SS hospital. Other books fit no genre at all: *Doskonala próżnia* (1971; *A Perfect Vacuum*, 1979) is totally original—a collection of reviews of books that have never been written. Another small book, *Prowokacja* (1984; partial trans. *One Human Minute*, 1986), is in the same category.

Beginning around 1970, Lem tried to abandon what he called the "ghetto" of traditional science fiction, constantly experimenting with new combinations of genres. In *Microworlds*, he enunciates his theories and criticizes other writers for squandering the intriguing and diverse potentials of science fiction by depending on clichéd patterns, plot devices, and themes. He argues that science fiction writers must discover or evolve new approaches and perspectives. Following his own advice, Lem created a blend of fiction, science fiction, and nonfiction, with each new book written in an experimental form and differing from those that preceded it. *Prowokacja* ("a kind of science fiction," says Lem) reviews a fictitious German historical/anthropological text on mass death as a recurring cultural phenomenon. The seriocomic robot "fairy tales" *Mortal Engines* (1977) and *Cyberiada* (1965; *The Cyberiad*, 1974) combine "Voltairean misanthropy" with dark humor as robot behavior mirrors human avarice, cruelty, and fallibility. *The Cosmic Carnival of Stanisław Lem* (1981) provides a panoramic selection of Lem's range, from realism to fantasy, from comedy to tragedy, from the technological to the poetic. Lem has engaged in broad satiric attacks on the governments, bureaucracies, militancy, science, and researchers of both East and West, Marxist and capitalist, and his perspective as a Polish scholar, scientist, and social critic has given his writings significance and distinction.

Lem's 1975 childhood memoir, *Wysoki Zamek*, provides a nostalgic, humorous, and meditative recreation of childhood memories of growing up in Lvov in the years between the two world wars. Lem begins his memoirs with his wish for a kaleidoscopic pattern to give meaning to his broken memories but

(Franz Rottensteiner)

ends with a wry commentary on the contrary nature of memory: the man of today and the child of memory are "a pair of horses eyeing each other distrustfully, pulling one wagon"—inseparable and impenetrable.

ACHIEVEMENTS

With books translated into forty languages, more than twenty titles in print in the United States, and sales of more than twenty-five million copies internationally, Lem is widely known as a significant science fiction writer and futurologist. Despite the inevitable loss of much innuendo, symbolism, and verbal gamesmanship in the translation from Polish to English, translators such as Michael Kandel and literary critics such as Stanisław Baranczak and Madison Davis have made Lem more accessible to English speakers.

Lem refashioned the genre of science fiction. His well-informed critical books, *Fantastyka i futurologia*, *Summa technologiae*, and *Microworlds*, and his many polemical essays written for Anglo-American science fiction magazines have expanded the limits of the genre and have solidified Lem's reputation among committed science fiction readers worldwide.

His own science fiction has brought to the genre linguistic inventiveness and intellectual versatility; it combines humanism with scientific accuracy and is commited to serious philosophical questions of science and of society. Generally rejecting conventional plots, Lem has organically blended real science with learned philosophic disquisitions on the nature of hummanity and the universe within a semifictive mode to transform science fiction into an intellectual tool for investigating human potentials and human limits (illusions, delusions, pretensions, and failures of imagination). In doing so, he has rebelled against the genre, calling it both "fossilized" and a "prison" and engaging in acerbic criticism of the "charlatans" who, he says, produce empty escapist pulp. He has been so critical of so much science fiction that his honorary membership in Science Fiction Writers of America was revoked in 1976.

The extent of Lem's revolt is not fully recognized by many English-language readers, partly because some of his critical works remain untranslated into English or have lost some of their verbal virtuosity and satiric edge in translation, and partly because Lem has become a cult figure, his readers only dimly aware that he is an apostate. Yet Lem brought science fiction into the domain of serious fiction, of belles lettres. He wedded the various components of the genre—an interest in science and technology, in different models of society and in other "species," as well as the exercise of the speculative imagination—to the devices and forms of serious literature. His innovative use of irony, humor, allegory, wordplay and verbal stylistics, suspense, narrative structure, and plot density have made him a foremost literary experimenter.

Lem's writing draws on a variety of nontraditional forms to expand the possibilities of science fiction. For example, a set of introductions to nonexistent books (including a literary history of nonhuman authors), a parody of encyclopedia advertisements, and two lectures by an arrogant computer named Golem XIV make up *Wielkść urojona* (1973; *Imaginary Magnitude*, 1984). *One Human Minute*, in turn, contains a statistical almanac of the frequency of occurrence of human activities (such as infant mortality, tumorous growths, and death by torture) in a period

of sixty seconds, reviews two volumes on twenty-first century weapons systems, and introduces a philosophical tract, "The World as Cataclysm," which asserts that humans give accidents meaning. Furthermore, Lem has contributed significantly to literary criticism, both through his critical books on science fiction and the horizons of science and through *A Perfect Vacuum*, with its clever reviews of nonexistent books (including a review of Lem's reviews) and its questioning of many of the assumptions of contemporary literary criticism.

No one has done more to bring together the domains of science and the humanities—C. P. Snow's "two cultures"—than Lem. He made science fiction a laboratory for testing new cognitive approaches and for exploring a surreal vision of human potential and dark, inescapable limitations. Above all, however, he is a figure of revolt and innovation. Dissatisfied with a literary genre, he tried to change it almost singlehandedly. Although he wrote that he believed his polemical efforts were wasted, his ultimate achievement is a major reorientation of contemporary literature.

Biography

Stanisław Lem was born in Lvov, in eastern Poland, shortly after the country regained its independence. His father, Samuel Lem, was a physician. (Stanisław, too, was to attend medical school; later he married a young student of medicine.) Lem's family shared a six-room apartment. Often lonely and resentful as a child, Lem has described his youthful self as a destructive terror. His father's medical library had a strong influence on Lem's youthful imagination, and he loved to read and browse at home—everything from his father's anatomy books to his hidden collection of erotic French novels. Lem was a good student, even something of a prodigy. His childhood was peaceful and relatively Arcadian: He enjoyed creating elaborate imaginary worlds and fantastic kingdoms, inventing new toys and instruments, mentally creating prehistoric animals unheard of in paleontology, dreaming about adventures aboard model ships, and drawing up identity papers, certificates, and passports for citizens of an imaginary community.

In Lvov, Lem finished "middle school" (similar to high school) and had begun his medical studies when World War II broke out in 1939. Lvov and eastern Poland were attacked by the Soviet Union on September 17. For twenty months, Lvov was in the hands of the Soviets, until June, 1941, when Adolf Hitler made a surprise attack against his Soviet allies. Lem survived the war by working as an automobile mechanic. It was only after the arrival of the Germans that Lem realized he was not an "Aryan." He knew that his ancestors were Jews, but his family was assimilated and knew nothing of either the Mosaic faith or Jewish culture. They managed to obtain false papers and avoided imprisonment in the ghetto. He has written that during this period he resembled more a hunted animal than a thinking human being, and he learned that the difference between life and death depended on the smallest of decisions—whether one found a door open or closed, whether one visited a friend at two o'clock or twenty minutes later. Lem had access to a depot of the German Luftwaffe and was able to give arms to members of the Polish Resistance.

After the war, Lvov was incorporated into the Soviet Union, and the Lem family moved to Krakow, where Lem resumed his medical studies. While he was a student, his first poems and stories were published in the Catholic weekly *Tygodnik powszechny* and in *Kuźnia*; these poems were collected and published in 1966 under the title *Wiersze młodzieńcze* (poems of youth). Lem also wrote dime-store thrillers to help support the family. In 1948, he completed his medical studies and wrote the first volume of *Czas nieutracony*, entitled *Hospital of the Transfiguration*, which was not published until several years later. In 1947, Lem had become a junior research assistant for an organization called The Circle for the Science of Science, which served as a clearinghouse for scientific literature from the United States and Canada to all the Polish universities. Lem read this material voraciously—one of the books he encountered in this fashion was Norbert Wiener's *The Human Use of Human Beings* (1950)—which was to influence later novels such as *Eden*, *Solaris*, and *The Invincible*. Lem also compiled surveys of scientific periodicals for the monthly *Życie nauki* (the life of science). In 1951, the publication of his first novel, *Astronauci* (the astronauts), brought him national fame; world fame followed with his subsequent books. In 1953, Lem married. His father died in 1954.

Toward the end of the 1950's, Lem bought a house on the outskirts of Krakow. There he would get up and begin writing at five each morning, then spend the afternoon waiting in food lines. However, he had trouble obtaining the foreign newspapers and scientific periodicals he liked to read at a daily rate of a dozen, and he worried about the effects of the local schools on his son Tomek. In the early 1980's, he moved to Vienna. There he enjoyed the new freedom and the physical comforts of life in the West (even trying psilocybin under a doctor's observation, but deciding that his own imagination was drug enough). After a while, however, he found the commercialism and the foreignness disturbing and distracting. Despite the restrictions of life in Poland, he felt more comfortable with the intellectual life there. Like his lonely, alienated protagonists, he discovered that physical comforts were not enough.

In 1988, he returned to the Krakow home where he had lived most of his life. In his seventies he entertained old friends such as noted Polish writer Jan Szczepanski. Wearing thick glasses and using a hearing aid in each ear, Lem played with his dachshund Proton, enjoyed his wife's cooking, and rejected invitations to travel abroad because of his dislike of hotels and the discomfort of dealing with strangers.

Lem once noted that he had lived under radically different social systems and that this circumstance has enabled him to understand the fragility that all systems share. He has also seen how human beings behave under extreme conditions—how their behavior, when they are under enormous pressure, is almost impossible to predict. These experiences have unquestionably influenced his fiction and his conception of individual psychology. World War II, moreover, transformed his way of looking at literature and traditional narration; as Lem put it in "Chance and Order," "The unfathomable futility of human life under the sway of mass murder cannot be conveyed by literary techniques in which individuals or small groups of persons form the core of the narrative."

The generation of Polish writers that began to write after World War II is often referred to as "Kolumbowie," or "Columbuses," because it was they who were the first to explore new political and social territory. Among them were poets such as Tadeusz Różewicz, Zbigniew Herbert, and Miron Białoszewski, and prose writers such as Tadeusz Borowski, Sławomir Mrożek, and Jerzy Andrzejewski. It is with these writers, who lived through experiences similar to Lem's, and many of whom came to reject traditional literary techniques, that Lem should be grouped.

ANALYSIS

Stanisław Lem has compared the effort of the first writers of science fiction (primarily Jules Verne, H. G. Wells, and Olaf Stapledon) to the exploration of a *terra incognita*. They had enormous room for maneuver because the field had only recently opened up and was still empty of both writers and books. The situation was similar to that in Poland and other Eastern European countries in 1945, and it was also, in large part, a continuation of the literature of exploration of the sixteenth, seventeenth, and eighteenth centuries. This was largely a European literature, and one of its major preoccupations was the New World of the Americas, although it also dealt with the other non-European continents. France, Spain, England—all Europe—became an insatiable market for such writings, some of which were firsthand accounts by authors who had been there but many of which were written at second or third hand. The bulk of this literature was based upon the psychological mechanism of projection. Instead of concentrating on the objective description of what was new about the recently discovered land and its peoples, with its real contours as they slowly came to be revealed, the writers maintained all their very European interests and concerns (with such things as wealth and gold mines, a trade link with China and India, and a desire to convert the American Indians) and simply projected these against the broad screen of the New World.

As a result, this literature is intensely subjective, and the mechanism of projection behind it is often crude and primitive, sometimes transparently serving the interests of publicists. It nevertheless reflected a strong desire to account for totally new experience, as with later science fiction. Few great writers devoted themselves to producing such literature, although its sheer bulk in all the European languages was enormous. The great writers could not ignore it, and they felt its attraction at one point or another of their lives, as evidenced by William Shakespeare's *The Tempest* (1611), whose setting appears to be based on the Bermuda islands, the writings of Michel de Montaigne and Chateaubriand, or, later, American literature dealing with the frontier.

As a genre, science fiction has had similar opportunities and similar liabilities—or traps to catch the naïve writer off guard. The market, or readership, is similarly large. Likewise, the temptation to employ a crude form of projection is very great. Under the guise of "speculation," much science fiction can be read in transparently psychological terms, and exotic creatures are readily translatable into the down-to-earth terms of the author's immediate biases, preoccupations, and obsessions. Science and technology, like the New World, are highly visible in their manifestations, impressive, and concrete, and, like the New World, they have the ability to catalyze the imagination. Bruno Bettelheim has written penetratingly about science fiction from the psychoanalytic point of view, demonstrating how it serves as an expression of the contemporary psyche and postwar anxieties. Some of its modes are regressive or neurotic, he claims, analogous to popular medieval preoccupations and superstitions about witchcraft and devils. Lem, too, was to point out some of the more regressive traits of science fiction—not from the point of view of an outsider, but from that of a practitioner of the genre with a superb command of modern science and the belief that science fiction presented a unique opportunity to explore the events and mechanisms of twentieth century history, to give them clear and cogent expression.

Lem has divided his own works into three main periods. During the first period, from about 1950 to 1956, Lem wrote what he now calls "purely secondary things," although they sold well throughout Europe and made him world-famous. *Astronauci*, for example, is about an expedition to the planet Venus from a simplistically utopian Earth. Why utopian? The plots of these early novels and the kind of life they depicted, Lem has said, were contrary to all his experiences of life at the time. The evil world of reality was supposed to have been mysteriously transformed into a good one. In the postwar years, there seemed to be only a single choice, according to Lem: between hope and despair, between a historically untenable optimism and a well-justified skepticism that easily slipped into nihilism.

In his books of this period, Lem wanted to embrace optimism and hope; by describing naïve utopias, he was expressing a desire for a world as peaceful as that described in his books. The books are bad, he has said, in the sense that a vain and erroneous expectation is stupid. At the time, however, Lem believed that science fiction could express "the direction in which the world is in fact moving" and that this conviction was based on a sense of reality. There was the belief that science fiction was able to deal with the whole species, not merely with specific individuals. Lem was optimistic about science fiction as a genre and expected it to expand, to become increasingly vital. "As a reader," he has written, "I expected something like what is called, in the evolutionary processes of nature, speciation—a new animal species generating a diverging, fanlike radiation of other new species. In my ignorance, I thought that the time of Verne, Wells, and Stapledon was the beginning, but not the beginning of the decline."

Astronauci, *Obłok Magellana* (the cloud of Magellan), and *Czas nieutracony* (time not lost) brought Lem enormous popularity; *Obłok Magellana* went through more than five large printings and was translated into Russian, German, Czech, Slovak, Hungarian, Rumanian, and Armenian. This was the Stalinist period, when the censors were applying the doctrines of Socialist Realism with rigor and when many serious writers were unable to publish. To a certain extent, Lem participated in the spirit of the times, and perhaps he did not care to look too closely at the world—the "Earth"—at his feet. The times encouraged neither criticism nor serious, analytical nonfiction.

During this early period, Lem's method of writing was characterized by trial and error. He would write spontaneously, often for eight or ten hours a day with hardly a break. Creative spontaneity, however, was not a guarantee that there would be a sure development of a whole narrative—that is, a plot that could be finished without applying force. Lem would often write something without the least idea of how its plot, characters, or problems would turn out. The early novels have a certain centripetal vigor that is attractive. They tend to be long; they suffer from a certain absence of form and, above all, from flatness of characterization.

The break between Lem's first and second stage occurred at about the time of the "thaw" of 1956, which followed upon the Polish and Hungarian revolts of that year. Lem's first volume of nonfiction, *Dialogi*, was published in 1957. Lem's second stage extends from 1956 to the end of the 1960's and includes some of his finest works of fiction, among them *Solaris* and *The Invincible*, as well as his best nonfiction. Lem aptly characterized his work of this period when he said that he reached the borders of a field that was already nearly completely mapped. At this time, Lem wrote without much regard for the continuity between his imagined worlds and the familiar world, but he did make an effort to understand them and integrate them. During this period, he continued to develop his works spontaneously, but the number of uncompleted novels was increasing. *Solaris*, one of Lem's most popular works (a film version under the same title, directed by André Tarkovsky, was released in 1971), was put aside for a year before he suddenly "learned" how it should end. (Lem claims that he sees no relation between the spontaneity with which a work is written and its quality.)

SOLARIS

Solaris is one of Lem's most successful books from the point of view of characterization; several of the characters are "well-rounded," in the lexicon of literary criticism. The book deals, in greater depth than his previous works, with the notion of what forms life might assume, or might not assume, in another world. Kelvin, the narrator, arrives at a station hovering over the planet Solaris and finds it empty of human beings; when he searches for its crew, he encounters the scientist Snow, who panics when he sees Kelvin. There is an "adversary" on Solaris, a "living ocean" that covers the whole planet. A colloidal-like sea functions as a homeostatic regulator of the gravitational fields exerted by the planet's two suns; it passes its eons creating huge, protean, mimetic structures from its waves. Scientists from Earth have tried to penetrate the mysteries of the planet for more than a century, finally bombarding the "sea" with X-rays. In retaliation, each of the scientists is visited by an exact, living model "read" from memory traces of the one person in the past about whom he feels most guilty. The situation is described with a rigor and complexity that make it compelling; the behavior of the beleaguered Earthmen is so finely attuned to their characters and so forcefully dramatized that the reader believes in their experience. The book ends with an account of "Solaristics" and a purely religious concept of "the sea" that give it unique depth.

Return from the Stars

Return from the Stars was one of Lem's first attempts to reconcile the other world of the stars with life on Earth. Lem has stated that he does not regard the book as a good one, but it is an intriguing book despite its faults. An astronaut who has been among the stars returns to Earth and finds it changed. At the beginning of the book, this future Earth is described in rich detail: its modes of public transportation, dress, nuclear power—all seen through the eyes of a first-person narrator who has left Earth at a time like the present and whose expectations therefore approximate the reader's. He encounters difficulties with the first people he meets, and there is a major difference between him and them. This difference is the result of a process called "betrization," a treatment that human beings in the future world have undergone to rid them of aggressive impulses. Lem believes that the book deals with the problem of social evil and its elimination in too primitive a fashion: "Even if the evil done to others with full intent could be suppressed pharmacologically—the book's main premise—no chemical or other influence upon the brain could cause the unintended evil effects of all social

dependencies, conflicts and contradictions to disappear from the world in the same manner that an insecticide can eliminate vermin." The book nevertheless remains a noble attempt to juxtapose two different worlds, to render the sustained sense of surprise of the narrator as he observes the New World (of Earth), and to describe it in dense, palpable, closely observed detail.

The Invincible

The Invincible, written several years after *Return from the Stars*, explores the theme of reliance—or overreliance—on monolithic military might. A mammoth space cruiser with an impregnable force field and "antimatter artillery" is defeated by hordes of flylike mechanisms on a planet where evolution has proceeded for some 500,000 years from the robots that colonized it. The political allegories of Lem are usually subtle and have diverse reverberations; the space cruiser may seem to resemble the Soviet Union, surrounded by smaller states, but it could as well be equated, for example, with the dinosaur. The description of the "flies" (their strictly symmetrical tripartite structures resembling the letter Y) is superb in its imaginative conception. The control system of the horde itself, its "mind," is baffling, and remains so, even as its power increases.

Memoirs Found in a Bathtub

Another book with political connotations is *Memoirs Found in a Bathtub*. Far in the future, a man wanders pointlessly in a vast underground labyrinth, the final stronghold of the American Pentagon. Pentagon III was buried in the Rocky Mountains sometime after the collapse of capitalist society; its center is controlled by a supremely complicated "brain," but one whose conduits of control, orders, tactics, codes, and chains of command are riddled with paranoid subterfuges to guard its secrets from an enemy that may, in fact, no longer exist. The nameless narrator, who spends his time scurrying from office to office, is caught in a maze of incidents that seem alternately fortuitous and part of an inscrutable plan. All the officials are like walking codes, their true purposes hidden behind their simulated advice and disguises, all of them creatures of the "brain." The book pushes the traditions of the spy novel to an extreme point of absurdity. It can be also read as a satire of the Cold War, a realistic depiction of bureaucracy, or an experiment in chance and design.

In most of the books of his second stage, Lem takes important themes of contemporary history and treats them with both complexity and philosophical depth. He tries to see basic *mechanisms* in society and its problems, and to universalize them. Sometimes this involves other worlds but sometimes not, as in *The Futurological Congress (from the Memoirs of Ijon Tichy)*, with its description of a synthetic paradise created by hallucinogenic drugs that completely falsify perceptions of the world. This permanently stoned world, ruled by a handful of "chemocrats," is remarkably close to home.

Lem's second period was also the time when he brought his revolt against traditional science fiction into the open. "My monograph on science fiction and futurology," he has written, "is an expression of my disappointment with a fiction and a non-fiction that pretend to be scientific, when neither of them turns the attention of the reader in the direction in which the world is in fact moving." In the late 1960's, Lem and Rottensteiner were protesting in public against the "common prison" of science fiction; "for me," Lem has written, "the scientific ignorance of most American science fiction writers was as inexplicable as the abominable literary quality of their output." His own nonfictional works and activities were having a decided influence on his fiction; as he has said, he was "oscillating" or "seesawing" between the two genres, and as he became more aware of that oscillation, cross-fertilization between the two increased.

A PERFECT VACUUM

The result was the beginning of the third period of Lem's career, extending from the end of the 1960's to the present. With *A Perfect Vacuum*, Lem felt that he had passed beyond the limits of science fiction as it had come to be known and was breaking entirely new ground. *A Perfect Vacuum* is one of the freest and most highly imaginative works Lem has written, but paradoxically the connecting links to the present—what Lem called "realism" in science fiction—are evident throughout the book. Here is the "turning toward" the familiar world, and the continuity between

it and imagined worlds, that he recommended for other writers of science fiction. It is a form of satire, not directed, however, at specific individuals as institutions but rather at tendencies, mechanisms, "species" that Lem concocts based on those that exist everywhere around us and at our very feet. Here was a whole new fictitious domain dependent not on the paraphernalia of spaceships, astronauts, and Martians, but on the even stranger, more exotic creatures of our own contemporary history.

HIS MASTER'S VOICE

Twenty-five thousand specialists in *His Master's Voice* declare a pulsating stream of life-promoting neutrino radiation to be a stellar code and convincingly detail totally divergent decoding strategies and messages that reflect human expectations: a technological gift from a dying civilization? a formula for the ultimate weapon? Lem cynically addresses the perils of scientific theories, scientific jealousies, and infighting, as well as the dangerous moral and social impact of blind adherence to pet theories. His central scientist dwells on Nazi atrocities and doomsday machines, on the philosophy of Immanuel Kant and Christianity. Ultimately, Lem once again argues the unlikelihood of communication with true aliens, suggests that humans respond as if the unknown were a giant Rorschach test, and describes humans as limited, "like snails, each stuck to his own leaf." *The Hunt* and *The Chain of Chance* continue to explore the human desire to find the familiar and meaningful in the alien and meaningless, to substitute theorizing and hypothesizing for observation and for acceptance of random chaos. In both, private investigators faced with bizarre mysteries deduce cause-effect relationships from a chain of coincidences but fail to explain the inexplicable.

THE IJON TICHY NOVELS

The Star Diaries, *The Futurological Congress (from the Memoirs of Ijon Tichy)*, *Memoirs of a Space Traveler*, and *Peace on Earth* record the reminiscences of Ijon Tichy, an average, mundane tourist of the universe, a futuristic Gulliver or Candide, whose name is a play on the Polish word for "quiet" and perhaps on the English word "cheeky." The delightfully informal tales of his outrageous misadventures, recorded in a free-wheeling, episodic diary, humorously ridicule human institutions (especially bureaucracies) and doctrines (especially repressive ones expressed in jargonate diction), and ideas about scientific laws, progress, and even human nature. (Baranczak compares these novels with George Orwell's 1945 satire *Animal Farm*.) Whether trying to speed up evolution to move humanoids to a more civilized level, caught in a time warp, split into multiple selves, experiencing the confusion wrought by the severing of the left and right hemispheres of his brain, or recounting how the creation of the universe was bungled or how the soul was invented, Tichy finds his assumptions challenged and life more complex than it at first seems.

In *The Star Diaries*, factions promoting different forms of genetic engineering (including sexual oddities) contend for dominance, and robot monks revive irrational religious beliefs. In *The Futurological Congress (from the Memoirs of Ijon Tichy)*, a parody of Lem's own genre, Tichy faces a "pitifully empty" world of revolution and chemical warfare in which terrorists become humanists thanks to mood-altering drugs, and in which grass becomes cheese without the cow. In *Memoirs of a Space Traveler* he finds the loss of body and social contact eternal hell. He encounters mechanical beings as real as the scientist who created them and self-destructive "Phools" who reflect the worst of free enterprise combined with social planning.

In *Peace on Earth*, a Cold War parable, the intrepid Tichy investigates the complex self-evolving lunar war machines that perpetuate the human arms race; these robotical machines have aggressive interplanetary ambitions, but their rising costs precipitate their end. The picaresque adventures of Ijon Tichy, like those of Pilot Pirx in later short stories, depict men and women as alienated and alone, misunderstanding their fellow creatures, destructively tampering with the unknowable, redeemed only when they respect other life forms and see into their own nature. Both Pirx and Tichy learn the inadequacy of human knowledge and the importance of sheer guts, and both are caught up in experiences that make them question even the value of their biological makeup.

Lem uses their experiences to satirize Stalinism, arms-race politics, military thinking, Cold War attitudes, and Marxist attempts to mold the New Man in reeducation camps, all with humor and wit.

FIASCO

Fiasco, which most critics find one of Lem's most accessible works, continues two themes that have recurred throughout his canon: human beings' self-absorption and lack of imagination—their inability to imagine the alien as uniquely different from themselves—and the absurdities of the arms race. Despite Lem's hallmark academic digressions (for example, on planet geology or the effects of sudden acceleration to the speed of light), the plot is fast-paced. An Earth expedition begins as a quest for knowledge through communication with a sentient, treelike fungus on the planet Quinta, but the quest fails because the humans project their own irrational passions and aggressive/defensive behavior patterns into the alien silence. They theorize about arms races and rival factions that mirror their own aggression and believe that the built-in computer responses of their spacecraft to the proximity of the alien confirm alien violence. Although one pilot wants to theorize less and use multiple approaches to understanding, and a Dominican monk suggests that the Quintans remain silent because they wish to be left alone, the other humans believe their own self-projections. They destroy Quinta's moon, project cartoons on the planet's clouds to stimulate contact, set up rings of elaborate defense systems, and finally elicit a Quintan response that reflects the novel's title.

LATER NOVELS

In Lem's third period, his method of composition changed somewhat. Only rarely did he sit down at the typewriter when he had a small and ready beginning; instead, he produced an increasing number of notes, "fictitious encyclopedias," and additional ideas, trying to get to know the "world" he was to create by first imagining the literature specific to it. He used these notes, he said, "to create my own "knowledge of another world, a knowledge entirely subservient to my literary program."

This research helped Lem to create links between the imagined world and the present. He published some of these notes, no doubt in an ironic form, in the appendix to *Wizja lokalna* (local vision). The use of this material gives rise to the question, What is the role of science in Lem's later science fiction? The question might be put in relief by comparing the "insects" in *The Invincible* with the insectlike inhabitants of Samuel Beckett's *Le Dépeupleur* (1971; *The Lost Ones*, 1972). Both works are imaginative, describing quasi-allegorical worlds that are self-contained and coherent within their own terms, at first glance different from our own. Beckett's floating cylinder even superficially resembles a mechanical contrivance in space. Both authors describe these worlds—their architecture, habitats, modes of locomotion and so on—with an attempt at rendering the psychology of the beings who live there. This technical detail is effective when it is informed by imaginative vision and concern for characterization, but when it leaves psychological perspective far behind, it becomes less functional, less dramatic and necessary.

Lem's later works occupy a domain in which science fiction and belles lettres (or serious literature) exist in uneasy balance. He integrates them in combinations that are always new. Whether his later works can be described as "science fiction" in the sense that the term is generally understood is unclear; Lem remains marked by his scientific background, yet he was never inclined to reduce a civilization to its lowest technological denominator. Culture has always been of the greatest importance to him. He has dealt with those scientists who would jettison culture once and for all in his fictitious review of a fictitious German tome, *Die Kultur als Fehler* (*Culture as Mistake*), in *A Perfect Vacuum*:

> "Culture, defender of Evolution's Causal Imbecilities," he writes ironically, "culture, shifty pettifogger of a lost cause, shyster mouthpiece of primitivism. . . . Technological development means the ruin of culture? But of course it does! And instead of shedding tears over the loss of our captivity, we should hasten our step to leave its dark house."

This savagely ironic passage, its invective mounting from page to page, reveals the Lem who attributes the highest values to liberal culture. The irony is expressed with the richness and imaginative wealth characteristic of the finest literature.

Lem's commitment to culture is beyond question, and any doubt about the matter is laid to rest once one has read the appendices to the 1984 edition of *Dialogi*. The essays on ethics and technology, on biology and values, are strong statements of the necessity to see science in the context of the other aspects of civilization that surround it, nourish it, and give rise to it, while the essay on the pathology of socialism is a blistering attack, written from the conviction that the health of a social organism requires a respect for pluralism and liberal values. Socialism (or communism) is described in terms of biological pathology. Lem analyzes with clarity and force the functional mechanisms of a regime that he believes is among the most destructive that have come into existence and that is fundamentally incapable of being reformed.

Lem's style is only partly perceptible in translations of his work, which have a tendency to streamline and sanitize his prose in order to emphasize plot and humor. Yet Lem's style always comes through as that of a literary artist; it is one of the most important features of his work. Lem's collection of short fiction *The Cyberiad*, for example, is a tour de force of verbal playfulness and stylistic high spirits; the English translation, although a very good one, permits only a partial appreciation of this book, which is as much about language as it is about cybernetics.

Lem's strong points as a writer are his imaginative style; his humor, which often assumes a mordant, satiric edge reminiscent of eighteenth century parodists such as Jonathan Swift and the Voltaire of *Candide* (1759) and *Le Micromégas* (1752; *Micromegas*, 1753); a gift for dramatic improvisation; and an ability to analyze situations, discerning their basic mechanisms, which he is then able to generalize and project in plot structures. His weak points are, perhaps, characterization, a fondness for the striking idea, with the result that his work is sometimes overly schematic, and a distance from the contours of concrete, everyday life. The concern for science and the intellect often results in a neglect of other human activities that are equally important. Yet Lem's work attempts a unique kind of literary synthesis, successfully fusing the best elements of science fiction and serious literature. Lem evokes universals—alienation, arrogance, obsession with trivia, blind commitment to theory, violence, self-reflective projections, fear of the unknown and unknowable, as well as resilience, resourcefulness, and the potential for understanding and humane behavior. He attacks scientists, bureaucrats, technicians, researchers, warmongers, theoreticians, and militarists alike, finding their activities more reflective of their own obsessions than of any reality.

John Carpenter, updated by Gina Macdonald

OTHER MAJOR WORKS

SHORT FICTION: *Sezam i inne opowiadania*, 1954; *Dzienniki gwiazdowe*, 1957, 1971 (*The Star Diaries*, 1976; *Memoirs of a Space Traveler: Further Reminiscences of Ijon Tichy*, 1982); *Inwazja z Aldebarana*, 1959 (partial translation, *Tales of Pirx the Pilot*, 1979); *Księga robotów*, 1961; *Bajki robotów*, 1964 (partial translation, *Mortal Engines*, 1977); *Cyberiada*, 1965 (*The Cyberiad: Fables for the Cybernetic Age*, 1974); *Ratujemy kosmos i inne opowiadania*, 1966; *Opowieści o pilocie Pirxie*, 1968 (*Tales of Pirx the Pilot*, 1979; *More Tales of Pirx the Pilot*, 1982); *Doskonała próżnia*, 1971 (*A Perfect Vacuum*, 1979); *Wielkść urojona*, 1973 (*Imaginary Magnitude*, 1984); *Maska*, 1976 (partial translation, *Mortal Engines*, 1977); *Suplement*, 1976; *Mortal Engines*, 1977; *Golem XIV*, 1981; *The Cosmic Carnival of Stanisław Lem: An Anthology of Entertaining Stories by the Modern Master of Science Fiction*, 1981; *Prowokacja*, 1984 (partial trans. *One Human Minute*, 1986); *Ciemność i pleśń*, 1988; *Apokryfy*, 1998.

PLAY: *Jacht Paradise*, pb. 1951 (with Roman Hussarski).

POETRY: *Wiersze młozieńcze*, 1966.

NONFICTION: *Dialogi*, 1957, 1984; *Wejście na orbitę*, 1962; *Summa technologiae*, 1964; *Wysoki Zamek*, 1966 (*Highcastle: A Remembrance*, 1995); *Filozofia przypadku*, 1968; *Fantastyka i futurologia*, 1970; *Rozprawy i szkice*, 1975; *Microworlds: Writings on Science Fiction and Fantasy*, 1984 (essays); *A Stanislaw Lem Reader*, 1997 (with Peter Swirski); *Bomba megabitorva*, 1999.

MISCELLANEOUS: *Noc księżycowa*, 1963; *Powtórka*, 1979.

BIBLIOGRAPHY

Baranczak, Stanisław. "Highcastle: A Remembrance." *The New Republic*, May 20, 1996, 39-41. Baranczak uses Lem's memoir as an excuse to explore the diversity of Lem's canon, the subtlety and humor of his political satire, and the underlying implications of his decision to focus on his lost youth in Lvov, a city with strong political resonances for Poles (it is now part of Ukraine). He calls Lem a twentieth century Chekhov and concludes that what seems a simple memoir is instead a statement about the imaginative nature of memory and the impossibility of truly recapturing a lost past.

_____. "Hospital of the Transfiguration." *The New Republic*, November 7, 1988, 39-41. Pointing out that the Polish term for science fiction is "scientific fantasy," Baranczak captures the politics and personal realities that make *Hospital of the Transformation* a realistic *Bildungsroman*, one superior to the trilogy in which it was written (*The Time Not Lost*). He praises the starkly realistic medical sections but explores why the novel as a whole is unsuccessful, concluding that Lem is more interested in human immutability than superficial historical evolution.

Davis, James Madison. *Stanisław Lem*. Borgo Press, 1990. A reader's guide to Lem. Provides an introduction to his life and writing; a survey of his major works, fiction and nonfiction; and annotated primary and secondary bibliographies. More up-to-date and extensive than the Richard Ziegfield guide, *Stanisław Lem*, published by Ungar in 1985.

Engel, Peter. "The Cosmic Carnival of Stanisław Lem." *The New Republic*, February 7, 1983, 37-41. Translator and editor Michael Kandal is the man most responsible for ensuring Lem's place in the English-speaking world, and his translation of selections from the comic/fable science fiction novels is particularly impressive. Ijon Tichy is probably the closest of all Lem's inventions to being the author's alter ego.

Lem, Stanisław. *A Stanisław Lem Reader*. Evanston,

Ill.: Northwestern University Press, 1997. In this collection of Lem's work, editor Peter Swirski provides two interviews with Lem, and Lem's own 1991 essay surveying thirty years of prognoses culled from his nonfiction works not yet translated into English. Included are Lem's attacks on what he sees as the abuses and misuses of the science fiction genre. A bibliography of primary and secondary sources completes the volume.

Santoro, Gene. "Eden." *The Nation*, April 2, 1990, 462-463. *Eden* proves an ironic, Crusoe-like encounter that provides Lem room to comment on the nature of consciousness and the human condition—the way experiences limit the human ability to perceive the new and alien. The novel could be read as a Stalinist dystopia, Santoro says, or, as "Lem's fantasy worlds come more and more to resemble our own," a Reaganist one, with public access to information curtailed, government spokespeople misspeaking, media complicity and a wearily passive populace.

Tierney, John. "A Mundane Master of Cosmic Visions." *Discover*, December, 1986, 56-66. Tierney provides an insightful overview of Lem's life and work. He marvels that Lem's novels postulate the truly bizarre. He finds even more marvelous the fact that such innovative cosmic visions, prophecies, and projections on everything from artificial intelligence to genetic engineering to quarks derive from a modern-day Voltaire from a nonprogressive city who wrote on a manual typewriter and had no desire to travel, preferring to tend his garden.

(Marc Hauser)

ELMORE LEONARD

Born: New Orleans, Louisiana; October 11, 1925

PRINCIPAL LONG FICTION

The Bounty Hunters, 1953
The Law at Randado, 1954
Escape from Five Shadows, 1956
Last Stand at Saber River, 1959 (also known as *Lawless River* and *Stand on the Saber*)
Hombre, 1961
The Big Bounce, 1969
The Moonshine War, 1969
Valdez Is Coming, 1970
Forty Lashes Less One, 1972
Mr. Majestyk, 1974
Fifty-two Pickup, 1974
Swag, 1976 (also known as *Ryan's Rules*)
The Hunted, 1977
Unknown Man No. 89, 1977
The Switch, 1978
Gunsights, 1979
City Primeval: High Noon in Detroit, 1980
Gold Coast, 1980
Split Images, 1981
Cat Chaser, 1982
Stick, 1983
LaBrava, 1983
Glitz, 1985
Elmore Leonard's Double Dutch Treat: Three Novels, 1986

Bandits, 1987
Touch, 1987
Freaky Deaky, 1988
Killshot, 1989
Get Shorty, 1990
Maximum Bob, 1991
Rum Punch, 1992 (also known as *Jackie Brown*)
Pronto, 1993
Riding the Rap, 1995
Out of Sight, 1996
Naked Came the Manatee, 1996 (with 12 other
    Florida writers)
Cuba Libre, 1998
Be Cool, 1999

OTHER LITERARY FORMS

Elmore Leonard published numerous Western short stories as well as several magazine articles on crime writing and police procedure. More significantly, he developed considerable expertise as a writer of screenplays, both originals and adaptations.

ACHIEVEMENTS

Leonard has come to be widely regarded as one of the best crime-fiction writers in the world and is ranked with Dashiell Hammett and Raymond Chandler as a writer who transcends the limitations of category fiction. He is one of those who made hard-boiled crime fiction "respectable," and his storytelling technique has influenced countless others. In 1984, *LaBrava* won the Mystery Writers of America (MWA) Edgar Allan Poe Award as the best novel of the year, and in 1992 the MWA named him a Grand Master, its highest accolade.

BIOGRAPHY

Elmore John Leonard, Jr., was born in New Orleans, Louisiana, but grew up in Detroit, Michigan, a city that forms the background for many of his crime novels. He attended Blessed Sacrament Elementary School and the University of Detroit High School and was drafted into the U.S. Navy in 1943, serving in the Admiralty Islands of New Guinea with the Seabees. After the war, he attended the University of Detroit on the G.I. Bill, majoring in English and phi-

losophy, and, following his graduation in 1950, went to work as a copywriter for a Detroit advertising agency. His growing family made it difficult for him to pursue his ambition to become a freelance writer, but he began writing Western short stories between 5:00 and 7:00 A.M. each day before going to work, and he published his first in 1951: "Trail of the Apache," in *Argosy* magazine. During the ensuing decade, he sold twenty-seven more such stories to pulp magazines and published four Western novels. Though he quit the advertising agency in 1959 to become a full-time writer, for several years he supplemented his fiction income by writing scripts for Encyclopædia Britannica educational films.

Hombre, his last Western novel, was published in 1961, and four years later Twentieth Century-Fox purchased the film rights for ten thousand dollars (it was made into a film starring Paul Newman in 1967). He also sold Columbia the film rights to "3:10 to Yuma," an early story, and *The Tall T* (1957), a novelette, during this period. At the same time, the market for Western fiction was drying up, perhaps because the genre had been overly exploited by television. Leonard, in characteristically pragmatic fashion, switched to writing crime fiction. This was the turning point in his career, for he had never felt entirely at ease with Westerns, and he made the transition effortlessly. His first non-Western novels, *The Big Bounce* and *The Moonshine War*, were published in 1969; Warner Bros. bought the film rights to the former, and Leonard wrote a screenplay (his first) of the latter and sold it. A few years later, in 1972, *Joe Kidd*, a film of his first original screenplay, was released. Thus began Leonard's long relationship with the film industry.

In 1974, after twenty years of heavy drinking, he joined Alcoholics Anonymous; in 1977 he and his wife divorced, and he remarried in 1979. He married his third wife in the early 1990's; they would make their home in Bloomfield Hills, Michigan.

Since the 1980's, Leonard's novels have received widespread critical praise, and he has been described as "the best American writer of crime fiction alive." When *LaBrava* won the Mystery Writers of America Edgar Allan Poe Award in 1984, his reputation as a major crime writer was secured, though he says he writes "novels, not mysteries." He has also been a popular success. In 1985, *Glitz* made *The New York Times* best-seller list, and Warner Books two years later published a first printing of 250,000 copies of *Bandits* in a one-million-dollar deal. A year later, he received three million dollars for *Freaky Deaky*. Film rights purchases continued to be a regular occurrence with Leonard novels, as 1995's *Get Shorty* was a success, and the 1998 film of *Out of Sight* was hailed as one of the year's best.

ANALYSIS

Elmore Leonard's early short stories and novels were conventional in terms of plot and characterization; however, writing Westerns was good training. Knowing nothing about the West, he learned to depend on research that he could embellish with his vivid imagination. This is essentially the method he has employed throughout his writing career. Furthermore, when he switched to crime fiction, he brought some of his hair-trigger, saloon-wrecking cowboy villains into urban settings with startling effects. Examples of these "redneck monsters" are Raymond Gidre in *Unknown Man No. 89*, Clement Mansell in *City Primeval*, Roland Crowe in *Gold Coast*, and Richard Nobles in *LaBrava*. Another type of displaced Western character is Armand Degas in *Killshot*, a half-breed American Indian turned Mafia hit man.

Placing cowboys and American Indians in modern cities such as Miami and Detroit is only one of the many types of contrast Leonard employs to produce effects. In his crime novels the most violent incidents occur in the most peaceful settings, such as family restaurants, supermarkets, and real estate offices, and the worst villainy is often directed against people whose lives had previously been conventional and uneventful. In *Killshot*, a working-class couple suddenly find themselves having their front windows blown out with shotgun blasts; the story ends with a double murder in the cozy breakfast nook of their model kitchen.

In 1959, there were thirty prime-time Western series on television. The public was bound to become surfeited with saloon brawls and shootouts on Main Street. It was not until this six-gun overkill forced Leonard to turn to crime fiction that he began to develop the distinctive approach to storytelling that brought him fame and fortune. That approach was influenced by his own involvement in filmmaking, which has one cardinal rule for writers: "Don't tell us: *Show* us."

Hollywood has long exerted a push-pull effect on fiction writers. The cinematic manner of telling stories through action and dialogue has had an incalculable influence on their conscious and unconscious minds, and the big money to be made from sales of motion-picture rights has provided an often irresistible temptation to structure novels so that adaptation from print to film would present no problems. The traits that distinguish Leonard's crime novels are those found in all good films: strong characterization, believable dialogue, and interesting visual effects.

The publication of his crime novel *Fifty-two Pickup* in 1974 was the turning point in his career. He says, "I started to realize that the way to describe anywhere, *anywhere*, was to do it from someone's point of view . . . and *leave me out of it*." Perhaps not entirely coincidentally, 1974 was also the year he separated from his first wife and began attending Alcoholics Anonymous meetings. In describing his recovery from alcoholism, he also said: "The key is getting out of yourself." Prior to *Fifty-two Pickup*, Leonard had written his fiction in a conventional manner—that is, mostly in the "voice" of an anonymous narrator who sets the scenes, describes his characters' appearance and behavior, and quotes their verbal interchanges. This objective technique was perfected by Ernest Hemingway, whose Spanish Civil War novel *For Whom the Bell Tolls* (1940) had a permanent effect on Leonard's approach to fiction writing. However, Leonard went beyond Hemingway, trying as much as possible to vanish as a narrator and to let his stories be told by the characters themselves. He describes the viewpoint characters see and hear as well as what they think and feel in language appropriate to each character, so that most of his narration and description reads like dialogue without the quotes.

It would be inaccurate to call this technique "stream of consciousness" or "interior monologue": It is a modification that Leonard describes as his unique "sound." There are no long passages in italics, no stream-of-consciousness ramblings. Nor are there "pebbles in the pond" or other old-fashioned flashback conventions. Since Leonard generally has the reader inside a character's mind, it is easy to move back and forth in time, as he frequently does. The character simply remembers an earlier event, and the reader is instantly transported back to the past.

Changing from past to present is simply another of Leonard's ways of deliberately keeping the reader off balance. The one consistent feature of a Leonard novel is that nothing ever stays the same. He imitates modern American films, which create the effect of being in continuous motion with changing camera angles, jump cuts, intercuts, tracking shots, aerial shots, flashbacks, and all the other tricks of the trade. His practice of constantly shifting viewpoints is analogous to modern filmmaking, in which scenes are shot simultaneously by several cameras, and strips of film are spliced together to provide visual variety as well as to highlight whatever the director considers most important. Typically, Leonard changes points of view from chapter to chapter; however, he does it within chapters as well, and with an effortlessness that makes lesser writers envious.

The average category fiction writer will describe his characters only once, when they first appear, and then rely largely on peculiarities of dialogue to differentiate them from one another for the rest of the book. A standard practice of commercial fiction writers is to give each character some "shtick"—a cane, a monocle, a pipe, a stammer, a foreign accent—to help the reader remember him or her; still, in many category novels the characters become a hopeless jumble in the reader's mind. The reader's interest in a novel depends on the credibility of its characters. Shootings, bombings, and other forms of violence are not effective unless the reader can believe they are happening to real people. In describing each character's appearance and actions through the eyes of another character, Leonard not only eliminates the need for the "intrusive author" but also characterizes both individuals at once. From beginning to end, he never stops characterizing. He also achieves a strong sense that his characters are actually interrelating, because each is seen in turn through the eyes of someone else. That is why Leonard's writing is so much more effective than most category fiction and why he has transcended his genre.

FIFTY-TWO PICKUP

In *Fifty-two Pickup*, Leonard was only partially successful in telling his story through the viewpoints of his characters. The "good guys," a middle-class husband and wife who are being victimized by blackmailers, come alive; however, the "bad guys" are two-dimensional characters exuding the all-too-familiar blend of sadism, cynical humor, and innuendo. Leonard knew that he needed to humanize his villains in order to give his novels balance. In his next novel, *Swag*, he tells the story from the points of view of the "bad guys," two likable young men who take up armed robbery for fun and profit.

SWAG

Swag may be the best novel Leonard has written, although it is far from being his best known. Held in the robbers' viewpoints like a fly in amber, the reader is helplessly but deliciously dragged into one holdup after another and lives out his own secret fantasies about walking into a store with a big Colt .45 automatic and walking out with a bag of cash. The reader experiences all the dangers of the profession and ponders all the intangibles: "What if the clerk dives for a gun?" "What if a customer starts screaming?" "What if an alarm goes off?" "What if a cop drives up?" Here, to quote horror writer Stephen King, is "the kind of book that if you get up to see if there are any chocolate chip cookies left, you take it with you so you won't miss anything."

This kind of story has drawbacks. For one thing, the reader is willing to identify with the "bad guys" only as long as they refrain from killing innocent people. Also, stories such as this one usually end with the protagonists being shot or sent to prison—as in the films *Bonnie and Clyde* (1967) and *Butch Cassidy and the Sundance Kid* (1969). In *Swag*, the antiheroes inevitably become overconfident and walk into disaster. Finally, the viewpoint characters in

Swag seem less like real criminals than like middle-class young men who are playing at being criminals. Such a "Robin Hood" plot might serve for a single novel but could not be extended to a career technique. Leonard realized that he needed to learn more about the criminal mentality.

In 1978, Leonard spent two and a half months haunting police headquarters in downtown Detroit, soaking up the atmosphere and listening to the way detectives, criminals, lawyers, and witnesses really talked. He also established contacts with working detectives, contacts that have continued to prove useful to him. His later novels show a much better balance between protagonists and antagonists.

FREAKY DEAKY

Leonard's highly successful *Freaky Deaky* is an example of his mature technique. A detective who specializes in bomb disposal is pitted against a beautiful but treacherous former convict plotting to extort a fortune from a pair of multimillionaire brothers, whom she suspects of informing on her back in the 1960's when they were antiwar activists together. The chapters alternate between the mind of the detective and that of the female extortionist, until all the principals are brought together at the end. The reader sees the world through the bomber's jaundiced eyes and sympathizes with her; however, the reader also sees the world through the detective's eyes and sympathizes with him a bit more. Leonard has become expert at manipulating the sympathies of his reader, which enables him to create more realistic characters. Like people in the real world, the characters in his best novels are not all good or all bad, but mixtures of both.

KILLSHOT

Leonard follows the same blueprint in *Killshot*. The main villain, a half-breed Native American, is a cold-blooded professional killer; however, the reader achieves a strong identification with and even affection for this lonely, unhappy individual, because the reader spends so much time in the killer's mind. Leonard seems to understand the criminal mentality so well that many people have labored under the erroneous impression that he must have an unsavory past. Whereas he once had trouble making his villains

seem credible, his problem later in his career has been making his law-abiding characters seem equally credible. In his next novel, *Get Shorty*, he did away with "good guys" altogether.

GET SHORTY

In *Get Shorty*, for the first time in his career, Leonard sets a novel in Hollywood, California. Here he reaps a rich harvest from his many years of experience as an author of original scripts, adaptations of other authors' novels, and adaptations of his own novels, and as an author of works that have been adapted by others. Among all of his novels, *Get Shorty* most clearly reveals his intention of making his fiction read like motion pictures. He even incorporates some pages of a screenplay that his sleazy characters are trying to peddle. Some of his Hollywood characters are so hopelessly immersed in the fantasy world of filmmaking that they see everyone as an actor and every event as a sequence of medium shots, closeups, and other types of camera shots with varied lighting effects—even when that other character might be coming to shoot them or throw them off a cliff. Leonard is suggesting that Americans are so brainwashed by films and television images that it is becoming impossible to distinguish between fantasy and reality.

MAXIMUM BOB

With *Maximum Bob*, his next novel, Leonard returned to familiar turf, southern Florida. The title character is a criminal court judge; though corrupt to the core professionally and personally, he metes out sentences that offenders deserve, and he easily wins reelection. In contrast to him, Leonard presents capable, dedicated, and honest policemen, assistant district attorneys, and probation officers; however, they fight a losing battle, buffeted not only by corrupt superiors like Judge Bob Isom Gibbs, but also by offenders who cannot be rehabilitated. The forces of good frequently confront this dilemma in Leonard novels, sometimes in a contrast between social haves and have nots. Also as in other Leonard books, *Maximum Bob* is peopled by assorted grotesques, notable among them the judge's wife, a onetime underwater dancing mermaid who has become a spiritualist with two personalities, one of which is a twelve-year-old

1850's slave with a voice like Butterfly McQueen of the 1939 film *Gone with the Wind*. The major character, though, is completely normal: Kathy Diaz Baker, a young probation officer with carefully honed people skills and analytical crime-solving ability who narrates most of the novel and is its moral conscience. Baker is not the only narrator, however; other characters also so serve, with the effect that a host of figures are developed more fully than they otherwise would have been. Also, in a curious turn, Leonard relates a portion of an episode from an alligator's point of view.

PRONTO

Leonard again criticizes aspects of law enforcement in *Pronto*, another novel with a Florida setting, though here he focuses primarily upon organized crime. The main theme of the book is interdependence. Be it Raylan Givens of the U.S. Marshals Service, Buck Torres of the Miami Beach police department, or FBI agent McCormick (whose lack of a first name depersonalizes him), success depends upon the cooperation of others, and all grit their teeth when they must enlist the aid of people they consider undesirables. Givens is the focus of a secondary theme, that of fundamental decency. Unimpressed by wealth earned through criminality and corruption, he has a refreshing naïveté tempered only by his determination to redeem a career-damaging error. He is the untainted person of the novel, and that he ultimately prevails—and gets the woman, too—presents an unmistakable thematic message. *Pronto* is of special interest in the Leonard canon for two reasons: It introduces Raylan Givens, who returns in the next novel, *Riding the Rap*, and it marks a singular Leonard reversion to a Western trademark. From start to finish, *Pronto* is a chase. The effect of this elementary plot technique is an immediate creation of tension, with momentum and suspense increasing without letup as the narrative moves to climactic shots two pages before the conclusion.

CUBA LIBRE

Leonard also returns to his fictional roots in *Cuba Libre*, a Western complete with a shoot-out and prison escape, albeit set in Cuba in 1898 at the time of the Spanish-American War. The protagonist is an Arizona Territory cowboy and erstwhile bank robber who heads to Cuba in order to sell horses and, not incidentally, to smuggle guns to Cuban rebels. This also is a novel with suspense, fast-paced action, and a collection of grotesque characters who somehow seem credible, no small tribute to Leonard's skills at characterization.

Bill Delaney, updated by Gerald H. Strauss

OTHER MAJOR WORKS

SCREENPLAYS: *The Moonshine War*, 1970; *Joe Kidd*, 1972; *Mr. Majestyk*, 1974; *Stick*, 1985 (with Joseph C. Stinson); *Fifty-two Pickup*, 1986 (with John Steppling); *The Rosary Murders*, 1987 (with Fred Walton).

TELEPLAYS: *High Noon Part 2: The Return of Will Kane*, 1980; *Desperado*, 1987.

BIBLIOGRAPHY

Geherin, David. *Elmore Leonard*. New York: Continuum, 1989. The first book-length study of Leonard, this volume provides a brief biography and then a critical evaluation of Leonard's works, beginning with his early Western short stories and concluding with more detailed discussions of his novels of the 1980's. It also includes a chronology, notes, a selected bibliography, and an index.

Millner, C. "Elmore Leonard: The Best Ear in the Business." *Writer's Digest*, June, 1997, 30-32. Many commentators call attention to Leonard's skill at creating realistic dialogue. Though this article does not offer much in the way of new insights, it is of interest because it is addressed primarily to writers, both professionals and those aspiring to become such.

Most, Glenn. "Elmore Leonard: Splitting Images." *Western Humanities Review* 41 (Spring, 1987): 78-86. This in-depth scholarly analysis of *Split Images* suggests some of the hidden psychological and sociological implications of Leonard's apparently simple writing. It also exemplifies the serious critical attention that Leonard's work has begun to receive.

Skinner, Robert E. "To Write Realistically: An Interview with Elmore Leonard." *Xavier Review* 7

(1987): 37-46. Less diffuse than most that have appeared in newspapers and magazines, this article deals primarily with Leonard's realism. The sources of this often praised quality are his extensive preliminary research into potential milieus (including visits and interviews by him or surrogates) and his keen ear for nuances of speech patterns.

Wholey, Dennis, ed. "Elmore Leonard." In *The Courage to Change: Personal Conversations About Alcohol with Dennis Wholey*. New York: Warner Books, 1986. This interview provides the best available information about Elmore Leonard as a human being. He describes his growing problem with alcohol over two decades and the psychological insights that enabled him to stop drinking. Leonard's hard-won victory over alcoholism has had an important influence on his writing technique and choice of subjects.

Wilkinson, A. "Elmore's Legs: Where Does Elmore Leonard Get His Atmosphere?" *The New Yorker*, September 30, 1996, 43-47. Writers for many years focused upon a few notable aspects of Leonard's novels; his creation of atmosphere is one of them. This piece is one of many, but it offers some different perspectives and insights into a career that spans decades and has produced more than two dozen novels.

(Ingrid Von Kruse)

Doris Lessing

Born: Kermanshah, Persia; October 22, 1919

Principal long fiction

The Grass Is Singing, 1950
Martha Quest, 1952
A Proper Marriage, 1954
Retreat to Innocence, 1956
A Ripple from the Storm, 1958
The Golden Notebook, 1962
Landlocked, 1965, 1991
The Four-Gated City, 1969
Briefing for a Descent into Hell, 1971
The Summer Before the Dark, 1973
The Memoirs of a Survivor, 1974
Shikasta, 1979
The Marriages Between Zones Three, Four, and Five, 1980
The Sirian Experiments, 1981
The Making of the Representative for Planet 8, 1982
Documents Relating to the Sentimental Agents in the Volyen Empire, 1983
The Diary of a Good Neighbour, 1983 (as Jane Somers)
If the Old Could . . . , 1984 (as Somers)
The Diaries of Jane Somers, 1984 (includes *The Diary of a Good Neighbour*, and *If the Old Could . . .*)
The Good Terrorist, 1985
The Fifth Child, 1988
Playing the Game, 1995

Love, Again, 1996
Mara and Dann, 1999

OTHER LITERARY FORMS

Doris Lessing has published numerous volumes of short stories. She has also written memoirs, documentaries, essays, plays, reviews, and a book of poems.

ACHIEVEMENTS

Lessing has been one of the most widely read and influential British novelists of the second half of the twentieth century. Her works have been translated into many languages and have inspired critical attention around the globe. Generally serious and didactic, Lessing's fiction repeatedly urges the human race to develop a wider consciousness that would allow for greater harmony and less violence. Although known particularly as a master of realism, Lessing is often experimental or deliberately fantastic, as shown in her science-fiction novels. Her interests are far-ranging, from Marxism and global politics to the mystical teachings of Sufism to the small personal voice of the individual. Her awards include the Somerset Maugham Award, the German Shakespeare Prize, the Austrian Prize for European Literature, and the French Prix Médicis for Foreigners. In 1995 she won the James Tait Black Prize and a *Los Angeles Times* Book Prize for her 1994 autobiography, *Under My Skin*.

BIOGRAPHY

Doris May Lessing was born in Kermanshah, Persia (later Iran), in 1919, the first child of Alfred Cook Tayler and Emily Maude McVeagh Tayler, who had immigrated from England to Persia shortly after World War I. A brother, Harry, was born two years later, and in 1925 the family moved to a farm in Southern Rhodesia (later Zimbabwe). Her parents were never financially successful. Her father was a dreamer who became a cynic after he failed at maize farming; her mother was domineering but ineffective. Despite Lessing's love of the African landscape and the isolated veld, she was eager to leave her family behind. She attended a Catholic convent school in Salisbury (now Harare) but left when she was fourteen, saying that she had eye problems, though she continued her voracious reading.

Lessing left home when she was fifteen to become a nursemaid and moved to Salisbury to work in various jobs, mostly clerical, and began writing fiction. She was married to Frank Charles Wisdom, a minor civil servant, in 1939, and had a son, John, and a daughter, Jean. Divorced in 1943, she was remarried two years later to a German-Jewish refugee, Gottfried Lessing. They had a son, Peter, in 1947. She divorced Gottfried Lessing in 1949 and that same year moved to England, settling in London; in 1950 she published her first novel. After that she continued to live in London and to make her living as a professional writer, writing reviews, media scripts, and nonfiction in addition to her novels, short stories, drama, and poetry.

Lessing's interest in politics began with a Marxist group in Rhodesia, and in England she was briefly a member of the Communist Party, leaving it officially in 1956. In the late 1950's she participated in mass demonstrations for nuclear disarmament and was a speaker at the first Aldermaston March in 1958. During the early 1960's she worked in the theater, helping to establish Centre 42, a populist art program, and writing her own plays. In the late 1960's Lessing's thinking began to be heavily influenced by the mystical teachings of Indries Shah and Sufism, which emphasizes conscious evolution of the mind in harmony with self and others. Although for many years Lessing resisted the role of public persona, in the mid-1980's she began to make numerous public appearances in many countries.

Lessing's work was recognized several times in 1995. She received an honorary degree from Harvard University that year and was also welcomed back into South Africa—she had been forced to leave in 1956. She went to visit her daughter and grandchildren and was received with open arms by the country. In 1995, her autobiography won the prestigious James Tait Black Memorial Prize for best biography and a *Los Angeles Times* Book Prize.

Lessing has remained one of the most prolific writers of the twentieth century, and many of her books have won critical acclaim. In the 1990's she made fewer public appearances, devoting herself to more writing. Although she made a fourteen-week tour to promote her autobiography, Lessing has stated that she is more useful to her publisher when she stays at home and writes. When her novel *Love, Again* was published in 1996, she made no public appearances to promote the book.

ANALYSIS

Doris Lessing is a powerful writer committed to the lofty goal of changing human consciousness itself. The narrative voice that weaves throughout her prolific fiction is that of an intense thinker who observes, explores, and describes the contemporary world but whose ultimate sense of human life is that the individual, and indeed the human race, is meant to go beyond mere recognition of perceived reality and to struggle with visions of the possible. Her novels repeatedly suggest that changes in the way humans view themselves, their world, and their relationships with others are imperative if life on this planet is to survive.

Lessing's scope is wide. Her creative imagination is able to provide a close analysis of a character—with all that individual's fears, longings, and contradictions—and to relate that individual not only to his or her circle of acquaintances but to patterns of global economics and politics as well, and then to sweep beyond even this planet to the cosmos and a perspective that encompasses the metaphysical questions of existence. Her fictional explorations are multiple, multidimensional, and overlapping, suggesting that no one viewpoint is adequate or complete. This range is also reflected in her varied narrative forms, which include realism, naturalism, science fiction, utopianism and dystopianism, fantasy, fable, transcultural postmodernism, and experimental combinations of these. This heterogeneity of themes, techniques, and perspectives illustrates Lessing's overriding premise that truth and substance cannot easily be compartmentalized or assigned fixed labels: existence is always process, always in flux.

Lessing's position as an exile is a prominent aspect of her work, both in content and in theme. Born in the Middle East of English parents, she spent her adolescence in Southern Rhodesia, first with her family on an isolated and impoverished farm whose workers were all native black Africans, and then on her own in Salisbury. In the city she became involved with a group interested in international politics whose most specific focus was increased rights for black Rhodesians. Her experiences there in the 1940's, including two marriages and three children, became material for nearly all of her novels for the first twenty years of her writing career.

THE GRASS IS SINGING

In 1949 Lessing arrived in London with her youngest son and the manuscript of *The Grass Is Singing*. In many ways this first book established a pattern for subsequent novels. Her manuscript was accepted for publication within three days of her submitting it to a publisher. The novel was well received and went through seven reprintings within five months. The title comes from part 5 of T. S. Eliot's *The Waste Land* (1922); Lessing's wide reading included the twentieth century writers as well as the great British, French, and Russian novelists of the nineteenth century. She most admired those writers with a sense of moral purpose, a sense of commitment to all humanity. *The Grass Is Singing* clearly shows the horrific effects of apartheid and racial prejudice on both the white colonial rulers and the black people who make up the overwhelming majority of the populations of southern Africa.

In a stylistic technique directly opposite to that of a stereotypical detective story, the third-person narrator reveals at the outset of *The Grass Is Singing* that Mary Turner, the wife of a poor farmer, has been killed by a houseboy, Moses, who confessed to the crime. The opening chapter shows the confusion and emotional collapse of Mary's husband, Dick Turner, and the reactions of Charlie Slatter, a neighbor, and Tony Marston, a young recent immigrant from England. The plot then becomes straightforward as it gives the background and chronology of events that led to the murder.

Mary grew up in the city and had established a pleasant though rather meaningless life after the death of her parents. At age thirty she begins to overhear acquaintances' disparaging remarks about the fact that she has never married. Suddenly seeing herself as a failure, she agrees to marry virtually the first man available, an impractical farmer who comes to town for supplies. Dick Turner immediately takes her to his isolated shack, where they are surrounded by black workers; the nearest white neighbor is many miles away. Mary is unprepared for marriage and totally inept at dealing with the series of houseboys Dick brings from the field to do cooking and housework. In exile from her city life, Mary is further hampered by the typical white Southern Rhodesian belief that natives are basically nonhuman, or at least subhuman and destined to inferiority. She cannot handle the intimate day-by-day contact with the native houseboys who seem so alien to her, and with the advent of the arrogant Moses, the many psychological strains lead inexorably to her almost invited death. Mary and all of white culture are guilty, but it is the black Moses who will be hanged.

Mary's failures are also a result of her inability to understand herself. She is not a reader. She has dreams and nightmares but makes no exploration of their possible significance. She has never examined social and political realities and has no one with whom to discuss her problems. She is unable to adjust to her current reality and unable to create any alternative reality.

THE CHILDREN OF VIOLENCE SERIES

Martha Quest, *A Proper Marriage*, *A Ripple from the Storm*, *Landlocked*, and *The Four-Gated City* trace in detail the growth and development of Martha Quest, an autobiographical character who, unlike Mary Turner, is intensely interested in knowing herself and making sense of the world. Together these novels make up the Children of Violence series. The first four are set in Africa, while *The Four-Gated City*, which nearly equals in length the preceding four, is set in London and traces Martha Quest's life from her arrival there around 1949 to the late 1990's. The novels set in Africa are categorized as social realism, while *The Four-Gated City* moves beyond that to discuss what are often considered paranormal capacities, and the work concludes after some unspecified disaster has destroyed much of life on earth. The

futurist world Lessing depicts here is neither entirely utopian nor dystopian, and despite forces beyond the control of the individual, Martha Quest and some of the other inhabitants of the postcatastrophic world epitomize the continuing need for individual responsibility and commitment to a more harmonious world.

Martha Quest, as her surname suggests, is a quintessential Lessing heroine, always examining the human condition and searching for a higher consciousness to change herself and her world. The characterization is detailed and frank, including descriptions of Martha's sexual relationships and, in *A Proper Marriage*, a lengthy and explicit description of childbirth. Yet Martha's perceptions and innermost thoughts also provide a historical overview of an entire era and a challenge to the status quo. Central to all Martha's struggles is her determination to grow and to envision a freer and more responsible world.

THE GOLDEN NOTEBOOK

It is good to note that Lessing interrupted the writing of the Children of Violence series to work on *The Golden Notebook*, published in 1962 and generally acknowledged as her most impressive and influential novel. "The two women were alone in the London flat," begins the long novel, and from this simple statement Lessing creates a fascinating portrait of the modern world. The protagonist is Anna Wulf, a writer who says that she is suffering from writer's block after a successful first novel about racial problems in Africa. Anna's friend Molly is a divorced mother trying to make a life for herself. Through them Lessing perceptively examines the problems of the intelligent and disillusioned modern woman. Anna tries to create order out of chaos by keeping a diary, which she divides into four notebooks: a black notebook recounting her experiences as a young woman in Africa; a red notebook for her Communist and political activities; a yellow notebook, which includes her fictional attempts to understand herself, including the creation of an autobiographical character named Ella, who is also writing a novel; and a blue notebook to record the factual details of her daily life and her relationships with men. Sections of these notebooks are repeated sequentially four times and are finally superseded by another notebook, the golden one of the novel's title, in which Anna attempts to integrate these compartmentalized and often-conflicting aspects of her life. In the golden notebook section, influenced by the mental breakdown of one of her lovers, Saul Green, Anna goes through layers of madness in herself and questions the idea of reality itself.

The shape of this pivotal metafictional novel is further complicated by sections called "Free Women," which open and close the book as well as separate the repeated sections of the black, red, yellow, and blue notebooks. The five "Free Women" sections together form a conventional novel about sixty thousand words long. Although it deals with the same characters and events recounted in the various notebook sections, it does so in a reductive and more structured way. It is as though the "Free Women" novel were what Anna is able to produce to end her writer's block, but a novel that shows that fiction is unable to capture the intricacies and complexities of actual existence. Since the sections of this conventional novel frame and appear throughout the larger work, the contrasts and variations with the notebook sections make *The Golden Notebook* as a whole a complex structural and stylistic achievement.

While *The Golden Notebook* elaborates Lessing's attitudes toward racism, sexism, and the interconnections between the personal and the political, it also shows the development of Lessing's thinking to include the benefits of the irrational and the necessity of exploring areas beyond the layers of social pretense and conventionality. These areas are further addressed in *The Four-Gated City* and in three subsequent novels, *Briefing for a Descent into Hell*, *The Summer Before the Dark*, and *The Memoirs of a Survivor*. Each of these novels breaks from traditional versions of realism and insists upon a wider definition of the possible.

BRIEFING FOR A DESCENT INTO HELL

Briefing for a Descent into Hell, one of the very few Lessing novels with a male as the central character, presents Charles Watkins, a classics professor at the University of Cambridge, who is found wandering incoherently in the streets and is hospitalized for treatment of a mental breakdown. While in the hospital, Watkins, who has forgotten even his name, imagines himself taken away in a spaceship, and most of the book relates his various encounters with unfamiliar creatures and situations that seem almost mythological. Many of these experiences are painful or frightening. Often he is alone, yet he feels a sense of urgency and intense anxiety: He must accomplish certain tasks or risk total failure for himself and others. He also has times of exceptional joy, as he sees the beauty of creation and has revelations of a harmony that could prevail if each creature accepted its part in the scheme of things and made its responsible contribution. In the final pages of the book, Watkins is given electroshock treatment and yanked back into his old life, but both he and the reader are left with the sense that compared to his previous insights he has been forced back to a shallow and hollow "normalcy."

THE SUMMER BEFORE THE DARK

In *The Summer Before the Dark*, Kate Brown, a woman in her early forties, also goes through a period of "madness," which reveals the extent to which she has previously succumbed to the pressures to become only roles: wife, mother, sex object, efficient organizer, selfless caregiver. During the summer that is the time frame of the novel, Kate's husband and grown children are away from home; at loose ends, Kate accepts a position as translator for an international food organization. She soon finds herself traveling and organizing global conferences. She spends some time in Spain with Jeffrey Merton, a young man whose psychosomatic and psychological illnesses spill over into her own life, and she returns to London to deal with her doubts and confusions. She stays for a while in a flat with Maureen, a twenty-two-year-old who is establishing her own identity. Through her reactions to Maureen, Kate comes to understand much about herself and her own family, and she finally grasps the relevance of a recurring dream about a seal. The seal dream appears fifteen times in the novel, and the basic image is of Kate struggling to return an abandoned seal to the ocean. When Kate is finally able to finish the dream and return the seal to water, she realizes that what she has been burdened with is her own ego and that she must fight against the power of repressive institutions and roles.

The Memoirs of a Survivor

Lessing again shows the conjunction between the individual and the larger society, including the importance of responsibility and direction, in *The Memoirs of a Survivor*. In this dystopian rendering of the "near future," the unnamed first-person narrator records her observations of a world in a state of cultural and social decline following an unexplained catastrophe. A stranger consigns into the narrator's care a girl of about twelve, Emily, who has with her Hugo, an ugly cat/dog creature. Much of the novel describes Emily's accelerated development through puberty and her association with Gerald, a young gang leader who, with Emily's help, tries to rebuild some semblance of order or at least some system of survival in a degenerated and nonfunctional society. From the window of her flat the narrator watches groups abandon the city, never to be heard of again, and she witnesses the collapse of civilization, demonstrated particularly in the very young children who fend for themselves and who have only fleeting connections to others for immediate gain. In these children, not only respect for others but also language itself has broken down, and they attack their victims or one another with barbaric yaps.

In the midst of all this collapse, the narrator has become aware of another layer of reality in and through the walls of her flat. When she enters this space, she is confronted with a variety of scenes from the past, not necessarily her own past, and usually she sees something that she must do. On one journey through the walls she glimpses a figure of a woman, perhaps a goddess or some aspect of herself, who fills her with a sense of hope. Surrounded by despair in the present world, the narrator constructs an alternative visionary world, and at the end of the novel, when even the air is unbreathable, the collapsed world is left behind as the narrator steps through the wall through both a willed and a magical transformation. She takes with her Emily and Gerald and their group of youngsters as well as Hugo, transformed from an ugly beast into something shining with hope and promise.

The Canopus in Argos Series

After a rare gap of five years without a novel, Doris Lessing burst forth with *Shikasta*, which she announced was the first in a series called Canopus in Argos: Archives, and in the next four years she published the other four books in the series. A number of loyal readers were disappointed with what Lessing called her "space fiction," with its undeveloped, stylized characters and strangely unexciting interplanetary rivalries. Yet the series attracted a new audience of science-fiction readers, and, taken as a whole, the series continues Lessing's themes: the individual versus the collective, political systems and their interference with racial and sexual equality, the interconnectedness of all life, and the need for a more enlightened consciousness.

Some of the terms used to describe the varied genres in the Canopus in Argos novels—outer space fiction, science fiction, fantasy, psychomyth, allegory, utopian—indicate the variety within and among these books. They do not even comfortably fit the classification of series, or *roman-fleuve*, since traditionally a series centers on a single character, as Lessing's Children of Violence had centered on Martha Quest. *Shikasta* is filled with reports, journals, and interviews by aliens who discuss the fate of Earth, or Shikasta. *The Marriages Between Zones Three, Four, and Five* does not seem to be set on another planet so much as in the realm of myth and legend as Al·Ith moves between the zones in search of her destiny. *The Sirian Experiments* is told by a woman named Ambien II, who is a leading administrator in the Sirian Colonial Service. She discovers that the rival Canopean Empire is actually in advance of Sirius in every way and more deserving of conducting experiments on Shikasta than is her own empire, though the Sirians certainly do not want to hear this. *The Making of the Representative for Planet 8* is the story of a small planet whose inhabitants live comfortably until the time of The Ice begins, with ice and snow covering most of the globe. The inhabitants are unable to emigrate, but a few of them survive in some nonphysical but essential existence. *Documents Relating to the Sentimental Agents in the Volyen Empire* uses testimonies and histories to show that the Volyen Empire has failed to keep its promises to its inhabitants and to the cosmos. The empire suffers a rhetoric-induced downfall, as its leaders had become enamored with the sound of their grand ideas rather than performing the actions that should have accompanied them.

None of the narrators and voices in the Canopus in Argos series is entirely reliable, and many questions are left unanswered. Perhaps this confusion is itself Lessing's goal: to make her readers question and reconsider ideas and actions. As Johor, an emissary to Shikasta, comments on the very first page of the series: "Things change. That is all we may be sure of. . . . This is a catastrophic universe, always; and subject to sudden reversals, upheavals, changes, cataclysms, with joy never anything but the song of substance under pressure forced into new forms and shapes."

THE DIARIES OF JANE SOMERS

The same year the final volume of Canopus in Argos was published, another novel appeared, titled *The Diary of a Good Neighbour*, purportedly by a new British writer, Jane Somers. It was not until the following year, and after the publication of another Jane Somers novel, *If the Old Could . . .*, that Lessing publicly revealed her authorship with the publication of the two novels together as *The Diaries of Jane Somers*. In her introduction to the book Lessing discusses some of her reasons for having used a pseudonym. One was to create a new persona as the narrator: How would a real Jane Somers write? Another was to show the difficulties unestablished writers have in getting published, and indeed the first manuscript was rejected by several publishers before it was printed by Michael Joseph in London, the same firm that had accepted the unknown Doris Lessing's *The Grass Is Singing* nearly four decades earlier. Lessing also says that she wanted the novels to be judged on their own merit, apart from the Lessing canon. When the Jane Somers novels first appeared, they sold in only modest numbers and received favorable but very limited attention from reviewers. Lessing notes that the modern publishing business markets high-volume, high-profile authors with the planned expectation that the novels will have a short

shelf life—big sellers for a few weeks but soon replaced and out of print; such policies do not favor new and experimental novelists.

The Diaries of Jane Somers focuses on old age, especially the relationship that develops between the middle-aged Jane Somers, head of a high-fashion magazine, and Maudie Fowler, a poor but proud woman in her nineties. Set in a realistic London, the novels, particularly *The Diary of a Good Neighbour*, give an insightful analysis of contemporary health-care services and again show the impact of social attitudes and governmental policies on the individual. The social realism of the novel, with its discussions of aging and dying, is given contrast by the summaries of novels Jane writes about Maudie's life. Maudie tells stories of her long, hard life, and Jane transforms them into successful romanticized fictions, which Maudie then enjoys hearing. Jane, whose friends call her Janna, is repeatedly mistaken for a "Good Neighbour," a social worker, as though there could be no other explanation for her friendship with Maudie. The layers of illusion and reality, fictions and lives, add to the emotional power of the novel and make it an important addition to Lessing's later works.

THE GOOD TERRORIST and THE FIFTH CHILD

The Good Terrorist shows rather stupid and totally unsympathetic would-be revolutionaries who move from city to city in England planning random bombings. Contrary to the title, there is no good terrorist in the novel, and it is just as well that these characters have a tendency to blow up themselves accidentally rather than killing others. A much more interesting novel is *The Fifth Child*, which can be read as an accurate and realistic account of an unfortunate English family, but which to other readers is a science-fiction fantasy, a tale of an alien being born into a human family. The novel hovers on some point that embraces both readings. The setting is England in the 1960's. Harriet and David Lovatt want a big family and a settled home life. Everything seems to be working according to their plan until the birth of their fifth child. Ben has nothing childlike about him: He is gruesome in appearance, insatiably hungry, abnormally strong, demanding, and violent. In no way does he fit into the happy home. Yet Harriet, steeped in the idea of motherhood, cannot bear to abandon him in some mental institution and insists on keeping him with her. As the years pass, the older children escape though already harmed by Ben's weirdness and violence, and even David finally recognizes that he cannot continue to live with such a creature. The novel ends in despair, the problems unresolved. Ben is well on his way to becoming a fully grown criminal, a rapist and murderer, with no one able to subdue him. The story of the Lovatts becomes a parable of the modern world, the vision of a simple and happy existence shattered within the family itself and a society unwilling to confront and unable to control its own most brutal aspects.

LOVE, AGAIN

Lessing's novel *Love, Again* confronts the uncertainty of love and the decisions made because of love. Sarah, an aging theater manager, writes a play based on the true story of a young, beautiful French mulatto named Julie Varion. Julie has many eligible suitors in her life, but none commits himself to her because of family pressures of status and community responsibility. Julie finally becomes engaged to an older gentleman, but she mysteriously dies before the wedding. Writing about this alluring character and her life is emotionally trying for Sarah, who feels she, unlike Julie, is unable to act upon her love interests because of her age. Unable to act on her feelings, Sarah suffers silently through her painful longings for a twenty-eight-year-old actor and a thirty-five-year-old director. Sarah eventually comes to terms with her age through painful moments of realization and acceptance.

All the characters are seen through the eyes of a narrator who focuses primarily on Sarah and reveals the characters as Sarah sees them. Like Julie and her suitors, Sarah and her friends are bound by obligations and social rules which affect the decisions they make for their own lives. Sarah is faced with decisions of loving but letting go. Sarah's brother, Hal, realizes that his future only holds loneliness because of his inability to see others and their needs. Stephen, a dear friend of Sarah's, ultimately commits suicide over his preoccupation and obsession with the deceased Julie Varion, which only become more intense as the production of the play about her continues.

MARA AND DANN

Mara and Dann is an exciting adventure story set thousands of years in the future. The two main characters, Mara and her brother Dann, were kidnapped from their home with the Mahondi tribe when Mara was seven and Dann was four. In order to stay alive, the two are forced to change their names when they are taken to a village of the Rock People, a tribe considered less advanced than the Mahondi. Mara stays in the village until she becomes a strong young woman who desires to learn as much as possible even as she faces starvation and drought; she is sold into slavery and taken prisoner to be a breeder for other tribes. Dann suffers through abductions and addictions and becomes divided in his desires and duties toward his sister. Through his dream world, Dann faces his fears and eventually accepts his past experiences. Although the two are separated many times, they never stop searching for each other even at the risk of slavery and death.

The novel is an interesting tale of survival of the human mind and spirit even through the most severe times a new world can encounter after an ice age. Mara and Dann's characters are well developed, and they change and learn from their experiences. Mara learns to love and to trust but also learns the price she must pay to survive in the world outside her home. Lessing portays issues of racism, greed, and power as they have affected every generation throughout time.

Lessing has had a wide readership. For many years she has been on best-seller lists, and her novels have been translated into many languages. Her work is widely anthologized and has been closely read by many contemporary authors, particularly women writers. The number of critical articles, books, and sections of books about her work is enormous and international in scope, reflecting the wide diversity of readers and the serious attention her work has commanded throughout her writing career.

Lessing's novels, far-ranging in scope and treatment, resist any easy labels. Still, her major themes, though presented in a variety of ways, have been remarkably consistent. The individual has responsibilities, Lessing always shows, not only to achieve self-knowledge and inner harmony but to contribute to the greater harmony of society as well. Human consciousness must expand, and people's attitudes and actions must change if human life is to survive.

Lois A. Marchino, updated by Mary A. Blackmon

OTHER MAJOR WORKS

SHORT FICTION: *This Was the Old Chief's Country*, 1951; *Five: Short Novels*, 1953; *The Habit of Loving*, 1957; *A Man and Two Women*, 1963; *African Stories*, 1964; *The Temptation of Jack Orkney and Other Stories*, 1972 (also known as *The Story of a Non-Marrying Man and Other Stories*); *This Was the Old Chief's Country: Volume 1 of Doris Lessing's Collected African Stories*, 1973; *The Sun Between Their Feet: Volume 2 of Doris Lessing's Collected African Stories*, 1973; *Sunrise on the Veld*, 1975; *A Mild Attack of Locusts*, 1977; *To Room Nineteen/Her Collected Stories*, 1978; *The Temptation of Jack Orkney/Her Collected Stories*, 1978; *Stories*, 1978; *London Observed: Stories and Sketches*, 1991 (pb. in U.S. as *The Real Thing: Stories and Sketches*, 1992); *Spies I Have Known and Other Stories*, 1995.

PLAYS: *Each His Own Wilderness*, pr. 1958; *Play with a Tiger*, pr., pb. 1962; *Making of the Representative for Planet 8*, pr. 1988 (libretto); *Play with a Tiger, and Other Plays*, pb. 1996.

POETRY: *Fourteen Poems*, 1959.

NONFICTION: *Going Home*, 1957; *In Pursuit of the English: A Documentary*, 1960; *Particularly Cats*, 1967; *A Small Personal Voice*, 1974; *Prisons We Choose to Live Inside*, 1987; *The Wind Blows Away Our Words*, 1987; *African Laughter: Four Visits to Zimbabwe*, 1992; *Under My Skin*, 1994; *A Small Personal Voice: Essays, Reviews, Interviews*, 1994; *Doris Lessing: Conversations*, 1994 (pb. in England as *Putting the Questions Differently*); *Shadows on the Wall of the Cave*, 1994; *Walking in the Shade*, 1997.

MISCELLANEOUS: *The Doris Lessing Reader*, 1988 (selections).

BIBLIOGRAPHY

Fishburn, Katherine. *The Unexpected Universe of Doris Lessing: A Study in Narrative Technique.* Westport, Conn.: Greenwood Press, 1985. This study considers Lessing's science fiction from *Briefing for a Descent into Hell* through the Canopus in Argos series. It argues that the science fiction has the purpose of transforming reality and involving the reader in ideas and the intricacies of the texts rather than in characterization. Fishburn also published *Doris Lessing: Life, Work, and Criticism* (Fredericton, New Brunswick, Canada: York Press, 1987), which provides a brief overview of Lessing's life and works, including literary biography, critical response, and an annotated bibliography.

Galen, Muge. *Between East and West: Sufism in the Novels of Doris Lessing.* Albany: State University of New York Press, 1997. This text applies the ideas of Sufism and its influence on Lessing and her novels. An introduction to Sufism and to Doris Lessing is included to help the reader understand the basic ideas of Sufism. Emphasis is placed on her space-fiction utopias as an alternative to the current Western lifestyles.

Greene, Gayle. *Changing the Story: Feminist Fiction and the Tradition.* Bloomington: Indiana University Press, 1991. Lessing's works are repeatedly referred to throughout the text. *The Golden Notebook* is covered extensively in a chapter titled "Naming a Different Way," which concentrates on how the novel was very differently received and understood by male and female readers. The essay focuses on the form and structure of the story as well as character development.

_____. *Doris Lessing: The Poetics of Change.* University of Michigan Press, 1997. Greene centers this study on how Lessing's novels are concerned with change. Several different critical approaches to Lessing's works, including Marxist, feminist, and Jungian, are included in the study.

Kaplan, Carey, and Ellen Cronan Rose, eds. *Doris Lessing: The Alchemy of Survival.* Ohio University Press, 1988. Eleven essays that display a variety of approaches to Lessing's works. The approaches and various perspectives are as diverse as her readership. The essays were gathered from Modern Language Association conventions from

1971 to 1985. The introduction includes a brief history of the development of the Doris Lessing Society and notes how Lessing criticism has grown within the MLA convention each year.

Robinson, Sally. *Engendering the Subject: Gender and Self-Representation in Contemporary Women's Fiction*. Albany: State University of New York Press, 1991. A chapter of this book is devoted to Lessing and her works. Primary focus is placed on the Children of Violence series: *Martha Quest*, *The Four-Gated City*, *Landlocked*, *A Proper Marriage*, and *A Ripple in the Storm*. Robinson focuses on Lessing's desire to present a humanist view in her characters and themes and how the female main characters tend to create contradictions when trying to reach their goals.

Rubenstein, Roberta. *The Novelistic Vision of Doris Lessing: Breaking the Forms of Consciousness*. Urbana: University of Illinois Press, 1979. This volume shows the cyclic design in Lessing's repeated themes, particularly the mind discovering, interpreting, and ultimately shaping its own reality. In a comprehensive chronological approach through 1978, it examines the relationship between fictional structure and meaning, the purpose of doubling, and the relationship between fiction and reality.

Seligman, Dee. *Doris Lessing: An Annotated Bibliography of Criticism*. Westport, Conn.: Greenwood Press, 1981. Seligman incorporates earlier checklists and bibliographies and provides a comprehensive annotated bibliography through 1978. She includes a bibliography of research and teaching suggestions, interviews with Lessing, and book reviews. Marshall Tymn draws on Seligman's bibliography and updates it to 1988 in the *Journal of the Fantastic in the Arts* special issue on Doris Lessing edited by Nicholas Ruddick (volume 2, no. 3, 1990).

Sprague, Claire, and Virginia Tiger, eds. *Critical Essays on Doris Lessing*. Boston: G. K. Hall, 1986. This collection includes review essays and various other articles plus a general introduction to Lessing and a chronology of her works. It is divided into sections entitled "Politics and Patterns," "Female (Other) Space," "Inner and Outer Space," and "Reception and Reputation."

Whittaker, Ruth. *Modern Novelists: Doris Lessing*. New York: St. Martin's Press, 1988. This resource provides a brief biography and insightful background information into Lessing and how her works have been influenced by her past. Major focus is given to her novels and a discussion of how Lessing excels as a modern novelist.

PRIMO LEVI

Born: Turin, Italy; July 31, 1919
Died: Turin, Italy; April 11, 1987

PRINCIPAL LONG FICTION

La chiave a stella, 1978 (*The Monkey's Wrench*, 1986)
Se non ora, quando?, 1982 (*If Not Now, When?*, 1985)

OTHER LITERARY FORMS

Associated with Holocaust literature, Primo Levi was a novelist, short-story writer, essayist, and poet, although he is known primarily for his memoirs. These include *Se questo è un uomo* (1947; *If This Is a Man*, 1959; revised as *Survival in Auschwitz: The Nazi Assault on Humanity*, 1961) and *La tregua* (1963; *The Reawakening*, 1965). Levi himself, in a preface, characterized his collection of stories *Moments of Reprieve* (1986) as a record of experiences left out of *If This Is a Man* and *The Reawakening*. (Most of these autobiographical short stories were previously published in 1981 in *Lilit e altri racconti*.) *Il sistema periodico* (1975; *The Periodic Table*, 1984), a collection of autobiographical pieces unified by its organization according to the chemical elements, mixes traditional genres. Levi's poems about his experiences during the Holocaust are collected in *Shema: Collected Poems* (1976). Additional poems are collected in *L'osteria di Brema* (1975). His early pseudonymous short-story collections *Storie naturali*

(1966) and *Vizio di forma* (1971) combine autobiography, science fiction, and fantasy to describe his experiences after the war. Levi's essays are collected in *La ricerca della radici* (1981).

ACHIEVEMENTS

An Italian Jew who survived Auschwitz, Levi is widely acclaimed as a fictional, historical, and auto-biographical chronicler of the Holocaust and its aftermath. Highly praised by such important writers as Umberto Eco, Italo Calvino, Studs Terkel, Claude Lévi-Strauss, Irving Howe, Alfred Kazin, Philip Roth, and Saul Bellow, Levi's work is distinguished by an attempt to understand his wartime experiences and by a compassionate, sensitive, and astonishingly optimistic view of humanity. Levi's epigraph for *The Periodic Table* is a Yiddish saying: "Troubles overcome are good to tell." Levi's works are ample proof of the proverb, his life a testament of the resiliency of the human spirit. In recognition of his many achievements, Levi won Italy's prestigious Premio Bagutta, Viareggio, Strega, and Campiello literary prizes.

BIOGRAPHY

Primo Levi was born on July 31, 1919, in Turin, Italy, to a cultured middle-class couple, Ester and Cesare Levi. Levi attended the University of Turin and in 1941 received his Ph.D. in chemistry. A Jew in occupied Italy during World War II, he joined the Italian Resistance and was soon arrested for anti-Fascist activities. Upon discovering that Levi was a Jew, the German SS deported him to their death facility in Auschwitz. There, where number 174517 was tattooed on his left arm, he remained until the concentration camp was liberated. For his survival, he credits luck, which manifested itself in terms of his health, which was good most of the time he was in Auschwitz and poor at precisely the right moment (when the Germans fled the concentration camp, taking with them all "healthy" prisoners). In addition, he worked as a chemist part of the time that he was in Auschwitz, and his friend, an Italian bricklayer, smuggled extra food to him.

After the war, Levi found employment as technical director of a paint factory. In 1947, Levi married

(Bernard Gotfryd/Archive Photos)

Lucia Morpurgo, a teacher, who helped him adjust to his new life. Still deeply depressed, he turned to writing in an attempt to understand his concentration-camp experience. The Holocaust turned the chemist into the writer. Levi describes his time in Auschwitz as "the fundamental experience of my life." He goes on to say, "I knew that if I survived, I would have to tell the story." In 1947, he chronicled his imprisonment at Auschwitz in *If This Is a Man*, and later, in *The Reawakening*, he described his bizarre, circuitous journey home from Poland. Many of his other works, including *Shema*, *Moments of Reprieve*, and *If Not Now, When?* were also inspired by the Holocaust. In 1977, Levi devoted himself to writing full-time. Levi died in his hometown of Turin on April 11, 1987, survived by a son, Renzo, a physicist, and a daughter, Lisa, a biologist.

ANALYSIS

Most of Primo Levi's work (with the exception of *The Monkey's Wrench*) can be placed within the genre of Holocaust literature. As a survivor of Auschwitz, Levi blended personal reminiscence and reflection to depict his major preoccupation, the unfathomable horror that was the Holocaust. Almost totally devoid of self-pity, Levi reserved his concern for others. He never indulged in luridness or melodrama. Rather, his tone is clear, straightforward, and moderate—his passion, muted. Although his writing deals with the deepest of human emotions and feelings, it remains restrained in a manner that makes for a quiet intensity, which is only emphasized by his subtle (if somewhat startling) humor. Through his unflinching and careful use of detail, he presents a picture of human degradation. Yet, despite the bleakness inherent in Levi's usual subjects, his portrayal leads not to bitterness, but, astoundingly, to a compelling affirmation of life, to a sense of faith in humanity, to a compassionate understanding of both victims and victimizers, and, finally, to a powerful and moving vision of the dignity of humankind.

THE MONKEY'S WRENCH

Although Levi's first piece of long fiction, *The Monkey's Wrench*, represents a divergence from his usual concerns (and therefore is lighter and even more amusing in tone), it still reflects Levi's life experiences, and Levi himself is one of the main characters. This work has been widely classified as a novel. In actuality, however, *The Monkey's Wrench* defies classification, being a combination of autobiography and long and short fiction. Indeed, in an interview with Philip Roth, Levi implied that he does not consider *The Monkey's Wrench* to be a novel. The work is, perhaps, best regarded as a collection of short stories linked by a narrative situation: The unnamed narrator/writer, who represents Levi, for the most part listens to and records stories related by Faussone, the protagonist and Levi's self-styled alter ego. This frame automatically emphasizes the complex relationship between storyteller and listener, between writer and reader.

In the street-smart, cocky, energetic Faussone, Levi created one of his most fully realized characters. An itinerant steelworker, Faussone (like Levi and the narrator) comes from Turin. In seemingly artless monologues, Faussone articulates his devotion to work, a passion he shares with the narrator, who finds, "If we except those miraculous and isolated moments fate can bestow on a man, loving your work (unfortunately, the privilege of a few) represents the best, most concrete approximation of happiness on earth." In fact, the central metaphor of the novel has to do with the relationship between life and work, whether the comparison is to rigging, to chemistry, or to writing.

Like Levi, the narrator is a chemist (a paint specialist) and author from Turin. Just as Levi became a full-time writer in 1977, the narrator (who, in describing his writing generally alternates between the languages of rigging and of chemistry) relates his last adventure as a chemist and marks his impending transition:

> With nostalgia, but without misgivings, I would choose another road . . . the road of the teller of stories. My own stories . . . then other people's stories . . . his [Faussone's], for example. . . . [I]t was possible that, having spent more than thirty years sewing together long molecules . . . I might have learned something about sewing together words and ideas.

IF NOT NOW, WHEN?

If in his previous works Levi depended primarily on his own individual experience, *If Not Now, When?* is based on the true story of Jewish partisans who banded together to fight the Nazis. Levi described this deliberate new direction in his writing in his interview with Roth: "I had made a sort of bet with myself: after so much plain or disguised autobiography, are you, or are you not, a full-fledged writer, capable of constructing a novel, shaping characters, describing landscapes you have never seen? Try it!" In *If Not Now, When?*, for the first time Levi imagines rather than recalls events surrounding the Holocaust. He reconstructs a people (Yiddish-speaking Eastern European Jews whom Levi had not known before his concentration camp experience), a period (World War II), a setting (the countryside of Eastern Europe), and even a language (Yiddish) to celebrate the active resistance of the Jews, arguing against the commonly held notion that all Jews passively submitted to their fate at the hands of their Nazi murderers. Levi outlined his intentions thus:

I wished to assault a commonplace still prevailing in Italy: a Jew is a mild person, a scholar (religious or profane), unwarlike, humiliated, who tolerated centuries of persecution without ever fighting back. It seemed to me a duty to pay homage to those Jews who, in desperate conditions, had found the courage and the skills to resist. . . . I cherished the ambition to be the first (perhaps only) Italian writer to describe the Yiddish world.

The story begins in 1943 as two Russian Jews—Mendel, one of the main characters, a resourceful and philosophic watchmaker whose wife has been slaughtered by the Nazis, and Leonid, an uncommunicative young concentration camp escapee—try to elude the Nazis. Living hand-to-mouth as they travel over marshes, forests, and countryside, they join with various ragged groups of refugees, stragglers, and partisans attempting both to survive and to fight the Germans. Eventually, the two meet a group of Jewish partisans, the Gedalists, named for their leader, Gedaleh. This courageous band—comprising a wide variety of Polish and Russian men and women, from former Soviet soldiers to fugitives of Nazi roundups and concentration camps—aims to survive, to harm the Germans, and eventually, to reach Palestine. Traveling over much of the same territory Levi himself crossed on his protracted journey home from Auschwitz (chronicled in his memoir, *The Reawakening*), the partisans get as far as Italy before the novel ends, as does the war in Europe, in August, 1945.

The novel oscillates in atmosphere from romantic to epic. The tone is not indignant, but rather reflective, understated, and at times quietly humorous. What distinguishes this work from most Holocaust literature is that Levi rarely details the German atrocities that form the backdrop of this story. Explicitly, "this story is not being told in order to describe massacres." Nevertheless, images of the grotesqueness of the Holocaust are a silent presence, almost more notable in their absence. As one character explains to another, "It's the first rule. . . . If we kept on telling one another what we've seen, we'd go crazy and instead we all have to be sane, children included."

Action-packed, tense, and suspenseful, the plot of this stirring war story is (like the plot of *The Re-awakening*) picaresque. Levi is a master of the episodic, a painter of poignant vignettes. As they travel westward from Russia to Italy, their springboard to Palestine, the Gedalists risk considerable danger to sabotage the Germans, engaging in a series of rearguard acts of harassment and guerrilla warfare—from ambushing trains to liberating concentration camps—that are variously amusing, frightening, exciting, and moving.

Yet *If Not Now, When?* is also a novel of character. In fact, as Levi confessed, "For the first and only time in my life as a writer, I had the impression (almost a hallucination) that my characters were alive, around me, behind my back, suggesting spontaneously their feats and their dialogues." Irrepressible and courageous, individual members of the Gedalists are sharply and insightfully drawn. The characters are made all the more vivid and striking through a series of elegant and wonderful metaphors.

Mendel's character is the most fully developed, and, as the third-person narrator, continually presents his innermost thoughts. This is in direct contrast to the presentation of the elusive Gedaleh, whose interior consciousness, and consequently his character, remains remote. Introduced as "the legendary leader" of the partisan group, Gedaleh, with his violin as talisman, is appropriately mysterious and heroic.

As for the group itself, the narrator presents the inner thoughts of the band as a whole, expressive of a developing Jewish collective consciousness. It is here that Levi strikes a chord of universality: The possibility for community, camaraderie, mutual responsibility, and unity emerges as the final lesson to be learned from the Holocaust and from all of Levi's works. Perhaps this lesson is best expressed in the words of Rabbi Hillel: "If I am not for myself, who will be for me? If I am for myself alone, what am I? If not now, when?"

Deborah D. Rogers

OTHER MAJOR WORKS

SHORT FICTION: *Storie naturali*, 1966; *Vizio di forma*, 1971; *Lilit e altri racconti*, 1981; *Moments of Reprieve*, 1986; *The Sixth Day and Other Tales*, 1990.

POETRY: *L'osteria di Brema*, 1975; *Shema: Collected Poems*, 1976; *Ad ora incerta*, 1984 (*Collected Poems*, 1988).

NONFICTION: *Se questo è un uomo*, 1947 (memoir; *If This Is a Man*, 1959; rev. as *Survival in Auschwitz: The Nazi Assault on Humanity*, 1961); *La tregua*, 1963 (memoir; *The Reawakening*, 1965); *Il sistema periodico*, 1975 (memoir; *The Periodic Table*, 1984); *La ricerca della radici*, 1981; *I sommersi e i salvati*, 1986 (*The Drowned and the Saved*, 1988); *L'altrui mestiere*, 1985 (*Other People's Trades*, 1989).

MISCELLANEOUS: *The Mirror Maker*, 1989 (stories and essays).

BIBLIOGRAPHY

Cicioni, Mirna. *Primo Levi: Bridges of Knowledge.* Oxford, England: Berg, 1995. This is a good general introduction to Levi's work. Because of Levi's family's reluctance to release biographical information about the writer, Cicioni has few biographical details to work with, but she does a fine job of outlining the social context of northern Italy in which Levi grew up and from which he was rudely wrenched in 1938. Her second chapter is devoted to Levi's experiences in Auschwitz, while the four that follow discuss the works that grew out of this period. An inclusive twenty-four-page bibliography lists primary and secondary materials written in English as well as foreign-language publications.

Langer, Lawrence. *The Holocaust and the Literary Imagination.* New Haven, Conn.: Yale University Press, 1975. Contains a discussion of Levi in the context of Holocaust literature, by one of the subject's principal authorities.

Rudolf, Anthony. *At an Uncertain Hour: Primo Levi's War Against Oblivion.* London: The Menard Press, 1990. This brief (fifty-six-page) homage to Levi by one of his publishers recycles some of Rudolf's earlier reviews and articles on Levi and includes a short bibliography.

Sodi, Risa B. *A Dante of Our Time: Primo Levi and Auschwitz.* New York: Peter Lang, 1990. Sodi's book is an academic exercise detailing the influence of Dante on Levi's *If This Is a Man* and *The*

Drowned and the Saved. Sodi makes liberal use of interviews in which Levi addresses the ethical concerns of other contemporary figures such as Sigmund Freud and Rudolf Hess.

Tarrow, Susan R., ed. *Reason and Light: Essays on Primo Levi.* Ithaca, N.Y.: Cornell University Press, 1990. Contains several essays on Levi's fiction and on his relationship to the Holocaust and its literature.

C. S. LEWIS

Born: Belfast, Northern Ireland; November 29, 1898
Died: Oxford, England; November 22, 1963

PRINCIPAL LONG FICTION

Out of the Silent Planet, 1938
Perelandra, 1943
That Hideous Strength: A Modern Fairy Tale for Grownups, 1945
The Lion, the Witch, and the Wardrobe, 1950
Prince Caspian, 1951
The Voyage of the Dawn Treader, 1952
The Silver Chair, 1953
The Horse and His Boy, 1954
The Magician's Nephew, 1955
The Last Battle, 1956
The Chronicles of Narnia, 1950-1956 (includes the seven previous titles)
Till We Have Faces: A Myth Retold, 1956

OTHER LITERARY FORMS

Though his novels for adults and children continue to be widely read and admired, C. S. Lewis is also well known as a religious essayist and literary scholar-critic. His religious writings of three decades include autobiography (*The Pilgrim's Regress*, 1933; *Surprised by Joy: The Shape of My Early Life*, 1955; *A Grief Observed*, 1961) and essays in varying lengths and forms. Some of his essays include *The Personal Heresy* (1939, with E. M. W. Tillyard), *Rehabilitations* (1939), *The Problem of Pain* (1940),

The Screwtape Letters (1942), *The Abolition of Man* (1943), *Miracles: A Preliminary Study* (1947), *Mere Christianity* (1952), *Reflections on the Psalms* (1958), and *The Four Loves* (1960). Posthumous works of a religious nature include *Letters to Malcolm: Chiefly on Prayer* (1964), *Letters to an American Lady* (1967), *God in the Dock* (1970), and *The Joyful Christian: 127 Readings from C. S. Lewis* (1977).

Lewis's criticism, focused primarily on medieval and Renaissance studies, includes *The Allegory of Love* (1936), *A Preface to "Paradise Lost"* (1942), *English Literature in the Sixteenth Century, Excluding Drama* (1954), *Studies in Words* (1960), *An Experiment in Criticism* (1961), and *The Discarded Image* (1964). Several posthumous volumes of criticism appeared, including *Spenser's Images of Life* (1967), *Selected Literary Essays* (1969), and *Present Concerns* (1986).

Less widely known are Lewis's early volumes of poetry, *Spirits in Bondage* (1919), a collection of lyrics; and *Dymer* (1926), a narrative. The posthumous *The Dark Tower and Other Stories* (1977) includes an unpublished fragment of a novel. This collection and one other, *Of Other Worlds: Essays and Stories* (1966), contain the only extant fictional pieces not printed during Lewis's lifetime. The Wade Collection at Wheaton College (Illinois) and the Bodleian Library, Oxford, hold many volumes of Lewis papers, including eleven volumes of Lewis family letters written from 1850 to 1930.

(CORBIS/Bettmann)

ACHIEVEMENTS

Lewis's achievements as a novelist are hard to separate from his role as a Christian apologist and from his impeccable literary scholarship. Many of Lewis's readers believe that his greatness lies in the unusually wide scope of his work: he wrote so much so well in so many forms. His *Mere Christianity*, for example, is a superb primer on Christian ideas, while *The Four Loves* and *A Grief Observed* are powerful explorations of the endurance of love despite doubt and deep pain. *The Screwtape Letters*, Lewis's most popular book in America, still enthralls new readers with its witty yet serious study of the war between good and evil in the contemporary world. Among his

critical writings, *The Allegory of Love* remains a classic study of medieval literature and society, while *The Discarded Image* is one of the very best discussions of the contrast between the medieval worldview and the modern mind.

The popularity of Lewis's novels for adults (*Out of the Silent Planet, Perelandra,* and *That Hideous Strength*—known as the space trilogy—and *Till We Have Faces*) owes more perhaps to their treatment of themes also developed in his nonfiction than to their literary excellence, although the space trilogy is widely read among devotees of fantasy and science fiction who have little acquaintance with Lewis's other works. The extraordinary appeal of Lewis's fiction for children, the Narnia books, is undisputed. Each year, these seven novels gain thousands of new readers of all ages and are, for many, the introduction to Lewis which inspires them to delve into his other works. Indeed, had Lewis never published another word, the Narnia books would have ensured his reputation with both critics and the public.

BIOGRAPHY

Born in Belfast in 1898, the son of Albert Lewis, a successful lawyer, and Flora Hamilton Lewis, a writer and mathematician, Clive Staples Lewis spent his early childhood in an atmosphere of learning and imagination. His mother tutored him in French and Latin before he was seven; his nurse, Lizzie Endicott, taught him the folktales of Ireland. Clive and his brother, Warren, devoted long, often rainy afternoons to exploring the book-lined corridors of Little Lea, their home. As small children, the brothers invented their own country, Boxen, for which they wrote a four-hundred-year chronicle and which they peopled with animal characters who became subjects of individual stories. These early childhood adventures were of incalculable influence on Lewis's long fiction, written almost half a century later.

With his mother's death from cancer in 1908, Lewis's life changed drastically and irrevocably. A disconsolate, bewildered Albert Lewis sent his sons to boarding school in England, the first of several cruel experiences before age sixteen that nurtured in Lewis a hatred for public-school education. At last persuading his father to place him with the demanding but kind tutor W. T. Kirkpatrick in 1914, Lewis developed his great scholarly talents and won a scholarship to University College, Oxford, two years later. Before taking his entrance exams, however, Lewis was recruited into the army and served as a second lieutenant on the front lines in France during World War I.

Surviving a wound and the mental shocks of war, Lewis happily entered Oxford life in 1919, his education financed by his father—whose support in other ways would always be lacking. Perhaps to compensate for this lack of parental affection, Lewis developed a steadfast friendship with a Mrs. Moore, the mother of a friend who had died fighting in France. With Mrs. Moore and her young daughter, Maureen, Lewis set up housekeeping, this arrangement continuing thirty years, until Mrs. Moore's death in 1951. Lewis's tenure at Oxford, as student, tutor, and fel-

low of Magdalen College, lasted even longer, ending in 1954 with his acceptance of the chair of Medieval and Renaissance Literature at Magdalene College, Cambridge. During the Oxford years, he wrote and published most of his fifty-eight books of adult and children's fiction, literary criticism, essays, Christian apologetics, and poetry. It was there also that Lewis, influenced by such close friends as J. R. R. Tolkien, underwent his conversion to Christianity.

Lewis's Christian fervor led to widely read publications and to a long series of radio talks before and during World War II. His faith also inspired fictional works, including his space trilogy, written during the war, and his Narnia books for children. Many of his Oxford colleagues, however, were offended by his overt religiousness—and his popularity. Through these years, they thus denied Lewis the Magdalen professorship that his eminence as a literary scholar warranted.

With his rise to a more esteemed position in the more congenial atmosphere of Cambridge, Lewis completed, among other projects, the books of Narnia, the first of which had been published in 1950, and wrote perhaps his finest novel, *Till We Have Faces*. This last work of fiction was dedicated to Joy Davidman Gresham, an American admirer with whom he had corresponded for several years and who came to England to join him in 1955. They were married in 1956, and, according to Lewis, "feasted on love" for the four years they shared before Joy's death from bone cancer in 1960. Despite his own worsening health, Lewis continued to produce autobiographical and critical works until suffering a heart attack in 1963. He died on November 22, the date of President John F. Kennedy's assassination and of the death of writer Aldous Huxley.

ANALYSIS

The happy fact of C. S. Lewis's creation of long fictional works is that the more of them he wrote, the better he became as a novelist. This is not to say that with each book from *Out of the Silent Planet* to *Till We Have Faces* he measurably improved, but from the early space trilogy (1938-1945) through the Narnia tales (1950-1956) to his last novel, there is a clear change in Lewis's conception of fiction. In the early books, characters exemplify definite sides in an ethical debate, and plot is the working out of victory for Lewis's side. In the later books, however, character becomes the battleground of ambiguous values, and plot takes place more and more within the minds of the characters.

THE SPACE TRILOGY

The hero of the space trilogy, Cambridge don Elwin Ransom, is often less the protagonist of novels than an embodiment of the Christian and intellectual virtues that Lewis recommended in his essays. Throughout the trilogy, Ransom represents Lewis's ideal of the relentless intellectual, his learning solidly founded on respect for great ideas from earlier ages, who valiantly maintains his integrity despite the powerful temptations posed by modern materialism. In both *Out of the Silent Planet* and *Perelandra*, Ransom's journeys to Mars (Malacandra) and Venus (Perelandra), respectively, Ransom's adversary is as clearly villainous as Ransom himself is heroic. The antagonist is Edward Weston, a brilliant physicist, who represents for Lewis that most insidious modern outgrowth of Renaissance humanism: the belief that the highest goal of humankind is to establish its dominance over all forms of life in as many worlds as it can conquer. This view, which Lewis saw as the root of the boundless ambition of political leaders Adolf Hitler, Joseph Stalin, and Benito Mussolini, is exemplified in Weston's misuse of technology to build a spacecraft that enables him to reach other planets, so that he might make them colonies of Earth.

By moving the scene of this attempt away from Earth, Lewis can manipulate material reality so that the limitations of Weston's philosophy become obvious and his actions ludicrous. Assuming the innate superiority of man over all other forms, and thus a perpetual state of war between man and nature, Weston fails to see the simplest, most significant facts of the new worlds he intends to conquer. As Ransom, the Christian student of myths and languages, easily perceives, the forces that rule Mars and Venus are both fully hospitable to humankind and infinitely more powerful. Thus, Weston shoots gentle creatures because they appear strange and, in a parody of the European explorers, tries to bribe with shiny trinkets the Oyarsa of Malacandra, who, as Ransom learns, is second only in power and wisdom to Maleldil, ruler of the universe. In contrast to Weston, Ransom—a far truer scientist than his opponent—befriends and learns the language of these extraterrestrials; hence, mysteries are opened to him. In *Out of the Silent Planet*, he learns that only Earth (Thulcandra), long under the dominance of the "bent eldil," is deprived of clear knowledge of the Oyarsa and Maleldil; Thulcandrans believe themselves enlightened above all others, when in reality they are the most benighted. He learns also that the universe is in a state of becoming: that the creatures of old worlds, such as Malacandra, can no longer be endangered by such forces as those which guide Weston, but that newer worlds, such as Thulcandra, are still theaters of contending principles, while the youngest worlds, such as Perelandra, have yet to achieve spiritual identity.

This is vital knowledge for Ransom, who realizes, in the second book, that he has been given wisdom because he has also been given the responsibility of helping to bring about Maleldil's reign on Perelandra, which places him in open confrontation with Weston, now clearly the mere instrument of the bent eldil. In a probing recapitulation of the temptation of Eve, Lewis has Ransom and Weston contend, somewhat in the mode of the medieval *psychomachia*, for the mind of Tinidril, the first woman of Perelandra. As the confoundingly subtle arguments of the Unman (the spirit that controls Weston) begin to conquer Tinidril, Ransom at last understands that he must physically fight, to the death, his adversary. Despite his slim chance of survival, Ransom attacks the Unman; he ultimately defeats him, though suffering wounds, incredible fatigue, and near despair. It is an epic battle, reminiscent of the Pearl-Poet's fourteenth century manuscript *Sir Gawain and the Green Knight* and Edmund Spenser's *The Faerie Queene* (1590, 1596); Ransom's faith and courage in the fight prepare the reader for his apotheosis in the final chapters, wherein Lewis's paradisiacally lush description of Perelandra takes on an almost beatific vividness and illumination.

In novelistic terms, *Perelandra* surpasses *Out of the Silent Planet* in its attention to the development of Ransom's awareness of his role and his struggle to maintain his integrity in the face of fears and misleading appearances. Nevertheless, its extraterrestrial setting and its clearly demarcated hero and villain make *Perelandra* more an epic romance than a novel. This is not to prefer one book to the other, but it is to distinguish them both from the third part of the trilogy, *That Hideous Strength*, which may be Lewis's most interesting fiction, although not his most consistent. *That Hideous Strength* tries to harmonize heterogeneous elements of romance, epic, and novel. Following the novelist's impulse, Lewis brings his setting back to earth and localizes it in the sort of place he knew best, a venerable English college town, which he calls Edgestow. He also centers the reader's interest on two authentic protagonists, Jane and Mark Studdock, whose story is their painful, humiliating, sometimes dangerous progress toward faith and self-awareness. They act bravely in the ultimate crisis, both risking torture and death, but they engage in nothing like the epic struggle of Ransom and the Unman.

Still, the events in which they engage are of epic magnitude, and in this thrust of the book Lewis returns to familiar fictional territory. The plot concerns a powerful conspiracy to turn Britain into a totalitarian state. This conspiracy is opposed most strenuously by a small underground directed by Elwin Ransom, now a heroic, almost godlike leader, whose powers are spiritual rather than physical. His main adversaries are men who, like Weston, call themselves scientists, but whose distinguishing traits are lust for power, deviousness, and cruelty. Having established a research institute called the National Institute of Co-ordinated Experiments (N.I.C.E.), these men use the press, political infiltrators, and their own "police" to avoid, placate, or squash opposition to their Nazi-like program of "social planning." Mark Studdock is one of the bright but indecisive minds easily co-opted by the N.I.C.E. Lewis shows convincingly how the leaders play on his ego and his fears of rejection in order to exploit his talent as a journalist. Conversely, Jane Studdock falls in with the resistance group; she weighs its values against those of her husband and gradually comes to see that whichever road she chooses will mean great danger for both of them. She chooses the resistance.

Had Lewis limited the book to the clash between political philosophies and its impact on two ordinary people, he would have had a conventional novel, but he wanted to portray this clash as occurring on a cosmic level, as a war between pure good and pure evil. Since the combatants in this novel are the human representatives of these supernatural forces, the reader necessarily finds himself once more in the realm of romance. Aware of his mixing of genres in *That Hideous Strength*, Lewis called the amalgam a fairy tale, arguing that his work fell into that long tradition in which supernatural events subsume the ordinary activities of realistic characters. What fairy tale means here is that when the N.I.C.E. performs such blatant works as the turning of rivers from their courses, the trapping of huge numbers of animals for vivisection, and the deforestation of ancient preserves, they call down on themselves the wrath of nature, personified in a resurrected Merlin, who pledges allegiance to Ransom as the spiritual successor of Arthur. His obedience allows Ransom to reinvest him with eldilic power, which enables him single-handedly to destroy the N.I.C.E. Add to the appearance of Merlin such important romantic elements as Jane Studdock's clairvoyance and the veneration of a talking head by the N.I.C.E., and *That Hideous Strength* seems almost more romance than novel.

The book should be judged as a fairy tale. Lewis warns the reader in his preface not to be deceived by the "hum-drum scenes and persons" into thinking this a realistic fiction. He merely intends the familiar names and places to heighten the reader's appreciation of the importance of the spiritual battles occurring around and within each individual. Indeed, one explicit purpose of the book is to warn England—here Lewis was prophetic—that radical social evil would not be eradicated with Hitler's defeat. The formal problem, however, is that a bit of realism begets the expectation of total realism, and so readers accustomed to novels will naturally look askance at Merlin's return and the survival of the severed head, while they will accept the generic consistency of the floating islands in *Perelandra*. Even if Lewis had deleted these effects from the third book, however, he would have had to substitute other supernatural manifestations in order to be consistent not only with the pattern of the first two books but also, more importantly, with his religious conviction of the immanence of the supernatural in everyday life. Viewing the book as a fairy tale, Lewis felt, would allow the reader sufficient suspension of disbelief to become involved with the characters. Nevertheless, the reader would still face, as in all of Lewis's other works, the challenge of accepting or rejecting Lewis's position on God, nature, and humanity.

THE CHRONICLES OF NARNIA

Lewis actually began the first book of the Narnia series, *The Lion, the Witch, and the Wardrobe*, in 1939, when four children, inspiration for the Pevensie children in the stories, were evacuated to his home at the start of the war. Returning ten years and many books later to the idea of writing for children, Lewis found the fictional form perhaps best suited to his genius. These tales of ordinary boys and girls transported to another world allowed Lewis to relive in some sense the childhood idyll at Little Lea that had been cut short by his mother's death; moreover, they let him put directly into prose the fantastic images—fauns, castles, golden lions—that came to him, without his having to adapt them, as he had in the space trilogy, to the narrower tastes of adult readers. The fairy-tale form restricted him to simpler vocabulary and syntax, as well as to a more exclusively narrative and descriptive mode, but these restrictions freed him to do what he did best in fiction: dialogue, action narrative, and vivid description of select detail. More than anything else, however, the form let him depict given characters as essentially good or evil, though careful readers will observe that these qualities are consistently dramatized in action, not merely posited by authorial fiat. One of the many virtues of these stories is that appearance never defines character; the reader likes or dislikes persons or animals in these books only when he has come to know them.

The seven books traverse some sixty years of English time, roughly between 1895 and 1955, and more than one thousand years of time in Narnia, a land which is the home of Aslan, the Golden Lion, as well as talking animals, dwarves, fauns, satyrs, witches, men and women, boys and girls. The chronicle begins with *The Magician's Nephew* (the sequence of publication differs from the internal chronology of the series), in which young Digory Kirke and Polly Plummer magically enter Narnia at the time of its creation by Aslan. Unfortunately, the curious Digory inadvertently breaks the spell that has bound Jadis, the White Witch, who becomes the main enemy of the Narnians.

In *The Lion, the Witch, and the Wardrobe*, almost fifty English years have passed, but an untold number in Narnia. The visitors are now the four Pevensie children, who enter Narnia through a magical wardrobe in the spacious country home of an old friend of their parents—Professor Digory Kirke. They find a cold world in terror of the Witch. The children eventually join those who are still rebelling against her, and their faith is rewarded when Aslan returns. His conquest is not complete, however, until he has been ritually murdered by the Witch, only to be reborn in far greater splendor. The four children are crowned kings and queens of Narnia.

The Horse and His Boy occurs during the reign of Peter Pevensie as High King of Narnia. It concerns Shasta, a boy of neighboring Calormen, who through various adventures is revealed to be the true prince of Archenland, another Narnian neighbor. The fourth part of the chronicle, *Prince Caspian*, takes place a thousand years forward in Narnian time, but only two or three years after the adventure through the wardrobe. The four children are transported to Narnia from a railway bench, only to find all record of their reign obliterated by time and by the purposeful lies told by invaders. The children's arrival, however, coincides with another coming of Aslan, who, aided by an alliance of all the creatures of Narnia, restores to the throne the true heir, Caspian. He is still king of Narnia when the fifth adventure, *The Voyage of the Dawn Treader*, occurs. This time, the two younger Pevensies, Edmund and Lucy, accompanied by a recalcitrant friend, Eustace Scrubb, reenter Narnia to help Caspian sail the farthest seas to find seven

Narnian lords banished by the invaders. On their voyage, they discover lands beyond imagining, including Aslan's country itself. The sixth chronicle, *The Silver Chair*, is another story of a search, this time by Eustace and a friend, Jill Pole, who are called to Narnia to find the dying Caspian's long-lost son, Rilian. Despite many deceptions and dangers, the children eventually discover the prince, by then the rightful king of Narnia.

The chronicles end with *The Last Battle*, the apocalypse of Narnia. King Tirian, Rilian's descendant, is joined by Eustace and Jill in a final battle to save Narnia from invading hordes of hostile neighbors. As they go to certain death, they are suddenly greeted by Aslan, who ushers them into the real Narnia, of which the mere parody is now disappearing as quickly as it had been born centuries before. There they are joined by all the friends of Narnia, including three of the four Pevensies, who, with their parents, have come to the real Narnia thanks to a railway accident in "their" world. Aslan tells them that this Narnia is forever, and that they need never leave: "The term is over; the holidays have begun. The dream is ended; this is the morning."

TILL WE HAVE FACES

Almost nothing of the style of the space trilogy is recognizable in *Till We Have Faces*, Lewis's first novel for adults after 1945, and the last of his career. Though Lewis here was reworking an ancient myth, that of Cupid and Psyche, this book can be unambiguously called a novel, in the full modern sense of that word. It begins and ends in the spiritual turmoil of the mind of the narrator, Orual, Queen of Glome, a tiny state somewhere north of Greece, sometime in the centuries just preceding the birth of Christ. The novel is the story of her life, told in two parts. The first, much the longer, is Orual's complaint against the gods for their hatred of humankind, hatred shown most obviously in their failure ever to make themselves clearly known. The second part, a few brief chapters hastily penned by the dying queen and ended in midsentence by her death, repents for the slanders of part 1 and tells of a few pivotal encounters and an extraordinary dream that have resolved her anger.

Part 1 recalls a lifelong source of her rage, her ugliness, which has made Orual hated by her father, the king, and shunned by most others. A far greater injury, however, is the sacrifice of her wonderfully beautiful sister, Psyche, whom the head priest of Glome offers to the god of the Grey Mountain in hopes of ending a drought. Orual cannot forgive the gods for taking the only joy of her life. What irritates her most, however, is her discovery that Psyche has not been devoured by the god of the mountain, as most people believe, but that he has wedded her. Moreover, Psyche is happy. Convincing herself that her sister's happiness can only be a fatal delusion, Orual persuades Psyche, with a threat of suicide, to disobey her lord's one command: that she never look at him. The result is that Psyche is banished and forced to undergo ordeals. Orual is also punished: The god tells her, cryptically, "You also will be Psyche." Never fully comprehending this sentence, and enraged by the ambiguity of the portent, Orual passes the years, eventually succeeding her father and distracting her thoughts by careful attention to government of her people. Orual becomes a wise and masterful ruler, but her mind remains troubled. When, by chance, she discovers that the story of Psyche has given rise to a cult of worshipers, she decides finally to spill her anger and doubt onto paper. The story the sect tells is false, she feels: In it, Psyche's sister is accused of deliberately plotting her fall. She feels that she must write to clear the record, to exonerate herself.

In part 2, she repents. She admits that the very writing of part 1 has brought back disquieting memories: Perhaps she had been jealous of Psyche. Her self-awareness grows when two meetings with longtime observers of her life convince her that her perspective on people and events has always been narrow and selfish. Finally, two terrible dreams—visions, she realizes—bring her crime before her eyes; she understands the sentence of the god. She has indeed been Psyche, in that while her sister has performed the ordeals assigned her, Orual, in her years of suffering, has borne all the anguish of them. Thus, she has both committed the crime and expiated the guilt. Her confession in part 2 gives way to thanksgiving, as she discovers that, washed clear of her guilt, she is as beautiful as the sister whom she is at last free to love.

The richness of Orual's character has been likened by critics to the increasing depth of compassion in Lewis's essays of these later years. The striking resonance of these works has been attributed, at least in part, to the influence on Lewis's life at this time of Joy Davidman, to whom he dedicated *Till We Have Faces*. That Lewis's renunciation of bachelorhood late in his life signaled an opening of himself, and his prose, to emotions and ways of seeing that he had not before allowed himself seems plausible; nevertheless, the simple design and straightforward nature of this last novel can as easily be explained as further developments of Lewis's style in the direction taken by the Narnia books. Perhaps the exploration of his own childhood necessitated by writing these books taught him lessons about his writing as profound as those Orual learned in trying to recapture her past. Perhaps he learned that he was truly happy as a writer when he could explore the curious corridors of his personality, just as he had loved to explore the rooms and passages of his boyhood home. It is surely no coincidence that the first part of his autobiography, *Surprised by Joy*, was published in 1955, while he was at work not only on *Till We Have Faces* but also on *The Last Battle*. All three books reveal an exquisite sensitivity which can be attributed to his deep introspection at this time. This sensitivity, this honesty, makes these books far more memorable in themselves than his more clever experiments in less traditional forms.

Christopher J. Thaiss

OTHER MAJOR WORKS

SHORT FICTION: *The Dark Tower and Other Stories*, 1977.

POETRY: *Spirits in Bondage*, 1919; *Dymer*, 1926; *Poems*, 1964; *Narrative Poems*, 1969.

NONFICTION: *The Pilgrim's Regress*, 1933; *The Allegory of Love*, 1936; *The Personal Heresy*, 1939 (with E. M. W. Tillyard); *Rehabilitations*, 1939; *The Problem of Pain*, 1940; *The Screwtape Letters*, 1942; *Broadcast Talks*, 1942; *A Preface to "Paradise Lost,"* 1942; *Hamlet: The Prince or the Poem*, 1942; *Christian Behaviour*, 1943; *The Abolition of Man*, 1943; *Beyond Personality*, 1944; *The Great Divorce*, 1945; *Miracles: A Preliminary Study*, 1947; *Arthurian Torso*, 1948; *The Weight of Glory, and Other Addresses*, 1949; *Mere Christianity*, 1952; *English Literature in the Sixteenth Century, Excluding Drama*, 1954; *Surprised by Joy: The Shape of My Early Life*, 1955; *Reflections on the Psalms*, 1958; *The Four Loves*, 1960; *The World's Last Night, and Other Essays*, 1960; *Studies in Words*, 1960; *An Experiment in Criticism*, 1961; *A Grief Observed*, 1961; *The Discarded Image*, 1964; *Letters to Malcolm: Chiefly on Prayer*, 1964; *Studies in Medieval and Renaissance Literature*, 1966; *Letters of C. S. Lewis*, 1966; *Christian Reflections*, 1967; *Letters to an American Lady*, 1967; *Spenser's Images of Life*, 1967; *Selected Literary Essays*, 1969; *God in the Dock*, 1970; *The Joyful Christian: 127 Readings from C. S. Lewis*, 1977; *They Stand Together: The Letters of C. S. Lewis to Arthur Greeves, 1914-1963*, 1979; *On Stories, and Other Essays on Literature*, 1982; *C. S. Lewis: Letters to Children*, 1985; *Present Concerns*, 1986; *Letters: C. S. Lewis and Don Giovanni Calabria, a Study in Friendship*, 1988.

MISCELLANEOUS: *Of Other Worlds: Essays and Stories*, 1966; *The Business of Heaven*, 1984; *Boxen: The Imaginary World of the Young C. S. Lewis*, 1985.

BIBLIOGRAPHY

Carpenter, Humphrey. *The Inklings: C. S. Lewis, J. R. R. Tolkien, Charles Williams, and Their Friends*. Boston: Houghton Mifflin, 1979. A major study of the lives and works of the "Inklings," a name first applied by Lewis, perhaps as early as 1933, to a group of literary friends who met regularly together at Oxford University. Capsule biographies of the Inklings, bibliographies of their major works, a section of photographs, extensive notes and an index enhance an illuminating exploration of Lewis's literary milieu.

Downing, David C. *Planets in Peril: A Critical Study of C. S. Lewis's Ransom Trilogy*. Amherst: University of Massachusetts Press, 1992. The introduction contains a concise, insightful view of

Lewis's varied career as literary critic, novelist, philosopher, and theologian. The first chapter shows how his early life influenced the writing of his trilogy. Subsequent chapters explore his Christian vision, his use of classicism and medievalism, his portraits of evil, his treatment of the spiritual pilgrimage, and the overall achievement of his trilogy. Includes notes and bibliography.

Gilbert, Douglas, and Clyde S. Kilby. *C. S. Lewis: Images of His World*. Grand Rapids, Mich.: Wm. B. Eerdmans, 1973. Photographer Gilbert's several hundred color and black-and-white portraits of friends of Lewis, as well as the British countryside that was his continual inspiration, are coupled with excerpts of Lewis's published and unpublished writings. Kilby, curator of the Lewis collection at Wheaton College in Illinois, has added a chronology of Lewis's life. Lewis family pictures and photographs of his juvenilia complement this visually impressive volume.

Holbrook, David. *The Skeleton in the Wardrobe: C. S. Lewis's Fantasies: A Phenomenological Study*. Lewisburg: Bucknell University Press, 1991. Of use mainly to advanced students, Holbrook provides a probing reading of Lewis's fiction for children and for adults. He explores the thesis that the Narnia stories make disturbing reading for children. Bibliography included.

Manlove, C. N. *C. S. Lewis: His Literary Achievement*. New York: St. Martin's Press, 1987. An explication of Lewis's major works of fiction, from *The Pilgrim's Regress* (1933) to *Till We Have Faces: A Myth Retold* (1956), including an analysis of each of the Narnia books (published between 1950 and 1956). Representative of a subgenre of Lewis studies and easily accessible is its consideration of narrative, structure, and theme in Lewis's stories. Finds Lewis's use of imagery and analogy a potent means of giving literary vitality to traditional Christian doctrines, though his complexly patterned works raise him above a facile religious apologist.

Sayer, George. *Jack: C. S. Lewis and His Times*. San Francisco: Harper & Row, 1988. An intimate biography by a former pupil and lifelong friend of Lewis. Assesses Lewis's experience of grade-school life as less abnormal than that portrayed in his own autobiography, suggests that Lewis and Mrs. Moore were not lovers, and provides a personal account of the last years of Lewis's life. Lewis emerges a gifted and sincere nonsectarian Christian. A section of black-and-white photographs, a classified bibliography, and an extensive index are included.

Smith, Robert Houston. *Patches of Godlight: The Pattern of Thought of C. S. Lewis*. Athens: University of Georgia Press, 1981. A scholarly but accessible analysis of Lewis's philosophy of religion, linking what is dubbed his Christian "Objectivism" to the profound influence of Platonism on his views of the nature, of man, and of God. A sympathetic treatment which nevertheless finds Lewis to have been flawed as a philosopher, a rational mystic torn between a romantic vision of the absolute and the boundaries of a reasoned faith. Extensive notes, a bibliography, and an index add to the worth of the study.

Wilson, A. N. *C. S. Lewis: A Biography*. New York: W. W. Norton, 1990. An important interpretation of Lewis and his work from a Freudian perspective. Paints Lewis as neither a saint nor a full-time Christian apologist but as a man of real passions and a contradictory nature unbefitting the cult following that developed after his death. The chronological biography traces many of his adult preoccupations to the sometimes traumatic experiences of his early childhood and comes to some controversial conclusions regarding several of Lewis's relationships (especially regarding Mrs. Moore). Black-and-white photographs, a select bibliography, and an index complete what turns out to be an iconoclastic portrait of the creator of Narnia.

MATTHEW GREGORY LEWIS

Born: London, England; July 9, 1775
Died: At sea, near Jamaica; May 14, 1818

(Library of Congress)

PRINCIPAL LONG FICTION

The Monk: A Romance, 1796 (also published as
Ambrosio: Or, The Monk)

OTHER LITERARY FORMS

Matthew Gregory Lewis's work in genres other
than fiction deserves more critical attention than it
has generally received. In his own day, his reputation
as a dramatist almost equaled his fame as the author
of *Ambrosio: Or, The Monk*, commonly referred to
simply as *The Monk*. *The Castle Spectre* (1797), a
gothic drama, was a major success. Clearly the work
of the author of *The Monk*, the drama is populated by
stock characters who move through an intricate plot
decorated with ghosts and spectacle. *The Castle
Spectre* allowed Lewis to show what *The Monk*
would only let him describe. *Alfonso, King of Castile*
(1801), a tragedy, was much hailed by critics, and
helped establish Lewis's reputation as a major figure
in the literary world of the early nineteenth century.

Lewis also wrote poetry. Some of his finer pieces
appear in the text of *The Monk*. One, "Alonzo the

Brave and the Fair Imogine," is still read as an excellent example of the then-popular gothic ballad and is
included in *The Oxford Book of Eighteenth Century
Verse* (1926). Lewis is also highly respected as a
writer of nonfiction. *Journal of a West India Proprietor, Kept During a Residence in the Island of Jamaica* (1834) is a detailed and vivid account of Jamaica in the days of slavery and of the reactions of a
genuinely humane person to this environment.

ACHIEVEMENTS

Lewis's outstanding achievement is his famous
novel, *The Monk*. Often mentioned but seldom read
today, this work helped to define a particular type of
gothic novel that is still popular today. Rather than
merely suggesting a dangerous supernatural presence
by the careful use of tone, *The Monk* relies upon
graphic description and bold action. Lewis's imagination worked with clear visual images rather than
with hints and elusive impressions. Indeed, he has
contributed more to the gothic conventions of stage
and cinema than he has to later horror fiction. The
great gothic writers of the nineteenth century—
Nathaniel Hawthorne, Edgar Allan Poe, Emily
Brontë—relied more on psychological effects and
less on graphic horror than did Lewis. Lewis's true
successors are contemporary novelists such as Stephen King and Peter Straub, who have taken the
graphic depiction of horror to new extremes.

Among the countless readers of *The Monk*, perhaps none has enjoyed the book so thoroughly as
Lewis himself did. In September, 1794, he announced in a letter to his mother that he had produced "a romance of between three and four hundred
pages octavo" in a mere ten weeks. With the outrageous immodesty of youth, he proclaimed, "I am myself so pleased with it, that, if the Booksellers will
not buy it, I shall publish it myself." Two years later,
the novel was published with a preface in imitation of
Horace: "Now, then, your venturous course pursue,/
Go, my delight! dear book, adieu!" *The Monk*'s
course has been "venturous" indeed. An immediate
success, it went into a second edition the same year it
was published, and by 1800, readers were buying the
fifth edition. The first edition had been published

anonymously; the second, however, not only bore the proud author's name but also his title of MP (Member of Parliament).

While the earliest reviews of *The Monk* had been generally favorable—the book was deemed artful, skillful, interesting—the second wave of criticism brought judgments less kind. *The Monk* was "a poison for youth, and a provocative for the debauchee," said poet Samuel Taylor Coleridge in the *Critical Review* for February, 1797. Moreover, the poison had been brewed by a Member of Parliament, the critics were fond of noting. Such criticism did no harm to the sale of the book, but an embarrassed Lewis expurgated later editions of *The Monk*.

BIOGRAPHY

Matthew Gregory Lewis was the oldest of four children born to Matthew Lewis and Frances Maria Sewell. Both families were quite prominent: Frances was the daughter of Sir Thomas Sewell, master of the rolls, and Matthew, born in Jamaica to a landed family, was deputy-secretary at war. They were an ill-matched pair, the elder Matthew being distant and austere, his wife delighting in gay times and the company of musical and literary people. The marriage failed, and the Lewises separated. While loyal to both parents, young Lewis was his mother's favorite, and he returned her affection in full.

From an early age, Lewis showed a great love for music and drama. At fifteen, he submitted a farce to the Drury Lane Theatre; it was rejected, but this did nothing to curb his industry. He sent his mother numerous songs and poems and outlined his plan to write a two-volume novel, burlesquing popular novels of sensibility. His father intended for him to have a diplomatic career, and in preparation, Lewis spent school vacations in Europe, where he soon mastered German. Through his father, he received a position as an attaché to the British embassy in Holland. While at The Hague, he completed *The Monk*. Lewis returned to England, and his novel was published in March, 1796.

Still in his early twenties, "Monk" Lewis became one of the most popular writers in England. In the following few years, this popularity was reinforced by some noteworthy successes on the stage. *The Castle Spectre* enjoyed a long run at Drury Lane; *Alfonso* played to enthusiastic audiences at Covent Garden. In the later years of his short life, Lewis turned away from literary effort. Having achieved great prominence at an early age, he seems to have found little reason to continue in an activity which could bring him no greater fame and which he did not need to pursue for a livelihood. "The act of composing has ceased to amuse me," he wrote in the preface to the play *Venoni* (1808).

Lewis's father provided more than adequate support, and after his death in 1812, the son inherited substantial fortune and property. Modest in his own needs and habits, he was known to his friends (who included poets Percy Bysshe Shelley, Lord Byron, and Sir Walter Scott) as a man of generosity and deep concern for the oppressed. In 1815, he sailed for Jamaica to do all he could to improve the conditions of the slaves on his estates. He was responsible for important reforms and improvements, including a hospital and a humane code regulating punishments for crimes. After a brief return to England and then to Italy to visit Shelley and Byron, Lewis sailed again for Jamaica. During a five-month stay, he continued to work for better conditions for slaves. He left the island on May 4, 1818. Already sick with yellow fever, his health declined over the next several days. He died on shipboard, on May 14, and was buried at sea. According to witnesses, the coffin was wrapped in a sheet with sufficient ballast to make it sink. The plunge caused the weights to fall out, however, and the loose sheet caught the wind. The body of "Monk" Lewis, the author of one of the most fantastic books in the English language, was last seen in a sailing coffin headed for Jamaica.

ANALYSIS

While *The Monk* is seldom read today, few students of English literature have not heard of this scandalous example of the gothic novel. While the modern devotee of popular gothic literature and film whose sensitivity has long since been dulled by graphic, technicolor horrors may find *The Monk* mild stuff indeed, the novel is not without excitement, and its relation to modern gothic cinema is closer than that of most other classic gothic novels, especially those of Ann Radcliffe. Radcliffe would not allow her imagination to break free from eighteenth century rationalism; the supernatural, in the end, had to be given a natural explanation. Matthew Gregory Lewis's gothic vision looked toward nineteenth century Romanticism. He endowed certain characters with total confidence in tangible reality only to deflate their skepticism with head-on encounters with the supernatural that defy reason's best efforts at explanation. Magic works in *The Monk*; the ghosts are real and interfere with human destiny; demons interact with men, and Satan himself, as a *deus ex machina*, finally resolves the plot.

THE MONK

The plot of *The Monk*, like the plot of most classic gothic novels, is not easily summarized. Father Ambrosio, a renowned priest and orator of Madrid who symbolizes all that is chaste and holy, falls in love with an innocent girl in his congregation, Antonia. He is, at the same time, pursued by the bolder Matilda, who enters the order disguised as a novice in order to be near Ambrosio. She and Ambrosio become passionate lovers, and Matilda, seeing that Ambrosio still pines for the young Antonia, promises to grant her to him by the aid of magic. Ambrosio bungles the staged seduction, kills Antonia's mother, Elvira, by mistake, and is forced to abduct Antonia to the dungeon of the monastery, where he drugs and rapes her. Seized with remorse and fear of exposure, he drives a knife in her heart when she returns to consciousness and begins to cry out. Imprisoned and faced with an Inquisitional investigation, he yields to Matilda's entreaties to sell his soul to the Devil in exchange for release from prison. He soon bitterly realizes that he faces far worse punishment at the Devil's hands than he would have, had he faced the Inquisitors, who were preparing to pardon him.

A subplot of the novel involves Agnes, a youthful nun who has given birth to the child of her lover, Raymond. She and the child are condemned to languish without food or water in the deepest part of the dungeon. In the final chapters of the book, she is discovered, half dead, and restored to Raymond.

Perhaps the most important thing to remember about Lewis the novelist is that he was also a successful playwright for the popular stage. Readers of *The Monk* do not have to concern themselves with questions of interpretation; they need not be bothered with understanding complex characters and subtle motivations. Lewis has made all the important decisions, principally that the supernatural is not only real but also a controlling force in human affairs, and with that decision, complex characterization becomes impossible and unnecessary. While Lewis denied his creation some of the elements that make a novel great, he added enough action to produce a good story.

Critics in Lewis's time generally agreed that the disreputable member of Parliament who authored *The Monk* had indiscriminately heaped immoral action upon blasphemous action to create a plot utterly devoid of moral purpose. Such a charge is not entirely fair, for *The Monk* obviously teaches a number of moral lessons. Antonia demonstrates that innocence alone is no defense against evil. The adventures of Agnes could hardly be said to promote promiscuity, and the decline and fall of Ambrosio, the monk, provides the major theme: Pride is a vice that can pervert all virtues, even religious piety.

Nevertheless, those early critics were not altogether unfair in their severe judgment, for Lewis's morality is only shallowly rooted in his plot. Antonia, a model of virtue, is forcibly raped and then stabbed to death by the panic-stricken monk. Agnes, in the heat of passion, gives herself to Raymond; her reward, after suffering the loss of her child and imprisonment in a subterranean crypt, is finally to be united in matrimony with her dashing and well-to-do lover. Ambrosio is proud of the spirituality and dedication to priestly celibacy that sets him above men bound to the flesh. A truly tragic Ambrosio would finally come to understand that his pride was misplaced, for, indeed, he is a man like his fellows. In fact, the events of the book viewed in the light of the revelations at the conclusion may even support Ambrosio's original pride. The monk is enticed to damnation by the personal attention of the Devil himself, who is apparently unwilling to trust this prize to the temptations that are sufficient to damn normal men.

Until the final two or three pages of the novel, Ambrosio seems quite capable of damning himself with no outside help, and more than one sentence would be helpful in understanding why this particular monk is deserving of such special demoniac effort. Lust, perfidy, rape, and murder so much direct his actions that the reader is at a loss to understand how Ambrosio has ever been considered virtuous. Those last pages, however, cast the preceding four-hundred in a quite different light. After revealing that Elvira and Antonia (the murdered mother and daughter) were, in fact, Ambrosio's own mother and sister, the Devil goes on to brag,

> "It was I who threw Matilda in your way; it was I who gave you entrance to Antonia's chamber; it was I who caused the dagger to be given you which pierced your sister's bosom; and it was I who warned Elvira in dreams of your designs upon her daughter, and thus, by preventing your profiting by her sleep, compelled you to add rape as well as incest to the catalogue of your crimes."

The prior existence of that virtue is suddenly given credibility by this surprise revelation of the total manipulation that was necessary for its destruction.

These concluding revelations come as such a surprise that some critics regard them as merely tacked on to the action of the novel. In particular, the revelation of Matilda's true nature suggests that the conclusion was a kind of afterthought. Early in the novel, disguised as a young monk, she wins the friendship of Ambrosio. When she reveals her true sex, friendship turns to lustful love, and when Ambrosio's lust cools, her love becomes utter dedication to satisfying his every desire, even his desire for Antonia. Matilda is, in some ways, the most interesting and complex character in the novel. In the conclusion, however, Lewis does his readers the dubious favor of unraveling her complexity by having the Devil finally announce that she is not a woman at all but a lesser demon in human form, whose every action has followed the Devil's own blueprint for Ambrosio's destruction. This is especially puzzling for the careful reader, who remembers that in earlier pages, Matilda professed love for Ambrosio while thinking him asleep, and that on more than one occasion, even the narrator presented her affection as sincere.

The Monk's conclusion, then, both damages the credibility of the narrator and clouds whatever moral might be found in the fall of Ambrosio. More accurately, he does not fall; he is pushed. Those late eighteenth and early nineteenth century critics for whom morality was a measure of artistic accomplishment had some cause for their attack on *The Monk*. A more generous interpretation will allow that Lewis did not construct his plot or characters to illustrate morals; he only tried to salvage what morality he could from a plot that was allowed to go its own way in search of excitement and adventure.

While there was much in *The Monk* to surprise and shock readers of the day, the novel was, in many ways, highly conventional. For example, the death of Antonia was demanded by convention. Once deflowered, an unmarried female character was useless as a symbol of virtue. Although the woman was raped against her will, her very participation in an extra-marital sex act destroyed her aura of purity for eighteenth century audiences. If the association of purity with that particular character was still needed to move the plot or motivate other characters, as Antonia's purity is clearly still needed as a contrast to Ambrosio's final sin, the selling of his soul, then something must be done to remove the taint of sex and reestablish the woman in her former symbolic role. She must pay for her unintentional sin through sacrifice, and Lewis's audience expected the ultimate sacrifice: death. After her rape, Antonia, alive, is of no use to the novel; her marriage to her sweetheart, Lorenzo, a man of wealth and breeding, would be unthinkable. Dead, however, her purity is restored and can effectively serve as a foil to Ambrosio's depravity. Antonia's fate could not have been otherwise.

Romantic conventions also demanded a happy ending for the characters left alive. Lorenzo's all too rapid recovery from the loss of his beloved Antonia and his speedy attachment to Virginia, a minor character introduced late in the plot as an obvious replacement, is perhaps Lewis's most awkward attempt to satisfy convention.

His handling of Agnes, the other major female

character, is considerably more skillful. In a cast of one-dimensional characters, Agnes stands out, if only as a slightly more believable human being. She displays moral frailty without becoming a caricature of lust; she is possessed of a sense of humor and at least enough intelligence to remind the reader that the quality is generally lacking among the other characters. Agnes, like Antonia, loses her virginity. That she does so with her own true love, Raymond, whom she hopes to marry, helps only a little. Lewis recognized that it would be awkward indeed to kill off Agnes in addition to Antonia. He would then be forced to end his story with a miserable Raymond or to find some way to kill him as well. Either solution would detract from the utter misery of the monk, whose fate is seen as all the more wretched in contrast to the final happiness of the other characters. Another Virginia created in the last pages to help Raymond forget his lost love would be more than even a reader of romances could accept. Forced by his plot to allow Agnes to live, Lewis at least attempted to satisfy his audience's predictable indignation at her indiscretion by bringing her as close to death as possible.

Before her happy reunion with Raymond, Agnes passes through a purgatory as horrible as any in literature. Thought dead by all but a very few, the pregnant Agnes is imprisoned by the evil prioress in a hidden dungeon under the convent's crypt. There, alone, with barely enough bread and water to sustain her, she gives birth. The child soon dies, and the nearly insane Agnes is left to lavish a mother's love on its putrefying corpse until her rescue by Lorenzo. Lewis was certainly aware that here he was walking a fine line between pity and disgust. If the audience reacts with repugnance, Agnes would acquire a new taint that would make her happy union with Raymond unacceptable. To avoid this, Lewis carefully chooses his words when Lorenzo comes upon the despairing Agnes. The dead baby is only a "bundle" with which Agnes refuses to part, and while the bundle's contents is obvious, Lewis wisely—and uncharacteristically—renders the scene vague and withholds description. Several pages later, a fully recovered and quite sane Agnes is allowed to tell her

own story, and she tells it with such sensitivity and self-understanding as to convince the audience that she has passed through the fire, learned from the experience, and is now a proper wife for Raymond.

The destinies of the individual characters—Antonia, Lorenzo, Agnes, the monk himself—show that Lewis was not naïve. He knew what his readers demanded to satisfy their moral expectations and sense of justice, and as far as was convenient, he was willing to comply, but if popular expectation conflicted with his own sense of what made a good story—adventure, graphic detail, action rather than characterization, and no rationalization of the fantastic—then he was committed to disappointing expectation.

William J. Heim

OTHER MAJOR WORKS

PLAYS: *Village Virtues*, pb. 1796; *The Castle Spectre*, pr. 1797; *The Twins: Or, Is It He or His Brother?*, pr. 1799, pb. 1962 (adaptation of Jean François Regnard's *Les Ménechmes: Ou, Les Jumeaux*); *The East Indian*, pr. 1799; *Adelmorn the Outlaw*, pr., pb. 1801; *Alfonso, King of Castile*, pb. 1801; *The Captive*, pr. 1803 (dramatic monologue); *The Harper's Daughter: Or, Love and Ambition*, pr. 1803 (adaptation of his play *The Minister*); *Rugantino: Or, The Bravo of Venice*, pr., pb. 1805 (two acts; adaptation of his play *The Bravo of Venice*); *Adelgitha: Or, The Fruits of a Single Error*, pb. 1806; *The Wood Daemon: Or, "The Clock Has Struck,"* pr. 1807; *Venoni: Or, the Novice of St. Mark's*, pr. 1808, pb. 1809 (adaptation of Jacques Marie de Monvel's play *Les Victimes cloîtrées*); *Temper: Or, The Domestic Tyrant*, pr. 1809 (adaptation of Sir Charles Sedley's translation, *The Grumbler*, of David Augustin Brueys and Jean Palaprat's play *Le Grondeur*); *Timour the Tartar*, pr., pb. 1811; *One O'Clock: Or, The Knight and the Wood Daemon*, pr., pb. 1811 (music by Michael Kelly and Matthew Peter King; adaptation of his play *The Wood Daemon*); *Rich and Poor*, pr., pb. 1812 (music by Charles Edward Horn; adaptation of his play *The East Indian*).

DRAMA TRANSLATIONS: *The Minister*, pb. 1797 (Friedrich Schiller's play *Kabale und Liebe*); *Rolla:*

Or, The Peruvian Hero, pb. 1799 (August von Kotzebue's play *Die Spanier in Peru: Oder, Rollas Tod*).

POETRY: *The Love of Gain: A Poem Initiated from Juvenal*, 1799; *Tales of Wonder*, 1801 (with Sir Walter Scott, Robert Southey, and John Leyden); *Monody on the Death of Sir John Moore*, 1809; *Poems*, 1812; *The Isle of Devils: A Metrical Tale*, 1827.

NONFICTION: *Journal of a West India Proprietor, Kept During a Residence in the Island of Jamaica*, 1834 (also as *Journal of a Residence Among the Negroes in the West Indies*, 1861).

TRANSLATIONS: *The Bravo of Venice: A Romance*, 1805 (of J. H. D. Zschokke's novel *Aballino der Grosse Bandit*); *Feudal Tyrants: Or, The Counts of Carlsheim and Sargans: A Romance, Taken from the German*, 1806 (four volumes; Christiane Benedicte Eugénie Naubert's novel *Elisabeth, Erbin von Toggenburg: Oder, Geschichte der Frauen in der Schweiz*).

EDITED TEXTS: *Tales of Terror*, 1799 (also as *An Apology for Tales of Terror*; includes work by Sir Walter Scott and Robert Southey); *Tales of Wonder*, 1801 (2 volumes; includes work by Scott, Southey, Robert Burns, Thomas Gray, John Dryden, and others).

MISCELLANEOUS: *Romantic Tales*, 1808 (4 volumes; includes poems, short stories, and ballads); *Twelve Ballads, the Words and Music by M. G. Lewis*, 1808; *The Life and Correspondence of M. G. Lewis, with Many Pieces Never Before Published*, 1839 (2 volumes; Margaret Baron-Wilson, editor).

BIBLIOGRAPHY

Cox, Jeffrey N. *Seven Gothic Dramas: 1789-1825*. Athens: Ohio University Press, 1992. See part 6 of Cox's introduction for a discussion of "Lewis and the Gothic Drama: Melodrama, Monodrama, and Tragedy."

Howard, Jacqueline. *Reading Gothic Fiction: A Bakhtinian Approach*. Oxford, England: Clarendon Press, 1994. See chapter 5, "Anticlerical Gothic: Matthew Lewis's *The Monk*." Recommended for advanced students with some grounding in literary theory.

Irwin, Joseph James. *M. G. "Monk" Lewis*. Boston: Twayne, 1976. Presents the life and writings of Lewis, with a concluding overview of his achievements. Discusses his family background, the beginning of his literary career in Paris, and the consequences of his second journey to Jamaica. Concentrates on *The Monk*, which brought Lewis fame and notoriety and set the standard for tales of terror. Also surveys his success and failure in the theater, with attention to his nongothic plays, such as *The East Indian*, and his poetry, praised by Sir Walter Scott and Samuel Taylor Coleridge. One chapter argues that *Journal of a West India Proprietor* is about self-discovery and has humanitarian and social importance, anticipating critical study of slavery. Includes notes, an annotated bibliography, and an index.

Kiely, Robert. *The Romantic Novel in England*. Cambridge, Mass.: Harvard University Press, 1972. An important book on Romantic prose fiction, including Lewis's gothic romances, which analyzes in depth twelve Romantic novels to define the intellectual context of the era. Notes that concepts of reality were tested and changed by Romantic novels and Edmund Burke's ideas of the sublime modified aesthetic forms. Lewis is given a prominent place in this general thesis, and *The Monk* is analyzed in detail as the focus of his chapter. Proposes that Ambrosio is a symbol of the artist and concludes that the novel is a nightmare vision of the chaos beneath the appearance of order. Finds a common drift toward death in most novels of this genre. Includes notes and an index.

Peck, Louis F. *A Life of Matthew G. Lewis*. Cambridge, Mass.: Harvard University Press, 1961. This first modern full-length biography of Lewis uses materials not available to earlier biographers, such as diaries, memoirs, and the correspondence of Lewis's contemporaries. Chapter 1 details his background and early life up to 1796 and devotes attention to *The Monk*, arguing that it was published in 1796 rather than 1795. Follows Lewis from his membership in Parliament in 1796 to the beginning of the Kelly affair in 1810, and also examines his dramas and his other prose and verse. Narrates Lewis's affairs in Jamaica and his death on board the ship returning him to England. Contains a collection of selected letters, a list of his principal works, a bibliography of works cited, notes, and an index.

Summers, Montague. *The Gothic Quest: A History of the Gothic Novel.* 1938. Reprint. New York: Russell & Russell, 1964. A pioneer study, placing gothic in the Romantic movement and examining its popularity from the success of publishers and circulating libraries. After cataloging the influences of Continental literature on English gothic writers, examines novels in the mode of the historical gothic. Gives sustained attention to Lewis's career, sketching his life, summarizing his plots, describing the public's response to each novel, and suggesting various works directly influenced by his novels and dramas. Lewis is also cited throughout the book as a major contributor to the gothic tradition. Contains sixteen illustrations, including as a frontispiece a portrait of Lewis, end notes for each chapter, and two indexes, one general and one for novels.

Varma, Devendra P. *The Gothic Flame.* London: Arthur Barker, 1957. A classic historical study of the gothic novel in England, which examines the origins of the gothic and analyzes Horace Walpole's *The Castle of Otranto* as the first novel in the genre. The study of Lewis is focused on, though not limited to, *The Monk,* showing how it derives from the taste for horror and how his writings influenced authors after him, including twentieth century American writers. Lewis was one of the earliest authors in the school of horror, emphasizing psychology, which combined with Sir Walter Scott's historical school and Ann Radcliffe's school of terror to produce Charles Robert Maturin and others. Includes three appendices, a bibliography, and an index.

(Library of Congress)

SINCLAIR LEWIS

Born: Sauk Centre, Minnesota; February 7, 1885
Died: Rome, Italy; January 10, 1951

PRINCIPAL LONG FICTION

Our Mr. Wrenn: The Romantic Adventures of a Gentle Man, 1914
The Trail of the Hawk: A Comedy of the Seriousness of Life, 1915
The Innocents: A Story for Lovers, 1917
The Job: An American Novel, 1917
Free Air, 1919
Main Street: The Story of Carol Kennicott, 1920
Babbitt, 1922
Arrowsmith, 1925
Mantrap, 1926
Elmer Gantry, 1927
The Man Who Knew Coolidge: Being the Soul of Lowell Schmaltz, Constructive and Nordic Citizen, 1928
Dodsworth, 1929
Ann Vickers, 1933
Work of Art, 1934
It Can't Happen Here, 1935
The Prodigal Parents, 1938

Bethel Merriday, 1940

Gideon Planish, 1943

Cass Timberlane: A Novel of Husbands and Wives, 1945

Kingsblood Royal, 1947

The God-Seeker, 1949

World So Wide, 1951

OTHER LITERARY FORMS

Sinclair Lewis started writing regularly during his freshman year at Yale University. His stories and poems imitating the manner of Alfred, Lord Tennyson and A. C. Swinburne appeared in the *Yale Literary Magazine*. His short stories began to appear in 1915 in *The Saturday Evening Post*. In 1934 *Jayhawker: A Play in Three Acts* was produced, and in 1935, Harcourt, Brace and Co. published the *Selected Short Stories of Sinclair Lewis*. During his lifetime, there were numerous stage and screen adaptations of many of his novels. The year after Lewis's death, Harcourt, Brace and Co. published *From Main Street to Stockholm: Letters of Sinclair Lewis, 1919-1930*, containing the novelist's correspondence with that publisher. In 1953, his miscellaneous writings appeared under the title *The Man from Main Street: Selected Essays and Other Writings, 1904-1950*.

ACHIEVEMENTS

In 1930, Lewis received the Nobel Prize in Literature, the first United States citizen so honored. He acknowledged in his acceptance address that the Swedish Academy honored American literature with this prize. By awarding it to the novelist who not only added the term "Babbitt" to the American language but also enriched the European vocabulary with his "Main Street," Europe acknowledged America's coming-of-age. There may have been a touch of condescension in the Academy's choice; the image of America that Lewis projected seemed to reinforce the European perception of the United States as a dollar-hunting, materialistic country, alien to cultural refinement.

Lewis's road to fame was stormy. He wrote five novels before he achieved his first big success with *Main Street* in 1920. Critics were divided: *The Dial* neglected his books, and academic critics Fred L. Pattee and Irving Babbitt rejected him, but, at the peak of Lewis's career, V. F. Parrington, T. K. Whipple, Constance Rourke, Walter Lippman, and Lewis Mumford acknowledged his strengths as a writer despite some reservations; H. L. Mencken enthusiastically supported him. English writers paid him tribute; among them were E. M. Forster, Rebecca West, Hugh Walpole, and John Galsworthy. They were joined by such fellow U.S. writers as F. Scott Fitzgerald and Vachel Lindsay. Lewis himself was generous with others; he helped young writers such as Thomas Wolfe and was quick to praise novelists of his own generation. In his Nobel Prize acceptance speech, which came to be called "The American Fear of Literature," he repudiated the genteel tradition, in which he included William Dean Howells, and praised Theodore Dreiser, Sherwood Anderson, and a score of younger writers. Like all his writings, this speech was regarded as controversial.

Each novel renewed the controversy; some considered him unworthy of the attention and overrated; others denounced his aggressive criticism of United States life, but after *Arrowsmith* he received favorable recognition even in *The Atlantic Monthly*, *The Nation*, *The New Republic*, *The New York Times*, the New York *Herald Tribune*, and *The Literary Review*. Indeed, his popularity in the United States reached unprecedented levels. In one decade, with the help of Harcourt, Brace and Co., he became the most widely known novelist in the country. An authentic interpreter of American life, he created self-awareness among people in the United States, yet this role was short-lived. In 1927, Walter Lippman called him a national figure, but by 1942, as Alfred Kazin pointed out, his importance was over. The short period of fame, preceded by long years of preparation, was followed by a painful period of decline marked by ten weak novels.

BIOGRAPHY

Harry Sinclair Lewis was born in Sauk Centre, Minnesota, on February 7, 1885. His father, Edwin J. Lewis, and his mother, Emma F. Kermorr, were both schoolteachers, but Edwin Lewis took a two-year medical course in Chicago and practiced as a country doctor, first in Wisconsin and later in Sauk Centre, a small Minnesota town with a population of 2,500. Harry Sinclair, nicknamed "Red" because of the color of his hair, was the third of three sons. His mother died of tuberculosis when he was three. Edwin Lewis remarried shortly after her death. The future novelist was an awkward, rather ugly, lonely child with little aptitude for sports or any type of physical exercise. He soon became an ardent reader; at an early age, he also started a diary and tried his hand at creative writing.

After a short preparation in the Oberlin Academy, Lewis became a freshman at Yale at the age of seventeen. There, too, he was a loner, even after he became a regular contributor of poems and short stories to the *Yale Literary Magazine*. In the summers of 1904 and 1906, he participated in cattle-boat trips to London, and in his senior year he left Yale. For a month, he worked as a janitor in Upton Sinclair's New Jersey commune, Helicon Hall. Since he had no financial support from his father at that time, he tried to make money, first in New York with his writing and then in Panama with work on the canal construction. Unsuccessful in both attempts, he returned to Yale and was graduated in 1908.

Between 1908 and 1915, Lewis traveled from New York to California in search of employment; he also sold story plots to other writers. From 1910 to 1915, he worked in New York for commercial publishers. In 1914, his first novel, *Our Mr. Wrenn*, was published, and on April 15, he married Grace Livingston Hegger. The couple settled in Long Island. In 1915, *The Saturday Evening Post* accepted one of Lewis's short stories for publication, the first of many to be published there. With some money at his disposal, he traveled around the country with Grace, publishing short stories and writing more novels.

The five novels following *Our Mr. Wrenn*, all published under pseudonyms, were unsuccessful, but *Main Street*, Lewis's first novel to be published by Harcourt, Brace and Co., suddenly made him famous. Never again did Lewis worry about money. With *Babbitt* his fame was firmly established. He went on a Caribbean tour in preparation for *Arrow-*

smith, and from 1923 to 1925 he traveled with Grace in Europe. It is interesting to note that Lewis loved publicity. In 1925, while working on *Elmer Gantry*, he defied God from a pulpit in Kansas City, giving God fifteen minutes to strike him down. His refusal of the Pulitzer Prize in 1926—an obvious act of anger over a previous disappointment—became an internationally broadcast event.

In 1927, Lewis separated from Grace and spent much of the next year in Europe. After Grace had obtained a Reno divorce, Lewis married Dorothy Thompson, whom he had met in Berlin, on May 14, 1928. At that time, Thompson was the best-known U.S. newspaperwoman in Europe; she also became the first U.S. journalist to be expelled from Nazi Germany. *It Can't Happen Here*, Lewis's novel about the possibility of fascism in America, was written under Thompson's influence. In 1929, Lewis published *Dodsworth*, a product of his long stay in Europe, which dealt with the American-in-Europe theme. In 1930, Lewis received the Nobel Prize and reached the peak of his fame.

After this period of renown, Lewis's life and career declined. A long-time drinking problem grew worse, and his health rapidly deteriorated. One sign of his restlessness was his break with Harcourt, Brace and Co.; he switched to Doubleday and Co. The world around him was changing rapidly; he became increasingly confused, unhappy, and lonely. In 1937, he separated from his second wife, and they were divorced in 1942. Lewis attempted to find a new career in acting and simultaneously had an affair with a young actress. His obsession with the theater is documented in *Bethel Merriday*. With *Kingsblood Royal*, a novel about racism, he once more tried his hand at an urgent contemporary issue, but his energy was decreasing. After World War II, he spent most of his time in Europe. He died in Rome, Italy, on January 10, 1951. His last novel, *World So Wide*, dedicated to "memories in Italy," was published posthumously in 1951.

ANALYSIS

Early reviews praised or condemned Sinclair Lewis for a blend of realism and optimism; indeed, a curious mixture of almost naturalistic realism and a kind of romance characterized Lewis's fiction throughout his career. He failed to solve the dichotomy in his novels, nor did he ever solve it for himself. If his characters sometimes behave as romantic rebels, so did Lewis, rebelling against a philistine lifestyle in which he was deeply rooted and to which he remained attached all his life. The five novels that made him famous, *Main Street, Babbitt, Arrowsmith, Elmer Gantry,* and *Dodsworth,* can be read as a series of variations on the same theme. Lewis exposed a United States dominated by business and petty bourgeois mentality. His characters, still full of nostalgia for the excitement of the frontier, persuade themselves that what they have at the present represents the zenith, the summit of human potential. Descendants of pious pioneer Puritans, Lewis's wealthy Americans of the 1920's are in desperate need of a civilization they can call their own. This transitory stage of the U.S. experience becomes the theme of Lewis's writings.

As Van Wyck Brooks described it, America's coming-of-age in the decade before World War I paved the way for a cultural and moral revolution, heralded by works such as Edgar Lee Masters's *Spoon River Anthology* (1915), Sherwood Anderson's *Winesburg, Ohio* (1919), and Lewis's *Main Street* and *Babbitt,* with its bitter attacks on "boobus Americanus." *Civilization in the U.S.* (1921), edited by Harold Stearns, gave a rather bleak picture of the average U.S. citizen in the 1920's—materialistic, hypocritical, and suffering from emotional and aesthetic starvation. At his best, Lewis portrayed this same world and became himself part of "the revolt from the village."

There were three distinct stages in Lewis's career. As a young novelist, he published five novels between 1914 and 1918, probing the problem of escape or the contradiction between easterners and midwesterners, favoring midwestern sincerity to eastern refinement. The 1920's were highlighted by five novels, extremely successful and ultimately winning Lewis the Nobel Prize in Literature. This glorious decade, however, was followed by a twenty-year period of decline during which he published ten inferior novels. With the passage of time, Lewis became increasingly out of touch with a rapidly changing world. While Lewis was still writing about the period of transition from exciting frontier life to small-town boredom, the United States rapidly proceeded to new phases, to radically different and exciting experiences.

The influences on him were many; he acknowledged a debt to Henry Thoreau, and among his contemporaries he had much in common with George Bernard Shaw and H. G. Wells. His ability for mimicry and for detailed observation made him a true "photographer" of life. Indeed, his novels are almost historical documents. He documented a fixed period in United States development, the frustrations and disillusionments of one generation. Unfortunately, Lewis never went beyond documentation; he re-created the symptoms but never analyzed them, never provided any formula for a meaningful life. The pattern in his books is always similar: There is a central character who—at any given moment—realizes the emptiness of his or her life and tries to break out of the mechanical boredom of the suffocating environment. The revolt is short-lived and leads nowhere. The escape ends in an impasse because Lewis himself could never solve the strange paradox of his own dislike of and attachment to Sauk Centre. If he was a loner in his native village, he remained lonely at Yale and in Europe as well. Unlike Mencken, who praised and encouraged him, Lewis was not a true iconoclast; deep down he remained attached to the values he exposed.

Lewis was an extremely hard worker; he did extensive research for each novel, carrying notebooks and drawing plans of streets, houses, furniture. All this made it possible for him to evoke a concrete world. This attention to realistic detail extended to the speech of his characters. More than any novelist of his time, Lewis made a systematic effort to record American speech from all levels of society, collecting examples of usage as if he were a student of linguistics. It is no surprise that Virginia Woolf claimed to have discovered the American language in Lewis's works. Lewis's creativity was that of a photographer with an admirable instinct for selecting his subjects but an inability to give a comprehensive evaluation of what he so diligently observed.

In his best novels, Lewis selected the most important issues of American life—villages/small towns in *Main Street*, business in *Babbitt*, science in *Arrowsmith*, religion in *Elmer Gantry*, politics in *It Can't Happen Here*, and finally, after World War II, racism in *Kingsblood Royal*—yet despite these successes, Lewis was not a great writer. As Lewis Mumford has pointed out, he was well aware of the limitations of his environment, of the lifestyle he depicted, but he lacked the strength and the imagination to overcome those very limitations in himself. The revolt in his fiction is always unsuccessful because it never presents any viable alternatives to the life Lewis opposed; he stopped at faithfully and photographically reproducing spiritual poverty.

MAIN STREET

In the year when Warren Harding was successfully campaigning for the presidency with the pledge of a "return to normalcy," Lewis captured the reading public with his *Main Street*. Stuart Sherman compared the book to Gustave Flaubert's *Madame Bovary* (1857), and Mencken praised the central characters, Carol Milford-Kennicott and her husband Dr. Will Kennicott as "triumphs of normalcy." While there are surface similarities between the plight of Emma Bovary and that of Carol Kennicott, the two characters are very different and the novels even more so. In Flaubert's novel, the emphasis is on the personal tragedy of the heroine; Lewis, on the other hand, as always, deals with a theme: the "village virus." In fact, Lewis had originally intended to give this title to the book. The village-virus syndrome was a characteristic of a certain period of U.S. life. Describing it with photographic accuracy, Lewis preserved the atmosphere of a short historical stage in U.S. development. Village novels were no rarity in literature before Lewis, but Lewis's sharp satirical approach marked a radical departure from that tradition.

Main Street, the most popular book of 1920, is deeply rooted in the author's life. Gopher Prairie, population three thousand, is modeled on Sauk Centre, Lewis's birthplace. Dr. William Kennicott is based in part on Lewis's father and on his brother Claude, who also became a doctor. Carol is partly Lewis himself, the romantic side of him. Born in Minnesota, she is not exactly a village girl when she first appears in the novel. It is 1906 and she is a student at Blodgett College near Minneapolis. Her studies in professional library work take her to Chicago, the center of a poetic revival in the twentieth century. There she is exposed to the benefits of America's coming-of-age: the Art Institute, classical music, intellectual discussions on Sigmund Freud, Romain Rolland, syndicates, feminism, radically new thinking in philosophy, politics, and art. She has a job at St. Paul's public library when she meets Dr. Kennicott. The bulk of the novel is about their married life in Gopher Prairie, where Will works as a country doctor; it covers the years 1912 to 1920, from World War I and the United States participation in the war to 1920, the cynical decade of the Jazz Age. The United States was passing into a new period in which the political and economic fiber of the country came to be shaped and determined in cities rather than rural communities. *Main Street* is not so much a chronicle of Carol Kennicott's life between 1912 and 1920 as it is a documentation of the national phenomenon of the village virus.

The village virus is best described by Gopher Prairie's frustrated liberal, Guy Pollock. He defines it as a vicious disease menacing ambitious people who stay too long in places such as Gopher Prairie. The small-town atmosphere breeds boredom, dullness, stupidity, complacency, and vulgarity, causing the inhabitants to wither away spiritually and become the living dead. Only a few of the inhabitants see Gopher Prairie as a menace. All the "important" people of the community—Ole Jensen, the grocer; Ezra Stowbody, the banker; Sam Clark, owner of a hardware store—take pride in Main Street. When she first sees Main Street, Carol is terrified by its repulsive ugliness, but to the others it constitutes the "climax of civilization."

All the people to whom Carol is drawn are outsiders in the community. Except for the resigned Guy Pollock, they all leave, disappointed and frustrated, or else die. Village atheist and political radical Miles Bjornstrom leaves after his wife and child die of typhoid. Before her death, his wife Bea, formerly Carol's maid, is Carol's only confidante in Gopher Prairie. The young, idealistic teacher Fern Mullins is cruelly driven out of town by Mrs. Bogart, the hypocritical watchdog of Puritan morality, and her son Cy Bogart, the village bully. Erik Valborg, an artistically minded eccentric with whom Carol almost engages in a love affair, leaves because of gossip. Those who always triumph are the Bogarts and Stowbodys; they succeed in slowly killing all of Carol's romantic ambitions.

When Carol arrives in Gopher Prairie, she is determined to bring about changes for the better. Much of the novel is about her frustrated reform efforts. Again and again she tries to initiate new and fresh ideas and plans, but all of them fail because of the all-pervasive spiritual emptiness of Gopher Prairie. People there are not interested in poetry nor in theater nor in intellectual discussions. Will Kennicott proves to be the gentle husband through all of his wife's efforts and failures. Though he does not understand Carol's frustration, he not only stands by her but also tries to help in every way he can.

Carol leaves Gopher Prairie with their son just as the war is ending. Will is there to wave good-bye as the train taking her to Washington, D.C., pulls out of the station. In the nation's capital, Carol is on her own; she tries to find her identity, tries to become a whole person, not simply a wife. She succeeds and enjoys the opportunity of a new life in which she can be active and in which she can use her brain once again, as she did in her girlhood, but she learns something else too: The radical changes in the behavior and attitudes of the young girls around her shock her as much as her behavior once had shocked a sleepy Gopher Prairie. In the end, she returns with Will to their home and settles down in Gopher Prairie, this time permanently. She still has dreams for her baby girl and likes to picture her as a future feminist or scientist; to the end, Carol remains a dreamer rather than a doer.

The last word in the novel belongs to the pragmatic Will Kennicott. He is Lewis's real favorite—the simple country doctor who performs acts of quiet heroism and worries about matters such as putting up storm windows. Lewis is unquestionably drawn to this stable, dependable, and reliable man, representing in his view the best of middle-class America.

Lewis only halfheartedly endorses Carol's romantic attempts at beautifying Gopher Prairie because he himself was of divided mind whom to prefer: the artistically minded Carol or the always commonsensical though unsophisticated Will. If the cigarette-smoking modern young girls of the 1920's shocked Carol, Lewis, too, was unable to catch up with new trends. In this sense, *Main Street*, a novel about the village virus, is also an autobiography of Sinclair Lewis's spiritual development or, rather, spiritual stagnation.

The year 1921 was highlighted by an outburst of favorable and unfavorable reactions to this novel. First, there emerged a series of Main Street literature, attacking, burlesquing, and imitating the original, among them Carolyn Wells's *Ptomaine Street*, Meredith Nicholson's *Let Main Street Alone*, and Donald Ogden Stewart's *A Parody Outline of History*. At the same time, dramatized by Harving O'Higgins and Harrier Ford, *Main Street* was performed at New York's National Theater.

BABBITT

Even before he finished *Main Street*, Lewis had started work on *Babbitt*, a novel about a land speculator. From Main Street, U.S.A., "the climax of civilization," the novelist moved to an imaginary city in the Middle West, satirically named Zenith, symbolizing the average U.S. city and its status-symbol-oriented population. Set in the boom decade of the 1920's, the novel concentrates on the new national disease, which came to be called "Babbittry," after the book's protagonist. Webster's dictionary would define a Babbitt as "a seemingly self-satisfied businessman who readily conforms to the norms and ideas of middle-class society." The term "seemingly" is important; it indicates that even in this realistic, satirical presentation of middle-class America and its business culture, Lewis's romantic side is present; it finds outlet in Babbitt's dissatisfaction with his life. Predominantly, though, the almost photographic portrayal of Zenith prevails. While President Harding was hoping to plant a Rotary Club in every city and village in the country to ensure the propagation of American ideals, Lewis was provoking the anger of those very Rotary Clubs by holding up a mirror to their Tartuffe-like hypocrisy and their materialistic culture.

Just as *Main Street* killed the friendly village novel by concentrating on the village virus, so *Babbitt* undercut the traditional business novel. With *Babbitt*, Lewis demonstrated that the era of the independent, creative tycoon was over. The tycoon gave way to the joiner, the conformist relying on status symbols and good public relations rather than daring and creative initiative. Babbitt, positively no giant, is almost a pathetic figure in his desperate need for approval. Far from being a tycoon, he lacks any individual ideas. He is a Booster, an Elk, a Presbyterian, a member of the chamber of commerce, a family man—nothing more. Senators of the Republican Party prescribe his political beliefs; national advertisers dictate his preferences in consumer goods. Without all these accessories, he is nobody; Babbitt is spiritually empty. While he relies on the sham values that make him a "solid citizen," he becomes a pitiful victim of mechanical gadgets; his identity depends on having a car, the most technologically advanced alarm clock, and a royal bathroom.

Lewis worked very hard on this novel, which some critics consider his best. He prepared detailed maps of Zenith, plans of the decoration and furniture of Babbitt's house. The mimicry of language is superb, culminating in Babbitt's famous address at the meeting of the Zenith Real Estate Board. In his speech, Babbitt pours scorn on moth-eaten, old-fashioned Europe and glorifies the city of Success, known "wherever condensed milk and paste-board cartons are known." The pitiful, empty world of Zenith is presented in loosely connected episodes, the sequence of which could almost be changed, and which are held together only by the presence of Babbitt. These episodes take the reader through the most important aspects of middle-class life: politics, leisure, clubs, class, labor, religion, and family.

This apparent contentment, however, is one side of the novel; Babbitt is only "seemingly" satisfied. In reality, this prosperous real estate agent passionately desires something more and different from mere material success. This desire leads to his unsuccessful, vague, romantic rebellion against the Zenith world.

Closely linked to his desire for escape is his long-standing friendship with Paul Riesling. Paul is one of those lonely, out-of-the-ordinary characters who emerge in all Lewis novels—creative, individualistic, nonconformist. With Paul, Babbitt escapes to Maine, but the escape does not help; his frustration remains.

Amid this frustration, crisis enters Babbitt's life. Paul is condemned to three years in prison for shooting his wife in what is described as temporary insanity. Without Paul, life seems impossible for Babbitt to bear; he tries to leave Zenith again but very soon returns. Zenith is the only thing in the world he knows; without it he is empty, a nobody. Like Lewis, who could never get rid of Sauk Centre, Babbitt takes Zenith with him wherever he goes. For a while, he tries to outrage Zenith society by drinking heavily and by associating with the wrong people—with the adventuress Tanis Judique and her bohemian friends, called the Bunch. At the same time, Vergil Gunch, one of the exemplary solid citizens, is organizing the Good Citizens' League. Babbitt shocks all his former friends and associates by defying Vergil's request to join their antilabor vigilante organization.

In *Main Street*, Lewis made Carol Kennicott return to Gopher Prairie. In a similar spirit of compromise, he finds a convenient way for Babbitt to give up his empty rebellion. His wife Myra has to undergo emergency surgery; her hospitalization pulls Babbitt back to his duties as a solid citizen. To seal his return to normalcy, he joins the Good Citizens' League. At the end of the novel, he is taken by surprise by his younger son; Ted drops out of school and elopes. In a private, man-to-man talk with his son, Babbitt acknowledges that he admires him for doing what he wants. He, Babbitt, never did that in all his life. In *Main Street*, Carol Kennicott's rebellion dwindles to romantic dreams for her daughter; all that remains of Babbitt's rebellion is his pleasure in his son's defiance and an encouragement not to let himself be bullied by Zenith. At the moment, however, Ted does not hold out much promise; rather than going to college he wants to be a mechanic at a factory.

Although *Babbitt* outraged certain sectors of the business community, the novel became an international success. Europeans loved it even more than

Main Street. They enjoyed seeing the United States portrayed as they believed it was: materialistic, vulgar, standardized, and hopelessly without culture. They enjoyed the language; the British edition even added a glossary of 125 "American" terms. It is interesting to note that even while the novel was being angrily attacked, a number of midwestern cities claimed to have been the model for Zenith. Without offering any cure, simply by diagnosing and photographically reproducing symptoms of a national phenomenon, Lewis promoted self-awareness among his many readers.

Critics who wondered whether Lewis himself was Babbitt, lacking all spiritual ideals, were surprised by *Arrowsmith*, which featured an idealistic hero with spiritual values. In 1922, while gathering material in Chicago for a labor novel, Lewis met Paul de Kruif, a University of Michigan teacher of bacteriology experienced in immunology research. They became friends, and Lewis changed his plans; assisted by Paul de Kruif's expertise, he decided to write a novel on the medical profession. Lewis had some personal experience on which to draw; his father, his brother Claude, an uncle, and a grandfather were doctors. He needed help, however, in the field of scientific research; that is what de Kruif provided. Because a plague in the West Indies was to be an important part of the novel, they took a tour in the Caribbean together. De Kruif stayed with Lewis in England while he was working on *Arrowsmith*, a well-researched novel and his best-plotted one.

ARROWSMITH

Arrowsmith was an instant success, being the first American novel about a medical researcher. The central character, Martin Arrowsmith, is a real hero with a purpose: He is wholly dedicated to pure science. The plot develops around the dramatic conflict between Martin, a few others of the same mind, and a society based on profit. Arrowsmith, Gottlieb, Sondelius, and Terry Wickett are akin to earlier idealists in Lewis's fiction, to Eric Valborg in *Main Street* and Paul Riesling in *Babbitt*, but there is a significant difference. Eric and Paul are lonely figures; Martin and his associates are not alone and they do not give up; they put up a fight against the commercial standards of a society that does not understand their ideals.

Martin Arrowsmith is introduced on the first page of the novel as a fourteen-year-old boy sitting in a country doctor's office. From his hometown of Elk Mills, the hero moves on to college to pursue his dreams; he regards himself as a "seeker of truth." At the University of Winnemac, young Martin associates with two kinds of people who symbolize the opposing forces of material versus purely scientific values. On one hand, there are the people involved in fraternity life; on the other, there is the German-born biologist, Max Gottlieb, modeled on Jacques Loeb, who allows Martin to work in his lab. Two events disrupt the smooth course of young Martin's drive to achieve his goal. First, he meets a nurse, Leora Tozer, and they fall in love; then, an irritable Gottlieb dismisses him from the laboratory. Martin and Leora marry, and, after an internship in Zenith General Hospital, they settle down in Wheatsylvania, North Dakota, responding to pressure from Leora's family.

As a country practitioner, Martin finds himself in a situation well known to Lewis. The young idealist who hopes to become another Robert Koch is increasingly in the position of a businessman in rivalry with other country doctors. At the same time, Martin's idol Gottlieb is undergoing a similar experience. After his defeat at Winnemac, he is faced with a new crisis in Pittsburgh when he refuses the request of a large pharmaceutical firm to have his antitoxin patented. Finally, a frustrated Martin escapes to Nautilus, Iowa, another Zenith, and then to the Rouncefield Clinic in Chicago. One of his articles catches the attention of Gottlieb, now associated with the McGurk Institute of Biology in New York, and the two are reunited. Martin even finds a new kindred spirit in Terry Wickett. Life at the Rouncefield Clinic and then at the McGurk Institute provides ample occasion for Lewis to describe the internal rivalry in such institutions, the pressures from outside and the search for power and fame.

When a severe plague erupts in the West Indies, Martin's recent discovery catches the attention of the outside world; this is the most dramatic part of the novel. Gottlieb's approach is not philanthropic but scientific. He wants Martin to use the antitoxin only with half of the patients so that its true value can be tested, but on the islands Martin is faced with real people. His faithful assistant Sondelius dies, and so does Leora. He initially intends to be a scientist and not a sentimentalist, but in the end he gives in, hoping to save more lives. On his return to New York, he finds changes at the Institute; Gottlieb is pensioned, and the new director is all for "practicalness." The frustrated Martin marries a wealthy socialite, Joyce Lanyon, and they have a baby; however, Martin and his friend Terry find themselves out of place in the Institute under the new direction, and Martin does not find in Joyce the companion he had in Leora. The two friends escape to Vermont to fish and to pursue their drive for pure science. While commercial society in Washington and elsewhere continues in its Babbitt-Zenith ways, Martin and Terry discuss quinine research in their boat.

The conclusion is rather romantic, sentimental, and unsatisfactory, but despite this flaw and some misgivings on the part of the medical community, *Arrowsmith* was universally acclaimed. Even the Pulitzer Prize, so far denied Lewis, was his, but he refused to accept it at that time. The retreat to Vermont in *Arrowsmith* was no real solution to the dilemma, but once again Lewis had presented, and called attention to, a genuine problem in American society. *Arrowsmith* celebrates an unwillingness to compromise and a dedication to ideals, which give this novel a heroic dimension missing in all other Lewis novels.

ELMER GANTRY

Lewis dedicated *Elmer Gantry* "with profound admiration" to Mencken, and rightly so, because in this novel the romantic side of the novelist is overshadowed by a brutal, iconoclastic, almost fanatical satire. From his idealistic excursion in *Arrowsmith*, Lewis returned to his former mood, except that this time he created in the central character a complete villain. Elmer Gantry is the American Tartuffe. The reader can feel compassion for Carol Kennicott and pity toward Babbitt, but there is absolutely no saving grace for Elmer Gantry, the fundamentalist preacher in Lewis's novel.

Elmer Gantry was probably Lewis's most thoroughly researched novel. In 1922, a preacher named William Stidger suggested to Lewis that he write a novel on the subject of religion. In the anti-Puritan 1920's, religious life was in disarray in America. When Lewis finally decided to write a novel on the topic, he went to Kansas City in search of Stidger, living there for a considerable time in order to prepare material for *Elmer Gantry*. In Kansas City, he visited churches, preached himself, and investigated and worked with a group of fifteen clergymen of various denominations in what he called "Sinclair Lewis's Sunday Work Class." There were tragic events in his own life while he was working on the novel: His father died, his marriage with Grace broke up, and he was literally drunk when writing the final pages in New York.

The most obvious characteristic of the novel is its brutality; there is no trace of that sympathy which mitigated the dark picture in *Main Street* or *Babbitt*; there is no trace of a love/hate relationship with Elmer Gantry. Neither he nor the novel's other major characters have many redeeming qualities. The novel, indeed, is an uncompromising indictment of American religious practices in the early century. This most devastating of Lewis's satires is similar to *Babbitt* in that it is loosely structured and episodic. Its three main parts concern Elmer Gantry's involvement with three different women. In no other Lewis novel is the sexual element as important as in this one; it is Gantry's sexual desire that threatens his rise in religious circles.

The young Elmer Gantry attends a Baptist college and is ordained a minister. As soon as he receives his first pulpit, he becomes sexually involved with a young girl. He gets rid of Lulu by casting doubt on her character, revealing the depths of falsehood and villainy of which he is capable. In the second phase of his religious career, he becomes an evangelist, the partner (religious and sexual) of the female evangelist Sharon Falcon. They are two of a kind who never consider "their converts as human beings"; they regard them as a surgeon regards his patients or as a fisherman regards trout. Sharon dies in a fire, and Elmer Gantry's adventures take him to the Methodist denomination. There, he rises quickly and is promoted to pastorates in larger and larger communities. He is made a Doctor of Divinity, marries, becomes the first preacher whose sermons are broadcast, and tours Europe. Suddenly his fame and position are almost destroyed by a new love affair. Hettie and her convict husband try to outwit Gantry; they set a trap for him. For a short time he is frightened, but influential and clever friends come to his rescue and he bounces back. At the end of the novel, he is leading his congregation in prayer, determined "to make these United States a moral nation." Like all true hypocrites, Gantry convinces himself of his sincerity.

Understandably, the novel outraged churches all over the United States. Some clergy even called Lewis "Satan's cohort," but the book sold 175,000 copies in less than six weeks, and a motion picture was made of the novel in 1960.

DODSWORTH

With *Dodsworth*, Lewis returned to Zenith. At the beginning of the novel, Sam Dodsworth, a successful businessman in his forties, undergoes a crisis similar to Babbitt's, but there the similarities end. Sam, a Yale graduate, is much better educated than Babbitt and is receptive to the arts. A self-made man, he built his own company, but, following the prevailing trend in America, his small business is bought by a conglomerate. This causes the active, enterprising Sam to believe himself to be a useless part of a big bureaucratic machine and provides an opportunity for his snobbish wife Fran to persuade him to go with her on a long European tour. This trip takes up the major part of the novel, which is a rather shallow treatment of Henry James's "international theme."

Sam Dodsworth does not know how to spend his wealth or his leisure time meaningfully; also, he is painfully gauche. In spite of these flaws, the author's sympathies are with him. Sam is trying hard to please his empty-headed wife. In her utter stupidity, Fran tries to imitate the worst symptoms of the decaying European aristocracy. At the end, she takes a lover and proposes divorce to Sam in hope of an exciting marriage. These plans fail, and Sam is there to rescue her, but their marriage cannot be saved. Lewis condemns the superficiality of European high society, but he is far from criticizing European culture; his satire is concentrated on Fran. Finally, Sam finds an understanding companion in a widow, Edith Cort-

right, who appreciates his honesty and integrity, likes him for what he is, and does not want to change him into something else. At the end of the novel, they are in Paris discussing marriage, but they are planning to return to the United States, where they know they belong.

Significantly, Lewis always turned back to the middle class for his subject matter. In *It Can't Happen Here* inspired by Dorothy Thompson's anti-Fascist stand, Lewis exposed the danger inherent in right-wing extremism in the United States; however, at the end of the 1930's, when the new left-wing writers hoped to see him write a proletarian novel, the essentially middle-class Lewis could not accommodate them.

During the long and painful years of his decline, Lewis tried to continue to focus on issues of importance—the career woman (*Ann Vickers*); organized philanthropy (*Gideon Planish*); American marriage (*Cass Timberlane*). American life was changing too rapidly for Lewis, however; he was never able to catch up with the changes. He did hit upon an important theme in *Kingsblood Royal*, but by that time his greatest ability—to re-create the world around him in photographic detail—seemed to have abandoned him.

Lewis's aesthetic shortcomings are obvious, but so are his merits. A writer of international reputation, he made American literature acceptable in Europe, becoming the first American winner of the Nobel Prize in Literature. His *Main Street* was one of the most sensational successes in U.S. publishing history. His biographer, Mark Schorer, describes him as a major force in the liberating of twentieth century American literature. Yet, by the turn of the twenty-first century, he was virtually ignored by critics. A well-balanced, objective evaluation of this controversial novelist is long overdue; the necessary distance in time should soon make it possible.

Anna B. Katona

OTHER MAJOR WORKS

SHORT FICTION: *Selected Short Stories of Sinclair Lewis*, 1935.

PLAY: *Jayhawker: A Play in Three Acts*, pr. 1934 (with Lloyd Lewis).

NONFICTION: *From Main Street to Stockholm: Letters of Sinclair Lewis, 1919-1930*, 1952 (Harrison Smith, editor); *The Man from Main Street: Selected Essays and Other Writings, 1904-1950*, 1953 (Harry E. Maule and Melville H. Crane, editors).

BIBLIOGRAPHY

Bloom, Harold, ed. *Modern Critical Views: Sinclair Lewis.* New York: Chelsea House, 1987. Bloom has gathered together an excellent spread of criticism on Lewis. Essays range from an analysis of *Arrowsmith* to discussion on the tension between romanticism and realism in his work. Bloom's introduction comments on the irony that the satirist Lewis should be remembered for the "idealizing romance" of *Arrowsmith*.

Bucco, Martin, ed. *Critical Essays on Sinclair Lewis.* Boston: G. K. Hall, 1986. Divided into two large sections of contemporary reviews of Lewis's novels and essay-length studies. The essays deal with the quality of the novels, Lewis's use of humor, his treatment of art and artists and of American businesses and philistinism. Bucco provides an introduction but no bibliography.

_____. *Main Street: The Revolt of Carol Kennicott.* New York: Twayne, 1993. One of Twayne's masterwork studies, this work explores closely the characterization in *Main Street* and its effects on literature.DiRenzo, Anthony. *If I Were Boss: The Early Business Stories of Sinclair Lewis.* Carbondale: Southern Illinois University Press, 1997. The introduction provides an excellent overview of Lewis's work in journalism, advertising, and public relations and shows how he developed in his early short fiction the themes that would distinguish his mature novels. The rest of the book makes available stories that have been out of print since their first publication.

Koblas, John J. *Sinclair Lewis: Home at Last.* Bloomington, Minn.: Voyageur Press, 1981. A look at Lewis's life and his midwestern roots, from which he tried to remove himself but to which he continually returned in his fiction. A valuable study, with much insight into the author and the places that were meaningful to him.

Light, Martin. *The Quixotic Vision of Sinclair Lewis.* West Lafayette, Ind.: Purdue University Press, 1975. A respected critic of Lewis, Light examines the conflict of realism and romance, which he terms the quixotic element, in Lewis's work. An invaluable and perceptive critical study of Lewis.

Love, Glen A. *Babbitt: An American Life.* New York: Twayne, 1993. Another in Twayne's masterwork studies, this volume examines *Babbitt* and its importance in U.S. society.

Parrington, Vernon Louis. *Sinclair Lewis: Our Own Diogenes.* Seattle: University of Washington Press, 1927. Reprint. New York: Haskell House, 1973. An essay on Lewis that discusses his role as the "bad boy of letters." Looks at Lewis's disillusionment through his novels *Babbitt* and *Arrowsmith*. A good example of critical thinking of the 1920's.

Schorer, Mark, ed. *Sinclair Lewis: A Collection of Critical Essays.* Englewood Cliffs, N.J.: Prentice-Hall, 1962. A compilation of criticism from H. L. Mencken's "Consolation" (1922) to Geoffrey Moore's "Sinclair Lewis: A Lost Romantic" (1959). A useful complement to the more current criticism available in Bloom's volume.

WYNDHAM LEWIS

Born: Amherst, Canada; November 18, 1882
Died: London, England; March 7, 1957

PRINCIPAL LONG FICTION
Tarr, 1918, 1928
The Childermass, 1928
The Apes of God, 1930
Snooty Baronet, 1932
The Revenge for Love, 1937
The Vulgar Streak, 1941
Self Condemned, 1954
The Human Age: Monstre Gai and Malign Fiesta, 1955
The Red Priest, 1956

(Library of Congress)

The Roaring Queen, 1973 (wr. 1936)
Mrs. Dukes' Million, 1977

OTHER LITERARY FORMS

In addition to ten book-length works of fiction (including the trilogy *The Human Age*), Wyndham Lewis published more than thirty other books in his lifetime; two novels, a volume of letters, and numerous collections of previously unpublished or uncollected material have appeared since his death. This mass of material is awesome in its diversity as well as in its bulk. It includes three volumes of short stories (*The Wild Body*, 1927; *Rotting Hill*, 1951; *Unlucky for Pringle*, 1973); two plays and a book of poems (*The Ideal Giant*, 1917; *Enemy of the Stars*, 1914, 1932; *One-Way Song*, 1933; these have been brought together in *Collected Poems and Plays*, 1979); and two autobiographies (*Blasting and Bombardiering*, 1937; *Rude Assignment: A Narrative of My Career Up-to-Date*, 1950). The bulk of Lewis's writing, however, is not fictional nor, strictly speaking, literary. He wrote enough art criticism to fill one

volume (*Wyndham Lewis on Art*, 1969) and enough literary criticism to fill several (*Men Without Art*, 1934; *The Writer and the Absolute*, 1952; *Enemy Salvos*, 1976), but even while writing such criticism he always focused on the political, cultural, and philosophical implications of the works of art. In keeping with this, Lewis wrote extensively on politics and philosophy, and his work of this kind should probably be called political, cultural, and philosophical criticism, as in these books he was always on the attack. Far and away the best known and most important of these works is *Time and Western Man* (1927); E. W. F. Tomlin's fine anthology, *Wyndham Lewis: An Anthology of His Prose* (1969), provides an excellent selection from the rest. A collection of essays, *Creatures of Habit, Creatures of Change*, appeared in 1989.

ACHIEVEMENTS

It is often, and probably correctly, said that Lewis's actual achievements fell far short of what he should have achieved, given his immense talents. Those talents were widely recognized by some of his most eminent contemporaries: T. S. Eliot called him "the most fascinating personality of our time" and "the greatest prose master of style of my generation—perhaps the only one to have invented a new style"; W. B. Yeats read his philosophical work "with ever-growing admiration and envy"; Ezra Pound thought that he should have won the Nobel Prize for his late novel *Self Condemned*. Yet he did not win, and, unlike these friends and admirers, he never became a household name. Lewis continues to appeal only to a small—if devoted—audience.

In a sense, Lewis had too much talent. Painter and writer, novelist and critic, philosopher and political thinker, he tried to do everything. He simply wrote too much and did too many different kinds of writing to achieve perfection in any one thing. In this, he is more like Ford Madox Ford or D. H. Lawrence than Eliot or James Joyce, who wrote little and therefore had time to perfect everything. Lewis's achievement is scattered across forty or fifty books, which makes it difficult to see his work as a whole or to find the right place to start. Each book has its interest; none is perfect.

Each book *does* have its interest, however, which is no mean achievement considering the size of Lewis's oeuvre. A constant source of interest is the personal nature of Lewis's work. No advocate of impersonality, in the manner of Gustave Flaubert, Henry James, or James Joyce, Lewis is on constant display in his work. More like a Victorian than a modern, in the tradition of, for example, Thomas Carlyle, he also resembles Carlyle in that the personality displayed is partisan, contentious, opinionated, domineering, and eccentric. This is probably why Lewis, virtually alone among modern British novelists, managed to write intellectually rich fiction. Ideas, far more than character or plot, are the fundamental material for Lewis's novels, which at times seem more like long arguments than narratives. Lewis wrote, of course, a great deal of nonfiction, and the fiction and the nonfiction interpenetrate. One finds in *The Childermass*, for example, essentially the same analysis of contemporary politics as that found in *The Art of Being Ruled* (1926).

Lewis's novels, however, are not simply *romans à thèse*, illustrations of points of view found in the nonfiction. In many cases, they are much more interesting and vital than the nonfiction. The reason for this is Lewis's unforgettable style, which Eliot rightly saw as strikingly original. The originality and achievement of his style also stem from his overwhelming presence in his works. Never striving for the objective representation of the familiar world, which is the aim of the realistic novelist, Lewis through his style uncompromisingly creates a world of his own. Some of his novels are what would today be called science fiction; the majority, set in contemporary society, are not. Whatever the genre of Lewis's novels, however, he always keeps one aware that one is reading a novel written by Wyndham Lewis. Many readers may find this irritating, preferring the pretense of the conventional novel that it is not a fiction, that it is about something that really happened. Indeed, one aspect of Lewis's considerable achievement as a novelist is that he anticipated by a full generation the self-conscious fiction of Jorge Luis Borges, Flann O'Brien, Alain Robbe-Grillet, John Barth, and others.

Lewis's achievement as a novelist, in short, is that, though he may not have written a single work of the stature of *Ulysses* (1922), he is always intelligent, always interesting; in the era of postmodernism, he is a contemporary to an extent that others of his generation such as Eliot or Joyce, let alone E. M. Forster or Lawrence, are not.

BIOGRAPHY

Percy Wyndham Lewis was born on his father's sailboat off Nova Scotia in 1882. His parents made an improbable couple, his father an independently wealthy American from upstate New York, his mother an Englishwoman who returned to England with her child after the marriage collapsed when Lewis was ten. Lewis then attended a number of schools, including Rugby, without distinction and finally went to the Slade School of Art in London from 1898 to 1901. After that came an extended period of wandering through Europe, particularly Germany, France, and Spain. The ostensible purpose of these travels was to paint and to study painting, but Lewis also saw himself as a writer, and his first appearance in print, in *The English Review* in 1909, was with a sketch drawn from his travels.

By 1912, the family finances could no longer support such travels, and Lewis returned to London to make his mark in the art world. He founded an art movement, vorticism, published a magazine, *Blast*, which caused a sensation though it only appeared twice, and created a distinctively vorticist style in both painting and writing. By 1914, the year of the vorticist movement, it looked as if he were on the verge of a brilliant career, but World War I interrupted these plans. Vorticism came to an end in the war, and Lewis fought in the trenches in France as a bombardier.

Keeping a much lower profile after the war, Lewis, though he continued to paint, saw himself and was seen more and more as a writer. He published twenty-six books between 1926 and the outbreak of World War II. These works aroused considerable controversy, both because of Lewis's satiric attacks on well-known literary figures and because of the often outrageous stands he took on political questions in the

1930's. This meant that he was increasingly isolated as a writer and painter, an isolation made absolute during World War II, when he and his wife, Anne, whom he had married in 1929, lived mostly in Canada.

This isolation lessened after World War II. Lewis became the regular art critic of *The Listener* until he went blind in 1951. He received various tributes, including an honorary D.Litt., a Civil List Pension, and a major Tate Gallery retrospective in 1956. In a final burst of energy, he published one book per year the last eight years of his life, some of his finest works among them, even though he was dying from the tumor which had first made him blind. Lewis died in March, 1957. It is reported that his last words, addressed to a nurse, were, appropriately enough for a man of his temperament, "Mind your own business."

Analysis

Wyndham Lewis published his first novel, *Tarr*, in 1918. *Tarr, The Childermass*, and *The Apes of God*—Lewis's first novels—are essentially about the satiric comment of someone committed to art and the intellect on the limitations of those committed to the values of life and the body.

Tarr

Tarr began as two separate stories which grew and were fused together, somewhat awkwardly, to form the novel. The first, which can be called "Tarr," is about Frederick Tarr, a young English painter living in bohemian Paris and engaged to a German, Bertha Lunken. Tarr is full of opinions about everything, and his part of the book is mostly taken up by his disquisitions, primarily on aesthetics. The other story, "Kreisler," is about an impoverished German sculptor, Otto Kreisler. Kreisler, as contemptible a failure in life as in art, runs out of money, rapes Bertha, gets in a duel, kills his opponent before the duel can take place, and finally commits suicide. The basic split between Tarr and Kreisler runs throughout Lewis's fiction. Mind and body, intellect and emotion, art and life—these are some of the obvious terms for expressing this split.

The Childermass

The Childermass and *The Apes of God* are considerably more dense, difficult, and ambitious works than *Tarr*. *The Childermass*, first published in 1928, is the first book of *The Human Age*, books 2 and 3 of which were not published until 1955, but it really stands on its own. Set in the life after death, it also divides into two parts. The first is about how James Pullman and Satterthwaite, a famous writer and his "fag" at school, make their way to the camp of the Bailiff outside what they take to be Heaven. The second half is a long debate, mostly between Hyperides, a Tarr-like figure who sounds remarkably like the Lewis who wrote *The Art of Being Ruled* and *Time and Western Man*, and the Bailiff, the political ruler of at least this corner of the afterlife, not Heaven at all, as Pullman slowly grasps.

The Apes of God

The Apes of God is set in contemporary London. A vicious satire in which most of the targets of Lewis's satire are recognizable, it is a prolonged attack on Bloomsbury, which Lewis saw as full of people aping their God, the artist, and in the process making the life of the genuine artist impossible. Everyone here is a follower of the Bailiff, or his worldly equivalent; the only person in the novel who does not seem to be an ape, Pierpoint, remains offstage, only speaking through disciples who, the reader should soon see, are as apelike as the rest.

Neither *The Childermass* nor *The Apes of God* can be taken lightly. One either takes their vision and judgment of contemporary society very seriously or one cannot take them at all. They have been praised very highly by Ezra Pound, I. A. Richards, and others, and they are probably Lewis's ultimate achievements in the sense of being the most unusual, the most personal, and the most Lewisian of his works. Nevertheless, most readers find them unreadable. They are, frankly, very difficult to read; W. B. Yeats, no stranger to difficult texts, called one passage in *The Childermass* "the most obscure piece of writing known to me." This difficulty is deliberate: Lewis is trying to defamiliarize the world for his readers, to present it, not as it is habitually seen, but as it should be seen. Lewis sees most people as little more than automata or machines, so he presents them in his fiction as such. This satiric strategy can have one of two effects on a reader; in neither case is Lewis left with much of an audience. Either the reader grasps the satiric point Lewis is trying to make, or he takes Lewis's novels as eccentric mythologies. Those who grasp the point are likely to feel insulted, for the reader is subsumed in Lewis's vision under the category of ape as well; those who appreciate mythological or fantastic fiction tend to prefer more genial mythologies.

Lewis himself must have sensed the problems inherent in *The Childermass* and *The Apes of God*, for the novels he wrote in the 1930's, *Snooty Baronet, The Roaring Queen*, and *Revenge for Love*, are very different. The first important difference is that in them Lewis abandons the attempt to write fiction as though no one else had written any before. There are no formal models for *Tarr, The Childermass*, and *The Apes of God*; they obey no generic laws of any kind, which is much of the reason why they seem so sprawling, so formless. Lewis's novels of the 1930's, by contrast, are generic parodies: *The Revenge for Love* is a political thriller, *Snooty Baronet* a travel book-cum-murder mystery, and *The Roaring Queen* a country house weekend novel, a parody of early Aldous Huxley and Evelyn Waugh. The second important difference is that none of these novels contains the all-knowing Lewis persona who comments on the action. They do express much the same vision of man: Human desires seem just as bizarre, as animalistic, as trivial in *Snooty Baronet* as they do in *The Apes of God*. What is missing is the eternal comment on this vision: Lewis abandons the static novel of ideas and presents his vision far more through what happens than what is said. These two changes make his novels of the 1930's far less intense and far more enjoyable to read.

How Lewis could have written *Snooty Baronet* two years after writing *The Apes of God* has long mystified critics. In 1977, however, *Mrs. Dukes' Million*, a novel Lewis began in 1908, about when he began *Tarr*, was published and made this shift far more comprehensible, though it made Lewis's beginnings as a novelist look much more complicated. *Mrs. Dukes' Million* is a fascinating if bizarre attempt at a detective thriller. Lewis frankly wrote it for money, but he could not quite write a straight example of the genre, so *Mrs. Dukes' Million* ends up being the same kind of parodic genre novel as *Snooty Baronet*. Thus, Lewis's impulses as a novelist were divided from the beginning: On the one hand, he wanted to be a serious novelist of ideas and a modernist innovator, which led to difficult, static works such as *The Apes of God*; on the other hand, he had a tremendous talent for narration and for a subversive handling of genre.

THE REVENGE FOR LOVE

In Lewis's greatest novel, *The Revenge for Love*, he manages to put these impulses together. *The Revenge for Love* is a satire on 1930's leftism, on the "parlour pinks" of London, and on the tremendous gap between the humanitarian idealism of these figures and the murderous nature of the ideology they espouse. It is as biting and incisive as *The Apes of God*, yet this commentary is embedded in a fast-moving thriller plot about smuggling arms into Republican Spain. Lewis's use of the thriller genre is perfectly opposite because *The Revenge for Love* is a meditation on the nature and value of action, and the thriller is the novel of action *par excellence*. Hence, the playful and the serious sides of Lewis's art come together perfectly in what is one of the most underrated novels of the twentieth century.

A new note is also struck in *The Revenge for Love*, a note that was to predominate in the major novels Lewis wrote after World War II, *Self Condemned* and books 2 and 3 of *The Human Age, Monstre Gai*, and *Malign Fiesta*. In the first part of his career, until *The Revenge for Love*, Lewis had been absolutely sure of his position, of his values, of his satirical critique of man. Lewis's role, as he saw it, was to castigate man for his lack of freedom and his deadness. In this role, he called himself the "Enemy" and set out to oppose virtually everything in the name of art, the intellect, and detachment. In *The Revenge for Love*, Lewis continues to attack most of what he portrays. The two major male characters are Percy Hardcaster, a professional Communist who holds the intellectual fellow travelers around him in contempt, and Victor Stamp, a hapless artist who gets drawn into the same gunrunning scheme as Hardcaster. These characters are not grotesques such as those in *The Apes of God*, but neither are they figures with whom the reader identifies. The third major character, however, is Victor's wife, Margot. Initially an object of caricature, a young devotee of Virginia Woolf, Margot grows in stature as the novel progresses. She stands in opposition to the world of action, politics, and men, portrayed in the rest of the novel, and stands for the bonds of love and human affection. In earlier Lewis novels, her feminine values, as Lewis labels them, would have been lumped in with the male values of activity and attacked from Lewis's detached, intellectual perspective. Here, though, Margot becomes a moral authority, and Lewis begins—tentatively, one must admit—to criticize his earlier position as excessively harsh and arid. Margot's death at the end is a real tragedy, inducing even in the tough Percy Hardcaster a tear that rolls down his cheek at the very end of the novel.

SELF CONDEMNED

Self Condemned continues this process of self-criticism, as should be obvious from the title. It is, obliquely, about Lewis's experiences during World War II in Canada, which he hated. René Harding, a distinguished English historian, and his wife, Hester, leave England for Canada, where they gradually deteriorate. Hester commits suicide rather than remain in Canada as René wishes, and at the end René has become "a glacial shell of a man." Hester, like Margot, is the moral center of the novel, and her suicide is an eloquent condemnation of René and his arid intellectualism. René may in part be Lewis's own sense of what he might have become had he similarly turned away from his wife; in any case, in *Self Condemned*, as in *The Revenge for Love*, women characters are the vehicles for an implicit critique of Lewis's earlier values.

THE HUMAN AGE

The Human Age covers the same ground, in a sense, but from a more profound and developed perspective. Male and female in *The Revenge for Love* and *Self Condemned* serve as a kind of shorthand for the values of selfish indifference and unselfish compassion, respectively. In *The Human Age*, this sexual symbolism is replaced by a religious perspective, and Lewis's art takes an explicitly theological turn. *The Human Age* is a continuation, after twenty-five years, of *The Childermass*, though written in the restrained style of his later years, not with the modernist pyrotechnics of *The Childermass*. In book 2, *Monstre Gai*, Pullman and Satterthwaite have entered Third City, which is neither Heaven nor Hell, but a bland third state reminiscent of the postwar Britain of the Welfare State. Pullman, who as *The Human Age* develops, grows to resemble Lewis more and more, does not dislike this state of affairs but, flattered by the Bailiff's attention and desirous of obtaining power, becomes a close ally of the Bailiff. *Monstre Gai* ends when the Bailiff has to flee Third City and goes to Hell, taking Pullman and Satterthwaite with him.

Malign Fiesta, book 3 of *The Human Age*, Lewis's most striking work of fiction after *The Revenge for Love*, is set in Hell. The Bailiff is rather a minor personage there, and Pullman soon becomes an important adviser to Sammael, Satan himself. Much of the artistic power of *The Human Age* stems from Lewis's ability to use the traditional conceptions of the afterlife to create his own special universe. The plot of *Malign Fiesta* centers on Pullman's and Sammael's plans to found a new human age. They want to humanize the angels in order to subvert the stark opposition between the human and the divine and between good and evil which, Sammael concludes, has always served God's aims. In order to do this, Pullman, the specialist in Man, draws on all the resources of modern publicity to set in motion a gigantic party for the angels, the malign fiesta that gives the book its title, the purpose of which is to interest the angels in such human activities as drunkenness and lechery. God does not like this at all, and after warning Pullman repeatedly, He invades Hell. The book ends as Pullman is carried off to Heaven by some of God's soldiers.

There was to be a fourth book which Lewis never finished, which would have concerned Pullman's turn to and acceptance of the divine. This had already begun in *Malign Fiesta*, as Pullman was becoming more and more convinced of the wickedness of what he was doing, even though he continued to work with Sammael. What links this to Lewis's other novels is that Pullman's self-critique is Lewis's: From the theological standpoint of *The Human Age*, Lewis criticizes the indifference and lack of compassion of his earlier work. He, too, has done the devil's work and now wishes to turn to the divine.

This shift toward the end of Lewis's life and career can, however, be overstated. Lewis did not go on to write the fourth volume of *The Human Age* set in Heaven. Instead, he completed *The Red Priest*, a minor if entertaining novel satirizing a Communist priest, and started on another novel, *Twentieth Century Palette*, about a young painter early in that century. The novel was unfinished at Lewis's death. A thoroughly affirmative Lewis, in any case, would have been a Lewis deprived of much of his interest. *The Revenge for Love, Self Condemned*, and books 2 and 3 of *The Human Age* are Lewis's greatest novels precisely because they continue the attack on the modern world begun in *The Childermass* and *The Apes of God* while qualifying and criticizing that attack as they articulate it. The resulting ambivalence is fascinating, far richer than the more single-minded earlier work. They also carry forward what was begun in *Snooty Baronet* and the other 1930's novels, as they are written in a more conventional and readable style and conform somewhat to generic expectations. The later Lewis, in short, writes in a way that acknowledges that others have written, which makes his work much more accessible; yet his work remains completely his own.

Lewis's novels form one of the most fascinating bodies of work written in the twentieth century. A less sympathetic account of his work could have pointed out many flaws not discussed here; nevertheless, the universe created in his oeuvre is a capacious if demanding one, a realm that many more readers should discover and explore.

Reed Way Dasenbrock

OTHER MAJOR WORKS

SHORT FICTION: *The Wild Body*, 1927; *Rotting Hill*, 1951; *Unlucky for Pringle*, 1973.

PLAYS: *Enemy of the Stars*, pb. 1914, 1932; *The Ideal Giant*, pb. 1917.

POETRY: *One-Way Song*, 1933.

NONFICTION: *The Art of Being Ruled*, 1926; *The Lion and the Fox: The Role of the Hero in Shakespeare's Plays*, 1927; *Time and Western Man*, 1927;

Paleface: The Philosophy of the Melting Pot, 1929; *Satire and Fiction*, 1930; *The Diabolical Principle and the Dithyrambic Spectator*, 1931; *Hitler*, 1931; *The Doom of Youth*, 1932; *Filibusters in Barbary*, 1932; *The Old Gang and the New Gang*, 1933; *Men Without Art*, 1934; *Left Wings over Europe*, 1936; *Count Your Dead, They Are Alive*, 1937; *Blasting and Bombardiering*, 1937; *Wyndham Lewis: The Artist from "Blast" to Burlington House*, 1939; *The Hitler Cult*, 1939; *The Jews, Are They Human?* 1939; *America, I Presume*, 1940; *America and Cosmic Man*, 1948; *Rude Assignment: A Narrative of My Career Up-to-Date*, 1950; *The Writer and the Absolute*, 1952; *Letters of Wyndham Lewis*, 1963 (W. K. Rose, editor); *Wyndham Lewis on Art*, 1969; *Hitler, the Germans, and the Jews*, 1973 (5 volumes); *Enemy Salvos*, 1976; *Creatures of Habit, Creatures of Change*, 1989.

BIBLIOGRAPHY

Ayers, David. *Wyndham Lewis and Western Man*. New York: St. Martin's Press, 1992. See especially Ayers's chapter on Lewis and Bergson and his chapter on *Tarr* and *The Apes of God*. Ayers is particularly concerned with Lewis's concept of self. Includes detailed notes and bibliography.

Foshay, Toby Avard. *Wyndham Lewis and the Avant-Garde: The Politics of Intellect*. Montreal: McGill-Queens University Press, 1992. See the chapter on *Tarr*. Foshay explores the reasons for Lewis's "perverse" opposition to modernism. Includes detailed notes and excellent bibliography.

Kenner, Hugh. *Wyndham Lewis*. Norfolk, Conn.: New Directions, 1954. Although relatively short, Kenner's work remains the standard account of Lewis. Stresses Lewis's opposition to the emphasis on time and change characteristic of most twentieth century thinkers, who instead believed in order and permanence. Rates Lewis's exposition of his views, *Time and Western Man*, as one of the key works of the twentieth century. Kenner's careful discussion of Lewis's work is based in part on his personal friendship with him.

Meyers, Jeffrey. *The Enemy*. London: Routledge & Kegan Paul, 1980. This long book is the standard biography, giving a full picture of Lewis's life and his work: fiction, painting, and criticism. Includes new information based on his access to Lewis's papers: for example, Lewis's activities in trying to secure Ezra Pound's release from prison. Contends that *Self Condemned* is Lewis's greatest novel.

_____, ed. *Wyndham Lewis: A Revaluation*. London: Athlone Press, 1980. Contains articles by leading authorities on Lewis on all aspects of his work. Among the essays are John Holloway's "Machine and Puppet: A Comparative View," which analyzes the theme of man's transformation into machinery and his reanimation. Marshall McLuhan discusses Lewis's prose style and Alistair Davies claims that *Tarr* is a Nietzschean novel.

Schenker, Daniel. *Wyndham Lewis: Religion and Modernism*. Tuscaloosa: University of Alabama Press, 1992. Compare chapter 1, "Wyndham Lewis in the Modernist Canon: Dissent, Division, and Displacement," to Foshay's study. Includes detailed notes and extensive bibliography.

CLARICE LISPECTOR

Born: Chechelnik, Ukraine, U.S.S.R.; December 10, 1925
Died: Rio de Janeiro, Brazil; December 9, 1977

PRINCIPAL LONG FICTION

Perto do coração selvagem, 1944
O lustre, 1946
A cidade sitiada, 1949
A maçã no escuro, 1961 (*The Apple in the Dark*, 1967)
A paixão segundo G. H., 1964 (*The Passion According to G. H.*, 1988)
Uma aprendizagem: Ou, O livro dos prazeres, 1969 (*An Apprenticeship: Or, The Book of Delights*, 1986)
Água viva, 1973 (*The Stream of Life*, 1989)
A hora da estrela, 1977 (*The Hour of the Star*, 1986)
Um sopro de vida: Pulsações, 1978

OTHER LITERARY FORMS

Clarice Lispector was a prominent short-story writer as well as a novelist; among her collections of stories are *Alguns contos* (1952; some stories) and *Laços de família* (1960; *Family Ties*, 1972). *A legião estrangeira* (1964; *The Foreign Legion*, 1986) is a collection of stories and brief miscellaneous prose pieces.

ACHIEVEMENTS

Lispector is regarded as one of the most influential and important Brazilian fiction writers. A member of the revisionist school of writers that emerged in the period following World War II, she was a force in the move, in Brazilian fiction, from the regionalism and sociological orientation of the 1930's to an intense interest in subjective experience.

She first achieved general acclaim with *Family Ties*, a collection of inward-looking short stories. *The Apple in the Dark* marked Lispector's major artistic breakthrough. Lengthy and complex, symbolic and mythic, its intense, lyrical style recalls the works of Djuna Barnes, Virginia Woolf, and Katherine Mansfield.

Lispector was the recipient of many literary prizes. In 1943, the publication of *Perto do coração selvagem* (close to the savage heart) won for her the Graça Aranha Prize. She received the Cármen Dolores Barbosa Prize for *The Apple in the Dark* in 1961, a prize from the Campanha Nacional da Criança for a children's story, "O mistério do coelho pensante" (the mystery of the thinking rabbit) in 1967, the Golfinho de Ouro Prize for *An Apprenticeship: Or, The Book of Delights* in 1969, and was awarded first prize in the tenth Concurso Literário Nacional for her overall contribution to Brazilian literature in 1976, one year before her death.

BIOGRAPHY

Clarice Lispector was born in Chechelnik, in the Ukraine, in 1925, of Jewish parents. The family moved to Brazil when the child was two months old. Lispector attended school first in Recife, then in Rio de Janeiro. In 1943, she was graduated from the Faculty of Law in Rio. She married a diplomat and lived in Italy, Switzerland, Great Britain, and the United States for many years. After her divorce, she settled permanently in Rio de Janeiro in 1959. She died from cancer in 1977.

ANALYSIS

Most, but not all, of Clarice Lispector's protagonists are female, and the author is keenly aware of women's problems and of the female side of the psyche. Her major works deal with internal guests. An occurrence in the protagonists' lives causes them to move out of their daily routines and enter into new types of relationship with themselves and with the physical world. They live each moment intensely, as if every breath of existence is a major experience, tightly connected to the pulsating rhythm of life itself. The protagonist's quest has no specific goal except to move forward, as in *The Apple in the Dark*:

> Still in his favor was the fact that he knew he should walk in a straight line because it would not be very practical to lose the thread of the maze. In his disfavor there was a danger he was on the lookout for: the fact that there were pleasure and beauty in a person's losing himself.

Lispector's major protagonists are all making their way through the maze of life, lost at times, but always eventually able to resume their journey toward enlightenment.

PERTO DE CORAÇÃO SELVAGEM

Perto de coração selvagem, Lispector's first novel, published when she was still a teenager, is considered a breakthrough in Brazilian literature because of its modernistic style. It is the story of Joana, a young orphan who, after an introspective adolescence, lives through a marriage and a subsequent divorce. In part 1, descriptions of Joana's childhood alternate with descriptions of her life as Octavio's wife. Part 2 tells the story of her marriage, her husband's infidelity, her divorce, and her ultimate encounter with herself as a free entity in the world. The epigraph for the novel, "He was alone. He was abandoned, happy, close to the savage heart of life" is taken from James Joyce's *A Portrait of the Artist as a Young Man* (1916).

(Courtesy of New Directions Publishing)

As a child, Joana is keenly aware of the cycle of life and death. Eating a chicken makes her think of the worm in the earth on which the chicken once nourished itself. Behind all life there is death, and the only thing that distinguishes human beings from other organisms is consciousness. A feeling of being connected with the physical world through a common destiny provides moments of profound pain and profound joy to Joana as well as to most of Lispector's later protagonists. "Oh, pity, that is what I sense then. Pity is my form of love. Of love and of communication."

Marriage proves to be a very disturbing experience for Joana, who as a child quizzed her teacher about the goal of happiness: "Be happy in order to obtain what?" she had wondered. While her need to touch another human being through love nevertheless remained strong, her marriage resulted in a sense of imprisonment. How does one tie oneself to another human being without becoming imprisoned by that person's construction of walls around one's body and soul? How is it possible to possess things without having things possess one? These are questions that will haunt all of Lispector's major protagonists. In her marriage, Joana's quest for self-fulfillment constantly comes into conflict with the bland happiness she finds with Octavio: "Lightly surprised she dilated her eyes, perceived her body plunged into a comfortable happiness. She did not suffer, but where was she?"

Part 2 describes Joana's long struggle to free herself from Octavio: "His presence, and more than his presence: knowing that he existed left her without liberty." Her time is no longer her own: "Now all her time was handed over to him and the minutes that were hers, she felt them allotted, distributed in small cubes of ice that she must swallow rapidly, before they melted." Marriage, she believes, is betrayal of herself and of the vision of life that she developed during adolescence. For Octavio, on the other hand, Joana's restlessness, which originally attracted him to her, proves too disturbing, and he seeks refuge in his former fiancée, Lidia, a woman whose dream is to create a conventional family. Victimized by irrational jealousy, Joana, too, takes a lover, at the same time attempting to retain Octavio. The drive toward self-fulfillment, however, proves stronger than the forces that link her to either her husband or her lover, and in the novel's last chapter Joana is alone. Her only goal now is to walk humbly down the road of life, without fear, receptive to the world and to death. Finally in harmony with the fluidity of life itself, Joana experiences within herself a burst of creative energy.

THE APPLE IN THE DARK

The Apple in the Dark is considered Lispector's most important novel. Martim, the protagonist, is fleeing a crime. At the beginning of the novel, he is in bed in a womblike hotel room. The balcony outside his room overlooks a garden bathed in darkness. Still half asleep, Martim walks out onto the balcony, observes that a car which has been parked in front of the hotel has disappeared, and suspects that a German who lives in the hotel has gone to turn him in to the police. Totally awake now, Martim jumps from the balcony into the garden and begins a long, slow walk into the dark.

The Apple in the Dark is a dreamlike narrative of Martim's quest for a side of the self with which he has lost contact while living as a married man in a conventional social setting. Unsure of where he is going, his only goal is to move in a straight line so as to avoid a circular return to the walls of the hotel. Martim's quest ends on an ambiguous note, since at the end of the novel he appears to have given up and is ready to be captured and returned to the world he left behind.

Nevertheless, Martim's journey has provided him with experiences and insights which he did not possess at the beginning of the book. "We don't know where we came from and we don't know where we're going; but we just experience things, we experience! And that's what we have, Ermelinda." Surrounded by stones and plants, Martim experiences exquisite moments of connection with the mystery of the natural world, as all of his senses open and his mind abdicates its power and accepts being merely a part of life "with the nakedness of his lack of understanding." He makes the surprising discovery that "the more stupid he was the more face to face with things he was." In his new state of consciousness, Martim replaces understanding with awareness. He senses the air he breathes with the delicate tension of a plant and attempts to adopt the patient rhythm of grazing cows.

The Apple in the Dark is a novel about love, both for the world itself and for other human beings. A significant part of the book describes Martim's stay at a farm and his encounter with two women, Ermelinda and Vitória. Ermelinda seeks, in her love for Martim, protection against her obsessive fear of death, only to discover that physical love, on the contrary, brings her closer to an experience of dying than does any other emotion. This newly won insight finally enables Ermelinda to accept her own mortality. Martim's encounter with Vitória is different, a communion of souls rather than bodies. In a moving description, Lispector shows how Martim's resistance to intimate contact with another person is gradually broken down, as Vitória for the first time in her life gives expression to her innermost thoughts and emotions. While communication does not last, the experience proves crucial to Martim, who is finally able to look upon himself with love and respect: "The man was loving himself for the first time, which meant that he was ready to love others. . . ." Martim no longer needs to flee, and he willingly consents to cut short his quest and return to society.

The title of the novel is important. *The Apple in the Dark* can be read as a commentary on the biblical myth on the tree of knowledge. The understanding of the world that Martim achieves is intuitive rather than rational. He never actually eats the apple, he merely reaches out for it in the dark, hoping that he will be able to hold onto the fruit: "And I have that clumsy way of reaching for an apple in the dark—and trying not to drop it."

THE PASSION ACCORDING TO G. H.

The quest for identity continues in *The Passion According to G. H.* While Martim's quest took the form of a voyage through external space, G. H.'s quest is wholly internal. The killing of a cockroach triggers in the protagonist an extensive and painful meditation on life, death, and writing, and on her own place within the order of things. Toward the end of the novel, G. H., like Martim, will emerge from her introspection with an increased awareness which will enable her to live her daily life in a more productive way than before.

AN APPRENTICESHIP

An Apprenticeship, written five years later, is Lispector's most optimistic novel. The novel has two protagonists, a woman and a man, engaged in an extensive dialogue. Lori, a physically attractive young teacher, lives an empty, nonreflective life until she falls in love with Ulysses, a professor of philosophy. Although Lori has had several affairs, Ulysses refuses to consummate their love until she has completed her "apprenticeship" and learned the secret meaning of life. Only then, he believes, is a permanent union of two people possible. Lori, feeling frustrated and rejected, reluctantly starts her slow, painful route toward self-discovery under his guidance.

Until the meeting with Ulysses, Lori had eliminated pain from her life, but she had also cut off any potential for meaningful contact with herself, with other people, or with life itself: "Without pain, she had been left without anything, lost in her own world and that of others without any means of contact."

Love, reduced to sex, failed to connect her to anything outside herself. Ulysses realizes this and decides that Lori must reestablish contact with her own body and soul before she will be able to love him or anybody else: "I could have possessed you already with my body and my soul, but I will wait even though it takes years, for you, too, to have a body and a soul to love with," he tells her.

During her apprenticeship, Lori experiences an increased sense of awareness of the world around her, and of the silence of death which perpetually lurks behind the bustling noises of life. Lori discovers that pain and pleasure, life and death, are inextricably linked. By attempting to escape from pain she has excluded pleasure from her life as well. Consequently, her new receptivity to pain will restore her ability to experience pleasure. It is only after having accepted the pain of death that she can start to feel a genuine joy of living.

The pleasure results from her growing ability to strip away façades and protective mechanisms and dare finally to be herself. Lori soon experiences flashes of communication and insights accompanied by a keen sense of genuinely existing. During this period of profound introspection, Lori needs to distance herself from society and from Ulysses as well, in order to be more fully with herself. Her ultimate goal, however, is connection, not isolation. First, she must be reattached to the earth itself. Then, she hopes to reestablish the link between herself and other people.

In an episode typical of Lispector's fiction, Lori is walking slowly and wearily down the street. She notices a girl waiting for the bus, and her heart begins to throb—she has decided to try to make contact with another person. After the brief encounter, Lori realizes that what she is looking for is more profound. She returns home and calls Ulysses. She bites into an apple and discovers that the eating of the fruit leads her to a state of grace rather than exile: "Unlike Eve, when she bit into the apple she entered paradise. . . . It was the beginning . . . of a state of grace." The state of grace is the state of someone who does not have to guess any longer, according to the narrator, someone who simply knows. The world around her acquires a kind of halo that radiates almost perfectly from things and people, a kind of energy consisting of very fine particles of light. Lori, at the same time, realizes that she does not want to experience grace often; she does not want to become addicted to it, because it would distance her from the struggle, from the perplexity and joy of an ordinary human destiny: "It was important not to forget that the state of grace was merely a small opening to the world which was like paradise—it was neither an entrance into it nor did it give one the right to eat from the fruits of its orchards."

Lori, then, does not stay in paradise but emerges from her experience of grace as a better human being. Ulysses, in the following chapter, tells her that she is now ready for love. Before leaving her apartment to join him, Lori stands by her window, watching the rain. She feels neither pain nor pleasure, only a keen sense of connection and release: "She and the rain were busy with their violent outpouring." She intuitively knows that she will be able to transfer her newly won intimacy with the world to her relationship with Ulysses, leaves her apartment without putting on her customary makeup, and takes a taxi to his place. Somehow, living and loving have finally become simple, as Lori has discovered that it is possible for her to give herself without losing herself. After a period of passionate lovemaking, she sees in a vision the fruit of the world, "And it was in midair that she placed her mouth on the fruit and managed to bite into it, yet leaving it intact gleaming in space." Ulysses is no longer a teacher to Lori. The two of them are equal, united through mutual love.

THE STREAM OF LIFE

An Apprenticeship, with its vision of a mature, passionate, conscious relationship between a man and a woman, is an exception within Lispector's total work, a pleasant detour along the road. In *The Stream of Life*, written four years later, the author returns once again to a solitary, questing protagonist. The novel is an intense, fluid monologue addressed to an absent *you*, a person with whom the narrator was once intimately involved. In the novel's first paragraph, the narrator bursts out in a cry of joy upon realizing that she is once again free. It is a joy mixed with the sadness of separation and the fear of an un-

known future. Nevertheless, she wants to capture the present moment, to connect with the spirit of life, and to sing out the joy she experiences from being in the world: "And I sing hallelujah in the air like the bird does."

The Stream of Life is a glorification of the self alone in the world, detached from material possessions and from other people. The prevailing emotion in the book is one of being intensely alive, bought at the price of separation from the person she loves. Her new lover is nature, a feminine principle both soothing and ferocious. This love affair with life itself is for the narrator a way of approaching God. Such a radical break is necessary for Lispector's narrator in order to escape from a society which flattens out emotional lives and turns people into automatons, unable ever to grasp the present moment. Separation, thus, becomes a gift of life that she, through her writing, wants to bestow upon her former lover as well. Separation is seen as a birth trauma, painful but necessary for the lover to experience the exquisite joy of liberty: "I give you liberty. First I break the waterbag. Then I cut the umbilical cord. And you are alive in your own right." On the book's final page, she addresses the lover for the last time: "Look at me and love me. No: you look at yourself and love you. And that is what is just."

The Stream of Life is a long meditation on love, separation, life, death, and God, seemingly inspired by Asian mysticism: "Profound prayer is a meditation on nothingness," according to the narrator. Faced with the pain of separation, analogous to the pain of dying, the narrator chooses to respond with joy: ". . . because it is too cruel, so I respond by the purity of indomitable joy. I refuse to be sad. Let us be joyous." The style of *The Stream of Life* is fluid and poetic, each sentence giving birth to the next with no preconceived structure, as Lispector attempts to capture the rhythm of her own respiration.

THE HOUR OF THE STAR

The Hour of the Star is also a detour. It is different from Lispector's other novels in that it focuses on a social rather than a metaphysical problem. Macabéa, the protagonist, is a young woman who moves from the poor northeast part of Brazil to the city. The novel deals with the problems of the rural North versus the urban South, of poverty and the dream of a better life, and, finally, of an uneducated woman's struggle to survive in a sexist society.

UM SOPRO DE VIDA

In her final novel, *Um sopro de vida* (a breath of life), Lispector returns for the last time to an intensely personal inquiry into the problems of life, death, and writing. Completed shortly before the author's own death, the novel is the ultimate statement of an artist whose own road has come to an end, for whom reality has caught up with her life's vision, and for whom each breath now literally encapsulates the essence of life itself. The novel was published posthumously.

Randi Birn

OTHER MAJOR WORKS

SHORT FICTION: *Alguns contos*, 1952; *Laços de família*, 1960 (*Family Ties*, 1972); *A legião estrangeira*, 1964 (*The Foreign Legion*, 1986); *Felicidade clandestina: Contos*, 1971; *A imitação da rosa*, 1973; *Onde estivestes de noite*, 1974; *A via crucis do corpo*, 1974; *A bela e a fera*, 1979; *Soulstorm*, 1989 (includes stories from *Onde estivestes de noite* and *A via crusis do corpo*).

NONFICTION: *Para não esquecer*, 1978.

CHILDREN'S LITERATURE: *O mistério do coelho pensante*, 1967; *A mulher que matou os peixes*, 1968 (*The Woman Who Killed the Fish*, 1982).

MISCELLANEOUS: *Seleta de Clarice Lispector*, 1975.

BIBLIOGRAPHY

Barbosa, Maria José Somerlate. *Clarice Lispector: Spinning the Webs of Passion*. New Orleans: University Press of the South, 1997. A good study of Lispector's works. Includes bibliographical references and an index.

Cixous, Helene. *Reading with Clarice Lispector*. Minneapolis: University of Minnesota Press, 1990. Chapters on *The Stream of Life*, *The Apple in the Dark*, "The Egg and the Chicken," and *The Hour of the Star*. The book includes an introduction by Verena Andermatt Conley, carefully explaining Cixous's critical approach to Lispector. Recommended for advanced students.

Coutinho, Afranio. *An Introduction to Literature in Brazil*. New York: Columbia University Press, 1960. A major Brazilian critic assesses Lispector's achievement, emphasizing her place in Brazilian literature and her powerful metaphorical and atmospheric fiction.

Fitz, Earl F. *Clarice Lispector*. Boston: Twayne, 1985. A useful introduction that includes a chapter of biography; a discussion of Lispector's place in Brazilian literature; a study of her style, structure, and point of view in her novels and short stories; and her nonfiction work. Includes chronology, detailed notes, and a well-annotated bibliography.

Lowe, Elizabeth. *The City in Brazilian Literature*. Rutherford, N.J.: Farleigh Dickinson University Press, 1982. Discusses Lispector as an urban writer, focusing mainly on *A cidade sitiada*, *The Passion According to G. H.*, and *The Stream of Life*.

Peixoto, Marta. *Passionate Fictions: Gender, Narrative, and Violence in Clarice Lispector*. Minneapolis: University of Minnesota Press, 1994. Written with a decidedly feminist bias, *Passionate Fictions* analyzes Lispector's frequently violent subject matter, juxtaposing it with her strange and original use of language. Special attention is paid to the nexus with Helene Cixous and to the autobiographical elements of *The Stream of Life* and *A via crucis do corpo*.

PENELOPE LIVELY

Born: Cairo, Egypt; March 17, 1933

PRINCIPAL LONG FICTION

The Road to Lichfield, 1977
Treasures of Time, 1979
Judgement Day, 1980
Next to Nature, Art, 1982

Perfect Happiness, 1983
According to Mark, 1984
Moon Tiger, 1987
Passing On, 1989
City of the Mind, 1991
Cleopatra's Sister, 1993
Heat Wave, 1996
Spiderweb, 1998

OTHER LITERARY FORMS

While Penelope Lively is known primarily as a novelist, she first earned an international reputation in the early 1970's as a writer of literature for children. Readers see in these early stories strong traces of the concerns subsequently explored in her adult fiction. The most widely known of her children's books, *The Ghost of Thomas Kempe* (1973), describes the experiences of young James Harrison as he encounters the ghost of a seventeenth century former inhabitant of the cottage in which James now lives. Blamed for the poltergeist's mischievous actions, James discovers the significance of historical perspective in explaining the world at large. Here, as in many of Lively's works for children, most notably *A Stitch in Time* (1976), the supernatural is the medium by which the past comes into contact with the present.

Along with many stories for older children, Lively has written one picture book for infants, *The Cat, the Crow, and the Banyan Tree* (1994; illustrated by Terry Milne). She has produced three short-story collections for adults and two full-length works of nonfiction: *The Presence of the Past* (1976), a study of landscape history, and *Oleander, Jacaranda* (1994), a personal memoir in which Lively looks back to her early childhood in Egypt. She has also written radio and television scripts, book reviews, and other articles for academic and nonacademic publications, including travel articles for *The New York Times*.

ACHIEVEMENTS

Lively's work has earned her a number of literary accolades. With *Moon Tiger*, she won Britain's most prestigious literary award, the Booker-McConnell Prize, an award for which two previous novels, *The Road to Lichfield* and *According to Mark*, were

shortlisted. *Moon Tiger* also received the 1988 *Los Angeles Times* Book Award. *Treasures of Time*, Lively's second work of long fiction for adults, received the British Arts Council's inaugural National Book Award in 1979. She won the Carnegie Medal, the top children's literature award in Britain, for *The Ghost of Thomas Kempe*, and the Whitbread Prize for *A Stitch in Time*. In 1985, Lively was named a Fellow of the Royal Society for Literature, and four years later, she became an officer of the Order of the British Empire (O.B.E.) by Queen Elizabeth II. In general, her body of work qualifies her as one of Britain's most popular, prolific, and influential late twentieth century novelists.

BIOGRAPHY

Born of British parents Vera and Roger Low, Lively spent her childhood in the suburbs of Cairo, where her father worked for the National Bank of Egypt. An only child, she received no formal education but was taught at home by a personal tutor in an apparently rather haphazard fashion. The young Lively was encouraged, however, to read voraciously the great classics of children's literature, as well as the Bible and ancient mythology. The ardent interest in the past that Lively exhibits in all her works may well have been engendered by the family's weekly visits to the Egyptian pyramids.

After her parents divorced in 1945, she was sent at the age of twelve to live with her paternal grandmother in rural Somerset, England, and soon after, to an austere English boarding school. Although the school emphasized physical over intellectual activity—she once was admonished by the headmistress for reading poetry outside of the classroom—Lively continued to read widely and obtained a place at St. Anne's College of Oxford University. Here, Lively felt a sense of liberation among Britain's best scholars and students. Her field was history, but she also read a good deal of contemporary fiction. She graduated in 1954 with a B.A. in modern history.

After working for a short time as a secretary for an Oxford University professor, in 1957 Lively married research fellow Jack Lively, who later became a professor of politics at the University of Warwick.

They had two children, Josephine and Adam, whom Lively stayed home to raise. She read to them often and soon became interested in writing children's stories of her own. Her first, *Astercote*, appeared in 1970, and others followed in quick succession. While continuing to publish works for children, in the late 1970's Lively turned to adult fiction—short stories and novels—and subsequently earned both critical acclaim and popular success. From 1985, Lively became active in the International Association of Poets, Playwrights, Editors, Essayists, and Novelists (PEN), and for a long period of time she chaired the Society of Authors. She also lectured in various countries for the British Arts Council. In the 1990's, Lively's time was divided between London and her farmhouse in Oxfordshire, and she continued to publish fiction for children and adults.

ANALYSIS

Lively is one of a number of British novelists who emerged in the late 1970's and early 1980's to reaffirm the English novel's capacity to express postmodernist themes without sacrificing its roots in the eighteenth and nineteenth century realist tradition. Her fictional worlds are predicated on the conventions of realist fiction, but these conventions are transformed both by perceptual shifts in the consciousness of her characters—a technique strongly reminiscent of modernists such as Virginia Woolf—and by her self-conscious examination of the nature of language.

In a manner characteristic of postmodernist British fiction, Lively's choice of characters demonstrates her fascination not only with the past but also with the ways in which it is reconstituted in and refracted by the present. Her novels introduce us to archaeologists, paleontologists, architects, biographers, historians, and teachers of history; all these occupations have in a common a concern for the meaning and the weight of the past. Lively is less experimental in terms of technique than some of her fellow writers in Britain and elsewhere; however, her theoretical interest in the workings of history and memory, and the intersections between the two, aligns her with such notable contemporaries as Julian Barnes, A. S. Byatt,

and Salman Rushdie. Collectively, then, her novels stress the palimpsest quality of a narrative present ineluctably underwritten by the presence of the past.

THE ROAD TO LICHFIELD

The Road to Lichfield marked Lively's shift from children's stories to adult fiction. The novel records the experiences of a middle-aged history teacher, Anne Linton, whose dying father, she learns, has been having an affair for many years. On train trips to visit her father, Anne meets schoolteacher David Fielding, and they begin an affair of their own. Her father's clandestine past, and her own clandestine activities in the present, force her to recognize the subjective quality of memory and perception. Marked by Lively's characteristically polished style, *The Road to Lichfield* employs a shifting third-person perspective to portray events from a number of different points of view. This technique recurs consistently in Lively's subsequent novels.

ACCORDING TO MARK

Lively's second novel earned her a second appearance on the Booker Prize shortlist. *According to Mark*, like much of Lively's subsequent work, is concerned with whether the attempt to re-create the past is closer to the order of fiction than to that of objective truth. Here, she tells the story of a literary biographer embarked on a project to write the life of a 1920's man of letters. The novel's title alludes to one of four biblical versions of the gospel, and her protagonist shares with Lively herself a concern for the nature and validity of historical evidence in re-creating the past. During the course of his research, the protagonist determines that uncovering the truth is impossible. The novel itself, though, qualifies this rather nihilistic conclusion in the sense that what the protagonist fails to re-create in the dead subject of his biographical research—"life"—he discovers for himself through his growing love for his subject's daughter.

MOON TIGER

"I am writing a history of the world," the elderly Claudia Hampton announces on her deathbed at the beginning of Lively's Booker Prize-winning novel, "and in the process my own." With these words, Lively's narrator, a former war correspondent and popular historian, establishes *Moon Tiger*'s preeminent concern: What is the relationship between world history and the span of an individual's life? As Claudia looks back on her past, she is periodically interrupted by the narrative present, in the form of the overheard voices of medical staff discussing her case. The rich and full life she fleshes out, though, during the course of the novel, stands in sharp contrast to their dismissive clinical remarks.

In typically postmodernist fashion, history is inescapable in this novel, but it takes on many diverse forms. Claudia's childhood interest in fossils and rock formations, for example, draws our attention to the scale of geological time, while in witnessing some of the crucial moments of World War II she points to the historical significance of global events and to those, such as German general field marshal Erwin Rommel, who apparently are history's central players. However, as the novel's opening lines suggest, these conventional conceptions of what constitutes history are overshadowed by the story of Claudia's own life. Combining personal recollections with ruminations on the nature and purpose of history, Claudia's story stresses the significance of imagination and memory over hard historical evidence. This is typified by Claudia's strategy of imagining "real" events from the different points of view of those involved; in such cases, the details remain broadly the same, but their meaning and context differ markedly according to the perspective from which they are perceived. In employing such techniques, Claudia's narration criticizes implicitly the conventional historian's faith in empirical evidence, objectivity, and linear cause-and-effect patterns.

The structure of *Moon Tiger* is, like memory itself, fragmentary and achronological, but the kaleidoscopic representation of Claudia's life is brought into focus when she recalls her brief affair in Egypt during World War II with Tom, a doomed British tank commander. This pivotal moment in the novel at once underscores and explains Claudia's perception of history: Tom's untimely death in a German air attack is in one respect utterly peripheral, hardly a footnote in the record of the twentieth century's central historical event, and yet Tom has, in effect, played the central role in Claudia's autobiography. In this way, the novel affirms the significance of the individual life in relation to history's larger forces. Such a conclusion is characteristic of Lively's work as a whole, but in *Moon Tiger* it receives perhaps its fullest and most evocative expression. *Moon Tiger* remains, for many readers, Lively's best novel, and it is certainly her most widely read and most widely taught.

CITY OF THE MIND

Following the enormous success of its predecessor, *City of the Mind* explores the history and geography of the city of London through the mind of the protagonist, Matthew Halland, an architect who contemplates the impact of his buildings on the centuries-old cityscape of England's capital city. Set against the backdrop of history on a grander scale—an array of the city's inhabitants going back to Elizabethan times—are the smaller experiences of an individual life: Halland's divorce, losing custody of his daughter, the commercial pressures imposed on him by a greedy developer, and his encounter with an expert glass engraver and Holocaust survivor. Ultimately, Halland's faith in human relations is restored when he meets and falls in love with the editor of an art magazine, Sarah Bridges. All these events influence in significant and unexpected ways Halland's minor contribution to the redevelopment of London's docklands that took place in the 1980's. *City of the Mind* examines the nature of historical continuity and historical change and asks, what is our debt to the past?

CLEOPATRA'S SISTER

This novel is in some ways Lively's most ambitious, in the sense that she creates an imaginary history not simply for her characters but for an entire country. *Cleopatra's Sister* tells the story of Lucy Faulkner, a relatively unsuccessful freelance journalist. On her way to Kenya, Lucy meets Howard Beamish, a paleontologist fascinated by different conceptions of time. Their airplane is grounded in the fictitious African nation of Callimbia and subsequently hijacked by Callimbian freedom fighters. The novel is concerned with the growing love between the two characters as they become enmeshed in unpredictable political circumstances. Interestingly, though, the narrative that traces this developing relationship periodically is interrupted by chapters such as "A Brief History of Callimbia," in which Lively creates a fictional history of the country from ancient times to the present day. Reviewers of *Cleopatra's Sister* found this element of the novel rather contrived or improbable, which is a fairly valid response. However, the novel does affirm the primacy of individual over national histories and individual relationships over political relationships, and in that sense it remains true to Lively's abiding concerns.

John L. Marsden

OTHER MAJOR WORKS

SHORT FICTION: *Nothing Missing but the Samovar and Other Stories*, 1978; *Corruption and Other Stories*, 1984; *Pack of Cards: Stories 1978-86*, 1986; *The Five Thousand and One Nights*, 1997.

NONFICTION: *The Presence of the Past: An Introduction to Landscape History*, 1976; *Oleander, Jacaranda: A Childhood Perceived, a Memoir*, 1994.

CHILDREN'S LITERATURE: *Astercote*, 1970; *The Whispering Knights*, 1971; *The Wild Hunt of Hagworthy*, 1971 (published in the U.S. as *The Wild Hunt of the Ghost Hounds*); *The Driftway*, 1972; *The Ghost of Thomas Kempe*, 1973; *The House in Norham Gardens*, 1974; *Boy Without a Name*, 1975; *Going Back*, 1975; *A Stitch in Time*, 1976; *The Stained Glass Window*, 1976; *Fanny's Sister*, 1976; *The Voyage of QV66*, 1978; *Fanny and the Monsters*, 1979; *Fanny and the Battle of Potter's Piece*, 1980; *The Revenge of Samuel Stokes*, 1981; *Fanny and the Monsters and Other Stories* (containing the three *Fanny* stories), 1982; *Uninvited Ghosts*, 1984; *Dragon Trouble*, 1984; *Debbie and the Little Devil*, 1987; *A House Inside Out*, 1988; *The Cat, the Crow, and the Banyan Tree*, 1994 (illustrated by Terry Milne).

BIBLIOGRAPHY

Jackson, Tony E. "The Consequences of Chaos: *Cleopatra's Sister* and Postmodern Historiography." *Modern Fiction Studies* 42, no. 2 (Summer, 1996). The theme of historiography in another of Lively's novels is taken up by Jackson.

LeMesurier, Nicholas. "A Lesson in History: The Presence of the Past in the Novels of Penelope Lively." *New Welsh Review* 2 (Spring, 1990). In a less theoretical vein than Jackson, LeMesurier discusses more generally the influence of the past on Lively's characters and settings.

Lively, Penelope. "An Interview with Penelope Lively." Interview by Amanda Smith. *Publishers Weekly* 232, no. 12 (March, 1988). Those interested in hearing what Lively has to say about her own life and work should begin by consulting this informative article.

Moran, Mary Hurley. *Penelope Lively*. New York: Twayne, 1993. Offers brief but useful critical readings of each of Lively's first nine novels for adults.

_____. "Penelope Lively's *Moon Tiger*: A Feminist 'History of the World.'" *Frontiers: A Journal of Women Studies* 11, no. 2/3 (1990). This essay takes a radical feminist approach to Lively's most well-known novel.

Raschke, Debrah. "Penelope Lively's *Moon Tiger*: Reexamining a 'History of the World.'" *ARIEL* 26, no. 4 (October, 1995). Examines Lively's treatment of history and personal identity as unstable. Raschke argues that the novel represents a liberation from the traditional limits of women's participation in historiography.

DAVID LODGE

Born: London, England; January 28, 1935

PRINCIPAL LONG FICTION

The Picturegoers, 1960
Ginger, You're Barmy, 1962
The British Museum Is Falling Down, 1965
Out of the Shelter, 1970
Changing Places: A Tale of Two Campuses, 1975
How Far Can You Go?, 1980 (also known as *Souls and Bodies*)
Small World, 1984
Nice Work, 1988

Paradise News, 1991
Therapy, 1995

OTHER LITERARY FORMS

Mediating between theory and practice, David Lodge has proved himself one of England's ablest and most interesting literary critics. Among his influential critical books are *The Language of Fiction* (1966) and *The Novelist at the Crossroads* (1971). In addition to his novels and criticism, he has written short stories, television screenplays of some of his novels, and (in collaboration with Malcolm Bradbury and Jim Duckett) several satirical revues.

ACHIEVEMENTS

As a novelist Lodge has made his mark in three seemingly distinct yet, in Lodge's case, surprisingly congruent areas: as a writer of Catholic novels, of "campus fiction," and of works that somehow manage to be at once realist and postmodern. The publication of *Changing Places* in 1975 and *Small World* nine years later brought Lodge to the attention of a much larger (especially American) audience. *Changing Places* won both the Yorkshire Post and Hawthornden prizes, *How Far Can You Go?* received the Whitbread Award, and *Nice Work* was shortlisted for Great Britain's prestigious Booker Prize.

BIOGRAPHY

David John Lodge was born on January 28, 1935, in London's lower-middle-class East End, the only son of a musician father and a staunchly Catholic mother. The family's straitened economic situation, his conservative Catholic upbringing, and the dangers of wartime London left their mark on young David. He began his first novel (unpublished) at eighteen while still a student at University College, London, where he received his B.A. in English (with first honors) in 1955 and an M.A. in 1959. Between times Lodge performed what was then an obligatory National Service (1955-1957). Although the two years were in a sense wasted, his stint in the army did give him time to complete his first published novel, *The Picturegoers*, and material for his second, *Ginger, You're Barmy*, as well as the impetus to continue

his studies. In 1959 he married to Mary Frances Jacob; they had three children. After a year working as an assistant at the British Council, Lodge joined the faculty at the University of Birmingham, where he completed his Ph.D. in 1969; he eventually attained the position of full professor of modern English literature in 1976.

The mid-1960's proved an especially important period in Lodge's personal and professional life. He became close friends with fellow critic and novelist Malcolm Bradbury (then also at Birmingham), under whose influence Lodge wrote his first comic novel, *The British Museum Is Falling Down*, for which the publisher, not so comically, forgot to distribute review copies; he was awarded a Harkness Commonwealth Fellowship to study and travel in the United States for a year (1964-1965); he published his first critical study, the influential *The Language of Fiction* (1966); and he learned that his third child, Christopher, suffered from Down syndrome (a biographical fact that manifests itself obliquely at the end of *Out*

(AP/Wide World Photos)

of the Shelter and more overtly in one of the plots of *How Far Can You Go?*). Lodge's second trip to the United States, this time as visiting professor of English at the University of California at Berkeley in 1969, during the height of the Free Speech Movement and political unrest, played its part in the conceiving and writing of his second comic novel, *Changing Places*, as did the critical essays he was then writing and would later collect in *The Novelist at the Crossroads* (1971) and *Working with Structuralism* (1981). The cash award that went along with the Whitbread Prize for his next novel, *How Far Can You Go?*, enabled Lodge to reduce his teaching duties to half-year and to devote himself more fully to his writing. He transformed his participation in the Modern Language Association's 1978 conference in New York, the 1979 James Joyce Symposium in Zurich, and a three-week world tour of conferences and British Council speaking engagements into his most commercially successful book, *Small World*, later adapted for British television.

His reputation growing and his financial situation brightening, Lodge donated all royalties from his next book, *Write On: Occasional Essays, '65-'85* (1986), to CARE (Cottage and Rural Enterprises), which maintains communities for mentally handicapped adults. In 1987 he took advantage of early retirement (part of Prime Minister Margaret Thatcher's austerity plan for British universities) so that he could work full time as a writer.

Lodge soon published *Paradise News* (1991) and *Therapy* (1995). He also published two collections of essays, *After Bakhtin: Essays on Fiction and Criticism* (1990) *The Art of Fiction* (1992), and a comedic play, *The Writing Game* (1991). Especially popular for his academic novels, Lodge enjoyed an increasingly strong critical reception in the 1990's. *The Writing Game* was adapted for television in 1996, and Lodge was named a Fellow of Goldsmith's College in London in 1992. In 1996 he published *The Practice of Writing*, a collection of seventeen essays on the creative process. In this text he treats fiction writers who have influenced him, from James Joyce to Anthony Burgess, and comments on the contemporary novelist and the world of publishing; the main focus, however, is on adapting his own work, as well as the work of Charles Dickens and Harold Pinter, for television.

Lodge remained a supporter of CARE and other organizations supporting the mentally handicapped (the subject of mental handicaps appears briefly in *Therapy* in a reference to the central character's sister's dedication to a mentally handicapped son). He retained the title of Honorary Professor of Modern English Literature at the University of Birmingham. In addition to interests in television, theater, and film, Lodge maintained an interest in tennis that is sometimes reflected in the novels.

ANALYSIS

In order to understand David Lodge's novels, it is necessary to place them in the context of postwar British literature—the "Movement" writers and "angry young men" of the 1950's, whose attacks on the English class system had an obvious appeal to the author of *The Picturegoers*, the English Catholic novel and "campus novel" traditions, and finally the postmodernism to which British fiction (it is often claimed) has proved especially resistant. In addition, Lodge's novels are significantly and doubly autobiographical. They draw not only on important events in the author's life, but also on his work as a literary critic. In *The Language of Fiction* Lodge defends the aesthetic validity and continuing viabilty of realist writing on the basis of linguistic mastery rather than fidelity to life, and in *The Novelist at the Crossroads* he rejects Robert Scholes's bifurcation of contemporary fiction into fabulistic and journalistic modes, positing the "problematic novel" in which the novelist innovatively builds his hesitation as to which mode to adopt into the novel. Lodge's own novels are profoundly pluralistic yet manifest the author's clear sense of aesthetic, social, and personal limitations as well as his awareness of working both within and against certain traditions and forms.

THE PICTUREGOERS

Set in a lower-middle-class area of London much like the one in which Lodge grew up, *The Picturegoers* is an interesting and even ambitious work marred by melodramatic excesses. As the plural of its title implies, *The Picturegoers* deals with a fairly large number of more or less main characters. Lodge's title also is indicative of his narrative method: abrupt cinematic shifts between the different plots, use of a similarly shifting focalizing technique, and a stylizing of the narrative discourse in order to reflect features of an individual character's verbal thought patterns. Of the seven main characters, Mark Underwood is the most important. A lapsed Catholic and aspiring writer, he arrives in London, rents a room in the home of a conservative Catholic family, the Mallorys, and falls in love with the daughter, Clare, formerly a Catholic novitiate. The affair will change them: Clare will become sexually awakened and then skeptical when Mark abandons her for the Catholicism from which she has begun to distance herself. Interestingly, his return to the Church seems selfish and insincere, an ironic sign not of his redemption but of his bad faith.

GINGER, YOU'RE BARMY

Dismissed by its author as a work of "missed possibilities" and an "act of revenge" against Great Britain's National Service, *Ginger, You're Barmy* continues Lodge's dual exploration of narrative technique and moral matters and largely succeeds on the basis of the solution Lodge found for the technical problem which the writing of the novel posed: how to write a novel about the tedium of military life without making the novel itself tedious to read. Lodge solved the problem by choosing to concentrate the action and double his narrator-protagonist Jonathan Browne's story. Lodge focuses the story on the first few weeks of basic training, particularly Jonathan's relationship with the altruistic and highly, though conservatively, principled Mike Brady, a poorly educated Irish Catholic, who soon runs afoul of the military authorities; on the accidental death or perhaps suicide of Percy Higgins; and on Jonathan's last days before being mustered out two years later. Lodge then frames this already-doubled story with the tale of Jonathan's telling, or writing, of these events three years later, with Jonathan now married (to Mike's former girlfriend), having spent the past three years awaiting Mike's release from prison. The novel's frame structure suggests that Jonathan has improved morally from the self-centered agnostic he was to

the selfless friend he has become, but his telling problematizes the issue of his development. Between Mike's naïve faith and Jonathan's intellectual self-consciousness and perhaps self-serving confession there opens up an abyss of uncertainty for the reader.

THE BRITISH MUSEUM IS FALLING DOWN

This moral questioning takes a very different form in Lodge's next novel. *The British Museum Is Falling Down* is a parodic pastiche about a day in the highly literary and (sexually) very Catholic life of Adam Appleby, a twenty-five-year-old graduate student trying to complete his dissertation before his stipend is depleted and his growing family overwhelms his slender financial resources. Desperate but by no means in despair, Adam begins to confuse literature and life as each event in the wildly improbable series that makes up his day unfolds in its own uniquely parodied style. The parodies are fun but also have a semiserious purpose, the undermining of all forms of authority, religious as well as literary. Parodic in form, *The British Museum Is Falling Down* is comic in intent in that Lodge wrote it in the expectation of change in the church's position on birth control. The failure of this expectation would lead Lodge fifteen years later to turn the comedy inside out in his darker novel, *How Far Can You Go?*

OUT OF THE SHELTER

Published after *The British Museum Is Falling Down* but conceived earlier, *Out of the Shelter* is a more serious but also less successful novel. Modeled on a trip Lodge made to Germany when he was sixteen, *Out of the Shelter* attempts to combine the *Bildungsroman* and the Jamesian international novel. In three parts of increasing length, the novel traces the life of Timothy Young from his earliest years in the London blitz to the four weeks he spends in Heidelberg in the early 1950's with his sister, who works for the American army of occupation. With the help of those he meets, Timothy begins the process of coming out of the shelter of home, conservative Catholicism, unambitious lower-middle-class parents, provincial, impoverished England, and sexual immaturity into a world of abundance as well as ambiguity. Lodge's Joycean stylization of Timothy's maturing outlook proves much less successful than his portrayal of

Timothy's life as a series of transitions in which the desire for freedom is offset by a desire for shelter, the desire to participate by the desire to observe. Even in the epilogue, Timothy, now thirty, married, and in the United States on a study grant, finds himself dissatisfied (even though he has clearly done better than any of the novel's other characters) and afraid of the future.

CHANGING PLACES

Lodge translates that fear into a quite different key in *Changing Places*. Here Lodge's genius for combining opposites becomes fully evident as the serious Timothy Young gives way to the hapless English liberal-humanist Philip Swallow, who leaves the shelter of the University of Rummidge for the expansive pleasures of the State University of Euphoria in Plotinus (Berkeley). Swallow is half of Lodge's faculty and narrative exchange program; the other is Morris Zapp, also forty, an academic Norman Mailer, arrogant and ambitious. Cartoonish as his characters—or rather caricatures—may be, Lodge makes them and their complementary as well as parallel misadventures in foreign parts humanly interesting. The real energy of *Changing Places* lies, however, in the intersecting plots and styles of this "duplex" novel. The first two chapters, "Flying" and "Settling," get the novel off to a self-consciously omniscient but otherwise conventional start. "Corresponding," however, switches to the epistolary mode, and "Reading" furthers the action (and the virtuosic display) by offering a series of newspaper items, press releases, flysheets, and the like. "Changing" reverts to conventional narration (but in a highly stylized way), and "Ending" takes the form of a filmscript. Set at a time of political activism and literary innovation, *Changing Places* is clearly a "problematic novel" written by a "novelist at the crossroads," aware of the means at his disposal but unwilling to privilege any one over any or all of the others.

HOW FAR CAN YOU GO?

Lodge puts the postmodern plays of *Changing Places* to a more overtly serious purpose in *How Far Can You Go?* It is a work more insistently referential than any of Lodge's other novels but also paradoxically more self-questioning: a fiction about the verifiably real world that nevertheless radically insists upon its own status as fiction. The novel switches back and forth between the sometimes discrete, yet always ultimately related stories of its ten main characters as freely as it does between the mimetic levels of the story and its narration. The parts make up an interconnected yet highly discontinuous whole, tracing the lives of its ten characters from 1952 (when nine are university students and members of a Catholic study group led by the tenth, Father Brierly) through the religious, sexual, and sociopolitical changes of the 1960's and 1970's to the deaths of two popes, the installation of the conservative John Paul II, and the writing of the novel *How Far Can You Go?* in 1978.

The authorial narrator's attitude toward his characters is at once distant and familiar, condescending and compassionate. Their religious doubts and moral questions strike the reader as quaintly naïve, the result of a narrowly Catholic upbringing. Yet the lives of reader and characters as well as authorial narrator are also strangely parallel in that (to borrow Lodge's own metaphor) each is involved in a game of Snakes and Ladders, moving narratively, psychologically, socially, and religiously ahead one moment, only to fall suddenly behind the next. The characters stumble into sexual maturity, marry, have children, have affairs, get divorced, declare their homosexuality, suffer illnesses, breakdowns, and crises of faith, convert to other religions, and join to form Catholics for an Open Church. All the while the authorial narrator of this most postmodern of post-Vatican II novels proceeds with self-conscious caution, possessed of his own set of doubts, as he moves toward the open novel. Exploring various lives, plots, voices, and styles, Lodge's artfully wrought yet ultimately provisional narrative keeps circling back to the question that troubles his characters: "How far can you go?" in the search for what is vital in the living of a life and the writing (or reading) of a novel.

SMALL WORLD

Lodge goes still further, geographically as well as narratively speaking, in his next novel. A campus fiction for the age of the "global campus," *Small World* begins at a decidedly provincial meeting in

Rummidge in 1978 and ends at a mammoth Modern Language Association conference in New York one year later, with numerous international stops in between as Lodge recycles characters and invents a host of intersecting stories (or narrative flight paths). The pace is frenetic and thematically exhaustive but, for the delighted reader, never exhausting. The basic plot upon which Lodge plays his add-on variations begins when Persse McGarrigle—poet and "conference virgin"—meets the elusive Angelica Pabst. As Angelica pursues literary theory at a number of international conferences, Persse pursues her, occasionally glimpsing her sister, a pornographic actress, Lily Papps, whom he mistakes for Angelica. Meanwhile, characters from earlier Lodge novels reappear to engage in affairs and rivalries, all in the international academic milieu. A parody of (among other things) the medieval quest, Lodge's highly allusive novel proves at once entertaining and instructive as it combines literary modes, transforms the traditional novel's world of characters into semiotics' world of signs, and turns the tables on contemporary literary theory's celebrated demystifications by demystifying it. At novel's end, Lodge makes a guest appearance, and Persse makes an exit, in pursuit of another object of his chaste desire. The quest continues, but that narrative fact does not mean that the novel necessarily endorses the kind of extreme open-endedness or inconclusiveness that characterizes certain contemporary literary theories. Rather, the novel seems to side with the reconstructed Morris Zapp, who has lost his faith in deconstruction, claiming that although the deferral of meaning may be endless, the individual is not: "Death is the one concept you can't deconstruct. Work back from there and you end up with the old idea of an autonomous self."

NICE WORK

Zapp's reduced expectations typify Lodge's eighth novel, *Nice Work*, set almost entirely in Rummidge but also—as in *How Far Can You Go?*—evidencing his interest in bringing purely literary and academic matters to bear on larger social issues. The essential doubleness of this geographically circumscribed novel manifests itself in a series of contrasts: between the nineteenth and twentieth centuries, literature and life,

the Industrial Midlands and Margaret Thatcher's economically thriving (but morally bankrupt) London, male and female, and the novel's two main characters. Vic Wilcox, age forty-six, managing director of a family-named but conglomerate-owned foundry, rather ironically embodies the male qualities his name implies. Robyn Penrose is everything Vic Wilcox is not: young, attractive, intellectual, cosmopolitan, idealistic, politically aware, sexually liberated, as androgynous as her name, and, as temporary lecturer in women's studies and the nineteenth century novel, ill-paid. The differences between the two are evident even in the narrative language, as Lodge takes pains to unobtrusively adjust discourse to character. The sections devoted to Vic, "a phallic sort of bloke," are appropriately straightforward, whereas those dealing with Robyn, a character who "doesn't believe in character," reflect her high degree of self-awareness. In order to bring the two characters and their quite different worlds together, Lodge invents an Industry Year Shadow Scheme that involves Robyn's following Vic around one workday per week for a semester. Both are at first reluctant participants. Displeasure slowly turns into dialogue, and dialogue eventually leads to bed, with sexual roles reversed. Along the way Lodge smuggles in a considerable amount of literary theory as Vic and Robyn enter each other's worlds and words: the phallo and logocentric literalmindedness of the one coming up against the feminist-semiotic awareness of the other. Each comes to understand, even appreciate, the other.

Lodge does not stop there. His ending is implausible, in fact flatly unconvincing, but deliberately so—a parody of the only solutions that, as Robyn points out to her students, the Victorian novelists were able or willing to offer to "the problems of industrial capitalism: a legacy, a marriage, emigration or death." Robyn will receive two proposals of marriage, a lucrative job offer, and an inheritance that will enable her to finance the small company Vic, recently fired, will found and direct and also enable her to stay on at Rummidge to try to make her utopian dream of an educated, classless English society a reality. The impossibly happy ending suggests just how slim her chances for success are, but the very existence of

Lodge's novel seems to undermine this irony, leaving *Nice Work* and its reader on the border between aspiration and limitation, belief and skepticism, the romance of how things should be and the reality, or realism, of how things are—a border area that is one of the hallmarks of Lodge's fiction.

PARADISE NEWS

Paradise News centers on the quest motif and the conflicts of a postmodern English Catholic. Bernard Walsh, a "sceptical theologican," was formerly a priest but now teaches theology at the University of Rummidge. Summoned, along with his father, to see his aunt, who left England after World War II and is now dying in Hawaii, Walsh signs up for a package tour to save money. The rumpled son and his curmudgeon father join a comic assortment of honeymooners, disgruntled families, and other eccentrics; Lodge calls an airport scene "carnivalesque." When the father breaks his leg on the first morning, Bernard must negotiate to bring his father and his aunt together so that his aunt can finally reveal and overcome the sexual abuse she suffered in childhood. Bernard's journey to Hawaii becomes a journey of discovery in his sexual initiation with Yolande, who gently leads him to know himself and his body.

A major theme, as the title suggests, is "paradise." Hawaii is the false paradise—paradise lost, fallen, or packaged by the tourist industry—yet a beautiful, natural backdrop is there, however worn and sullied. Paradise emerges from within the individuals who learn to talk to one another. The "news" from paradise includes Bernard's long letter to himself, which he secretly delivers to Yolande, and letters home from members of the tour group. As with Lodge's other novels, prominent themes are desire and repression in English Catholic families and a naïve academic's quest for self. In a complex tangle of human vignettes, Bernard moves from innocence and repression to an awakening of both body and spirit—an existential journey that is both comic and poignant.

THERAPY

Therapy centers on another spiritual and existential quest. Lawrence (Tubby) Passmore, successful writer of television comedies, is troubled by knee pains and by anxiety that leads him, after reading the works of Søren Kierkegaard, to consider himself the "unhappiest man." Seeking psychotherapy, aromatherapy, massage therapy, and acupuncture, Tubby moves through a haze of guilt and anxiety. When his wife of thirty years asks for a divorce, he seeks solace with a series of women, with each quest ending in comic failure. Obsessed with Kierkegaard's unrequited love, Tubby launches a quest for the sweetheart whom he feels he wronged in adolescence.

Lodge's concern with the blurring of literary forms is evident in Tubby's preoccupation with writing in his journal, sometimes writing Browningesque monologues for other characters. Opening with an epigraph from Graham Greene asserting that writing itself is "therapy," Lodge takes Tubby through a quest for self through writing that coincides with a literal pilgrimage when he joins his former sweetheart, Maureen, on a hiking pilgrimage in Spain. When Tubby at last finds Maureen, her recollections of their teenage romance minimize his guilt, and his troubles seem trivial in comparison with her losing a son and surviving breast cancer. At the end, Tubby is planning a trip (a pilgrimage) to Kierkegaard's home with Maureen and her husband. Tubby's real therapy has been self-discovery through writing in his journal; other therapies and journeys have failed. Intertwined with existential angst, Tubby's physical and psychological journeys are both comic and sad, with an underlying sense of the power of human goodness and the need to overcome repressions.

Robert A. Morace, updated by Mary Ellen Pitts

OTHER MAJOR WORKS

PLAYS: *Between These Four Walls*, pr. 1963 (with Malcolm Bradbury and James Duckett); *Slap in the Middle*, pr. 1965 (with Duckett and David Turner); *The Writing Game*, pr. 1990.

NONFICTION: *Graham Greene*, 1966; *The Language of Fiction*, 1966; *Evelyn Waugh*, 1971; *The Novelist at the Crossroads*, 1971; *Modes of Modern Writing: Metaphor and Metonymy and the Typology of Modern Literature*, 1977; *Working with Structuralism*, 1981; *Write On: Occasional Essays, '65-'85*, 1986; *After Bakhtin*, 1990; *The Art of Fiction*, 1992; *The Practice of Writing*, 1996.

EDITED TEXTS: *Jane Austen: "Emma," a Casebook*, 1968; *Scenes of Clerical Life*, 1971 (by George Eliot); *Twentieth Century Literary Criticism: A Reader*, 1972; *The Woodlanders*, 1974 (by Thomas Hardy); *The Best of Ring Lardner*, 1984; *Modern Criticism and Theory: A Reader*, 1988.

BIBLIOGRAPHY

Acheson, James. "The Small Worlds of Malcolm Bradbury and David Lodge." In *The British and Irish Novel Since 1960*, edited by James Acheson. New York: St. Martin's Press, 1991. Examines similarities in Bradbury's and Lodge's treatment of liberal academics, with the theme of *Small World* as the starting point of study.

Bouchard, Norma. "'Critifictional' Epistemes in Contemporary Literature: The Case of *Foucault's Pendulum*." *Comparative Literature Studies* 32, no. 4 (1995): 497-513. Addresses Lodge's treatment of academic subject and his use of deconstruction as both theory and technique. Compares Lodge's techniques to those of Malcolm Bradbury and Umberto Eco, specifically comparing Lodge's postmodern experiments with Eco's story of Milanese editors who, toying with a mysterious code, initiate wide-ranging effects in the real world, including mysterious disappearances.

Friend, Joshua. "'Every Decoding Is Another Encoding': Morris Zapp's Poststructural Implication on Our Postmodern World." *English Language Notes* 33, no. 3 (March, 1996): 61-67. Situates the globe-trotting Zapp of the academic novels (*Changing Places*, *Small World*, and *Nice Work*) in the context of Lodge's complex understanding of poststructural/postmodern literary theory. Argues that Lodge parodies postmodernist theory and criticism through Zapp.

Honan, Park. "David Lodge and the Cinematic Novel in England." *Novel: A Forum on Fiction* 5 (Winter, 1982): 167-173. Placing Lodge at one pole of avant-garde English writing (the new realist) and B. S. Johnson at the other, Honan analyzes Lodge's use of impressionistic-cinematic techniques, especially the limiting of dialogue and the cinematizing of "the language of fiction so that varied 'styles' cling completely to the thing represented."

Laing, Stuart. "The Three Small Worlds of David Lodge." *Critical Survey* 3, no. 3 (1991): 24-30. Examines the structure of Lodge's narrative in *Small World*. Argues that it parallels television serial drama and discusses the episodic techniques of serial drama.

Mews, Siegfried. "The Professor's Novel: David Lodge's *Small World*." *Modern Language Notes* 104 (April, 1989): 713-726. Mews begins by placing *Small World* within the context of American, British, Canadian, and German campus fiction. He then analyzes specific features of Lodge's novel that support his conclusion that despite its playful surface, *Small World* presents a serious questioning of contemporary literary theories from an essentially Arnoldian point of view.

Morace, Robert A. *The Dialogical Novels of Malcolm Bradbury and David Lodge*. Carbondale: Southern Illinois University Press, 1989. Provides chapter-length readings of all Lodge's novels through *Small World* in terms of Mikhail Bakhtin's theory of the dialogical novel. As a novelist, Lodge (like Bradbury) works simultaneously within and against the English novel tradition, as he seeks neither to perpetuate old forms and their ideological assumptions nor to surrender to the new (particularly American postmodernism and Continental poststructualist theories) but instead to renegotiate the terms upon which the English novel can remain viable.

Widdowson, Peter. "The Anti-History Men: Malcolm Bradbury and David Lodge." *Critical Quarterly* 26 (1984): 5-32. Argues that the progressive postmodern surface of Lodge's and Bradbury's fiction serves to mask a reactionary ideology and to protect "English culture against charges of provincialism." In support of his position, Widdowson discusses the vague values Lodge espouses, Lodge's typically liberal fear of history and politics, and the willed closure of his novels in which the return to home and family and the liberal freedom of having it both ways often play especially important parts.

JACK LONDON

Born: San Francisco, California; January 12, 1876
Died: Glen Ellen, California; November 22, 1916

PRINCIPAL LONG FICTION

A Daughter of the Snows, 1902
The Call of the Wild, 1903
The Sea-Wolf, 1904
The Game, 1905
White Fang, 1906
Before Adam, 1906
The Iron Heel, 1907
Martin Eden, 1908
Burning Daylight, 1910
Adventure, 1911
The Abysmal Brute, 1913
The Valley of the Moon, 1913
The Mutiny of the Elsinore, 1914
The Scarlet Plague, 1915
The Star Rover, 1915
The Little Lady of the Big House, 1916
Jerry of the Islands, 1917
Michael, Brother of Jerry, 1917
Hearts of Three, 1920
The Assassination Bureau, Ltd., 1963 (completed by Robert L. Fish)

OTHER LITERARY FORMS

Jack London's fifty-nine published works include plays, children's fiction, sociological studies, essays, short stories, and novels. Although generally known as a writer of short fiction, London is also remembered for his pioneering work in tramp nonfiction (*The Road*, 1907) and the science-fiction novel (*The Star Rover*). London was also a journalist, serving as a newspaper correspondent for the San Francisco *Examiner* during the Russo-Japanese War in 1904 and, later, during the Mexican conflict in Veracruz in 1915. His accounts of these wars were published in 1970 under the title *Jack London Reports*. London's correspondence was first published in one volume in 1965.

ACHIEVEMENTS

Called at one time the "Kipling of the Klondike," London was in the forefront of the move toward naturalistic fiction and realism. His social fiction, which included the first sympathetic and realistic treatment of the convict and the tramp, gave him credence as a spokesman for the working class. As a folk hero, London has achieved a popularity that may make him, along with Mark Twain, a permanent figure in American mythology. London is also extremely popular in Europe and the Soviet Union. His work has been translated into more than fifty languages, and his stories appear in countless anthologies of short fiction. Complete editions of London's work have been published in French, German, and Russian. London's novels, especially *The Sea-Wolf* and *The Call of the Wild*, are taught each year in high school and college English courses; a number of his books remain in print year after year. London's reputation

(Library of Congress)

as a solid craftsman—especially of short stories—has now been established firmly, even among literary critics. His novels, still regarded by many as weak and unpolished, gained in stature in the late twentieth century as more and more critics found London's work a subject worthy of discussion.

BIOGRAPHY

A sometime tramp, oyster pirate, seaman, Socialist, laundryman, and miner, Jack (John Griffith) London is as famous for the life he lived and the myths he wove around it as he is for the short stories and novels he wrote. Largely self-educated, London was the product of California ranches and the working-class neighborhoods of Oakland. His rise to literary fame came as a result of the Klondike gold rush. Unsuccessful in his attempt to break into the magazine market, London joined the flood of men rushing toward instant riches in the Yukon. He found little gold but returned after the winter of 1897 with a wealth of memories and notes of the northland, the gold rush, and the hardships of the trail. By 1900, London had firmly established himself as a major American writer.

Also in 1897, London married Elizabeth May Maddern. The couple settled in Oakland, soon adding two daughters to their family. In 1904, seeking new material for his stories and escape from his marriage, which by this time had gone sour, London signed with publisher William Randolph Hearst to cover the impending Russo-Japanese War for Hearst's newspaper the San Francisco *Examiner.* His photographs and accounts of that war were among the first to be published, and he returned to California in triumph, only to face a divorce action.

London's next years were marked by further adventures and travels. In 1905, he journeyed across the United States, lecturing on the need for a socialist revolution. He married Clara Charmian Kittredge that same year, and together they planned a seven-year voyage around the world on a yacht they named *Snark* after Lewis Carroll's mock epic. Ill health forced abandonment of the adventure after only two years, however, and London returned once more to California, this time to create a large ranch complex in Sonoma County.

To support his travels and building program, as well as an extravagant lifestyle, London wrote at a furious pace, publishing fifty books by his fortieth year. His body could not withstand the brutal treatment it received, however, and shortly before his forty-first birthday, Jack London died. His death, officially labeled uremic poisoning and renal colic, was widely rumored to have been suicide. The mysterious circumstances surrounding it have never been explained satisfactorily.

ANALYSIS

Jack London's fame as a writer came about largely through his ability to realistically interpret humanity's struggle in a hostile environment. Early in his career, London realized that he had no talent for invention, that in his writing he would have to be an interpreter of the things that are, rather than a creator of the things that might be. Accordingly, he drew his plots, characters, themes, and settings from real-life experiences and published accounts.

London's career as a novelist began shortly after the turn of the twentieth century with the publication of *A Daughter of the Snows.* It ended nineteen novels later with the posthumous publication of *The Assassination Bureau, Ltd.* in 1963. The novels vary widely in length, subject matter, and (especially) artistic quality, for while London could write bold, violent, and sometimes primitive short stories of immense power, depicting the frontier environment and man's struggle within it in memorable fashion, his novels oftentimes suffered from weakness of structure and excessive didacticism. London's failure of invention, never a significant problem in his short stories, all too often surfaced in his longer works. Some critics have complained that a few of his novels (such as *Burning Daylight,* for example) are not novels at all, but merely strings of short stories hung together by the merest contrivance.

London's novels characteristically contain at least one of three different settings: the Canadian northland, where he began his literary apprenticeship; the primitive South Seas and Hawaii, where his career began anew following a short decline; and the California wilderness—particularly the Sonoma Valley—

where London retreated during the last years of his life.

Each novel also generally contains a philosophical focus. Popular at the time were Charles Darwin's theory of evolution, as interpreted by Herbert Spencer; Friedrich Nietzsche's version of the superman, and, much later, the new psychology of Sigmund Freud and Carl Jung, as well as Karl Marx's theories of a new social order. All fired London's imagination and provided fuel for his characters and plots, and their presence—particularly London's version of the Darwinian "survival of the fittest" motif—lends credence to London's claim for membership in the naturalistic school of fiction.

THE CALL OF THE WILD

London was at the height of his powers when he wrote *The Call of the Wild*. He was dealing with the kind of subject matter, theme, and setting with which he was most comfortable. Written with vigor and intensity, the novel was intended originally only as a companion story to "Batard," an earlier short story. The story literally "got away from him," as he explained in a letter to a friend, and he was forced to expand it to its present length. The book was written shortly after his return from the slums of London. Wanting to escape the degradation and poverty he had witnessed there, London returned to the clean, frozen, beautiful world of the North, where the struggle for survival was elemental, uncomplicated, and fierce. The story is that of a dog, Buck, who is kidnapped from his home on a California ranch and taken to the Yukon, where he is forced to pull heavily laden sleds for inhumane masters. In order to survive, Buck must adapt, falling back on primitive instincts. With domesticity stripped from him, Buck learns the ways of his ancestors; he learns the law of the club—that he will be beaten but will survive. Gradually, as he completes his initiation into the primitive, Buck learns to respond. He learns the law of the fang: that he must be quick to use his own fangs, before others use theirs on him. By adapting to his new environment, Buck survives, learns the instincts of his forebears, and finally, hears the true call of the wild.

Incredibly, London's most successful novel was the one least understood by its author. He did not foresee its popularity, and he sold it outright to his publisher for two thousand dollars. He did not like its title, which now has become a recognizable phrase in the English language, nor did he understand the most powerful element in the book—the human allegory.

In *The Call of the Wild*, London was able to incorporate to good advantage the popular notion of the fierce Darwinian struggle for survival of the fittest. Curiously, he modified the Darwinian theme slightly. Buck must struggle to survive, but his survival is not predicated upon ultimate triumph. He must learn how to use his instincts, he must learn to be a good sled dog, but he need not become the team leader in order to survive. Struggle for its own sake also appears in *The Call of the Wild* and in other London novels. The team does not have to kill the snowshoe rabbit; at the time they are sleek and well fed. Yet, they chase after the animal anyway for the sheer sport of the kill. Struggle for its own sake reappears in *The Iron Heel*, *Martin Eden*, and *The Valley of the Moon*.

THE SEA-WOLF

The Sea-Wolf drew on London's youthful adventures in the sealing grounds off Japan. The novel concerns the survival of upper-class Humphrey Van Weyden, a man who finds himself, through means beyond his control, aboard *The Ghost*, a sealing schooner on its way to Japan. Van Weyden soon finds that the captain of the schooner, Wolf Larsen, has created a hell-ship, filled with brutality and sordidness, where even the ship's practical purpose—to hunt seals—is lost in the misery of mere survival. Van Weyden survives this environment because, like Buck, he is able to adapt to it, learning new codes of survival, drawing upon unknown instincts, and using to best advantage all the benefits of his upbringing and status: intelligence, optimism, and a capacity to love. Van Weyden's growth is the focus of the novel.

If Van Weyden survives because he, too, has learned the law of the club and the fang, the ship's captain, Wolf Larsen, dies precisely because he cannot adapt. At least, that was London's intention, but it was lost upon many early critics. "I attacked Nietzsche and his super-man idea," London wrote to Mary Austin. "Lots of people read *The Sea-Wolf*, [but] no one discovered that it was an attack upon the superman philosophy."

The Sea-Wolf is a fine example of literary naturalism. Larsen, a sensitive, intelligent, domineering man, treats his crew with arrogance. He has no inhibitions and also no friends. Alone, his life lacks purpose and direction, and his aloneness and alienation from nature and from humankind, and, in fact, from himself, lead to his inevitable destruction. Without Van Weyden's ability to adapt, Larsen dies.

If London fails to convince his reader that Larsen died because he was a superman, perhaps it is because London did not fully subscribe to the idea himself. The world is full of supermen—London fancied himself one in many ways—and the socialist alternative that London supported intellectually was one he could not accept emotionally. This conflict between the superman idea and socialism erupts full-scale in *Martin Eden*, when London again takes Nietzsche to task.

While *The Sea-Wolf* may have failed to convey its point to the critics, it did not fail to capture the fancy of the reading public. Next to *The Call of the Wild*, it was (and is) London's most popular book, and it gave the author the financial security he so desperately needed.

The last third of the book is concerned not only with the powerful element of Larsen's degeneration (which Ambrose Bierce called "unforgettable") but also with the introduction of Maud Brewster. London generally had trouble with female characters in his fiction—his editors demanded strict Victorian morals, and London was happy to oblige—and following Maud's introduction, the book is reduced to a sentimental shambles. While the love story, in great part, ensured the critical failure of the book, it also ensured the book's popular success. As soon as Maud steps aboard, Van Weyden reverts to his earlier stature, as if wholly unaffected by the events that have thus transpired: His growth and adaptation are cast aside. The contradictions of *The Sea-Wolf* mirror the contradictions of London's own times. The novel is successful in depicting the turn-of-the-century society in which London lived, which was shaking off the morals and ways of the last century yet still was holding on to vestiges and customs of the earlier time.

WHITE FANG

If *The Call of the Wild* is a novel about a dog who reacquaints himself with his ancestral instincts and learns survival by adaptation, *White Fang* is both its sequel and reverse. *White Fang* is the story of a wolf-dog brought from the Alaskan wilderness to California civilization. Just as Buck used his civilized intelligence to survive, so White Fang uses his primitive strength and endurance to survive in a new environment—the world of civilized humanity. Environment is London's primary focus in this novel, as he traces the changes in the animal's behavior as it moves first from the wolf pack to an American Indian village, then to the white settler, and, finally, to the Santa Clara Valley in California. White Fang is tamed by love, and he successfully makes the transition from savage wolf to loving house pet. While the book does not have the power of *The Call of the Wild*, it does show White Fang's struggle with nature as represented by Native Americans, dogs, white men, and finally, after critical injuries suffered while defending his new benevolent master, death itself.

London was intensely interested in sociology and sociological studies. He wrote one himself, *The People of the Abyss* (1903), and planned another one about the slums of New York City. Much of his interest in the subject can be explained by his belief in socialism, an answer to the problems many sociologists revealed. Thus it is not surprising that he would write *The Iron Heel*, a novel espousing a Marxist solution.

THE IRON HEEL

Like *The Valley of the Moon*, *The Iron Heel* is a novel set in the California wilderness. The similarities end there, however, for while London would later see his agrarian vision as a solution to the economic troubles of his time, in 1905, he still believed that a socialist revolution was necessary and inevitable. He documented it in this futuristic novel of social science fiction—a twentieth century vision of blood, fire, and destruction.

Basing his story on a small book by W. J. Ghent entitled *Our Benevolent Feudalism* (1902), London poured out his private dreams of revolution and glory. If Martin Eden would later die because he was Jack London without socialist fervor, Ernest Everhard, the hero of *The Iron Heel*, cannot live because he lacks the depth and conviction of his own cause. London preaches in *The Iron Heel* without dramatizing his beliefs in convincing action. Indeed, he tried to convince his audience of the righteousness of a cause in which he did not fully believe. Everhard is too superhuman to be credible; Avis Everhard, the widow of the leader of the revolt, is disembodied. Not until the struggle in the book reaches a climax and the battle in the street begins does the novel start to take life.

London used a number of complicated plot structures to convey his point in *The Iron Heel*, and, as usual when dealing with fiction of greater length, he was not entirely successful in sustaining the plot or action. *The Iron Heel* is supposed to be a copy of the Everhard manuscript, a fragment of a paper hidden away by Avis Everhard. This paper was supposed to have been found, some seven centuries later, edited by Anthony Meredith, and then brought to publication as *The Iron Heel*. Covering the period 1912-1913 when the oligarchy rises to power and destroys all forms of free speech and opposition, the paper tells of Everhard's struggle against the oppression and his final flight underground, where he continues the fight, sometimes, as in *The Call of the Wild*, for the sheer sport of it. The novel reaches a bloody climax in Chicago when the mob is slaughtered by the Iron Heel mercenaries.

As might be expected, London's novel was not particularly popular with the reading public. His vision was not accepted by the Socialists, either, perhaps because they sensed that the book was written as a halfhearted attempt at reaffirmation. The struggle between man and nature, so convincingly portrayed in *The Call of the Wild*, becomes a struggle between man and man, oppressed and oppressor, and even London was unsure who would really win the battle.

MARTIN EDEN

While sailing around the world on his yacht *Snark*, London attempted a novel to bolster his career, which was sagging badly in 1907. The result, *Martin Eden*, was a profoundly moving novel, but also, as literary critic Franklin Walker would later

note, a most puzzling work. Called alternately London's finest and his worst novel, *Martin Eden* was meant as another attack on individualism and the Nietzschean superhero. As in *The Sea-Wolf*, London was only partially able to convey this intention. The rags-to-riches motif runs so strongly through the book that the reader is compelled to identify and sympathize with Martin, a lowly seaman, who without education or culture is thrown into the world of the educated and cultured. His introduction to their world fires his mind, and he yearns for their sophisticated ways, their knowledge, and the woman who brings this world to him. Like London himself, Martin decides that the path to social betterment lies through his writing talent, and the novel masterfully describes Martin's (and London's) literary apprenticeship, early failure, and final success.

Martin Eden is a *Bildungsroman*—a novel of education. It employs the potent cultural myth of rags to riches and masterfully depicts Martin's painful transition from the innocence of unknowing to the power of knowledge. As Martin grows and learns, he finds himself embroiled in the battle of the Iron Heel, pitting man against man, oppressed against oppressor. London offers Martin the key to salvation through the poet Brissenden—socialism—but Martin rejects it, and in so doing seals his fate. By the time Martin's road to success ends, it is too late. Without a reason for living, Martin rejects all that he has sought and, finally, takes his own life.

Martin Eden was written aboard ship and is about a sailor. It is therefore not surprising that the paramount symbol in the novel is water. Beginning life as a sailor, coming from the ocean, Martin must return to his beginnings, and he does so by booking passage on an ocean liner and then committing suicide by drowning in the sea.

London returns to the theme of *The Call of the Wild* in *Martin Eden*, with one peculiar twist. Like Buck, Martin begins life unconscious of himself. He does not know that his grammar is imperfect, that his dress is slovenly, or that his manners are uncouth until Ruth Morse educates him. As he learns about himself, he becomes self-conscious. No longer do the instincts that Buck uses to adapt and survive work for

Martin. Unable to adapt to his new environment, Martin returns to the only thing he knows best—the sea—and, fulfilling the paradox of knowing and unknowing, dies.

Martin Eden is a profoundly moving work of imaginative realism, but, like much of London's longer work, it suffers from an uneven structure and sometimes clumsy expression. The major flaw of the book, however, is London's failure to convey his point. Readers are so caught by the potent myth, so sympathetic toward Martin and his fight to the top, that they cannot understand Martin's inevitable death and feel cheated by it. There is too much of Jack London in Martin Eden, too much of London's own confusion over individualism versus Marxism, to carry the novel, and so it fails, as London did, in the attempt.

THE VALLEY OF THE MOON

In a May, 1911, letter to editor Roland Phillips, London outlined his plan for *The Valley of the Moon*: The theme of the book would be back to the land, a likely motif, for it paralleled London's own life story. The agrarian vision, London wrote, would be accomplished by a man and a woman, both wage earners, who meet and grow to love each other in the confines of a big city. Hard times befall them, and the woman, in an attempt to regain the good times they had had together, leads them both on a pilgrimage through California which ends, finally, in Jack London's own valley, the Valley of the Moon.

As London matured, he saw a return to the soil as the solution to the great economic problems of the age. He used this agrarian vision to advantage in his writings and also on the acres of his own expanding ranch. The theme runs through much of his work, including not only *The Valley of the Moon* but also *Burning Daylight* and *The Little Lady of the Big House*.

To solve the problems of the city, Saxon and Billy, the two characters in *The Valley of the Moon*, flee, as they must. London saw the strikes, the fierce struggles for economic and human survival, as symptomatic of the greater problem of humankind out of touch with itself. To return to the soil, to gain salvation, men and women must restore rural America. Billy and Saxon set out to do this, but first they must

be reborn; London did not advocate an escape to the wilderness, but a return to the goodness of nature. To return to Eden, Billy and Saxon must first gain salvation so that they do not spoil Eden as their ancestors once did.

Eden, in this case, is London's own ranch, and once Billy and Saxon arrive they begin applying the principles of agrarian success London fancied himself to be applying. They bring with them the good intentions, motivation, good character, and knowledge necessary to treat the land gently. They do not make the same mistakes the old-style American farmer made; they do not use the land up or wear it out; they apply new methods they have learned from foreigners, Portuguese farmers, to restore the land to its former richness. London realized there was no longer a vast American West. The land beyond the horizon had long been conquered and ruined. It was up to enlightened men and women to restore the land for the reruralization of America that was to come.

Although much more successful as a short-story writer than as a novelist, London's best novels remain alive and vibrant even to this day. His longer fiction was often episodic, disjointed, and loosely structured; his plots were often weak, and many times he let his characters preach rather than act out their philosophy. Nevertheless, London offered a compelling vision of the human condition. The Darwinian struggle for survival was at the forefront of American thought at the turn of the twentieth century; London's fiction mirrored his society, including its contradictions, and led his readers to the primitive arenas where the struggle for survival is best laid bare. London's contribution to the naturalistic tradition and his raw power as a storyteller ensure his continued place in the American literary heritage.

David Mike Hamilton

OTHER MAJOR WORKS

SHORT FICTION: *The Son of the Wolf*, 1900; *The God of His Fathers and Other Stories*, 1901; *Children of the Frost*, 1902; *The Faith of Men and Other Stories*, 1904; *Moon-Face and Other Stories*, 1906; *Love of Life and Other Stories*, 1906; *Lost Face*, 1910; *When God Laughs and Other Stories*,

1911; *South Sea Tales*, 1911; *The House of Pride and Other Tales of Hawaii*, 1912; *Smoke Bellew Tales*, 1912; *A Son of the Sun*, 1912; *The Night-Born*, 1913; *The Strength of the Strong*, 1914; *The Turtles of Tasman*, 1916; *The Human Drift*, 1917; *The Red One*, 1918; *On the Makaloa Mat*, 1919; *Dutch Courage and Other Stories*, 1922.

PLAYS: *Scorn of Women*, pb. 1906; *Theft*, pb. 1910; *The Acorn-Planter*, pb. 1916.

NONFICTION: *The Kempton-Wace Letters*, 1903 (with Anna Strunsky); *The People of the Abyss*, 1903; *The War of the Classes*, 1905; *The Road*, 1907; *Revolution and Other Essays*, 1910; *The Cruise of the Snark*, 1911; *John Barleycorn*, 1913; *Letters from Jack London*, 1965 (King Hendricks and Irving Shepard, editors).

CHILDREN'S LITERATURE: *The Cruise of the Dazzler*, 1902; *Tales of the Fish Patrol*, 1905.

BIBLIOGRAPHY

Auerbach, Jonathan. *Male Call: Becoming Jack London*. Durham: Duke University Press, 1996. Auerbach reverses the trend of earlier London studies, emphasizing how London used his writing to reinvent himself. Above all, Auerbach argues, London wanted to become a successful author, and in that respect he shaped his life to suit his art. Includes detailed notes but no bibliography.

Cassuto, Leonard, and Jeanne Campbell Reesman, eds. *Rereading Jack London*. Stanford: Stanford University Press, 1996. Essays on London as "representative man," his commitment to authorship, his portrayal of American imperialism, his handling of power, gender, and ideological discourse, his relationship to social Darwinism, and his status as writer/hero. Includes end notes, but no bibliography.

Hedrick, Joan D. *Solitary Comrade: Jack London and His Work*. Chapel Hill: University of North Carolina Press, 1982. A Marxist-feminist interpretation of London's life and work. An interesting book with a distinct point of view: that London used his writing to search for "selfhood."

Kershaw, Alex. *Jack London: A Life*. New York: St. Martin's Press, 1997. Concentrates on the "powerful drama" of London's life. Includes notes, illustrations, bibliography, and several helpful maps.

Labor, Earle, and Jeanne Campbell Reesman. *Jack London*, Rev. ed. New York: Twayne, 1994. This clear introduction, first published in 1974, takes into account the twenty years of scholarship after the volume first appeared. This volume also takes issue with the widespread belief that the quality of London's work declined in the last decade of his life. Includes chronology, notes, and an annotated bibliography.

Stasz, Clarice. *American Dreamers: The Story of Charmain and Jack London*. New York: St. Martin's Press, 1988. Jack London and his wife, Charmain—his "mate-woman," as he called her—were married for eleven years. This study, largely based on forty years of Charmain's unpublished diaries, focuses on their relationship.

Watson, Charles N. *The Novels of Jack London: A Reappraisal*. Madison: University of Wisconsin Press, 1982. A very good critical overview of London's fiction. Highly readable and accessible to students of all levels.

MALCOLM LOWRY

Born: Liscard, England; July 28, 1909
Died: Ripe, England; June 27, 1957

PRINCIPAL LONG FICTION

Ultramarine, 1933, revised 1962
Under the Volcano, 1947
Lunar Caustic, 1968
Dark as the Grave Wherein My Friend Is Laid, 1968
October Ferry to Gabriola, 1970

OTHER LITERARY FORMS

All but two of the volumes now attributed to Malcolm Lowry were published after his death at the age of forty-seven. During the last decade of his life, after the publication of *Under the Volcano*, Lowry worked more or less concurrently on numerous projects but was unable to finish any of them before his death. The one closest to completion when he died was *Hear Us O Lord from Heaven Thy Dwelling Place* (1961), a collection of seven interrelated tales. Additional short fiction has been collected in *Malcolm Lowry: Psalms and Songs* (1975), edited by Margerie Bonner Lowry. A selection of poems, edited by Earle Birney, appeared in 1962. *Lunar Caustic*, a novella edited from two earlier versions by Birney and Margerie Bonner Lowry, was published in 1968. Throughout his career, Lowry elaborated and reelaborated a massive scheme of interlocking narratives called, collectively, "The Voyage That Never Ends," which, had he lived to complete it, would have included all of his longer works, with *Under the Volcano* at the center of the "bolus," as he called it. The *Selected Letters of Malcolm Lowry*, edited by Harvey Breit and Margerie Bonner Lowry, appeared in 1965 and played a large part in the revival of interest in Lowry during the 1960's and 1970's. Lowry was also much interested in the cinema and, in collaboration with his second wife Margerie Bonner (herself a published novelist), prepared a screenplay for an adaptation of F. Scott Fitzgerald's *Tender Is the Night* (1934); the film was never produced, but the Lowrys' notes for the film script were published in 1976. Malcolm Lowry's life is the subject of the film *Volcano: An Inquiry into the Life and Death of Malcolm Lowry* (1977), directed by Donald Brittain.

Since so many of Lowry's works were left unfinished at his death, and since even the works published posthumously are selections from numerous versions Lowry left behind, selections made and pieced together by editors, the authenticity of the texts published after 1957 is at least questionable. The special collection of Lowry manuscripts housed at the University of British Columbia Library in Vancouver is, therefore, very important.

Achievements

The only Lowry novel to attract any notable attention during his lifetime was *Under the Volcano*, which was in general very warmly received (in France and the United States at any rate, though curiously it was all but ignored in England) upon its appearance in 1947. During the ten years following, however, no extended works of fiction by Lowry appeared in English, and by the time of his death, even *Under the Volcano* was out of print. Nevertheless, an underground following quietly persisted in its admiration for what must then have seemed, to most, a cometlike blaze of genius revealed in that one novel, appearing out of nowhere and as suddenly disappearing from sight.

The situation altered with the posthumous publication of other Lowry works in the 1960's, beginning with *Hear Us O Lord from Heaven Thy Dwelling Place*. By 1965, a selection of poems had appeared, *Ultramarine* and *Under the Volcano* had been reissued, the *Paris Review* offered a new edition (the first to appear in English) of *Lunar Caustic*, and *Selected Letters of Malcolm Lowry* was published to largely favorable reviews. Lowry was belatedly "discovered" in England, and *Under the Volcano* was hailed as "one of the great English novels of this century" (Philip Toynbee). With the appearance at the end of the decade of the heavily edited, fragmentary novels *Dark as the Grave Wherein My Friend Is Laid* and October Ferry to Gabriola, however, a reaction set in. Both books were widely regarded as failures, and Lowry's tendency toward solipsism was judged to have gotten the better of him in his abortive later works. This view probably does an injustice to Lowry. First, works never brought to completion by Lowry cannot be justly measured against a fully realized work on which the author lavished almost ten years of concerted labor. Even so, Douglas Day's long awaited authorized biography, published to nearly universal acclaim in 1973, seemed to legitimize the view of Lowry as an artist *manqué* whose single triumph amounted to a kind of fluke accomplished despite its author's compulsive tendencies to self-destruction and willed failure. In the late twentieth century, there were salutary signs of a reassessment of the Lowry canon as a whole, with such critics as Muriel C. Bradbrook, Ronald Binns, and Sherrill Grace arguing persuasively against the distortions of the "one-book author" label.

BIOGRAPHY

The youngest of four brothers, Clarence Malcolm Lowry was born at Warren Crest, North Drive, Liscard, Cheshire, England, on July 28, 1909. His father, Arthur O. Lowry, was a wealthy cotton broker of sturdy Victorian probity; his mother, Evelyn Boden, was the daughter of Captain Lyon Boden of Liverpool. A prominent shipowner and mariner, Captain Boden had died of cholera while homeward bound from Calcutta in 1880. This part of the family legacy, so unlike that of the paternal side, would provide Malcolm Lowry with the doom-tinged romantic yearning for the sea much in evidence in his fiction.

At fourteen, Lowry was sent to a public school, The Leys, from which he was expected to proceed to Cambridge University, as his brothers had done. It was during his four years at The Leys, however, that he began to engage in what amounted to a subtle subterfuge of the respectable middle-class life that his father had prescribed for him. He became infatuated with jazz and took up playing the "taropatch," or tenor ukulele. Enthusiastic readings of Herman Melville, Joseph Conrad, Jack London, and the early Eugene O'Neill fed his dreams of adventure at sea. Meanwhile, encouraged by one of his schoolmasters (the model for James Hilton's "Mr. Chips"), he began to write his own stories for the school's literary magazine. At this time, too, he began, surreptitiously at first, what would become another of his lifelong infatuations: alcohol.

By 1927, the conflict with his father had become overt, but Lowry finally agreed to go to Cambridge—after going to sea. In May, he shipped as deckboy aboard the SS *Pyrrhus*, bound for the Far East. This experience, which lasted about six months and was to provide the raw material for *Ultramarine*, punctured at least some of his youthful illusions about the sea. It was followed, in the summer of 1928, by another pilgrimage, this time to New England, where he went to pay homage to Conrad Aiken. The American writer's experimental novel of the sea, *Blue Voyage* (1927), was the catalyst of a kind of private tutorial (Lowry being already engaged in the writing of *Ultramarine*). The two got on famously, beginning a literary kinship—and, later a competition—as of father

and son, which would last in one form or another for thirty years.

At Cambridge, Lowry scarcely applied himself to his formal studies. Instead, he plumped the role of the loutish yet brilliant sailor, took up jazz again, became a connoisseur of avant-garde German silent films, drank, ran with an "advanced" circle of friends, and continued to work on *Ultramarine*. In November, 1929, one of his friends, Paul Fitte, committed suicide. The circumstances remain uncertain, but it is clear from the obsessive references to this event in his later fiction that Lowry felt partly responsible for it. The other significant occurrence of this time came in the summer of 1930, when Lowry again shipped out, this time as fireman on a Norwegian tramp steamer bound for Archangel in the White Sea. His purpose was to pay a visit to Norwegian author Nordahl Grieg, whose novel *The Ship Sails On* (translated in 1927) seemed to Lowry as important a precursor as Aiken's *Blue Voyage*. This journey and the eventual meeting between the two men gave Lowry the idea for another novel, *In Ballast to the White Sea*, on which he worked intermittently for the next fourteen years until the manuscript (running to some one thousand pages) was destroyed in a fire at his home in Canada in 1944.

After graduating with third-class honors in English, Lowry traveled on the Continent, meeting Aiken in Spain in the spring of 1933. There he also met and soon married Jan Gabrial, formerly a stunt woman in Hollywood films. It was an unhappy match, and Jan left him only a few weeks after their marriage in January, 1934. She returned to the United States, Lowry following her by ship the next autumn. In June, 1935, after a particularly severe bout of drinking, he was admitted to the psychiatric ward of Bellevue Hospital in New York. Upon his release ten days later, he began, between further drinking marathons, to write the first draft of *Lunar Caustic*. When an attempt to find a job in Hollywood proved fruitless, Jan and Lowry sailed to Mexico in November, 1936, settling soon after in Cuernavaca, where he began to write *Under the Volcano*. In December of the following year, Jan, who had never been faithful to the unstable Lowry, left him permanently. He drifted south to Oaxaca, where he spent some days in jail and formed an important friendship with a Mexican named Juan Fernando Márquez. Almost continually drunk, Lowry, with the assistance of "agents" sent by his father, was at length put on a train out of the country in July, 1938.

Back in California, Lowry met and fell in love with another American, Margerie Bonner. By the end of 1940, divorced from Jan and remarried to Margerie, Lowry had moved with Margerie into a squatter's shack in Dollarton, on Burrard Inlet, British Columbia. Here they would remain, with occasional trips to Mexico, Haiti, and Europe, for the next fourteen years. It was by far the happiest, most sober (comparatively speaking), and most productive period of Lowry's life. By December, 1944, he had completed the fourth and final version of *Under the Volcano*. A five-month return visit to Mexico between 1944 and 1945 had nearly disastrous consequences—a suicide attempt, more drinking, the discovery that his Mexican friend, Juan Fernando Márquez, had been killed, trouble with the Mexican authorities, and finally deportation—but from these experiences Lowry gained most of the materials for *Dark as the Grave Wherein My Friend Is Laid* and the unpublished fragment *La Mordida*. By 1950, he was working, as it were, simultaneously on these novels, the stories to be collected in *Hear Us O Lord from Heaven Thy Dwelling Place*, the film script for *Tender Is the Night*, his poems, and *October Ferry to Gabriola*.

This period of intense creative effort came to an end in 1954, when Lowry's American publisher, out of patience with his proliferating but seemingly unproductive schemes for his "bolus," severed their contract. Another severance occurred when the Lowrys left their "northern paradise" in Dollarton. After a final, brief reunion with Aiken in New York, they sailed for Italy. In late 1955, Lowry was admitted to a hospital in London for psychiatric treatment. Released in February, 1956, he settled with Margerie in the village of Ripe, Sussex, where he resumed his work. His sudden death, on June 27, 1957, caused by a fatal combination of alcohol and barbiturates, was officially termed "death by misadventure." Not sur-

prisingly, Lowry had long since arrived at his own verdict:

> Malcolm Lowry
> Late of the Bowery
> His prose was flowery
> And often glowery
> He lived, nightly, and drank, daily,
> And died playing the ukulele.

ANALYSIS

Like most artists, Malcolm Lowry was always fascinated by the mystery of the creative process. Unlike many other modern writers, however, he was little inclined to the explicit formulation of aesthetic theories. Still, his attitudes toward art, particularly his own art, are frequently embodied in his fiction. In the opening chapter of *Under the Volcano*, for example, one of the main characters, a film director named Jacques Laruelle, sees a drunken horseman "sprawling all over his mount, his stirrups lost, . . . barely managing to hold on by the reins, though not once . . . [grasping] the pommel to steady himself." Hurtling at breakneck speed through the narrow, winding streets of a Mexican village, the rider slips to one side, nearly falls, rights himself, almost slides off backward, and barely regains his balance, "just saving himself each time, but always with the reins, never the pommel." A closer look reveals a machete in one of the rider's hands, used to beat the horse's flanks furiously. It is, as M. Laruelle reflects, a "maniacal vision of senseless frenzy, but controlled, not quite uncontrolled, somehow almost admirable." This image serves, *mutatis mutandis*, as an epitome of Lowry's art: full of high risk, willfully unstable, disdainful of conventional controls, precariously balanced—but balanced all the same.

Obviously, such balance is achieved, when it is achieved, with great difficulty. This was particularly true for Lowry, whose inclination was always to follow the minutest divagations of the mind. His is an art of excess, in several senses. The composition of a novel, for him, meant continual amplification and expansion, patiently adding layer after layer of meaningful reference and telling detail, until the structure of the whole fairly exploded with a rich profusion of reverberating meanings. Such "overloading," to use Lowry's own word describing his technique, is felt at every level. His prose style, for example, is characterized by wheeling complex sentences, rife with qualifications, suspensions, and parentheses. Brian O'Kill has aptly described this style as "expansive" and "centrifugal," persistently "avoiding the closed unit of the periodic sentence in favor of an open form with an almost infinite capacity for addition and reduplication."

Lowry's range of tone is also unusually wide and varied. As Robert B. Heilman observed,

> In recording a disaster of personality that is on the very edge of the tragic, [Lowry] has an extravagant comic sense that creates an almost unique tension among moods. Desperation, the ludicrous, nightmare, the vulgar, the appalling, the fantastic, the nonsensical, and the painfully pathetic coexist in an incongruous melange that is still a unity.

In a famous letter defending *Under the Volcano* against various suggestions for further revision, Lowry argued that the book could be regarded as a symphony, an opera, a jazz break, a poem, a tragedy, a comedy, a farce, a Churrigueresque cathedral, a wheel, a cryptogram, a prophecy, a film, and a kind of machine. If this claim sounds extravagant, it should be remembered that Lowry believed, with Charles Baudelaire, that "life is a forest of symbols." Virtually everything in this novel—from a theater marquee to items on a menu, newspaper advertisements, an armadillo digging a hole, a cat chasing a dragonfly, amusement park rides, a travel brochure, a urinal—*everything* signifies. Appearing amid profuse allusions to the Bible, Christopher Marlowe, Dante, the Cabbala, John Bunyan, Sophocles, William Shakespeare, Herman Melville, and T. S. Eliot, among many others, these "found objects" in the setting gradually develop into a vast network of the protagonist's plight, elevating it to the level of a modern myth, indeed a tragedy for modern times.

In these respects, as in many others, Lowry resembles no one so much as Melville. (Lowry once admitted, characteristically with irony at his own expense, that he identified himself with the American novelist for several reasons but "mostly because of

his failure as a writer and his whole outlook generally." Both novelists were acutely aware of the monstrous potencies of the human imagination, which could envision—and proceed resolutely to enact—apocalyptic destruction as readily as it could create life-serving works of art. Both knew well the dangers involved in unleashing those potencies, particularly in the service of a narcissistic quest for what Melville's Ishmael calls "the ungraspable phantom of life," the self.

Such a view of the imagination, overtly Romantic and possessed by the seductive demoness of an artistic ego of leviathan, of volcanic, proportions, is clearly fraught with risk. Lowry, like Melville, accepted the risks involved, not the least of which was the gamble that the reader would go along, entertaining the terms of the risk. There are times when, inevitably, the gamble fails. "Overloading"—the Melvillian tendency in Lowry to pile on six portents or allusions or symbols to evoke something that another writer would either summarize in a simple declarative sentence or else not attempt to say at all—sometimes threatens to sink the vessel. Reading the work of both men requires the granting of far more than the usual share of indulgences before the bountiful aesthetic rewards can be reaped.

Some readers, however, do not find such tolerance of unevenness to their taste, and *Under the Volcano* is on the way to becoming one of the least read of great novels, in company with *Moby Dick* (1851). Lowry's other works (like Melville's *Pierre*, 1852, and *The Confidence Man*, 1857) are so much the more neglected, despite the efforts of later critics to call attention to their worth. One can only regret this aesthetic stinginess, along with the more commonplace preference for readily accessible, streamlined fictions. In Lowry's case, the reader who gives himself to the experience proffered, accepting the terms of risk including the excesses involved, and the occasional failings, is likely to find that the gamble more than justifies itself. For, as Matthew Corrigan has aptly observed, when such "writing works for us, it does so . . . because it entails a vision of a higher order of creative existence altogether than we ordinarily get in modern literature."

UNDER THE VOLCANO

Under the Volcano is a book of wonders, a grand testament to the undiminished plentitude of the English language and the prodigious powers—both creative and destructive—of the human imagination. Not the least of its wonders is that Malcolm Lowry began writing it while he was in Mexico suffering through the personal anguish of a failed marriage, chronic alcoholism, and a terror of life so pervasive that it is a minor miracle he survived at all, much less that he was able to write. The novel went through at least four complete drafts in nine years (the third draft having been rejected by no fewer than thirteen publishers) and was finally completed in December, 1944. By that time, Lowry, from the far more stable perspective provided by living simply on the beach in Dollarton with his second wife Margerie, had succeeded in sufficiently harnessing his inner demons so as to transform his earlier sufferings into art. He described the work in an important letter to his British publisher, Jonathan Cape, as a "drama of . . . man's struggle between the powers of darkness and light," but it would be more precise to call it a "Bible of Hell" written by one who had been a member of the Devil's party and knew it well.

One index of Lowry's ability to amplify his experience, transmuting it into a pattern with universal implications, is his management of setting. While the fictional village of Quauhnahuac is loosely modeled on Cuernavaca, where Lowry lived between 1936 and 1938, there is no attempt at documentary realism. To be sure, Lowry selects elements from the real town—the surrounding mountains dominated by the great volcano, Popocatepetl, the Cortes palace with its revolutionary frescoes, the Hotel Casino de la Selva, the dilapidated Borda Gardens of Maximilian and Carlota, the winding cobbled streets, the quaintly named cantinas, the fetid barranca or ravine winding through the town—but his rendering of them emphasizes not mere "local color" but the power of the mind to metamorphose external reality into an interlocking set of correspondences to the inner life of man. One of Lowry's strongest convictions was that life was, as Charles Baudelaire said, a forest of symbols. Thus, Hernando Cortes's palace and the Diego Rivera frescoes adorning it suggest the Spanish Conquest and the Mexican Revolution of 1910-1920, which in turn suggest both the endless internecine conflicts of history and the perpetual battle of the individual human soul against the powers of darkness. The Borda Gardens embody similar meanings, along with the aura of doomed love.

The volcano literally looms large over the entire novel, its snowy summit serving as a symbol of the characters' spiritual aspiration toward ascent, while at its base winds the ubiquitous barranca, suggestive of an alternative destination awaiting the wayward soul. The proximity of the barranca to the totemic volcano and to the many gardens in the novel (most of them, like the Borda Gardens, overgrown, untended, and ruined) calls attention to one of Lowry's central themes: the "infernal paradise" that is the essence of Mexico and, by extension, the modern world itself. This oxymoronic image owes something to D. H. Lawrence, whose novel *The Plumed Serpent* (1926) similarly links the contradictions endemic to revolutionary Mexico with the struggle of his protagonist to undergo a kind of rebirth of spirit. In Lowry, however, the allure of the infernal paradise does not liberate his protagonist from the despoiled garden of life and propel him toward redemption; rather, it arrests him in a state of prolonged inertia, a paralysis of will which renders him finally incapable of actively pursuing the spiritual ascent he so often imagines for himself. In Lowry's version of the myth, at least in *Under the Volcano*, man is condemned to inhabit a garden gone to seed, bereft of its creator: Paradise, surviving only as an image of longing, is irretrievably lost. Solipsistic dreams of ascent succeed only in preventing the upward progress of the soul and, indeed, in promoting its gradual descent into the infernal abyss.

Lowry's narrative, like his setting, is designed to encourage the reader to view the events in broadly symbolic terms. Apart from the opening chapter, which is set one year to the day after the events recounted in the rest of the novel, the narrative's present action is confined to the events of a single day, November 2, 1938, the last day in the life of the protagonist Geoffrey Firmin, a British ex-Consul and an alcoholic's alcoholic. It is also the last day in the life of his wife, Yvonne. The Firmins have been divorced for nearly a year, but on this holiday, known to all in Mexico as the Day of the Dead (All Soul's Day), Yvonne has returned to try to reconcile with Geoffrey. He realizes, however, that such a reconciliation—which he himself has desperately longed for during her absence—would require that he give up drinking, and this he cannot bring himself to do. They quarrel, fail at making love, and part for a time, the Consul to the company of a bottle, Yvonne to that of Geoffrey's half brother Hugh, formerly her lover. Later, the threesome make a day trip "downhill" by bus to Tomalín, where, as Hugh makes a spectacle of himself at an event called a "bull-throwing," Yvonne fervently proposes to Geoffrey that they leave Mexico and try to make a new life together in some "northern paradise" (clearly a reference to Dollarton).

At length, after more drinking and more quarreling, the Consul emphatically refuses and runs off alone, claiming that he prefers "hell" to her offer of a "sober" northern paradise. Pursuing Geoffrey in the darkness through the woods, Yvonne encounters a spooked horse and is trampled to death. The Consul, meanwhile, has gone to the lurid Farolito cantina in Parián, where, after a series of misunderstandings and mescal-inspired blunders—culminating in his freeing of a tethered horse (the same animal that tramples Yvonne in the forest), an act of fuddled yet genuine protest—he is accused of being a Communist spy and is shot to death by Fascist "irregular police." His body is thrown down into the barranca along with that of a dead dog. In the novel's opening chapter, these tragic events, along with many earlier incidents in the lives of the doomed Firmins, are recollected on the Day of the Dead one year later by Jacques Laruelle, a retired French film director who had once been the Consul's closest friend as well as another of Yvonne's lovers.

Such a summary is inevitably misleading, for *Under the Volcano*, like most of Lowry's fiction, really offers little in the way of conventional plot. For one thing, the story is deliberately deprived of any ordinary sort of suspense by the disclosure of its tragic outcome in the first chapter. What this curiously epiloguelike prologue accomplishes, among other things, is a displacement of emphasis away from the sequence of events themselves to their causes and, in the grief of M. Laruelle, some of their effects. Other disruptions of the superficial story interest stem from the frequent use of flashbacks (although strictly speaking, the entire novel after the first chapter is a flashback), as the characters brood on their past lives leading up to this day of crisis; from ellipses caused by the Consul's passing out or hallucinating; and from the constantly shifting narrative viewpoint. Five of the novel's twelve chapters are presented from the Consul's perspective, three from Yvonne's, three from Hugh's, and one from Laruelle's. The focus is thus chiefly inward, on the embattled consciousness of the characters.

Even the characters' surroundings in the external world—Laruelle's bizarre mosquelike house with the oracular inscription on one of the towers (*no se puede vivir sin amar*—"one cannot live without loving"); the municipal garden with its equally oracular warning sign (*¿Le gusta este jardín que es suyo? ¡Evite que sus hijos lo destruyan!*—"Do you like this garden that is yours? See that your children do not destroy it!"); the amusement park rides, including a loop-the-loop contraption called (after a play by Jean Cocteau) *La Máquina Infernal* and a "luminous wheel" that is as much time or fortune as a ferris wheel; the advertisements for a horror film, *The Hands of Orlac*, about an artist-turned-murderer; a cantina called *La Sepultura*, and another called *Salón Ofelia*; the forest around Quauhnahuac and Parián equated repeatedly with Dante's dark wood—all of these external places or objects (and there are many other examples) are essentially coordinates on the map of the mind that the novel traces. Indeed, so densely overgrown is Lowry's "forest of symbols" that one can sometimes lose sight of the immediate or human level of the story. At such junctures, time seems to be arrested or abolished by the "self-reflexive" play of images and motifs, just as it does in *The Waste Land* (1922) and other great "spatializing" works in the modernist tradition. Yet in *Under the Volcano*, the force of time is powerfully affirmed at the bottom of the reeking barranca.

Despite the novel's inward focus, Lowry manages to achieve an ironic detachment from his characters. This is no mean feat, not only because of the autobiographical origins of the story, but also because the Consul himself lays claim to ironic detachment even as he observes his own downfall. Lowry's detachment is achieved precisely through the form of the novel, an exceedingly complex design which includes but is finally larger than even the Consul and his remarkably resourceful capacity to transform his life into species of "quixotic oral fiction." Even though the Consul's tragedy in a moral sense is of his own making, it is made by Lowry to resonate like a central melodic pattern within an enormous surrounding symphonic structure. In part, this resonance derives from the novel's frequent echoing of its own infernal music—the leitmotifs mentioned previously. Equally important are the allusive echoes to literature, myth, and history.

The novel teems with allusions direct and implicit to the Bible, the Cabala, Sophocles, Ovid, Dante, Christopher Marlowe, William Shakespeare, Johann Wolfgang von Goethe, William Blake, Percy Bysshe Shelley, Edgar Allan Poe, Herman Melville, Joseph Conrad, and T. S. Eliot, among others. Persistently, the Consul's situation is compared (often by the Consul himself) with that of Oedipus, Prometheus, Adam, Christ, Judas, the Fisher King, Faust, and Hamlet. These allusions, moreover, are not gratuitous. Individually and collectively, they amount to a kind of running commentary on the pattern of heroism to which the Consul, and sometimes the other characters, aspire, and against which his downfall may be measured. What is one to make, for example, of a hero who, at one moment, proclaims in impressive Promethean tones that "the will of man is unconquerable. Even God cannot conquer it," and who collapses "with a crash," unconscious, the next?

Even more tellingly ironic are the historical analogues that Lowry draws between the Consul and such figures as Cortes, William Blackstone the explorer, Maximilian, and General Victoriano Huerta. All of the latter were men of action, which the Consul emphatically is not; yet, like him, they all became involved, sooner or later, in nefarious political in-

trigues whose result—sometimes unwittingly—was the exploitation of a subject people, usually of another nation or race. During World War I, Geoffrey, then lieutenant commander of a Q-boat, the SS *Samaritan*, was obscurely implicated in the murder of captured German officers; and as Lowry wrote to Cape, "you can even see the German submarine officers taking revenge on the Consul in the form of the *sinarquistas* and semi-fascist *brutos* at the end." However absurd on the face of it, the political pretexts for the murder of the Consul by the pro-Fascists carry a certain underlying truth.

In an important episode in chapter 8, a wounded Mexican Indian is found by the roadside. Because of a Mexican law prohibiting any interference in a crime, even after the fact, the Consul prevents Hugh from attempting to help the dying man. *"Compañero,"* the Indian says, appealing to them, but all they can do is ruminate on the horror of it all, even as another traveler on the bus to Tomalín openly steals the dying man's money. Clearly, there is but a small difference between this sin of commission, the theft, and the Consul's sin of omission, so that in the last chapter, it is fitting that *he* should be "the one dying by the wayside and no good Samaritan would halt." "We evict those who destroy," warns the terrible sign in the garden (as meaningfully mistranslated by the Consul) and, like Cortes, Huerta, and no doubt every other man, in one diluted way or another, Geoffrey Firmin stands guilty at heart: *"No se puede vivir sin amar."*

Yet while Lowry more than encourages the reader to see his characters against this elaborate backdrop of interrelated allusions, symbols, and motifs, it would be a mistake to overemphasize the backdrop at the expense of the foreground figures. The Consul, Hugh, Yvonne, and Laruelle are the cynosures through whose eyes the reader is allowed to glimpse the "massive interests" of a world sliding into the abyss beneath the volcano. At the same time, there is admittedly a deficiency in Lowry's portrayal of character, if by "portrayal" one has in mind the conventions of realistic characterization such as found in Henry James. Lowry was well aware of this deficiency. "The truth is," he wrote to Jonathan Cape, "that the character drawing [in *Under the Volcano*] is not only weak but virtually nonexistent, save with certain minor characters, the four main characters being intended, in one of the book's meanings, to be aspects of the same man, or of the human spirit." Lowry seems almost to be opting for a kind of allegorist's stance when he adds that there "are a thousand writers who can draw adequate characters till all is blue for one who can tell you something new about hell fire. And I am telling you something new about hell fire." This is, as it were, Lowry's *donnée*. He is not particularly interested in his characters as fully realized individuals whose development over the course of time is gradually presented.

The four main characters are all, as he said to Cape, "aspects of the same man." Hugh is "Everyman tightened up a screw . . . the youth of Everyman"; Yvonne is "the eternal women," the anima principle; Laruelle is the Consul's *Doppelgänger*, a surrogate for the artist/betrayer with blood on his hands. Although Lowry has provided glimpses into these characters' past lives, his purpose is less to trace the etiology of, for example, the Consul's alcoholism, than it is to locate key moments that chime with the present situation or offer ironic contrast to it. As Terence Wright has noted, "Lowry is not concerned with the Consul's fall as a *process*, nor with the attempts to save him as a thing which may or may not be accomplished, but with the *contemplation* of a state of affairs—the state of affairs being that a man is in Hell."

Notwithstanding the Consul's grandiose gestures toward Promethean rebellion, what is really most remarkable about him is his readiness to embrace his own death and damnation. This is perhaps what Lowry was referring to when he claimed to be teaching the world "something new about hell fire." The Consul *knows*, as his very utterance indicates ("A corpse will be transported by express!"), that his "glorious" descent is nearing its conclusion and that death is imminent, just as the reader knows, from the opening chapter, that Geoffrey has *already* succeeded in finding the disaster he has so ardently courted. This curious sense that everything has already happened conditions the whole feeling of the book and makes possible a range of effects—including moments of wild comedy and soaring lyricism—that one would not ordinarily expect to find in a tragic tale. It is as if the Consul, having resigned himself to the inevitability of his downfall, having indeed long since chosen the "hell" of addiction, solipsism, and despair represented for him by the Farolito, can undergo his descent and simultaneously observe himself descending, even deriving a certain amusement from the spectacle. The Consul's semidetachment from his own suffering derives in part from his very awareness of the paradigms of tragic downfall in literature, above all Marlowe's Doctor Faustus, whose despairing quest for forbidden knowledge he deliberately emulates. At the same time, indulging in this "heroic" despair, he seems to harbor the illusion (derived this time from Blake) that "right through hell there is a path" leading to a "new life" beyond: By sinking as low as it is possible for a man to sink, giving himself over to complete damnation, he will somehow be saved in the end.

Salvation, however, will come, if it comes, not in the form of a loving union with Yvonne in some sober northern paradise but in the form of mystical vision—a state of mind for which, he believes, alcohol is *"absolutamente necesario."* The Consul regards his drinking as a religious exercise comparable to the partaking of an eternal sacrament. His determination to resist the meddling "salvage operations" of Hugh and Yvonne takes on the significance of a kind of holy war, an anticrusade, so to speak. As he tells Jacques Laruelle, he is fighting for nothing less than "the survival of the human consciousness." The fact that these are, on one level, an alcoholic's rationalizations, does not alter the issue. Drink, as the principal means of access to the visionary state, has become an integral part of his quest for occult knowledge and as such is immutably associated with a peculiar kind of fulfillment that the Consul has actually known, ". . . how, unless you drink as I do, can you hope to understand the beauty of an old woman from Tarasco who plays dominoes [in the cantina] at seven o'clock in the morning?"

This mixture of attitudes accounts for the "tragic joy" that, for a time, mitigates the gathering darkness of *Under the Volcano*. The Consul's vision at such moments is of genuinely heroic proportions, for he succeeds not merely in embracing Faustian despair but in transcending it, albeit fleetingly. The Consul is a man of awesome imaginative energies and tremendous resources of humor and intelligence, so that when he dies, the reader experiences that sense of immense waste that accompanies the deaths of great tragic heroes such as Doctor Faustus. Yet the very qualities that set him apart contribute directly to his downfall. The ultimate irony here is that even though he succeeds in finding at the Farolito the "hell" he has sought all along, he succeeds "in a manner somewhat outside his calculations." He finds that damnation is not so ennobling—much less is it an amusing object for detached contemplation—after all. Knocked flat on his face by the shots of a Chief of Rostrums (of all people), the Consul is disappointed, as he was bound to be: "Christ . . . this is a dingy way to die," he tells himself. At this point, the Consul in effect sloughs off the trappings of a borrowed literary heroism and achieves his own "autochthonous" stature as a hero. He dies not as a modern-day Faustus but as Geoffrey Firmin, self-evicted from the potential satisfaction of living in even an infernal paradise. Nevertheless, as he lies dying, shorn of all vestiges of grandiosity, he recognizes what, in his solipsism, he has become. He acknowledges the tragic error of attempting to live without loving—faces, that is, his own essential humanity—though, as his final vision of climbing the volcano only to find himself hurtling down into it makes clear, it is too late for him to act on this new awareness. Moreover, even if he could somehow act, Yvonne is no longer attainable, thanks to his last defiant gesture of releasing the horse.

The novel closes with the Consul's final vision (chorically echoed by the oracular warning sign in the ruined garden), at once the culminating comment on his life of solipsistic denial and a vision of apocalyptic destruction:

> The world itself was bursting, bursting into black spouts of villages catapulted into space, with himself falling through it all, through the inconceivable pandemonium of a million tanks, through the blazing of ten million burning bodies, falling, into a forest, falling.

Although *Under the Volcano* is Lowry's best and most highly regarded work, his other pieces have received more sympathetic treatment. Muriel C. Bradbrook was the first to call attention to Lowry's early experiences on the Wirral Peninsula, in public school, and at Cambridge as in many ways the crucial source of his mature vision, an emphasis that nicely balances Douglas Day's excessive dwelling on the last, doom-haunted years. Ronald Binns is one of several critics to examine Lowry's fiction after *Under the Volcano* both seriously and sympathetically, finding in it evidence of a new direction toward the metafictional mode of such postmodernists as Samuel Beckett, Vladimir Nabokov, and Jorge Luis Borges, rather than mere failed attempts to repeat the "high modernist" performance that links *Under the Volcano* with the older tradition of James Joyce and Marcel Proust. For her part, Sherrill Grace maintains that *Under the Volcano* is "best viewed as the magnificent Popocatepetl among lesser, but by no means uninteresting, peaks." In short, although *Under the Volcano* still stands as Lowry's undisputed masterpiece, an adequate appreciation of his complex achievement finally depends on a firm understanding of his "bolus" as a whole. When this understanding occurs, there is reason to believe that Lowry will be recognized as one of the greatest of modern visionary artists.

Ronald G. Walker

OTHER MAJOR WORKS

SHORT FICTION: *Hear Us O Lord from Heaven Thy Dwelling Place*, 1961; *Malcolm Lowry: Psalms and Songs*, 1975 (Margerie Bonner Lowry, editor).

POETRY: *Selected Poems*, 1962 (Earle Birney, editor).

NONFICTION: *Selected Letters of Malcolm Lowry*, 1965 (Harvey Breit and Margerie Bonner Lowry, editors).

MISCELLANEOUS: *Notes on a Screenplay for F. Scott Fitzgerald's "Tender Is the Night,"* 1976 (with Margerie Bonner Lowry).

BIBLIOGRAPHY

Asals, Frederick. *The Making of Malcolm Lowry's "Under the Volcano."* Athens: University of Georgia Press, 1997. Discusses Lowry's themes in his major work. Includes bibliographical references and an index.

Binns, Ronald. *Contemporary Writers: Malcolm Lowry.* London: Methuen, 1984. Discusses the Lowry "myth," with emphasis given to *Under the Volcano* and the autobiographical elements in his writing. The chapter on metafictions is a particularly useful survey of Lowry's late experimental novels and stories. A valuable guide for the beginning reader of Lowry.

Bowker, Gordon. *Malcolm Lowry Remembered.* London: British Broadcasting Corp., 1985. A readable collection of reminiscences that attempt to "penetrate the myth and reach the man." Some of the essays are published here for the first time. Also includes interviews with Lowry's two wives and many of his friends and admirers.

_____. *Pursued by Furies: A Life of Malcolm Lowry.* New York: HarperCollins, 1993. A comprehensive, scholarly biography. See especially the preface for pithy comments on the relationship between Lowry's life and fiction. Includes a brief bibliography.

Costa, Richard Hauer. *Malcolm Lowry.* New York: Twayne, 1972. The second half of this study deals with Lowry's work during his fifteen years in Canada. Costa approaches his study of Lowry from a Jungian perspective and looks at this author's "mystical-messianic aspects."

Grace, Sherrill, ed. *Swinging the Maelstrom: New Perspectives on Malcolm Lowry.* Montreal: McGill-Queen's University Press, 1992. Grace's introduction is a useful guide to Lowry's reputation. Part 1 contains essays on the relationship between his life and his fiction. Part 2 concentrates on *Under the Volcano*; part 3 on Lowry's subsequent fiction; part 4 on assessments of his body of work. Includes notes but no bibliography.

Markson, David. *Malcolm Lowry's Volcano: Myth, Symbol, Meaning.* New York: Times Books, 1978. An in-depth critical study of Lowry's *Under the Volcano*, considered his masterpiece and recognized by many critics as a major novel of this century. Indispensable to the serious scholar of Lowry.

ALISON LURIE

Born: Chicago, Illinois; September 3, 1926

PRINCIPAL LONG FICTION

Love and Friendship, 1962
The Nowhere City, 1965
Imaginary Friends, 1967
Real People, 1969
The War Between the Tates, 1974
Only Children, 1979
Foreign Affairs, 1984
The Truth About Lorin Jones, 1988
Women and Ghosts, 1994
The Last Resort, 1998

OTHER LITERARY FORMS

Besides writing fiction, Alison Lurie distinguished herself in two other areas, children's literature and the semiotics of dress, and her novels reflect both concerns as well. Her interest in children's literature is reflected in *Only Children*, in which two little girls pose their fantasies against the shocking reality exposed to them by their parents, and in *Foreign Affairs*, in which one of the two central characters, Vinnie Miner, spends her sabbatical in England collecting playground rhymes. Real children's rhymes, Lurie observes, are surprisingly subversive, not like the "safe" literature written for children by adults. She developed this insight in a nonfiction work, *Don't Tell the Grown-Ups: Subversive Children's Literature* (1990). Lurie's fascination with the semiotics of clothing (*The Language of Clothes*, 1981) is reflected frequently in the novels, where she pursues the relationship between clothing and personal identity. An especially provocative example can be found in *Imaginary Friends*, where Roger Zimmern, forced by a strange religious group to abandon his normal academic dress in favor of cheap suits, loses his sense of identity.

ACHIEVEMENTS

Lurie's fiction has received much praise from critics, and her work has been very popular with the

(Jimm Roberts/Orlando)

broader reading public. Her first novel, *Love and Friendship*, appeared in 1962 and was followed by several prestigious grants and fellowships: Yaddo Foundation Fellowships in 1963, 1964, and 1966; a Guggenheim grant in 1965-1966; a Rockefeller Foundation grant in 1967-1968; a New York State Cultural Council Foundation grant in 1972-1973. *The War Between the Tates* in 1974 brought Lurie a popular audience and more critical acclaim. An American Academy of Arts and Letters award followed in 1978, and for *Foreign Affairs* she was awarded a Pulitzer Prize in 1985. All of Lurie's fiction displays a remarkable control of language, a style which surprises and amuses. Both for her wit and for her sharp-edged, satiric depiction of human follies, she has often been compared to Jane Austen.

BIOGRAPHY

Alison Lurie was born September 3, 1926, in Chicago, Illinois, but grew up in White Plains, New York. Her Latvian-born father was a scholar, a teacher, and a socialist who later became the founder and executive director of the Council of Jewish Federations. Lurie's mother, also a socialist, was a former journalist for the Chicago Free Press. Lurie suffered a minor birth injury that affected the hearing in her left ear and also caused some damage to her facial muscles. An avid reader as a child, she began at about the age of thirteen to read such authors as Charles Dickens, George Bernard Shaw, and Jane Austen. In 1947, she graduated from Radcliffe, where she met many people who later became important literary figures, including Jonathan Peale Bishop, a teacher, critic, and essayist. She married Bishop in 1948, and they had three children. In 1975, Lurie separated from Bishop, divorcing him ten years later.

Struggling with many discouraging rejections of her writing in her twenties, the turning point in her life came in 1966, when she wrote a memoir of an eccentric friend, V. R. (Bunny) Lang. Thereafter came a succession of novels that garnered high praise, including a Pulitzer Prize for *Foreign Affairs*. A professor of children's literature at Cornell University in Ithaca, New York, where she began teaching in 1969, Lurie divided her time between Ithaca, Key West, and London.

ANALYSIS

Alison Lurie's novels are known for their comedy and satire, and her acute observation is most often trained on the complications of love, marriage, and friendship as they affect the lives of the upper classes, the educated, the academic. Many of her novels take place at the fictional Convers College in New England or at Corinth University in upstate New York (based on Cornell University, where Lurie taught for many years) or concern characters who teach at or have been associated with Corinth. These novels are not, however, all academic satire; the academics often travel to other places or become involved in issues beyond the campus.

Lurie's style is most often detached and ironic, a treatment that has won for her both blame and praise.

Her novels, except for *Only Children*, explore the time in which they are written and reflect the events and culture of Lurie's own adult years. The novels typically cover a short space of time, a crisis point in the lives of the characters, but several of the characters are seen at different points in their lives because of Lurie's use of the same characters in different novels—sometimes as major, sometimes as minor characters. Lurie works successfully with a variety of narrative points of view: omniscient narration in *The War Between the Tates*, first-person narration in *Real People*, third-person focus narration in *Imaginary Friends* (expanded to include two focus characters in *Foreign Affairs*). She shows no penchant for either the happy or the unhappy ending, realistically leaving her characters to continue to work out their lives as best they can.

LOVE AND FRIENDSHIP

At the heart of Lurie's first two novels are couples trying to work out their relationships. Her first novel, *Love and Friendship* (a title taken from Jane Austen), draws out the main lines of the issue. What is love and what is friendship? Are they different in what is best and most enduring? In this novel, the main character, Emmy Turner, "loves" her lover more than she does her husband. In the end, however, she chooses her husband over her lover because he needs her and to him she can be a friend. Indeed, what first led her to enter into a love affair was a frustration with her husband's failure to make a friend of her, to discuss with her his work and his concerns. Ultimately, Lurie suggests, friendship is more satisfying and lasting than love; indeed, love at its best is friendship at its best.

THE NOWHERE CITY

In her second novel, *The Nowhere City*, the ending is the opposite, but the implication seems the same. Paul Cattleman rediscovers his wife at the end after much neglect and many adulteries. It is too late, however: Friendship is lost, and with it love; she tells him that she is not angry with him, but she just does not know him anymore.

REAL PEOPLE

While the love and friendship theme becomes a secondary issue in *Imaginary Friends*, the novel Lurie published after *The Nowhere City*, she made it once again the central focus of *Real People*. In this novel, Janet Belle Spencer, a writer, has taken up residence at Illyria, a haven for writers and artists. She has gone there primarily to work, since she cannot seem to writLagerkvisthe is also drawn there by her love for an artist, Ken, with whom she believes she has much more in common than with her insurance-executive husband. The artists' colony of Illyria is an unreal world, however, and Janet discovers that she and Ken are not really friends; she learns much about her writing that she resolves to change. It is at home with her husband, Clark, not at Illyria, she finally realizes, that she will be able to put to work her new understandings.

THE WAR BETWEEN THE TATES

Love and friendship in marriage are explored most intensively in Lurie's next and most celebrated novel, *The War Between the Tates*. Erica and Brian Tate, a young academic couple, are in their own eyes and in the eyes of their friends the perfect couple, but as middle age looms, Brian becomes increasingly frustrated at not being famous, while the children become rebellious teenagers. True love and friendship appear to be lacking. Finally, Brian has an affair with a student whom he makes pregnant, Erica befriends the student, and both Brian and Erica, but especially Erica, wander through a bewildering maze of events that leave their earlier sense of themselves and their marriage damaged. As the novel ends, they drift back together, confused, "out of love," but basically seeking a peace they can find only with each other.

ONLY CHILDREN

Love and friendship in marriage is the topic once again of *Only Children*, but this time the actions of the adults are seen through the eyes of two little girls, Lolly and Mary Ann, who respond to what they see in the behavior of their elders, especially their parents. In each set of parents there is one serious, deeply dedicated person (Lolly's mother, Mary Ann's father) and one shallow, egotistic, flamboyant hunter of the other sex. The two sets of parents ultimately stay together, but, lacking a love based on friendship, they are merely maintaining a façade, and their example will cripple their children's ability to love.

Foreign Affairs

The love and friendship theme appears again in *Foreign Affairs*, which juxtaposes two main characters, one married and one not. Vinnie Miner, a middle-aged professor, finds love surprisingly where she had least expected it, in a friendship with a man totally unlike her, a retired sanitary engineer. The other main character, a handsome young man in Vinnie's academic department, begins the novel estranged from his wife, is temporarily dazzled and infatuated by a far more glamorous Englishwoman, but returns to his wife at the end, finding her superior in trust, honesty, and common decency.

The Truth About Lorin Jones

Love and friendship are very complicated and contradictory in *The Truth About Lorin Jones*, a novel that is a departure from her earlier novels for a number of reasons. Instead of an academic setting, the setting is the contemporary art world, and the primary relationship in the novel is one that essentially exists within the mind of Polly Alter, a failed painter who is researching the life of the late Lorin Jones, an artist whose life and loves seem to speak to Polly's own situation. Lorin, who was once Lauren "Lolly" Zimmern, one of the little girls in *Only Children*, has lived a life of professional and personal frustration and is possibly still haunted by the demons of her childhood. The contemporary issues of feminism and lesbianism complicate the lives of both Polly and Lorin, but Lurie adds a new twist to the feminist argument by suggesting that it was Lorin who exploited the men in her life, using them as a means to serve her own ambitions. Polly's discovery of the truth about Lorin permits her a new lease on life, as does her romance with Hugh Cameron, a onetime hippie poet who had been Lorin's first husband.

The Last Resort

In Lurie's tenth novel, *The Last Resort*, Jenny Walker, formerly a subservient wife to her distinguished academic husband, faces a crisis in her marriage when she increasingly comes under the sway of the charismatic lesbian Lee Weiss. Jenny's attraction to Lee is heightened by the respect and attention Lee accords her, whereas her husband, Wilkie, is content to see her merely as a passive supporter of his plans.

Wilkie himself, under the impression that he is terminally ill, begins to detach himself emotionally from his wife but has a brief flirtation with a young female admirer even as he prepares to commit suicide. Although the couple are reunited at the end of the novel, their relationship has changed. Jenny acquires greater self-confidence and feels she is now in charge of her own life. Wilkie's "greatness" is no longer allowed to dominate their relationship as it once did.

The Academic Microcosm

Lurie's novels concern themselves with relationships between people, and these relationships are at the center of all of her work. Yet the lives of Lurie's characters are affected by more than personal forces alone. Context, temporal and physical alike, is also central to these novels, and the direction of the lives of Lurie's characters is profoundly affected by the times and the places in which they live. The most persistent context, moreover, is academic, since many of these characters, like Lurie herself, are university professors or members of their families. In this case again, *Love and Friendship* sets a pattern which other novels will follow. Emmy Turner's husband, Holman Turner, is a young instructor at Convers, a small, exclusive liberal arts college in New England. Emmy wants to share her husband's academic interests but he shuts her out, treasuring her as an ideal wife and mother but bored by her attempts to enter into his intellectual concerns. Ironically, Emmy should be more at home at Convers (her wealthy father is a trustee, and two brothers are alumni), while Holman has come from a very different background, yet it is he, not Emmy, who seems the "Convers type." Emmy's love affair flaunts the Convers traditions, while Holman seems the perfect instructor. In the end, however, he falls afoul of those same Convers traditions, and it is Emmy who must stay to save him.

The academic world is also a factor in *The Nowhere City*, although the story takes place in a Los Angeles setting which dominates the novel. Paul, in the end, will retreat to the eastern academic world that he knows (remaking his relationships with his old Harvard friends and taking a teaching post at Convers College), while Katherine, who had initially seemed the more eastern academic of the two, refuses to return there with him and seems to find a new self in Los Angeles.

The War Between the Tates again makes the academy not only a strong backdrop but also an actor in the events. Brian Tate is a highly successful sociology professor at Corinth University in upstate New York; his wife, Erica, is a faculty wife. Their two closest friends, who divorce in the novel, are Leonard Zimmern, an English professor, and Danielle Zimmern, Erica's closest female friend, a part-time faculty member in the French department. The convulsions of American academe in the late 1960's interfere directly in Brian's and Erica's lives. Brian, though very successful academically, has always dreamed of fame as an adviser to governments and presidents, and his middle-aged frustration makes him susceptible to trying to recover his lost youth by mixing socially with his graduate students, increasingly adapting his clothing and other styles to theirs, finally indulging in his affair with Wendy. Erica, like Katherine Cattleman in *The Nowhere City*, attempts to preserve her traditional moral values in the face of all this upheaval and tries not only to adapt herself to these values but also to give direction to Brian and Wendy, even to the point of insisting that Brian divorce her and marry Wendy. She becomes peripherally involved, through her friend Danielle, in the Hens, a local feminist group, and finding the local Hare Krishna guru of the students to be an old school friend, under his guidance has her own adventure with LSD. Brian and Erica, then, experience their marital troubles amid the student rebellions of the 1960's. Though the novel does not probe as deeply as *Imaginary Friends* into the political and intellectual doubts and troubles of academe, these influences are present, shaping their reaction.

In *Foreign Affairs*, the two main characters are again college professors, both from the English department at Corinth University: the middle-aged, internationally famous expert in children's literature, Vinnie Miner, and the young specialist in the eighteenth century, Fred Turner, both on leave to do scholarly work in London. The novel for the most part tells their stories separately, their paths crossing

significantly only twice. While their common background does make their lives cross in significant ways, and while both their lives are shaped by their academic backgrounds, the primary focus of the novel is on other aspects of their lives, which will be discussed below.

THE AMERICAN MACROCOSM

The university campus, then, demonstrates the importance of time and place in Lurie's novels. This is also true in a larger sense, since American culture itself, with its regional and sociological tensions, plays just as important a role as the characters do. If *Love and Friendship*, the first novel, works off a Jane Austen theme, it also echoes a peculiarly American, Fitzgeraldian theme in which the different regions and classes of America become important players in the conflicts of the novel. Emmy is New Jersey rich, her lover Will Thomas southern shabby genteel, and her husband Holman Chicago shabby but respectable poor. As the marital couple work out their conflicts with traditions of Convers College playing an important role, these different regional and class conflicts do much to shape their actions and reactions. In *The Nowhere City*, 1960's America, with its new and strange customs and dress, almost overpowers its characters' ability to work out their human problems. Here, Los Angeles is the city in which "nowhere" comes to mean "present but lacking history and future." Strange and mixed new forms of architecture in both house and public building design, styles of hair and dress, sexual lifestyles, artistic forms, even subjects being studied in the universities are all strange, macabre, and new, dividing Katherine and Paul Cattleman as they respond to them so differently. Setting plays just as important a role in *Imaginary Friends*, which brings two very traditional strongholds, the enclosed small town and the principles of academic inquiry, together with the strains of the world without.

Real People, again, though it removes its main characters to an isolated, protected, ideal world of the artists' colony, nevertheless shows that the best work cannot be done in an artificial atmosphere but only when the artists are living and writing truthfully about the world in which they are "real people."

Again, too, despite all the 1960's campus shenanigans of *The War Between the Tates* (drugs; strange new lifestyles, clothes, and hairstyles) the novel presents a strong sense that the campus is only reflecting all the major movements, confusions, and displacements of the society at large. In *Only Children*, which is set during the Great Depression, the characters reflect the concerns of that time, including its powerful economic and political conflicts. Bill Hubbard, for example, is an example of the President Franklin Roosevelt-type liberal democrat, dedicated to social reforms that will lift the poor, while Dan Zimmern represents the nascent Madison Avenue type, flamboyant and driven to succeed. *Foreign Affairs*, in the experiences of both Vinnie Miner and Fred Turner, discloses the tensions of many cultural mores, especially different class and sexual expectations, complicated further by differences between Great Britain and the United States.

In her ninth and tenth novels, Lurie abandons both the international theme and an academic setting, returning to the world of art and the artist that was her subject in *Real People*. In *The Truth About Lorin Jones*, which explores the art world and the lesbian feminist subculture, the closest we come to a traditional intellectual is the character of Garrett Jones, a powerful art critic and patron. In *The Last Resort*, the academic world is reflected only in the character of Wilkie Walker, a prominent plant botanist who has branched out into writing best-selling works for the general public. He is very widely respected, although there are some doubts about the thoroughness of his research. In this novel, academic and cultural achievement is seen as a dangerous booster of the male ego, giving older men the illusion of a control over their lives they in fact lack. Another side of cultural life in *The Last Resort* is represented by the poet Gerald Grass, an aging survivor of the beatnik and hippie movements of earlier decades, who is a variation on the character of Hugh Cameron in *The Truth About Lorin Jones*.

The Truth About Lorin Jones and *The Last Resort* introduce another setting into Lurie's work, namely Key West, the southernmost point in the continental United States and the site of Lurie's second home.

Lurie uses the remoteness and luxury of Key West to place her characters in a distinct setting where they can work out their problems before returning, altered and refreshed, to the "real" world. In this way, Key West operates much like the island in William Shakespeare's *The Tempest* (1611). Lurie also sketches cultural and political differences on the island, delineating the way Key West's sizable homosexual community comes under attack from wealthy, right-wing Republicans who also reside in the area. Issues such as aging and AIDS also are given extended, if sometimes light-hearted, examination.

LITERARY INFLUENCES

The lives of the individual characters are additionally set against the backdrop of the world of literature itself. In *Real People*, Janet Belle Spencer images Ken as the ideal reader of her fiction, largely because he recognizes every literary reference—which in turn is reminiscent of Lurie's own rich texture of literary reference. In this regard, as already observed, she uses the "love and friendship" theme from Jane Austen. Another novelist to whom Lurie is greatly indebted is Henry James, especially in *Imaginary Friends* and *Foreign Affairs*. Indeed, *Imaginary Friends* in many ways duplicates the plot of James's *The Bostonians* (1885-1886), in which a young woman named Verena leads a band of truth-seekers by an extraordinary gift of public speaking, which seems to proceed from a trancelike ability to contact higher powers. Lurie's Verena, like James's heroine, is torn between her group and her believers there, and a young man in love with her who wishes to carry her away. This role, taken by Basil Ransom in James's novel, is split in *Imaginary Friends* between the narrator, Roger, and the young man Ted, who does finally marry Verena and carry her off to the University of Arizona, where they are last seen as student agitators.

Foreign Affairs enlarges on the Jamesian theme not only by explicitly introducing James's work by name but also by exploring one of his most insistent themes: what happens when basically good, decent Americans encounter a far more culturally sophisticated European society. In James's novels of this type, the balance is struck in favor finally of the basic, honest decency of Americans against the more sophisticated but possibly corrupt world of the Europeans, and Lurie's novel arrives at the same resolution. This exploration is complicated by the fact that, of the two Americans, Vinnie Miner is very sophisticated in the ways of the English, knowing their ways and customs so well that she really feels more culturally at home there than in the United States. Fred Turner, on the other hand, despite his great physical charms and handsomeness and his knowledge of eighteenth century literature, is basically a raw recruit to European culture. Both, however, have "foreign affairs": Vinnie, with an almost illiterate Oklahoman whom she meets on the plane on the way over, so embarrasingly crude that she dreads presenting him to her friends; Fred, with an English aristocrat and actress so elegant and sophisticated that his American life appears crude by comparison. Despite this structural converse, in which Vinnie loves an American far less presentable than her European friends, and in which Fred loves an Englishwoman far more sophisticated than his American wife and friends, both find, despite all of their differences, their American loves superior after all, and their European friends, for all of their sophistication, less satisfying morally as friends and lovers than their American friends. Thus, the pattern of James's international novels, in which superior American decency confronts and ultimately wins out over superior European elegance and sophistication, is repeated here in Lurie's fiction.

The influence of James can also be discerned in *The Truth About Lorin Jones*, which, like *Imaginary Friends*, recalls James's *The Bostonians*. In this case, the competition between male and female for the loyalty of a talented woman is enlarged into an exploration of the politics of lesbian feminist separatism, something only hinted at in the James novel.

CHARACTERS

If Lurie's readers often spot resonances from other fiction, they also have the pleasure of recognizing characters they have met in other Lurie novels, for Lurie frequently works with recurring characters. Emmy Turner's four-year-old boy Freddy from *Love and Friendship* is one of the grown-up main charac-

ters in *Foreign Affairs*, while Fred's wife Roo in that same novel appeared as a child in the earlier *The War Between the Tates*. Sometimes Lurie will, in a later novel, go back to an earlier period in a character's life: Miranda, the grown-up, married mother of three children in *Love and Friendship*, is seen as a child in the later novel *Only Children*. Of all the characters that recur, the most persistent one is Leonard Zimmern, first seen in *Real People* as a middle-aged, distinguished critic of American literature living in New York; later, in *The War Between the Tates*, as a friend of Brian and Erica. He is also the father of Roo, a child here but an adult in *Foreign Affairs*. In *Only Children*, the Depression-era story, Zimmern is a teenager, and in *Foreign Affairs* he is the father of a grown-up Roo, the famous critic whose harsh article on Vinnie Miner's work in children's literature haunts Vinnie as she goes to England. Roger Zimmern of *Imaginary Friends* is mentioned briefly in *The War Between the Tates* as Leonard Zimmern's cousin. L. D. Zimmern also surfaces in *The Truth About Lorin Jones* as the legal owner of his half-sister Lorin's unsold paintings. In addition, *The Truth About Lorin Jones* features the return of Lorin's father, Dan Zimmern of *Only Children*, and Danielle Zimmern, divorced wife of Leonard and Erica's best friend in *The War Between the Tates*. In her next novel, *The Last Resort*, L. D. Zimmern returns as the cousin of Lee Weiss, the lesbian who befriends Jenny Walker. Another continuity in *The Last Resort* is the return of the character of Barbara Mumpson, who first appeared in *Foreign Affairs*. This remarkable amount of recurrence suggests Lurie's strong interest in understanding how her characters came to be who they are, despite her novels' time frames. Her novels, as noted before, cover only short periods of time—one, *Only Children*, takes place in a single weekend. In order to continue her characters' development, then, Lurie often spreads out their lives over several novels, the recurrence of her characters in different novels doing much to tie their lives together.

IMAGINARY FRIENDS

As in the other novels, all the themes discussed so far are treated as well in *Imaginary Friends*. Their treatment in this novel, however, represents perhaps

Lurie's broadest and deepest effort, for the academic backdrop she uses so often elsewhere is broadened here to embrace the most fundamental of human questions, questions of knowledge, of identity, of sanity, and finally of madness. The main character in this novel, sociologist Roger Zimmern—a young, brand-new Ph.D. at a large, upstate New York university—goes to Sophis, a nearby small town, as the research assistant of Thomas McMann, a famous senior professor in his department whom Roger admires despite rumors he has heard about him from other young faculty members and despite the realization that McMann's form of empirical sociology (the case-study method) is passé. To investigate McMann's hypothesis that small groups can build a belief system so powerful that it can withstand, rationalize, and incorporate doubting attacks from within and without, Roger infiltrates, under the cover of a public opinion seeker, a group of religious fundamentalists called the Truth-seekers, whose young leader, Verena, leads and directs through automatic writing from superior beings on another planet, named Varna. McMann is introduced as a businessman friend, also interested in their theories. Roger's secure identity is overset by his mentor's unscientific attempt to control the experiment in the direction of his hypothesis rather than merely to observe and record. Also tormented by his sexual attraction for Verena, he reaches a point where he no longer knows what he believes in, no longer knows who he is, no longer knows whether there is in his discipline any objective basis for scientific inquiry. He believes that he is going mad but decides that it is, rather, his mentor who is insane, and he unwillingly becomes the primary witness whose testimony results in McMann's being committed to an asylum. The novel ends with Roger maintaining a tenuous but commonsensical hold on his own sanity. Here, Lurie has touched upon questions central not only to academic life but to the lives of everyone else as well: How can one truly observe and know? How real is our own sense of self?

Taken as a whole, Lurie's novels reveal a remarkable uniformity. Her own background in academe provides the most common setting for her novels, and frequently this setting is broadened to reflect the central questions with which Lurie is concerned. Her interest in clothing and identity, in the lives of children, indeed in the lives of all of her characters, is unusual. Her work is best considered not as a series of separate novels but as a continuity in which her characters' lives continue, not ceasing with the end of a particular novel but continuing as do all our lives—growing and changing through time.

June M. Frazer, updated by Margaret Boe Birns

OTHER MAJOR WORKS

NONFICTION: *The Language of Clothes*, 1981; *Don't Tell the Grown-Ups: Subversive Children's Literature*, 1990.

CHILDREN'S LITERATURE: *The Heavenly Zoo: Legends and Tales of the Stars*, 1979; *Clever Gretchen and Other Foreign Folktales*, 1980; *Fabulous Beasts*, 1981.

EDITED TEXT: *The Oxford Book of Modern Fairy Tales*, 1993.

BIBLIOGRAPHY

Costa, Richard Hauer. *Alison Lurie*. New York: Twayne, 1992. The first book-length study of Lurie, this overview is an essential resource. Written with Lurie's cooperation, the book includes a biographical sketch and discussion of all her writing, including a thorough examination of her major novels. Also features an extensive bibliography.

Dear, Pamela, ed. *Contemporary Authors*. Rev. series, vol. 50. Detroit: Gale Research, 1996. Contains a useful overview of all of Lurie's work, up to and including *The Truth About Lorin Jones*. Includes a brief biography and a brief but useful discussion of the novels. Also lists critical sources.

Hite, Molly. *The Other Side of the Story: Structures and Strategies of Contemporary Feminist Literature*. Ithaca, N.Y.: Cornell University Press, 1989. A brief entry on Lurie with reference to her novel *Foreign Affairs*. Places Lurie in the genre of women writing in the margins, the metaphor in their novels being minor characters playing major roles.

Newman, Judie. "Paleface into Redskin: Cultural Transformations in Alison Lurie's *Foreign Affairs.*" In *Forked Tongues: Comparing Twentieth Century British and American Literature*, edited by Ann Massa and Alistair Stead. London: Longman, 1994. Particularly valuable for its discussion of Lurie's theme of transatlantic cultural differences. Offers insights into why Lurie is so popular in England.

Rogers, Katherine M. "Alison Lurie: The Uses of Adultery." In *American Women Writing Fiction: Memory, Identity, Family, Space*, edited by Mickey Pearlman. Lexington: University of Kentucky Press, 1989. An important study of Lurie's novels through *Foreign Affairs*. A feminist analysis, it especially concentrates on the theme of self-examination on the part of Lurie's heroines.

M

ROSE MACAULAY

Born: Rugby, England; August 1, 1881
Died: London, England; October 30, 1958

PRINCIPAL LONG FICTION

Abbots Verney, 1906
The Furnace, 1907
The Secret River, 1909
The Valley Captives, 1911
The Lee Shore, 1912
Views and Vagabonds, 1912
The Making of a Bigot, 1914
Non-Combatants and Others, 1916
What Not: A Prophetic Comedy, 1918
Potterism: A Tragi-farcical Tract, 1920
Dangerous Ages, 1921
Mystery at Geneva, 1922
Told by an Idiot, 1923
Orphan Island, 1924
Crewe Train, 1926
Keeping up Appearances, 1928 (pb. in U.S. as *Daisy and Daphne*, 1928)
Staying with Relations, 1930
They Were Defeated, 1932 (pb. in U.S. as *The Shadow Flies*, 1932)
Going Abroad, 1934
I Would Be Private, 1937
And No Man's Wit, 1940
The World My Wilderness, 1950
The Towers of Trebizond, 1956

OTHER LITERARY FORMS

Though principally a novelist, Rose Macaulay wrote prolifically in several genres. Early in her career, she published two slim volumes of verse, *The Two Blind Countries* (1914) and *Three Days* (1919), both of which earned favorable reviews in the British press. For many years, Macaulay contributed reviews and essays to such publications as *The Spectator, The Guardian*, and the *New Statesman*; she produced two generally well-received book-length critical studies, *Milton* (1934, revised 1957) and *The Writings of E. M. Forster* (1938). Some of Macaulay's best prose can be found in two of her widely acclaimed travel books, *Fabled Shore: From the Pyrenees to Portugal* (1949) and *Pleasure of Ruins* (1953).

ACHIEVEMENTS

Throughout much of her lifetime, Macaulay was one of Great Britain's best-known authors. Many of her lighter sketches and essays appeared in the *Daily Mail*, the *Evening Standard*, and other newspapers and periodicals aimed at large, general audiences; some of her fiction appeared in serialized form in *Eve*, a popular English magazine aimed at women and filled mainly with froth. Yet Macaulay's more serious works consistently earned high praise in Great Britain's most respected literary publications; her twenty-third and final novel, *The Towers of Trebizond*, won the prestigious James Black Tait Memorial Prize. In 1951, Macaulay was awarded an honorary doctorate of letters from Cambridge University; in 1958, she was named a dame commander of the British Empire. Her death from heart seizure in 1958 brought forth warm and respectful tributes from many leading literary figures, including Harold Nicolson, Rosamond Lehmann, and Anthony Powell.

BIOGRAPHY

Emilie Rose Macaulay was born in Rugby, England, on August 1, 1881. Her father, George Macaulay, was a schoolmaster and Latin scholar; her mother, the former Grace Conybeare, was a bright, energetic, but rather severe woman who sought to impart to her children a High Church interpretation of Anglican Christianity. Rose Macaulay was related to a long line of ministers, teachers, and authors (the celebrated historian Thomas Babington Macaulay was her paternal grandfather's first cousin); not surprisingly, she was so well schooled by her parents that, by early adolescence, she was already on very familiar terms with, among other classics, Dante's *Divine Comedy* (c. 1320) and Shakespeare's plays.

Because doctors prescribed warmth and sunshine as a means of treating her mother's tuberculosis, Macaulay spent the better part of her childhood in Varazzo, Italy—a place she would later recall with considerable fondness. In 1900, she entered Oxford's Somerville College, where she studied modern history and became—as her biographer Constance Babington Smith records—"a chatterbox who gabbled away so fast that at times she was hardly intelligible, a ready speaker who made lively contributions to undergraduate debates." Soon after completing her studies at Oxford, Macaulay—while living with her parents in Wales—began work on her first novel, *Abbots Verney*, which critics praised for its artistic promise. In 1915, Macaulay acquired a flat of her own in London, where she quickly developed friendships with such influential literary figures as J. C. Squire, Hugh Walpole, and Walter de la Mare, and where, in 1917, she entered into what became a twenty-five-year love affair with Gerald O'Donovan, a married man and a former Catholic priest who was himself well known in London's literary circles as the author of the highly autobiographical and anticlerical novel *Father Ralph* (1913). Though she traveled frequently, widely, and often intrepidly to locations that saw little tourist activity, Macaulay continued to make her home in London, where even in old age she was seen—as one friend recalled—"at every party, every private view, protest meeting, cruise, literary luncheon, or ecclesiastical gathering." Macaulay openly began to identify herself as an agnostic during her university days; much of her fiction pokes generally gentle fun at organized religion. After O'Donovan's death in 1942, however, she experienced a renewed interest in orthodox Christianity, an interest much in evidence in her later novels.

ANALYSIS

Over a writing career that spanned fifty years, Rose Macaulay produced twenty-three novels. She understandably came to regard the earliest of these—including *The Furnace, The Secret River,* and *The Valley Captives*—as immature and rather badly made, and she did nothing to encourage their republication. In her novels, Macaulay utilizes a wide variety of carefully rendered settings (some of which are quite exotic); her prose is beautifully cadenced and richly detailed. Occasionally, however, the exuberance and ornateness of Macaulay's prose can be distracting, and, occasionally, her plots bog down beneath the weight of the descriptive digressions and authorial intrusions that pepper her texts. Many of Macaulay's characters are both convincing and memorable. Some, however, are both stereotypical and stiff and appear to be exchanging speeches rather than engaging in spontaneous conversation. Macaulay recognized that, as a novelist, she was least skilled at characterization; indeed, she was sometimes urged by friends and critics to concentrate on the essay form. Yet Macaulay also recognized that her fiction had a large and rather devoted readership and that, moreover, fiction could provide her with an entertaining vehicle for disseminating, and dissecting, a wide range of stimulating ideas.

As a novelist, Macaulay returned again and again to the same provocative themes. It is plain that, on the whole, she very much liked human beings. Still, she was severely critical of the intellectual laziness that she found epidemic in the human race. Repeatedly, her novels mock and sometimes savage characters who unthinkingly digest easy answers to the questions of life and who are prone, then, to sentimentality and cant. Though she is not generally ranked among her generation's more overtly feminist authors, Macaulay frequently reveals in her work a deep disdain for a social system that continued to deny women equal access to education and adventure. She regularly features as central figures young women who are witty, well read, and intellectually ambitious.

Many of Macaulay's recurring concerns are overtly stated in *Potterism*, one of her most enduring novels—and the first to sell impressively in the United States. *Potterism* is, in fact, dedicated to "the unsentimental precisians in thought, who have, on this confused, inaccurate, and emotional planet, no fit habitation." It features among its five epigraphs Dr. Johnson's injunction to "clear your mind of cant. . . . Don't *think* foolishly." At the core of *Potterism* is the abrupt death of a young newspaper editor recently wed to Jane Potter, whose father is the publisher of a string of superficial, cant-spewing newspapers, and whose mother, under the pseudonym of Leila Yorke, churns out foolish and schmaltzy novels that enjoy huge sales. In order to discuss and analyze this somewhat suspicious demise from varying perspectives, Macaulay presents "extracts" from the "private journals" of several characters who knew the young editor, including his novel-writing mother-in-law. Employing clichéd and rather empurpled prose, Mrs. Potter shows herself to be quite capable of the sort of overemotionalism and muddled thinking that Macaulay, throughout her career, so thoroughly disdained. The three authors of the other journal entries are the friends of the Potter twins, Johnny and Jane, who have sought to distance themselves from what they disparagingly refer to as the "Potterism" of their parents. Macaulay demonstrates that Johnny and Jane and their university-trained friends are not without their own pretensions and illusions, but she makes it clear that their crusade against vulgarity and stupidity—though quite probably quixotic—is well worth the taking.

TOLD BY AN IDIOT

Macaulay's thirteenth novel, the highly praised *Told by an Idiot*, is set in England between 1879 and 1927 and takes its title, and its epigraph, from Macbeth's well-known observation that life is a "tale told by an idiot, full of sound and fury,/ Signifying nothing. . . ." In this work, Macaulay focuses on the family of Maurice Garden, whose continuing struggles with faith and doubt have made him at various times a Catholic, a Baptist, a Positivist, an Anglican, "a plain agnostic," and, when the novel opens, an enthusiastic member of the Ethical Society. Garden's theological gyrations are well tolerated by his calm wife and his bright children, whose ranks include lively daughters named Imogen, Stanley, and Rome. Through her portrait of Maurice, Macaulay not only conveys something of her sense of the futility of most conflicting "isms" but also provides an acute portrait of the mental landscape of Victorian England. Through her depiction of the Gardens' daughters, she is able to portray young women who, though by no means perfect, possess energy, perspicacity, and a desire for independence.

ORPHAN ISLAND

In *Orphan Island*, perhaps Macaulay's most satisfactorily plotted novel, she harshly satirizes the sort of narrow-minded smugness that was not uncommon among influential people in the Victorian age. In the novel's early chapters, Macaulay describes how in 1855 a ship carrying dozens of young English orphans is blown off its California-bound course during a violent storm and winds up wrecked along the coast of a small, uncharted island in the South Pacific. In succeeding chapters, she shows how the prim and proper Miss Charlotte Smith—the orphans' supervisor—gradually turns the island into a model of Victorian England and establishes herself as its stern and platitudinous queen. In the 1920's, Miss Smith's island is rediscovered by a team headed by Mr. Thinkwell, a Cambridge lecturer in sociology. Thinkwell is astonished to discover that, in the remotest part of the South Pacific, Victorian England—complete with pronounced social inequities and an obsession with propriety—is, in effect, frozen in time. Still, Thinkwell enjoys the island's remarkable beauty, which Macaulay effectively renders through frequent and detailed descriptions of its sunny skies, lush plant life, and exotic vegetation. He also becomes attached to his growing status as a man of great intelligence and learning. In fact, near the novel's close and soon after the ancient Miss Smith's long-expected death, he becomes the island's prime minister, bent on reforming the corrupt monarchy into a republic where freedom and social justice can thrive. Macaulay does not reveal whether Thinkwell succeeds, though she does point out that, in the end, human folly has a way of winning out, and that the island is "likely" to become "as tyrannous, as unfair, as oligarchic in constitution and economic condition" as it was during Miss Smith's curious reign.

THEY WERE DEFEATED

Macaulay's sole historical novel is *They Were Defeated*, called *The Shadow Flies* in its American edition, which takes place in England and covers an eight-month period beginning in the fall of 1640. Essentially, the novel centers on the often bloody and self-defeating religious conflicts that were then taking place between Puritans, Anglicans, and Roman

Catholics. Among its characters are several well-known historical and literary figures, including the poets Robert Herrick, John Cleveland, and John Suckling. The scholarly and highly analytical Dr. Conybeare, himself based on one of Macaulay's distant relations, is one of the many central characters in her fiction who finds himself struggling with religious doubts. Similarly, his daughter Julian is a recognizable Macaulay "type": She bears what is commonly regarded as a male name and desires for herself the male prerogative to ask questions and obtain knowledge. In a prefatory note to this long, intricately plotted and largely convincing book, Macaulay explains,

> I have done my best to make no person in this novel use in conversation any words, phrases, or idioms that were not demonstrably used at the time in which they lived; though I am aware, for all the constant and stalwart aid of the Oxford Dictionary, and the wealth of literature, letters and journals of the period that we possess for our guidance, that any such attempt must be extremely inadequate; or, at least, that mine is so.

In fact, after the publication of *The Shadow Flies*, Macaulay received assurances from several students of the language that her errors in word usage were both minor and few.

GOING ABROAD

Going Abroad, Macaulay's next novel, represents a decided change of pace. Dedicated to two friends "who desired a book of unredeemed levity," *Going Abroad* is set largely in Zarauz, a coastal resort town in the Basque country of Spain. It features a large cast of British eccentrics, including a Dante scholar, a young aesthete, a rigid colonel, and a woman schooled in the classics who seeks to relocate and recreate the Garden of Eden. Also featured in *Going Abroad* is a pair of vulgarians who run a string of beauty parlors and a group of hearty Oxford students who seek to spread goodness and religion through the Moral Re-armament Movement, and who are successfully portrayed by Macaulay as both foolish and, in their own sort of way, admirable. By focusing on the often strained interaction of these diverse types, Macaulay created a highly successful comic novel set in an appealingly sunny climate—one that deserves

to be ranked among the most amusing of its time.

THE WORLD MY WILDERNESS

During the 1950's, Rose Macaulay produced two novels that are generally placed among her most accomplished. The first of these, *The World My Wilderness*, draws heavily upon the recent events of World War II. Its central figure, a seventeen-year-old girl named Barbary, spent the war years in France, where she witnessed or was touched by a host of brutalities, including her stepfather's murder by Resistance fighters who believed, wrongly, that he collaborated regularly with the Nazis. After the war, Barbary moves to London to live with her father, a wealthy barrister. She studies art and tries to start a more ordered life. As Macaulay repeatedly emphasizes, however, the ruins of war still dominate London: Blocks and blocks of buildings have been shattered, and so have innumerable lives. Thus, Barbary and her brother Raoul eventually fall in with a group of young Londoners who have been similarly affected by the recent violence and chaos and who spend their days wandering around in the city's many ruins, their energies focused on petty crime. During the war, Macaulay's small flat was itself destroyed by German bombs; she lost all of her letters, manuscripts, and books. Certainly, much of her sense of loss and despair informs *The World My Wilderness*.

THE TOWERS OF TREBIZOND

The Towers of Trebizond, Macaulay's final novel, begins with the delightful and arresting words, "Take my camel, dear." This work—which is set principally in Turkey, along the Mediterranean coast—seems at first glance to be an outrageous and funny farce in the manner of *Going Abroad*. For example, one of its main characters, the camel-riding Aunt Dot, is immediately recognizable as yet another of Macaulay's eccentric—and harmless—fanatics. Her goal is to spread single-handedly the doctrine of female emancipation throughout Islamic Turkey, while along the way bringing wayward Muslims into the Anglican fold. She is accompanied on her trip by a priggish, relic-scavenging High Church priest, and by a niece, Laurie, who relates the novel's action.

Like many of Macaulay's earlier novels, *The Towers of Trebizond* pokes gentle, rather affectionate fun at zealous churchgoers. Like many of her novels, it displays a subtle, complex, and rhythmical prose style that sometimes dazes and more frequently dazzles. Laurie, its narrator, is certainly very much in keeping with Macaulay's earlier central figures. She is witty, intelligent, and widely read. In the final analysis, Laurie's observations on many serious matters give *The Towers of Trebizond* a far less farcical tone than *Going Abroad*. Indeed, Laurie—Macaulay's last heroine—is, perhaps appropriately, her most autobiographical. She not only freely expresses a mixture of guilt and joy at having maintained a long and intimate relationship with a married man, but—like Macaulay after Gerald O'Donovan's death—she repeatedly reveals a deep desire to return to the Church that she denied for so many years. Even more revealing, however, is her zest for life. Like Macaulay, Laurie has read and traveled and carefully observed because, as she points out,

> life, for all its agonies of despair and loss and guilt, is exciting and beautiful, amusing and artful and endearing, full of liking and of love, at times a poem and a high adventure, at times very gay; and whatever (if anything) is to come after it, we shall not have this life again.

Brian Murray

OTHER MAJOR WORKS

POETRY: *The Two Blind Countries*, 1914; *Three Days*, 1919.

NONFICTION: *A Casual Commentary*, 1925; *Catchwords and Claptrap*, 1926; *Some Religious Elements in English Literature*, 1931; *Milton*, 1934, revised 1957; *Personal Pleasures*, 1935; *The Writings of E. M. Forster*, 1938; *Life Among the English*, 1942; *They Went to Portugal*, 1946; *Fabled Shore: From the Pyrenees to Portugal*, 1949; *Pleasure of Ruins*, 1953; *Letters to a Friend, 1950-1952*, 1961; *Last Letters to a Friend, 1952-1958*, 1962; *Letters to a Sister from Rose Macaulay*, 1964.

BIBLIOGRAPHY

Bensen, Alice. *Rose Macaulay*. New York: Twayne, 1969. This standard account is especially valuable because there are few books devoted to Macaulay. Offers a survey of her widely varied output: novels, short stories, historical works, travel books, essays, and book reviews. Her tolerance for and sympathy with others are brought out. Macaulay belonged to the species of "gifted amateurs," and her carefully wrought style was sometimes too arch.

Crawford, Alice. *Paradise Pursued: The Novels of Rose Macaulay*. Madison, N.J.: Fairleigh Dickinson University Press, 1995. Explores Macaulay's beginnings as an Edwardian novelist, her World War I novels, her treatment of women and civilization in the 1920's, her novels of the 1930's, and her final novels. Includes appendices on Macaulay's childhood reading and on other writings. Provides notes and bibliography.

Emery, Jane. *Rose Macaulay: A Writer's Life*. London: John Murray, 1991. The standard biography of Macaulay, written with grace and sensitivity to the life and the work. See especially the introduction, "Three Voices of Rose Macaulay." Includes notes and bibliography.

Passty, Jeanette. *Eros and Androgyny: The Legacy of Rose Macaulay*. London: Associated University Presses, 1988. Sees Macaulay as a feminist pioneer who repudiated the traditional pattern of the male-dominated family in favor of an androgynous ideal, arguing that people should pursue their aims in a gender-free way. Gives an account of Macaulay's work, the most comprehensive available, with the feminist theme always in the forefront. Her correspondence with Father Hamilton Johnston and its importance for her work receive detailed attention.

Smith, Constance Babington. *Rose Macaulay*. London: Collins, 1972. The standard (and only) biography of Macaulay. Presents a detailed account of her family background and sheds light on key episodes in her life, such as her unrequited love for Rupert Brooke. Gives synopses of most of her major works. A useful feature is an appendix that contains tributes to Macaulay from a number of her friends, including Harold Nicolson and Rosamond Lehmann.

Cormac McCarthy

Born: Providence, Rhode Island; July 20, 1933

PRINCIPAL LONG FICTION

The Orchard Keeper, 1965
Outer Dark, 1968
Child of God, 1973
Suttree, 1979
Blood Meridian: Or, The Evening Redness in the West, 1985
All the Pretty Horses, 1992
The Crossing, 1994
Cities of the Plain, 1998
The Border Trilogy, 1999 (includes *All the Pretty Horses*, *The Crossing*, and *Cities of the Plain*)

OTHER LITERARY FORMS

Cormac McCarthy is known almost exclusively as a writer of novels. Short excerpts from his novels in progress sometimes appeared in such literary magazines as *Yale Review*, *Sewanee Review*, and *Tri-Quarterly*. He also wrote the script for *The Gardener's Son*, a teleplay in the *Visions* series shown on public television. First broadcast in January, 1977, the drama is based on an actual murder in 1876 in Graniteville, South Carolina. In a story full of dark implications, crippled Rob McEvoy, son of a poor working family, kills the son of the local textile mill owner. The story was adapted for the big screen in 1996.

ACHIEVEMENTS

Few writers have received such critical acclaim as McCarthy without also gaining wide popularity. He has consistently been praised for his carefully crafted work; his unflinching, dark vision; his immense range of vocabulary; and his powers of observation and description. These qualities also won for him rich recognition in the form of prizes and grants. *The Orchard Keeper* won the 1965 William Faulkner Foundation Award as the best first novel by an American writer and helped win for McCarthy an American Academy of Arts and Letters traveling fellowship to Europe in 1965-1966. The following years brought him grants

from the Rockefeller, Guggenheim, Lyndhurst, and MacArthur foundations. McCarthy has been compared to Faulkner, Edgar Allan Poe, and Mark Twain.

The same qualities in McCarthy that have been praised have also been the cause of criticism and help to explain why he has not been more popular. A slow writer, he took at least twenty years to produce his first five books; thus, McCarthy faded from the public eye between books. His subjects—killings, incest, necrophilia, Knoxville lowlife, and scalp-hunting Western marauders—may repel some readers, and others may find his dark vision too unrelenting and morbid. Finally, his tendencies to ransack the dictionary for unusual words and to describe his dripping horrors in overwritten prose make him sound occasionally like gothic writer H. P. Lovecraft.

In 1992, *All the Pretty Horses* won the National Book Award and the National Book Critics Circle Award for fiction. Although many readers do not enjoy McCarthy's lurid subject matter, his work has been much praised by critics. He is respected for his unflinching moral vision and his sense of humanity.

(David Styles)

Biography

Cormac McCarthy was born into a middle-class Catholic family—about as far as one can get from the background of most of his characters (with the notable exception of Suttree). He was born in Providence, Rhode Island, in 1933. When McCarthy was four, his family moved to the Knoxville, Tennessee, area, where his father was chief legal counsel to the Tennessee Valley Authority (TVA). There, McCarthy grew up, attending parochial school, Catholic High School, and the University of Tennessee. He dropped out of the university after one year, traveled for a year, and then joined the United States Air Force, in which he served for four years. Afterward, he attended the University of Tennessee for three more years but finally left in 1959 without getting a degree.

McCarthy did discover his writing vocation at the University of Tennessee, where he began work on a novel. After the publication of *The Orchard Keeper*, he traveled in Europe for three years, living in London, in Paris, and on the Spanish island of Ibiza. While in Europe, he married Anne de Lisle of Hamble, England. Later, they lived on a small farm in Rockford, Tennessee, just outside Knoxville. McCarthy moved to El Paso, Texas, during the time he was writing *Blood Meridian*.

As *Blood Meridian* and his East Tennessee novels show, McCarthy's work is influenced by the landscape around him, and McCarthy absorbed local talk, color, and tradition. Whether he was more directly influenced by his father's work with the TVA is an interesting question. For many families who had been living in the mountain valleys for generations, the TVA was their first contact with big government—a traumatic one that has still not been forgiven. The permanent flooding of their land by TVA projects, despite "compensation," resulted in massive dislocations within the traditional mountain culture. One of the more gruesome aspects was transferring the contents of cemeteries to higher ground—a scene of the restless dead that seems to be echoed repeatedly in McCarthy's work, as is the theme of the government's bringing of change. Tennessee would continue to be a special place to McCarthy, though in his later years he traveled frequently, living and writing in motels.

Analysis

Like British Catholic writer Graham Greene, Cormac McCarthy is reluctant to develop any optimistic themes. He is also reluctant about stating his themes, although some of his titles offer strong hints. For the most part, he merely tells his stories and leaves it up to the reader to interpret their meanings. As a result, one critic has judged McCarthy to be nihilistic, but surely this judgment is incorrect. McCarthy's reluctance to preach about the good news masks a profoundly moral sensibility that is forced to face the worst in human nature and to recognize the power of evil. In this way, his novels are comparable to the medieval morality play or to such films by Ingmar Bergman as *The Seventh Seal* (1957).

There is also a softer, more modern side to McCarthy's morality. Few writers identify so thoroughly with people beyond the pale—the poor, the homeless and dispossessed, the criminal and degenerate, the outcasts. He manages to find some humanity even in the worst of these and to ascribe their conditions partly to contingency, bad luck, or the operations of respectable society. Their nemesis (besides themselves) is often the law and its officers, who, for them, become additional embodiments of the death and destruction that pursue everyone. McCarthy's refusal to avert his sympathies from the outcasts thus raises some complex social and theological issues.

The Orchard Keeper

McCarthy's first novel, *The Orchard Keeper*, introduces the outcasts as members of the disappearing mountain culture of East Tennessee. Young Marion Sylder lives by bootlegging, and in self-defense he kills a man and disposes of the body in an abandoned peach orchard that symbolizes the dying culture. Old Arthur Ownby, who fondly watches over the orchard, finds the body, but he does not report it. He lets it rest in peace for seven years. The old man also believes in his own peace and privacy, and when these are disturbed by a government holding tank erected on a nearby hill, he shoots his *X* on the tank's side. Both the men live by old mountain codes which, by definition, are outside the law of the intruding modern world. Yet the enforcers of the law, who finally arrest and beat Sylder and send the old man to a mental institution, seem degenerate in comparison to them. The novel's theme is also represented in John Wesley Rattner (ironically, the son of the dead man), a boy who hunts and traps, is befriended by the two men, and comes of age in the novel. He decides to cast his loyalties with the old ways even if they have become anachronistic.

Oᴜᴛᴇʀ Dᴀʀᴋ

The episodic converging stories and italicized flashbacks of *The Orchard Keeper* recall Faulkner's narrative techniques, and McCarthy's second novel, *Outer Dark*, also owes a debt to Faulkner. The novel takes place in some vaguely Deep South setting early in the twentieth century and deals with the horrible consequences of incest between Culla and Rinthy Holme, brother and sister. Rinthy delivers a baby boy, and Culla abandons it in the woods, where a passing tinker finds and takes it. Culla tells Rinthy that the baby died, but Rinthy digs up the shallow grave, discovers his lie, and intuitively goes in search of the tinker. Culla goes after Rinthy to bring her back. Their wanderings on the roads recall those of Lena Grove and Joe Christmas in Faulkner's *Light in August* (1932). Everyone she encounters befriends Rinthy, who moves along dripping mother's milk for over six months, but Culla meets nothing except suspicion and trouble. These episodes also recall the journey down the river in Mark Twain's *The Adventures of Huckleberry Finn* (1884), particularly a wild incident in which a loose ferry is swept down a raging river.

McCarthy's most original and unforgettable creation in *Outer Dark* is a set of three avenging angels, or devils, who rove about the landscape murdering people. On a realistic level, they are lawless, asocial drifters who have gone totally beyond the pale into the "outer dark." They have lost all caring. Appropriately, Culla meets this unholy trio of blood brothers near the novel's end. The three hang the tinker and dispose of the baby (now symbolically scarred as in a Nathaniel Hawthorne story) before Culla's eyes: One slits the baby's throat and another sucks its blood.

Cʜɪʟᴅ ᴏꜰ Gᴏᴅ

If *Outer Dark* does not contain horror enough, McCarthy followed it with *Child of God*, which returns to a rural East Tennessee setting. Here, mountain man Lester Ballard loses his farm for failure to pay taxes; embittered and alone, he sinks gradually into necrophilia and then murder. His degeneration is marked by movement from the farm to an abandoned shack that burns, to a cave where he stores his supply of dead women. He is finally captured, dies in a state mental hospital, and is dissected in a medical laboratory. His neighbors, whose choruslike, folksy comments are interspersed throughout the story, always thought him a bit strange, with bad blood. McCarthy suggests that all Lester ever needed, however, was a home and love. Lester was only "a child of God much like yourself perhaps."

Sᴜᴛᴛʀᴇᴇ

A short, tightly unified work, *Child of God* contrasts with McCarthy's next novel, *Suttree*, usually considered his masterpiece. *Suttree* displays the variety and range of McCarthy's talent. Set in Knoxville during the 1950's, the novel is a long, rambling work rich in incident, character, language, and mood, including some surprisingly amusing, bawdy humor. Yet *Suttree* has certain features in common with *Child of God*. Misery and unhappiness also predominate here, and instead of one child of God, *Suttree* has hundreds—drunks, prostitutes, perverts, petty criminals, and the poor generally, black and white—all dumped together in a slum known as McAnally Flats. The characters have such names as Hoghead, Gatemouth, Worm, and Trippin Through The Dew, and their dialogue is spiced with slang and expletives.

The central character is Cornelius "Buddy" Suttree, scion of a prominent local family. He has deliberately chosen to live in this slum on a houseboat moored in the Tennessee River, from whose filthy waters he catches a few carp and catfish to sell. Why he has made this strange choice gradually becomes clear. On the one hand, he has made a mess of his life. He and his parents are no longer on speaking terms, and his wife left him long ago, taking their child (who dies in the novel). Suttree sank to drink and served a term in the prison workhouse. Now he lives in McAnally Flats because, on the other hand, he feels at home there. There, he can find the company of like-minded, fun-loving pals who can help him pass the time and avoid involvement in the pain of life. There he sits, the fisher king in his wasteland, and with dread and longing he awaits the oblivion of death.

A happy flaw in Suttree's character, however, prevents his nihilistic scheme from taking effect: compassion. He cannot avoid feeling compassion for the people around him, such as the ignorant but irrepressible Gene Harrogate, a country boy who serves a term in the workhouse for having sex with a farmer's watermelons and who dynamites the city's sewer system down on himself trying to rob a bank (the "country mouse," as he is first called, soon becomes the "city rat"). Further involvement with people leads to further pain for Suttree—a girl he falls in love with is killed, his long affair with a rich prostitute breaks up, and most of his pals are killed or imprisoned. Deeper emotional commitment on Suttree's part, however, might have saved both the girl and the affair with the prostitute. After a solitary retreat to the Great Smoky Mountains and a near-fatal illness, Suttree decides to embrace life—pain and all—and to leave Knoxville. He leaves just as the McAnally Flats are being torn down to make room for an expressway. His parting words of advice concern the hounds of death: "Fly them."

Blood Meridian

McCarthy's fifth book, *Blood Meridian*, is a historical novel set in the American Southwest and northern Mexico around the middle of the nineteenth century. The novel's protagonist is a nameless character known only as "the kid" (with suggested parallels perhaps to Billy the Kid), who runs away from his Tennessee home when he is fourteen and heads west. His story might be that of Huck Finn after Huck "lit out for the territory" and left civilization behind. After repeated scrapes, always moving west, the kid joins a band of scalping bounty hunters who hunt the Apaches when the Apaches are not hunting them. The massacres go on endlessly, all duly noted in the running summaries that head each chapter.

In some ways, *Blood Meridian* provides a useful retrospective view of McCarthy's work. It returns to the horrors of his earlier novels but seems to relate these to the social themes of *Suttree*. The scalp hunters are, after all, the advance guard of Western civilization. They suggest a terrible moral ambiguity at the heart of civilization, as in the hearts of individuals, that enables it to stamp out Apaches and backward mountaineers and to create such slums as McAnally Flats. Judge Holden, the repulsive and evil philosopher of *Blood Meridian*, argues that God made humanity thus, that morality is irrelevant, and that superior violence shall triumph. The naked judge finally embraces the kid with an apparent death hug inside a privy behind a whorehouse in Fort Griffin, Texas. Readers can probably find a warning in this to flee such philosophers.

The Border Trilogy

The American Southwest and northern Mexico also serve as the setting for McCarthy's most ambitious work, *The Border Trilogy*, the sweeping saga of two boys' initiation into manhood immediately before, during, and after the Second World War. With this work the author sheds the label of southern regional writer by combining universal themes and postmodernist thought with the bold experimental style he exhibited in *Blood Meridian*.

In the opening book, *All the Pretty Horses*, McCarthy paints a splendid yet harsh landscape populated by an equally noble yet coarse cast of characters. Among them are John Grady Cole and Billy Parham, who spend much of their time in search of a cultural identity and Western way of life that is on the verge of extinction. A sense of restlessness permeates the tale as Cole and Parham, despite their determination, seem incapable of attaching themselves to a particular time or place, other than the disappearing open range.

In *The Crossing*, a prequel to *All the Pretty Horses*, the sense of homelessness is similarly pervasive, starting with the opening sequence when Parham becomes obsessed with trapping a renegade she-wolf. Once he has captured the animal, he decides to release her back into the wild, a symbolic act indicating the wild-at-heart temperaments McCarthy instills in his characters. It is the first of a series of losses experienced by Parham, a list that later would include his parents, brother, and dog.

The thematic "quest" continues in *Cities of the Plain*, as Cole and Parham are united while working as a pair of hired hands on a New Mexico cattle ranch where they quickly become inseparable friends, bound by a love of horses and life on the range. Soon, Cole finds another love in the figure of Magdalena, a Mexican prostitute. In an attempt to rescue her from an abusive pimp, both Cole and Magdalena wind up dead, leaving Parham alone to wander the land, performing odd jobs, before finding himself back in New Mexico an elderly man.

The Border Trilogy is unconventional in word and deed and filled with an imaginative succession of contrasts and conflicts that drive the author's narrative to its conclusion. Throughout his story he is able to juxtapose competing cultures, languages, and moral codes to create a milieu which spawns extraordinary actions and stretches of dialogue, such as the series of tales by the priest, the blind man, and the gypsy in *The Crossing*. The mystic element of these exchanges underscores the thread of the natural versus the supernatural running through the story. Yet, whenever otherworldly elements edge closer to becoming the balm for his protagonists' troubles, there is always the landscape to return them to reality. As critics have noted, the surrounding land becomes another of McCarthy's characters with contrasting features of its own, from august mountains to desolate plains. It is not an oversimplification to conclude that much of the trilogy becomes a matter of when man and nature meet and that the author's characters do not change or grow over the course of his story. Rather, they are blended into the ever present landscape which, in the end, is destined to unite them.

Harold Branam, updated by William Hoffman

OTHER MAJOR WORKS

PLAY: *The Stonemason*, pb. 1994.
SCREENPLAY: *The Gardener's Son*, 1996.
TELEPLAY: *The Gardener's Son*, 1977.

BIBLIOGRAPHY

Arnold, Edwin T., and Dianne C. Luce, eds. *Perspectives on Cormac McCarthy*. Oxford: University Press of Mississippi, 1993. This collection of ten essays examining the works of McCarthy serves as an excellent introduction to his novels. A thorough bibliography is included.

Bell, Vereen M. *The Achievement of Cormac McCarthy*. Baton Rouge: Louisiana State University Press, 1988. The first thorough critical study of McCarthy, in which Bell explains McCarthy's unconventional methods and his emphasis on language as responses to the fact that the real world is tainted by evil. The vivid description of that world can in some sense underline the value of life. Interestingly, Bell points out that McCarthy's literate readers would be better able to transcend reality through language than most of his characters. Contains a good bibliography and a full index.

_____. "The Ambiguous Nihilism of Cormac McCarthy." *Southern Literary Journal* 15 (Spring, 1983): 31-41. Focuses on what Bell sees as the central conflict in McCarthy's fiction: the impossibility of fitting the self, which yearns for purpose, into a world which is meaningless and miserable, filled with alienation, suffering, and violence.

Ditsky, John. "Further into Darkness: The Novels of Cormac McCarthy." *The Hollins Critic* 18 (April, 1981): 1-11. Ditsky argues that McCarthy carries grotesque action and obscure prose even further than William Faulkner did. Much of the essay describes what Ditsky sees as the gradual change in McCarthy's work, from the description of a barbaric but rich primitive world, which finds meaning in ritual or magic, to a more naturalistic view of life, without even the illusion of meaning.

Jarrett, Robert L. *Cormac McCarthy*. New York: Twayne, 1997. Contains the most information on McCarthy. Includes bibliography and index.

Woodward, Richard B. "Cormac McCarthy's Venomous Fiction." *The New York Times Magazine*, April 19, 1992, 28-31. In one of his rare interviews, McCarthy discusses his views on the nature of evil and the allure of violence. His belief is that an independent life and a life of harmony are incompatible.

MARY McCARTHY

Born: Seattle, Washington; June 21, 1912
Died: New York, New York; October 25, 1989

PRINCIPAL LONG FICTION
The Oasis, 1949
The Groves of Academe, 1952
A Charmed Life, 1955
The Group, 1963
Birds of America, 1971
Cannibals and Missionaries, 1979

OTHER LITERARY FORMS

First known as a book reviewer, drama critic, and essayist, Mary McCarthy also wrote short stories, collected in *The Company She Keeps* (1942), *Cast a Cold Eye* (1950), and *The Hounds of Summer and Other Stories* (1981). Her drama criticism is collected in *Sights and Spectacles, 1937-1956* (1956) and in *Mary McCarthy's Theatre Chronicles, 1937-1962* (1963). *Venice Observed* (1956) and *The Stones*

(Jerry Bauer)

of Florence (1959) are books of travel and art history. *The Writing on the Wall and Other Literary Essays* (1970) and *Ideas and the Novel* (1980) are literary essays and lectures. *On the Contrary: Articles of Belief* (1961) contains autobiographical essays and literary criticism. *Memories of a Catholic Girlhood* (1957) and *How I Grew* (1987) are memoirs of her childhood and youth. Her books *Vietnam* (1967) and *Hanoi* (1968) oppose United States involvement in the Vietnam War, an interest that she continued in *Medina* (1972) and in *The Seventeenth Degree* (1974). *The Mask of State* (1974) presents impressions of the Watergate affair hearings.

ACHIEVEMENTS

From the appearance of her first book reviews, when she was just out of college, to the time of her death, Mary McCarthy was one of the leading figures on the American literary scene. In her novels as much as in her essays and reviews, she was above all a critic, a sharp observer of contemporary society. For students of twentieth century American culture her work is indispensable.

BIOGRAPHY

Born into an affluent family of mixed Irish and Jewish heritage on June 21, 1912, in Seattle, Washington, Mary Therese McCarthy had a segmented childhood. After six years of what she called a "fairy-tale" existence of happiness, both parents died of influenza in 1918 during a move to Minneapolis. Mary and her three younger brothers, placed with their grandaunt and uncle, then entered a bleak phase of intense, strict Catholicism, which McCarthy described in *Memories of a Catholic Girlhood*. In 1923, McCarthy's grandparents moved her to a convent school in Seattle for the seventh and eighth grades; she spent her ninth grade year in a public school and then her remaining high school years at the Annie Wright Seminary in Tacoma, from which she was graduated in 1929 at the top of her class. In the same year of her graduation as a Phi Beta Kappa from Vassar College in 1933, she married Harold Johnsrud, a marriage that lasted three years. She reviewed novels and biographies for *The New Republic* and *The*

Nation, worked for the left-wing publishers Covici Friede, and, in 1937, involved herself in Trotskyite politics. In 1937, she became drama editor for the *Partisan Review*.

The next year, Mary McCarthy married Edmund Wilson and gave birth to a son, Reuel Wilson; also, at Wilson's urging, she wrote her first fiction, a short story. Thereafter, the stories she wrote for *Southern Review*, *Partisan Review*, and *Harper's Bazaar* were collected in 1942 in the book *The Company She Keeps*. She separated from Edmund Wilson in 1945, the same year that she was teaching literature at Bard College, and in 1946, she married Bowden Broadwater. In 1948, she taught one semester at Sarah Lawrence College and, in 1949, was a Guggenheim Fellow, an award which was repeated in 1959. Also in 1949, she received the *Horizon* literary prize from the publishers of her novel *The Oasis*. In 1961, she was divorced from Bowden Broadwater, married James Raymond West—a State Department official assigned to Paris—and went to live with him in France.

Two events dominated the 1960's for McCarthy. The first was the enormous popular success of her novel *The Group*, which became a number-one best-seller. The second was the Vietnam War; she was an outspoken critic of United States policy in Vietnam. In the 1970's she published two novels with social and political themes: *Birds of America* in 1971 and *Cannibals and Missionaries* in 1979; the latter, she said, would be her last novel.

In 1980, an offhand remark on *The Dick Cavett Show* embroiled McCarthy in a prolonged legal battle that became a *cause célèbre* in the literary community. McCarthy said of dramatist Lillian Hellman that "every word she writes is a lie, including 'and' and 'the.'" Hellman sued. The resulting legal maneuvering was costly for McCarthy (in contrast, the wealthy Hellman did not count the cost), ending only in 1984, when, after Hellman's death, the suit was dropped before going to trial. Meanwhile, legal issues aside, the controversy brought several of Hellman's autobiographical works under close scrutiny, and the consensus was that McCarthy's judgment, clearly stated in hyperbolic terms, was vindicated.

In 1987, McCarthy published *How I Grew*, the first installment in what was projected to be a multi-volume intellectual autobiography. In general, critics found it inferior to *Memoirs of a Catholic Girlhood*, which had covered some of the same territory from a different perspective. McCarthy died in New York on October 25, 1989.

ANALYSIS

Mary McCarthy's novels often feature herself, with an assumed name, as protagonist; she also exploited her husbands and other people close to her for fictional purposes. Her characters generally have a superior education and/or intellect so that citations and quotations from learned sources—mainly classical or artistic—spring into their conversations. This heightened discourse promotes compact paragraphs of dialogue, in which several persons speak to the same topic, in contrast with the usual fictional technique of a separate paragraph for each speaker. Yet, in the close conceptual unity of McCarthy's novels, lengthy paragraphs of extensive character analyses frequently fill several pages without interruption. As a result, the technique of several speakers in one paragraph seems to support the general schema. It supports, also, the paradigm of the group.

Structurally, the three novels preceding *The Group* develop around separate chapters, each presenting the viewpoints and the consciousness of the different characters; their point of unity is the common awareness of the social group. A protagonist, often a reflection of the author, generally emerges from among these peripheral persons, but the effect of each chapter remains that of the portrait or sketch.

Several factors of McCarthy's work can be inferred from this structure. As an orphan and a Catholic among Protestants, she no doubt had an early sensitivity to the significance of the group and the outsider. Furthermore, the intensely autobiographical nature of her work blurs the lines of genre, so that her essays read like short stories and her short stories like essays. Genre distinction, then, becomes a problem in any analysis of her work. An example is *The Company She Keeps*, short stories which are pulled into book form and revolve around a central theme—

the quest—and parallel the structure of her novels. Furthermore, McCarthy did not term *The Oasis* a "novel" but called it a *conte philosophique*. Also, several chapters of her novels were published individually as short stories before being incorporated in the novels. The effect of this technique raises the question of whether she pushed the boundaries of the traditional novel outward or merely retreated to its earliest phases of development. She lamented the loss of a "sense of character" in modern novels, saying it began to fade with D. H. Lawrence. She admired Leo Tolstoy, Gustave Flaubert, George Eliot, Charles Dickens, and "all the Elizabethans."

The dominant quality of McCarthy's work is satire, and much of it is achieved by exaggeration and generalization. The dominant organization is the pairing of a separate character with each chapter, infused with an occasional chorus of viewpoints. McCarthy compared the technique to ventriloquism: The author throws her voice into various characters who speak for her. The long paragraphs of explication or character analysis tend to minimize plot; the concentration is on the psychological effects of what are frequently trivial incidents—as in *The Oasis*, when a couple illegally picking berries on the group's farm destroys the group.

The themes of McCarthy's novels generally concern the social failures of a group—of utopian communities in *The Oasis*, of progressive education in *The Groves of Academe*, or of cultural progress in *The Group*. The interest in group attitudes can be best observed in the political content of McCarthy's novels, many of which feature a person who had some affiliation with the Communist party and defected or failed to become a member. Her work also shows a persistent aversion to the efforts of Senator Joseph McCarthy to eradicate communists in the United States.

The Oasis

McCarthy's first novel, *The Oasis*, was published in *Horizon* under the title *A Source of Embarrassment* and puts into practice the theories of Arthur Koestler about "oases," small libertarian groups that would try, as McCarthy said, "to change the world on a small scale." Set at Pawlet, Vermont, at an abandoned hotel on an isolated mountain in 1946 or 1947,

the novel brings together a group of about fifty people of varying backgrounds and motives. The characters seek to revive the concept of utopian communities and welcome defectors from Europe. Their efforts, however, remain confined to the daily problems of food gathering and management and fall short of the larger goals.

First, the group fails to agree on its purpose. The purists aspire to a millennium but the realists seek only a vacation or a retreat from atomic warfare. They disagree, also, about who should be permitted to join the group, and some oppose the admission of businessman Joe Lockman. Next, they find that intellect, good intentions, and the simple life without electricity do not bring about moral reform: Personal relationships and property ownership intrude. Joe Lockman leaves oil in the kitchen stove which singes the eyebrows of Katy Norell, and then, as a prank, he frightens Will Taub by pointing a gun at him. Later, when intruders pick their wild strawberries (the stolen fruit in their Eden), Katy is highly offended at the theft of *her* property, and Joe is indignant about the other colonists' attempts to drive away the berry pickers, until he realizes that it was his property, the gun, they used in the assault.

The first to defect from the community is Will Taub, in whom many readers recognized Philip Rahv, and Katy, who resembles Mary McCarthy, dreams of the dissolution of the community at the book's end. With Joe Lockman cast in the role of the outsider, with little plot and with incident minimized, and with much explication of philosophical theory and discussion of ideals and goals, the book sets the style for McCarthy's other novels.

The Groves of Academe

Suspense is greatly improved in McCarthy's next novel, *The Groves of Academe*, set in a small Pennsylvania college called Jocelyn and resembling Bard College. Directing its satire at progressive education, this novel pits the progressive against the classical, satirizes the small college in general, and exposes the evils of McCarthyism, focused in Senator Joseph McCarthy's House Committee on Un-American Activities. The group here is the English department faculty, from which Professor Henry Mulcahy finds himself dismissed. He rallies the faculty to his support, although he is a poor academician and deserves dismissal, and gains it through an appeal for sympathy for his wife and children. McCarthyism brought him to the position—the president hired him because he had been unjustly accused of being a Communist sympathizer—and, finally, it accounts for his retention. Mulcahy loses his chief faculty supporter when she discovers that he lied about his wife's illness, but he gains another weapon through a visiting poet who recognizes him from Communist party meetings. At the climax of the novel, the McCarthy scare is shown at its most evil: Protecting the college, the well-meaning president conducts an interview into Mulcahy's past, which results in his being charged with libel. The unstable Mulcahy triumphs and secures his position at Jocelyn—certain to continue bullying students and colleagues alike—and the president resigns.

A CHARMED LIFE

In *A Charmed Life*, Martha Sinnott returns to a group of artistic people at New Leeds, a small New England village based on Wellfleet, Cape Cod, where she had lived with her former husband (much like McCarthy had lived at Wellfleet and returned with a second husband). Martha returns determined to be different from and independent of the New Leedsians who live a charmed life of many accidents, none of which kills them. Here, time, which signifies the mortal, is askew and awry, as indicated by the many problems with clocks and calendars. Part of Martha's anxiety about her return to New Leeds is the possibility of meeting her former husband (based on Edmund Wilson) with his new wife and child and the fear that he will reestablish domination over her. When he seduces her and she later finds herself pregnant, she cannot remember the date well enough to determine whether her former or present husband is the father. Her moral decision to have an abortion because she cannot live a lie results in her death; returning from borrowing money for the abortion, she drives on the right side of the road, contrary to New Leeds custom, and meets another car head-on. The charmed life of New Leeds goes on, but Martha lives and dies an outsider.

McCarthy called this novel a fairy tale. Loosely analogous to "Sleeping Beauty," Martha Sinnott pricks her hand at the beginning of the novel, lives in self-doubt on the fringes of the immortality of New Leeds (the timelessness of a century of sleep), and is awakened to the new existence of pregnancy and decision. The prince who wakens her with a kiss (the seduction), however, is an evil prince.

THE GROUP

With a theme of the failure of modern progress, *The Group* was published in November, 1963. At that time, Betty Friedan's *Feminine Mystique* (1962) and other feminist writings had focused on the problems of women, and the public was responsive to works focused on the problems of the emancipated woman. Although the novel is set in the seven years from 1933 to 1940, the progressiveness of the eight *cum* nine young Vassar women seemed to be the progress which was engulfing women of the 1960's. Like gleanings from an alumnae bulletin, the random appearances, different voices, and loose ends are not expected to be resolved. The undistinguished occupations of the group, also, confirm the alumnae magazine reports of most women graduates, but somehow more is expected of Vassar women. Not only the money but also increased competition for admission meant that, by 1963, most women could not get into Vassar. For the general public, there is some comfort in the failure of the culturally advantaged.

The novel begins with the wedding of Kay Strong in 1933 and ends with her death seven years later at the age of twenty-nine. Of the eight members of the group who had lived in the same dormitory, plus one outsider, Kay seemed to be most forward-looking and progressive. Like McCarthy, she comes from the West and, immediately upon graduation, she marries her lover of some time, a mostly unemployed playwright named Harald Petersen who resembles Harold Johnsrud. Part of McCarthy's personality is dispersed among the other characters, especially Libby Mac-Ausland, a woman of formidable intellect who writes book reviews and becomes a literary agent.

The elegant, beautiful, and wealthy Elinor Eastlake disappears into Europe and reemerges a lesbian prior to Kay's death. Polly Andrews becomes attached to a married man who is obviously well adjusted except that he pays twenty-five dollars a week for psychiatric counseling. Working in a hospital, Polly becomes engaged to another man, a psychiatrist who has defected from the profession and thus augments the satiric attack on psychiatry. Helena Davison, in Cleveland, remains the stable rich girl, highly intelligent and analytic. Priss Hartshorn marries a pediatrician, and, attempting to breast-feed her son and train him by modern theories, provides the satire on this aspect of progressivism. Pokey Prothero, from a household organized and represented by an invaluable butler, plans to become a veterinarian.

Kay, during a fight with Harald, gets a black eye and finds herself committed to a mental hospital. Despite Harald's admission that she does not belong there, she decides to stay for a rest and then disappears from the story until she reemerges after a divorce and a year in the West. Back East, ready to start a career again, she falls to her death while spotting planes from her window and becomes the first casualty of the war.

Representing a culmination of the group philosophy and the disjointed voices of the earlier novels, *The Group* with its timely feminist content earned for McCarthy a great deal of money and many appearances on talk shows and in magazines. Some Vassar alumnae were recognizable in it, and the film version omitted naming the college. This novel established McCarthy as a popular writer, but she did not attempt to capitalize on it with a follow-up novel. Instead, eight years later, she brought out a novel of a different sort altogether.

Birds of America

Departing from the group structure, McCarthy's next novel, *Birds of America*, begins in 1964 with Peter Levi's return at age nineteen to Rocky Port, Maine, after an absence of five years. During his absence, his favorite horned owl died. With his divorced and remarried mother Rosamund, he searches for a waterfall that they cannot find—the victim of a highway project. In their respective ways, the village and the mother cling to fashions of the past but rapidly succumb to modernity.

Peter goes to the Sorbonne for his junior year in college but finds his ideals of French culture in conflict with the realities. His friends are American; he

has a painful Thanksgiving dinner at an American general's home discussing vegetarianism and the war in Vietnam; he runs afoul of the French police while watching a demonstration; and he spends Christmas vacation in Rome where the masses of tourists interfere with his appreciation of the Sistine Chapel. Returned to Paris, he attempts in his Kantian way—"Behave as if thy maxim could be a universal law"—to help the street drunkards. Everywhere he goes, he tangles with human refuse, which is best revealed in a long letter home about the filth of Parisian toilets. Clinging to his preferences for nature, however, he grows vegetables and other plants in his apartment and joins a bird study group. At a zoo at the close of the novel, he is attacked by a swan while attempting to feed it from his hand. He wakens, later, in a hospital recovering from a reaction to a penicillin shot. At this point, Kant speaks to him, saying that "nature is dead, my child."

Peter (obviously modeled on Reuel Wilson) calls his father "babbo," is familiar with Italy, speaks both French and Italian, and is an intellectual like his mother. This novel, much different from the other seven, is the only one with a clear and unmistakable protagonist. The group Peter satirizes are tourists as a group; but the group does not make up the novel's characters.

Cannibals and Missionaries

The group of *Cannibals and Missionaries*, originally formed as a committee of six to fly by Air France to Iran to investigate reports of the Shah's torturing of prisoners, expands, by the time the plane is hijacked to Holland, to twenty-four hostages and eight terrorists. Set during the administration of President Gerald Ford, the novel takes its title from the puzzle in which three cannibals and three missionaries must cross a river in a boat that will hold only two people, and if the cannibals outnumber the missionaries, they might eat the missionaries. In the novel, however, there is no clear indication as to which group represents the cannibals and which the missionaries.

In one passage of explication, McCarthy points out that the terrorists' demands accomplish nothing but the reabsorption into the dominant society of whatever they demanded; prisoners released, for example, are eventually returned to prison. Confined in a Dutch farmhouse, hostages learn of their terrorists' demands from television: $1.25 million, Holland's withdrawal from the North Atlantic Treaty Organization (NATO), the breaking of relations with Israel, and the release of "class war" prisoners from Dutch jails. Like the other groups in McCarthy's fiction, the members of this group are pulled together in a common cause; even though divided between hostages and terrorists, the hostages willingly aid the terrorists in some efforts and feel triumphant in the successful completion of a task, such as hiding the helicopter that brought them to the farmhouse. At the novel's conclusion, however, all but four are killed, one of whom claims that she has not been changed by the experience.

The European settings of the last two novels reflect McCarthy's travel experiences and utilize her interest in art. In *Cannibals and Missionaries*, McCarthy returned to her early interest in communism and to the group structure with separate narrative voices.

While *The Groves of Academe* is still highly esteemed as an example of the academic novel, and *The Group* is read by students of popular fiction and women's issues, McCarthy's novels considered by themselves do not make up a lasting body of work. Rather, they derive their lasting significance from their place in the life and work of an exemplary woman of letters.

Grace Eckley

OTHER MAJOR WORKS

SHORT FICTION: *The Company She Keeps*, 1942; *Cast a Cold Eye*, 1950; *The Hounds of Summer and Other Stories*, 1981.

NONFICTION: *Sights and Spectacles, 1937-1956*, 1956; *Venice Observed*, 1956; *Memories of a Catholic Girlhood*, 1957; *The Stones of Florence*, 1959; *On the Contrary: Articles of Belief*, 1961; *Mary McCarthy's Theatre Chronicles, 1937-1962*, 1963; *Vietnam*, 1967; *Hanoi*, 1968; *The Writing on the Wall and Other Literary Essays*, 1970; *Medina*, 1972; *The Seventeenth Degree*, 1974; *The Mask of State*, 1974; *Ideas and the Novel*, 1980; *Occasional Prose*, 1985; *How I Grew*, 1987.

BIBLIOGRAPHY

Auchincloss, Louis. *Pioneers and Caretakers: A Study of Nine American Novelists*. Minneapolis: University of Minnesota Press, 1961. Auchincloss regards McCarthy the novelist as a caretaker of American culture. Covers McCarthy's transition from novellas ("a perfect medium for [her]") to longer works such as *The Oasis*. Considers *The Groves of Academe* the apex of her satirical art. A valuable guide to McCarthy.

Brightman, Carol. *Writing Dangerously: Mary McCarthy and Her World*. New York: Clarkson Potter, 1992. This work supplements but does not supersede Carol W. Gelderman's earlier biography. Like Gelderman, Brightman was able to interview her subject, and her book reflects not only inside knowledge but (as its subtitle suggests) also a strong grasp of the period in which McCarthy published. Includes a biographical glossary and notes.

Gelderman, Carol W. *Mary McCarthy: A Life*. New York: St. Martin's Press, 1988. Probably the most thorough study available on McCarthy and a must for scholars of her work as well as fans of good biography. Essentially a biography, but includes much valuable criticism of her novels and extracts from her letters and other writings. The material is arranged chronologically and is well organized. No bibliography, but includes extensive notes.

_____, ed. *Conversations with Mary McCarthy*. Jackson: University Press of Mississippi, 1991. A series of interviews with the author, dating from 1962 to 1989.

Grumbach, Doris. *The Company She Kept*. New York: Coward, McCann, 1967. A full-length study of McCarthy with special emphasis on her Catholic upbringing. In a personal and accessible style, Grumbach skillfully interweaves biography with criticism of McCarthy's novels, stressing her profoundly feminine approach. Follows McCarthy's development as a writer, including her involvement with the *Partisan Review* circle in the late 1930's, her time in Europe, the elusiveness of critical acclaim for her work, and the popular success of The Group.

Stock, Irvin. *Mary McCarthy*. Minneapolis: University of Minnesota Press, 1968. A pamphlet that offers accessible, readable criticism with insight into McCarthy's motives as a writer. Takes the point of view that McCarthy's work is loyal to the life that she lived—that the mind's accomplishments are worth little in the face of life's difficulties. Includes discussion of McCarthy's nonfiction as well as her novels, in particular her controversial piece *Vietnam*. Selected bibliography.

Stwertka, Eve, and Margo Viscusi, eds. *Twenty-four Ways of Looking at Mary McCarthy: The Writer and Her Work*. Westport, Conn.: Greenwood Press, 1996. Part of the Contributions to the Study of World Literature series, this volume is based on essays presented at a conference on the author at Bard College in 1993.

CARSON MCCULLERS

Born: Columbus, Georgia; February 19, 1917
Died: Nyack, New York; September 29, 1967

PRINCIPAL LONG FICTION
The Heart Is a Lonely Hunter, 1940
Reflections in a Golden Eye, 1941
The Member of the Wedding, 1946
The Ballad of the Sad Café, 1943 (serial), 1951 (book)
Clock Without Hands, 1961

OTHER LITERARY FORMS
Carson McCullers published a number of short stories, some of which are included in the volume containing *The Ballad of the Sad Café* and some in a collection of short works, *The Mortgaged Heart* (1971), edited by her sister, Margarita G. Smith. The latter also contains some magazine articles and notes of her writing. McCullers adapted *The Member of the Wedding* for the stage in 1950 (a film version appeared in 1952). She wrote two plays, including *The Square Root of Wonderful* (1957). McCullers's poetry is published in *The Mortgaged Heart* and in a

children's book, *Sweet as a Pickle and Clean as a Pig* (1964).

ACHIEVEMENTS
Like William Faulkner, McCullers has literary kinship with those older, midnight-haunted writers—Edgar Allan Poe, Nathaniel Hawthorne, and Herman Melville among them—who projected in fable and with symbol the story of America's unquiet mind. Against her southern background she created a world of symbolic violence and tragic reality, indirectly lighted by the cool Flaubertian purity of her style. Of the writers of her generation, none was more consistent or thorough in achieving a sustained body of work.

Several of McCullers's works received critical acclaim. "A Tree, a Rock, a Cloud," a short story sometimes compared in theme to Samuel Taylor Coleridge's "The Rime of the Ancient Mariner" (1798), was chosen for the O. Henry Memorial Prize in 1942. The dramatic version of *The Member of the Wedding* was extremely successful, running on Broadway continuously for nearly fifteen months, and it was named for both the Donaldson Award and the New York Drama Critics Circle Award in 1950. In addition, McCullers was a Guggenheim fellow in 1942 and 1946, and she received an award from the American Academy of Arts and Letters in 1943.

BIOGRAPHY
Carson McCullers was born Lula Carson Smith on February 19, 1917, in Columbus, Georgia. Marguarite Smith, McCullers's mother, was very early convinced that her daughter was an artistic genius and sacrificed herself and, to some extent, McCullers's father, brother, and sister, to the welfare of her gifted child. McCullers grew up, therefore, with a peculiar kind of shyness and emotional dependence on her mother, combined with supreme self-confidence about her ability. McCullers announced early in life that she was going to be a concert pianist, and she indeed displayed a precocious talent in that direction. Smith placed her daughter under the tutelage of Mary Tucker, a concert musician, who agreed that McCullers was talented.

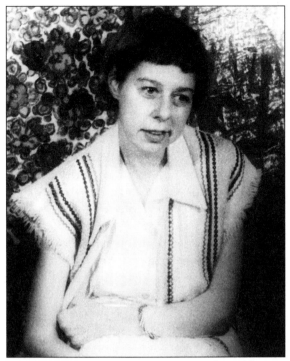

(Library of Congress)

ots and a mean old woman of one hundred years." Her next opus was a play in rhymed verse called *The Fire of Life*, starring Jesus Christ and Friedrich Nietzsche. Soon after, she became enthralled by the great Russian writers Fyodor Dostoevski, Anton Chekhov, and Leo Tolstoy—a fascination she never outgrew. Years later, she was to suggest, with considerable cogency, that modern southern writing is most indebted to the Russian realists.

The Smith household, while never wealthy, was not so hard pressed for money as McCullers sometimes later pretended. Lamar Smith, her father, was a respected jeweler in Columbus, Georgia, and a skilled repairer of clocks and watches. There was enough money, at least, to send the seventeen-year-old McCullers to New York City to attend the famous Juilliard School of Music. There was not enough, however, to replace the tuition money she had lost in the subway. Perhaps she was too moritified to ask for help, foreseeing that her father would simply send her a ticket to return home.

Whether through carelessness or naïveté, McCullers found herself almost penniless in New York. Having already paid her tuition for night classes at Columbia University, however, she intended to survive as best she could with whatever odd jobs she could find. Her inexperience and ineptness led to her being fired repeatedly from whatever employment she could find. One way or another, McCullers managed to support herself through the school term. By the time she came home in the summer, she had begun to write in earnest, and the dream of being a concert pianist was entirely displaced by the vision of becoming a great writer. She had launched her publishing career by selling two short stories to *Story* magazine: "Wunderkind" and "Like That." Her first novel, *The Heart Is a Lonely Hunter*, was in its formative stages.

Back home, McCullers met a handsome young soldier Reeves McCullers, who shared both her ambitions of living in New York and of becoming a writer. In 1936, Reeves left the army and traveled to New York to attend Columbia University, as McCullers was doing. His college career lasted only a few weeks, however, before he withdrew entirely to

McCullers came to love Mrs. Tucker and her family with an all-consuming passion, a pattern she was to follow with a number of other close friends during her life. Dr. Mary Mercer, a psychiatrist friend of McCullers's during her later years, suggested that the emotional devastation of the adolescent girl in *The Member of the Wedding*, when she was not allowed to accompany her beloved brother and his bride on their honeymoon, was an expression of McCullers's despair when the Tuckers moved away from her hometown. She seemed to experience every break in human contact as personal betrayal or tragedy.

Writing was also an early enthusiasm of McCullers. As a child, she created shows to be acted by herself and her siblings in the sitting room. Her mother would gather in neighbors or relatives for an appreciative audience. In an article entitled "How I Began to Write" (*Mademoiselle*, September, 1948), McCullers said that these shows, which she described as anything from "hashed-over movies to Shakespeare," stopped when she discovered Eugene O'Neill. She was soon writing a three-act play "about revenge and incest" calling for a cast of a "blind man, several idi-

escort McCullers back home to Georgia to recover from one of her many serious illnesses.

In 1937, Carson and Reeves were married, although Reeves was financially in no condition to support a wife. Though idyllically happy at first, their marriage became increasingly troubled. While McCullers's first novel, published when she was twenty-two, brought her immediate recognition in the literary world of New York, her husband met with continual frustration in his own ambitions.

Their problems did not derive simply from the professional dominance of McCullers. Both she and her husband were sexually ambivalent. The repressed homosexuality and odd love triangles that are so characteristic of McCullers's fiction had some correlation to real-life situations. McCullers had a disconcerting tendency to fall in love with either men or women, and to suffer inordinately when such attentions were repulsed. As her fiction suggests, she believed that one of the central problems of living was to love and be loved in equal measure.

McCullers often left Reeves to his own devices when professional opportunities or invitations came her way. She was offered a fellowship, for example, in the prestigious Bread Loaf Writers' Conference, where she consorted with such persons as Robert Frost, Louis Untermeyer, John Marquand, and Wallace Stegner. That same summer, she also met Erika and Klaus Mann, Thomas Mann's children, and Annemarie Clarac-Schwartzenbach, a prominent Swiss journalist and travel writer. McCullers fell deeply in love with the stunning Annemarie. When Annemarie left the country, it was another terrible "desertion" for McCullers. *Reflections in a Golden Eye*, McCullers's second novel, was dedicated to Annemarie.

In 1940, McCullers and her husband separated, and McCullers moved into a two-room apartment in a large Victorian house in Brooklyn Heights, owned by George Davis, editor of *Harper's Bazaar*. The old house became the temporary home for a stimulating group of artists, including poets Wystan Auden and Louis MacNeice; the composer Benjamin Britten; Peter Pears, tenor; Gypsy Rose Lee, fan dancer and writer; and novelist Richard Wright. These were only the earlier residents. A group of musicians and composers, including Aaron Copland, Leonard Bernstein, and David Diamond, joined the ranks at one time or another. Diamond was to become another of those fateful friends who was emotionally involved with both McCullers and Reeves. Also temporarily in residence were Salvador Dali and his wife Gala, as well as other prominent Surrealist painters.

A new and terrifying illness drove McCullers back to the South to her mother's care. She was afraid this time that she was going blind. Years later, doctors declared that this episode, when she was barely twenty-four years old, was her first cerebral stroke. There was no paralysis, but her recovery was slow.

McCullers and Reeves tried again to live together in New York and for a time took comfort in a new intimacy with their friend David Diamond. McCullers was invited to Yaddo, a retreat for resident artists situated a few miles from Saratoga Springs, New York. The motherly overseer of the colony, Elizabeth Ames, became almost a second mother to McCullers, who returned again and again to this peaceful setting and considered it the place most conducive to writing.

McCullers eventually divorced Reeves; he went back into the service, became a much-decorated war hero, was wounded several times in action, and finally returned as an officer beloved by his men. McCullers was so admiring of his new role that they were remarried. As a civilian husband, however, Reeves could not maintain the independence and pride he had so hardily won as a soldier. He turned increasingly to drink and eventually expressed the desire to commit suicide. When, in Europe, he seemed determined that they should both hang themselves, McCullers fled from him in terror and returned home alone. Shortly thereafter, Reeves was found dead in a Paris hotel.

After McCullers finished *The Member of the Wedding*, which proved immensely popular, her friendship with dramatist Tennessee Williams encouraged her to attempt a stage adaptation of the work. After many trials in deciding on an agreeable version for the stage, the play finally was produced, starring Ethel Waters and Julie Harris. McCullers wrote one other play, *The Square Root of Wonderful*, which was not nearly so successful. *The Member of the Wedding* was eventually adapted into a motion picture with the original cast. John Huston produced a film version of another of McCullers's works, *Reflections in a Golden Eye*, shortly before her death.

McCullers's last years were a nightmare of pain, though she continued to maintain a fairly cheerful social life while partially paralyzed and often bedridden. She had two strokes; underwent several operations on her paralyzed left arm, leg, and hand; had a cancerous breast removed; broke her hip and elbow in a fall; and finally died after another massive stroke. She was fifty years old.

ANALYSIS

Carson McCullers's fiction has a childlike directness, a disconcerting exposure of unconscious impulses in conjunction with realistic detail. She is like the candid child who announces that the emperor in his new clothes is really naked. She sees the truth, or at least a partial truth of the human psyche, then inflates or distorts that truth into a somewhat grotesque fable which is sometimes funny, but always sad.

Such a tragicomic effect derives, apparently, from an unusual openness to subconscious direction, combined with conscious cultivation of a style that best exploits such material, weaving into it just enough objectively observed reality to achieve plausibility. McCullers herself explained the technique by which she achieved the fusion of objective reality with symbolic, psychic experience. In "The Russian Realists and Southern Literature," first published in *Decision*, July, 1941 (now available in *The Mortgaged Heart*), she speaks of the charge of cruelty which was brought against both Russian writers (particularly Fyodor Dostoevski) and southern writers such as William Faulkner and herself, though she does not refer to her own works.

> No single instance of "cruelty" in Russian or Southern writing could not be matched or outdone by the Greeks, the Elizabethans, or, for that matter, the creators of the Old Testament. Therefore it is not the specific "cruelty" itself that is shocking, but the manner in which it is presented. And it is in this approach to life and suffering that the southerners are so indebted to

the Russians. The technique briefly is this: a bold and outwardly callous juxtaposition of the tragic with the humorous, the immense with the trivial, the sacred with the bawdy, the whole soul of a man with a materialistic detail.

What is peculiar to the Russians and the southerners is not the inclusion of farce and tragedy in the same work, but the fusion of the two so that they are experienced simultaneously. McCullers uses Faulkner's *As I Lay Dying* (1930) as an example of this technique. She could as effectively have demonstrated it with her own *Ballad of the Sad Café*, which is a masterpiece of tragicomedy. The relative lack of success of the earlier *Reflections in a Golden Eye* results partly, perhaps, from her inability to balance the sadomasochistic elements with elements of satire or farce. She reportedly claimed that incidents such as the rejected wife cutting off her nipples with garden shears were "hilariously funny." This may demonstrate an oddly warped sense of humor, a failure of craft, or simply ignorance about her own creative processes, or it may simply be a way of shunting off rational explanations of a work of art, a red herring to confuse critics. As a novelist, McCullers operates like a poet or perhaps like a Surrealist painter, who tells the truth but "tells it slant."

The thematic content of McCullers's works is consistent: All her stories deal with the metaphysical isolation of individuals and their desperate need to transcend this isolation through love. Love is the key to a magnificent transformation of leaden existence into gold, but the exalted state is doomed because love is so seldom reciprocated. Though this feeling (and it is more feeling than thought) may stem from McCullers's early fears and dependence on her mother, it strikes a universal chord. That McCullers projects this terrible sense of unrequited love into all kinds of human relationships except that between mother and daughter may be suggestive in itself. In an interview with Virginia Spencer Carr, Lamar Smith, Jr., said that his sister did not depict a meaningful mother-daughter relationship in her fiction because she did not want to strip herself bare and show the utter dependency that she felt for her mother.

The Heart Is a Lonely Hunter

Nevertheless, McCullers successfully universalizes the state of metaphysical isolation as a perennial human condition, not merely a neurotic regression to childhood. Her first novel, *The Heart Is a Lonely Hunter*, has Mick Kelly as its child character, who clings to John Singer, the deaf-mute, who, she fancies, understands and sympathizes with her problems. McCullers's own definition of the character in "Author's Outline of 'The Mute'" (*The Mortgaged Heart*) reveals an almost transparent self-dramatization: "Her story is that of the violent struggle of a gifted child to get what she needs from an unyielding environment." Only metaphorically is Mick's struggle "violent," but even when McCullers presents physical violence in fiction it often seems to function as the objective correlative to mental anguish.

McCullers casts Jake Blount, the ineffectual social agitator, as a would-be Marxist revolutionary, but he may seem more like an overgrown frustrated child. Her outline says, "His deepest motive is to do all that he can to change the predatory, unnatural social conditions existing today. . . . He is fettered by abstractions and conflicting ideas. . . . His attitude vacillates between hate and the most unselfish love."

Dr. Benedict Copeland is the more believable character, representing the peculiar plight of the educated African American in the South, who has internalized the white man's condemnation of black cultural traits. His daughter's black dialect and careless posture embarrass him, and he frowns on what he considers the irresponsible fecundity and emotionality of the black youth. What McCullers calls his "passionate asceticism" has driven away even his own family.

Biff Brannon, the proprietor of the local restaurant, is the dispassionate observer of men, sympathetic, in a distant way, with all human oddities. Like Mick, he seems almost a part of McCullers, a grown-up version of the child who sat silently in the corners of stores watching people, who loved to listen to the voices of African Americans, and who paid her dimes repeatedly to see the freaks in the side shows. Brannon is also sexually impotent, with homosexual leanings. He is cold and withdrawn with his wife and

has a repressed attraction for Mick in her tomboyish prepuberty—an impulse that fades as soon as she shows sexual development.

All of these characters pivot around the deaf-mute, John Singer, who is the central symbol of man's metaphysical isolation. They take his silence as wisdom and pour out their hearts to his patient but unreceptive ears. He does lip-read, so he knows what they are saying, but he has no way to communicate with them in reply. Moreover, the experiences they confide to him seem so alien to his own that he does not really understand. Mick talks about music, which he has never heard; Jake Blount rants about the downtrodden working classes; Dr. Copeland speaks of his frustrations as a racial leader without any followers; and Biff Brannon simply looks on with no project of his own.

Yet, John Singer shares their universal need to love and communicate with a kindred soul. The object of his adoration is another mute, a sloppy, retarded Greek named Antonopoulos, who loves nothing but the childish pleasure of a full stomach. When the Greek dies in an institution, Singer commits suicide. The whole pyramid of illusion collapses.

This bleak tale suggests that the beloved is created in the lover's mind out of the extremity of his need and projected upon whomever is available. Singer drew the love of these desperate souls on account of his polite tolerance of their advances coupled with an essential blankness. They looked into his eyes and saw their own dreams reflected there, just as Singer himself read a secret sympathy and understanding in the blank round face of Antonopoulos, who was actually incapable of such sentiments.

The haunting quality of this story may derive partly from the impression of getting an inside look at a multiple personality. McCullers displays a curious ability to divide her ambivalent psyche to create new, somewhat lopsided beings. McCullers had never seen a deaf-mute, for example, and when Reeves wanted to take her to a convention of deaf-mutes, she declined, saying she already knew John Singer. Marxist political agitators may have been just as foreign to her actual experience, but she could create one from the jumble of liberal sentiment she acquired through educated friends and through reading. If the issues were not clear in her own mind, it did not really matter, because Jake was a confused and drunken loser. McCullers has been praised by black writers for her sensitive portrayal of African Americans, yet the peculiar warmth of the relationship between Dr. Copeland's daughter Portia, her husband, and her brother suggests the triangular love affairs McCullers sometimes acted out in her own life and dramatized several times in other fiction.

REFLECTIONS IN A GOLDEN EYE

McCullers wrote *Reflections in a Golden Eye* in a short period of time, "for fun," she said, after the long session with *The Heart Is a Lonely Hunter*. The idea for the story germinated when, as an adolescent, she first went to Fort Benning, but she also drew on her experience of Fayetteville, where she and Reeves lived for a while, and nearby Fort Bragg. The story caused considerable shock in conservative southern communities. Americans generally were not prepared for a fictional treatment of homosexuality. A perceptive reader might suspect the latent homosexuality in Biff Brannon, but there is no doubt about Captain Penderton's sexual preferences. Moreover, the sadomasochism, the weird voyeurism, and the Freudian implications of horses and guns are unmistakable. If *The Heart Is a Lonely Hunter* is about love, *Reflections in a Golden Eye* is about sex and its various distortions. These characters are lonely, isolated people, driven by subconscious impulses. The story concerns two army couples, a houseboy, a rather primitive young man, all of them somewhat abnormal, and a horse. One suspects the horse is akin to a dream symbol for the ungovernable libido.

Captain Penderton is impotent with his beautiful wife Leonora but is drawn to her lover, Major Langdon. The major's wife is sickly and painfully aware of her husband's affair with Leonora. Mrs. Langdon is solicitously attended by a Filipino houseboy, who is also maladjusted. The other character is Private Williams, an inarticulate young man who seems to be a fugitive from somebody's unconscious (probably Captain Penderton's). He has a mystical affinity for nature, and he is the only person who can handle Leonora's high-spirited stallion, Firebird. Captain

Penderton is afraid of the horse, and he both loves and hates Private Williams.

D. H. Lawrence's *The Prussian Officer* (1914) may have provided a model for Penderton's relationship to Private Williams, since McCullers was an admirer of Lawrence. Private Williams is quite different, however, from the perfectly normal, healthy orderly who is the innocent victim of the Prussian officer's obsession. The silent Private Williams enacts a psychodrama that repeats, in different terms, the sexual impotence of Penderton. Having seen Leonora naked through an open door, he creeps into the Penderton house each night to crouch silently by her bedside, watching her sleep. When Penderton discovers him there, he shoots him. The scene in the dark bedroom beside the sleeping woman is loaded with psychological overtones. Not a word is spoken by either man. In one sense, the phallic gun expresses the captain's love-hate attraction to the private; in another sense, Penderton is killing his impotent shadow-self.

Technically speaking, *Reflections in a Golden Eye* is superior to McCullers's first novel; at least, it has an admirable artistic unity. Its four-part structure has the precision of a tightly constructed musical composition. In content, the story line seems as gothic as Edgar Allan Poe's "The Fall of the House of Usher" (1839), yet the style is objective and nonjudgmental—like the impersonal eye of nature in which it is reflected. McCullers was perfecting the kind of perception and style she spoke of in her essay on the Russian realists, presenting human action starkly without editorial comment.

THE BALLAD OF THE SAD CAFÉ

McCullers's next work, *The Ballad of the Sad Café*, was a more successful treatment of archetypal myth, with its psychodramatic overtones tempered this time by humor. Like the true folk ballad, it is a melancholy tale of love. The setting is an isolated southern village—little more than a trading post with a few dreary, unpainted buildings. The most prominent citizen is known as Miss Emelia, a strong, mannish, cross-eyed woman with a sharp business sense. She runs the general store and operates a still that produces the best corn liquor for miles around. There is nothing to do for entertainment in town except drink her brew, follow the odd career of this sexless female, and listen to the melancholy singing of the chain gang, which suggests a universal entrapment in the dreary reality of one's life.

The story concerns a temporary hiatus from boredom when Miss Emelia and the observing townspeople become a real community. Love provides the means for a temporary transcendence of Miss Emelia's metaphysical isolation and, through her, sheds a reflected radiance on all. Like John Singer, Miss Emelia chooses an odd person to love, a homeless dwarf who straggles into town, claiming to be her cousin and hoping for a handout. Although Miss Emelia had thrown out her husband, the only man who had ever loved her, because he expected sexual favors when they were married, she unaccountably falls in love with this pathetic wanderer. She takes Cousin Lymon in and, because he likes company, begins a restaurant, which becomes the social center of the entire community. All goes well until the despised husband, Marvin Macy, is released from the penitentiary and returns to his hometown, bent on revenge for the monstrous humiliation Miss Emelia had visited upon him.

Another unusual threesome develops when Cousin Lymon becomes infatuated with Marvin Macy. The competition between Macy and Miss Emelia for the attention of Cousin Lymon comes to a tragicomic climax in a fistfight between the rivals. Miss Emelia, who has been working out with a punching bag, is actually winning when the treacherous Cousin Lymon leaps on her back, and the two men give her a terrible drubbing. Macy and Cousin Lymon flee after they vandalize Miss Emelia's store and her still in the woods. Miss Emelia is left in a more desolate isolation than she has ever known and becomes a solitary recluse thereafter. The coda at the end recalls again the mournful song of the chain gang.

There is no more somber image of spiritual isolation than the glimpse of the reclusive Miss Emelia at the window of her boarded-up café: "It is a face like the terrible, dim faces known in dreams—sexless and white, with two gray crossed eyes which are turned inward so sharply that they seem to be exchanging with each other one long and secret gaze of grief." This story, written in a style that precludes sentimentality, is surely McCullers's most successful treatment of unrequited love and betrayal. The fight scene is a satire of all traditionally masculine brawls for the love of a woman, witnessed by the entire community as a battle larger than life, for a prize both morally and physically smaller than life. Besides the satire on all crude American substitutes for the duel of honor, this story may also call to mind Faulkner's famous gothic tale, "A Rose for Emily," about the genteel aristocratic lady who murdered her lover to keep him in her bed. Miss Emelia is certainly the absolute opposite to all conventions about the beautiful but fragile southern lady, who is entirely useless.

The Member of the Wedding

The Member of the Wedding is possibly the most popular of McCullers's novels, partly because it was converted into a successful Broadway play—in defiance of one critic's judgment that the novel is entirely static, totally lacking in drama. In fact, the story has a quality somewhat akin to closet drama, such as George Bernard Shaw's "Don Juan in Hell," which is performed by readers with no attempt at action. The endless conversation occurs in one spot, the kitchen of a lower-middle-class home in the South. There are occasional forays into the outer world, but always the principals return to the kitchen, where real experience and visionary ideals blend in an endless consideration of human possibilities.

The protagonist, a motherless adolescent girl named Frankie Addams, is the central quester for human happiness, foredoomed to disappointment. She is similar to Mick in *The Heart Is a Lonely Hunter*. It is no accident that both their names reflect the genderless state of prepuberty; moreover, neither has been indoctrinated into the attitudes and conventional expectations of little girls. In the isolation and boredom of Frankie's life, the only exciting event is the upcoming marriage of her older brother. Frankie conceives of the dream that will sustain her in the empty weeks of the long, hot summer: She will become a member of the wedding and join her brother and his bride on their honeymoon and new idyllic life of love and communion.

This impossible dream is the central issue of those long conversations in the kitchen where the girl is flanked by a younger cousin, John Henry, who represents the childhood from which Frankie is emerging, and the black maid, Berenice, who tries to reason with Frankie without stripping her of all solace. Ignorant as she is of the dynamics of sexual love, what Frankie aspires to is not a love so self-seeking as eros, nor quite so all-encompassing as agape. She envisions an ideal love that establishes a permanent and free-flowing communication among the members of a small, select group. This imagined communion seems to express an unvoiced dream of many, sometimes situated in a visionary future or an equally visionary past. Berenice, for all her gentle earthiness, shows that her vision of a golden age is in the past, when she was married to her first husband. She admits that after that man died, her other two marriages were vain attempts to recapture the rapport she had known with her first husband.

A curious irony of the story is that Frankie, with her persistent goal of escaping her isolated personal identity in what she calls the "we of me," actually comes closest to that ideal in the course of these endless conversations with the child and the motherly black woman. This real communion also passes away, as surely as the imagined communion with the wedded pair never materializes. John Henry dies before the end of the story, symbolic perhaps of the passing of Frankie's childhood. Reality and banality seem to have conquered in a world unsuited to the dreams of sensitive human beings.

CLOCK WITHOUT HANDS

McCullers's last novel, *Clock Without Hands*, written during a period of suffering and ill health, moves beyond the not quite adult problems of adolescence at the cost of much of her lyricism. Perhaps the novel is a somewhat feeble attempt to emulate the moral power of Leo Tolstoy's *The Death of Ivan Ilyich* (1886). It concerns a very ordinary man who faces death from leukemia and suspects that he has never lived on his own terms. The theme is still loneliness and spiritual isolation, but it has taken on existential overtones. The protagonist, J. T. Malone, like Tolstoy's Ivan, discovers too late that moral dignity

requires some kind of commitment to action. In his new and painful awareness of his own moral vacuity, there are few decisions left to make. He does make one small gesture, however, to redeem an otherwise meaningless life. He refuses to accept the community's order to bomb the home of an African American who had dared to move into a white neighborhood. McCullers's description of Judge Clane, Malone's aging friend, reveals with precision the peculiar combination of sentimentality and cruelty that characterizes conventional white racism of the old southern variety.

Although Carson McCullers will probably endure as a writer with a very special talent for describing the in-between world before a child becomes an adult, the no-man's-land of repressed homosexuality, and the irrational demands of love in the absence of any suitable recipient of love, the range of her fiction is quite limited. Somehow, the "child genius" never quite achieved maturity. Nevertheless, all people are immature or maimed in some secret way; in that sense, every reader must admit kinship to Carson McCullers's warped and melancholy characters.

Katherine Snipes

OTHER MAJOR WORKS

SHORT FICTION: *The Ballad of the Sad Café: The Novels and Stories of Carson McCullers*, 1951; *The Ballad of the Sad Café and Collected Short Stories*, 1952, 1955.

PLAYS: *The Member of the Wedding*, pr. 1950; *The Square Root of Wonderful*, pr. 1957.

CHILDREN'S LITERATURE: *Sweet as a Pickle and Clean as a Pig*, 1964.

MISCELLANEOUS: *The Mortgaged Heart*, 1971 (short fiction, poetry, and essays; Margarita G. Smith, editor).

BIBLIOGRAPHY

Bloom, Harold, ed. *Carson McCullers*. New York: Chelsea House, 1986. Essays on McCullers's novels and major short stories. Includes introduction, chronology, and bibliography.

Carr, Virginia Spencer. *The Lonely Hunter: A Biography of Carson McCullers*. Garden City, N.Y.:

Anchor Press, 1975. The most complete biographical study of McCullers. An impressive volume, based on interviews and research into published and unpublished materials over a period of seven years. Includes a preface by Tennessee Williams. Also contains numerous illustrations, a complete list of sources, and a helpful index.

_____. *Understanding Carson McCullers*. Columbia: University of South Carolina Press, 1990. A thoughtful guide to McCullers's works. Includes bibliographical references.

Clark, Beverly Lyon, and Melvin J. Friedman, eds. *Critical Essays on Carson McCullers*. New York: G. K. Hall, 1996. Divided into sections on reviews of the novels, tributes, and extended essays reflecting a variety of interpretations of individual novels, stories, and McCullers's relationship with the South. Includes introduction but no bibliography.

Evans, Oliver. *The Ballad of Carson McCullers: A Biography*. New York: Coward, McCann, 1966. Although this work is fairly short, it is particularly valuable for the critical analysis of McCullers's works. Along with his own thoughtful comments, Evans includes references to major critical studies. Contains illustrations, a good index, and a bibliography which is helpful, although dated.

_____. "The Theme of Spiritual Isolation in Carson McCullers." In *South: Modern Southern Literature in Its Cultural Setting*, edited by Louis D. Rubin, Jr. and Robert D. Jacobs. Westport, Conn.: Greenwood Press, 1961. Although one of the major themes in southern literature, it is significant that spiritual isolation is the topic specifically illustrated by McCullers in this important collection. This essay, which is clearly written and carefully supported by specific references, would be an ideal starting point for any study of McCullers's works.

Graver, Lawrence. *Carson McCullers*. Minneapolis: University of Minnesota Press, 1969. This monograph is a good brief introduction to McCullers which integrates biographical details with excellent discussions of her major works. Contains a thorough bibliography.

James, Judith Giblin. *Wunderkind: The Reputation of Carson McCullers, 1940-1990*. Columbia, S.C.: Camden House, 1995. Examines McCullers's place in literature as a southern female author. Bibliographical references and an index are provided.

McDowell, Margaret B. *Carson McCullers*. Boston: Twayne, 1980. This volume provides a sound biographical outline. Its chief value, however, is that it has a full, carefully balanced discussion of differing critical interpretations of specific works and of differing assessments by critics of the author's artistic intentions and accomplishments. The bibliography, which is partially annotated, is especially helpful.

ROSS MACDONALD
Kenneth Millar

Born: Los Gatos, California; December 13, 1915
Died: Santa Barbara, California; July 11, 1983

PRINCIPAL LONG FICTION

The Dark Tunnel, 1944 (as Kenneth Millar; pb. in Britain as *I Die Slowly*, 1955)

Trouble Follows Me, 1946 (as Millar; pb. in Britain as *Night Train*, 1955)

Blue City, 1947 (as Millar)

The Three Roads, 1948 (as Millar)

The Moving Target, 1949 (as John Macdonald; reissued as *Harper*, 1966)

The Drowning Pool, 1950 (as John Ross Macdonald)

The Way Some People Die, 1951 (as John Ross Macdonald)

The Ivory Grin, 1952 (as John Ross Macdonald; reissued as *Marked for Murder*, 1953)

Meet Me at the Morgue, 1953 (as John Ross Macdonald; pb. in Britain as *Experience with Evil*, 1954)

Find a Victim, 1954 (as John Ross Macdonald)

The Barbarous Coast, 1956

The Doomsters, 1958
The Galton Case, 1959
The Ferguson Affair, 1960
The Wycherly Woman, 1961
The Zebra-Striped Hearse, 1962
The Chill, 1964
The Far Side of the Dollar, 1965
Black Money, 1966
The Instant Enemy, 1968
The Goodbye Look, 1969
The Underground Man, 1971
Sleeping Beauty, 1973
The Blue Hammer, 1976

(Hal Boucher)

OTHER LITERARY FORMS

Ross Macdonald's reputation is based primarily on his twenty-four published novels, particularly on the eighteen which feature private detective Lew Archer. He also published a collection of short stories, *Lew Archer, Private Investigator* (1977), which includes all the stories from an earlier collection, *The Name Is Archer* (1955). *Self-Portrait: Ceaselessly into the Past* (1981) gathers a selection of his essays, interviews, and lectures about his own work and about other writers, including two essays first published in his *On Crime Writing* (1973). Macdonald wrote dozens of book reviews and several articles on conservation and politics.

ACHIEVEMENTS

Macdonald was recognized early in his career as the successor to Dashiell Hammett and Raymond Chandler in the field of realistic crime fiction, and his detective, Lew Archer, was recognized as the successor to Sam Spade and Philip Marlowe. Macdonald's advance over his predecessors was in the greater emphasis he placed on psychology and character, creating a more humane and complex detective and more intricate plotting. He is generally credited with raising the detective novel to the level of serious literature. The Mystery Writers of America awarded him Edgar Allan Poe scrolls in 1962 and 1963. In 1964, *The Chill* was awarded the Silver Dagger by the Crime Writers' Association of Great Britain. The same organization gave his next novel, *The Far Side*

of the Dollar, the Golden Dagger as the best crime novel of the year. Macdonald served as president of the Mystery Writers of America in 1965 and was made a Grand Master of that organization in 1974. In a review of *The Goodbye Look* in *The New York Times Book Review*, William Goldman called the Lew Archer books "the finest series of detective novels ever written by an American." His work has gained popular as well as critical acclaim: *The Goodbye Look*, *The Underground Man*, *Sleeping Beauty*, and *The Blue Hammer* were all national best-sellers. Three of his books have been made into successful motion pictures, two starring Paul Newman as Lew Archer: *The Moving Target* was made into the film *Harper* (1966) and *The Drowning Pool* was filmed in 1975. *The Three Roads* was filmed as *Double Negative* in 1979.

BIOGRAPHY

Ross Macdonald, whose real name is Kenneth Millar, was born in Los Gatos, California, on December 13, 1915. He published his early novels as Kenneth Millar or as John (or John Ross) Macdonald, but settled on the pseudonym Ross Macdonald by the time he wrote *The Barbarous Coast*, in order to avoid being confused with two other famous mystery writers: his wife, Margaret Millar, whom he had married in 1938, and John D. Macdonald. His family moved to Vancouver, British Columbia, soon after he was born, and he was reared and educated in Canada. After he was graduated with honors from the University of Western Ontario in 1938, he taught English and history at a high school in Toronto and began graduate work at the University of Michigan in Ann Arbor during the summers. He returned to the United States permanently in 1941, when he began full-time graduate studies at Ann Arbor, receiving his M.A. in English in 1943. During World War II, he served as communications officer aboard an escort carrier in the Pacific and participated in the battle for Okinawa. In 1951, he was awarded a Ph.D. in English from the University of Michigan, writing his dissertation on the psychological criticism of Samuel Taylor Coleridge. Macdonald belonged to the American Civil Liberties Union and, a dedicated conservationist, was a member of the Sierra Club and helped found the Santa Barbara chapter of the National Audubon Society. He lived in Santa Barbara, California, from 1946 until his death from Alzheimer's disease on July 11, 1983.

ANALYSIS

Ross Macdonald's twenty-four novels fall fairly neatly into three groups: Those in which Lew Archer does not appear form a distinct group, and the Archer series itself, which may be separated into two periods. His first four books, *The Dark Tunnel, Trouble Follows Me, Blue City*, and *The Three Roads*, together with two later works, *Meet Me at the Morgue* and *The Ferguson Affair*, do not feature Lew Archer. These six novels, especially the first three, are rather typical treatments of wartime espionage or political corruption and are primarily of interest to the extent that they prefigure the concerns of later works: *The Three Roads*, for example, contains Macdonald's first explicit use of the Oedipus myth as a plot structure and of California as a setting.

The first six Archer books, *The Moving Target, The Drowning Pool, The Way Some People Die, The*

Ivory Grin, Find a Victim, and *The Barbarous Coast*, introduce and refine the character of Archer, build the society and geography of California into important thematic elements, and feature increasingly complex plots, with multiple murders and plot lines. Archer still shows traces of the influence of the hard-boiled detectives of Hammett and Chandler (he is named after Miles Archer, Sam Spade's partner in Hammett's *The Maltese Falcon*, 1930, but closely patterned after Philip Marlowe), but he also shows marks of the sensitivity and patience, the reliance on understanding and analysis, that separate him from his models. Even in these early books, Archer is more often a questioner than a doer.

THE DOOMSTERS

The next twelve Archer novels constitute Macdonald's major achievement. Crimes in these books are not usually committed by professional criminals but rather by middle-class people going through emotional crises. They followed a period of personal crisis in Macdonald's own life, during which he underwent psychotherapy; all these novels deal more or less explicitly with psychological issues. *The Doomsters*, although begun before his psychoanalysis, presents his first extended treatment of the plot of intrafamilial relations that dominates all the later books. Carl Hallman, a psychologically disturbed young man, appears at Archer's door after escaping from the state mental hospital. He has been confined there as a murder suspect in the mysterious death of his father. Although he knows himself to be legally innocent, he feels guilty for having quarreled violently with his father on the night of his death. This Oedipal tension between father and son, following the pattern of Sigmund Freud's famous interpretation, often serves as the mainspring of the plot in Macdonald's later novels. After hiring Archer to investigate the death, Carl panics and escapes again as Archer is returning him to the hospital. Carl's brother, Jerry, and sister-in-law, Zinnie, are subsequently murdered under circumstances which appear to incriminate Carl.

As it turns out, the case really began three years earlier, with the apparently accidental drowning of Carl's mother, Alicia. She had forced Carl's wife,

Mildred, to undergo an abortion at gunpoint at the hands of Dr. Grantland. Mildred hit Alicia over the head with a bottle when she came out of anesthesia and assumed that she had killed her. Dr. Grantland actually killed Alicia and made it look like drowning, but he conceals this fact and uses his power over Mildred, who is becoming psychologically unstable, to persuade her to kill Carl's father. He has designs on the family's money, and Mildred is greedy herself. She is also influenced, however, by her hatred of her own father, who deserted her mother, and by her desire to possess Carl entirely, to gain his love for herself by eliminating conflicting familial claims to it. She murders his brother and sister-in-law, his only remaining family, as she increasingly loses touch with sanity. Women are frequently the murderers in Macdonald's books, and he analyzed the reasons behind this in an interview. He considered that people who have been victims tend to victimize others in turn, and he regarded American society as one which systematically victimizes women. Mildred's difficult childhood and gunpoint abortion provide a clear illustration of this theme.

THE GALTON CASE

While the focus on family psychology constituted a clean break with the Hammett and Chandler school as well as with most of his own early work, the next Archer novel, *The Galton Case*, was of even greater importance for Macdonald's career. In *The Doomsters*, the case is rooted in a crime committed three years earlier; in *The Galton Case*, as in most of the novels to follow, the present crime is rooted deeper in the past, in the preceding generation. This gives Macdonald the means to show the long-term effects of the influence of the family upon each of its members. The elderly Maria Galton hires Archer to trace her son Anthony, who had stolen money from his father after a quarrel (reminiscent of that between Carl Hallman and his father) and run off to the San Francisco area with his pregnant wife, Teddy, twenty-three years before. Archer discovers that Anthony, calling himself John Brown, was murdered not long after his disappearance. He also finds a young man calling himself John Brown, Jr., who claims to be searching for his long-lost father. Events lead Archer

to Canada, where he learns that the young man is Theo Fredericks, the son of Nelson Fredericks and his wife. Mrs. Galton's lawyer, Gordon Sable, has planned Theo's masquerade as her grandson to acquire her money when she dies. Yet a further plot twist reveals that Theo really is Anthony Galton's son. Fred Nelson had murdered Anthony twenty-three years before for the money he had stolen from his father and had taken Anthony's wife and son as his own under the name Fredericks.

This summary does not reflect the true complexity of the novel, which ties together a number of other elements, but does bring out the major theme of the son searching for his father, a theme which will recur in later works such as *The Far Side of the Dollar, The Instant Enemy, The Goodbye Look, The Underground Man*, and *The Blue Hammer*. As Macdonald explains in his essay "Writing *The Galton Case*" (1973), this plot is roughly shaped on his own life. His own father left him and his mother when he was three years old. Like Macdonald, John Brown, Jr., was born in California, grew up in Canada, and attended the University of Michigan before returning to California. It is interesting that each man assumed his lost father's name: Macdonald was Kenneth Millar's father's middle name. This transformation of personal family history into fiction seems to have facilitated the breakthrough that led him to write the rest of his novels about varying permutations of the relations between parents and children.

THE ZEBRA-STRIPED HEARSE

The exploration of the relations between three generations of fathers and sons in *The Galton Case* was followed by examinations of father and daughter relationships in *The Wycherly Woman* and *The Zebra-Striped Hearse*. Macdonald always counted the latter among his favorites for its intensity and range. In *The Zebra-Striped Hearse*, Archer is hired by Mark Blackwell to investigate his daughter Harriet's fiancé, Burke Damis, with a view to preventing their marriage. The implication is made that Mark sees Damis as a rival for his daughter's love. Archer discovers that Damis is really Bruce Campion and is suspected of having murdered his wife, Dolly, and another man, Quincy Ralph Simpson. Suspicion shifts to Mark when it is revealed that he is the father of Dolly's baby and then to Mark's wife, Isobel, who knew Dolly as a child. Harriet disappears and Mark confesses to murdering her, Dolly, and Simpson before committing suicide. Yet Archer believes that Harriet is still alive and tracks her down in Mexico. She had killed Dolly to clear the way for her marriage to Bruce and had also killed Simpson when he discovered her crime. Underlying her motive for Dolly's murder, however, is another Freudian pattern. The child of Mark and Dolly is Harriet's half brother, making Dolly a sort of mother figure and, by extension, making her husband, Bruce, a sort of father figure. Harriet thus symbolically kills her mother and marries her father.

THE CHILL

The Chill features one of Macdonald's most complex plots, but at its center is another basic family relationship, this time between a mother and son. Archer is brought into the case by Alex Kincaid, who hires him to find his wife, Dolly, who has disappeared the day after their wedding after a visit from an unknown man. The visitor turns out to have been her father, Thomas McGee, who has just been released from prison after serving a ten-year sentence for the murder of his wife and Dolly's mother, Constance. Later it is revealed that he had convinced her of his innocence and told her that Constance was having an affair with Roy Bradshaw. To learn more about Roy, Dolly has left Alex to go to work for Roy's mother, Mrs. Bradshaw, as a driver and companion. Shortly thereafter, she is found, hysterical, at the Bradshaws', talking about the murder of her college counselor, Helen Haggerty. Helen is soon discovered murdered and the weapon used is found under Dolly's mattress, though under circumstances that suggest that it may have been planted there. Archer learns from Helen's mother that she had been deeply affected by a death that occurred twenty years before. Luke Deloney had been killed in a shooting that was ruled accidental on the basis of an investigation that was conducted by Helen's father, but Helen was convinced that the facts had been covered up. Luke's widow admits to Archer that there had been a cover-up, that her husband committed suicide. Ar-

cher later discovers another connection between the recent death and those of ten and twenty years ago: Roy Bradshaw was the elevator boy at the building in which Luke died.

Investigation of Roy reveals that he has been secretly married to Laura Sutherland, having recently obtained a divorce from a woman named Letitia Macready. Archer confronts Mrs. Bradshaw with the latter fact (though not the former), and after an initial denial she confirms that twenty years ago Roy had briefly been married to a much older woman. Letitia turns out to have been the sister of Luke's wife, and it was rumored that she was having an affair with her sister's husband. Letitia apparently died in Europe during World War II, shortly after Luke's death. Archer eventually draws a fuller story out of Roy: Luke, who was indeed Letitia's lover, found her in bed with Roy. There had been a violent struggle, during which Letitia accidentally shot and killed Luke. Roy married her and took her to Europe, later returning with her to America. He had been leading a secret double life ever since, concealing Letitia, now quite old and sick, from all of his friends as well as from the police and, especially, from his possessive mother. During this confession, Archer answers a telephone call and hears Laura, who believes that she is speaking to Roy, tell him that "she" has discovered their secret marriage. Roy attacks Archer at this news and escapes in his car to attempt to intercept the other woman, who had vowed to kill Laura. Roy is killed when Mrs. Bradshaw's car crashes into his. Archer knows by now that Mrs. Bradshaw is not Roy's mother, but his first wife: She is Letitia Macready. Roy has acted out the Oedipal drama of the death of a father figure, Letitia's lover Luke, and the marriage to a mother figure, the older woman who posed as his real mother. (Macdonald develops the obverse of this plot in *Black Money*, which pairs a young woman with a much older man.) Letitia murdered Constance McGee because Roy had been having an affair with her and murdered Helen Haggerty in the belief that it was she rather than Laura Sutherland whom Roy was currently seeing.

This unraveling of the plot has come a long way from Alex Kincaid's request that Archer find his wife, but one of the characteristics of Macdonald's later novels is the way in which seemingly unrelated events and characters come together. The deeper Archer goes into a set of circumstances involving people who know one another, the more connectedness he finds. These novels all have large casts of characters and a series of crimes, often occurring decades apart. Once the proper connections are made, however, there is usually only one murderer and one fundamental relationship at the center of the plot. All the disparate elements, past and present, hang together in one piece.

While Freudian themes continued to dominate Macdonald's work, he often combined them with elements adapted from other stories from classical mythology or the Bible. *The Far Side of the Dollar* has been seen as a modern, inverted version of the story of Ulysses and Penelope. Jasper Blevins, the fratricidal murderer of *The Instant Enemy*, explicitly draws the analogy between his story and that of Cain and Abel. He has also murdered one of his stepfathers, adding the Oedipal masterplot to the biblical plot, and murdered his own wife in one of the series' most violent books, perhaps reflecting the violence of the wartime period during which the book was written. The complex events of *The Goodbye Look* are catalyzed by the search for a gold box which is specifically compared to Pandora's box. Again the myth is combined with the primal story of the parricide, this time committed by a child. All three of these books also repeat the quintessential Macdonald plot of a young man's search for his missing father.

THE UNDERGROUND MAN

The search for the absent father also sets in motion the events of *The Underground Man*, probably the most admired of Macdonald's works. This novel, together with his next, *Sleeping Beauty*, also reflects its author's abiding concern with conservation. Each novel examines an ecological crime as well as a series of crimes committed against individuals. In *Sleeping Beauty*, Macdonald uses an offshore oil spill, inspired by the 1967 spill near his home in Santa Barbara, as a symbol of the moral life of the society responsible for it, in particular that of the Lennox family, which runs the oil corporation and is

also the locus of the series of murders in the book. In *The Underground Man*, the disaster of a human-made forest fire serves similar ends. The story begins unexceptionally: Archer is taking a day off at home, feeding the birds in his yard. He strikes up an acquaintance with young Ronny Broadhurst and Ronny's mother, Jean, who are staying at the home of Archer's neighbors. The boy's father, Stanley, disrupts the meeting when he drives up with a young girl, later identified as Sue Crandall, and takes his son to visit Stanley's mother, Elizabeth Broadhurst. They never pay the planned visit, and when Jean hears that a fire has broken out in that area, she enlists Archer to help her look for them. On the way there, Jean explains that her husband has gradually become obsessed by his search for his father, Leo, who apparently ran away with Ellen Kilpatrick, the wife of a neighbor, Brian, some fifteen years ago. It turns out that Stanley, accompanied by Ronny and Sue, obtained a key from Elizabeth's gardener, Fritz Snow, and had gone up to her cabin on a mountain nearby. There, Archer finds Stanley, murdered and half-buried. The fire originated from a cigarillo Stanley dropped when he was killed, creating a causal as well as symbolic link between the personal and ecological disasters.

After an investigation that is complex even by Macdonald's standards, Archer is able to reconstruct the past events that explain those of the present. The seeds of the present crimes are found in the previous generation. Eighteen years ago, Leo Broadhurst impregnated Martha Nickerson, an underage girl. She ran away with Fritz Snow and Al Sweetner in a car they stole from Lester Crandall. The incident was planned by Leo and Martha to provide a scapegoat to assume the paternity of her coming child. When they were tracked down, Al went to jail for three years, Fritz was sentenced to work in a forestry camp for six months, and Martha married Lester Crandall. Three years later, Leo was having an affair with Ellen Kilpatrick. She went to Reno to obtain a divorce from her husband, Brian, and waited there for Leo to join her. While she was gone, however, Leo went up to the cabin with Martha and their child, Sue. Brian, who knew about his wife's affair with Leo and

wanted revenge, discovered the renewal of this earlier affair and informed Leo's wife, Elizabeth. She
went up to the mountain cabin and shot her husband,
believing that she killed him. Stanley, who had followed his mother that night, was an aural witness to
the shooting of his father, as was Susan, also Leo's
child. Yet Leo had not been killed by the bullet. He
was stabbed to death, as he lay unconscious, by Edna
Snow, Fritz's mother, in revenge for the trouble that
Leo and Martha's affair had caused her son and also
as a self-appointed agent of judgment on Leo's adulteries. She forced Fritz and Al to bury Leo near the
cabin. Fifteen years later, on almost the same spot,
she murders Stanley, who is on the verge of discovering his father's body and Edna's crime. Life moves in
a circle as Ronny witnesses Stanley's death in the
same place that Stanley witnessed Leo's shooting.
The connection is reinforced by Sue's presence at
both events.

THE BLUE HAMMER

The last novel Macdonald wrote is *The Blue Hammer*, and whether he consciously intended it to be the
last, it provides in certain ways an appropriate conclusion to the series. It is the first time, apart from a
brief interlude in *The Goodbye Look*, that Archer has
a romantic interest. The effects of a lack of love preoccupy all the Archer novels, and Archer recognizes
in this book that the same lack has had its effects on
him. He has been single since his divorce from his
wife, Sue, which took place before the first book begins. In the last book, he meets and soon falls in love
with Betty Jo Siddon, a young newspaper reporter.
Yet Macdonald knew that Raymond Chandler was
unable to continue the Philip Marlowe novels after
marrying off his detective, and perhaps he intended
to end his own series similarly. It seems that the
genre requires a detective who is himself without
personal ties, who is able to and perhaps driven to
move freely into and then out of the lives of others.
Indeed, the involvement of Betty in the case does create a tension between Archer's personal and professional interests. Another suggestion that *The Blue
Hammer* may have been intended to be the last of the
Archer novels lies in its symmetry with the first, *The
Moving Target*. In the earlier book, Archer kills a

man in a struggle in the ocean, the only such occurrence in the eighteen books and an indication of
the extent to which the compassionate Archer differs from his more violent predecessors. In the last
book, he finds himself in a similar struggle, but this
time manages to save his adversary. Archer specifically parallels the two events and feels that he has
balanced out his earlier sin, somehow completing a
pattern.

The plot of *The Blue Hammer* is built around the
Dostoevskian theme of the double, a theme that Macdonald treated before in *The Wycherly Woman*, in
which Phoebe Wycherly assumes the identity of
her murdered mother, and in *The Instant Enemy*, in
which Jasper Blevins takes on the role of his murdered half brother. The motif is developed here in its
most elaborate form and combined with the familiar
themes of the crimes of the past shaping those of the
present and of the son's search for his true father,
forming an appropriate summation of the major
themes of MacDonald's entire Archer series.

Thirty-two years ago, Richard Chantry stole the
paintings of his supposed half brother, William
Mead, then serving in the army, and married William's girlfriend Francine. William murdered Richard when he returned and assumed his identity as
Francine's husband, though he had already married a
woman named Sarah and had a son, Fred, by her.
Seven years later, Gerard Johnson, a friend of William from the army, appears at William's door with
Sarah and Fred, threatening to blackmail him. William kills Gerard and then takes his name, in a doubling of the theme of doubleness. He returns to
live with Sarah and Fred and remains a recluse for
twenty-five years to hide his crimes.

The case begins for Archer when he is called in to
locate a painting that has been stolen from Jack
Biemeyer. He learns that it was taken by Fred Johnson, who wanted to study it to determine whether it
was a recent work by the famous artist Richard Chantry, who had mysteriously vanished twenty-five years
before. If genuine, it would establish that the painter
was still alive. Fred had seen similar pictures in the
Johnson home and had formed the idea that Chantry
might be his real father. William steals the painting,

which is one of his own works, in a doubling of his earlier theft of his own paintings from Richard. The painting had been sold by Sarah to an art dealer, and William is forced to kill again to prevent the discovery of his true identity and his earlier murders. By the book's guardedly positive resolution, three generations of men—Fred Johnson; his father, William Mead; and Jack Biemeyer, who turns out to be William's father—have all come to the admission or recognition of their previously concealed identities and have come to a kind of redemption through their suffering.

Macdonald's work, in terms of quantity as well as quality, constitutes an unparalleled achievement in the detective genre. The twenty-four novels, particularly the eighteen which feature Lew Archer, form a remarkably coherent body of work both stylistically and thematically. The last twelve Archer books have received especially high critical as well as popular acclaim and have secured Macdonald's standing as the author of the finest series of detective novels ever written, perhaps the only such series to have bridged the gap between popular and serious literature.

William Nelles

OTHER MAJOR WORKS

SHORT FICTION: *The Name Is Archer*, 1955 (as John Ross Macdonald); *Lew Archer, Private Investigator*, 1977.

NONFICTION: *On Crime Writing*, 1973; *Self-Portrait: Ceaselessly into the Past*, 1981.

BIBLIOGRAPHY

Bruccoli, Matthew J. *Ross Macdonald*. San Diego: Harcourt Brace Jovanovich, 1984. Describes the development of Macdonald's popular reputation as a prolific author of detective fiction and his critical reputation as a writer of literary merit. Includes illustrations, an appendix with an abstract of his Ph.D. thesis, notes, a bibliography, and an index.

Mahan, Jeffrey H. *A Long Way from Solving That One: Psycho/Social and Ethical Implications of Ross Macdonald's Lew Archer Tales*. Lanham: University Press of America, 1990. Explores the Archer stories and their importance in the detective-fiction canon. Includes bibliographical references.

Nolan, Tom. *Ross Macdonald: A Biography*. New York: Scribner, 1999. The first full-length biography of Macdonald. Discusses the origins of the novels and critical responses to them.

Schopen, Bernard A. *Ross Macdonald*. Boston: Twayne, 1990. A sound introductory study, with a chapter on Macdonald's biography ("The Myth of One's Life"), on his handling of genre, his development of the Lew Archer character, his mastery of the form of the detective novel, and the maturation of his art culminating in *The Underground Man*. Provides detailed notes and an annotated bibliography.

Sipper, Ralph B., ed. *Ross Macdonald: Inward Journey*. Santa Barbara, Calif.: Cordelia Editions, 1984. This collection of twenty-seven articles includes two by Macdonald, one a transcription of a speech about mystery fiction and the other a letter to a publisher which discusses Raymond Chandler's work in relation to his own. Contains photographs and notes on contributors.

Skinner, Robert E. *The Hard-Boiled Explicator: A Guide to the Study of Dashiell Hammett, Raymond Chandler, and Ross Macdonald*. Metuchen, N.J.: Scarecrow Press, 1985. An indispensable volume for the scholar interested in tracking down unpublished dissertations as well as mainstream criticism. Includes brief introductions to each author, followed by annotated bibliographies of books, articles, and reviews.

South Dakota Review 24 (Spring, 1986). This special issue devoted to Macdonald, including eight articles, an editor's note, photographs, and notes, is a valuable source of criticism.

Speir, Jerry. *Ross Macdonald*. New York: Frederick Ungar, 1978. Serves as a good introduction to Macdonald's work, with a brief biography and a discussion of the individual novels. Includes chapters on his character Lew Archer, on alienation and other themes, on Macdonald's style, and on the scholarly criticism available at the time. Contains a bibliography, notes, and an index.

Wolfe, Peter. *Dreamers Who Live Their Dreams: The World of Ross Macdonald's Novels*. Bowling Green, Ohio: Bowling Green University Press, 1976. This detailed study contains extensive discussions of the novels and a consideration of the ways in which Macdonald's life influenced his writing. Includes notes.

Joseph McElroy

Born: Brooklyn, New York; August 21, 1930

Principal long fiction

A Smuggler's Bible, 1966
Hind's Kidnap: A Pastoral on Familiar Airs, 1969
Ancient History: A Paraphrase, 1971
Lookout Cartridge, 1974
Plus, 1977
Women and Men, 1987
The Letter Left to Me, 1988

Other literary forms

Joseph McElroy's reputation stands on his achievements as a novelist. A number of excerpts from his massive novel *Women and Men* first appeared in short-story form; the excellence of three of these pieces ("The Future," "The Message for What It Was Worth," and "Daughter of the Revolution") was acknowledged by their selection for the *O. Henry Prize Stories* and *Best American Short Stories*. In addition, McElroy published a number of uncollected essays on topics as various as the Apollo 17 launch, the influence on his generation of Vladimir Nabokov's fiction, and autobiographical aspects of his own work. Between 1971 and 1976 he was also a regular reviewer for *The New York Times Book Review*.

Achievements

From the start, McElroy was received as one of the generation of American novelists that includes Robert Coover, Thomas Pynchon, and William Gaddis—writers of long and technically demanding fic-

tions. Among them, McElroy remains the dark star, outshone by their well-publicized brilliance while being acknowledged among his peers as the writer's writer, one who is committed to giving fictional order to a complex "information society" by optimistically recognizing its possibilities for narrative art and human growth. In 1977, McElroy's writing was acclaimed by an Award in Literature from the American Academy of Arts and Letters. Still, the regard of critics was slow in coming, and reviewers have argued that the complexity of internal reference and detail in McElroy's work is too demanding of the reader. In a 1979 interview, McElroy countered that he continued to "hope . . . for readers who would be willing to commit themselves to a strenuous, adventurous fiction." The reissue of several of McElroy's novels, in addition to blooming scholarly acclaim, suggests that this hope is well placed.

Biography

Joseph Prince McElroy was born in Brooklyn, New York, on August 21, 1930, and has lived near there for most of his life. He received a baccalaureate from Williams College in 1951 and a master of arts degree from Columbia University in 1952. After two years with the United States Coast Guard (1952-1954), he returned to graduate studies at Columbia, completing the Ph.D. in 1962 with a dissertation on seventeenth century poet Henry King. From 1956 to 1961, he held positions as instructor and assistant professor of English at the University of New Hampshire. Beginning in 1964, he was a full professor of English at Queens College, City University of New York. McElroy was a visiting professor or a writer-in-residence at a number of major universities, received a wide range of fellowships and awards, and served editorial terms on several literary magazines. He would make his home in New York City.

Analysis

Joseph McElroy's novels unfold in the topographies of mind. He has called them "neural neighborhoods." Within those imaginary spaces, McElroy's fictions grow from a profound desire for order, for a meaningful landscape of human intentions and actions. Also, they grow from a profound recognition that such orders may be unobtainable amid the fragmenting stresses of advanced machine culture. The point, as his books illustrate, is not to kick against this crux but to set the mind in motion within it, thus to create form and meaning. This precept is the source of both difficulty and great achievement in McElroy's writing.

Not that McElroy's neural landscapes stand apart from ordinary surroundings. It is quite the opposite: His novels are saturated with the stuff of contemporary society, with references to and metaphors from urban culture, and from such wide-ranging pursuits as cinematography, information processing, linguistics, and the space program. Richly detailed and technically specific, these familiar endeavors illustrate the fragmentary nature of human knowledge. At the same time they point out unsuspected possibilities for human growth. McElroy's narrator-protagonists are imbued with an almost claustrophobic variety of concise memories and everyday desires. Yet within these mental topographies they are driven to discover order, or "plot," for novels are also "plotted," and it is of the essence of McElroy's novels that the action, the narrators' attempted discoveries, be seen as contemporary variations on the detective plot. They solve no significant enigmas. Not "representations" of events that have been rarefied by memory, McElroy's fictions are instead "demonstrations" of the complexities involved in reconstructing any past event. Inevitably the character's memory involves his own categories of feeling and linguistic mapping, which themselves become objects of scrutiny. The best one can do, suggests McElroy, is to "smuggle" or "kidnap" a perception or idea over the received boundary of some other. By thus learning to manipulate them, one surmounts the inadequacies and paradoxes of human knowledge.

This brief sketch of McElroy's principal concerns will suggest the interests he shares with many modern and contemporary writers. With modernists such as Marcel Proust and André Gide, he is concerned to show both the complexity and the potential illicitness of narratively reconstructed events, which are "counterfeit" creations precisely to the degree that they

recognize themselves as ordered rememberings of life's dismembered orderings. With contemporaries such as Michel Butor, William Gaddis, Nicholas Moseley, and Thomas Pynchon, he reflects on the linguistic nature of this narrative activity. Like them, he sees the ability to manipulate hypothetical, alternative structures—for example, the worlds of "stories"—as a condition of social existence, and he reflects on how we too hastily suppose that continuity and causality are absolute requirements of that structuring work.

A SMUGGLER'S BIBLE

A Smuggler's Bible was a brilliant first articulation of these themes. By McElroy's own account, this novel was not his first, but it developed after several aborted attempts at a rather conventionally sequential, causal type of long narrative. Its title describes the book's main emblem: A "smuggler's Bible" is a hollowed-out volume designed for carrying contraband over borders. Similarly, McElroy's narrative develops by making illicit leaps. Even though its eight parts are essentially disconnected, the reader still "smuggles" bits of information across their boundaries to reconstruct a "story" about its narrator-protagonist, David Brooke. In fact, readers are encouraged in this by another, omniscient narrative voice, which appears in short interchapters. This voice advertises itself as David's "creator" and comments on his task, itself also the reader's, which is to "analyze, synthesize, [and] assimilate" details gleaned by "projecting" oneself into others' experience. This is the task framed by a conventional, "realistic" novel. Yet a smuggler's Bible is also a clever deception: an illegal, profane business tucked inside an authorized, holy cover. In similar ways, David's eightfold story, a kind of experimental writing, can be read as trying, and failing, to disguise itself as an artistically conventional novel replete with causal plot.

The essentials of that inner narrative are as follows. David and his wife, Ellen, are passengers aboard a ship, the *Arkadia*, bound for London. There he must deliver to a mysterious "Old Man" the manuscript of a book he has written, each of its eight parts the story of an event or of characters with special significance in his own life. The ship's passage takes eight days. During that time, at the rate of a story per day, David struggles to give the manuscript continuity. He provides narrative transitions and "smuggles" characters from one narrative into another. He even attempts to structure each story according to some mythic subtext, such as those of Oedipus, Midas, or the Golden Ass. This technique of highly self-conscious parody—what poet T.S. Eliot called the "mythic method" in reference to James Joyce's *Ulysses* (1922)—is revealed as yet another mode of smuggling, which has lost that sacred magic it once promised to modernist writers. Thus, while David may think of himself as "an epistemological reuniac" attempting an integral, totalizing reconstruction of the past, *A Smuggler's Bible*, especially in its interchapters, tends contrariwise toward disjunction and incompleteness. McElroy has said that it "was designed to fracture."

Throughout this long, stylistically brilliant performance, the image one gets (not a "picture" but an immanence or field theory) is of women and men existing in a grand relational network. Yet only David's acts of memory hold that web in balance. This field of charged particles did exist, and had "reality," but only when a single mind was composing it, and that mind is, in the best sense of the term, *trivial*: It finds pattern and meaning in the accidental minutiae of ordinary lives.

A few examples: In the fourth of his "principal parts," David recounts the story of his acquaintance, at the University of New Hampshire, with an intellectual con artist named Duke Amerchrome. An immensely popular historian and theorist of American culture, Duke engineered his fame on forged sources and blustering rhetoric. He is an exemplar of the literati who smuggle themselves into positions of "authority." Tony Tanner thinks that the character is patterned on Norman Mailer, yet almost any other (such as Marshall McLuhan) would do, and one could also point to the autobiographical aspects and note that McElroy may have been exorcising personal as well as professional demons. In any event, much of Duke's story is transmitted to David through his son Michael, who discloses the man's use of counter-

feited trivia about the Battle of Ticonderoga. Michael, however, has selfish motives for these disclosures, such as coveting his father's nubile young wife (Duke's third). This Oedipal motif broadens; the idea of "shadowing" a (supposed) father, tracking him and absorbing the minutiae of his days until one knows enough to expose and supplant him, recurs in other chapters. The first memory concerns a bored rare-book dealer named Peter St. John who is being followed by a boy who thinks that the man resembles his father. In the second, David's association with a group of eccentric fellow boarders eventually centers on a rare-coin dealer named Pennitt, who may be a counterfeiter; whether he is is never certain, because the old man brushes David off before disclosing any conclusive evidence. In the final part, David's father spins through his last, trivial thoughts while dying of angina and rectal cancer. David *inhabits* these memories, seeking safe harbor between antinomies: the imploding heart of humanity, symbolizing powers of empathy and connection, versus the exploding rectum, David's symbol of dispersal and "apartness." The book ends there, with the mind shuttling in between, never resolving that antinomy but finding art in the act of composing.

Hind's Kidnap

Hind's Kidnap, McElroy's next novel, takes these ideas a step further. Once again the concern is with detection, with the mind moving inside a labyrinthine network of information that points equally to integral order and to zeros of disorder. Yet this novel falls short of its ambition. Critics have aptly noted that the book succeeds better in its idea than in its stylistic performance, which often becomes tiresome.

The reasons are several. One is that the narrator's attention to matters of trivial but feasibly significant detail achieves a still closer focus than in *A Smuggler's Bible*, but this attention must be borne by units of narrative (sentences on up to chapters) that strain from sheer length, and hence from the span of attention demanded of readers. Another reason, and doubtless an attempt to explain (that is, to naturalize) the first, is that in *Hind's Kidnap* the narrator-protagonist is virtually obsessed with the dialectic of detection.

The story is related by Jack Hind, a six-foot, seven-inch, lookout tower of a man who, for years, has been intermittently tracking his way back and forth through the same case. A four-year-old boy, Hershey Laurel, was kidnapped from his rural home, and for seven years there has been no trace of the boy. Desperate to solve the enigma, Hind tells and retells the known facts to everyone he knows; in time, his auditors become so knowledgeable as to seem implicated in the original crime. Hind's recollections thus become a labyrinth without boundaries, as if all were "suspicioned" into the plot, often on the slightest of linguistic associations, such as a name. Midway through the narrative, with the book's reader now equally knowledgeable of the main "facts," it becomes necessary for Hind to "de-kidnap" everyone, to extricate them from the paranoid plottings of his own mind. Thus, Hind, too, becomes implicated. In the novel's second part, he turns his detective skills onto his own past: the early deaths of both parents, his childhood with a guardian (a linguist, as it happens), and the question of his own paternity (the guardian appears to have been his actual father). These matters explain his obsession. Jack's quest for the boy is a means of asserting his own guardianship, and so of questing into the self, of separating illusion from reality and discovering how he was misled by language. As the novel's subtitle implies, Jack thereby seeks to become a truer shepherd of both memories and the discourses used to shape them.

ANCIENT HISTORY

The discourse of *Hind's Kidnap* is often so meditative, so far removed from the pitch and flow of narrative, as to read like a poetic anatomy. This tendency continues in *Ancient History*, McElroy's third (and least satisfying) novel, in which the narrator, Cy, searches to explain the evident suicide of his friend, Dom. Like Hind, he discovers that every force expended in the effort of detection tends to reverberate throughout the web of his friend's associations, and eventually through his own memories. Yet the stylistic and technical demands of this novel also bring diminishing returns to the reader. The book becomes, at the last, a poetic demonstration of the spatial possibilities in linguistically organized memory. It has little in it of narrative action.

LOOKOUT CARTRIDGE

Lookout Cartridge, arguably McElroy's best work, resolves these problems. The plot crackles with action and the style surges ahead in a more declarative mode, while never weakening the complex power of its main idea. A further "demonstration" of the dynamics and the essential incompleteness of memory in an information society, *Lookout Cartridge* asks to be read as a mystery-thriller.

The narrator-protagonist, Cartwright, a filmmaker who has been collaborating with a director named Dagger DiGorro on a politically radical documentary project, is literally pushed into his detective research. The narrative opens with the momentary fall (as a result of mechanical failure) of a helicopter hovering over a terrorist explosion in New York, itself partly explained at the novel's end. This recollection spins Cartwright into another beginning: an unseen hand that pushed him violently down an escalator, a fall he transforms by half-coordinated steps into a self-preserving forward stagger. In the narrative order, Cartwright's second "fall" thus redeems the mindless near-accident of his first. It also eventually emblematizes the detective activity, as a type of half-random, half-volitional motion. For a novel preoccupied with kinds of drive (physical and cinematic, social and narrational, epistemological and historical), this paradox is crucial.

Persons unknown, for reasons that are never fully explained, want Cartwright and Dagger's film destroyed, along with Cartwright's shooting diary, Cartwright himself, and perhaps even members of Cartwright's family who have knowledge of the film at second hand. All of this is apparently necessary because the film may have inadvertently recorded minute details of "an international power struggle." It may have, but without replaying or at least mentally reconstructing the footage, Cartwright can never know for certain. Therefore he sets to work. Like McElroy's previous detectives, he takes up the fragmentary evidence: the remaining chunks of the diary, recollections (often prompted) of friends and associates, material objects, whatever comes to hand during his headlong plunge through England, where much of the footage was shot, and New York City.

This urgency of self-survival gives *Lookout Cartridge* a sense of immediate purpose missing from the more abstract plots of *Hind's Kidnap* and *Ancient History*, and is something McElroy would capitalize on again, in *Plus*. As Cartwright shuttles back and forth between London and New York, and between pieces of contrary evidence, his in-betweenness becomes the basis for an uncannily creative power. Though he imagines himself as a "lookout cartridge" of film inserted "in someone else's system," still Cartwright discovers how, "between blind coghood" (the camera as simple recording instrument) and "that sinister hint of godhead" (in the conspiracies of unknown others), he himself has the power—even by using purest accident—of pushing events toward disclosure. Indeed, Cartwright finally nails both his assailants and their banal secrets. This resolution is the result, equally, of his power to manipulate details of story and his power simply to act by lunging forward, by reacting. Through it all, readers "have" only this Cartwright-Cartridge: the mind as recording machine, the machine as uncanny intercessor for the mind. What the lens records will depend entirely on where one is, what one wants to see, how long one rolls the film, and, later, how it is spliced. The camera thus becomes, like the remembering human subject, part of a relational system or associational grid whose power is greater than its parts.

This idea underwrites the lexicons of cinematography and information processing evident on the novel's every page. There is much, much more. Cartwright's narrative also includes speculations on Mayan calendars, on Mercator maps, and on Stonehenge or the standing stones of Callanish as ancient data-processing systems; details about the topographies of Corsica, London, or New York; and countless oblique references to the conspiracy-racked politics of the 1960's and 1970's. Involving readers in this labyrinth of events, representation techniques, and forms of knowledge, *Lookout Cartridge* surpasses the excesses and the feigned completion of other contemporary encyclopedic novels, such as Pynchon's *Gravity's Rainbow* (1973) or Coover's *The Public Burning* (1977).

By comparison to these, *Lookout Cartridge* makes far more demands on the reader. As the title suggests,

the reader is also inserted into this survival-experience and discovers that what matters is not a final why, but how one might manipulate the journey. Yet many of the novel's critics were so taken by its profusion of reference and detail that they missed commenting on one of its completed enigmas, a palpable bit of political absurdity worthy of Joseph Conrad's *The Secret Agent* (1907). That explosion in chapter 1 was set off by a faction of Cartwright's assailants, who were terrorizing the city for towing their illegally parked car. This detail points to a wry, detached satire of a contemporary society in which politics is managed as sequences of media events.

PLUS

At first glance, that potential for satire would also seem to be the motive force of McElroy's fifth novel, *Plus*, one of his most accessible works of fiction. Given the novel's premise, the chances for targeting the absurdities of contemporary "information society" were numerous. Its story concerns a disembodied brain inserted, cartridgelike, in an orbiting space platform called Imp, whose computer he—or it—was programmed to be. The engineers dubbed the combination "Imp Plus." Relaying technical data, controlling Imp's self-sustaining internal environment, with its glucose-producing algae—these are its simple programmed functions. Yet as a relational network, an ecosystem, Imp Plus is more than a mere machine. It has the power of self-induced growth. In sum, once more the narration unfolds in the topography, now absolute, of mind, and the primary action again involves the composition of self from fragments of memory.

In a reconstruction of its past and present states (made difficult by its linguistic limitations), Imp Plus forms a new identity. Looking backward from this perspective, its story is simple. Exposed to lethal doses of radiation, a space scientist donates his brain, and Imp Plus is launched as an experiment in photosynthesis and symbiosis—the algae providing necessary glucose for the brain, the brain respiring carbon dioxide necessary for the algae, the brain and its mechanical platform interpreting and relaying data. Then, however, the brain begins re-forming itself. Imp Plus expands inwardly by recovering discrete sensual memories and thereby reconstructing language. (In an elegantly structured argument, Brooke-Rose shows how this develops from a hypothetically "nonsensical" sentence by linguist Noam Chomsky: "Colorless green ideas sleep furiously.") Imp Plus also expands outwardly by linking the neural sites of previous sensory activity, such as vision, to the platform's circuitry. It thereby realizes the practical and virtual reciprocity of mind and matter, a discovery tantamount to the age-old philosopher's stone. It also begins disregarding and disobeying signals from Earth, and when Ground Control threatens fiery destruction, Imp Plus carries out a ploy which will carom the platform off Earth's atmosphere and into deep space. There Imp Plus envisions further growth—leaving matter behind to become pure light, the wholly disembodied "Plus" of McElroy's title.

Plus can be read as a recapitulation of the principal themes of McElroy's previous books—a work of summary and consolidation. With *Plus*, he had published five challenging novels in just over a decade; his sixth novel, *Women and Men*, was itself ten years in the writing.

WOMEN AND MEN

Everything about *Women and Men* proclaims its enormous ambition. Its title has the immodest sweep of Fyodor Dostoevski's *Prestupleniye i nakazaniye* (1866; *Crime and Punishment*, 1886) or Leo Tolstoy's *Voyna i mir* (1865-1869; *War and Peace*, 1886). In sheer bulk, nearly twelve hundred pages, it easily outweighs any of McElroy's earlier books. In the complexity of its structure, the density of information it conveys, it is even more daunting than *Lookout Cartridge*. Reviewing the novel in *The Washington Post Book World*, Tom LeClair suggested that "*Women and Men* is the single book—fiction or nonfiction—that best manifests what human beings can know and be and imagine now and, just as importantly, in the future."

Whether such claims will stand up is a matter for time to tell. A first reading of *Women and Men* is essentially a reconnaissance mission. The action of the novel is set primarily in the mid-1970's. The two central characters—James Mayn, a journalist specializing in science and technology and economic issues,

and Grace Kimball, a radical feminist guru—live in the same apartment building in New York. They do not know each other, but they have mutual acquaintances, and they are connected in more subtle ways as well. This pattern of coincidence is a model for the novel as a whole, which traces a multitude of unexpected connections both in the private lives and family histories of the characters and in the life of the planet.

While the intertwining stories of Mayn and Kimball constitute a loose narrative line, many chapters are self-contained vignettes that illuminate, from diverse perspectives, the relation between women and men at a time of significant change: change in assumptions concerning sexual roles, but also more broadly change in the assumptions by which we organize our experience. "The ways in which we embrace the world and embrace other people," McElroy has said, "can be more precise and clear than we sometimes think." Weather patterns, body chemistry, economic cycles—these are not merely esoteric academic subjects but rather the stuff of everyday life. All that is required is attentiveness to available knowledge.

Much of the knowledge that informs *Women and Men* is scientific, but this is complemented by a strong emphasis on what has been called New Age spirituality. Native American lore plays an important role in the book; Grace Kimball frequently invokes the Goddess (the primeval Earth Mother who, many feminists contend, was universally worshipped by humankind before the onset of patriarchy); and there are hints of reincarnation throughout the novel.

Indeed, several long sections, set in the future, are given to a chorus of disembodied spirits who comment on the action and the characters of the main narrative. Here McElroy seems to suggest a collective consciousness in which individual identity is subsumed. It is not clear how literally this vision is to be taken; even readers who find it unpersuasive will be left with a vivid sense of intricate order within the dizzying multiplicity of things.

THE LETTER LEFT TO ME

Though McElroy's *The Letter Left to Me* is his shortest novel, in several aspects it is also his most complicated. On its surface the story is simple enough. A mother delivers to her son a letter from his recently deceased father, which was written three years before the father's death. Soon, the boy's mother and step-grandfather, impressed with the letter's contents, decide to distribute copies of it to friends and relatives. Eventually, a copy even ends up in the hands of a dean at the small New England college the boy attends. The dean, in turn, disseminates a copy to the entire freshmen class for analysis, believing it contains lessons in survival.

As narrator, the son draws a parallel between the range of reactions to the letter and the pattern of events in his life. The letter itself is simple in style and replete with paternal platitudes, the most important of which is the father's admonition to his son to make something of himself, as he had failed to do while at college. For McElroy the letter serves as a starting point to explore the intricate connections between the past and the present. By the time the letter leaves home, it has taken on a life of its own. No longer is it merely an inanimate object but instead a mysterious metaphor.

As an object of interpretation, the letter in McElroy's novel represents the intrinsic distinction the author sees between the spoken word and the written word. The writing process, he intimates, requires a degree of detachment from the body as words are transformed into the graphic form. As a consequence, the product (letter) and interpreter (reader) are distanced from the agent (writer). On the other hand, the words engaged in conversation are part of a collaborative effort between the speaker and listener. The written word in effect moves beyond the author's control, where it easily can be appropriated and re-created by successive subjective explications. Ownership thus becomes an issue, as it does in *The Letter Left to Me* when the original letter evolves into something akin to a communal piece of property for all to claim through a process of interpretation. In the end the letter becomes a metaphor for the culture, with all its diversities and complexities.

There is no mistaking the autobiographical elements in *The Letter Left to Me*. Like the boy-narrator, McElroy grew up in the 1940's in Brooklyn and at-

tended a small New England college; like the narrator's father, McElroy's went to Harvard University. As critics have noted, the novel embraces nearly all of the major themes McElroy addressed in his earlier works. Among them are how the interdependence between people, and particularly families, can be at once suffocating and comforting, how the continuities of life are connected, and how the reliance on the written word causes the culture to become a prisoner of vocabulary and of the convolutions of syntax. As a leading practitioner of postmodern fiction, McElroy's aim is to identify the forces shaping society and connect them in ways that are consistent with the truth.

Steven Weisenburger,
updated by William Hoffman

BIBLIOGRAPHY

Campbell, Gregor. "Processing *Lookout Cartridge*." *The Review of Contemporary Fiction* (Spring, 1990): 112-118. Explores *Lookout Cartridge*'s closed fictional system, modeled on physics and cybernetics, and mentions McElroy's use of film technology. Notes his love of abstraction and the complexity of the plot. Campbell praises the novel as a "triumph of information-processing design and technology," and claims that it can be viewed as a 1960's novel concerned with historical change.

Hanke, Steffen. *Conspiracy and Paranoia in Contemporary American Fiction: The Works of Don DeLillo and Joseph McElroy*. New York: Lang, 1994. Offers an in-depth analysis and comparative view of the postmodern themes of two leading American novelists.

LeClair, Tom. "Opening Up Joseph McElroy's *The Letter Left to Me*." *The Review of Contemporary Fiction* (Spring, 1990): 258-267. Contains McElroy's statement on his use of the word "attention" in *The Letter Left to Me*. LeClair gives critical commentary on this novel, noting that McElroy's use of language has "opened up sensibility for anyone to read. Everyone who cares about mastery in American letters should." Also discusses *Women and Men* and its peeling away of layers and obstacles.

LeClair, Tom, and Larry McCaffrey. *Anything Can Happen: Interviews with Contemporary American Novelists*. Chicago: University of Illinois Press, 1983. A thoughtful interview with McElroy by LeClair that provides much valuable information and insight into McElroy's work and vision as a writer. Includes a brief introduction by LeClair which is helpful in summing up the main themes in McElroy's writing.

McHale, Brian. *Constructing Postmodernism*. New York: Routledge, 1992. McHale provides passages from the works of several postmodern authors, including McElroy, to illustrate the evolutionary aspect of the literary movement from modernism to postmodernism.

Mathews, Harry. "We for One: An Introduction to Joseph McElroy's *Women and Men*." *The Review of Contemporary Fiction* 10 (Spring, 1990): 199-226. Examines the novel's interchange between men and women and vice versa, noting its use of language and double entendres. Mathews makes liberal use of extracts from the novel and diagrams to illustrate his commentary. A complex piece of criticism that probes the function of the narrative in McElroy's work.

The Review of Contemporary Fiction 10 (Spring, 1990). This special issue is devoted to the work of McElroy, with a collection of important critical essays and a bibliographical essay. Includes an introduction by Stanley Elkin and a piece by McElroy entitled "Midcourse Corrections," followed by an interview with McElroy conducted by John Graham. A valuable resource for McElroy scholars and readers alike.

Pᴀᴛʀɪᴄᴋ MᴄGɪɴʟᴇʏ

Born: Killaned, County Donegal, Ireland; February 8, 1937

Pʀɪɴᴄɪᴘᴀʟ ʟᴏɴɢ ꜰɪᴄᴛɪᴏɴ
Bogmail, 1978
Goosefoot, 1982
Foxprints, 1983
Foggage, 1983
The Trick of the Ga Bolga, 1985
The Red Men, 1987
The Devil's Diary, 1988
The Lost Soldier's Song, 1994

Oᴛʜᴇʀ ʟɪᴛᴇʀᴀʀʏ ꜰᴏʀᴍs
Patrick McGinley is known primarily for his long fiction.

Aᴄʜɪᴇᴠᴇᴍᴇɴᴛs
From the outset, McGinley's fiction enjoyed an enthusiastic reception from reviewers, particularly in the United States, where critics, inadequately acquainted with some of his background material, misleadingly drew attention to the work's Irishness. Reviews in England and Ireland, though less generous, were generally favorable, if somewhat resistant to McGinley's prolificity. McGinley's first novel, *Bogmail*, was nominated for several awards, including the prestigious Edgar Award for Best Novel of 1981, an award presented by the Mystery Writers of America.

Bɪᴏɢʀᴀᴘʜʏ
Although his books received such popular success, little is known about Patrick Anthony McGinley's life; indeed, at a time when Irish fiction is receiving an increasing amount of academic attention, this author could be called the most anonymous Irish novelist of his generation. McGinley was born to a farming family in a comparatively remote area of County Donegal, Ireland's northwesternmost county. He was educated locally and at University College, Galway, from which he graduated with a bachelor's degree in commerce in 1957. For five years after his graduation he taught secondary school in Ireland before emigrating to England and entering the publishing profession. Apart from a year in Australia (1965-1966), he remained in publishing and became managing director of Europa Publications in 1980. McGinley married Kathleen Frances Cuddy in 1967 and had one son, Myles Peter. His family made its home in Kent, outside London.

ANALYSIS

Because of lack of serious critical attention until the late 1990's, it had been difficult to assess Patrick McGinley's status as a contemporary Irish novelist. Beginning in the early 1960's, Irish writing in all forms underwent major self-interrogation, accompanied by the new thematic and formal considerations. While, unlike many Irish writers, McGinley was anything but vocal in this sustained period of reappraisal, it is instructive to see his work in such a context. Its individuality is arguably its most significant feature and, by a paradox more apparent than real, is the attribute that makes his novels symptomatic of new departures in Irish writing. At the same time, the representations of nature, the sense of the uncanny, the choice of traditional and relatively unchanging rural communities as settings, the focus on death, and the use of the romance form all reveal McGinley as being interestingly related to a long tradition of such preoccupations in Irish writing, from the seventh century writings of Saint Columkille, for whom McGinley's native place is named, to the modern era. More particularly, his fascination with reason's frailty and the fact of death makes his work an intriguing pendant to that of one of the most important Irish novelists of the twentieth century, Flann O'Brien.

Although McGinley is usually classified as a crime novelist, to consider him one in the conventional sense is both accurate and misleading. While it is true that, until the publication of *The Lost Soldier's Song* in 1994, McGinley had not deviated from the path signposted in the opening paragraph of his first published novel, *Bogmail*, where poisonous toadstools are being introduced to a mushroom omelette, and while it is also true that his publishers have tended to emphasize the murderous mysteriousness of his plots, there is both more and less than meets the eye to the convenient classification. This state of affairs is of significance because it draws attention to the fact that it is impossible to approach McGinley's work without drawing attention to its bifocal character. McGinley's fiction evinces more interest in mystery than in solution—his work has only one detective, McMyler in *Goosefoot*, and the few policemen who crop up in the other novels are somewhat less

than a credit to the force and have thoroughly earned their status as minor characters. The works' focus is directed gently but ineluctably toward those areas of existence that may not be brought within stable frameworks of perception. In particular, the unreasonable fact of death is so much more to the fore than is any power to counteract it that it is tempting to attach to the whole of this author's output the quotation from Robert Southey that is the epigraph to *Foggage*: "My name is Death: the last best friend am I."

SETTINGS

For the most part, McGinley's novels are set in the author's native County Donegal. An exception to this general rule is *Foxprints*, which is largely set in the suburban Home Counties of England, a context that the author fails to enliven, perhaps because of its excessively social character. Typically, McGinley feels at home in remoteness, and Donegal settings possess a variety of strategic advantages for a writer of his proclivities. In the first place, by selecting Donegal as the scene of the action, McGinley is clearly presenting settings that he can treat with authority. So faithful is he to the fastidious recreation of locales clearly maintained in his mind's eye by a deep attachment to his native area that he establishes a very palpable sense of place, and in every McGinley novel there are quietly rapturous descriptive passages that seem to hymn the landscapes they depict.

Situating his plots so squarely in a felt environment—in which the play of light, natural features, the oscillations of the sea, the weather's vagaries, and the presence of wildlife continually recur—seems to enable McGinley to virtually dispense with time. The exigencies of plot naturally require that time pass, but generally speaking there is little specific sense of period. Before *The Lost Soldier's Song*, which is set during the Black and Tan War and focuses on the events of the war itself, as well as its impact on character, long historical perspectives had little or no part to play in the assessing of the characters' problematic destinies. What exceptions there are to this rule—the setting of *The Trick of the Ga Bolga* in the early years of World War II, or the rather boldly stated observations on the spurious development of rural Ireland propounded by the protagonist of *The Devil's Di-*

ary—seem rather to underline how watertight the rule is, since neither note of contemporaneity contributes significantly to the balance of forces at the center of either of these novels.

One effect of McGinley's obviation of cultural conceptions of time, and a general relaxation of time-consciousness, is that it assists in the creation of atmosphere but inhibits in the creation of thrills. Such a result accentuates the all-enveloping quality of the rural setting, while at the same time drawing both the characters' and the readers' attention from event to perception of event. The mystery deepens to the degree that it becomes as much part of the nature of things as the landscape in which it is situated. Any tension that results from the distressingly arbitrary and violent events of the plot—often as much the result of accidents as of articulated intentions—are to be found, unreleased, within the consciousness of McGinley's protagonists, and its psychological repercussions fail, with what the protagonists understandably find to be a maddening consistency, to have an objective correlative in the natural world around them. Remoteness of setting therefore, is not merely an occasion of picturesqueness for McGinley. On the contrary, it is one of his fundamental means of lending plausibility to the sense of the inscrutable and uncanny that bedevils the mental landscapes of his protagonists, the majority of whom traverse the dual terrains of these novels like lost souls.

By virtue of its very naturalness, setting is experienced by McGinley's protagonists as a primary instance of otherness, of a set of conditions that are not comprehensible, tractable, alterable, or humanly amenable in any particular—conditions that are, strictly speaking, mysterious. Yet it is important to note that McGinley is sufficiently resourceful to prevent his approach from becoming too schematic. The rich farming country of County Tipperary, which provides the setting for *Foggage* and in which its main characters are ostensibly firmly established, engenders as much distress and destruction as County Donegal ever did, revealing unsuspected psychic remotenesses, while in *Goosefoot* ungenial Dublin exposes the unsuspecting and vital Patricia Teeling to

malevolences that are the antithesis of her winning sense of life.

McGinley's protagonists, settled or unsettled, are peculiarly susceptible to the atmosphere of their environments. For the most part they are unsettled, and it is generally this condition that has brought them to the locale of the story. Once arrived, they seem to believe, however, that they have found a secure haven: To a degree, the enclosed and remote character of their landfall—typified by the Glenkeel in *The Devil's Diary*, which has the same road into it as out—seduces them into thinking that now they are safe, they have come to the end of a particular phase of their lives and are permitted by their new circumstances to live lives that are at once both self-engrossed and detached. In a number of cases—*Foxprints* and *The Trick of the Ga Bolga* are the most significant—the progatonists are on the run from unsatisfactory marriages. The protagonists' status as outsiders, however, gives them novelty value to the locals, and before long they are involved in local affairs, often in a very literal sense, one of the principal means of involvement being that of sexual attraction. The inability to deny the presence of their sexuality has the effect of replicating in more intense form the substance of earlier distressing experiences, with the result that settings that seemed to be escapes end up as terminuses. Aiming for simplicity, McGinley's protagonists find it only to discover its essential mysteriousness.

Cʜᴀʀᴀᴄᴛᴇʀs

The repetition and duplication of experience, the unforsakable and evidently unforgiving character of one's own nature, are particularly crucial in *The Devil's Diary* and *The Trick of the Ga Bolga*. Yet more important than their presence, and raising their significance beyond that of mere plot devices, is the fact that the protagonists perceive their condition for what it is. The typical McGinley protagonist is well educated and sometimes dauntingly well read. The unwitting choice of a volume of the *Encyclopædia Britannica*, eleventh edition, as a murder weapon seems virtually natural in *Bogmail*, whereas in most murder mysteries it would seem at least eccentric. There seems nothing unusual in Father Jerry Mc-

Sharry taking down a volume of patristic theology for a little bedtime reading in *The Devil's Diary*. Likewise, Florrie McColl's burning of Frank Ganly's copy of *A Short History of the English People* leads to Maureen Sheehy's only criticism of his barbaric tactics in *The Lost Soldier's Song*. In addition, circumstances generally conspire to aggravate what seems to be the protagonists' natural predilection for self-scrutiny. Discrepancies between self and world begin to proliferate, and the capacity for consciousness to keep pace with them is frequently stretched unreasonably. A quest for pattern, for coherence, for congruity and perception bedevils McGinley's characters, who, for all of their learning, persist in giving the impression of innocence. The evil that their presence inadvertently uncovers strikes them as a force that cannot be reasoned away, and they become embroiled in a double bind: The more they see, the less they are able to believe. No satisfactory denouement results from their existential and epistemological entanglements. McGinley's apparent indifference to a resonant denouement has the effect of rendering his protagonists as occasions of authorial game-playing rather than more familiar, "well-rounded" characters. This ostensible deficiency must be considered, however, in the context of the essentially experimental nature of McGinley's work.

Not only do repetition and replication feature to a significant degree within each of McGinley's novels, but they are also notably present in his output as a whole. As a result, while resourceful variations in setting and protagonist occur—a female protagonist in *Goosefoot*, three protagonists in *The Red Men*, a suburban never-never land as the setting for *Foxprints*—and while these changes effectively vary the angle of approach from novel to novel, each work's ultimate preoccupations remain essentially unchanged. McGinley's output has a consistency of focus and pliability of approach that are crucially denied its characters. It hardly seems to matter that the English engineer Potter in *Bogmail* is a prototype for Coote, the protagonist of *The Trick of the Ga Bolga*, or that Coote's mistress has a formidable avatar in the insistently incestuous Maureen Hurley of *Foggage*. Story line is more ornament than staple, and while

McGinley's plots are richly woven and colorfully peopled, they seem to be considered as no more than edifices of superficial plausibility to an investigation of whose inscrutable foundations the protagonist is, through no fault of his own (McGinley's fiction is resolutely amoral), condemned.

McGinley's sense of setting draws heavily on the elements—the motion of the seasons, the cloudscapes of the often protean Irish sky, the world of crag, pool, bog, and seashore. His sense of protagonist reproduces this concentration on the elemental. These characters seldom have a specific social role, or if they do—as in the case of Father Jerry in *The Devil's Diary*—it produces rather than defends against existential dread. On the other hand, the protagonists, for all the author's concentration on them and his use of them as both embodiments and victims of a unique optic on themselves and their world, are not sufficiently well endowed to render considerations of social role by functioning in a recognizable manner. Deprived of the safeguards that social and literary convention provide, they appear to have no choice but to assume a more fundamental, vulnerable, and elementary condition of selfhood—or rather, the plot lines of McGinley's novels show that fall taking place. In addition, the creation of mysteries without solution and the commissioning of crime without reproducing the social machinery of incrimination that is its normal, or generic, accompaniment, take at face value the genre to which these novels superficially belong, and by doing so subvert it, reducing it to such a bare embodiment of its elements that it only nominally maintains its presence.

Themes

The unemphatic but omnipresent concentration on a sense of the elemental in McGinley's fiction is nowhere seen to better advantage than in the works' recurring themes. Having brought his unsuspecting protagonists, who without knowing it are at the end of their tether, to what seems like the end of the world, the author subjects them to other experiences of the terminal. The most obvious one of these is death. Yet although its literal presence is of prime importance to sustaining these works' fragmentary figment of plot, death is not merely present in a literal sense. It also exists as the pun for sexual climax familiar to students of English Renaissance poetry, where it helps to make a familiar and typically antithetical conjunction for McGinley (the fact of death is frequently deeply implicated in the act of love). In addition, its presence denotes a primary instance of the chaos and nullity to which a protagonist's perception of life may in any case be reduced—a state of perception that is frequently the aftermath of the violent and unexpected deaths that punctuate the duration of the McGinley protagonist's rustication. Rather than describe McGinley as a writer of mysteries, it seems more appropriate to consider his works as those of a parablist, who utters in story what cannot be otherwise so readily articulated. At least one McGinley novel, *The Red Men* (commonly taken as a retelling of the parable of the talents in the New Testament, seems to support such a view. More broadly, a strong case may be made for McGinley's novels to be considered as sophisticated romances of consciousness, in which the romantic quest, for all its pastoral trappings, is ironized by succeeding in finding that with which it cannot live.

What the quest locates reveals the philosophical undertow of McGinley's fiction. It would be misleading to consider McGinley a philosophical novelist of the school of, for example, Albert Camus, as is implied by his works' pleasing lightness of tone and deftness of manner. In all McGinley's works prior to *The Lost Soldier's Song*, philosophical themes, however fundamental to the extreme conditions to which action and character are reduced, are treated with no more intensity or deliberation than is any other feature of McGinley's fictional universe, possibly as a result of his having no ideological ax to grind. At the same time, the clearly existentialist scenarios, the manner in which action preys on mind in order to elicit meaning, the emphasis on the mutability of fate as a standby of plot, the frequent epiphanic encounters between humanity and nature, the quietly satirical allusions to mind-body problems, and the impetus toward pattern forming and pattern recognition that initially stimulates and ultimately frustrates the inquirer all suggest works of a speculative, philosophizing, intellectual character.

This omnipresent preoccupation with perception, cognition, and the impossibility to stabilize or normalize them that bemuses McGinley's protagonist seems to amuse the author. Not only is his style, for the most part, wry, succinct, and supple, but its tone is also frequently one of comic detachment. A great strength of his work is his ability to create compelling minor characters, all of them gifted talkers, whose presence both diffuses and enhances the works' central preoccupations. In addition, McGinley is not averse to placing the reader in the lexical equivalent of his protagonists' opacity of perception by the inclusion of archaic and unfamiliar terminology. Here again, however, this tactic is employed in a spirit of play rather than one of dogmatism, just as his works as a whole resist to an exemplary degree didacticism and moralizing, preferring to articulate consciousness as a field of forces too vivid to be ignored and too broad to be disciplined. The greatest pleasure to be derived from McGinley's fiction, therefore, is not merely from its undoubtedly attractive and distracting stories, locales, and characters but also from the ruminative cast of mind that sets the various fictive effects in motion.

THE LOST SOLDIER'S SONG

All these elements are present in part or in full before *The Lost Soldier's Song*, and many of them remain important even in this novel, which represents a departure from McGinley's previous fiction. Far from being a crime novel, except perhaps in the sense that the criminality of war is expressed in its pages, this novel focuses on the experiences of Declan Osborne and Maureen Sheehy during the Black and Tan War and the war's repercussions. As in his previous novels, however, McGinley continues his poetic attachment to place with his descriptions of locales such as the enchanted Chalice, his deft creation of minor characters in such figures as the enigmatic Owney Muldowney, his preoccupation with death, and his refusal to moralize.

Some of the most memorable and significant passages in this novel center on what is elemental, and they ably unite place, character, and philosophical concern. After having the prisoners he had taken at Loganboy murdered by McColl, for instance, Declan

ı that had attracted him one sum-
ᵣiteness from a distance. However,
ₛely its corruption was revealed, giv-
son in Irish history," for he had en-
ₑlf in the midst of something "best
ı firm ground and from afar." Maureen's
"shadow of redness in the air" left by a
ᵣox in the rural countryside brings to mind
ᵣd brother, who would have made up a tale to
ᵢn the fox's phantom, making her recognize that
ᵢat you miss about people is the way they put
ᵢngs. When they've gone, you realise that they've
ₑft a little bit of their mind in yours." Declan's own
vision of a running fox, "fully and superbly alive,"
forces him to realize that the courage he showed at
Loganboy may never be duplicated; he can never
again take anything for granted. As this example
shows and as is true of McGinley's earlier novels, his
characters are totally cognizant of their true condition. This is especially true of Declan, who clearly
understands his motive for becoming and remaining
involved in the war—to find a place for himself in the
world, ironically comparable to the safe haven sought
by McGinley's characters in previous novels. He unmistakably realizes that luck, not courage, led to his
spur-of-the-moment heroism at Fiachra's Well. Like
McGinley's other protagonists, Declan is an existential hero who relentlessly follows his course, despite
the fact that he is never quite sure he believes in it.

What makes this novel different from McGinley's
previous fiction is the necessary importance of the
historical perspective, for none of the events would
occur without the presence of the war. It is the war
that also serves as the philosophical core of the book,
as is seen when Declan and Ganly come to realize
that they are "fighting high-handed imperialism with
high-minded barbarism." Before she drowns herself
in the Black Pool, the emotionally wounded Maureen
appropriately writes the epitaph for the war: "It was a
strange victory. . . . For some it was more like a defeat." Indeed, the final pages of the novel lead the
reader to wonder what has improved for the heroes of
the war who return to the brickyards or to the farms
they had so wanted to escape. Sober, philosophical,
poetic, and yet permeated with irony, *The Lost Sol-*

dier's Song lies firmly in the mainstream of Irish fiction, while at the same time continuing to be stylistically and philosophically connected to McGinley's
previous fiction.

George O'Brien, updated by Jaquelyn W. Walsh

BIBLIOGRAPHY

Brown, Richard E. "Patrick McGinley's Novels of
Detection." *Colby Quarterly* 33 (September,
1997): 209-222. Discusses McGinley's mystery
novels as parodies of the detective novel.

Cahalan, James M. *The Irish Novel: A Critical History.* Boston: Twayne, 1988. The concluding chapter of this study is a survey of contemporary Irish
fiction, which provides a good sense of McGinley's context. There are also stimulating, though
necessarily brief, asides on McGinley's works up
to and including *The Red Men.*

Clissmann, Anne. *Flann O'Brien: A Critical Introduction to His Writings.* New York: Barnes & Noble Books, 1975. Chapters 2 and 3 of this work offer a useful means of assessing the imaginative
terrain upon which much of McGinley's fiction
rests.

Kenner, Hugh. "A Deep and Lasting Mayonnaise."
The New York Times Book Review, July 21, 1985,
20. A review of *The Trick of the Ga Bolga* by a
very influential commentator on Irish literary
themes. Many of McGinley's interests and orien-
tations are succinctly brought to the fore.

McGinley, Patrick. Interview by Jean W. Ross. In
Contemporary Authors, edited by Susan M.
Trosky. Vol. 127. Detroit: Gale Research, 1989. A
wide-ranging response by McGinley to questions
concerning his background, life as a writer, and
writing methods.

Shea, Thomas F. "Patrick McGinley's Impressions of
Flann O'Brien: *The Devil's Diary* and *At Swim-
Two-Birds*." *Twentieth Century Literature* 40
(Summer, 1994): 272-281. Taking a cue from
Hugo McSharry, the novelist-character in the work,
Shea examines McGinley's novel as a palimpsest,
a parchment partially erased yet retaining traces
of the original inscriptions, with the echoes of
other writers, particularly Flann O'Brien.